Principles of Microeconomics (ECON121) / Macroeconomics (ECON123)

SIXTH EDITION

Compiled by:
Bip Banerji
Shalini Mitra
Gary Cook

University of Liverpool
Management School

ISBN 13: 9781308243832

McGraw-Hill Custom Publishing

www.mcgrawhillcreate.co.uk

Published by McGraw-Hill Education (UK) Ltd an imprint of McGraw-Hill Education, 2 Penn Plaza, New York, NY 10121.

This McGraw-Hill Custom text may include materials submitted to McGraw-Hill for publication by the instructor of this course. The instructor is solely responsible for the editorial content of such materials.

Cover image: ©iStock.com/ter_minus

ISBN: 9781308243832

Principles of

Microeconomics (ECON121) / Macroeconomics (ECON123)

SIXTH EDITION

Contents

Credits

PART ONE: PRINCIPLES OF MICROECONOMICS

CHAPTER 1

THINKING LIKE AN ECONOMIST

Much of microeconomics entails the study of how people choose under conditions of scarcity. Many people react to this description by saying that the subject is of little real relevance in developed countries, where material scarcity is largely a thing of the past.

This reaction, however, takes too narrow a view of scarcity, for there are *always* important resources in short supply. At his death, Aristotle Onassis was worth several billion dollars. He had more money than he could possibly spend and used it for such things as finely crafted whale ivory footrests for the barstools on his yacht. And yet he confronted the problem of scarcity much more than most of us will ever have to. Onassis was the victim of *myasthenia gravis,* a debilitating and progressive neurological disease. For him, the scarcity that mattered was not money but time, energy, and the physical skill needed to carry out ordinary activities.

Time is a scarce resource for everyone, not just the terminally ill. In deciding which films to see, for example, it is time, not the price of admission, that constrains most of us. With only a few free nights available each month, seeing one film means not being able to see another, or not being able to have dinner with friends.

Time and money are not the only important scarce resources. Consider the economic choice you confront when a friend invites you to a buffet lunch. You must decide how to fill your plate. Even if you are not rich, money would be no object, since you can eat as much as you want for free. Nor is time an obstacle, since you have all afternoon and would enjoy spending it in the company of your friend. The important scarce resource here is the capacity of your stomach. A smorgasbord of your favourite foods lies before you, and you must decide which to eat and in what quantities. Eating another slice of pizza necessarily means having less room for more pasta. The fact that no money changes hands here does not make your choice any less an economic one.

Every choice involves important elements of scarcity. Sometimes the most relevant scarcity will involve money, but not always. Coping with scarcity is the essence of the human condition. Indeed, were it not for the problem of scarcity, life would be stripped of much of its intensity. For someone with an infinite lifetime and limitless material resources, hardly a single decision would ever matter.

In this chapter we examine some basic principles of microeconomic theory and see how an economist might apply them to a wide variety of choices involving scarcity. Later chapters more formally develop the theory. For now, our only goal is to get an intuitive feel for that distinctive mind-set known as 'thinking like an economist'. And the best way to do that is to work through a series of problems familiar from actual experience.

THE COST-BENEFIT APPROACH TO DECISIONS

Many of the choices economists study can be posed as the following question:

Should I do activity x?

If the benefit of an activity exceeds its cost, do it.

For the choice confronting a filmgoer, '. . . do activity x?' might be, for example, '. . . see *Casablanca* tonight?' For the person attending the buffet lunch, it might be '. . . eat another slice of pizza?' Economists answer such questions by comparing the costs and benefits of doing the activity in question. The decision rule we use is disarmingly simple. If $C(x)$ denotes the costs of doing x and $B(x)$ denotes the benefits, it is:

If $B(x) > C(x)$, do x; otherwise don't.

To apply this rule, we must define and measure costs and benefits. Monetary values are a useful common denominator for this purpose, even when the activity has nothing directly to do with money. We define $B(x)$ as the maximum monetary amount you would be willing to pay to do x. Often $B(x)$ will be a hypothetical magnitude, the amount you would be willing to pay if you had to, even though no money will change hands. $C(x)$, in turn, is the value of all the resources you must give up in order to do x. Here, too, $C(x)$ need not involve an explicit transfer of money.

For most decisions, at least some of the benefits or costs will not be readily available in monetary terms. To see how we proceed in such cases, consider the following simple decision.

EXAMPLE 1.1 Should I turn down my stereo?

You have settled into a comfortable chair and are listening to your stereo when you realize that the next two tracks on the CD are ones you dislike. If you had a programmable player, you would have programmed it not to play them. But you don't, and so you must decide whether to get up and turn the music down or to stay put and wait it out.

The benefit of turning it down is not having the songs you don't like blare away at you. The cost, in turn, is the inconvenience of getting out of your chair. If you are extremely comfortable and the music is only mildly annoying, you will probably

stay put. But if you haven't been settled for long or if the music is really bothersome, you are more likely to get up.

Even for simple decisions like this one, it is possible to translate the relevant costs and benefits into a monetary framework. Consider first the cost of getting out of your chair. If someone offered you 1 cent to get up out of a comfortable chair and there were no reason other than the penny to do it, would you take the offer? Most people would not. But if someone offered you €1000, you would be on your feet in an instant. Somewhere between 1 cent and €1000 lies your **reservation price,** the minimum amount it would take to get you out of the chair.

reservation price of activity x the price at which a person would be indifferent between doing *x* and not doing *x*.

To see where the threshold lies, imagine a mental auction with yourself in which you keep boosting the offer by small increments from 1 cent until you reach the point at which it is barely worthwhile to get up. Where this point occurs will obviously depend on circumstance. If you are rich, it will tend to be higher than if you are poor, because a given amount of money will seem less important; if you feel energetic, it will be lower than if you feel tired; and so on. For the sake of discussion, suppose your reservation price for getting out of the chair turns out to be €1. You can conduct a similar mental auction to determine the maximum sum you would be willing to pay someone to turn the music down. This reservation price measures the benefits of turning the music down; let us suppose it turns out to be 75 cents.

In terms of our formal decision rule, we then have x = 'turn my stereo down', with $B(x) = €0.75 < C(x) = €1$, which means that you should remain in your chair. Listening to the next two songs will be unpleasant, but less so than getting up would be. A reversal of these cost and benefit figures would imply a decision to get up and turn the music down. If $B(x)$ and $C(x)$ happened to be equal, you would be indifferent between the two alternatives. ◆

THE ROLE OF ECONOMIC THEORY

The idea that anyone might actually calculate the costs and benefits of turning down a stereo may sound absurd. Economists have been criticized for making unrealistic assumptions about how people behave, and outsiders are quick to wonder what purpose is served by the image of a person trying to decide how much he would pay to avoid getting up from his chair.

There are two responses to this criticism. The first is that economists don't assume that people make such calculations explicitly. Rather, many economists argue, we can make useful predictions by assuming people act *as if* they made such calculations. This view was forcefully expressed by Nobel laureate Milton Friedman, who illustrated his point by looking at the techniques expert pool players use.[1] He argued that the shots they choose, and the specific ways they attempt to make them, can be predicted extremely well by assuming that players take careful account of all the relevant laws of Newtonian physics. Of course, few expert pool players have had formal training in physics, and hardly any can recite such laws as 'the angle of incidence equals the angle of reflection'. Nor are they likely to know the definitions of 'elastic collisions' and 'angular momentum'. Even so, Friedman argued, they would never have become expert players in the first place *unless* they played as dictated by the laws of physics. Our theory of pool player behaviour assumes, unrealistically, that players know the laws of physics. Friedman urged us to judge this theory not by how accurate its central assumption is but by how well it predicts behaviour. And on this score, it performs very well indeed.

People do not always behave as predicted by economic models, but the models provide useful insights about how to achieve important goals.

Professional pool champion Corey Deuel, from the USA, may not know all the formal laws of Newtonian physics, but the quality of his play suggests that he has a deep understanding of them.

Like pool players, we must also develop skills for coping with our environments. Many economists, Friedman among them, believe that useful insights into our behaviour can be gained by assuming that we act as if governed by the rules of rational decision making. By trial and error we eventually absorb these rules, just as pool players absorb the laws of physics.

A second response to the charge that economists make unrealistic assumptions is to concede that behaviour does often differ from the predictions of economic models. Thus, as economist Richard Thaler puts it, we often behave more like novice than expert pool players—ignoring bank shots and having no idea about putting the proper spin on the cue ball to position it for the next shot. Considerable evidence supports this second view.

But even where economic models fail on descriptive grounds, they often provide useful guidance for decisions. That is, even if they don't always predict how we *do* behave, they may often give useful insights into how to achieve our goals more efficiently. If novice pool players have not yet internalized the relevant physical laws, they may nonetheless consult those laws for guidance about how to improve. Economic models often play an analogous role with respect to ordinary consumer and business decisions. Indeed, this role alone provides a compelling reason for learning economics.

[1]Milton Friedman, 'The Methodology of Positive Economics', *Essays in Positive Economics*, Chicago: University of Chicago Press, 1953.

COMMON PITFALLS IN DECISION MAKING

Some economists are embarrassed if an outsider points out that much of what they do boils down to an application of the principle that we should perform an action if and only if its benefits exceed its costs. That just doesn't sound like enough to keep a person with a PhD busy all day! There is more to it, however, than meets the eye. People who study economics quickly discover that measuring costs and benefits is as much an art as a science. Some costs seem almost deliberately hidden from view. Others may seem relevant but, on a closer look, turn out not to be.

Economics teaches us how to identify the costs and benefits that really matter. An important goal of this book is to teach you to become a better decision maker. A good starting point is to examine some common pitfalls in decision making. The relevant economic principles are simple and commonsensical, but many people ignore them.

Pitfall 1. Ignoring Implicit Costs

One pitfall is to overlook costs that are not explicit. If doing activity x means not being able to do activity y, then the value to you of doing y (had you done it) is an **opportunity cost** of doing x. Many people make bad decisions because they tend to ignore the value of such forgone opportunities. This insight suggests that it will almost always be instructive to translate questions such as 'Should I do x?' into ones such as 'Should I do x or y?' In the latter question, y is simply the most highly valued alternative to doing x. The following example helps drive this important point home.

opportunity cost of activity the value of all that must be sacrificed to do the activity.

EXAMPLE 1.2 Should I go skiing today or work as a research assistant?

There is a ski area near your campus. From experience you know that a day on the slopes is worth €60 to you. The charge for the day is €40 (which includes bus fare, lift ticket and equipment). However, this is not the only cost of going skiing. You must also take into account the value of the most attractive alternative you will forgo by heading for the slopes. Suppose the best alternative is your new job as a professor's research assistant. The job pays €45 per day, and you like it just well enough to be willing to do it for free. The question you face is, 'Should I go skiing or work as a research assistant?'

Here the cost of skiing is not just the explicit cost of the ski package (€40) but also the opportunity cost of the lost earnings (€45). The total costs are therefore €85, which exceeds the benefits of €60. Since $C(x) > B(x)$, you should stay on campus and work for your professor. Someone who ignored the opportunity cost of the forgone earnings would decide incorrectly to go skiing. ◆

The fact that you liked the research job just well enough to have been willing to do it for free is another way of saying there were no psychic costs associated with doing it. This is important because it means that by not doing the job you would not have been escaping something unpleasant. Of course, not all jobs fall into this category. Suppose instead that your job is to wash dishes in the dining hall for the same pay, €45/day, and that the job is so unpleasant that you would be unwilling to do it for less than €30/day. Assuming your manager at the dining hall permits you to take a day off whenever you want, let us now reconsider your decision about whether to go skiing.

EXAMPLE 1.3 Should I go skiing today or wash dishes?

There are two equivalent ways of looking at this decision. One is to say that one benefit of going skiing is not having to wash dishes. Since you would never be willing to wash dishes for less than €30/day, avoiding that task is worth that amount to you. Going skiing thus carries the indirect benefit of not washing dishes. When we add that indirect benefit to the €60 direct benefit of the skiing, we get $B(x) = €90$. In this view of the problem, $C(x)$ is the same as before, namely, the €40 ski charge plus the €45 opportunity cost of the lost earnings, or €85. So now $B(x) > C(x)$, which means you should go skiing.

Alternatively, we could have viewed the unpleasantness of the dish-washing job as an offset against its salary. By this approach, we would subtract €30/day from your €45/day earnings and say that the opportunity cost of not working is only €15/day. Then $C(x) = €40 + €15 = €55 < B(x) = €60$, and again the conclusion is that you should go skiing.

It makes no difference in which of these two ways you handle the valuation of the unpleasantness of washing dishes. It is critically important, however, that you do it either one way or the other. Don't count it twice! ◆

As Example 1.3 makes clear, costs and benefits are reciprocal. Not incurring a cost is the same as getting a benefit. By the same token, not getting a benefit is the same as incurring a cost.

Obvious as this sounds, it is often overlooked. A case in point was a foreign graduate student who got his degree some years ago in the US and was about to return to his home country. The trade regulations of his nation permitted people returning from abroad to bring back a new automobile without having to pay the normal 50 per cent tariff. The student's father-in-law asked him to bring him back a new $20,000 Chevrolet and sent him a cheque for exactly that amount. This put the student in a quandary. He had been planning to bring back a Chevrolet and sell it in his home country. Because, as noted, new cars normally face a 50 per cent import tax, such a car would sell at a dealership there for $30,000. The student estimated that he could easily sell it privately for $28,000, which would net him an $8000 gain. Thus the opportunity cost of giving the car to his father-in-law for $20,000 was going to be $8000! Not getting this big benefit was a big cost. In the end, it was one the student elected to bear because he valued keeping peace in the family even more. As the cost-benefit principle makes clear, the best decision is not always the one that leaves you with the most money in your pocket.

EXAMPLE 1.4 Should I work first or go to university first?

University costs are not limited to tuition fees, housing, food, books, supplies, and the like. They also include the opportunity cost of earnings forgone while studying. Earnings increase with experience. Thus the more experience you have, the more you must forgo to attend university. This opportunity cost is therefore lowest when you are right out of secondary school.

On the benefit side, one big gain of a university education is sharply higher earnings. The sooner you graduate, the longer you will reap this benefit. Another benefit is the pleasantness of going to university as opposed to working. In general, the kinds of jobs people hold tend to be less unpleasant (or more pleasant) the more education they have. By going to university right away, you thus avoid having to work at the least pleasant jobs. For most people, then, it makes sense to go to university first and work afterward. Certainly it makes more sense to attend university at age 20 than at age 50.

A common exception involves people who are too immature right out of secondary school to reap the benefits of university work, who often do better by working a year or two before university. ◆

The university example is a perfect illustration of Friedman's argument about how to evaluate a theory. School leavers do not decide when to attend university on the basis of sophisticated calculations involving opportunity costs. On the contrary, most start right out of secondary school simply because that is what most of their peers do. It is the thing to do.

But this begs the question of how it got to *be* the thing to do. Customs do not originate out of thin air. A host of different societies have had centuries to experiment with this decision. If there were a significantly better way of arranging the learning and working periods of life, some society should have long since discovered it. Our current custom has survived because it is efficient. People may not make explicit calculations about the opportunity cost of forgone earnings, but they often behave *as if* they do.[2]

As simple as the opportunity cost concept is, it is one of the most important in microeconomics. The art in applying the concept correctly lies in being able to recognize the most valuable alternative that is sacrificed by the pursuit of a given activity.

Pitfall 2. Failing to Ignore Sunk Costs

An opportunity cost may not seem to be a relevant cost when in reality it is. On the other hand, sometimes an expenditure may seem relevant when in reality it is not. Such is often the case with *sunk costs,* costs that are beyond recovery at the moment a decision is made. Unlike opportunity costs, these costs *should be* ignored. Not ignoring them is a second pitfall in decision making. The principle of ignoring sunk costs emerges clearly in the following example.

EXAMPLE 1.5 Should I drive to Berlin or take the train?

You are planning a 250-km trip to Berlin. Except for the cost, you are completely indifferent between driving and taking the train. Train fare is €100. You don't know how much it would cost to drive your car, so you call Hertz for an estimate. Hertz tells you that for your make of car the costs of a typical 10,000-km driving year are as follows:

Insurance	€1000
Interest	2000
Fuel and oil	1000
Maintenance	1000
Total	€5000

If a cost has already been incurred and cannot be recovered, it is irrelevant for all decisions about the future.

Suppose you calculate that these costs come to €0.50/km and use this figure to compute that the 250-km trip will cost you €125 by car. And since this is more than the €100 bus fare, you decide to take the train.

If you decide in this fashion, you fall victim to the sunk cost pitfall. Insurance and interest payments do not vary with the number of kilometres you drive each year. Both are sunk costs and will be the same whether or not you drive to Berlin. Of the costs listed, fuel and oil and maintenance are the only ones that vary with kilometres driven. These come to €2000 for each 10,000 kilometres you drive, or €0.20/km. At €0.20/km, it costs you only €50 to drive to Berlin, and since this is less than the train fare, you should drive. ◆

[2]This does not mean that all customs necessarily promote efficiency. For example, circumstances may have changed in such a way that a custom that promoted efficiency in the past no longer does so. In time, such a custom might change. Yet many habits and customs, once firmly entrenched, are very slow to change.

In Example 1.5, note the role of the assumption that, costs aside, you are indifferent between the two modes of transport. If you had preferred one mode to the other, we would also have had to weigh that preference. For example, if you were willing to pay €60 to avoid the hassle of driving, the real cost of driving would be €110, not €50, and you should take the train.

Exercises such as the one below are sprinkled throughout the text to help you make sure that you understand important analytical concepts. You will master microeconomics more effectively if you do these exercises as you go along.

EXERCISE 1.1 How, if at all, would your answer to the question in Example 1.5 be different if the worth of avoiding the hassle of driving is €20 and you average one €28 traffic fine for every 200 kilometres you drive?

As a check, the answers to the in-chapter exercises are at the end of each chapter. Naturally, the exercises will be much more useful if you work through them before consulting the answers.

EXAMPLE 1.6 The pizza experiment

A pizzeria near Cornell University offers an all-you-can-eat lunch for $5. You pay at the door, then the waiter brings you as many slices of pizza as you like. A former colleague performed this experiment: An assistant served as the waiter for one group of tables.[3] The 'waiter' selected half the tables at random and gave everyone at those tables a $5 refund before taking orders. Diners at the remaining tables got no refund. He then kept careful count of the number of slices of pizza each diner ate. What difference, if any, do you predict in the amounts eaten by these two groups?

Eating additional food just to get your money's worth is not a sensible decision strategy.

Diners in each group confront the question 'Should I eat another slice of pizza?' Here, the activity x consists of eating one more slice. For both groups, $C(x)$ is exactly zero: even members of the group that did not get a refund can get as many additional slices as they want at no extra charge. Because the refund group was chosen at random, there is no reason to suppose that its members like pizza any more or less than the others. For everyone, the decision rule says keep eating until there is no longer any extra pleasure in eating another slice. Thus, $B(x)$ should be the same for each group, and people from both groups should keep eating until $B(x)$ falls to zero.

By this reasoning, the two groups should eat the same amount of pizza, on average. The $5 admission fee is a sunk cost and should have no influence on the amount of pizza one eats. *In fact, however, the group that did not get the refund consumed substantially more pizza.* ◆

Although our cost-benefit decision rule fails the test of prediction in this experiment, its message for the rational decision maker stands unchallenged. The two groups logically *should* have behaved the same. The only difference between them, after all, is that patrons in the refund group have lifetime incomes that are $5 higher than the others'. Such a trivial difference should have no effect on pizza consumption. Members of the no-refund group seemed to want to make sure they 'got their money's worth'. In all likelihood, however, this motive merely led them to overeat.[4]

[3]See Richard Thaler, 'Toward a Positive Theory of Consumer Choice', *Journal of Economic Behavior and Organization* 1, 1980.

[4]An alternative to the 'get-your-money's-worth' explanation is that $5 is a significant fraction of the amount of cash many diners have available to spend *in the short run*. Thus members of the refund group might have held back in order to save room for the dessert they could now afford to buy. To test this alternative explanation, the experimenter could give members of the no-refund group a $5 cash gift earlier in the day and then see if the amount of pizza consumed by the two groups still differed.

What is wrong with being motivated to 'get your money's worth'? Absolutely nothing, as long as the force of this motive operates *before* you enter into transactions. Thus it makes perfectly good sense to be led by this motive to choose one restaurant over an otherwise identical competitor that happens to cost more. Once the price of your lunch has been determined, however, the get-your-money's-worth motive should be abandoned. The satisfaction you get from eating another slice of pizza should then depend only on how hungry you are and on how much you like pizza, not on how much you paid. Yet people often seem not to behave in this fashion. The difficulty may be that we are not creatures of complete flexibility. Perhaps motives that make sense in one context are not easily abandoned in another.

EXERCISE 1.2 Jim wins a ticket from a radio station to see a jazz band perform at an outdoor concert. Mike has paid €18 for a ticket to the same concert. On the evening of the concert there is a tremendous thunderstorm. If Jim and Mike have the same tastes, which of them will be more likely to attend the concert, assuming that each decides on the basis of a standard cost-benefit comparison?

Pitfall 3. Measuring Costs and Benefits as Proportions Rather Than Absolute Monetary Amounts

When a boy asks his mother 'Are we almost there yet?' how will she answer if they are ten kilometres from their destination? Without some knowledge of the context of their journey, we cannot say. If they are near the end of a 300-km journey, her answer will almost surely be yes. But if they have just embarked on a 12-km journey, she will say no.

Contextual clues are important for a variety of ordinary judgements. Thinking about distance as a percentage of the total amount to be travelled is natural and informative. Many also find it natural to think in percentage terms when comparing costs and benefits. But as the following pair of simple examples illustrates, this tendency often causes trouble.

EXAMPLE 1.7*a* Should you drive to the superstore to save €10 on a €20 clock radio?

You are about to buy a clock radio at the nearby campus store for €20 when a friend tells you that the very same radio is on sale at the local superstore for only €10. If the superstore is a 15-minute drive away, where would you buy the radio? (If it fails under warranty, you must send it to the manufacturer for repairs, no matter where you bought it.)

EXAMPLE 1.7*b* Should you drive to the superstore to save €10 on a €1000 television set?

You are about to buy a new television set at the nearby campus store for €1010 when a friend tells you that the very same set is on sale at the local superstore for only €1000. If the superstore is a 15-minute drive away, where would you buy the television? (Again, repairs under warranty would entail sending the set to the manufacturer in each case.)

There is no uniquely correct answer to either of these questions, both of which ask whether the benefit of driving to the supermarket is worth the cost. Most people say the trip would definitely be worth making for the clock radio, but definitely not worth making for the television. When pressed to explain, they say driving yields a 50 per cent saving on the radio but less than a 1 per cent saving on the television.

When comparing costs and benefits, always use absolute monetary amounts, not proportions.

These percentages, however, are irrelevant. In each case the benefit of driving to the superstore is exactly the €10 saving from the lower purchase price. What is the cost of driving to the superstore? Some might be willing to make the drive for as little as €5, while others might not be willing to do it for less than €50. But whatever the number, it should be the same in both cases. So your answers to the questions just posed should be the same. If you would be willing to make the drive for, say, €8, then you should buy both the clock radio and the television at the superstore. But if your reservation price for making the drive is, say, €12, then you should buy both appliances at the nearby campus store. ◆

When using the cost-benefit test, you should express costs and benefits in absolute euro terms. Comparing percentages is not a fruitful way to think about decisions like these.

EXERCISE 1.3 You are holding a discount coupon that will entitle you to a fare reduction on only one of the two trips you are scheduled to take during the coming month. You can get €100 off the normal €200 airfare to Barcelona, or you can get €120 off the normal €2400 airfare to New Delhi. On which trip should you use your coupon?

Pitfall 4. Failure to Understand the Average-Marginal Distinction

So far we have looked at decisions about whether to perform a given action. Often, however, the choice is not whether to perform the action but the extent to which it should be performed. In this more complex case, we can apply the cost-benefit principle by reformulating the question. Instead of asking 'Should I do activity x?', we repeatedly pose the question 'Should I increase the level by which I am currently engaging in activity x?'

To answer this question, we must compare the benefit and cost of an *additional* unit of activity. The cost of an additional unit of activity is called the **marginal cost** of the activity, and the benefit of an additional unit is called its **marginal benefit**.

marginal cost the increase in total cost that results from carrying out one additional unit of an activity.

marginal benefit the increase in total benefit that results from carrying out one additional unit of an activity.

The cost-benefit rule tells us to keep increasing the level of an activity as long as its marginal benefit exceeds its marginal cost. But as the following example illustrates, people often fail to apply this rule correctly.

EXAMPLE 1.8 Should Tom launch another boat?

Tom manages a small fishing fleet of three boats. His current daily cost of operations, including boat rentals and fishermen's wages, is €300, or an average of €100 per boat launched. His daily total revenue, or benefit, from the sale of fish is currently €600, or an average of €200 per boat launched. Tom decides that since his cost per boat is less than his revenue per boat, he should launch another boat. Is this a sound decision?

To answer this question, we must compare the marginal cost of launching a boat with its marginal benefit. The information given, however, tells us only the **average cost** and **average benefit** of launching a boat—which are, respectively, one-third of the total cost of three boats and one-third of the total revenue from three boats. Knowing the average benefit and average cost per boat launched does not enable us to decide whether launching another boat makes economic sense. For although the average benefit of the three boats launched thus far *might*

average cost the average cost of undertaking n units of an activity is the total cost of the activity divided by n.

average benefit the average benefit of undertaking n units of an activity is the total benefit of the activity divided by n.

be the same as the marginal benefit of launching another boat, it might also be either higher or lower. The same statement holds true regarding average and marginal costs.

To illustrate, suppose the marginal cost of launching a boat and crew is constant at €100 per boat per day. Then Tom should launch a fourth boat only if doing so will add at least €100 in daily revenue from his total fish catch. The mere fact that the current average revenue is €200 per boat simply doesn't tell us what the marginal benefit of launching the fourth boat will be.

Suppose, for example, that the relationship between the number of boats launched and the daily total revenue is as described in Table 1.1. With three boats per day, the average benefit per boat would then be €200, just as indicated above. If Tom launched a fourth boat, the *average* daily revenue would fall to €160 per boat, which is still more than the assumed marginal cost of €100. Note, however, that in the second column the total revenue from four boats is only €40 per day more than the total revenue from three boats. That means that the marginal revenue from launching the fourth boat is only €40. And since that is less than its marginal cost (€100), launching the fourth boat makes no sense. ◆

TABLE 1.1
How Total Cost Varies with the Number of Boats Launched

Number of boats	Daily total benefit (€)	Daily average benefit (€/boat)
0	0	0
1	300	300
2	480	240
3	600	200
4	640	160

The following example illustrates how to apply the cost-benefit principle correctly in this case.

EXAMPLE 1.9 How many boats should Tom launch?

The marginal cost of launching a boat and crew is again constant at €100 per day. If total daily revenue from the catch again varies with the number of boats launched as shown in Table 1.1, how many boats should Tom launch?

Tom should keep launching boats as long as the marginal benefit of doing so is at least as great as the marginal cost. With marginal cost constant at €100 per launch, Tom should thus keep launching boats as long as the marginal benefit is at least €100.

Applying the definition of marginal benefit to the total benefit entries in the second column of Table 1.1 yields the marginal benefit values in the third column of Table 1.2. (Because marginal benefit is the change in total benefit that results when we change the number of boats by one, we place each marginal benefit entry midway between the rows showing the corresponding total benefit entries.) For example, the marginal benefit of increasing the number of boats from one to two is €180, the difference between the €480 total revenue with two boats and the €300 with one.

TABLE 1.2
How Marginal Benefit Varies with the Number of Boats Launched

Number of boats	Daily total benefit (€)	Daily marginal benefit (€/boat)
0	0	
		300
1	300	
		180
2	480	
		120
3	600	
		40
4	640	

Comparing the €100 marginal cost per boat with the marginal benefit entries in the third column of Table 1.2, we see that the first three launches satisfy the cost-benefit test, but the fourth does not. Tom should thus launch three boats. ◆

EXERCISE 1.4 **If the marginal cost of launching each boat had not been €100 but €150, how many boats should Tom have launched?**

The cost-benefit principle tells us that *marginal* costs and benefits—measures that correspond to the *increment* of an activity under consideration—are the relevant ones for choosing the level at which to pursue the activity. Yet many people compare the *average* cost and benefit of the activity when making such decisions. As Example 1.8 should have made clear, however, increasing the level of an activity may not be justified, even though its average benefit at the current level is significantly greater than its average cost.

USING MARGINAL BENEFIT AND MARGINAL COST GRAPHICALLY

The examples just discussed entail decisions about an activity that could take place only on specific levels—no boats, one boat, two boats, and so on. The levels of many other activities, however, can vary continuously. One can buy petrol, for example, in any quantity one wishes. For activities that are continuously variable, it is often convenient to display the comparison of marginal benefit and marginal cost graphically.

EXAMPLE 1.10 **How much should Susan talk to Hal each month?**

Susan has a telephone plan for which the charge is 4 cents per minute for a long-distance call to her boyfriend Hal. (Fractional minutes are billed at the same rate, so a 30-second call would cost her 2 cents.) The value to Susan, measured in terms of her willingness to pay, of an additional minute of conversation with Hal is shown on curve *MB* in Figure 1.1. How many minutes should she spend on the phone with Hal each month?

The downward slope of curve *MB* reflects the fact that the value of an additional minute declines with the total amount of conversation that has occurred thus far.

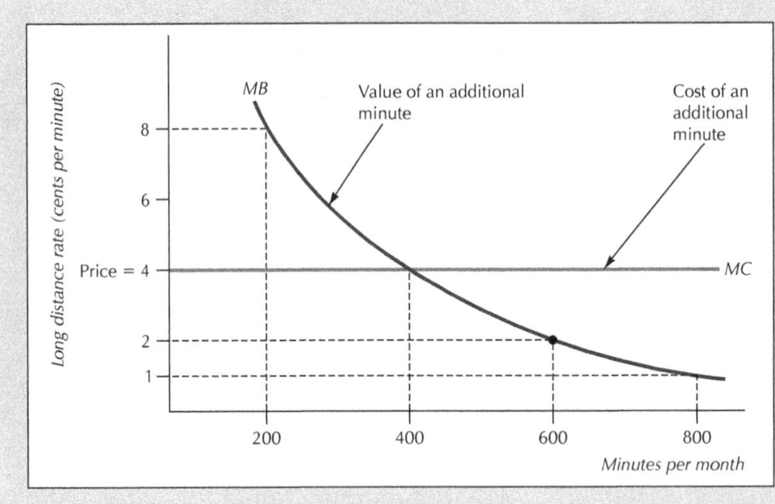

FIGURE 1.1
The Optimal Quantity of Conversation
The optimal amount of a continuously variable activity is the quantity for which its marginal benefit is just equal to its marginal cost.

(As we will see in Chapter 3, it is a common pattern that the more someone has of a good, the less value he assigns to having additional units of it.) Curve *MC* in the diagram measures the cost of each additional minute, assumed to be constant at €0.04. The optimal quantity of conversation is the quantity for which these two curves cross—namely, 400 minutes per month. If Susan speaks with Hal for less than that amount, the marginal benefit from adding another minute would exceed the marginal cost, so she should talk longer. But if they speak for more than 400 minutes per month, the amount she would save by speaking less would exceed the benefit she would sacrifice, which means they should speak less. ◆

EXERCISE 1.5 If her marginal benefit curve is again as given in Figure 1.1, how many minutes should Susan speak with Hal each month if the long-distance rate falls to 2 cents per minute?

THE INVISIBLE HAND

One of the most important insights of economic analysis is that the individual pursuit of self-interest is often not only *consistent* with broader social objectives, but actually even *required* by them. Wholly unaware of the effects of their actions, self-interested consumers often act as if driven by what Adam Smith called an *invisible hand* to produce the greatest social good. In perhaps the most widely quoted passage from *The Wealth of Nations,* Smith wrote:

> It is not from the benevolence of the butcher, the brewer, or the baker that we expect our dinner, but from their regard of their own interest. We address ourselves not to their humanity, but to their self-love, and never talk to them of our necessities, but of their advantage.

Smith observed that competition among sellers fostered attempts to develop better products and cheaper ways of producing them. The first to succeed in those attempts enjoyed higher profits than their rivals, but only temporarily. As others copied the new products and methods, their offerings put inevitable downward pressure on prices. Smith's insight, in a nutshell, was that although sellers were seeking only to promote their own advantage, the ultimate beneficiaries were consumers.

Adam Smith: 1723–1790. Smith's modern disciples often oversimplify his message.

Modern economists sometimes lose sight of the fact that Smith did not believe that *only* selfish motives are important. In his earlier treatise, *The Theory of Moral Sentiments,* for example, he wrote movingly about the compassion we feel for others:

> How selfish soever man may be supposed, there are evidently some principles in his nature, which interest him in the fortune of others, and render their happiness necessary to him, though he derives nothing from it, except the pleasure of seeing it. Of this kind is pity or compassion, the emotion which we feel for the misery of others, when we either see it, or are made to conceive it in a very lively manner. That we often derive sorrow from the sorrow of others, is a matter of fact too obvious to require any instances to prove it; for this sentiment, like all the other original passions of human nature, is by no means confined to the virtuous and humane, though they perhaps may feel it with the most exquisite sensibility. The greatest ruffian, the most hardened violator of the laws of society, is not altogether without it.

Smith was well aware, moreover, that the outcome of unbridled pursuit of self-interest is sometimes far from socially benign. As the following example illustrates, the invisible hand mechanism breaks down when important costs or benefits accrue to people other than the decision makers themselves.

EXAMPLE 1.11 Should I burn my leaves or haul them into the woods?

Suppose the cost of hauling the leaves is €20 and the cost to the homeowner of burning them is only €1. If the homeowner cares only about costs that accrue directly to herself, she will burn her leaves. The difficulty is that burning leaves entails an important **external cost,** which means a cost borne by people who are not directly involved in the decision. This external cost is the damage done by the smoke from the fire. That cost accrues not to the homeowner who makes the decision about burning the leaves but to the people downwind. Suppose the smoke damage amounts to €25. The good of the community then requires that the leaves be hauled, not burned. From the perspective of the self-interested homeowner, however, it seems best to burn them.[5] ◆

external cost of an activity a cost that falls on people who are not directly involved in the activity.

External costs and benefits often motivate laws that limit individual discretion. (External costs and benefits will be our focus in Chapter 16.) Most communities, for example, now have laws prohibiting the burning of leaves within city limits. Such laws may be viewed as a way of making the costs and benefits seen by individuals more nearly resemble those experienced by the community as a whole. With a law against burning leaves in effect, the potential leaf burner weighs the penalty of breaking the law against the cost of hauling the leaves. Most people conclude it is cheaper to haul them.

[5] Of course, if the homeowner interacts frequently with the people downwind, self-interest may still dictate hauling the leaves, to preserve goodwill for future interactions. But where the people downwind are anonymous strangers, this motive will operate with less force.

WOULD PARENTS WANT THEIR DAUGHTER OR SON TO MARRY *HOMO ECONOMICUS*?

Many economists and other behavioural scientists remain sceptical about the importance of duty and other unselfish motives. They feel that the larger material payoffs associated with selfish behaviour so strongly dominate other motives that, as a first approximation, we may safely ignore non-egoistic motives.

With this view in mind, the stereotypical decision maker in the self-interest model is often given the label *Homo economicus,* or 'economic man'. *Homo economicus* does not experience the sorts of sentiments that motivate people to vote, or to return lost wallets to their owners with the cash intact. On the contrary, personal material costs and benefits are the only things he cares about. He does not contribute voluntarily to private charities, keeps promises only when it pays to do so, and if the pollution laws are not carefully enforced, disconnects the catalytic converter on his car to save on fuel. And so on.

Self-interest is one of the most important human motives. But it is not the only important motive.

Obviously, many people do not fit the me-first caricature of the self-interest model. They donate bone marrow to strangers with leukaemia. They endure great trouble and expense to see justice done, even when it will not undo the original injury. At great risk to themselves, they pull people from burning buildings and jump into icy rivers to rescue people who are about to drown. Soldiers throw their bodies atop live grenades to save their comrades.

To be sure, selfish motives are important. When a detective investigates a murder, for example, her first question is, 'Who stood to benefit from the victim's death?' When an economist studies a government regulation, he wants to know whose incomes it enhances. When a politician proposes a new spending project, the political scientist tries to discover which of his constituents will be its primary beneficiaries.

Our goal in much of this text is to understand the kinds of behaviours to which selfish motives give rise in specific situations. But throughout this process, it is critical to remember that the self-interest model is not intended as a prescription for how to conduct your own affairs. On the contrary, we will see in later chapters that *Homo economicus* is woefully ill suited to the demands of social existence as we know it. Each of us probably knows people who more or less fit the *Homo economicus* caricature. And our first priority, most of the time, is to steer clear of them.

The irony here is that being a purely self-interested person entails a degree of social isolation that is not only bad for the soul but also harmful to the pocketbook. To succeed in life, even in purely material terms, people must form alliances and relationships of trust. But what sensible person would be willing to trust *Homo economicus*? Later chapters present specific examples of how unselfish motives confer material rewards on those who hold them. For the present, however, bear in mind that the self-interest model is intended only to capture one part of human behaviour, albeit an important one.

THE ECONOMIC NATURALIST

Studying biology enables people to observe and marvel at many details of life that would otherwise escape them. For the naturalist, a walk in a quiet wood becomes an adventure. In much the same way, studying microeconomics enables someone to become an 'economic naturalist', a person who sees the mundane details of ordinary existence in a sharp new light. Each feature of the manmade landscape is no longer an amorphous mass but the result of an implicit cost-benefit calculation. Following are some examples of economic naturalism.

Why is airline food so bad?

ECONOMIC NATURALIST 1.1

Everyone complains about airline food. Indeed, if any serious restaurant dared to serve such food, it would quickly go bankrupt. Our complaints seem to take for granted that airline meals should be just as good as the ones we eat in restaurants. But why should they? The cost-benefit perspective says that airlines should increase the quality of their meals if and only if the benefit would outweigh the cost. The benefit of better food is probably well measured by what passengers would be willing to pay for it, in the form of higher ticket prices. If a restaurant-quality meal could be had for, say, a mere €10 increase in fares, most people would probably be delighted to pay it. The difficulty, however, is that it would be much more costly than that to prepare significantly better meals at 39,000 feet in a tiny galley with virtually no time. It could be done, of course. An airline could remove 20 seats from the plane, install a modern, well-equipped kitchen, hire extra staff, spend more on ingredients, and so on. But these extra costs would be more like €100 per passenger than €10. For all our complaints about the low quality of airline food, few of us would be willing to bear this extra burden. The sad result is that airline food is destined to remain unpalatable. ■

The time and effort required to become a championship tennis player rule out the possibility of simultaneously becoming a leading concert pianist.

Many of us respond warmly to the maxim 'Anything worth doing is worth doing well'. After all, it encourages a certain pride of workmanship that is often sadly lacking. Economic Naturalist 1.1 makes clear, however, that if the maxim is interpreted literally, it does not make any sense. To do something well requires time, effort and expense. But these are scarce resources. To devote them to one activity makes them unavailable for another. Increasing the quality of one of the things we do thus necessarily means to reduce the quality of others—yet another application of the concept of opportunity cost. Every intelligent decision must be mindful of this trade-off.

Everything we see in life is the result of some such compromise. For Rafael Nadal, playing championship tennis rules out becoming a concert pianist. Yet this obviously does not mean he should not spend any time playing the piano. It just means that he should hold himself to a lower standard there than in the tennis arena.

Why do manual transmissions have five forward speeds, automatics only four?

ECONOMIC NATURALIST 1.2

The more forward speeds a car's transmission has, the better its fuel economy will be. The additional gears act like the 'overdrive' of cars of the 1940s, conserving fuel by allowing cars to cruise at motorway speeds at lower engine speeds. Historically, most cars offer five forward speeds on their manual transmissions, only three or four on their automatics. Since fuel economy is obviously a good thing, why limit the number of speeds on automatics?

The reason is that fuel economy is not our only objective. We also want to keep the price of the car within limits. Automatic transmissions are more complex than manual ones, and the cost of adding an extra speed is accordingly much greater in automatics. The benefits of adding an extra speed, by contrast, are the same in both cases. If carmakers follow the rule 'Add an extra speed if its benefit outweighs its cost', then we can understand why automatics have historically had fewer speeds than manuals.

In recent years automatic transmissions with five or six speeds have become more common. This suggests that technology has advanced to the point where the cost of adding an extra speed is less than the benefit of doing so. ■

The reasoning in Economic Naturalist 1.2 also helps make clear why many manual transmissions now have five forward speeds when 50 years ago most had only three (and many automatic transmissions only two). The benefit of adding an extra speed, again, is that it increases fuel economy. The value of this benefit, in monetary terms, thus depends directly on the price of fuel. The price of petrol relative to other goods is much higher than it was 50 years ago, which helps explain why transmissions have more speeds than they used to.

POSITIVE QUESTIONS AND NORMATIVE QUESTIONS

To understand the objectives and role of microeconomics it is important to understand the distinction between positive and normative questions. An example helps illustrate this distinction.

Commercial fishing is a traditional way of life for much of coastal Europe. That way of life has, however, come under increasing threat due to overfishing and the depletion of fish stocks. Numerous ways have been tried to solve the problem including the EU's Common Fisheries Policy. The main component of this policy is the annual setting of Total Allowable Catches (TACs) that put a quota on how much a fisherman can catch. For example, Danish and UK fishermen were restricted to catching 32,500 tonnes and 23,700 tonnes of cod in 2012, respectively. To cut a long story short, the Common Fisheries Policy does not seem to work well.[6] Is there a better solution?

Overfishing is caused by an excess demand for fish and over-employment in the fishing industry. The problem is, therefore, as much an economic as ecological problem. Finding a viable solution requires asking two very different types of questions—positive and normative.

A **positive question** is one that has a definitive answer. Questions about the consequences of specific policies or institutional arrangements are positive questions. If we decrease the size of TACs what will happen to the price of fish? How will employment in fishing towns and villages be affected? If the price of fish increases, by how much will demand for fish decrease? These are all positive economic questions. Economic analysis is primarily about answering such questions, with a mix of theoretical and empirical analysis. This book will give you some of the tools you need to answer positive economic questions.

positive question a question about the consequences of specific policies or institutional arrangements.

normative question a question about what policies or institutional arrangements lead to the best outcomes.

A **normative question** is one that does not have a definitive answer. It is a question that involves value judgements about what *ought* to be or *should* be. Is it important to preserve fish stocks for future generations? Is it important to preserve the fishing industry because of its value to society and historical importance? Is it more important to preserve the fishing industry than to spend money on better health care? These are all normative questions. By itself, economic analysis cannot answer such questions. It is for society to decide, and two different societies that hold different values may come to different conclusions, even though members of both societies are in complete agreement about all the relevant economic facts and theories.

[6]See S. Villasante et al., 'Sustainability of Deep-sea Fish Species under the European Union Common Fisheries Policy', *Ocean and Coastal Management*, 2012.

There is an important connection between positive and normative questions. Positive economic questions, and the answers to them, are clearly relevant to our thinking about the underlying normative question. They put us in a more informed position to say what ought or should be. Knowing, for instance, how employment will be affected if TACs are reduced allows us to better judge the benefits of preserving the fishing industry. Conversely, it is the normative questions of most interest to society that prompt the positive questions that economists need to answer. The problem of overfishing has prompted a lot of analysis on the consequences of TACs.

MICROECONOMICS AND MACROECONOMICS

Our focus in this chapter is on issues confronting the individual decision maker. As we proceed, we will also consider economic models of groups of individuals—for example, the group of all buyers or all sellers in a market. The study of individual choices and the study of group behaviour in individual markets both come under the rubric of microeconomics. Macroeconomics, by contrast, is the study of broader aggregations of markets. For example, it tries to explain the national unemployment rate, the overall price level, and the total value of national output.

Economists are much better at predicting and explaining what happens in individual markets than in the economy as a whole. When prominent economists disagree in the press or on television, the issue is more likely to be from macroeconomics than from microeconomics. But even though economists still have trouble with macroeconomic questions, macroeconomic analysis is undeniably important. After all, recessions and inflation disrupt millions of lives.

Economists increasingly believe that the key to progress in macroeconomics lies in more careful analysis of the individual markets that make up broader aggregates. As a result, the distinction between micro and macro has become less clear in recent years. The graduate training of all economists, micro and macro alike, is increasingly focused on microeconomic analysis.

SUMMARY

- Microeconomics entails the study of choice under scarcity. Scarcity is ever present, even when material resources are abundant. There are always important limitations on time, energy, and the other things we need to pursue our goals.
- Much of the economist's task is to try to answer questions of the form 'Should I do activity *x*?' The approach to answering them is disarmingly simple. It is to do *x* if and only if its costs are smaller than its benefits. Not incurring a cost is the same as getting a benefit.
- The cost-benefit model sometimes fails to predict how people behave when confronted with everyday choices. The art of cost-benefit analysis lies in being able to specify and measure the relevant costs and benefits, a skill many decision makers lack. Some costs, such as sunk costs, often seem relevant but turn out not to be. Others, such as implicit costs, are sometimes ignored, even though they are important. Benefits, too, are often difficult to measure. Experience has taught that becoming aware of the most common pitfalls helps most people become better decision makers.
- When the question is not whether to perform an activity but rather at what level to perform it, marginal analysis draws our attention to the importance of marginal benefits and marginal costs. We should increase the level of an activity whenever its marginal benefit exceeds its marginal cost.
- The principles of rational choice are by no means limited to formal markets for goods and services. Indeed, some form of implicit or explicit cost-benefit calculation lies behind almost every human action, object and behaviour. Knowledge of the underlying principles casts our world in a sharp new light, not always flattering, but ever a source of stimulating insight.

QUESTIONS FOR REVIEW

1. What is your opportunity cost of reading a novel this evening?
2. Your roommate is thinking of dropping out of university this semester. If his tuition payment for this semester is non-refundable, should he take it into account when making his decision?
3. Give three examples of activities accompanied by external costs or benefits.
4. Why is the opportunity cost of attending university higher for a 50-year-old than for a 20-year-old?
5. Why should sunk costs be irrelevant for current decisions?
6. How can the cost-benefit model be useful for studying the behaviour of people who do not think explicitly in terms of costs and benefits?

PROBLEMS

1. Jamal has a flexible summer job. He can work every day but is allowed to take a day off anytime he wants. His friend Don suggests they go to the amusement park on Tuesday. The admission charge for the park is €15 per person, and it will cost them €5 each for petrol and parking. Jamal loves amusement parks and a day at the park is worth €45 to him. However, Jamal also enjoys his job so much that he would actually be willing to pay €10 per day to do it.

   a. If Jamal earns €10 if he works, should he go to the amusement park?
   b. If Jamal earns €15 . . . ?
   c. If Jamal earns €20 . . . ?

2. Tom is a mushroom farmer. He invests all his spare cash in additional mushrooms, which grow on otherwise useless land behind his barn. The mushrooms double in size during their first year, after which time they are harvested and sold at a constant price per kilogram. Tom's friend Dick asks Tom for a loan of €200, which he promises to repay after 1 year. How much interest will Dick have to pay Tom in order for Tom to be no worse off than if he had not made the loan?

3. The meal plan at University A lets students eat as much as they like for a fixed fee of €500 per semester. The average student there eats 250 kg of food per semester. University B charges students €500 for a book of meal tickets that entitles the student to eat 250 kg of food per semester. If the student eats more than 250 kg, he or she pays extra; if the student eats less, he or she gets a refund. If students are rational, at which university will average food consumption be higher?

4. You are planning a 1000-km trip to Lisbon. Except for cost, you are indifferent between driving and taking the train. Train fare is €260. The costs of operating your car during a typical 10,000-km driving year are as follows:

Insurance	€1000
Interest	2000
Fuel and oil	1200
Tyres	200
Licence and registration	50
Maintenance	1100
Total	€5550

   Should you drive or take the train?

5. Al and Jane have rented a banquet hall to celebrate their wedding anniversary. Fifty people have already accepted their invitation. The caterers will charge €5 per person for food and €2 per person for drinks. The band will cost €300 for the evening, and the hall costs €200. Now Al and Jane are considering inviting 10 more people. By how much will these extra guests increase the cost of their party?

6. You loan a friend €1000, and at the end of 1 year she writes you a cheque for €1000 to pay off this loan. If the annual interest rate on your savings account is 6 per cent, what was your opportunity cost of making this loan?

7. Bill and Joe live in Dover, England. At 2 p.m. Bill goes to the local Ticketmaster and buys a £30 ticket to a football game to be played that night in London (80 kilometres west). Joe plans to attend the same game, but doesn't purchase his ticket in advance because he knows from experience that it is always possible to buy just as good a seat at the stadium. At 4 p.m. a heavy, unexpected snowstorm begins, making the prospect of the drive to London much less attractive than before. If both Bill and Joe have the same tastes and are rational, is one of them more likely to attend the game than the other? If so, say who and explain why. If not, explain why not.

8. Two types of radar weather-detection devices are available for commercial passenger aircraft: the 'state-of-the-art' machine and another that is significantly less costly, but also less effective. The European Aviation Safety Agency (EASA) has hired you for advice on whether all passenger planes should be required to use the state-of-the-art machine. After careful study, your recommendation is to require the more expensive machine only in passenger aircraft with more than 200 seats. How would you justify such a recommendation to an EASA member who complains that all passengers have a right to the best weather-detecting radar currently available?

9. A group has chartered a bus to Paris. The driver costs €100, the bus costs €500, and tolls will cost €75. The driver's fee is non-refundable, but the bus may be cancelled a week in advance at a charge of only €50. At €18 per ticket, how many people must buy tickets so that the trip need not be cancelled?

10. Residents of your city are charged a fixed weekly fee of €6 for refuse collection. They may put out as many refuse sacks as they wish. The average household puts out three sacks per week.

    Now, suppose your city changes to a 'tag' system. Each sack of refuse must have a tag affixed to it. The tags cost €2 each.

    What effect will the introduction of the tag system have on the total quantity of refuse collected?

11. Suppose that random access memory (RAM) can be added to your computer at a cost of €100 per gigabyte. Suppose also that the value to you, measured in terms of your willingness to pay, of an additional gigabyte of memory is €800 for the first gigabyte, and then falls by one-half for each additional gigabyte. Draw a graph of marginal cost and marginal benefit. How many gigabytes of memory should you purchase?

12. Suppose in Problem 11 the cost of RAM falls to €50 per gigabyte. How many gigabytes of memory should you purchase now? Suppose additionally that your benefit for an additional gigabyte of memory rises to €1600 for the first gigabyte, also falling by one-half for each additional gigabyte. How many gigabytes of memory should you purchase now, with both the lower price and the larger benefit?

*13. Dana has purchased a €40 ticket to a rock concert. On the day of the concert she is invited to a welcome-home party for a friend returning from abroad. She cannot attend both the concert and the party. If she had known about the party before buying the ticket, she would

*Problems marked with an asterisk (*) are more difficult.

have chosen the party over the concert. *True or false*: It follows that if she is rational, she will go to the party anyway. Explain.

*14. Yesterday you were unexpectedly given a free ticket to a Muse concert scheduled for April 1. The market price of this ticket is €75, but the most you could sell it for is only €50. Today you discover that Lady Gaga will be giving a concert that same evening. Tickets for the Lady Gaga concert are still available at €75. Had you known before receiving your Muse ticket yesterday that Lady Gaga would be coming, you definitely would have bought a ticket to see her, not Muse. *True or false*: From what we are told of your preferences, it follows that if you are rational, you should attend the Lady Gaga concert. Explain.

*15. Mr Smith recently faced a choice between being (*a*) an economics professor, which pays €60,000/yr, or (*b*) a safari leader, which pays €50,000/yr. After careful deliberation, Smith took the safari job, but it was a close call. 'For a euro more,' he said, 'I'd have gone the other way.'

Now Smith's brother-in-law approaches him with a business proposition. The terms are as follows:

- Smith must resign his safari job to work full-time in his brother-in-law's business.
- Smith must give his brother-in-law an interest-free loan of €100,000, which will be repaid in full if and when Smith leaves the business. (Smith currently has much more than €100,000 in the bank.)
- The business will pay Smith a salary of €70,000/yr. He will receive no other payment from the business.

The interest rate is 10 per cent per year. Apart from salary considerations, Smith feels that working in the business would be just as enjoyable as being an economics professor. For simplicity, assume there is no uncertainty regarding either Smith's salary in the proposed business or the security of his monetary investment in it. Should Smith join his brother-in-law and, if so, how small would Smith's salary from the business have to be to make it NOT worthwhile for him to join? If not, how large would Smith's salary from the business have to be to make it worthwhile for him to join?

*16. You have just purchased a new Ford Mondeo for €20,000, but the most you could get for it if you sold it privately is €15,000. Now you learn that Toyota is offering its Yaris, which normally sells for €25,000, at a special sale price of €20,000. If you had known before buying the Mondeo that you could buy a Yaris at the same price, you would have definitely chosen the Yaris. *True or false*: From what we are told of your preferences, it follows that if you are rational, you should definitely not sell the Mondeo and buy the Yaris. Explain.

ANSWERS TO IN-CHAPTER EXERCISES

1.1. Someone who gets a €28 traffic ticket every 200 kilometres driven will pay €35 in fines, on average, for every 250 kilometres driven. Adding that figure to the €20 hassle cost of driving, and then adding the €50 fuel, oil and maintenance cost, we have €105. This is more than the €100 bus fare, which means taking the bus is best.

1.2. The €18 Mike paid for his ticket is a sunk cost at the moment he must decide whether to attend the concert. For both Jim and Mike, therefore, the costs and benefits should be the same. If the benefit of seeing the concert outweighs the cost of sitting in the rain, they should go. Otherwise they should stay home.

*Problems marked with an asterisk (*) are more difficult.

1.3. You should use your coupon for the New Delhi trip, because it is more valuable to save €120 than to save €100.

1.4. Two boats. Referring to Table 1.2, note that if marginal cost is €150, it now pays to launch the second boat (marginal benefit = €180) but not the third.

1.5. At 2 cents per minute, Susan should talk for 600 minutes per month.

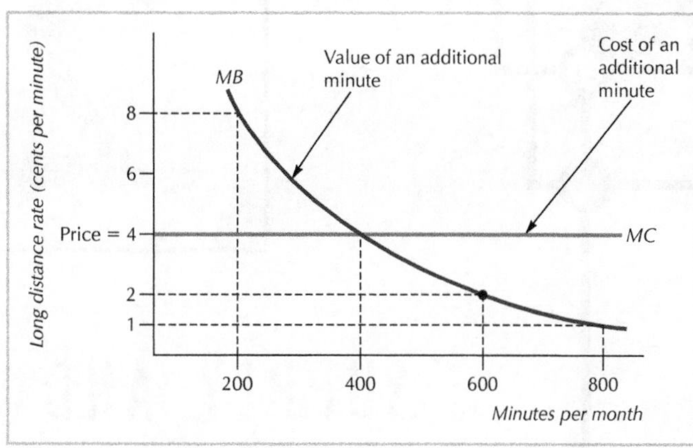

CHAPTER 2

SUPPLY AND DEMAND

In 1979 one of us (Robert) was working for the US government and living in Washington, DC. Outside the apartment window stood a petrol station. With 16 pumps, it was larger than most, but otherwise typical of the modern urban self-serve station.

In April of that year, a major oil supply interruption occurred in the US Mideast, which sent petrol prices skyrocketing. To keep prices from rising further, the Carter administration implemented a complex system of fuel allocations and price controls. One result was that many urban markets got substantially less petrol than motorists wanted to buy at the regulated prices. At the station outside the apartment window, a line of cars regularly stretched for several blocks.

Quarrels over position in such queues were common, and many motorists got into fistfights and shouting matches. One was shot and killed for butting into line. Tensions continued until the petrol lines dwindled with the passing of the summer travel months.

The government's system of price controls and allocations tried to accomplish a task we usually relegate to markets. The Washington experience was typical of similar interventions in other times and places. These programmes typically produce confusion and conflict. Of course, the unfettered market can itself produce outcomes we don't like. But rarely does it fail to allocate available supplies in a smooth, efficient manner.

CHAPTER PREVIEW

In this chapter we will explore why markets function so smoothly most of the time and why attempts at direct allocation are so often problematic. The early part of the chapter will look at basic supply and demand analysis. First, we will review the usual descriptive features of supply and demand analysis covered in the introductory course. Next, we will see that, for given attributes of buyers and sellers, the unregulated competitive market yields the best attainable outcome, in the sense that any other combination of price and quantity would be worse for at least some buyers or sellers.

Despite this attractive feature, market outcomes often do not command society's approval. Concern for the well-being of the poor has motivated the governments of every Western society to intervene in a variety of ways—for instance, by adopting laws that peg prices above or below their equilibrium levels. Such laws, we will see, almost always generate harmful, if unintended, consequences.

A generally more efficient solution to the problems of the poor is to boost their incomes directly. The law of supply and demand cannot be repealed by the legislature. But legislatures can alter the underlying forces that govern the shape and position of supply and demand schedules.

Finally, we will explore supply and demand analysis as a useful device for understanding how taxes affect equilibrium prices and quantities. In particular, it helps dispel the myth that a tax is paid primarily by the party on whom it is directly levied; rather, the burden of a tax falls most heavily on whichever side of the market is least able to avoid it.

SUPPLY AND DEMAND CURVES

Our basic tool for analysing market outcomes is supply and demand analysis, already familiar to most of you from your introductory course. Let us begin with the following working definition of a market.

> **Definition:** A market consists of the buyers and sellers of a good or service.

Some markets are confined to a single specific time and location. For example, all the participating buyers and sellers (or at least their designated representatives) gather together in the same place for an antiques auction. Other markets span vast geographic territory, and most participants in them never meet or even see one another. The London Stock Exchange is such a market. The Internet provides access to markets of this type for many goods.

Sometimes the choice of market definition will depend on the bias of the observer. EU competition law, for example, prevents mergers between companies that would impede competition. One important measure of competition is market share. Accordingly, the European Commission may define markets narrowly, thereby making the combined market share as large as possible. The merging companies, by contrast, will tend to view their markets in much broader terms, which naturally makes their combined market share smaller. Consider, for example, a merger between two airlines such as that between British Airways and Spanish airline, Iberia in 2011. The combined airline has a relatively small share of the airline market. The European Commission, however, needed to be reassured that there would be sufficient competition in the market for flights between the UK and Spain. In general, as in this particular instance, the best market definition will depend on the purpose at hand.

Over the years, economists have increasingly recognized that even subtle product differences matter a great deal to some consumers, and the trend in analysis has been toward ever narrower definitions of goods and markets. Two otherwise identical products are often classified as separate if they differ only with respect to the times or places they are available. An umbrella on a sunny day, for example, is in this sense a very different product from an umbrella during a downpour. And the markets for these two products behave very differently indeed.

To make our discussion concrete, let us consider the workings of a specific market—say, the one for a yellow tulip at the Aalsmeer Flower Auction near

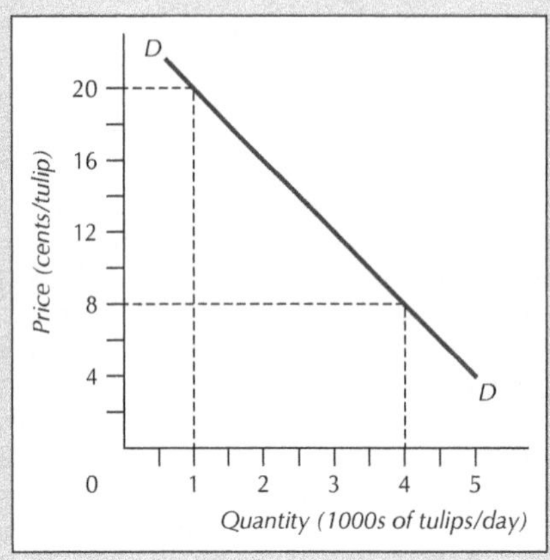

FIGURE 2.1 The Demand Curve for Yellow Tulips at the Aalsmeer Flower Auction, 20 March 2012 The demand curve tells the quantities buyers will wish to purchase at various prices. Its key property is its downward slope; when price falls, the quantity demanded increases. This property is called the law of demand.

Amsterdam on 20 March 2012.[1] For this market, our task is to explain both the price of tulips and the quantity traded. We begin with the basic *demand curve,* a simple mathematical relationship that tells how many tulips buyers wish to purchase at various possible prices (holding all else constant). The curve *DD* depicted in Figure 2.1, for example, tells us that 4000 tulips will be demanded at a price of 8 cents each, 1000 at a price of 20 cents, and so on.

If a visitor from Mars were told only that tulips sell for 8 cents each, he would have no way of knowing whether they were cheap or expensive. In 1900, an 8 cent tulip would have been out of reach of all but the wealthiest consumers. In 2011, by contrast, a tulip would have been considered affordable at that price. Unless otherwise stated, the price on the vertical axis of the demand curve diagram will refer to the **real price** of the good, which means its price relative to the prices of all other goods and services. Thus, the prices on the vertical axis of Figure 2.1 represent tulip prices on 20 March 2012, and the context within which those prices are interpreted by buyers is the set of prices of all other goods on that same date.

real price of a product its price relative to the prices of other goods and services.

The discussion above describes the demand curve as a schedule telling how much of a product consumers wish to purchase at various prices. This is called the *horizontal interpretation* of the demand curve. Under this interpretation, we start with price on the vertical axis and read the corresponding quantity demanded on the horizontal axis. For instance, at a price of 20 cents per tulip, the demand curve in Figure 2.1 tells us that the quantity demanded will be 1000 tulips per day.

A second interpretation of the demand curve is to start with quantity on the horizontal axis and then read the marginal buyer's reservation price on the vertical axis. Thus when the quantity of tulips sold is 4000 per day, the demand curve in Figure 2.1 tells us that the marginal buyer's reservation price is 8 cents per tulip. This second way of reading the demand curve is called the *vertical interpretation.*

The demand curve shown in Figure 2.1 happens to be linear, but demand curves in general need not be. The key property assumed of them is that they are downward sloping: the quantity demanded rises as the price of the product falls. This property

[1]The Aalsmeer Flower Auction is the world's biggest market for flowers with millions of flowers selling every day. It is also one of the largest buildings in the world by floor space, and a great place to be a microeconomics tourist.

law of demand the empirical observation that when the price of a product falls, people demand larger quantities of it.

is often called the **law of demand.** Although we will see in Chapter 4 that it is theoretically possible for a demand curve to be upward sloping, such exceptions are virtually never encountered in practice. To be sure, the negative slope of the demand curve accords in every way with our intuitions about how people respond to rising prices.

As we will see in more detail in Chapter 4, there are normally two independent reasons for the quantity demanded to fall when price rises. One is that many people switch to a close substitute. Thus, when yellow tulips get more expensive, some consumers may switch to red tulips, others to roses. A second reason is that people are not *able* to buy as much as before. Incomes, after all, go only so far. When price goes up, it is not possible to buy as much as before unless we purchase less of something else.

The demand curve for a good is a summary of the various cost-benefit calculations that buyers make with respect to the good, as we will see in greater detail in the next chapter. The question each person faces is, 'Should I buy the product?' (and usually, 'If so, how much of it?'). The cost side of the calculation is simply the price of the product (and implicitly, the other goods or services that could be bought with the same money). The benefit side is the satisfaction provided by the product. The negative slope of the demand schedule tells us that the cost-benefit criterion will be met for fewer and fewer potential buyers as the price of the product rises.

On the seller's side of the market, the corresponding analytical tool is the supply schedule. A hypothetical schedule for our tulip market is shown as line *SS* in Figure 2.2. Again, the linear form of this particular schedule is not a characteristic feature of supply schedules generally. What these schedules do tend to have in common is their upward slope: the quantity supplied rises as the price of a product rises. This property can be called the **law of supply.** For a supplier to be willing to sell a product, its price must cover the marginal cost of producing or acquiring it. As we will see in detail in Chapter 9, the cost of producing additional units often tends to rise as more units are produced, especially in the short run. When this is the case, increased production is profitable only at higher prices.

law of supply the empirical observation that when the price of a product rises, firms offer more of it for sale.

In our tulip market, the reasons for this are clear. Suppliers plant and harvest in the best areas first, and then progressively extend to less ideal areas. So, the more they plant and the more they harvest the more it costs.

Another factor contributing to the upward slope of the supply curve is substitution on the part of flower growers. As the price of yellow tulips increases, more growers switch to yellow tulips, rather than red tulips, or roses.

FIGURE 2.2
A Supply Schedule for Yellow Tulips at the Aalsmeer Flower Auction, 20 March 2012
The upward slope of the supply schedule reflects the fact that costs tend to rise when producers expand production in the short run.

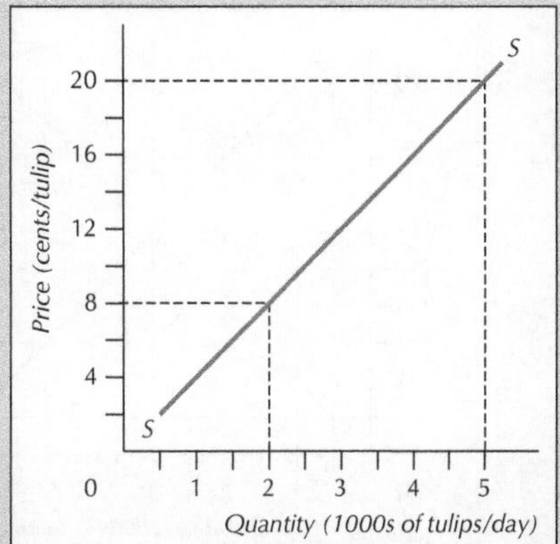

Like demand curves, supply curves can be interpreted either horizontally or vertically. Under the horizontal interpretation, we begin with a price, then go over to the supply curve to read the quantity that sellers wish to sell at that price on the horizontal axis. For instance, at a price of 8 cents per tulip, sellers in Figure 2.2 wish to sell 2000 tulips per day.

Under the vertical interpretation, we begin with a quantity, then go up to the supply curve to read the corresponding marginal cost on the vertical axis. For example, if sellers in Figure 2.2 are currently supplying 5000 tulips per day, the opportunity cost of the last tulip supplied by the marginal seller would be 20 cents. In other words, the supply curve tells us that the marginal cost of delivering the 5000th tulip is 20 cents. If someone could deliver a 5001st tulip for less than 20 cents, she would have had an incentive to do so, in which case the quantity of tulips supplied at a price of 20 cents would not have been 5000 per day to begin with. By similar reasoning, when the quantity of tulips supplied is 2000 per day, the marginal cost of delivering another tulip must be 8 cents.

An alternative way of describing the supply schedule is to call it the set of price-quantity pairs for which suppliers are satisfied. The term 'satisfied' has a technical meaning here, which is that any point on the supply schedule represents the quantity that suppliers want to sell, *given the price they face*. They would obviously be happy to get even higher prices for their offerings. But for any given price, suppliers would consider themselves worse off if forced to sell either more or less than the corresponding quantity on the supply schedule. If, for example, the price of tulips in Figure 2.2 were 8 cents, suppliers would not be satisfied selling either more or fewer than 2000 tulips a day.

The demand schedule may be given a parallel description. It is the set of price-quantity pairs for which buyers are satisfied in precisely the same sense. At any given price, they would consider themselves worse off if forced to purchase either more or less than the corresponding quantity on the demand schedule.

EQUILIBRIUM QUANTITY AND PRICE

With both the supply and demand schedules in hand, we can describe the *equilibrium quantity and price* of tulips. It is the price-quantity pair at which both buyers and sellers are satisfied. Put another way, it is the price-quantity pair at which the supply and demand schedules intersect. Figure 2.3 depicts the equilibrium in our tulip market, at which a total of 3000 tulips are traded at a price of 12 cents each.

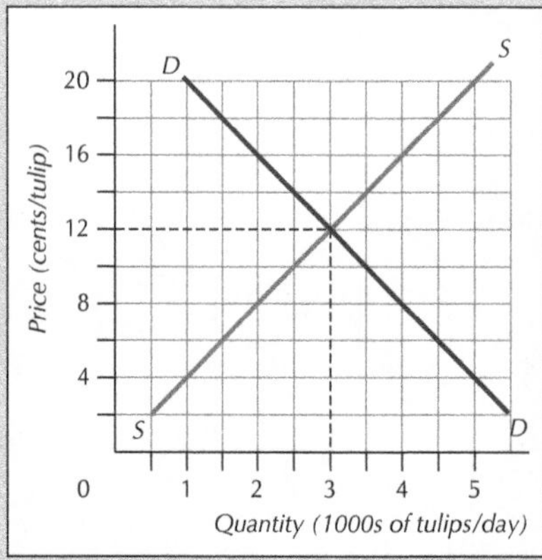

FIGURE 2.3
Equilibrium in the Tulip Market
The intersection of the supply and demand curves represents the price-quantity pair at which all participants in the market are 'satisfied': buyers are buying the amount they want to buy at that price, and sellers are selling the amount they want to sell.

FIGURE 2.4
Excess Supply and Excess Demand
When price exceeds the equilibrium level, there is excess supply, or surplus. When price is below the equilibrium level, there is excess demand, or shortage.

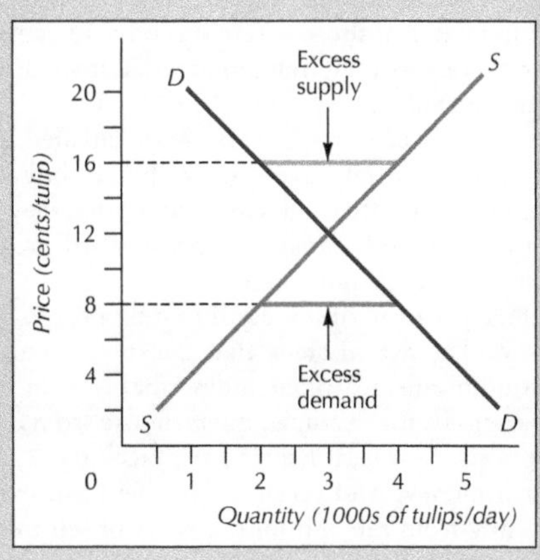

If we were at any price-quantity pair other than the one in Figure 2.3, either buyers or sellers, or both, would be dissatisfied in the sense described above. If the price happened for some reason to lie above the 12 cents equilibrium level, sellers would tend to be the ones who are frustrated. At a price of 16 cents, for example, buyers would purchase only 2000 tulips, whereas sellers would offer 4000. (See Figure 2.4.) Buyers would be satisfied at a price of 16 cents, but sellers would not. A situation in which price exceeds its equilibrium value is called one of **excess supply**, or *surplus*. At 16 cents, there is an excess supply of 2000 tulips.

excess supply the amount by which quantity supplied exceeds quantity demanded.

If, by contrast, the price happened to lie below the equilibrium price of 12 cents, then buyers would be the ones dissatisfied. At a price of 8 cents, for example, they would want to purchase 4000 tulips, whereas suppliers would be willing to sell only 2000. A situation in which price lies below its equilibrium value is referred to as one of **excess demand**, or *shortage*. At a price of 8 cents in this tulip market, there is an excess demand of 2000 tulips. At the market equilibrium price of 12 cents, both excess demand and excess supply are exactly zero.

excess demand the amount by which quantity demanded exceeds quantity supplied.

EXERCISE 2.1 At a price of 4 cents in this hypothetical tulip market, how much excess demand for tulips will there be? How much excess supply will there be at a price of 20 cents?

ADJUSTMENT TO EQUILIBRIUM

When price differs from the equilibrium price, trading in the marketplace will be constrained—by the behaviour of buyers if the price lies above equilibrium, by the behaviour of sellers if below. At any price other than the equilibrium price, one side or the other of the market is dissatisfied. This will put pressure on prices to move towards the equilibrium.

At prices above equilibrium, for example, sellers are not selling as much as they want to. The impulse of a dissatisfied seller is to reduce the price. In the tulip business, after all, stock not sold today can be worthless tomorrow. At a price of 16 cents each, 2000 tulips are being sold, but another 2000 go unclaimed. Each seller reasons, correctly, that if the price of his tulips were reduced to 15 cents, while others remained at 16 cents, he could move all his unsold tulips. Buyers can also reason that they are paying too high a price. Buyers will abandon sellers where the price is 16 cents in favour of those where it is only 15 cents. Downward pressure on price will persist as long as there remain any dissatisfied sellers—that is, until price falls to its equilibrium value.

When price is below 12 cents, buyers are dissatisfied. At a price of 8 cents each, 2000 tulips are being sold, but buyers are willing to buy another 2000. Buyers will start bidding against each other, increasing the price they are willing to pay, in the hope of seeing their demands satisfied. This upward pressure on price will persist until price reaches its equilibrium value.

An extraordinary feature of this equilibrating process is that no one consciously plans or directs it. The actual steps that consumers and producers must take to move toward equilibrium are often indescribably complex. Suppliers looking to expand their operations, for example, must choose from a bewilderingly large menu of equipment options. Buyers, for their part, face literally millions of choices about how to spend their money. And yet the adjustment toward equilibrium results more or less automatically from the natural reactions of self-interested individuals facing either surpluses or shortages.

Why do people not haggle in supermarkets?

ECONOMIC NATURALIST 2.1

All marketplaces are different. In fact, there is a dazzling array of different ways that buyers and sellers have found to meet, trade and agree a price. To give just a few examples: Prices at the Aalsmeer Flower Auction are determined by a, so-called, Dutch or clock auction; the price ticks down until a buyer indicates his willingness to buy. Traders on the Paris Bourse input bids and asks to a computer system. Buyers at the Grand Bazaar in Istanbul haggle face-to-face with market traders. And customers of a superstore are offered take it or leave it prices.

Despite the huge array of different ways to trade, the basic pressure on prices to move toward equilibrium always remains the same. Sometimes, it might seem as though the price is being determined only by buyers, such as the Flower Auction, or by the seller, such as a superstore. But this is an illusion. If flower growers don't bring their flowers to auction, or customers don't go to the superstore, the price will change.

So, why do we see such different ways to trade? Clearly, history and tradition play their part. The inevitable logic of cost-benefit calculation is also at work, however. The Aalsmeer Flower Auction is an efficient way to sell a huge amount of flowers very quickly. The Grand Bazaar is a great way to bring together a large number of buyers and sellers. A superstore offers time-pressed customers a convenient way to do the weekly shop in less than an hour. ■

SOME WELFARE PROPERTIES OF EQUILIBRIUM

Given the attributes—tastes, abilities, knowledge, incomes, and so on—of buyers and sellers, the equilibrium outcome has some attractive properties. Specifically, we can say that no reallocation can improve some people's position without harming the position of at least some others. *If price and quantity take anything other than their equilibrium values, however, it will always be possible to reallocate so as to make at least some people better off without harming others.*

Sticking with the tulip example, suppose the price is 8 cents, with suppliers therefore offering only 2000 tulips. As indicated in Figure 2.5, the vertical interpretation of the demand curve tells us that when only 2000 tulips are available, buyers are willing to pay 16 cents. Similarly, the vertical interpretation of the supply curve tells us that when 2000 tulips a day are supplied, the marginal cost of delivering another tulip is only 8 cents. When the value to the buyer of the last tulip grown (16 cents) is higher than the cost of supplying it (8 cents), there is room to cut a deal.

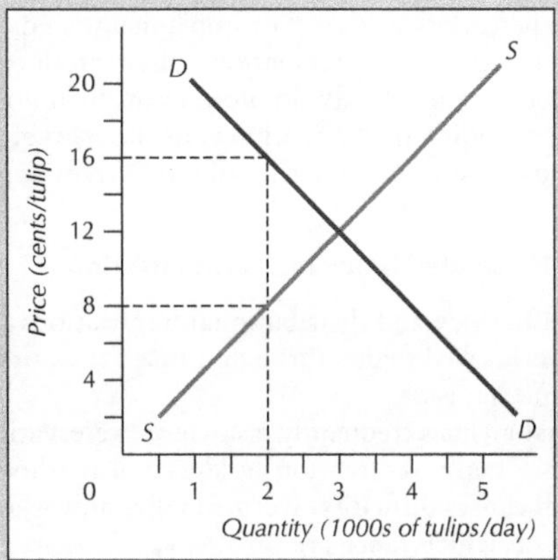

FIGURE 2.5
An Opportunity for Improvement in the Tulip Market
When the quantity traded in the market is below (or above) the equilibrium quantity, it is always possible to reallocate resources in such a way that some people are made better off without harming others. Here, a dissatisfied buyer can pay a seller 10 cents for an additional tulip, thus making both parties better off.

Suppose, for example, a dissatisfied buyer were to offer a supplier 10 cents for a tulip. The supplier would gladly sell an additional tulip at this price (since, at 2000 tulips, an additional tulip costs only 8 cents to harvest). This transaction would improve the buyer's position by 6 cents (the difference between the 16 cents value he attaches to the tulip and the 10 cents he paid for it). It would also improve the seller's position by 2 cents (the difference between the 10 cents she got and the 8 cents cost of supplying the extra tulip). No one suffers any harm from this transaction, and the participants reap 8 cents of additional benefit from it (6 cents for the buyer, 2 cents for the seller). A similar argument can be made concerning any price below the equilibrium value. For any such price, it is always possible to make some people better off without hurting others.

What if the price had been higher than the equilibrium price to begin with? Suppose price is 16 cents with trading therefore limited by buyers' demands for 2000 tulips. (Again, see Figure 2.5.) Now a dissatisfied seller can propose a transaction that will make both the seller and some buyers better off. Suppose, for example, a seller offers an additional tulip for sale for 14 cents. Since buyers value additional tulips at 16 cents, whoever buys it will be better off by 2 cents. And since tulips cost only 8 cents to supply, the seller will be better off by 6 cents. Again, no one is injured by this transaction, and again the two parties gain a total of 8 cents.

Thus, no matter whether price starts out above or below its equilibrium value, a mutually beneficial transaction will always be possible. We will examine the welfare properties of the market system in much greater detail in later chapters. But for now, suffice it to say that the equilibrium price and quantity constitute the best outcome attainable, given the initial attributes and endowments of buyers and sellers.

FREE MARKETS AND THE POOR

The fact that market equilibrium is efficient in the sense just described does not mean that it is necessarily desirable in any absolute sense. All markets may be in perfect equilibrium, for example, and yet many people may lack sufficient incomes to purchase even the bare necessities of life. Saying market equilibrium is efficient does not challenge the notion that being poor is difficult, often even painful. Efficiency says merely that, *given the low incomes of the poor,* free exchange enables them to do the best they can. One can hold this view and still believe it desirable to provide public assistance to poor people.

Concern for the well-being of the poor motivates most societies to try to intervene, as in the petrol price control example mentioned earlier. The difficulty, as in that example, is that these interventions often produce unintended harmful consequences. Indeed, many clearly do more harm than good. As we will see, a more thorough understanding of the workings of the market mechanism would prevent many of the most costly consequences of our current approach.

EXAMPLE 2.1 Denied boarding compensation

What are the efficiency and distributional implications of handling excess demand for seats on overbooked flights through a first-come, first-served policy as opposed to an auction mechanism?

Commercial airlines frequently issue more reservations than there are seats on a flight. Because many reservation holders fail to show up for their flights, this practice seldom causes difficulty. Occasionally, however, 160 passengers will show up for a flight on which there are only, say, 150 seats. Before the late 1970s, airlines dealt with overbooked flights by boarding passengers on a first-come, first-served basis.

This solution gives insufficient weight to the interests of passengers with pressing needs who may be a bit late to arrive at their final destinations on time. With this problem clearly in mind, the Civil Aeronautics Board (CAB), the government agency that used to regulate the commercial aviation industry in the US, proposed a simple regulation. When too many people showed up for a flight, the airline would be required to call for volunteers to abandon their seats in return for either a cash payment or an in-kind payment, such as a free air ticket. The airline would be required to keep increasing its offer until it got enough volunteers.

The advantage of the CAB proposal was that it would allow passengers to decide for themselves how pressing their schedules were. People with important meetings could simply refuse to volunteer. Others could agree to wait a few hours, often in return for several hundred dollars or a free trip to Hawaii. By comparison with the first-come, first-served solution, the CAB proposal promised a better outcome for all passengers.

Or at any rate, so it seemed. A consumer-action group immediately objected to the CAB's proposal on the grounds that it was unfair to low-income passengers. The group's complaint was that the auction method of soliciting volunteers would almost always result in the poorest ticket holders being the ones to wait for the next flight.

© InkkStudios

Why is an auction a better way to allocate seats on an over-booked flight than first-come, first-served?

Now, a poor person will surely be more likely to find a cash payment a compelling reason to volunteer. But by volunteering, a person says that the cash payment is *worth* the wait. The world would indeed be a better place if poor people had higher incomes and were not tempted by their poverty to give up their seats on airplanes. But the consumer group was not proposing to give the poor higher incomes. Rather, it wanted the industry to stick with a system that bumped passengers from overbooked flights irrespective of the value they attached to remaining on board.

It is hard to see how poor people's interests would be served by preventing them from earning extra cash by volunteering to wait for the next flight. And in the end, the CAB adopted its denied-boarding-compensation proposal, to the benefit of air travellers at all income levels. ◆

Many critics of the market system complain that it is unfair to ration goods and services by asking how much people are willing to pay for them. This criterion, they point out, gives short shrift to the interests of the poor. But as Example 2.1 clearly illustrates, serious contradictions plague alternative schemes of allocation. Consider again our hypothetical tulip market. Suppose we are concerned that the equilibrium price of 12 cents will exclude many deserving poor persons from experiencing the pleasure of receiving flowers from a loved one. And suppose that, with this in mind, we adopt a system that periodically gives free tulips to the poor. Wouldn't such a system represent a clear improvement in the eyes of any person who feels compassion for the poor?

The answer, as in Example 2.1, is that for the same cost we can do even better. When a poor person, or indeed even a rich person, does not buy tulips because the price is too high, she is saying, in effect, that she would prefer to spend her money on other things. If we gave her a bunch of 10 tulips, what would she want to do with it? In an ideal world, she would immediately sell it to someone willing to pay the €1.20 equilibrium price. We know there will be such persons because some of the tulips that would have been bought for 12 cents were instead given to the poor. The poor person's sale of the tulips to one of these people will bring about a clear improvement for both parties—for the buyer, or else he would not have bought it, and for the seller because the tulips are worth less than €1.20 to her.

The practical difficulty, as we will see in detail in later chapters, is that it would take time and effort for our hypothetical poor person to find a buyer for the tulips. In the end, she would probably find a vase for them. True enough, she might enjoy looking at them. But by her own reckoning, she would have enjoyed the €1.20 even more.

The problem is the same with petrol price controls. The controls were implemented in the sincere belief they were needed to protect the poor from sharply higher petrol prices. Their effect, however, was to induce a host of behaviours that helped neither rich nor poor.

Despite statements to the contrary by critics of the market system, people are highly responsive to energy prices when they make decisions about how to spend their incomes. If petrol costs €3.00/litre, for example, many people will form car pools or purchase fuel-efficient cars, even though they would do neither if the price were only €1.50/litre. Whether a long trip is considered worth taking also clearly depends on the price of petrol.

Regardless of whether fuel is in short supply, it is in everyone's interest—rich or poor—to use it for the activities people value most. But the costs of a policy that does not do this are particularly high when fuel is scarce. Selling petrol for less than the equilibrium price is just such a policy. It encourages people to use petrol in wasteful ways.

Rent Controls

Rent control is used in one form or another in most European countries to protect households from unaffordable rent hikes. Such laws, like so many others, are motivated by an honest concern for the well-being of low-income citizens. But their economic consequences are no less damaging for being unintended. Indeed, it has been said that the surest way to destroy a city, short of dropping a nuclear bomb on it, is to pass a rent control law.

Basic supply and demand analysis is again all we need to see clearly the nature of the difficulties. Figure 2.6 depicts the supply and demand schedules for a hypothetical urban apartment market. The equilibrium rent in this market would be €600/

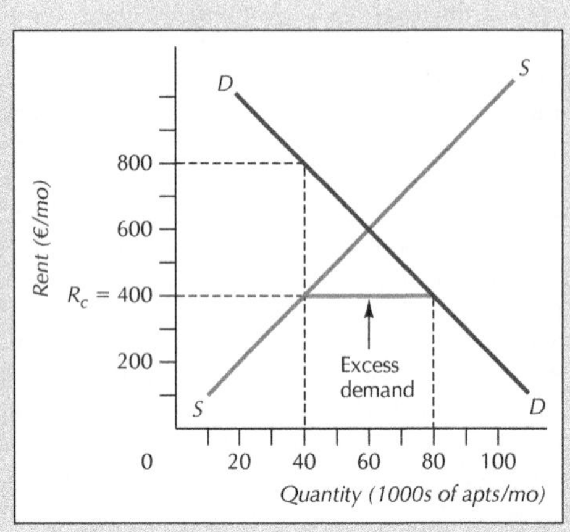

FIGURE 2.6
Rent Controls
With the rent control level set at €400 a month, there is an excess demand of 40,000 apartments a month.

month, and at this level there would be 60,000 apartments rented. The government, however, has passed a law that holds rents at R_c = €400/month, or €200 below the market-clearing value. R_c in this example constitutes a **price ceiling** for rents, a level beyond which rents are not permitted to rise. At €400/month, buyers would like to rent 80,000 apartments, but suppliers are willing to offer only 40,000. There is an excess demand of 40,000 units. And if the rent control level remains fixed at €400/month, excess demand will grow over time as population grows and inflation reduces the value of money.

price ceiling level above which the price of a good is not permitted by law to rise.

In an unregulated market, the immediate response would be for rents to rise sharply. But here the law prevents them from rising above R_c. Yet there are other ways the pressures of excess demand can make themselves felt. One is for owners to spend less on maintaining their rental units. If there are two renters knocking at the door of each vacant apartment, clogged drains, peeling paint, broken thermostats, and the like are not apt to receive prompt attention.

Nor are these the most serious difficulties. With an offering of only 40,000 apartments per month, we see in Figure 2.6 that renters would be willing to pay as much as €800/month for an apartment (again, the vertical interpretation of the demand curve). This pressure almost always finds ways, legal or illegal, of expressing itself. In Stockholm, for example, it is not unheard of to see 'finder's fees' or 'key deposits' as high as a thousand euros. Owners who cannot charge a market-clearing rent for an apartment also have the option of converting it to a co-op, which enables them to sell their asset for a price much closer to its true economic value.

Even when rent-controlled apartment owners do not hike their prices in these various ways, serious misallocations result. A widow steadfastly remains in her seven-room apartment even after her children have left home because it is cheaper than alternative dwellings not covered by rent control. It would be better for all concerned if she relinquished that space to a larger family. But under rent controls, she has no economic incentive to do so.

© pidjoe

Why are rent-controlled apartments less well maintained than unregulated units?

EXAMPLE 2.2 Suppose the rent control is lowered (strengthened) to €200/month. What is the excess demand, and how does it compare with the excess demand when rents were limited (more loosely) to €400/month?

At €200/month, buyers would like to rent 100,000 apartments, but suppliers are willing to offer only 20,000. Thus there is an excess demand of 80,000 units. The excess demand is greater than the excess demand of 40,000 units at the €400/month rent control. ◆

EXERCISE 2.2 In the market for apartments described in Figure 2.6, what would happen if the rent control level were set at €625/mo?

In response to the kinds of problems described above, some rent-control programmes have been modified to allow landlords to raise rents when a tenant moves out of an apartment. Such changes reduce, but do not eliminate, misallocations. And they may even create new problems. For example, a landlord who knows that a tenant's departure would permit a rent increase may take any available lawful steps to make the tenant's life unpleasant if he remains.

The main problem confronting the poor is that they have too little money. Transferring additional money to the poor does more to help them than attempting to control the prices of things they buy.

There are much more effective ways to help poor people than to give them cheap petrol, rent-controlled apartments, or free tulips. One would be to give them additional income and let them decide for themselves how to spend it. Chapter 17 examines some of the practical difficulties involved in transferring additional purchasing power into the hands of the poor. In brief, the most pressing problem is that it is hard to target cash to the genuinely needy without attracting others who could fend for themselves. But as we will see, economic reasoning also suggests practical ways to overcome this difficulty. There are no simple or easy solutions. But given the enormous losses caused by policies that keep prices below their equilibrium levels, these issues deserve our most serious attention.

PRICE SUPPORTS

Rent controls are an example of a price ceiling that prevents the price from rising to its equilibrium level. For the converse we can look at the EU's Common Agricultural Policy which imposes *price supports,* or **price floors**, which keep agricultural prices above their equilibrium levels. While price ceilings merely require the announcement of a level beyond which prices could not rise, price supports require the government to become an active buyer in the market.

price floor a minimum price for a good, established by law, and supported by government's offer to buy the good at that price.

Figure 2.7, for example, depicts a price support level of P_s in the market for wheat. Because P_s is above the equilibrium price, there is an excess supply of 200,000 tonnes/yr. To maintain the price at P_s = €100/tonne, the EU must purchase 200,000 tonnes/yr of wheat. Otherwise farmers would face powerful incentives to cut their prices.

An important purpose of farm price supports is to ensure prices high enough to provide adequate incomes for farm families. In practice, however, the supports have proved a costly and inefficient instrument. One problem is the disposition of the surplus bought by governments. To produce this surplus requires valuable labour, capital, fertilizer and other inputs. Yet often it is simply left to decay in storage bins. Another difficulty is that much of the surplus is produced by large corporate farms, whose owners have no need for support. For every euro that price supports put into the hands of a needy family farmer, several more go into the coffers of prosperous

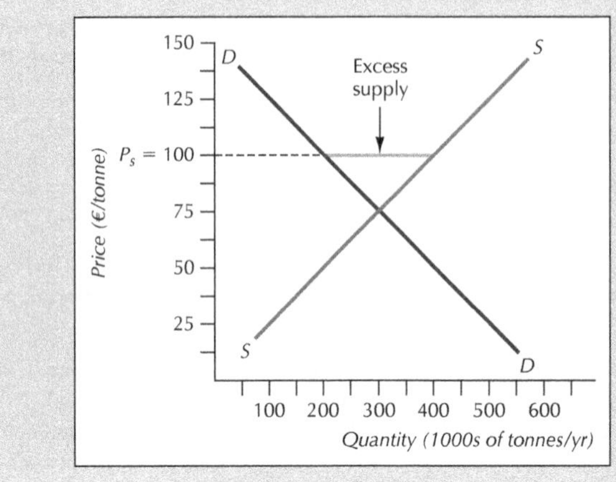

FIGURE 2.7
A Price Support in the Wheat Market
For a price support to have any impact, it must be set above the market-clearing price. Its effect is to create excess supply, which governments then purchase.

agribusinesses. Price supports also raise the food bills of all families, and often raise prices of goods not directly supported. (See Example 2.3 later in this chapter.) If society wants to subsidize small family farms, there are more efficient and direct means than agricultural price supports.

THE RATIONING AND ALLOCATIVE FUNCTIONS OF PRICES

Prices serve two important and distinct functions. First, they ration existing supplies of goods. Scarcity is the universal feature of economic life. People want more of virtually everything than could be supplied at a price of zero. Equilibrium prices curtail these excessive claims by rationing scarce supplies to the users who place the highest value on them. This is the **rationing function of price.** It is a short-run function, in the sense that its focus is the distribution of output that already exists.

rationing function of price the process whereby price directs existing supplies of a product to the users who value it most highly.

The second function of price is that of a signal to direct productive resources among the different sectors of the economy. In industries in which there is excess demand, firms are able to charge more than they need to cover their costs of production. The resulting profits act as a carrot that lures additional resources into these industries. The other side of this coin is that losses act as the stick that drives resources out of those industries in which there is excess supply. This is the so-called **allocative function of price,** the driving force behind Adam Smith's invisible hand. It is a long-run function in the sense that its focus is to induce resources to migrate from industries with excess supply to those with excess demand.

allocative function of price the process whereby price acts as a signal that guides resources away from the production of goods whose prices lie below cost toward the production of goods whose prices exceed cost.

Rent controls subvert both functions of the price mechanism. The rationing function is undercut by the alternative mechanisms that distribute housing with little regard to the value people place on it. The underlying needs of renters are relegated to secondary status. Both luck and the people you happen to know are often decisive. Artificially low rents undercut the allocative function of price by sending a false signal to investors about the need for additional housing. Under rent controls, apartment builders earn less than they could by investing their money elsewhere. The cruel irony is that the pressing need in many communities with rent controls is for more low-income housing units, not fewer—which is precisely what the market would produce on its own if the poor were given more money.

DETERMINANTS OF SUPPLY AND DEMAND

Supply and demand analysis is useful not only for the normative insight it offers into questions of public policy but also for a rich variety of descriptive purposes. Most important, it predicts how equilibrium prices and quantities will respond to changes in market forces. Because supply and demand curves intersect to determine equilibrium prices and quantities, anything that shifts these curves will alter equilibrium values in a predictable way. In the next several chapters, we investigate in detail the forces that determine the shape and position of market demand curves. For the moment, let us discuss a few whose roles are intuitively clear.

Determinants of Demand

Incomes For most goods, the quantity demanded at any price rises with income. Goods that have this property are called *normal goods.* So-called *inferior goods* (such as ground beef with high fat content) are the exception. For such goods, the quantity demanded at any price falls with income. The idea is that consumers abandon these goods in favour of higher-quality substitutes (such as leaner grades of meat in the ground beef case) as soon as they can afford to.

Tastes Tastes vary across people and over time. In Western societies, culture instils a taste for sitting on padded furniture, whereas in many Eastern societies, people are conditioned to favour sitting cross-legged on the floor. The demand for armchairs thus tends to be larger in the West than in the East. By the same token, the demand for skirts with hemlines above the knee tends to vary sharply from one decade to another.

Prices of Substitutes and Complements Bacon and eggs play a complementary role in the diets of some people. For them, a sharp increase in the price of bacon leads not only to a reduction in the quantity of bacon demanded but also to a reduction in the demand for eggs. Such goods are considered *complements*: an increase in the price of one good decreases demand for the other good. In the case of close *substitutes,* such as coffee and tea, an increase in the price of one will tend to increase the demand for the other.

Expectations Expectations about future income and price levels also affect current purchase decisions. For example, someone who expects higher future income is likely to spend more today than an otherwise identical person who expects lower future income. (After all, with higher expected future income, the need to save diminishes.) Similarly, people will often accelerate their current purchases of goods whose prices are expected to rise in the months to come.

Population In general, the number of people who buy a product grows as the number of potential buyers grows. Thus, in cities with growing populations, the demand for housing increases from year to year, whereas it tends to fall in cities with declining populations.

Figure 2.8 graphically displays some factors that shift demand curves. We will revisit these factors in more detail in Chapter 4.

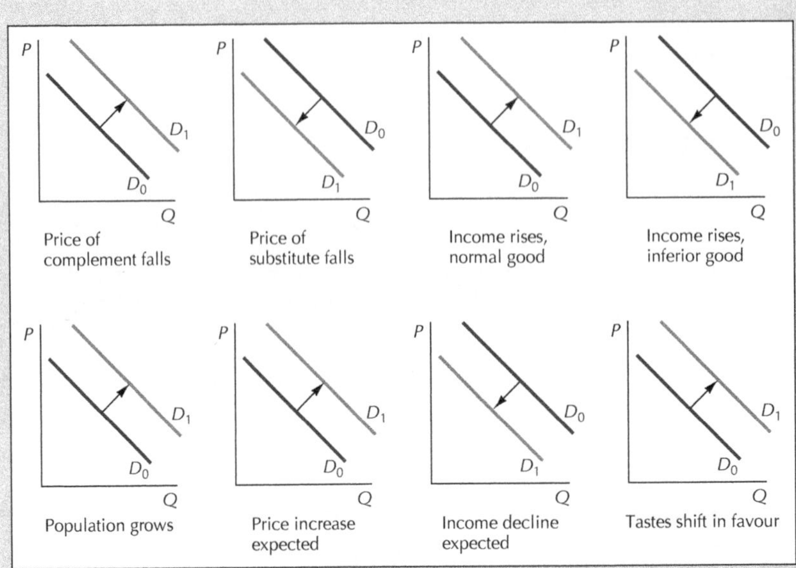

FIGURE 2.8
Factors that Shift Demand Curves
Prices of substitutes and complements, incomes, population, expectation of future price and income changes, and tastes all influence the position of the current demand curve for a product.

Determinants of Supply

Technology The amount suppliers are willing to offer at any price depends primarily on their costs of production. These costs, in turn, are closely linked to technology. For instance, the discovery of a more efficient way of making computer chips will reduce the cost of producing them, which results in a rightward shift in the supply schedule.

Factor Prices A supplier's costs also depend on the payment it must make to its factors of production: labour, capital, and so on. If the price of combine harvesters rises, or if the wage paid to farm labourers goes up, the supply schedule for wheat shifts to the left.

The Number of Suppliers The more firms that can supply a good, the greater will be the quantity supplied of it at any given price. The supply schedule of personal computers has shifted sharply to the right as more and more companies have begun producing them.

Expectations Suppliers too take expected changes in prices into account in their current production decisions. For example, if farmers expect beef prices to rise sharply in the future because of an epidemic affecting young cattle, they are likely to withhold current supplies of mature livestock to take advantage of the higher future prices.[2]

Weather For some products, particularly agricultural ones, nature has significant effects on the supply schedule. In years of drought, for example, the supply schedule for many foodstuffs shifts to the left.

[2]Note that supply is the quantity offered for sale at various prices, not necessarily current production (when suppliers are able to store inventory). Hence, the farmers reduce sales of cattle in the current period, since they can sell them in a later period when prices are higher.

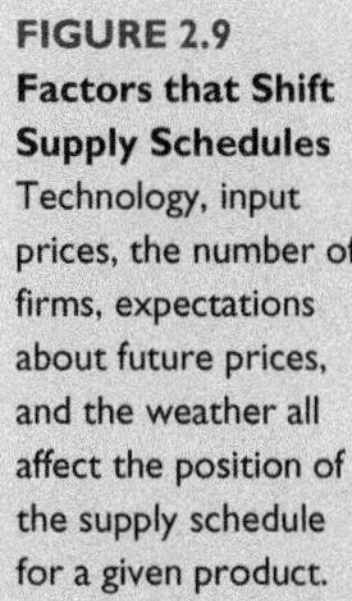

FIGURE 2.9
Factors that Shift Supply Schedules
Technology, input prices, the number of firms, expectations about future prices, and the weather all affect the position of the supply schedule for a given product.

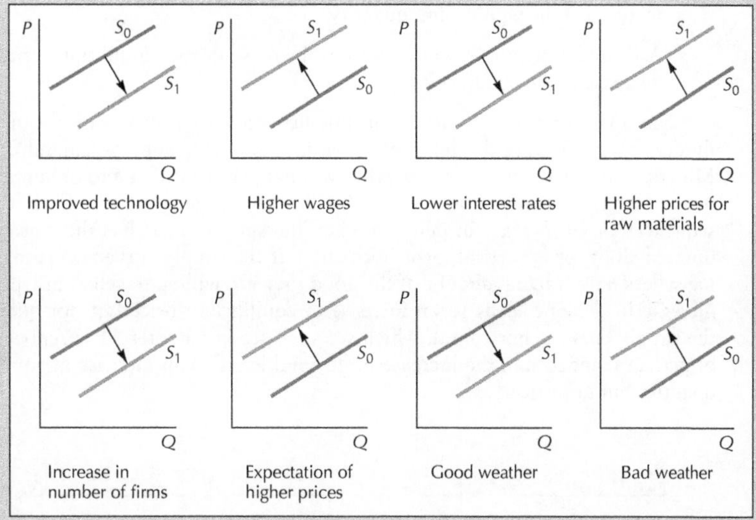

Figure 2.9 shows the effects of some factors that shift supply schedules.

Neither of the preceding lists of supply and demand shifters is meant to be exhaustive.

Changes in Demand versus Changes in the Quantity Demanded

When economists use the expression *change in demand,* they mean a shift in the entire demand curve. Thus, when the average income level of buyers changes, the demand curve shifts—there is a change in demand. When we say *change in the quantity demanded,* we mean a movement along the demand curve. When the price of a good falls, for example, the result is an increase in the quantity demanded, not an increase in demand.

Analogous interpretations attach to the expressions *change in supply* and *change in the quantity supplied.* These terminological distinctions are important for clear communication both in classroom discussion and in exams. And if the experience of previous generations of students is any guide, it requires effort to keep them straight.

PREDICTING AND EXPLAINING CHANGES IN PRICE AND QUANTITY

To predict or explain changes in equilibrium prices and quantities, we must predict or account for the shifts in the relevant supply and/or demand schedules. When supply and demand curves have the conventional slopes, the following propositions about equilibrium prices and quantities will hold:

- An increase in demand will lead to an increase in both the equilibrium price and quantity.
- A decrease in demand will lead to a decrease in both the equilibrium price and quantity.

- An increase in supply will lead to a decrease in the equilibrium price and an increase in the equilibrium quantity.
- A decrease in supply will lead to an increase in the equilibrium price and a decrease in the equilibrium quantity.

There is no point in memorizing this list, since each proposition can be easily derived by shifting the relevant curve in a standard supply-demand diagram. Moreover, it is easy enough to see what will happen if the demand or supply curve does not have a conventional slope. To illustrate, Figure 2.10 looks at the consequences of an increase in demand when the supply curve has the conventional upward slope, or is vertical, or is horizontal. If the supply curve is vertical, meaning sellers have a fixed amount of the good they are willing to sell at any price, the increase in demand leads to an increase in equilibrium price but not quantity. If the supply curve is horizontal, which we shall see in Chapter 11 is representative of perfect competition, the increase in demand leads to an increase in equilibrium quantity but not price.

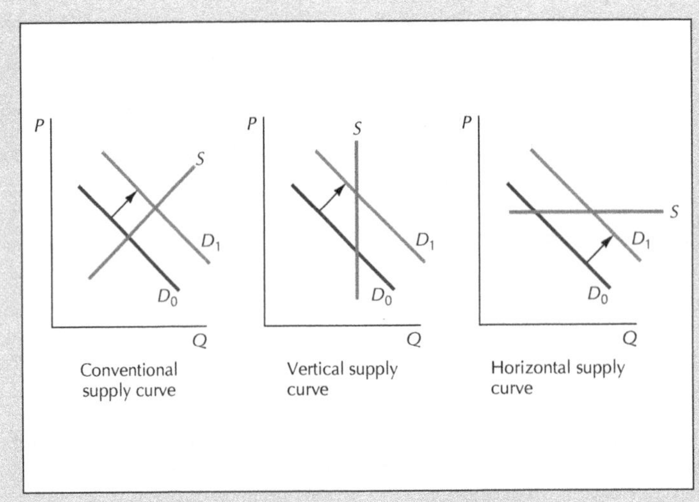

FIGURE 2.10
The Consequences of a Shift in the Demand Curve
If the supply curve has the conventional slope, an increase in demand causes the equilibrium price and quantity to increase. If the supply curve is vertical, an increase in demand causes the equilibrium price to increase but not quantity. If the supply curve is horizontal, an increase in demand causes the equilibrium quantity to increase but not price.

Why do the prices of some goods, like apples, go down during the months of heaviest consumption while others, like beachfront cottages, go up?

ECONOMIC NATURALIST 2.2

The answer is that the seasonal consumption increase is the result of a supply increase in the case of apples, a demand increase in the case of cottages. As shown in Figure 2.11, these shifts produce the observed seasonal relationships between equilibrium prices and quantities. (The subscripts w and s in Figure 2.11 are used to denote winter and summer values, respectively.) When demand increases (as for cottages), the increase in the equilibrium quantity occurs concurrently with an increase in the equilibrium price. When supply increases (as for apples), the increase in the equilibrium quantity occurs concurrently with a decrease in the equilibrium price. ■

FIGURE 2.11
Two Sources of Seasonal Variation
The quantities consumed of both apples and beachfront cottages are highest in the summer months. (*a*) Apple prices are at their lowest during the summer because the quantity increase is the result of increased supply. (The subscripts *w* and *s* denote winter and summer values, respectively.) (*b*) Cottage prices are at their highest in summer because the quantity increase is the result of an increase in demand.

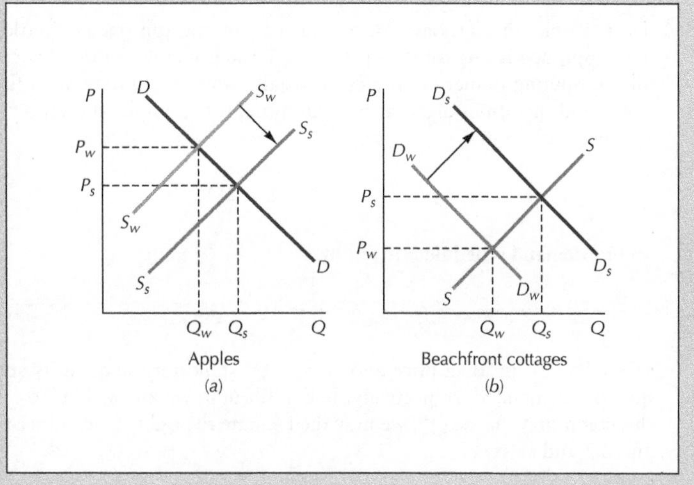

EXERCISE 2.3 What will happen to the equilibrium price and quantity in the fresh seafood market if each of the following events occurs: (1) a scientific report is issued saying that fish contains mercury, which is toxic to humans, and (2) the price of diesel fuel (used to operate fishing boats) falls significantly?

EXAMPLE 2.3 If soybeans are one of the ingredients in cattle feed, how does a price support programme in the soybean market affect the equilibrium price and quantity of beef?

The price support programme raises the price of cattle feed, which causes a leftward shift in the supply schedule for beef. (See Figure 2.12.) This, in turn, results in an increase in the equilibrium price and a reduction in the equilibrium quantity of beef. ◆

FIGURE 2.12
The Effect of Soybean Price Supports on the Equilibrium Price and Quantity of Beef
By raising the price of soybeans, an input used in beef production, the price supports produce a leftward shift in the supply curve of beef. The result is an increase in the equilibrium price and a reduction in the equilibrium quantity.

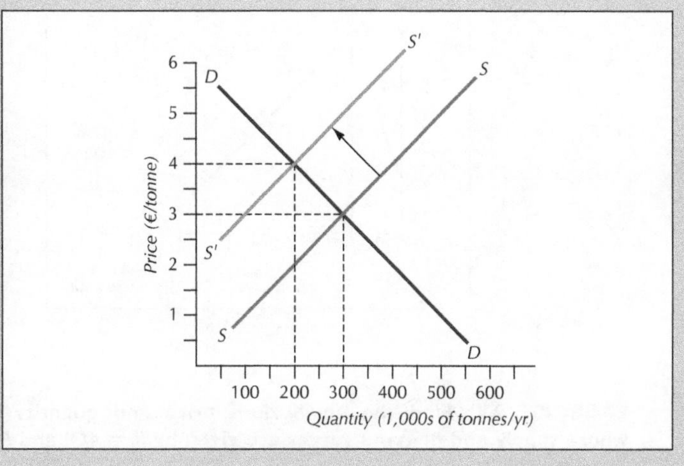

THE ALGEBRA OF SUPPLY AND DEMAND

The examples thus far have focused on a geometric approach to market equilibrium. This approach is fine for illustrating the basic principles of the theory. But for actually computing numerical values, it usually is more convenient to find equilibrium prices and quantities algebraically. Suppose, for example, the supply schedule for a product is given by

$$P = 2 + 3Q^s \qquad (2.1)$$

and its demand schedule is given by

$$P = 10 - Q^d \qquad (2.2)$$

where P is the product price and Q^s and Q^d stand for the quantity supplied and the quantity demanded, respectively. In equilibrium, we know that $Q^s = Q^d$. Denoting this common value as Q^*, we may then equate the right-hand sides of Equations 2.1 and 2.2 and solve:

$$2 + 3Q^* = 10 - Q^* \qquad (2.3)$$

which gives $Q^* = 2$. Substituting $Q^* = 2$ back into either the supply or demand equation gives the equilibrium price, $P^* = 8$.

Needless to say, we could have graphed Equations 2.1 and 2.2 to arrive at precisely the same solution (see Figure 2.13). The advantage of the algebraic approach is that it is much less painstaking than having to produce accurate drawings of the supply and demand schedules.

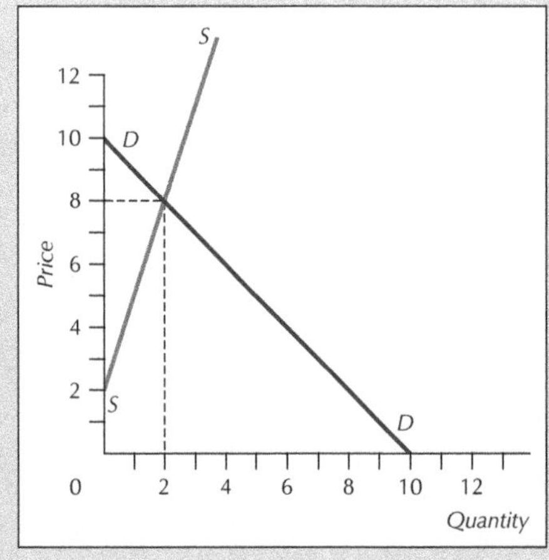

FIGURE 2.13
Graphs of Equations 2.1 and 2.2
The algebraic and geometric approaches lead to exactly the same equilibrium prices and quantities. The advantage of the algebraic approach is that exact numerical solutions can be achieved more easily. The geometric approach is useful because it gives a more intuitively clear description of the supply and demand curves.

EXERCISE 2.4 Find the equilibrium price and quantity in a market whose supply and demand curves are given by $P = 4Q^s$ and $P = 12 - 2Q^d$, respectively.

SUMMARY

- The supply curve is generally an upward-sloping line that tells what quantity sellers will offer at any given price. The demand curve is a downward-sloping line that tells what quantity buyers will demand at any given price. In an unregulated market, the equilibrium price and quantity are determined by the intersection of these two curves.
- If price is above its equilibrium, there will be dissatisfied sellers, or excess supply. This condition motivates sellers to cut their prices. By contrast, when prices are below equilibrium, there will be dissatisfied buyers, or excess demand. This condition motivates sellers to charge higher prices. The only stable outcome is the one in which excess demand and excess supply are exactly zero.
- Given the attributes of buyers and sellers, the equilibrium price and quantity represent the best attainable outcome, in the sense that any other price-quantity pair would be worse for at least some buyers or sellers.
- The fact that market outcomes are efficient in this sense does not mean they necessarily command society's approval. On the contrary, we often lament the fact that many buyers enter the market with so little income. Concern for the well-being of the poor has motivated the governments of almost every society to intervene in a variety of ways to alter the outcomes of market forces.
- Sometimes these interventions take the form of laws that peg prices above or below their equilibrium levels. Such laws often generate harmful, if unintended, consequences. Rent controls, for example, interfere with both the rationing and allocative functions of the price mechanism. They lead to black marketeering and a rapid deterioration of the stock of rental housing. By the same token, price support laws in agriculture tend to enrich large corporate farms while doing little to ease the plight of the small family farm. In almost every instance, it is possible to design an alternative intervention that is better in every respect.
- If the difficulty is that the poor have too little money, the solution is to discover ways of boosting their incomes directly. Legislatures cannot repeal the law of supply and demand. But legislatures do have the capacity to alter the underlying forces that govern the shape and position of supply and demand schedules.
- Supply and demand analysis is the economist's basic tool for predicting how equilibrium prices and quantities will change in response to changes in market forces. Four simple propositions guide this task: (1) an increase in demand will lead to an increase in both the equilibrium price and quantity; (2) a decrease in demand will lead to a decrease in both the equilibrium price and quantity; (3) an increase in supply will lead to a decrease in the equilibrium price and an increase in the equilibrium quantity; and (4) a decrease in supply will lead to an increase in the equilibrium price and a decrease in the equilibrium quantity.
- Incomes, tastes, the prices of substitutes and complements, expectations, and population are among the factors that shift demand schedules. Supply schedules, in turn, are governed by such factors as technology, input prices, the number of suppliers, expectations, and, for agricultural products, the weather.

QUESTIONS FOR REVIEW

1. What is the difference between 'scarcity' and 'shortage'?
2. What would the supply curve look like for a good that is not scarce? Assuming the good is useful, what would its demand curve look like? Explain why a positive price for a commodity implies that it is scarce.
3. Give two examples of actions taken by the administration of your college or university whose effect is to prevent specific markets from reaching equilibrium. What evidence of excess supply or excess demand can you cite in these examples?
4. What is the difference between 'a reduction in supply' and 'a reduction in the quantity supplied'?
5. Identify each of the following as (1) a change in demand or (2) a change in the quantity demanded.
   a. Grape consumption falls because of a consumer boycott.
   b. Grape consumption falls because of a tax on grape producers.
   c. Grape consumption rises because of a good harvest.
   d. Grape consumption rises because of a change in tastes.
6. When there is excess supply, why is any single seller able to sell all she wants to by offering only a small reduction below the current market price?
7. Give an example of a market in which the allocative function of price is not very important.
8. Suppose you are a government official and need to collect revenue by taxing a product. For political reasons, you want the burden of the tax to fall mostly on consumers, not firms (who have been substantial contributors to your campaign fund). What should you look for when picking a product to tax?
9. Which would a rational poor person be more likely to accept and why?
   a. A €50,000 Mercedes (immediate resale value = €30,000)
   b. €35,000 cash.

PROBLEMS

1. Assume that tea and lemons are complements and that coffee and tea are substitutes.
   a. How, if at all, will the imposition of an effective ceiling price on tea affect the price of lemons? Explain.
   b. How, if at all, will the imposition of an effective ceiling price on tea affect the price of coffee? Explain.
2. The market for DVDs has supply and demand curves given by $P' = 2Q^s$ and $P = 42 - Q^d$, respectively.
   a. How many units will be traded at a price of €35? At a price of €14? Which participants will be dissatisfied at these prices?
   b. What quantity of DVDs at what price will be sold in equilibrium?
   c. What is the total revenue from DVD sales?
3. Hardware and software for computers are complements. Discuss the effects on the equilibrium price and quantity:
   a. In the software market, when the price of computer hardware falls.
   b. In the hardware market, when the price of computer software rises.
4. Suppose a newly released study shows that battery-powered toys harm a child's development and recommends that parents adjust their purchasing behaviour accordingly. Use diagrams to show the effect on price and quantity in each of the following markets:
   a. The market for battery-powered toys.
   b. The market for D batteries.
   c. The market for yo-yos (which do not require batteries).
5. Using diagrams, show what changes in price and quantity would be expected in the following markets under the scenarios given:
   a. *Crude oil*: As petroleum reserves decrease, it becomes more difficult to find and recover crude oil.
   b. *Air travel*: Worries about air safety cause travellers to shy away from air travel.
   c. *Rail travel*: Worries about air safety cause travellers to shy away from air travel.
   d. *Hotel rooms in Hawaii*: Worries about air safety cause travellers to shy away from air travel.
   e. *Milk*: A genetically engineered hormone enables large milk producers to cut production costs.
6. For each scenario in Problem 5, state whether the effect is a change in demand or just a change in quantity demanded.
7. Suppose demand for seats at football games is $P = 1900 - (1/50)Q$ and supply is fixed at $Q = 90{,}000$ seats.
   a. Find the equilibrium price and quantity of seats for a football game (using algebra and a graph).
   b. Suppose the government prohibits tickets scalping (selling tickets above their face value), and the face value of tickets is €50 (this policy places a price ceiling at €50). How many consumers will be dissatisfied (how large is excess demand)?
   c. Suppose the next game is a major rivalry, and so demand jumps to $P = 2100 - (1/50)Q$. How many consumers will be dissatisfied for the big game?
   d. How do the distortions of this price ceiling differ from the more typical case of upward-sloping supply?
8. The demand for apartments is $P = 1200 - Q$ while the supply is $P = Q$ units. The government imposes rent control at $P =$ €300/month. Suppose demand grows in the market to $P = 1400 - Q$.
   a. How is excess demand affected by the growth in demand for apartments?
   b. At what price would the government have to set the rent control to keep excess demand at the same level as prior to the growth in demand?
9. Suppose demand is $P = 600 - Q$ and supply is $P = Q$ in the wheat market, where Q is tonnes of wheat per year. The EU sets a price support at $P =$ €500/tonne and purchases any

excess supply at this price. In response, as a long-run adjustment, farmers switch their crops from corn to wheat, expanding supply to $P = (1/2)Q$.

a. How does excess supply with the larger supply compare to excess supply prior to the farmers switching crops?
b. How much more does the EU have to spend to buy up the excess supply?

10. How would the equilibrium price and quantity change in the market depicted below if the marginal cost of every producer were to increase by €2/kg? (Hint: Recall the vertical interpretation of the supply curve discussed in Chapter 1.)

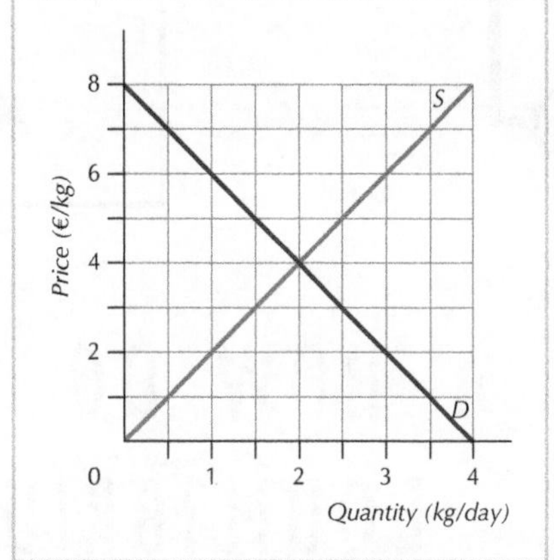

ANSWERS TO IN-CHAPTER EXERCISES

2.1. At a price of 4 cents/tulip, the quantity demanded is 5000 tulips/day and the quantity supplied is 1000 tulips/day, making excess demand equal to 4000 tulips/day. At a price of 20 cents/tulip, excess supply is 4000 tulips/day.

2.2. A rent control level set above the equilibrium price has no effect. The rent will settle at its equilibrium value of €600/mo.

2.3. The fall in the price of diesel fuel shifts the supply curve to the right. The report on mercury shifts the demand curve to the left. As shown in the following diagrams, the equilibrium price will go down (both panels) but the equilibrium quantity may go either up (panel *b*) or down (panel *a*).

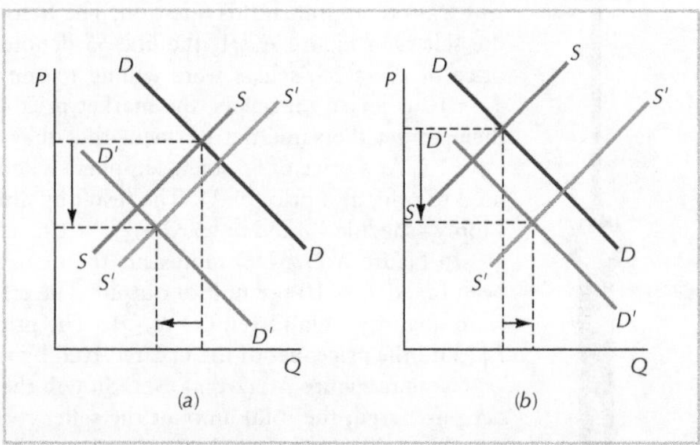

2.4. $4Q^* = 12 - 2Q^*$, which yields $Q^* = 2$ and $P^* = 4Q^* = 8$.

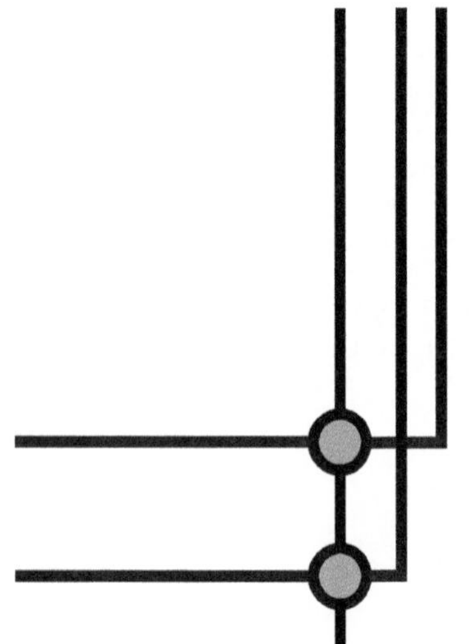

APPENDIX

2

HOW DO TAXES AFFECT EQUILIBRIUM PRICES AND QUANTITIES?

Supply and demand analysis is also a useful tool for analysing the effects of various taxes. In this section we consider a constant tax per unit of output. How will the equilibrium price and quantity of a product be affected if a tax of $T = 10$ is levied on each unit sold by the producer? There are two equivalent ways to approach this question. The first is to suppose that the tax is levied on the seller. In Figure A.2.1, the line *SS* denotes the original supply schedule. At a price of $P_0 = 25$, sellers were willing to supply Q_0 units of output. When a tax $T = 10$ is levied on sellers, the market price would have to be $P_0 + 10 = 35$ for them to get the same net payment that they used to receive when the price was $P_0 = 25$. At a price of 35, then, suppliers will offer the same amount of output they used to offer at a price of 25. The resulting after-tax supply schedule is the original supply schedule shifted upward by $T = 10$.

In Figure A.2.2, *DD* represents the demand curve facing the sellers who have been taxed $T = 10$ per unit of output. The effect of the tax is to cause the equilibrium quantity to fall from Q^* to Q_1^*. The price paid by the buyer rises from P^* to P_1^*; and the price, net of the tax, received by the seller falls to $P_1^* - 10$.

Note in Figure A.2.2 that even though the seller pays a tax of T on each product purchased, the total amount the seller receives per unit lies less than T below the old equilibrium price. Note also that even though the tax is collected from the seller, its effect is to increase the price paid by buyers. The burden of the tax is thus divided between the buyer and the seller.

FIGURE A.2.1
A Tax of $T = 10$ Levied on the Seller Shifts the Supply Schedule Upward by T Units
The original supply schedule tells us what price suppliers must charge in order to cover their costs at any given level of output. From the seller's perspective, a tax of $T = 10$ units is the same as a unit-cost increase of 10 units. The new supply curve thus lies 10 units above the old one.

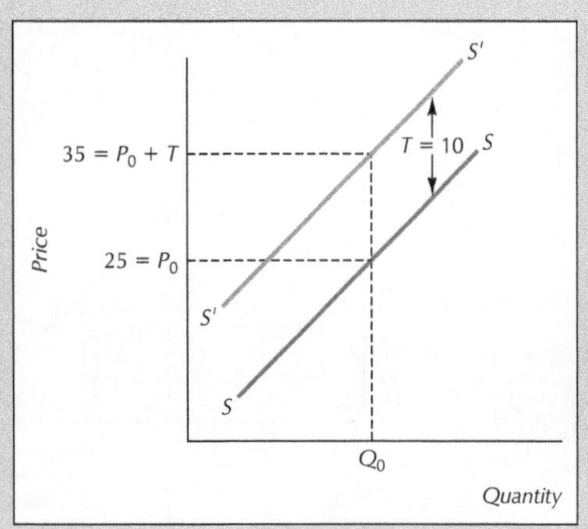

Algebraically, the seller's share of the tax, denoted t_s, is the reduction in the price the seller receives, divided by the tax:

$$t_s = \frac{P^* - (P_1^* - T)}{T} \qquad (A.2.1)$$

Similarly, the buyer's share of the tax, t_b, is the increase in price (including tax) divided by the tax:

$$t_b = \frac{P_1^* - P^*}{T} \qquad (A.2.2)$$

EXERCISE A.2.1 Verify that $t_s + t_b = 1$.

In general, t_b and t_s depend on the shapes of the supply and demand schedules. If, for example, supply is highly unresponsive to changes in price, t_b will be close to zero, t_s close to 1. Conversely, if demand is highly unresponsive to price, t_b will be

FIGURE A.2.2
Equilibrium Prices and Quantities When a Tax of $T = 10$ Is Levied on the Seller
The tax causes a reduction in equilibrium quantity from Q^* to Q_1^*. The new price paid by the buyer rises from P^* to P_1^*. The new price received by the seller falls from P^* to $P_1^* - 10$.

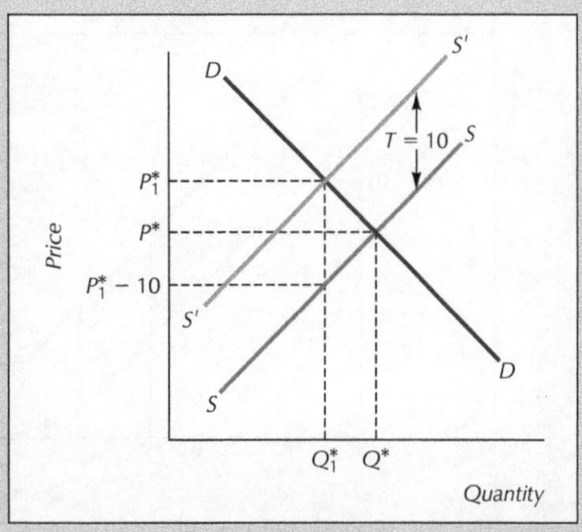

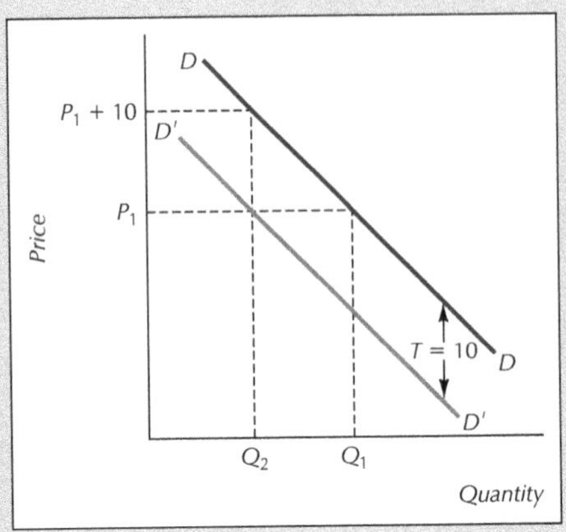

FIGURE A.2.3
The Effect of a Tax of $T = 10$ Levied on the Buyer
Before the tax, buyers would buy Q_1 units at a price of P_1. After the tax, a price of P_1 becomes $P_1 + 10$, which means buyers will buy only Q_2. The effect of the tax is to shift the demand curve downward by 10 units.

close to 1, t_s close to zero. These claims amount to a statement that a tax tends to fall most heavily on the side of the market that can least escape it. If buyers have no substitute products to which they are prepared to turn, the lion's share of the tax will be passed on to them by suppliers. But if suppliers have no alternative other than to go on supplying a product, most of the burden of a tax will fall on them. As long as the supply curve is positively sloped and the demand curve is negatively sloped, however, both t_s and t_b will be positive.

The second way of analysing the effect of a tax of $T = 10$ per unit of output is to imagine that the tax is collected directly from the buyer. How would that affect the demand curve for the product? In Figure A.2.3, *DD* is the demand curve before the imposition of the tax. At a price of P_1, buyers would demand a quantity of Q_1. After imposition of the tax, the total amount that buyers have to pay if the product price is P_1 will be $P_1 + 10$. Accordingly, the quantity they demand falls from Q_1 to Q_2. In like fashion, we can reckon the quantity demanded at any other price after imposition of the tax. $D'D'$ is the resulting after-tax demand curve in Figure A.2.3. It is the original demand curve translated downward by 10 units.

If *SS* in Figure A.2.4 denotes the supply schedule for this market, we can easily trace out the effects of the tax on the equilibrium price and quantity. The

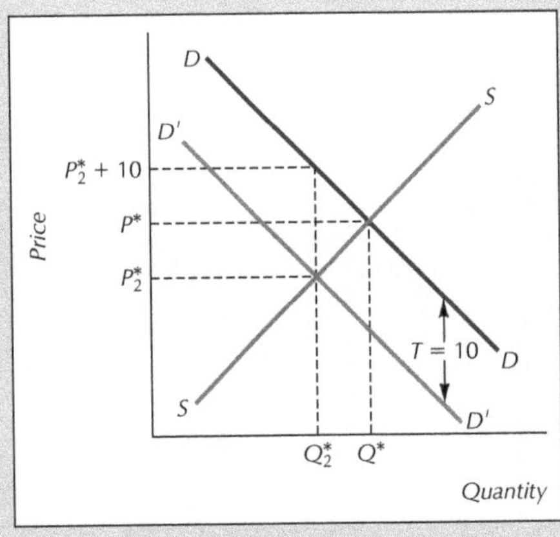

FIGURE A.2.4
Equilibrium Prices and Quantities after Imposition of a Tax of $T = 10$ Paid by the Buyer
The tax causes a reduction in equilibrium quantity from Q^* to Q_2^*. The new price paid by the buyer rises from P^* to $P_2^* + 10$. The new price received by the seller falls from P^* to P_2^*.

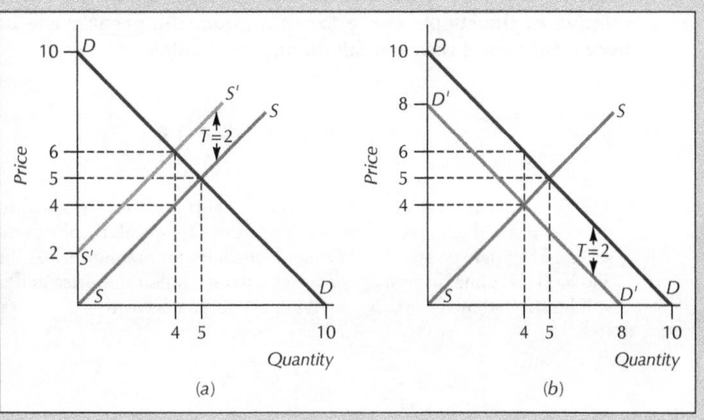

FIGURE A.2.5
A Tax on the Buyer Leads to the Same Outcome as a Tax on the Seller
The price received by sellers (net of the tax), the price paid by buyers (including tax), and the equilibrium quantity will all be the same when the tax is collected from sellers (panel *a*) as when it is collected from buyers (panel *b*).

equilibrium quantity falls from Q^* to Q_2^*, and the equilibrium pretax price falls from P^* to P_2^*. The total price paid by the buyer after imposition of the tax rises to $P_2^* + 10$.

Is the effect of a tax on the seller any different from the effect of a tax on the buyer? Not at all. To illustrate, suppose the supply and demand curves for a market are given by $P = Q^s$ and $P = 10 - Q^d$, respectively, and consider first the effect of a tax of 2 per unit of output imposed on the seller. Figure A.2.5(*a*) shows the original supply and demand curves and the new after-tax supply curve, $S'S'$. The original equilibrium price and quantity are both equal to 5. The new equilibrium price to the buyer (inclusive of tax) and quantity are 6 and 4, respectively. The price received by sellers, net of the tax, is 4.

Now, consider a tax of 2 per unit of output imposed on the buyers. Figure A.2.5(*b*) shows the original supply and demand curves and the new after-tax demand curve, $D'D'$. Note that the effects on price and quantity are exactly the same as in the case of the tax levied on sellers shown in panel *a*.

EXERCISE A.2.2 Consider a market whose supply and demand curves are given by $P = 4Q^s$ and $P = 12 - 2Q^d$, respectively. How will the equilibrium price and quantity in this market be affected if a tax of 6 per unit of output is imposed on sellers? If the same tax is imposed on buyers?

When tax revenues must be raised, many political leaders find it expedient to propose a sales tax on corporations because 'they can best afford to pay it'. But careful analysis of the effects of a sales tax shows that its burden will be the same whether it is imposed on buyers or sellers. The *legal incidence of the tax* (whether it is imposed on buyers or on sellers) has no effect on the *economic incidence* of the tax (the respective shares of the tax burden borne by buyers and sellers). Economically speaking, the entity from which the tax is actually collected is thus a matter of complete indifference.

A word of caution: When we say that the economic burden of the tax does not depend on the party from whom the tax is directly collected, this does not mean that buyers and sellers always share the burden of taxes equally. Their respective shares may, as noted, be highly unequal. The independence of legal incidence and economic incidence simply means that the burden will be shared in the same way no matter where the tax is placed.

EXERCISE A.2.3 ***True or false?*** **The steeper the demand curve for a good relative to the supply curve for that good, the greater the proportion of a tax on that good that will fall on buyers. Explain.**

PROBLEMS

1. The government, fearful that a titanium shortage could jeopardize national security, imposes a tax of €2/g on the retail price of this rare metal. It collects the tax from titanium sellers. The original supply and demand schedules for titanium are as shown in the diagram. Show, in the same diagram, how the short-run equilibrium price and quantity of titanium will be affected by the tax. Label all important points clearly.

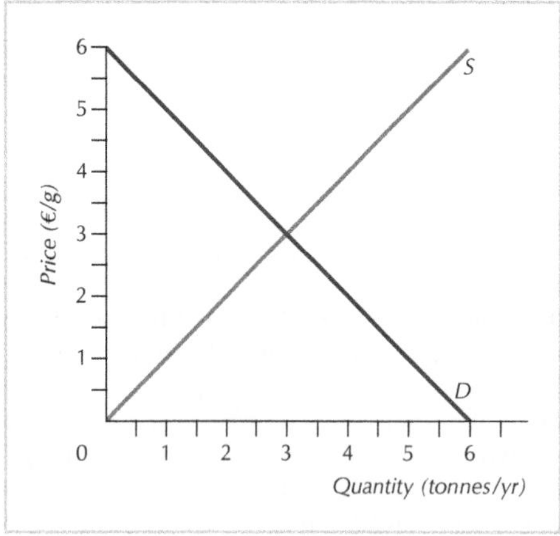

2. In the market for titanium described in Problem 1 (with no tax), suppose that a price floor of €4/g results in sales of only 2 tonnes/yr (with no tax). Describe a transaction that will make some buyers and sellers better off without harming others.

3. Suppose the titanium market in Problem 1, with a tax of €2/g, experiences growth in the demand for titanium because of new-found medical uses. The new demand curve is $P = 8 - Q$. Find the change in government tax revenue due to the heightened demand for titanium.

4. Suppose instead the titanium market in Problem 2, with no tax but a price floor at €4/g, suffers a reduction in supply because of dwindling titanium reserves. The new supply curve is $P = 2 + Q$. How does excess supply change due to the reduction in supply? Is the price floor still binding (does it cause price to rise from its equilibrium level)?

5. Suppose state government levies a tax of €9 on each DVD sold, collected from sellers.

   a. What quantity of DVDs will be sold in equilibrium?
   b. What price do buyers pay?
   c. How much do buyers now spend in total?
   d. How much money goes to the government?
   e. Show the above results graphically.

6. For the tax described in Problem 5,

   a. What fraction of the tax does the seller bear?
   b. What fraction of the tax does the buyer bear?

7. US President Ronald Reagan negotiated a 'voluntary' import quota on Japanese cars sold in the United States in the early 1980s. Some of his advisers had recommended that he impose a higher import tax (tariff) instead. Assuming the tariff was in the form of a constant tax T per Japanese car sold in the US and that T was chosen to produce the same quantity

reduction as the quota, how will the prices paid for Japanese cars by US consumers compare under the two policies?

8. Many studies on rats and mice have established that charred meat grilled over hot coals causes cancer. Since the government cannot easily regulate home cooking methods, an alternative method has been proposed to discourage the consumption of barbecued meat. The proposal is to place a 100 per cent tax at the retail level on charcoal briquets. Suppose the daily demand for charcoal was $P = 120 - 2Q$ and the supply was $P = 30 + Q$, where P is in euros per bag and Q is the number of 10kg bags of charcoal sold weekly.
   a. What is the before- and after-tax price of charcoal?
   b. What is the before- and after-tax quantity of charcoal?
   c. How is the tax divided among sellers and buyers?

9. Supply is $P = 4Q$, while demand is $P = 20$, where P is price in euros per unit and Q is units of output per week.
   a. Find the equilibrium price and quantity (using both algebra and a graph).
   b. If sellers must pay a tax of $T =$ €4/unit, what happens to the quantity exchanged, the price buyers pay, and the price sellers receive (net of the tax)?
   c. How is the burden of the tax distributed across buyers and sellers and why?

10. Repeat Problem 9, but instead suppose the buyer pays the tax, demand is $P = 28 - Q$, and supply is $P = 20$.

ANSWERS TO IN-APPENDIX EXERCISES

A.2.1. $t_s + t_b = [(P^* - P_1^* + T) + (P_1^* - P^*)]/T = T/T = 1.$

A.2.2. The original price and quantity are given by $P^* = 8$ and $Q^* = 2$, respectively. The supply curve with the tax is given by $P = 6 + 4Q^s$. Letting P' and Q' denote the new equilibrium values of price and quantity, we now have $6 + 4Q' = 12 - 2Q'$, which yields $Q' = 1$, $P' = 10$, where P' is the price paid by buyers. $P' - 6 = 4$ is the price received by sellers. Alternatively, the demand curve with a tax of 6 levied on buyers is given by $P = 6 - 2Q^d$, and we have $4Q' = 6' - 2Q'$, which again yields $Q' = 1$. $P'' = 4$, where P'' is the price received by sellers. $P'' + T = P'' + 6 = 10$ is the price paid by buyers.

A.2.3. True.

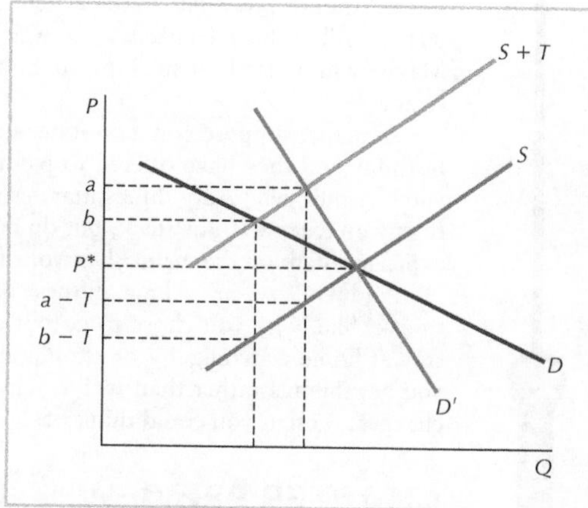

Buyer's share for tax with $D' = (a - P^*)/T$

Buyer's share for tax with $D = (b - P^*)/T$

RATIONAL CONSUMER CHOICE

It is Saturday night and you have decided to eat out at a new restaurant in town. The waitress hands you the menu, and there is a lot of choice. How are you going to decide what to eat?

The more you analyse this seemingly simple problem the less simple it can seem. You need to think about which dish looks most tasty, what is best for your diet etc. All of this then needs to be weighed against the relative prices of the dishes. Maybe you prefer beef steak to pizza, but are you willing to pay an extra €10 for steak?

Actually, suppose you do not need to worry about price because it is a friend's birthday and they have offered to pay the bill. Is the problem any easier? Despite your friend's generosity things may have got a bit trickier. What if you are willing to pay an extra €10 for steak, but do not want to feel guilty for choosing the most expensive item on the menu? It is your friend's birthday after all.

And while we are asking all these questions, there is a lot more we might want to ask, like, why you chose to go out to your friend's birthday party rather than stay at home watching TV or reading more of your economic textbooks. Why did you get the bus rather than walk? Why, after much deliberation, did you buy the cheapest present you could think of?

CHAPTER PREVIEW

Our task in this chapter is to set forth the economist's basic model for answering questions such as the ones posed above. This model is known as the theory of *rational consumer choice*. It underlies all individual purchase decisions, which in turn add up to the demand curves we worked with in the preceding chapter.

Rational choice theory begins with the assumption that consumers enter the marketplace with well-defined preferences. Taking prices as given, their task is to allocate their incomes to best serve these preferences. Two steps are required to carry out this task. Step 1 is to describe the various combinations of goods the consumer is *able* to buy. These combinations depend on both her income level and the prices of the goods. Step 2 then is to select from among the feasible combinations the particular one that she *prefers* to all others. Analysis of step 2 requires some means of describing her preferences, in particular, a summary of her ranking of the desirability of all feasible combinations. Formal development of these two elements of the theory will occupy our attention throughout this chapter. Because the first element—describing the set of possibilities—is much less abstract than the second, let us begin with it.

THE OPPORTUNITY SET OR BUDGET CONSTRAINT

bundle a particular combination of two or more goods.

For simplicity, we start by considering a world with only two goods,[1] shelter and food. A **bundle** of goods is the term used to describe a particular combination of shelter, measured in square metres per week, and food, measured in kilograms per week. Thus, in Figure 3.1, one bundle (bundle *A*) might consist of 5 sq. m/wk of shelter and 7 kg/wk of food, while another (bundle *B*) consists of 3 sq. m/wk of shelter and 8 kg/wk of food. For brevity, we use (5, 7) to denote bundle *A* and (3, 8) to denote bundle *B*. More generally, (S_0, F_0) will denote the bundle with S_0 sq. m/wk of shelter and F_0 kg/wk of food. By convention, the first number of the pair in any bundle represents the good measured along the horizontal axis.

Note that the units on both axes are *flows*, which means physical quantities per unit of time—kilograms per week, square metres per week. Consumption is always measured as a flow. It is important to keep track of the time dimension because without it there would be no way to evaluate whether a given quantity of consumption was large or small. (Suppose all you know is that your food consumption is 4 kg. If that is how much you eat each day, it is a lot. But if that is all you eat in a month, you are not likely to survive for long.)[2]

FIGURE 3.1
Two Bundles of Goods
A bundle is a specific combination of goods. Bundle *A* has 5 units of shelter and 7 units of food. Bundle *B* has 3 units of shelter and 8 units of food.

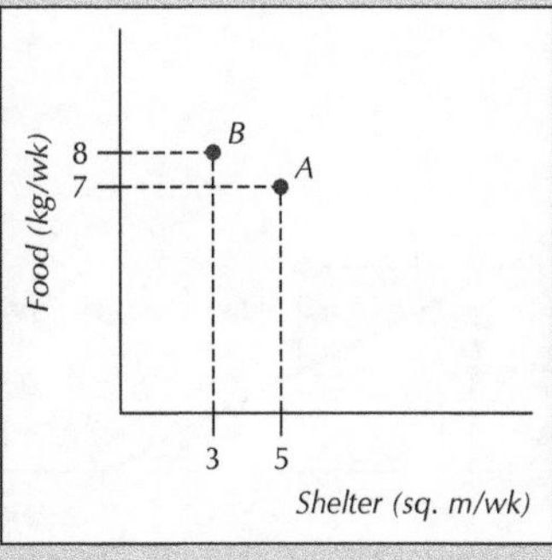

[1]As economists use the term, a 'good' may refer to either a product or a service.
[2]The flow aspect of consumption also helps us alleviate any concern about goods not being divisible. If you consume 1.5 kg/mo, then you consume 18 kg/yr, which is a whole number.

Suppose the consumer's income is M = €100/wk, all of which she spends on some combination of food and shelter. (Note that income is also a flow.) Suppose further that the prices of shelter and food are P_S = €5/sq. m and P_F = €10/kg, respectively. If the consumer spent all her income on shelter, she could buy M/P_S = (€100/wk) ÷ (€5/sq. m) = 20 sq. m/wk. That is, she could buy the bundle consisting of 20 sq. m/wk of shelter and 0 kg/wk of food, denoted (20, 0). Alternatively, suppose the consumer spent all her income on food. She would then get the bundle consisting of M/P_F = (€100/wk) ÷ (€10/kg), which is 10 kg/wk of food and 0 sq. m/wk of shelter, denoted (0, 10).

Note that the units in which consumption goods are measured are subject to the standard rules of arithmetic. For example, when we simplify the expression on the right-hand side of the equation M/P_S = (€100/wk) ÷ (€5/sq. m), we are essentially dividing one fraction by another, so we follow the standard rule of inverting the fraction in the denominator and multiplying it by the fraction in the numerator: (sq. m/€5) × (€100/wk) = (€100 × sq. m)/(€5 × wk). After dividing both the numerator and denominator of the fraction on the right-hand side of this last equation by €5, we have 20 sq. m/wk, which is the maximum amount of shelter the consumer can buy with an income of €100/wk. Similarly, M/P_F = (€100/wk) ÷ (€10/kg) simplifies to 10 kg/wk, the maximum amount of food the consumer can purchase with an income of €100/wk.

In Figure 3.2 these polar cases are labelled K and L, respectively. The consumer is also able to purchase any other bundle that lies along the straight line that joins points K and L. [Verify, for example, that the bundle (12, 4) lies on this same line.] This line is called the **budget constraint** and is labelled B in the diagram.

budget constraint the set of all bundles that exactly exhausts the consumer's income at given prices. Also called the *budget line*.

Recall the maxim from high school algebra that the slope of a straight line is its 'rise' over its 'run' (the change in its vertical position divided by the corresponding change in its horizontal position). Here, note that the slope of the budget constraint is its vertical intercept (the rise) divided by its horizontal intercept (the corresponding run): −(10 kg/wk)/(20 sq. m/wk) = $-\frac{1}{2}$ kg/sq. m. (Note again how the units obey the standard rules of arithmetic.) The minus sign signifies that the budget line falls as

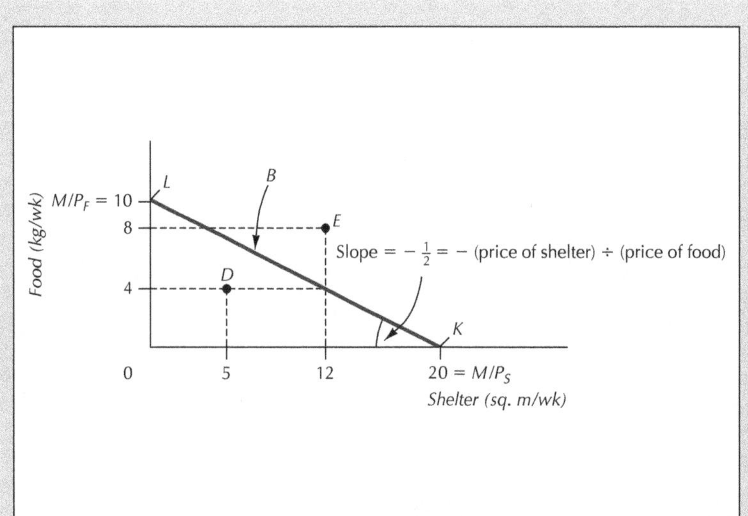

FIGURE 3.2
The Budget Constraint, or Budget Line
Line B describes the set of all bundles the consumer can purchase for given values of income and prices. Its slope is the negative of the price of shelter divided by the price of food. In absolute value, this slope is the opportunity cost of an additional unit of shelter—the number of units of food that must be sacrificed in order to purchase one additional unit of shelter at market prices.

it moves to the right—that it has a negative slope. More generally, if M denotes the consumer's weekly income, and PS and PF denote the prices of shelter and food, respectively, the horizontal and vertical intercepts will be given by (M/P_S) and (M/P_F), respectively. Thus the general formula for the slope of the budget constraint is given by $-(M/P_F)/(M/P_S) = -P_S/P_F$, which is simply the negative of the price ratio of the two goods. Given their respective prices, it is the rate at which food can be exchanged for shelter. Thus, in Figure 3.2, 1 kg of food can be exchanged for 2 sq. m of shelter. In the language of opportunity cost from Chapter 1, we would say that the opportunity cost of an additional square metre of shelter is $P_S/P_F = \frac{1}{2}$ kg of food.

In addition to being able to buy any of the bundles along her budget constraint, the consumer is also able to purchase any bundle that lies within the *budget triangle* bounded by it and the two axes. D is one such bundle in Figure 3.2. Bundle D costs €65/wk, which is well below the consumer's income of €100/wk. The bundles on or within the budget triangle are also referred to as the *feasible set,* or **affordable set.** Bundles like E that lie outside the budget triangle are said to be *infeasible,* or *unaffordable.* At a cost of €140/wk, E is simply beyond the consumer's reach.

affordable set bundles on or below the budget constraint; bundles for which the required expenditure at given prices is less than or equal to the income available.

If S and F denote the quantities of shelter and food, respectively, the budget constraint must satisfy the following equation:

$$P_S S + P_F F = M \tag{3.1}$$

which says simply that the consumer's weekly expenditure on shelter ($P_S S$) plus her weekly expenditure on food ($P_F F$) must add up to her weekly income (M). To express the budget constraint in the manner conventionally used to represent the formula for a straight line, we solve Equation 3.1 for F in terms of S, which yields

$$F = \frac{M}{P_F} - \frac{P_S}{P_F}S \tag{3.2}$$

Equation 3.2 is another way of seeing that the vertical intercept of the budget constraint is given by M/P_F and its slope by $-(P_S/P_F)$. The equation for the budget constraint in Figure 3.2 is $F = 10 - \frac{1}{2}S$.

Budget Shifts Due to Price or Income Changes

Price Changes The slope and position of the budget constraint are fully determined by the consumer's income and the prices of the respective goods. Change any one of these factors and we have a new budget constraint. Figure 3.3 shows the effect of an increase in the price of shelter from P_{S1} = €5/sq. m to P_{S2} = €10. Since both weekly income and the price of food are unchanged, the vertical intercept of

FIGURE 3.3
The Effect of a Rise in the Price of Shelter
When shelter goes up in price, the vertical intercept of the budget constraint remains the same. The original budget constraint rotates inward about this intercept.

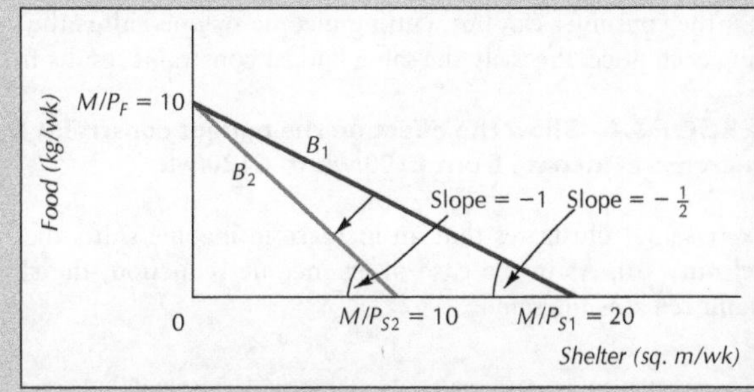

the consumer's budget constraint stays the same. The rise in the price of shelter rotates the budget constraint inward about this intercept, as shown in the diagram.

Note in Figure 3.3 that even though the price of food has not changed, the new budget constraint, $B2$, curtails not only the amount of shelter the consumer can buy but also the amount of food.[3]

EXERCISE 3.1 Show the effect on the budget constraint B_1 in Figure 3.3 of a fall in the price of shelter from €5/sq. m to €4/sq. m.

In Exercise 3.1, you saw that a fall in the price of shelter again leaves the vertical intercept of the budget constraint unchanged. This time the budget constraint rotates outward. Note also in Exercise 3.1 that although the price of food remains unchanged, the new budget constraint enables the consumer to buy bundles that contain not only more shelter but also more food than she could afford on the original budget constraint.

The following exercise illustrates how changing the price of the good on the vertical axis affects the budget constraint.

EXERCISE 3.2 Show the effect on the budget constraint B_1 in Figure 3.3 of a rise in the price of food from €10/kg to €20/kg.

When we change the price of only one good, we necessarily change the slope of the budget constraint, $-P_S/P_F$. The same is true if we change both prices by different proportions. But as Exercise 3.3 will illustrate, changing both prices by exactly the same proportion gives rise to a new budget constraint with the same slope as before.

EXERCISE 3.3 Show the effect on the budget constraint B_3 in Figure 3.3 of a rise in the price of food from €10/kg to €20/kg and a rise in the price of shelter from €5/sq. m to €10/sq. m.

Note from Exercise 3.3 that the effect of doubling the prices of both food and shelter is to shift the budget constraint inward and parallel to the original budget constraint. The important lesson of this exercise is that the slope of a budget constraint tells us only about *relative prices,* nothing about prices in absolute terms. When the prices of food and shelter change in the same proportion, the opportunity cost of shelter in terms of food remains the same as before.

Income Changes The effect of a change in income is much like the effect of an equal proportional change in all prices. Suppose, for example, that our hypothetical consumer's income is cut by half, from €100/wk to €50/wk. The horizontal intercept of the consumer's budget constraint then falls from 20 sq. m/wk to 10 sq. m/wk, and the vertical intercept falls from 10 kg/wk to 5 kg/wk, as shown in Figure 3.4. Thus the new budget, B_2, is parallel to the old, B_1, each with a slope of $-\frac{1}{2}$. In terms of its effect on what the consumer can buy, cutting income by one-half is thus no different from doubling each price. Precisely the same budget constraint results from both changes.

EXERCISE 3.4 Show the effect on the budget constraint B_1 in Figure 3.4 of an increase in income from €100/wk to €120/wk.

Exercise 3.4 illustrates that an increase in income shifts the budget constraint parallel outward. As in the case of an income reduction, the slope of the budget constraint remains the same.

[3]The single exception to this statement involves the vertical intercept (0, 10), which lies on both the original and the new budget constraints.

FIGURE 3.4
The Effect of Cutting Income by Half
Both horizontal and vertical intercepts fall by half. The new budget constraint has the same slope as the old but is closer to the origin.

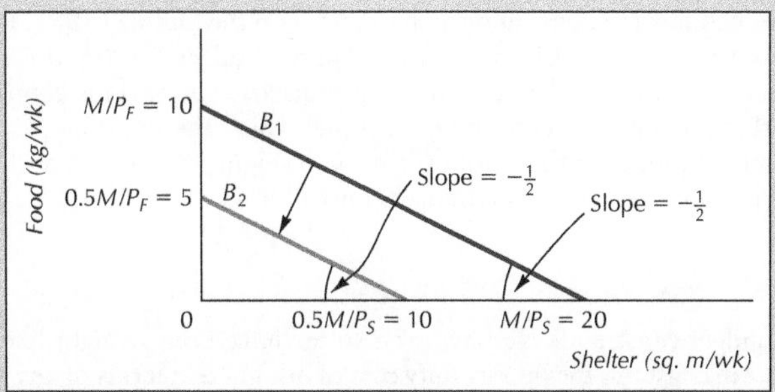

Budgets Involving More Than Two Goods

In the examples discussed so far, the consumer could buy only two different goods. No consumer faces such narrow options. In its most general form, the consumer budgeting problem can be posed as a choice between not two but N different goods, where N can be an indefinitely large number. With only two goods ($N = 2$), the budget constraint is a straight line, as we just saw. With three goods ($N = 3$), it is a plane. When we have more than three goods, the budget constraint becomes what mathematicians call a *hyperplane,* or *multidimensional plane.* It is difficult to represent this multidimensional case geometrically. We are just not very good at visualizing surfaces that have more than three dimensions.

The nineteenth-century economist Alfred Marshall proposed a disarmingly simple solution to this problem. It is to view the consumer's choice as being one between a particular good—call it X—and an amalgam of other goods, denoted Y. This amalgam is generally called the **composite good.** By convention, the units of the composite good are defined so that its price is €1 per unit. This convention enables us to think of the composite good as the amount of income the consumer has left over after buying the good X. Equivalently, it is the amount the consumer spends on goods other than X. For the moment, all the examples we consider will be ones in which consumers spend all their incomes. In Chapter 5 we will use the rational choice model to analyse the decision to save.

> ***composite good*** in a choice between a good X and numerous other goods, the amount of money the consumer spends on those other goods.

To illustrate how the composite good concept is used, suppose the consumer has an income of €M/wk, and the price of X is P_X. The consumer's budget constraint may then be represented as a straight line in the X, Y plane, as shown in Figure 3.5. Because the price of a unit of the composite good is €1, a consumer who devotes all his income to it will be able to buy M units. All this means is that he will have €M

FIGURE 3.5
The Budget Constraint with the Composite Good
The vertical axis measures the amount of money spent each week on all goods other than X.

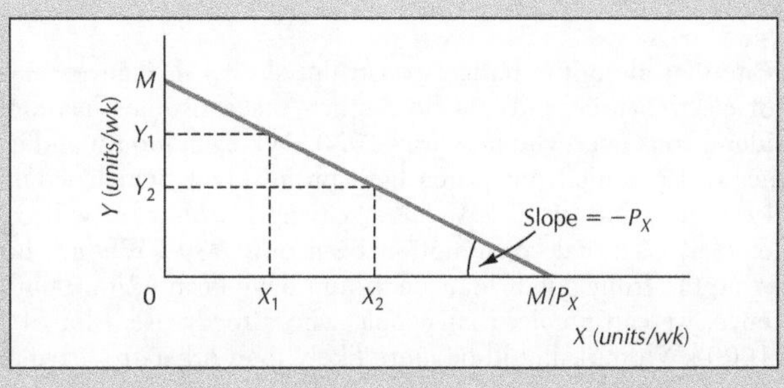

available to spend on other goods if he buys no X. Alternatively, if he spends his entire income on X, he will be able to purchase the bundle $(M/P_X, 0)$. Since the price of Y is assumed to be €1/unit, the slope of the budget constraint is simply $-P_X$.

As before, the budget constraint summarizes the various combinations of bundles that exhaust the consumer's income. Thus, the consumer can have X_1 units of X and Y_1 units of the composite good in Figure 3.5, or X_2 and Y_2, or any other combination that lies on the budget constraint.

Non-Linear Budget Constraints

The budget constraints we have seen so far have been straight lines. When relative prices are constant, the opportunity cost of one good in terms of any other is the same, no matter what bundle of goods we already have. But often budget constraints are not straight lines. To illustrate, consider the following example of quantity discounts.

EXAMPLE 3.1 **The Gigawatt Power Company charges €0.10 per kilowatt-hour (kWh) for the first 1000 kWh of power purchased by a residential customer each month, but only €0.05/kWh for all additional kWh. For a residential customer with a monthly income of €400, graph the budget constraint for electric power and the composite good.**

If the consumer buys no electric power, he will have €400/mo to spend on other goods. Thus the vertical intercept of his budget constraint is (0, 400). As shown in Figure 3.6, for each of the first 1000 kWh he buys, he must give up €0.10, which means that the slope of his budget constraint starts out at $-\frac{1}{10}$. At 1000 kWh/mo, the price falls to €0.05/kWh, which means that the slope of his budget constraint from that point rightward is only $-\frac{1}{20}$. ◆

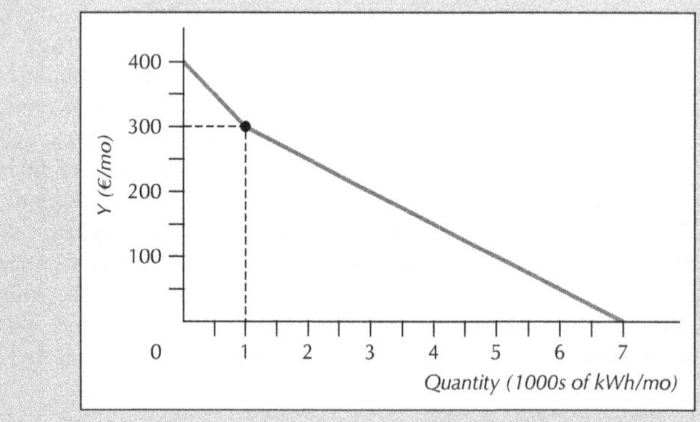

FIGURE 3.6 A Quantity Discount Gives Rise to a Non-Linear Budget Constraint Once electric power consumption reaches 1000 kWh/mo, the opportunity cost of additional power falls from €0.10/kWh to €0.05/kWh.

Note that along the budget constraint shown in Figure 3.6, the opportunity cost of electricity depends on how much the consumer has already purchased. Consider a consumer who now uses 1020 kWh each month and is trying to decide whether to leave his front porch light on all night, which would result in additional consumption of 20 kWh/mo. Leaving his light on will cost him an extra €1/mo. Had his usual consumption been only 980 kWh/mo, however, the cost of leaving the front porch light on would have been €2/mo. On the basis of this difference, we can predict that people who already use a lot of electricity (more than 1000 kWh/mo) should be more likely than others to leave their porch lights burning at night.

EXERCISE 3.5 Suppose instead Gigawatt Power Company charged €0.05/kWh for the first 1000 kWh of power purchased by a residential consumer each month, but €0.10/kWh each for all additional kilowatt-hours. For a residential consumer with a monthly income of €400, graph the budget constraint for electric power and the composite good. What if the rate jumps to €0.10/kWh for *all* kilowatt-hours if power consumption in a month exceeds 1000 kWh (where the higher rate applies to all, not just the additional, kilowatt-hours)?

Non-linear budget constraints are not uncommon. For instance, any offers of the form, 'buy one get one free', 'free delivery if you spend over €50', or '20% off if you spend over €50', cause the budget constraint to be non-linear. Two-part tariffs where there is a lump sum to use the service, for example a gym or phone network, as well as cost per unit used also cause the budget constraint to be non-linear. In Chapters 5 and 12 we shall look at why it may be in a firm's interest to price in this way.

If the Budget Constraint Is the Same, the Decision Should Be the Same

Even without knowing anything about the consumer's preferences, we can use budgetary information to make certain inferences about how a rational consumer will behave. Suppose, for example, that the consumer's tastes do not change over time and that he is confronted with exactly the same budget constraint in each of two different situations. If he is rational, he should make exactly the same choice in both cases. After all, if the budget constraint is the same as before, the consumer has exactly the same menu of possible bundles available as before; and since we have no reason to believe that his ranking of the desirability of these bundles has changed, the most desirable bundle should also be the same. As the following example makes clear, however, it may not always be immediately apparent that the budget constraints are in fact the same.

EXAMPLE 3.2 On one occasion, Gowdy fills his car's tank with diesel on the evening before his departure on a fishing trip. He awakens to discover that a thief has siphoned out all but 1 litre from his 61-litre tank. On another occasion, he plans to stop for diesel on his way out the next morning before he goes fishing. He awakens to discover that he has lost €60 from his wallet. If diesel sells for €1/litre and the round trip will consume 15 litres, how, if at all, should Gowdy's decision about whether to take the fishing trip differ in the two cases? (Assume that, monetary costs aside, the inconvenience of having to refill his tank is negligible.)

Suppose Gowdy's income is €M/mo. Before his loss, his budget constraint is B_1 in Figure 3.7. In both instances described, his budget constraint at the moment he discovers his loss will shift inward to B_2. If he does not take the trip, he will have M − €60 available to spend on other goods in both cases. And if he does take the trip, he will have to purchase the required diesel at €1/litre in both cases. No matter what the source of the loss, the remaining opportunities are exactly the same. If Gowdy's budget is tight, he may decide to cancel his trip. Otherwise, he may go despite the loss. But because his budget constraint and tastes are the same in the lost-cash case as in the stolen-diesel case, it would not be rational for him to take the trip in one instance but not in the other. ◆

If your preferences are stable and your opportunities are the same in two situations, you should make the same choice in each case.

Although the rational choice model makes clear that the decisions *should* be the same if the budget constraints and preferences are the same, people sometimes choose differently. The difficulty is often that the way the different situations are

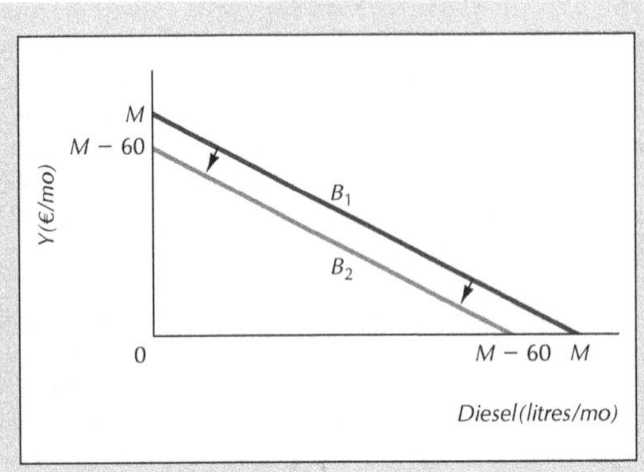

FIGURE 3.7
Budget Constraints Following Theft of Diesel, Loss of Cash
A theft of €60 worth of diesel has exactly the same effect on the budget constraint as the loss of €60 in cash. The bundle chosen should therefore be the same, irrespective of the source of the loss.

described sometimes causes people to overlook the essential similarities between them. For instance, in Example 3.2, many people erroneously conclude that the cost of taking the trip is higher in the stolen-diesel case than in the lost-money case, and so they are less likely to take the trip in the former instance. We shall return to similar issues in Chapter 8.

To recapitulate briefly, the budget constraint or budget line summarizes the combinations of bundles that the consumer is able to buy. Its position is determined jointly by income and prices. From the set of feasible bundles, the consumer's task is to pick the particular one she likes best. To identify this bundle, we need some means of summarizing the consumer's preferences over all possible bundles she might consume. We now turn to this task.

CONSUMER PREFERENCES

preference ordering a ranking of all possible consumption bundles in order of preference.

For simplicity, let us again begin by considering a world with only two goods: shelter and food. A **preference ordering** enables the consumer to rank any two bundles of goods in terms of their desirability, or order of preference. Consider two bundles, *A* and *B*. For concreteness, suppose that *A* contains 12 sq. m/wk of shelter and 8 kg/wk of food, while *B* has 10 sq. m/wk of shelter and 10 kg/wk of food. Knowing nothing about a consumer's preferences, we can say nothing about which of these bundles he will prefer. *A* has more shelter but less food than *B*. Someone who spends a lot of time at home would probably choose *A*, while someone with a rapid metabolism might be more likely to choose *B*.

The preference ordering enables the consumer to rank pairs of bundles but not to make more precise quantitative statements about their relative desirability. Thus, the consumer might be able to say that he prefers bundle *A* to *B* but not that *A* provides twice as much satisfaction as *B*.

Preference orderings often differ widely among consumers. One person will like Rachmaninoff, another the Red Hot Chili Peppers. Despite these differences, however, most preference orderings share several important features. Economists generally assume five simple properties of preference orderings. These properties allow us to construct the concise analytical representation of preferences we need for the budget allocation problem. We shall introduce these five properties over the next couple of pages. Here are the first two.

1. Completeness A preference ordering is *complete* if it enables the consumer to rank all possible combinations of goods and services. For any two bundles *A* and *B*, the consumer is able to make one of three possible statements: (1) *A* is preferred to *B*, (2) *B* is preferred to *A*, or (3) *A* and *B* are equally attractive. Taken literally, the completeness assumption is never satisfied, for there are many goods we know too little about to be able to evaluate. It is nonetheless a useful simplifying assumption for the analysis of choices among bundles of goods with which consumers are familiar. Its real intent is to rule out instances like the one portrayed in the fable of Buridan's ass. The hungry animal was unable to choose between two bales of hay in front of him and starved to death as a result.

2. Transitivity If you like steak better than hamburger and hamburger better than hot dogs, you are probably someone who likes steak better than hot dogs. To say that a consumer's preference ordering is *transitive* means that, for any three bundles *A*, *B* and *C*, if he prefers *A* to *B* and prefers *B* to *C*, then he always prefers *A* to *C*.

The preference relationship is thus assumed to be like the relationship used to compare heights of people. If O'Neal is taller than Nowitzki and Nowitzki is taller than Bryant, we know that O'Neal must be taller than Bryant. Not all comparative relationships are transitive. This is shown by the relationship 'defeats in football'. Some seasons, Manchester United beat Arsenal, and Arsenal beat Chelsea, but that does not tell us that Manchester United will necessarily beat Chelsea.

Transitivity is a simple consistency property and applies as well to the relation 'equally attractive as' and to any combination of it and the 'preferred to' relation. For example, if *A* is equally attractive as *B* and *B* is equally attractive as *C*, it follows that *A* is equally attractive as *C*. Similarly, if *A* is preferred to *B* and *B* is equally attractive as *C*, it follows that *A* is preferred to *C*.

The transitivity assumption can be justified as eliminating the potential for a 'money pump' problem. To illustrate, suppose you prefer *A* to *B* and *B* to *C*, but you also prefer *C* over *A*, so that your preferences are intransitive. If you start with *C*, you would trade *C* for *B*, trade *B* for *A*, and then trade *A* for *C*. This cycle could continue forever. If in each stage you were charged a tiny fee for the trade, you would eventually transfer all your money to the other trader. Clearly, such preferences are problematic.

As reasonable as the transitivity property sounds, we will see examples in later chapters of behaviour that seems inconsistent with it. But it is an accurate description of preferences in most instances. Unless otherwise stated, we will adopt it.

Taken together, the completeness and more-is-better properties are very important and useful. Their main implication is that we can put different bundles in order from the least preferred to most preferred. This allows us to use a utility function to represent the consumer's preferences (as discussed in the Appendix). More fundamentally, it means that the budget allocation problem is going to have a solution. Without either of these properties our task would look impossible. For instance, if the consumer's preference ordering is not complete, and he cannot tell us whether he prefers bundle *A* to *B*, then how are we to know what bundle its best for him to choose.

Indifference Curves

The two properties of preference orderings we have discussed so far enable us to generate a graphical description of the consumer's preferences. To see how, consider first the bundle *A* in Figure 3.8, which has 12 sq. m/wk of shelter and 10 kg/wk of food. What we want to do is to find bundles that are equally attractive as *A*. To make our task easier we introduce the next property we shall assume of preference orderings.

3. More-Is-Better The more-is-better property means simply that, other things equal, more of a good is preferred to less. We can, of course, think of examples of more of something making us worse off rather than better (as with someone who has overeaten). But these examples usually contemplate some sort of practical difficulty, such as having a self-control problem or being unable to store a good for

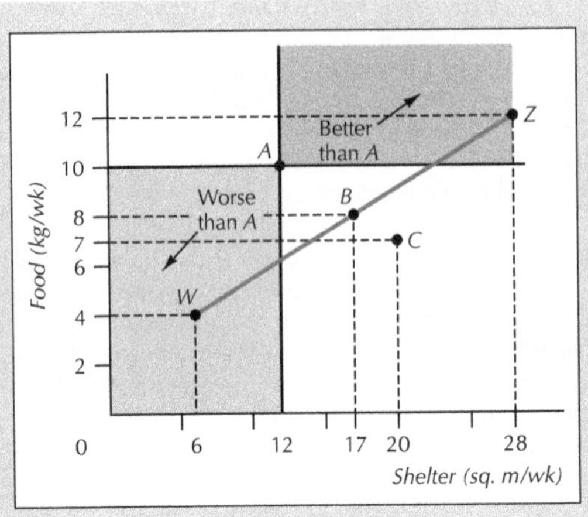

FIGURE 3.8
Generating Equally Preferred Bundles
Z is preferred to *A* because it has more of each good than *A* has. For the same reason, *A* is preferred to *W*. It follows that on the line joining *W* and *Z* there must be a bundle *B* that is equally attractive as *A*. In similar fashion, we can find a bundle *C* that is equally attractive as *B*.

future use. As long as people can freely store or dispose of goods they don't want, having more of something can't make them worse off.

As an example of the application of the more-is-better assumption, consider two more bundles: *W*, which has 6 sq. m/wk of shelter and 4 kg/wk of food, and *Z*, which has 28 sq. m/wk of shelter and 12 kg/wk of food. The assumption tells us that *Z* is preferred to *W* because it has more food and no less shelter. We can also tell that *A* is preferred to *W*, and, consistent with transitivity, *Z* is preferred to *A*.

Now consider the set of bundles that lie along the line joining *W* and *Z*. To say something about these bundles we need the fourth property of preference orderings.

4. Continuity Small changes in the quantity of a good should not lead to sudden 'jumps' in preferences. For instance, we would not expect the consumer to have a strong preference over 12 sq. m/wk shelter compared to 11.999 sq. m/wk. A consumer's preference ordering is *continuous* if, for any two bundles *Z* and *W*, the consumer prefers *Z* to *W* then any bundle sufficiently close to *Z* is also preferred to *W*.

Because *Z* is preferred to *A* and *A* is preferred to *W*, the continuity assumption means that as we move from *Z* to *W* we must encounter a bundle that is equally attractive as *A*. (The intuition behind this claim is the same as the intuition that tells us that if we climb on any continuous path on a mountainside from one point at 1000 metres above sea level to another at 2000 metres, we must pass through every intermediate altitude along the way.) Let *B* denote the bundle that is equally attractive as *A*, and suppose it contains 17 sq. m/wk of shelter and 8 kg/wk of food. (The exact amounts of each good in *B* will of course depend on the specific consumer whose preferences we are talking about.) The more-is-better assumption also tells us that there will be only one such bundle on the straight line between *W* and *Z*. Points on that line to the northeast of *B* are all better than *B*; those to the southwest of *B* are all worse.

In precisely the same fashion, we can find another point—call it *C*—that is equally attractive as *B*. *C* is shown as the bundle (20, 7), where the specific quantities in *C* again depend on the preferences of the consumer under consideration. By the transitivity assumption, we know that *C* is also equally attractive as *A* (since *C* is equally attractive as *B*, which is equally attractive as *A*).

We can repeat this process as often as we like, and the end result will be an **indifference curve,** a set of bundles all of which are equally attractive as the original bundle *A*, and hence also equally attractive as one another. This set is shown as the curve labelled *I* in Figure 3.9. It is called an indifference curve because the consumer is indifferent among all the bundles that lie along it.

indifference curve a set of bundles among which the consumer is indifferent.

FIGURE 3.9
An Indifference Curve
An indifference curve is a set of bundles that the consumer considers equally attractive. Any bundle, such as *L*, that lies above an indifference curve is preferred to any bundle on the indifference curve. Any bundle on the indifference curve, in turn, is preferred to any bundle, such as *K*, that lies below the indifference curve.

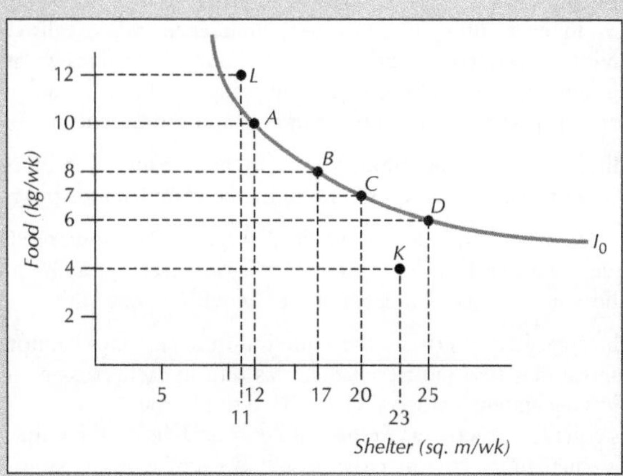

An indifference curve also permits us to compare the satisfaction implicit in bundles that lie along it with those that lie either above or below it. It permits us, for example, to compare bundle *C* (20, 7) to bundle *K* (23, 4), which has less food and more shelter than *C* has. We know that *C* is equally attractive as *D* (25, 6) because both bundles lie along the same indifference curve. *D*, in turn, is preferred to *K* because of the more-is-better assumption: it has 2 sq. m/wk more shelter and 2 kg/wk more food than *K* has. Transitivity, finally, tells us that since *C* is equally attractive as *D* and *D* is preferred to *K*, *C* must be preferred to *K*.

By analogous reasoning, we can say that bundle *L* is preferred to *A*. *In general, bundles that lie above an indifference curve are all preferred to the bundles that lie on it. Similarly, bundles that lie on an indifference curve are all preferred to those that lie below it.*

The completeness property of preferences implies that there is an indifference curve that passes through every possible bundle. That being so, we can represent a consumer's preferences with an **indifference map**, an example of which is shown in Figure 3.10. This indifference map shows just four of the infinitely many indifference curves that, taken together, yield a complete description of the consumer's preferences.

indifference map a representative sample of the set of a consumer's indifference curves, used as a graphical summary of her preference ordering.

The numbers $I_1, \ldots, I_4$ in Figure 3.10 are index values used to denote the order of preference that corresponds to the respective indifference curves.

FIGURE 3.10
Part of an Indifference Map
The entire set of a consumer's indifference curves is called the consumer's indifference map. Bundles on any indifference curve are less preferred than bundles on a higher indifference curve, and more preferred than bundles on a lower indifference curve.

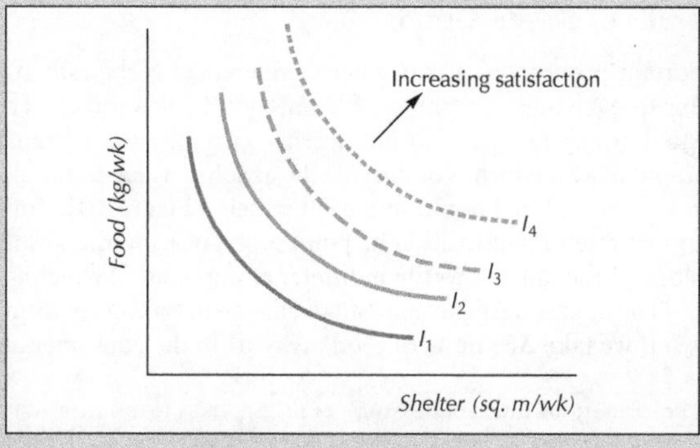

Any index numbers would do equally well provided they satisfied the property $I_1 < I_2 < I_3 < I_4$. In representing the consumer's preferences, what really counts is the *ranking* of the indifference curves, not the particular numerical values we assign to them.[4]

The four properties of preference orderings we have looked at so far imply three important properties of indifference curves and indifference maps:

1. Indifference curves are ubiquitous. Any bundle has an indifference curve passing through it. This property is assured by the completeness property of preferences.
2. Indifference curves are downward-sloping. An upward-sloping indifference curve would violate the more-is-better property by saying a bundle with more of both goods is equivalent to a bundle with less of both.
3. Indifference curves (from the same indifference map) cannot cross. To see why, suppose that two indifference curves did, in fact, cross as in Figure 3.11. The following statements would then have to be true:
   E is equally attractive as *D* (because they each lie on the same indifference curve).
   D is equally attractive as *F* (because they each lie on the same indifference curve).
   E is equally attractive as *F* (by the transitivity assumption).
   But we also know that
   F is preferred to *E* (because more is better).
   Because it is not possible for the statements *E is equally attractive as F* and *F is preferred to E* to be true simultaneously, the assumption that two indifference curves cross thus implies a contradiction. The conclusion is that the original proposition must be true, namely, two indifference curves cannot cross.

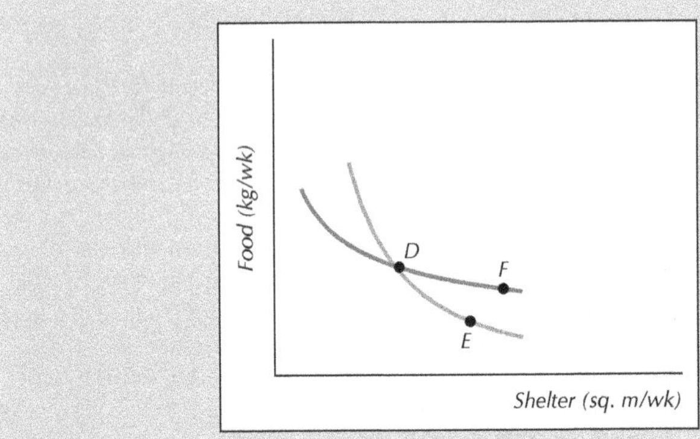

FIGURE 3.11 Why Two Indifference Curves Do Not Cross
If indifference curves were to cross, they would have to violate at least one of the assumed properties of preference orderings.

Trade-offs between Goods

An important property of a consumer's preferences is the rate at which he is willing to exchange, or 'trade off', one good for another. This rate is represented at any point on an indifference curve by the **marginal rate of substitution (MRS)**, which is defined as the absolute value of the slope of the indifference curve at that point. In the left panel of Figure 3.12, for example, the marginal rate of substitution at point *A* is given by the absolute value of the slope of the tangent to the indifference curve at *A*, which is the ratio $\Delta F_A/S_A$.[5] (The notation ΔF_A means 'small change in food from the amount at point *A*'.) If we take ΔF_A units of food away from the consumer at point *A*,

marginal rate of substitution (MRS) at any point on an indifference curve is the rate at which the consumer is willing to exchange the good measured on the vertical axis for the good measured along the horizontal axis; equal to the absolute value of the slope of the indifference curve.

[4]For a more complete discussion of this issue, see the Appendix to this chapter.
[5]More formally, the indifference curve may be expressed as a function $Y = Y(X)$ and the MRS at point *A* is defined as the absolute value of the derivative of the indifference curve at that point: $MRS = |dY(X)/dX|$.

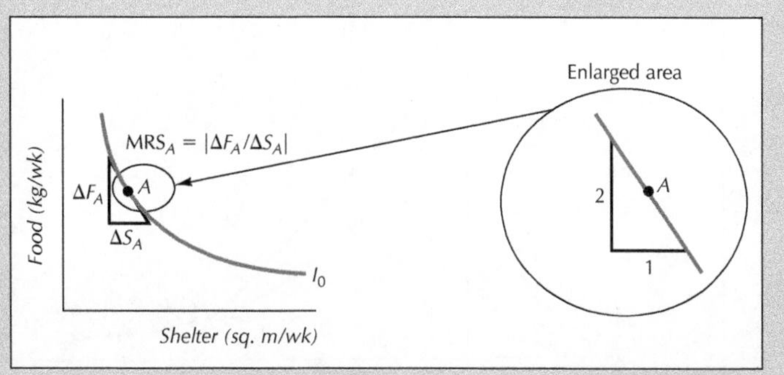

FIGURE 3.12
The Marginal Rate of Substitution
MRS at any point along an indifference curve is defined as the absolute value of the slope of the indifference curve at that point. It is the amount of food the consumer must be given to compensate for the loss of 1 unit of shelter.

we have to give him ΔS_A additional units of shelter to make him just as well off as before. The right panel of the figure shows an enlargement of the region surrounding bundle *A*. If the marginal rate of substitution at *A* is 2, this means that the consumer must be given 2 kg/wk of food to make up for the loss of 1 sq. m/wk of shelter.

Whereas the slope of the budget constraint tells us the rate at which we can substitute food for shelter without changing total expenditure, the MRS tells us the rate at which we can substitute food for shelter without changing total satisfaction. Put another way, the slope of the budget constraint is the marginal cost of shelter in terms of food, and the MRS is the marginal benefit of shelter in terms of food.

It is now time to introduce the fifth property of preference orderings.

5. Convexity Mixtures of goods are preferable to extremes. If you are indifferent between two bundles *A* and *D*, your preferences are convex if you prefer a bundle that contains half of *A* and half of *D* (or any other mixture) to either of the original bundles. For example, suppose you are indifferent between $A = (3, 17)$ and $D = (16, 3)$. If your preferences are convex, you will prefer the bundle $E = (9.5, 10)$ to each of the more extreme bundles. This property conveys the sense that we like balance in our mix of consumption goods.

The convexity property of preferences tells us that along any indifference curve, the more a consumer has of one good, the more she must be given of that good before she will be willing to give up a unit of the other good. Stated differently, MRS declines as we move downward to the right along an indifference curve. Indifference curves with diminishing rates of marginal substitution are thus convex—or bowed outward—when viewed from the origin. The indifference curves shown in Figures 3.9, 3.10 and 3.12 have this property, as does the curve shown in Figure 3.13.

Figure 3.13 shows why they are bowed out. If we pick any two bundles on the same indifference curve, like *A* and *D* and draw a line between them then we obtain all possible mixtures of *A* and *D*. For example, we get bundle *E* half way along the line. Convexity tells us that all the bundles along this line are preferred to bundles *A* and *D*. The indifference curve, therefore, passing through *A* and *D* needs to bow below the straight line that connects *A* and *D*.

In Figure 3.13, note that at bundle *A* food is relatively plentiful and the consumer would be willing to sacrifice 3 kg/wk of it in order to obtain an additional square metre of shelter. Her MRS at *A* is 3. At *C*, the quantities of food and shelter are more balanced, and there she would be willing to give up only 1 kg/wk to obtain an additional square metre of shelter. Her MRS at *C* is 1. Finally, note that food is relatively scarce at *D*, and there she would be willing to give up only $\frac{1}{4}$ kg/wk of food to obtain an additional unit of shelter. Her MRS at *D* is $\frac{1}{4}$.

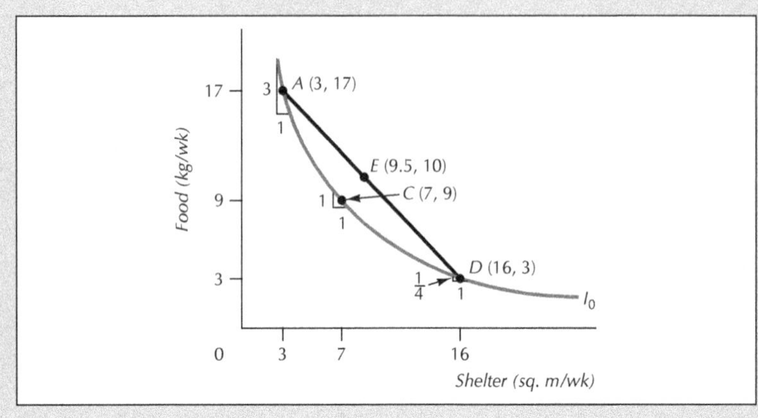

FIGURE 3.13 Diminishing Marginal Rate of Substitution The more food the consumer has, the more she is willing to give up to obtain an additional unit of shelter. The marginal rates of substitution at bundles *A*, *C* and *D* are 3, 1 and 1/4, respectively. Convexity implies that bundle *E* is preferred to bundles *A* and *D*.

Intuitively, diminishing MRS means that consumers like variety. We are usually willing to give up goods we already have a lot of to obtain more of those goods we now have only a little of.

Using Indifference Curves to Describe Preferences

To get a feel for how indifference maps describe a consumer's preferences, let us see how indifference maps can be used to portray differences in preferences between two consumers. Suppose, for example, that both Tex and Mohan like potatoes but that Mohan likes rice much more than Tex does. This difference in their tastes is captured by the differing slopes of their indifference curves in Figure 3.14. Note in Figure 3.14(*a*), which shows Tex's indifference map, that Tex would be willing to exchange 1 kg of potatoes for 1 kg of rice at bundle *A*. But at the corresponding bundle in Figure 3.14(*b*), which shows Mohan's indifference map, we see that Mohan would trade 2 kg of potatoes for 1 kg of rice. Their difference in preferences shows up clearly in this difference in their marginal rates of substitution of potatoes for rice.

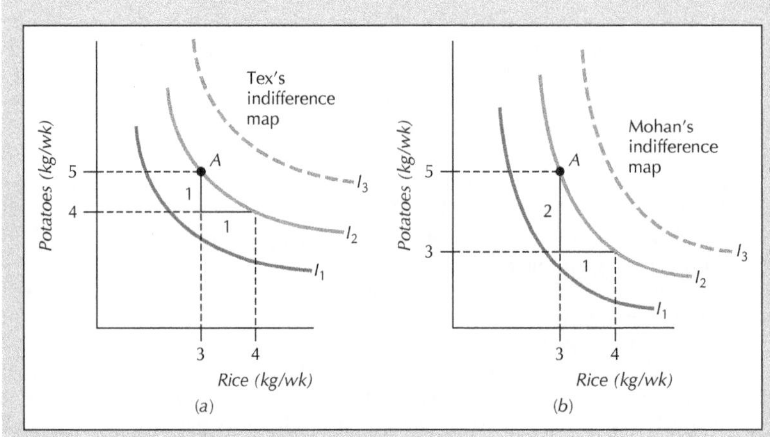

FIGURE 3.14 People with Different Tastes Relatively speaking, Tex is a potato lover; Mohan, a rice lover. This difference shows up in the fact that at any given bundle Tex's marginal rate of substitution of potatoes for rice is smaller than Mohan's.

More-Is-Worse and Satiation Points

Preferences do not have to satisfy the five properties we have assumed so far. As long, however, as the preference ordering satisfies completeness, transitivity and continuity we can still represent preferences using an indifference map. To illustrate, consider Mohan at his favourite restaurant. He has ordered a dish containing fish and potatoes. Figure 3.15 shows his indifference map.

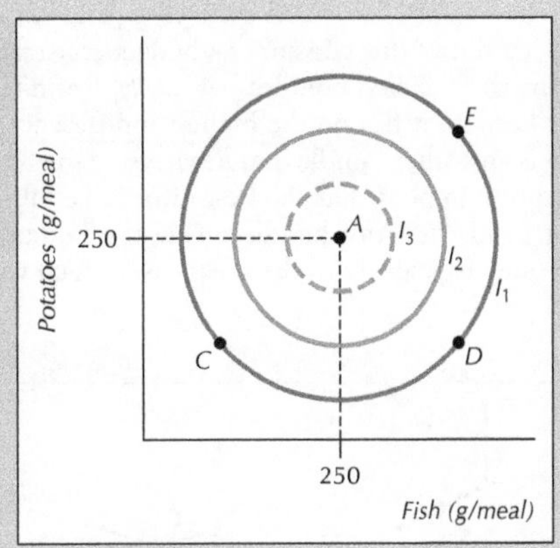

FIGURE 3.15
Preferences with a Satiation Point
The best outcome for Mohan is bundle *A*. At bundle *D* he has too much fish and so the indifference curve slopes up. At bundle *E* he has too much fish and potato and so points below the indifference curve are preferred to points on it.

Mohan's perfect meal contains 250 g of fish and 250 g of potatoes. This is bundle *A* and is called his satiation point. To the bottom left of *A*, near bundle *C*, the indifference curves look 'standard' because Mohan would like more fish and potato. The indifference curve slopes down because Mohan is willing to trade off more fish for less potato.

Things are not so standard to the bottom right of *A*. With bundle *D* Mohan's meal has too much fish. The more-is-better property assumes that he can either store or dispose of the fish he does not want, but in an expensive restaurant neither option may be all that viable. Thus, to the right of *A*, more-is-worse in terms of fish. This is captured by an upward sloping indifference curve at *D*. Mohan is no longer willing to trade off more fish for less potato. He is only willing to trade off more fish (the good he has too much of) for more potato (the good he has too little of). The marginal rate of substitution is measuring the rate at which Mohan is willing to exchange potato for more fish.

Bundle *E* means that Mohan has too much fish and potato. The indifference curve is sloping down but things are still not standard. Less-is-better, and so bundles that lie below the indifference curve are preferred to the bundles that lie on it.

EXERCISE 3.6 Gary likes food but dislikes cigarette smoke. The more food he has, the more he would be willing to give up to achieve a given reduction in cigarette smoke. If food and cigarette smoke are the only two goods, draw Gary's indifference curves.

THE BEST AFFORDABLE BUNDLE

We now have the tools we need to determine how the consumer should allocate his income between two goods. The indifference map tells us how the various bundles are ranked in order of preference. The budget constraint, in turn, tells us which bundles are affordable. The consumer's task is to put the two together and to choose the **best affordable bundle.** (Recall from Chapter 1 that we need not suppose that consumers think explicitly about budget constraints and indifference maps when deciding what to buy. It is sufficient to assume that people make decisions *as if* they were thinking in these terms, just as expert pool players choose between shots as if they knew all the relevant laws of Newtonian physics.)

best affordable bundle the most preferred bundle of those that are affordable.

Let us again consider the choice between food and shelter that confronts a consumer with an income of M = €100/wk facing prices of P_F = €10/kg and P_S = €5/sq. m. Figure 3.16 shows this consumer's budget constraint and part of his indifference map. Of the five labelled bundles—*A, D, E, F* and *G*—in the diagram, *G* is the most preferred because it lies on the highest indifference curve. *G*, however, is not affordable, nor is any other bundle that lies beyond the budget constraint. The more-is-better assumption implies that the best affordable bundle must lie *on* the budget constraint, not inside it. (Any bundle inside the budget constraint would be less preferred than one just slightly to the northeast, which would also be affordable.)

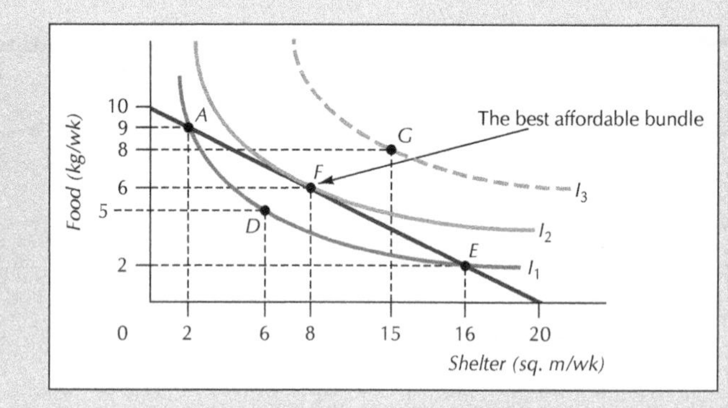

FIGURE 3.16
The Best Affordable Bundle
The best the consumer can do is to choose the bundle on the budget constraint that lies on the highest attainable indifference curve. Here, that is bundle *F*, which lies at a tangency between the indifference curve and the budget constraint.

Where exactly is the best affordable bundle located along the budget constraint? We know that it cannot be on an indifference curve that lies partly inside the budget constraint. On the indifference curve I_1, for example, the only points that are even candidates for the best affordable bundle are the two that lie on the budget constraint, namely, *A* and *E*. But *A* cannot be the best affordable bundle because it is equally attractive as *D*, which in turn is less desirable than *F* by the more-is-better assumption. So by transitivity, *A* is less desirable than *F*. For the same reason, *E* cannot be the best affordable bundle.

Since the best affordable bundle cannot lie on an indifference curve that lies partly inside the budget constraint, and since it must lie on the budget constraint itself, we know it has to lie on an indifference curve that intersects the budget constraint only once. In Figure 3.16, that indifference curve is the one labelled I_2, and the best affordable bundle is *F*, which lies at the point of tangency between I_2 and the budget constraint. With an income of €100/wk and facing prices of €5/sq. m for shelter and €10/kg for food, the best this consumer can do is to buy 6 kg/wk of food and 8 sq. m/wk of shelter.

The choice of bundle *F* makes perfect sense on intuitive grounds. The consumer's goal, after all, is to reach the highest indifference curve he can, given his budget constraint. His strategy is to keep moving to higher and higher indifference curves until he reaches the highest one that is still affordable. For indifference maps for which a tangency point exists, as in Figure 3.16, the best affordable bundle will always lie at the point of tangency.

In Figure 3.16, note that the marginal rate of substitution at F is exactly the same as the absolute value of the slope of the budget constraint. This will always be so when the best affordable bundle occurs at a point of tangency. The condition that must be satisfied in such cases is therefore

$$MRS = \frac{P_S}{P_F} \tag{3.3}$$

The right-hand side of Equation 3.3 represents the opportunity cost of shelter in terms of food. Thus, with P_S = €5/sq. m and P_F = €10/kg, the opportunity cost of an additional square metre of shelter is $\frac{1}{2}$ kg of food. The left-hand side of Equation 3.3 is $|\Delta F/\Delta S|$, the absolute value of the slope of the indifference curve at the point of tangency. It is the amount of additional food the consumer must be given in order to compensate him fully for the loss of 1 sq. m of shelter. In the language of cost-benefit analysis discussed in Chapter 1, the slope of the budget constraint represents the opportunity cost of shelter in terms of food, while the slope of the indifference curve represents the benefits of consuming shelter as compared with consuming food. Since the slope of the budget constraint is $-\frac{1}{2}$ in this example, the tangency condition tells us that $\frac{1}{2}$ kg of food would be required to compensate for the benefits given up with the loss of 1 sq. m of shelter.

If the consumer were at some bundle on the budget line for which the two slopes are not the same, then it would always be possible for him to purchase a better bundle. To see why, suppose he were at a point where the slope of the indifference curve (in absolute value) is less than the slope of the budget constraint (also in absolute value), as at point E in Figure 3.16. Suppose, for instance, that the MRS at E is only $\frac{1}{4}$. This tells us that the consumer can be compensated for the loss of 1 sq. m of shelter by being given an additional $\frac{1}{4}$ kg of food. But the slope of the budget constraint tells us that by giving up 1 sq. m of shelter, he can purchase an additional $\frac{1}{2}$ kg of food. Since this is $\frac{1}{4}$ kg more than he needs to remain equally satisfied, he will clearly be better off if he purchases more food and less shelter than at point E. The opportunity cost of an additional pound of food is less than the benefit it confers.

EXERCISE 3.7 Suppose that the marginal rate of substitution at point *A* in Figure 3.16 is 1.0. Show that this means the consumer will be better off if he purchases less food and more shelter than at *A*.

Corner Solutions

The best affordable bundle need not always occur at a point of tangency. In some cases, there may simply *be* no point of tangency—the MRS may be everywhere greater, or less, than the slope of the budget constraint. In this case we get a **corner solution,** like the one shown in Figure 3.17, where M, P_F and P_S are again given by €100/wk, €10/kg and €5/sq. m, respectively. The best affordable bundle is the one labelled A, and it lies at the upper end of the budget constraint. At A the MRS is less than the absolute value of the slope of the budget constraint. For the sake of illustration, suppose the MRS at $A = \frac{1}{4}$, which means that this consumer would be willing to give up $\frac{1}{4}$ kg of food to get an additional square metre of shelter. But at market prices the opportunity cost of an additional square metre of shelter is $\frac{1}{2}$ kg of food. He increases his satisfaction by continuing to give up shelter for more food until it is no longer possible to do so. Even though this consumer regards shelter as a desirable commodity, the best he can do is to spend all his income on food. Market prices are such that he would have to give up too much food to make the purchase of even a single unit of shelter worthwhile.

corner solution in a choice between two goods, a case in which the consumer does not consume one of the goods.

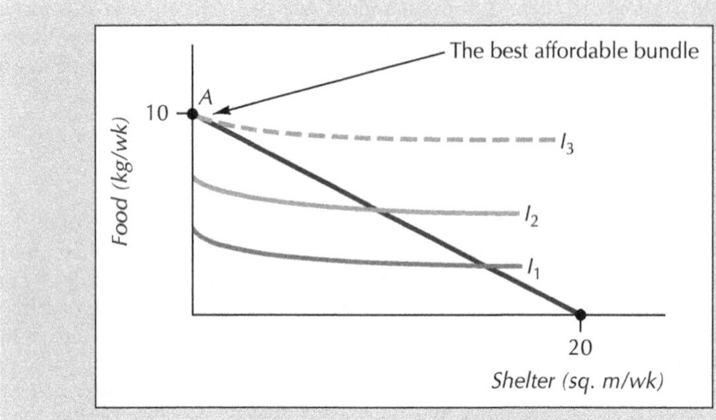

FIGURE 3.17
A Corner Solution
When the MRS of food for shelter is always less than the slope of the budget constraint, the best the consumer can do is to spend all his income on food.

The indifference map in Figure 3.17 satisfies the property of diminishing marginal rate of substitution—moving to the right along any indifference curve, the slope becomes smaller in absolute terms. But because the slopes of the indifference curves start out smaller than the slope of the budget constraint the two never reach equality. The condition that must be satisfied in such cases is therefore

$$MRS < \frac{P_S}{P_F} \tag{3.4}$$

when the amount of shelter is zero.

Why do people not consume most goods?

ECONOMIC NATURALIST 3.1

How many bottles of English sparkling wine have you drunk in the past week? How many times have you been to watch football at Old Trafford this year, or to experience ballet at the Mariinsky Theatre? How many Boeing 747s, speedboats, Porsches, four-bedroom houses and tins of baked beans do you own? Hopefully, you have answered none to at least one of these questions. More generally, there are millions of products and services available and the typical consumer will consume only a very, very small fraction of these. So, do not think that Figure 3.16 captures the 'normal' situation and Figure 3.17 more 'extreme' situations. If anything, it is the other way around.

This tells us something useful about the likely slopes of the budget constraint and indifference curves. To illustrate, consider the demand for English sparkling wine. Some English wine is nice, but it is also relatively expensive (even for someone living in England). For most people the opportunity cost of buying English wine is everywhere greater than the willingness to exchange, say, champagne for English wine. So they do not buy any English wine. Those who do consume English wine must have a greater willingness to exchange champagne for English wine. ■

Indifference curves that are not strongly convex are characteristic of goods that are easily substituted for one another. Corner solutions are more likely to occur for such goods, and indeed are almost certain to occur when goods are perfect substitutes. (See Example 3.3.) For such goods, the MRS does not diminish at all; rather, it is everywhere the same. With perfect substitutes, indifference curves are straight lines. If they happen to be steeper than the budget constraint, we get a corner solution on the horizontal axis; if less steep, we get a corner solution on the vertical axis.

EXAMPLE 3.3 **Mattingly is a caffeinated-cola drinker who spends his entire soft drink budget on Coca-Cola and Jolt cola and cares only about total caffeine content. If Jolt has twice the caffeine of Coke, and if Jolt costs €1/litre and Coke costs €0.75/litre, how will Mattingly spend his soft drink budget of €15/wk?**

For Mattingly, Jolt and Coke are *perfect substitutes,* which means that his indifference curves will be linear. The top line in Figure 3.18 is the set of all possible Coke-Jolt combinations that provide the same satisfaction as the bundle consisting of 0 litres of Jolt per day and 30 litres of Coke per day. Since each litre of Jolt has twice the caffeine of a litre of Coke, all bundles along this line contain precisely the same amount of caffeine. The first green line down is the indifference curve for bundles equivalent to bundle (0, 20); and the second green line down is the indifference curve corresponding to (0, 10). Along each of these indifference curves, the marginal rate of substitution of Coke for Jolt is always $\frac{2}{1}$, that is, 2 litres of Coke for every litre of Jolt.

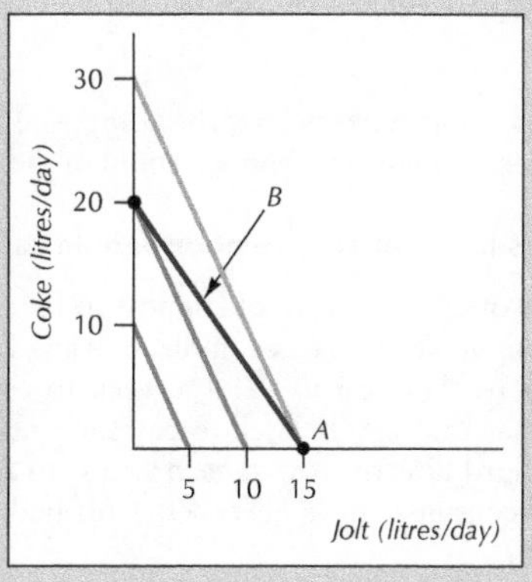

FIGURE 3.18 Equilibrium with Perfect Substitutes Here, the MRS of Coke for Jolt is 2 at every point. Whenever the price ratio P_J/P_C is less than 2, a corner solution results in which the consumer buys only Jolt. On the budget constraint *B*, the consumer does best to buy bundle *A*.

In the same diagram, Mattingly's budget constraint is shown as *B*. The slope of his indifference curves is -2; of his budget constraint, $-\frac{4}{3}$. The best affordable bundle is the one labelled *A*, a corner solution in which he spends his entire budget on Jolt. This makes intuitive sense in light of Mattingly's peculiar preferences: he cares only about total caffeine content, and Jolt provides more caffeine per euro than Coke does. If the Jolt-Coke price ratio, P_J/P_C had been 3 (or any other amount greater than 2) Mattingly would have spent all his income on Coke. That is, we would again have had a corner solution, only this time on the vertical axis. Only if the price ratio had been exactly $\frac{2}{1}$ might we have seen Mattingly spend part of his income on each good. In that case, any combination of Coke and Jolt on his budget constraint would have served equally well. ◆

Most of the time we will deal with problems that have *interior solutions*—that is, with problems where the best affordable bundle will lie at a point of tangency. An interior solution, again, is one where the MRS is exactly the same as the slope of the budget constraint.

EXERCISE 3.8 **Suppose Albert always uses exactly two pats of butter on each piece of toast. If toast costs €0.10/slice and butter costs €0.20/pat, find Albert's best affordable bundle if he has €12/mo to spend on toast and butter. Suppose Albert starts to watch his cholesterol and therefore alters his preference to using exactly one pat of butter on each piece of toast. How much toast and butter would Albert then consume each month?**

Indifference Curves When There Are More Than Two Goods

In the examples thus far, the consumer cared about only two goods. Where there are more than two, we can construct indifference curves by using the same device we used earlier to represent multigood budget constraints. We simply view the consumer's choice as being one between a particular good X and an amalgam of other goods Y, which is again called the composite good. As before, the composite good is the amount of income the consumer has left over after buying the good X.

In the multigood case, we may thus continue to represent the consumer's preferences with an indifference map in the XY plane. Here, the indifference curve tells the rate at which the consumer will exchange the composite good for X. As in the two-good case, equilibrium occurs when the consumer reaches the highest indifference curve attainable on his budget constraint.

AN APPLICATION OF THE RATIONAL CHOICE MODEL

As the following example makes clear, the composite good construct enables us to deal with more general questions than we could in the two-good case.

EXAMPLE 3.4 Is it better to give poor people cash or rent support?

Most governments offer some form of support to families with low income to help them pay for accommodation. For example, housing benefit in the UK entitles low income consumers to claim up to £290 a week to cover rent for a two-bedroom property. This money can only be used to pay for rent; indeed, the government will often pay the landlord directly. Any rent in excess of £290/wk must be paid by the family. Would the consumer have been better off had he instead been given £290/wk directly in cash?

We can try to answer this question by investigating which alternative would get him to a higher indifference curve. Suppose Y denotes the composite good and X denotes rent. If the consumer's income is £500/wk, his initial equilibrium is the bundle J in Figure 3.19. The effect of housing benefit is to increase the total amount of rent he can afford each week from £500 to £790. In terms of the maximum amount of rent he can afford, housing benefit is thus exactly the same as a cash grant of £290.

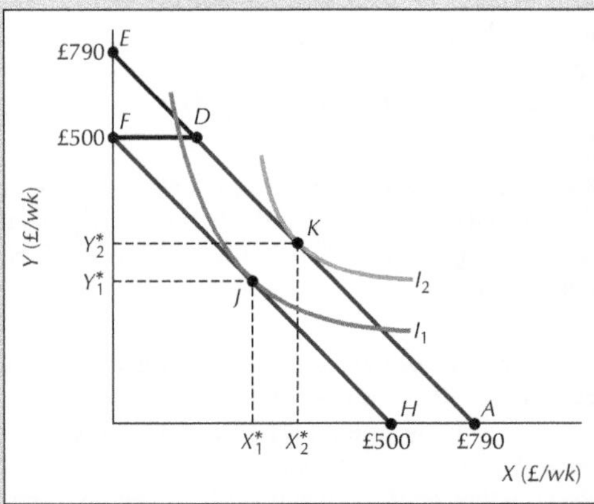

FIGURE 3.19
Housing Benefit versus Cash Grant
By comparison with the budget constraint under a cash grant (*AE*), the budget constraint under housing benefits (*ADF*) limits the amount that can be spent on non-housing goods. But for the consumer whose indifference map is shown, the equilibrium bundles are the same under both alternatives.

Where the two alternatives differ is in terms of the maximum amounts of other goods he can buy. With a cash grant of £290, he has a total weekly income of £790, and this is, of course, the maximum amount of other goods (the composite good) he can buy. His budget constraint in this case is thus the line labelled *AE* in Figure 3.19.

With housing benefit, by contrast, the consumer is not able to buy £790/wk of other goods because his £290 in housing benefit can be used only for rent. The maximum amount of other goods he can purchase is £500. In Figure 3.19, his budget constraint with housing benefit is labelled *ADF*. For values of *Y* less than £500, it is thus exactly the same as his budget constraint with a cash grant. For values of *Y* larger than £500, however, his budget constraint with housing benefit is completely flat.

Note that the consumer whose indifference curves are shown in Figure 3.19 buys exactly the same bundle—namely, bundle *K*—under both options. The effect of housing benefit here is precisely the same as the effect of the cash grant. In general, this will be true whenever the consumer with a cash grant would have spent more on rent anyway than the amount of housing benefit he would have received.

Figure 3.20 depicts a consumer for whom this is *not* the case. With a cash grant, he would choose the bundle *L*, which would put him on a higher indifference curve than he could attain with housing benefit, which would lead him to buy bundle *D*. Note that bundle *D* contains exactly £290 worth of rent, the amount of housing benefit he received. Bundle *L*, by contrast, contains less than £290 worth of rent. Here, the effect of housing benefit is to cause the recipient to spend more on rent than he would have if he had instead been given cash. ◆

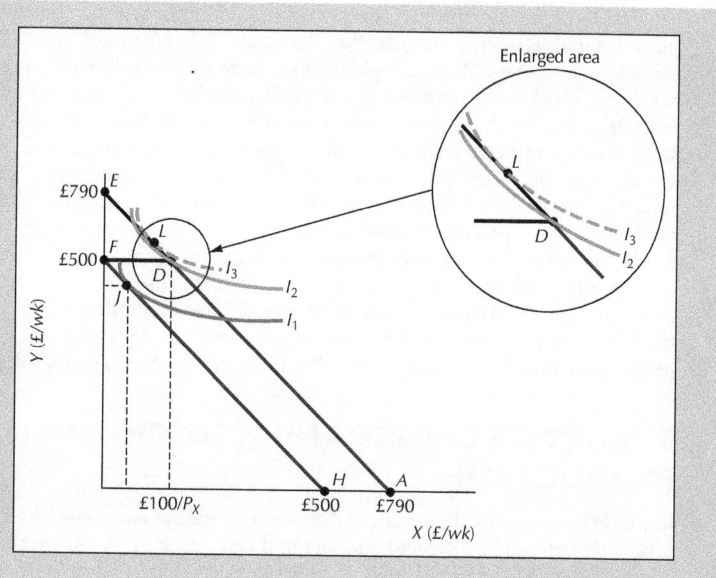

FIGURE 3.20 Where Housing Benefit and Cash Grants Yield Different Outcomes
For the consumer whose indifference map is shown, a cash grant would be preferred to housing benefit, which forces him to devote more to rent than he would choose to spend on his own.

The analysis in Example 3.4 raises the question of why governments do not just give poor people cash grants in the first place. The ostensible reason is that they want to help poor people rent suitable accommodation, not buy luxury items or even cigarettes and alcohol. And yet if most participants would have spent at least as much on rent as they received in housing benefit, not being able to use housing benefit to buy other things is a meaningless restriction. For instance, if someone would have spent £300 on rent anyway, getting £290 in housing benefit simply lets him take some of the money he would have spent on rent and spend it instead on whatever else he chooses.

On purely economic grounds, there is thus a strong case for replacing housing benefit—and all other benefits—with a much simpler programme of cash grants to the poor. At the very least, this would eliminate the cumbersome step of applying for housing benefit after having agreed a rental contract with a landlord.

As a political matter, however, it is easy to see why governments might have set things up the way they did. Many taxpayers would be distressed to see their tax used to buy illicit substances. If housing benefit prevents even a tiny minority of participants from spending more on such goods, it spares many political difficulties.

Example 3.4 calls our attention to a problem that applies not just to housing benefit but to all other forms of in-kind transfers as well: although the two forms of transfer are sometimes equivalent, gifts in cash seem clearly superior on those occasions when they differ.

Why do people often give gifts in kind instead of cash?

ECONOMIC NATURALIST 3.2

Occasionally someone receives a gift that is exactly what he would have purchased for himself had he been given an equivalent amount of money. But we are all far too familiar with gifts that miss the mark. Who has never been given an article of clothing that he was embarrassed to wear? The logic of the rational choice model seems to state unequivocally that we could avoid the problem of useless gifts if we followed the simple expedient of giving cash. And yet virtually every society continues to engage in ritualized gift giving.

The fact that this custom has persisted should not be taken as evidence that people are stupid. Rather, it suggests that the rational choice model may fail to capture something important about gift giving. One purpose of a gift is to express affection for the recipient. A thoughtfully chosen gift accomplishes this in a way that cash cannot. Or it may be that some people have difficulty indulging themselves with even small luxuries and would feel compelled to spend cash gifts on purely practical items. For these people, a gift provides a way of enjoying a small luxury without having to feel guilty about it.[6] This interpretation is supported by the observation that we rarely give purely practical gifts like plain cotton underwear or laundry detergent.

Whatever the real reasons people may have for giving in kind rather than in cash, it seems safe to assume that we do not do it because it never occurred to us to give cash. On the contrary, occasionally we do give cash gifts, especially to young relatives with low incomes. But even though there are advantages to gifts in cash, people seem clearly reluctant to abandon the practice of giving in kind. ■

THEORY OF CHOICE AND HOUSEHOLD PRODUCTION

In the 1960s and 70s the traditional model of rational consumer choice was independently criticized by Kelvin Lancaster and Gary Becker.[7] A look at the alternative approaches they proposed allows us to better understand the traditional model and appreciate how it can be extended.

Kelvin Lancaster emphasized that the consumption of goods gives rise to *characteristics* and it is these characteristics, not the goods themselves, that consumers care about. For example, a meal gives rise to nutritional and taste characteristics. A dinner

[6]For a discussion of this interpretation, see R. Thaler, 'Mental Accounting and Consumer Choice', *Marketing Science*, 4, Summer 1985.

[7]See, for instance, K. L. Lancaster, 'A New Approach to Consumer Theory', *The Journal of Political Economy*, 74, April 1966, and R. T. Michael and G. S. Becker, 'On the New Theory of Consumer Behavior', *Swedish Journal of Economics*, 75, December 1973.

party, combining the goods of a meal and social setting, gives rise to nutritional, taste and intellectual characteristics. It is the nutritional, taste and intellectual characteristics that matter to the consumer. The relationship between goods, or a collection of goods, and the characteristics they lead to was called *consumption technology*.

Gary Becker emphasized that a consumer often puts his own time and effort into converting goods into characteristics (or what Becker called commodities). When cooking pancakes, for instance, the consumer combines goods like flour, eggs, milk and time to produce the pancakes which, when consumed, give rise to nutritional and taste characteristics. This process is captured by a *household production function*.

Embracing these approaches means we should think of a preference ordering as ranking pairs of bundles of characteristics, and not bundles of goods. Bundles of goods are only ranked indirectly through the characteristics they give. Moreover, the budget constraint should take into account the time of the consumer as well as their ability to produce characteristics. Some are better at making pancakes than others.

The advantage of modelling consumer choice this way is that it allows a more natural interpretation of consumer behaviour. To illustrate, consider David deciding whether to drink black tea or green tea. With the standard approach we interpret black tea and green tea either as two different goods or as the same good. There is no in-between. In particular, there is no way to recognize that black tea and green tea are more similar than, say, black tea and a trip to the zoo. That seems a little weird. A consumption technology approach solves the problem because it allows us to say that black tea and green tea are two different goods that give rise to very similar characteristics.

Next consider Fred, who consumes more heating in winter and more shorts in summer. The traditional approach can only explain this by saying Fred's preferences for heating and shorts must have changed between winter and summer. Again, that seems a little weird. A consumption technology approach allows us to say that preferences for the temperature characteristic remain the same during winter and summer. It is the consumption technology that changes with the seasons.

If the consumption technology and household production function approach to consumer choice make so much sense, why bother with the traditional approach? The answer is primarily one of analytical convenience. If we embrace these alternative approaches then preferences need to be drawn on a graph with characteristics on the axes, for example nutrition and taste, as in panel (*a*) of Figure 3.21. The budget constraint, however, still needs to be plotted on a graph with goods on the axes, for example restaurant meal and the composite good, as in panel (*b*) of Figure 3.21. The consumption technology or household production function connects the two, but we cannot obtain the convenient budget constraint-indifference map diagram we have used so often in this chapter, as in Figure 3.16.

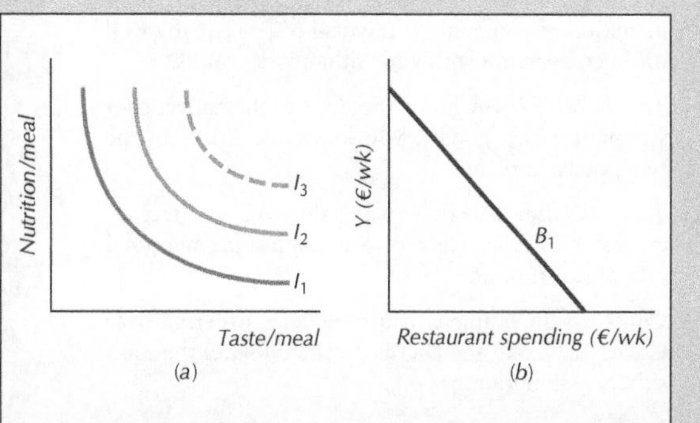

FIGURE 3.21
Representing the Budget Allocation Problem with Consumption Technology
The preferences of the consumer are defined relative to characteristics, like nutrition and taste, as in panel (*a*). The budget constraint is defined relative to goods, like restaurant meals, as in panel (*b*). The consumption technology relates these two together.

This complication means the traditional model is still the primary tool used to understand consumer choice. Both the consumption technology and household production function approach have, however, been applied to answer questions the traditional model cannot. Indeed, Gary Becker won the 1992 Nobel Prize in Economics for work that encompasses the household production function approach. He demonstrated that models of consumer choice can inform on household decisions, such as, getting married and having children.

The Appendix to this chapter develops the utility function approach to the consumer budgeting problem. Topics covered include cardinal versus ordinal utility, algebraic construction of indifference curves, and the use of calculus to maximize utility.

SUMMARY

- Our task in this chapter was to set forth the basic model of rational consumer choice. In all its variants, this model takes consumers' preferences as given and assumes they will try to satisfy them in the most efficient way possible.
- The first step in solving the budgeting problem is to identify the set of bundles of goods the consumer is able to buy. The consumer is assumed to have an income level given in advance and to face fixed prices. Prices and income together define the consumer's budget constraint, which, in the simple two-good case, is a downward-sloping line. Its slope, in absolute value, is the ratio of the two prices. It is the set of all possible bundles that the consumer might purchase if he spends his entire income.
- The second step in solving the consumer budgeting problem is to summarize the consumer's preferences. Here, we begin with a preference ordering by which the consumer is able to rank all possible bundles of goods. This ranking scheme is assumed to be complete, transitive and continuous and to exhibit the more-is-better property. Preference orderings that satisfy these restrictions give rise to indifference maps, or collections of indifference curves, each of which represents combinations of bundles among which the consumer is indifferent. Preference orderings are also assumed to exhibit a diminishing marginal rate of substitution, which means that, along any indifference curve, the more of a good a consumer has, the more he must be given to induce him to part with a unit of some other good. The diminishing MRS property accounts for the characteristic convex shape of indifference curves.
- The budget constraint tells us what combinations of goods the consumer can afford to buy. To summarize the consumer's preferences over various bundles, we use an indifference map. In most cases, the best affordable bundle occurs at a point of tangency between an indifference curve and the budget constraint. At that point, the marginal rate of substitution is exactly equal to the rate at which the goods can be exchanged for one another at market prices.

QUESTIONS FOR REVIEW

1. If the prices of all products are rising at 20 per cent per year and your employer gives you a 20 per cent salary increase, are you better off, worse off, or equally well off in comparison with your situation a year ago?
2. *True or false*: If you know the slope of the budget constraint (for two goods), you know the prices of the two goods. Explain.
3. *True or false*: The downward slope of indifference curves is a consequence of the diminishing marginal rate of substitution.
4. Construct an example of a preference ordering over Coke, Diet Coke and Diet Pepsi that violates the transitivity assumption.
5. Explain in your own words how the slope of an indifference curve provides information about how much a consumer likes one good relative to another.
6. Explain why a consumer will often buy one bundle of goods even though he prefers another.
7. Why are corner solutions especially likely in the case of perfect substitutes?
8. *True or false*: If the indifference curve map is concave to the origin, then the optimal commodity basket must occur at a corner equilibrium, except possibly when there are quantity discounts.
9. If Ralph were given €10, he would spend none of it on tuna fish. But when asked, he claims to be indifferent between receiving €10 worth of tuna fish and a €10 note. How could this be?

PROBLEMS

1. The Acme Seed Company charges €2/kg for the first 10 kg you buy of marigold seeds each week and €1/kg for every kilogram you buy thereafter. If your income is €100/wk, draw your budget constraint for the composite good and marigold seeds.
2. Same as Problem 1, except now the price for every kilogram after 10 kg/wk is €4/kg.
3. Smith likes cashews better than almonds and likes almonds better than walnuts. He likes pecans equally well as macadamia nuts and prefers macadamia nuts to almonds. Assuming his preferences are transitive, which does he prefer:
   a. Pecans or walnuts?
   b. Macadamia nuts or cashews?
4. Originally P_X is €120 and P_Y is €80. *True or false*: If P_X increases by €18 and P_Y increases by €12, the new budget line will be shifted inward and parallel to the old budget line. Explain.
5. Martha has €150 to spend each week and cannot borrow money. She buys Malted Milk Balls and the composite good. Suppose that Malted Milk Balls cost €2.50 per bag and the composite good costs €1 per unit.
   a. Sketch Martha's budget constraint.
   b. What is the opportunity cost, in terms of bags of Malted Milk Balls, of an additional unit of the composite good?
6. In Problem 5, suppose that in an inflationary period the price of the composite good increases to €1.50 per unit, but the price of Malted Milk Balls remains the same.
   a. Sketch the new budget constraint.
   b. What is the opportunity cost of an additional unit of the composite good?
7. In Problem 6, suppose that Martha demands a pay raise to fight inflation. Her boss raises her salary to €225/wk.
   a. Sketch the new budget constraint.
   b. What is the opportunity cost of an additional unit of the composite good?
8. Picabo, an aggressive skier, spends her entire income on skis and bindings. She wears out one pair of skis for every pair of bindings she wears out.
   a. Graph Picabo's indifference curves for skis and bindings.
   b. Now draw her indifference curves on the assumption that she is such an aggressive skier that she wears out two pairs of skis for every pair of bindings she wears out.
9. Suppose Picabo in Problem 8 has €3600 to spend on skis and bindings each year. Find her best affordable bundle of skis and bindings under both of the preferences described in the previous problem. Skis are €480/pr and bindings are €240/pr.
10. For Alexi, coffee and tea are perfect substitutes: one cup of coffee is equivalent to one cup of tea. Suppose Alexi has €90/mo to spend on these beverages, and coffee costs €0.90/cup while tea costs €1.20/cup. Find Alexi's best affordable bundle of tea and coffee. How much could the price of a cup of coffee rise without harming her standard of living?
11. Eve likes apples but doesn't care about pears. If apples and pears are the only two goods available, draw her indifference curves.
12. If you were president of a conservation group, which rate structure would you prefer the Gigawatt Power Company to use: the one described in Example 3.1, or one in which all power sold for €0.08/kWh? (Assume that each rate structure would exactly cover the company's costs.)
13. Paula, a former actress, spends all her income attending plays and movies and likes plays exactly three times as much as she likes movies.
    a. Draw her indifference map.
    b. Paula earns €120/wk. If play tickets cost €12 each and movie tickets cost €4 each, show her budget line and highest attainable indifference curve. How many plays will she see?
    c. If play tickets are €12, movie tickets €5, how many plays will she attend?

14. For each of the following, sketch:
    a. A typical person's indifference curves between garbage and the composite good.
    b. Indifference curves for the same two commodities for Oscar the Grouch on *Sesame Street,* who loves garbage and has no use for the composite good.
15. Boris budgets €9/wk for his morning coffee with milk. He likes it only if it is prepared with 4 parts coffee, 1 part milk. Coffee costs €1/100 g, milk €0.50/100 g. How much coffee and how much milk will Boris buy per week? How will your answers change if the price of coffee rises to €3.25/100 g? Show your answers graphically.
16. The US government wants to support education but must not support religion. To this end, it gives the University of Notre Dame $2 million with the stipulation that this money be used for secular purposes only. The accompanying graph shows Notre Dame's pre-federal-gift budget constraint and best attainable indifference curve over secular and non-secular expenditures. How would the university's welfare differ if the gift came without the secular-use restriction?

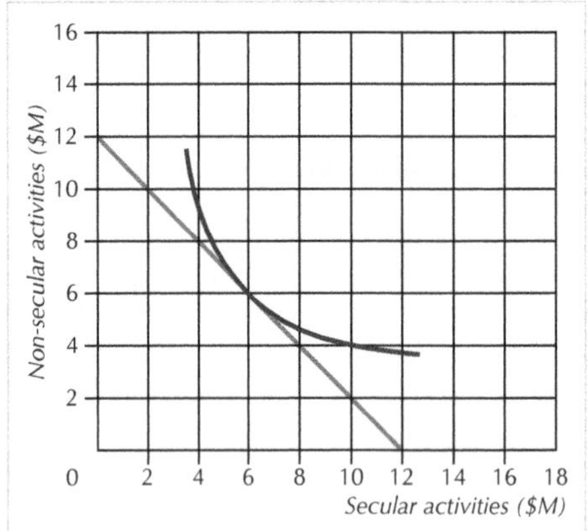

17. A telephone company offers an optional package for local calls whereby each month the subscriber gets the first 50 min of local calls free, the next 100 min at €0.25/min, and any additional time at the normal rate of €0.50/min. Draw the budget constraint for local phone calls and the composite good for a subscriber with an income of €400/mo.
18. For the telephone subscriber in Problem 17, what is the opportunity cost of making an additional 20 min of calls if he currently makes:
    a. 40 min of calls each month?
    b. 140 min of calls each month?
19. You have the option of renting a car on a daily basis for €40/day or on a weekly basis for €200/wk. Draw your budget constraint for a budget of €360/trip.
    a. Find your best affordable bundle if your travel preferences are such that you require exactly €140 worth of other goods for each day of rental car consumption.
    b. Alternatively, suppose you view a day of rental car consumption as a perfect substitute for €35 worth of other goods.
20. Howard said that he was exactly indifferent between consuming four slices of pizza and one beer versus consuming three slices of pizza and two beers. He also said that he prefers a bundle consisting of one slice of pizza and three beers to either of the first two bundles. Do Howard's preferences exhibit diminishing marginal rates of substitution?
21. Your local telephone company has offered you a choice between the following billing plans:
    Plan A: Pay €0.05 per call.
    Plan B: Pay an initial €2/wk, which allows you up to 30 calls per week at no charge. Any calls over 30/wk cost €0.05 per call.
    If your income is €12/wk and the composite good costs €1, graph your budget constraints for the composite good and calls under the two plans.

*22. At your school's fund-raising picnic, you pay for soft drinks with tickets purchased in advance—one ticket per bottle of soft drink. Tickets are available in sets of three types:
Small: €3 for 3 tickets
Medium: €4 for 5 tickets
Large: €5 for 8 tickets
If the total amount you have to spend is €12 and fractional sets of tickets cannot be bought, graph your budget constraint for soft drinks and the composite good.

*23. Consider two Italian restaurants located in identical towns 200 miles apart. The restaurants are identical in every respect but their tipping policies. At one, there is a flat €15 service charge, but no other tips are accepted. At the other, a 15 per cent tip is added to the bill. The average food bill at the first restaurant, exclusive of the service charge, is €100. How, if at all, do you expect the amount of food eaten in the two restaurants to differ?

*24. Vincent, a retired college administrator, consumes only grapes and the composite good $Y(P_Y = €1)$. His income consists of €10,000/yr from a pension, plus the proceeds from whatever he sells of the 2000 bushels of grapes he harvests annually from his vineyard. Last year, grapes sold for €2/bushel, and Vincent consumed all 2000 bushels of his grapes in addition to 10,000 units of Y. This year the price of grapes is €3/bushel, while P_Y remains €1. If his indifference curves have the conventional shape, will this year's consumption of grapes be greater than, smaller than, or the same as last year's? Will this year's consumption of Y be greater than, smaller than, or the same as last year's? Explain.

ANSWERS TO IN-CHAPTER EXERCISES

3.1. *Food (kg/wk)*

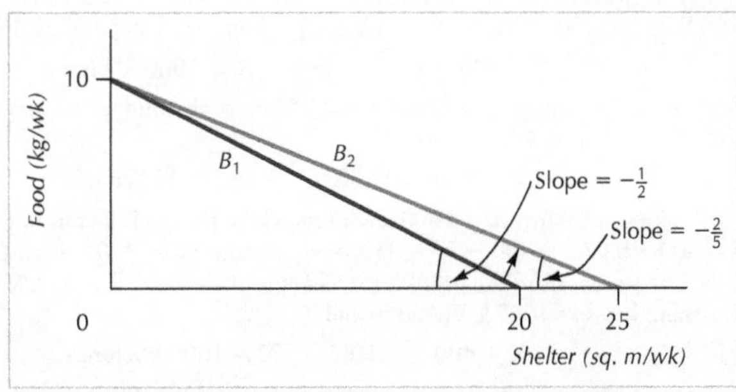

3.2. *Food (kg/wk)*

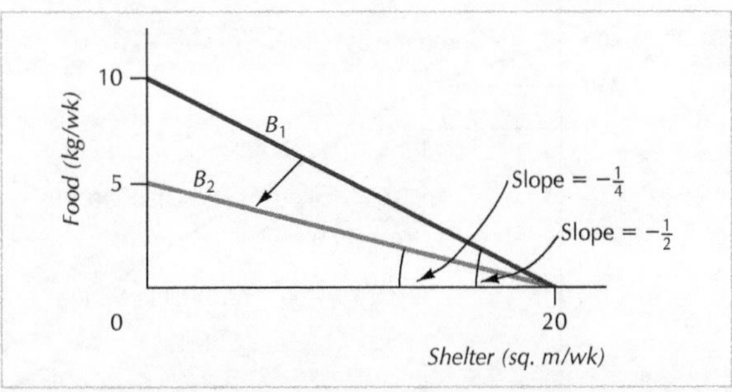

*Problems marked with an asterisk (*) are more difficult.

3.3. *Food (kg/wk)*

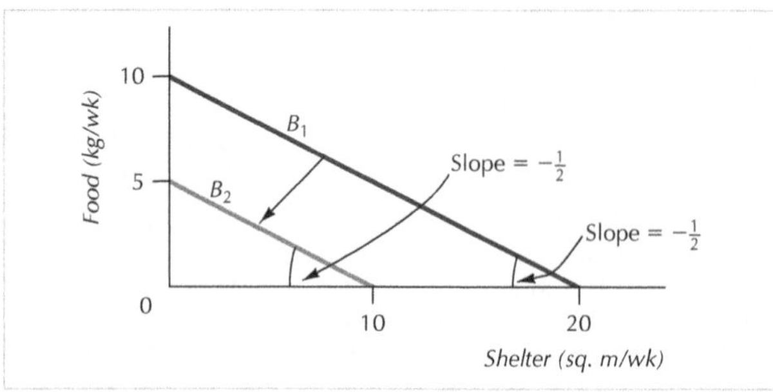

3.4. *Food (kg/wk)*

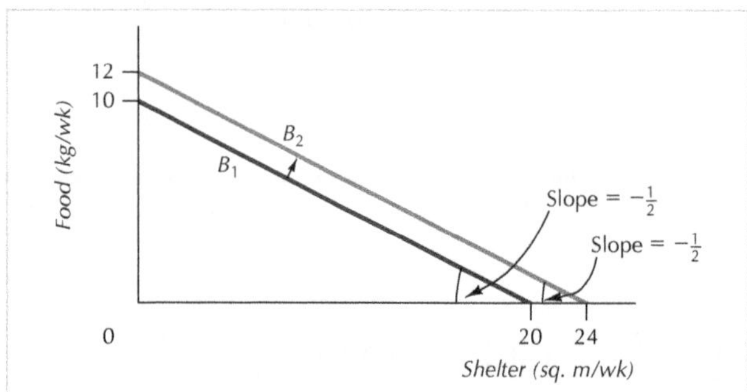

3.5. The budget constraint for a residential consumer with Gigawatt Power Company would be kinked outward, as the initial rate for the first 1000 kWh/mo is lower. For power consumption X up to 1000 kWh/mo, the budget constraint has a slope of the lower rate €0.05/kWh.

$$Y = 400 - 0.05X \qquad 0 \le X \le 1000 \text{ kWh/mo}$$

For power consumption X above 1000 kWh/mo, the budget constraint has a slope of the higher rate €0.10/kWh.

$$Y = 450 - 0.10X \qquad X > 1000 \text{ kWh/mo}$$

The kink occurs when $X = 1000$ kWh/mo, where the level of consumption of other goods is $Y = 400 - 0.05X = 400 - 50 = 350$, or equivalently, $Y = 450 - 0.10X = 450 - 100 = 350$. If the rate were instead €0.10/kWh for all kWh that exceeded 1000 kWh/mo, then the budget constraint for $X > 1000$ kWh/mo would be

$$Y = 400 - 0.10X \qquad X > 1000 \text{ kWh/mo}$$

and would have a discrete jump from $Y = 350$ to $Y = 300$ at $X = 1000$ kWh/mo.

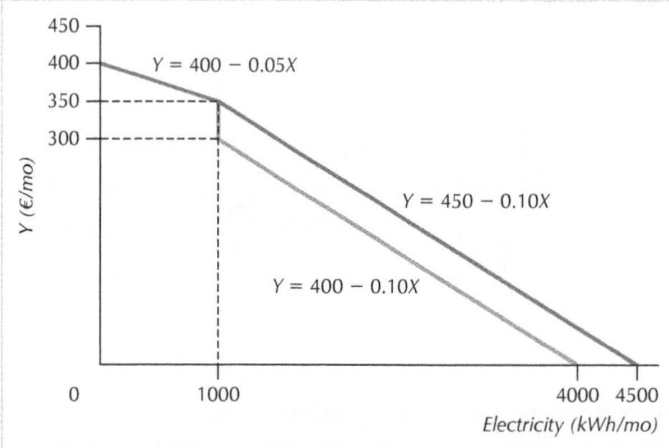

3.6.

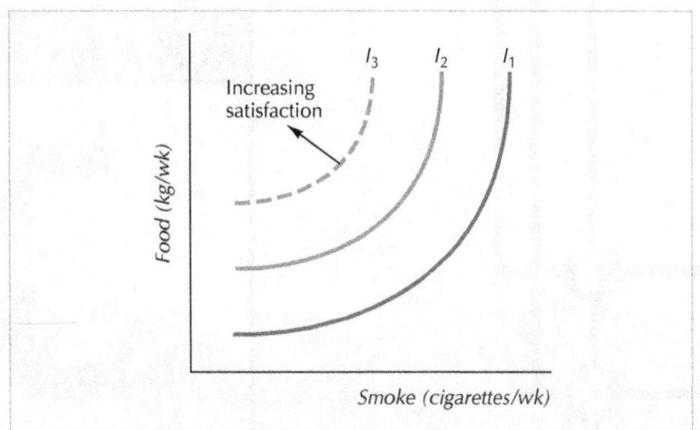

3.7. At bundle A, the consumer is willing to give up 1 kg of food to get an additional square metre of shelter. But at the market prices it is necessary to give up only $\frac{1}{2}$ kg of food to buy an additional square metre of shelter. It follows that the consumer will be better off than at bundle A if he buys 1 kg less of food and 2 sq. m more of shelter.

3.8. Albert's budget constraint is $T = 120 - 2B$. Albert's initial preferences are for two pats of butter for every slice of toast $B = 2T$. Substituting this equation into his budget constraint yields $T = 120 - 4T$, or $5T = 120$, which solves for $T = 24$ slices of toast, and thus $B = 48$ pats of butter each month. Albert's new preferences are for one pat of butter for every slice of toast $B = T$. Substituting this equation into his budget constraint yields $T = 120 - 2T$, or $3T = 120$, which solves for $T = 40$ slices of toast, and thus $B = 40$ pats of butter each month. Not only has Albert cut the fat, but he is consuming more fibre too!

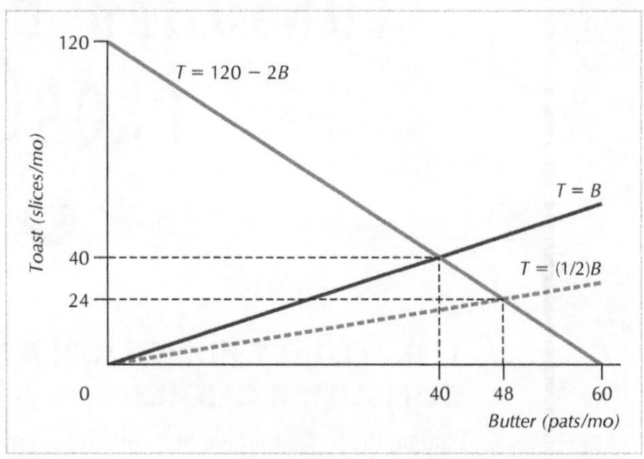

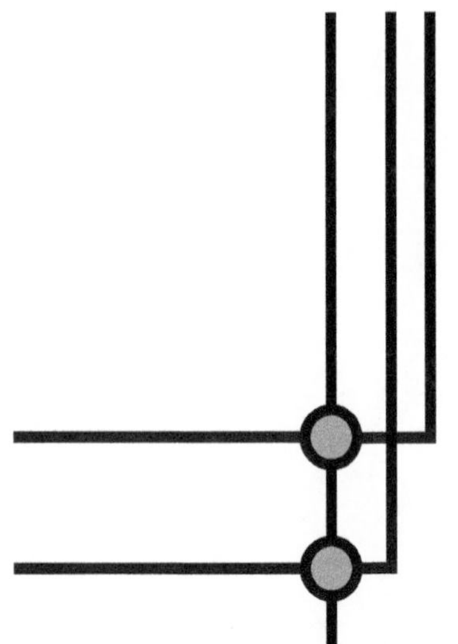

THE UTILITY FUNCTION APPROACH TO THE CONSUMER BUDGETING PROBLEM

THE UTILITY FUNCTION APPROACH TO CONSUMER CHOICE

Finding the highest attainable indifference curve on a budget constraint is just one way that economists have analysed the consumer choice problem. For many applications, a second approach is also useful. In this approach we represent the consumer's preferences not with an indifference map but with a *utility function.*

For each possible bundle of goods, a utility function yields a number that represents the amount of satisfaction provided by that bundle. Suppose, for example, that Tom consumes only food and shelter and that his utility function is given by $U(F, S) = FS$, where F denotes the number of kilograms of food, S the number of square metres of shelter he consumes per week, and U his satisfaction, measured in 'utils' per week.[1] If $F = 4$ kg/wk and $S = 3$ sq. m/wk, Tom will receive 12 utils/

[1]The term 'utils' represents an arbitrary unit. As we will see, what is important for consumer choice is not the actual number of utils various bundles provide, but the rankings of the bundles based on their associated utilities.

wk of utility, just as he would if he consumed 3 kg/wk of food and 4 sq. m/wk of shelter. By contrast, if he consumed 8 kg/wk of food and 6 sq. m/wk of shelter, he would receive 48 utils/wk.

The utility function is analogous to an indifference map in that both provide a complete description of the consumer's preferences. In the indifference curve framework, we can rank any two bundles by seeing which one lies on a higher indifference curve. In the utility-function framework, we can compare any two bundles by seeing which one yields a greater number of utils. Indeed, as the following example illustrates, it is straightforward to use the utility function to construct an indifference map.

EXAMPLE A.3.1 If Tom's utility function is given by $U(F, S) = FS$, graph the indifference curves that correspond to 1, 2, 3, and 4 utils, respectively.

In the language of utility functions, an indifference curve is all combinations of F and S that yield the same level of utility—the same number of utils. Suppose we look at the indifference curve that corresponds to 1 unit of utility—that is, the combinations of bundles for which $FS = 1$. Solving this equation for S, we have

$$S = \frac{1}{F} \tag{A.3.1}$$

which is the indifference curve labelled $U = 1$ in Figure A.3.1. The indifference curve that corresponds to 2 units of utility is generated by solving $FS = 2$ to get $S = 2/F$, and it is shown by the curve labelled $U = 2$ in Figure A.3.1. In similar fashion, we generate the indifference curves to $U = 3$ and $U = 4$, which are correspondingly labelled in the diagram. More generally, we get the indifference curve corresponding to a utility level of U_0 by solving $FS = U_0$ to get $S = U_0/F$. ◆

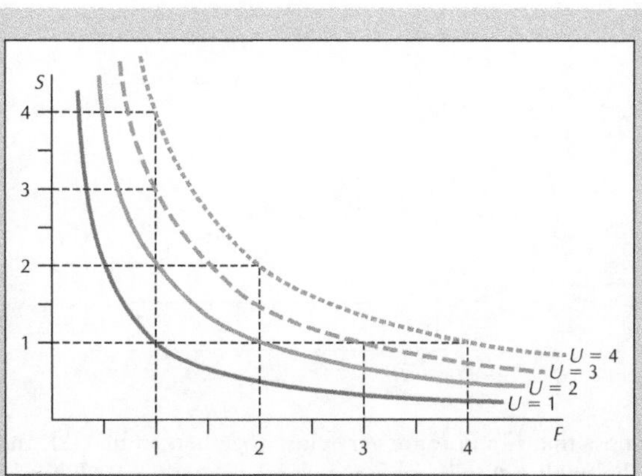

FIGURE A.3.1 Indifference Curves for the Utility Function $U = FS$
To get the indifference curve that corresponds to all bundles that yield a utility level of U_0, set $FS = U_0$ and solve for S to get $S = U_0/F$.

In the indifference curve framework, the best affordable bundle is the bundle on the budget constraint that lies on the highest indifference curve. Analogously, the best affordable bundle in the utility-function framework is the bundle on the budget constraint that provides the highest level of utility. In the indifference curve framework, the best affordable bundle occurs at a point of tangency between an indifference curve and the budget constraint. At the optimal bundle, the slope of the indifference curve, or MRS, equals the slope of the budget constraint. Suppose food and shelter are again our two goods, and PF and PS are their respective prices.

If $\Delta S/\Delta F$ denotes the slope of the highest attainable indifference curve at the optimal bundle, the tangency condition says that $\Delta S/\Delta F = P_F/P_S$. What is the analogous condition in the utility-function framework?

To answer this question, we must introduce the concept of *marginal utility* (the marginal utility of a good is the rate at which total utility changes with consumption of the good), which is the rate at which total utility changes as the quantities of food and shelter change. More specifically, let MU_F denote the number of additional utils we get for each additional unit of food and MU_S denote the number of additional utils we get for each additional unit of shelter. If we change the quantities of both food and shelter, the change in total utility is given by the total derivative of U,

$$\Delta U = MU_F \Delta F + MU_S \Delta S \tag{A.3.2}$$

This simply says that the change in total utility is equal to the change in utility from consuming a different amount of food plus the change in utility from consuming a different amount of shelter.

In Figure A.3.2, note that bundle K has ΔF fewer units of food and ΔS more units of shelter than bundle L. Thus, if we move from bundle K to bundle L, we gain $MU_F \Delta F$ utils from having more food, but we lose $MU_S \Delta S$ utils from having less shelter. Because K and L both lie on the same indifference curve, we know that both bundles provide the same level of utility. Thus $\Delta U = 0$ and the utility we lose from having less shelter must be exactly offset by the utility we gain from having more food. This tells us that

$$MU_F \Delta F = MU_S \Delta S \tag{A.3.3}$$

Cross-multiplying terms in Equation A.3.3 gives

$$\frac{MU_F}{MU_S} = \frac{\Delta S}{\Delta F} \tag{A.3.4}$$

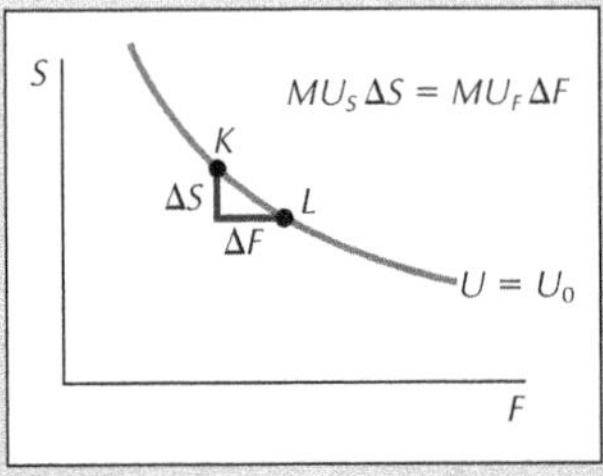

FIGURE A.3.2
Utility Along an Indifference Curve Remains Constant
In moving from K to L, the loss in utility from having less shelter, $MU_S \Delta S$, is exactly offset by the gain in utility from having more food, $MU_F \Delta_F$.

Suppose that K and L are very close together, so that ΔF and ΔS are both very small. The smaller they become the closer the ratio $\Delta S/\Delta F$ becomes to the slope of the indifference curve. We know that the slope of the indifference curve is equal to the marginal rate of substitution. This gives us an important formula

$$\frac{MU_F}{MU_S} = MRS \tag{A.3.5}$$

The marginal rate of substitution is equal to the ratio of the marginal utilities of the two goods. To illustrate why, suppose that $MU_F = 2$ and $MU_S = 1$. If the consumer gets one more unit of food their utility will increase by 2. If they give up 2 units of shelter their utility will decrease by 2. The consumer would be willing to exchange 2 units of shelter for 1 unit of food. Thus, his MRS is 2.

Excluding the possibility of corner solutions, we know that the slope of the indifference curve at the optimal bundle is the same as that of the budget constraint; the following condition must hold for the optimal bundle:

$$\frac{MU_F}{MU_S} = \frac{P_F}{P_S} \tag{A.3.6}$$

Equation A.3.6 is the condition in the utility-function framework that is analogous to the $MRS = P_F/P_S$ condition in the indifference curve framework. If we cross-multiply terms in Equation A.3.6, we get an equivalent condition that has a very straightforward intuitive interpretation:

$$\frac{MU_F}{P_F} = \frac{MU_S}{P_S} \tag{A.3.7}$$

In words, Equation A.3.7 tells us that the ratio of marginal utility to price must be the same for all goods at the optimal bundle. The following examples illustrate why this condition must be satisfied if the consumer has allocated his budget optimally.

EXAMPLE A.3.2 Suppose that the marginal utility of the last euro John spends on food is greater than the marginal utility of the last euro he spends on shelter. For example, suppose the prices of food and shelter are €1/kg and €2/sq. m, respectively, and that the corresponding marginal utilities are 6 and 4. Show that John cannot possibly be maximizing his utility.

If John bought 1 sq. m/wk less shelter, he would save €2/wk and would lose 4 utils. But this would enable him to buy 2 kg/wk more food, which would add 12 utils, for a net gain of 8 utils. ◆

Abstracting from the special case of corner solutions, a necessary condition for optimal budget allocation is that the last euro spent on each commodity yields the same increment in utility.

EXAMPLE A.3.3 Mary has a weekly allowance of €10, all of which she spends on newspapers (*N*) and magazines (*M*), whose respective prices are €1 and €2. Her utility from these purchases is given by *U*(*N*) + *V*(*M*). If the values of *U*(*N*) and *V*(*M*) are as shown in the table, is Mary a utility maximizer if she buys 4 magazines and 2 newspapers each week? If not, how should she reallocate her allowance?

N	U(N)	M	V(M)
0	0	0	0
1	12	1	20
2	20	2	32
3	26	3	40
4	30	4	44
5	32	5	46

For Mary to be a utility maximizer, extra utility per euro must be the same for both the last newspaper and the last magazine she purchased. But since the second newspaper provided 8 additional utils per euro spent, which is four times the 2 utils per euro she got from the fourth magazine (4 extra utils at a cost of €2), Mary is not a utility maximizer.

N	U(N)	MU(N)	MU(N)/PN	M	U(M)	MU(M)	MU(M)/PM
0	0			0	0		
		12	12			20	10
1	12			1	20		
		8	8			12	6
2	20			2	32		
		6	6			8	4
3	26			3	40		
		4	4			4	2
4	30			4	44		
		2	2			2	1
5	32			5	46		

To see clearly how she should reallocate her purchases, let us rewrite the table to include the relevant information on marginal utilities. From this table, we see that there are several bundles for which $MU(N)/P_N = MU(M)/P_M$—namely, 3 newspapers and 2 magazines; or 4 newspapers and 3 magazines; or 5 newspapers and 4 magazines. The last of these bundles yields the highest total utility but costs €13, and is hence beyond Mary's budget constraint. The first, which costs only €7, is affordable, but so is the second, which costs exactly €10 and yields higher total utility than the first. With 4 newspapers and 3 magazines, Mary gets 4 utils per euro from her last purchase in each category. Her total utility is 70 utils, which is 6 more than she got from the original bundle. ◆

In Example A.3.3, note that if all Mary's utility values were doubled, or cut by half, she would still do best to buy 4 newspapers and 3 magazines each week. This illustrates the claim that consumer choice depends not on the absolute number of utils associated with different bundles, but instead on the ordinal ranking of the utility levels associated with different bundles. If we double all the utils associated with various bundles, or cut them by half, the ordinal ranking of the bundles will be preserved, and thus the optimal bundle will remain the same. This will also be true if we take the logarithm of the utility function, the square root of it, or add 5 to it, or transform it in any other way that preserves the ordinal ranking of different bundles.

CARDINAL VERSUS ORDINAL UTILITY

In our discussion about how to represent consumer preferences, we assumed that people are able to rank each possible bundle in order of preference. This is called the *ordinal utility* approach to the consumer budgeting problem. It does not require that people be able to make quantitative statements about how much they like various bundles. Thus it assumes that a consumer will always be able to say whether he prefers A to B, but that he may not be able to make such statements as 'A is 6.43 times as good as B'.

In the nineteenth century, economists commonly assumed that people could make such statements. Today we call theirs the *cardinal utility* approach to the consumer choice problem. In the two-good case, it assumes that the satisfaction provided by any bundle can be assigned a numerical, or cardinal, value by a utility function of the form

$$U = U(X, Y) \qquad (A.3.8)$$

where X and Y are the two goods.

In three dimensions, the graph of such a utility function will look something like the one shown in Figure A.3.3. It resembles a mountain, but because of the more-is-better assumption, it is a mountain without a summit. The value on the U axis measures the height of the mountain, which continues to increase the more we have of X or Y.

FIGURE A.3.3
A Three-Dimensional Utility Surface

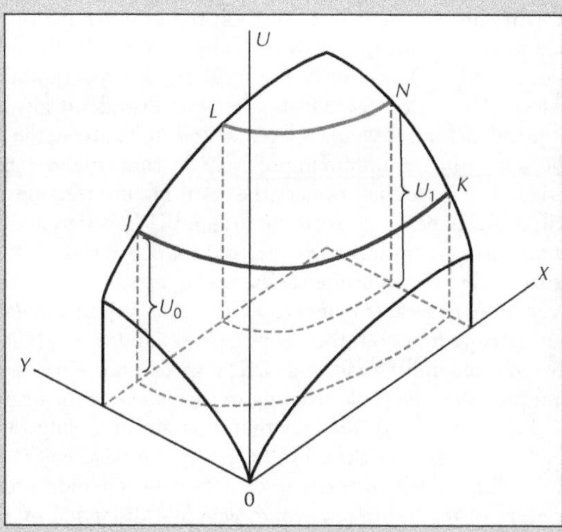

Suppose in Figure A.3.3 we were to fix utility at some constant amount, say, U_0. That is, suppose we cut the utility mountain with a plane parallel to the XY plane, U_0 units above it. The line labelled JK in Figure A.3.3 represents the intersection of that plane and the surface of the utility mountain. All the bundles of goods that lie on JK provide a utility level of U_0. If we then project the line JK downward onto the XY plane, we have what amounts to the U_0 indifference curve, shown in Figure A.3.4.

FIGURE A.3.4
Indifference Curves as Projections

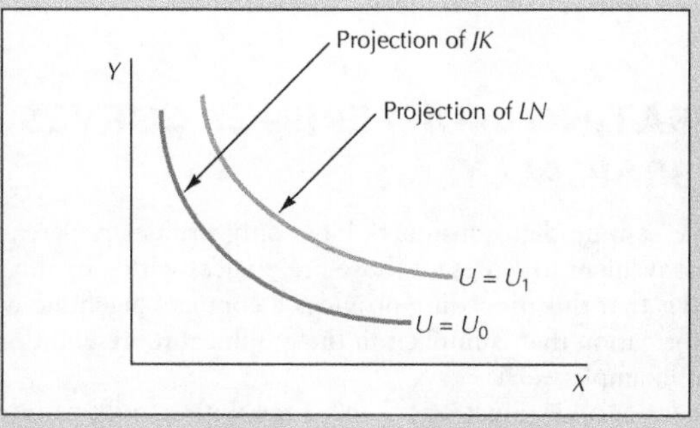

Suppose we then intersect the utility mountain with another plane, this time U_1 units above the XY plane. In Figure A.3.3, this second plane intersects the utility mountain along the line labelled LN. It represents the set of all bundles that confer the utility level U_1. Projecting LN down onto the XY plane, we thus get the indifference curve labelled $U1$ in Figure A.3.4. In like fashion, we can generate an entire indifference map corresponding to the cardinal utility function $U(X, Y)$.

Thus we see that it is possible to start with any cardinal utility function and end up with a unique indifference map. *But it is not possible to go in the other direction!* That is, it is not possible to start with an indifference map and work backward to a unique cardinal utility function. The reason is that there will always be infinitely many such utility functions that give rise to precisely the same indifference map.

To see why, just imagine that we took the utility function in Equation A.3.8 and doubled it, so that utility is now given by $V = 2U(X, Y)$. When we graph V as a function of X and Y, the shape of the resulting utility mountain will be much the same as before. The difference will be that the altitude at any X, Y point will be twice what it was before. If we pass a plane $2U_0$ units above the XY plane, it would intersect the new utility mountain in precisely the same manner as the plane U_0 units high did originally. If we then project the resulting intersection down onto the XY plane, it will coincide perfectly with the original U_0 indifference curve.

All we do when we multiply (divide, add to, or subtract from) a cardinal utility function is to relabel the indifference curves to which it gives rise. Indeed, we can make an even more general statement: if $U(X, Y)$ is any cardinal utility function and if V is any increasing function, then $U = U(X, Y)$ and $V = V[U(X, Y)]$ will give rise to precisely the same indifference maps. The special property of an increasing function is that it preserves the rank ordering of the values of the original function. That is, if $U(X_1, Y_1) > U(X_2, Y_2)$, the fact that V is an increasing function assures that $V[U(X_1, Y_1)]$ will be greater than $V[U(X_2, Y_2)]$. And as long as that requirement is met, the two functions will give rise to exactly the same indifference curves.

The concept of the indifference map was first discussed by Francis Edgeworth, who derived it from a cardinal utility function in the manner described above. It took the combined insights of Vilfredo Pareto, Irving Fisher and John Hicks to establish that Edgeworth's apparatus was not uniquely dependent on a supporting cardinal utility function. As we have seen, the only aspect of a consumer's preferences that matters in the standard budget allocation problem is the shape and location of his indifference curves. Consumer choice turns out to be completely independent of the labels we assign to these indifference curves, provided only that higher curves correspond to higher levels of utility.

Modern economists prefer the ordinal approach because it rests on much weaker assumptions than the cardinal approach. That is, it is much easier to imagine that people can rank different bundles than to suppose that they can make precise quantitative statements about how much satisfaction each provides.

GENERATING INDIFFERENCE CURVES ALGEBRAICALLY

Even if we assume that consumers have only ordinal preference rankings, it will often be convenient to represent those preferences with a cardinal utility index. The advantage is that this procedure provides a compact algebraic way of summarizing all the information that is implicit in the graphical representation of preferences, as we saw in Example A.3.1.

Consider another illustration, this time with a utility function that generates straight-line indifference curves: $U(X, Y) = (\frac{2}{3})X + 2Y$. The bundles of X and Y that yield a utility level of U_0 are again found by solving $U(X, Y) = U_0$ for Y. This time we get $Y = (U_0/2) - (\frac{1}{3})X$. The indifference curves corresponding to $U = 1$, $U = 2$, and $U = 3$ are shown in Figure A.3.5. Note that they are all linear, which tells us that this particular utility function describes a preference ordering in which X and Y are perfect substitutes.

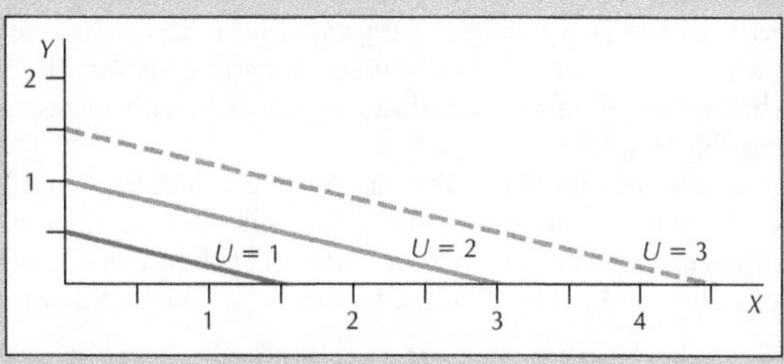

FIGURE A.3.5 Indifference Curves for the Utility Function $U(X,Y) = (\frac{2}{3})X + 2Y$
The indifference curve that corresponds to all bundles yielding a utility level of U_0 is given by $Y = (U_0/2) - (\frac{1}{3})X$.

Using Calculus to Maximize Utility

Students who have had calculus are able to solve the consumer's budget allocation problem without direct recourse to the geometry of indifference maps. Let $U(X, Y)$ be the consumer's utility function; and suppose M, P_X and P_Y denote income, the price of X, and the price of Y, respectively. Formally, the consumer's allocation problem can be stated as follows:

$$\underset{X,\,Y}{\text{Maximize}}\; U(X, Y) \text{ subject to } P_X X + P_Y Y = M \tag{A.3.9}$$

The appearance of the terms X and Y below the 'maximize' expression indicates that these are the variables whose values the consumer must choose. The price and income values in the budget constraint are given in advance.

The Method of Lagrangian Multipliers

As noted earlier, the function $U(X, Y)$ itself has no maximum; it simply keeps on increasing with increases in X or Y. The maximization problem defined in Equation A.3.9 is called a *constrained maximization problem,* which means we want to find the values of X and Y that produce the highest value of U *subject to the constraint that the consumer spend only as much as his income.* We will examine two different approaches to this problem.

One way of making sure that the budget constraint is satisfied is to use the so-called method of *Lagrangian multipliers.* In this method, we begin by transforming the constrained maximization problem in Equation A.3.9 into the following unconstrained maximization problem:

$$\underset{X,\,Y,\,\lambda}{\text{Maximize}}\; L = U(X, Y) - \lambda(P_X X + P_Y Y - M) \tag{A.3.10}$$

The term λ is called a Lagrangian multiplier, and its role is to assure that the budget constraint is satisfied. (How it does this will become clear in a moment.) The first-order conditions for a maximum of L are obtained by taking the first partial derivatives of L with respect to X, Y and λ and setting them equal to zero:

$$\frac{\partial L}{\partial X} = \frac{\partial U}{\partial X} - \lambda P_X = 0 \tag{A.3.11}$$

$$\frac{\partial L}{\partial Y} = \frac{\partial U}{\partial Y} - \lambda P_Y = 0 \tag{A.3.12}$$

and

$$\frac{\partial L}{\partial \lambda} = M - P_X X - P_Y Y = 0 \tag{A.3.13}$$

The next step is to solve Equations A.3.11–A.3.13 for X, Y and λ. The solutions for X and Y are the only ones we really care about here. The role of the equilibrium value of λ is to guarantee that the budget constraint is satisfied. Note in Equation A.3.13 that setting the first partial derivative of L with respect to λ equal to zero guarantees this result.

Specific solutions for the utility-maximizing values of X and Y require a specific functional form for the utility function. We will work through an illustrative example in a moment. But first note that an interesting characteristic of the optimal X and Y values can be obtained by dividing Equation A.3.11 by Equation A.3.12 to get

$$\frac{\partial U/\partial X}{\partial U/\partial Y} = \frac{\lambda P_X}{\lambda P_Y} = \frac{P_X}{P_Y} \qquad \text{(A.3.14)}$$

Equation A.3.14 is the utility function analogue to Equation 3.3 from the text, which says that the optimal values of X and Y must satisfy MRS = P_X/P_Y. The terms $\partial U/\partial X$ and $\partial U/\partial Y$ from Equation A.3.14 are called the *marginal utility of* X and the *marginal utility of* Y, respectively. In words, the marginal utility of a good is the extra utility obtained per additional unit of the good consumed. Equation A.3.14 tells us that the ratio of these marginal utilities is simply the marginal rate of substitution of Y for X.

If we rearrange Equation A.3.14 in the form

$$\frac{\partial U/\partial X}{P_X} = \frac{\partial U/\partial Y}{P_Y} \qquad \text{(A.3.15)}$$

another interesting property of the optimal values of X and Y emerges. In words, the left-hand side of Equation A.3.15 may be interpreted as the extra utility gained from the last euro spent on X. Equation A.3.15 is thus the calculus derivation of the result shown earlier in Equation A.3.7.

An Example To illustrate the Lagrangian method, suppose that $U(X, Y) = XY$ and that $M = 40$, $P_X = 4$, and $P_Y = 2$. Our unconstrained maximization problem would then be written as

$$\underset{X,\,Y,\,\lambda}{\text{Maximize}}\ L = XY - \lambda(4X + 2Y - 40) \qquad \text{(A.3.16)}$$

The first-order conditions for a maximum of L are given by

$$\frac{\partial L}{\partial X} = \frac{\partial(XY)}{\partial X} - 4\lambda = Y - 4\lambda = 0 \qquad \text{(A.3.17)}$$

$$\frac{\partial L}{\partial Y} = \frac{\partial(XY)}{\partial Y} - 2\lambda = X - 2\lambda = 0 \qquad \text{(A.3.18)}$$

and

$$\frac{\partial L}{\partial \lambda} = 40 - 4X - 2Y = 0 \qquad \text{(A.3.19)}$$

Dividing Equation A.3.17 by Equation A.3.18 and solving for Y, we get $Y = 2X$; substituting this result into Equation A.3.19 and solving for X, we get $X = 5$, which in turn yields $Y = 2X = 10$. Thus (5, 10) is the utility-maximizing bundle.[2]

An Alternative Method

There is an alternative way of making sure that the budget constraint is satisfied, one that involves less cumbersome notation than the Lagrangian approach. In this alternative method, we simply solve the budget constraint for Y in terms of X and

[2]Assuming that the second-order conditions for a local maximum are also met.

substitute the result wherever Y appears in the utility function. Utility then becomes a function of X alone, and we can *maximize* it by taking its first derivative with respect to X and equating that to zero.[3] The value of X that solves that equation is the optimal value of X, which can then be substituted back into the budget constraint to find the optimal value of Y.

To illustrate, again suppose that $U(X, Y) = XY$, with $M = 40$, $P_X = 4$ and $P_Y = 2$. The budget constraint is then $4X + 2Y = 40$, which solves for $Y = 20 - 2X$. Substituting this expression back into the utility function, we have $U(XY) = X(20 - 2X) = 20X - 2X^2$. Taking the first derivative of U with respect to X and equating the result to zero, we have

$$\frac{dU}{dX} = 20 - 4X = 0 \qquad \text{(A.3.20)}$$

which solves for $X = 5$. Plugging this value of X back into the budget constraint, we discover that the optimal value of Y is 10. So the optimal bundle is again (5, 10), just as we found using the Lagrangian approach. For these optimal values of X and Y, the consumer will obtain $5 \times 10 = 50$ units of utility.

Both algebraic approaches to the budget allocation problem yield precisely the same result as the graphical approach described in the text. Note in Figure A.3.6 that the $U = 50$ indifference curve is tangent to the budget constraint at the bundle (5, 10).

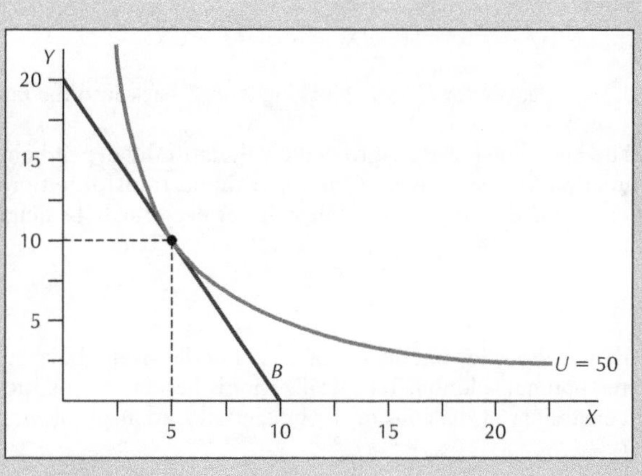

FIGURE A.3.6 The Optimal Bundle when $U = XY$, $P_x = 4$, $P_y = 2$ and $M = 40$.

A Simplifying Technique

Suppose our constrained maximization problem is of the general form

$$\underset{X,\,Y}{\text{Maximize}}\; U(X, Y) \text{ subject to } P_X X + P_Y Y = M \qquad \text{(A.3.21)}$$

If (X^*, Y^*) is the optimum bundle for this maximization problem, then we know it will also be the optimum bundle for the utility function $V[U(X, Y)]$, where V is any increasing function.[4] This property often enables us to transform a computationally difficult maximization problem into a simple one. By way of illustration, consider the following example:

$$\underset{X,\,Y}{\text{Maximize}}\; X^{1/3}Y^{2/3} \text{ subject to } 4X + 2Y = 24 \qquad \text{(A.3.22)}$$

[3]Here, the second-order condition for a local maximum is that $d^2U/dX^2 < 0$.
[4]Again, an increasing function is one for which $V(X_1) > V(X_2)$ whenever $X_1 > X_2$.

First note what happens when we proceed with the untransformed utility function given in Equation A.3.20. Solving the budget constraint for $Y = 12 - 2X$ and substituting back into the utility function, we have $U = X^{1/3}(12 - 2X)^{2/3}$. Calculating dU/dX is a bit tedious in this case, but if we carry out each step carefully, we get the following first-order condition:

$$\frac{dU}{dX} = (\tfrac{1}{3})X^{-2/3}(12 - 2X)^{2/3} + X^{1/3}(\tfrac{2}{3})(12 - 2X)^{-1/3}(-2) = 0 \quad \text{(A.3.23)}$$

which, after a little more tedious rearrangement, solves for $X = 2$. And from the budget constraint we then get $Y = 8$.

Now suppose we transform the utility function by taking its logarithm:

$$V = \ln[U(X, Y)] = \ln(X^{1/3}Y^{2/3}) = (\tfrac{1}{3}) \ln X + (\tfrac{2}{3}) \ln Y \quad \text{(A.3.24)}$$

Since the logarithm is an increasing function, when we maximize V subject to the budget constraint, we will get the same answer we got using U. The advantage of the logarithmic transformation here is that the derivative of V is much easier to calculate than the derivative of U. Again, solving the budget constraint for $Y = 12 - 2X$ and substituting the result into V, we have $V = (\tfrac{1}{3}) \ln X + (\tfrac{2}{3}) \ln (12 - 2X)$. This time the first-order condition follows almost without effort:

$$\frac{dV}{dX} = \frac{\tfrac{1}{3}}{X} - \frac{2(\tfrac{2}{3})}{12 - 2X} = 0 \quad \text{(A.3.25)}$$

which solves easily for $X = 2$. Plugging $X = 2$ back into the budget constraint, we again get $Y = 8$.

The best transformation to make will naturally depend on the particular utility function you start with. The logarithmic transformation greatly simplified matters in the example above, but will not necessarily be helpful for other forms of U.

Corner Solutions

The two methods for finding the optimal bundle given above are not guaranteed to find the optimal solution. Technically that is because we omitted two other important constraints of the consumer's budget allocation problem, namely, $X \geq 0$ and $Y \geq 0$.

An Example Suppose that $U(X, Y) = (\tfrac{2}{3})X + 2Y$ and that $M = 40$ and $P_X = 4$. We leave P_Y unspecified. Our unconstrained maximization problem would then be written as

$$\underset{X,\, Y,\, \lambda}{\text{Maximize}}\ L = (\tfrac{2}{3})X + 2Y - \lambda(4X + P_Y Y - 40) \quad \text{(A.3.26)}$$

The first-order conditions for a maximum of L are given by

$$\frac{\partial L}{\partial X} = \frac{\partial((\tfrac{2}{3})X + 2Y)}{\partial X} - 4\lambda = \frac{2}{3} - 4\lambda = 0 \quad \text{(A.3.27)}$$

$$\frac{\partial L}{\partial Y} = \frac{\partial((\tfrac{2}{3})X + 2Y)}{\partial Y} - P_Y\lambda = 2 - P_Y\lambda = 0 \quad \text{(A.3.28)}$$

and

$$\frac{\partial L}{\partial \lambda} = 40 - 4X - P_Y Y = 0 \quad \text{(A.3.29)}$$

Dividing Equation A.3.27 by Equation A.3.28 gives

$$\frac{1}{3} = \frac{4}{P_Y} \tag{A.3.30}$$

This can only be satisfied if $P_Y = 12$. So, what if P_Y does not equal 12? In that case we must have a corner solution. To solve the problem we can go back and look at the indifference map as given in Figure A.3.7. If P_Y is more than 12, say 20, the budget constraint is B_1 and the consumer will consume only good X. Thus (10, 0) is the utility maximizing bundle. If P_Y is less than 12, say 10, the budget constraint is B_2 and the consumer will consume only good Y. Thus (0, 4) is the utility maximizing bundle.

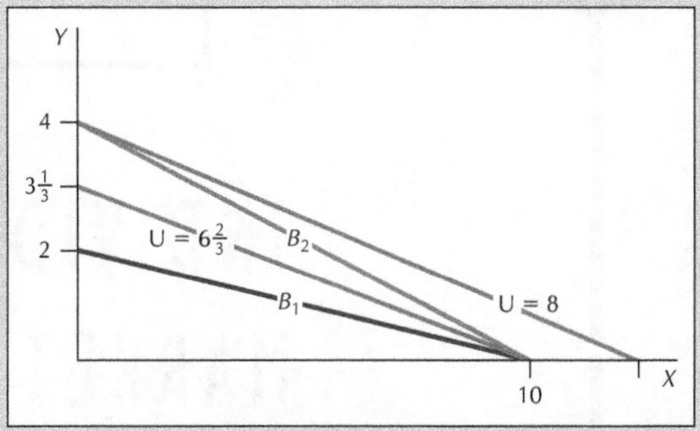

FIGURE A.3.7
The Optimal Bundle when $U = (\frac{2}{3})X + 2Y$, $P_x = 4$ and $M = 40$
The optimal bundle depends on whether the price of good Y is more or less than 12. If it is more than 12 the consumer should consume only good X. If it is less than 12 the consumer should consume only good Y.

PROBLEMS

1. Tom spends all his €100 weekly income on two goods, X and Y. His utility function is given by $U(X, Y) = XY$. If $P_X = 4$ and $P_Y = 10$, how much of each good should he buy?
2. Same as Problem 1, except now Tom's utility function is given by $U(X, Y) = X^{1/2}Y^{1/2}$.
3. Note the relationship between your answers in Problems 1 and 2. What accounts for this relationship?
4. Sue consumes only two goods, food and clothing. The marginal utility of the last euro she spends on food is 12, and the marginal utility of the last euro she spends on clothing is 9. The price of food is €1.20/unit, and the price of clothing is €0.90/unit. Is Sue maximizing her utility?
5. Albert has a weekly allowance of €17, all of which he spends on used CDs (C) and movie rentals (M), whose respective prices are €4 and €3. His utility from these purchases is given by $U(C) + V(M)$. If the values of $U(C)$ and $V(M)$ are as shown in the table, is Albert a utility maximizer if he buys 2 CDs and rents 3 movies each week? If not, how should he reallocate his allowance?

C	U(C)	M	V(M)
0	0	0	0
1	12	1	21
2	20	2	33
3	24	3	39
4	28	4	42

INDIVIDUAL AND MARKET DEMAND

A kilogram of salt costs about 30 pence in the UK. Would the average UK consumer buy more salt if the price was only 5 pence/kg? Would they buy less if it was 60 pence/kg? Would they buy more if they got a new job that doubled their income? The answer to all three questions is: probably not.

Salt is an unusual case. The amounts we buy of many other goods are much more sensitive to prices and incomes. For instance, the average rent on a two-bedroom property in London is more than £2000 a week. Two hundred kilometres north, in Birmingham, the average rent on a four-bedroom property is less than £1000 a week. It would be a real surprise if someone moving from London to Birmingham did not upsize and rent a bigger property.

CHAPTER PREVIEW

Viewed within the framework of the rational choice model, the differences between salt and housing are perfectly intelligible. Our focus in this chapter is to use the tools from Chapter 3 to shed additional light on why, exactly, the responses of various purchase decisions to changes in income and price differ so widely. In Chapter 3, we saw how changes in prices and incomes affect the budget constraint. Here we will see how changes in the budget constraint affect actual purchase decisions. More specifically, we will use the rational choice model to generate an individual consumer's demand curve for a product and employ our model to construct a relationship that summarizes how individual demands vary with income.

We will see how the total effect of a price change can be decomposed into two separate effects: (1) the substitution effect, which denotes the change in the quantity demanded that results because the price change alters the attractiveness of substitute goods, and (2) the income effect, which denotes the change in quantity demanded that results from the change in purchasing power caused by the price change.

Next we will show how individual demand curves can be added to yield the demand curve for the market as a whole. A central analytical concept we will develop in this chapter is the price elasticity of demand, a measure of the responsiveness of purchase decisions to small changes in price. We will also consider the income elasticity of demand, a measure of the responsiveness of purchase decisions to small changes in income. And we will see that, for some goods, the distribution of income, not just its average value, is an important determinant of market demand.

A final elasticity concept in this chapter is the cross-price elasticity of demand, which is a measure of the responsiveness of the quantity demanded of one good to small changes in the prices of another good. Cross-price elasticity is the criterion by which pairs of goods are classified as being either substitutes or complements.

These analytical constructs provide a deeper understanding of a variety of market behaviours as well as a stronger foundation for intelligent decision and policy analysis.

THE EFFECTS OF CHANGES IN PRICE

The Price-Consumption Curve

Recall from Chapter 2 that a market demand curve tells how much of a good the market as a whole wants to purchase at various prices. Suppose we want to generate a demand schedule for a good—say, shelter—not for the market as a whole but for only a single consumer. Holding income, preferences and the prices of all other goods constant, how will a change in the price of shelter affect the amount of shelter the consumer buys? To answer this question, we begin with this consumer's indifference map, plotting shelter on the horizontal axis and the composite good Y on the vertical axis. Suppose the consumer's income is €120/wk, and the price of the composite good is again €1 per unit. The vertical intercept of her budget constraint will then be 120. The horizontal intercept will be $120/P_S$, where P_S denotes the price of shelter. Figure 4.1 shows four budget constraints that correspond to four different prices of shelter, namely, €24/sq. m, €12/sq. m, €6/sq. m and €4/sq. m. The corresponding best affordable bundles contain 2.5, 7, 15 and 20 sq. m/wk of shelter, respectively. If we were to repeat this procedure for indefinitely many prices,

FIGURE 4.1
The Price-Consumption Curve
Holding income and the price of Y fixed, we vary the price of shelter. The set of optimal bundles traced out by the various budget lines is called the price-consumption curve, or PCC.

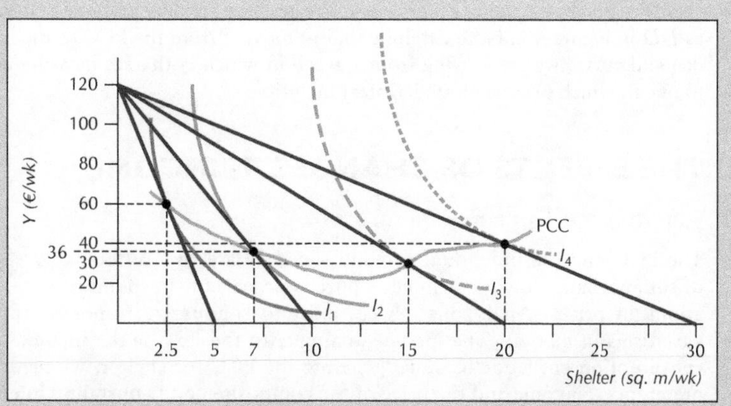

the resulting points of tangency would trace out the line labelled PCC in Figure 4.1. This line is called the **price-consumption curve,** or **PCC.**

price-consumption curve (PCC) holding income and the price of *Y* constant, the PCC for a good *X* is the set of optimal bundles traced on an indifference map as the price of *X* varies.

For the particular consumer whose indifference map is shown in Figure 4.1, note that each time the price of shelter falls, the budget constraint rotates outward, enabling the consumer to purchase not only more shelter but more of the composite good as well. And each time the price of shelter falls, this consumer chooses a bundle that contains more shelter than in the bundle chosen previously. Note, however, that the amount of money spent on the composite good may either rise or fall when the price of shelter falls. Thus, the amount spent on other goods falls when the price of shelter falls from €24/sq. m to €12/sq. m but rises when the price of shelter falls from €6/sq. m to €4/sq. m. Below, we will see why this is a relatively common purchase pattern.

The Individual Consumer's Demand Curve

An individual consumer's demand curve is like the market demand curve in that it tells the quantities the consumer will buy at various prices. All the information we need to construct the individual demand curve is contained in the price-consumption curve. The first step in going from the PCC to the individual demand curve is to record the relevant price-quantity combinations from the PCC in Figure 4.1, as in Table 4.1. (Recall from Chapter 3 that the price of shelter along any budget constraint is given by income divided by the horizontal intercept of that budget constraint.)

TABLE 4.1
A Demand Schedule

Price of shelter (€/sq. m)	Quantity of shelter demanded (sq. m/wk)
24	2.5
12	7
6	15
4	20

To derive the individual's demand curve for shelter from the PCC in Figure 4.1, begin by recording the quantities of shelter that correspond to the shelter prices on each budget constraint.

The next step is to plot the price-quantity pairs from Table 4.1, with the price of shelter on the vertical axis and the quantity of shelter on the horizontal. With sufficiently many price-quantity pairs, we generate the individual's demand curve, shown as *DD* in Figure 4.2. Note carefully that in moving from the PCC to the individual demand curve, we are moving from a graph in which both axes measure quantities to one in which price is plotted against quantity.

THE EFFECTS OF CHANGES IN INCOME

The Income-Consumption Curve

The PCC and the individual demand schedule are two different ways of summarizing how a consumer's purchase decisions respond to variations in prices. Analogous devices exist to summarize responses to variations in income. The income analogue to the PCC is the **income-consumption curve,** or **ICC.** To generate the PCC for shelter, we held preferences, income and the price of the composite good constant while tracing out the effects of a change in the price of shelter. In the case

income-consumption curve (ICC) holding the prices of *X* and *Y* constant, the ICC for a good *X* is the set of optimal bundles traced on an indifference map as income varies.

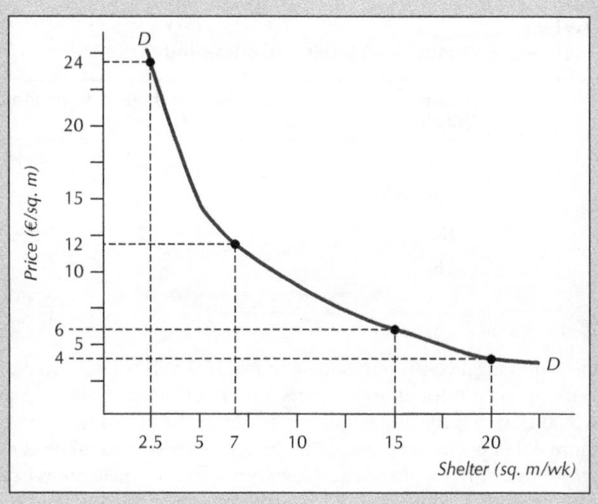

FIGURE 4.2
An Individual Consumer's Demand Curve
Like the market demand curve, the individual demand curve is a relationship that tells how much the consumer wants to purchase at different prices.

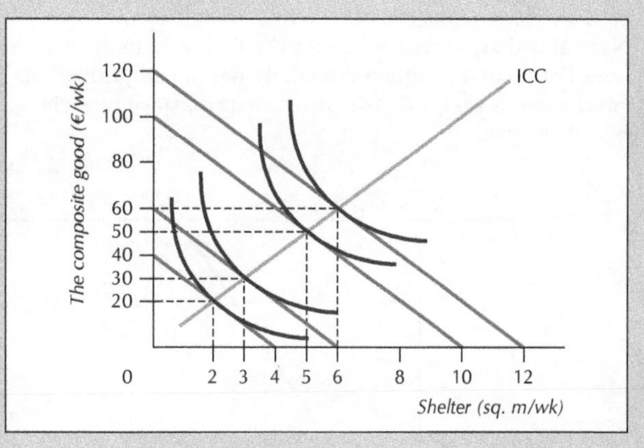

FIGURE 4.3
An Income-Consumption Curve
As income increases, the budget constraint moves outward. Holding preferences and relative prices constant, the ICC traces out how these changes in income affect consumption. It is the set of all tangencies as the budget line moves outward.

of the ICC, we hold preferences and relative prices constant and trace out the effects of changes in income.

In Figure 4.3, for example, we hold the price of the composite good constant at €1 per unit and the price of shelter constant at €10/sq. m and examine what happens when income takes the values €40/wk, €60/wk, €100/wk and €120/wk. Recall from Chapter 3 that a change in income shifts the budget constraint parallel to itself. As before, to each budget there corresponds a best affordable bundle. The set of best affordable bundles is denoted as ICC in Figure 4.3. For the consumer whose indifference map is shown, the ICC happens to be a straight line, but this need not always be the case.

The Engel Curve

The analogue to the individual demand curve in the income domain is the individual **Engel curve.** It takes the quantities of shelter demanded from the ICC and plots them against the corresponding values of income. Table 4.2 shows the income-shelter pairs

TABLE 4.2
Income and Quantity of Shelter Demanded

Income (€/wk)	Quantity of shelter demanded (sq. m/wk)
40	2
60	3
100	5
120	6

for the four budget constraints shown in Figure 4.3. If we were to plot indefinitely many income-consumption pairs for the consumer shown in Figure 4.3, we would trace out the line *EE* shown in Figure 4.4. The Engel curve shown in Figure 4.4 happens to be linear, but Engel curves in general need not be.

Engel curve a curve that plots the relationship between the quantity of *X* consumed and income.

Note carefully the distinction between what we measure on the vertical axis of the ICC and what we measure on the vertical axis of the Engel curve. On the vertical axis of the ICC, we measure the amount the consumer spends each week on all goods other than shelter. On the vertical axis of the Engel curve, by contrast, we measure the consumer's total weekly income.

Note also that, as was true with the PCC and individual demand curves, the ICC and Engel curves contain essentially the same information. The advantage of the Engel curve is that it allows us to see at a glance how the quantity demanded varies with income.

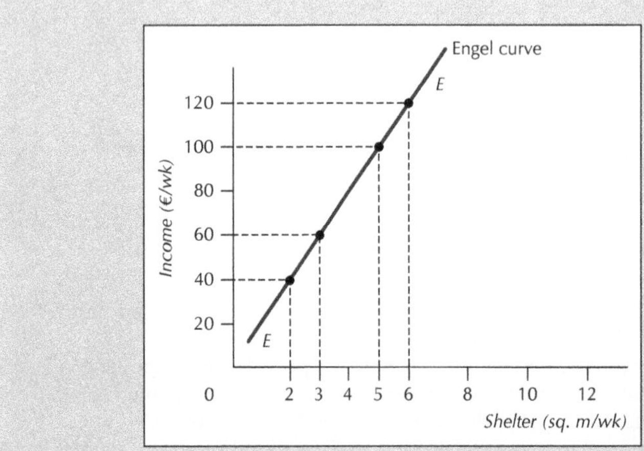

FIGURE 4.4
An Individual Consumer's Engel Curve
Holding preferences and relative prices constant, the Engel curve tells how much shelter the consumer will purchase at various levels of income.

Normal and Inferior Goods

Note that the Engel curve in Figure 4.5(*a*) is upward-sloping, implying that the more income a consumer has, the more tenderloin steak he will buy each week. Most things we buy have this property, which is the defining characteristic of a **normal good.** Goods that do not have this property are called **inferior goods.** For such goods, an increase in income leads to a reduction in the

normal good one whose quantity demanded rises as income rises.

FIGURE 4.5
The Engel Curves for Normal and Inferior Goods
(*a*) This Engel curve is for a normal good. The quantity demanded increases with income. (*b*) This Engel curve for hamburger has the negative slope characteristic of inferior goods. As the consumer's income grows, he switches from hamburger to more desirable cuts of meat.

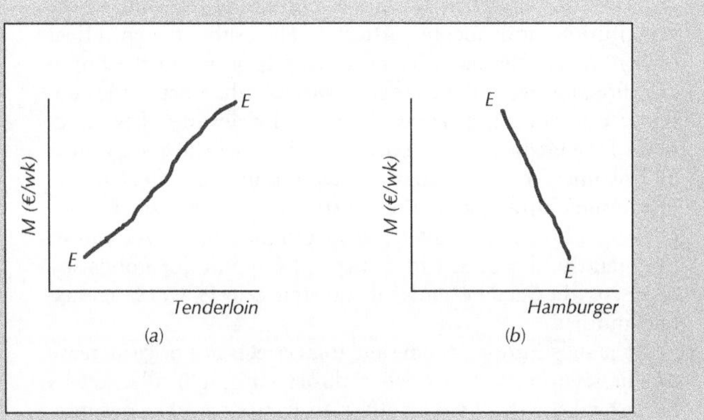

inferior good one whose quantity demanded falls as income rises.

quantity demanded. Figure 4.5(*b*) is an example of an Engel curve for an inferior good. The more income a person has, the fewer hamburgers he will buy each week.

Why would someone buy less of a good following an increase in his income? The prototypical inferior good is one with several strongly preferred, but more expensive, substitutes. Supermarkets, for example, generally carry several different grades of ground beef, ranging from hamburger, which has the highest fat content, to ground sirloin, which has the lowest. A consumer trying to restrict the amount of fat in his diet will switch to a leaner grade of meat as soon as he can afford it. For such a consumer, hamburger is an inferior good.

For any consumer who spends all her income, it is a matter of simple arithmetic that not all goods can be inferior. After all, when income rises, it is mathematically impossible to spend less on all goods at once. It follows that the more broadly a good is defined, the less likely it is to be inferior. Thus, while hamburger is an inferior good for many consumers, there are probably very few people for whom 'meat' is inferior, and fewer still for whom 'food' is inferior.[1]

THE INCOME AND SUBSTITUTION EFFECTS OF A PRICE CHANGE

substitution effect that component of the total effect of a price change that results from the associated change in the relative attractiveness of other goods.

income effect that component of the total effect of a price change that results from the associated change in real purchasing power.

In Chapter 2 we saw that a change in the price of a good affects purchase decisions for two reasons. Consider the effects of a price increase. (The effects of a price reduction will be in the opposite direction.) When the price of a good rises, close substitutes become more attractive than before. For example, when the price of rice increases, wheat becomes more attractive. This is the so-called **substitution effect** of a price increase.

The second effect of a price increase is to reduce the consumer's purchasing power. For a normal good, this will further reduce the amount purchased. But for an inferior good, the effect is just the opposite. The loss in purchasing power, taken by itself, increases the quantity purchased of an inferior good. The change in the quantity purchased attributable to the change in purchasing power is called the **income effect** of the price change.

[1]Another useful way to partition the set of consumer goods is between so-called *necessities* and *luxuries*. A good is defined as a luxury for a person if he spends a larger proportion of his income on it when his income rises. A necessity, by contrast, is one for which he spends a smaller proportion of his income when his income rises. (More on this distinction follows.)

The *total effect* of the price increase is the sum of the substitution and income effects. The substitution effect always causes the quantity purchased to move in the opposite direction from the change in price—when price goes up, the quantity demanded goes down, and vice versa. The direction of the income effect depends on whether the good is normal or inferior. For normal goods, the income effect works in the same direction as the substitution effect—when price goes up (down), the fall (rise) in purchasing power causes the quantity demanded to fall (rise). For inferior goods, by contrast, the income and substitution effects work against one another.

When incomes rise, many consumers switch from low-priced ground beef with high fat content . . .

. . . to leaner, more expensive, cuts of meat.

The substitution, income and total effects of a price increase can be seen most clearly when displayed graphically. Let us begin by depicting the total effect. In Figure 4.6, the consumer has an initial income of €120/wk and the initial price of shelter is €6/sq. m. This gives rise to the budget constraint labelled B_0, along which the optimal bundle is *A*, which contains 10 sq. m/wk of shelter. Now let the price of shelter increase from €6/sq. m to €24/sq. m, resulting in the budget labelled B_1. The new optimal bundle is *D*, which contains 2 sq. m/wk of shelter. The movement from *A* to *D* is called the total effect of the price increase. Naturally, the price increase causes the consumer to end up on a lower indifference curve (I_1) than the one he was able to attain on his original budget (I_0).

To decompose the total effect into the income and substitution effects, we begin by asking the following question: How much income would the consumer need to reach his original indifference curve (I_0) after the increase in the price of shelter? Note in Figure 4.7 that the answer is €240/wk. If the consumer were given a total income of that amount, it would undo the injury caused by the loss in purchasing power resulting from the increase in the price of shelter. The budget constraint labelled B' is purely hypothetical, a device constructed for the purpose at hand. It has the same slope as the new budget constraint (B_1)—namely, −24—and is just far enough

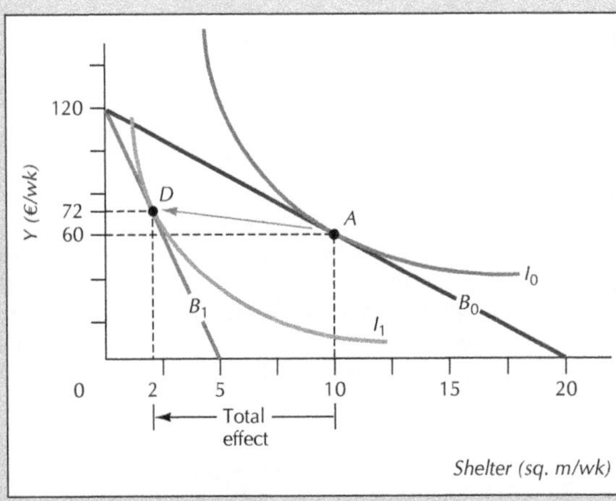

FIGURE 4.6
The Total Effect of a Price Increase
With an income of €120/wk and a price of shelter of €6/sq. m, the consumer chooses bundle *A* on the budget constraint B_0. When the price of shelter rises to €24/sq. m, with income held constant at €120/wk, the best affordable bundle becomes *D*. The movement from 10 to 2 sq. m/wk of shelter is called the total effect of the price increase.

out to be tangent to the original indifference curve, I_0. With the budget constraint B', the optimal bundle is *C*, which contains 6 sq. m/wk of shelter. The movement from *A* to *C* gives rise to the substitution effect of the price change—here a reduction of 4 sq. m/wk of shelter and an increase of 36 units/wk of the composite good.

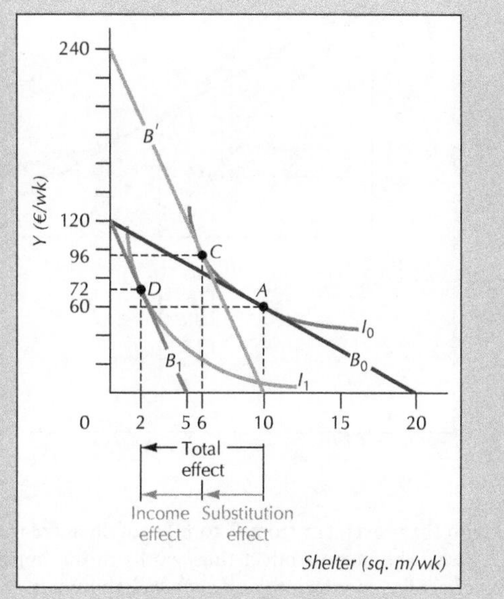

FIGURE 4.7
The Substitution and Income Effects of a Price Change
To get the substitution effect, slide the new budget B_1 outward parallel to itself until it becomes tangent to the original indifference curve, I_0. The movement from *A* to *C* gives rise to the substitution effect, the reduction in shelter due solely to the fact that shelter is now more expensive relative to other goods. The movement from *C* to *D* gives rise to the income effect. It is the reduction in shelter that results from the loss in purchasing power implicit in the price increase.

The hypothetical budget constraint B' tells us that even if the consumer had enough income to reach the same indifference curve as before, the increase in the price of shelter would cause him to reduce his consumption of it in favour of other goods and services. *For consumers whose indifference curves have the conventional convex shape, the substitution effect of a price increase will always reduce consumption of the good whose price increased.*

The income effect stems from the movement from C to *D*. The particular good shown in Figure 4.7 happens to be a normal good. The hypothetical movement of the consumer's income from €240/wk to €120/wk accentuates the reduction of his consumption of shelter, causing it to fall from 6 sq. m/wk to 2 sq. m/wk.

Whereas the income effect reinforces the substitution effect for normal goods, the two effects tend to offset one another for inferior goods. In Figure 4.8, B_0 depicts the budget constraint for a consumer with an income of €24/wk who faces a price of hamburger of €1/kg. On B_0 the best affordable bundle is *A*, which contains 12 kg/wk of hamburger. When the price of hamburger rises to €2/kg, the resulting budget constraint is B_1 and the best affordable bundle is now *D*, which contains 9 kg/wk of hamburger. The total effect of the price increase is thus to reduce hamburger consumption by 3 kg/wk. Budget constraint B' once again is the hypothetical budget constraint that enables the consumer to reach the original indifference curve at the new price ratio. Note that the substitution effect (the change in hamburger consumption associated with movement from *A* to *C* in Figure 4.8) is to reduce the quantity of hamburger consumed by 4 kg/wk—that is, to reduce it by more than the value of the total effect. The income effect by itself (the change in hamburger consumption

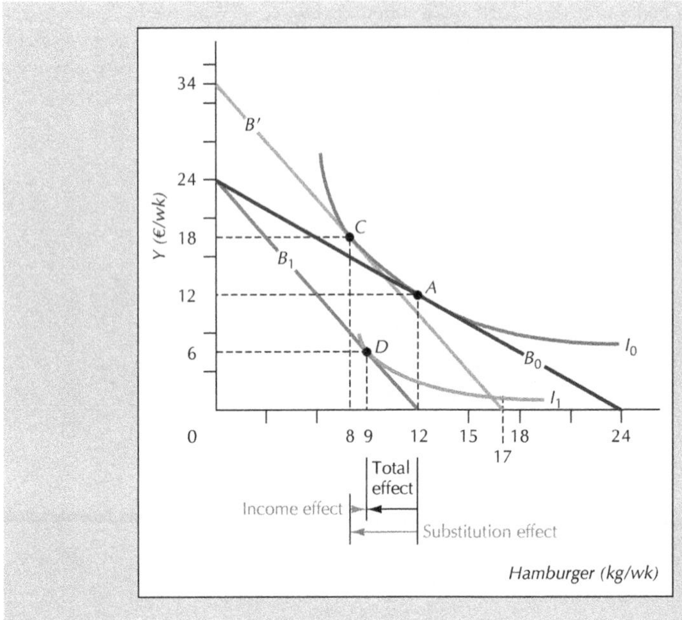

FIGURE 4.8 Income and Substitution Effects for an Inferior Good
By contrast to the case of a normal good, the income effect acts to offset the substitution effect for an inferior good.

associated with the movement from *C* to *D*) actually increases hamburger consumption by 1 kg/wk. The income effect thus works in the opposite direction from the substitution effect for an inferior good such as hamburger.

Giffen Goods

A **Giffen good** is one for which the total effect of a price increase is to increase, not reduce, the quantity purchased. Since the substitution effect of a price increase is always to reduce the quantity purchased, the Giffen good must be one whose income effect offsets the substitution effect. That is, the Giffen good must be an inferior good—so strongly inferior, in fact, that the income effect is actually larger than the substitution effect.

Giffen good one for which the quantity demanded rises as its price rises.

A much-cited example of a Giffen good was the potato during the Irish potato famine of the nineteenth century. The idea was that potatoes were such a large part of poor people's diets to begin with that an increase in their price had a severe adverse effect on the real value of purchasing power. Having less real income, many families responded by cutting back on meat and other more expensive foods, and buying even more potatoes. (See Figure 4.9.) Or so the story goes.

Modern historians dispute whether the potato ever was really a Giffen good. Whatever the resolution of this dispute, the potato story does illustrate the characteristics that a Giffen good would logically have to possess. First, it would not only have to be inferior, but also have to occupy a large share of the consumer's budget. Otherwise, an increase in its price would not create a significant reduction in real purchasing power. (Doubling the price of keyrings, for example, does not make anyone appreciably poorer.) The second characteristic required of a Giffen good is that it has a relatively small substitution effect, one small enough to be overwhelmed by the income effect.

In practice, it is extremely unlikely that a good will satisfy both requirements. Most goods, after all, account for only a tiny share of the consumer's total expenditures. Moreover, as noted, the more broadly a good is defined, the less likely it is

FIGURE 4.9
The Demand Curve for a Giffen Good
If a good is so strongly inferior that the income effect of a price increase dominates the substitution effect, the demand curve for that good will be upward sloping. Giffen goods are a theoretical possibility, but are seldom, if ever, observed in practice.

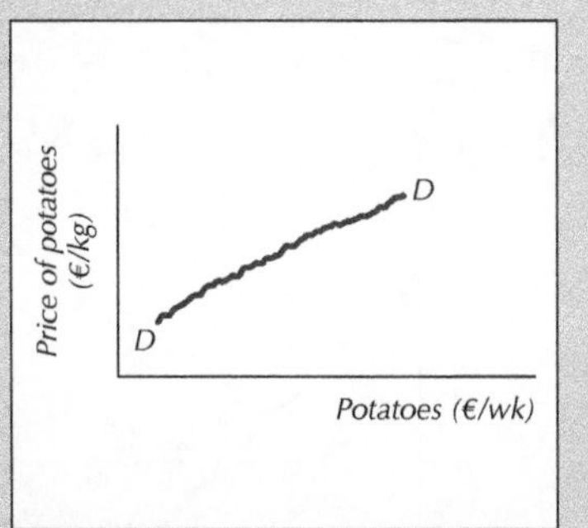

to be inferior. Finally, inferior goods by their very nature tend to be ones for which there are close substitutes. The consumer's tendency to substitute ground sirloin for hamburger, for example, is precisely what makes hamburger an inferior good.

The Giffen good is an intriguing anomaly, chiefly useful for testing students' understanding of the subtleties of income and substitution effects. Unless otherwise stated, all demand curves used in the remainder of this text will be assumed to have the conventional downward slope.

EXAMPLE 4.1 Income and substitution effects for perfect complements. Suppose skis and bindings are perfect, one-for-one complements and Paula spends all her equipment budget of €1200/yr on these two goods. Skis and bindings each cost €200. What will be the income and substitution effects of an increase in the price of bindings to €400 per pair?

Since our goal here is to examine the effect on two specific goods (skis and bindings), we proceed by devoting one axis to each good and dispense with the composite good. On the original budget constraint, B_0, the optimal bundle is denoted A in Figure 4.10. Paula buys three pairs of skis per year and three pairs of bindings. When the price of bindings rises from €200 per pair to €400 per pair, we get the new budget constraint, B_1, and the resulting optimal bundle D, which contains two pairs of skis per year and two pairs of bindings. An equipment budget of €1800/yr is what the consumer would need at the new price to attain the same indifference curve she did originally (I_0). (To get this figure, slide B_1 out until it hits I_0, then calculate the cost of buying the bundle at the vertical intercept—here, nine pairs of skis per year at €200 per pair.) Note that because perfect complements have right-angled indifference curves, the budget B' results in an optimal bundle C that is exactly the same as the original bundle A. For perfect complements, the substitution effect is zero. So for this case, the total effect of the price increase is exactly the same as the income effect of the price increase. ◆

Example 4.1 tells us that if the price of ski bindings goes up relative to the price of skis, people will not alter the proportion of skis and bindings they purchase. But because the price increase lowers their real purchasing power (that is, because it limits the quantities of both goods they can buy), they will buy fewer units of ski equipment. The income effect thus causes them to lower their consumption of both skis and bindings by the same proportion.

EXERCISE 4.1 Repeat Example 4.1 with the assumption that pairs of skis and pairs of bindings are perfect two-for-one complements. (That is, assume that Paula wears out two pairs of skis for every pair of bindings she wears out.)

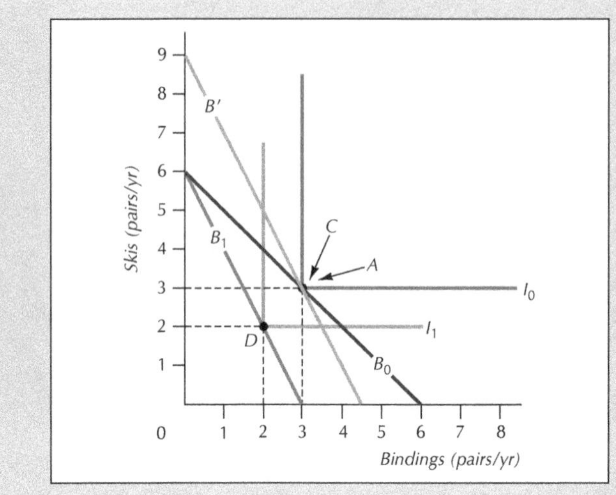

FIGURE 4.10 Income and Substitution Effects for Perfect Complements For perfect complements, the substitution effect of an increase in the price of bindings (the movement from *A* to *C*) is equal to zero. The income effect (the movement from *A* to *D*) and the total effect are one and the same.

EXAMPLE 4.2 Income and substitution effects for perfect substitutes. Suppose Pam considers tea and coffee to be perfect one-for-one substitutes and spends €12/wk on these two beverages. Coffee costs €1/cup, while tea costs €1.20/cup. What will be the income and substitution effects of an increase in the price of coffee to €1.50/cup?

Pam will initially demand 12 cups of coffee per week and no cups of tea (point *A* in Figure 4.11), since each good contributes equally to her utility but tea is more expensive. When the price of coffee rises, Pam switches to consuming only tea, buying 10 cups per week and no coffee (point *D*). Pam would need a budget of €14.40/wk to afford 12 cups of tea (point C), which she likes as well as the 12 cups of coffee she originally consumed. The substitution effect (comparing point *A* and C) is 12 and the income effect (comparing point C and *D*) is 0. The total effect is, therefore, equal to the substitution effect. With perfect substitutes, the substitution effect can be very large: for small price changes (near MRS), consumers may switch from consuming all one good to consuming only the other. ◆

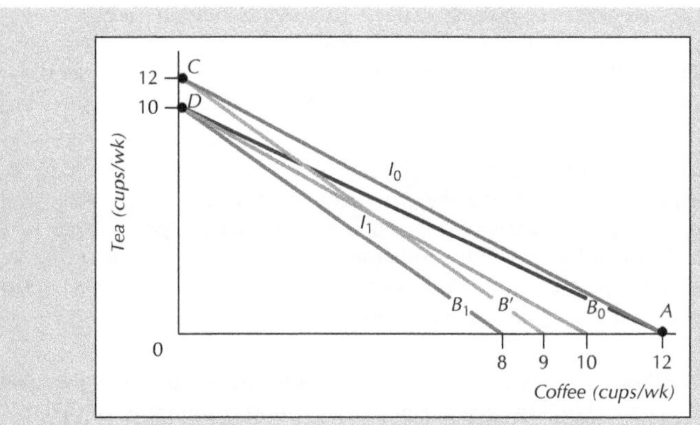

FIGURE 4.11 Income and Substitution Effects for Perfect Substitutes For perfect substitutes, the substitution effect of an increase in the price of coffee (the movement from *A* to *C*) can be very large.

EXERCISE 4.2 Starting from the original price in Example 4.2, what will be the income and substitution effects of an increase in the price of tea to €1.50/cup?

CONSUMER RESPONSIVENESS TO CHANGES IN PRICE

The quantity of salt demanded is highly insensitive to price for two reasons: (1) For many people, there are no attractive substitutes for salt, and (2) salt is so cheap that its price simply isn't worth worrying about.

We began this chapter with the observation that for certain goods, such as salt, consumption is highly insensitive to changes in price while for others, such as housing, it is much more sensitive. The principal reason for studying income and substitution effects is that they help us understand such differences.

Consider first the case of salt. When analysing substitution and income effects, there are two salient features to note about salt. First, for most consumers, it has no close substitutes. If someone were forbidden to shake salt onto his steak, he might respond by shaking a little extra pepper, or even by squeezing some lemon juice onto it. But for most people, these alternatives would fall considerably short of the real thing. Salt's second prominent feature is that it occupies an almost imperceptibly small share of total expenditures. An extremely heavy user of salt might consume a kilogram every month. If this person's income were €1200/mo, a doubling of the price of salt—say, from €0.30/kg to €0.60/kg—would increase the share of his budget accounted for by salt from 0.00025 to 0.0005. For all practical purposes, the income effect for salt is negligible.

In Figure 4.12, the fact that salt has no close substitutes is represented by indifference curves with a nearly right-angled shape. Salt's negligible budget share is captured by the fact that the cusps of these indifference curves occur at extremely small quantities of salt.

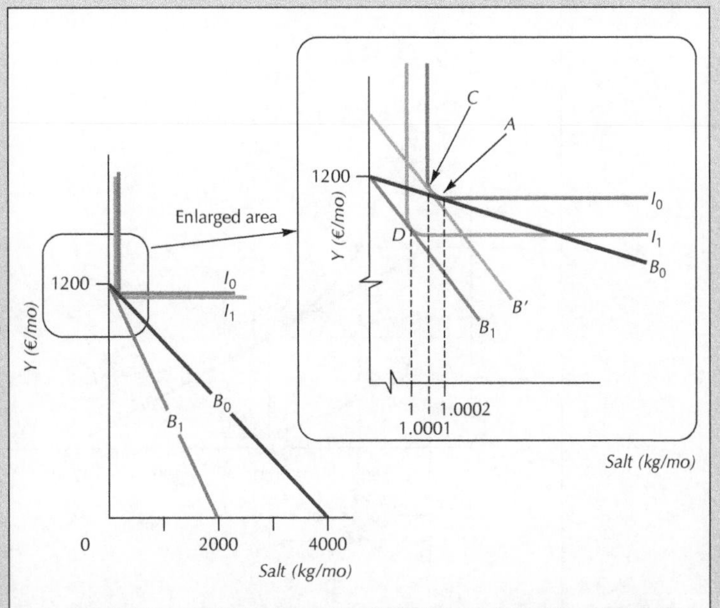

FIGURE 4.12
Income and Substitution Effects of a Price Increase for Salt
The total effect of a price change will be very small when (1) the original equilibrium bundle lies near the vertical intercept of the budget constraint, and (2) the indifference curves have a nearly right-angled shape. The first factor causes the income effect (the reduction in salt consumption associated with the movement from *C* to *D*) to be small; the second factor causes the substitution effect (the reduction in salt consumption associated with the movement from *A* to *C*) to be small.

Suppose, as in Figure 4.12, the price of salt is originally €0.30/kg, resulting in the equilibrium bundle *A* in the enlarged region, which contains 1.0002 kg/mo of salt. A price increase to €0.60/kg results in a new equilibrium bundle *D* with 1 kg/mo of salt. The income and substitution effects are measured in terms of the intermediate bundle C. Geometrically, the income effect is small because the original tangency occurred so near the vertical intercept of the budget constraint. When we are near the pivot point of the budget constraint, even a very large rotation produces only a small movement. The substitution effect, in turn, is small because of the nearly right-angled shape of the indifference curves.

Let us now contrast salt with housing. The two salient facts about housing are that (1) it accounts for a substantial share of total expenditures (more than 30 per cent for many people), and (2) most people have considerable latitude to substitute other goods for housing. Many Londoners, for example, can afford to live in apartments larger than the ones they now occupy, yet they prefer to spend what they save in rent on restaurant meals, theatre performances, and the like. Another substitution possibility is to consume less conveniently located housing. Someone who works in London can live near her job and pay high rent; alternatively, she can live in Birmingham and pay considerably less. Or she can choose an apartment in a less fashionable neighbourhood, or one not quite as close to a convenient underground station. The point is that there are many different options for housing, and the choice among them depends strongly on income and relative prices.

In Figure 4.13, the consumer's income is €120/wk and the initial price of shelter is €0.60/sq. m. The resulting budget constraint is B_0, and the best affordable bundle on it is *A*, which contains 100 sq. m/wk of shelter. An increase in the price of shelter to €2.40/sq. m causes the quantity demanded to fall to 20 sq. m/wk. The smooth

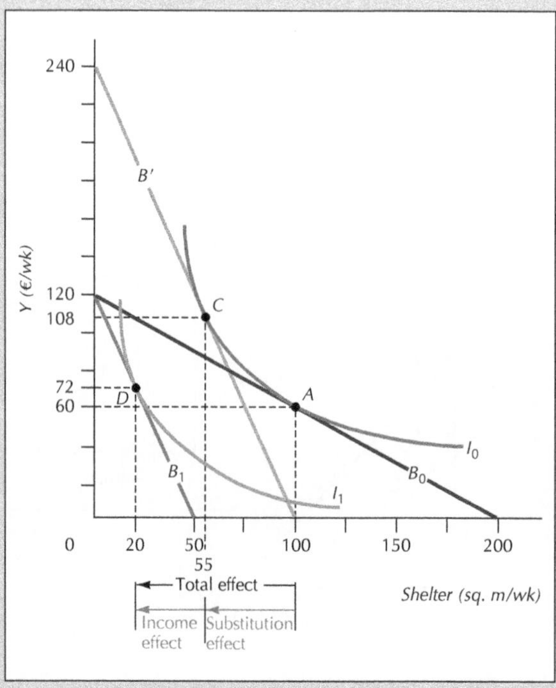

FIGURE 4.13 Income and Substitution Effects for a Price-Sensitive Good Because shelter occupies a large share of the budget, its income effect tends to be large. And because it is practical to substitute away from shelter, the substitution effect also tends to be large. The quantities demanded of goods with both large substitution and large income effects are highly responsive to changes in price.

convex shape of the indifference curves represents the high degree of substitution possibilities between housing and other goods and accounts for the relatively large substitution effect (the fall in shelter consumption associated with the movement from *A* to C). Note also that the original equilibrium bundle, *A*, was far from the vertical pivot point of the budget constraint. By contrast to the case of salt, here the rotation in the budget constraint caused by the price increase produces a large movement in the location of the relevant segment of the new budget constraint. Accordingly, the income effect for shelter (the fall in shelter consumption associated with the movement from *C* to *D*) is much larger than for salt. With both a large substitution and a large income effect working together, the total effect of an increase in the price of shelter (the fall in shelter consumption associated with the movement from *A* to *D*) is very large.

EXAMPLE 4.3 Deriving the individual demand curve for perfect complements. James views car washes and petrol as perfect complements in a 1-to-10 ratio, requiring one car wash for every 10 litres of petrol. Petrol costs €3/litre, and James has €144/mo to spend on petrol and car washes. (See Figure 4.14.) Construct James's demand curve for car washes by considering his quantity demanded of car washes at various prices (such as €6, €18 and €42; see Figure 4.15).

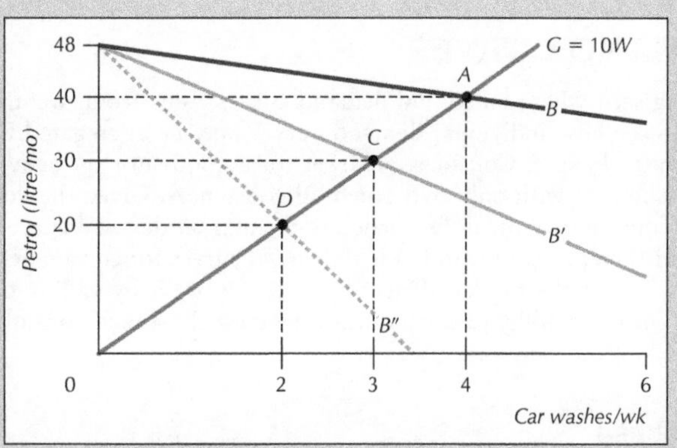

FIGURE 4.14
A Price Increase for Car Washes
With €144/mo, James buys 4 washes/mo when the price is €6/wash (budget constraint *B*), 3 washes/mo when the price is €18/wash (budget constraint *B*′), and 2 washes/mo when the price is €42/wash (budget constraint *B*″).

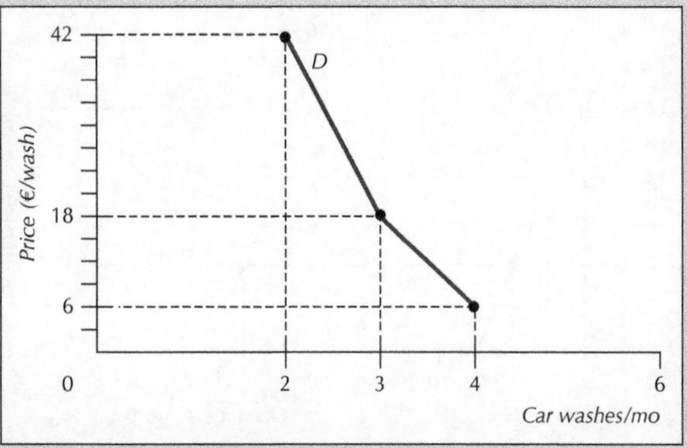

FIGURE 4.15
James's Demand for Car Washes
The quantity of car washes James demands at various prices forms his demand curve for car washes.

James's preferences dictate that his optimal bundle must satisfy $G = 10W$, as his indifference curves are L-shaped. James's budget constraint is $3G + P_W W = 144$, or $G = 48 - \frac{P_W}{3}W$. Substituting $G = 10W$, his budget constraint is $30W + P_W W = 144$, which implies $(30 + P_W)W = 144$. At $P_W = 6$, $W = 4$; at $P_W = 18$, $W = 3$; at $P_W = 42$, $W = 2$, as summarized in Table 4.3. ◆

TABLE 4.3
A Demand Schedule for Car Washes

Price of car wash (€/wash)	Quantity of car washes demanded (washes/mo)
6	4
18	3
42	2
114	1

MARKET DEMAND: AGGREGATING INDIVIDUAL DEMAND CURVES

Having seen where individual demand curves come from, we are now in a position to see how individual demand curves may be aggregated to form the market demand curve. Consider a market for a good—for the sake of concreteness, again shelter—with only two potential consumers. Given the demand curves for these consumers, how do we generate the market demand curve? In Figure 4.16, D_1 and D_2 represent the individual demand curves for consumers 1 and 2, respectively. To get the market demand curve, we begin by calling out a price—say, €4/sq. m—and adding the quantities demanded by each consumer at that price.

FIGURE 4.16
Generating Market Demand from Individual Demands
The market demand curve (D in the right panel) is the horizontal sum of the individual demand curves, D_1 (left panel) and D_2 (centre panel).

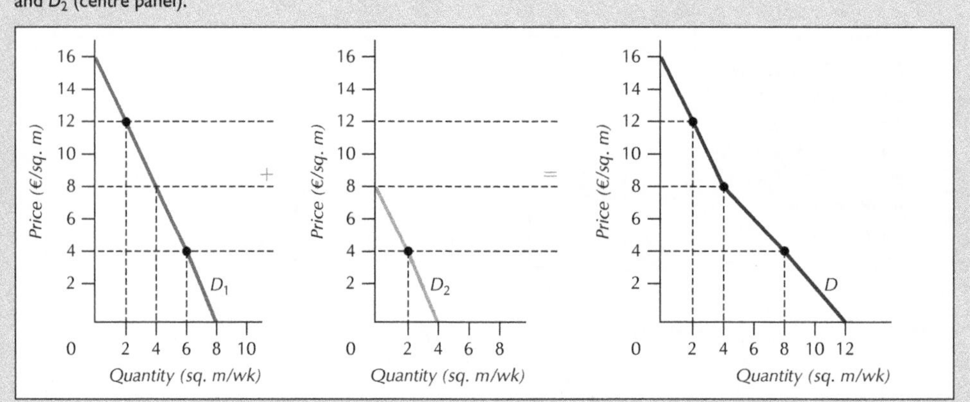

This sum, 6 sq. m/wk + 2 sq. m/wk = 8 sq. m/wk, is the total quantity of shelter demanded at the price €4/sq. m. We then plot the point (8, 4) as one of the quantity-price pairs on the market demand curve D in the right panel of Figure 4.16. To generate additional points on the market demand curve, we simply repeat this process for other prices. Thus, the price €8/sq. m corresponds to a quantity of 4 + 0 = 4 sq. m/wk on the market demand curve for shelter. Proceeding in like fashion for additional prices, we trace out the entire market demand curve. Note that for prices above €8/sq. m, consumer 2 demands no shelter at all, and so the market demand curve for prices above €8 is identical to the demand curve for consumer 1.

The procedure of announcing a price and adding the individual quantities demanded at that price is called *horizontal summation*. It is carried out the same way whether there are only two consumers in the market or many millions. In both large and small markets, the market demand curve is the horizontal summation of the individual demand curves.

In Chapter 2 we saw that it is often easier to generate numerical solutions when demand and supply curves are expressed algebraically rather than geometrically. Similarly, it will often be convenient to aggregate individual demand curves algebraically rather than graphically. When using the algebraic approach, a common error is to add individual demand curves vertically instead of horizontally. A simple example makes this danger clear.

EXAMPLE 4.4 Smith and Jones are the only consumers in the market for lamb chops in a small town in Wales. Their demand curves are given by $P = 30 - 2Q_J$ and $P = 30 - 3Q_S$ where Q_J and Q_S are the quantities demanded by Jones and Smith, respectively. What is the market demand curve for lamb chops in their town?

When we add demand curves horizontally, we are adding quantities, not prices. Thus it is necessary first to solve the individual demand equations for the respective quantities in terms of price. This yields $Q_J = 15 - (P/2)$ for Jones, and $Q_S = 10 - (P/3)$ for Smith. If the quantity demanded in the market is denoted by Q, we have $Q = Q_J + Q_S = 15 - (P/2) + 10 - (P/3) = 25 - (5P/6)$. Solving back for P, we get the equation for the market demand curve: $P = 30 - (6Q/5)$. We can easily verify that this is the correct market demand curve by adding the individual demand curves graphically, as in Figure 4.17.

FIGURE 4.17

The Market Demand Curve for Lamb Chops

When adding individual demand curves algebraically, be sure to solve for quantity first before adding.

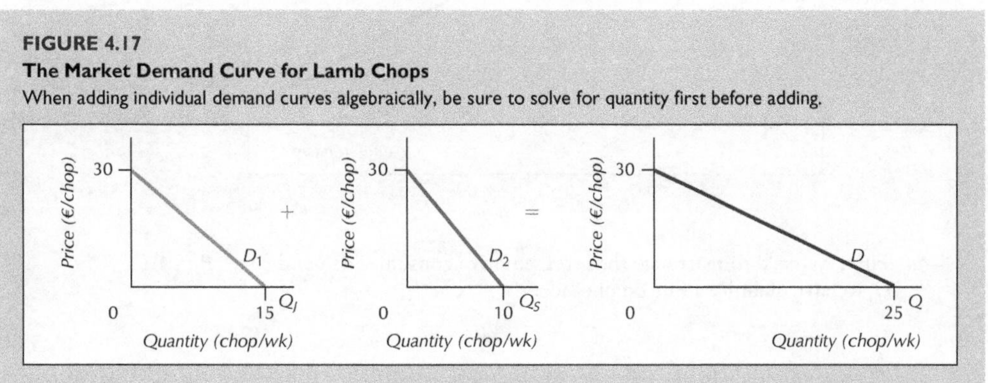

The common pitfall is to add the demand functions as originally stated and then solve for P in terms of Q. Here, this would yield $P = 30 - (5Q/2)$, which is obviously not the market demand curve we are looking for. ◆

EXERCISE 4.3 Write the individual demand curves for shelter in Figure 4.16 in algebraic form, then add them algebraically to generate the market demand curve for shelter. (*Caution*: Note that the formula for quantity along D_2 is valid only for prices between 0 and 8.)

The horizontal summation of individual consumers' demands into market demand has a simple form when the consumers in the market are all identical. Suppose n consumers each have the demand curve $P = a - bQ_i$. To add up the quantities for the n consumers into market demand, we rearrange the consumer demand curve $P = a - bQ_i$ to express quantity alone on one side $Q_i = a/b - (1/b)P$. Then market demand is the sum of the quantities demanded Q_i by each of the n consumers.

$$Q = nQ_i = n\left(\frac{a}{b} - \frac{1}{b}P\right) = \frac{na}{b} - \frac{n}{b}P$$

We can then rearrange market demand $Q = na/b - n(P/b)$ to get back in the form of price alone on one side $P = a - (b/n)Q$. The intuition is that each one unit demanded by the market is $1/n$ unit for each consumer. These calculations suggest a general rule for constructing the market demand curve when consumers are identical. If we have n individual consumer demand curves $P = a - bQ_i$, then the market demand curve is $P = a - (b/n)Q$.

EXAMPLE 4.5 Suppose a market has 10 consumers, each with demand curve $P = 10 - 5Q_i$, where P is the price in euros per unit and Q_i is the number of units demanded per week by the *i*th consumer (Figure 4.18). Find the market demand curve.

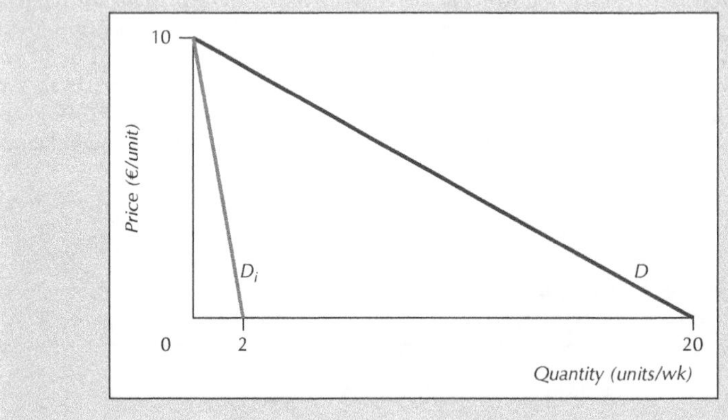

FIGURE 4.18 Market Demand Curve with Identical Consumers When 10 consumers each have demand curve $P = 10 - 5Q_i$ the market demand curve is the horizontal summation $P = 10 - (\frac{1}{2})Q$, with the same price intercept and $\frac{1}{10}$ the slope.

First, we need to rearrange the representative consumer demand curve $P = 10 - 5Q_i$ to have quantity alone on one side:

$$Q_i = 2 - \tfrac{1}{5}P$$

Then we multiply by the number of consumers, $n = 10$:

$$Q = nQ_i = 10Q_i = 10(2 - \tfrac{1}{5}P) = 20 - 2P$$

Finally, we rearrange the market demand curve $Q = 20 - 2P$ to have price alone on one side, $P = 10 - (\frac{1}{2})Q$, to return to the slope-intercept form. ◆

EXERCISE 4.4 Suppose a market has 30 consumers, each with demand curve $P = 120 - 60Q_i$, where P is price in euros per unit and Q_i is the number of units demanded per week by the ith consumer. Find the market demand curve.

PRICE ELASTICITY OF DEMAND

price elasticity of demand the percentage change in the quantity of a good demanded that results from a 1 per cent change in its price.

An analytical tool of central importance is the price elasticity of demand. It is a quantitative measure of the responsiveness of purchase decisions to variations in price, and as we will see in both this and later chapters, it is useful for a variety of practical problems. *Price elasticity of demand is defined as the percentage change in the quantity of a good demanded that results from a 1 per cent change in price.* For example, if a 1 per cent rise in the price of shelter caused a 2 per cent reduction in the quantity of shelter demanded, then the price elasticity of demand for shelter would be −2. The price elasticity of demand will always be negative (or zero) because price changes always move in the opposite direction from changes in quantity demanded.

The demand for a good is said to be *elastic* with respect to price if its price elasticity is less than −1. The good shelter mentioned in the preceding paragraph would thus be one for which demand is elastic with respect to price. The demand for a good is *inelastic* with respect to price if its price elasticity is greater than −1 and *unit elastic* with respect to price if its price elasticity is equal to −1. These definitions are portrayed graphically in Figure 4.19.

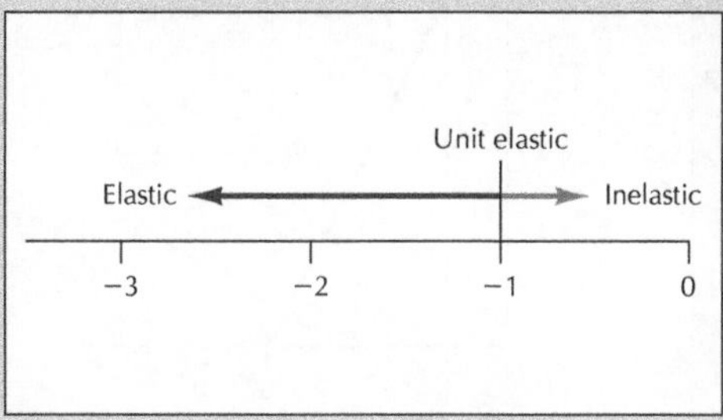

FIGURE 4.19
Three Categories of Price Elasticity
With respect to price, the demand for a good is elastic if its price elasticity is less than −1, inelastic if its price elasticity exceeds −1, and unit elastic if its price elasticity is equal to −1.

When interpreting actual demand data, it is often useful to have a more general definition of price elasticity that can accommodate cases in which the observed change in price does not happen to be 1 per cent. Let P be the current price of a good and let Q be the quantity demanded at that price. And let ΔQ be the change in the quantity demanded that occurs in response to a very small change in price, ΔP. The price elasticity of demand at the current price and quantity will then be given by

$$\epsilon = \frac{\Delta Q/Q}{\Delta P/P} \tag{4.1}$$

The numerator on the right side of Equation 4.1 is the proportional change in quantity. The denominator is the proportional change in price. Equation 4.1 is exactly the same as our earlier definition when ΔP happens to be a 1 per cent change in current price. The advantage is that the more general definition also works when ΔP is any other small percentage change in current price.

A Geometric Interpretation of Price Elasticity

Another way to interpret Equation 4.1 is to rewrite it as

$$\epsilon = \frac{\Delta Q}{\Delta P}\frac{P}{Q} \tag{4.2}$$

Equation 4.2 suggests a simple interpretation in terms of the geometry of the market demand curve. When ΔP is small, the ratio $\Delta P/\Delta Q$ is the slope of the demand curve, which means that the ratio $\Delta Q/\Delta P$ is the reciprocal of that slope. Thus the price elasticity of demand may be interpreted as the product of the ratio of price to quantity and the reciprocal of the slope of the demand curve:[2]

$$\epsilon = \frac{P}{Q}\frac{1}{\text{slope}} \tag{4.3}$$

Equation 4.3 is called the *point-slope method* of calculating price elasticity of demand. By way of illustration, consider the demand curve for shelter shown in Figure 4.20. Because this demand curve is linear, its slope is the same at every point, namely, -2. The reciprocal of this slope is $-\frac{1}{2}$. The price elasticity of demand at point A is therefore given by the ratio of price to quantity at A $(\frac{12}{2})$ multiplied by the reciprocal of the slope at A $(-\frac{1}{2})$, so we have $\epsilon_A = (\frac{12}{2})(-\frac{1}{2}) = -3$.

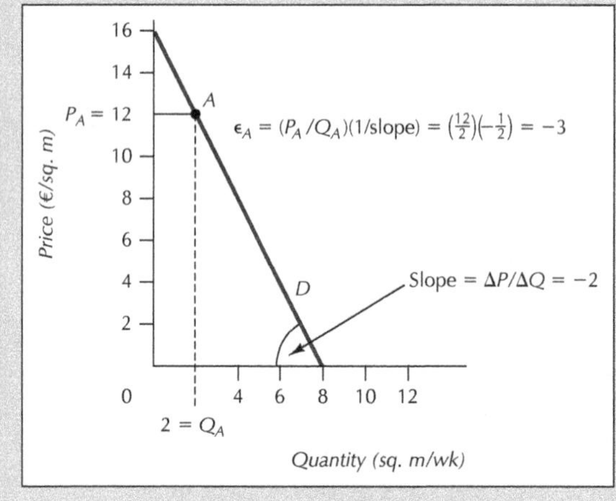

FIGURE 4.20
The Point-Slope Method
The price elasticity of demand at any point is the product of the price-quantity ratio at that point and the reciprocal of the slope of the demand curve at that point. The price elasticity at A is thus $(\frac{12}{2})(-\frac{1}{2}) = -3$.

When the market demand curve is linear, as in Figure 4.20, several properties of price elasticity quickly become apparent from this interpretation. The first is that the price elasticity is different at every point along the demand curve. More specifically, we know that the slope of a linear demand curve is constant throughout, which means that the reciprocal of its slope is also constant. The ratio of price to quantity, by contrast, takes a different value at every point along the demand curve. As we approach the vertical intercept, it approaches infinity. It declines steadily as we move downward along the demand curve, finally reaching a value of zero at the horizontal intercept.

A second property of demand elasticity is that it is never positive. As noted earlier, because the slope of the demand curve is always negative, its reciprocal must also be negative; and because the ratio P/Q is always positive, it follows that

[2]In calculus terms, price elasticity is defined as $\epsilon = (P/Q)[dQ(P)/dP]$.

the price elasticity of demand—which is the product of these two—must always be a negative number (except at the horizontal intercept of the demand curve, where P/Q, and hence elasticity, is zero). For the sake of convenience, however, economists often ignore the negative sign of price elasticity and refer simply to its absolute value. When a good is said to have a 'high' price elasticity of demand, this will always mean that its price elasticity is large in absolute value, indicating that the quantity demanded is highly responsive to changes in price. Similarly, a good whose price elasticity is said to be 'low' is one for which the absolute value of elasticity is small, indicating that the quantity demanded is relatively unresponsive to changes in price.

A third property of price elasticity at any point along a straight-line demand curve is that it will be inversely related to the slope of the demand curve. The steeper the demand curve, the less elastic is demand at any point along it. This follows from the fact that the reciprocal of the slope of the demand curve is one of the factors used to compute price elasticity.

EXERCISE 4.5 Use the point-slope method (Equation 4.3) to determine the elasticity of the demand curve $P = 32 - Q$ at the point where $P = 24$.

Two polar cases of demand elasticity are shown in Figure 4.21. In Figure 4.21(*a*), the horizontal demand curve, with its slope of zero, has an infinitely high price elasticity at every point. Such demand curves are often called *perfectly elastic* and, as we will see, are especially important in the study of competitive firm behaviour. In Figure 4.21(*b*), the vertical demand curve has a price elasticity everywhere equal to zero. Such curves are called *perfectly inelastic.*

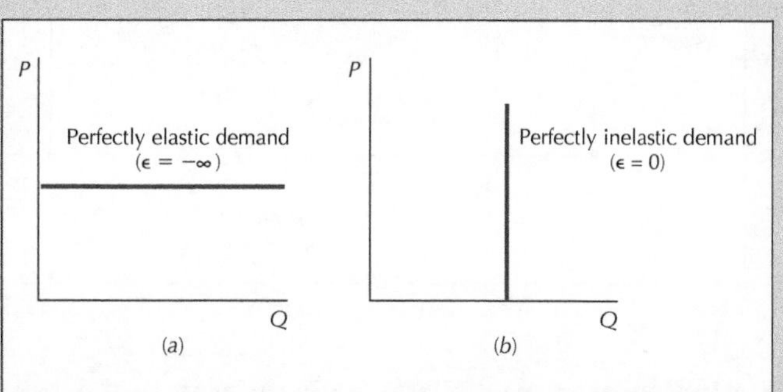

FIGURE 4.21
Two Important Polar Cases
(*a*) The price elasticity of the demand curve is equal to $-\infty$ at every point. Such demand curves are said to be perfectly elastic. (*b*) The price elasticity of the demand curve is equal to 0 at every point. Such demand curves are said to be perfectly inelastic.

As a practical matter, it would be impossible for any demand curve to be perfectly inelastic at all prices. Beyond some sufficiently high price, income effects must curtail consumption, even for seemingly essential goods with no substitutes, such as surgery for malignant tumours. Even so, the demand curve for many such goods and services will be perfectly inelastic over an extremely broad range of prices (recall the salt example discussed earlier in this chapter).

The Unit-Free Property of Elasticity

Another way of measuring responsiveness to changes in price is to use the slope of the demand curve. Other things equal, for example, we know that the quantity demanded of a good with a steep demand curve will be less responsive to changes in price than will one with a less steep demand curve.

Since the slope of a demand curve is much simpler to calculate than its elasticity, it may seem natural to ask, 'Why bother with elasticity at all?' One reason is that the slope of the demand curve is sensitive to the units we use to measure price and quantity, while elasticity is not. By way of illustration, notice in Figure 4.22(*a*) that when the price of petrol is measured in €/litre, the slope of the demand curve at point C is −0.02. By contrast, in Figure 4.22(*b*), where price is measured in €/gallon, the slope at C is −0.0909 (because there are around 4.55 litres in a gallon). In both cases, however, note that the price elasticity of demand at C is −3. This will be true no matter how we measure price and quantity. And most people find it much more informative to know that a 1 per cent cut in price will lead to a 3 per cent increase in the quantity demanded than to know that the slope of the demand curve is −0.0909.

When weighing costs and benefits, always compare absolute monetary amounts, not proportions. But when describing how quantity demanded responds to changes in price, it is generally best to speak in terms of proportions.

FIGURE 4.22
Elasticity Is Unit-Free
The slope of the demand curve at any point depends on the units in which we measure price and quantity. The absolute magnitude of the slope at point *C* when we measure the price of petrol in euros per litre (*a*) is more than when we measure the price in euros per gallon (*b*). The price elasticity at any point, by contrast, is completely independent of units of measure.

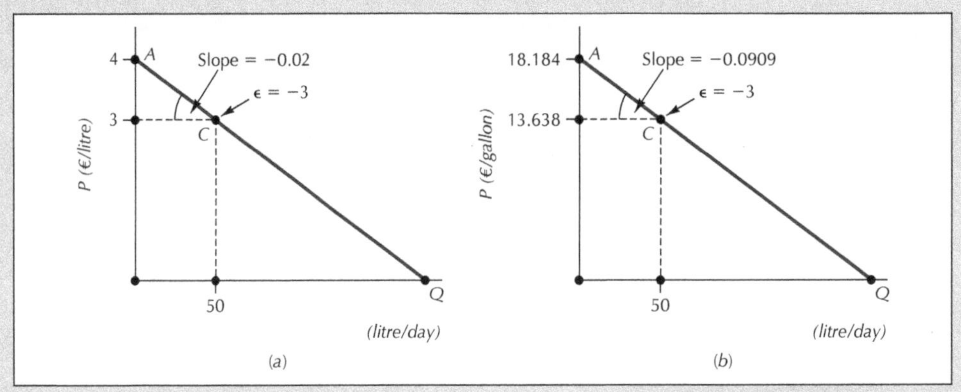

Some Representative Elasticity Estimates

As the entries in Table 4.4 show, the price elasticities of demand for different products often differ substantially. The low elasticity for theatre and opera performances probably reflects the fact that buyers in this market have much larger than average incomes, so that income effects of price variations are likely to be small. Income effects for green peas are also likely to be small even for low-income consumers, yet the price elasticity of demand for green peas is more than 14 times larger than for theatre and opera performances. The difference is that there are many more close substitutes for green peas than for theatre and opera performances. Later in this chapter we investigate in greater detail the factors that affect the price elasticity of demand for a product.

Elasticity and Total Expenditure

Suppose you are the administrator in charge of setting tolls for the Oresund Bridge, which links Copenhagen to Malmo. Suppose that with the toll at €30/trip, 100,000 trips per day are taken across the bridge. If the price elasticity of demand for trips is

TABLE 4.4
Price Elasticity Estimates for Selected Products*

Good or service	Price elasticity
Green peas	−2.8
Air travel (vacation)	−1.9
Frying chickens	−1.8
Beer	−1.2
Marijuana	−1.0
Movies	−0.9
Air travel (non-vacation)	−0.8
Shoes	−0.7
Cigarettes	−0.3
Theatre, opera	−0.2
Local telephone calls	−0.1

*Some of these short-run elasticity estimates represent the midpoint of the corresponding range of estimates. Sources: Fred Nordhauser and Paul L. Farris, 'An Estimate of the Short-Run Price Elasticity of Demand for Fryers', *Journal of Farm Economics,* November 1959; H. S. Houthakker and Lester Taylor, *Consumer Demand in the United States: Analyses and Projections,* 2nd edn, Cambridge, MA: Harvard University Press, 1970; Charles T. Nisbet and Firouz Vakil, 'Some Estimates of Price and Expenditure Elasticities of Demand for Marijuana among UCLA Students', *Review of Economics and Statistics,* November 1972; L. Taylor, 'The Demand for Electricity: A Survey', *Bell Journal of Economics,* Spring 1975; K. Elzinga, 'The Beer Industry', in Walter Adams (ed.), *The Structure of American Industry,* New York: Macmillan, 1977; Rolla Edward Park, Bruce M. Wetzel, and Bridger Mitchell, *Charging for Local Telephone Calls: Price Elasticity Estimates from the GTE Illinois Experiment,* Santa Monica, CA: Rand Corporation, 1983; Tae H. Oum, W. G. Waters II, and Jong Say Yong, 'A Survey of Recent Estimates of Price Elasticities of Demand for Transport', World Bank Infrastructure and Urban Development Department Working Paper 359, January 1990; M. C. Farrelly and J. W. Bray, 'Response to Increases in Cigarette Prices by Race/Ethnicity, Income, and Age Groups—United States, 1976–1993', *Journal of the American Medical Association,* 280, 1998.

−2.0, what will happen to the number of trips taken per day if you raise the toll by 10 per cent? With an elasticity of −2.0, a 10 per cent increase in price will produce a 20 per cent reduction in quantity. Thus the number of trips will fall to 80,000/day. Total expenditure at the higher toll will be (80,000 trips/day)(€33/trip) = €2,640,000/day. Note that this is smaller than the total expenditure of €3,000,000/day that occurred under the €30 toll.

Now suppose that the price elasticity had been not −2.0 but −0.5. How would the number of trips and total expenditure then be affected by a 10 per cent increase in the toll? This time the number of trips will fall by 5 per cent to 95,000/day, which means that total expenditure will rise to (95,000 trips/day) (€33/trip) = €3,135,000/day. If your goal as an administrator is to increase the total revenue collected from the bridge toll, you need to know something about the price elasticity of demand before deciding whether to raise the toll or lower it.

This example illustrates the important relationships between price elasticity and total expenditure. The questions we want to be able to answer are of the form, 'If the price of a product changes, how will total spending on the product be affected?' and 'Will more be spent if we sell more units at a lower price or fewer units at a

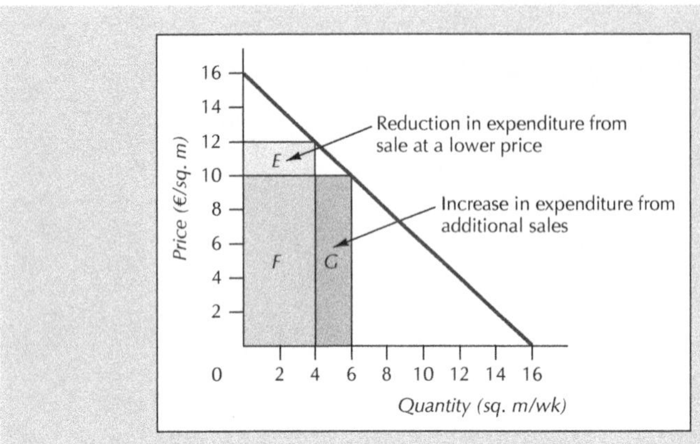

FIGURE 4.23 The Effect on Total Expenditure of a Reduction in Price When price falls, people spend less on existing units (*E*). But they also buy more units (*G*). Here, *G* is larger than *E*, which means that total expenditure rises.

higher price?' In Figure 4.23, for example, we might want to know how total expenditures for shelter are affected when the price falls from €12/sq. m to €10/sq. m.

The total expenditure, *R*, at any quantity-price pair (*Q*, *P*) is given by the product

$$R = PQ \tag{4.4}$$

In Figure 4.23, the total expenditure at the original quantity-price pair is thus (€12/sq. m)(4 sq. m/wk) = €48/wk. Geometrically, it is the sum of the two shaded areas *E* and *F*. Following the price reduction, the new total expenditure is (€10/sq. m) (6 sq. m/wk) = €60/wk, which is the sum of the shaded areas *F* and *G*. These two total expenditures have in common the shaded area *F*. The change in total expenditure is thus the difference in the two shaded areas *E* and *G*. The area *E*, which is (€2/sq. m)(4 sq. m/wk) = €8/wk, may be interpreted as the reduction in expenditure caused by selling the original 4 sq. m/wk at the new, lower price. *G*, in turn, is the increase in expenditure caused by the additional 2 sq. m/wk of sales. This area is given by (€10/sq. m)(2 sq. m/wk) = €20/wk. Whether total expenditure rises or falls thus boils down to whether the gain from additional sales exceeds the loss from lower prices. Here, the gain exceeds the loss by €12, so total expenditure rises by that amount following the price reduction.

If the change in price is small, we can say how total expenditure will move if we know the initial price elasticity of demand. Recall that one way of expressing price elasticity is the percentage change in quantity divided by the corresponding percentage change in price. If the absolute value of that quotient exceeds 1, we know that the percentage change in quantity is larger than the percentage change in price. And when that happens, the increase in expenditure from additional sales will always exceed the reduction from sales of existing units at the lower price. In Figure 4.23, note that the elasticity at the original price of €12 is 3.0, which confirms our earlier observation that the price reduction led to an increase in total expenditure. Suppose, on the contrary, that price elasticity is less than unity. Then the percentage change in quantity will be smaller than the corresponding percentage change in price, and the additional sales will not compensate for the reduction in expenditure from sales at a lower price. Here, a price reduction will lead to a reduction in total expenditure.

EXERCISE 4.6 For the demand curve in Figure 4.23, what is the price elasticity of demand when *P* = €4/sq. m? What will happen to total expenditure on shelter when price falls from €4/sq. m to €3/sq. m?

The general rule for small price reductions, then, is this: *A price reduction will increase total revenue if and only if the absolute value of the price elasticity of demand is greater than 1.* Parallel reasoning leads to an analogous rule for small price increases: *An increase in price will increase total revenue if and only if the absolute value of the price elasticity is less than 1.* These rules are summarized in the top panel of Figure 4.24, where the point *M* is the midpoint of the demand curve.

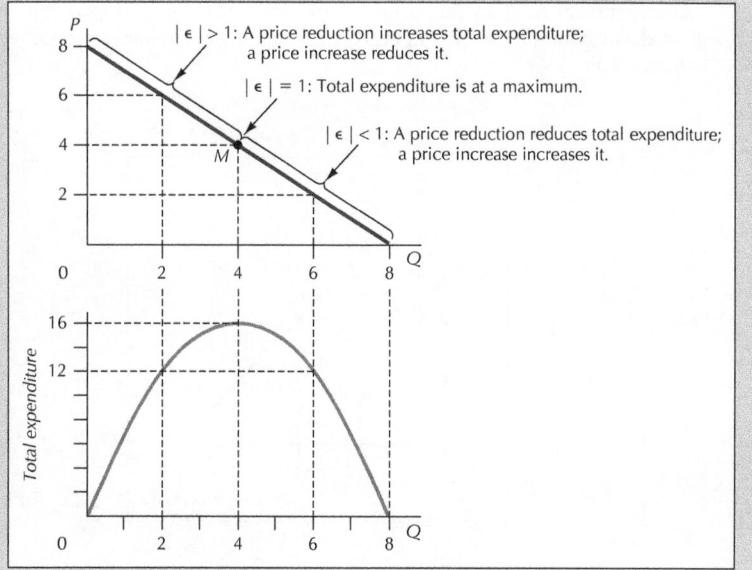

FIGURE 4.24
Demand and Total Expenditure
When demand is elastic, total expenditure changes in the opposite direction from a change in price. When demand is inelastic, total expenditure and price both move in the same direction. At the midpoint of the demand curve (*M*), total expenditure is at a maximum.

The relationship between elasticity and total expenditure is spelled out in greater detail in the relationship between the top and bottom panels of Figure 4.24. The top panel shows a straight-line demand curve. For each quantity, the bottom panel shows the corresponding total expenditure. As indicated in the bottom panel, total expenditure starts at zero when *Q* is zero and increases to its maximum value at the quantity corresponding to the midpoint of the demand curve (point *M* in the top panel). At that quantity, price elasticity is unity. Beyond that quantity, total expenditure declines with output, reaching zero at the horizontal intercept of the demand curve.

EXAMPLE 4.6 The market demand curve for bus rides in a small community is given by $P = 100 - (Q/10)$, where P is the fare per ride in cents and Q is the number of rides each day. If the price is 50 cents/ride, how much revenue will the bus system collect each day? What is the price elasticity of demand for rides? If the system needs more revenue, should it raise or lower the price? How would your answers have differed if the initial price had been not 50 cents/ride but 75?

Total revenue for the bus system is equal to total expenditure by riders, which is the product PQ. First we solve for Q from the demand curve and get $Q = 1000 - 10P$. When P is 50 cents/ride, Q will be 500 rides/day and the resulting total revenue will be €250/day. To compute the price elasticity of demand, we can use the formula $\epsilon = (P/Q)(1/slope)$. Here the slope is $-\frac{1}{10}$, so $1/\text{slope} = -10$.[3] P/Q takes the value

[3]The slope here is from the formula $P = 100 - (Q/10)$.

50/500 = $\frac{1}{10}$. Price elasticity is thus the product $(-\frac{1}{10})$ (10) = −1. With a price elasticity of unity, total revenue attains its maximum value. If the bus company either raises or lowers its price, it will earn less than it does at the current price.

At a price of 50 cents, the company was operating at the midpoint of its demand curve. If the price had instead been 75 cents, it would be operating above the midpoint. More precisely, it would be halfway between the midpoint and the vertical intercept (point *K* in Figure 4.25). Quantity would be only 250 rides/day, and price elasticity would have been −3 (computed, for example, by multiplying the price-quantity ratio at *K*, $\frac{3}{10}$, by the reciprocal of the demand curve slope, $-\frac{1}{10}$) Operating at an elastic point on its demand curve, the company could increase total revenue by cutting its price. ◆

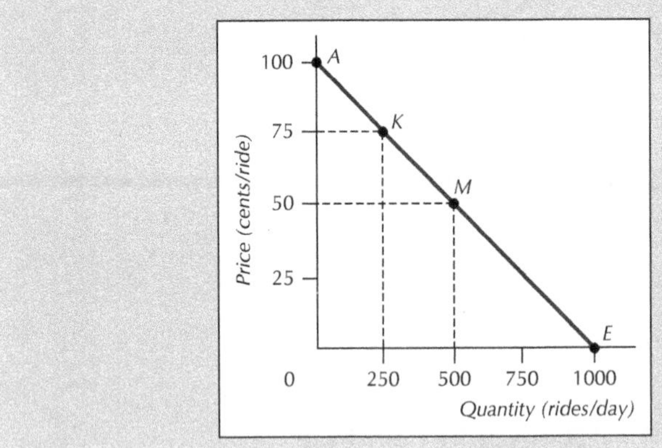

FIGURE 4.25
The Demand for Bus Rides
At a price of 50 cents/ride, the bus company is maximizing its total revenues. At a price of 75 cents/ride, demand is elastic with respect to price, and so the company can increase its total revenues by cutting its price.

Determinants of Price Elasticity of Demand

What factors influence the price elasticity of demand for a product? Our earlier discussion of substitution and income effects suggests primary roles for the following factors:

- **Substitution possibilities.** The substitution effect of a price change tends to be small for goods with no close substitutes. Consider, for example, the vaccine against rabies. People who have been bitten by rabid animals have no substitute for this vaccine, so demand for it is highly inelastic. We saw that the same was true for a good such as salt. But consider now the demand for a particular brand of salt, say, Morton's. Despite the advertising claims of salt manufacturers, one brand of salt is a more-or-less perfect substitute for any other. Because the substitution effect between specific brands is large, a rise in the price of one brand should sharply curtail the quantity of it demanded. In general, the absolute value of price elasticity will rise with the availability of attractive substitutes.

- **Budget share.** The larger the share of total expenditures accounted for by the product, the more important will be the income effect of a price change. Goods such as salt, rubber bands, cellophane wrap, and a host of others account for such small shares of total expenditures that the income effects of a price change are likely to be negligible. For goods like housing and higher education, by contrast, the income effect of a price increase is likely to be large. In general, the smaller the share of total expenditure accounted for by a good, the less elastic demand will be.

© George Clerk

The price of elasticity of demand for petrol is higher in the long run because when the price of petrol rises, it takes time for people to switch from inefficient vehicles . . .

. . . to more efficient ones.

- **Direction of income effect.** A factor closely related to the budget share is the direction—positive or negative—of its income effect. While the budget share tells us whether the income effect of a price change is likely to be large or small, the direction of the income effect tells us whether it will offset or reinforce the substitution effect. Thus, a normal good will have a higher price elasticity than an inferior good, other things equal, because the income effect reinforces the substitution effect for a normal good but offsets it for an inferior good.
- **Time.** Our analysis of individual demand did not focus explicitly on the role of time. But it too has an important effect on responses to changes in prices. Consider the oil price increases of recent years. One possible response is simply to drive less. But many car trips cannot be abandoned, or even altered, very quickly. A person cannot simply stop going to work, for example. He can cut down on his daily commute by joining a car pool or by purchasing a house closer to where he works. He can also curtail his petrol consumption by trading in his current car for one that gets better mileage. But all these steps take time, and as a result, the demand for petrol will be much more elastic in the long run than in the short run.

The short- and long-run effects of a supply shift in the market for petrol are contrasted in Figure 4.26. The initial equilibrium at *A* is disturbed by a supply reduction from *S* to *S'*. In the short run, the effect is for price to rise to P_{SR} = €2.80/litre and for quantity to fall to Q_{SR} = 5 million litres/day. The long-run demand curve is more elastic than the short-run demand curve. As consumers have more time to adjust, therefore, price effects tend to moderate while quantity effects tend to become more pronounced. Thus the new long-run equilibrium in Figure 4.26 occurs at a price of P_{LR} = €2.60/litre and a quantity of Q_{LR} = 4 million litres/day.

We see an extreme illustration of the difference between short- and long-run price elasticity values in the case of natural gas used in households. The price elasticity for this product is only −0.1 in the short run but a whopping −10.7 in the long run![4] This difference reflects the fact that once consumers have chosen appliances to heat and cook with, they are virtually locked in for the short run. People aren't going to cook their rice for only 10 minutes just because the price of natural gas has gone up. In the long run, however, consumers can and do switch between fuels when there are significant changes in relative prices.

[4]H. S. Houthakker and Lester Taylor, *Consumer Demand in the United States: Analyses and Projections*, 2nd edn, Cambridge, MA: Harvard University Press, 1970.

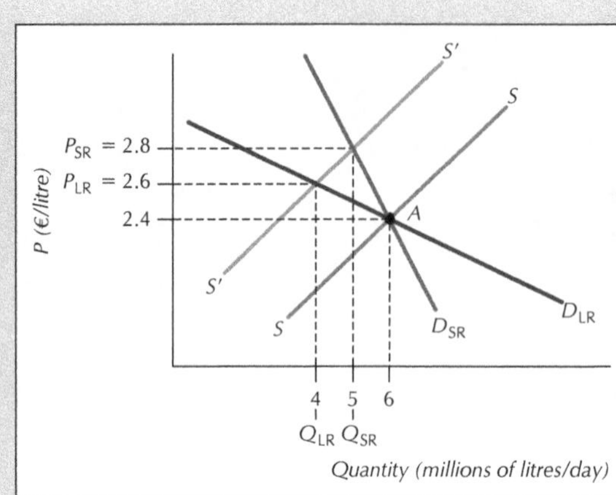

FIGURE 4.26
Price Elasticity Is Greater in the Long Run Than in the Short Run
The more time people have, the more easily they can switch to substitute products. The price effects of supply alterations are therefore always more extreme in the short run than in the long run.

THE DEPENDENCE OF MARKET DEMAND ON INCOME

As we have seen, the quantity of a good demanded by any person depends not only on its price but also on the person's income. Since the market demand curve is the horizontal sum of individual demand curves, it too will be influenced by consumer incomes. In some cases, the effect of income on market demand can be accounted for completely if we know only the average income level in the market. This would be the case, for example, if all consumers in the market were alike in terms of preference and all had the same incomes.

In practice, however, a given level of average income in a market will sometimes give rise to different market demands depending on how income is distributed. A simple example helps make this point clear.

EXAMPLE 4.7 **Two consumers, *A* and *B*, are in a market for food. Their tastes are identical, and each has the same initial income level, €120/wk. If their individual Engel curves for food are as given by *EE* in Figure 4.27, how will the market demand curve for food be affected if *A*'s income goes down by 50 per cent while *B*'s goes up by 50 per cent?**

The non-linear shape of the Engel curve pictured in Figure 4.27 is plausible considering that a consumer can eat only so much food. Beyond some point, increases in income should have no appreciable effect on the amount of food consumed. The implication is that *B*'s new income (€180/wk) will produce an increase in his consumption (2 kg/wk) that is smaller than the reduction in *A*'s consumption (4 kg/wk) caused by *A*'s new income (€60/wk).

What does all this say about the corresponding individual and market demand curves for food? Identical incomes and tastes give rise to identical individual demand curves, denoted D_A and D_B in Figure 4.28. Adding D_A and D_B horizontally, we get the initial market demand curve, denoted D. The nature of the individual Engel curves tells us that *B*'s increase in demand will be smaller than *A*'s reduction in demand following the shift in income distribution. Thus, when we add the new individual demand curves (D'_A and D'_B), we get a new market demand for food (D') that lies to the left of the original demand curve. ◆

FIGURE 4.27
The Engel Curve for Food of *A* and *B*
When individual Engel curves take the non-linear form shown, the increase in food consumption that results from a given increase in income will be smaller than the reduction in food consumption that results from an income reduction of the same amount.

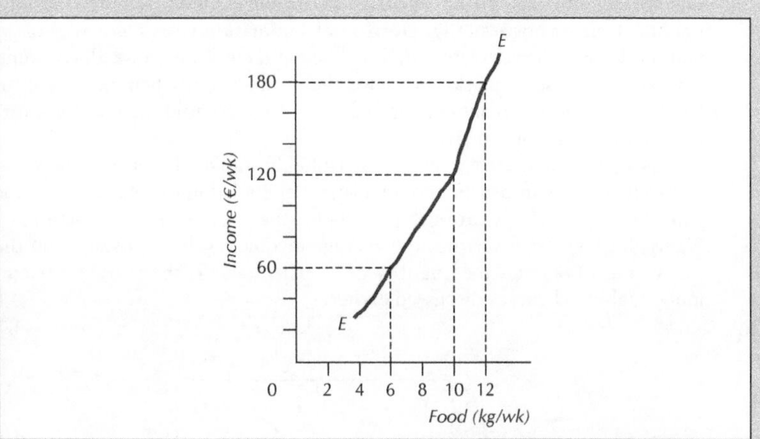

FIGURE 4.28
Market Demand Sometimes Depends on the Distribution of Income
A given increase in income produces a small demand increase for *B* (*b*); an income reduction of the same size produces a larger demand reduction for *A* (*a*). The redistribution from *A* to *B* leaves average income unchanged but reduces market demand (*c*).

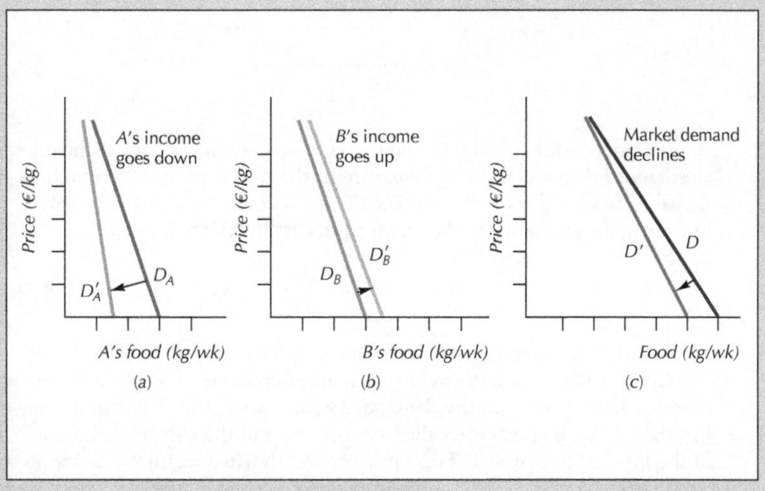

The dependence of market demands on the distribution of income is important to bear in mind when the government considers policies to redistribute income. A policy that redistributes income from rich to poor, for example, is likely to increase demand for goods like food and reduce demand for luxury items, such as jewellery and foreign travel.

Demand in many other markets is relatively insensitive to variations in the distribution of income. In particular, the distribution of income is not likely to matter much in markets in which individual demands tend to move roughly in proportion to changes in income.

Engel curves at the market level are schedules that relate the quantity demanded to the average income level in the market. The existence of a stable relationship between average income and quantity demanded is by no means certain for any given product because of the distributional complication just discussed. In particular, note that we cannot construct Engel curves at the market level by simply adding individual Engel curves horizontally. Horizontal summation works as a way of generating market demand curves from individual demand curves because all consumers in the market face the same market price for the product. But when incomes differ widely from one consumer to another, it makes no sense to hold income constant and add quantities across consumers.

As a practical matter, however, reasonably stable relationships between various aggregate income measures and quantities demanded in the market may nonetheless exist. Suppose such a relationship exists for the good X and is as pictured by EE in Figure 4.29, where Y denotes the average income level of consumers in the market for X, and Q denotes the quantity of X. This locus is the market analogue of the individual Engel curves discussed earlier.

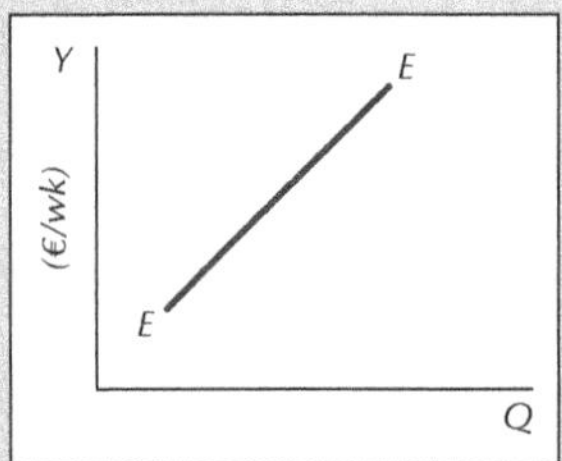

FIGURE 4.29
An Engel Curve at the Market Level
The market Engel curve tells what quantities will be demanded at various average levels of income.

income elasticity of demand the percentage change in the quantity of a good demanded that results from a 1 per cent change in income.

If a good exhibits a stable Engel curve, we may then define its **income elasticity of demand**, a formal measure of the responsiveness of purchase decisions to variations in the average market income. Denoted η, it is given by a formula analogous to the one for price elasticity:[5]

$$\eta = \frac{\Delta Q/Q}{\Delta Y/Y} \tag{4.5}$$

where Y denotes average market income and ΔY is a small change therein.

Goods such as food, for which a change in income produces a less than proportional change in the quantity demanded at any price, thus have an income elasticity less than 1. Such goods are called *necessities,* and their income elasticities must lie in the interval $0 < \eta < 1$. Food is a commonly cited example. *Luxuries* are those goods for which $\eta > 1$. Common examples are expensive jewellery and foreign travel. Inferior goods are those for which $\eta < 0$. Goods for which $\eta = 1$ will have Engel curves that are straight lines through the origin, as pictured by the locus EE in Figure 4.30*(a)*. The market Engel curves for luxuries, necessities and inferior goods, where these exist and are stable, are pictured in Figure 4.30*(b)*.

The income elasticity formula in Equation 4.5 is easier to interpret geometrically if we rewrite it as

$$\eta = \frac{Y}{Q}\frac{\Delta Q}{\Delta Y} \tag{4.6}$$

The first factor on the right side of Equation 4.6 is simply the ratio of income to quantity at a point along the Engel curve. It is the slope of the line from the origin (a ray) to that point. The second factor is the reciprocal of the slope of the Engel

[5]In calculus terms, the corresponding formula is $\eta = (Y/Q)\,[dQ(Y)/dY]$.

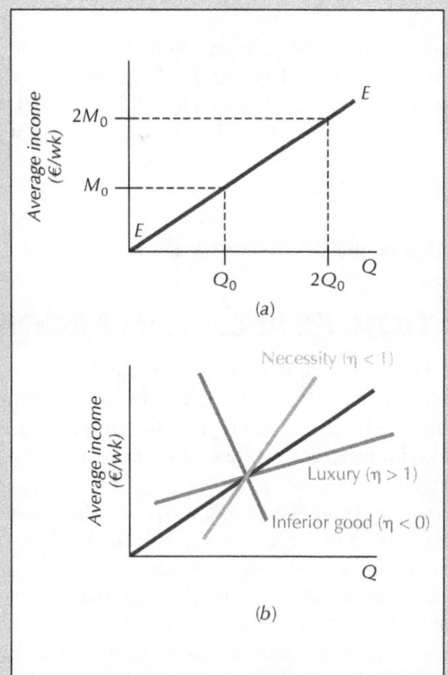

FIGURE 4.30
Engel Curves for Different Types of Goods
(*a*) The good whose Engel curve is shown has an income elasticity of 1. For such goods, a given proportional change in income will produce the same proportional change in quantity demanded. Thus when average income doubles, from M_0 to $2M_0$, the quantity demanded also doubles, from Q_0 to $2Q_0$. (*b*) The Engel curves show that consumption increases more than in proportion to income for a luxury and less than in proportion to income for a necessity, and it falls with income for an inferior good.

curve at that point. If the slope of the ray exceeds the slope of the Engel curve, the product of these two factors must be greater than 1 (the luxury case). If the ray is less steep, η will be less than 1 but still positive, provided the slope of the Engel curve is positive (the necessity case). Thus, in distinguishing between the Engel curves for necessities and luxuries, what counts is not the slopes of the Engel curves themselves but how they compare with the slopes of the corresponding rays. Finally, if the slope of the Engel curve is negative, η must be less than zero (the inferior case).

Why have pubs become good at cooking food?

ECONOMIC NATURALIST 4.1

The public house, or pub, has long been a cornerstone of British and Irish community life. It's a place to go for fine ale, boisterous conversation, and a smoke. But, times change. Now you are more likely to see a children's play area than people smoking. And you are more likely to go to the pub for a meal than a drink. In 2003 the proportion of pubs selling food was 90 per cent, up from 60 per cent only ten years before. This dramatic increase in the proportion of pubs selling food has coincided with equally dramatic increases in the quality and price of food. In the 1990s, 'pub grub' was likely to consist of 'steak and ale pie' for £5. Now you are likely to find 'Walmerstone tomato tarte fine' for £25.

The rise of the so-called 'gastropub' epitomizes this change in focus. The term was first used in 1991 by the owners of the Eagle Pub to capture the idea of fine dining within a pub. In 2001 the Stagg Inn became the first gastropub to earn the coveted Michelin Star. In 2011 the Hand and Flowers went one better by becoming the first gastropub to earn two Michelin stars. There are not many restaurants that can boast two Michelin stars and so things have clearly come a long way from the days of 'pub grub'.

What spawned this dramatic boom in pub food? The short answer is that incomes have increased a lot and pubs have adapted accordingly. Median after-tax income in the UK increased by 70 per cent between 1992 and 2010. For the top 1 per cent of earners it has increased by 132 per cent.[6] Dining in fine restaurants is clearly a luxury good. Drinking ale in a smoke-filled room is arguably an inferior good. As incomes have risen, therefore, pubs have had to adapt to changes in consumer demand. Rapid income growth among those with already high incomes spawned demand for a broad spectrum of other luxury goods as well. ■

APPLICATION: FORECASTING ECONOMIC TRENDS

If the income elasticity of demand for every good and service were 1, the composition of GNP would be completely stable over time (assuming technology and relative prices remain unchanged). Each year, the proportion of total spending devoted to food, travel, clothing, and indeed to every other consumption category would remain unchanged.

As the entries in Table 4.5 show, however, the income elasticities of different consumption categories differ markedly. And therein lies one of the most important applications of the income elasticity concept, namely, forecasting the composition of future purchase patterns. Ever since the industrial revolution in the West, real purchasing power per capita has grown at roughly 2 per cent per year. Our knowledge of income elasticity differences enables us to predict how consumption patterns in the future will differ from the ones we see today.

Thus, a growing share of the consumer's budget will be devoted to goods like restaurant meals and automobiles, whereas ever smaller shares will go to tobacco,

TABLE 4.5
Income Elasticities of Demand for Selected Products*

Good or service	Income elasticity
Automobiles	2.46
Furniture	1.48
Restaurant meals	1.40
Water	1.02
Tobacco	0.64
Petrol and oil	0.48
Electricity	0.20
Margarine	−0.20
Pork products	−0.20
Public transportation	−0.36

*These estimates come from H. S. Houthakker and Lester Taylor, *Consumer Demand in the United States: Analyses and Projections*, 2nd edn, Cambridge, MA: Harvard University Press, 1970; L. Taylor and R. Halvorsen, 'Energy Substitution in U.S. Manufacturing', *Review of Economics and Statistics*, November 1977; H. Wold and L. Jureen, *Demand Analysis*, New York: Wiley, 1953.

[6] HM Revenue and Customs.

fuel and electricity. And if the elasticity estimates are correct, the absolute amounts spent per person on margarine, pork products and public transportation will be considerably smaller in the future than they are today.

CROSS-PRICE ELASTICITIES OF DEMAND

cross-price elasticity of demand the percentage change in the quantity of one good demanded that results from a 1 per cent change in the price of the other good.

The quantity of a good purchased in the market depends not only on its price and consumer incomes but also on the prices of related goods. **Cross-price elasticity of demand** is the percentage change in the quantity demanded of one good caused by a 1 per cent change in the price of the other. More generally, for any two goods, X and Z, the cross-price elasticity of demand may be defined as follows:[7]

$$\epsilon_{XZ} = \frac{\Delta Q_X/Q_X}{\Delta P_Z/P_Z} \tag{4.7}$$

where ΔQ_X is a small change in Q_X, the quantity of X, and ΔP_Z is a small change in P_Z, the price of Z. ϵ_{XZ} measures how the quantity demanded of X responds to a small change in the price of Z.

Unlike the elasticity of demand with respect to a good's own price (the *own-price elasticity*), which is never greater than zero, the cross-price elasticity may be either positive or negative. X and Z are defined as *complements* if $\epsilon_{XZ} < 0$. If $\epsilon_{XZ} > 0$, they are *substitutes*. Thus, a rise in the price of ham will reduce not only the quantity of ham demanded, but also, because ham and eggs are complements, the demand for eggs. A rise in the price of coffee, by contrast, will tend to increase the demand for tea. Estimates of the cross-price elasticity of demand for selected pairs of products are shown in Table 4.6.

EXERCISE 4.7 Would the cross-price elasticity of demand be positive or negative for the following pairs of goods: (*a*) apples and oranges, (*b*) airline tickets and car tyres, (*c*) computer hardware and software, (*d*) pens and paper, (*e*) pens and pencils?

TABLE 4.6
Cross-Price Elasticities for Selected Pairs of Products*

Good or service	Good or service with price change	Cross-price elasticity
Butter	Margarine	+0.81
Margarine	Butter	+0.67
Natural gas	Fuel oil	+0.44
Beef	Pork	+0.28
Electricity	Natural gas	+0.20
Entertainment	Food	−0.72
Cereals	Fresh fish	−0.87

*From H. Wold and L. Jureen, *Demand Analysis*, New York: Wiley, 1953; L. Taylor and R. Halvorsen, 'Energy Substitution in U.S. Manufacturing', *Review of Economics and Statistics*, November 1977; E. T. Fujii et al., 'An Almost Ideal Demand System for Visitor Expenditures', *Journal of Transport Economics and Policy*, 19, May 1985, 161–171; and A. Deaton, 'Estimation of Own- and Cross-Price Elasticities from Household Survey Data', *Journal of Econometrics*, 36, 1987, 7–30.

[7] In calculus terms, the corresponding expression is given by $\epsilon_{XZ} = (P_Z/Q_X)(dQ_X/dP_Z)$.

SUMMARY

- Our focus in this chapter was on how individual and market demands respond to variations in prices and incomes. To generate a demand curve for an individual consumer for a specific good *X*, we first trace out the price-consumption curve in the standard indifference curve diagram. The PCC is the line of optimal bundles observed when the price of *X* varies, with both income and preferences held constant. We then take the relevant price-quantity pairs from the PCC and plot them in a separate diagram to get the individual demand curve.

- The income analogue to the PCC is the income-consumption curve, or ICC. It too is constructed using the standard indifference curve diagram. The ICC is the line of optimal bundles traced out when we vary the consumer's income, holding preferences and relative prices constant. The Engel curve is the income analogue to the individual demand curve. We generate it by retrieving the relevant income-quantity pairs from the ICC and plotting them in a separate diagram.

- Normal goods are those the consumer buys more of when income increases, and inferior goods are those the consumer buys less of as income rises.

- The total effect of a price change can be decomposed into two separate effects: (1) the substitution effect, which denotes the change in the quantity demanded that results because the price change makes substitute goods seem either more or less attractive, and (2) the income effect, which denotes the change in quantity demanded that results from the change in real purchasing power caused by the price change. The substitution effect always moves in the opposite direction from the movement in price: price increases (reductions) always reduce (increase) the quantity demanded. For normal goods, the income effect also moves in the opposite direction from the price change and thus tends to reinforce the substitution effect. For inferior goods, the income effect moves in the same direction as the price change and thus tends to undercut the substitution effect.

- The fact that the income and substitution effects move in opposite directions for inferior goods suggests the theoretical possibility of a Giffen good, one for which the total effect of a price increase is to increase the quantity demanded. There have been no documented examples of Giffen goods, and in this text we adopt the convention that all goods, unless otherwise stated, are demanded in smaller quantities at higher prices.

- Goods for which purchase decisions respond most strongly to price tend to be ones that have large income and substitution effects that work in the same direction. For example, a normal good that occupies a large share of total expenditures and for which there are many direct or indirect substitutes will tend to respond sharply to changes in price. For many consumers, housing is a prime example of such a good. The goods least responsive to price changes will be those that account for very small budget shares and for which substitution possibilities are very limited. For most people, salt has both of these properties.

- There are two equivalent techniques for generating market demand curves from individual demand curves. The first is to display the individual curves graphically and then add them horizontally. The second is algebraic and proceeds by first solving the individual demand curves for the respective *Q* values, then adding those values, and finally solving the resulting sum for *P*.

- A central analytical concept in demand theory is the price elasticity of demand, a measure of the responsiveness of purchase decisions to small changes in price. It is defined as the percentage change in quantity demanded that is caused by a 1 per cent change in price. Goods for which the absolute value of elasticity exceeds 1 are said to be elastic; those for which it is less than 1, inelastic; and those for which it is equal to 1, unit elastic.

- Another important relationship is the one between price elasticity and the effect of a price change on total expenditure. When demand is elastic, a price reduction will increase total expenditure; when inelastic, total expenditure falls when the price goes down. When demand is unit elastic, total expenditure is at a maximum.

- The price elasticity of demand depends largely on four factors: substitutability, budget share, direction of income effect, and time. (1) *Substitutability.* The more easily consumers may switch to other goods, the more elastic demand will be. (2) *Budget share.* Goods that account for a large share of total expenditures will tend to have higher price elasticity. (3) *Direction of income effect.* Other factors the same, inferior goods will tend to be less elastic with respect to price than normal goods. (4) *Time.* Habits and existing commitments limit the extent to which consumers can respond to price changes in the short run. Price elasticity of demand will tend to be larger, the more time consumers have to adapt.

- Changes in the average income level in a market generally shift the market demand curve. The income elasticity of demand is defined analogously to price elasticity. It is the percentage change in quantity that results from a 1 per cent change in income. Goods whose income elasticity of demand exceeds zero are called normal goods; those for which it is less than zero are called inferior; those for which it exceeds 1 are called luxuries; and those for which it is less than 1 are called necessities. For normal goods, an increase in income shifts market demand to the right; and for inferior goods, an increase in income shifts demand to the left. For some goods, the distribution of income, not just its average value, is an important determinant of market demand.

- The cross-price elasticity of demand is a measure of the responsiveness of the quantity demanded of one good to a small change in the price of another. It is defined as the percentage change in the quantity demanded of one good that results from a 1 per cent change in the price of the other. If the cross-price elasticity of demand for X with respect to the price of Z is positive, X and Z are substitutes; and if negative, they are complements. In remembering the formulas for the various elasticities—own price, cross-price, and income—many people find it helpful to note that each is the percentage change in an effect divided by the percentage change in the associated causal factor.
- The Appendix to this chapter examines additional topics in demand theory, including the constant elasticity demand curve and the income-compensated demand curve.

QUESTIONS FOR REVIEW

1. Why does the quantity of salt demanded tend to be unresponsive to changes in its price?
2. Why is the quantity of education demanded in private universities much more responsive than salt is to changes in price?
3. Draw Engel curves for both a normal good and an inferior good.
4. Give two examples of what are, for most students, inferior goods.
5. Can the price-consumption curve for a normal good ever be downward-sloping?
6. To get the market demand curve for a product, why do we add individual demand curves horizontally rather than vertically?
7. Summarize the relationship between price elasticity, changes in price, and changes in total expenditure.
8. Why don't we measure the responsiveness of demand to price changes by the slope of the demand curve instead of using the more complicated expression for elasticity?
9. For a straight-line demand curve, what is the price elasticity at the revenue maximizing point?
10. Do you think an education at a specific university has a high or low price (tuition) elasticity of demand?
11. How can changes in the distribution of income across consumers affect the market demand for a product?
12. If you expected a long period of declining GNP, what kinds of companies would you invest in?
13. *True or false*: For a budget spent entirely on two goods, an increase in the price of one will necessarily decrease the consumption of both, unless at least one of the goods is inferior. Explain.
14. Mike spends all his income on tennis balls and football tickets. His demand curve for tennis balls is elastic. *True or false*: If the price of tennis balls rises, he consumes more tickets. Explain.
15. *True or false*: If each individual in a market has a straight-line demand curve for a good, then the market demand curve for that good must also be a straight line. Explain.
16. Suppose your budget is spent entirely on two goods: bread and butter. If bread is an inferior good, can butter be inferior as well?

PROBLEMS

1. Sam spends €6/wk on orange juice and apple juice. Orange juice costs €2/cup while apple juice costs €1/cup. Sam views 1 cup of orange juice as a perfect substitute for 3 cups of apple juice. Find Sam's optimal consumption bundle of orange juice and apple juice each week. Suppose the price of apple juice rises to €2/cup, while the price of orange juice remains constant. How much additional income would Sam need to afford his original consumption bundle?

2. Bruce has the same income and faces the same prices as Sam in Problem 1, but he views 1 cup of orange juice as a perfect substitute for 1 cup of apple juice. Find Bruce's optimal consumption bundle. How much additional income would Bruce need to be able to afford his original consumption bundle when the price of apple juice doubles?

3. Maureen has the same income and faces the same prices as Sam and Bruce, but Maureen views 1 cup of orange juice and 1 cup of apple juice as perfect complements. Find Maureen's optimal consumption bundle. How much additional income would Maureen need to afford her original consumption bundle when the price of apple juice doubles?

4. The market for lemonade has 10 potential consumers, each having an individual demand curve $P = 101 - 10Q_i$, where P is price in euros per cup and Q_i is the number of cups demanded per week by the ith consumer. Find the market demand curve using algebra. Draw an individual demand curve and the market demand curve. What is the quantity demanded by each consumer and in the market as a whole when lemonade is priced at $P =$ €1/cup?

5. a. For the demand curve $P = 60 - 0.5Q$, find the elasticity at $P = 10$.
   b. If the demand curve shifts parallel to the right, what happens to the elasticity at $P = 10$?

6. Consider the demand curve $Q = 100 - 50P$.
   a. Draw the demand curve and indicate which portion of the curve is elastic, which portion is inelastic, and which portion is unit elastic.
   b. Without doing any additional calculation, state at which point of the curve expenditures on the goods are maximized, and then explain the logic behind your answer.

7. Suppose the demand for crossing the Oresund Bridge is given by $Q = 10{,}000 - 100P$.
   a. If the toll (P) is €30, how much revenue is collected?
   b. What is the price elasticity of demand at this point?
   c. Could the bridge authorities increase their revenues by changing their price?
   d. Scandlines and HH Ferries offer a ferry service that competes with the Oresund Bridge. Suppose they improve the onboard cafeteria and duty free shop. How would this affect the elasticity of demand for trips across the Oresund Bridge?

8. Consumer expenditures on safety are thought to have a positive income elasticity. For example, as incomes rise, people tend to buy safer cars (larger cars with side air bags), they are more likely to fly on trips rather than drive, they are more likely to get regular health tests, and they are more likely to get medical care for any health problems the tests reveal. Is safety a luxury or a necessity?

9. Professors Adams and Brown make up the entire demand side of the market for summer research assistants in the economics department. If Adams's demand curve is $P = 50 - 2Q_A$ and Brown's is $P = 50 - Q_B$, where Q_A and Q_B are the hours demanded by Adams and Brown, respectively, what is the market demand for research hours in the economics department?

10. Suppose that at a price of €400, 300 tickets are demanded to fly from Madrid to Oslo. Now the price rises to €600, and 280 tickets are demanded. Assuming the demand for tickets is linear, find the price elasticities at the quantity-price pairs (300, 400) and (280, 600).

11. The monthly market demand curve for calculators among engineering students is given by $P = 100 - Q$, where P is the price per calculator in euros and Q is the number of calculators purchased per month. If the price is €30, how much revenue will calculator makers get each month? Find the price elasticity of demand for calculators. What should calculator makers do to increase revenue?

12. What price maximizes total expenditure along the demand curve $P = 27 - Q^2$?

13. A hot dog vendor faces a daily demand curve of $Q = 1800 - 15P$, where P is the price of a hot dog in cents and Q is the number of hot dogs purchased each day.

    a. If the vendor has been selling 300 hot dogs each day, how much revenue has he been collecting?
    b. What is the price elasticity of demand for hot dogs?
    c. The vendor decides that he wants to generate more revenue. Should he raise or lower the price of his hot dogs?
    d. At what price would he achieve maximum total revenue?

14. Rank the absolute values of the price elasticities of demand at the points *A, B, C, D* and *E* on the following three demand curves.

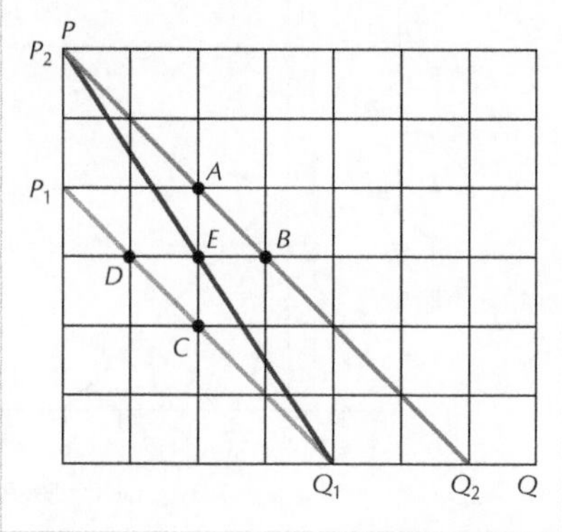

15. Draw the Engel curves for the following goods: food, Hawaiian vacations, peanuts, budget sports trainers (€4.99/pair).

16. Is the cross-price elasticity of demand positive or negative for the following pairs of items?

    a. Tennis rackets and tennis balls
    b. Bread and jam
    c. Hot dogs and hamburgers

*17. In 2001, *X* cost €3 and sold 400 units. That same year, a related good *Y* cost €10 and sold 200 units. In 2002, *X* still cost €3 but sold only 300 units, while *Y* rose in price to €12 and sold only 150 units. Other things the same, and assuming that the demand for *X* is a linear function of the price of *Y*, what was the cross-price elasticity of demand for *X* with respect to *Y* in 2001?

*18. Smith cannot tell the difference between rice and wheat and spends all her food budget of €24/wk on these foodstuffs. If rice costs €3/kg, draw Smith's price-consumption curve for wheat and the corresponding demand curve.

*19. Repeat the preceding problem on the assumption that rice and wheat are perfect, one-for-one complements.

*20. Suppose your local espresso bar makes the following offer: People who supply their own half-litre carton of milk get to buy a cup of cappuccino for only €1.50 instead of €2.50. Half-litre cartons of milk can be purchased in the adjacent convenience store for €0.50. In the wake of this offer, the quantity of cappuccino sold goes up by 60 per cent and the convenience store's total revenue from sales of milk exactly doubles.

    a. *True or false*: If there is a small, but significant, amount of hassle involved in supplying one's own milk, it follows that absolute value of the price elasticity of demand for cappuccino is 3. Explain.
    b. *True or false*: It follows that demand for the convenience store's milk is elastic with respect to price. Explain.

*Problems marked with an asterisk (*) are more difficult.

ANSWERS TO IN-CHAPTER EXERCISES

4.1. On Paula's original budget, B_0, she consumes at bundle A. On the new budget, B_1, she consumes at bundle D. (To say that D has 1.5 pairs of bindings per year means that she consumes 3 pairs of bindings every 2 years.) The substitution effect of the price increase (the movement from A to C) is zero.

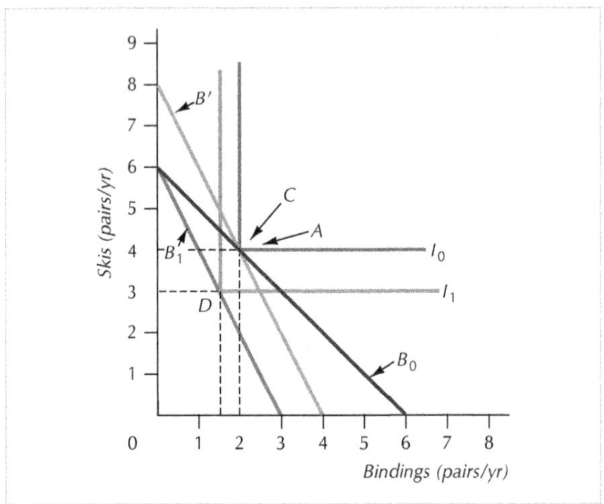

4.2. The income effect, substitution effect, and total effects are all zero because the price change does not alter Pam's optimal consumption bundle.

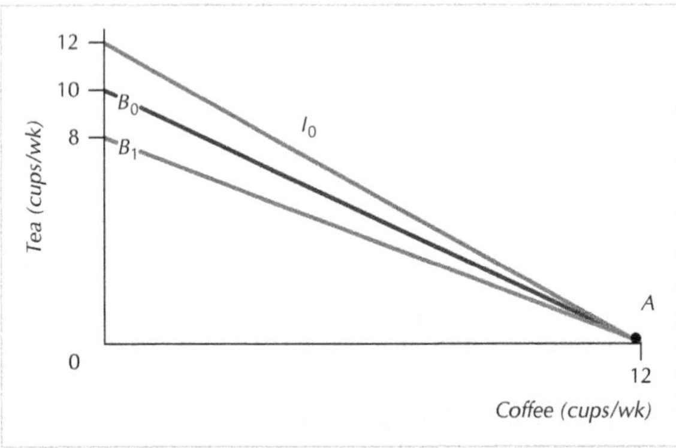

4.3. The formulas for D_1 and D_2 are $P = 16 - 2Q_1$ and $P = 8 - 2Q_2$, respectively. For the region in which $0 \le P \le 8$, we have $Q_1 = 8 - (P/2)$ and $Q_2 = 4 - (P/2)$. Adding, we get $Q_1 + Q_2 = Q = 12 - P$, for $0 \le P \le 8$. For $8 < P \le 16$, the market demand curve is the same as D_1, namely, $P = 16 - 2Q$.

4.4. First, we need to rearrange the representative consumer demand curve $P = 120 - 60Q_i$ to have quantity alone on one side:

$$Q_i = 2 - \tfrac{1}{60}P$$

Then we multiply by the number of consumers, $n = 30$,

$$Q = nQ_i = 30Q_i = 30(2 - \tfrac{1}{60}P) = 60 - \tfrac{1}{2}P$$

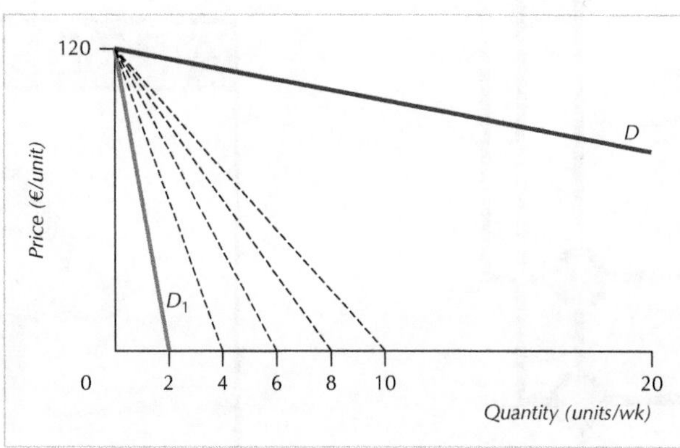

Finally, we rearrange the market demand curve $Q = 60 - \frac{1}{2}P$ to have price alone on one side, $P = 120 - 2Q$, to return to the slope-intercept form.

4.5. Since the slope of the demand curve is -1, we have $\epsilon = -P/Q$. At $P = 24$, $Q = 8$, and so $\epsilon = -P/Q = -\frac{24}{8} = -3$.

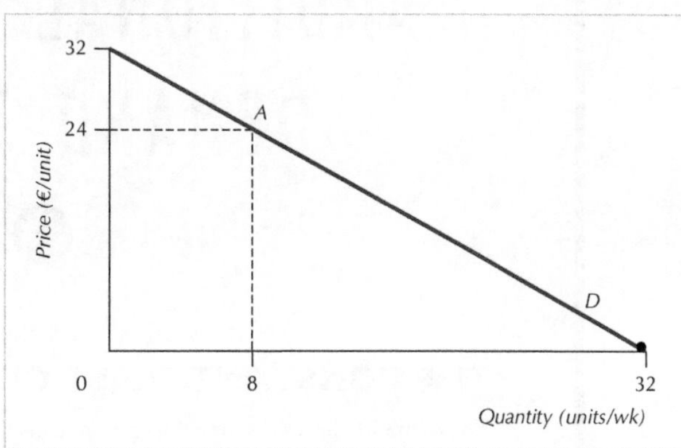

4.6. Elasticity when $P =$ €4/sq. m is $\frac{1}{3}$, so a price reduction will reduce total expenditure. At $P = 4$, total expenditure is €48/wk, which is more than the €39/wk of total expenditure at $P = 3$.

4.7. Substitutes, such as *a*, *b* and *e*, have positive cross-price elasticity (an increase in price of one good raises quantity demanded of the other good). Complements, such as *c* and *d*, have negative cross-price elasticity (an increase in price of one good lowers quantity demanded of the other good).

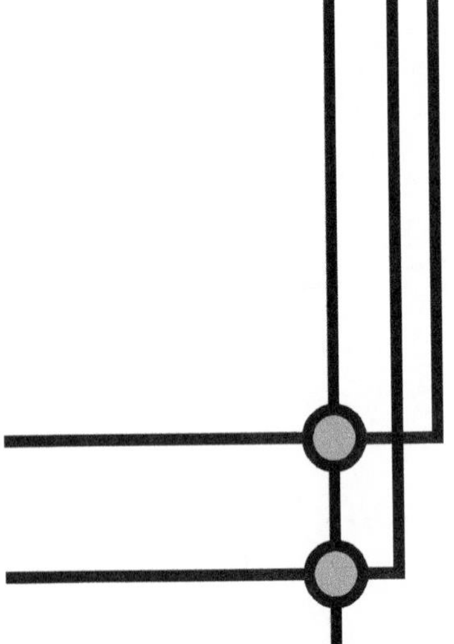

APPENDIX 4

ADDITIONAL TOPICS IN DEMAND THEORY

THE CONSTANT ELASTICITY DEMAND CURVE

The demand curves discussed so far have been linear, for which, as noted, price elasticity declines as we move down the demand curve. Not all demand curves have this property, however; on the contrary, there are others for which price elasticity can remain constant or even rise with movements down the demand curve. The *constant elasticity demand curve* is the name given to a demand curve for which elasticity does not vary with price and quantity. Whereas the linear demand curve has the general form $P = a - bQ$, the constant elasticity demand curve is instead written

$$P = \frac{k}{Q^{1/\epsilon}} \tag{A.4.1}$$

where k and ϵ are positive numbers, specific values of which determine the exact shape and position of the curve.[1] An example with $k = 2$ and $\epsilon = 1$ is pictured in Figure A.4.1.

Let us examine some points on the curve pictured in Figure A.4.1 and verify that they do indeed have the same price elasticity. Consider first the point $P = 2$, $Q = 1$, and calculate price elasticity as the product of the ratio P/Q and the

[1]Using the formal definition of elasticity, it is easy to show that the elasticity at any price-quantity pair along this demand curve is $-\epsilon$:

$$\frac{P}{Q}\frac{dQ(P)}{dP} = \frac{k/Q^{1/\epsilon}}{Q}\frac{1}{(-1/\epsilon)kQ^{1/\epsilon-1}} = -\epsilon$$

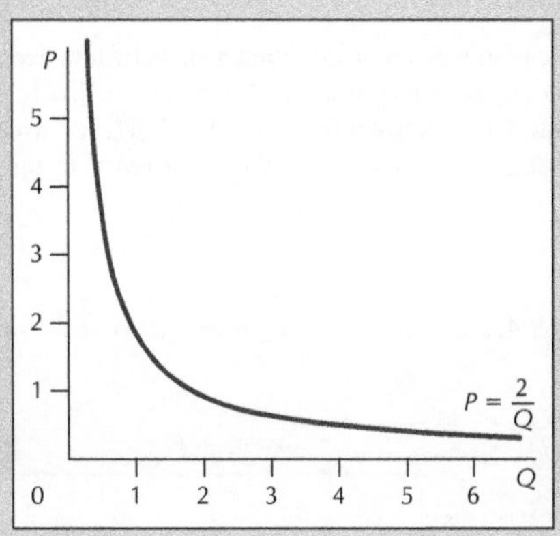

FIGURE A.4.1
A Constant Elasticity Demand Curve
Whereas the price elasticity along a linear demand curve declines as quantity increases, it remains the same along a constant elasticity demand curve.

reciprocal of the slope of the demand curve. To calculate the slope of the demand curve, we need to calculate the ΔQ that occurs in response to a very small ΔP near the point (1, 2). Suppose, for example, we use a price change of +0.001. If $P = 2.001$, we can solve from the demand curve (that is, from the equation $P = 2/Q$) to get the corresponding $Q = 2/2.001 = 0.9995$. Thus $\Delta Q = 0.9995 - 1 = -0.0005$, and the slope of the demand curve at (1, 2) may be calculated as $\Delta P/\Delta Q$, or $0.001/(-0.0005) = -2$. The reciprocal of the slope is $-\frac{1}{2}$, and so the price elasticity is $2\,(-\frac{1}{2}) = -1$.

Consider now the point (2, 1). Again using a ΔP of 0.001, we get a new Q of $2/1.001 = 1.998$, or a ΔQ of -0.002. Thus the slope of the demand curve at (2, 1) is $0.001/(-0.002) = -\frac{1}{2}$, and its reciprocal is -2. The price elasticity at (2, 1) is therefore $(\frac{1}{2})(-2)$, or again -1.

EXERCISE A.4.1 Try several other points along the demand curve in Figure A.4.1 and verify that the price elasticity in every instance is equal to −1. [The answer at the end of the chapter uses the points (0.5, 4) and (4, 0.5).]

The demand curve given by $P = k/Q$ is a special case of the constant elasticity demand curve called the *constant expenditure demand curve.* At every point along such a demand curve, total expenditure is given by the product $PQ = k$, where k is again a positive constant. Thus, unlike the case of the straight-line demand curve, here people spend exactly the same amount when price is high as they do when price is low. Someone who spends her entire allowance on compact discs (CDs) each month, for example, would have a constant expenditure demand curve for CDs. The constant k would be equal to the amount of her allowance.

As we move downward along any constant elasticity demand curve ($P = k/Q^{1/\epsilon}$), the fall in the ratio P/Q is exactly counterbalanced by the rise in the reciprocal of the slope. A constant elasticity demand curve with $\epsilon > 1$ has the property that a price cut will always increase total expenditures. For one with $\epsilon < 1$, by contrast, a price cut will always reduce total expenditures.

EXERCISE A.4.2 What happens to total expenditure when price falls from 4 to 3 along the demand curve given by $P = 4/Q^{1/2}$?

Segment-Ratio Method

The price elasticity at a given point along a straight-line demand curve may be given one other useful geometric interpretation. Suppose we divide the demand curve into two segments AC and CE, as shown in Figure A.4.2. The price elasticity of demand (in absolute value) at point C, denoted $|\epsilon_c|$, will then be equal to the ratio of the two segments.[2]

$$|\epsilon_c| = \frac{CE}{AC} \qquad \text{(A.4.2)}$$

Equation A.4.2 is called the *segment-ratio* for calculating price elasticity of demand.

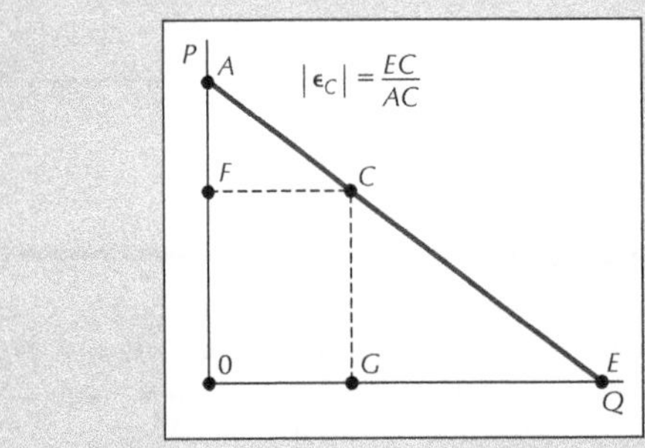

FIGURE A.4.2
The Segment-Ratio Method
The absolute value of price elasticity at any point is the ratio of the two demand curve segments from that point. At point C, the absolute value of the price elasticity of demand is equal to CE/AC.

Knowing that the price elasticity of demand at any point along a straight-line demand curve is the ratio of two line segments greatly simplifies the task of making quantitative statements about it. Consider the demand curve shown in the top panel of Figure A.4.3. At the midpoint of that demand curve (point M), for example, we can see at a glance that the value of price elasticity is -1. One-fourth of the way down the demand curve (point K in Figure A.4.3), the elasticity is -3; three-fourths of the way down (point L), $-\frac{1}{3}$; and so on. The bottom panel of Figure A.4.3 summarizes the relation between position on a straight-line demand curve and the price elasticity of demand.

GENERATING DEMAND AND ENGEL CURVES ALGEBRAICALLY

The Appendix of Chapter 3 showed how to use calculus to solve the consumer's budget allocation problem. It is a simple step from this to solve for the demand curve, Engel curve, and income and substitution effects.

As previously, suppose there are two goods, X and Y. Let $U(X, Y)$ be the consumer's utility function; and suppose M, P_X and P_Y denote income, the price of X, and the price of Y, respectively.

[2]To see why this is so, we can make use of some simple high school geometry. First, note that the reciprocal of the slope of the demand curve in Figure A.4.2 is the ratio GE/GC and that the ratio of price to quality at point C is GC/FC. Multiplying these two, we get $|\epsilon_c| = (GE/GC)(GC/FC) = GE/FC$. Now note that the triangles AFC and CGE are similar, which means that the ratios of their corresponding sides must be the same. In particular, it means that the ratio GE/FC, which we just saw is equal to the price elasticity of demand at point C, must also be equal to the ratio CE/AC. And this, of course, is just the result we set out to establish.

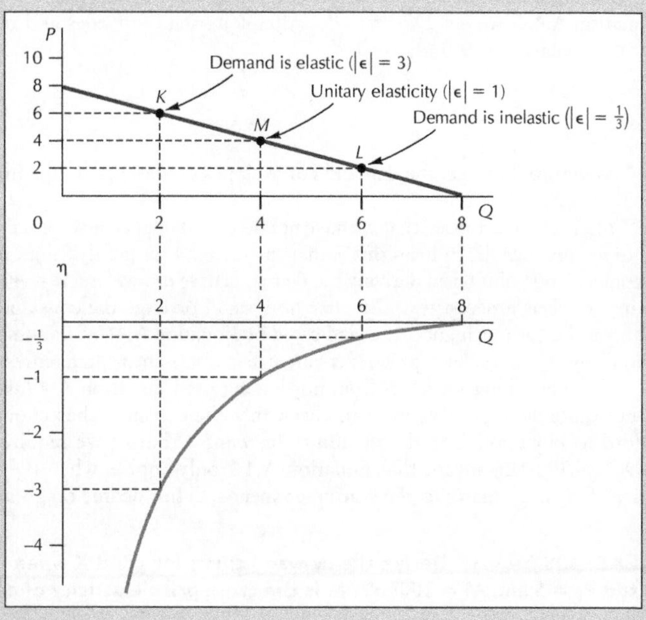

FIGURE A.4.3 Elasticity at Different Positions along a Straight-Line Demand Curve Using the segment-ratio method, the price elasticities at points *K*, *M* and *L* (top panel) can be calculated in an instant.

Deriving the Demand Curve for Good *X*

When solving the consumer's budget allocation problem we assumed the price and income values in the budget constraint, *M*, P_X and P_Y, are given in advance. Solving the allocation problem for a specific value of P_X gives us one point on the demand curve for good X. To derive the full demand curve we need to solve the allocation problem for a non-specific value of P_X. For this we can use the Method of Lagrangian Multipliers, or any other way of solving the allocation problem.

An Example To illustrate how to use the Lagrangian method to derive a demand curve, suppose that $U(X, Y) = 2X^{1/2} + Y$ and that $M = 400$ and $P_Y = 2$. Note that P_X has not been specified. Our unconstrained maximization problem is written as

$$\underset{X,\,Y,\,\lambda}{\text{Maximize}}\ L = 2X^{1/2} + Y - \lambda(P_X X + 2Y - 400) \qquad \text{(A.4.3)}$$

The first-order conditions for a maximum of L are given by

$$\frac{\partial L}{\partial X} = \frac{\partial(2X^{1/2} + Y)}{\partial X} - P_X\lambda = X^{-1/2} - P_X\lambda = 0 \qquad \text{(A.4.4)}$$

$$\frac{\partial L}{\partial Y} = \frac{\partial(2X^{1/2} + Y)}{\partial Y} - 2\lambda = 1 - 2\lambda = 0 \qquad \text{(A.4.5)}$$

and

$$\frac{\partial L}{\partial \lambda} = 400 - P_X X - 2Y = 0 \qquad \text{(A.4.6)}$$

Solving Equation A.4.5, we get $\lambda = 1/2$. Substituting this value for λ into Equation A.4.4, we get $2X^{-1/2} = P_X$. After squaring both sides and rearranging we get the demand curve for good X

$$X = \frac{4}{P_X^2} \tag{A.4.7}$$

As we would hope, the demand curve slopes down because the higher is P_X the smaller is X.

You may have noticed that we have not used the budget constraint, Equation A.4.6, yet. One thing we learn from this is that the demand for good X does not depend on income. At no point when deriving the demand curve did we use $M = 400$. This means that good X is a necessity. No matter how small or large the consumer's income he wants to buy as much good X as indicated by Equation A.4.7. Salt and toothpaste are two likely examples. Such preferences are called quasi-linear preferences.

The other thing we learn from not having used Equation A.4.6 is that our job is not quite done yet. We need to check that the consumer has enough income to afford to buy good X in the quantities he wants. That is, we require $M = 400 \geq P_X X = 4/P_X$. This means that Equation A.4.7 only applies when $P_X \geq 0.01$. If the price of X is less than this the consumer spends all his income on good X.

EXERCISE A.4.3 Derive the demand curve for good X when $U(X, Y) = XY$ and $P_Y = 5$ and $M = 200$? What is the cross-price elasticity of demand?

Deriving the Engel Curve for Good X

To derive the demand curve for good X we solved the allocation problem for a non-specific value of P_X. To derive the Engel curve for good X we need to solve the allocation problem for a non-specific value of M. For this we can again use the Method of Lagrangian Multipliers.

An Example Suppose that $U(X, Y) = 2X^{1/2} + 4Y^{1/2}$ and that $P_X = 2$ and $P_Y = 4$. Note that M has not been specified. Our unconstrained maximization problem is written as

$$\underset{X,\,Y,\,\lambda}{\text{Maximize}}\; L = 2X^{1/2} + 4Y^{1/2} - \lambda(2X + 4Y - M) \tag{A.4.8}$$

The first-order conditions for a maximum of L are given by

$$\frac{\partial L}{\partial X} = \frac{\partial(2X^{1/2} + 4Y^{1/2})}{\partial X} - 2\lambda = X^{-1/2} - 2\lambda = 0 \tag{A.4.9}$$

$$\frac{\partial L}{\partial Y} = \frac{\partial(2X^{1/2} + 4Y^{1/2})}{\partial Y} - 4\lambda = 2Y^{-1/2} - 4\lambda = 0 \tag{A.4.10}$$

and

$$\frac{\partial L}{\partial \lambda} = M - 2X - 4Y = 0 \tag{A.4.11}$$

Dividing Equation A.4.9 by A.4.10, squaring both sides and rearranging, gives the Engel curve

$$X = M/6$$

The Engel curve is a straight line. The consumer spends $P_X X = M/3$, or a third of income, on good X.

EXERCISE A.4.4 Derive the Engel curve for good X when $U(X, Y) = 2X^{1/2} + Y$ and $P_X = 1$ and $P_Y = 5$. What about the Engel curve for good Y?

Deriving the Substitution and Income Effects of a Price Change

Once we know the Engel curve it is relatively easy to derive the income and substitution effects of a price change. To see how, suppose that the price of good X increases from an initial value of P_X^0 to a new value of P_X^1. Let M and P_Y continue to denote income and the price of Y.

We can work out demand for good X before and after the price change. Let X_0 be the initial demand and X_1 the new demand. We can also work out the initial utility of the consumer. Denote this by U_0. To derive the substitution effect we need to know how much the consumer would demand of good X if the price were the *new price* P_X^1 and his income were increased to the point where he can achieve his *initial utility* U_0. Algebraically, this requires solving the following problem,

$$\underset{X,\,Y}{\text{Minimize}}\ P_X^1 X + P_Y Y \text{ subject to } U(X, Y) = U_0 \qquad \text{(A.4.12)}$$

This problem says that we need to find demand for good X when we give the consumer the minimum necessary to achieve utility U_0. Let X_S denote this demand.

Recall, that X_0 is initial demand for good X, X_1 is new demand for good X, and X_S is the demand if we shift the budget constraint. The total effect of the price rise is $X_0 - X_1$. The substitution effect is $X_0 - X_S$ and the income effect is $X_S - X_1$.

Fortunately, the Engel curve is all we need to solve problem A.4.12.

An Example Let $U(X, Y) = XY$. Also, suppose that income is $M_0 = 40$, the price of good Y is $P_Y = 2$, and the price of good X increases from $P_X^0 = 4$ and $P_X^1 = 5$. We know (see the Appendix to Chapter 3) that initially demand is $X_0 = 5$ and $Y_0 = 10$. This means that $U_0 = 5 \times 10 = 50$. After the price increase, you can work out that demand will be $X_1 = 4$ and $Y_1 = 10$.

Focus now on prices $P_X^1 = 5$ and $P_Y = 2$. You can work out that the Engel curve for good X is $X = M/10$ and for good Y is $Y = M/4$. This allows us to write,

$$U = XY = \left(\frac{M}{10}\right)\left(\frac{M}{4}\right) = \frac{M^2}{40}$$

If we put $U = U_0 = 50$ then we need $M = 44.7$. This tells us that the consumer needs an income of at least 44.7 to attain the initial utility with the higher price. Given his income is 40 he needs an extra 4.7. The final thing we need to do is work out demand for good X when $P_X^1 = 5$, $P_Y = 2$ and $M = 44.7$. You should find that $X_S = 4.47$.

The total change in demand is, therefore, $5 - 4 = 1$. The substitution effect is $5 - 4.47 = 0.53$ and the income effect is $4.47 - 4 = 0.47$. This is depicted in Figure A.4.4.

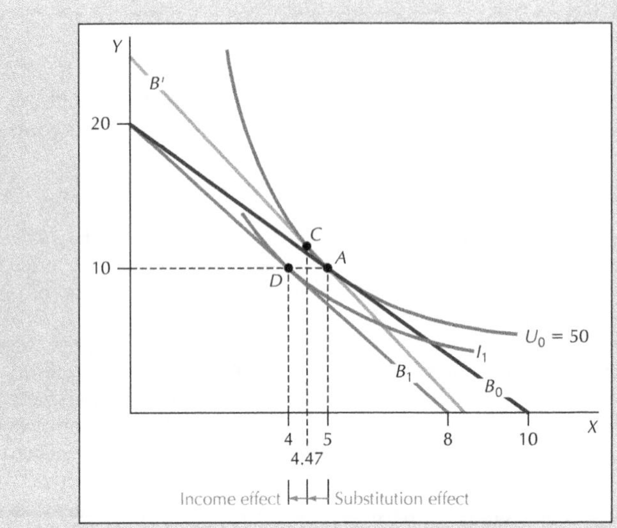

FIGURE A.4.4
The Substitution and Income Effects of a Price Change for the Example
To get the substitution effect, slide the new budget B_1 outward parallel to itself until it becomes tangent to the original indifference curve, $U_0 = 50$. The movement from *A* to *C* gives rise to the substitution effect. The movement from *C* to *D* gives rise to the income effect.

ANSWERS TO IN-APPENDIX EXERCISES

A4.1. First consider the point (0.5, 4). If we again let ΔP be 0.001 so that the new P is 4.001, the resulting Q is 2/4.001 = 0.499875, which means that ΔQ is −0.000125. Price elasticity is therefore equal to (4/0.5)(−0.000125/0.001) = −1. Now consider the point (4, 0.5). If we again let ΔP be 0.001, so that the new P is 0.501, the resulting Q is 2/0.501 = 3.992, which means that ΔQ is −0.008. Price elasticity is therefore equal to (0.5/4)(−0.008/0.001) = −1.

A4.2. For $P = 4$, we have $4 = 4/\sqrt{Q}$, which yields $Q = 1$, so total expenditure is 4(1) = 4. For $P = 3$, we have $3 = 4/\sqrt{Q}$, which yields $Q = \frac{16}{9}$, so total expenditure is $(3)\frac{16}{9} = (\frac{16}{3})$. So with $\epsilon = 2$ total expenditure rises with a decrease in price.

A4.3. The demand curve for good X is $X = 100/P_X$. The cross-price elasticity of demand is 0 because the demand for good X does not depend on the price of good Y.

A4.4. The Engel curve for good X is $X = 25$. Demand does not, therefore, depend on income. The budget constraint becomes $M = 25 + 5Y$. So, the Engel curve for good Y is $Y = (M - 25)/5$.

CHAPTER 5

APPLICATIONS OF RATIONAL CHOICE AND DEMAND THEORIES

In the 2009–2010 academic year, annual tuition and fees at Cornell University passed the $36,000 level. The university has a special policy whereby children of its faculty who attend Cornell are required to pay only fees, which come to approximately $2500/yr. Needless to say, this policy provides a strong financial incentive for faculty children to attend Cornell.

The faculty committee on compensation argued for many years that the university should extend the same tuition benefits to faculty children who attend universities other than Cornell. The traditional response of the university was that it could not afford to make such an offer. Under prodding by economists on the committee, however, the administration eventually took a tentative step in this direction by offering to pay one-third of tuition and fees at other universities. To its surprise, this new policy not only did not cost the university any money, it actually saved a great deal because the number of faculty children attending Cornell went down significantly once the new policy was in effect. This drop opened up an equivalent number of new positions in the freshman class, and because most of these were filled by tuition-paying students, Cornell actually came out ahead. Faculty families who received the new financial aid also came out ahead, and so did the new students who otherwise would have been unable to attend Cornell. The university had overlooked the opportunity cost of allocating positions to faculty children and had failed to anticipate that so many of them would be vacated because of the new offer.

CHAPTER PREVIEW

Cornell's tuition policy provides yet another lesson that prices affect behaviour. Many government policies affect not only the incomes that people receive but also the prices they pay. Sometimes these effects are the deliberate aim of government policy, but on other occasions they are unintended consequences of policies directed toward other ends. In either case, both common sense and our analysis of the rational choice model tell us that changes in incomes and prices can normally be expected to alter the ways in which consumers spend their money.

In this chapter we consider a variety of applications and examples involving the rational choice and demand theories developed in Chapters 3 and 4. We will see that the rational choice model can yield crucial insights not always available to policy analysts armed with only common sense.

We begin with two examples—school finance and a tax and rebate policy—that illustrate how the rational choice model can shed light on important economic policy questions. In looking at a tax and rebate policy we introduce income-compensated demand curves. Next we consider the concept of consumer surplus, a measure of how much the consumer benefits from being able to buy a given product at a given price. And we will see how the rational choice model can be used to examine how price and income changes affect welfare. Next on our agenda are two case studies that illustrate the role of price elasticity in policy analysis. Finally, we consider how the rational choice model can be adapted to choices that have future consequences.

APPLICATION: FINANCING OF PRIVATE SCHOOLS

Every developed country in the world has a public education system that offers free education to all children, and is financed through general taxation. Alongside this is typically an alternative private or independent school system.[1] Parents, therefore, have the choice whether to send their child to a public school or a private school. In Germany, Sweden, Denmark and the UK, around 10 per cent of parents choose private schools. In the Netherlands the number is a lot higher, around 70 per cent.

The choice facing a parent is a complicated one, but the cost of attending a private school is clearly an important factor in the decision. And the cost of attending a private school varies enormously from country to country. In the UK, private schools receive no government funding and so the fees for attending such a school are high, averaging around £11,500 per year (or approximately €14,000). In Germany, Denmark and the Netherlands private schools receive government funding and so the fees are much lower, typically less than $1000. In Sweden there is no fee for attending a private school.

Many agree that school vouchers would expand choice and increase competition in the education sector. But what would be their impact on total education spending?

What are the implications of such a huge difference in price and policy? To get some insight on this question, let us start by modelling the UK system where private schools receive no government funding and consequently charge high fees.

For simplicity, suppose that the quantity of education measured in terms of classroom hours per year is fixed, and that when we speak of spending more on education, we mean not buying more hours of education but buying education of higher quality. Suppose the current tax system charges each family P_e of tax for 1 unit of public education, whether or not the family uses it, where '1 unit' is defined as a year's worth of education of the quality currently offered in the public schools. If it does not send its child to public school, the family has the option

[1]For historical reasons private schools in the UK are also called public schools. Public schools are called state schools. Here, public school means state school!

to purchase 1 or more units of education at a private school, also at the price of P_e per unit. For example, to buy 1.2 units of education at a private school would mean to purchase education of 20 per cent higher quality than is currently offered in the public schools. Families are required by law to provide their child with at least 1 unit of education, public or private.

Given these values, we can now derive the current budget constraint for education and other goods for a representative family whose pretax income is *Y*. If there were no taxes and no public schools, the family's budget constraint would be the line labelled *ABD* in Figure 5.1. But because each family must pay P_e in school taxes, the vertical intercept of the current budget constraint is not *Y* but $Y - P_e$. Since 1 unit of public education is 'free', the family's budget constraint is horizontal out to 1 unit. If the family then wants to buy more than 1 unit of education under the current system, it must withdraw its child from the public school and enrol her in a private school at an additional cost of P_e per unit. This explains why the current budget constraint drops vertically by P_e at 1 unit of education. Thereafter the budget constraint continues to slope downward at the rate of P_e per unit. Thus the budget constraint for a family considering how much education to purchase is denoted by *A'BCE* in Figure 5.1.

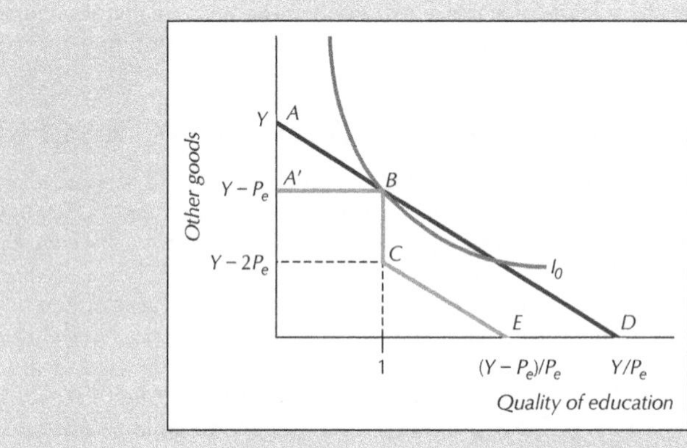

FIGURE 5.1
Educational Choice under the UK System
The family has a pretax income of *Y*, out of which it must pay P_e in school taxes. It is entitled to 1 unit of tuition-free public education. In lieu of public education, it may purchase at least 1 unit of private education at the price of P_e per unit. Its budget constraint is thus *A'BCE*, and its optimal bundle is *B*, which contains 1 unit of public education.

Note in Figure 5.1 that the non-linear budget constraint makes a tangency solution unlikely for a family with indifference curves like the one shown. For such a family, the optimal bundle is, in effect, a corner solution in which exactly 1 unit of public education is chosen.

Let us contrast this result with what happens in Sweden and the Netherlands. Both countries, either implicitly or explicitly, use a voucher system. Under that system, families again pay P_e in school tax, but then get a voucher worth P_e, which may be used toward the purchase of either public or private education. The budget constraint under a voucher system is given by *A'BD* in Figure 5.2. Compare Figures 5.1 and 5.2. Note that the principal difference produced by the voucher system is to eliminate the discontinuity at point *B* of the budget constraint. Parents no longer have to forfeit their school taxes when they switch from public to private schools.

The law requires that families provide at least 1 unit of education for their children. But are parents free to choose a quality of education above 1? This depends on whether private schools are allowed to charge fees, in addition to the voucher. In Sweden they are not. This constrains the family to consume 1 unit of education at point B. In the Netherlands, private schools can charge fees but only to a very limited extent. This constrains the family to be near point B. The system used in Sweden and the Netherlands does, therefore, restrict choice on the quality of education. This is motivated on equality grounds but is a constraint nonetheless. In principle, families in the UK are able to buy a quality of education well above 1, but at a cost. Families in Sweden and the Netherlands are not able to do so (unless they send their child to the UK).

The main advantage of a voucher system is that it encourages competition amongst private and public schools. This hopefully makes schools more efficient in their production of educational services. This can increase the quality of education—meaning the minimum quality of education in Sweden and the Netherlands is above that in the UK. A possibility, most actively discussed in the US, is to allow unlimited fees on top of the voucher. Parents could then purchase increments of education well beyond 1 unit without having to 'pay double'. The family in Figure 5.2 would choose bundle *G*, which contains more than 1 unit of education. Spending on education would increase. Inequality would likely also increase, but it is by no means clear that a goal of public policy should be to prevent parents from spending more on education.

FIGURE 5.2
Educational Choice under a Voucher System
A voucher system allows parents to provide small increases above 1 unit of education at the price of P_e per unit. The budget constraint is now *A′BD*, and the family shown now chooses bundle *G*, which contains more than 1 unit of education.

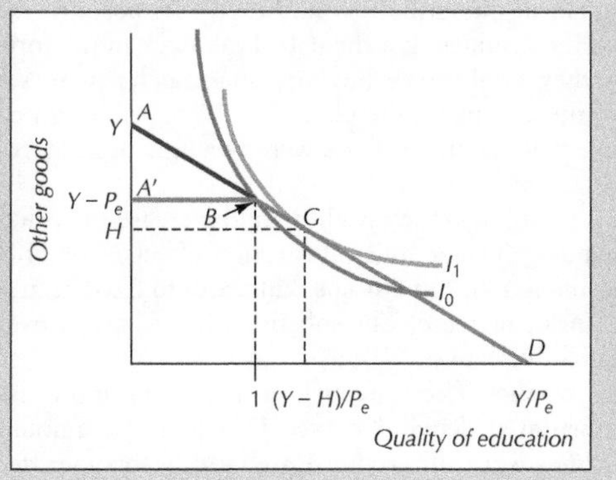

And what of Denmark and Germany? These two countries operate a 'quasi'-voucher system in which the government offers less than full funding to private schools. Essentially, a voucher is worth P_e to a public school but only, say, $0.75P_e$ to a private school. The difference is made up by fees at private schools. Fees are still, however, limited in order to maintain equality between private and public schools. That parents are willing to send their children to a private school under such a system tells us that public and private schools are not perfect substitutes.

THE INCOME-COMPENSATED DEMAND CURVE

The individual demand curves we saw in the previous chapter take into account both the substitution and income effects of price changes. For many applications, such demand curves will be the relevant tool for predicting people's response to a change in price. Suppose, for example, that petrol prices rise because of a new OPEC agreement. Such a price increase will have both income and substitution effects, and the individual demand curve described earlier will be the appropriate device for predicting a person's response.

In other situations, however, this demand curve will not be the right tool. Evaluating the impact of a tax change is one important example. Put simply, governments take money through taxes and give it back through state benefits or publicly funded services. So, when a government increases the tax on a good the revenue from that tax should trickle back to consumers one way or another. Because of redistribution from, say, the rich to the poor, the revenue from a tax rise does not necessarily go back directly to those who paid the taxes. But, often it does. Finance ministers typically play on this fact, softening the news of a tax rise with promises of all the things the revenue will be spent on.

In 1979, critics used economically flawed arguments to defeat US President Carter's proposed tax on petrol.

Sometimes, governments go further by explicitly saying that money raised from a tax will be given back in benefits. As an interesting historical case in point consider a proposal in the US in the late 1970s to tax petrol. The aim was to make the US less dependent on foreign oil. A modern view would also look at the possible reduction in carbon emissions. One immediate objection to the proposal was that the resulting rise in petrol prices would impose economic hardship on the poor. Anticipating this objection, the government proposed to ease the burden on the poor by using the proceeds of the petrol tax to reduce the tax on wage earnings. Critics immediately responded that to return the proceeds of the tax in this fashion would defeat its purpose. These critics believed that if consumers got the petrol tax back in the form of higher paycheques, they would go on buying just as much petrol as before. The critics 'won' the argument, the plans were dropped, and petrol is still cheap in the US. But as we will see, these critics were woefully in need of instruction in the basic principles of rational choice.

A tax on petrol, taken by itself, would increase the price of petrol and produce the corresponding income and substitution effects. The effect of the simultaneous earnings tax reduction, roughly speaking, would have been to eliminate the income effect of the price increase. The substitution effect, however, still remains. This is what the critics overlooked.

To analyse the effect of such a policy in more detail, we can use the **income-compensated demand curve**. This tells the amounts consumers would buy if they were fully compensated for the income effects of changes in price. To generate this curve for an individual, we simply eliminate the income effect from the total effect of price changes.

income-compensated demand curve demand curve that tells how much consumers would buy at each price if they were fully compensated for the income effects of price changes.

The top panel of Figure 5.3 shows the income and substitution effects of an increase in the price of petrol from €0.75/litre to €1.50/litre for a consumer whose weekly income is €120. The ordinary demand curve for petrol for the individual pictured here would associate €0.75 with 70 litre/wk and €1.50 with 45 litre/wk.

The income-compensated demand curve is always constructed relative to a fixed reference point, the current price. Thus like the ordinary demand curve, it too associates 70 litre/wk with the price €0.75. But with the price €1.50 it associates not 45 litre/wk but 55 litre/wk, which is the amount of petrol the consumer would have bought at €1.50/litre if he had been given enough income to remain on the original indifference curve, I_0.

The critical point is that C lies well to the left of the original bundle A, which means that, despite his income being compensated, the consumer substantially curtails his petrol consumption. If petrol is a normal good, the effect of the rebate is to offset partially the income effect of the price increase. It does nothing to alter the substitution effect.

The individual whose responses are described in Figure 5.3 happens to regard petrol as a normal good, one for which the quantity demanded increases as income rises. For normal goods, the income-compensated demand curve will necessarily be steeper than the ordinary demand curve. In the case of an inferior good, however,

FIGURE 5.3
Income-Compensated Demand Curve for a Normal Good
The ordinary demand curve plots the substitution and income effects of a price change. The income-compensated demand curve plots only the substitution effect. For a normal good, the income-compensated demand curve will always be steeper than the ordinary demand curve.

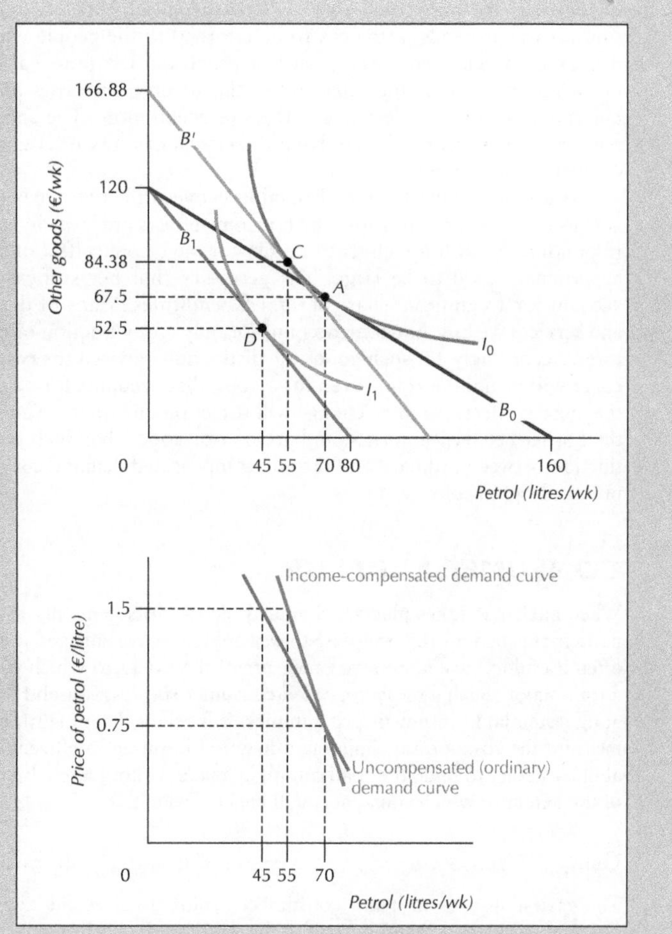

the ordinary demand curve will always be the steeper of the two. The relationship between the two demand curves for an inferior good is as pictured in Figure 5.4.

In applications, the distinction between ordinary and income-compensated demand curves turns out to be particularly important for questions of tax policy.

FIGURE 5.4
Income-Compensated Demand Curves for an Inferior Good
The income effect offsets the substitution effect for an inferior good. The income-compensated demand curve, which omits the income effect, is therefore less steep than the ordinary demand curve in the case of an inferior good.

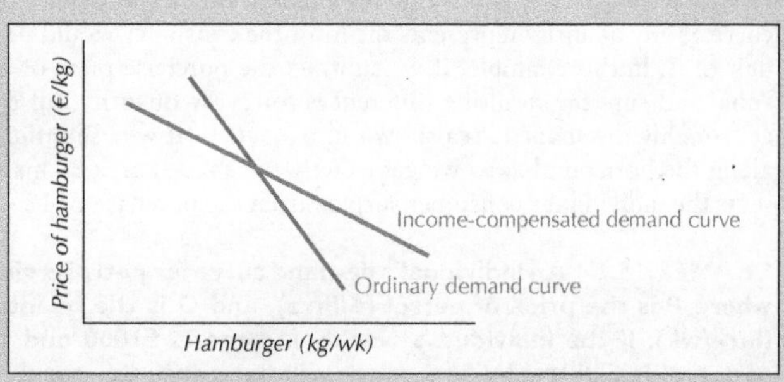

In the case of Jimmy Carter's petrol tax proposal, there was an explicit provision for the proceeds of the tax to be returned to the people who paid it. But, as discussed earlier, even without such a provision, the practical impact of a new tax would be roughly the same. When the government raises more revenue from one source it can raise less from others or spend more. The end result is that the relevant demand curve for studying the effects of a tax on a good is the income-compensated demand curve.

As a practical matter, the distinction between the two types of demand curves is relevant only for goods for which income effects are large in relation to the corresponding substitution effects. In order for the income effect of a price change for a particular good to be large, it is necessary (but not sufficient) that the good account for a significant share of total expenditures. Many of the individual goods and services we buy, however, account for only a tiny fraction of our total expenditures. Accordingly, for such goods the distinction between the two types of demand curve will be unimportant. Even for a good that accounts for a large budget share, the income effect of a price change will sometimes be small. (The good might lie on the border between a normal and an inferior good.) For such goods, too, the distinction between ordinary and income-compensated demand curves will be of little practical significance.

CONSUMER SURPLUS

When exchange takes places voluntarily, economists generally assume it makes all participants better off. Otherwise they would not have engaged in the exchange. It is often useful to have a monetary measure of the extent to which people benefit from a transaction. Such a measure, called **consumer surplus,** is useful for evaluating potential government programmes. It is relatively straightforward to measure the costs of, say, building a new road. But an intelligent decision about whether to build the road cannot be made without a reliable estimate of the extent to which consumers will benefit from it.

consumer surplus a monetary measure of the extent to which a consumer benefits from participating in a transaction.

Using Demand Curves to Measure Consumer Surplus

The easiest way to measure consumer surplus involves the consumer's ordinary (uncompensated) demand curve for the product. In both panels in Figure 5.5, the line labelled *D* represents an individual's demand curve for shelter, which sells for a market price of €3/sq. m. In panel (*a*), note that the most the consumer would have been willing to pay for the first square metre of shelter is €14. Since shelter costs only €3/sq. m, this means that he obtains a surplus of €11 from his purchase of the first square metre of shelter each week. The most he would be willing to pay for the second square metre of shelter is €13, so his surplus from the purchase of that unit will be smaller, only €10. His surplus from the third unit is smaller still, at €9. For shelter or any other perfectly divisible good, the height of the individual's demand curve at any quantity represents the most the consumer would pay for an additional unit of it. In this example, if we subtract the purchase price of €3/sq. m from that value and sum the resulting differences for every quantity out to 12 sq. m/wk, we get roughly the shaded area shown in panel (*b*). (If we use infinitesimal increments along the horizontal axis, we get exactly the shaded area.) This shaded area represents the individual's consumer surplus from the purchase of 12 sq. m/wk of shelter.

EXAMPLE 5.1 **An individual's demand curve for petrol is given by $P = 10 - Q$, where P is the price of petrol (€/litre), and Q is the quantity she consumes (litre/wk). If the individual's weekly income is €1000 and the current price of petrol is €2/litre, by how much will her consumer surplus decline if an oil import restriction raises the price to €3/litre?**

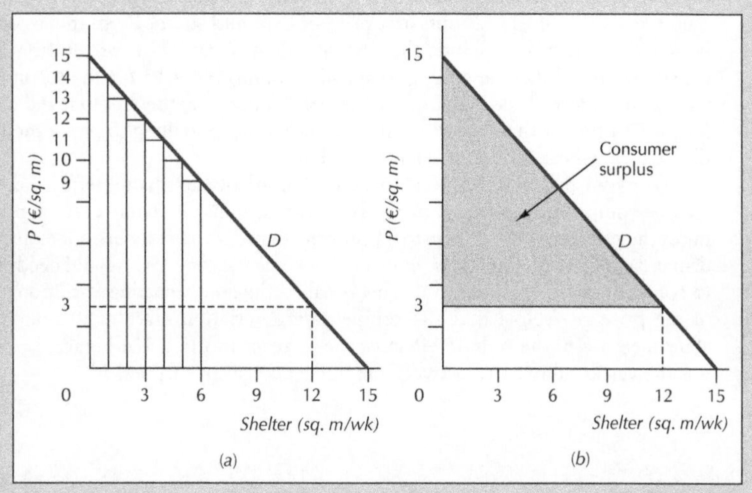

FIGURE 5.5
The Demand Curve Measure of Consumer Surplus
(*a*) The height of the demand curve at any quantity measures the most the consumer would be willing to pay for an extra unit of shelter. That amount minus the market price is the surplus he gets from consuming the last unit. (*b*) The total consumer surplus is the shaded area between the demand curve and the market price.

Figure 5.6 displays her demand curve. At a price of €2/litre, she consumes 8 litres of petrol per week. Her consumer surplus at the price of €2/litre is given by the area of the triangle *AEF* in Figure 5.6, CS = $\frac{1}{2}(10 - 2)8$ = €32/wk. Following the price increase, her consumption falls from 8 to 7 litre/wk, and her surplus shrinks to the area of the triangle *ACD*, CS′ = $\frac{1}{2}(10 - 3)7$ = €24.50/wk. Her loss in consumer surplus is the difference between these two areas, which is the area of the trapezoid *DCEF*, the shaded region in Figure 5.6. This area is equal to CS − CS′ = 32 − 24.5 = €7.50/wk. ◆

EXERCISE 5.1 By how much would consumer surplus shrink in Example 5.1 if the price of petrol rose from €3/litre to €4/litre?

Compensating Variation

We measure consumer surplus using the ordinary (or uncompensated) demand curve. This creates a slight bias in our measure of how much someone benefits from a transaction. To see why, let us revisit the logic used in explaining Figure 5.5.

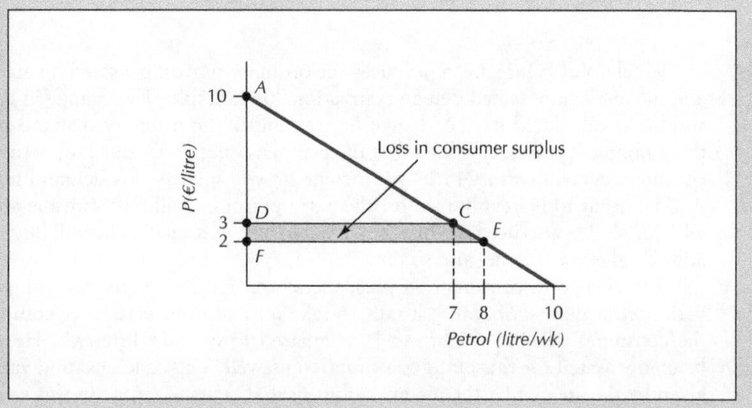

FIGURE 5.6
The Loss in Consumer Surplus from an Oil Price Increase
At a price of €2/litre, consumer surplus is given by the area of triangle *AEF*. At a price of €3/litre, consumer surplus shrinks to the area of triangle *ACD*. The loss in consumer surplus is the difference between these two areas, which is the area of the shaded region.

The ordinary demand curve tells us that the consumer would be willing to buy 1 unit at a price of €14, 2 units at a price of €13, and so on. From this it would not be strictly correct to conclude that, having already paid €14 for the first unit, the consumer would then be willing to spend an *additional* €13 for the second unit. If the income effect of the demand for the good is positive, the fact that the consumer is now €14 poorer than before means that he would be willing to pay somewhat less than €13 for the second unit. Hence, the bias.

To avoid this bias we need to take account of the income effect and use an income-compensated demand curve. To illustrate, consider again a tax on petrol that raises the price from €0.75/litre to €1.50/litre. In order to use an income-compensated demand curve we need to know how much income the consumer would need to compensate for the price rise. This is called the **compensating variation** of the price rise. Note that the compensating variation gives us a monetary measure of the welfare effect of the increase in price. On Figure 5.7 it is the vertical difference between the budget constraint B_1 and B'.

compensating variation the amount of money a consumer would need to compensate for a price change.

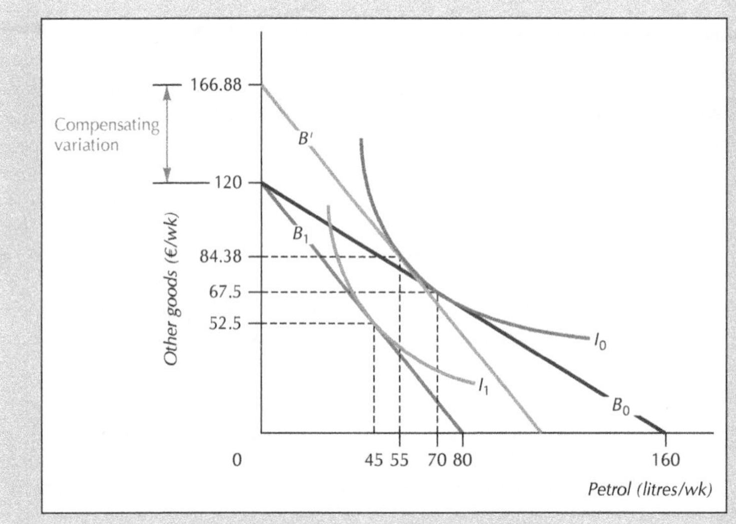

FIGURE 5.7
The Compensating Variation of a Petrol Price Increase
In order to compensate for the rise in price from €0.75/litre to €1.50/litre the consumer needs an extra €46.88/wk.

Panel (*a*) of Figure 5.8 reproduces the ordinary (uncompensated) demand curve and income-compensated demand curve for this example. The change in consumer surplus is calculated by the change in area under the ordinary demand curve. In this example it is €43.13/wk. Is that the compensating variation? No, because if the consumer gets an extra €43.13/wk income he will increase his demand for petrol. And he needs to be reimbursed for the extra petrol he will buy with the additional €43.13/wk. He also needs to be reimbursed for the extra petrol he will buy with any additional extra income, and so on.

The change in consumer surplus, therefore, underestimates the compensating variation. It does so, because it fails to take into account that, once compensated, the consumer will buy 55 litres/wk, compared to only 45 litres/wk. He needs to be compensated for this extra consumption as well. The compensating variation is given by the area under the income-compensated demand curve. In this example, it is €46.88/wk.

FIGURE 5.8
The Demand Curve Measure of Compensating Variation
The compensating variation of a price rise is the area under an income-compensated demand curve. For a normal good, the compensating variation will be larger than the change in consumer surplus.

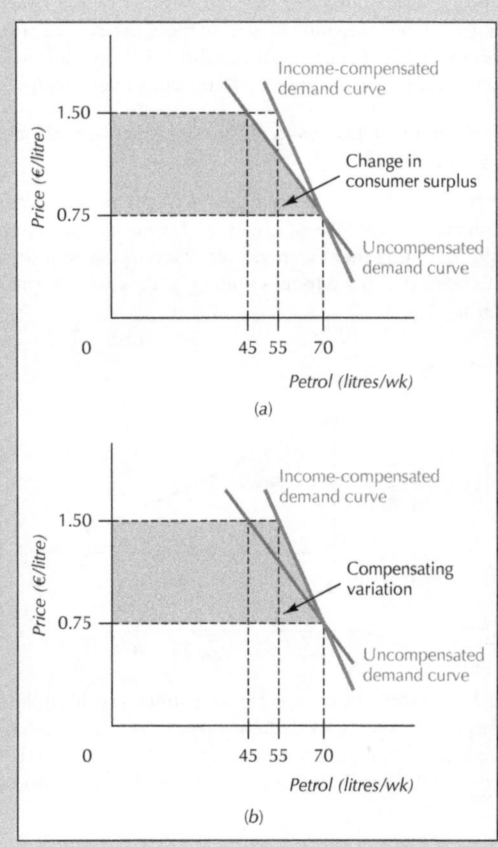

In this case, the loss in consumer surplus is smaller than the compensating variation. So, one could argue that the loss in consumer surplus underestimates the effects of the tax rise. This will always be the case if the price of a normal good rises. If the good is inferior, the loss in consumer surplus will be larger than the compensating variation.

The loss in consumer surplus differs from the compensating variation because it does not take into account what the consumer will do with the extra income he gets from being compensated. If the income effect is small this bias will be negligible. Since income effects for most goods are small, it will generally be an acceptable approximation to equate consumer surplus and compensating variation. For goods where the income effect is potentially large, however, it is important to consider compensating variation.

Why do many tennis clubs have both annual membership fees and court rental fees?

Application: Two-Part Pricing

Economic reasoning suggests that a voluntary exchange will take place between a buyer and a seller if and only if that exchange makes both parties better off. On the buyer's side, we may say that willingness to exchange depends on the buyer's expectation of receiving consumer surplus from the transaction.

Economic theory does not tell us much about how the gains from exchange will be divided between the buyer and the seller. Sometimes the buyer will be in an advantageous bargaining position, enabling her to capture most of the benefits. Other times the buyer's options will be more limited, and in these cases, her consumer surplus is likely to be smaller. Indeed, as Economic Naturalist 5.1 illustrates, the seller can sometimes design a pricing strategy that captures *all* the consumer surplus.

Why do many tennis clubs have an annual membership charge in addition to their hourly court fees?

ECONOMIC NATURALIST 5.1

A suburban tennis club rents its courts for €25 per person per hour. John's demand curve for court time, $P = 50 - \frac{1}{4}Q$, where Q is measured in hours per year, is given in Figure 5.9. Assuming there were no other tennis clubs in town, what is the maximum annual membership fee John would be willing to pay for the right to buy court time for €25/hr?

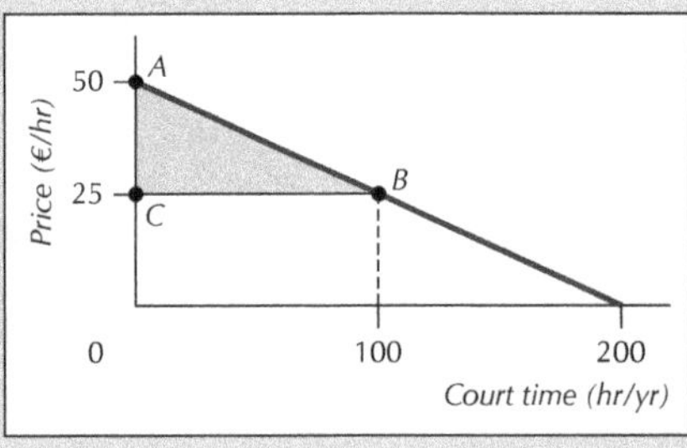

FIGURE 5.9
An Individual Demand Curve for Tennis Court Time
At a price of €25/hr, John receives €1250/yr (the shaded area) of consumer surplus from renting court time. The maximum annual membership fee the club can charge is €1250.

The answer to this question is the consumer surplus John receives from being able to buy as much court time as he wants at the €25/hr price. This is equal to the area of triangle ABC in Figure 5.9, which is $CS = \frac{1}{2}(50 - 25)100 =$ €1250/yr. If the club charged a fee higher than that, John would be better off not renting any court time at all. ■

EXERCISE 5.2 In Economic Naturalist 5.1 how much would the maximum annual membership fee be if the club charged only €20/hr for court time?

Economic Naturalist 5.1 sheds light on many of the pricing practices we observe throughout the economy. Many amusement parks, for example, charge a fixed admission fee in addition to a charge for each ride. Many telephone companies charge a fixed monthly fee in addition to charges based on actual calls made. And some shopping clubs charge a fixed membership fee for the right to buy items carried in their stores or catalogues. Pricing schemes like these are often called **two-part pricing.** Their effect is to transfer a portion of the consumer surplus from the buyer to the seller.

two-part pricing a pricing scheme that consists of a fixed fee and a marginal charge for each unit purchased (also called two-part tariffs).

Why do some amusement parks charge *only* a fixed admission fee, with no additional charge even for rides with long lines?

ECONOMIC NATURALIST 5.2

The price of a one-day pass at Disneyland Paris is €55 for children under 11. This pass includes unlimited access to all rides and attractions in the theme park, the only catch being that on certain rides—such as the popular Space Mountain roller coaster—waiting lines can be more than an hour long. Given persistent excess demands for some rides at a price of zero, why doesn't Disney charge an additional fee for each use of its most popular rides?

Economic theory predicts that the price of any good or service will rise in the face of excess demand. Long waiting lines like the ones described above thus pose a challenge for economists. In this case, a possible explanation may be that the people who have to pay for the rides (parents) are different from the ones who demand them (their children). Since their parents are paying, children want to ride the most thrilling rides whether the price is €0 or €5 per ride. At a price high enough to eliminate waiting lines, it would be possible to go on the most popular rides dozens of times a day, and many children would want to do exactly that. Parents could always ration access by saying no, of course. But not many parents look forward to a vacation in which they must spend the entire day saying no to their children. For these parents, Disney's current pricing policy is perhaps an ideal solution. It enables them to say to their children, 'Go on whichever rides you want, as many times as you want', and then allow waiting lines to perform the essential rationing function. ■

OVERALL WELFARE COMPARISONS

The concept of consumer surplus helps us identify the benefits (or costs) of changes that occur in particular markets. Often we will want to assess whether consumers are better or worse off as a result of changes not just in one market but in many. Here, too, our model of rational choice lets us draw a variety of useful inferences. Consider the following example.

EXAMPLE 5.2 **Jones spends all his income on two goods: X and Y. The prices he paid and the quantities he consumed last year are as follows: $P_X = 10$, $X = 50$, $P_Y = 20$, and $Y = 25$. This year P_X and P_Y are both 10, and Jones's income is €750. Assuming his tastes do not change, in which year was Jones better off, last year or this?**

To answer this question, begin by comparing Jones's budget constraints for the 2 years. Note first that his income last year was equal to what he spent, namely, $P_XX + P_YY = 1000$. For the prices given, we thus have the budget constraints shown in Figure 5.10(*a*).

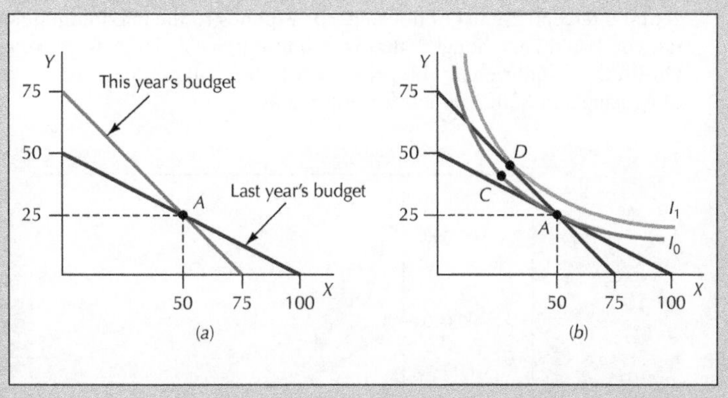

FIGURE 5.10
Budget Constraints for Two Years
(*a*) If the consumer's budget constraint for this year contains the same bundle he bought last year (bundle *A*), he will be at least as well off this year as last. (*b*) If, in addition, relative prices are different in the two years, he will necessarily be able to buy a better bundle this year (bundle *D*).

In Figure 5.10*(a)*, we see that Jones's budget constraint for this year contains the very same bundle he bought last year. Since his tastes have not changed, this tells us he cannot be worse off this year than last. After all, he can still afford to buy the same bundle as before. But our standard assumptions about preference orderings enable us to draw an even stronger inference. If his indifference curves have the usual convex shape, we know that an indifference curve—call it I_0—was tangent to last year's budget constraint at the point *A* in Figure 5.10*(b)*. We also know that this year's budget constraint is steeper than last year's, which tells us that part of I_0 must lie inside this year's budget triangle. On I_0, bundle *A* is equally preferred to bundle *C*. And because more is better, we know that *D* is preferred to *C*. It thus follows that *D* is preferred to *A*, and so we know that Jones was able to purchase a bundle of goods this year that he likes better than the one he bought last year. It follows that Jones was better off this year than last. ◆

EXERCISE 5.3 Jones spends all his income on two goods: X and Y. The prices he paid and the quantities he consumed last year are as follows: $P_X = 15$, $X = 20$, $P_Y = 25$, and $Y = 30$. This year the prices have changed ($P_X = 15$ and $P_Y = 20$), and Jones's income is now €900. Assuming his tastes have not changed, in which year was Jones better off, last year or this?

Application: The Welfare Effects of Changes in Housing Prices

Consider the following two scenarios:

1. You have just purchased a house for €200,000. The very next day, the prices of all houses, including the one you just bought, double.
2. You have just purchased a house for €200,000. The very next day, the prices of all houses, including the one you just bought, fall by half.

In each case, how does the price change affect your welfare? (Are you better off before the price change or after?)

The overwhelming majority of people typically respond that you are better off as a result of the price increase in scenario 1, but worse off as a result of the price drop in scenario 2. Although most seem confident about these two responses, only one turns out to be correct.

To see why, first consider the case in which all housing prices double. Suppose your total wealth just before purchasing your house was €400,000. Let the size of your current house correspond to 1 unit of housing and let the price of other goods (the composite good) be 1. Your original budget constraint under scenario 1 will then correspond to the line labelled B_1 in Figure 5.11. Its vertical intercept, €400,000, is the maximum amount you could have spent on other goods. Its horizontal intercept, 2 units of housing, corresponds to the maximum quantity of housing you could have bought (that is, a house twice as large as your current house). On B_1, the equilibrium at A represents your original purchase. At A, you have 1 unit of housing and €200,000 left for other goods.

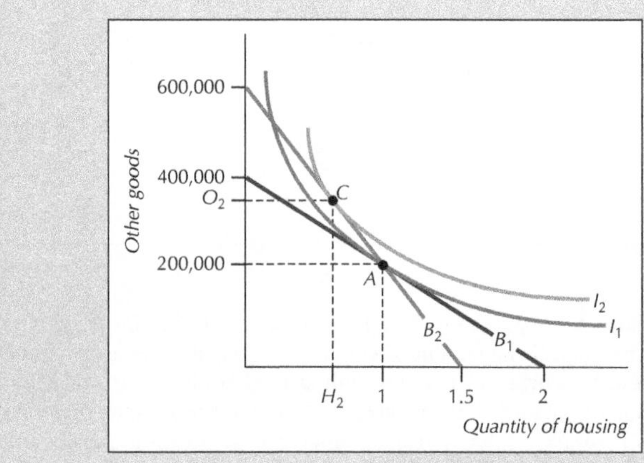

FIGURE 5.11
Rising Housing Prices and the Welfare of Homeowners
When the price of housing doubles, your budget constraint becomes B_2, which also contains your original bundle A. Because C, the optimal bundle on B_2, lies on a higher indifference curve than A, the effect of the housing price increase is to make you better off.

After the price of your house doubles, your budget constraint becomes the line labelled B_2 in Figure 5.11. To calculate the vertical intercept of B_2, note that your current house can now be sold for €400,000, which, when added to the €200,000 you had left over after buying your house, yields a maximum of €600,000 available for other goods. The horizontal intercept of B_2 tells us that when the price of housing doubles to €400,000/unit, your €600,000 will buy a maximum of only 1.5 units of housing. Note finally that on B_2 your optimal bundle is *C*, which contains $H_2 < 1$ units of housing and $O_2 >$ €200,000 worth of other goods. And since bundle *C* lies on a higher indifference curve than bundle *A*, you are better off than before the price increase.

Not surprisingly, when the price of housing goes up, your best response is to buy fewer units of housing and more units of other goods. Note that you are insulated from the harm of the income effect of the price increase because the price increase makes the house you own more valuable.

So far, so good. Now consider the more troubling case—namely, scenario 2, in which housing prices fall by half. Again adopting the units of measure used in scenario 1, your budget constraint following the fall in housing prices is the line labelled B_3 in Figure 5.12. To get its vertical intercept, note that sale of your current house will now yield only €100,000, which, when added to the €200,000 you already have, makes a maximum of €300,000 available for the purchase of other goods. To calculate the horizontal intercept of B_3, note that when the price of housing falls to €100,000, your €300,000 will now buy a maximum of 3 units of housing. Given the budget constraint B_3, the best affordable bundle is the one labelled *D*, which contains $H_3 > 1$ units of housing and $O_3 < 200{,}000$ units of other goods. As in scenario 1, the effect of the relative price change is again to move you to a higher indifference curve. This time, however, your direction of substitution is the opposite of the one in scenario 1: because housing is now cheaper than before, you respond by purchasing more units of housing and fewer units of other goods.

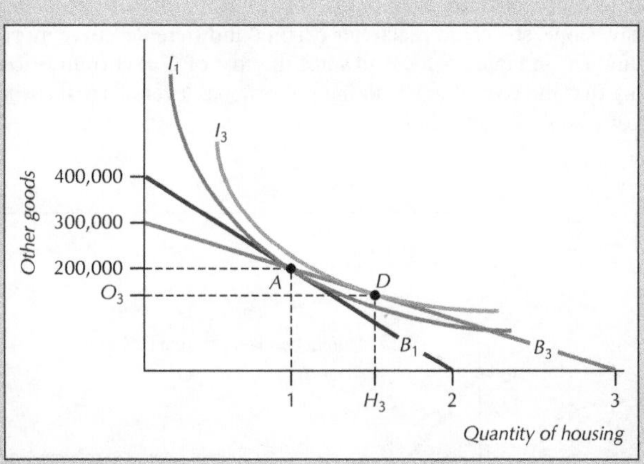

FIGURE 5.12
Falling Housing Prices and the Welfare of Homeowners
When the price of housing falls by half, your budget constraint becomes B_3, which also contains your original bundle *A*. Because *D*, the optimal bundle on B_3, lies on a higher indifference curve than *A*, the effect of the housing price drop is to make you better off.

In each scenario, note that your new budget constraint contains your original bundle, which means that you have to be at least as well off after the price change as before. Note also that in each case the change in relative prices means your new budget constraint contains bundles beyond your original indifference curve, making it possible to achieve a better outcome in each scenario.

Application: A Bias in the Consumer Price Index

A consumer price index (CPI) measures changes in the 'cost of living', the amount a consumer must spend to maintain a given standard of living. In the Euro area, for instance, Eurostat publishes a monthly Monetary Union Index of Consumer Prices that aggregates indices from Euro area countries. A CPI is calculated by first computing the cost of a representative bundle of goods and services during a reference period and then dividing that cost into the current cost of the same bundle. Thus, if it cost €100 to buy the representative bundle in the reference period and €150 to buy the same bundle today, the CPI would be 1.5. Announcing this figure, spokespersons would explain that it meant the cost of living had increased by 50 per cent compared with the reference period.

What the CPI fails to take into account, however, is that when prices of different goods rise by different proportions, consumers do not generally buy the same bundle of goods as before. Typically, they substitute away from those goods whose prices have risen most. By reallocating their budgets, consumers are able to escape at least part of the harmful effects of price increases. Because the CPI fails to take substitution into account, it overstates increases in the cost of living.

A simple example using the rational choice model makes this point unmistakably clear. Suppose the only goods in the economy were rice and wheat and that the representative consumer consumed 20 kg/mo of each in the reference period. If rice and wheat each cost €1/kg in the reference period, what will be the CPI in the current period if rice now costs €2/kg and wheat costs €3/kg? The cost of the reference period bundle at reference period prices was €40, while at current prices the same bundle now costs €100. The CPI thus takes the value of €100/€40 = 2.5. But is it really correct to say that the cost of living is now 2.5 times what it was?

To consider an extreme case, suppose our representative consumer regarded rice and wheat as perfect one-for-one substitutes, meaning that her indifference curves are negatively sloped 45° lines. In Figure 5.13, her original bundle is A and her original indifference curve (which coincides exactly with her original budget constraint) is I_0. How much income would she need in the current period to achieve the same level of satisfaction she achieved in the reference period? At the new prices, the slope of her budget constraint is no longer -1, but $-3/2$. With a budget constraint with this new slope, she could reach her original indifference curve most cheaply by buying bundle C in Figure 5.13. And since the cost of C at current prices is only €80, we can say that the cost of maintaining the original level of satisfaction has gone up by a factor of only 2.0, not 2.5.

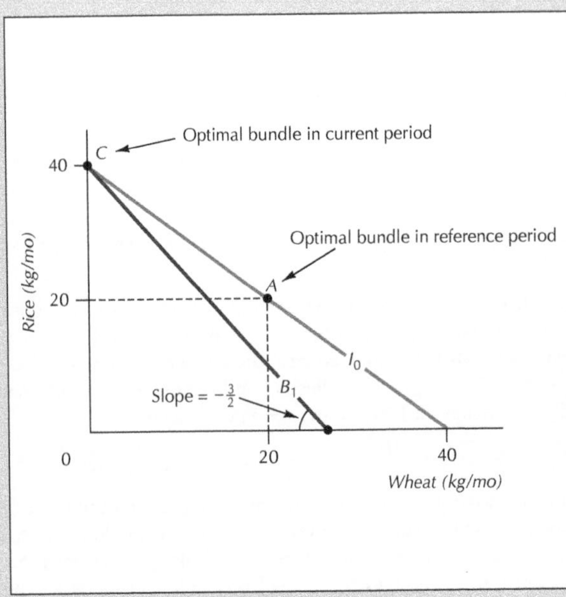

FIGURE 5.13
The Bias Inherent in a Consumer Price Index
For this consumer, rice and wheat are perfect substitutes. When the price of each was €1/kg, she bought 20 kg/mo of each in the reference period, for a total expenditure of €40/mo. If the current prices of rice and wheat are €2/kg and €3/kg, respectively, the expenditure required to buy the original bundle is €100/mo. The CPI is the ratio of these two expenditures, €100/€40 = 2.5. But the consumer can attain her original indifference curve, I_0, by buying bundle C, which costs only €80 at current prices. The cost of maintaining the original level of satisfaction has thus risen by a factor of only 2.0.

In general, we can say that the extent to which the CPI overstates the cost of living will go up as substitution possibilities increase. The bias will also be larger when there are greater differences in the rates of increase of different prices.

Quality Change: Another Bias in the CPI?

Gathering data on the prices of goods and services might seem like a straightforward task. In practice, however, it is complicated by the existence of discounts, rebates and other promotional offers in which the actual transaction price may be substantially different from the official list price.

Yet important as they are, accurate price data are not sufficient for estimating changes in the cost of living. We must also account for changes in quality. And this, unfortunately, turns out to be a far more complicated task than measuring changes in prices.

A brief look at the automobile industry illustrates the difficulty. The US Department of Commerce reported that the average price for a new vehicle in 1994 was \$19,675, a 5.1 per cent increase over 1993 and a 72.8 per cent increase over 1984.[2] During that same 10-year span, the US CPI rose only 42.6 per cent. Does this mean that the prices of cars rose much more rapidly during that period than those of other goods and services? Not necessarily. After all, cars produced in 1994 came with many features not found on earlier models. For example, whereas approximately 90 per cent of cars sold in the United States in 1994 came equipped with air bags and about 40 per cent with antilock brakes, virtually none had these features in 1984. The number of cars with convenience equipment such as rear window defrosters and power windows once confined to luxury models rose more than 50 per cent during the same decade.

The Department of Commerce now calculates a special automotive CPI, which deducts the cost of such additional features in an effort to measure changes in the prices of comparably equipped cars. This index rose only 32.2 per cent between 1984 and 1994—or about 10 per cent *less* than the overall CPI.

Although these adjustments obviously help, they capture only a small part of the automobile quality changes that have been occurring in recent years. For example, the automotive CPI made no allowance for the fact that 1994 cars had achieved a 40 per cent reduction in hydrocarbon emissions and a 60 per cent reduction in oxides of nitrogen relative to 1984 cars. Nor did the index allow for the fact that 1994 cars were much more reliable, crashworthy, and corrosion resistant than cars from a decade earlier.

The pace of auto quality improvement is vividly illustrated by a comparison of the 1995 Honda Civic DX sedan—one of the company's smallest and cheapest cars during that model year—with Honda's top-of-the-line Accord sedan from 1982. Besides having a bevy of safety features not found on the older Accord, the '95 Civic had a larger interior; a quieter, cleaner-burning, yet more powerful engine (102 horsepower versus 75); better tyres and brakes; and a much more sophisticated suspension. The '95 Civic accelerated from 0 to 60 mph in 9.1 seconds, compared with 12.2 seconds for the '82 Accord. Whereas the '95 Civic's finish will survive six northern winters in near-showroom condition, similar exposure left the '82 Accord riddled with rust. The '82 Accord had a sticker price of \$8995, but since it was in short supply, many dealers sold it for about \$10,000. The '95 Civic had a sticker price of \$12,360, and most dealers sold it at a substantial discount. So even with the passage of 13 years, the nominal dollar transaction price was not much higher for the Civic than for the older Accord. The '95 Civic's sticker price, adjusted for changes in the overall CPI, translates into \$8852 in 1982 dollars—in effect, a much better car for less money.

[2]The data in this section are drawn from Csaba Csere, 'Do Cars Cost Too Much, or Do We Just Like Costly Cars?', *Car and Driver*, June 1995, p. 9.

If the Civic–Accord comparison is representative, it seems that the US government's attempts to adjust for automobile quality improvements have fallen short. This is unlikely to be a historical one-off. With the growth of global competition, quality has been improving rapidly not just in automobiles but in other goods and services as well. And we may be sure that many of the relevant changes will have escaped attempts to adjust for quality in the US, Europe and elsewhere.

Failure to account fully for quality of improvements has the same effect as failure to account for substitution. Both cause the official cost-of-living index to overstate the true increase in prices.

This bias matters. A nation's CPI is almost always used to index the cost-of-living adjustments received by social security recipients and beneficiaries of other government programmes. Even a slight upward bias in the CPI can swell the budget deficit by many millions of euros.

USING PRICE ELASTICITY OF DEMAND

In the sphere of applied economic analysis, few tools are more important than the concept of price elasticity of demand. In this section we examine applications of this concept in two very different settings.

Application: London Underground Fare Increases

Fares on the London transport system increased by around 6 per cent in January 2012. London Mayor, Boris Johnson, said that the fare increase was essential in order to fund upgrades in the existing transport infrastructure. But, how much extra revenue could Transport for London expect from the increase in fares? And what will be the effect on demand for public transport?

In order to answer these questions we need to know the elasticity of demand for public transport in London. Fortunately, we have some reliable estimates.[3] For example, the elasticity of demand for the London Underground is estimated at around –0.3 in the short term (one to two years) and –0.6 in the long term (more than two years). The distinction between short-term and long-term elasticity captures the fact that it may take time for passengers to substitute to an alternative.

Given a fare increase of 6 per cent and an elasticity of demand of –0.3, demand should fall by 1.8 per cent. Note that demand is estimated to be relatively inelastic and so the drop in demand is relatively small. In 2011 there were around 1171 million passenger journeys on the London Underground.[4] So, we should expect around 1150 million journeys after the price rise. Revenue from the London Underground in 2011 was £1981 million suggesting an average fare per journey of £1.69. If the average fare increases by 6 per cent or, equivalently, 10 pence then extra revenue of 1150×0.1 = £117 million will be raised from the London Underground.

Clearly, this estimate is a very crude one. A much more thorough analysis is needed to get a more precise estimate of the extra revenue. Knowing the elasticity of demand is, however, crucial to doing that.

EXERCISE 5.4 Suppose that prices on the London Underground were raised by 10 per cent. How much extra revenue would have been raised?

What if we tell you that the number of journeys made on the London Underground increased after the price rise? Does that mean our calculations were wrong? Not at all. Passenger numbers increase, year on year, on the London Underground for a variety of reasons. Without the fare increase passenger numbers would almost certainly have

[3]R. Balcombe et al., 'The Demand for Public Transport: A Practical Guide', TRL Report 593, 2004.
[4]Transport for London Annual Report and Statement of Accounts for 2012.

increased by more than they did. So, we still need to know how much demand will fall, everything else the same, in order to calculate the effect of the price rise.

Application: The Price Elasticity of Demand for Alcohol

How does the consumption of alcoholic beverages respond to changes in their price? For many decades, the conventional wisdom on this subject responded, 'not much'. Unfortunately, however, estimates of the price elasticity of demand for alcohol tend to be unreliable. The problem is that liquor prices usually do not vary sufficiently to permit accurate estimates.

In a careful study,[5] Philip Cook made use of some previously unexploited data on significant changes in alcohol prices. He suggested that the price elasticity of demand for alcohol may be much higher than we thought.

Cook's method was to examine changes in alcohol consumption that occur in response to changes in liquor taxes. Of the 48 contiguous states of the US, 30 license and tax the private sale of liquor. Periodically, most of these states increase their nominal liquor taxes to compensate for the effects of inflation. The pattern is for the real value of a state's liquor tax to be highest right after one of these tax increases, then to erode steadily as the cost of living rises. The fact that taxes are not adjusted continuously to keep their real value constant provides the real price variability we need to estimate the responsiveness of alcohol purchases to price changes.

There were 39 liquor tax increases in Cook's 30-state sample during the period 1960–1975. In 30 of these 39 cases, he found that liquor consumption declined relative to the national trend in the year following the tax increase. His estimate of the price elasticity of demand was -1.8, a substantially higher value than had been found in previous studies.

Cook's interpretation of his findings provides an interesting case study in the factors that govern price elasticity. One salient fact about the alcohol market, he noted, is that heavy drinkers, though a small fraction of the total population, account for a large fraction of the total alcohol consumed. This fact had led many people to expect that alcohol consumption would be unresponsive to variations in price. The common view of heavy drinkers, after all, is that they drink primarily out of habit, not because of rational deliberations about price. Stated another way, analysts always expected the substitution effect to be small for these people. But even if the substitution effect were zero for heavy drinkers, there would remain the income effect. The budget share devoted to alcohol tends to be large among heavy drinkers for two reasons. The obvious one is that heavy drinkers buy a lot of liquor. Less obvious, perhaps, is that their incomes tend to be significantly smaller than average. Many heavy drinkers have difficulty holding steady jobs and often cannot work productively in the jobs they do hold. The result is that the income effect of a substantial increase in the price of liquor forces many heavy drinkers to consume less. In support of this interpretation, Cook observed that mortality from cirrhosis of the liver declines sharply in the years following significant liquor tax increases. This is a disease that for the most part afflicts only people with protracted histories of alcohol abuse, and clinical experience reveals that curtailed drinking can delay or prevent its onset in long-term heavy drinkers.

THE INTERTEMPORAL CHOICE MODEL

The choices we have considered thus far have involved trade-offs between alternatives in the present—the choice between food now and clothing now, between travel now and stereo equipment now, and so on. There was no hint that the alternative chosen today might affect the menu of alternatives available in the future.

[5]Philip J. Cook, 'The Effect of Liquor Taxes on Drinking, Cirrhosis, and Auto Accidents', in *Alcohol and Public Policy,* Mark Moore and Dean Gerstein (eds.), Washington, DC: National Academy Press, 1982.

Yet such effects are a prominent feature of many important decisions. Our task in this section is to enlarge the basic consumer choice model in Chapter 3 to accommodate them.

Intertemporal Consumption Bundles

People may either consume all their income now or save part for the future. How would rational consumers distribute their consumption over time? To keep the analysis manageable, suppose there are only two time periods, *current* and *future.* In the standard, or *atemporal,* choice model in Chapter 3, the alternatives were different goods that could be consumed in the current period—apples now versus oranges now, etc. In our simple *intertemporal choice model,* the alternatives instead will be *current consumption* (C_1) versus *future consumption* (C_2). Each of these is an amalgam—the functional equivalent of the composite good (see Chapter 3). For simplicity, we set aside the question of how to apportion current and future consumption among specific consumption goods.

In the atemporal choice model, any bundle of goods can be represented as a point in a simple two-dimensional diagram. We use an analogous procedure in the intertemporal choice model. In Figure 5.14, for example, current consumption of €6000 combined with future consumption of €6000 is represented by the bundle *E.* Bundle *D* represents current consumption of €3000 and future consumption of €9000.

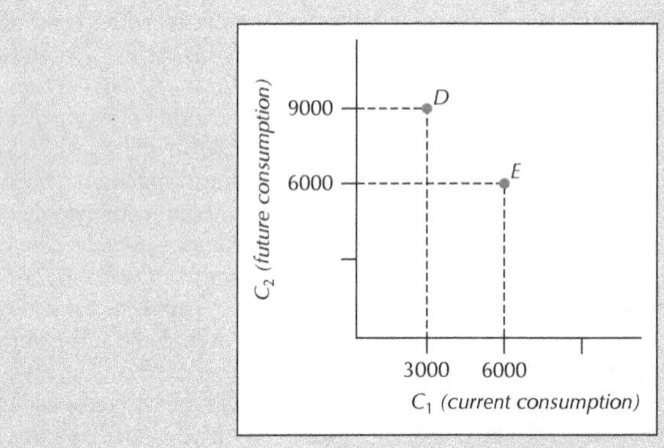

FIGURE 5.14
Intertemporal Consumption Bundles
Alternative combinations of current and future consumption are represented as points in the C_1, C_2 plane. By convention, the horizontal axis measures current consumption; the vertical axis, future consumption.

The Intertemporal Budget Constraint

Suppose you receive €50,000 income now and €60,000 in the future. Suppose also that if you deposit some of your current income in a bank, you can receive your principal plus 20 per cent in the future period. Similarly, if you wish to borrow against your future income, you may receive €1 now for every €1.20 you must repay in the future. (See Figure 5.15.) To construct your intertemporal budget constraint, first note that you can always merely consume your income in each period, so C_1 = €50,000 and C_2 = €60,000 must be a point on your intertemporal budget constraint. Another option is to deposit all €50,000 (maximum lending) and thus receive 1.2(50,000) = €60,000 in addition to your €60,000 future income for C_2 = €120,000 future consumption with no current consumption ($C_1 = 0$). Yet another option is to borrow €60,000/1.2 = €50,000 (maximum borrowing) in addition to your €50,000 current income for C_1 = €100,000 current consumption with no future consumption ($C_2 = 0$). The equation for your intertemporal budget constraint is C_2 = €120,000 − $1.2C_1$, or, equivalently, $1.2C_1 + C_2$ = €120,000.

FIGURE 5.15
The Intertemporal Budget Constraint
For every euro by which current consumption is reduced, it is possible to increase future consumption by €1.2.

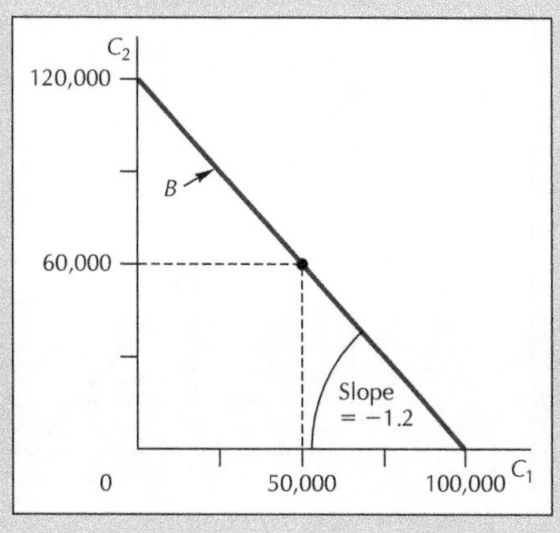

In general, suppose you receive M_1 of your income in the first period and M_2 in the second, and can either borrow or lend at the interest rate r. What is the most you can consume in the future period? Maximum future consumption occurs when you set all your current income aside for future use. Setting aside M_1 in the current period at the interest rate r means your deposit will grow to $M_1(1 + r)$ by the future period. So the most you can possibly consume in the future is that amount plus your future income, or $M_1(1 + r) + M_2$.

What is the most you could consume in the current period? The answer is your current income plus the maximum amount you can borrow against your future income. The most you can borrow against a future income of M_2 is called the **present value** of M_2, denoted PV(M_2). It is the amount that, if deposited today at the interest rate r, would be worth exactly M_2 in the future period. Accordingly, we can find the present value of M_2 by solving $\text{PV}(M_2)(1 + r) = M_2$ for PV(M_2):

present value the present value of a payment of X euros T years from now is $X/(1 + r)^T$, where r is the annual rate of interest.

$$\text{PV}(M_2) = \frac{M_2}{1 + r} \tag{5.1}$$

For example, if M_2 were €110,000 and the interest rate were 10 per cent (that is, $r = 0.10$), the present value of M_2 would be €110,000/1.1 = €100,000. Present value is a simple equivalence relationship between sums of money that are payable at different points in time. If $r = 0.10$, then €100,000 today will be worth €110,000 in the future. By the same token, €110,000 in the future is worth €100,000 today when the interest rate is 10 per cent.

It is not necessary, of course, to borrow or save the maximum amounts possible. The consumer who wishes to shift some of her future income into the current period can borrow any amount up to the maximum at the rate of $1/(1 + r)$ euros today for every euro given up in the future. Or, she can save any amount of her current income and get back $(1 + r)$ euros in the future for every euro not consumed today. The intertemporal budget constraint, shown as B in Figure 5.16, is thus again the straight line that joins the maximum current consumption and maximum future consumption points. And its slope will again be $-(1 + r)$. As in the atemporal model, here too the slope of the budget constraint may be interpreted as a relative price ratio. This time it is the ratio of the prices of current and future consumption. Current consumption has a higher price than future consumption because of the opportunity cost of the interest forgone when money is spent rather than saved. It is conventional to refer to the horizontal intercept of the intertemporal budget constraint as the *present value of lifetime income*.

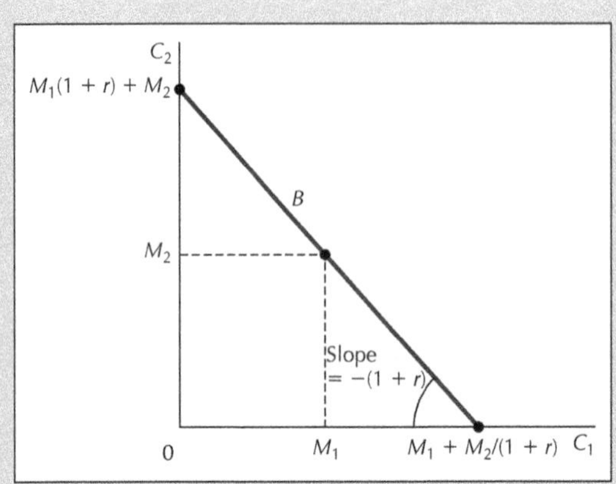

FIGURE 5.16
Intertemporal Budget Constraint with Income in Both Periods, and Borrowing or Lending at the Rate *r*
The opportunity cost of €1 of present consumption is $(1 + r)$ euros of future consumption. The horizontal intercept of the intertemporal budget constraint is the present value of lifetime income, $M_1 + M_2/(1 + r)$.

EXERCISE 5.5 You have €50,000 of current income and €42,000 of future income. If the interest rate between the current and future period is 5 per cent, what is the present value of your lifetime income? What is the maximum amount you could consume in the future? What is the equation describing your intertemporal budget constraint?

As in the atemporal case considered in Chapter 3, the intertemporal budget constraint is a convenient way of summarizing the consumption bundles that someone is *able* to buy. And again as before, it tells us nothing about which particular combination a person will *choose* to buy.

Intertemporal Indifference Curves

To discover which bundle the consumer will select from those that are feasible, we need some convenient way of representing the consumer's preferences over current and future consumption. Here again the analytical device is completely analogous to one we used in the atemporal case. Just as a consumer's preferences over two current consumption goods may be captured by an indifference map, so too may his preferences over current and future goods be represented in this fashion. In Figure 5.17, the consumer is indifferent between the bundles on I_1, which are less desirable than those on I_2, and so on.

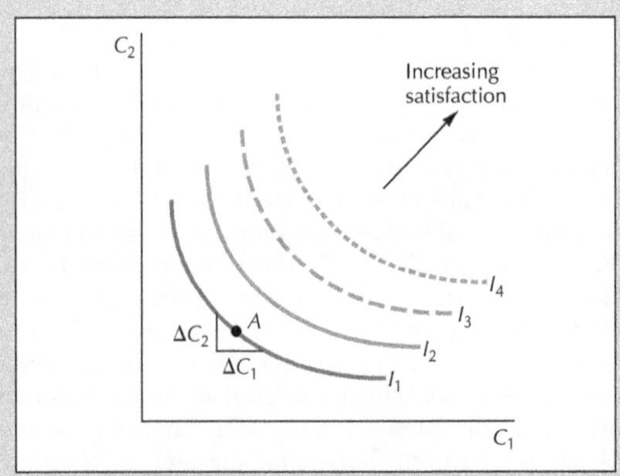

FIGURE 5.17
An Intertemporal Indifference Map
As in the atemporal model, movements to the northeast represent increasing satisfaction. The absolute value of the slope of an indifference curve at a point is called the marginal rate of time preference (MRTP) at that point. The MRTP at *A* is $|\Delta C_2/\Delta C_1|$.

The absolute value of the slope of the intertemporal indifference curve at any point is the marginal rate of substitution between future and current consumption. At point A in Figure 5.17, it is given by $|\Delta C_2/\Delta C_1|$, and this ratio is also referred to as the **marginal rate of time preference (MRTP)** at A.[6] If $|\Delta C_2/\Delta C_1| > 1$ at A, the consumer is said to exhibit *positive time preference* at that point. This means that he requires more than 1 unit of future consumption to compensate him for the loss of a unit of current consumption. If $|\Delta C_2/\Delta C_1| < 1$ at a point, he is said to exhibit *negative time preference* at that point. Such a person is willing to forgo 1 unit of current consumption in return for less than 1 unit of future consumption. Finally, if $|\Delta C_2/\Delta C_1| = 1$ at a point, the consumer is said to have *neutral time preference* at that point. With neutral time preference, present and future consumption trade off against one another at the rate of 1 to 1.

marginal rate of time preference the number of units of consumption in the future a consumer would exchange for 1 unit of consumption in the present.

As in the atemporal case, it appears justified to assume that the marginal rate of time preference declines as one moves downward along an indifference curve. The more current consumption a person already has, the more she will be willing to give up in order to obtain an additional unit of future consumption. For most of us, then, the question of whether time preference is positive, negative, or neutral will be a matter of where we happen to be on our indifference maps. The scion of a wealthy family who is unable to borrow against the €5 billion he is due to inherit in 2 years very likely has strongly positive time preference. By contrast, the primitive farmer whose food stocks are perishable is likely to have negative time preference in the wake of having harvested a bumper crop.

The optimal allocation between current and future consumption is determined exactly as in the atemporal model. The consumer selects the point along his budget constraint that corresponds to the highest attainable indifference curve. If the intertemporal indifference curves have the conventional convex shape, we ordinarily get a tangency solution like the one shown in Figure 5.18. If the MRTP is everywhere larger than (or everywhere smaller than) the slope of the budget constraint, corner solutions result, just as in the atemporal case.

Note in Figure 5.18 that the marginal rate of time preference at the optimal bundle (C_1, C_2) is positive, because the absolute value of the slope of the budget constraint is $1 + r > 1$. In the example pictured in the diagram, the consumer has the same income in each time period, but consumes slightly more in period 2.

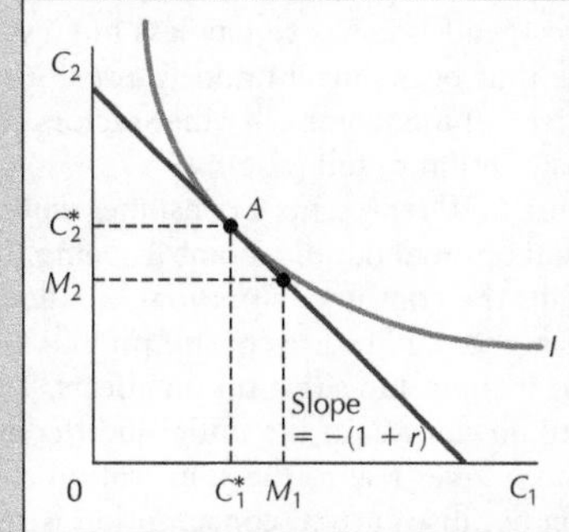

FIGURE 5.18
The Optimal Intertemporal Allocation
As in the atemporal model, the optimal intertemporal consumption bundle (bundle *A*) lies on the highest attainable indifference curve. Here, that occurs at a point of tangency.

[6] In calculus terms, the marginal rate of time preference is given by $|dC_2/dC_1|$.

The optimal allocation will of course be different for different consumers. The optimum shown in Figure 5.19*(a)*, for example, is for a consumer whose preferences are much more heavily tilted in favour of future consumption. The one shown in Figure 5.19*(b)*, by contrast, is for a consumer who cares much more about present consumption. But in each case, note that the slope of the indifference curve at the optimal point is the same. As long as consumers can borrow and lend at the interest rate r, the marginal rate of time preference at the optimal bundle will be $(1 + r)$ (except, of course, in the case of corner solutions). For interior solutions, positive time preference is the rule, regardless of the consumer's preferences.

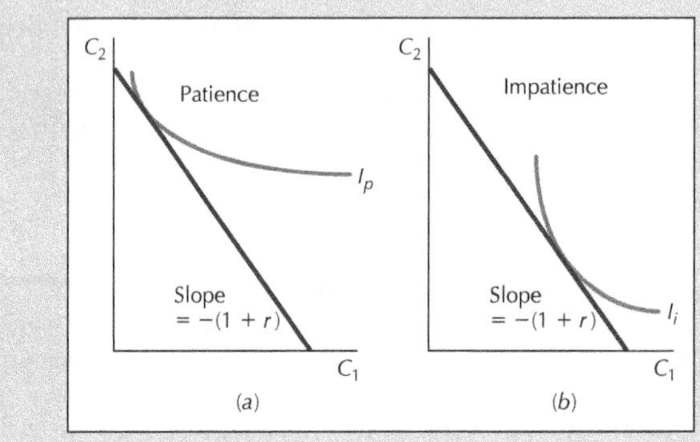

FIGURE 5.19
Patience and Impatience
(a) The patient consumer postpones the bulk of consumption until the future period. *(b)* The impatient consumer consumes much more heavily in the current period. But in equilibrium, the marginal rate of time preference $(1 + r)$ is the same for both types of consumers.

Application: Monetary Policy

Changing interest rates is the main tool of monetary policy. Following the 2008 financial crises, for instance, the ECB and Bank of England dropped interest rates to historic lows in order to stimulate demand. The intertemporal choice model can help explain the logic, and potential pitfalls, behind this policy.

A fall in the interest rate will make current consumption relatively cheaper and future consumption relatively more expensive. This causes the intertemporal budget constraint to become flatter, as depicted in Figure 5.20. To see the consequences of this we consider and compare a consumer who was a saver before the rate change with someone who was a borrower.

This distinction is important because a saver will have *less* money to spend after the interest rate fall—he will get less return on his saving—while a borrower will have *more* money to spend—he has to pay less interest on his borrowing. It is conventional to assume that both current and future consumption are normal goods. Thus a decrease (increase) in income, all other factors constant, will cause both current and future consumption to fall (rise).

Panel (a) of Figure 5.20 represents a consumer who is saving for the future. This is shown by the initial optimal bundle, point A, being to the left of income, point E. When the interest falls the consumer's optimal bundle becomes point D where current consumption is higher and future consumption lower. This overall effect can be decomposed into the income and substitution effects. To do so, we increase the consumer's income until he can attain the initial indifference curve I_0, at point F. The movement from A to F gives rise to the substitution effect; the consumer increases current consumption because current consumption is relatively cheaper. The movement from F to D gives rise to the income effect; the consumer decreases current consumption and future consumption because he has less money to spend. Combining these two effects we can say with certainty that future consumption will fall. The consequences for current consumption are ambiguous.

Panel (b) of Figure 5.20 represents a consumer who is borrowing. This is shown by the initial optimal bundle, point A, being to the right of income, point E. When the interest falls the consumer's optimal bundle becomes point D where current consumption is higher and future consumption lower. To decompose this overall effect into the substitution and income effects we decrease the consumer's income until he attains the initial indifference curve I_0, at point F. The movement from A to F gives rise to the substitution effect; as before, the consumer increases current consumption because current consumption is relatively cheaper. The movement from F to D gives rise to the income effect; this time the consumer increases current and future consumption because he has more money to spend. Combining these two effects we can say with certainty that current consumption will increase. The consequences for future consumption are ambiguous.

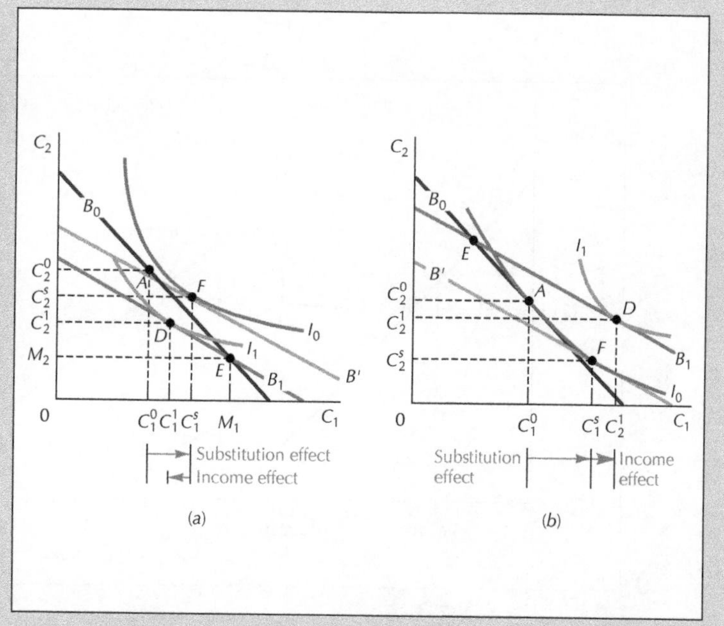

FIGURE 5.20
The Effect of a Fall in the Interest Rate
When the interest rate goes down, the intertemporal budget constraint rotates about the current endowment point. A consumer who was saving before the rate fall, panel (a), will decrease future consumption, point A to point D. The income effect causes current and future consumption to fall, point F to D. A consumer who was borrowing before the rate fall, panel (b), will increase current consumption, point A to point D. The income effect causes current and future consumption to increase, point F to D.

To summarize: A consumer who was saving before the rate fall will decrease future consumption and may or may not decrease current consumption. A consumer who was borrowing before the rate fall will increase current consumption and may or may not increase future consumption.

For an interest rate fall to stimulate current consumption we need most consumers to be borrowers. Given that many consumers are indebted, particularly those that own property, this is likely. Hence, the policy of the ECB and Bank of England, following the 2008 crisis. The logic behind a rate drop is by no means foolproof, however. In particular, we see that future consumption is predicted to fall. That can have a knock-on effect on the incentive of firms to invest for the future. We shall analyse the effects of an interest rate fall on the decisions of firms in subsequent chapters.

EXAMPLE 5.3 You have current income of €100,000 and future income of €154,000, and can borrow and lend at the rate $r = 0.1$. Under these conditions, you consume exactly your income in each period. *True or false*: An increase in r to $r = 0.4$ will cause you to save some of your current income.

Line B in Figure 5.21 is the original budget constraint. Its horizontal intercept is the present value of lifetime income when $r = 0.1$: €100,000 + €154,000/1.1 = €240,000. Its vertical intercept is future income plus $(1 + r)$ times current income: €154,000 + (1.1)(€100,000) = €264,000. The optimal bundle occurs at A, by assumption, which implies that the MRTP at A is 1.1. When the interest rate rises to 0.4, the intertemporal budget constraint becomes B'. Its horizontal intercept is €100,000 + €154,000/1.4 = €210,000. Its vertical intercept is €154,000 + (1.4) (€100,000) = €294,000. Because the MRTP at A is less than the absolute value of the slope of the budget constraint B', it follows that the consumer will be better off by consuming less now and more in the future than he did at A. The new bundle is shown at D in Figure 5.21. ◆

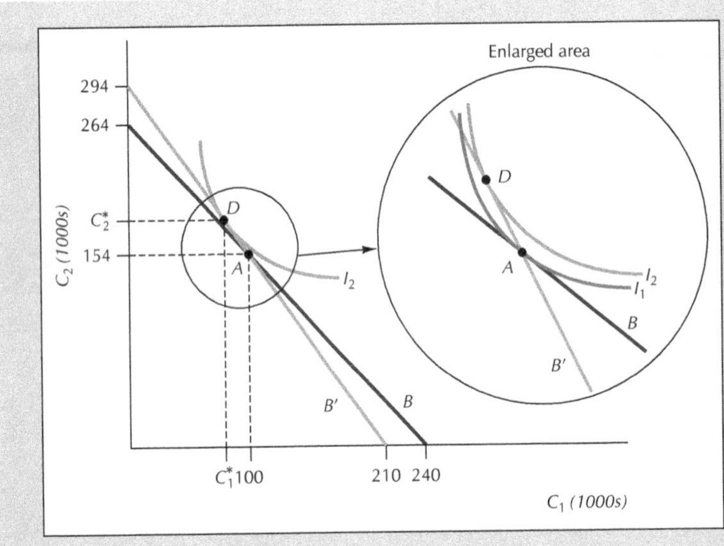

FIGURE 5.21
The Effect of a Rise in the Interest Rate
When the interest rate goes up, the intertemporal budget constraint rotates about the current endowment point. If the current endowment point (A) was optimal at the lower interest rate, the new optimal bundle (D) will have less current consumption and more future consumption.

Application: The Permanent Income and Life-Cycle Hypotheses

Economists once assumed that a person's current consumption depends primarily on her current income. Thus if a consumer received a windfall roughly equal to her current income, the prediction was that her consumption would roughly double.

In the 1950s, however, Milton Friedman, Franco Modigliani, Richard Brumberg and others argued that the intertemporal choice model suggests otherwise.[7] To illustrate, consider a consumer with current and future incomes both equal to 120, who can borrow and lend at the rate $r = 0.2$. Line B in Figure 5.22 is the consumer's intertemporal budget constraint, and the optimal bundle along it is A. Note that

[7]See Franco Modigliani and R. Brumberg, 'Utility Analysis and the Consumption Function: An Interpretation of Cross-Section Data', in K. Kurihara (ed.), *Post Keynesian Economics*, London: Allen & Unwin, 1955; and Milton Friedman, *A Theory of the Consumption Function*, Princeton, NJ: Princeton University Press, 1957.

FIGURE 5.22
Permanent Income, Not Current Income, Is the Primary Determinant of Current Consumption
The effect of a rise in current income (from 120 to 240) will be felt as an increase not only in current consumption (from 80 to 150), but also in future consumption (from 168 to 228).

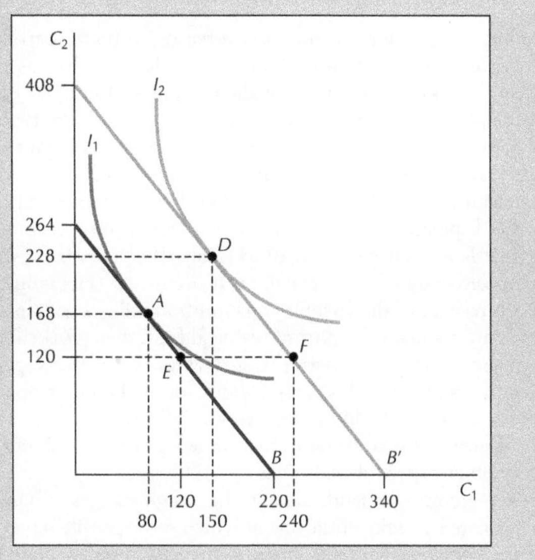

the horizontal intercept of B is the present value of lifetime income, namely, $120 + (120/1.2) = 220$.

Notice what happens when this consumer's current income rises from 120 to 240. His budget constraint is now B', and the optimal bundle is D. The effect of increasing current income is thus to increase not only current consumption (from 80 to 150) but future consumption as well (from 168 to 228). Because intertemporal indifference curves exhibit diminishing marginal rates of time preference,[8] the consumer generally does best not to concentrate too much of his consumption in any one period. By spreading his windfall over both periods, he is able to achieve a better outcome.

permanent income the present value of lifetime income.

Friedman's *permanent income hypothesis* says that the primary determinant of current consumption is not current income but what he called **permanent income.** In terms of our simple intertemporal choice model, permanent income is simply the present value of lifetime income. (Following the increase in current income in Figure 5.22, permanent income is $240 + 120/1.2 = 340$.) When we consider that in reality the future consists of not just one but many additional periods, it becomes clear that current income constitutes only a small fraction of permanent income. (If there were 10 future periods we were concerned about, for example, then a 10 per cent increase in current income would cause permanent income to increase by just over 2 per cent.)[9] Accordingly, Friedman argued, a given proportional change in current income should give rise to a much smaller proportional change in current consumption, just as we saw in Figure 5.22. (The *life-cycle hypothesis* of Modigliani and Brumberg tells essentially the same story.)

[8]Diminishing marginal rate of time preference is the intertemporal analogue of diminishing marginal rate of substitution in the atemporal model.
[9]Again, we assume an interest rate of $r = 0.2$.

Factors Accounting for Differences in Time Preference

Uncertainty regarding the future is one reason to prefer current to future consumption. In countries at war, for example, people often live as though there were no tomorrow, as indeed for many of them there will not be. By contrast, a peaceful international climate, secure employment, stable social networks, good health, and a variety of similar factors tend to reduce uncertainty about the future, in the process justifying greater weight on future consumption.

Intertemporal indifference maps, like the atemporal variety, also vary according to the disposition of the individual. Parents soon become aware of this when comparing their children as one of us (Robert) can explain. My first son will have a strongly positive time preference in most situations. (His indifference curves are very steep with respect to the current consumption axis.) Ever since he was a small boy, he always ate his favourite part of his meal first, then worked his way through to his least favoured items. Only with pressure would he eat his vegetables at all, and even then he always ate them last. My second son is the polar opposite case. He always starts with the foods he likes least, carefully husbanding his favourite items for the end of his meal. This contrast in their behaviour at the dinner table pervades virtually every other aspect of their lives.

Time preference depends also on the circumstances at hand. Experimental studies have isolated certain situations in which most people have strongly positive time preference, others in which they show strongly negative time preference. Carnegie-Mellon University economist George Loewenstein, for example, told experimental subjects to imagine they had won a kiss from their favourite movie star and then asked them when they would most like to receive it. Even though getting it right away was one of the options, most subjects elected to wait an average of several days. These choices imply negative time preference, and Loewenstein explained that most subjects simply wanted a little while to savour the anticipation of the kiss.[10]

Loewenstein also told a group of subjects to imagine that they were going to receive a painful electric shock and then asked them when they would like to receive it. This time most subjects chose to get it right away. They apparently wanted to spend as little time as possible dreading the shock. But since an electric shock is a 'bad' rather than a 'good', these choices also imply negative time preference.

While negative time preferences are occasionally observed in individual cases and can be invoked among many people by suitably chosen experiments, a preference for present over future consumption is more common. For example, if we put a can of honey-roasted cashews in front of Loewenstein's experimental subjects, not many of them would want to wait a few days to anticipate the pleasure of eating them. On the contrary, the nuts would probably disappear in short order, even if that meant spoiling dinner an hour away.

Nineteenth-century economist Eugen von Böhm-Bawerk suggested that one reason for such behaviour is that current consumption opportunities confront our senses directly, whereas future ones can only be imagined. The pleasure of eating the roasted nuts, for example, is both intense and immediate. Even those people who would strongly prefer the meal to the nuts often lack the self-control to wait. Böhm-Bawerk believed that our 'faulty telescopic faculty' was no good reason to assign greater weight to current than to future pleasures. Uncertainty aside, he felt that people would reap greater satisfaction from their lives if they weighed the present and the future equally.

[10]See George Loewenstein, 'Anticipation and the Valuation of Delayed Consumption', *Economic Journal*, 97, September 1987: 666–684.

SUMMARY

- In this chapter our primary focus was on applications of the rational choice and demand theories developed in Chapters 3 and 4. We also considered the concept of consumer surplus, which measures the amount by which a consumer benefits by being able to buy a given product at a given price. We saw that consumer surplus is well approximated by the area bounded above by the individual demand curve and below by the market price. Two-part pricing structures are a device by which a portion of consumer surplus is transferred from the buyer to the seller.
- The rational choice model is also useful for evaluating the welfare effects of price and income changes. It suggests why the consumer price index, the government's measure of changes in the cost of living, may often overstate the true cost of achieving a given level of satisfaction.
- The intertemporal choice model is analogous to the atemporal choice model in Chapter 3. In the two-dimensional case, it begins with a commodity graph that depicts current and future consumption levels of a composite good. The consumer's initial endowment is the point, (M_1, M_2), that corresponds to current and future income. If the consumer can borrow and lend at the rate r, his intertemporal budget constraint is then the line passing through the endowment point with a slope of $-(1 + r)$. The opportunity cost of a unit of current consumption is $1 + r$ units of future consumption. The horizontal intercept of the intertemporal budget constraint is the present value of all current and future income, which is also called the present value of lifetime wealth.
- The consumer's intertemporal preferences are represented with an indifference map with the same properties as in the atemporal case. A consumer is said to exhibit positive, neutral, or negative time preference at a point if his marginal rate of time preference (the absolute value of the slope of his indifference curve) at that point is greater than 1, equal to 1, or less than 1, respectively. In the case of interior solutions, equilibrium occurs at a tangency between the intertemporal budget constraint and an indifference curve. Because the slope of the intertemporal budget constraint exceeds 1 when $r > 0$, consumers exhibit positive time preference in equilibrium, irrespective of the shape of their indifference curves.
- An important application of the intertemporal choice model is to the study of decisions about how much to save. The permanent income and life-cycle hypotheses employ the model to demonstrate that it is the present value of lifetime wealth, not current income alone, that governs current consumption (and hence current savings).

QUESTIONS FOR REVIEW

1. Explain in your own words why a petrol tax whose proceeds are refunded to the consumer in a lump-sum amount will nonetheless reduce the consumption of petrol.
2. Explain in your own words what a two-part pricing scheme is and why sellers might use one.
3. Do you think a university education has a high- or low-price (tuition) elasticity of demand?
4. Explain in your own words why even long-term heavy drinkers might be highly responsive to increases in the price of alcohol.
5. Explain why 1 plus the interest rate in the intertemporal choice model is analogous to the relative price ratio in the consumer choice model discussed in Chapter 3.
6. Bus services are generally more energy efficient than cars yet the trend over the past 30 years has been a decline in the proportion of commuters taking buses despite an increase in real energy prices. Why?
7. Jennifer, who earns an annual salary of €20,000, wins €25,000 in the lottery. Explain why she most likely will not spend all her winnings during the next year.

PROBLEMS

1. Using a diagram like Figure 5.1, explain why, under the current method of educational finance, a rich family in the UK is much more likely than a poor family to send its children to a private school.
2. When the price of petrol is €1/litre, you consume 1000 litre/yr. Then two things happen: (1) The price of petrol rises to €2/litre, and (2) a distant uncle dies, with the instruction to

his executor to send you a cheque for €1000/yr. If no other changes in prices or income occur, do these two changes leave you better off than before?

3. Larry demands strawberries according to the schedule $P = 4 - (Q/2)$, where P is the price of strawberries (€/kg) and Q is the quantity (kg/wk). Assuming that the income effect is negligible, how much will he be hurt if the price of strawberries goes from €1/kg to €2/kg?

4. The only DVD rental club available to you charges €4 per movie per day. If your demand curve for movie rentals is given by $P = 20 - 2Q$, where P is the rental price (€/day) and Q is the quantity demanded (movies per year), what is the maximum annual membership fee you would be willing to pay to join this club?

5. Jane spent all her income on hot dogs and caviar. Her demand curve for caviar was inelastic at all prices for caviar. Unfortunately, an accident at a nuclear power plant caused the supply of caviar to fall and the price to rise. What happened to Jane's consumption of hot dogs? Explain. (*Note:* You should assume that the accident had no effect on the price of hot dogs or Jane's preference for caviar.)

6. Jones spends all his income on two goods, X and Y. The prices he paid and the quantities he consumed last year are as follows: $P_X = 15$, $X = 20$, $P_Y = 25$ and $Y = 30$. If the prices next year are $P_X = 6$ and $P_Y = 30$, and Jones's income is 1020, will he be better or worse off than he was in the previous year? (Assume that his tastes do not change.)

7. Smith lives in a world with two time periods. His income in each period, which he receives at the beginning of each period, is €210. If the interest rate, expressed as a fraction, is 0.05 per time period, what is the present value of his lifetime income? Draw his intertemporal budget constraint. On the same axes, draw Smith's intertemporal budget constraint when $r = 0.20$.

8. Suppose Smith from Problem 7 views current and future consumption as perfect, one-for-one substitutes for one another. Find his optimal consumption bundle.

9. Suppose Smith from Problem 7 views current and future consumption as one-to-one complements. Find his optimal consumption bundle.

10. Karen earns €75,000 in the current period and will earn €75,000 in the future.

    a. Assuming that these are the only two periods, and that banks in her country borrow and lend at an interest rate $r = 0$, draw her intertemporal budget constraint.
    b. Now suppose banks offer 10 per cent interest on funds deposited during the current period, and offer loans at this same rate. Draw her new intertemporal budget constraint.

11. Find the present value of €50,000 to be received after 1 year if the annual rate of interest is:

    a. 8 per cent
    b. 10 per cent
    c. 12 per cent.

12. Crusoe will live this period and the next period as the lone inhabitant of his island. His only income is a crop of 100 coconuts that he harvests at the beginning of each period. Coconuts not consumed in the current period spoil at the rate of 10 per cent per period.

    a. Draw Crusoe's intertemporal budget constraint. What will be his consumption in each period if he regards future consumption as a perfect, one-for-one substitute for current consumption?
    b. What will he consume each period if he regards 0.8 units of future consumption as being worth 1 unit of current consumption?

13. Kathy earns €55,000 in the current period and will earn €60,000 in the future period. What is the maximum interest rate that would allow her to spend €105,000 in the current period? What is the minimum interest rate that would allow her to spend €120,500 in the future period?

14. Smith receives €100 of income this period and €100 next period. At an interest rate of 10 per cent, he consumes all his current income in each period. He has a diminishing marginal rate of time preference between consumption next period and consumption this period.

True or false: If the interest rate rises to 20 per cent, Smith will save some of his income this period. Explain.

15. At current prices, housing costs €50 per unit and the composite good has a price of €1 per unit. A wealthy benefactor has given Joe, a penniless person, 1 unit of housing and 50 units of the composite good. Now the price of housing falls by half. *True or false*: Joe is better off as a result of the price change. Explain.

*16. Tom and Karen are economists. In an attempt to limit their son Harry's use of the family car, they charge him a user fee of 20 cents/mile. At that price he still uses the car more than they would like, but they are reluctant to antagonize him by simply raising the price further. So Tom and Karen ask him the following question: What is the minimum increase in your weekly allowance you would accept in return for having the fee raised to 40 cents/mile? Harry, who is a known truth-teller and has conventional preferences, answers €10/wk.

a. If Tom and Karen increase Harry's allowance by €10/wk and charge him 40 cents/mile, will he drive less than before? Explain.
b. Will the revenue from the additional mileage charges be more than, less than, or equal to €10/wk? Explain.

*17. All book buyers have the same preferences, and under current arrangements, those who buy used books at €22 receive the same utility as those who buy new books at €50. The annual interest rate is 10 per cent, and there are no transaction costs involved in the buying and selling of used books. Each new textbook costs €m to produce and lasts for exactly 2 years.

a. What is the most a buyer would pay for the use of a new book for 1 yr?
b. How low would m have to be before a publisher would find it worthwhile to print books with disappearing ink—ink that vanishes 1 yr from the point of sale of a new book, thus eliminating the used-book market? (Assume that eliminating the used-book market will exactly double the publisher's sales.)

*18. Herb wants to work exactly 12 hr/wk to supplement his graduate fellowship. He can either work as a clerk in the library at €6/hr or tutor first-year graduate students in economics. Pay differences aside, he is indifferent between these two jobs. Each of three first-year students has a demand curve for tutoring given by $P = 10 - Q$, where P is the price in euros per hour, and Q is the number of hours per week. If Herb has the option of setting a two-part tariff for his tutoring services, how many hours per week should he tutor and how many hours should he work in the library? If he does any tutoring, what should his rate structure be?

†19. Cornell is committed to its current policy of allowing the children of its faculty to attend the university without paying tuition. Suppose the demand curve of Cornell faculty children (CFCs) for slots in other universities is given by $P = 30 - 5Q_0$, where P is the tuition price charged by other universities (in thousands of dollars) and Q_0 is the number of CFCs who attend those universities. Cornell is now considering a proposal to subsidize some proportion k of the tuition charged to CFCs who attend other universities. Suppose Cornell knows that it can fill all its available slots with non-CFCs who pay tuition at the rate of €45,000/yr. Assuming that all CFCs who do not attend other universities will go to Cornell, what value of k will maximize Cornell's tuition revenues, net of outside subsidies, if the tuition price at all other universities is €24,000/yr?

†20. How will your answer to the preceding problem differ if the tuition charged by outside universities is €12,000/yr? What is the economic interpretation of a value of k greater than 1?

*21. Harry runs a small movie theatre, whose customers all have identical tastes. Each customer's reservation price for the movie is €5, and each customer's demand curve for popcorn at his concession stand is given by $P_c = 4 - Q_c$, where P_c is the price of popcorn in euros and Q_c is the amount of popcorn in quarts. If the marginal cost of allowing another patron to watch the movie is zero, and the marginal cost of popcorn is €1, at what price should Harry sell tickets and popcorn if his goal is to maximize his profits? (Assume that Harry is able to costlessly advertise his price structure to potential patrons.)

*Problems marked with an asterisk (*) are more difficult.
†Problems marked with a dagger (†) are most easily solved using calculus.

ANSWERS TO IN-CHAPTER EXERCISES

5.1. Initial consumer surplus at P = €3 (and Q = 7 litre/wk) is CS = $\frac{1}{2}(10 - 3)7$ = €24.50/wk. Consumer surplus at the higher price P' = €4 (and Q' = 6 litre/wk) is CS′ = $\frac{1}{2}(10 - 4)6$ = €18/wk. The loss in consumer surplus is given by the area of *DCEF*, which equals 24.5 − 18 = €6.50/wk.

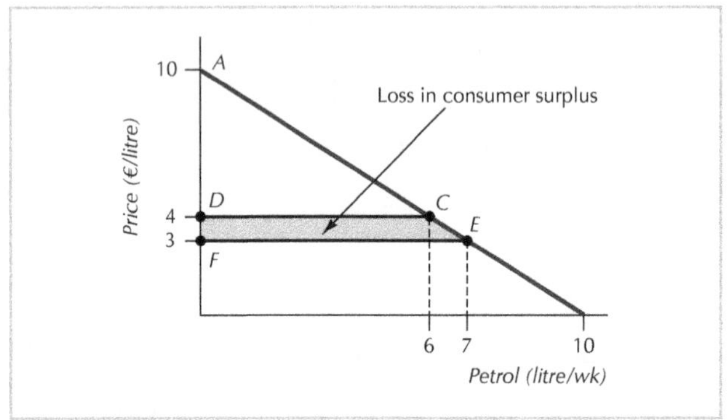

5.2. The maximum membership fee is now given by the area of triangle $AB'C'$, which is CS = $\frac{1}{2}(50 - 20)120$ = €1800/yr.

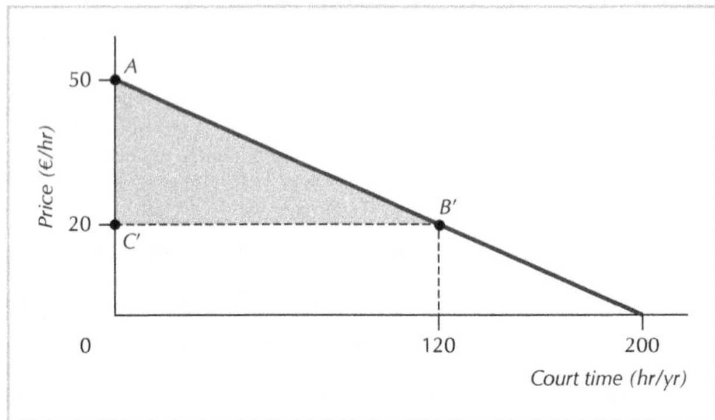

5.3. The two budget lines and last year's optimal bundle are shown in the following diagram. A closer look at the tangency point (enlarged area) shows that this year Jones can now afford to purchase a bundle he prefers to the one he bought last year.

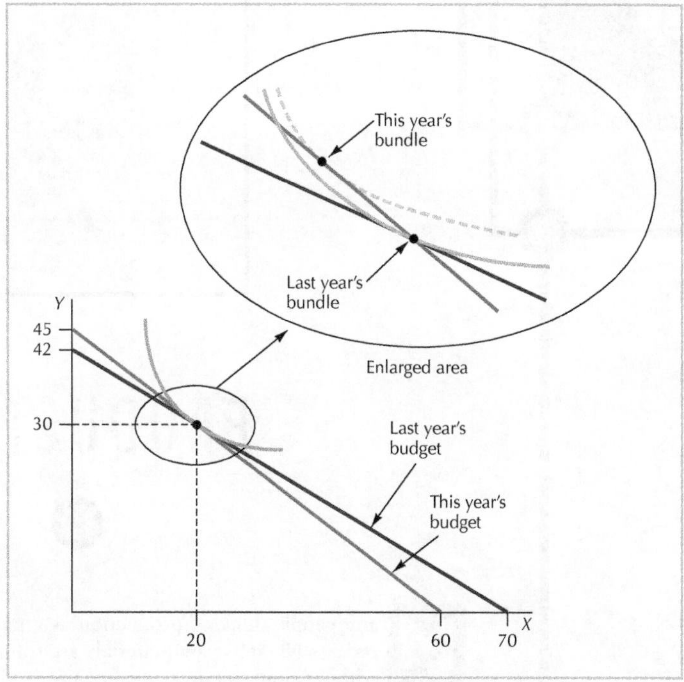

5.4. Demand will fall by 3 per cent to around 1136 million journeys. The price will increase by around 17 pence. So, the increase in revenue is around £193 million.

5.5. PV = €50,000 + €42,000/1.05 = €90,000. Maximum future consumption = 50,000(1.05) + €42,000 = €94,500. The equation for your intertemporal budget constraint is C_2 = €94,500 − $1.05C_1$.

CHAPTER 9

PRODUCTION

Many people think of production as a highly structured, often mechanical process whereby raw materials are transformed into finished goods. And without doubt, a great deal of production—like a mason's laying bricks for the walls of a house—is of roughly this sort. Economists emphasize, however, that production is also a much more general concept, encompassing many activities not ordinarily thought of as such. We define it as *any activity that creates present or future utility*.

Thus, the simple act of telling a joke constitutes production. Woody Allen (Figure 9.1) tells the story of the man who complains to his analyst that his brother thinks he's a chicken. 'Why don't you tell him he's *not* a chicken?' asks the analyst, to which the man responds, 'I can't, I need the eggs.' Once a joke is told, it leaves no more tangible trace than a pleasant memory. But under the economic definition of production, Woody Allen is as much a production worker as the welder putting together a containership at the Odense Steel Shipyard. The person who delivers a singing telegram is also engaged in production; so is the doctor who gives a child a tetanus shot; the lawyer who draws up a will; the people who collect the garbage on Wednesday mornings; the postal worker who delivers a tax return to the government; and even the economists who write about production.

CHAPTER PREVIEW

In our discussions of consumer choice during the preceding chapters, an existing menu of goods and services was taken for granted. But where do these goods and services come from? In this chapter we will see that their production involves a decision process very similar to the one we examined in earlier chapters. Whereas our focus in earlier chapters was on the economic decisions that underlie the demand side of the market relationship, our focus in the next seven chapters is on the economic decisions that underlie the supply side.

FIGURE 9.1
A Production Worker
© Associated Press

In this chapter we describe the production possibilities available to us for a given state of technology and resource endowments. We want to know how output varies with the application of productive inputs in both the short run and the long run. Answers to these questions will set the stage for our efforts in the next chapter to describe how firms choose among technically feasible alternative methods of producing a given level of output.

THE INPUT-OUTPUT RELATIONSHIP, OR PRODUCTION FUNCTION

There are several ways to define production. One definition, mentioned above, is that it is any activity that creates present or future utility. Production may be equivalently described as a process that transforms inputs (factors of production) into outputs. (The two descriptions are equivalent because output is something that creates present or future utility.) Among the inputs into production, economists have traditionally included land, labour, capital, and the more elusive category called entrepreneurship.[1] To this list, it has become increasingly common to add such factors as knowledge or technology, organization, and energy.

production function the relationship that describes how inputs like capital and labour are transformed into output.

A **production function** is the relationship by which inputs are combined to produce output. Schematically, it may be represented as the box in Figure 9.2. Inputs are fed into it, and output is discharged from it. The box implicitly embodies the existing state of technology, which has been improving steadily over time. Thus, a given combination of productive inputs will yield a larger number of cars with today's technology than with the technology of 1970.

A production function may also be thought of as a cooking recipe. It lists the ingredients and tells you, say, how many pancakes you will get if you manipulate the ingredients in a certain way.[2]

[1]'Entrepreneurship' is defined as 'the process of organizing, managing, and assuming responsibility for a business enterprise' (*Random House College Dictionary*). An entrepreneur is thus, by definition, a risk-taker.

[2]In some recipes, the ingredients must be mixed in fixed proportions. Other recipes allow substitution between ingredients, as in a pancake recipe that allows milk and oil to be substituted for eggs. Production functions can be of either of these two types.

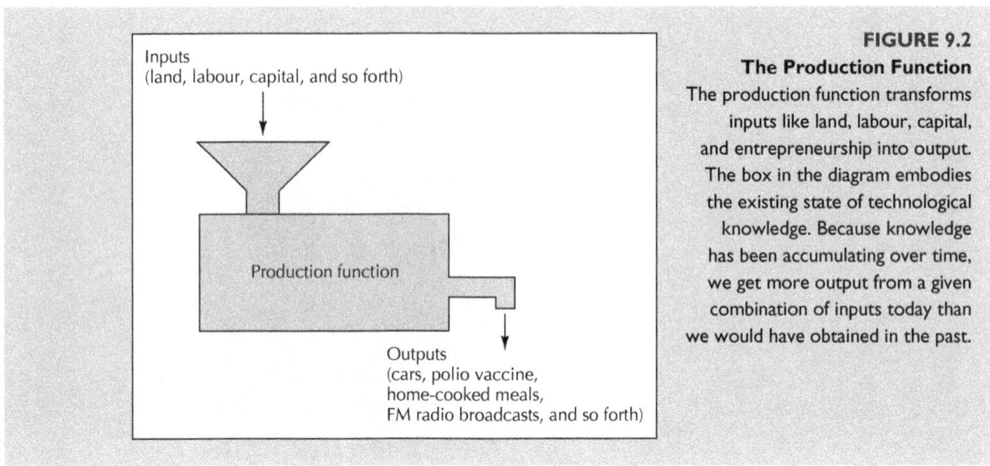

FIGURE 9.2
The Production Function
The production function transforms inputs like land, labour, capital, and entrepreneurship into output. The box in the diagram embodies the existing state of technological knowledge. Because knowledge has been accumulating over time, we get more output from a given combination of inputs today than we would have obtained in the past.

Yet another way of describing the production function is to cast it in the form of a mathematical equation. Consider a production process that employs two inputs, capital (K) and labour (L), to produce meals (Q). The relationship between K, L, and Q may be expressed as

$$Q = F(K, L) \tag{9.1}$$

where F is a mathematical function that summarizes the process depicted in Figure 9.2. It is no more than a simple rule that tells how much Q we get when we employ specific quantities of K and L. By way of illustration, suppose the production function for meals is given by $F(K, L) = 2KL$, where K is measured in equipment-hours per week,[3] L is measured in person-hours per week, and output is measured in meals per week. For example, 2 equipment-hr/wk combined with 3 person-hr/wk would yield $2(2)(3) = 12$ meals/wk with this particular production function. The relationship between K, L, and weekly output of meals for the production function $Q = 2KL$ is summarized in Table 9.1.

TABLE 9.1
The Production Function $Q = 2KL$

		Labour (person-hours/wk)				
		1	**2**	**3**	**4**	**5**
	1	2	4	6	8	10
Capital	**2**	4	8	12	16	20
(equipment-hours/wk)	**3**	6	12	18	24	30
	4	8	16	24	32	40
	5	10	20	30	40	50

The entries in the table represent output, measured in meals per week, and are calculated using the formula $Q = 2KL$.

[3]Here, 1 frying pan-hr/wk is 1 frying pan used for 1 hour during the course of a week. Thus, a frying pan that is in use for 8 hr/day for each day of a 5-day workweek would constitute 40 frying pan-hr/wk of capital input.

Intermediate Products

Capital (as embodied, for example, in the form of stoves and frying pans) and labour (as embodied in the services of a chef) are clearly by themselves insufficient to produce meals. Raw foodstuffs are also necessary. The production process described by Equation 9.1 is one that transforms raw foodstuffs into the finished product we call meals. In this process, foodstuffs are *intermediate products,* which many economists treat as inputs like any others. For the sake of simplicity, we will ignore intermediate products in the examples we discuss in this chapter. But this feature could be built into all these examples without changing any of our essential conclusions.

Fixed and Variable Inputs

The production function tells us how output will vary if some or all of the inputs are varied. In practice, there are many production processes in which the quantities of at least some inputs cannot be altered quickly. The FM radio broadcast of classical music is one such process. To carry it out, complex electronic equipment is needed, and also a music library and a large transmission tower. Records and compact discs can be purchased in a matter of hours. But it may take weeks to acquire the needed equipment to launch a new station, and months or even years to purchase a suitable location and construct a new transmission tower.

The **long run** for a particular production process is defined as the shortest period of time required to alter the amounts of *every* input. The **short run,** by contrast, is defined as that period during which one or more inputs cannot be varied. An input whose quantity can be altered in the short run is called a **variable input.** One whose quantity cannot be altered—except perhaps at prohibitive cost—within a given time period is called a **fixed input.** In the long run, all inputs are variable inputs, by definition. In the classical music broadcast example, compact discs are variable inputs in the short run, but the broadcast tower is a fixed input. If sufficient time elapses, however, even it becomes a variable input. In some production activities, like those of a street-corner hot dog stand, even the long run does not involve an extended period of time. We begin in the next section by considering short-run production and then we move on to long-run production in the following section.

long run the shortest period of time required to alter the amounts of all inputs used in a production process.

short run the longest period of time during which at least one of the inputs used in a production process cannot be varied.

variable input an input that can be varied in the short run.

fixed input an input that cannot vary in the short run.

PRODUCTION IN THE SHORT RUN

Consider again the production process described by $Q = F(K, L) = 2KL$, the simple two-input production function described in Table 9.1. And suppose we are concerned with production in the short run—here, a period of time in which the labour input is variable but the capital input is fixed, say, at the value $K = K_0 = 1$. With capital held constant, output becomes, in effect, a function of only the variable input, labour: $F(K, L) = 2K_0L = 2L$. This means we can plot the production function in a two-dimensional diagram, as in Figure 9.3(*a*). For this particular $F(K, L)$, the short-run production function is a straight line through the origin whose slope is 2 times the fixed value of K: thus, $\Delta Q/\Delta L = 2K_0$. In Figure 9.3(*b*), note that the short-run production rotates upward to $F(K_1, L) = 6L$ when K rises to $K_1 = 3$.

EXERCISE 9.1 Graph the short-run production function for $F(K, L) = \sqrt{K}\sqrt{L}$ when K is fixed at $K_0 = 4$.

As you saw in Exercise 9.1, the graphs of short-run production functions will not always be straight lines. The short-run production function shown in Figure 9.4 has several properties that are commonly found in production functions observed in practice. First, it passes through the origin, which is to say that we get no output if we

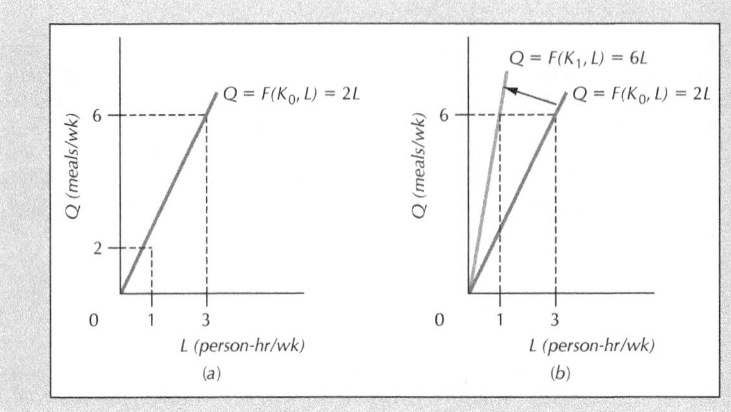

FIGURE 9.3
A Specific Short-Run Production Function
Panel (*a*) shows the production function, $Q = 2KL$, with K fixed at $K_0 = 1$. Panel (*b*) shows how the short-run production function shifts when K is increased to $K_1 = 3$.

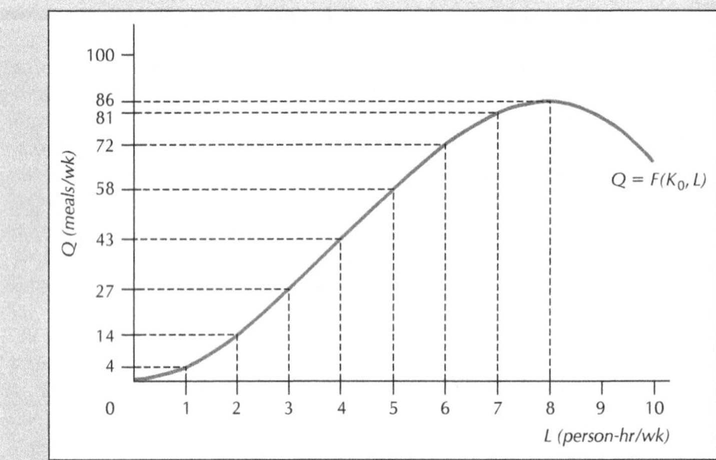

FIGURE 9.4
Another Short-Run Production Function
The curvilinear shape shown here is common to many short-run production functions. Output initially grows at an increasing rate as labour increases. Beyond $L = 4$, output grows at a diminishing rate with increases in labour.

use no variable input. Second, initially the addition of variable inputs augments output at an increasing rate: moving from 1 to 2 units of labour yields 10 extra units of output, while moving from 2 to 3 units of labour gives 13 additional units. Finally, the function shown in Figure 9.4 has the property that beyond some point ($L = 4$ in the diagram), additional units of the variable input give rise to smaller and smaller increments in output. Thus, the move from 5 to 6 units of labour yields 14 extra units of output, while the move from 6 to 7 units of labour yields only 9. For some production functions, the level of output may actually decline with additional units of the variable input beyond some point, as happens here for $L > 8$. With a limited amount of capital to work with, additional workers may eventually begin to get in one another's way.

The property that output initially grows at an increasing rate may stem from the benefits of division of tasks and specialization of labour. With one employee, all tasks must be done by the same person, while with two or more employees, tasks may be divided and employees may better perform their dedicated tasks. (Similar logic applies to specializing in one task within any period of time.)

The final property noted about the short-run production function in Figure 9.4—that beyond some point, output grows at a diminishing rate with increases in the

law of diminishing returns if other inputs are fixed, the increase in output from an increase in the variable input must eventually decline.

variable input—is known as the **law of diminishing returns.** And although it too is not a universal property of short-run production functions, it is extremely common. The law of diminishing returns is a short-run phenomenon. Formally, it may be stated as follows:

> As equal amounts of a variable input are sequentially added while all other inputs are held fixed, the resulting increments to output will eventually diminish.

Why can't all the world's people be fed from the amount of grain grown in a single flowerpot?

ECONOMIC NATURALIST 9.1

The law of diminishing returns suggests that no matter how much labour, fertilizer, water, seed, capital equipment, and other inputs were used, only a limited amount of grain could be grown in a single flowerpot. With the land input fixed at such a low level, increases in other inputs would quickly cease to have any effect on total output. ■

Employing the logic of Economic Naturalist 9.1, the British economist Thomas Malthus argued in 1798 that the law of diminishing returns implied eventual misery for the human race. The difficulty is that agricultural land is fixed and, beyond some point, the application of additional labour will yield ever smaller increases in food production. The inevitable result, as Malthus saw it, is that population growth will drive average food consumption down to the starvation level.

Whether Malthus's prediction will be borne out in the future remains to be seen. But he would never have imagined that food production per capita would grow more than twenty-fold during the ensuing two centuries. Note carefully, however, that the experience of the last 200 years does not contradict the law of diminishing returns. What Malthus did not foresee was the explosive growth in agricultural technology that has far outstripped the effect of a fixed supply of land. Still, the ruthless logic of Malthus's observation remains. No matter how advanced our technology, if population continues to grow, it is just a matter of time before limits on arable land spell persistent food shortages.

Thomas Malthus failed to anticipate the capacity of productivity growth to keep pace with population growth. But his basic insight—that a planet with fixed resources can support only so many people—remains valid.

The world's population has grown rapidly during the years since Malthus wrote, more than doubling during the last 50 years alone. Are we in fact doomed to eventual starvation? Perhaps not. As the late economist Herbert Stein once famously remarked, 'If something can't go on forever, it won't.' And indeed, population specialists now predict that the earth's population will peak by the year 2070 and then begin to decline.[4] If we don't blow ourselves up in the meantime, there is thus a good chance that we will escape the dire fate that Malthus predicted.

Technological improvements in production are represented graphically by an upward shift in the production function. In Figure 9.5, for example, the curves labelled F_1 and F_2 are used to denote the agricultural production functions in 1808 and 2008, respectively. The law of diminishing returns applies to each of these curves, and yet the growth in food production has kept pace with the increase in labour input during the period shown.

[4]See Wolfgang Lutz, Warren Sanderson and Sergei Sherbov, 'The End of World Population Growth', *Nature*, 412, 2 August 2001: 543–545.

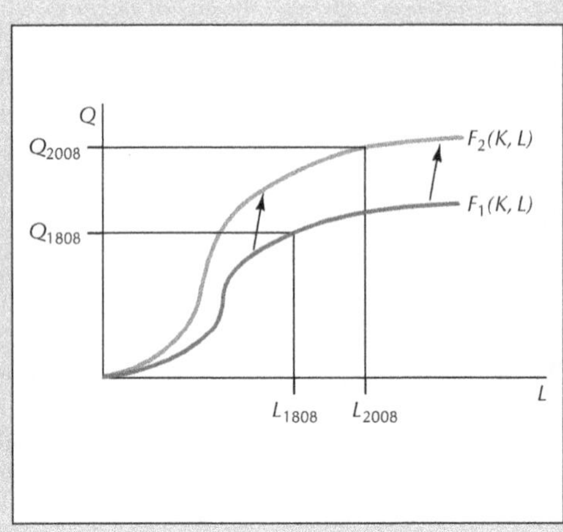

FIGURE 9.5
The Effect of Technological Progress in Food Production
F_1 represents the production function for food in the year 1808. F_2 represents the corresponding function for 2008. The effect of technological progress in food production is to cause F_2 to lie above F_1. Even though the law of diminishing returns applies to both F_1 and F_2, the growth in food production between 1808 and 2008 has more than kept pace with the growth in labour inputs over the same period.

Total, Marginal and Average Products

Short-run production functions like the ones shown in Figures 9.4 and 9.5 are often referred to as **total product curves.** They relate the total amount of output to the quantity of the variable input. Also of interest in many applications is the *marginal product* of a variable input. It is defined as *the change in the total product that occurs in response to a unit change in the variable input (all other inputs held fixed).* A business manager trying to decide whether to hire or fire another worker has an obvious interest in knowing what the **marginal product** of labour is.

total product curve a curve showing the amount of output as a function of the amount of variable input.

marginal product change in total product due to a 1-unit change in the variable input.

More formally, if ΔL denotes a small change in the variable input, and ΔQ denotes the resulting change in output, then the marginal product of L, denoted MP_L, is defined as

$$MP_L = \frac{\Delta Q}{\Delta L} \tag{9.2}$$

Geometrically, the marginal product at any point is simply the slope of the total product curve at that point, as shown in the top panel of Figure 9.6.[5] For example, the marginal product of labour when $L = 2$ is $MP_{L=2} = 12$. Likewise, $MP_{L=4} = 16$ and $MP_{L=7} = 6$ for the total product curve shown in Figure 9.6. Note, finally, that MP_L is negative for values of L greater than 8.

The marginal product curve itself is plotted in the bottom panel in Figure 9.6. Note that it rises at first, reaches a maximum at $L = 4$, and then declines, finally becoming negative for values of L greater than 8. Note also that the maximum point on the marginal product curve corresponds to the inflection point on the total product curve, the point where its curvature switches from convex (increasing at an increasing rate) to concave (increasing at a decreasing rate). Note also that the marginal product curve reaches zero at the value of L at which the total product curve reaches a maximum.

As we will see in greater detail in later chapters, the importance of the marginal product concept lies in the fact that decisions about running an enterprise most naturally arise in the form of decisions about *changes*. Should we hire another

[5]The formal definition of the marginal product of a variable input is given by $MP(L) = \partial F(K, L)/\partial L$.

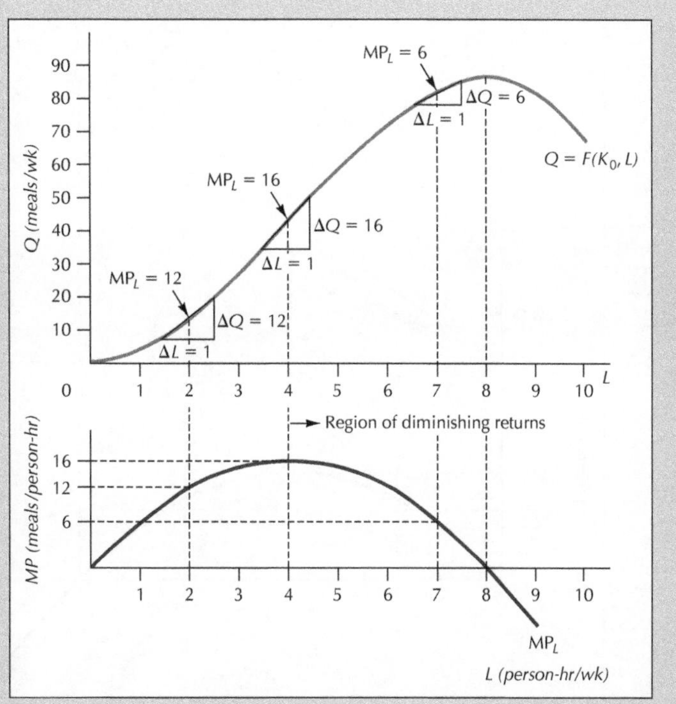

FIGURE 9.6
The Marginal Product of a Variable Input
At any point, the marginal product of labour, MP_L, is the slope of the total product curve at that point (top panel). For the production function shown in the top panel, the marginal product curve (bottom panel) initially increases as labour increases. Beyond $L = 4$, however, the marginal product of labour decreases as labour increases. For $L > 8$ the total product curve declines with L, which means that the marginal product of labour is negative in that region.

engineer or accountant? Should we reduce the size of the maintenance staff? Should we install another copier? Should we lease another delivery truck?

To answer such questions intelligently, we must compare the benefit of the change in question with its cost. And as we will see, the marginal product concept plays a pivotal role in the calculation of the benefits when we alter the level of a productive input. Looking at Figure 9.6, we may identify a range of values of the variable input that a rational manager would never employ. In particular, as long as labour commands a positive wage, such a manager would never want to employ the variable input in the region where its marginal product is negative ($L > 8$ in Figure 9.6). Equivalently, he would never employ a variable input past the point where the total product curve reaches its maximum value (where $MP_L = 0$).

EXERCISE 9.2 What is the marginal product of labour when $L = 3$ in the short-run production function shown in Figure 9.3(*a*)? When $L = 1$? Does this short-run production function exhibit diminishing returns to labour?

average product total output divided by the quantity of the variable input.

The average product of a variable input is defined as the total product divided by the quantity of that input. Denoted AP_L, it is thus given by

$$AP_L = \frac{Q}{L} \tag{9.3}$$

When the variable input is labour, the average product is also called labour productivity.

Geometrically, the average product is the slope of the line joining the origin to the corresponding point on the total product curve. Three such lines, R_1, R_2 and

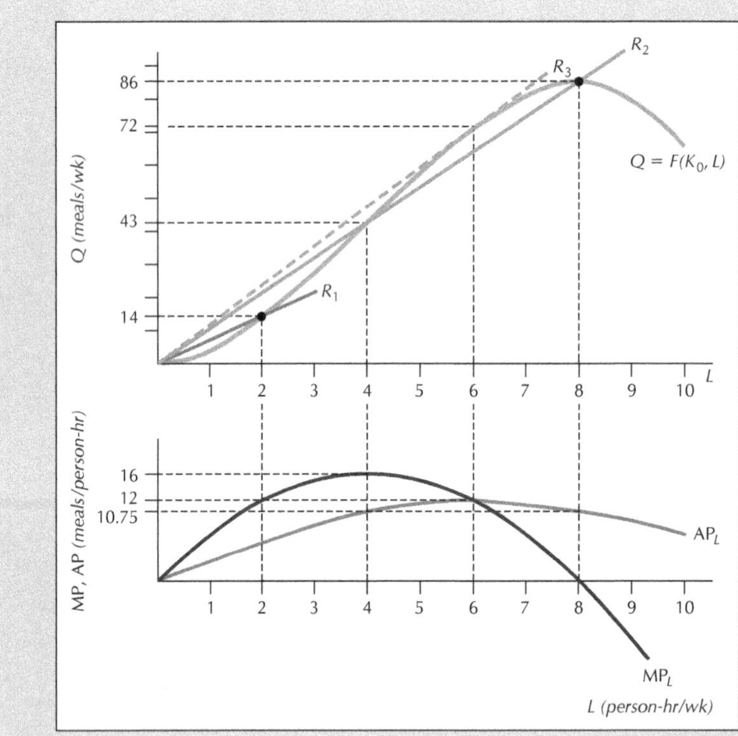

FIGURE 9.7
Total, Marginal and Average Product Curves
The average product at any point on the total product curve is the slope of the ray to that point. For the total product curve shown in the top panel, AP_L rises with $L = 6$, then declines. At $L = 6$, $MP_L = AP_L$. For any $L < 6$, $MP_L > AP_L$, and for any $L > 6$, $MP_L < AP_L$.

R_3, are drawn to the total product curve shown in the top panel in Figure 9.7. The average product at $L = 2$ is the slope of R_1, which is $\frac{14}{2} = 7$. Note that R_2 intersects the total product curve in two places—first, directly above $L = 4$, and then directly above $L = 8$. Accordingly, the average products for these two values of L will be the same—namely, the slope of R_2, which is $\frac{43}{4} = \frac{86}{8} = 10.75$. R_3 intersects the total product curve at only one point, directly above $L = 6$. The average product for $L = 6$ is thus the slope of R_3, $\frac{72}{6} = 12$.

EXERCISE 9.3 For the short-run production function shown in Figure 9.3(*a*), what is the average product of labour at $L = 3$? At $L = 1$? How does average product compare with marginal product at these points?

The Relationships between Total, Marginal and Average Product Curves

Because of the way the total, marginal and average products are defined, systematic relationships exist among them. The top panel in Figure 9.7 shows a total product curve and three of the rays whose slopes define the average product of the variable input. The steepest of the three rays, R_3, is tangent to the total product curve at $L = 6$. Its slope, $\frac{72}{6} = 12$, is the average product of labour at $L = 6$. The marginal product of labour at $L = 6$ is defined as the slope of the total product curve at $L = 6$, which happens to be exactly the slope of R_3, since R_3 is tangent to the total product curve. Thus $AP_{L=6} = MP_{L=6}$, as shown in the bottom panel by the fact that the AP_L curve intersects the MP_L curve for $L = 6$.

Whenever the last unit of an activity exceeds the average level of the activity, the average must be rising. Conversely, when the last unit is smaller than the average, the average must be falling.

For values of L less than 6, note in the top panel in Figure 9.7 that the slope of the total product curve is larger than the slope of the ray to the corresponding point. Thus, for $L < 6$, $MP_L > AP_L$, as reflected in the bottom panel. Note also in the top panel that for values of L greater than 6, the slope of the total product curve is smaller than the slope of the ray to the corresponding point. This means that for $L > 6$, we have $AP_L > MP_L$, as shown in the bottom panel in Figure 9.7.

Note finally in Figure 9.7 that for extremely small values of L, the slope of the ray to the total product curve becomes indistinguishable from the slope of the total product curve itself. This tells us that for $L = 0$, average and marginal products are the same, which is reflected in the bottom panel in Figure 9.7 by the fact that both curves emanate from the same point.[6]

The relationship between the marginal and average product curves may be summarized as follows: *When the marginal product curve lies above the average product curve, the average product curve must be rising; and when the marginal product curve lies below the average product curve, the average product curve must be falling. The two curves intersect at the maximum value of the average product curve.* A moment's reflection on the definitions of the two curves makes the intuitive basis for this relationship clear. If the contribution to output of an additional unit of the variable input exceeds the average contribution of the variable inputs used thus far, the average contribution must rise. This effect is analogous to what happens when a student who is 2 metres tall joins a class with an average height of 1.8 metres: the new student's presence causes the group's average height to rise. Conversely, adding a variable input whose marginal product is less than the average product of existing units is like adding a new student with a height of 1.7 metres. Here, the effect is for the existing average to fall.[7]

EXERCISE 9.4 Consider a short-run production process for which $AP_{L=10} = 7$ and $MP_{L=10} = 12$. Will $AP_{L=10.1}$ be larger or smaller than $AP_{L=10}$ for this process?

The Practical Significance of the Average-Marginal Distinction

The distinction between average and marginal products is of central importance to anyone who must allocate a scarce resource between two or more productive activities. The specific question is, 'how should the resource be allocated in order to maximize total output?' The following examples make clear the issues posed by this problem and the general rule required to solve it.

Read through the following scenario carefully and try to answer the question posed at the end:

> Suppose you own a fishing fleet consisting of a given number of boats, and can send your boats in whatever numbers you wish to either of two ends of an extremely wide lake, east or west. Under your current allocation of boats, the ones fishing at the east end return daily with 100 kilograms of fish each, while those in the west return daily

[6] For the production function shown, that point happens to be the origin, but in general it need not be.

[7] Mathematically, the result that MP intersects AP at the maximum value of AP can be shown by noting that the necessary condition for a maximum of AP is that its first partial derivative with respect to L be zero:

$$\partial(Q/L)/\partial L = [L(\partial Q/\partial L) - Q]/L^2 = 0$$

from which it follows that $\partial Q/\partial L = Q/L$.

with 120 kilograms each. The fish populations at each end of the lake are completely independent, and your current yields can be sustained indefinitely. Should you alter your current allocation of boats?

Most people, especially those who have not had a good course in microeconomics, answer confidently that the current allocation should be altered. Specifically, they say that the fishing fleet owner should send more boats to the west side of the lake. Yet, as the following example illustrates, even a rudimentary understanding of the distinction between the average and marginal products of a productive resource makes clear that this response is not justified.

EXAMPLE 9.1 **In the fishing fleet scenario just described, suppose the relationship between the number of boats sent to each end and the number of kilograms caught per boat is as summarized in Table 9.2. Suppose further that you have four boats in your fleet, and that two currently fish the east end while the other two fish the west end. (Note that all of these suppositions are completely consistent with the facts outlined in the scenario.) Should you move one of your boats from the east end to the west end?**

TABLE 9.2
Average Product, Total Product and Marginal Product (kg/day) for Two Fishing Areas

Number of boats	East end			West end		
	AP	TP	MP	AP	TP	MP
0	0	0		0	0	
			100			130
1	100	100		130	130	
			100			110
2	100	200		120	240	
			100			90
3	100	300		110	330	
			100			70
4	100	400		100	400	

The average catch per boat is constant at 100 kilograms per boat for boats sent to the east end of the lake. The average catch per boat is a declining function of the number of boats sent to the west end.

From the entries in Table 9.2, it follows that your total output under the current allocation is 440 kilograms of fish per day (100 kilograms from each of the two boats at the east end, 120 from each of the two at the west end). Now suppose you transfer one boat from the east end to the west end, which means you now have three boats in the west and only one in the east. From the figures in Table 9.2, we see that your total output will now be only 430 kilograms per day, or 10 kilograms per day less than under the current allocation. So, no, you should not move an extra boat to the west end. Neither, for that matter, should you send one of the west end boats to the east end. Loss of a boat from the west end would reduce the total daily catch at that end by 110 kilograms (the difference between the 240 kilograms caught by two boats and the 130 that would be caught by one), which is more than the extra 100 kilograms you would get by having an extra boat at the east end. The current allocation of two boats to each end is optimal. ◆

Example 9.1 is an instance of an important class of problems in which managers must decide how to allocate an input across several alternative processes used for producing a given product. *The general rule for allocating an input efficiently in such cases is to allocate the next unit of the input to the production activity where its marginal product is highest.* This form of the rule applies to resources, such as boats, that are not perfectly divisible, and also to cases in which the marginal product of a resource is always higher in one activity than in another.[8] For a resource that is perfectly divisible, and for activities for which the marginal product of the resource is not always higher in one than in the others, the rule is to *allocate the resource so that its marginal product is the same in every activity*.

Many people, however, 'solve' these kinds of problems by allocating resources to the activity with the highest *average* product, or by trying to equalize *average* products across activities. The reason that this particular wrong answer often has appeal is that people often focus on only part of the relevant production process. By sending only two boats to the west end, the average catch at that end is 20 kilograms per day greater than the average catch per boat at the east end. But note that if you send a third boat to the west end, that boat's contribution to the total amount of fish caught at the west end will be only 90 kilograms per day (the difference between the 330 kilograms caught by three boats and 240 kilograms caught by two). What people often tend to overlook is that the third boat at the west end catches some of the fish that would otherwise have been caught by the first two.

As the figures in Table 9.2 illustrate, the opportunity cost of sending a third boat to the west end is the 100 kilograms of fish that will no longer be caught at the east end. But since that third boat will add only 90 kilograms to the daily catch at the west end, the best that can be done is to keep sending two boats to each end of the lake. The fact that either of the two boats currently fishing at the east end could catch 10 kilograms per day more by moving to the west end is no cause for concern to a fishing fleet owner who understands the distinction between average and marginal products.

Example 9.1 produced what economists call an *interior solution*—one in which each of the production activities is actually employed. But not all problems of this sort have interior solutions. As the next example will make clear, one activity sometimes dominates the other.

EXAMPLE 9.2 Same as the fishing fleet Example 9.1, except now the marginal product of each boat sent to the west end of the lake is equal to 120 kg/day.

The difference between this example and Example 9.1 is that this time there is no drop-off in the rate at which fish are caught as more boats are sent to the west end of the lake. So this time the average product of any boat sent to the west end is identical to its marginal product. And since the marginal product is always higher for boats sent to the west end, the optimal allocation is to send all four boats to that end. ◆

Cases such as the one illustrated in Example 9.2 are by no means unusual. But by far the more common, and more interesting, production decisions are the ones that involve interior solutions such as the one we saw in Example 9.1, where some positive quantity of the productive input must be allocated to each activity.

EXAMPLE 9.3 Suppose that from the last seconds you devoted to Problem 1 on your first economics exam you earned 4 extra points, while from the last seconds devoted to Problem 2 you earned 6 extra points. The total number of points you earned on these two questions were 20 and 12, respectively, and the total time you spent on each was the same. The total number of points possible on each problem was 40. How—if at all—should you have reallocated your time between problems?

The rule for efficient allocation of time spent on exams is the same as the rule for efficient allocation of any resource: the marginal product of the resource should be

[8]See Example 9.2.

the same in each activity. From the information given, the marginal product of your time spent on Problem 2 was higher than the marginal product of your time spent on Problem 1. Even though the average product of your time spent on Problem 1 was higher than on Problem 2, you would have scored more points if you had spent a few seconds less on Problem 1 and a few seconds more on Problem 2. ◆

PRODUCTION IN THE LONG RUN

The examples discussed thus far have involved production in the short run, where at least one productive input cannot be varied. In the long run, by contrast, all factors of production are by definition variable. In the short run, with K held fixed in the production function $Q = F(K, L)$, we were able to describe the production function in a simple two-dimensional diagram. With both K and L variable, however, we now require three dimensions instead of two. And when there are more than two variable inputs, we require even more dimensions.

This creates a problem similar to the one we encountered in Chapter 3 when the consumer was faced with a choice between multiple products: we are not very adept at graphical representations involving three or more dimensions. For production with two variable inputs, the solution to this problem is similar to the one adopted in Chapter 3.

To illustrate, consider again the production function discussed earlier in this chapter:

$$Q = F(K, L) = 2KL \tag{9.4}$$

and suppose we want to describe all possible combinations of K and L that give rise to a particular level of output—say, $Q = 16$. To do this, we solve $Q = 2KL = 16$ for K in terms of L, which yields

$$K = \frac{8}{L} \tag{9.5}$$

The (L, K) pairs that satisfy Equation 9.5 are shown by the curve labelled $Q = 16$ in Figure 9.8. The (L, K) pairs that yield 32 and 64 units of output are shown in Figure 9.8 as the curves labelled $Q = 32$ and $Q = 64$, respectively. Such curves are called **isoquants,** and are defined formally as *all combinations of variable inputs that yield a given level of output.*[9]

isoquant the set of all input combinations that yield a given level of output.

Note the clear analogy between the isoquant and the indifference curve of consumer theory. Just as an indifference map provides a concise representation of a consumer's preferences, an *isoquant map* provides a concise representation of a production process.

On an indifference map, movements to the northeast correspond to increasing levels of satisfaction. Similar movements on an isoquant map correspond to increasing levels of output. A point on an indifference curve is preferred to any point that lies below that indifference curve, and less preferred than any point that lies above it. Likewise, any input bundle on an isoquant yields more output than any input bundle that lies below that isoquant, and less output than any input bundle that lies above it. Thus, bundle C in Figure 9.8 yields more output than bundle A, but less output than bundle D.

The only substantive respect in which the analogy between isoquant maps and indifference maps is incomplete is the significance of the labels attached to the two types of curves. From Chapter 3 recall that the actual numbers assigned

[9]'Iso' comes from the Greek word for 'same', which also appears, for example, in the meteorological term 'isobars', meaning lines of equal barometric pressure.

FIGURE 9.8
Part of an Isoquant Map for the Production Function $Q = 2KL$
An isoquant is the set of all (L, K) pairs that yield a given level of output. For example, each (L, K) pair on the curve labelled $Q = 32$ yields 32 units of output. The isoquant map describes the properties of a production process in much the same way as an indifference map describes a consumer's preferences.

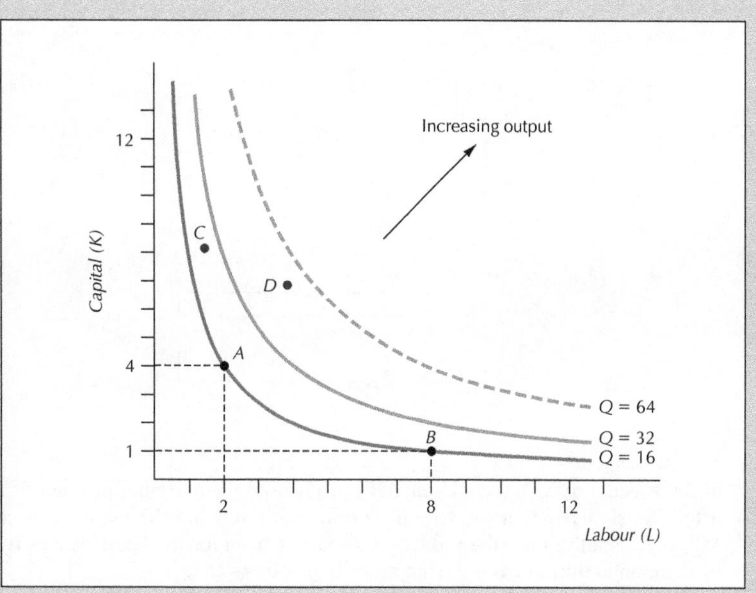

to each indifference curve were used to indicate only the relative rankings of the bundles on different indifference curves. The number we assign to an isoquant, by contrast, corresponds to the actual level of output we get from an input bundle along that isoquant. With indifference maps, we are free to relabel the indifference curves in any way that preserves the original ranking of bundles. But with isoquant maps, the labels are determined uniquely by the production function.

The Marginal Rate of Technical Substitution

Recall from our discussion of consumer theory in Chapter 3 that the marginal rate of substitution is the rate at which the consumer is willing to exchange one good for another along an indifference curve. The analogous concept in production theory is called the **marginal rate of technical substitution**, or **MRTS**. It is the rate at which one input can be exchanged for another without altering output. In Figure 9.9, for example, the MRTS at A is defined as the absolute value of the slope of the isoquant at A, $|\Delta K/\Delta L|$.

marginal rate of technical substitution (MRTS) the rate at which one input can be exchanged for another without altering the total level of output.

In consumer theory, we assumed that the marginal rate of substitution diminishes with downward movements along an indifference curve. For most production functions, the MRTS displays a similar property. Holding output constant, the less we have of one input, the more we must add of the other input to compensate for a one-unit reduction in the first input.

A simple but important relationship exists between the MRTS at any point and the marginal products of the respective inputs at that point. In a small neighbourhood of point A in Figure 9.9, suppose we reduce K by ΔK and augment L by an amount ΔL just sufficient to maintain the original level of output. If MP_{KA} denotes the marginal product of capital at A, then the reduction in output caused by the loss

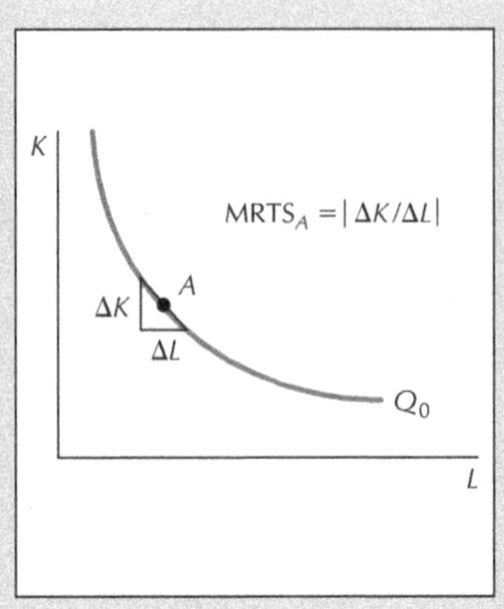

FIGURE 9.9
The Marginal Rate of Technical Substitution
The MRTS is the rate at which one input can be exchanged for another without altering total output. The MRTS at any point is the absolute value of the slope of the isoquant that passes through that point. If ΔK units of capital are removed at point A, and ΔL units of L are added, output will remain the same at Q_0 units.

of ΔK is equal to $MP_{KA}\Delta K$. Using MP_{LA} to denote the marginal product of L at A, it follows similarly that the gain in output resulting from the extra ΔL is equal to $MP_{LA}\Delta L$. Finally, since the reduction in output from having less K is exactly offset by the gain in output from having more L, it follows that

$$MP_{KA}\Delta K = MP_{LA}\Delta L \tag{9.6}$$

Cross-multiplying, we get

$$\frac{MP_{LA}}{MP_{KA}} = \frac{\Delta K}{\Delta L} \tag{9.7}$$

which says that the MRTS at A is simply the ratio of the marginal product of L to the marginal product of K. This relationship will have an important application in the next chapter, where we will take up the question of how to produce a given level of output at the lowest possible cost.

EXERCISE 9.5 Given a firm's current level of capital and labour inputs, the marginal product of labour for its production process is equal to 3 units of output. If the marginal rate of technical substitution between *K* and *L* is 9, what is the marginal product of capital?

In consumer theory, the shape of the indifference curve tells us how the consumer is willing to substitute one good for another. In production theory, an essentially similar story is told by the shape of the isoquant. Figure 9.10 illustrates the extreme cases of inputs that are perfect substitutes (*a*) and perfect complements (*b*). Figure 9.10(*a*) describes a production process in which cars and petrol are combined to produce trips. The input of petrol comes in two brands, Texaco and BP, which are perfect substitutes for one another. We can substitute 1 litre of BP petrol for 1 litre of Texaco petrol and still produce the same number of trips as before. The MRTS between Texaco and BP remains constant at 1 as we move downward along any isoquant.

Figure 9.10(*b*) describes a production process for typing letters using the two inputs of typewriters and typists. In this process, the two inputs are perfect complements. Here, inputs are most effectively combined in fixed proportions. Having more than one typewriter per typist doesn't augment production, nor does having more than one typist per typewriter.

FIGURE 9.10
Isoquant Maps for Perfect Substitutes and Perfect Complements
In panel (*a*), we get the same number of trips from a given total quantity of petrol, no matter how we mix the two brands. BP and Texaco are perfect substitutes in the production of car trips. In panel (*b*), typewriters and typists are perfect complements in the process of typing letters.

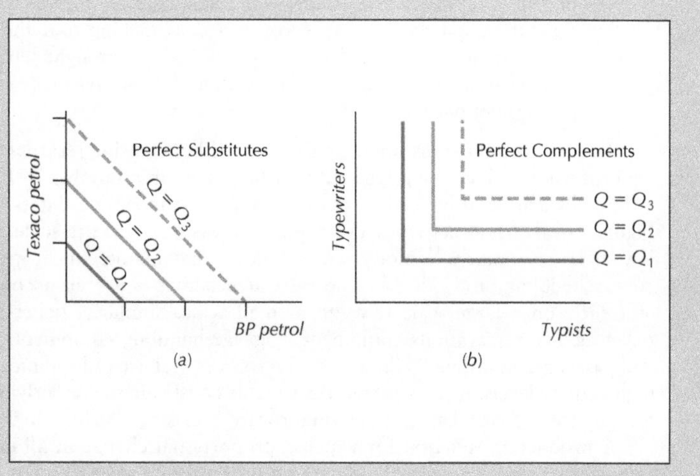

RETURNS TO SCALE

A question of central importance for the organization of industry is whether production takes place most efficiently at large scale rather than small scale (where 'large' and 'small' are defined relative to the scale of the relevant market). This question is important because the answer dictates whether an industry will end up being served by many small firms or only a few large ones.

The technical property of the production function used to describe the relationship between scale and efficiency is called *returns to scale.* The term tells us what happens to output when all inputs are increased by exactly the same proportion. Because returns to scale refer to a situation in which all inputs are variable, *the concept of returns to scale is an inherently long-run concept.*

A production function for which any given proportional change in all inputs leads to a more than proportional change in output is said to exhibit **increasing returns to scale.** For example, if we double all inputs in a production function with increasing returns to scale, we get more than twice as much output as before. As we will see in Chapters 12 and 13, such production functions generally give rise to conditions in which a small number of firms supply most of the relevant market.

increasing returns to scale the property of a production process whereby a proportional increase in every input yields a more than proportional increase in output.

Increasing returns to scale often result from the greater possibilities for specialization in large organizations. Adam Smith illustrated this point by describing the division of labour in a pin factory.[10]

> One man draws out the wire, another straightens it, a third cuts it, a fourth points it, a fifth grinds it at the top for receiving the head; to make the head requires two or three distinct operations. . . . I have seen a small manufactory . . . of this kind where only ten men were employed . . . [who] could, when they exerted themselves, make among them about twelve pounds of pins in a day. There are in a pound upwards of four thousand pins of middling size. Those ten persons, therefore, could make among them upwards of forty-eight thousand

[10]Adam Smith, *The Wealth of Nations,* New York: Everyman's Library, 1910 (1776), Book 1, p. 5.

pins in a day. Each person, therefore, making a tenth part of forty-eight thousand pins might be considered as making four thousand eight hundred pins in a day. But if they had all wrought separately and independently . . . they could not each of them have made twenty, perhaps not one pin in a day. . . .

The airline industry is often cited as one with increasing returns to scale. Industry professionals have long stressed that having a large number of flights helps an airline fill each flight by feeding passengers from its incoming flights to its outgoing flights. Local airport activities also exhibit increasing returns to scale. Because of the law of large numbers,[11] moreover, it follows that maintenance operations, flight crew scheduling, and other inventory-related activities are all accomplished more efficiently on a large scale than on a small scale. Similarly, ticket-counter space, ticket agents, reservations equipment, baggage-handling equipment, ground crews and passenger-boarding facilities are all resources that are utilized more efficiently at high activity levels. Increasing returns to scale constitute the underlying explanation for why the industry has been moving toward ever larger airlines in the last decade.

A production function for which a proportional change in all inputs causes output to change by the same proportion is said to exhibit **constant returns to scale.** In such cases, doubling all inputs results in a doubling of output. In industries in which production takes place under constant returns to scale, large size is neither an advantage nor a disadvantage.

constant returns to scale the property of a production process whereby a proportional increase in every input yields an equal proportional increase in output.

Finally, a production function for which a proportional change in all inputs causes a less than proportional change in output is said to exhibit **decreasing returns to scale.** Here large size is a handicap, and we do not expect to see large firms in an industry in which production takes place with decreasing returns to scale. As we will see in Chapter 11, the constant and decreasing returns cases often enable many sellers to coexist within the same narrowly defined markets.

decreasing returns to scale the property of a production process whereby a proportional increase in every input yields a less than proportional increase in output.

A production function need not exhibit the same degree of returns to scale over the entire range of output. On the contrary, there may be increasing returns to scale at low levels of output, followed by constant returns to scale at intermediate levels of output, followed finally by decreasing returns to scale at high levels of output.

ECONOMIC NATURALIST 9.2

Why do builders use prefabricated frames for roofs but not for walls?

When construction crews build a wood-frame house, they usually construct framing for the walls at the construction site. By contrast, they often buy prefabricated framing for the roof. Why this difference?

There are two key differences between wall framing and roof framing: (1) cutting the timber for roof framing involves many complicated angle cuts, whereas the right-angle cuts required for wall framing are much simpler; and (2) sections of roof framing of a given size are all alike, whereas wall sections differ according to the placement of window and door openings. Both properties of roof framing lead to substantial economies of scale in production. First, the angle cuts they require can be made much more rapidly if a frame or 'jig' can be built that guides the lumber past the saw-blade at just the proper angle. It is economical to set up such jigs in a factory where thousands of cuts are made each day, but it usually does not pay to use this method for the limited number of cuts required at any one construction site. Likewise, automated methods are easy to employ for roof framing by virtue of its uniformity. The idiosyncratic nature of wall framing, by contrast, militates against the use of automated methods.

[11]See Chapter 6.

Why do builders build custom frames for walls but use prefabricated frames for roofs?

So the fact that there are much greater economies of scale in the construction of roof framing than wall framing helps account for why wall framing is usually built at the construction site while roof framing is more often prefabricated. ■

Showing Returns to Scale on the Isoquant Map

A simple relationship exists between a production function's returns to scale and the spacing of its isoquants.[12] Consider the isoquant map in Figure 9.11. As we move outward into the isoquant map along the ray labelled *R*, each input grows by exactly the same proportion. The particular production function whose isoquant map is shown in the diagram exhibits increasing returns to scale in the region from *A* to *C*. Note, for example, that when we move from *A* to *B*, both inputs double while output goes up by a factor of 3; likewise, when we move from *B* to *C*, both inputs grow by 50 per cent while output grows by 100 per cent. In the region from *C* to *F*, this same production function exhibits constant returns to scale. Note, for example, that when we move from *D* to *E*, both inputs grow by 25 per cent and output also grows by 25 per cent. Finally, the production function whose isoquant map is shown in Figure 9.11 exhibits decreasing returns to scale in the region to the northeast of *F*. Thus, when we move from *F* to *G*, both inputs increase by 16.7 per cent while output grows by only 11.1 per cent.

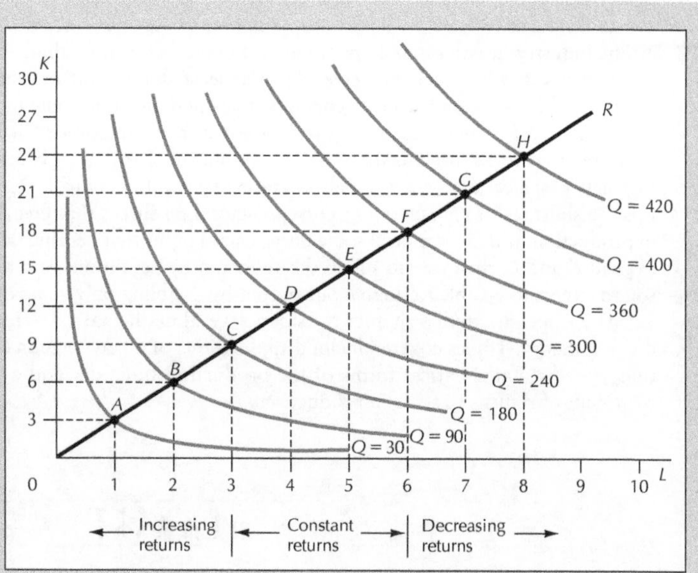

FIGURE 9.11
Returns to Scale Shown on the Isoquant Map
In the region from *A* to *C*, this production function has increasing returns to scale. Proportional increases in input yield more than proportional increases in output. In the region from *C* to *F*, there are constant returns to scale. Inputs and output grow by the same proportion in this region. In the region northeast of *F*, there are decreasing returns to scale. Proportional increases in both inputs yield less than proportional increases in output.

[12]The discussion in this section applies to *homothetic* production functions, an important class of production functions defined by the property that the slopes of all isoquants are constant at points along any ray.

The Distinction between Diminishing Returns and Decreasing Returns to Scale

It is important to bear in mind that decreasing returns to scale have nothing whatsoever to do with the law of diminishing returns. Decreasing returns to scale refer to what happens when *all* inputs are varied by a given proportion. The law of diminishing returns, by contrast, refers to the case in which one input varies while all others are held fixed. As an empirical generalization, it applies with equal force to production functions having increasing, constant or decreasing returns to scale.

To illustrate the difference, consider again an airline company. If the company increases the number of pilots it employs while leaving unchanged everything else there will clearly come a point of diminishing returns to pilots. This does not, in any way, rule out increasing returns to scale. If we increase the number of pilots *and* the number of planes, ticket agents etc., then there may be increasing returns to scale.

The Logical Puzzle of Decreasing Returns to Scale

If the production function $Q = F(K, L)$ is a complete description of the corresponding production process, it is difficult to see how any production function could ever exhibit decreasing returns to scale in practice. The difficulty is that we ought to be able to duplicate the process used to produce any given level of output, and thereby achieve constant returns to scale. To illustrate, suppose first that $Q_0 = F(K_0, L_0)$. If we now want to produce $2Q_0$ units of output, we can always do so by again doing what we did the first time—namely, by again combining K_0 and L_0 to get Q_0 and adding that to the Q_0 we already have. Similarly, we can get $3Q_0$ by carrying out $F(K_0, L_0)$ three times in succession. Simply by carrying out the process again and again, we can get output to grow in the same proportion as inputs, which means constant returns to scale. And for reasons similar to the ones discussed above for the airline industry, it will often be possible to do even better than that.

In cases in which it is not possible to at least double our output by doubling both K and L, we seem forced to conclude that there must be some important input besides K and L that we are failing to increase at the same time. This input is variously referred to as ‘organization’ or ‘communication’, the idea being that when a firm gets past a certain size, it somehow starts to get out of control. Others claim that it is the shortage of managerial or entrepreneurial resources that creates bottlenecks in production. If there is indeed some unmeasured input that is being held fixed as we expand K and L, then we are still in the short run by definition. And there is no reason to expect to be able to double our output by doubling only *some* of our inputs.

The Appendix to this chapter considers several mathematical extensions of production theory. Topics covered include applications of the average-marginal distinction, specific mathematical forms of the production function, and a mathematical treatment of returns to scale in production.

SUMMARY

- Production is any activity that creates current or future utility. A production function summarizes the relationship between inputs and outputs. The short run is defined as that period during which at least some inputs are fixed. In the two-input case, it is the period during which one input is fixed, the other variable.
- The marginal product of a variable input is defined as the change in output brought forth by an additional unit of the variable input, all other inputs held fixed. The law of diminishing returns says that beyond some point the marginal product declines with additional units of the variable input.

- The average product of a variable input is the ratio of total output to the quantity of the variable input. Whenever marginal product lies above average product, the average product will increase with increases in the variable input. Conversely, when marginal product lies below average product, average product will decline with increases in the variable input.
- An important practical problem is that of how to allocate an input across two productive activities to generate the maximum possible output. In general, two types of solutions are possible. A corner solution occurs when the marginal product of the input is always higher in one activity than in the other. In that case, the best thing to do is to concentrate all the input in the activity where it is more productive.
- An interior solution occurs whenever the marginal product of the variable input, when all of it is placed in one activity, is lower than the marginal product of the first unit of the input in the other activity. In this case, the output-maximizing rule is to distribute the input across the two activities in such a way that its marginal product is the same in both. Even experienced decision makers often violate this simple rule. The pitfall to be on guard against is the tendency to equate not marginal but average products in the two activities.
- The long run is defined as the period required for all inputs to be variable. The actual length of time that corresponds to the short and long runs will differ markedly in different cases. In the two-input case, all of the relevant information about production in the long run can be summarized graphically by the isoquant map. The marginal rate of technical substitution is defined as the rate at which one input can be substituted for another without altering the level of output. The MRTS at any point is simply the absolute value of the slope of the isoquant at that point. For most production functions, the MRTS will diminish as we move downward to the right along an isoquant.
- A production function is said to exhibit constant returns to scale if a given proportional increase in all inputs produces the same proportional increase in output, decreasing returns to scale if a given proportional increase in all inputs results in a smaller proportional increase in output, and increasing returns to scale if a given proportional increase in all inputs causes a greater proportional increase in output. Production functions with increasing returns to scale are also said to exhibit economies of scale. Returns to scale constitute a critically important factor in determining the structure of industrial organization.

QUESTIONS FOR REVIEW

1. List three examples of production that a non-economist might not ordinarily think of as production.
2. Give an example of production in which the short run lasts at least 1 year.
3. Why should a person in charge of hiring productive inputs care more about marginal products than about average products?
4. A wag once remarked that when a certain government official moved from New York to California, the average IQ level in both states went up. Interpret this remark in the context of the average-marginal relationships discussed in the chapter.
5. How is an isoquant map like an indifference map? In what important respect do the two constructs differ?
6. Distinguish between diminishing returns to a variable input and decreasing returns to scale.
7. *True or false*: If the marginal product is decreasing, then the average product must also be decreasing. Explain.
8. A factory adds a worker and subsequently discovers that the average product of its workers has risen. *True or false*: The marginal product of the new worker is less than the average product of the plant's workers before the new employee's arrival.
9. Currently, 2 units of labour and 1 unit of capital produce 1 unit of output. If you double both the inputs (4 units of labour and 2 units of capital), what can you conclude about the output produced under constant returns to scale? Decreasing returns to scale? Increasing returns to scale?

PROBLEMS

1. Graph the short-run total product curves for each of the following production functions if K is fixed at $K_0 = 4$.

   a. $Q = F(K, L) = 2K + 3L$.
   b. $Q = F(K, L) = K^2L^2$.

2. Do the two production functions in Problem 1 obey the law of diminishing returns?

3. Suppose the marginal product of labour is currently equal to its average product. If you were one of ten new workers the firm was about to hire, would you prefer to be paid the value of your average product or the value of your marginal product? Would it be in the interests of an employer to pay you the value of your average product?

4. The following table provides partial information on total product, average product, and marginal product for a production function. Using the relationships between these properties, fill in the missing cells.

Labour	Total product	Average product	Marginal product
0		0	
1	180		
2			140
3	420		
4		120	

5. The London Metropolitan Police Service (the Met) must decide how to allocate police officers between East London and City Centre. Measured in arrests per hour, the average product, total product and marginal product in each of these two areas are given in the table below. Currently the Met allocates 200 police officers to City Centre and 300 to East London. If police can be redeployed only in groups of 100, how, if at all, should the Met reallocate its officers to achieve the maximum number of arrests per hour?

Number of police	East London			City Centre		
	AP	TP	MP	AP	TP	MP
0	0	0		0	0	
100	40	40	40	45	45	45
200	40	80	40	40	80	35
300	40	120	40	35	105	25
400	40	160	40	30	120	15
500	40	200	40	25	125	5

6. Suppose a crime wave hits East London, so that the marginal product and average product of police officers are now 60 arrests per hour for any number of police officers. What is the optimal allocation of 500 police officers between the two areas now?

7. A firm's short-run production function is given by

$$Q = \tfrac{1}{2}L^2 \qquad \text{for } 0 \leq L \leq 2$$

and

$$Q = 3L - \tfrac{1}{4}L^2 \qquad \text{for } 2 < L \leq 7$$

a. Sketch the production function.
b. Find the maximum attainable production. How much labour is used at that level?
c. Identify the ranges of L utilization over which the marginal product of labour is increasing and decreasing.
d. Identify the range over which the marginal product of labour is negative.

8. Each problem in an exam is worth 20 points. Suppose that from the last seconds you devoted to Problem 10 in the exam you earned 2 extra points, while from the last seconds

devoted to Problem 8 you earned 4 extra points. The total number of points you earned on these two problems were 8 and 6, respectively, and the total time you spent on each was the same. How—if at all—should you have reallocated your time between them?

9. Suppose capital is fixed at 4 units in the production function $Q = KL$. Draw the total, marginal, and average product curves for the labour input.

10. Identify the regions of increasing, constant and decreasing returns to scale on the isoquant map shown.

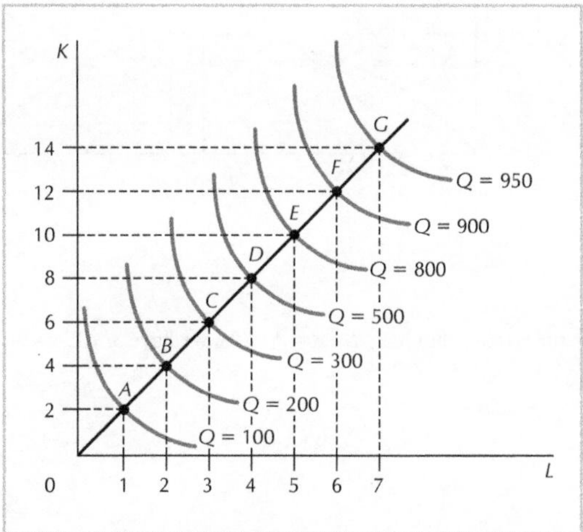

11. When Paul Samuelson switched from physics to economics, Robert Solow is said to have remarked that the average IQ in both disciplines went up. A bystander responded that Solow's claim must be wrong because it implies that the average IQ for academia as a whole (which is a weighted average of the average IQ levels for each discipline) must also have gone up as a result of the switch, which is clearly impossible. Was the bystander right? Explain.

ANSWERS TO IN-CHAPTER EXERCISES

9.1. For $K = 4$, $Q = \sqrt{4}\sqrt{L} = 2\sqrt{L}$

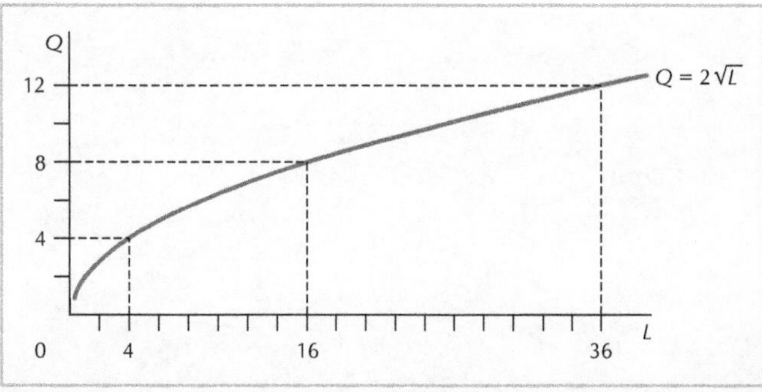

9.2. The slope of the total product curve in Figure 9.3(*a*) is 2 for all values of *L*. So $MP_{L=3} = 2$.

9.3. The slope of the ray to any point on the total product curve is 2, and so $AP_{L=3} = 2$. When the total product curve is a ray, as here, $AP_L = MP_L$ is constant for all values of *L*.

9.4. Because $AP_{L=10} < MP_{L=10}$, AP will rise when *L* increases, and so $AP_{L=10.1} > AP_{L=10}$.

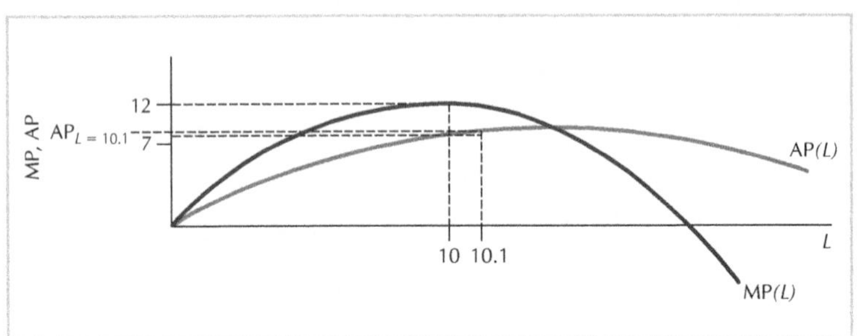

9.5. From the relationship MP_L/MP_K = MRTS, we have $3/MP_K = 9$, which yields $MP_K = \frac{1}{3}$.

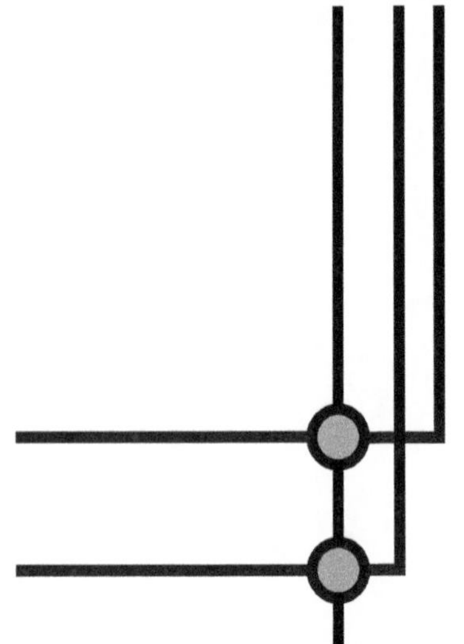

MATHEMATICAL EXTENSIONS OF PRODUCTION THEORY

APPLICATION: THE AVERAGE-MARGINAL DISTINCTION

Suppose that when your tennis opponent comes to the net, your best response is either to lob (hit the ball over his head) or to pass (hit the ball out of reach on either side). Each type of shot is more effective if it catches your opponent by surprise. Suppose someone who lobs all the time will win a given point only 10 per cent of the time with a lob, but that someone who virtually never lobs wins the point on 90 per cent of the rare occasions when he does lob. Similarly, suppose someone who tries passing shots all the time wins any given point only 30 per cent of the time with a passing shot, but someone who virtually never tries to pass wins 40 per cent of the time when he does try. Suppose, finally, that the rate at which each type of shot becomes less effective with use declines linearly with the proportion of times a player uses it. What is the best proportion of lobs and passing shots to use when your opponent comes to the net?[1]

The payoffs from the two types of shots are summarized graphically in Figure A.9.1. Here, the 'production' problem is to produce the greatest possible percentage of winning shots when your opponent comes to the net. $F(L)$ tells you

[1]This example was suggested by Harvard psychologists Richard Herrnstein and James Mazur, in 'Making Up our Minds: A New Model of Economic Behavior', *The Sciences*, November/December 1987: 40–47.

FIGURE A.9.1
Effectiveness versus Use: Lobs and Passing Shots

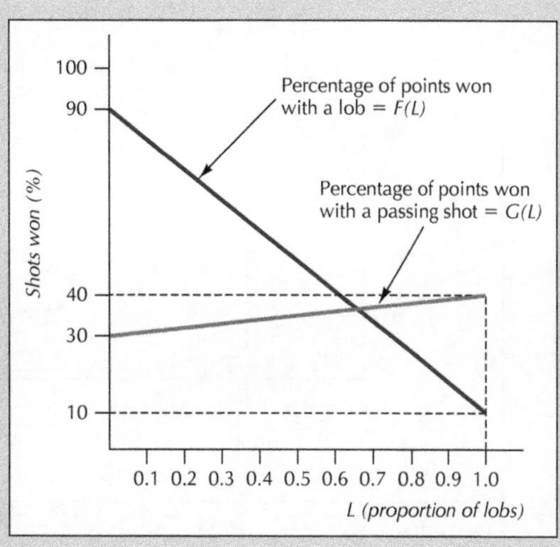

the percentage of points you will win with a lob as a function of the proportion of times you lob (L). $F(L)$ is thus, in effect, the average product of L. $G(L)$ tells you the percentage of points you will win with a passing shot, again as a function of the proportion of times you lob. The negative slope of $F(L)$ reflects the fact that lobs become less effective the more you use them. Similarly, the positive slope of $G(L)$ says that passing shots become more effective the more you lob. Your problem is to choose L^*, the best proportion of times to lob.

To find the optimal value of L, we must first discover how the percentage of total points won, denoted P, varies with L. For any value of L, P is simply a weighted average of the percentages won with each type of shot. The weight used for each type of shot is simply the proportion of times it is used. Noting that $(1 - L)$ is the proportion of passing shots when L is the proportion of lobs, we have

$$P = LF(L) + (1 - L)G(L) \tag{A.9.1}$$

The expression $LF(L)$ is the percentage of total points won on lobs. $(1 - L)G(L)$, similarly, is the percentage of total points won on passing shots. From Figure A.9.1, we see that the algebraic formulas for $F(L)$ and $G(L)$ are given by $F(L) = 90 - 80L$ and $G(L) = 30 + 10L$. Substituting these relationships into Equation A.9.1 gives

$$P = 30 + 70L - 90L^2 \tag{A.9.2}$$

which is plotted in Figure A.9.2. The value of L that maximizes P turns out to be $L^* = 0.389$, and the corresponding value of P is 43.61 per cent.[2]

Note in Figure A.9.3 that at the optimal value of L, the likelihood of winning with a lob is almost twice as high (58.9 per cent) as that of winning with a passing shot (33.9 per cent). Many people seem to find this state of affairs extremely uncomfortable—so much so that they refuse to have anything to do with it. In extensive experimental studies, Harvard psychologists Richard Herrnstein and James Mazur found that people tend to divide their shots not to maximize their

[2]The calculus-trained student can find L^* without having to plot P as a function of L simply by solving

$$dP/dL = 70 - 180L = 0$$

which yields $L^* = 7/18 = 0.389$, which, upon substitution into Equation A.9.2, yields $P = 43.61$.

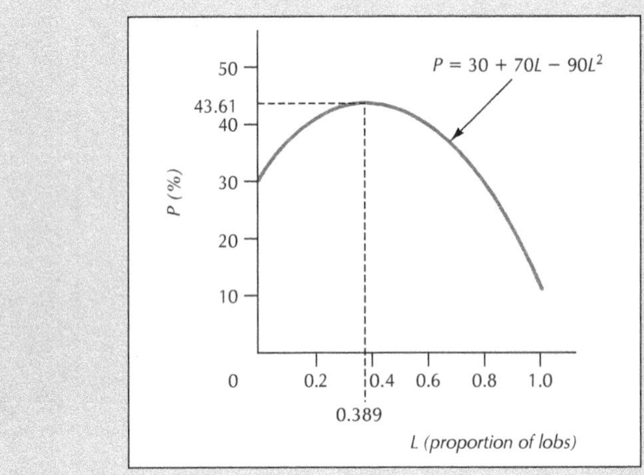

FIGURE A.9.2 The Optimal Proportion of Lobs

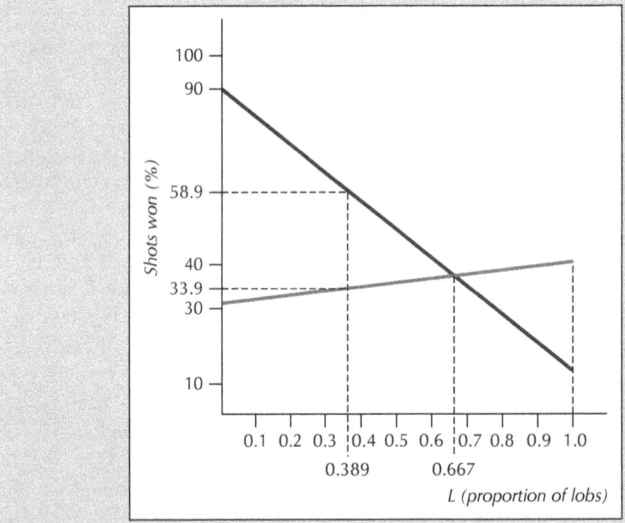

FIGURE A.9.3 At the Optimizing Point, the Likelihood of Winning with a Lob is Much Greater Than of Winning with a Passing Shot

overall chances of winning, but to equate the *average product* of each type. Note in Figure A.9.3 that this occurs when $L = 2/3$, at which point the percentage of points won with either shot is 36.7. At this value of L, however, the *marginal product* of a passing shot will be much higher than for a lob, because it will strongly increase the effectiveness of all your *other* lobs. (Of course, an extra passing shot will also reduce the effectiveness of your other passing shots, but by a much smaller margin.)

The situation here is analogous to the allocation example involving the fishing boats mentioned in Chapter 9. There is no more reason to want the average return to each tennis shot to be the same than there is to want the average product on each end of the lake to be the same. And yet the tendency to equate average rather than marginal products is a very common pitfall, one that even experienced maximizers have to be on guard against. Let us consider one final example.

EXAMPLE A 9.1 Suppose that there are two supermarkets in town. You are the manager of one of them. Each Monday morning you must decide prices for the following week. You can either price aggressively, by offering discounts, or non-aggressively. An analyst tells you that in weeks you price aggressively you make an average profit of €20,000. In weeks you price non-aggressively you make an average profit of €30,000. *True or false*: you should price non-aggressively each week?

If you answered 'true', you have not been paying attention. We need to know how often the supermarket has been pricing aggressively, and we need to know how a change in this proportion would affect profitability. Pricing aggressively less often may lower the profitability, not only of the additional weeks where non-aggressive pricing is used, but all other weeks where it is used. ◆

ISOQUANT MAPS AND THE PRODUCTION MOUNTAIN

Previously, we derived isoquants algebraically by holding output constant in the production function and then solving for K in terms of L. But there is also a geometric technique for deriving the isoquant map, one that is similar to the derivation of the indifference map discussed in the Appendix to Chapter 3. This approach begins with a three-dimensional graph of the production function, perhaps something like the one shown in Figure A.9.4. It resembles the sloping surface of a mountain. The value on the Q axis measures the height of the mountain, or total output, which continues to increase as we employ more of K or L.

Suppose in Figure A.9.4 we were to fix output at some constant amount, say, Q_0. That is, suppose we cut the production mountain with a plane parallel to the KL plane, Q_0 units above it. The line labelled AB in Figure A.9.4 represents the intersection of that plane and the surface of the production mountain. All the input bundles that lie on AB yield an output level of Q_0. If we then project line AB downward onto the KL plane, we get the Q_0 isoquant shown in Figure A.9.5. As defined in Chapter 9, an isoquant is a locus of K, L pairs that produce the same level of output.

FIGURE A.9.4 The Production Mountain

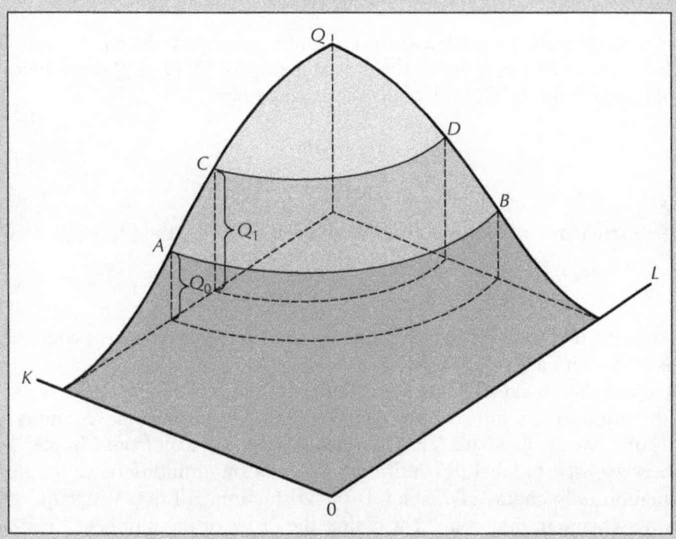

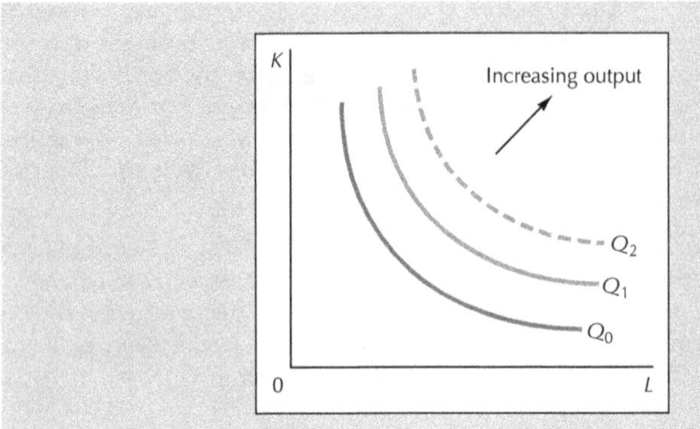

FIGURE A.9.5 The Isoquant Map Derived from the Production Mountain

Suppose we then intersect the production mountain with another plane, this time Q_1 units above the KL plane. In Figure A.9.4, the second plane intersects the production mountain along the line labelled CD. It represents all input bundles that yield Q_1. Projecting CD down onto the KL plane, we thus get the isoquant labelled Q_1 in Figure A.9.5. In like fashion, we can generate an entire isoquant map corresponding to the production function $Q = F(K, L)$.

SOME EXAMPLES OF PRODUCTION FUNCTIONS

In this section we will examine two of the many different production functions that are commonly used in economic analysis.

The Cobb-Douglas Production Function

Perhaps the most widely used production function of all is the Cobb-Douglas, which in the two-input case takes the form

$$Q = mK^{\alpha}L^{\beta} \tag{A.9.3}$$

where α and β are numbers between zero and 1, and m can be any positive number.

To generate an equation for the Q_0 isoquant, we fix Q at Q_0 and then solve for K in terms of L. In the Cobb-Douglas case, this yields

$$K = \left(\frac{m}{Q_0}\right)^{-1/\alpha}(L)^{-\beta/\alpha} \tag{A.9.4}$$

For the particular Cobb-Douglas function $Q = K^{1/2}L^{1/2}$, the Q_0 isoquant will be

$$K = \frac{Q_0^2}{L} \tag{A.9.5}$$

A portion of the isoquant map for this particular Cobb-Douglas production function is shown in Figure A.9.6.

The number assigned to each particular isoquant in Figure A.9.6 is exactly the level of output to which it corresponds. For example, when we have 2 units of K and 2 units of L, we get $Q = \sqrt{2}\sqrt{2} = 2$ units of output. Recall from Chapter 3 that the numbers we used to label the indifference curves on an indifference map conveyed information only about *relative* levels of satisfaction. All that was required of our indexing scheme in that context was that the *order* of the numbers we assigned to the indifference curves reflects the proper ranking of the corresponding satisfaction

FIGURE A.9.6
Isoquant Map for the Cobb-Douglas Production Function $Q = K^{1/2} L^{1/2}$

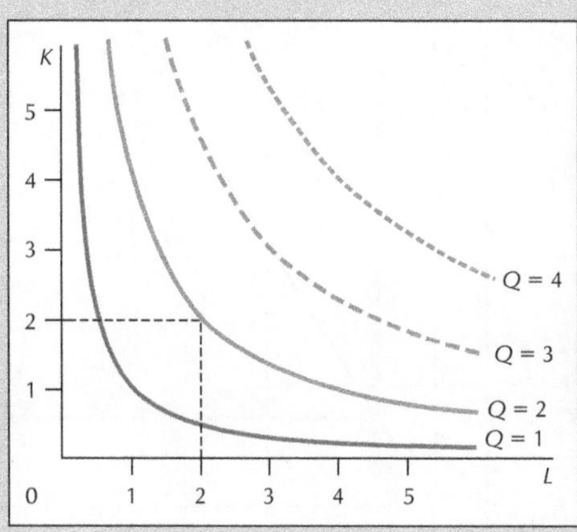

levels. With isoquants, the situation is altogether different. We have, in effect, no choice about what labels to assign to them.

Calculus-trained students can easily verify the following expressions for the marginal products of labour and capital in the Cobb-Douglas case:

$$MP_K = \frac{\partial Q}{\partial K} = \alpha m K^{\alpha-1} L^{\beta} \qquad \text{(A.9.6)}$$

and

$$MP_L = \frac{\partial Q}{\partial L} = \beta m K^{\alpha-1} L^{\beta-1} \qquad \text{(A.9.7)}$$

The Leontief, or Fixed-Proportions, Production Function

The simplest among all production functions that are widely used is the *Leontief*, named for the Nobel laureate Wassily Leontief, who devised it. For the two-input case, it is given by

$$Q = \min\,(aK, bL) \qquad \text{(A.9.8)}$$

If you are unfamiliar with this curious functional form, its interpretation is simply that Q is equal to either aK or bL, whichever is smaller. Suppose, for example, that $a = 2$, $b = 3$, $K = 4$, and $L = 3$. Then, $Q = \min(2 \times 4, 3 \times 3) = \min\,(8, 9) = 8$. The isoquant map for $Q = \min\,(2K, 3L)$ is shown in Figure A.9.7.

To see why the Leontief is also called the fixed-proportions production function, note first in Figure A.9.7 that if we start with 3 units of K and 2 units of L, we get 6 units of output. If we then add more L—so that we have, say, 3 units of L instead of 2—we still get only $Q = \min\,(2 \times 3, 3 \times 3) = \min\,(6, 9) = 6$ units of output. By the same token, adding more K when we are at $K = 3$ and $L = 2$ will not lead to any additional output. In the Leontief case, K and L are used most effectively when $aK = bL$—in the example at hand, when $2K = 3L$. In Figure A.9.7, the locus of points for which $2K = 3L$ is shown as the ray $K = (\frac{3}{2})L$. It is along this ray that the cusps of all the right-angled isoquants of this Leontief production function will lie.

Recall from Chapter 3 that in the case of perfect complements, the indifference curves had the same right-angled shape as the isoquants for the Leontief production

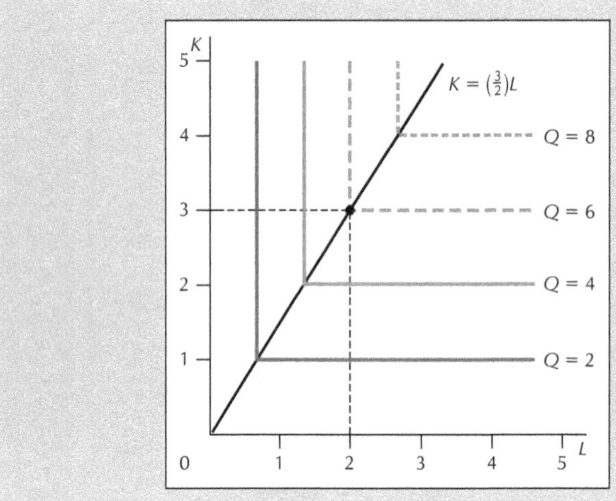

FIGURE A.9.7
Isoquant Map for the Leontief Production Function $Q = \min(2K, 3L)$

function. This meant that the MRS was infinite on the vertical arm of the indifference curve, zero on the horizontal arm, and undefined at the cusp. For exactly parallel reasons, the MRTS in the Leontief case will be infinite on the vertical arm of the isoquant, zero on the horizontal, and undefined at the cusp.

A MATHEMATICAL DEFINITION OF RETURNS TO SCALE

Mathematically, to increase all inputs in the same proportion means simply to multiply all inputs by the same number $c > 1$. By way of illustration, consider the production function we discussed in Chapter 9, $Q = F(K, L) = 2KL$. For this particular function, when we multiply each input by c we get

$$F(cK, cL) = 2(cK)(cL) = c^2 2KL = c^2 F(K, L) \tag{A.9.9}$$

The result of multiplying each input by c in this production function is thus to multiply the original output level by c^2. Output thus grows more than in proportion to input growth in this case [with proportional growth, we would have had output equal to $cF(K, L)$], so this production function has increasing returns to scale. Thus, for example, if $c = 2$ (a doubling of each input), we get $F(2K, 2L) = 2(2K)(2L) = 4(2KL)$, a quadrupling of output.

Drawing on these observations, the definitions of our three cases may be summarized as follows:

$$\text{Increasing returns: } F(cK, cL) > cF(K, L) \tag{A.9.10}$$

$$\text{Constant returns: } F(cK, cL) = cF(K, L) \tag{A.9.11}$$

and

$$\text{Decreasing returns: } F(cK, cL) < cF(K, L) \tag{A.9.12}$$

The following two exercises will help cement your ability to apply these definitions to specific examples.

EXERCISE A.9.1 Does the production function $Q = \sqrt{K}\sqrt{L}$ have increasing, constant or decreasing returns to scale?

EXERCISE A.9.2 Does the production function $Q = K^{1/3}L^{1/3}$ have increasing, constant or decreasing returns to scale?

In the case of the Cobb-Douglas production function, $Q = mK^{\alpha}L^{\beta}$ Equations A.9.10 to A.9.12 imply a simple relationship between the parameters α and β and the degree of returns to scale. Specifically, if $\alpha + \beta > 1$, there are increasing returns to scale; $\alpha + \beta = 1$ means constant returns to scale; and $\alpha + \beta < 1$ means decreasing returns to scale. To illustrate for the constant returns case, suppose $Q = F(K, L) = mK^{\alpha}L^{\beta}$, with $\alpha + \beta = 1$. Then we have

$$F(cK, cL) = m(cK)^{\alpha}(cL)^{\beta} \quad \text{(A.9.13)}$$

which reduces to

$$c^{(\alpha + \beta)}\, mK^{\alpha}L^{\beta} = cmK^{\alpha}L^{\beta} = cF(K, L) \quad \text{(A.9.14)}$$

which, by Equation A.9.11, is the defining characteristic of constant returns to scale.

PROBLEMS

*1. Do the following production functions have increasing, decreasing or constant returns to scale? Which ones fail to satisfy the law of diminishing returns?

a. $Q = 4K^{1/2}Lb^{1/2}$
b. $Q = aK^2 + bL^2$
c. $Q = \min(aK, bL)$
d. $Q = 4K + 2L$
e. $Q = K^{0.5}\,L^{0.6}$
f. $Q = K_1^{0.3}K_2^{0.3}L^{0.3}$

*2. What is the marginal product of labour in the production function $Q = 2K^{1/3}L^{1/3}$ if K is fixed at 27?

3. Can the Cobb-Douglas production function be used to portray a production process in which returns to scale are increasing at low output levels and are constant or decreasing at high output levels?

4. Suppose that a firm with the production function

$$Q = \min(2K, 3L)$$

is currently using 6 units of capital and 5 units of labour. What are the marginal products of K and L in this case?

5. The average profit of a supermarket that prices aggressively is $8 + 12r$, where r is the fraction of weeks they price aggressively. Their average profit in weeks they price non-aggressively is $10 - 8r$. What is their optimal fraction of weeks they should price aggressively? At this value of r, what is the average profit in weeks they price aggressively? And non-aggressively? (This problem and the next one are similar to the tennis example considered earlier.)

6. Suppose you are the manager of a supermarket trying to compete against a new entrant. The entrant's profits are shown below. If your goal is to minimize the entrant's profit, what is the optimal proportion of weeks you should price aggressively? At this proportion, what are the entrant's profits if you price aggressively, and non-aggressively?

*This problem is most easily solved using the calculus definition of marginal product.

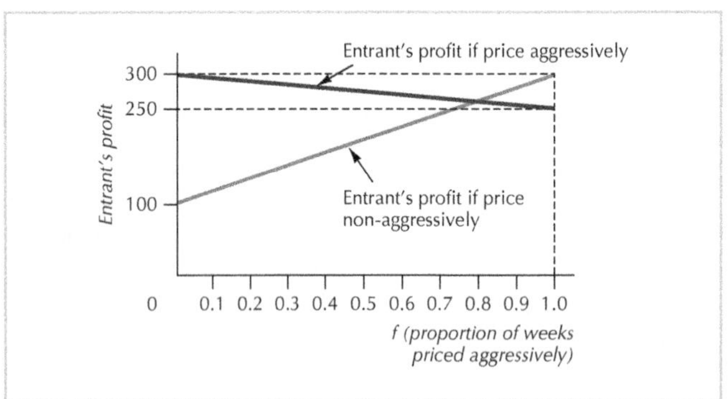

ANSWERS TO IN-APPENDIX EXERCISES

A.9.1. $F(K,L) = \sqrt{K}\sqrt{L}$, so $F(cK,cL) = \sqrt{cK}\sqrt{cL} = \sqrt{c^2}\sqrt{K}\sqrt{L} = cF(K,L)$, and so it has constant returns to scale.

A.9.2. $F(K, L) = K^{1/3} L^{1/3}$, so $F(cK, cL) = (cK)^{1/3}(cL)^{1/3} = c^{2/3}K^{1/3}L^{1/3} = c^{2/3}F(K, L) < cF(K, L)$, and so it has decreasing returns to scale.

CHAPTER 10

COSTS

Just after finishing college, one of us (Robert) was a high school maths and science teacher in Sanischare, a small village in eastern Nepal. During the two years spent there, one of the country's few roads was in the process of being built through Sanischare. Once the right-of-way was cleared and the culverts and bridges laid in, the next step was to spread gravel over the roadbed. As at almost every other stage of the process, the methods employed at this step were a page torn from another century. The Nepalese workmen squatted by the side of the road in the blazing sun, tapping away at large rocks with their hammers. In a 12-hour day, each worker would produce a small mound of gravel, not enough to cover even one running foot of roadbed. But there were a lot of people working, and eventually the job was done.

© Martial Colomb/Getty Images/DAL

In Europe, of course, we do not hire people to hammer rocks into gravel by hand. Instead, we have huge machines that pulverize several tons of rock each minute. The reason for this difference may seem obvious: Nepal, being a very poor country, simply could not afford the expensive equipment used in industrialized nations. But this explanation is wrong. As we will see, it still would have made sense for Nepal to make gravel with manual labour even if it had had vast surplus revenues in its national treasury, because labour is very cheap relative to capital equipment there.

CHAPTER PREVIEW

In this chapter our goal is to translate the theory of production developed in Chapter 9 into a coherent theory of costs. In Chapter 9 we established the relationship between the quantities of inputs employed and the corresponding level of output. Here, we will forge the link between the quantity of output produced and the cost of producing it.

Our first step will be to tackle the question of how costs vary with output in the short run. This question turns out to be more involved than it sounds, for there are seven different types of costs to keep track of—total cost, variable cost, fixed cost, marginal cost, average total cost, average variable cost and average fixed cost. This array sounds bewildering at first, but the links between the different cost concepts are actually clear and simple. And each turns out to be important for the study of firm behaviour, our principal concern in the chapters to follow.

Of even greater importance for the structure and conduct of industry is the question of how costs vary with output in the long run. Here, we will begin with the question of how to produce a given level of output—say, a mile of road—at the lowest possible cost. A given quantity can be produced many ways: we need to find the cheapest way, the most appropriate method for existing factor prices. The answer to this question enables us to explore how costs are related to returns to scale in production.

COSTS IN THE SHORT RUN

To see how costs vary with output in the short run, it is convenient to begin with a simple production example of the sort we discussed in Chapter 9. Suppose Kelly's Cleaners washes bags of laundry using labour (L) and capital (K). Labour is purchased in the open market at a wage rate w = €10/person-hr.[1] Capital is fixed in the short run. The relationship between the variable input and the total number of bags washed per hour is summarized in Table 10.1. Note that output initially grows at an increasing rate with additional units of the variable input (as L grows from 0 to 4 units), then grows at a diminishing rate (as L grows from 4 to 8 units).

The total cost of producing the various levels of output is simply the cost of all the factors of production employed. If Kelly owns his own capital, its implicit rental value is an opportunity cost, the money Kelly could have earned if he had sold his capital and invested the proceeds in, say, a government bond (see Chapter 1). Suppose Kelly's capital is fixed at 120 machine-hr/hr, the rental value of each of which is r = €0.25/machine-hr,[2] for a total capital rental of €30/hr. This cost is **fixed cost** (FC), which means that it does not vary in the short run as the level of output varies. More generally, if K_0 denotes the amount of capital and r is its rental price per unit, we have

fixed cost (FC) cost that does not vary with the level of output in the short run (the cost of all fixed factors of production).

$$FC = rK_0 \tag{10.1}$$

[1]A person-hour is one person working for 1 hour. In Chapter 14 we will consider how input prices are determined. For the present, we simply take them as given.

[2]A machine-hour is one machine working for 1 hour. To say that Kelly's capital is fixed at 120 machine-hr/hr means that he has 120 machines that can operate simultaneously.

TABLE 10.1
The Short-Run Production Function for Kelly's Cleaners

Quantity of labour (person-hr/hr)	Quantity of output (bags/hr)
0	0
1	4
2	14
3	27
4	43
5	58
6	72
7	81
8	86

The entries in each row of the right column tell the quantity of output produced by the quantity of variable input in the corresponding row of the left column. This production function initially exhibits increasing, then diminishing, returns to the variable input.

Other examples of fixed cost might include property taxes, insurance payments, interest on loans and other payments to which the firm is committed in the short run and which do not vary as the level of output varies. Business managers often refer to fixed costs as *overhead costs.*

Variable cost (VC) is defined as the total cost of the variable factor of production at each level of output.[3] To calculate VC for any given level of output in this example, we simply multiply the amount of labour needed to produce that level of output by the hourly wage rate. Thus, the variable cost of 27 bags/hr is (€10/person-hr) (3 person-hr/hr) = €30/hr. More generally, if L_1 is the quantity of labour required to produce an output level of Q_1 and w is the hourly wage rate, we have

variable cost (VC) cost that varies with the level of output in the short run (the cost of all variable factors of production).

$$\mathrm{VC}_{Q_1} = wL_1 \tag{10.2}$$

Note the explicit dependence of VC on output in the notation on the left-hand side of Equation 10.2, which is lacking in Equation 10.1. This is to emphasize that variable cost depends on the output level produced, whereas fixed cost does not.

Total cost (TC) is the sum of FC and VC. If Kelly wishes to wash 43 bags/hr, the total cost of doing so will be €30/hr + (€10/person-hr) (4 person-hr/hr) = €70/hr. More generally, the expression for total cost of producing an output level of Q_1 is written

total cost (TC) all costs of production: the sum of variable cost and fixed cost.

$$\mathrm{TC}_{Q_1} = \mathrm{FC} + \mathrm{VC}_{Q_1} = rK_0 + wL_1 \tag{10.3}$$

Table 10.2 shows fixed, variable and total cost for corresponding output levels for the production function given in Table 10.1. The relationships among the various cost categories are most clearly seen by displaying the information graphically, not in tabular form. The short-run production function from Table 10.1 is plotted in Figure 10.1. Recall from Chapter 9 that the initial region of upward curvature ($0 \leq L \leq 4$) of the production function corresponds to increasing returns to the variable input. Beyond the point $L = 4$, the production function exhibits diminishing returns to the variable input.

[3]In production processes with more than one variable input, variable cost refers to the cost of *all* such inputs.

TABLE 10.2
Outputs and Costs

The fixed cost of capital is €30/hr, and the cost per unit of the variable factor (L) is €10/hr. Total cost is calculated as the sum of fixed cost and variable cost.

Q	FC	VC	TC
0	30	0	30
4	30	10	40
14	30	20	50
27	30	30	60
43	30	40	70
58	30	50	80
72	30	60	90
81	30	70	100
86	30	80	110

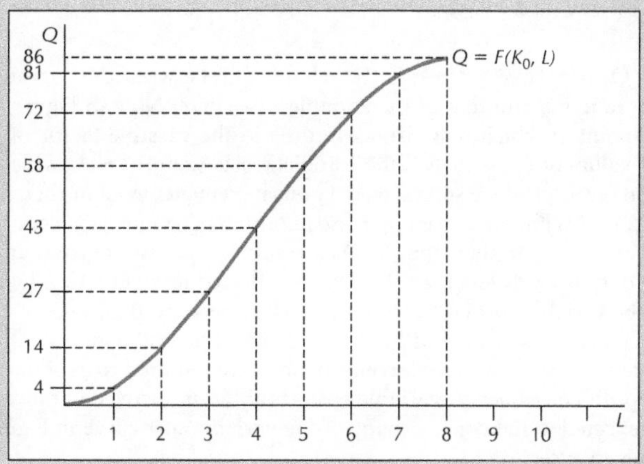

FIGURE 10.1
Short-Run Production Function
This production process shows increasing returns to the variable input up to $L = 4$, and diminishing returns thereafter.

Graphing the Total, Variable and Fixed Cost Curves

Not surprisingly, the shape of the variable cost curve is systematically related to the shape of the short-run production function. The connection arises because the production function tells us how much labour we need to produce a given level of output, and this quantity of labour, when multiplied by the wage rate, gives us variable cost. Suppose, for example, we want to plot the variable cost of producing 58 units of output. (See Figures 10.1, 10.2.) We first note from the production function shown in Figure 10.1 that 58 units of output require 5 units of labour, which, at a wage rate of €10/person-hr, gives rise to a variable cost of (5)(10) = €50/hr. So in Figure 10.2, the output level of 58 is plotted against a variable cost of €50/hr. Similarly, note from the production function that 43 units of output require 4 units of labour, which, at the €10 wage rate, gives rise in Figure 10.2 to a variable cost of €40/hr. In like fashion, we can generate as many additional points on the variable cost curve as we choose.

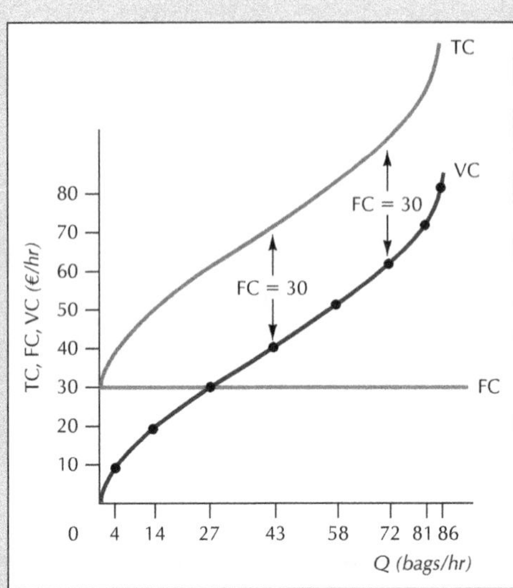

FIGURE 10.2
The Total, Variable and Fixed Cost Curves
These curves are for the production function for Kelly's Cleaners, shown in Figure 10.1. The variable cost curve passes through the origin, which means that the variable cost of producing zero units of output is equal to zero. The TC curve, which is the sum of the FC and VC curves, is parallel to the VC curve and lies FC = 30 units above it.

Of particular interest is the relationship between the curvature of the production function and that of the variable cost curve. Note in Figure 10.1 that $L = 4$ is the point at which diminishing returns to the variable factor of production set in. For values of L less than 4, there are increasing returns to L, which means that increments in L produce successively larger increments in Q in that region. Put another way, in this region a given increase in output, Q, requires successively smaller increments in the variable input, L. As a result, variable cost grows at a diminishing rate for output levels less than 43. This is reflected in Figure 10.2 by the concave shape of the variable cost curve for output levels between 0 and 43.

Once L exceeds 4 in Figure 10.1, we enter the region of diminishing returns. Here, successively larger increments in L are required to produce a given increment in Q. In consequence, variable cost grows at an increasing rate in this region. This is reflected in the convex shape of the variable cost curve in Figure 10.2 for output levels in excess of 43.

Because fixed costs do not vary with the level of output, their graph is simply a horizontal line. Figure 10.2 shows the fixed, variable and total cost curves (FC, VC and TC) for the production function shown in Figure 10.1. Note in the figure that the variable cost curve passes through the origin, which means simply that variable cost is zero when we produce no output. The total cost of producing zero output is equal to fixed costs, FC. Note also in the figure that the vertical distance between the VC and TC curves is everywhere equal to FC. This means that the total cost curve is parallel to the variable cost curve and lies FC units above it.

EXAMPLE 10.1 **Suppose the production function is given by $Q = 3KL$, where K denotes capital and L denotes labour. The price of capital is €2/machine-hr, the price of labour is €24/person-hr, and capital is fixed at 4 machine-hr/hr in the short run. Graph the TC, VC and FC curves for this production process.**

Unlike the production process shown in Figure 10.1, the process in this example is one in which there are everywhere constant returns to the variable factor of production. As shown in Figure 10.3, output here is strictly proportional to the variable input.

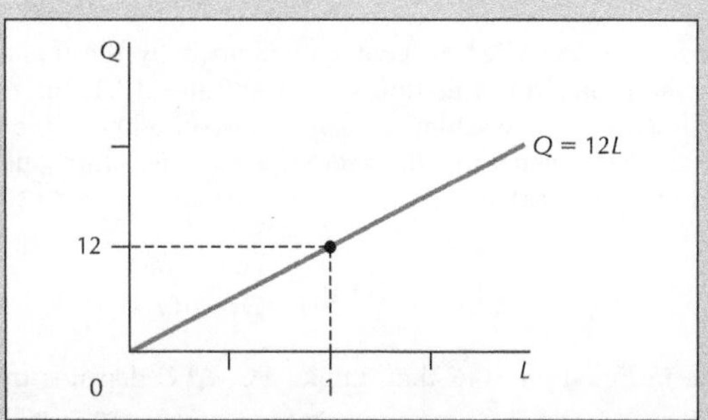

FIGURE 10.3
The Short-Run Production Function $Q = 3KL$, with $K = 4$
This short-run production function exhibits constant returns to L over the entire range of L. There is neither a region of increasing returns nor a region of diminishing returns to L.

To derive the total cost function from this production function, we must first discover how much capital and labour are required to produce a given level of output in the short run. Since K is fixed at 4 machine-hr/hr, the required amount of labour input is found by solving $Q = 3KL = 3(4)L$ for $L = Q/12$. The total cost of producing Q units of output per hour is therefore given by

$$\text{TC}(Q) = (€2/\text{machine-hr})(4\ \text{machine-hr/hr}) + (€24/\text{person-hr})\left(\frac{Q}{12}\ \text{person-hr/hr}\right) = €8/\text{hr} + €2Q/\text{hr} \qquad (10.4)$$

The €8/hr expenditure on capital constitutes fixed cost. Variable cost is total cost less fixed cost, or

$$\text{VC}_Q = 2Q \qquad (10.5)$$

The total, variable and fixed cost curves are plotted in Figure 10.4. ◆

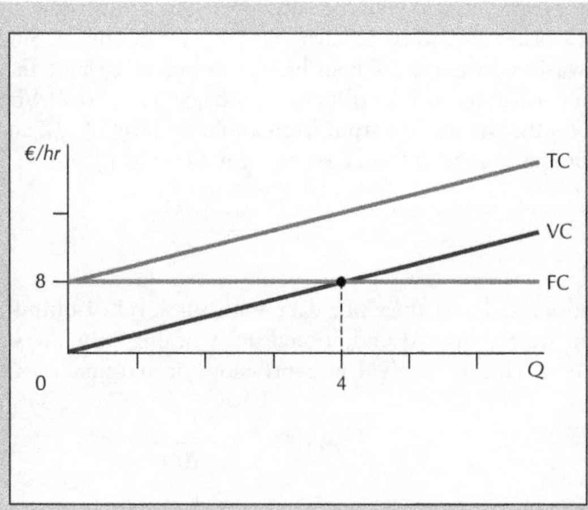

FIGURE 10.4
The Total, Variable and Fixed Cost Curves for the Production Function $Q = 3KL$
With K fixed at 4 machine-hr/hr in the short run and a price of K of r = €2/machine-hr, fixed costs are €8/hr. To produce Q units of output per hour requires $Q/12$ person-hr/hr of labour. With a price of labour of €24/person-hr, variable cost is €2Q/hr. Total cost is €8/hr + €2Q/hr.

EXERCISE 10.1 Same as Example 10.1 except the price of capital r = €4/machine-hr.

Other Short-Run Costs

Average fixed cost (**AFC**) is fixed cost divided by the quantity of output. For the production function shown in Table 10.1, for example, the average fixed cost of washing 58 bags/hr is (€30/hr) ÷ (58 bags/hr) = €0.517/bag. More generally, the average fixed cost of producing an output level of Q_1 is written

average fixed cost (AFC) fixed cost divided by the quantity of output.

$$AFC_{Q_1} = \frac{FC}{Q_1} = \frac{rk_0}{Q_1} \tag{10.6}$$

Note in Equation 10.6 that, unlike FC, AFC depends on the level of output produced.

Average variable cost (**AVC**) is variable cost divided by the quantity of output. If Kelly washes 72 bags/hr, his AVC will be (€10/person-hr) (6 person-hr/hr) ÷ 72 bags/hr = €0.833/bag. The average variable cost of producing an output level Q_1 may be written as

average variable cost (AVC) variable cost divided by the quantity of output.

$$AVC_{Q_1} = \frac{VC_{Q_1}}{Q_1} = \frac{wL_1}{Q_1} \tag{10.7}$$

Average total cost (**ATC**) is total cost divided by the quantity of output. And since total cost is the sum of total fixed cost and total variable cost, it follows that ATC is the sum of AFC and AVC. For example, the ATC of washing 58 bags/hr is (€30/hr) ÷ (58 bags/hr) + (€10/person-hr) (5 person-hr/hr) ÷ (58 bags/hr) = €0.517/bag + €0.862/bag = €1.379/bag. The average total cost of producing Q_1 units of output is given by

average total cost (ATC) total cost divided by the quantity of output.

$$ATC_{Q_1} = AFC_{Q_1} + AVC_{Q_1} = \frac{rK_0 + wL_1}{Q_1} \tag{10.8}$$

Marginal cost (**MC**), finally, is the change in total cost that results from producing an additional unit of output.[4] In going from 58 to 72 bags/hr, for example, total costs go up by €10/hr, which is the cost of hiring the extra worker needed to achieve that increase in output. Since the extra worker washes an extra 14 bags/hr, the marginal cost of the additional output in per-bag terms is (€10/hr) ÷ (14 bags/hr) = €0.714/bag. More generally, if ΔQ denotes the change in output from an initial level of Q_1, and ΔTC_{Q_1} denotes the corresponding change in total cost, marginal cost at Q_1 is given by

marginal cost (MC) change in total cost that results from a 1-unit change in output.

$$MC_{Q_1} = \frac{\Delta TC_{Q_1}}{\Delta Q} \tag{10.9}$$

Because fixed cost does not vary with the level of output, the change in total cost when we produce ΔQ additional units of output is the same as the change in variable cost. Thus an equivalent expression for marginal cost is

$$MC_{Q_1} = \frac{\Delta VC_{Q_1}}{\Delta Q} \tag{10.10}$$

where ΔVC_{Q_1} represents the change in variable cost when we produce ΔQ units of additional output.

[4]In calculus terms, the definition of marginal cost is simply $MC_Q = dTC_Q/dQ$.

Graphing the Short-Run Average and Marginal Cost Curves

Since FC does not vary with output, average fixed cost declines steadily as output increases. Suppose McGraw-Hill's fixed costs in producing this textbook were approximately €200,000. If only 1000 copies were produced, its average fixed cost would be €200/book. But if the publisher produces 20,000 copies, AFC will fall to €10/book. McGraw-Hill's best-selling economics principles text, by Campbell McConnell and Stanley Brue, is considerably longer than this book, and yet its average fixed cost comes to little more than €1/book. The process whereby AFC falls with output is often referred to as 'spreading overhead costs'.

For the fixed cost curve FC shown in the top panel in Figure 10.5, the corresponding average fixed cost curve is shown in the bottom panel as the curve labelled AFC. Like all other AFC curves, it takes the form of a rectangular hyperbola. As output shrinks toward zero, AFC grows without bounds, and it falls ever closer to zero as output increases. Note that the units on the vertical axis of the AFC curve

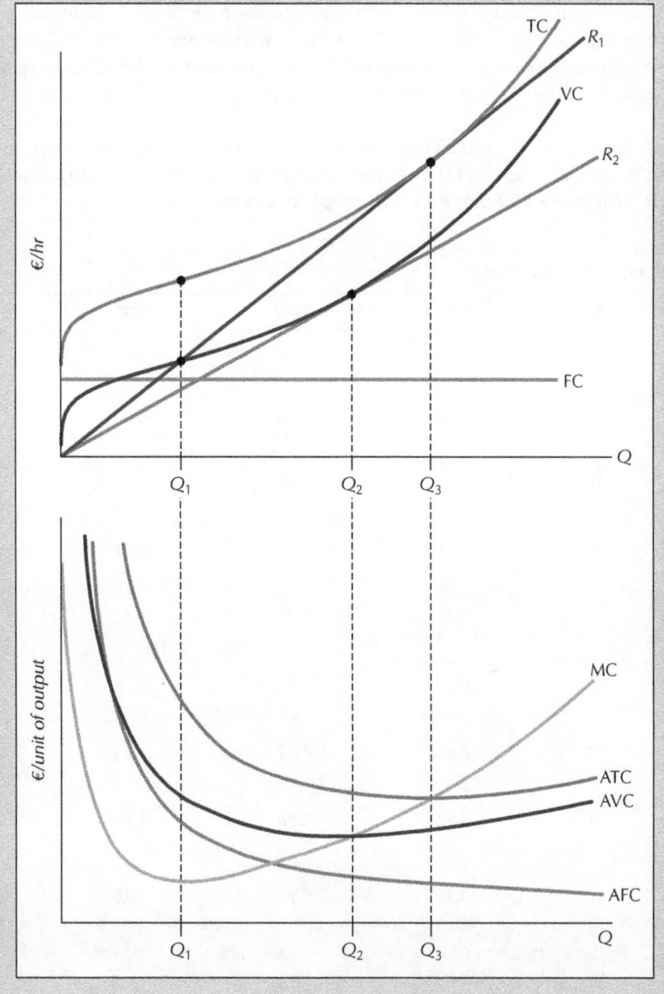

FIGURE 10.5 The Marginal, Average Total, Average Variable and Average Fixed Cost Curves
The MC curve intersects the ATC and AVC curves at their respective minimum points.

are euros per unit (€/unit) of output, and that the vertical axis of the FC curve, by contrast, is measured in euros per hour(€/hr).

Geometrically, average variable cost at any level of output Q, which is equal to VC/Q, may be interpreted as the slope of a ray to the variable cost curve at Q. Notice in the top panel in Figure 10.5 that the slope of a ray to the VC curve declines with output up to the output level Q_2; thereafter it begins to increase. The corresponding average variable cost curve, shown in the bottom panel in Figure 10.5, therefore reaches its minimum value at Q_2, the output level at which the ray R_2 is tangent to the variable cost curve. Beyond that point, the AVC curve increases with output.

The graph of the ATC curve is generated in an analogous fashion. For any level of output, ATC is the slope of the ray to the total cost curve at that output level. For the total cost curve in the top panel in Figure 10.5, the corresponding ATC curve is plotted in the bottom panel of the diagram. Note that the minimum point on ATC in the bottom panel occurs at Q_3, the output level for which the ray R_1 is tangent to the TC curve in the top panel.

Recall that because TC = FC + VC, it follows that ATC = AFC + AVC (simply divide both sides of the former equation by output). This means that the vertical distance between the ATC and AVC curves at any level of output will always be the corresponding level of AFC. Thus the vertical distance between ATC and AVC approaches infinity as output declines toward zero, and shrinks toward zero as output grows toward infinity. Note also in Figure 10.5 that the minimum point on the AVC curve occurs for a smaller unit of output than does the minimum point on the ATC curve. Because AFC declines continuously, ATC continues falling even after AVC has begun to turn upward.

EXAMPLE 10.2 Construct a table showing average fixed cost, average variable cost, average total cost and marginal cost using the information in Table 10.1 for Kelly's Cleaners. Then graph these average costs.

Outputs and Costs

Q	AFC	AVC	ATC	MC*
0	∞	–	∞	
				2.50
4	7.50	2.50	10.00	
				1.0
14	2.14	1.43	3.57	
				0.77
27	1.11	1.11	2.22	
				0.63
43	0.70	0.93	1.63	
				0.67
58	0.52	0.86	1.38	
				0.71
72	0.42	0.83	1.25	
				1.11
81	0.37	0.86	1.23	
				2.0
86	0.35	0.93	1.28	

*The marginal cost entries are placed between the lines of the table to indicate that each entry represents the cost per bag of moving from the preceding output level to the next.

We calculate average fixed cost as fixed cost divided by quantity AFC = FC/Q, average variable cost as variable cost divided by quantity AVC = VC/Q, and average total cost as total cost divided by quantity ATC = TC/Q. We calculate marginal cost by finding the difference in total cost and dividing by the difference in quantity: MC = $\Delta TC/\Delta Q$ to fill in the table above. The average cost curves are illustrated in Figure 10.6. ◆

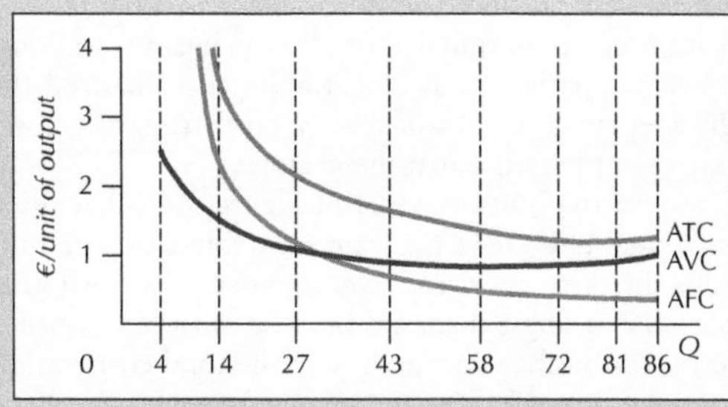

FIGURE 10.6
Quantity versus Average Costs
ATC is the sum of AVC and AFC. AFC is declining for all values of Q.

EXERCISE 10.2 If FC takes the value 20, what is the vertical distance between the ATC and AVC curves in Figure 10.5 when Q = 10?

In terms of its role in the firm's decision of how much output to produce, by far the most important of the seven cost curves is the *marginal cost curve.* The reason, as we will see in the coming chapters, is that the firm's typical operating decision involves the question of whether to expand or contract its current level of output. To make this decision intelligently, the firm must compare the relevant costs and benefits. The cost of expanding output (or the savings from contracting) is by definition equal to marginal cost.

Geometrically, marginal cost at any level of output may be interpreted as the slope of the total cost curve at that level of output. And since the total cost and variable cost curves are parallel, marginal cost is also equal to the slope of the variable cost curve. (Recall that the variable cost component is all that varies when total cost varies, which means that the change in total cost per unit of output must be the same as the change in variable cost per unit of output.)

Notice in the top panel in Figure 10.5 that the slope of the total cost curve decreases with output up to Q_1, and rises with output thereafter.[5] This tells us that the marginal cost curve, labelled MC in the bottom panel, will be downward sloping up to Q_1 and upward sloping thereafter. Q_1 is the point at which diminishing returns set in for this production function, and diminishing returns are what account for the upward slope of the short-run marginal cost curve.

At the output level Q_3, the slope of the total cost curve is exactly the same as the slope of the ray to the total cost curve (the ray labelled R_1 in the top panel in Figure 10.5). This tells us that marginal cost and average total cost will take precisely the same value at Q_3. To the left of Q_3, the slope of the total cost curve is smaller than the slope of the corresponding ray, which means that marginal cost will be smaller than average total cost in that region. For output levels in excess of Q_3, the slope of the total cost curve is larger than the slope of the corresponding ray, so marginal cost will be larger than average total cost for output levels larger than Q_3. These relationships are reflected in the average total cost and marginal cost curves shown

[5]A point at which the curvature changes is called an *inflection point.*

in the bottom panel in Figure 10.5. Notice that the relationship between the MC and AVC curves is qualitatively similar to the relationship between the MC and ATC curves. One common feature is that MC intersects each curve at its minimum point. Both average cost curves have the additional property that *when MC is less than average cost (either ATC or AVC), the average cost curve must be decreasing with output; and when MC is greater than average cost, average cost must be increasing with output.*

Note also that both of these relationships are very much like the ones among marginal and average product curves discussed in Chapter 9. They follow directly from the definition of marginal cost. Producing an additional unit whose cost exceeds the average (either total or variable) cost incurred thus far has the effect of pulling the average cost up. Conversely, an extra unit whose cost is less than the average will necessarily pull down the average.

Finally, note in the bottom panel in Figure 10.5 that the units on the vertical axis of the marginal cost curve diagram are again euros per unit (€/unit) of output, the same as for the three short-run average cost curves. All four of these curves can thus be displayed in a single diagram. But you must never, *ever,* attempt to place any of these four curves on the same axes with the total cost, variable cost or fixed cost curves. The units measured along the vertical axes are simply not compatible.

EXAMPLE 10.3 **Suppose output is given by the production function $Q = 3KL$, where K denotes capital and L denotes labour. The price of capital is €2/machine-hr, the price of labour is €24/person-hr, and capital is fixed at 4 units in the short run (this is the same production function and input prices as in Example 10.1). Graph the ATC, AVC, AFC and MC curves.**

Recall from Example 10.1 that the total cost curve for this process is given by

$$TC_Q = 8 + 2Q \tag{10.11}$$

Marginal cost is the slope of the total cost curve, which here is equal to €2/unit of output:

$$MC_Q = \frac{\Delta TC_Q}{\Delta Q} = 2 \tag{10.12}$$

Average variable cost is given by VC_Q/Q, which is also €2/unit of output:

$$AVC_Q = \frac{2Q}{Q} = 2 \tag{10.13}$$

When marginal cost is constant, as in this production process, it will always be equal to AVC.

Average fixed cost is given by

$$AFC_Q = \frac{8}{Q} \tag{10.14}$$

and average total cost is given by

$$ATC_Q = 2 + \frac{8}{Q} \tag{10.15}$$

in this example. The marginal and average cost curves are as shown in the bottom panel in Figure 10.7, where the top panel reproduces the corresponding total, variable and fixed cost curves. ◆

FIGURE 10.7
Cost Curves for a Specific Production Process
For production processes with constant marginal cost, average variable cost and marginal cost are identical. Marginal cost always lies below ATC for such processes.

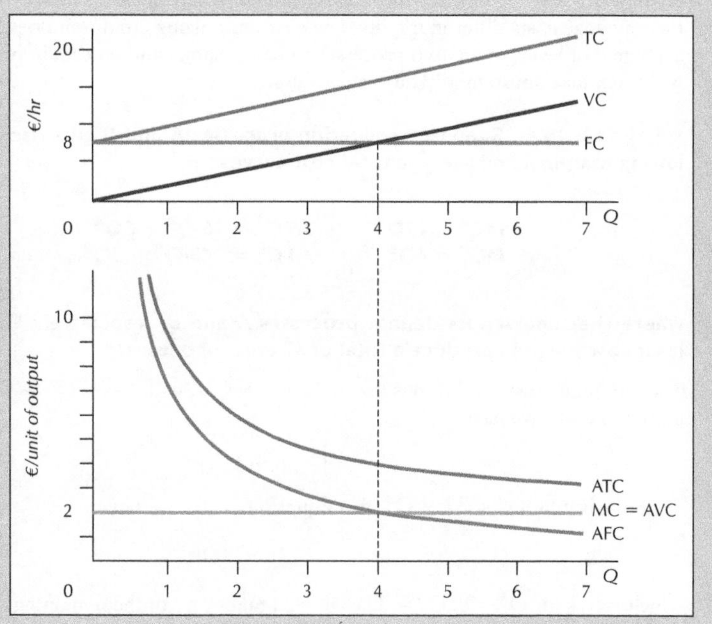

ALLOCATING PRODUCTION BETWEEN TWO PROCESSES

In Chapter 9, we saw that the problem of allocating a fixed resource between two production activities is solved by equating the marginal product of the resource in each. A closely related problem can be solved with the cost concepts developed in this chapter. Here, the problem is to divide a given production quota between two production processes in such a way as to produce the quota at the lowest possible cost.

Let Q_T be the total amount to be produced, and let Q_1 and Q_2 be the amounts produced in the first and second processes, respectively. And suppose the marginal cost in either process at very low levels of output is lower than the marginal cost at Q_T units of output in the other (which ensures that both processes will be used).[6] *The values of Q_1 and Q_2 that solve this problem will then be the ones that result in equal marginal costs for the two processes.*

To see why, suppose the contrary—that is, suppose that the cost-minimizing allocation resulted in higher marginal cost in one process than in the other. We could then shift one unit of output from the process with the higher marginal cost to the one with the lower. Because the result would be the same total output as before at a lower total cost, the initial division could not have been the cost-minimizing one.

In Chapter 9 we saw that two production processes could have equal marginal products even though their average products differed substantially. Here, too, it is

[6]Suppose the marginal cost at $Q = Q_T$ using production function A were less than the marginal cost at $Q = 0$ for production process B: $MC^A_{Q_T} < MC^B_{Q_T}$. Then the cheapest way of producing Q_T would be to use only process A.

possible for two production processes to have equal marginal costs even though their average costs differ markedly. The cost-minimizing condition does not require average cost levels in the two processes to be the same, and indeed, in practice, they will often take substantially different values.

EXAMPLE 10.4 Suppose production processes *A* and *B* give rise to the following marginal and average total cost curves:

$$MC^A = 12Q^A \qquad ATC^A = 16/Q^A + 6Q^A$$
$$MC^B = 4Q^B \qquad ATC^B = 240/Q^B + 2Q^B$$

where the superscripts denote processes *A* and *B*, respectively. What is the least costly way to produce a total of 32 units of output?

The minimum-cost condition is that $MC^A_{Q^A} = MC^B_{Q^B}$, with $Q^A + Q^B = 32$. Equating marginal costs, we have

$$12\,Q^A = 4Q^B \qquad (10.16)$$

Substituting $Q^B = 32 - Q^A$ into Equation 10.16, we have

$$12\,Q^A = 128 - 4Q^A \qquad (10.17)$$

which solves for $Q^A = 8$. $Q^B = 32 - 8 = 24$ takes care of the remaining output, and at these output levels, marginal cost in both plants will be €96/unit of output (see Figure 10.8). The line $MC^T = 3Q^T$ is the horizontal sum of MC^A and MC^B.[7]

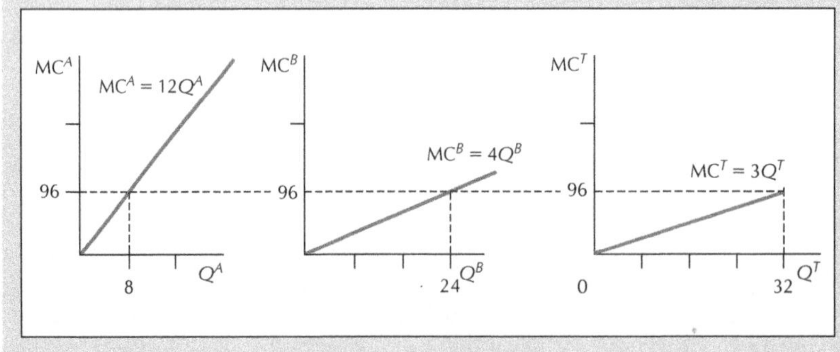

FIGURE 10.8 The Minimum-Cost Production Allocation
To produce a given total output at minimum cost, it should be allocated across production activities so that the marginal cost of each activity is the same.

The average total cost values that correspond to this allocation are ATC^A = €50/unit of output and ATC^B = €58/unit of output. From the average total cost curves we can deduce total cost curves in this example (just multiply ATC by Q).[8] They are given by $TC^A = 16 + 6(Q^A)^2$ and $TC^B = 240 + 2(Q^B)^2$. The cost-minimizing allocation results in TC^A = €400 and TC^B = €1392, illustrating that the cost-minimizing allocation does not require equality of total costs either. ◆

EXERCISE 10.3 Same as Example 10.4 except the total output is 12.

[7] MC^T is found by solving $Q^T = Q^A + Q^B = MC/12 + MC/4 = MC/3$ for $MC^T = 3Q^T$.
[8] Note that $MC^A = dTC^A/dQ^A = d[16 + 6(Q^A)^2]/dQ^A = 12Q^A$ and $MC^B = dTC^B/dQ^B = d[240 + 2(Q^B)^2]/dQ^B = 4Q^B$.

THE RELATIONSHIP BETWEEN MP, AP, MC AND AVC

In Chapter 9, we saw that the marginal product curve cuts the average product curve at the maximum value of the AP curve. And in this chapter, we saw that the marginal cost curve cuts the average variable cost curve at the minimum value of the AVC curve. There is a direct link between these relationships. To see the connection, note first that from the definition of marginal cost we have MC = ΔVC/ΔQ. When labour is the only variable factor, ΔVC = ΔwL so that ΔVC/ΔQ is equal to ΔwL/ΔQ. If wage rates are fixed, this is the same as $w\Delta L/\Delta Q$. And since $\Delta L/\Delta Q$ is equal to 1/MP, it follows that

$$\mathrm{MC} = \frac{w}{\mathrm{MP}} \tag{10.18}$$

In similar fashion, note from the definition of average variable cost that AVC = VC/Q = wL/Q, and since L/Q is equal to 1/AP, it follows that

$$\mathrm{AVC} = \frac{w}{\mathrm{AP}} \tag{10.19}$$

From Equation 10.18, we see that the minimum value of marginal cost corresponds to the maximum value of MP. Likewise, it follows from Equation 10.19 that the minimum value of AVC corresponds to the maximum value of AP. The top panel in Figure 10.9 plots the AP and MP curves as functions of L. The bottom panel uses Equations 10.18 and 10.19 to plot the corresponding MC and AVC curves as functions of L. (Normally, the MC and AVC curves are plotted as functions of Q. The value of Q that corresponds to a given value of L in the bottom panel may be

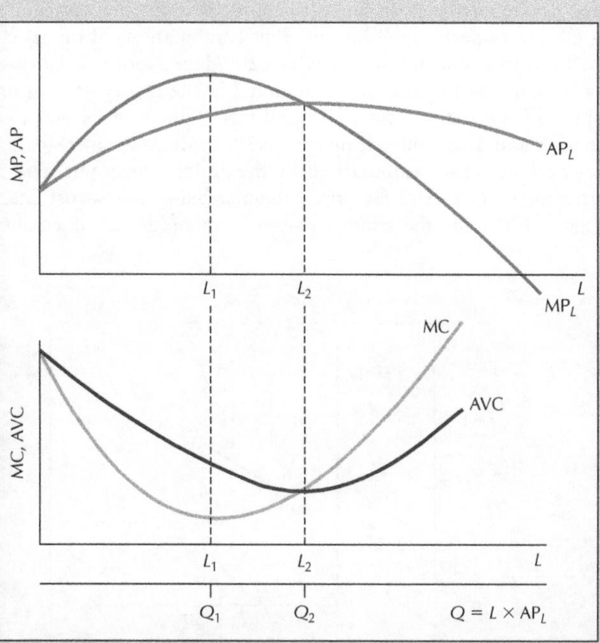

FIGURE 10.9
The Relationship between MP, AP, MC and AVC
Normally, the MC and AVC curves are plotted with Q on the horizontal axis. In the bottom panel, they are shown as functions of L. The value of Q that corresponds to a given value of L is found by multiplying L times the corresponding value of AP$_L$. The maximum value of the MP curve, at $L = L_1$, top panel, corresponds to the minimum value of the MC curve, at $Q = Q_1$, bottom panel. Similarly, the maximum value of the AP curve, at $L = L_2$, top panel, corresponds to the minimum value of the AVC curve, at $Q = Q_2$, bottom panel.

calculated by multiplying L times the corresponding value of AP_L.) Note that the MP curve in the top panel takes its maximum value at $L = L_1$, and that the minimum value of the MC curve in the bottom panel occurs at the output level (Q_1) that corresponds to $L = L_1$. Note also that the AP curve in the top panel takes its maximum value at $L = L_2$, and that the minimum value of the AVC curve in the bottom panel occurs at the output level (Q_2) that corresponds to $L = L_2$.

EXERCISE 10.4 For a production function at a given level of output in the short run, the marginal product of labour is greater than the average product of labour. How will marginal cost at that output level compare with average variable cost?

COSTS IN THE LONG RUN

In the long run all inputs are variable by definition. If the manager of the firm wishes to produce a given level of output at the lowest possible cost and is free to choose any input combination she pleases, which one should she choose? As we will see in the next section, the answer to this question depends on the relative prices of capital and labour.

Choosing the Optimal Input Combination

No matter what the structure of industry may be—monopolistic or atomistically competitive, capitalist or socialist, industrialized or less developed—the objective of most producers is to produce any given level and quality of output at the lowest possible cost. Equivalently, the producer wants to produce as much output as possible from any given expenditure on inputs.

Let us begin with the case of a firm that wants to maximize output from a given level of expenditure. Suppose it uses only two inputs, capital (K) and labour (L), whose prices, measured in euros per unit of input per day, are r = €2/day and w = €4/day, respectively. What different combinations of inputs can this firm purchase for a total expenditure of C = €200/day? Notice that this question has the same structure as the one we encountered in the theory of consumer behaviour in Chapter 3 ('With an income of M, and facing prices of P_X and P_Y, what combinations of X and Y can the consumer buy?'). In the consumer's case, recall, the answer was easily summarized by the budget constraint. The parallel information in the case of the firm is summarized by the **isocost line**, shown in Figure 10.10 for the example given. Any of the input combinations

isocost line a set of input bundles each of which costs the same amount.

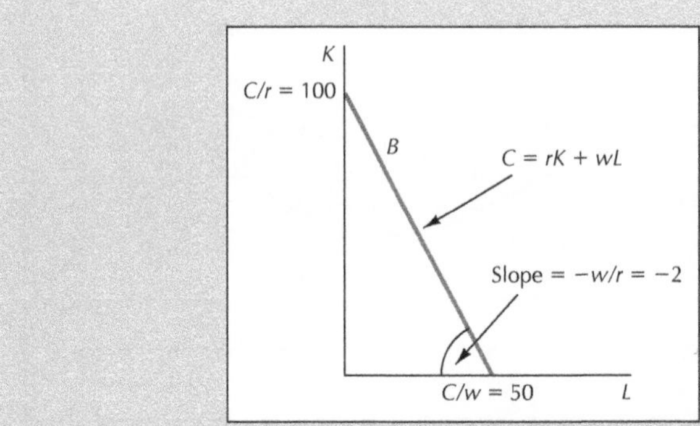

FIGURE 10.10
The Isocost Line
For given input prices (r = 2 and w = 4 in the diagram), the isocost line is the locus of all possible input bundles that can be purchased for a given level of total expenditure C (€200 in the diagram). The slope of the isocost line is the negative of the input price ratio, $-w/r$.

on the locus labelled *B* can be purchased for a total expenditure of €200/day. Analogously to the budget constraint case, the slope of the isocost line is the negative of the ratio of the input prices, $-w/r$.

EXERCISE 10.5 If $w = 3$ and $r = 6$, draw the isocost lines that correspond to total expenditure of €90 and €180 per unit of time.

The analytic approach for finding the maximum output that can be produced for a given cost turns out to be similar to the one for finding the optimal consumption bundle. Just as a given level of satisfaction can be achieved by any of a multitude of possible consumption bundles (all of which lie on the same indifference curve), so too can a given amount of output be produced by any of a host of different input combinations (all of which lie on the same isoquant). In the consumer case, we found the optimum bundle by superimposing the budget constraint onto the indifference map and locating the relevant point of tangency.[9] Here, we superimpose the isocost line onto the isoquant map. In Figure 10.11, the tangency point (L^*, K^*) is the input combination that yields the highest possible output (Q_0) for an expenditure of *C*.

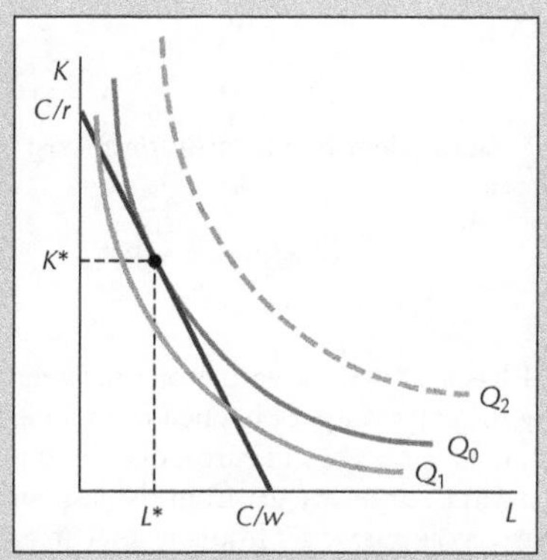

FIGURE 10.11
The Maximum Output for a Given Expenditure
A firm that is trying to produce the largest possible output for an expenditure of *C* will select the input combination at which the isocost line for *C* is tangent to an isoquant.

As noted, the problem of producing the largest output for a given expenditure is solved in essentially the same way as the problem of producing a given level of output for the lowest possible cost. The only difference is that in the latter case we begin with a specific isoquant (the one that corresponds to the level of output we are trying to produce), then superimpose a map of isocost lines, each corresponding to a different cost level. In our first exercise, cost was fixed and output varied; this time, output is fixed and costs vary. As shown in Figure 10.12, the least-cost input bundle (L^*, K^*) corresponds to the point of tangency between an isocost line and the specified isoquant (Q_0).

Recall from Chapter 9 that the slope of the isoquant at any point is equal to $-MP_L/MP_K$, the negative of the ratio of the marginal product of *L* to the marginal product of *K* at that point. (Recall also from Chapter 9 that the absolute value of this ratio is called the marginal rate of technical substitution.) Combining this with

[9]Except, of course, in the case of corner solutions.

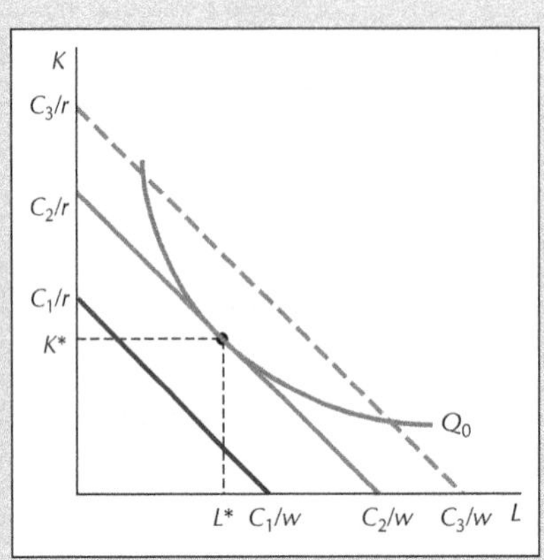

FIGURE 10.12
The Minimum Cost for a Given Level of Output
A firm that is trying to produce a given level of output, Q_0, at the lowest possible cost will select the input combination at which an isocost line is tangent to the Q_0 isoquant.

the result that minimum cost occurs at a point of tangency with the isocost line (whose slope is $-w/r$), it follows that

$$\frac{MP_{L^*}}{MP_{K^*}} = \frac{w}{r} \tag{10.20}$$

where K^* and L^* again denote the minimum-cost values of K and L. Cross-multiplying, we have

$$\frac{MP_{L^*}}{w} = \frac{MP_{K^*}}{r} \tag{10.21}$$

Equation 10.21 has a straightforward economic interpretation. Note first that MP_{L^*} is simply the extra output obtained from an extra unit of L at the cost-minimizing point. w is the cost, in euros, of an extra unit of L. The ratio MP_{L^*}/w is thus the extra output we get from the last euro spent on L. Similarly, MP_{K^*}/r is the extra output we get from the last euro spent on K. In words, Equation 10.21 tells us that when costs are at a minimum, the extra output we get from the last euro spent on an input must be the same for all inputs.

If you get a larger increase in output from the last euro you spent on one input than from the last euro you spent on another, you should be spending more on the first input and less on the second.

It is easy to show why, if that were not the case, costs would not be at a minimum. Suppose, for example, that the last units of both labour and capital increased output by 4 units. That is, suppose $MP_L = MP_K = 4$. And again, suppose that $r =$ €2/day and $w =$ €4/day. We would then have achieved only 1 unit of output for the last euro spent on L, but 2 units for the last euro spent on K. We could reduce spending on L by a euro, increase spending on K by only 50 cents, and get the same output level as before, saving 50 cents in the process. Whenever the ratios of marginal products to input prices differ across inputs, it will always be possible to make a similar cost-saving substitution in favour of the input with the higher MP/P ratio.[10]

More generally, we may consider a production process that employs not two but N inputs, $X_1, X_2, \ldots, X_N$. In this case, the condition for production at minimum cost is a straightforward generalization of Equation 10.21:

$$\frac{MP_{X_1}}{P_{X_1}} = \frac{MP_{X_2}}{P_{X_2}} = \cdots \frac{MP_{X_N}}{P_{X_N}} \tag{10.22}$$

[10]Again, this statement is true except in the case of corner solutions.

Why is gravel made by hand in Nepal but by machine in Europe?

ECONOMIC NATURALIST 10.1

For simplicity, suppose that capital (K) and labour (L) are employed to transform rocks into gravel. And suppose that any of the input combinations on the isoquant labelled $Q = 1$ tonne in Figure 10.13 will yield 1 tonne of gravel. Thus, the combination labelled ($L^*_{Germany}$, $K^*_{Germany}$) might correspond to the highly capital-intensive technique used in Germany and (L^*_{Nepal}, K^*_{Nepal}) to the highly labour-intensive technique used in Nepal.

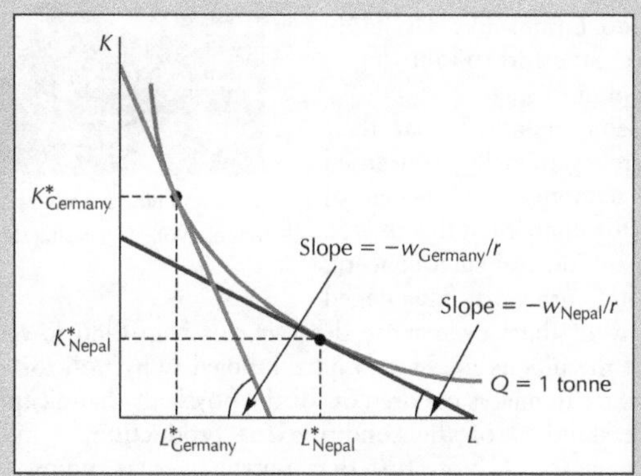

FIGURE 10.13 Different Ways of Producing One Tonne of Gravel Countries where labour is cheap relative to capital will select labour-intensive techniques of production. Those where labour is more expensive will employ relatively more capital-intensive techniques.

The reason the chosen techniques differ between countries is not that Germany is richer; rather, it is that the relative prices of labour and capital differ so dramatically in the two countries. In Nepal, labour is cheaper than in almost any other nation. Wages in Germany, by contrast, are among the highest in the world. Construction equipment is traded in world markets and, aside from shipping costs, its price does not differ much from one country to another. If the price of capital, r, is roughly the same in the two countries and the price of labour, w, is much higher in Germany, it follows that the isocost line is much flatter in Nepal. And as shown in Figure 10.13, this fact alone is sufficient to account for the dramatic difference in production techniques. ■

EXERCISE 10.6 Suppose capital and labour are perfect complements in a one-to-one ratio. That is, suppose that $Q = \min(L, K)$. Currently, the wage is $w = 5$ and the rental rate is $r = 10$. What is the minimum cost and method of producing $Q = 20$ units of output? Suppose the wage rises to $w' = 20$. If we keep total cost the same, what level of output can now be produced and what method of production (input mix) is used?

EXERCISE 10.7 Repeat the previous exercise but now suppose capital and labour are perfect substitutes in a one-to-one ratio: $Q = K + L$.

Why do unions support minimum wage laws so strongly?

ECONOMIC NATURALIST 10.2

Labour unions have historically been among the most outspoken proponents of minimum wage legislation. They favour not only higher levels of the minimum wage, but also broader coverage. UNISON, for example, represents well over a million public sector workers in the UK. It campaigned strongly for a minimum wage to be introduced in the UK (it was in 1998). And it continues to campaign strongly for a higher minimum, and greater enforcement of the legislation. For instance, it expresses concern that migrant workers are not being paid the minimum. Most union members, however, earn substantially more than the minimum wage, and hardly any union members are migrant workers. Why, then, do unions like UNISON devote such great effort to lobbying in favour of minimum wages?

Why do union members, who earn substantially more than the minimum wage, favour increasing the minimum wage?

One reason might be that their members are genuinely concerned about the economic well-being of workers less fortunate than themselves. No doubt many do feel such concern. But there are other disadvantaged groups—many of them even more deserving of help than low-wage workers—on whose behalf the unions might also have lobbied. Why not, for example, try to get extra benefits for homeless children or for the physically handicapped?

An understanding of the condition for production at minimum cost helps answer these questions. Note first that, on the average, union workers tend to be more skilled than non-union workers. Unskilled labour and skilled labour are substitutes for one another in many production processes, giving rise to isoquants shaped something like the one shown in Figure 10.14. What mix of the two skill categories the firm chooses to use will depend strongly on relative prices. Figure 10.14 shows the least costly mix for producing $Q = Q_0$ both before and after the enactment of the minimum wage statute. The wage rate for skilled labour is denoted by w. The pre-legislation price of unskilled labour is w_1, which rises to w_2 after enactment of the law. The immediate effect is to increase the absolute value of the slope of the isocost line from w_1/w to w_2/w, causing the firm to increase its employment of skilled labour from S_1 to S_2, simultaneously reducing its employment of unskilled (non-union) labour from U_1 to U_2.

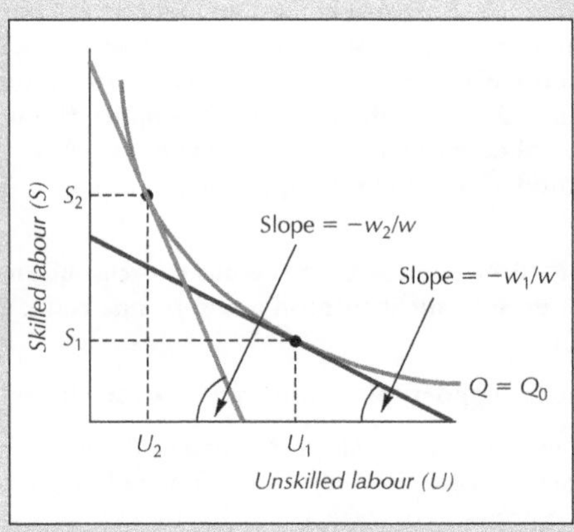

FIGURE 10.14
The Effect of a Minimum Wage Law on Employment of Skilled Labour
Unskilled labour and skilled labour are substitutes for one another in many production processes. When the price of unskilled labour rises, the slope of the isocost line rises, causing many firms to increase their employment of skilled (unionized) labour.

Although most union workers are not affected directly by the minimum wage laws, these laws have the indirect consequence of increasing the demand for union labour.[11] Even if unions lacked their avowed concern for the well-being of unskilled, largely non-union workers, there would thus be little mystery as to why unions devote so much of their resources in support of extensions of minimum wage legislation. ■

ECONOMIC NATURALIST 10.3

Why would a bathroom equipment manufacturer bake the image of a housefly onto the centre of its ceramic urinals?

The substitution of capital for labour is sometimes motivated not by a change in factor prices, but by the introduction of new ideas. Consider, for example, the 'official toilet project' initiated by Jos van Bedaf, then head manager of cleaning for the Schiphol airport in Amsterdam.[12] His problem was that the men's toilets at the airport, which were used by more than 100,000 patrons a year, had a tendency to become messy and smelly despite frequent cleanings. Mr van Bedaf's solution was not to intensify the efforts of maintenance crews but to make a minor change in the restroom equipment. Specifically, he requested that his sanitation equipment manufacturer supply the airport with urinals with the image of a housefly baked onto the centre of each fixture's glazed ceramic surface. His theory was that the presence of this target would cause patrons to be much more accurate in their use of the facilities. The result? Dramatically cleaner facilities and a 20 per cent reduction in cleaning costs. A national newspaper in the Netherlands rated the Schiphol facilities first on a list of clean toilets. ■

The Relationship between Optimal Input Choice and Long-Run Costs

Given sufficient time to adjust, the firm can always buy the cost-minimizing input bundle that corresponds to any particular output level and relative input prices. To see how the firm's costs vary with output in the long run, we need only compare the costs of the respective optimal input bundles.

output expansion path the locus of tangencies (minimum-cost input combinations) traced out by an isocost line of given slope as it shifts outward into the isoquant map for a production process.

The curve labelled *EE* in Figure 10.15 shows the firm's **output expansion path.** It is the set of cost-minimizing input bundles when the input price ratio is fixed at w/r. Thus, when the price of K is r and the price of L is w, the cheapest way to produce Q_1 units of output is to use the input bundle S, which contains K_1^* units of K, L_1^* units of L, and costs TC_1. The bundle S is therefore one point on the output expansion path. In like fashion, the output level Q_2 is associated with bundle T, which has a total cost of TC_2; Q_3 is associated with U, which costs TC_3; and so on. In the theory of firm behaviour, the long-run expansion path is the analogue to the income-consumption curve in the theory of the consumer.

To go from the long-run expansion path to the long-run total cost curve, we simply plot the relevant quantity-cost pairs from Figure 10.15. Thus, the output level Q_1 corresponds to a long-run total cost of TC_1, Q_2 to TC_2, and so on. The result is the curve labelled LTC in the top panel in Figure 10.16. In the long run there is no need to distinguish between total, fixed and variable costs, since all costs are variable.

The LTC curve will always pass through the origin because in the long run the firm can liquidate all of its inputs. If the firm elects to produce no output, it need not retain,

[11]Note that this example assumes that the firm will produce the same level of output after the minimum wage hike as before. As we will see in the next chapter, however, the firm will generally produce less output than before. If the output reduction is large enough, it could offset the firm's switch to skilled labour.
[12]This example is based on Stefan Verhagen, 'Fly in the Pot', *Cornell Business,* 21 April 1992.

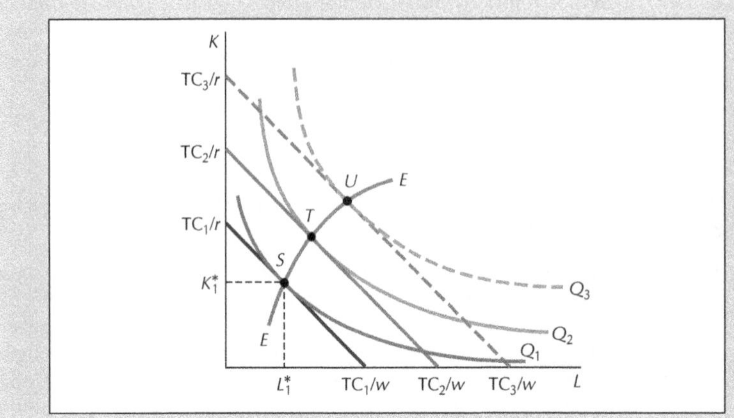

FIGURE 10.15 The Long-Run Expansion Path With fixed input prices *r* and *w*, bundles *S*, *T*, *U* and others along the locus *EE* represent the least costly ways of producing the corresponding levels of output.

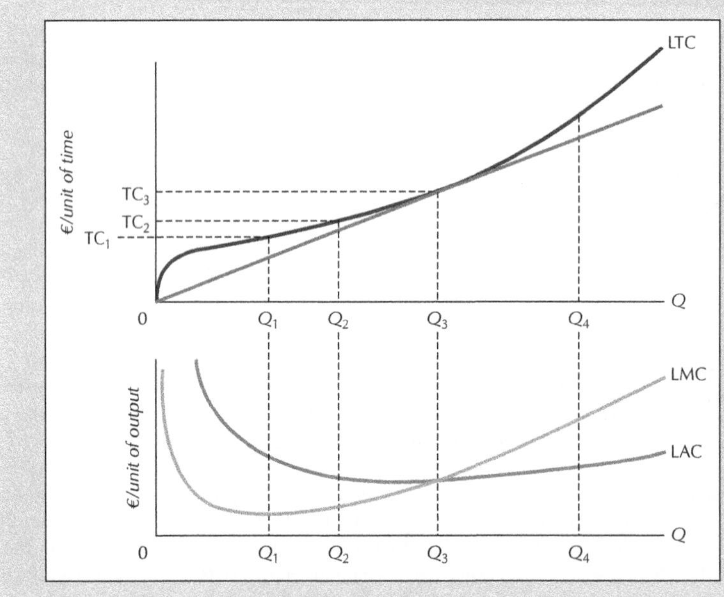

FIGURE 10.16 The Long-Run Total, Average and Marginal Cost Curves In the long run, the firm always has the option of ceasing operations and ridding itself of all its inputs. This means that the long-run total cost curve (top panel) will always pass through the origin. The long-run average and long-run marginal cost curves (bottom panel) are derived from the long-run total cost curves in a manner completely analogous to the short-run case.

or pay for, the services of any of its inputs. The shape of the LTC curve shown in the top panel looks very much like that of the short-run total cost curve shown in Figure 10.2. But this need not always be the case, as we will presently see. For the moment, though, let us take the shape of the LTC curve in the top panel in Figure 10.16 as given and ask what it implies for the long-run average and marginal cost curves.

Analogously to the short-run case, long-run marginal cost (LMC) is the slope of the long-run total cost curve:

$$\text{LMC}_Q = \frac{\Delta \text{LTC}_Q}{\Delta Q} \tag{10.23}$$

In words, LMC is the cost to the firm, in the long run, of expanding its output by 1 unit.

Long-run average cost (LAC) is the ratio of long-run total cost to output:

$$\mathrm{LAC}_Q = \frac{\mathrm{LTC}_Q}{Q} \tag{10.24}$$

Again, there is no need to discuss the distinctions between average total, fixed and variable costs, since all long-run costs are variable.

The bottom panel in Figure 10.16 shows the LAC and LMC curves that correspond to the LTC curve shown in the top panel. The slope of the LTC curve is diminishing up to the output level Q_1 and increasing thereafter, which means that the LMC curve takes its minimum value at Q_1. The slope of LTC and the slope of the ray to LTC are the same at Q_3, which means that LAC and LMC intersect at that level of output. And again as before, the traditional average-marginal relationship holds: LAC is declining whenever LMC lies below it, and rising whenever LMC lies above it.

For a constant returns to scale production function, doubling output exactly doubles costs.[13] Tripling all inputs triples output and triples costs, and so on. For the case of constant returns to scale, long-run total costs are thus exactly proportional to output. As shown in Figure 10.17(*a*), the LTC curve for a production function with constant returns to scale is a straight line through the origin. Because the slope of LTC is constant, the associated LMC curve is a horizontal line, and is exactly the same as the LAC curve, as in Figure 10.17(*b*).

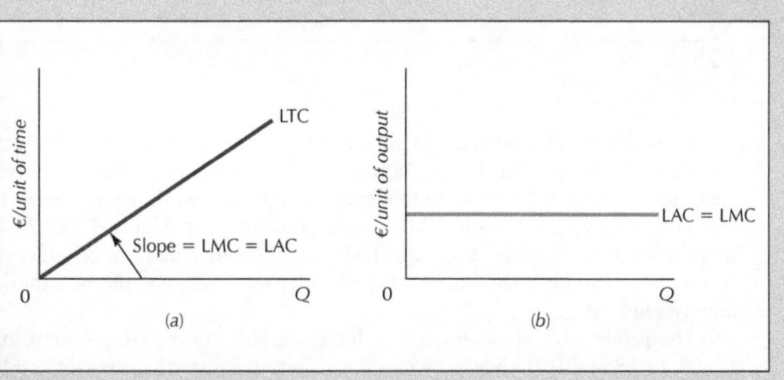

FIGURE 10.17
The LTC, LMC and LAC Curves with Constant Returns to Scale
(*a*) With constant returns, long-run total cost is strictly proportional to output. (*b*) Long-run marginal cost is constant and equal to long-run average cost.

When the production function has decreasing returns to scale, a given proportional increase in output requires a greater proportional increase in all inputs and hence a greater proportional increase in costs. The LTC, LMC and LAC curves for a production function with decreasing returns to scale are shown in Figure 10.18. For the particular LTC curve shown in Figure 10.18(*a*), the associated LAC and LMC curves happen to be linear, as in Figure 10.18(*b*), but this need not always happen. The general property of the decreasing returns case is that it gives rise to an upward-curving LTC curve and upward-sloping LAC and LMC curves. Note yet another application of the average-marginal relationship: the fact that LMC exceeds LAC ensures that LAC must rise with output.

[13]Assuming, of course, that input prices remain the same as output varies.

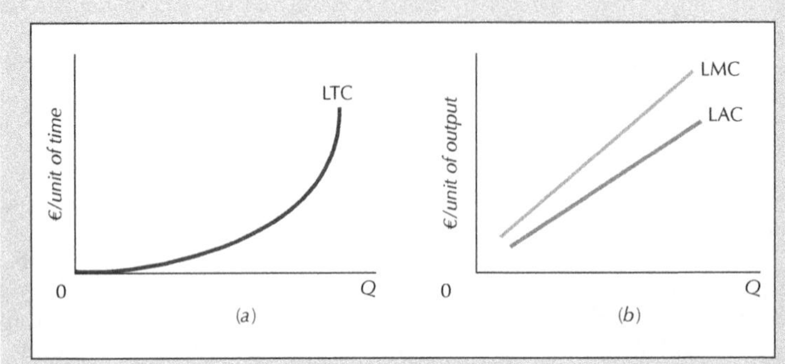

FIGURE 10.18
The LTC, LAC and LMC Curves for a Production Process with Decreasing Returns to Scale
Under decreasing returns, output grows less than in proportion to the growth in inputs, which means that total cost grows more than in proportion to growth in output.

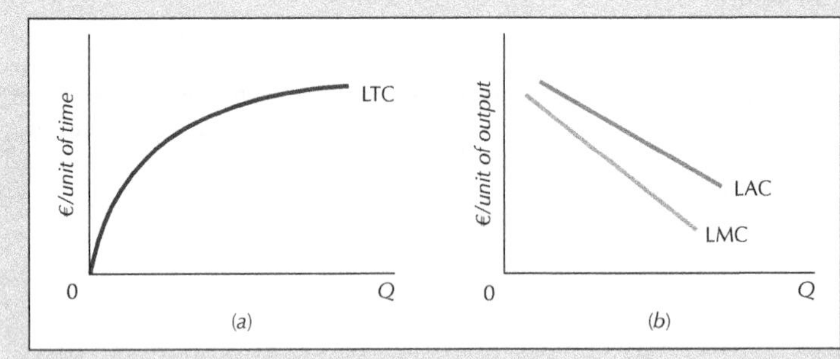

FIGURE 10.19
The LTC, LAC and LMC Curves for a Production Process with Increasing Returns to Scale
With increasing returns, the large-scale firm has lower average and marginal costs than the smaller-scale firm.

Consider, finally, the case of increasing returns to scale. Here, output grows more than in proportion to the increase in inputs. In consequence, long-run total cost rises less than in proportion to increases in output, as shown in Figure 10.19(*a*). The accompanying LAC and LMC curves are shown in Figure 10.19(*b*). The distinguishing feature of the LAC and LMC curves under increasing returns to scale is not the linear form shown in this particular example, but the fact that they are downward sloping.

The production processes whose long-run cost curves are pictured in Figures 10.17, 10.18 and 10.19 are 'pure cases', exhibiting constant, decreasing and increasing returns to scale, respectively, over their entire ranges of output. As discussed in Chapter 9, however, the degree of returns to scale of a production function need not be the same over the whole range of output.

LONG-RUN COSTS AND THE STRUCTURE OF INDUSTRY

As noted in the preview to this chapter, long-run costs are important because of their effect on the structure of industry. A detailed elaboration of this role will be the subject of the coming chapters. Here, a brief overview of the key issues will help set the stage for that discussion.

When, as in Figure 10.20(*a*), there are declining long-run average costs throughout, the tendency will be for a single firm to serve the market. If two firms attempted to serve such a market, with each producing only part of the total output sold, each

natural monopoly an industry whose market output is produced at the lowest cost when production is concentrated in the hands of a single firm.

would have higher average costs than if one of them alone served the market. The tendency in such a market will be for the firm that happens to grow larger to have a cost advantage that enables it to eliminate its rival. Markets characterized by declining long-run average cost curves are for this reason often referred to as **natural monopolies.**

FIGURE 10.20
LAC Curves Characteristic of Highly Concentrated Industrial Structures
(*a*) LAC curves that slope downward throughout tend to be characteristic of natural monopolies. Unit costs are lowest when only one firm serves the entire market. (*b*) U-shaped LAC curves whose minimum points occur at a substantial share of total market output are characteristic of markets served by only a small handful of firms.

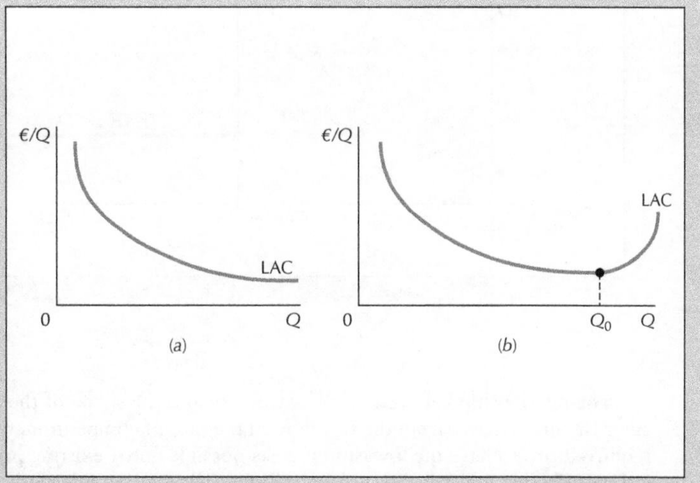

Consider now the LAC curve shown in Figure 10.20(*b*). The minimum point on this curve occurs at the output level Q_0. At that output level, the firm achieves its lowest possible unit cost of production. The output level Q_0 may be called the *minimum efficient scale*: the level of production required for LAC to reach its minimum level. If Q_0 constitutes a substantial share of industry output—more than, say, 20 per cent—the industry will tend to be dominated by a small handful of firms. As in the natural monopoly case, a large number of small firms would be unlikely to survive in such a market, since each would have much higher average costs than larger firms. By contrast to the natural monopoly case, however, the upturn in the LAC beyond Q_0 will make it difficult for a single firm to serve the entire market. Markets served by firms with LACs like the one in Figure 10.20(*b*) are likely to be 'highly concentrated', which means that a small number of firms will tend to account for the lion's share of all output sold.

The long-run average cost curve associated with a market served by many firms is likely to take one of the three forms shown in Figure 10.21. If Q_0, the minimum point on the U-shaped average cost curve in panel (*a*), constitutes only a small fraction of total industry output, we expect to see an industry populated by numerous firms, each of which produces only a small percentage of total industry output. Small size is also not a disadvantage when the production process is one that gives rise to a horizontal LAC curve like the one shown in panel (*b*). For such processes, all firms—large or small—have the same unit costs of production. For the upward-sloping LAC curve shown in panel (*c*) in Figure 10.21, small size is not only compatible with survival in the marketplace but positively required, since large firms will always have higher average costs than smaller ones. As a practical matter, however, it is very unlikely that there could ever be an LAC curve that is upward sloping even at extremely small levels of output. (Imagine, for example, the unit costs of a firm that tried to produce $\frac{1}{100}$ of a pound of sugar.)

FIGURE 10.21
LAC Curves Characteristic of Unconcentrated Industry Structures
The requirement for survival in any market is that a firm have the lowest possible unit costs. If the minimum point of a U-shaped LAC (Q_0 in panel *a*) occurs at a small fraction of market output, or if LAC is everywhere flat or rising (panels *b* and *c*, respectively), then small size and survival are compatible. Each firm will tend to produce only a small share of total market output.

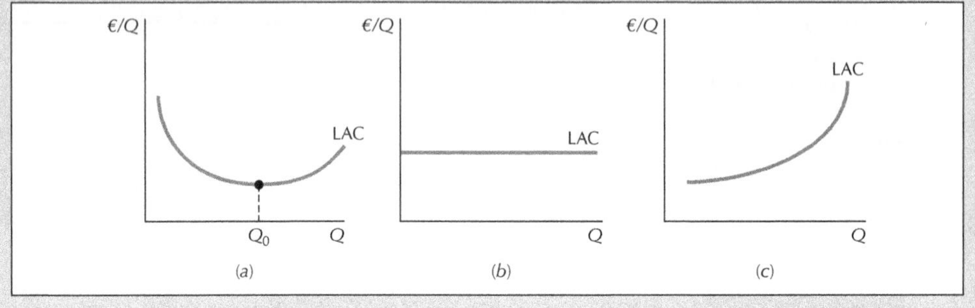

The relationship between market structure and the shape of the long-run average cost curve derives from the fact that, in the face of competition, market survival requires firms to have the lowest unit costs possible under existing production technology. Whether that happens at low or high levels of output depends entirely on the shape of the LAC curve.

THE RELATIONSHIP BETWEEN LONG-RUN AND SHORT-RUN COST CURVES

Let us return again to the example of Kelly's Cleaners with which we began the chapter. Earlier we derived the short-run cost curves with capital fixed at 120 machine-hr/hr. These curves were depicted in Figure 10.6. Figure 10.22 shows again the short-run marginal cost curve, labelled SMC_{120}, and short-run average total cost curve, labelled ATC_{120}.

In the long run we know that capital need not be fixed at 120 machine-hr/hr. What if capital is 200 machine-hr/hr? We can derive a new set of short-run cost curves. Figure 10.22 depicts the SMC and ATC curves when capital is fixed at 200 machine-hr/hr. Because of the larger amount of capital it is more expensive to wash a relatively small amount of laundry but cheaper to wash a relatively large amount of laundry. Figure 10.22 also depicts the SMC and ATC curves when capital is fixed at 240 machine-hr/hr.

Clearly, there is no reason to consider only 120, 200 or 240 machine-hr/hr. We can derive short-run cost functions for any amount of capital.

Suppose, again, the capital is fixed at 120 machine-hr/hr. For most levels of output Kelly would wish it had either more or less than 120 machine-hr/hr. The only reason Kelly does not change capital is because he cannot. There should, however, be some output level where capital of 120 machine-hr/hr is optimal. That is, there must be some output level where Kelly would choose to have 120 machine-hr/hr. In Figure 10.22 this is output Q_1. To the left of Q_1 Kelly has 'too much' capital. To the right of Q_1 he has 'too little' capital. But, at Q_1 it would be optimal to employ exactly 120 machine-hr/hr.

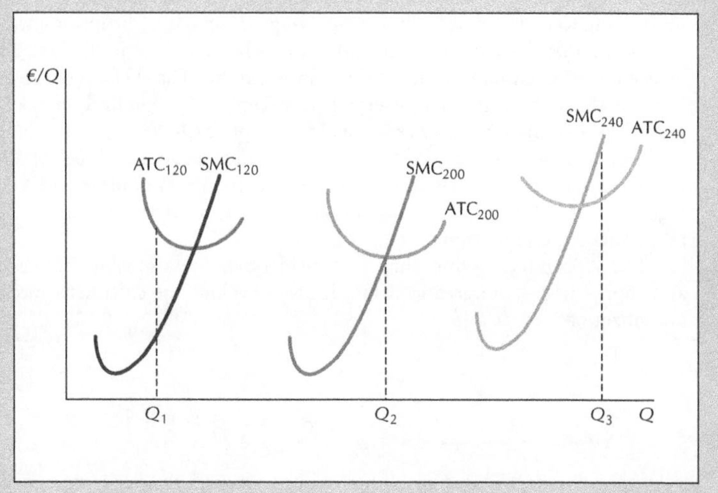

FIGURE 10.22 Short-Run Cost Curves for Different Amounts of Fixed Capital
The SMC and ATC curves when capital is fixed at 120 or 200 or 240 machine-hr/hr. With a larger amount of capital it is relatively cheaper to produce a larger output. The output level where it is optimal to employ 120, 200 or 240 machine-hr/hr is given by Q_1 Q_2 and Q_3.

There must be levels of output where it is optimal to have 200 machine-hr/hr and 240 machine-hr/hr. These are given by outputs Q_2 and Q_3 in Figure 10.22.

Given that Kelly would choose to have 120 machine-hr/hr when producing output Q_1 we know that the short-run and long-run marginal and average total cost must equal at this point. There is no way to decrease costs in the long run because Kelly is already choosing the optimal amount of capital. He can do no better. Point A in Figure 10.23 must, therefore, lie on the long-run average cost curve and point B must lie on the long-run marginal cost curve. Similarly, points C and D must lie on the LAC curve and points C and E on the LMC curve. If we drew the ATC and SMC curves for 10,000 different levels of capital and joined the dots we would get something like Figure 10.23.

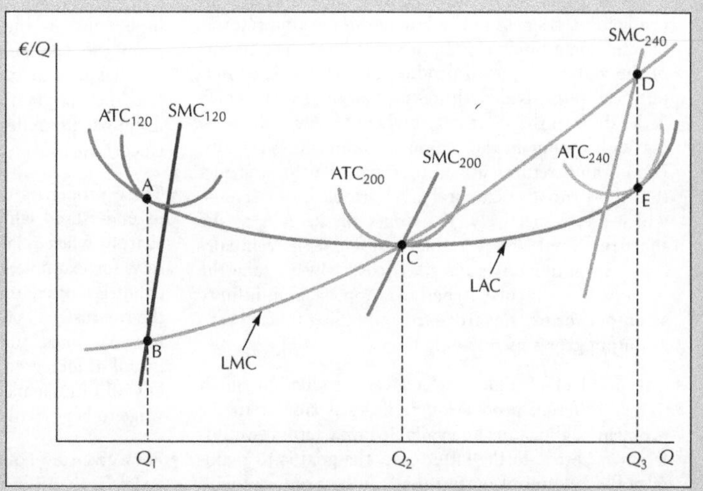

FIGURE 10.23 The Family of Cost Curves Associated with a U-Shaped LAC
The LAC curve is the 'outer envelope' of the ATC curves. LMC = SMC at the Q value for which the ATC is tangent to the LAC. At the minimum point on the LAC, LMC = SMC = ATC = LAC.

This allows us to relate short-run and long-run cost curves. There is just one more thing to mention. If Kelly is employing 120 machine-hr/hr and not producing output Q_1 then his costs must be higher than they could be in the long run, because he is employing either too much or too little capital. The ATC_{120} curve must, therefore, lie above the LAC curve everywhere except at Q_1. Similarly the ATC_{200} curve must lie above the LAC curve everywhere except at Q_2.

One way of thinking of the LAC curve is thus as an 'envelope' of all the short-run average total cost curves. Note that at the minimum point on the LAC curve in Figure 10.23 ($Q = Q_2$), the long-run and short-run marginal and average costs all take exactly the same value.

The Appendix to this chapter considers the relationship between long-run and short-run costs in greater detail. It also develops the calculus approach to cost minimization.

SUMMARY

- Of all the topics covered in an intermediate microeconomics text, students usually find the material on cost curves by far the most difficult to digest. And for good reason, since the sheer volume of specific concepts can easily seem overwhelming at first encounter. It is important to bear in mind, therefore, that all the various cost curves can be derived from the underlying production relationships in a simple and straightforward manner.

- Short-run cost curves, for example, all follow directly from the short-run production function. All short-run production functions we have discussed involved one fixed factor and one variable factor, but the theory would be exactly the same in the case of more than one fixed input. Short-run total costs are decomposed into fixed and variable costs, which correspond, respectively, to payments to the fixed and variable factors of production. Because of the law of diminishing returns, beyond some point we require ever larger increments of the variable input to produce an extra unit of output. The result is that short-run marginal cost, which is the slope of the short-run total cost curve, is increasing with output in the region of diminishing returns. Diminishing returns are also responsible for the fact that short-run average total and variable cost curves—which are, respectively, the slopes of the rays to the short-run total and variable cost curves—eventually rise with output. Average fixed costs always take the form of a rectangular hyperbola, approaching infinity as output shrinks toward zero, and falling toward zero as output grows increasingly large.

- The problem of allocating a given production quota to two different production facilities is similar to the problem of allocating an available input across two different facilities. In the latter case, the goal is to maximize the amount of output that can be produced with a given amount of input. In the former, it is to produce a given level of output at the lowest total cost. The solution is to allocate the production quota so that the marginal cost is the same in each production process. This solution does not require that average costs be the same in each process, and in practice, they often differ substantially.

- The optimal input bundle for producing a given output level in the long run will depend on the relative prices of the factors of production. These relative prices determine the slope of the isocost line, which is the locus of input bundles that can be purchased for a given total cost. The optimal input bundle will be the one that lies at the point of tangency between an isocost line and the desired isoquant. At the cost-minimizing point, the ratio of the marginal product of an input to its price will be the same for every input. Put another way, the extra output obtained from the last euro spent on one input must be the same as the extra output obtained from the last euro spent on any other input. Still another way of stating the minimum-cost condition is that the marginal rate of technical substitution at the optimizing bundle must be the same as the slope of the isocost line.

- These properties of production at minimum cost help us understand why methods of production often differ sharply when relative factor prices differ sharply. We saw, for example, that it helps explain why developing countries often use labour-intensive techniques while their industrial counterparts choose much more capital-intensive ones, and why labour unions often lobby on behalf of increased minimum wages, even though virtually all of their members earn more than the minimum wage to begin with.

- For a given level of output, long-run total costs can never be larger than short-run total costs for the simple reason that we have the opportunity to adjust all inputs in the long run, only some of them in the short run. The slope of the long-run average cost curve is a direct reflection of the degree of returns to scale in production. When there are increasing returns, LAC declines with output. With decreasing returns, by contrast, LAC rises with output. And finally, constant returns in production give rise to a horizontal LAC. A U-shaped LAC is one that corresponds to a production process that exhibits first increasing, then constant, and finally decreasing returns to scale. No matter what its shape, the LAC curve will always be an envelope of the corresponding family of ATC curves, each of which will be tangent to the LAC at one and only one point. At the output levels that correspond to these points of tangency, LMC and the corresponding SMC will be the same.

- The relationship between market structure and long-run costs derives from the fact that survival in the marketplace requires firms to have the lowest costs possible with available production technologies. If the LAC curve is downward sloping, lowest costs occur when only one firm serves the market. If the LAC curve is U-shaped and its minimum point occurs at a quantity that corresponds to a substantial share of total market output, the lowest costs will occur when only a few firms serve the market. By contrast, if the minimum point on a U-shaped LAC curve corresponds to only a small fraction of total industry output, the market is likely to be served by many competing firms. The same will be true when the LAC curve is either horizontal or upward sloping.

QUESTIONS FOR REVIEW

1. What is the relationship between the law of diminishing returns and the curvature of the variable cost curve?
2. What is the relationship between the law of diminishing returns and the slope of the short-run marginal cost curve?
3. In which production process is fixed cost likely to be a larger percentage of short-run total costs, book publishing or landscape gardening?
4. Why does the short-run MC curve cut both the ATC and AVC curves at their minimum points?
5. If the LAC curve is rising beyond some point, what can we say about the degree of returns to scale in production?
6. Why should the production of a fixed amount of output be allocated between two production activities so that the marginal cost is the same in each?

PROBLEMS

1. The Preservation Embalming Company's cost data have been partially entered in the table below. Following the sudden and unexpected death of the company's accountant, you are called on to fill in the missing entries.

Bodies embalmed	Total cost	Fixed cost	Variable cost	ATC	AVC	AFC	MC
0	24			–	–	–	
1						–	16
2			50				
3	108						
4							
5					39.2		52
6				47			

2. Sketch the short-run TC, VC, FC, ATC, AVC, AFC and MC curves for the production function

$$Q = 3KL$$

where K is fixed at 2 units in the short run, with $r = 3$ and $w = 2$.

3. When the average product of labour is the same as the marginal product of labour, how will marginal cost compare with average variable cost?

4. A firm has access to two production processes with the following marginal cost curves: $MC_1 = 0.4Q$ and $MC_2 = 2 + 0.2Q$.

   a. If it wants to produce 8 units of output, how much should it produce with each process?
   b. If it wants to produce 4 units of output?

5. A firm uses two inputs, K and L, in its production process and finds that no matter how much output it produces or how input prices vary, it always minimizes its costs by buying only one or the other of the two inputs. Draw this firm's isoquant map.

6. A firm finds that no matter how much output it produces and no matter how input prices vary, it always minimizes its costs by buying half as many units of capital as of labour. Draw this firm's isoquant map.

7. A firm purchases capital and labour in competitive markets at prices of $r = 6$ and $w = 4$, respectively. With the firm's current input mix, the marginal product of capital is 12 and the marginal product of labour is 18. Is this firm minimizing its costs? If so, explain how you know. If not, explain what the firm ought to do.

8. A firm has a production function $Q = F(K, L)$ with constant returns to scale. Input prices are $r = 2$ and $w = 1$. The output-expansion path for this production function at these input prices is a straight line through the origin. When it produces 5 units of output, it uses 2 units of K and 3 units of L. How much K and L will it use when its long-run total cost is equal to 70?

9. A firm with the production function $Q = F(K, L)$ is producing an output level Q^* at minimum cost in the long run. How will its short-run marginal cost when K is fixed compare with its short-run marginal cost when L is fixed?

10. A firm employs a production function $Q = F(K, L)$ for which only two values of K are possible, K_1 and K_2. Its ATC curve when $K = K_1$ is given by $ATC_1 = Q^2 - 4Q + 6$. The corresponding curve for $K = K_2$ is $ATC_2 = Q^2 - 8Q + 18$. What is this firm's LAC curve?

11. If a firm's LMC curve lies above its SMC curve at a given level of output, what will be the relationship between its ATC and LAC curves at that output level?

*12. A firm has a long-run total cost function:

$$LTC(Q) = Q^3 - 20Q^2 + 220Q$$

Derive expressions for long-run average cost and marginal cost, and sketch these curves.

*13. For the long-run total cost function

$$LTC(Q) = Q^2 + 10$$

sketch ATC, AVC, AFC and MC.

*These problems are most easily solved using the calculus definition of marginal cost.

ANSWERS TO IN-CHAPTER EXERCISES

10.1. The variable cost curve is the same as before; the FC and TC curves are shifted upward by 8 units. (See the following graph.)

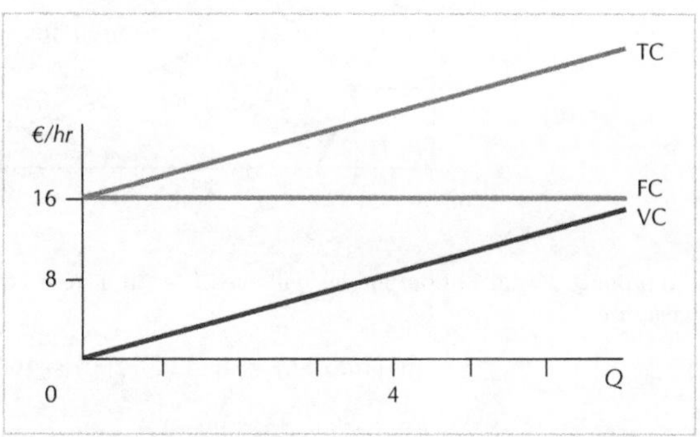

10.2. The vertical distance between the ATC and AVC curves is AFC. So we have $ATC_{10} - AVC_{10} = FC/10 = 20/10 = 2$.

10.3. Equating marginal costs, we have $12Q^A = 4Q^B$. Substituting $Q^B = 12 - Q^A$ yields $12Q^A = 48 - 4Q^A$, which solves for $Q^A = 3$. $Q^B = 12 - 3 = 9$ takes care of remaining output, and at these output levels, marginal cost in both plants will be €36/unit of output.

10.4. When marginal product lies above average product, marginal cost lies below average variable cost. (See Figure 10.9.)

10.5.

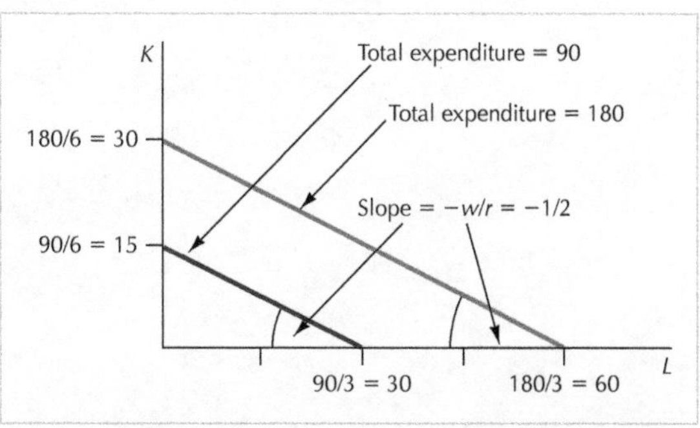

10.6. To produce 20 units of output, we will need $L = K = 20$. As $r = 10$ and $w = 5$, costs are

$$C = 10K + 5L = 200 + 100 = 300$$

which may be rewritten as $K = 30 - \frac{1}{2}L$ in slope-intercept form. When the wage rises $w = 20$, keeping costs at $C = 300$ requires that we find the point at which $K = L$ on the new isocost curve

$$C = 10K + 20L = 300$$

which may be rewritten as $K = 30 - 2L$ in slope-intercept form. Setting $K = L$, we have

$$10K + 20L = 300 = 10L + 20L = 300 = 30L = 300, \text{ so } L = 10$$

Thus, $L = K = 10$ and we produce $Q = 10$.

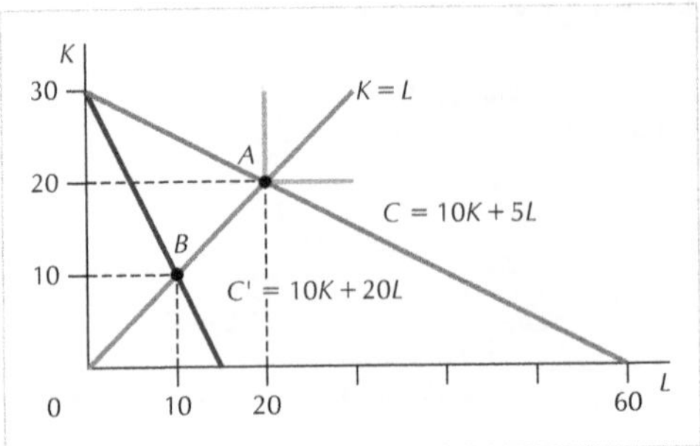

10.7. To produce 20 units of output, we will need $L = 20$ or $K = 20$. Since $r = 10$ and $w = 5$, costs are

$$C = \min\{10K, 5L\} = \min\{200, 100\} = 100$$

When the wage rises to $w = 20$, keeping costs at $C = 100$ implies that

$$Q = \max\left\{\frac{100}{r}, \frac{100}{w}\right\} = \max\{10, 5\} = 10$$

Thus, we use no labour ($L = 0$), all capital ($K = 10$), and produce $Q = 10$.

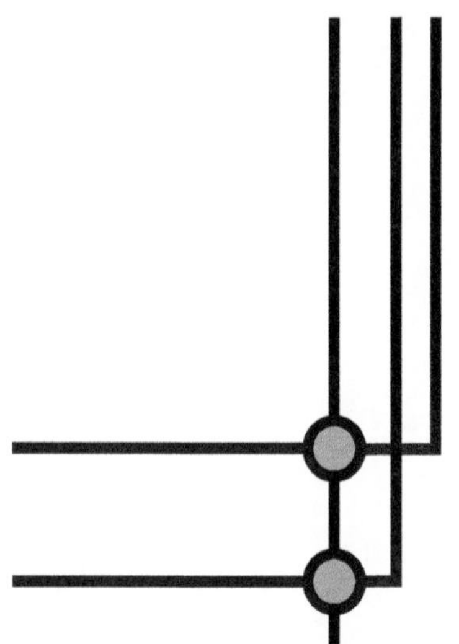

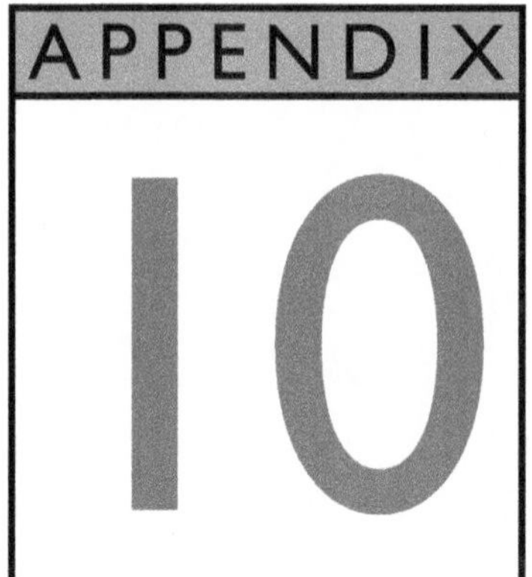

MATHEMATICAL EXTENSIONS OF THE THEORY OF COSTS

THE RELATIONSHIP BETWEEN LONG-RUN AND SHORT-RUN COST CURVES

Let us consider first in greater detail the relationship between long- and short-run total costs. Recall that the LTC curve is generated by plotting the Q value for a given isoquant against the corresponding total cost level for the isocost line tangent to that isoquant. Thus, for example, in Figure A.10.1, $Q = 1$ is associated with a long-run total cost of LTC_1, $Q = 2$ with LTC_2, and so on.

When K is variable, as it and all other factors are in the long run, the expansion path is given by the line $0E$. Now suppose, however, that K is fixed at K_2^*, the level that is optimal for the production of $Q = 2$. The short-run expansion path will then be the horizontal line through the point $(0, K_2^*)$, which includes the input bundles X, T and Z. The short-run total cost of producing a given level of output—say, $Q = 1$—is simply the total cost associated with the isocost line that passes through the intersection of the short-run expansion path and the $Q = 1$ isoquant (point X in Figure A.10.1), namely, STC_1.

Note in Figure A.10.1 that short- and long-run total costs take the same value for $Q = 2$, the output level for which the short- and long-run expansion paths cross. For all other output levels, the isocost line that passes through the intersection of the corresponding isoquant and the short-run expansion path will lie above the isocost line that is tangent to the isoquant. Thus, for all output levels other than $Q = 2$, short-run total cost will be higher than long-run total cost.

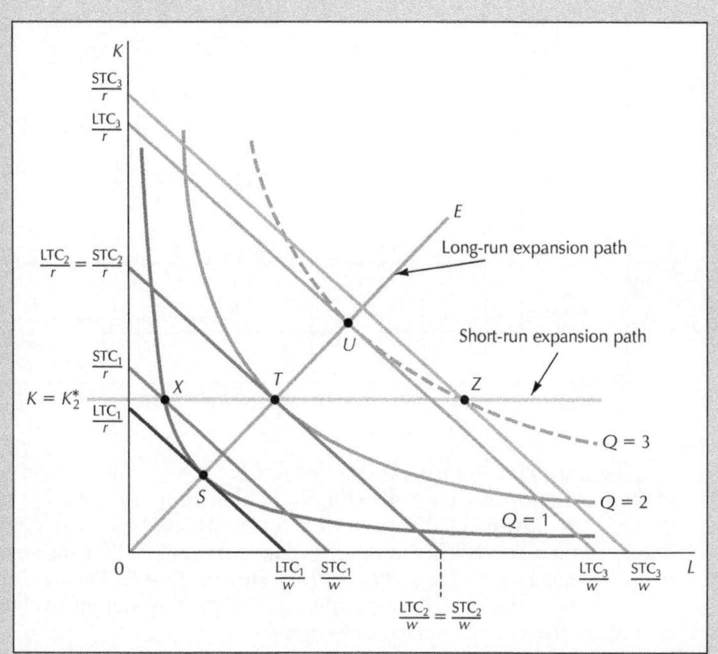

FIGURE A.10.1
The Short-Run and Long-Run Expansion Paths
The long-run expansion path is the line of 0*E*. With *K* fixed at the short-run expansion path is a horizontal line through the point $(0, K_2^*)$. Because K_2^*, is the optimal amount of *K* for producing 2 units of output, the long-run and short-run expansion paths intersect at *T*. The short-run total cost of producing a given level of output is the cost associated with the isocost line that passes through the intersection of the relevant isoquant and the short-run expansion path. Thus, for example, STC_3 is the short-run total cost of producing 3 units of output.

The short- and long-run total cost curves that correspond to the isoquant map of Figure A.10.1 are shown in Figure A.10.2. Note in Figure A.10.1 that the closer output is to $Q = 2$, the smaller the difference will be between long-run and short-run total cost. This property is reflected in Figure A.10.2 by the fact that the STC curve is tangent to the LTC curve at $Q = 2$: the closer Q is to 2, the closer STC_Q is to STC_2. Note also in Figure A.10.2 that the STC curve intersects the vertical axis at $rK_2^*$the fixed cost associated with K_2^* units of *K*.

The production process whose isoquant map is shown in Figure A.10.1 happens to be one with constant returns to scale. Accordingly, its long-run average and marginal cost curves will be the same horizontal line. The position of this line is determined by the slope of the LTC curve in Figure A.10.2. The associated ATC curve will be U-shaped and tangent to the LAC curve at $Q = 2$, as shown in Figure A.10.3.

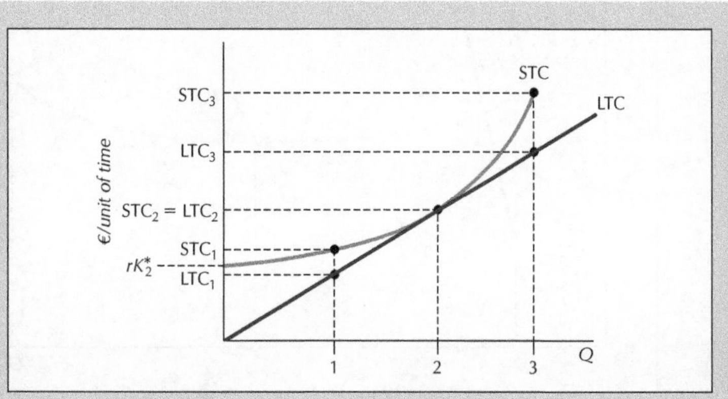

FIGURE A.10.2
The LTC and STC Curves Associated with the Isoquant Map in Figure A.10.1
As Q approaches 2, the level of output for which the fixed factor is at its optimal level, STC_Q approaches LTC_Q. The two curves are tangent at $Q = 2$.

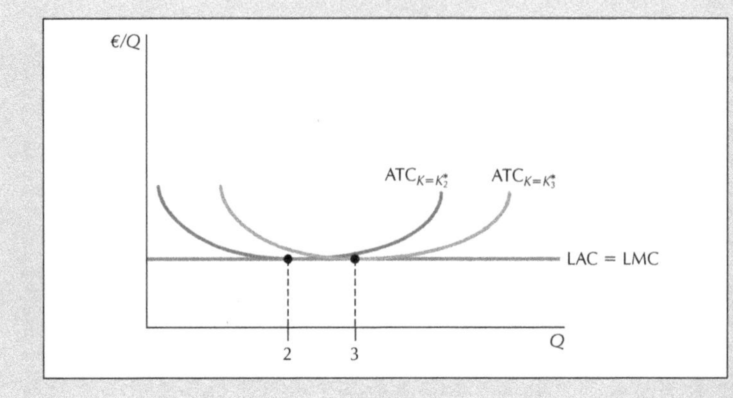

FIGURE A.10.3 The LAC, LMC and Two ATC Curves Associated with the Cost Curves from Figure A.10.2
Short-run average cost is tangent to long-run average cost at the same output level for which the corresponding LTC and STC curves are tangent.

There are short-run cost curves not just for $K = K_2^*$, but for every other level of the fixed input as well. For example, the short-run average cost curve when K is fixed at K_3^* (the optimal amount of K for producing $Q = 3$) is shown in Figure A.10.3 as the curve labelled $ATC_{K=K_3^*}$. Like the ATC curve associated with K_2^*, it too is U-shaped, and is tangent to the LAC curve at $Q = 3$. The ATC curves will in general be U-shaped and tangent to the LAC curve at the output level for which the level of the fixed input happens to be optimal.

A similar relationship exists in the case of production processes that give rise to U-shaped LAC curves. For such a process, the LAC curve and three of its associated ATC curves are shown in Figure A.10.4. When the LAC curve is U-shaped, note that the tangencies between it and the associated ATC curves do not in general occur at the minimum points on the ATC curves. The lone exception is the ATC curve that is tangent to the minimum point of the U-shaped LAC (ATC_2 in Figure A.10.4). On the downward-sloping portion of the LAC curve, the tangencies will lie to the left of the minimum points of the corresponding ATC curves; and on the upward-sloping portion of the LAC curve, the tangencies will lie to the right of the minimum points.

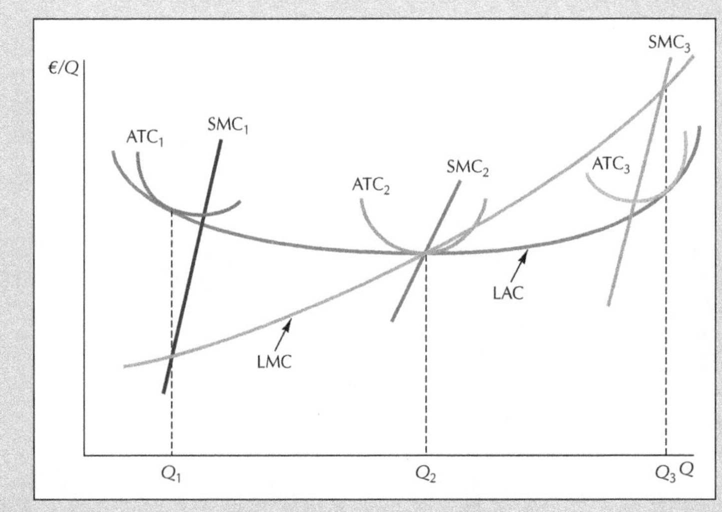

FIGURE A.10.4 The Family of Cost Curves Associated with a U-shaped LAC
The LAC curve is the 'outer envelope' of the ATC curves. LMC = SMC at the Q value for which the ATC is tangent to the LAC. At the minimum point on the LAC, LMC = SMC = ATC = LAC.

In the text, we noted that one way of thinking of the LAC curve is as an 'envelope' of all the ATC curves, like the one shown in Figure A.10.4. At the output level at which a given ATC is tangent to the LAC, the long-run marginal cost (LMC) of producing that level of output is the same as the short-run marginal cost (SMC). To see why this is so, recall that the tangency point represents the quantity level that is optimal for the fixed factor level that corresponds to the particular ATC curve. If we change output by a very small amount in the short run—by either increasing or reducing the amount of the variable input—we will end up with an input mix that is only marginally different from the optimal one, and whose cost is therefore approximately the same as that of the optimal mix. Accordingly, for output levels very near the relevant tangency point, SMC and LMC are approximately the same.

Note also in Figure A.10.4 that the SMC curves are always steeper than the LMC curve. The reason is implicit in our discussion of why LMC and SMC are nearly the same in a neighbourhood of the tangency points. Starting at a tangency point—say, at Q_1 in Figure A.10.4—suppose we want to produce an extra unit of output in the short run. To do so, we will have to move from an input mix that is optimal to one that contains slightly more L and slightly less K than would be optimal for producing $Q_1 + 1$ in the long run. So the cost of that extra unit will be higher in the short run than in the long run, which is another way of saying $SMC_{Q_1+1} > LMC_{Q_1+1}$.

Now suppose that we start at Q_1 and want to produce 1 unit of output less than before. To do so, we will have to move to an input bundle that contains less L and more K than would be optimal for producing $Q_1 - 1$. In consequence, our cost savings will be smaller in the short run than they would be in the long run, when we are free to adjust both L and K. This tells us that $LMC_{Q_1-1} > SMC_{Q_1+1}$. To say that LMC exceeds SMC whenever output is less than Q_1, but is less than SMC when output is greater than Q_1, is the same thing as saying that the LMC curve is less steep than the SMC curve at Q_1.

EXERCISE A.10.1 Consider a production function $Q = F(K, L)$ for which only two values of K are possible. These two values of K give rise to the ATC curves shown in the diagram. What is the LAC curve for this firm?

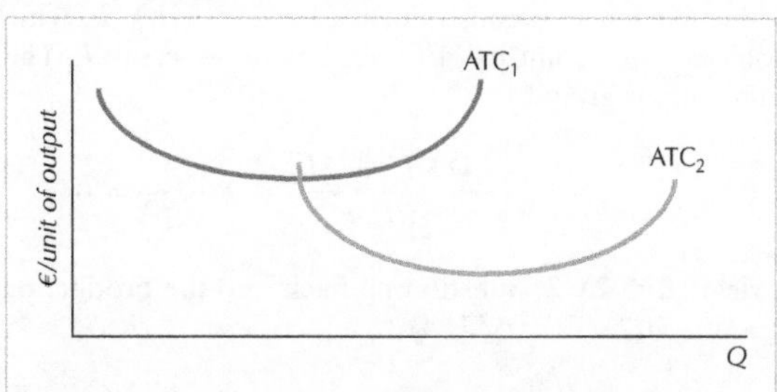

THE CALCULUS APPROACH TO COST MINIMIZATION

Using the Lagrangian technique discussed in the Appendix to Chapter 3, we can show that the equality of MP/P ratios (Equation 10.22) emerges as a necessary condition for the following cost-minimization problem:

$$\min_{K,\,L} P_K K + P_L L \quad \text{subject to} F(K, L) = Q_0 \tag{A.10.1}$$

To find the values of K and L that minimize costs, we first form the Lagrangian expression (we will use LG to denote the Lagrangian to avoid confusion over Ls):

$$LG = P_K K + P_L L + \lambda\,[F(K, L) - Q_0] \tag{A.10.2}$$

The first-order condition for a minimum is given by

$$\frac{\partial LG}{\partial K} = P_K + \lambda\frac{\partial F}{\partial K} = 0 \tag{A.10.3}$$

$$\frac{\partial LG}{\partial L} = P_L + \lambda\frac{\partial F}{\partial L} = 0 \tag{A.10.4}$$

and

$$\frac{\partial LG}{\partial \lambda} = F(K, L) - Q_0 = 0 \tag{A.10.5}$$

Dividing Equation A.10.3 by Equation A.10.4 and rearranging terms, we have

$$\frac{\partial F/\partial K}{P_K} = \frac{\partial F/\partial L}{P_L} \tag{A.10.6}$$

which is the result of Equation 10.21. (As an exercise, derive the same result by finding the first-order conditions for a maximum level of output subject to a cost limit of C.)

An alternative to the Lagrangian technique is to solve the production function constraint in Equation A.10.1 for K in terms of L, then substitute the result back into the expression for total cost. To illustrate this alternative approach, consider the following example.

EXAMPLE A.10.1 For the production function $Q = F(K, L) = \sqrt{K}\sqrt{L}$ with $P_K = 4$ and $P_L = 2$, find the values of K and L that minimize the cost of producing 2 units of output.

Our problem here is to minimize $4K + 2L$ subject to $F(K, L) = \sqrt{K}\sqrt{L} = 2$. Here the production function constraint is $Q = 2 = \sqrt{K}\sqrt{L}$, which yields $K = 4/L$. So our problem is to minimize $4(4/L) + 2L$ with respect to L. The first-order condition for a minimum is given by

$$\frac{d[(16/L) + 2L]}{dL} = 2 - \frac{16}{L^2} = 0 \tag{A.10.7}$$

which yields $L = 2\sqrt{2}$. Substituting back into the production function constraint, we have $K = 4/(2\sqrt{2}) = \sqrt{2}$. ◆

PROBLEMS

1. A firm produces output with the production function

$$Q = \sqrt{K}\sqrt{L}$$

where K and L denote its capital and labour inputs, respectively. If the price of labour is 1 and the price of capital is 4, what quantities of capital and labour should it employ if its goal is to produce 2 units of output?

2. Sketch LTC, LAC and LMC curves for the production function given in Problem 2. Does this production function have constant, increasing or decreasing returns to scale?
3. Suppose that a firm has the following production function:

$$Q(K, L) = 2L\sqrt{K}$$

   a. If the price of labour is 2 and the price of capital is 4, what is the optimal ratio of capital to labour?
   b. For an output level of $Q = 1000$, how much of each input will be used?
4. A firm with the production function

$$Q(K, L) = 2L\sqrt{KL}$$

is currently utilizing 8 units of labour and 2 units of capital. If this is the optimal input mix, and if total costs are equal to 16, what are the prices of capital and labour?
5. For a firm with the production function

$$Q(K, L) = 3 \ln K + 2 \ln L$$

find the optimal ratio of capital to labour if the price of capital is 4 and the price of labour is 6.

ANSWER TO IN-APPENDIX EXERCISE

A.10.1. The LAC curve (bottom panel) is the outer envelope of the two ATC curves (top-panel).

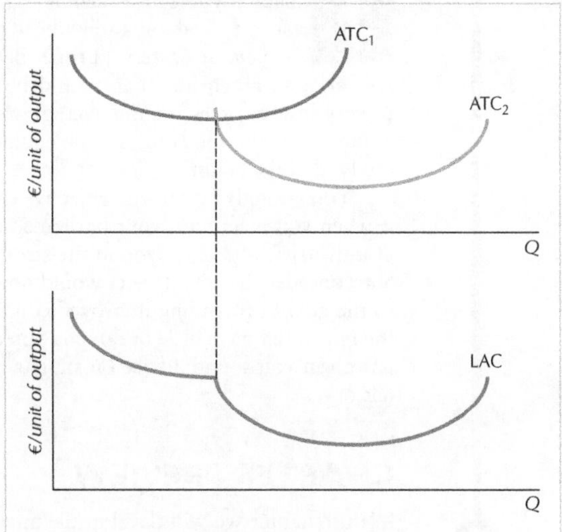

PERFECT COMPETITION

Imagine yourself a member of the European Parliament. You have been asked to vote on a bill whose purpose is to alleviate poverty among rural farmers in Eastern Europe. Because of limited equipment, crops are usually meagre, much less than would be achieved in Western Europe. This results in very low incomes for the average worker. The bill under consideration would authorize public funds to provide equipment that would double the crop yields on the land in the country.

You strongly favour the objective of the bill and are about to vote in favour of it when you meet with your parliamentary aide, an intern who studied economics at university. She urges you in the strongest possible terms not to vote for the bill. She concedes that the project would double crop yields, and she too is sympathetic to the goal of providing improved conditions for farmers. Even so, she insists that the bill would have little or no long-run effect on the earnings of farmers. Your aide has given you sound advice on similar matters in the past, and you decide to hear her out.

CHAPTER PREVIEW

In this chapter we will develop the analytical tools necessary for our hypothetical parliamentarian to assess his aide's advice, including a model of price and output determination in perfectly competitive markets. Our first step will be to characterize the competitive firm's objective as that of earning the highest possible profit. This is clearly not the only goal a firm might pursue, but we will see several reasons why firms might often behave as if profit were all they cared about.

We will then consider the four conditions that define a perfectly competitive market: (1) the existence of a standardized product, (2) price-taking behaviour on the part of firms, (3) perfect long-run mobility of factors of production, and (4) perfect information on the part of consumers and firms. It turns out that none of these conditions is likely to be satisfied in practice for any industry. Nonetheless, we will see that the economic model of perfect competition often generates useful insights even when its structural preconditions are only approximately satisfied.

Next, using the cost curves discussed in Chapter 10, we will derive the necessary condition for profit maximization in the short run. The rule calls for the firm to produce an output level at which its short-run marginal cost is equal to the price of the product. We will see that implementation of this rule fortunately does not require that firms have a detailed understanding of the economist's concept of marginal cost.

From the individual firm's supply decision, we will move to the issue of industry-wide supply. The technique for generating the industry supply schedule turns out to be closely analogous to the one for aggregating individual demand curves into a market demand curve: we simply add the individual firms' supply curves horizontally.

The industry short-run supply and demand curves interact to determine the short-run market price, which forms the basis for output decisions by individual firms. We will see that a firm's short-run profitability acts as a signal governing the movement of resources into and out of the industry—more specifically, that profits prompt resources to enter while losses prompt them to leave.

We will see that in the long run, if tastes and technology are unchanging, a competitive industry whose firms have U-shaped LAC curves will settle at an equilibrium price equal to the minimum value of the LAC curve. And we will also see that, under certain conditions, it will not be possible in such a market for anyone to enter into additional transactions that would benefit some people without at the same time harming some others.

THE GOAL OF PROFIT MAXIMIZATION

In studying not only perfect competition but also a variety of other market structures, economists traditionally assume that the firm's central objective is to maximize profit. Two things must be said about this assumption. The first is to clarify just what is meant by the term 'profit', and the second is to explain why it often makes sense to assume that firms try to maximize it.

Profit—or, more precisely, *economic profit*—is defined as the difference between total revenue and total cost, where total cost includes all costs—both explicit and implicit—associated with resources used by the firm. This definition is significantly different from the one used by accountants and many other non-economists, which does not subtract opportunity or implicit costs from total revenue. *Accounting profit* is simply total revenue less all explicit costs incurred.

To illustrate the distinction, suppose a firm produces 100 units of output per week by using 10 units of capital and 10 units of labour. Suppose the weekly price of each factor is €10/unit, and the firm owns its 10 units of capital. If output sells for €2.50/unit, the firm's total revenue will be €250/wk. To calculate the week's economic profit, we subtract from €250 the €100 spent on labour (an explicit cost) and the €100 opportunity cost of capital (an implicit cost), which leaves €50. (Under the assumption that the firm could have rented its capital to some other firm at the weekly rate of €10/unit, the €100 opportunity cost is simply the earnings forgone by using the capital in its own operation.) The week's accounting profit for this firm, by contrast, is €150, the difference between the €250 total revenue and the €100 out-of-pocket expenditure for labour.

Accounting profit may be thought of as the sum of two components: (1) *normal profit*, which is the opportunity cost of the resources owned by the firm (in this example, €100), and (2) economic profit, as defined above (here, €50). Economic profit is profit over and above the normal profit level.

The importance of the distinction between accounting and economic profits is driven home forcefully—if a bit fancifully—by the following example.

EXAMPLE 11.1 Cullen Gates runs a miniature golf course in the traditional English seaside resort of Margate. He rents the course and equipment from a large recreational supply company and supplies his own labour. His monthly earnings, net of rental payments, are £800, and he considers working at the golf course just as attractive as his only other alternative, working in a supermarket for £800/mo.

Now Cullen learns that his Uncle Bill has given him some land in Knightsbridge in the centre of London. The land has been cleared, and Cullen discovers that a construction company is willing to install and maintain a miniature golf course on it for a payment of £4000/mo. Cullen also commissions a market survey, which reveals that he would collect £16,000/mo in revenue by operating a miniature golf course there. (A mini-golf course in the centre of London would no doubt be very popular.) After deducting the £4000/mo payment to the construction company, this would leave him with £12,000/mo free and clear. Given these figures, and assuming Cullen's living costs will remain the same, should Cullen, a profit maximizer, switch his operation to London?

Since he is a profit maximizer, he should switch to London only if his economic profit there will be higher than in Margate. Suppose, however, that Cullen is unfamiliar with the concept of economic profit and instead compares his accounting profits in the two locations. In Margate, his accounting profit is £800/mo, the amount he has left over after paying all his bills. In London, the corresponding figure will be £12,000/mo. On this comparison, he would quickly forsake Margate for London.

If he compares economic profits, however, he will reach precisely the opposite conclusion. In Margate, his economic profit is zero once we account for the opportunity cost of his labour. (He could have earned £800/mo as a grocery clerk, exactly the amount of his accounting profit.) To calculate what his economic profits would be in London, we must deduct from his £12,000/mo accounting profits not only the £800 monthly opportunity cost of his labour, but also the opportunity cost of his land. Few locations on earth command higher land prices than Knightsbridge. Suppose we conservatively estimate that Cullen's land would sell for £100,000,000 in today's real estate market, and suppose that the interest rate is 1 per cent/mo. The opportunity cost of devoting the land to a miniature golf course will then be (0.01) × (£100,000,000) = £1,000,000/mo, which makes his monthly economic profit in London equal to £12,000 − £800 − £1,000,000 = −£988,800. Thus, if we assign any reasonable value to the opportunity cost of his land, it will obviously be better for Cullen to sell or rent it to someone else and remain in Margate. The reason London real estate is so expensive is that people can build luxury apartments on it and charge high rents to a multitude of tenants. To build a miniature golf course in Knightsbridge would be like wearing diamonds on the soles of your shoes. ◆

EXERCISE 11.1 In Example 11.1, how low would the monthly interest rate have to be before Cullen should relocate to London?

Let us turn now to the assumption of profit maximization. To predict what any entity—a firm, person, committee or government—will do under specific conditions, some sort of assumption must be made about its goals. After all, if we know where people want to go, it is much easier to predict what they will do to get there. Economists assume that the goal of firms is to maximize economic profit; then they try to discover what specific behaviours promote that goal.

Numerous challenges have been raised to the profit-maximization assumption. Some critics say the firm's goal is to maximize its chances of survival; others believe that it wants to maximize total sales or total revenues; and some even claim that firms do not try to maximize anything at all.

One reason for such scepticism is that examples abound in which the managers of firms appear unqualified to take the kinds of actions required for maximizing profit. It is important to understand, however, that the assumption of profit maximization is not refuted by the existence of incompetent managers. On the contrary, a case can be made that, even in a world in which the actions of firms are initially random, a long-run tendency for profit-maximizing behaviour will eventually dominate.[1]

The argument is analogous to Charles Darwin's theory of evolution by natural selection, and it goes roughly as follows. First, in a world of random action, some firms will, purely by chance, come much closer than others to profit-maximizing behaviour. The former firms will have greater surplus revenues at their disposal, which will enable them to grow faster than their rivals. The other side of this coin is that firms whose behaviour deviates most sharply from profit maximization are the ones most likely to go bankrupt. In the animal kingdom, food is an essential resource for survival, and profit plays a parallel role in the competitive marketplace. Those firms with the highest profits are often considerably more likely to survive. The evolutionary argument concludes that, over long periods of time, behaviour will tend toward profit maximization purely as a result of selection pressures in the competitive environment.

But the forces in support of profit maximization are not limited to the unintentional pressures of natural selection. They also include the actions of people who are very consciously pursuing their own interests. Bankers and other moneylenders, for example, are eager to keep their risks to a minimum, and for this reason, they prefer to do business with highly profitable firms. In addition to having more internal resources, such firms thus have easier access to external sources of capital to finance their growth. Another important force supporting profit-maximizing behaviour is the threat of an outside takeover. The price of shares of stock in a firm is based on the firm's profitability (more on this point in Chapter 15), with the result that shares of stock of a non-profit-maximizing firm will often sell for much less than their potential value. This creates an opportunity for an outsider to buy the stock at a bargain price and then drive its price upward by altering the firm's behaviour.

Another pressure in favour of profit maximization is that the owners of many firms compensate their managers in part by giving them a share of the firm's profits. This provides a clear financial incentive for managers to enhance profitability whenever opportunities arise for them to do so.

Let us note, finally, that the assumption of profit maximization does not imply that firms conduct their operations in the most efficient conceivable manner at all times. In the world we live in there are not only many intelligent, competent managers, but also a multitude who possess neither of these attributes. Needless to say, not every task can be assigned to the most competent person in the universe. In a sensible world, the most important tasks will be carried out by the best managers, the less important tasks by less competent ones. So the mere fact that we often observe firms doing silly things does not establish that they are not maximizing profits. To maximize profits means simply to do the best one can under the circumstances, and that will sometimes mean having to muddle along with uninspired managers.

Taken as a whole, the foregoing observations lend support to the assumption of profit maximization. We might even say that they place the burden of proof on those

[1]See, for example, Armen Alchian, 'Uncertainty, Evolution, and Economic Theory', *Journal of Political Economy,* 1950.

who insist that firms do not maximize profits. But they obviously do not establish conclusively that firms always pursue profit at the expense of all other goals. This remains an empirical question, and in the chapters to come we will see some evidence that firms sometimes fall short. Even so, the assumption of profit maximization is a good place to begin our analysis of firm behaviour, and there is no question but that it provides useful insights into how firms respond to changes in input or product prices, taxes and other important features of their operating environments.

THE FOUR CONDITIONS FOR PERFECT COMPETITION

To predict how much output a competitive firm will produce, economists have developed the *theory of perfect competition*. Four conditions define the existence of a perfectly competitive market. Let us consider each of them in turn.

1. **Firms Sell a Standardized Product** In a perfectly competitive market, the product sold by one firm is assumed to be a perfect substitute for the product sold by any other. Interpreted literally, this is a condition that is rarely if ever satisfied. Connoisseurs of fine wines, for example, insist that they can tell the difference between wines made from the same variety of grape grown on estates only a few hundred metres apart. It is also difficult to speak of a market for even such a simple commodity as shirts, because shirts come in so many different styles and quality levels. If we define the market sufficiently narrowly, however, it is sometimes possible to achieve a reasonable degree of similarity among the products produced by competing firms. For instance, 'French spring wheat' may not be exactly the same on different farms, but it is close enough that most buyers do not care very much which farm the wheat comes from.

© Kyoungil Jeon

Few product markets fully satisfy the conditions required for perfect competition, but the markets for many agricultural products come close.

2. **Firms Are Price Takers** This means that the individual firm treats the market price of the product as given. More specifically, it must believe that the market price will not be affected by how much output it produces. This condition is likely to be satisfied when the market is served by a large number of firms, each one of which produces a negligible fraction of total industry output. But a large number of firms are not always necessary for price-taking behaviour. Even with only two firms in the market, for example, each may behave as a price taker if it believes that other firms stand ready to enter its market at a moment's notice.

3. **Free Entry and Exit, with Perfectly Mobile Factors of Production in the Long Run** One implication of this condition is that if a firm perceives a profitable business opportunity at a given time and location, it will be able to hire the factors of production required to take advantage of it. Similarly, if its current venture no longer appears attractive in relation to alternative business ventures, it is free to discharge its factors of production, which will then move to industries in which opportunities are stronger. Of course, no one believes that resources are perfectly mobile. Labour, in particular, is not likely to satisfy this condition. People buy homes, make friends, enrol their children in schools, and establish a host of other commitments that make it difficult to move from one place to another. Nonetheless, the perfect mobility assumption is often reasonably well satisfied in practice, especially if we take into account that it is not always necessary for labour to move geographically in order for it to be mobile in an economic sense. Indeed, the firm can often move to the worker, as happens when textile companies outsource to India or the Far East.

4. **Firms and Consumers Have Perfect Information** A firm has no reason to leave its current industry if it has no way of knowing about the existence of more profitable opportunities elsewhere. Similarly, a consumer has no motive to switch from a high-priced product to a lower-priced one of identical quality unless she knows about the existence of the latter. Here too the required condition is never satisfied in a literal sense. The world is sufficiently complex that there will inevitably be relevant features of it hidden from view. As a practical matter, the assumption of perfect information is usually interpreted to mean that people can acquire most of the information that is most relevant to their choices without great difficulty. Even this more limited condition will fail in many cases. As we saw in Chapter 8, people often have the relevant information right at their fingertips and yet fail to make sensible use of it. These observations notwithstanding, we will see that the state of knowledge is often sufficient to provide a reasonable approximation to the perfect information condition.

To help assess whether the assumptions underlying the model of perfect competition are hopelessly restrictive, it is useful to compare them to the assumptions that underlie the physicist's model of objects in motion. If you have taken a high school or college physics course, then you know (or once knew) that a force applied to an object on a frictionless surface causes that object to accelerate at a rate inversely proportional to its mass. Thus, a given force applied to a 10-kilogram object will cause that object to accelerate at twice the rate we observe when the same force is applied to a 20-kilogram object.

To illustrate this theory, physics teachers show us films of what happens when various forces are applied to a hockey puck atop a large surface of dry ice. These physicists understand perfectly well that there is an easily measured amount of friction between the puck and the dry ice. But they are also aware that the friction levels are so low that the model still provides reasonably accurate predictions.

In the kinds of situations we are most likely to encounter in practice, friction is seldom as low as between a puck and a dry ice surface. This will be painfully apparent to you, for example, if you have just taken a spill from your Harley Sportster motorcycle on an asphalt road. But even here the physicist's laws of motion apply, and we can make adjustments for friction in order to estimate just how far a fallen rider will slide. And even where the model cannot be calibrated precisely, it tells us that the rider will slide farther the faster he was going when he fell, and that he will slide farther if the pavement is wet or covered with sand or gravel than if it is clean and dry.

With the economic model of perfect competition, the issues are similar. In some markets, most notably those for agricultural products, the four conditions come close to being satisfied. The predictions of the competitive model in these cases are in many ways as precise as those of the physicist's model applied to the puck on dry ice. In other markets, such as those for garbage trucks or earth-moving equipment, at least some of the conditions are not even approximately satisfied. But even in these cases, the competitive model can tell us something useful if we interpret it with care.

THE SHORT-RUN CONDITION FOR PROFIT MAXIMIZATION

The first question we want our model of competitive firm behaviour to be able to answer is, 'How does a firm choose its output level in the short run?' Under the assumption that the firm's goal is to maximize economic profit, it will choose that level of output for which the difference between total revenue and total cost is largest.

Consider a firm with the short-run total cost curve labelled TC in the top panel in Figure 11.1. Like many of the firms we discussed in Chapter 10, this firm experiences first increasing, then decreasing, returns to its variable input, which produces the familiar pattern of curvature in its total cost curve. Suppose this firm can sell its output at a price of P_0 = €18/unit. Its total revenue per week will then be €18/unit of output times the number of units of output sold each week. For example, if the firm sells no output, it earns zero total revenue; if it sells 10 units of output per week, it earns €180/wk; if it sells 20 units/wk, it earns €360/wk; and so on. So for the perfectly competitive firm, which can sell as much or as little output as it chooses at a constant market price, total revenue is exactly proportional to output. For the firm in this example, the total revenue curve is the line labelled TR in the top panel in Figure 11.1. It is a ray whose slope is equal to the product price, $P_0 = 18$.

The bottom panel in Figure 11.1 plots the difference between TR and TC, which is the curve labelled Π_Q, the notation traditionally used in economics to represent

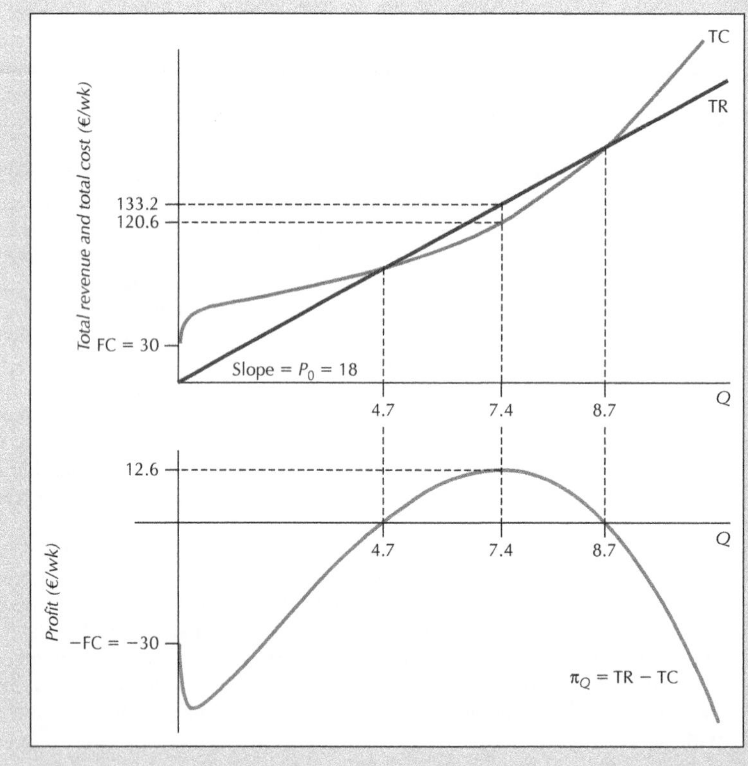

FIGURE 11.1 Revenue, Cost and Economic Profit The total revenue curve is the ray labelled TR in the top panel. The difference between it and total cost (TC in the top panel) is economic profit (Π_Q in the bottom panel). At $Q = 0$, $\Pi_Q = -\text{FC} = -30$. Economic profit reaches a maximum (€12.60/wk) for $Q = 7.4$.

economic profit. Here, Π_Q is positive for output levels between $Q = 4.7$ and $Q = 8.7$, and reaches a maximum at $Q = 7.4$. For output levels less than 4.7 or greater than 8.7, the firm is earning economic losses, which is simply another way of saying that its economic profits are negative for those values of Q.

In the bottom panel in Figure 11.1, note also that the vertical intercept of the profit curve is equal to −€30/wk, the negative of the firm's fixed cost. When the firm produces no output, it earns no revenue and incurs no variable cost but must still pay its fixed costs, so its profit when $Q = 0$ is simply $-FC$. If there were no positive output level for which the firm could earn higher profit than $-FC$, its best option would be to produce zero output in the short run.

The maximum profit point can also be characterized in terms of the relationship between output price and short-run marginal cost. Output price, which is equal to the slope of the total revenue curve, is also called **marginal revenue (MR)**.[2] Marginal revenue is formally defined as *the change in revenue that occurs when the sale of output changes by 1 unit*. In the cost-benefit language of Chapter 1, MR is the benefit to the firm of selling an additional unit of output. If the firm wants to maximize its profit, it must weigh this benefit against the cost of selling an extra unit of output, which is its marginal cost.

marginal revenue the change in total revenue that occurs as a result of a 1-unit change in sales.

The short-run marginal and average variable cost curves that correspond to the TC curve in Figure 11.1 are shown in Figure 11.2, where we again suppose that the firm can sell its output at a price of P_0 = €18/unit. To maximize its economic profit, the firm should follow this rule: provided P_0 is larger than the minimum value of AVC (more on the reason for this condition below), *the firm should produce a level of output for which marginal revenue, $P_0 = 18$, is equal to marginal cost on the rising portion of the MC curve.* For the particular cost curves shown in Figure 11.2, $P_0 = 18$ is indeed larger than the minimum value of AVC, and is equal to marginal cost at the quantity level $Q^* = 7.4$. The requirement that marginal revenue intersect marginal cost on the rising portion of marginal cost implies that marginal revenue intersects marginal cost from above. Thus marginal revenue lies below marginal cost past this point of intersection, and the firm has no incentive to expand output beyond this point (additional units would reduce profits).

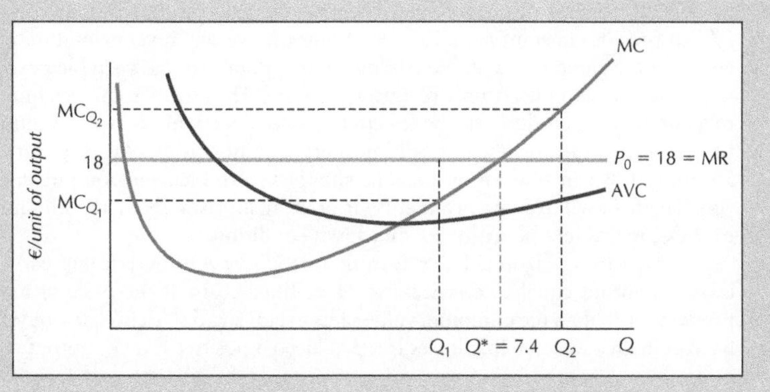

FIGURE 11.2
The Profit-Maximizing Output Level in the Short Run
A necessary condition for profit maximization is that price equal marginal cost on the rising portion of the marginal cost curve. Here, this happens at the output level $Q^* = 7.4$.

As the following exercise demonstrates, the definitions of MR and MC tell us something about the relative values of the slopes of the TR and TC curves at the maximum-profit point in Figure 11.1.

EXERCISE 11.2 How do the slopes of the TC and TR curves compare at Q = 7.4 in Figure 11.1?

Why is 'price = marginal cost' a necessary condition for profit maximization? Suppose we picked some other level of output, say, Q_1, that is less than $Q^* = 7.4$.

[2] As we will see in the next chapter, output price and marginal revenue are *not* the same for a monopolist.

The benefit to the firm of selling an additional unit of output will be P_0 = €18 (its marginal revenue).

The addition to total cost of producing an extra unit of output at Q_1 will be its marginal cost at the level of output, MC_{Q_1}, which in Figure 11.2 is clearly less than €18. It follows that for any level of output on the rising portion of the MC curve to the left of $Q^* = 7.4$, the benefit of expanding (as measured by marginal revenue) will be greater than the cost of expanding (as measured by marginal cost). This amounts to saying that profit will increase when we expand output from Q_1.

Now consider any level of output to the right of $Q^* = 7.4$, such as Q_2. At Q_2, the benefit of contracting output by 1 unit will be the resulting cost savings, which is marginal cost at that level of output, namely, MC_{Q_2}. (Note here that we are using the term 'benefit' to refer to the avoidance of a cost.) The cost to the firm of contracting output by 1 unit will be its marginal revenue, $P_0 = 18$, the loss in total revenue when it sells 1 unit less. (Here, not getting a benefit is a cost.) Since MC_{Q_2} > €18, the firm will save more than it loses when it contracts output by 1 unit. It follows that for any output level greater than $Q^* = 7.4$, the firm's profit will grow when it contracts output. The only output level at which the firm cannot earn higher profit by either expanding or contracting is $Q^* = 7.4$, the level for which the cost of any move is exactly equal to its benefit.[3]

The Shutdown Condition

Recall that the rule for short-run profit maximization is to set price equal to marginal cost, provided price exceeds the minimum value of average variable cost. Why must price be greater than the minimum point of the AVC curve? The answer is that unless this condition is met, the firm will do better to shut down—that is, to produce no output—in the short run. To see why, note that the firm's *average revenue (AR)* per unit of output sold is simply the price at which it sells its product. (When price is constant for all levels of output, average revenue and marginal revenue are the same.)[4] If average revenue is less than average variable cost, the firm is taking a loss on each unit of output it sells. The firm's total revenue (average revenue times quantity) will be less than its total variable cost (AVC times quantity), and this means that it would do better by not producing any output at all. Shutting down in this context means simply to produce zero output in the short run. The firm will resume production if price again rises above the minimum value of AVC, the trigger point for its **shutdown condition.**

shutdown condition if price falls below the minimum of average variable cost, the firm should shut down in the short run.

As we saw in Figure 11.1, a firm that produces zero output will earn economic profit equal to the negative of its fixed costs. If the price of its product is less than the minimum value of its average variable costs, it would have even greater economic losses if it produced a positive level of output.

[3]The firm's problem is to maximize $\Pi = PQ - TC_Q$, where TC_Q is the short-run total cost of producing Q units of output. The first-order condition for a maximum is given by

$$\frac{d\Pi}{dQ} = P - \frac{dTC_Q}{dQ} = P - MC_Q = 0$$

which gives the condition $P = MC_Q$. The second-order condition for a maximum is given by

$$\frac{d^2\Pi}{dQ^2} = \frac{-dMC_Q}{dQ} < 0$$

or

$$\frac{dMC_Q}{dQ} > 0$$

which tells us why we must be at a point on the rising portion of the marginal cost curve.

[4]Note that AR = TR/Q = $PQ/Q = P$.

The two rules—(1) that price must equal marginal cost on a rising portion of the marginal cost curve and (2) that price must exceed the minimum value of the average variable cost curve—together define the short-run supply curve of the perfectly competitive firm. The firm's supply curve tells how much output the firm wants to produce at various prices. As shown by the heavy red locus in Figure 11.3, it is the rising portion of the short-run marginal cost curve that lies above the minimum value of the average variable cost curve (which is €12/unit of output in this example). Below $P = 12$, the supply curve coincides with the vertical axis, indicating that the firm supplies zero output when price is less than min AVC. For prices above 12, the firm will supply the output level for which $P =$ MC. Thus, prices of 14 and 20 will cause this firm to supply 6.4 and 7.8 units of output, respectively. The competitive firm acts here as both a price taker and a profit maximizer: taking the market price as given, it chooses the level of output that maximizes economic profit at that price.

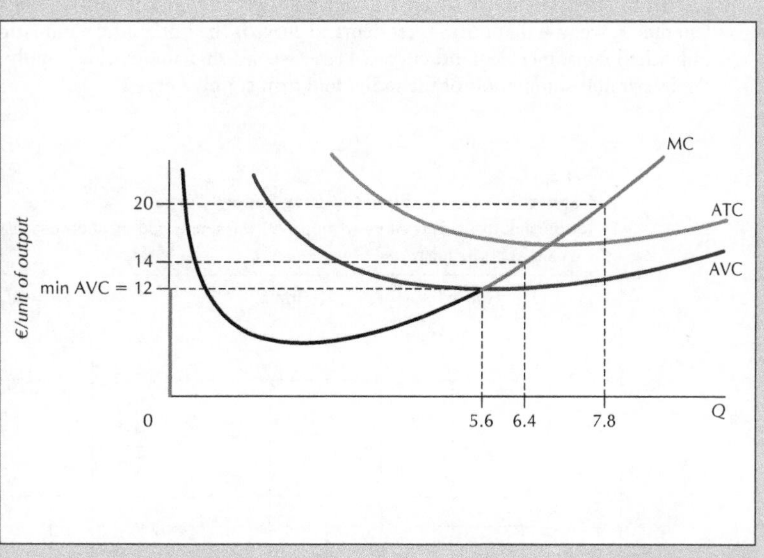

FIGURE 11.3 The Short-Run Supply Curve of a Perfectly Competitive Firm When price lies below the minimum value of average variable cost (here €12/unit of output), the firm will make losses at every level of output, and will keep its losses to a minimum by producing zero. For prices above min AVC, the firm will supply that level of output for which $P =$ MC on the rising portion of its MC curve.

Note in Figure 11.3 that the firm supplies positive output whenever price exceeds min AVC, and recall that average variable cost is less than average total cost, the difference being average fixed cost. It follows that no matter how small AFC is, there will be a range of prices that lie between the AVC and ATC curves. For any price in this range, the firm supplies the level of output for which $P =$ MC, which means that it will lose money because P is less than ATC. For example, the firm whose cost curves are shown in Figure 11.3 cannot cover all its costs at a price of €14. Even so, its best option is to supply 6.4 units of output per week, because it would lose even more money if it were to shut down. Being able to cover variable costs does not assure the firm of a positive level of economic profit. But it is sufficient to induce the firm to supply output in the short run.

Note also in Figure 11.3 that the firm's short-run supply curve is upward sloping. This is because the relevant portion of the firm's short-run marginal cost curve is upward sloping, which, in turn, is a direct consequence of the law of diminishing returns.

THE SHORT-RUN COMPETITIVE INDUSTRY SUPPLY

The short-run supply curve for a competitive industry is generated in a manner analogous to the one we used to generate the market demand curve in Chapter 5. In this case we simply announce a price and then add together the amounts each firm wishes to supply at that price. The resulting sum is industry supply at that price. Additional points on the industry supply curve are generated by pairing other prices with the sums of individual firm supplies at those prices.

Figure 11.4 illustrates the procedure for one of the simplest cases, an industry consisting of only two firms. At a price of €2/unit of output, only firm 1 (left panel) wishes to supply any output, and so its offering, $Q_1 = 2$ units of output per week, constitutes the entire industry supply at $P = 2$ (right panel). At $P = 3$, firm 2 enters the market (centre panel) with an offering of $Q_2 = 4$. Added to firm 1's offering at $P = 3$—namely, $Q_1 = 3$—the resulting industry supply at $P = 3$ is $Q = 7$ (right panel). In like fashion, we see that industry supply at $P = 7$ is $Q = 7 + 8 = 15$. In Chapter 5, we saw that the market demand curve is the horizontal summation of the individual consumer demand curves. Here, we see that the market supply curve is the horizontal summation of the individual firm supply curves.

FIGURE 11.4
The Short-Run Competitive Industry Supply Curve
To get the industry supply curve (right panel), we simply add the individual firm supply curves (left and centre panels) horizontally.

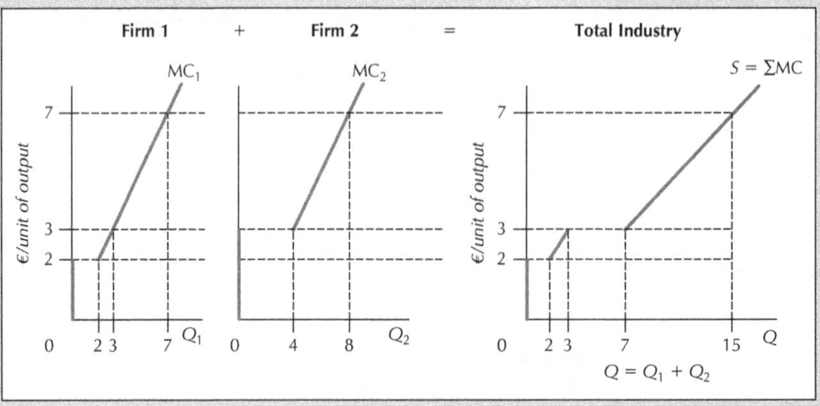

The horizontal summation of an individual firm's supplies into industry supply has a simple form when the firms in the industry are all identical. Suppose n firms each have supply curve $P = c + dQ_i$. To add up the quantities for the n firms into industry supply, we rearrange the firm supply curve $P = c + dQ_i$ to express quantity alone on one side: $Q_i = -(c/d) + (1/d)P$. Then industry supply is the sum of the quantities supplied Q_i by each of the n firms,

$$Q = nQ_i = n\left(-\frac{c}{d} + \frac{1}{d}P\right) = \frac{nc}{d} + \frac{n}{d}P$$

We can then rearrange industry supply $Q = -(nc/d) + (n/d)P$ to get it back in the form of price alone on one side: $P = c + (d/n)Q$. The intuition is that each one unit supplied by the industry is $1/n$ unit for each firm to supply. These calculations suggest a general rule for constructing the industry supply curve when firms are identical. If we have n individual firm supply curves $P = c + dQ_i$, then the industry supply curve is $P = c + (d/n)Q$.

EXAMPLE 11.2 Suppose an industry has 200 firms, each with supply curve $P = 100 + 1000Q_i$. What is the industry supply curve?

First, we need to rearrange the representative firm supply curve $P = 100 + 1000Q$ to have quantity alone on one side:

$$Q_i = -\frac{1}{10} + \frac{1}{1000}P$$

Then we multiply by the number of firms $n = 200$:

$$Q = nQ_i = 200Q_i = 200\left(-\frac{1}{10} + \frac{1}{1000}P\right) = -20 + \frac{1}{5}P$$

Finally, we rearrange the industry supply curve $Q = -20 + (\frac{1}{5})P$ to have price alone on one side $P = 100 + 5Q$ to return to the slope-intercept form. ◆

EXERCISE 11.3 Suppose an industry has 30 firms, each with supply curve $P = 20 + 90Q_i$. What is the industry supply curve?

SHORT-RUN COMPETITIVE EQUILIBRIUM

The individual competitive firm must choose the most profitable level of output to produce in response to a given price. But where does that price come from? As we saw in Chapter 2, it comes from the intersection of the supply and demand curves for the product. Recall that at the equilibrium price sellers are selling the quantity they wish to sell and buyers are buying the quantity they wish to buy.

In the left panel in Figure 11.5, the curve labelled D is the market demand curve for a product sold in a perfectly competitive industry. The curve labelled S is the corresponding short-run industry supply curve, the horizontal summation of the relevant portions of the individual short-run marginal cost curves.[5] These two curves intersect to establish the short-run competitive equilibrium price, here denoted $P^* =$ €20/unit of output. $P^* = 20$, in turn, is the price on which individual firms base their output decisions.

The conditions confronting a typical firm are shown in the right panel in Figure 11.5. The demand curve facing this firm is a horizontal line at $P^* = 20$. This means that it can sell as much or as little as it chooses at the market price of €20/unit. Put another way, any single firm can sell as much as it wants to without affecting the market price. If a firm charged more than €20, it would sell no output at all because buyers would switch to a competing firm that sells for €20. A firm could charge less than €20, of course, but would have no motive to do so if its objective were to maximize economic profit, since it can already sell as much as it wants to at €20. The result is that even though the market demand curve is downward sloping, the demand curve facing the individual firm is perfectly elastic. (Recall from the definition of price elasticity in Chapter 5 that a horizontal demand curve has infinite price elasticity, which is what 'perfectly elastic' means.)

In the right panel in Figure 11.5, the representative firm maximizes its profit by equating $P^* =$ €20/unit to marginal cost at an output level of $Q_1^* = 80$ units/

[5]Here, the 'relevant portions' are those that lie above the respective values of min AVC.

FIGURE 11.5
Short-Run Price and Output Determination under Pure Competition
The short-run supply and demand curves intersect to determine the short-run equilibrium price, $P^* = 20$ (left panel). The firm's demand curve is a horizontal line at $P^* = 20$ (right panel). Taking $P^* = 20$ as given, the firm maximizes economic profit by producing $Q_1^* = 80$ units/wk, for which it earns an economic profit of $\Pi_i =$ €640/wk (the shaded rectangle in the right panel)

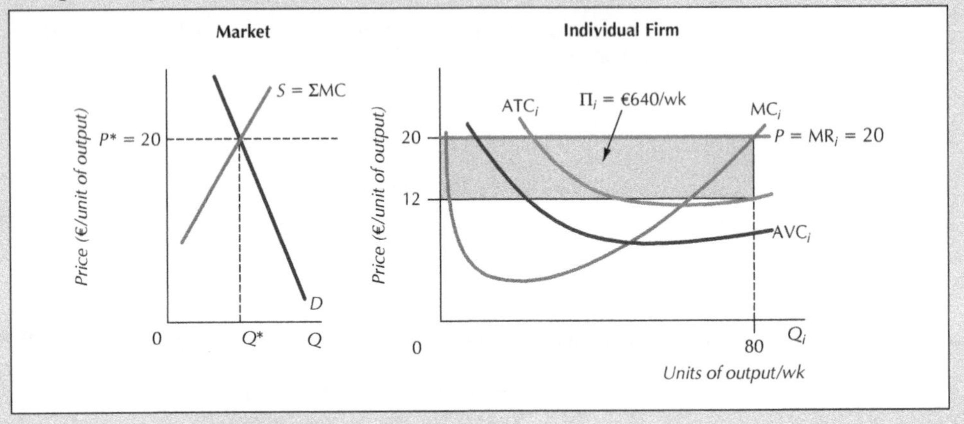

wk. At that output level its total revenue is $P^*Q_1^* =$ €1600/wk and its total costs are $\text{ATC}_{Q_i^*} Q_1^* =$ (€12/unit) (80 units/wk) = €960/wk. Its economic profit is the difference between total revenue and total cost, €1600/wk − €960/wk = €640/wk, and is represented by the shaded rectangle denoted Π_i. Equivalently, profits can be calculated as the difference between price (€20/unit) and average total cost (€12/unit) times the quantity sold (80 units/week).

Recall that the opportunity cost of resources owned by the firm constitutes part of the cost included in its average total cost curve. This is why we say that total revenues over and above total costs constitute economic profit. If the firm's revenue were exactly equal to its total cost, it would earn only a normal profit—which is to say, zero economic profit.

Facing a price equal to average total cost implies that total cost equals total revenue, and the firm earns zero economic profits. Thus price equal to the minimum of average total cost can be called the breakeven point—the lowest price at which the firm will not suffer negative profits in the short run.

The situation portrayed in Figure 11.5 and Table 11.1 is one in which the short-run equilibrium price enables the firm to make a positive economic profit. Another possibility is that the short-run supply and demand curves will intersect at an equilibrium price that is sufficiently high to induce firms to supply output, but not high enough to enable them to cover all their costs. This situation is shown in Figure 11.6 and Table 11.1. In the left panel, supply and demand intersect at a price $P^* =$ €10/unit of output, which lies above the minimum value of the AVC curve of the firm shown in the right panel, but below that firm's ATC curve at the profit-maximizing level of output, $Q_1^* = 60$ units of output per week. The result is that the firm makes an economic loss of $P^*Q_i^* - \text{ATC}_{Q_i^*} Q_i^* =$ −€120/wk. This loss is shown in the right panel in Figure 11.6 by the shaded rectangle labelled Π_i. Note that this loss is less than −TFC, the value of economic profit when output is zero. Thus it makes sense to produce even when economic profit falls below zero in the short run.

TABLE 11.1
Economic Profits versus Economic Losses

Q	ATC	MC	$\Pi(P = 20)$	$\Pi(P = 10)$
40	14	6	240	−160
60	12	10	480	−120
80	12	20	640	−160
100	15	31	500	−500

At a price of 20, the firm earns economic profits, but at a price of 10, it suffers economic losses.

FIGURE 11.6
A Short-Run Equilibrium Price that Results in Economic Losses
The short-run supply and demand curves sometimes intersect to produce an equilibrium price $P^* = €10$/unit of output (left panel) that lies below the minimum value of the ATC curve for the typical firm (right panel), but above the minimum point of its AVC curve. At the profit-maximizing level of output, $Q_i^* = 60$ units/wk, the firm earns an economic loss of $\Pi_i = -€120$/wk.

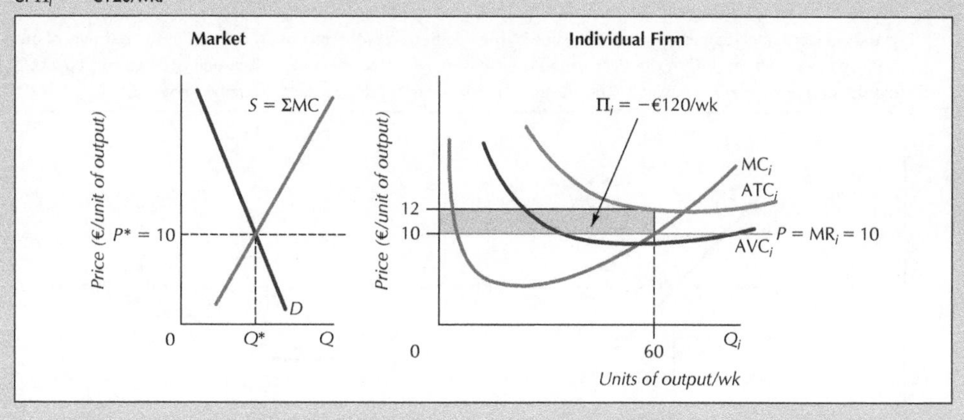

EXERCISE 11.4 If the short-run marginal and average variable cost curves for a competitive firm are given by MC = 2Q and AVC = Q, how many units of output will the firm produce at a market price of P = 12? At what level of fixed cost will this firm earn zero economic profit?

THE EFFICIENCY OF SHORT-RUN COMPETITIVE EQUILIBRIUM

One of the most attractive features of competitive markets is the fact that they result in **allocative efficiency**, which means that they fully exploit the possibilities for mutual gains through exchange. To illustrate, let us consider the short-run equilibrium pictured in the left panel of Figure 11.7, and suppose that the cost curves pictured in the right panel are the same for each of 1000 firms in the industry.

allocative efficiency a condition in which all possible gains from exchange are realized.

In a competitive market in the short run, consumers give firms money, which firms use to buy variable inputs to produce the output that goes to consumers. To say that the competitive equilibrium leaves no room for further mutually beneficial exchange is the same thing as saying that there is no way for any producer and consumer to agree to a private transaction at any price other than €10. Of course, consumers would gladly pay less than €10 for an additional unit of output. But since €10 is equal to the value of the resources required to produce another unit (MC_i in the right panel of Figure 11.7), no firm would be willing to respond. Firms, for their part, would gladly produce an extra unit of output if the price were higher than €10. But with 100,000 units of output already in the market, there are no consumers left who are willing to pay more than €10 (left panel of Figure 11.7). At the short-run competitive equilibrium price and quantity, the value of the resources used to produce the last unit of output (as measured by short-run marginal cost) is exactly equal to the value of that unit of output to consumers (as measured by the price they are willing to pay for it). Firms may wish that prices were higher, and consumers may complain that prices are too high already. But two parties have no incentive to trade at any price other than the equilibrium price.

FIGURE 11.7
Short-Run Competitive Equilibrium Is Efficient
At the equilibrium price and quantity, the value of the additional resources required to make the last unit of output produced by each firm (MC in the right panel) is exactly equal to the value of the last unit of output to buyers (the demand price in the left panel). This means that further mutually beneficial trades do not exist.

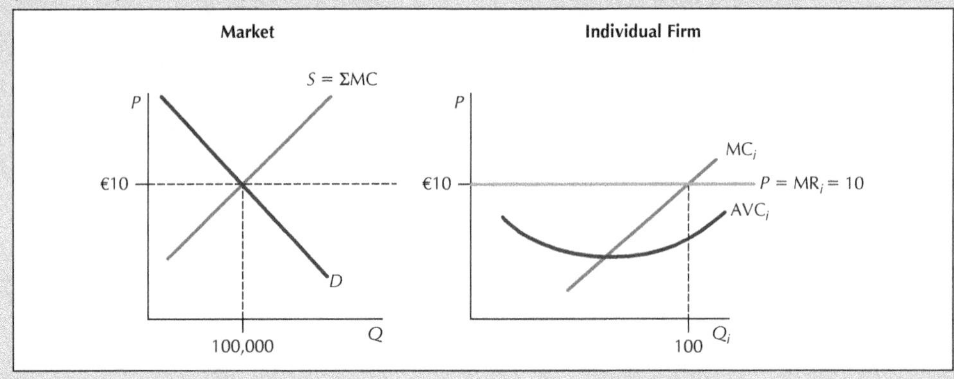

PRODUCER SURPLUS

To say that a competitive market is efficient is to say that it maximizes the net benefits to its participants. In policy analysis, it is often useful to estimate the actual amount by which people and firms gain from their participation in specific markets. Suppose, for example, that the government of a developing country knows it can open up new markets for seafood by building a road from its coast to an interior region. If its goal is to use the country's resources as efficiently as possible, its decision about whether to build the road will depend on whether the benefits people and firms reap from these new markets exceed the cost of building the road.

In Chapter 4 we discussed the concept of consumer surplus as a measure of the benefit to the consumer of engaging in a market exchange. An analogous measure exists for producers. Economists call it **producer surplus,** and it measures how much better off the firm is as a result of having supplied its profit-maximizing level of output. It may seem tempting to

producer surplus the euro amount by which a firm benefits by producing a profit-maximizing level of output.

say that the firm's producer surplus is simply its economic profit, but surplus and profit often differ. To see why, first recall that in the short run if the firm produces nothing, it will sustain a loss equal to its fixed cost. If the price exceeds the minimum value of AVC, however, it can do better by supplying a positive level of output. How much better? The firm's gain compared with the alternative of producing nothing is the difference between total revenue and total variable cost at the output level where P = MC. Now recall that economic profit is the difference between total revenue and total cost and that total cost differs from variable cost by fixed cost; it follows that producer surplus is the sum of economic profit and fixed cost.[6] Diagrammatically, it is the area of the shaded rectangle shown in the left panel in Figure 11.8. In the short run, producer surplus is thus larger than economic profit, because the firm would lose more than its economic profit if it were prevented from participating in the market. In the long run, all costs are variable. So producer surplus is the same as economic profit in the long run.

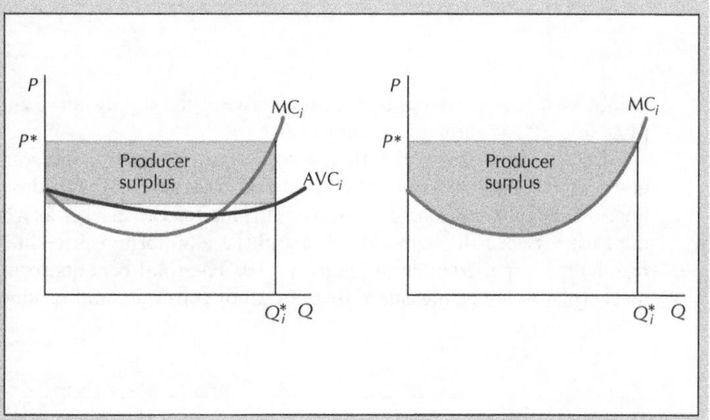

FIGURE 11.8
Two Equivalent Measures of Producer Surplus
The difference between total revenue and total variable cost is a measure of producer surplus, the gain to the producer from producing Q_i^* units of output rather than zero. It can be measured as the difference between $P^*Q_i^*$ and $AVC_{Q_i^*}Q_i^*$ (shaded rectangle, left panel), or as the difference between $P^*Q_i^*$ and the area under the marginal cost curve (upper shaded area, right panel).

The right panel in Figure 11.8 shows an equivalent way of representing producer surplus. The alternative measure makes use of the fact that variable cost at any level of output is equal to the area under the marginal cost curve (below the shaded area in the right panel). To see why this is so, note that the variable cost of producing 1 unit of output is equal to marginal cost at 1 unit, MC_1; VC for 2 units is the sum of MC_1 and MC_2, and so on, so that $VC_Q = MC_1 + MC_2 + \cdots + MC_Q$, which is just the area under the MC curve. Hence the difference between the total revenue and total variable cost may also be expressed as the upper shaded area in the right panel in Figure 11.8.

Which of the two ways of measuring producer surplus is most useful will depend on the specific context at hand. If we are interested in the change in an existing producer surplus, the method shown in the right panel in Figure 11.8 will usually be easiest to work with. But when we want to measure total producer surplus, it will often be easier to calculate the surplus by using the method shown in the left panel.

To measure aggregate producer surplus for a market, we simply add the producer surplus for each firm that participates. In cases where each firm's marginal cost curve is upward sloping for the bulk of its range, aggregate producer surplus

[6]If $\Pi = TR - TC$ and $TC = VC + FC$, then producer surplus $= TR - VC = TR - TC + FC = \Pi + FC$.

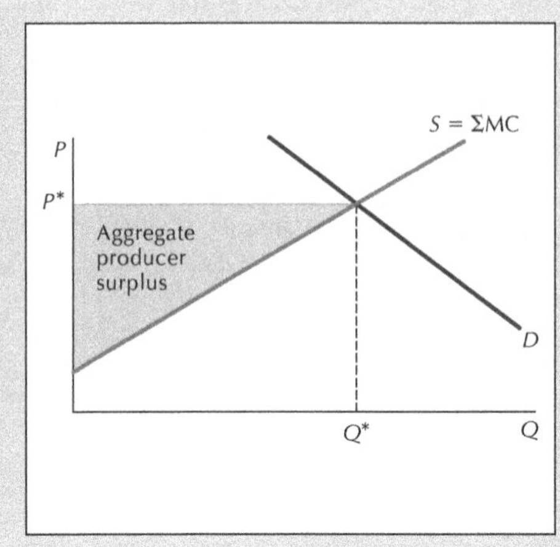

FIGURE 11.9
Aggregate Producer Surplus When Individual Marginal Cost Curves Are Upward Sloping Throughout
For any quantity, the supply curve measures the minimum price at which firms would be willing to supply it. The difference between the market price and the supply price is the marginal contribution to aggregate producer surplus at that output level. Adding these marginal contributions up to the equilibrium quantity Q^*, we get the shaded area, which is aggregate producer surplus.

will be well approximated by the area between the supply curve and the equilibrium price line, P^*, as shown in Figure 11.9.

Recall from Chapter 4 that a rough approximation of consumer surplus is given by the area between the consumer's demand curve and the equilibrium price line.[7] An approximation of consumer surplus for the market as a whole is given by the area between the demand curve and the equilibrium price line, as indicated by the shaded upper triangle in Figure 11.10. The total benefits from exchange in the marketplace may be measured by the sum of consumer and producer surpluses.

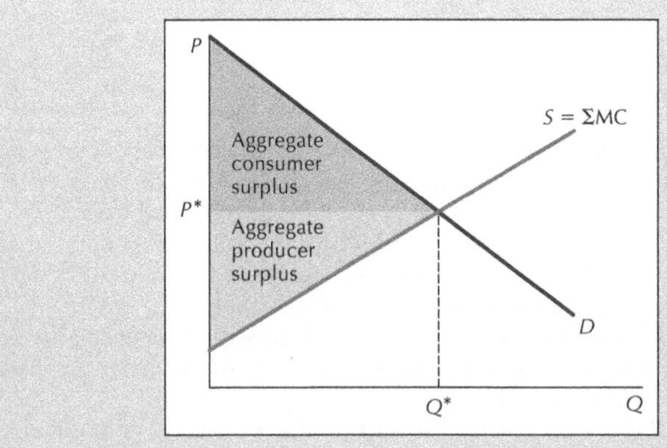

FIGURE 11.10
The Total Benefit from Exchange in a Market
The sum of aggregate producer surplus (shaded lower triangle) and consumer surplus (shaded upper triangle) measures the total benefit from exchange.

EXAMPLE 11.3 **Suppose there are two types of users of fireworks: careless and careful. Careful users never get hurt, but careless ones sometimes injure not only themselves, but also innocent bystanders. The short-run marginal cost curves of each of the 1000 firms in the fireworks industry are given by MC = 10 + Q, where Q is measured in number of cherry bombs per year and**

[7]Recall that this measure of consumer surplus is most accurate when income effects are small.

MC is measured in euros per cherry bomb. The demand curve for fireworks by careful users is given by $P = 50 - 0.001Q$. Legislators would like to continue to permit careful users to enjoy fireworks. But since it is impractical to distinguish between the two types of users, they have decided to outlaw fireworks altogether. How much better off would consumers and producers be if legislators had the means to effect a partial ban?

If the entire fireworks market is banned completely, the total of consumer and producer surplus will be zero. So to measure the benefits of a partial ban, we need to find the sum of consumer and producer surplus for a fireworks market restricted to careful users. To generate the supply curve for this market, we simply add the marginal cost curves of the individual firms horizontally, which results in the curve labelled *S* in Figure 11.11. The demand curve for careful users would intersect *S* at an equilibrium price of €30 and an equilibrium quantity of 20,000 bombs/yr.

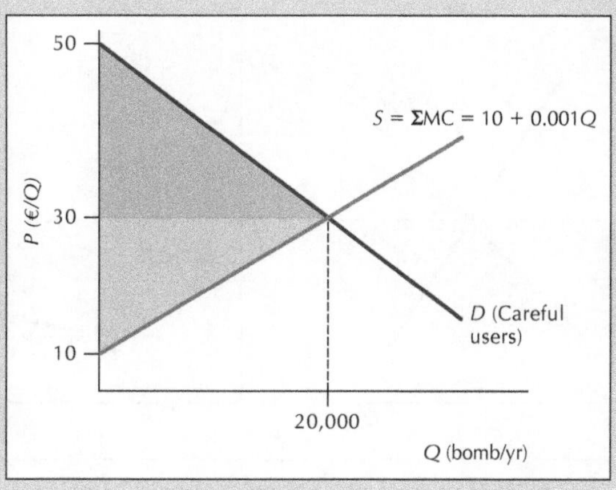

FIGURE 11.11 Producer and Consumer Surplus in a Market Consisting of Careful Fireworks Users The upper shaded triangle is consumer surplus (€200,000/yr). The lower shaded triangle is producer surplus (€200,000/yr). The total benefit of keeping this market open is the sum of the two, or €400,000/yr.

By outlawing the sale of fireworks altogether, legislators eliminate producer and consumer surplus values given by the areas of the two shaded triangles in Figure 11.11, which add to €400,000/yr. In the language of cost-benefit analysis, this is the cost imposed on producers and careful users. The benefit of the ban is whatever value the public assigns to the injuries prevented (net of the cost of denying careless users the right to continue). It is obviously no simple matter to put a monetary value on the pain and suffering associated with fingers blown off by cherry bombs. In Chapter 14, we will discuss how at least rough estimates have been attempted in similar situations. But even in the absence of a formal quantitative measure of the value of injuries prevented, the public can ask itself whether the forgone surplus of €400,000/yr is a reasonable price to pay.

Many countries ban the private use of fireworks—Australia, Ireland, and most states in the US. Some countries have hardly any restrictions on private use—the UK and France. Whether or not this reflects differences in the estimated value of injuries prevented or of the proportion of careless users we leave for you to judge. ◆

EXERCISE 11.5 What would the sum of consumer and producer surplus be in Example 11.3 if the demand curve for careful users were instead given by $P = 30 - 0.001Q$?

ADJUSTMENTS IN THE LONG RUN

The firm's objective in the long run is the same as in the short run, to earn the highest economic profit it can. But, there are two things the firm can do in the long run that it cannot do in the short run. (1) It can change fixed inputs. This will change its short-run marginal costs and, therefore, will change its short-run supply curve. (2) The firm can leave the industry or decide to enter a new industry. This will change the industry supply curve.

To illustrate, suppose that industry supply and demand intersect at the price level $P = 10$, as shown in the left panel in Figure 11.12. The cost curves for a representative firm are shown in the right panel in Figure 11.12. At $Q = 200$, the price of €10/unit of output exceeds ATC_2, with the result that the firm earns economic profit of €600 each time period. This profit is indicated by the shaded rectangle.

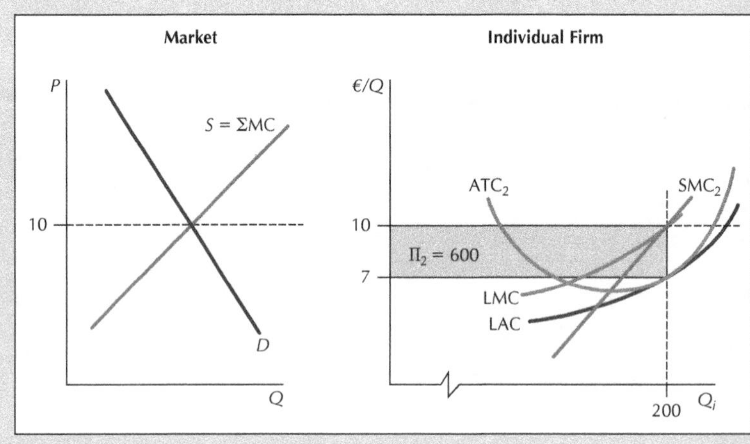

FIGURE 11.12 A Price Level that Generates Economic Profit At the price level $P =$ €10/unit, the firm has adjusted its plant size so that $SMC_2 = LMC = 10$. At the profit-maximizing level of output, $Q = 200$, the firm earns an economic profit equal to €600 each time period, indicated by the area of the shaded rectangle.

The situation depicted in Figure 11.12 is inherently unstable. The reason is that positive economic profit creates an incentive for outsiders to enter the industry. Recall that the average total cost curves already include the opportunity cost of the capital that a firm requires to do business. This means that an outsider can buy everything needed to duplicate the operations of one of the existing firms in the industry, and in the process earn an economic profit of €600 each time period.

So, let us suppose that at least one new firm enters the industry. As shown in the right hand panel of Figure 11.13, this will cause a rightward shift in the industry supply curve. The new supply schedule, S', intersects the demand schedule at $P = 7.80$. At a price of €7.80 the existing firm, given its short-run supply curve, will reduce output to 190 and make less profit.

The situation depicted in Figure 11.13 is still inherently unstable. The reason this time is that the old firm is not employing the optimal quantity of fixed inputs. At an output of 190 the firm would want to employ less capital stock than it did when producing 200. As the firm readjusts its capital stock downwards we get new short-run cost curves ATC_3 and SMC_3 in Figure 11.14. Note that as the SMC curve shifts to the left so does the industry supply curve. In terms of its effect on the industry supply curve, this adjustment thus works in the opposite direction from

FIGURE 11.13
First Step along the Path toward Long-Run Equilibrium
Entry of new firms causes supply to shift rightward, lowering price from €10 to €7.80. This lowers the profit of existing firms in the industry.

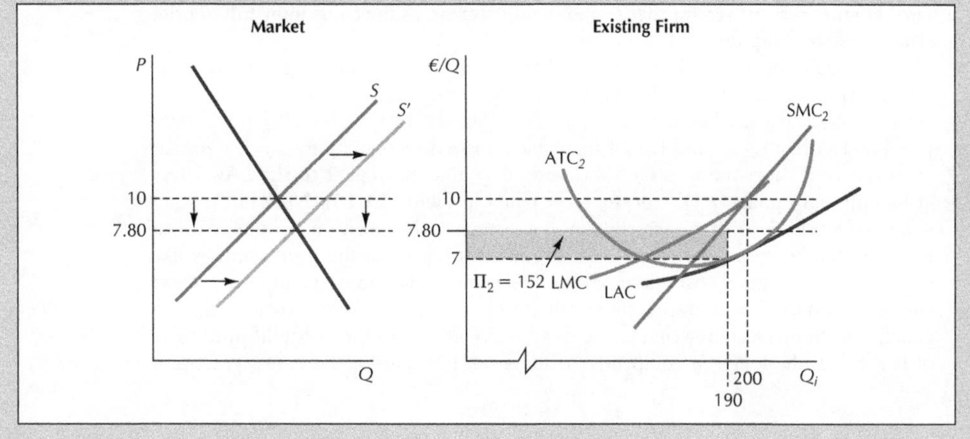

the adjustment caused by the entry of new firms. But the *net* effect of the two adjustments must be to shift industry supply to the right. If it were not, price would not have fallen in the first place, and there would have been no reason for existing firms to reduce their capital stocks. The net effect, in this case, leaves us with industry supply curve S'' and an equilibrium price of €8.

After adjusting its capital stock the firm has lowered output to 180 but increased profit. Profits are higher because the firm has readjusted its capital stock to the

FIGURE 11.14
Second Step along the Path toward Long-Run Equilibrium
Entry of new firms causes supply to shift rightward, lowering price from 10 to 8. The lower price causes existing firms to adjust their capital stocks downward, giving rise to the new short-run cost curves ATC_3 and SMC_3.

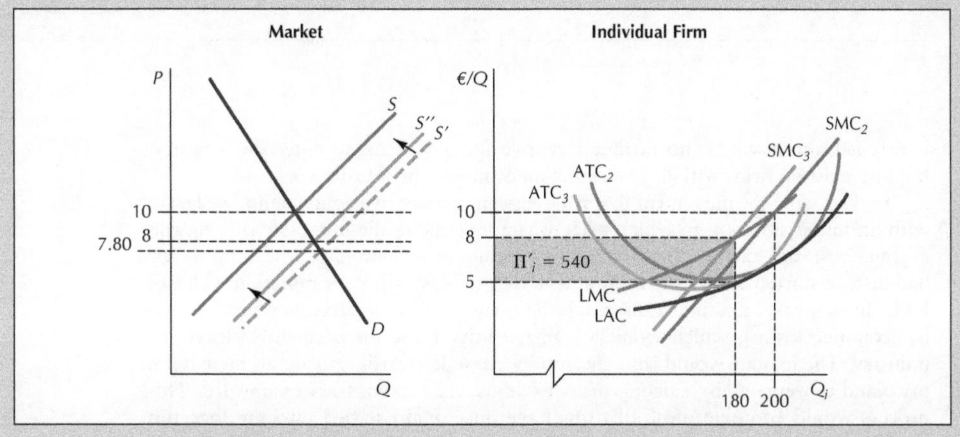

optimal level. Profits are still lower, however, following the entry of the new firm, €540 per time period, than before, €600 per time period.

Even after the adjustments described above take place, new and existing firms in the industry continue to earn positive economic profits. The new profit level is lower than before, but still acts as an incentive for additional entry into the industry. Further entry sets off yet another round of adjustment, as the continuing fall in price renders existing capital stocks too large.

For industries whose firms have U-shaped long-run average cost curves, entry, falling prices and capital stock adjustment will continue until these two conditions are met: (1) Price reaches the minimum point on the LAC curve (P^* in the right panel in Figure 11.15), and (2) all firms have moved to the capital stock size that gives rise to a short-run average total cost curve that is tangent to the LAC curve at its minimum point (ATC* in the right panel in Figure 11.15). Note in the right panel in Figure 11.15 that once all firms have reached this position, economic profit for each will be zero. The short-run marginal cost curve in the right panel is like the short-run marginal cost curve of all other firms in the industry, and when these curves are added horizontally, we get the industry supply curve shown in the left panel, which intersects the market demand curve at the long-run equilibrium price of P*. This is the long-run competitive equilibrium position for the industry. Once it

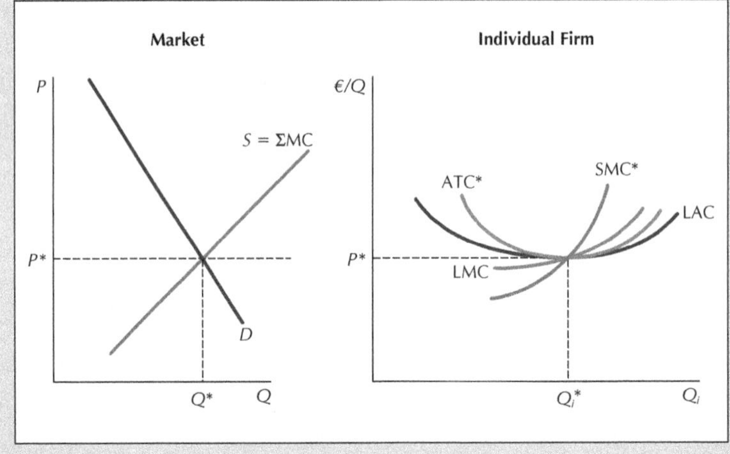

FIGURE 11.15
The Long-Run Equilibrium under Perfect Competition
If price starts above P^*, entry keeps occurring and capital stocks of existing firms keep adjusting until the rightward movement of the industry supply curve causes price to fall to P^*. At P^*, the profit-maximizing level of output for each firm is Q_i^*, the output level for which P^* = SMC* = LMC = ATC* = LAC. Economic profits of all firms are equal to zero.

is reached, there will be no further incentive for new firms to enter the industry, because existing firms will all be earning an economic profit of zero.

In discussing the movement toward long-run competitive equilibrium, we began with an initial situation in which price was above the minimum value of long-run average cost and existing firms were all earning an economic profit. Suppose we had instead started with a situation in which price was below the minimum value of LAC. In that case, existing firms would be earning negative economic profits (that is, economic losses), which would be an incentive for some of them to leave the industry. The exodus would shift the supply curve leftward, causing an increase in price and movements by existing firms to adjust their capital stocks upward. This process would continue until all firms have once again settled into the long-run equilibrium position portrayed in the right panel in Figure 11.15.

THE INVISIBLE HAND

As Adam Smith saw clearly more than two centuries ago, it is the invisible hand of the self-interest motive—in particular, the carrot of economic profit, or the stick of economic losses—that drives competitive industries to their respective long-run equilibrium positions. But even though no firm consciously intends to promote the general social welfare, there are some remarkably attractive features of long-run competitive equilibrium. Thus, as Smith described the actions of an industrialist,

> he intends only his own security; and by directing that industry in such a manner as its produce may be of the greatest value, he intends only his own gain; and he is in this, as in many other cases, led by an invisible hand to promote an end which was no part of his intention. Nor is it always the worse for the society that it was no part of it. By pursuing his own interest, he frequently promotes that of the society more effectually than when he really intends to promote it.[8]

In what sense is the long-run equilibrium in competitive markets attractive from the perspective of society as a whole? For one thing, price is equal to marginal cost, both long-run and short-run, which means that the equilibrium is efficient in the sense previously discussed: it exhausts all possibilities for mutually beneficial trades. The last unit of output consumed is worth exactly the same to the buyer as the resources required to produce it. Moreover, price is equal to the minimum point on the long-run average cost curve, which means that there is no less costly way of producing the product. Finally, all producers earn only a normal rate of profit, which is the opportunity cost of the resources they have invested in their firms. The public pays not a cent more than what it cost the firms to serve them.

Even more remarkable than these efficiency properties is the sheer volume of activity that is coordinated by the market mechanism. Throughout the dead of Ithaca winters, a food truck sits parked outside the Cornell dormitories all night, so that at 3 a.m. any student can take a few steps outside and purchase a fresh cup of coffee for a dollar. No student had to instruct the operator of that truck to be there, or tell him where to buy paper cups or propane gas for his portable stove. Similarly, a student can go to a nearby store and buy a new cartridge for their printer at a moment's notice. The local supermarket has fresh rabbit on Fridays and Saturdays, and a truck arrives each morning at dawn carrying fresh swordfish. On only a few hours' notice, several airlines stand ready to carry the student to New York, Los Angeles or Paris. All this activity, and much, much more, takes place without any central coordination at all, the result of a multitude of people each striving to earn an economic profit.

In controlled economies, resources are allocated not by markets but by central planning committees. Because of natural limits on the amount of information such committees can process, they are unable to specify in exact detail the characteristics of the goods called for by their plans. Workers and managers in controlled economies are therefore often able to interpret their production orders in self-serving ways.

A famous Russian cartoon, for example, shows the response of the manager of a roofing nail factory who was called on by the plan to deliver 10,000 pounds of roofing nails for the month of August. He alertly discovered that the easiest way to fulfil his quota was to produce a single 10,000-pound nail.

---

[8]Adam Smith, *The Wealth of Nations,* Chapter 2, http://www.online-literature.com/view.php/wealth_nations/24?term = invisible%20hand.

Whatever other faults it may have, the market system cannot be accused of producing products that people do not want to buy. In the market system, the consumer is sovereign, and firms that fail to provide what consumers want face economic extinction.[9] The question of whether central plans are more efficient than market incentives was a hotly debated issue for most of the twentieth century. But no longer. Before their demise in the late 1980s, controlled economies all over the globe introduced market-like incentives in a desperate attempt to revive their lagging production totals.

This is not to say that competitive markets lead to the best possible outcome in every instance. On the contrary, in later chapters we will see that market systems fall short in a variety of ways.

Moreover, the efficiency claims on behalf of competitive allocations are conditional on the initial distribution of resources among members of society. Markets are efficient at producing what people demand in the marketplace, and what gets produced depends on how much income specific people have. If you do not believe that the underlying distribution of resources is fair, there is no compelling reason for you to approve of the pattern of goods and services served up by competitive markets. But one need not take a naively optimistic view of the competitive process to appreciate its truly awesome power to draw order from complexity.

Why does an airline ticket from London to Frankfurt cost only €10?

ECONOMIC NATURALIST 11.1

After the Second World War the airline industry in Europe was very heavily regulated. National governments have rights over airspace and they used this to restrict which airlines could operate. Moreover, national airlines were typically government owned. In short, the airline history was a heavily controlled market.

Through the 1970s and 80s competition in the industry, slowly but surely, increased as governments lowered restrictions. British Airways was privatized in 1987. And finally, in the 1990s came an official EU policy to deregulate the industry. This removed all restrictions on flights within the EU. Since then, many national airlines have been privatized, or part-privatized. The latest trend is competition between airports. All this has made the airline industry much more competitive than it was before.

So, what are the consequences of this liberalization? Fares are dramatically lower, passenger numbers are far higher, and the possibilities for travel within Europe have expanded enormously. Airlines such as Ryanair and EasyJet have transformed the market. Even the old national carriers like British Airways, Lufthansa, KLM and Air France have adapted to the increased competition, become more efficient, and maintained a substantial presence in the market.

Today, if you want to fly from London to Frankfurt, you have at least four airports to choose from in London and two in Frankfurt. And there are at least 10 airlines offering to take you. It is because of such competition that you can get a ticket for only €10. ■

Application: The Cost of Extraordinary Inputs

The Project to Increase Crop Yields We are in a position now to return to the question with which we began this chapter, namely, whether an EU-financed investment that doubles crop yields will raise the incomes of poor farmers.

[9]The late Harvard economist John Kenneth Galbraith challenged this view. We will consider his arguments in Chapter 13.

First, let us consider the current situation. Farmers here may be viewed as the operators of small competitive firms. They supply their own labour, and keep the proceeds from selling their grain in a market so large that their own offerings have no appreciable effect on the price of grain, which is, say, €10/bushel. Suppose that an individual farmer can farm 40 acres and the land will yield 30 bushels of grain per acre per year. His total revenue from the sale of his grain will then be €12,000/yr.

Let us suppose that the only cost the farmer incurs is buying seeds. The seeds need to be bought every year (they do not reproduce) and are supplied by a multinational company that has an effective monopoly on the supply of seeds in the country. What will be the cost of seeds?

Suppose the alternative to working as a farmer is to work in a factory for €6000/yr, and that factory work is generally regarded as neither more nor less pleasant than farming. If the price of seeds were only, say, €5000/yr for a 40-acre parcel, then all the country's workers would prefer farming to working in the factories, because their net earnings would be €7000 instead of €6000. Everyone would want to be a farmer. If the price of seeds were, say, €7000/yr for a 40-acre parcel, then all the country's workers would prefer working in the factories and earning €6000 instead of €5000. We would expect, therefore, the price of seeds to be €6000/yr for a 40-acre parcel. This is the price that farmers are willing to pay.

Now let us see what happens after the EU investment. With grain yields now 60 bushels/acre instead of 30, a 40-acre farm will produce €24,000 in annual total revenue instead of €12,000. If the price of seeds remained at its original €6000/yr level, a farmer would earn €18,000/yr instead of €6000. Indeed, it was the prospect of such a dramatic rise in farm incomes that has attracted so much support for the investment in the first place.

What supporters of the bill have failed to recognize, however, is that the price of seeds will not remain at €6000/yr after the investment. Both farmers and factory workers would be willing to pay a lot more than €6000/yr for seeds. Needless to say, the price of seeds will rise from €6000 to €18,000/yr for a 40-acre farm. Once the price of seeds for a 40-acre parcel reaches €18,000, the balance between farm and factory opportunities is restored.

Recall that our hypothetical parliamentary aide recommended against the investment project on the grounds that it would not raise the incomes of farmers in the long run. She perceived correctly that the beneficiaries of the project would be not the impoverished farmers but the multinational company that supplies seeds. On the view that the owners of the company already have high incomes, there is no social purpose served by spending tax euros to increase their incomes further.[10] Despite these arguments, EU money has been spent in countries like Romania, and it is the multinational seed companies that appear to have benefited more than rural farmers.

This example illustrates the important idea that strong forces tend to equalize the average total costs of different firms in a competitive industry. Here, seed prices adjusted to bring the return to farming in line with the return from other employments. It also illustrates that a company with monopoly power can extract profits from competitive firms (more on this in the next chapter).

An Efficient Manager Suppose one firm is like all others except that it employs an extraordinarily efficient manager. This manager is so efficient that the firm earns

[10]Of course, the project would still be attractive if its cost were less than the value of the extra grain that resulted.

€500,000 of economic profit each year in an industry in which the economic profit of the other firms hovers close to zero. Because this manager receives the same salary as all other managers, the firm that employs her has much lower costs than all other firms in the industry. But that creates a strong incentive for some other firm to bid this manager away by offering her a higher salary.

Suppose a new firm offered her €300,000 more than her current annual salary and she accepted. That new firm would then earn an economic profit of €200,000/yr. That's not as good as an economic profit of €500,000/yr, but it is €200,000/yr better than the normal profit her original employer will earn without her.

Still other firms would have an incentive to offer even more for this manager. Theory tells us that the bidding should continue until the cost savings for which she is responsible are entirely incorporated into her salary—that is, until her salary is €500,000/yr higher than the salary of an ordinary manager. And once her salary is bid up to that level, the firm that hires her will no longer enjoy a cost advantage over the other firms in the industry. The existence of such competitive bidding for inputs makes it plausible to assume that all the firms in a competitive industry have roughly the same average total costs in equilibrium.

Apple co-founder and long-time CEO Steve Jobs has been described as the main reason for the firm's financial success. Was he compensated accordingly?

EXERCISE 11.6 Suppose all firms in an industry have 'competent' managers and earn zero economic profit. The manager of one of the firms suddenly leaves and the firm finds that only incompetent applicants respond when the position is advertised at the original salary of €50,000/yr (which is the going rate for competent managers in this industry). Under an incompetent manager paid this salary, the firm will experience an economic loss of €20,000/yr. At what salary would it make sense for this firm to hire an incompetent manager?

THE LONG-RUN COMPETITIVE INDUSTRY SUPPLY CURVE

We saw that the short-run supply curve for a perfectly competitive industry is the horizontal summation of the short-run marginal cost curves of its individual firms. But the corresponding long-run supply curve for a competitive industry is not the horizontal summation of the long-run marginal cost curves of individual firms. Our task in the next sections is to derive the long-run supply curve for competitive industries operating under a variety of different cost conditions.

Long-Run Supply Curve with U-Shaped LAC Curves

What does the long-run supply curve look like in an industry in which all firms have identical U-shaped long-run average cost (LAC) curves? Suppose, in particular, that these LAC curves are like the one labelled LAC_i in the right panel in Figure 11.16. Suppose the demand curve facing the industry is initially the one labelled D_1 in the left panel. Given this demand curve, the industry will be in long-run equilibrium when each firm installs the capital stock that gives rise to the short-run marginal cost curve labelled SMC_i in the right panel. The number of firms in the industry will adjust so that the short-run supply curve, denoted S_{SR} in the left panel, intersects D_1 at a price equal to the minimum value of LAC_i.

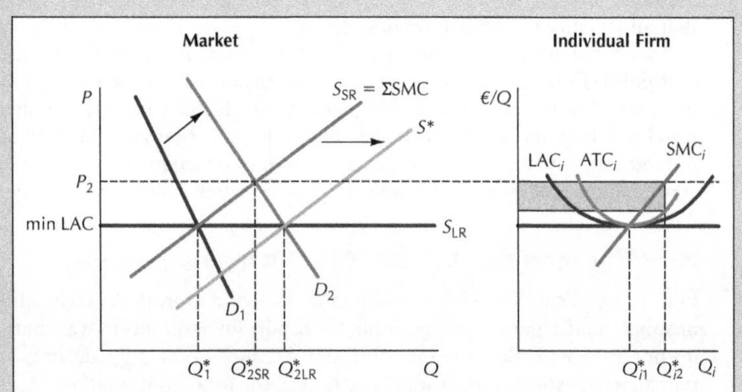

FIGURE 11.16
The Long-Run Competitive Industry Supply Curve
When firms are free to enter or leave the market, price cannot depart from the minimum value of the LAC curve in the long run. If input prices are unaffected by changes in industry output, the long-run supply curve is S_{LR}, a horizontal line at the minimum value of LAC.

(If there were more firms than that or fewer, each would be making either an economic loss or a profit.)

Now suppose demand shifts rightward from D_1 to D_2, intersecting the short-run industry supply curve at the price P_2. The short-run effect will be for each firm to increase its output from Q_{i1}^* to Q_{i2}^*, which will lead to an economic profit measured by the shaded rectangle in the right panel in Figure 11.16. With the passage of time, these profits will lure additional firms into the industry until the rightward supply shift (to S* in the left panel) again results in a price of min LAC. The long-run response to an increase in demand, then, is to increase industry output by increasing the number of firms in the industry. As long as the expansion of industry output does not cause the prices of capital, labour and other inputs to rise, there will be no long-run increase in the price of the product.[11]

If demand had shifted to the left from D_1, a parallel story would have unfolded: price would have fallen in the short run, firms would have adjusted their offerings, and the resulting economic losses would have induced some firms to leave the industry. The exodus would shift industry supply to the left until price had again risen to min LAC. Here again the long-run response to a shift in demand is accommodated by a change in the number of firms. With U-shaped LAC curves, there is no tendency for a fall in demand to produce a long-run decline in price.

In summary, the long-run supply curve for a competitive industry with U-shaped LAC curves and constant input prices is a horizontal line at the minimum value of the LAC curve. In the long run, all the adjustment to variations in demand occurs not through changing prices but through variations in the number of firms serving the market. Following possibly substantial deviations in the short run, price shows a persistent tendency to gravitate to the minimum value of long-run average cost.

Industry Supply When Each LAC Curve Is Horizontal

As in the case of U-shaped LAC curves, the long-run industry supply curve when each firm's LAC curve is horizontal will again be a horizontal line (again assuming that input prices do not change with changes in industry output). But there is one salient difference between the two cases: When firms have identical U-shaped LAC curves, we can predict that each firm will produce the quantity that corresponds to

[11]More follows on what happens when changes in industry output cause changes in input prices.

the minimum point on its LAC curve. We thus get an industry composed of firms that all produce the same level of output.

With horizontal LAC curves, by contrast, there is simply no unique minimum-cost point. LAC is the same at any level of output, which leads to an indeterminacy not present in the earlier case. We just cannot predict what the size distribution of firms will look like in the case of horizontal LAC curves. There may be a handful of large firms, many small ones, or a mixture of different sizes. All we can say with confidence is that price in the long run will gravitate towards the value of LAC.

How Changing Input Prices Affect Long-Run Supply

In our analysis of cost curves in Chapter 10, which forms the basis of our analysis of supply under perfect competition, an important assumption was that input prices do not vary with the amount of output produced. For a single firm whose input purchases constitute only a small fraction of the total input market, this assumption is plausible. In many cases, moreover, even the entire industry's demands for inputs constitute only a small share of the overall input market. For example, even if the insurance industry issues 20 per cent more policies this year than last, it employs such a small percentage of the total available supplies of secretaries, computers, executives and other inputs that the prices of these inputs should not be significantly affected. So here too we may reasonably assume that input prices do not depend on output.

But there are at least some industries in which the volume of inputs purchased constitutes an appreciable share of the entire input market. The market for commercial airliners, for example, consumes a significant share of the total amount of titanium sold each year. In such cases, a large increase in industry output will often be accompanied by significant increases in input prices.

When that happens, we have what is known as a **pecuniary diseconomy,** a bidding up of input prices when industry output increases.[12] Even though the industry can expand output indefinitely without using more inputs per unit of output, the minimum point on each firm's LAC curve is nonetheless a rising function of industry output. For example, note in the left panel in Figure 11.17 that the firm's LAC curve for an industry output of Q_2 lies above its LAC curve for an industry output of $Q_1 < Q_2$, and that the LAC curve for an industry output of $Q_3 > Q_2$ lies higher still. To each industry output level there corresponds a different LAC curve, because input prices are different at every level of industry output. The long-run supply curve for such an industry will trace out the minimum points of these LAC curves. Thus, on the long-run industry supply curve (S_{LR}, right panel), Q_1 corresponds to the minimum point on the firm's LAC curve when industry output is Q_1 (left panel); Q_2 corresponds to the minimum point for the LAC curve for Q_2; and so on. With pecuniary diseconomies, the long-run supply curve will be upward sloping even though each individual firm's LAC curve is U-shaped. Pecuniary diseconomies also produce an upward-sloping industry supply curve when each firm's LAC curve is horizontal. Competitive industries in which rising input prices lead to upward-sloping supply curves are called *increasing cost industries.*

> ***pecuniary diseconomy*** a rise in production cost that occurs when an expansion of industry output causes a rise in the prices of inputs.

There are also cases in which the prices of inputs may fall significantly with expanding industry output. This will happen, for example, if inputs are manufactured using technologies in which there are substantial economies of scale. A dramatic increase in road building, for example, might facilitate greater exploitation of economies of scale in the production of earthmoving equipment, resulting in a lower price for that input. Such cases are called *pecuniary economies,* and give rise

[12] A *pecuniary diseconomy* thus implies that input prices will fall when industry output contracts.

FIGURE 11.17
Long-Run Supply Curve for an Increasing Cost Industry
When input prices rise with industry output, each firm's LAC curve will also rise with industry output (left panel). Thus the firm's LAC curve when industry output is Q_2 lies above its LAC curve when industry output is Q_1 (left panel). Firms will still gravitate to the minimum points on their LAC curves (Q_i^* left panel), but because this minimum point depends on industry output, the long-run industry supply curve (S_{LR}, right panel) will now be upward sloping.

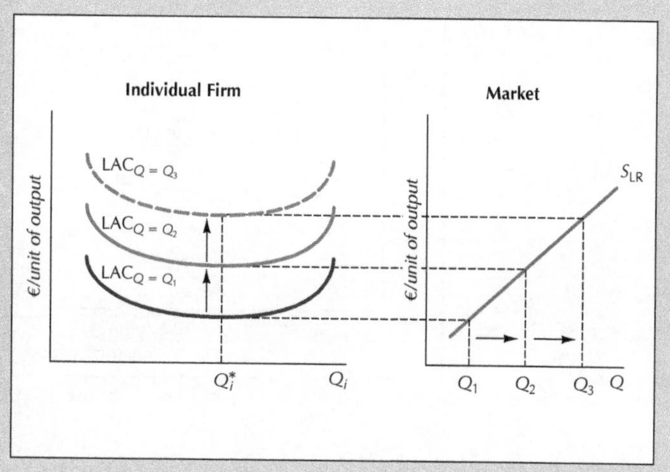

to a downward-sloping long-run industry supply curve, even where each firm's LAC curve is either horizontal or U-shaped. Competitive industries in which falling input prices lead to downward-sloping supply curves are called *decreasing cost industries.*

THE ELASTICITY OF SUPPLY

In Chapter 5 we defined the price elasticity of demand as a measure of the responsiveness of the quantity demanded to variations in price. An analogous concept exists for measuring the responsiveness of the quantity supplied to variations in price. Naturally, it is called the **price elasticity of supply.** Suppose we are at a point (Q, P) on the industry supply curve shown in Figure 11.18, where a change in price of ΔP gives rise to a change of ΔQ in the quantity supplied. The price elasticity of supply, denoted ϵ^S, is then given by

price elasticity of supply the percentage change in quantity supplied that occurs in response to a 1 per cent change in product price.

$$\epsilon^S = \frac{\Delta Q}{\Delta P}\frac{P}{Q} \text{ (see footnote 13 below)} \tag{11.1}$$

As in the case of elasticity of demand, supply elasticity has a simple interpretation in terms of the geometry of the industry supply curve. When ΔP is small, the ratio $\Delta P/\Delta Q$ is the slope of the supply curve, which means that the ratio $\Delta Q/\Delta P$ is the reciprocal of that slope. Thus the price elasticity of supply may be interpreted as the product of the ratio of price to quantity and the reciprocal of the slope of the supply curve:

$$\epsilon^S = \frac{P}{Q}\frac{1}{\text{slope}} \tag{11.2}$$

Because of the law of diminishing returns, the short-run competitive industry supply curve will always be upward sloping, which means that the short-run

[13]In calculus terms, supply elasticity is defined by

$$\epsilon^S = \frac{P}{Q}\frac{dQ}{dP}$$

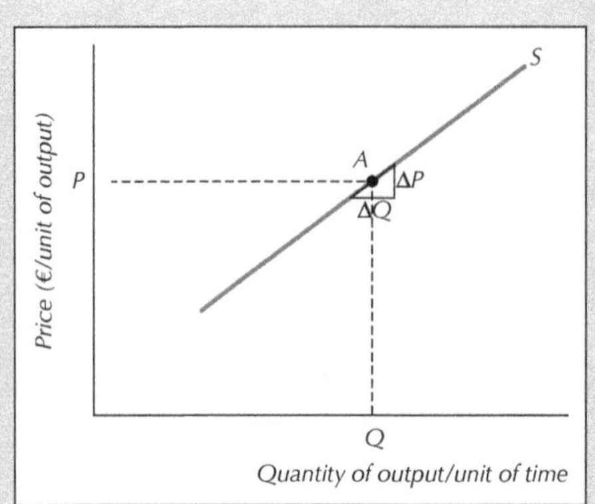

FIGURE 11.18
The Elasticity of Supply
At point *A*, the elasticity of supply is given by $\epsilon^s = (\Delta Q/\Delta P)(P/Q)$. Because the short-run supply curve is always upward sloping, the short-run elasticity of supply will always be positive. In the long run, elasticity of supply can be positive, zero or negative.

elasticity of supply will always be positive. For industries with a horizontal long-run supply curve, the long-run elasticity of supply is infinite. Output can be expanded indefinitely without a change in price. Because of pecuniary economies and diseconomies, long-run competitive industry supply curves may also be either downward or upward sloping in specific cases. The corresponding long-run elasticities of supply in these cases will be either negative or positive.

As noted earlier, most industries employ only a relatively small share of the total volume of inputs traded in the marketplace, which means that modest variations in industry output should have no significant effect on input prices in most industries. In practical applications of the competitive model, therefore, most economists adopt the working hypothesis that long-run supply curves are horizontal. Of course, this hypothesis can always be modified when there is evidence that pecuniary economies or diseconomies are important.

APPLYING THE COMPETITIVE MODEL

As noted earlier in the chapter, economists recognize that no industries strictly satisfy the four requirements for perfect competition—a standardized product, firms as price takers, perfect factor mobility and perfect information. For practical purposes, the important question is how far an industry can fall short of these conditions before general tendencies of the competitive model fail to apply. Unfortunately, there are no hard-and-fast rules for making this judgement. In industries where entry and exit are especially easy—such as the airline industry—a firm may behave as a price taker even in a market in which it is the only competitor.[14] In industries in which entry and exit are more difficult, even the existence of a relatively large number of established firms does not guarantee price-taking behaviour. In the short run, especially, firms may be able to work out tacit agreements to restrain price competition even when there are extra-normal profits.

Despite this difficulty, experience has shown that many of the most important long-run properties of the competitive model apply in most industries, with the notable exception of those where the government erects legal barriers to entry (for example, by requiring a government licence in order to participate in a market, as used to be the case in the airline industry).

[14]At a limited number of large airports, entry is difficult even in the airline industry. For these airports to accommodate carriers, new capacity will have to be built, which could take years or even decades.

By way of illustration, let us consider three brief applications that highlight some of the insights afforded by the perfectly competitive model.

Price Supports as a Device for Saving Family Farms

In 1900, over 10 per cent of the UK labour force earned its living in farming; today, less than 2 per cent do. In 1980, around 30 per cent of the Polish labour force was earning its living in farming; today, less than 15 per cent do. Similar declines in employment in farming can be seen across Europe. This change is obviously not the result of a dramatic decline in food consumption. Rather, it is one of the many consequences of farming methods having become vastly more productive.

In Western Europe farming methods became more productive as farm machinery grew larger and more sophisticated. In Eastern Europe farming methods changed more abruptly following the fall of the Iron Curtain. The consequences, however, are the same. As productivity increases, the size of land parcels at which long-run average cost curves cease declining has grown ever larger. Where family farms were once common, large corporate farms have increasingly become the norm.

In terms of the competitive model developed in this chapter, the family farm may be thought of as a firm whose capital stock gives rise to the short-run cost curves denoted ATC_F and SMC_F in Figure 11.19. The corresponding cost curves for the corporate farm are denoted ATC_C and SMC_C. Competition has the effect of driving the long-run equilibrium price toward P^*, the minimum point on the LAC curve. At P^*, corporate farms earn a normal profit while family farms, with their higher costs, earn economic losses of Π_F, as measured by the shaded rectangle in Figure 11.19.

FIGURE 11.19 Cost Curves for Family and Corporate Farms With the availability of modern farming methods, large farms have much lower unit costs than small ones. A price that covers cost for large corporate farms will produce large economic losses for family farms.

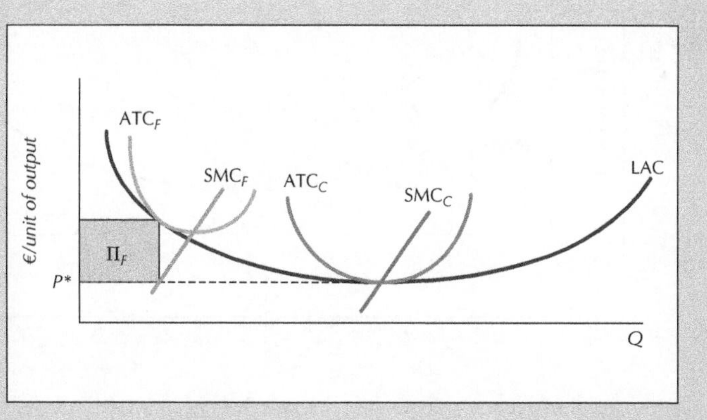

Despite the intense determination of many family farmers to remain on the land, large losses are simply not sustainable over a period of many years. Most farmers remain well past the time they are no longer able to earn a profit equal to the opportunity cost of their land. Many remain even long after they have ceased to earn the opportunity cost of their own labour. And a substantial number hang on by borrowing away most of the value of their only significant asset, their farmland. But credit cannot be extended without limit, and in the absence of government intervention, the long-run tendency has been for family farmers to leave the industry, selling whatever land they still own to the more efficient corporate farms.

Contrary to the stylized assumptions of the model of perfect competition, this process of resource mobility is far from perfect. Family farming is a way of life, one that people do not readily abandon when the terms of trade turn against them. There is great sympathy for the plight of family farmers. This sympathy currently finds its voice in the Common Agricultural Policy (CAP). One of the initial objectives set out for the CAP was to 'ensure a fair standard of living for the agricultural population'.

The CAP has gone through various iterations since its inception and the latest reform is never far away. Historically, a main component of the CAP was a system of price support. Essentially, the EU announces a price for a given product and then national governments stand ready to buy whatever private buyers fail to purchase. This is coupled with high import tariffs. One of the most important, if not always explicitly stated, goals of these policies is to keep prices high enough to prevent small family farms from going bankrupt.

Sad to say, these policies have failed miserably. Sadder still, even the most cursory understanding of competitive market dynamics would have made clear why this outcome was inevitable. To illustrate, suppose the price support is set at P_G in a market in which the unsupported price would have been P^*. In Figure 11.20, we see that the short-run effect is to cause family farms to increase their output to Q_F, and to cause corporate farms to increase theirs to Q_C. At these output levels, family farms will earn an economic loss labelled Π_F in Figure 11.20, while corporate farms earn an economic profit indicated by the shaded rectangle Π_C.

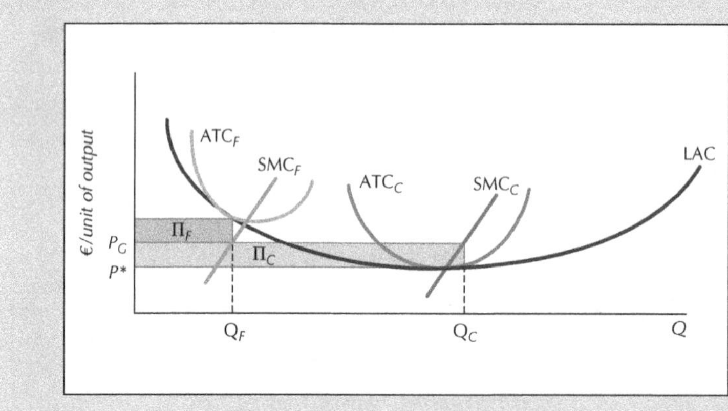

FIGURE 11.20
The Short-Run Effect of Agricultural Price Supports
Price supports initially reduce the losses of family farms, while creating economic profits for corporate farms. In the long run, however, they serve only to bid up land prices.

In the short run, to the extent the new loss is smaller than the previous loss suffered by family farmers, the price support has had the intended effect of helping the family farmer. But the relief is destined to be transitory. To see why, note first that the same price support that reduces the short-run losses of family farms generates positive profits for corporate farms. We know, however, that positive profits are not sustainable in an industry with freedom of entry. They will lure outsiders to bid for farmland so that they too may earn more than a normal rate of return. The effect of this bidding will be to cause land prices to rise to the point where corporate farms no longer earn economic profits. But with land prices higher than before, the cost curves of all farms, corporate and family, shift upward. The only mitigating factor for family farms is that the value of their land has increased.

In recent years the CAP has moved away from price support towards direct subsidies. In particular, the Single Payment Scheme, begun in 2003, pays farms a subsidy based on the size and quality of their land. Clearly, a subsidy can cover the loss being made by family farmers and thus help them to survive. The relief is again destined, however, to be transitory. Given that all farms receive the subsidy, whether small or not, the logic of the proceeding discussion follows through just as before. Corporate farms will make positive profits that are not sustainable in an industry with freedom of entry.

Economists are not in a position to tell the EU whether trying to preserve the existence of the family farm is a worthwhile goal. That is a political question. But given that the EU has decided to pursue this objective, economists can give advice about what policies are most likely to be effective. Price supports and the single payment scheme failed because of the competitive bidding for land that was induced by them. Their long-run effect was to drive up the price of land, while doing little to ensure the survival of small family farms. There are much more direct ways to support family farming.

ECONOMIC NATURALIST 11.2

Is there not a better way to support family farms?

It would be fair to say that the Common Agricultural Policy has never been particularly popular in the UK. Politicians of all shapes and sizes have queued up to lament its failings. But have they been able to come up with a better way of supporting family farms?

Natural England runs an Environmental Stewardship Scheme that offers payments to farmers for managing their land in a way that enhances the environment and wildlife. Things like the replanting of hedgerows, the creation of ponds and areas of grassland, the keeping of rare livestock, and free access to the public are encouraged. Large corporate farms are unlikely to be attracted by such things and so the scheme more directly helps family farms.

The reason this scheme has some chance of success is that it essentially creates a new market, rather than trying to manipulate an existing market. Family farms in the UK are increasingly seen as 'protectors' of the natural environment rather than mass producers of food. Family farms can, therefore, survive because they offer a different product—protection of the natural environment—compared to large corporate farms. Family farms have a natural advantage in the market for protecting the natural environment. ■

The Illusory Attraction of Taxing Business

As noted in Chapter 2, political leaders often find it easier to propose new taxes on business than to collect additional taxes from individuals. Proposals to tax business usually include statements to the effect that 'wealthy corporations can better afford to pay extra taxes than struggling workers can'. But as we saw in Chapter 2, a tax placed on the product sold by an industry will in general be passed on, at least in part, to consumers.

Let us examine a perfectly competitive industry in which individual firms have identical U-shaped LAC curves like the one labelled LAC_i in the right panel in Figure 11.21. In the most common case, moderate variations in the industry's output will have no appreciable effect on its input prices, with the result that the long-run supply curve for this industry will be a horizontal line at the minimum point of LAC_i (the curve labelled S_{LR} in the left panel). If D is the market demand curve, then the equilibrium price will be P^*.

Now suppose a tax of T euros is collected on each unit of output sold in the market. The effect of this tax is to shift the LAC and SMC curves of each firm upward by T euros (right panel in Figure 11.21). The new long-run industry supply curve is again a horizontal line at the minimum value of the LAC curve—this

FIGURE 11.21
The Effect of a Tax on the Output of a Perfectly Competitive Industry
A tax of T euros per unit of output raises the LAC and SMC curves by T euros (right panel). The new long-run industry supply curve is again a horizontal line at the minimum value of LAC (left panel). Equilibrium price rises by T euros (left panel), which means that 100 per cent of the tax is passed on to consumers.

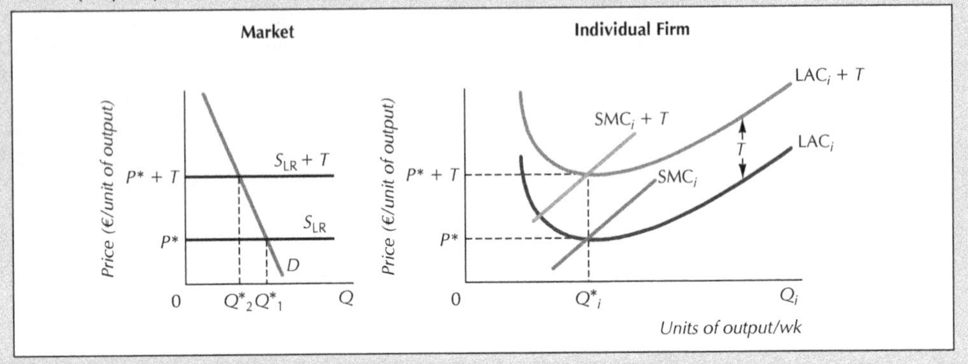

time the curve $S_{LR} + T$ in the left panel in Figure 11.21. The effect of the tax is to increase the price of the product by exactly T euros. Industry output contracts from Q_1^* to Q_2^* (left panel), and this contraction is achieved by firms leaving the industry.

Thus we see that, for competitive industries whose firms have U-shaped LAC curves, and whose input prices are fixed (the most empirically relevant case), the burden of a tax on output falls entirely on consumers. As we will see in later chapters, there are a variety of legitimate reasons for taxing the output of specific industries. But the claim that corporations have more money than people do is simply not one of these reasons. Claims to the contrary are fraudulent, and an economically literate population would be unlikely to re-elect politicians who defend taxing business on this ground.

If constant-cost competitive industries are able to pass on 100 per cent of taxes to buyers, why do industry lobbyists oppose taxes so strongly? Note in Figure 11.21 that one effect of a tax is to reduce total industry output. This reduction is achieved by some firms going out of business. Bankruptcy is never a pleasant experience for the owners of a firm, and on this account it is far from surprising that industry trade associations are so strongly opposed to new taxes.

The Adoption of Cost-Saving Innovations

The economist's emphasis on the competitive firm as a price taker sometimes creates the impression that competitive firms do little more than passively respond to impersonal price signals served up by the environment. This impression is deeply misleading. While it is true, for example, that an individual trucker can do little to affect trucking rates set in the open market, there is a great deal he can and must do to ensure his continued survival.

The short-run response to the dramatic fuel price increases of the 1970s automatically led to just the sorts of adjustments predicted by the competitive model: short-term losses, exit from the industry, gradually rising prices, and a gradual restoration of profitability for surviving firms. But the change in the environment also created opportunities that some firms actively exploited to their own advantage. A case in point is illustrated in the following Economic Naturalist.

Why did 18-wheel cargo trucks suddenly begin using airfoils in the mid-1970s?

ECONOMIC NATURALIST 11.3

Before 1970, the profile of the typical 18-wheel semi tractor-trailer truck was like the one shown in the top drawing below. The broad, flat expanse of the top of the trailer was directly exposed to the force of the oncoming wind, which at motorway speeds was substantial. But diesel fuel cost was relatively cheap in 1970, and so the penalty from having to run the engine a little harder was not large in those days.

With diesel prices much higher by the early 1980s, however, that penalty became much more important—so much so that entrepreneurs devised ways of reducing it. One of the most successful innovations was the simple airfoil that now adorns the cab of virtually every large truck on the road. Shown in the bottom drawing, its purpose is to deflect the wind to the top of the trailer. The profile of today's semi is still no aerodynamic masterpiece, but truckers estimate that the reduced wind resistance increases their mileage by 15 per cent at motorway speeds.

The truckers who were first to install the airfoils did so at a time when the industry price level was determined by the higher costs of running trucks that lacked them. As a result, these early adopters earned economic profits from their efforts. As time passed, however, more and more trucks began to sport the devices, and the industry price level gradually declined in response to the lower costs they made possible. At this point in history, it is rare to see an 18-wheeler that lacks an airfoil. By now it is safe to assume that the resultant cost savings have been fully reflected in lower trucking rates. The result is that the owner of a truck must now install an airfoil merely to be able to earn a normal rate of profit. Those who fail to install them pay the penalty of earning economic losses. ■

The lesson of this example is that the entrepreneur who earns economic profits is the one who adopts cost-saving innovations ahead of the competition. It is the search for such innovations that keeps even the price-taking firm from being merely a passive reactor to economic forces beyond its control.

■ SUMMARY ■

- The assumed objective of the firm is to maximize its economic profit. Competitive pressures in the marketplace may render this a plausible assumption, even though it seems to impute an unrealistically high degree of purposefulness to the actions of many managers. Economic profit is the difference between total revenue and cost—both explicit and implicit—of all resources used in production. Economic profit is not to be confused with accounting profit, which is the difference between total revenue and the explicit cost of resources used.
- The economic model of perfect competition assumes a standardized product, price-taking behaviour on the part of the firms, perfect mobility of resources, and perfect information on the part of buyers and firms. In this sense, it is similar to the physicist's model of motion on frictionless surfaces. Both models describe idealized conditions that are rarely if ever met in practice, and yet each generates useful predictions and explanations of events we observe in the world.
- The rule for profit maximization in the short run is to produce the level of output for which price is equal to short-run marginal cost on the rising portion of that curve. If price falls below the minimum value of average variable cost, the firm does best to produce no output

in the short run. The individual firm's short-run supply curve is thus the rising portion of its short-run marginal cost curve that lies above the minimum point of its average variable cost curve.

- The short-run industry supply curve is the horizontal summation of the individual firms' supply curves. It intersects the industry demand curve to determine the short-run equilibrium price. The individual competitive firm's demand curve is a horizontal line at the equilibrium price. If that price happens to lie above the minimum value of the long-run average cost curve, each firm will earn positive economic profit. If price is less than that value, each will suffer economic losses.
- Long-run adjustments consist not only of alterations in the size of existing firms' capital stocks, but also of entry and exit of firms. Where firms have identical U-shaped LAC curves, the long-run equilibrium price will be the minimum value of that LAC curve, and each firm will produce the corresponding quantity.
- Both long-run and short-run equilibrium positions are efficient in the sense that the value of the resources used in making the last unit of output is exactly equal to the value of that output to the buyer. This means that the equilibrium position exhausts all possibilities for mutually beneficial exchange. The long-run equilibrium has two additional attractive features: (1) Output is produced at the lowest possible unit cost, and (2) the seller is paid only the cost of producing the product. No economic profit is extracted from the buyer.
- Under perfect competition with constant input prices, the long-run industry supply curve is a horizontal line, not only when LAC curves are horizontal, but also when they are U-shaped. When input prices are an increasing function of industry output, the industry supply curves in both cases will be upward sloping. When input prices decline with industry output, the competitive industry supply curve will be downward sloping.
- The effect of competition for the purchase of unusually high-quality inputs is to raise the price of those inputs until they no longer enable the firm that employs them to earn an economic profit. This is an extremely important part of the long-run adjustment process, and failure to account for it lies behind the failure of many well-intended economic policies.
- Even price-taking firms must actively seek out means of reducing their costs of doing business. To the early adopters of cost-saving innovations goes a temporary stream of economic profit, while late adopters must suffer through periods of economic losses.

QUESTIONS FOR REVIEW

1. What is the difference between economic profit and accounting profit, and how does this difference matter for actual business decisions?
2. Under what conditions will we expect firms to behave as price takers even though there are only a small number of other firms in the industry?
3. Would the market for dry cleaning be perfectly competitive in large cities such as Paris or London? Why or why not? How about in a small town?
4. A firm's total revenue curve is given by $TR = aQ - 2Q^2$. Is this a perfectly competitive firm? Explain why or why not.
5. Does the fact that a business manager may not know the definition of marginal cost contradict the theory of perfect competition?
6. *True or false*: If marginal cost lies below average fixed cost, the firm should shut down in the short run. Explain.
7. What do economists mean when they say that the short-run competitive equilibrium is efficient?
8. *True or false*: In a constant-cost industry, a tax of a constant, fixed amount on each unit of output sold will not affect the amount of output sold by a perfectly competitive firm in the long run. Explain.
9. Suppose all firms in a competitive industry are operating at output levels for which price is equal to long-run marginal cost. *True or false*: This industry is necessarily in long-run equilibrium.
10. *True or false*: Consumer surplus is the area between the demand curve and the price line. For a perfectly competitive firm the demand curve equals the price line. Thus, a perfectly competitive industry produces no consumer surplus.
11. Why are pecuniary economies and diseconomies said to be the exception rather than the rule?
12. Would you expect a firm that adopts cost-saving innovations faster than 80 per cent of all firms in its industry to earn economic profits? If so, will there be any tendency for these profits to be bid away?

PROBLEMS

1. A competitive firm has the cost structure described in the following table. Graph the marginal cost, average variable cost, and average total cost curves. How many units of output will it produce at a market price of 32? Calculate its profits and show them in your graph.

Q	ATC	AVC	MC
1	44	4	8
2	28	8	16
4	26	16	32
6	31	24	48
8	37	32	64

2. If the short-run marginal and average variable cost curves for a competitive firm are given by SMC = 2 + 4Q and AVC = 2 + 2Q, how many units of output will it produce at a market price of 0? At what level of fixed cost will this firm earn zero economic profit?

3. Each of 1000 identical firms in the competitive peanut butter industry has a short-run marginal cost curve given by

$$\text{SMC} = 4 + Q$$

If the demand curve for this industry is

$$P = 10 - \frac{2Q}{1000}$$

what will be the short-run loss in producer and consumer surplus if an outbreak of aflatoxin suddenly makes it impossible to produce any peanut butter?

4. Assuming the aflatoxin outbreak in Problem 3 persists, will the long-run loss in producer and consumer surplus be larger than, smaller than, or the same as the short-run loss?

5. A perfectly competitive firm faces a price of 10 and is currently producing a level of output at which marginal cost is equal to 10 on a rising portion of its short-run marginal cost curve. Its long-run marginal cost is equal to 12. Its short-run average variable cost is equal to 8. The minimum point on its long-run average cost curve is equal to 10. Is this firm earning an economic profit in the short run? Should it alter its output in the short run? In the long run, what should this firm do?

6. All firms in a competitive industry have long-run total cost curves given by

$$\text{LTC}_Q = Q^3 - 10Q^2 + 36Q$$

where Q is the firm's level of output. What will be the industry's long-run equilibrium price? (*Hint*: Use either calculus or a graph to find the minimum value of the associated long-run average cost curve.) What will be the long-run equilibrium output level of the representative firm?

7. Same as Problem 6, except now

$$\text{LTC}_Q = Q^2 + 4Q$$

Could any firm actually have this particular LTC curve? Why or why not?

8. The marginal and average cost curves of taxis in Metropolis are constant at €0.20/mile. The demand curve for taxi trips in Metropolis is given by $P = 1 - 0.00001Q$, where P is the fare, in euros per mile, and Q is measured in kilometres per year. If the industry is perfectly competitive and each cab can provide exactly 10,000 kilometres/yr of service, how many cabs will there be in equilibrium and what will be the equilibrium fare?

9. Now suppose that the city council of Metropolis decides to curb congestion in the city centre by limiting the number of taxis to 6. Applicants participate in a lottery, and the six winners get a medallion, which is a permanent licence to operate a taxi in Metropolis. What will the equilibrium fare be now? How much economic profit will each medallion holder earn? If medallions can be traded in the marketplace and the rate of interest is 10 per cent/yr, how much will the medallions sell for? (*Hint*: How much money would you have to deposit in a bank to earn annual interest equal to the profit made by a taxi medallion?) Will the person who buys a medallion at this price earn a positive economic profit?

10. Merlin is like all other managers in a perfectly competitive industry except in one respect: Because of his great sense of humour, people are willing to work for him for half the going wage rate. All other firms in the industry have short-run total cost curves given by

$$STC_Q = M + 10Q + wQ^2 \text{ (see footnote 15)}$$

where M is the salary paid to ordinary managers and w is the going wage rate for the industry. If all firms in the industry face an output price of 28, and if $w = 2$, how much more will Merlin be paid than the other managers in the industry?

11. You are the owner/manager of a small competitive firm that manufactures house paints. You and all your 1000 competitors have total cost curves given by

$$TC = 8 + 2Q + 2Q^2$$

and the industry is in long-run equilibrium.

Now you are approached by an inventor who holds a patent on a process that will reduce your costs by half at each level of output.

a. What is the most you would be willing to pay for the exclusive right to use this invention?
b. Would the inventor be willing to sell at that price?

12. In the short run, a perfectly competitive firm produces output using capital services (a fixed input) and labour services (a variable input). At its profit-maximizing level of output, the marginal product of labour is equal to the average product of labour.

a. What is the relationship between this firm's average variable cost and its marginal cost? Explain.
b. If the firm has 10 units of capital and the rental price of each unit is €4/day, what will be the firm's profit? Should it remain open in the short run?

13. A firm in a competitive industry has a total cost function of $TC = 0.2Q^2 - 5Q + 30$, whose corresponding marginal cost curve is $MC = 0.4Q - 5$. If the firm faces a price of 6, what quantity should it sell? What profit does the firm make at this price? Should the firm shut down?

14. The demand for petrol is $P = 5 - 0.002Q$ and the supply is $P = 0.2 + 0.004Q$, where P is in euros and Q is in litres. If a tax of €1/litre is placed on petrol, what is the incidence of the tax? What is the lost consumer surplus? What is the lost producer surplus?

15. Suppose that bicycles are produced by a perfectly competitive, constant-cost industry. Which of the following will have a larger effect on the long-run price of bicycles: (1) a government programme to advertise the health benefits of bicycling, or (2) a government programme that increases the demand for steel, an input in the manufacture of bicycles that is produced in an increasing cost industry?

16. Suppose a representative firm in a perfectly competitive, constant-cost industry has a cost function $TC = 4Q^2 + 100Q + 100$.

a. What is the long-run equilibrium price for this industry?
b. If market demand is given by the function $Q = 1000 + P$, where P denotes price, how many firms will operate in this long-run equilibrium?
c. Suppose the government grants a lump-sum subsidy to each firm that manufactures the product. If this lump-sum subsidy equals 36, what would be the new long-run equilibrium price for the industry?

17. The domestic supply and demand curves for Jolt coffee beans are given by $P = 10 + Q$ and $P = 100 - 2Q$, respectively, where P is the price in euros per bushel, and Q is the quantity

[15] The associated marginal cost curve is $dSTC_Q/dQ = MC_Q = 10 + 2wQ$.

in millions of bushels per year. The EU produces and consumes only a trivial fraction of world Jolt bean output, and the current world price of €30/bushel is unaffected by events in the EU market. Transportation costs are also negligible.

a. How much will EU consumers pay for Jolt coffee beans, and how many bushels per year will they consume?
b. How will your answers to part (a) change if the EU enacts a tariff of €20/bushel?
c. What total effect on domestic producer and consumer surplus will the tariff have? How much revenue will the tariff raise?

18. An Australian researcher has discovered a drug that weakens a sheep's wool fibres just above the sheep's skin. The drug sharply reduces the cost of shearing (cutting the wool off) sheep because the entire coat pulls off easily in one piece. The world wool market is reasonably close to the model of perfect competition in both the product and factor sides. Trace out all of the effects of the introduction of this new drug.

ANSWERS TO IN-CHAPTER EXERCISES

11.1. Let r^* be the monthly interest rate for which Cullen's economic profit would be zero. Then r^* must satisfy £16,000 − £4000 − £800 − r^* (£100,000,000) = 0, which yields $r^* = 0.000112$, or 0.0112 per cent/mo. Cullen should relocate only if the interest rate is lower than r^*.

11.2. Marginal cost is the slope of the total cost curve, and marginal revenue is the slope of the total revenue curve. At the maximum profit point, $Q = 7.4$, the slopes of these two curves are exactly the same.

11.3. First, we need to rearrange the representative firm supply curve $P = 20 + 90Q_i$ to have quantity alone on one side.

$$Q_i = -\frac{2}{9} + \frac{1}{90}P$$

Then we multiply by the number of firms $n = 30$.

$$Q = nQ_i = 30Q_i = 30\left(-\frac{2}{9} + \frac{1}{90}P\right) = -\frac{20}{3} + \frac{1}{3}P$$

Finally, we rearrange the industry supply curve in order to get $P = 20 + 3Q$.

11.4. Short-run profit maximization for a perfectly competitive firm occurs at the quantity where price equals marginal cost, P = MC, provided P > min AVC (otherwise, the firm shuts down). Since marginal cost is MC = $2Q$, the market price $P = 12$ equals marginal cost $12 = 2Q$ at quantity $Q = 6$. Note that min AVC = 0 here. We can express profits (with fixed costs separated out) as p = (P − AVC)Q − FC. Since average variable cost is $AVC = Q = 6$, the firm would earn profits of

$$\pi = (12 - 6)6 - \text{FC} = 36 - \text{FC}$$

Thus, with fixed cost FC = 36, the firm would earn zero profits.

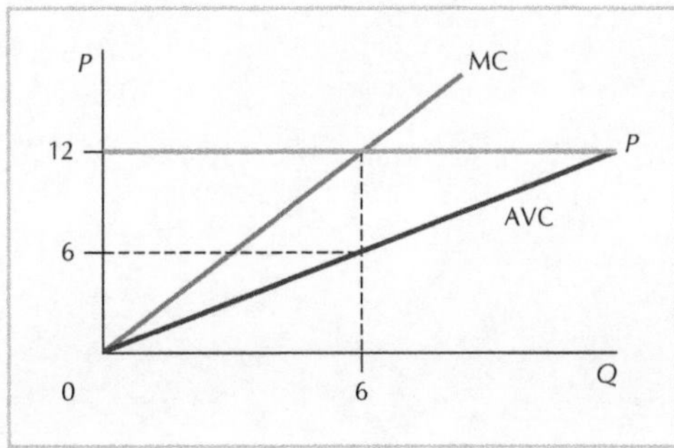

11.5. Total surplus is equal to the sum of the two shaded triangles shown below, which is €100,000/yr.

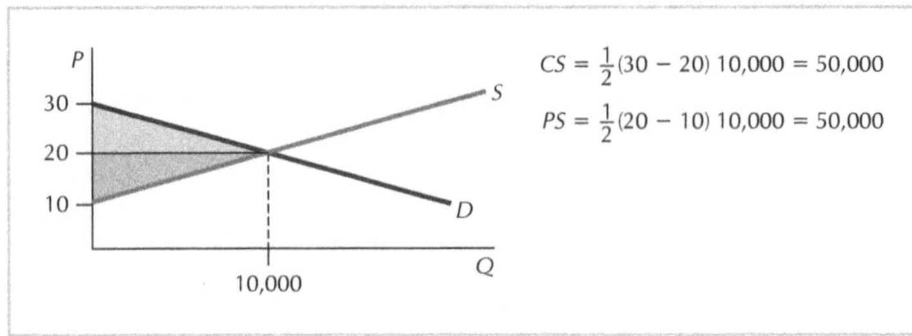

11.6. If the firm pays an incompetent manager only €30,000, it will continue to earn zero economic profit. It cannot pay any more than that without suffering an economic loss.

MONOPOLY

Virtually every cinema charges different admission prices to moviegoers who belong to different groups. Students pay one price, adults another, senior citizens still another. Some cinemas sell 'ten-packs' of movie tickets at a lower unit price than the tickets they sell at the door. And people who attend showings at the dinner hour sometimes pay much less than those who attend evening showings. None of these practices would be expected under our model of perfect competition, which holds that all buyers pay a single price for a completely standardized product (the so-called *law of one price*).

The same cinema operators who charge different ticket prices to different groups follow quite another practice when it comes to the sale of concession items. Here, the law of one price almost always prevails. Students, adults, senior citizens, international football stars, the clergy, service station attendants and all other patrons pay exactly the same price for their popcorn. The same observation applies to the prices of soft drinks and coffee. These prices, however, are usually much higher than we see for the same items sold in grocery stores and other retail establishments, certainly far greater than any reasonable measure of the marginal cost of providing them.

Both behaviours—charging differential admission prices on the one hand and uniformly high concession prices on the other—are, as we will see, perfectly consistent with what the economic model predicts about the single seller of a good or service.

CHAPTER PREVIEW

In this chapter, our task will be to examine the market structure that least resembles perfect competition—namely, *monopoly,* a market served by a single seller of a product with no close substitutes. We will discuss five factors that lead to this market structure: (1) control over key inputs, (2) economies of scale, (3) patents, (4) network economies, and (5) government licences. We will then see that the monopolist's rule for maximizing profits in the short run is the same as the one used by perfectly competitive firms. The monopolist will expand output if the gain in revenue exceeds the increase in costs, and will contract output if the loss in revenue is smaller than the reduction in costs.

Next, we will examine the monopolist's behaviour when confronted with the options of selling in several separate markets. Here again, the logic of cost-benefit analysis will provide a convenient framework for analysing the firm's decision about whether to alter its current behaviour.

Our next step will be to examine the efficiency properties of the standard monopoly equilibrium. Unlike the perfectly competitive case, the monopoly equilibrium does not exhaust the potential gains from exchange. In general, the value to society of an additional unit of output will exceed the cost to the monopolist of the resources required to produce it. This finding has often been interpreted to mean that monopoly is less efficient than perfect competition. But this interpretation, we will see, is of only limited practical significance because the conditions that give rise to monopoly are rarely compatible with those required for perfect competition.

Our policy focus in the chapter will be on the question of how the government should treat natural monopolies—markets characterized by downward-sloping long-run average cost curves. We will consider five policy alternatives: (1) state ownership, (2) private ownership with government price regulation, (3) competitive bidding by private firms for the right to be the sole provider of service, (4) vigorous enforcement of antitrust laws designed to prevent monopoly, and finally, (5) a complete *laissez-faire,* or hands-off, policy. Because problems are inherent in each alternative, the best policy generally will be different in different circumstances.

DEFINING MONOPOLY

Monopoly is a market structure in which a single seller of a product with no close substitutes serves the entire market. This definition could hardly appear any simpler, and yet it turns out to be exceedingly difficult to apply in practice. Consider the example of cinemas with which the chapter began. Is a local cinema a monopoly under our definition? In smaller cities, at least, it is likely to be the only one showing a given film at a given time. Whether it is a monopoly obviously depends on what we mean by a close substitute. If, for example, the cinema is currently showing *Halloween Part 8,* there is likely to be a rich variety of close substitutes for its product. Indeed, literally hundreds of low-grade blood-and-gore films are released each year, and the potential patrons of such films generally do not have to look far if they are dissatisfied with the films available at any particular cinema.

But what about a cinema that is in the midst of an exclusive six-month, first-run engagement of the latest *Spiderman* film? For fans of this series, there is really no close substitute. Those who want to see it while the excitement level surrounding its release is still high have only one seller to deal with.

The key feature that differentiates the monopoly from the competitive firm is the price elasticity of demand facing the firm. For the perfectly competitive firm, recall, price elasticity is infinite. If a competitive firm raises its price only slightly, it will lose all its sales. A monopoly, by contrast, has significant control over the price it charges.

Empirically, one practical measure for deciding whether a firm enjoys significant monopoly power is to examine the cross-price elasticity of demand for its closest substitutes. In one famous antitrust case, the DuPont Corporation was charged with having an effective monopoly on the sale of cellophane. Even though the company sold more than 80 per cent of all cellophane traded, it was able to defend itself against this charge by arguing that the cross-price elasticities between cellophane and its close substitutes—at the time, mainly waxed paper and aluminium foil—were sufficiently high to justify lumping all of these flexible-wrap products into a single market. DuPont sold less than 20 per cent of total industry output under this broader market definition. In a controversial decision, the court deemed that small enough to sustain effective competition.

This is not to say, however, that cross-price elasticity provides a clear, unambiguous measure that distinguishes a product with close substitutes from one without. While there may not be anything quite like the latest *Spiderman* movie, there have always been lots of alternative ways to entertain oneself for 2 hours. For the person whose heart is set on seeing *Spiderman,* the cinema is a monopolist, but for the person merely out in search of a good movie, the same cinema faces stiff competition. The difference between perfect competition and monopoly often boils down to the question of which of these two types of buyers is more numerous. As in so many other cases in economics, the task of distinguishing between competition and monopoly remains as much an art as a science.

Note carefully that the distinction between monopoly and competition does not lie in any difference between the respective price elasticities of the *market* demand curves for the two cases. On the contrary, the market price elasticity of demand for products supplied by competitive firms is often much smaller than the price elasticity of demand facing a monopolist. The price elasticity of demand is smaller for wheat than for Polaroid cameras, even though wheat is produced under nearly perfectly competitive conditions while Polaroid's patents make it the only legal seller in most of its markets. *The important distinction between monopoly and competition is that the demand curve facing the individual competitive firm is horizontal (irrespective of the price elasticity of the corresponding market demand curve), while the monopolist's demand curve is simply the downward-sloping demand curve for the entire market.*

FIVE SOURCES OF MONOPOLY

How does a firm come to be the only one that serves its market? Economists discuss five factors, any one or combination of which can enable a firm to become a monopoly. Let us consider these factors in turn.

1. Exclusive Control over Important Inputs The Perrier Corporation of France sells bottled mineral water. It spends millions of euros each year advertising the unique properties of this water, which are the result, it says, of a once-in-eternity confluence of geological factors that created their mineral spring. In New York State, the Adirondack Soft Drink Company offers a product that is essentially tap water saturated with carbon dioxide gas. Most are unable to tell the difference between Adirondack Seltzer and Perrier. But others feel differently, and for many of them there is simply no satisfactory substitute for Perrier. Perrier's monopoly position with respect to these buyers is the result of its exclusive control over an input that cannot easily be duplicated.

A similar monopoly position has resulted from the deBeers Diamond Mines' exclusive control over most of the world's supply of raw diamonds. Synthetic diamonds have now risen in quality to the point where they can occasionally fool even an experienced jeweller. But for many buyers, the preference for a stone that was mined from the earth is not a simple matter of greater hardness and refractive brilliance. They want *real* diamonds, and deBeers is the company that has them.

Exclusive control of key inputs is not a guarantee of permanent monopoly power. The preference for having a real diamond, for example, is based largely on the fact that mined diamonds have historically been genuinely superior to synthetic ones. But assuming that synthetic diamonds eventually do become completely indistinguishable from real ones, there will no longer be any basis for this preference. And as a result, deBeers' control over the supply of mined diamonds will cease to confer monopoly power. New ways are constantly being devised of producing existing products, and the exclusive input that generates today's monopoly is likely to become obsolete tomorrow.

2. Economies of Scale When the long-run average cost curve (given fixed input prices) is downward sloping, the least costly way to serve the market is to concentrate production in the hands of a single firm. In Figure 12.1, for example, note that a single firm can produce an industry output of Q^* at an average cost of LAC_{Q^*}, while with two firms sharing the same market, average cost rises to $LAC_{Q^*/2}$. A market that is most cheaply served by a single firm is called a *natural monopoly*. A frequently cited example is the provision of local telephone landlines.

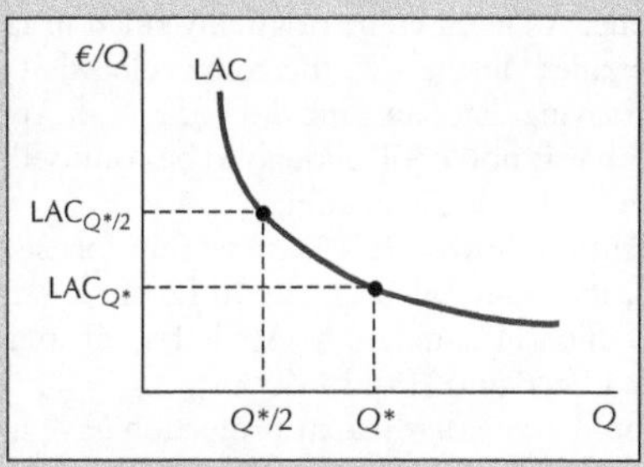

FIGURE 12.1
Natural Monopoly
When the LAC curve is declining throughout, it is always cheaper for a single firm to serve the entire industry.

Recall from Chapter 11 that it is possible for the LAC curve to be downward sloping even in the absence of economies of scale. This can happen, for example, if the price of an important input falls significantly when industry output expands (a *pecuniary economy,* in the language of Chapter 11). Note carefully, however, that this case is *not* one that gives rise to natural monopoly. Input prices here depend on the level of industry output, not on the output of any one firm. Pecuniary economies will apply with equal force whether one or many firms serve the market.

Strictly speaking, then, it is the degree of returns to scale, not the slope of the LAC curve, that determines whether we have a natural monopoly. With fixed input prices, of course, there is always a one-to-one relationship between returns to scale and the slope of the LAC curve (see Chapter 10).

3. Patents Most countries protect inventions through some sort of patent system. A patent typically confers the right to exclusive benefit from all exchanges involving the invention to which it applies. There are costs as well as benefits to patents. On the cost side, the monopoly it creates usually leads, as we will see, to higher prices for consumers. On the benefit side, the patent makes possible a great many inventions that would not otherwise occur. Although some inventions are serendipitous, most are the result of long effort and expense in sophisticated research laboratories. If a firm were unable to sell its product for a sufficiently high price to recoup these outlays, it would have no economic reason to undertake research and development in the first place. Without a patent, competition would force price down to marginal cost, and the pace of innovation would be slowed dramatically. The protection from competition afforded by a patent is what makes it possible for the firm to recover its costs of innovation. In the EU, the life of a patent is 20 years, a compromise figure that is too long for many inventions, too short for many others. In particular, there is a persuasive argument that the patent life should be extended in the prescription drug industry, where the testing and approval process often consumes all but a few years of the current patent period.[1]

[1]Henry Grabowski, *Drug Regulation and Innovation,* Washington, DC: American Enterprise Institute, 1976.

What is a just reward for designing the iPhone or finding a treatment for cancer?

ECONOMIC NATURALIST 12.1

In 2011 Apple launched a series of lawsuits against competitors for patent infringement. Companies, including Samsung and Motorola, were accused of using patented technology on smartphones and tablets. It was not long before Samsung countersued—arguing that Apple had infringed its patents. Expensive legal battles in the US, Europe and Far East ensued.

To illustrate the complexity consider just one product—Samsung's Galaxy Tab 10.1 tablet computer. A German court ruled in favour of Apple and banned the tablet from sale. A Dutch court originally ruled in favour of Apple, but the verdict was later overruled. In the UK, the court ruled that Apple should put a disclaimer on its website saying that Samsung did not breech Apple's patent; the judge said that the Galaxy Tab was not 'cool' enough to be confused with the iPad. Very confusing! Needless to say, appeals are pending.

Most attention, however, was inevitably focused on the much broader case in the US. Here, the court ruled largely in favour of Apple. Samsung was ordered to pay over $1 billion in damages to Apple for infringing various patents such as the 'Bounce-Back Effect' and 'Tap to Zoom'.

Apple would argue that patent protection gave it the incentive to be innovative. Its lawyer Harold McElhinny told the jury that 'In ... three months, Samsung was able to copy and incorporate the result of Apple's four-year investment in hard work and ingenuity—without taking any of the risks'. The key thing here is risk—many projects fail and so a firm must be confident that on the successful projects they can recoup not only the costs from the successful project but also all the unsuccessful projects. Without patent protection we may never have seen the iPhone or iPad.

Others, however, would argue that Apple has done pretty well out of the iPhone and iPad. Patent protection is now merely stifling competition, and keeping lawyers happy. Was patent protection key in Apple's decision to invest in the iPhone? It was possibly not all that important. But that is only because Apple operates in markets where there is significant brand loyalty. When the latest iPad or iPhone is released customers queue for hours to get their hands on one. These customers will clearly buy the iPhone and iPad even if Samsung offers a similar, cheaper product. Apple profits, therefore, from being a market leader, irrespective of patent laws.

Things are different in markets with no brand loyalty. In the prescription drug industry, for example, patent protection is crucial. In this market customers can easily substitute to cheaper brands. There would, therefore, be no incentive for Pfizer, Novartis or AstraZeneca to discover a treatment for cancer if they knew that their rivals could undercut them and run away with all the profits. ■

4. Network Economies On the demand side of many markets, a product becomes more valuable as greater numbers of consumers use it.[2] A vivid early illustration was the VHS technology's defeat of the competing Beta format in home video recorders. The attraction of VHS over the initial versions of Beta was that it permitted longer recording times. Beta later corrected this deficiency, and on most important technical dimensions became widely regarded by experts as superior to VHS. Yet the initial sales advantage of VHS proved insuperable. Once the fraction of consumers owning VHS passed a critical threshold, the reasons for choosing it became compelling—variety and availability of tape rentals, access to repair facilities, the capability to exchange tapes with friends, and so on.

[2]See, for example, Joseph Farrell and Garth Saloner, 'Standardization, Compatibility, and Innovation', *Rand Journal of Economics,* 16, 1985: 70–83; and M. L. Katz and Carl Shapiro, 'Systems Competition and Network Effects', *Journal of Economic Perspectives,* Spring 1994: 93–115.

In extreme cases, such *network economies* function like economies of scale as a source of natural monopoly. Microsoft's Windows operating system, for example, achieved its dominant market position on the strength of powerful network economies. Because Microsoft's initial sales advantage gave software developers a strong incentive to write for the Windows format, the inventory of available software in the Windows format is by now vastly larger than for any competing operating system. And although general-purpose software such as word processors and spreadsheets continues to be available for multiple operating systems, specialized professional software and games usually appear first in the Windows format and often only in that format. This software gap has given people a good reason for choosing Windows, even if, as in the case of many Apple Macintosh users, they believe a competing system is otherwise superior. The end result is that more than 90 per cent of the world's personal computers now run Microsoft's Windows operating system. If that's not a pure monopoly, it comes awfully close.

5. Government Licences or Franchises In many markets, the law prevents anyone but a government-licensed firm from doing business. At service areas on motorways, for example, not just any fast-food restaurant is free to set up operations. The motoring authorities negotiate with several companies, choose one, and then grant it an exclusive licence to serve a particular area. The authorities' purpose in restricting access in the first place is that there is simply not room for more than one establishment in these locations. In such cases, the government licence as a source of monopoly is really a scale economy acting in another form. But government licences are also required in a variety of other markets, such as the one for taxis, where scale economies do not seem to be an important factor.

Government licences are sometimes accompanied by strict regulations that spell out what the licensee can and cannot do. Where the government gives a chain restaurant an exclusive licence, for example, the restaurant will often be required to charge prices no more than, say, 10 per cent higher than it charges in its unregulated outlets. In other cases, the government simply charges an extremely high fee for the licence, virtually forcing the licensee to charge premium prices. This is the practice of some airport authorities, who essentially auction their terminal counter space to the highest bidders. Your annoyance at having to pay £5 for a coffee in London's Heathrow or Gatwick Airport is thus more properly focused on Heathrow Airport Holdings or GIP, who owns Gatwick.

By far the most important of the five factors for explaining monopolies that endure is economies of scale. Production processes change over time, which makes exclusive control over important inputs only a transitory source of monopoly. Patents too are inherently transitory. Network economies, once firmly entrenched, can be as persistent a source of natural monopoly as economies of scale. Strictly speaking, network economies work through the demand side of the market by affecting what buyers are willing to pay for a product. But they may be equivalently conceptualized on the supply side as yet another feature of product quality. The more people who own the product, the higher its effective quality level. It may thus be said of a product that benefits from network economies that any given quality level can be produced at lower cost as sales volume increases. Viewed in this way, network economies are just another form of economies of scale in production, and that is how we shall view them in the discussion that follows. Government licences can persist for extended periods, but many of these licences are themselves merely an implicit recognition of scale economies that would lead to monopoly in any event.

Information as a Growing Source of Economies of Scale

In 1984, at the dawn of the personal computing age, approximately 80 per cent of the cost of a personal computer was accounted for by its hardware, only 20 per cent by its software. Only six years later, those percentages were exactly reversed. Now all but a tiny fraction of the total costs of bringing a personal computer to market are associated in one way or another with the production of information. Although this transformation has been especially dramatic in the case of personal computers, similar ones have been occurring for most other products as well.

The distinctive feature about information is that virtually all costs associated with the production of it are fixed—in contrast to hardware, for which a large share of production costs are roughly proportional to the volume of production. The upshot is that the production of information-rich products is often characterized by enormous economies of scale.

Because the concept of economies of scale refers to the long run by definition, the preceding paragraph's reference to economies of scale and fixed costs in the same breath might seem inconsistent. After all, fixed costs are expenditures associated with fixed inputs, and as we saw in Chapter 9, no inputs are fixed in the long run.

As a practical matter, however, large one-time costs, including product research and other costs associated with generating information, are often incurred before a product is launched. Typically these costs never recur, even during a product life cycle spanning several decades. Strictly speaking, these costs are not fixed, since the inputs used for generating the information could be varied in principle. Yet when the product is launched, there is simply no economic reason for varying them. So for practical purposes these costs are essentially fixed. In any case, the important point is that the firm's long-run average cost curve is likely to be downward sloping whenever a substantial share of its total cost is associated with initial investments in information.

A case in point is the microprocessor that powers personal computers and a growing array of other products. The fixed investment required to produce the latest Intel chip is roughly €2 billion. Once the chip has been designed and the manufacturing facility built, however, the marginal cost of producing each chip is only a few cents. It is hardly a surprise, therefore, that Intel currently supplies more than 80 per cent of all microprocessors sold today.

Economies of scale have always been an important feature of the modern industrial landscape. But as more and more of the value embedded in products consists of information, the importance of economies of scale can only grow further.

With this brief overview of the causes of monopoly in mind, let us turn now to the question of what the consequences of monopoly are. In order to do this, we will proceed in much the same fashion as we did in our study of the competitive firm. That is, we will examine the firm's output decision and ask whether it leads to a situation in which all possible gains from exchange are exhausted. The answer is generally no. But in formulating a government policy to improve on the results of unregulated monopoly, we will see that it is critical to understand the original source of monopoly.

THE PROFIT-MAXIMIZING MONOPOLIST

As in the competitive case, we assume that the monopolist's goal is to maximize economic profit. And again as before, in the short run this means to choose the level of output for which the difference between total revenue and short-run total cost is greatest. The case for this motive is less compelling than in the case of perfect competition. After all, the monopolist's survival is less under siege than the competitor's, and so the evolutionary argument for profit maximization applies with less force in the monopoly case. Nonetheless, we will explore just what behaviours follow from the monopolist's goal of profit maximization.

The Monopolist's Total Revenue Curve

The key difference between the monopolist and the perfect competitor is the way in which total, and hence marginal, revenue varies with output. Recall from Chapter 11 that the demand curve facing the perfect competitor is simply a horizontal line at the short-run equilibrium market price—call it P^*. The competitive firm is a price taker, typically because its own output is too small to have any discernible influence on the market price. Under these circumstances, the perfectly competitive firm's total revenue curve is a ray with slope P^*, as shown in Figure 12.2.

FIGURE 12.2
The Total Revenue Curve for a Perfect Competitor
Price for the perfect competitor remains at the short-run equilibrium level P^* irrespective of the firm's output. Its total revenue is thus the product of P^* and the quantity it sells: TR = P^*Q.

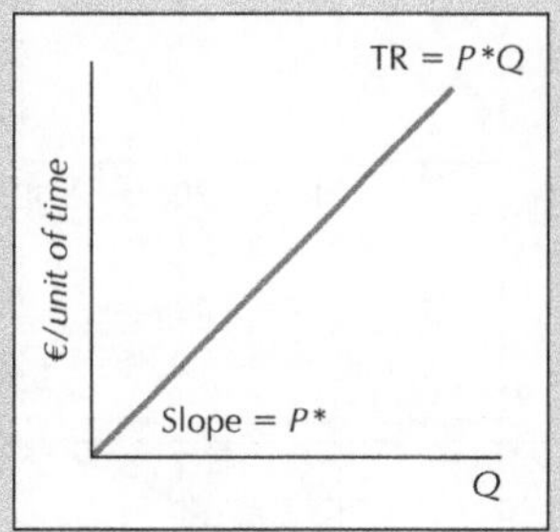

Now consider a monopolist with the downward-sloping demand curve $P = 80 - (\frac{1}{5})Q$ pictured in the top panel in Figure 12.3. For this firm as well, total revenue is the product of price and quantity. At point *A* on its demand curve, for example, it sells 100 units of output per week at a price of €60/unit, giving a total revenue of €6000/wk. At *B*, it sells 200 units at a price of €40, so its total revenue at *B* will be €8000/wk, and so on. The difference between the monopolist and the competitor is that for the monopolist to sell a larger amount of output, it must cut its price—not only for the marginal unit but for all preceding units as well. As we saw in Chapter 5, the effect of a downward-sloping demand curve is that total revenue is no longer proportional to output sold. As in the competitive case, the monopolist's total revenue curve (middle panel in Figure 12.3) passes through the origin, because in each case selling no output generates no revenue. But as price falls, total revenue for the monopolist does not rise linearly with output. Instead, it reaches a maximum value at the quantity corresponding to the midpoint of the demand curve (*B* in the top panel), after which it again begins to fall. The corresponding values of the price elasticity of demand are shown in the bottom panel in Figure 12.3. Note that total revenue reaches its maximum value when the price elasticity of demand is unity.

EXERCISE 12.1 Sketch the total revenue curve for a monopolist whose demand curve is given by P = 100 − 2Q.

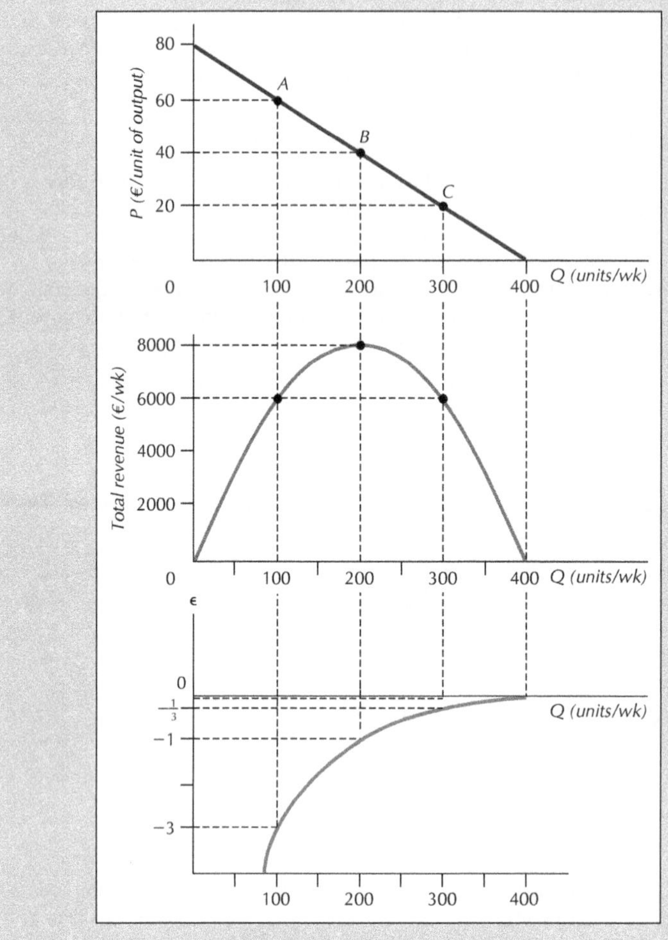

FIGURE 12.3
Demand, Total Revenue and Elasticity
For the monopolist to increase sales, it is necessary to cut price (top panel). Total revenue rises with quantity, reaches a maximum value, and then declines (middle panel). The quantity level for which the price elasticity of demand is unity corresponds to the midpoint of the demand curve, and at that value total revenue is maximized.

The top panel in Figure 12.4 portrays the short-run total cost curve and total revenue curve for a monopolist facing the demand curve shown in Figure 12.3. Economic profit, plotted in the bottom panel, is positive in the interval from $Q = 45$ to $Q = 305$, and is negative elsewhere. The maximum profit point occurs at $Q^* = 175$ units/wk, which lies to the left of the output level for which total revenue is at a maximum ($Q = 200$).

Notice in Figure 12.4 that the vertical distance between the short-run total cost and total revenue curves is greatest when the two curves are parallel (when $Q = 175$). Suppose this were not the case. For example, suppose that at the maximum-profit point the total cost curve were steeper than the total revenue curve. It would then be possible to earn higher profits by producing less output, because costs would go down by more than the corresponding reduction in total revenue. Conversely, if the total cost curve were less steep than the total revenue curve, the monopolist could earn higher profits by expanding output, because total revenue would go up by more than total cost.

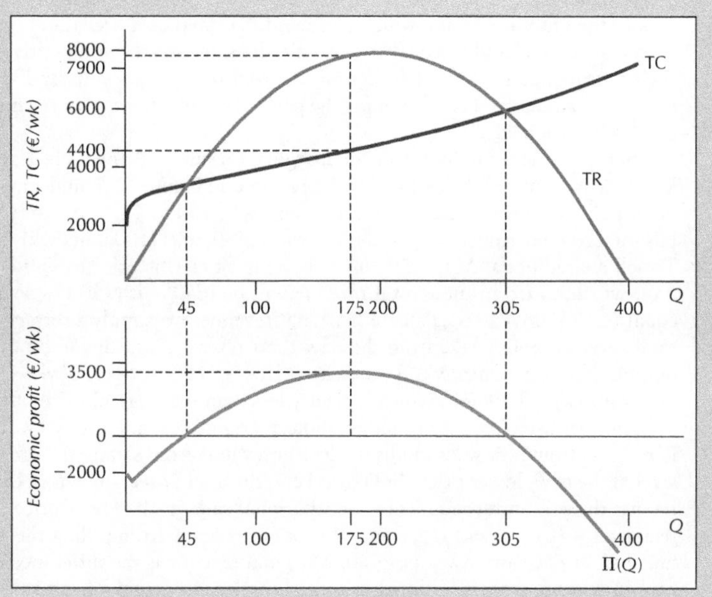

FIGURE 12.4
Total Cost, Revenue and Profit Curves for a Monopolist
Economic profit [Π(Q) in the bottom panel] is the vertical distance between total revenue and total cost (TR and TC in the top panel). Note that the maximum-profit point, $Q^* = 175$, lies to the left of the output level at which TR is at a maximum ($Q = 200$).

Marginal Revenue

The slope of the total cost curve at any level of output is by definition equal to marginal cost at that output level. By the same token, the slope of the total revenue curve is the definition of *marginal revenue*.[3] As in the case of the perfectly competitive firm, we can think of marginal revenue as the change in total revenue when the sale of output changes by 1 unit. More precisely, suppose ΔTR_Q is the change in total revenue that occurs in response to a small change in output, ΔQ. Marginal revenue, denoted MR_Q, is then given by

$$MR_Q = \frac{\Delta TR_Q}{\Delta Q} \tag{12.1}$$

Using this definition, a profit-maximizing monopolist in the short run will choose that level of output Q^* for which

$$MC_{Q^*} = MR_{Q^*} \text{ (see footnote 4)} \tag{12.2}$$

provided marginal revenue intersects marginal cost from above. Equation 12.2 defines the **optimality condition for a monopolist.** The monopolist wants to sell all units for which marginal revenue exceeds marginal cost, so marginal revenue should lie above marginal cost prior to the intersection (for some cost structures, marginal cost may decline initially and then increase, leading to two intersections of marginal cost and marginal revenue).

optimality condition for a monopolist a monopolist maximizes profit by choosing the level of output where marginal revenue equals marginal cost.

[3]In calculus terms, marginal revenue is defined as the derivative $d\text{TR}/dQ$.

[4]This condition can also be justified by noting that the first-order condition for maximum profit is given by

$$\frac{d\Pi}{dQ} = \frac{d(\text{TR} - \text{TC})}{dQ} = \text{MR} - \text{MC} = 0$$

Recall that the analogous condition for the perfectly competitive firm is to choose the output level for which price and marginal cost are equal. Recalling that marginal revenue and price (P) are exactly the same for the competitive firm (when such a firm expands output by 1 unit, its total revenue goes up by P), we see that the profit-maximizing condition for the perfectly competitive firm is simply a special case of Equation 12.2.

In the case of the monopoly firm, marginal revenue will always be less than price.[5] To see why, consider the demand curve pictured in Figure 12.5, and suppose that the monopolist wishes to increase output from $Q_0 = 100$ to $Q_0 + \Delta Q = 150$ units/wk. His total revenue from selling 100 units/wk is (€60/unit) (100 units/wk) = €6000/wk. To sell an additional $\Delta Q = 50$ units/wk, he must cut his price to €60 − ΔP = €50/unit, which means his new total revenue will be (€50/unit)(150 units/wk), which is equal to €7500/wk. To calculate marginal revenue, we simply subtract the original total revenue, €6000/wk, from the new total revenue, and divide by the change in output, $\Delta Q = 50$ units/wk. This yields $MR_{Q_0} = 100$ = (€7500/wk − €6000/wk)/(50 units/wk) = €30/unit, which is clearly less than the original price of €60/unit.

Another useful way of thinking about marginal revenue is to view it as the gain in revenue from new sales minus the loss in revenue from selling the previous output level at the new, lower price. In Figure 12.5, the area of rectangle B (€2500/wk) represents the gain in revenue from the additional sales at the lower price. The area of rectangle A (€1000/wk) represents the loss in revenue from selling the original 100 units/wk at €50/unit instead of €60. Marginal revenue is the difference between the gain in revenue from additional sales and the loss in revenue from sales at a lower price, divided by the change in quantity. This yields (€2500/wk − €1000/wk)/(50 units/wk), which is again equal to €30/unit.

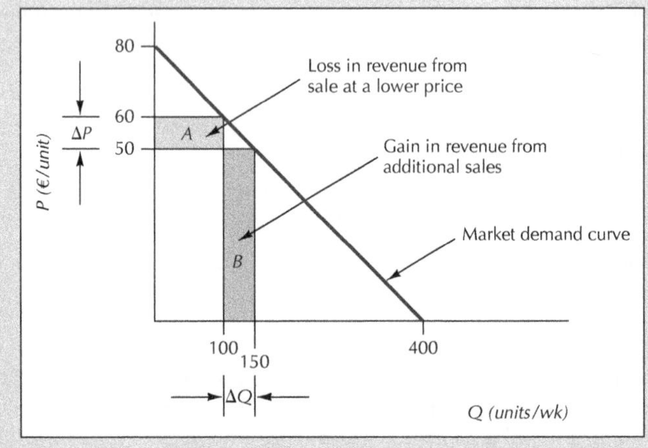

FIGURE 12.5
Changes in Total Revenue Resulting from a Price Cut
The area of rectangle A (€1000/wk) is the loss in revenue from selling the previous output level at a lower price. The area of rectangle B (€2500/wk) is the gain in revenue from selling the additional output at the new, lower price. Marginal revenue is the difference between these two areas (€2500 − €1000 = €1500/wk) divided by the change in output (50 units/wk). Here MR equals €30/unit, which is less than the new price of €50/unit.

To explore how marginal revenue varies as we move along a straight-line demand curve, consider the demand curve pictured in Figure 12.6, and suppose that the monopolist wishes to increase output from Q_0 to $Q_0 + \Delta Q$ units. His total revenue from selling Q_0 units is P_0Q_0. To sell an additional ΔQ units, he must cut his

[5]There is actually one exception to this claim, namely, the case of the perfectly discriminating monopolist, discussion of which follows.

price to $P_0 - \Delta P$, which means his new total revenue will be $(P_0 - \Delta P)(Q_0 + \Delta Q)$, which is equal to $P_0Q_0 + P_0\Delta Q - \Delta PQ_0 - \Delta P\Delta Q$. To calculate marginal revenue, simply subtract the original total revenue, P_0Q_0, from the new total revenue, and divide by the change in output, ΔQ. This leaves $MR_{Q_0} = P_0 - (\Delta P/\Delta Q)Q_0 - \Delta P$, which is clearly less than P_0. As ΔP approaches zero, the expression for marginal revenue thus approaches[6]

$$MR_{Q_0} = P_0 - \frac{\Delta P}{\Delta Q}Q_0 \tag{12.3}$$

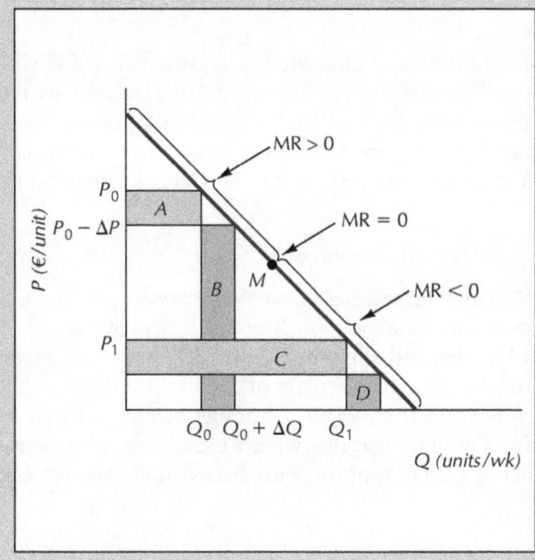

FIGURE 12.6
Marginal Revenue and Position on the Demand Curve
When Q is to the left of the midpoint (M) of a straight-line demand curve (for example, $Q = Q_0$), the gain from added sales (area B) outweighs the loss from a lower price for existing sales (area A). When Q is to the right of the midpoint (for example, $Q = Q_1$), the gain from added sales (area D) is smaller than the loss from a lower price for existing sales (area C). At the midpoint of the demand curve, the gain and the loss are equal, which means marginal revenue is zero.

Equation 12.3 makes intuitive sense if we think of ΔQ as being a 1-unit change in output; P_0 would then be the gain in revenue from the sale of that extra unit, and $(\Delta P/\Delta Q)Q_0 = \Delta PQ_0$ would be the loss in revenue from the sale of the existing units at the lower price. We see again in Equation 12.3 that marginal revenue is less than price for all positive levels of output.

The fact that area B is larger than area A in Figure 12.6 means that marginal revenue is positive at Q_0. Once output moves past the midpoint (M in Figure 12.6) on a straight-line demand curve, however, the marginal revenue of a further expansion will be negative. Thus, the area of rectangle C is larger than the area of rectangle D in Figure 12.6, which means that marginal revenue at the output level Q_1 is less than zero.

Marginal Revenue and Elasticity

Yet another useful relationship links marginal revenue to the price elasticity of demand at the corresponding point on the demand curve. Recall from Chapter 5 that the price elasticity of demand at a point (Q, P) is given by

$$\epsilon = \frac{\Delta Q}{\Delta P}\frac{P}{Q} \tag{12.4}$$

In Equation 12.4, the terms ΔQ and ΔP have opposite signs, because the demand curve is downward sloping. By contrast, recall that the ΔQ and ΔP terms

[6]Note that when ΔP shrinks toward zero, the corresponding ΔQ does so as well. Because ΔP and ΔQ are both positive here, the ratio $\Delta P/\Delta Q$ is simply the negative of the slope of the demand curve.

in Equation 12.3, which also represent changes in P and Q as we move along the demand curve, are both positive. Suppose we redefine ΔQ and ΔP from Equation 12.4 so that both of these terms are positive. That equation then becomes

$$|\epsilon| = \frac{\Delta Q}{\Delta P}\frac{P}{Q} \tag{12.5}$$

The purpose of making both ΔQ and ΔP positive is to be able to relate Equation 12.5 back to Equation 12.3. If we now solve Equation 12.5 for $\Delta P/\Delta Q\,|\epsilon|$ and substitute into Equation 12.3, we get

$$\text{MR}_Q = P\left(1 - \frac{1}{|\epsilon|}\right) \tag{12.6}$$

Equation 12.6 tells us that the less elastic demand is with respect to price, the more price will exceed marginal revenue.[7] It also tells us that in the limiting case of infinite price elasticity, marginal revenue and price are exactly the same. (Recall from Chapter 11 that price and marginal revenue are the same for the competitive firm, which faces a horizontal, or infinitely elastic, demand curve.)

Graphing Marginal Revenue

Equation 12.6 also provides a convenient way to plot the marginal revenue values that correspond to different points along a demand curve. To illustrate, consider the straight-line demand curve in Figure 12.7, which intersects the vertical axis at a price value of $P = 80$. The elasticity of demand is infinite at that point, which means that $\text{MR}_0 = 80(1 - 1/|\epsilon|) = 80$. Although marginal revenue will generally be less than price for a monopolist, the two are exactly the same when quantity is zero. The reason is that at zero output there are no existing sales for a price cut to affect.

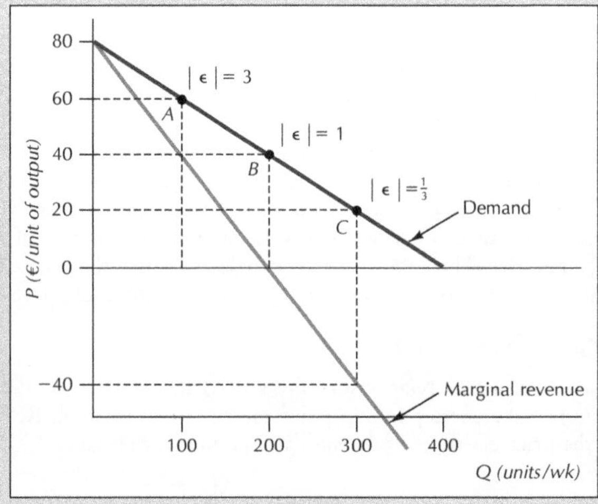

FIGURE 12.7
The Demand Curve and Corresponding Marginal Revenue Curve
For the case of a straight-line demand curve, the corresponding marginal revenue curve is also a straight line. It has the same vertical intercept as the demand curve, and its horizontal intercept is half that of the demand curve.

[7]Equation 12.6 can be derived using calculus as follows:

$$\text{MR} = \frac{d\text{TR}}{dQ} = \frac{d(PQ)}{dQ} = P + Q\frac{dP}{dQ} = P\left(1 + \frac{QdP}{PdQ}\right) = P\left(1 + \frac{1}{\epsilon}\right) = P\left(1 - \frac{1}{|\epsilon|}\right)$$

Now suppose we move, say, one-quarter of the way down the demand curve to point *A*, (100, 60). At that point, $|\epsilon| = 3$. Thus we have $MR_{100} = (60)(1 - \frac{1}{3}) = 40$.

Halfway down the demand curve, at point *B*, (200, 40), $|\epsilon| = 1$, which gives us $MR_{200} = (40)(1 - \frac{1}{1}) = 0$. This confirms our earlier finding (Chapter 5) that total revenue is at a maximum at the midpoint of a straight-line demand curve, where elasticity is unity.

Finally, consider point C, (300, 20), which is three-fourths of the way down the demand curve. Here $|\epsilon| = \frac{1}{3}$, so we have $MR_{300} = (20)\,[1 - (1/\frac{1}{3})] = (20)(-2) = -40$. Thus, at $Q = 300$, the effect of selling an extra unit of output is to reduce total revenue by €40/wk.

Filling in additional points in the same fashion, we quickly see that the marginal revenue curve associated with a straight-line demand curve is itself a straight line, one whose slope is twice that of the demand curve. The marginal revenue curve cuts the horizontal axis just below the midpoint of the demand curve, and for all quantities larger than that marginal revenue is negative. Note that all points to the right of the midpoint of the demand curve have price elasticity values less than 1 in absolute value. The fact that marginal revenue is negative in this region thus fits our observation from Chapter 5 that a cut in price will reduce total revenue whenever demand is inelastic with respect to price.

EXAMPLE 12.1 Find the marginal revenue curve that corresponds to the demand curve $P = 12 - 3Q$.

The marginal revenue curve will have the same intercept as and twice the slope of the demand curve, which gives us $MR = 12 - 6Q$, as plotted in Figure 12.8.

The general formula for a linear demand curve is $P = a - bQ$, where a and b are positive numbers. The corresponding marginal revenue curve will be $MR = a - 2bQ$.[8] ◆

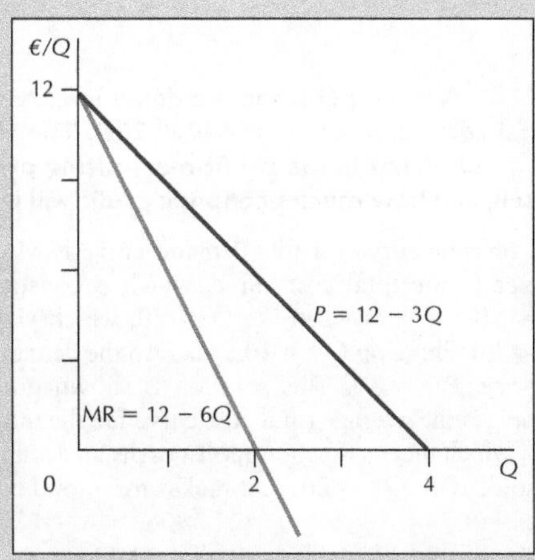

FIGURE 12.8
A Specific Linear Demand Curve and the Corresponding Marginal Revenue Curve
The marginal revenue curve has the same vertical intercept and twice the slope of the corresponding linear demand curve.

EXERCISE 12.2 Sketch demand and marginal revenue curves for a monopolist whose market demand curve is given by $P = 100 - 2Q$.

[8]Note that total revenue for the demand curve $P = a - bQ$ is given by $TR = aQ - bQ^2$. The corresponding marginal revenue curve is

$$MR = \frac{dTR}{dQ} = a - 2bQ$$

Graphical Interpretation of the Short-Run Profit Maximization Condition

Recall from Chapter 11 the graphical representation of the maximum-profit point for the competitive firm in the short run. An analogous graphical representation exists for the monopolist. Consider a monopolist with the demand, marginal revenue and short-run cost curves pictured in Figure 12.9. The profit-maximizing level of output for this firm is Q^*, the one for which the marginal revenue and marginal cost curves intersect. At that quantity level, the monopolist can charge a price of P^*, and by so doing will earn an economic profit equal to the shaded rectangle labelled Π.

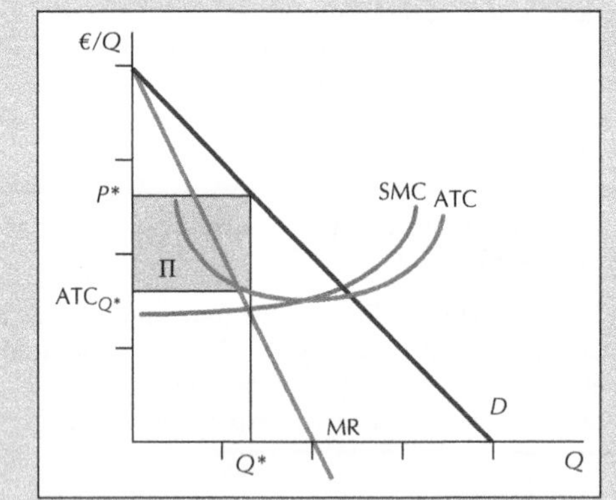

FIGURE 12.9
The Profit-Maximizing Price and Quantity for a Monopolist
Maximum profit occurs at the output level Q^*, where the gain in revenue from expanding output (or loss in revenue from contracting output), MR, is exactly equal to the cost of expanding output (or the savings from contracting output), SMC. At Q^*, the firm charges P^* and earns an economic profit of Π.

EXAMPLE 12.2 A monopolist faces a demand curve of $P = 100 - 2Q$ and a short-run total cost curve of $TC = 640 + 20Q$. The associated marginal cost curve is $MC = 20$. What is the profit-maximizing price? How much will the monopolist sell, and how much economic profit will it earn at that price?

The marginal revenue curve for this demand curve is $MR = 100 - 4Q$. Marginal cost is the slope of the total cost curve, which is constant at 20 in this example. Setting $MR = MC$, we have $100 - 4Q = 20$, which yields the profit-maximizing quantity, $Q^* = 20$. Plugging $Q^* = 20$ back into the demand curve, we get the profit-maximizing price, $P^* = 60$. This solution is shown graphically in Figure 12.10, which also displays the average total cost curve for the monopolist. Note that at Q^* the ATC is 52, which means the monopolist earns an economic profit of $60 - 52 = 8$ on each unit sold. With $Q^* = 20$, that makes for a total economic profit of 160. ◆

Note in Figure 12.10 that the monopolist's fixed cost was irrelevant to the determination of the profit-maximizing output level and price. This makes sense intuitively, because fixed cost has no bearing on the gains and losses that occur when output changes.

EXERCISE 12.3 How would the profit-maximizing price and quantity change in Example 12.2 if the monopolist's total cost curve were instead given by $TC = 640 + 40Q$? The associated marginal cost curve is $MC = 40$.

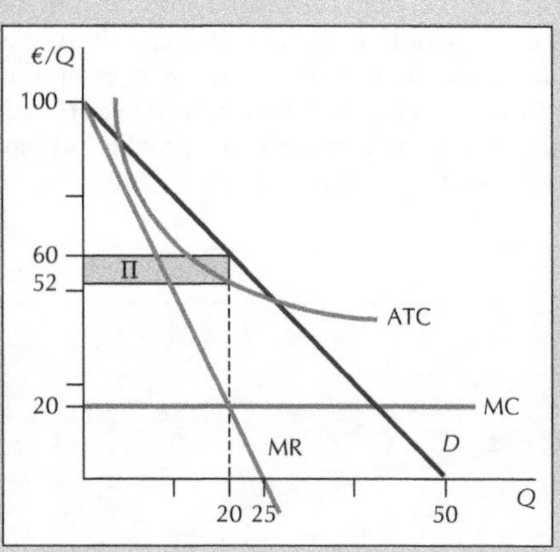

FIGURE 12.10
The Profit-Maximizing Price and Quantity for Specific Cost and Demand Functions

A Profit-Maximizing Monopolist Will Never Produce on the Inelastic Portion of the Demand Curve

If a monopolist's goal is to maximize profits, it follows directly that she will never produce an output level on the inelastic portion of her demand curve. If she were to increase her price at such an output level, the effect would be to increase total revenue. The price increase would also reduce the quantity demanded, which, in turn, would reduce the monopolist's total cost. Since economic profit is the difference between total revenue and total cost, profit would necessarily increase in response to a price increase from an initial position on the inelastic portion of the demand curve. The profit-maximizing level of output must therefore lie on the elastic portion of the demand curve, where further price increases would cause both revenue and costs to go down.

The Profit-Maximizing Mark-up

The profit-maximization condition MR = MC can be combined with Equation 12.6, which says MR = $P[1 - (1/|\epsilon|)]$, to derive the profit-maximizing mark-up for the monopolist:

$$\frac{P - \text{MC}}{P} = \frac{1}{|\epsilon|} \tag{12.7}$$

which is the difference between price and marginal cost, expressed as a fraction of the profit-maximizing price. For example, if the price elasticity of demand facing a monopolist were equal to −2, the profit-maximizing mark-up would be $\frac{1}{2}$, which implies that the profit-maximizing price is twice marginal cost. Equation 12.7 tells us that the profit-maximizing mark-up grows smaller as demand grows more elastic. In the limiting case of infinitely elastic demand, the profit-maximizing mark-up is zero (which implies P = MC), the same as in the perfectly competitive case.

The Monopolist's Shutdown Condition

In the case of the perfectly competitive firm, we saw that it paid to shut down in the short run whenever the price fell below the minimum value of average variable cost (AVC). The analogous condition for the monopolist is that there exists no quantity for which the demand curve lies above the average variable cost curve. The monopolist whose demand, marginal revenue, SMC and AVC curves are shown in Figure 12.11, for example, has no positive level of output for which price exceeds AVC, and so the monopolist does best by ceasing production in the short run. He will then sustain a short-run economic loss equal to his fixed costs, but he would do even worse at any positive level of output.

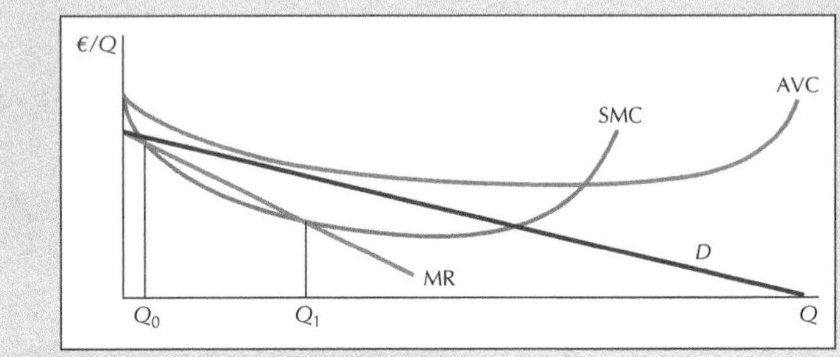

FIGURE 12.11
A Monopolist Who Should Shut Down in the Short Run
Whenever average revenue (the price value on the demand curve) is lower than average variable cost for every level of output, the monopolist does best to cease production in the short run.

Another way of stating the shutdown condition for a monopolist is to say that he should cease production whenever average revenue is less than average variable cost at every level of output. Average revenue is simply another name for price—the value of *P* along the monopolist's demand curve.[9]

Figure 12.11 also illustrates the important point that MR = MC is a necessary, but not sufficient, condition for maximum profit. Note in the figure that marginal revenue is equal to marginal cost at the output level Q_0. Why isn't this the maximum-profit point? Recall that in the case of the perfectly competitive firm, the maximum-profit condition called for price to equal marginal cost on a rising portion of the marginal cost curve, above the minimum point on the AVC curve. A somewhat different condition applies in the case of the monopolist. In Figure 12.11, note that at Q_0 the MR curve intersects the MC curve from below.[10] This means not only that Q_0 is not the maximum-profit point, but that it actually corresponds to a *lower* profit level than any of the other output levels nearby. For example, consider an output level just less than Q_0. At any such output level the gains from contracting output (MC) will exceed the losses (MR), so the firm does better to contract from Q_0. Now consider an output level just slightly larger than Q_0. For such an output level, the gains from expanding (MR) exceed the costs (MC), so the firm does better to expand. Thus, when the firm is at Q_0, it can earn higher profits by either contracting *or* expanding. Q_0 is called a *local minimum* profit point.[11]

Note also in Figure 12.11 that the MR curve intersects the MC curve a second time at the output level Q_1. This time the intersection occurs from above, and you can easily show as an exercise that Q_1 yields higher profits than any of the other output

[9]More formally, note that average revenue = TR/Q = PQ/Q = P.
[10]To 'intersect from below at Q_0' means that as Q approaches Q_0 from the left, MR lies below MC and then crosses MC when $Q = Q_0$.
[11]The second-order condition for maximum profit is given by

$$\frac{d(\mathrm{MR} - \mathrm{MC})}{dQ} = \frac{d\mathrm{MR}}{dQ} - \frac{d\mathrm{MC}}{dQ} < 0$$

which says simply that the slope of the marginal revenue curve must be less than the slope of the marginal cost curve.

levels close by. (The argument runs exactly parallel to the one in the preceding paragraph.) We refer to points like Q_1 as *local maximum* profit points. But although Q_1 yields more profit than any nearby output level, the firm fails to cover its average variable cost at the level of output, and so does better simply to produce nothing at all. The point Q^* we saw earlier in Figure 12.9 is both a local maximum profit point and a *global maximum* profit point, the latter designation indicating that no other output level, including zero, yields higher profit. For a monopolist, a global maximum profit point might occur either on the rising or on the falling portion of the MC curve. But it must be at a point where the MR curve intersects the MC curve from above.

EXERCISE 12.4 Find the optimal price and quantity for the monopolist described by the information in the following table.

Q	P	MR	SMC	AVC
0	100	100	150	150
15	86	71	71	107
25	75	50	41	84
34	66	33	33	72
50	50	0	63	63

To recapitulate briefly, we have seen that the monopolist behaves like a perfectly competitive firm in the sense that each chooses an output level by weighing the benefits of expanding (or contracting) output against the corresponding costs. For both the perfect competitor and the monopolist, marginal cost is the relevant measure of the cost of expanding output. Fixed costs are irrelevant for short-run output decisions in both cases. For both the monopolist and the perfect competitor, the benefits of expanding output are measured by their respective values of marginal revenue. For the competitor, marginal revenue and price are one and the same. For the monopolist, by contrast, marginal revenue is less than price. The competitor maximizes profit by expanding output until marginal cost equals price. The monopolist maximizes profit by expanding output until marginal cost equals marginal revenue, and thus chooses a lower output level than if he had used the competitor's criterion. Both the monopolist and the perfect competitor do best to shut down in the short run if price is less than average variable cost for all possible levels of output.

A MONOPOLIST HAS NO SUPPLY CURVE

As we saw in Chapter 11, the competitive firm has a well-defined supply curve. It takes market price as given and responds by choosing the output level for which marginal cost and price are equal. At the industry level, a shifting demand curve will trace out a well-defined industry supply curve, which is the horizontal summation of the individual firm supply curves.

There is no similar supply curve for the monopolist. The reason is that the monopolist is not a price taker, which means that there is no unique correspondence between price and marginal revenue when the market demand curve shifts. Thus, a given marginal revenue value for one demand curve can correspond to one price, while the same value of marginal revenue for a second demand curve corresponds to a different price. As a result, it is possible to observe the monopolist producing Q_1^* and selling at P^* in one period, and then selling Q_2^* at P^* in another period.

To illustrate, consider a monopolist with a demand curve of $P = 100 - Q$ and with the same cost curves as in Example 12.2, in particular with MC = 20. The marginal revenue curve for this monopolist is given by MR = $100 - 2Q$, and equating MR to MC yields a profit-maximizing output level of $Q^* = 40$. The corresponding profit-maximizing price is $P^* = 60$. Note that this is the same as the profit-maximizing price we saw for the monopolist in Example 12.2, even though the demand curve here lies to the right of the earlier one.

When the monopolist's demand curve shifts, the price elasticity of demand at a given price generally will also shift. But these shifts need not occur in the same direction. When demand shifts rightward, for example, elasticity at a given price may either increase or decrease, and the same is true when demand shifts leftward. The result is that there can be no unique correspondence between the price a monopolist charges and the amount she chooses to produce. And hence we say that the monopolist has no supply curve. Rather, she has a *supply rule,* which is to equate marginal revenue and marginal cost.

ADJUSTMENTS IN THE LONG RUN

In the long run, the monopolist is of course free to adjust all inputs, just as the competitive firm is. What is the optimal quantity in the long run for a monopolist with a given technology? The best the monopolist can do is to produce the quantity for which long-run marginal cost is equal to marginal revenue. In Figure 12.12, that will mean choosing a capital stock that gives rise to the short-run average and marginal cost curves labelled ATC* and SMC*. For that level of capital stock, the short-run marginal cost curve passes through the intersection of the long-run marginal cost and marginal revenue curves. Q^* will be the profit-maximizing quantity in the long run, and it will sell at a price of P^*. For the conditions pictured in Figure 12.12, the long-run economic profit level, Π, will be positive, and is indicated by the area of the shaded rectangle.

As we saw in Chapter 11, economic profits tend to vanish in the long run in perfectly competitive industries. This tendency will sometimes be present for monopoly. To the extent that the factors that gave rise to the firm's monopoly position come under attack in the long run, there will be downward pressure on its profits. For example, competing firms may develop substitutes for important inputs that were previously under the control of the monopolist. Or in the case of patented products,

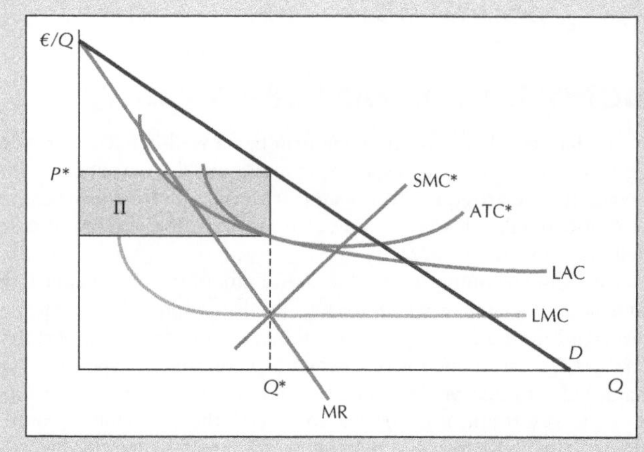

FIGURE 12.12
Long-Run Equilibrium for a Profit-Maximizing Monopolist
The profit-maximizing quantity in the long run is Q^*, the output level for which LMC = MR. The profit-maximizing price in the long run is P^*. The optimal capital stock in the long run gives rise to the short-run marginal cost curve SMC*, which passes through the intersection of LMC and MR.

competitors may develop close substitutes that do not infringe on existing patents, which are in any event only temporary.

But in other cases there may be a tendency for monopoly profits to persist. The firm shown in Figure 12.12, for example, has a declining long-run average cost curve, which means that it may enjoy a persistent cost advantage over potential rivals. In such natural monopolies, economic profits may be highly stable over time. And the same, of course, may be true for a firm whose monopoly comes from having a government licence. Persistent economic profits are indeed one of the major policy concerns about monopoly, as we will discuss later in the chapter.

PRICE DISCRIMINATION

Our discussion thus far has assumed that the monopolist sells all its output at a single price. In reality, however, monopolists often charge different prices to different buyers, a practice that is known as *price discrimination*. The cinema discount tickets discussed at the beginning of this chapter constitute one example. In the following sections, we analyse how the profit-maximizing monopolist behaves when it is possible to charge different prices to different buyers. When price discrimination is possible, a monopolist can transfer some of the gains from consumers into its own profits. However, we will see that not all the higher profits under price discrimination come at the expense of consumers. Efficiency is enhanced as the monopolist expands output toward the level at which demand intersects marginal cost.

Third-Degree Price Discrimination

Suppose the monopolist has two completely distinct markets in which she can sell her output. Perhaps she is the only supplier in the domestic market for her product, and the only one in a foreign market as well. If she is a profit maximizer, what prices should she charge and what quantities should she sell in each market?

Suppose the demand and marginal revenue curves for the two markets are as given in the left and middle panels in Figure 12.13. First note that if the monopolist is maximizing profit, her marginal revenue should be the same in each market. (If

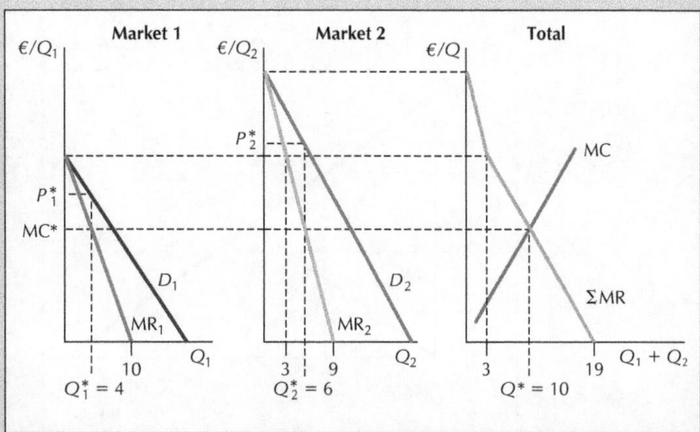

FIGURE 12.13
The Profit-Maximizing Monopolist Who Sells in Two Markets
For a monopolist who sells in two markets, the profit-maximizing output level is where the ΣMR curve intersects the MC curve, here, $Q^* = 10$. Marginal revenue in each market will be the same when $Q_1^* = 4$ and $Q_2^* = 6$ are sold in markets 1 and 2, respectively.

it weren't, she could sell 1 unit less in the market with lower MR and 1 unit more in the market with higher MR, thereby increasing her profit.) Given that MR in the two markets must be the same, the profit-maximizing total quantity will be the one for which this common value is the same as marginal cost. Graphically, the solution is to add the marginal revenue curves horizontally across the two markets, and produce the level of output for which the resulting curve intersects the marginal cost curve. In the right panel in Figure 12.13, the optimal total output is indicated by $Q^* = 10$ units. $Q_1^* = 4$ of it is sold in market 1 at a price of P_1^*, and the remaining $Q_2^* = 6$ in market 2 at a price of P_2^*.

EXAMPLE 12.3 A monopolist has marginal costs MC = Q and home market demand P = 30 − Q. The monopolist can also sell to a foreign market at a constant price P_F = 12. Find and graph the quantity produced, quantity sold in the home market, quantity sold in the foreign market, and price charged in the home market. Explain why the monopolist's profits would fall if it were to produce the same quantity but sell more in the home market.

The linear demand curve $P = 30 - Q$ has associated marginal revenue $MR = 30 - 2Q$. The profit-maximizing level of output for a monopolist selling to segmented markets occurs where $\Sigma MR = MC$. The horizontal sum of the marginal revenues across markets is the home marginal revenue function MR_H up to home output where $MR_F = MR_H$, and then the foreign marginal revenue function $MR_F = 12$ for any further units (see Figure 12.14). Total marginal revenue equals marginal cost at $MR_F = MC$, which solves for $Q = 12$. Marginal cost for this level of output equals home marginal revenue at $30 - 2Q_H = 12$, so $Q_H = 9$, with the remaining units sold abroad:

$$Q_F = Q - Q_H = 12 - 9 = 3$$

In the home market, the monopolist charges

$$P_H = 30 - Q_H = 30 - 9 = 21$$

Any further units sold at home would yield marginal revenue less than 12. Since sales to the foreign market yield a constant marginal revenue of 12, shifting sales to the home market would decrease profits due to the lost marginal revenue for each unit shifted. ◆

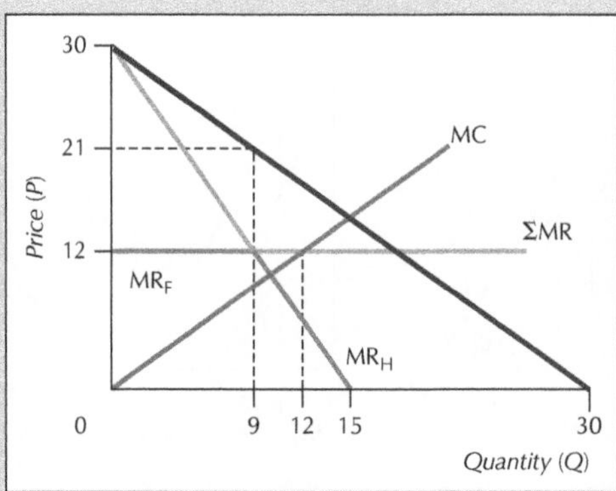

FIGURE 12.14
A Monopolist with a Perfectly Elastic Foreign Market
The curve ΣMR follows MR_H as long as $MR_H \geq MR_F$, and then follows MR_F. The profit-maximizing output level is where the ΣMR curve intersects the MC curve, here $Q^* = 12$.

EXERCISE 12.5 Suppose a monopolist sells in two separate markets, with demand curves given by $P_1 = 10 - Q_1$ and $P_2 = 20 - Q_2$, respectively. If her total cost curve is given by $TC = 5 + 2Q$ (for which the associated marginal cost curve is given by $MC = 2$), what quantities should she sell and what prices should she charge in the two markets?

Note in Exercise 12.5 that the monopolist who sells in two markets charges a higher price in the market where demand is less elastic with respect to price.[12] Charging different prices to buyers in completely separate markets is often referred to as **third-degree price discrimination**. There is no special significance to the term 'third-degree' beyond the fact that this type of price discrimination happened to have been the third one that appeared in an early taxonomy.

third-degree price discrimination different prices are charged in different markets, or to different categories of consumer.

By charging different prices in different markets the monopolist increases their profit. They will, therefore, look to distinguish markets wherever possible. Typically, this involves distinguishing between different categories of buyer. For example, the university sports centre might distinguish between students, faculty and local residents. Examples of such discrimination abound. Any discount for students, old-age pensioners, children or local residents is an example of third-degree price discrimination.

Why do some doctors and lawyers offer discounts to people with low incomes?

ECONOMIC NATURALIST 12.2

In medicine, law, dentistry and other professions, many practitioners set their fees on a 'sliding scale'—in effect, selling their services to low-income consumers at significant discounts. This practice is often said to stem from professionals' concerns about the economic hardships confronting the poor. Such concerns are no doubt often heartfelt. But note also that the services offered by these professionals are normal goods, which means that the demand curves of low-income customers lie well below those of their wealthier counterparts. Sliding-scale fees may thus also be viewed as attempts by professionals to increase their profits by tailoring their prices to elasticity differences among different groups of buyers. A similar pattern is observed in the market for movie tickets, in which it is common for cinema owners to set lower prices for students, senior citizens and other groups believed to have higher price elasticities of demand. ■

Notice also that price discrimination is feasible if two conditions hold. First, it needs to be possible to distinguish categories of consumer. For instance, to get a student discount it is necessary to show a student ID card. Furthermore, it must be impossible, or at least impractical, for buyers to trade among themselves. If a product costs €20 for students and €30 for non-students then entrepreneurial students would buy €20 books and sell them for, say, €25 to non-students; others, hoping to get in on the action, would cut price even further, and eventually the price differential would vanish. Buying at a low price from one source and reselling at a higher price is often called **arbitrage**. Where arbitrage is practical, large price differentials for a single product cannot persist. Arbitrage ensures, for example, that the price of gold in London can never differ significantly from the price of gold in New York.

arbitrage the purchase of something for costless risk-free resale at a higher price.

[12]This result follows from Equation 12.6, which says that $MR = P(1 - 1/|\epsilon|)$. Setting $MR_1 = MR_2$ yields $P_1/P_2 = (1 - 1/|\epsilon_2|)/(1 - 1/|\epsilon_1|)$. Hence the higher price will be charged to customers with the lower price elasticity of demand.

Why do cinema owners offer student discounts on admission tickets but not on popcorn?

ECONOMIC NATURALIST 12.3

Arbitrage is practical in some cases but not in others. Student discounts on tickets enable cinemas to segment their markets because it is not possible for one person to see a movie at a low price and then sell the experience to someone else at a higher price. By the same token, it is practical for lawyers and doctors to charge different people different prices on the basis of differences in price elasticity of demand. But such market segmentation is more difficult for products like popcorn. If cinemas attempted to sell popcorn for €1 to students and for €3 to adults, some enterprising student would seize the arbitrage opportunity, selling popcorn to disgruntled adults for only €2. And under the pressure of competition from other arbitrageurs, the price differential would fall until the price differential was barely sufficient to make it worth the students' while to engage in the transaction. ■

The Perfectly Discriminating Monopolist

Third-degree price discrimination allows the monopolist to increase profit. But, it is not the best it can do. **First-degree price discrimination** is the term used to describe the largest possible extent of discrimination. To understand one way in which this may work recall the examples of two-part tariffs given in Chapter 5. We looked at a tennis club that charges an annual membership fee in addition to hourly court fees. To refresh your memory consider Figure 12.15. This shows the demand curve of a particular consumer. With hourly court fees of P' the consumer would demand Q' hours of tennis and receive a consumer surplus equal to area EFG. This means the consumer is willing to pay an annual membership fee of $M = \frac{1}{2}Q'(P^1 - P')$. By charging an annual membership fee of M and hourly fee of P' the tennis club captures all consumer surplus.

first-degree price discrimination consumers are charged individual prices that capture all consumer surplus.

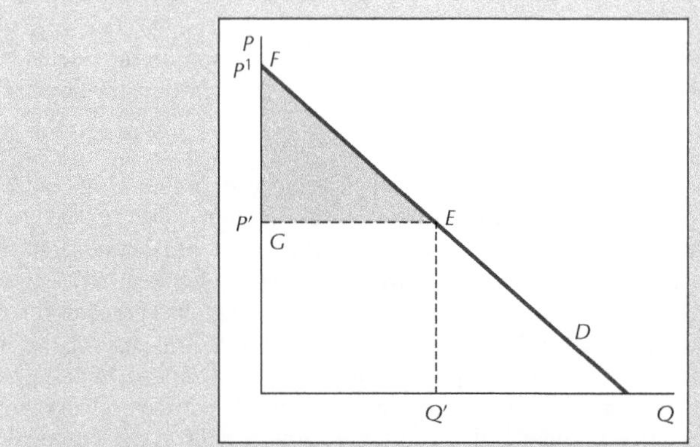

FIGURE 12.15
Two-Part Tariff
If the monopolist charges an hourly rate of P' and annual membership fee equal to the area EFG he can capture all consumer surplus.

So far, nothing new. What we need to do next is add into the mix other consumers and the costs of the tennis club. Suppose that there are two consumers—one a student and one a member of faculty. Because they carry a university ID card the tennis club can easily distinguish them. Figure 12.16 shows the individual and total demand curves, and the marginal cost curve. To find the optimal hourly fee we look to the total demand curve and the point where the marginal cost curve crosses the demand curve. It does so at price P^*. The tennis club should charge an hourly court fee of P^*. We then work out the maximum membership fee that each consumer is willing to pay. The student is willing to pay $M_s = \frac{1}{2}Q_1^*(P_S - P^*)$ and the professor is willing to pay $M_f = \frac{1}{2}Q_2^*(P_F - P^*)$.

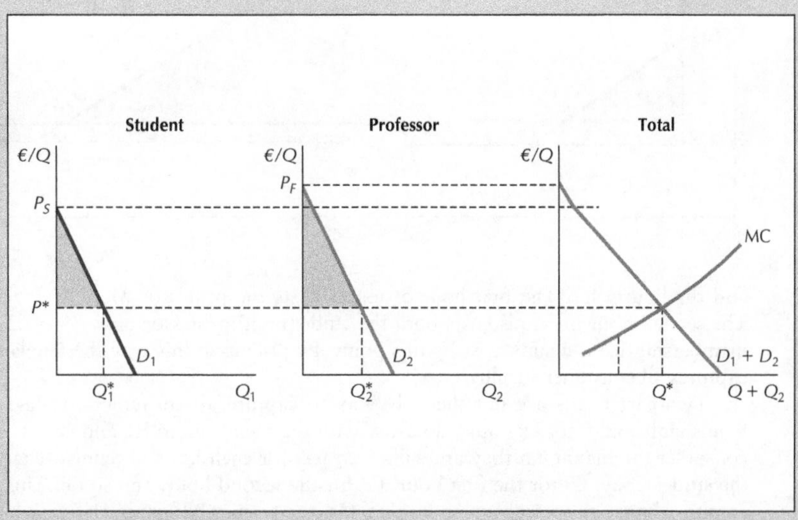

FIGURE 12.16 First-Degree Price Discrimination If the monopolist charges an hourly rate of P^* he then charges the student and professor an annual membership fee equal to their respective consumer surplus. The hourly rate is the same for both consumers, but the membership fee is not.

By charging an hourly fee of P^* and annual membership fees of M_s and M_f the tennis club extracts the consumer surplus of both the student and professor. This is an example of first-degree price discrimination.

EXAMPLE 12.4 A tennis club has two customers. One is a student with demand curve P = 10 − Q. The other is a professor with demand curve P = 20 − Q. The tennis club has marginal costs MC = 2. Find and graph the optimal hourly court fee and annual membership fees for the student and professor. Explain why there is a difference in membership fee for the student and professor.

We find the optimal hourly fee by setting $P = MC$. Thus, the optimal hourly fee is $P^* = 2$. With an hourly fee of €2 the student will demand 8 hours of tennis and the professor will demand 18 hours of tennis (see Figure 12.17). The student is willing to pay an annual membership fee of up to $M_s = \frac{1}{2}(8)(10 - 2) = €32$. The professor is willing to pay an annual membership fee of up to $M_f = \frac{1}{2}(18)(20 - 2) = €162$.

The professor pays a higher annual membership fee than the student because of his higher demand. The higher demand may reflect the professor's greater income or greater love of tennis.◆

First-degree price discrimination is characterized by the firm charging different consumers different prices *and* charging different prices for different units of output. To see how this works in the example, observe that the first hour of tennis costs the student $M_s + P^* = €34$ because he needs to pay both the annual membership

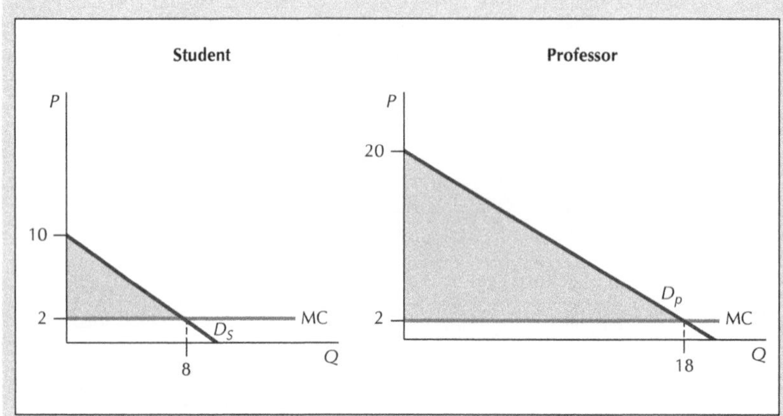

FIGURE 12.17 First-Degree Price Discrimination with Constant Marginal Cost The monopolist can charge an hourly rate of $P^* = MC$. He then charges the student and professor an annual membership fee equal to their respective consumer surplus of €32 and €162.

and the hourly fee. The first hour of tennis costs the professor $M_f + P^* =$ €164. The second hour of tennis costs both the student and professor only $P^* =$ €2; the membership fee is a sunk cost by this point. By pricing in this way the tennis club captures all consumer surplus.

Two-part tariffs are not the only way to capture all consumer surplus. The tennis club could, for example, do away with the membership fee and charge each consumer the maximum they are willing to pay for each hour of tennis—charging the student, say, €9 for the first hour, €8 for the second hour, and so on. This will capture almost all the consumer surplus. Or, the tennis club could charge a bigger membership fee and scrap the hourly fee but limit use of the court. For example, it could charge the student a €48 membership fee and limit him to 8 hours of court time. This again captures all consumer surplus.

No matter what the monopolist does, there are two salient points of comparison between the perfectly discriminating monopolist and the monopolist who cannot discriminate at all. The first is that the perfect discriminator produces a higher level of output because he need not be concerned with the effect of a price cut on the revenue from output produced thus far. He can cut price to the people who would not otherwise buy, and maintain higher prices to those who are willing to pay them. And he can cut prices on some units of the good without lowering prices on others. Price and marginal revenue are one and the same, just as in the case of perfect competition.

A second important difference is that there generally is positive consumer surplus under the non-perfectly discriminating monopolist, but none under the perfect discriminator. With third-degree price discrimination, for instance, consumer surplus exists. If the monopolist must charge a buyer the same price for all units of the good then he cannot capture consumer surplus. Similarly, if he must charge the same price to all consumers the least elastic demanders end up paying a price well below their respective reservation prices—hence the consumer surplus.

Perfect price discrimination is a never-attained theoretical limit. If a customer's demand curve were tattooed on his forehead, it might be possible for a seller to tailor each price to extract the maximum possible amount from every buyer. But in general, the details of individual demand are only imperfectly known to the seller. The tennis club cannot charge each different consumer an individually tailored membership fee. Firms do, however, often estimate individual elasticity on the basis of information known about groups to which the individual belongs. Tennis clubs do charge different membership fees to different groups. This is a step towards perfect price discrimination.

Perhaps the closest thing we see to an in-depth assessment of individual elasticities is in the behaviour of merchants in bazaars in the Middle East. The shrewd camel trader has had many years of experience in trying to assess how much a buyer with a given demographic and psychological profile is willing to pay. His stock in trade is to interpret the incongruous gesture, the furtive eye movement. But even here, the wily buyer may know how to conceal his eagerness to own the camel.

Second-Degree Price Discrimination

Given that we have covered first- and third-degree price discrimination there are no prizes for guessing that second-degree price discrimination is next. But can you work out what characterizes second-degree price discrimination?

Third-degree price discrimination is where firms charge different prices in different markets, or to different categories of consumer. First-degree price discrimination is where firms charge different prices to different categories of consumer *and* charge different prices for different units of the good. **Second-degree price discrimination** is where firms charge difference prices for different units of the good.

second-degree price discrimination different quantities of the good sell for different prices.

Two-part tariffs are an example of second-degree price discrimination. Two-for-one offers are another example. Many electric utilities employ what are called *declining tail-block rate structures* by which the first, say, 300 kilowatt-hours per month are billed at 10 cents each, the next 700 at 8 cents, and all quantities over 1000 kilowatt-hours/mo at 5 cents each. Such rate structures are also a form of second-degree price discrimination. Figure 12.18 illustrates the effect of such a rate structure for a consumer with the demand curve labelled D_i. In comparison with the alternative of charging a price of P_3 for every unit, the quantity discount scheme increases the consumer's total payment by an amount equal to the shaded area.

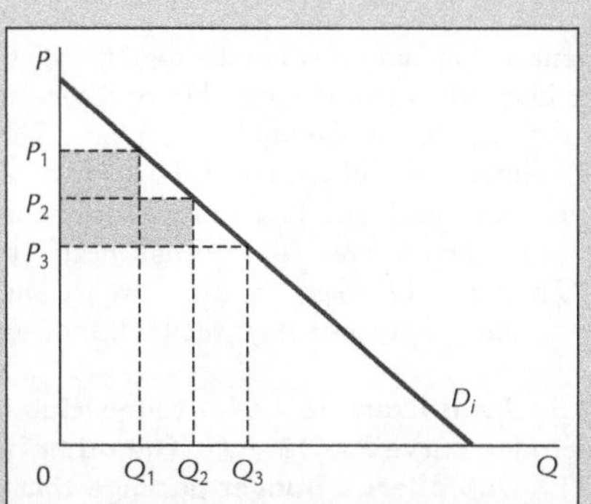

FIGURE 12.18
Second-Degree Price Discrimination
The seller offers the first block of consumption (0 to Q_1) at a high price (P_1), the second block (Q_1 to Q_2) at a lower price (P_2), the third block (Q_2 to Q_3) at a still lower price (P_3), and so on. This enables the monopolist to capture a substantial share of consumer surplus (the shaded area).

Second-degree price discrimination is distinguished from first-degree discrimination by the inability to charge different categories of consumer different prices. It is easy enough to tell apart student and faculty if they have a university ID card. It is less easy to tell apart 'rich' and 'poor' or 'tennis lovers' and 'occasional players'. And it is clearly not enough to just ask customers what category they fall into. If the tennis club announces a lower price, or lower membership fee, for 'poor' people then everyone clearly has an incentive to say they are poor.

The fact that the firm cannot directly distinguish categories does not mean, however, that they cannot do so indirectly. To illustrate let us look again at the tennis club. Suppose that the club can no longer directly distinguish student from professor.

Figure 12.19 reproduces the demand curve of the student and professor in one diagram. The perfectly price-discriminating monopolist would charge an hourly fee P^* and a low membership fee M_s, equal to area *EFG*, for the student, and a high membership fee M_f, equal to area *EHJ*, for the professor. This pricing plan will not work if there is no way to distinguish the student from the professor. The professor would clearly prefer to pay the low fee and save some money. How can the tennis club avoid this?

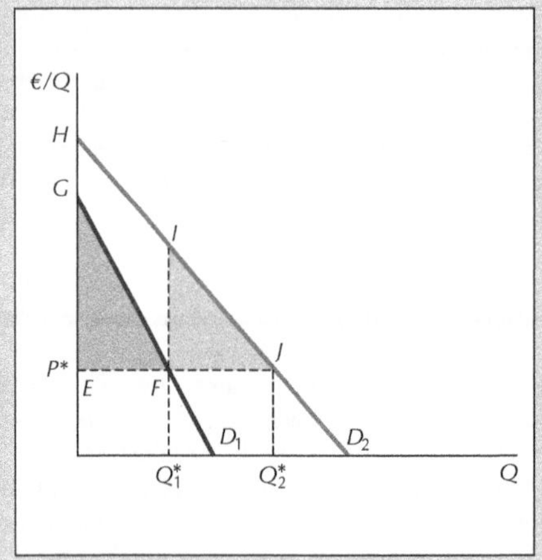

FIGURE 12.19
Second-Degree Price Discrimination with Two-Part Tariffs
The monopolist offers a budget membership package and allows users up to Q_1^* of court time. Each hour is charged at price P^*. The membership fee is equal to area *EFG*. If the professor chooses this package then he gets consumer surplus equal to area *FGHI*. The monopolist can offer an executive package that allows unlimited use and has membership fee equal to area *EFG* plus *FJI*.

What the tennis club can do is bundle together quantity and price. In particular, suppose the club offers two membership packages. The 'budget package' costs M_s and allows the member to play up to Q_1^* hours. The 'executive package' costs M' and allows unlimited use of the court. How high can M' be for the professor to choose the executive package? If the professor chooses the budget package his consumer surplus is equal to area *HGFI*. That means the professor will be willing to pay area *EFG* plus area *FJI* to get the executive package. He would then have the same consumer surplus whether he buys the budget or executive package.

EXAMPLE 12.5 As in Example 12.4 a tennis club has two customers. One is poor with demand curve $P = 10 - Q$. The other is rich with demand curve $P = 20 - Q$. The club offers a budget package that costs €32 and allows up to 8 hours of court time at cost €2 per hour. It also offers an executive package that costs €M and allows unlimited court time at cost €2 per hour. What is the maximum the rich customer will pay for the executive package? How does this amount compare to the fee that can be charged if the club can distinguish between the rich and poor customer?

The budget package is clearly aimed towards the poor customer. If the rich consumer buys the budget package then his consumer surplus will equal area *FGHI* (Figure 12.20). This works out at $(10)(8) = €80$. If the executive package costs an amount equal to area *EFG* plus *FIJ* he would be indifferent between the executive and budget package. This gives a membership fee of $M = €32 + \frac{1}{2}(18 - 8)(12 - 2) = €82$. At this price the rich consumer still gets consumer surplus equal to area *FGHI* if he buys the executive package.

FIGURE 12.20
Second-Degree Price Discrimination Example
The monopolist charges an hourly rate of €2. The budget package costs €32, area *EFG*, and limits use to 8 hours. If the rich consumer were to buy this package his consumer surplus would be €80, area *GHIF*. He is willing to pay €82, areas *EFG* plus *FIJ*, to get an executive package offering unlimited use of the court.

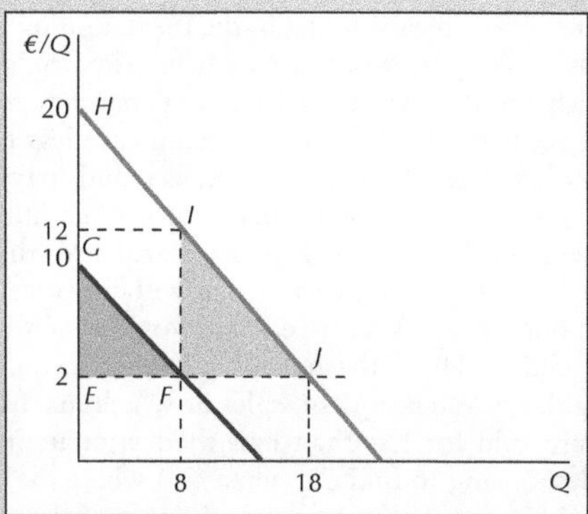

We saw in Example 12.4 that the rich consumer would be willing to pay a membership fee of €162 if he is not allowed to buy the budget package. If he can buy the budget package he is no longer willing to pay €162 for the executive package—he would switch to the budget package. Consequently the fee is set at only €82 and the rich consumer gets a consumer surplus of €80. ◆

Bundling quantity and price together like this means different units of the good cost different prices. In the previous example, it costs (8)(2) + 32 = €48 to use the court for 8 hours, or €6 per hour. It costs (18)(2) + 82 = €118 to use the court for 18 hours, or €6.56 per hour. Because different units of the good cost different prices it is second-degree price discrimination, even though the objective is partly to distinguish between different categories of customer as in third-degree price discrimination.

Bundling quantity and price together is very common. British Telecom, for instance, offers a broadband package that costs £13 per month and allows 10 GB of downloads, or an unlimited package that costs £26 per month and allows unlimited downloads. Builders merchants also typically bundle together quantity and price to distinguish professional, trade customers from domestic, DIY customers.

Hardcover €25 Paperback €15
Readers who are willing to wait a year can buy the paperback edition at a substantial discount.

The Hurdle Model of Price Discrimination

Bundling together price and quantity is not the only possibility open to the monopolist. They can also bundle together price and quality. In this case price discrimination is being used as a technique whereby the firm induces the most elastic buyers to identify themselves. This is the *hurdle model of price discrimination.* The basic idea is that the seller sets up a hurdle of some sort and makes a discount price available to those buyers who elect to jump over it. The logic is that those buyers who are most sensitive to price will be more likely than others to jump the hurdle.

One example of a hurdle is a rebate form included in the product package. Here, jumping over the hurdle means filling in the form, finding a stamp and an envelope, and then getting to the post office to mail it in. The firm's hope is that people who do not care much about price will be less likely than others to bother going through this process. If so, then people whose demands are less elastic end up paying the 'regular' price, while those with more elastic demands pay the lower discount price.

It is a rare product whose seller does not use the hurdle model of differential pricing. Booksellers offer only high-priced hardback editions in the first year of publication. Buyers who do not care strongly about price buy these editions when they first come out. Others wait a year or two and then buy the much less expensive softcover edition. Here, the hurdle is having to endure the wait. Appliance sellers offer regular 'scratch-'n-dent' sales at which machines with trivial cosmetic imperfections are sold for less than half their regular price. Here, there are two common hurdles: having to find out when and where the sale takes place and having to put up with a scratch or dent (which most of the time will be out of sight). Airlines offer 'super-saver' discounts of up to half off the regular standard fare. Here also there are two common hurdles: having to make reservations a week or more in advance and having to stay over a Saturday night. Many retailers include discount coupons in their newspaper ads. Here, the hurdles are having to read the ads, clip the coupons, and get to the store before they expire. Some sellers post signs behind the counter saying 'Ask about our special low price'. Here, the hurdle is merely having to do the asking. But even this trivial hurdle can be remarkably effective, because many well-heeled buyers would find asking about a special price too unseemly even to contemplate.

None of these schemes perfectly segregates high-elasticity from low-elasticity buyers. For instance, there are some people who wait for the January white sales to buy their towels even though they would buy just as many if the sales were not offered. But on the whole, the hurdles seem to function much as intended. A perfect hurdle would be one that imposes only a negligible cost on the buyers who jump it, yet perfectly separates buyers according to their elasticity of demand. Analytically, the effect of such a hurdle is portrayed in Figure 12.21, where P_H represents the 'regular' price and P_L represents the discount price. With a perfect hurdle, none of the people who pay the discount price has a reservation price greater than or equal to the regular price, which means that all of them would have been excluded from the market had only the regular price been available.

The hurdle model need not be limited to the two-price version depicted in Figure 12.21. On the contrary, many sellers have developed it into a highly complex art form involving literally dozens of price-hurdle combinations. On its Los Angeles–Honolulu route alone, for example, United Airlines offers dozens of different fares, each with its own set of restrictions. But no matter how simple or complex

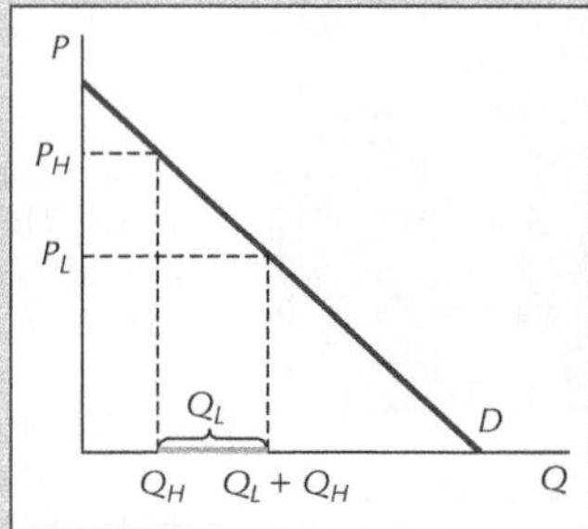

FIGURE 12.21
A Perfect Hurdle
When a hurdle is perfect, the only buyers who become eligible for the discount price (P_L) by jumping it are those who would not have been willing to pay the regular price (P_H). A perfect hurdle also imposes no significant costs on those who jump it.

the scheme may be, its goal is the same—to give discounts to customers who would not otherwise buy the product.

The hurdle model is like first-degree price discrimination in that it tries to tailor prices to the elasticities of individual buyers. The principal difference is that even in its most sophisticated form, the hurdle model cannot hope to capture all the consumer surplus.

THE EFFICIENCY LOSS FROM MONOPOLY

Recall from Chapter 11 the claim that perfect competition led to an efficient allocation of resources. This claim was based on the observation that in long-run competitive equilibrium, there are no possibilities for additional gains from exchange. The value to buyers of the last unit of output is exactly the same as the market value of the resources required to produce it.

How does the long-run equilibrium under monopoly measure up by the same criteria? Not very well, it turns out. To illustrate, consider a monopolist with constant long-run average and marginal costs and the demand structure shown in Figure 12.22. The profit-maximizing quantity for this monopolist is Q^*, which he will sell at a price of P^*. Note that at Q^*, the value of an additional unit of output to buyers is P^*, which is greater than the cost of producing an additional unit, LMC. This means that the single-price monopolist does not exhaust all possible gains from exchange. As we saw earlier, if it were possible for the monopolist to charge different prices to every buyer, output would expand to Q_C, which is the same amount we would see in a perfectly competitive industry under the same demand and cost conditions. If output did expand from Q^* to Q_C because of perfect price discrimination, the gain in producer surplus would be equal to the combined areas of the triangles labelled S_1 and S_2. Under perfect competition, the triangle S_1 would be part of consumer surplus. The cost to society of having such an industry served by a single-price monopolist, rather than by perfectly competitive sellers, will be the loss of that consumer surplus.

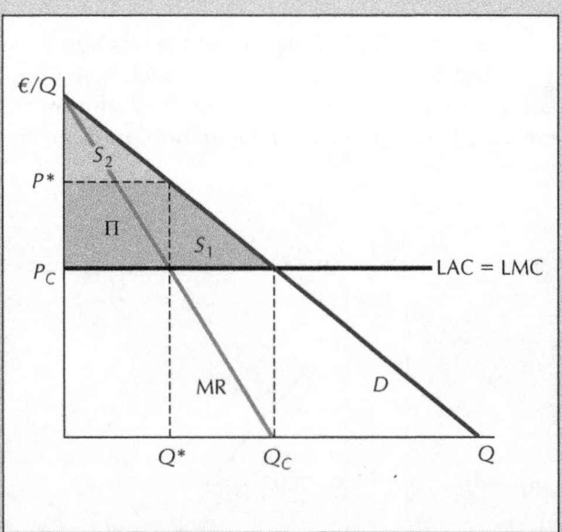

FIGURE 12.22
The Welfare Loss from a Single-Price Monopoly
A monopolist who charges a single price to all buyers will produce Q^* and sell at P^*. A competitive industry operating under the same cost conditions would produce Q_C and sell at P_C. In comparison with the perfectly competitive outcome, single-price monopoly results in a loss of consumer surplus equal to the area of $\Pi + S_1$. Since the monopolist earns Π, the cost to society is S_1—called the deadweight loss from monopoly.

Thus, in pure efficiency terms, the perfectly discriminating monopolist and the perfectly competitive industry lead to the same result. The difference is that in the former case all the benefit comes in the form of producer surplus, in the latter case all in the form of consumer surplus. The efficiency loss from monopoly is the result of failure to price discriminate perfectly. This loss (the area of triangle S_1 in Figure 12.22) is called the *deadweight loss from monopoly*.

In the preceding analysis, it made sense to speak of the welfare loss from having monopoly rather than competition because the cost structure was one that is compatible with the existence of perfect competition. But with that kind of cost structure, only legal barriers could prevent the emergence of competition. The existence of economic profits (Π in Figure 12.22) would lure competitors into the industry until price and quantity were driven to P_C and Q_C, respectively.

Suppose the reason for having a monopoly with a flat LAC curve is that the firm enjoys patent protection for its product. Can we now say that the welfare loss from having a single-price monopoly is equal to the lost consumer surplus measured in Figure 12.22? Before answering, we must first ask, 'What is the alternative to the current situation?' If it is a society without patent protection, we may well have never got the product in the first place, so it hardly makes sense to complain that, compared with pure competition, monopoly produces a welfare loss. True enough, the patent-protected single-price monopoly does not exhaust all possible gains from trade. But with the patent-protected monopoly, we do get a consumer surplus plus producer surplus of $S_2 + \Pi$, whereas we might have got nothing at all without the patent protection.

PUBLIC POLICY TOWARD NATURAL MONOPOLY

These observations make clear that the relevant question is not whether monopoly is efficient in comparison with some unattainable theoretical ideal, but how it compares with the alternatives we actually confront. This question is nowhere more important than in the case of natural monopoly.

To keep the analysis simple, consider a technology in which total cost is given by

$$TC = F + MQ \qquad (12.8)$$

where Q is the level of output. And suppose the demand and marginal revenue curves for a single-price monopolist producing with this technology are as shown in Figure 12.23.

The theoretical ideal allocation for this market would be to produce a quantity of Q^{**} and sell it at marginal cost, which here is equal to M. Note that this is only possible if there is a monopoly firm. It is efficient that only one firm pays the large fixed costs F. Hence we refer to 'natural' monopoly.

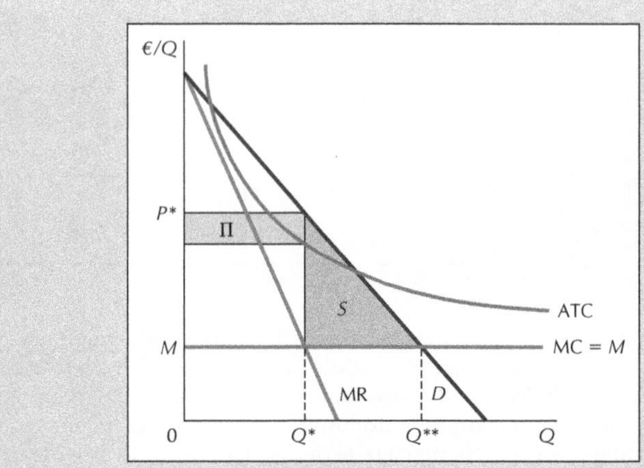

FIGURE 12.23
A Natural Monopoly
The two main objections to single-price natural monopoly are that it earns economic profit (Π) and that it results in the loss of consumer surplus (S).

A non-discriminating monopoly producer would, however, produce Q^* and sell it for P^*. There are basically two objections to the outcome: (1) the *fairness objection,* which is that the producer earns an economic profit (Π), and (2) the *efficiency objection,* which is that price is above marginal cost, resulting in lost consumer surplus (S).

Policymakers may respond in a variety of ways to the fairness and efficiency objections. The five options considered below account for the most important alternatives.

1. State Ownership and Management

Efficiency requires that price be equal to marginal cost. The difficulty this creates is that, for natural monopoly, marginal cost is below average total cost. Because private firms are not able to charge prices less than average cost and remain in business in the long run, the single-price firm has no alternative but to charge more than marginal cost. An option for getting around this particular difficulty is to have the state take over the industry. The attractive feature of this option is that the government is not bound, the way a private firm is, to earn at least a normal profit. It would thus be able to set a price equal to marginal cost, and absorb the resulting economic losses out of general tax revenues.

Traditionally many natural monopolies have been state owned. Utility companies, for example, that provide water, electricity or gas are often state owned. As are telecom companies, postal services, railway and road providers, television services. In each case state ownership can be motivated by the large fixed costs that would make private provision inefficient.

But there are also unattractive features of state ownership. Foremost among them is the fact that it often seems to weaken incentives for cost-conscious, efficient management. As the late Harvard University economist Harvey Leibenstein emphasized, an organization's costs depend not just on its technology, but also on the vigour with which it pursues efficiency. In Leibenstein's phrase, an organization that does not act energetically to curb costs is said to exhibit **X-inefficiency.**[13]

X-inefficiency a condition in which a firm fails to obtain maximum output from a given combination of inputs.

X-inefficiency is by no means the exclusive province of government. In widely varying degrees, it is found in private firms as well. Leibenstein argued that the extent to which X-inefficiency is a problem will depend on economic incentives, which suggests a theoretical reason for believing that it is likely to be more widespread in government. When a private firm cuts a euro from its costs, its profit goes up by a euro. By contrast, when the person in charge of a government agency cuts a euro from her agency's budget, the effect is merely to shrink her fiefdom.

Several noted scholars have argued that the goal of most bureaucrats is to maximize their operating budgets.[14] This is not to deny that bureaucrats are for the most part sincere, dedicated public servants. But it is perhaps only human nature for a bureaucrat to think that her particular agency has the most important mission in government, and to lobby accordingly on its behalf.

Persuaded by these arguments, the trend in Europe has been towards the privatization of state-owned natural monopolies. The telecom sector, for instance, has largely passed from public to private hands. British Telecom was privatized in 1984, Deutsche Telecom in 1995, and France Telecom in 2004. Electricity and gas

[13]Harvey Leibenstein, 'Allocative Efficiency vs. X-Efficiency', *American Economic Review,* June 1966: 392–415.

[14]See, for example, William Niskanen, *Bureaucracy and Representative Government,* Chicago: Aldine-Atherton, 1971; and Gordon Tullock, *The Politics of Bureaucracy,* Washington, DC: Public Affairs Press, 1965. But for a contrasting view, see Albert Breton and Ronald Wintrobe, *The Logic of Bureaucratic Conduct,* Cambridge: Cambridge University Press, 1982.

markets were next with state-owned monopolies such as British Gas, Electricité de France, and Gaz de France passing to at least partial private ownership. The European Commission has been instrumental in the liberalization of both telecom and energy markets, requiring the opening up of national markets to competition.

The liberalization of the telecom sector is typically heralded as a success. Prices were reduced, efficiency increased, and companies like British Telecom, Deutsche Telecom and France Telecom are competing successfully on a global scale. This success stems partly from a reduction in X-inefficiency caused by privatization. It also stems, however, from an interesting property of natural monopolies—they are often temporary. As technology improves, cost curves change, and natural monopolies can stop being natural monopolies. This is arguably what has happened in the telecom sector, particularly with the advent of mobile phones. Competition is now natural within the telecom sector making it difficult to gauge how much of the improvement in efficiency is due to privatization or the change in market structure.

The evidence on liberalization within industries that are unambiguously still natural monopolies is more mixed. Prices in the energy sector remain high. And there is no convincing evidence that efficiency is higher in the UK and the Netherlands, where markets are more competitive, than France or Germany, where the state maintains a larger presence. This has led to concerns over further liberalization—as the following economic naturalist illustrates.

Why are British railways so bad compared to European railways?

ECONOMIC NATURALIST 12.4

In 1994 British Rail was privatized. This followed an EU directive requiring the *decoupling* of track and infrastructure management from the provision of passenger services. British Rail was split into a company called Railtrack, that would have ownership of things like track, signalling and stations, and 25 passenger train operating units. The basic idea was that the train operating units compete to operate services on a rail system maintained and operated by Railtrack.

Anyone who travels by British Rail cannot but notice that things have improved since privatization. Indeed, some trains now run on time. Privatization has not, however, been without its problems. Following financial difficulties and a fatal train crash, Railtrack was renationalized. And most acknowledge that breaking up the industry into so many companies has pushed up the cost of running the railway.

Having observed the UK's troubles, the German and French governments have shown reluctance to go along with the European Commission's plans for liberalizing rail services. France, for instance, created a new company RFF with ownership of track, and an agency DCF to manage access. The old state monopoly SNCF would maintain the track and run its own services. The latest plans, however, are to bring everything back under SNCF with enough internal separation to satisfy the EU directive on decoupling. This is how things are already done in Germany.

To put things in context consider Figure 12.24 with a stylized comparison of British Rail and Deutsche Bahn. Suppose that demand is equal to Q^*. This is not to say that demand for trains is perfectly price inelastic—it is not. It more recognizes that rail users and the government typically share the cost of providing rail services. We will suppose the government fixes user prices so that demand is Q^*. British Rail has average total cost curve ATC_{BR} and Deutsche Bahn has curve ATC_{DB}. Clearly costs are a lot higher with British Rail. This is because of X-inefficiency. It means that providing Q^* costs ATC^*_{BR} rather than ATC^*_{DB} resulting in extra spending equal to area $ABCD$. This spending goes on higher salaries, extra staff, bureaucracy, the manager's new office etc.

After privatization X-inefficiency is removed, meaning the average total cost curve in the UK is the same as that of Deutsche Bahn. Fragmentation of the industry, however, means that average costs will be relatively high because firms cannot

FIGURE 12.24
Cost on European Railways Compared
Costs are significantly higher with the old British Rail (BR) than with Deutsche Bahn (DB). This is due to X-inefficiency. With privatization, costs in the UK become similar to those in Germany. But, the UK market is fragmented resulting in a higher average cost than Germany.

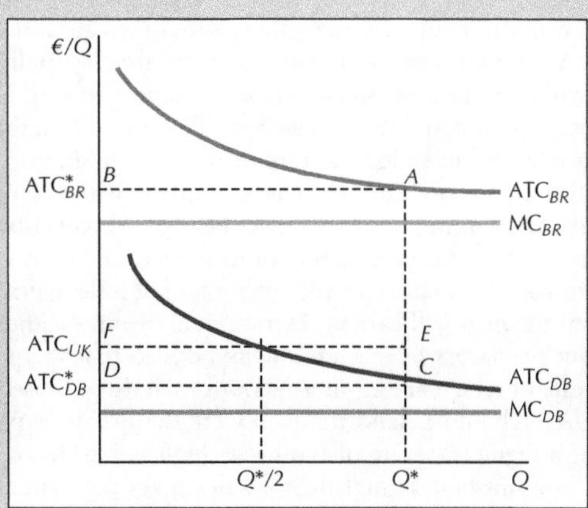

benefit from economies of scale. Figure 12.24 depicts what happens as the industry is split into two firms, each providing $Q^*/2$. Average costs become ATC^*_{UK}. These are substantially lower than with British Rail but still higher than in Germany. The extra cost is now equal to area *CDEF*.

This example emphasizes that the best scenario with a natural monopoly is state ownership and efficient marginal cost pricing. If that is what Deutsche Bahn and SNCF are achieving then why mess around with it? Privatization may have helped in the UK but it still leaves a 'second best' outcome. ■

If state-owned companies can avoid X-inefficiency then state-ownership is best.[15] Recent experience arguably shows that X-inefficiency can be avoided in state-owned companies. This helps explain why the tide appears to be turning against the privatization of natural monopolies. Indeed, in the UK, privatization is fast becoming a word that politicians dare not use, which is an abrupt change from 10 or 20 years ago. But, there are several alternatives to state ownership that will still need to be considered.

2. State Regulation of Private Monopolies

One such alternative is to put ownership in private hands, while providing guidelines or regulations that limit pricing discretion. Most of the formerly state-owned monopolies that have been privatized within Europe have been regulated to some extent. In the UK, for instance, Ofwat, Ofgem and Ofcom regulate, respectively, water, energy and telecommunication companies. National regulators cooperate on a European level through associations such as the European Council of European Energy Regulators and Agency for the Cooperation of Energy Regulators.

Price regulation has a long history in the US. Historically *rate-of-return regulation* has been used in which prices are set to allow the firm to earn a predetermined rate of return on its invested capital. Ideally, this rate of return would allow the firm to recover exactly the opportunity cost of its capital. The firm is, thus, constrained to earn zero economic profit, while still having the incentive to reduce X-inefficiency. We do not get price equal to marginal cost, but we can hope for the next best thing of price equal to average cost.

[15]See Elliott D. Sclar, *You Don't Always Get What You Pay For*, Ithaca, NY: Cornell University Press, 2000.

That is, if it works. In practice rate-of-return regulation has not proved very successful. European countries have, therefore, opted for alternatives such as a cap on prices or a cap on revenues. These, however, are essentially equivalent to a rate-of-return regulation, because in each case the objective is to limit the profits of the firm and obtain price equal to average cost. To understand, therefore, the pitfalls of regulation it is sufficient to look at rate-of-return regulation.

In practice a regulator can never be certain what the competitive rate of return will be in any period. If the rate they set lies below the competitive return, the firm will have an incentive to reduce the quality of its service, and eventually to go out of business. By contrast, if regulators set too high a rate of return, prices will be higher than necessary and the firm will earn an extranormal profit. Neither of these outcomes is attractive, but regulators have traditionally decided that the problems caused by an insufficient rate of return are far more serious than those caused by an excessive one.

Harvey Averch and Leland Johnson were the first to explore in detail the consequences of a regulatory rate of return set higher than the cost of capital.[16] Their conclusion, in a nutshell, is that this practice gives the firm an incentive to substitute capital for other inputs in a way that inflates the cost of doing business. If the regulated utility's goal is to maximize profit, the behavioural path it will follow will be to make its 'rate base'—the invested capital on which it earns the allowed rate of return—as large as possible. If the regulated monopolist can borrow capital at 8 per cent/yr and is allowed to earn 10 per cent/yr on each euro invested, it can clear €20,000 of extra profit for every extra €1,000,000 of borrowed funds it invests.

At least two important distortions follow from the discrepancy between the allowed rate of return and the actual cost of capital. The first we may call the *gold-plated water cooler effect.* It refers to the fact that the regulated monopolist has an incentive to purchase more capital equipment than is actually necessary to produce any given level of output. Faced with a choice between buying a regular water cooler, for example, and a more expensive gold-plated one, the regulated monopolist has an incentive to opt for the latter. To illustrate, suppose that the allowed rate of return on capital were 10 per cent a year and the actual cost of capital only 8 per cent. If a gold-plated water cooler costs €1000 more than a regular one, the monopolist would then earn €20 higher profit each year by installing the more expensive water cooler. Regulatory commissions try to prevent the purchase of unnecessary equipment, but the complexities of day-to-day operations are too great to allow every decision to be monitored carefully.

A second distortion induced by rate-of-return regulation is peculiar to the monopolist who serves more than one separate market, and we may call it the *cross-subsidy effect.* Because the allowed rate of return exceeds the cost of capital, such a monopolist has an incentive to sell below cost in the more elastic market, and cross-subsidize the resulting losses by selling above cost in the less elastic market. The idea is that the below-cost price in the elastic market boosts sales by more than the above-cost price in the less elastic market curtails them. The resulting increase in output increases the requirements for capital to produce it, and hence increases the profits allowed by regulation.

To illustrate, consider the regulated monopolist whose demand and cost curves for two markets are shown in Figure 12.25. The ATC curves are constructed to include the allowed rate of profit, which exceeds the cost of capital. Thus, when the monopolist is earning a zero profit in terms of the cost curves shown in Figure 12.25, he is really earning

$$\Pi = (r^a - r^c)K \tag{12.9}$$

[16]Harvey Averch and Leland Johnson, 'Behavior of the Firm under Regulatory Constraint', *American Economic Review,* December 1962: 1052–1069. See also R. M. Spann, 'Rate of Return Regulation and Efficiency in Production: An Empirical Test of the Averch-Johnson Thesis', *Bell Journal of Economics,* Spring 1974: 38–52.

where r^a is the allowed rate of return, r^c the actual cost of capital, and K the size of the total capital stock. To maximize profit, the monopolist thus wants to make K as big as possible, which in turn means making the sum of the outputs sold in the two markets as large as possible. To do that, he will set MR = MC in the market with the less elastic demand (market 1 in panel *a*) and use the profits earned in that market (Π_1) to subsidize a price below average cost in the market with more elastic demand (market 2 in panel *b*). The aim, again, is to boost sales in the latter market by more than they are curtailed in the former. By selling the largest possible output, the monopolist is able to employ the largest possible capital stock, and thereby is able to earn the largest possible profit.

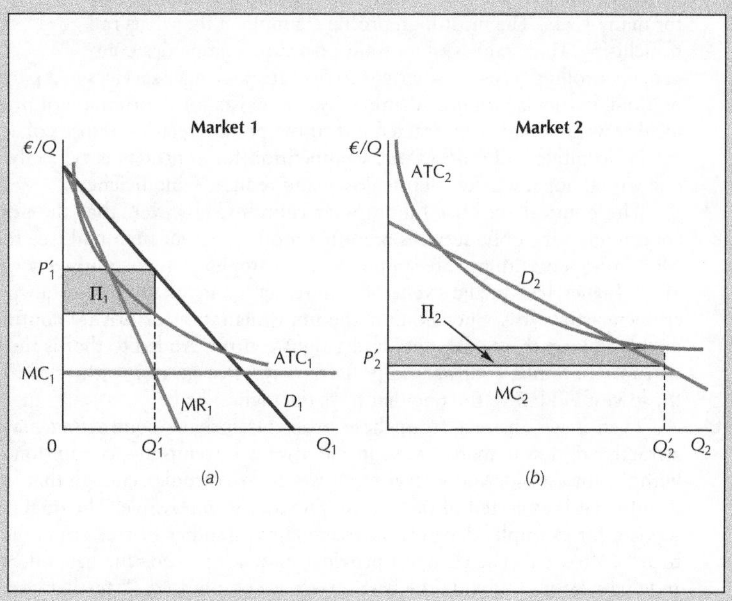

FIGURE 12.25
Cross-Subsidization to Boost Total Output
A regulated monopolist is generally allowed to earn a rate of return that exceeds the actual cost of capital, which provides an incentive to acquire as much capital as possible. To increase output (thereby to increase the required capital stock), the monopolist can sell above cost in his less elastic market (market 1 in panel *a*) and use the resultant profits ($\Pi_1 > 0$) to subsidize the losses ($\Pi_2 < 0$) sustained by selling below cost in his more elastic market.

Regulatory pitfalls have not prevented governments in virtually every part of the world from continuing to intervene in the price and output decisions of important natural monopolies like electric and gas utilities. Whether these interventions do more good than harm, in purely economic terms, remains an unsettled question. But they clearly seem to serve an important psychological function on behalf of a public that feels understandably uncomfortable about not having a buffer between itself and the sole supplier of a critical good or service.

3. Exclusive Contracting for Natural Monopoly

The basic problem with regulation is that the firm knows a lot more than the regulator. In particular, the firm knows its cost function, the regulator does not. This constrains the regulator's ability to control the firm. Is there not a way to force the firm to reveal its cost function?

In the title of a widely quoted article, UCLA economist Harold Demsetz asked the disarmingly simple question, 'Why Regulate Monopoly?'[17] His point was that

[17]Harold Demsetz, 'Why Regulate Monopoly?' *Journal of Law and Economics*, April 1968: 55–65.

even though cost conditions may dictate that a market be served by a single supplier, there can still be vigorous competition to see who gets to *be* that supplier. In Demsetz's proposal, the government would specify in detail the service it wanted provided—fire protection, garbage collection, postal delivery, whatever—and then call for private companies to submit bids to supply the service. And to the low bidder would then go the contract. The advantage of this contracting out approach is that firms have an incentive to bid the true value of operating in the market. There are not the distorted incentives that we see with regulation.

Rural-Metro, a private, for-profit company, has provided fire protection services in Scottsdale, Arizona, since 1952.

This scheme has been widely used in the US and the UK for many years. The most high profile example in the UK is rail franchising. Under this system train operating companies compete on a rolling basis for the right to operate passenger services in a particular area, or along particular routes. A similar system exists for the running of prisons. Many local services are also contracted out to the private sector—refuse collection, catering in hospitals and schools etc. Competition for contracts is typically high. This, one would hope, will keep costs down and reduce X-inefficiency.[18]

The political scientist Elliott Sclar cautions, however, that the advantages of contracting for public services are often more apparent than real (see footnote 15). Most contracts with private suppliers, for example, contain contingency clauses that allow higher fees in the event of unforeseen changes in circumstances. The government employees who monitor the implementation of private contracts may be unable to keep these extra fees under tight control. Added to that is the problem of corruption. Public contracts in practice may often go not to the firm that submits the lowest bid but to the one that pays the highest bribe.

Even if we abstract from these problems, private contracting may not be an attractive option in many cases. It will always be tempting, corruption aside, to go with the lowest bid. Many services, however, are complex enough that setting out in detail what is expected of the private provider is impossible. The quality of railway service, for example, depends on punctuality, number of free seats, quality of on-board coffee, etc. The cheapest provider may not provide the best on-board coffee. Judging who will provide the best service is complicated. A further complication is the potential for the provider to go bankrupt mid contract because they underestimated the costs of providing the service. These problems are all too familiar to those who have followed the rail franchising experience of the UK.

So, while the franchising and contracting out of services to the private sector is a neat idea in principle, it may not always be the best answer in practice. The simpler the service, the more effective contracting out is likely to be.

4. Vigorous Enforcement of Antitrust Laws

A major element in the policy arsenal for dealing with monopoly are antitrust laws. Article 102 of the Treaty on the Functioning of the European Union prohibits firms holding a dominant position on a determined market to abuse that position, for example by charging unfair prices, by limiting production, or by refusing to innovate. Article 101 limits agreements between companies that would restrict competition. The European Commission enforces these Articles.

In the case of industries with declining long-run average cost curves, the cost of production will be much higher if we are served by many firms rather than by only a few. The most vigorous supporters of the antitrust laws insist that the laws will

[18]For an extended survey of studies comparing private costs and public costs, see E. S. Savas, *Privatizing the Public Sector,* Chatham, NJ: Chatham House Publishers, 1982.

not impede the formation of natural monopolies. But as we will see in Chapter 13, they may substantially postpone the time when economies of scale are fully realized.

One response to this difficulty would be to apply the antitrust laws to prevent only those mergers where significant cost savings would not be realized. The European Commission is not in a good position, however, to distinguish one type of case from another. The result is that antitrust policy impedes all consolidations, even those that would lead to substantial reductions in cost.

Is the EU powerless against Microsoft?

ECONOMIC NATURALIST 12.5

We have already mentioned that over 90 per cent of the world's personal computers run Microsoft's Windows operating system. Microsoft's monopoly position clearly gives it power to manipulate the market towards its own ends. The job of competition authorities is to stop it abusing that power.

The easiest way to do that is to stop such a dominant market position from being established in the first place. And the EU competition authorities do regularly stop mergers to prevent this happening. The Microsoft example illustrates, however, how difficult it can be to stop a firm obtaining a monopoly. Microsoft's initial success came from giving customers what they wanted—and that is the supposed benefit of competition. Its continued success reflects the network economies that undoubtedly exist in the market. These network economies create a natural monopoly.

The competition authorities are left, therefore, with the task of making sure Microsoft does not abuse the power it has. Since the turn of the century, Microsoft has been fined well over a billion euros by the EU for anti-competitive behaviour. It has been ordered to make its operating system available to open source software developers. And, it was ordered to unbundle various software from its operating system.[19] These measures check the power of Microsoft, but arguably not much.

The greater threat to Microsoft's dominant position is probably the widening use of tablets, e-readers, smartphones and the like. These typically do not use Microsoft operating systems. A new market has, therefore, provided a level playing field for firms to compete with Microsoft. This is another illustration that natural monopolies can be temporary. ■

5. A Laissez-Faire Policy toward Natural Monopoly

As a fifth and final alternative for dealing with natural monopoly, let us consider the possibility of laissez faire, or doing nothing—just letting the monopolist produce whatever quantity she chooses and sell it at whatever price the market will bear. The obvious objections to this policy are the two we began with, namely, the fairness and efficiency problems. In this section, however, we will see that there may be at least some circumstances in which these problems are of only minimal importance.

Consider, in particular, a natural monopolist who uses the hurdle model of differential pricing. To keep the discussion simple, let's suppose she charges a regular price and also a discount price, the latter available to customers who clear some hurdle, such as mailing in a rebate form. How does the presence of this differential pricing device affect the fairness and efficiency objections to natural monopoly?

Consider first the efficiency objection. Recall that the problem is that the single-price monopolist charges a price above marginal cost, which excludes many potential buyers from the market, ones who value the product more highly than the value of the resources required to produce it.

For illustrative purposes, let us examine a natural monopolist with a total cost curve given by $F + MQ$ and a linear demand curve given by $P = A - BQ$.

[19]See case number 37792 on the EU competition website (http://ec.europa.eu/competition).

Figure 12.26(*a*) shows the demand and marginal cost curves for such a monopolist. If she is a single-price profit maximizer, she will produce Q^* and sell for P^*. But if she is able to charge one price to the buyers along the upper part of the demand curve and a lower price to all other buyers (Figure 12.26*b*), her profit-maximizing strategy will be to sell Q_H at the price P_H and Q_L at the price P_L.[20]

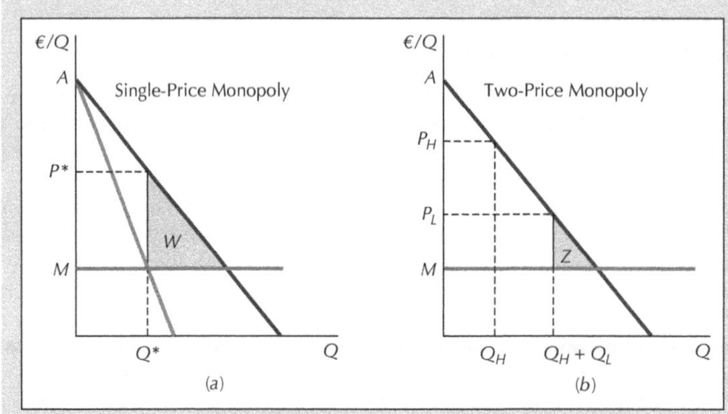

FIGURE 12.26
The Efficiency Losses from Single-Price and Two-Price Monopoly
By being able to offer a discount price to the most elastic portion of the demand curve, the two-price monopolist (panel *b*) expands the market, thereby causing a much smaller efficiency loss (area *Z*, panel *b*) than in the case of the single-price monopolist (area *W*, panel *a*).

Note that the efficiency loss associated with the two-price monopolist (lost consumer surplus, which is the area of triangle *Z* in panel *b*) is much smaller than the corresponding loss for the single-price monopolist (the area of triangle *W* in panel *a*).

In general, the more finely the monopolist can partition her market under the hurdle model, the smaller the efficiency loss will be. As noted earlier, it is common

[20]For the single-price monopolist the profit function is given by

$$\Pi_1 = (A - BQ)Q - F - MQ$$

The first-order condition for a maximum is given by

$$\frac{d\Pi_1}{dQ} = A - 2BQ - M = 0$$

which yields a profit-maximizing quantity of $Q' = (A - M)/2B$, and a corresponding price of $P' = (A + M)/2$.
The profit function for the two-price monopolist, by contrast, is given by

$$\Pi_2 = (A - BQ_H)Q_H + (A - BQ_H - BQ_L)Q_L - F - M(Q_H + Q_L)$$

The first-order conditions for a maximum are given by

$$\frac{\partial \Pi_2}{\partial Q_H} = A - 2BQ_H - BQ_L - M = 0$$

and

$$\frac{\partial \Pi_2}{\partial Q_L} = A - BQ_H - 2BQ_L - M = 0$$

which can be solved for

$$Q_H = \frac{A - M}{3B} = Q_L \text{ and } P_L = \frac{A + 2M}{3} \text{ and } P_H = \frac{2A + M}{3}$$

in most firms to see not one but a whole menu of different discount prices, each with a different set of restrictions (the deeper the discount, the more stringent the restriction). Given the wide latitude many firms have to expand their markets through hurdle pricing, the efficiency problem of natural monopoly will often be of only secondary importance.

What about the fairness problem? First, what *is* this problem? The popular perception of it is that the monopolist transfers resources from people who desperately need them (namely, poor consumers) to others who have more than they need to begin with (namely, wealthy shareholders). We will see below that, defined in this particular way, the problem is sometimes less serious than it appears.

The more general question of what constitutes a fair distribution of society's resources is a deep philosophical one, well beyond the scope of our discussion here. At the very least, however, we can say that no firm is entitled to acquire, through force or coercion, the power to extract excessive resources from other persons. But suppose the monopolist has become the lone seller in her market through completely benevolent means. This is not implausible. As a natural monopolist, her costs are by definition lower than if other firms also served the same market. And perhaps her cheerful and courteous service has also helped entrench her position. Does she then create an injustice by charging prices in excess of marginal cost?

Certainly consumers would be happier to pay only the marginal cost of production. But marginal cost is less than average cost in a natural monopoly, and so it is not possible for *everyone* to pay marginal cost and have the supplier remain in business. At best, *some* consumers can pay prices close to marginal cost, but others will have to pay substantially more. Even so, if the monopolist is earning an economic profit, we know that buyers are paying more, on the average, than the cost of the resources required to serve them. How can this be defended in the name of fairness?

Earlier we saw that hurdle pricing makes the monopoly allocation more efficient. It would be an exaggeration to say that the same hurdle model makes the existence of monopoly profits seem completely fair. But it does help mitigate some of the most serious objections to them.

Consider first the source of a given euro of monopoly profit. From which buyers does this euro come? It is straightforward to show that it cannot have come from the discount price buyer. Typical discount prices range from 15 to 50 per cent off the so-called regular price, and seldom do more than half of all buyers pay the discount price. Taking an illustrative case in which the discount is 30 per cent and half of all buyers receive it, we see that the monopolist's revenue would fall by 15 per cent if everyone paid the discount price. Very few firms would remain profitable in the face of a 15 per cent decline in total revenue.

It follows that if the monopolist is earning economic profit, the source of that profit is the buyer who pays the regular price. The fact that this buyer could have paid a discount price if he had been willing to jump the requisite hurdle tells us that the burden imposed on him is no greater than the trouble of jumping the hurdle. This is obviously not the same as saying that the regular-price buyer makes a voluntary charitable contribution to the monopolist. But it does take at least some of the sting out of the notion that the monopolist's customers are being cruelly victimized.

So much for the source of monopoly profit. What about its disposition? Who gets it? If we assume a corporate income tax rate of 40 per cent, 40 cents of each euro of monopoly profits goes to the government. The remainder is paid out to shareholders, either directly through dividends or indirectly by reinvesting it into the company. Granted, the average income of shareholders is greater than that of citizens as a whole. But there are many low-income shareholders in Europe. Most employee pension funds, for example, are invested in the stock market, as are the private insurance holdings of many low-income individuals. So a considerable fraction of any euro of monopoly profit will wind up in the hands of low-income shareholders.

But to take the worst possible case from a distributional point of view, let us suppose that what is left of the euro of monopoly profit goes entirely to the wealthiest resident of Berlin. Assume that she pays income tax at the rate of 45 per cent on the 60 cents that the government has not already taken, leaving 33 cents. Local and sales taxes will claim an additional 7 cents or so, leaving only 26 cents in the hands of our wealthy shareholder.

To summarize, then, the source of a euro in monopoly profit is the regular-price buyer, someone who could have paid a discount price had he but taken a little extra trouble. Of that euro, 74 cents goes to the government. The disposition of more than two-thirds of the euro is thus subject to governmental control. The remainder becomes income in the hands of shareholders, at least some of whom have low incomes to begin with. So it is by no means clear that the economic profit associated with natural monopoly creates distributional inequities of the sort commonly perceived.

Hurdles, of course, are seldom perfect. Inevitably they screen out some buyers who will not buy at the regular price. And much of the time, real resources must be expended in order to jump over these hurdles. Mailing in a rebate coupon may not take a lot of time, but the time it takes could certainly be better spent. And in at least some cases, tax avoidance will keep the government from collecting as much as the tax tables specify.

So what are we to conclude from this brief analysis of the five policy options for dealing with natural monopoly? The short answer is that each has problems. None completely eliminates the difficulties that arise when a single seller serves the market. Sometimes the least costly solution will be competitive contracting, other times direct state ownership. Regulation will continue to play a role in specific industries, particularly the traditional public utilities. And despite their many shortcomings, antitrust laws serve the public well by discouraging price-fixing and other anticompetitive practices. But in some cases, particularly those in which the monopolist has devised means of richly segmenting the market, the best option may be simply not to intervene at all.

Does Monopoly Suppress Innovation?

One of the most enduring topics of conversation among economic conspiracy buffs is the notion that monopolists deprive consumers of a spectrum of enormously valuable technological innovations. Who has not heard, for example, of how the light bulb manufacturers have conspired to prevent revolutionary new designs for long-lasting light bulbs from reaching the market?

Is the suppression of innovation yet another cost of monopoly that we ought to have considered in our analysis of public policy options? As the following example will make clear, the logic of profit maximization suggests that monopolists may not always be so eager to suppress innovation.

EXAMPLE 12.6 Suppose the current light bulb design lasts 1000 hours. Now the light bulb monopolist discovers how to make a bulb that lasts 10,000 hours for the same per-bulb cost of production. Will the monopolist introduce the new bulb?

Suppose we measure the quantity produced by the monopolist not as light bulbs per se, but as the number of bulb-hours of lighting services. Thus, if the cost of producing the current design is, say, €1.00/bulb-hr, then the cost of the new design is only €0.10/bulb-hr. In Figure 12.27, *D* represents the market demand curve for lighting and MR the associated marginal revenue curve.

FIGURE 12.27
Does Monopoly Suppress Innovation?
The cost of producing the new, efficient light bulb, at €0.10/bulb-hr, is only one-tenth the cost of producing the current design, €1/bulb-hr. Because the monopolist's profits with the efficient design (area of *FGHK*) exceed its profits with the current design (area of *ABCE*), it will offer the new design.

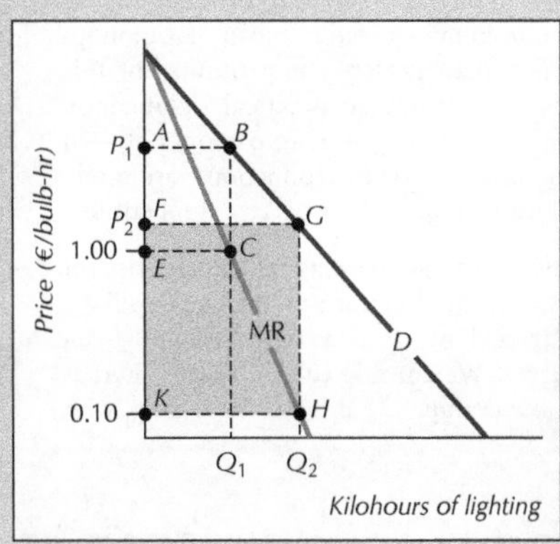

Note that the profit-maximizing price and quantity for the current design, whose marginal cost is €1/bulb-hr, are P_1 and Q_1, respectively. For the new design, whose marginal cost is €0.10/bulb-hr, the profit-maximizing price and quantity are P_2 and Q_2. The monopolist's profit under the current design is the area of the rectangle *ABCE*. For the new design, the corresponding profit value is the area of the rectangle *FGHK*. And because the monopolist's profit is higher under the new design, it has every incentive to make that design available. Indeed, as some of you may recall, the availability of just such an efficient new light bulb was announced several years ago. ◆

This example does not imply that the monopolist's incentives to introduce innovations will always and everywhere be the same as a competitive firm's. But it should caution us against uncritical acceptance of claims that monopolists always deprive consumers of the benefits of the latest available technology.

SUMMARY

- Monopoly is the name given to the market structure in which a single firm serves the entire market. Five factors, acting alone or in combination, give rise to monopoly: (1) control over key inputs, (2) economies of scale, (3) patents, (4) network economies, and (5) government licences. In the long run, by far the most important of these is economies of scale, in part because it also helps explain network economies and government licences.
- Because the monopolist is the only seller in the market, his demand curve is the downward-sloping market demand curve. Unlike the perfect competitor, who can sell as much as he chooses at the market price, the monopolist must cut price in order to expand his output. The monopolist's rule for maximizing profits is the same as the one used by perfectly competitive firms. It is to expand output if the gain in revenue (marginal revenue) exceeds the increase in costs (marginal cost), and to contract if the loss in revenue is smaller than the reduction in costs. The pivotal difference is that marginal revenue is less than price for the monopolist, but equal to price for the perfect competitor.
- When the monopolist can sell in several separate markets, he distributes output among them so that marginal revenue is the same in each. Here again, the familiar logic of cost-benefit analysis provides a convenient framework for analysing the firm's decision about whether to alter its current behaviour.
- Unlike the perfectly competitive case, the monopoly equilibrium generally does not exhaust the potential gains from exchange. In general, the value to society of an additional unit of output will exceed the cost to the

monopolist of the resources required to produce it. This finding has often been interpreted to mean that monopoly is less efficient than perfect competition. But this interpretation is of only limited practical significance, because the conditions that give rise to monopoly—in particular, economies of scale in production—are rarely compatible with those required for perfect competition.

- Our policy focus in the chapter was on the question of how the government should treat natural monopolies—markets characterized by downward-sloping long-run average cost curves. We considered five policy alternatives: (1) state ownership, (2) private ownership with government price regulation, (3) competitive bidding by private firms for the right to be the sole provider of service, (4) vigorous enforcement of antitrust laws designed to prevent monopoly, and finally (5) a complete laissez-faire, or hands-off, policy. Problems arise with each of these alternatives, and the best policy will in general be different in different circumstances. The laissez-faire stance is most attractive in markets where the monopolist is able to employ the hurdle model of differential pricing. Allowing buyers to decide for themselves whether to become eligible for a discount price softens both the efficiency and fairness objections to natural monopoly.

QUESTIONS FOR REVIEW

1. What five factors give rise to monopoly? In the long run, why are economies of scale the most important factor?
2. If the United States has thousands of cement producers but a small town has only one, is this cement producer a monopolist? Explain.
3. When is marginal revenue less than price for a monopolist? Explain.
4. Why does a profit-maximizing monopolist never produce on an inelastic portion of the demand curve? Would a revenue-maximizing monopolist ever produce on the inelastic portion of the demand curve?
5. Why is an output level at which MR intersects MC from below never the profit-maximizing level of output?
6. What effect will the imposition of a 50 per cent tax on economic profit have on a monopolist's price and output decisions? (*Hint*: Recall that the assumed objective is to choose the level of output that maximizes economic profit.)
7. Suppose the elasticity of demand is $\epsilon = -3$. By how much will a profit-maximizing monopolist's price exceed marginal cost? How does this mark-up of price over marginal cost compare with perfect competition?
8. *True or false*: A lump-sum tax on a monopolist will always increase the price charged by the monopolist and lower the quantity of output sold.
9. *True or false*: If a monopolist faces a perfectly horizontal demand curve, then the deadweight loss to the economy is zero.
10. What forces work against X-inefficiency in privately owned monopolies?
11. How does the hurdle method of price discrimination mitigate both the efficiency and fairness problems associated with monopoly?

PROBLEMS

1. You are a self-employed profit-maximization consultant specializing in monopolies. Five single-price, profit-maximizing monopolies are currently seeking your advice, and although the information they have supplied to you is incomplete, your expert knowledge allows you to go back and make a definite recommendation in each case. Select one of the following recommendations for each firm in the short run:

   a. Remain at the current output level.
   b. Increase output.
   c. Reduce output.
   d. Shut down.
   e. Go back and recalculate your figures because the ones supplied cannot possibly be right.

Firm	P	MR	TR	Q	TC	MC	ATC	AVC	Your recommendation
A	3.90	3.00		2000	7400	2.90		3.24	
B	5.90			10000		5.90	4.74	4.24	
C		9.00	44000	4000		9.00	11.90	10.74	
D	35.90	37.90		5000		37.90	35.90		
E	35.00		3990	1000	3300		at min value	23.94	

2. A monopolist has a demand curve given by $P = 100 - Q$ and a total cost curve given by $TC = 16 + Q^2$. The associated marginal cost curve is $MC = 2Q$. Find the monopolist's profit-maximizing quantity and price. How much economic profit will the monopolist earn?

3. Now suppose the monopolist in Problem 2 has a total cost curve given by $TC = 32 + Q^2$. The corresponding marginal cost curve is still $MC = 2Q$, but fixed costs have doubled. Find the monopolist's profit-maximizing quantity and price. How much economic profit does the monopolist earn?

4. Now suppose the monopolist in Problem 2 has a total cost curve given by $TC = 16 + 4Q^2$. The corresponding marginal cost curve is now $MC = 8Q$, and fixed costs are back to the original level. Find the monopolist's profit-maximizing quantity and price. How much economic profit does the monopolist earn?

5. Now suppose the monopolist in Problem 2 also has access to a foreign market in which he can sell whatever quantity he chooses at a constant price of 60. How much will he sell in the foreign market? What will his new quantity and price be in the original market?

6. Now suppose the monopolist in Problem 2 has a long-run marginal cost curve of $MC = 20$. Find the monopolist's profit-maximizing quantity and price. Find the efficiency loss from this monopoly.

7. Suppose a perfectly discriminating monopolist faces market demand $P = 100 - 10Q$ and has constant marginal cost $MC = 20$ (with no fixed costs). How much does the monopolist sell? How much profit does the monopolist earn? What is the maximum per-period licence fee the government could charge the firm and have the firm still stay in business?

8. The demand by senior citizens for showings at a local cinema has a constant price elasticity equal to -4. The demand curve for all other patrons has a constant price elasticity equal to -2. If the marginal cost per patron is €1 per showing, how much should the cinema charge members of each group?

9. During the Iran–Iraq war, the same arms merchant often sold weapons to both sides of the conflict. In this situation, a different price could be offered to each side because there was little danger that the country offered the lower price would sell arms to its rival to profit on the difference in prices. Suppose a French arms merchant has a monopoly of Exocet air-to-sea missiles and is willing to sell them to both sides. Iraq's demand for Exocets is $P = 400 - 0.5Q$ and Iran's is $P = 300 - Q$, where P is in millions of euros. The marginal cost of Exocets is $MC = Q$. What price will be charged to each country?

10. If you have ever gone grocery shopping on a weekday afternoon, you have probably noticed some elderly shoppers going slowly down the aisles checking their coupon book for a coupon that matches each of their purchases. How is this behaviour explained by the hurdle model of price discrimination?

11. A monopolist's price is €10. At this price the absolute value of the elasticity of demand is 2. What is the monopolist's marginal cost?

12. Suppose the government imposed a price ceiling on a monopolist (an upper bound on the price the monopolist can charge). Let $\overline{P}$ denote the price ceiling, and suppose the monopolist incurs no costs in producing output. *True or false*: If the demand curve faced by the monopolist is inelastic at the price $\overline{P}$, then the monopolist would be no better off if the government removed the price ceiling.

13. *The Times,* a profit-maximizing newspaper, faces a downward-sloping demand schedule for advertisements. When advertising for itself in its own pages (for example, an ad saying 'Read Maureen Dowd in the *Sunday Times*'), is the opportunity cost of a given-size ad simply the price it charges its outside advertisers? Explain.

*14. Crazy Harry, a monopolist, has a total cost curve given by TC = $5Q + 15$. He sets two prices for his product, a regular price, P_H, and a discount price, P_L. Everyone is eligible to purchase the product at *PH*. To be eligible to buy at P_L, it is necessary to present a copy of the latest Crazy Harry newspaper ad to the sales clerk. Suppose the only buyers who present the ad are those who would not have been willing to buy the product at P_H.

a. If Crazy Harry's demand curve is given by $P = 20 - 5Q$, what are the profit-maximizing values of P_H and P_L?
b. How much economic profit does Harry make?
c. How much profit would he have made if he had been forced to charge the same price to all buyers?
d. Are buyers better or worse off as a result of Harry's being able to charge two prices?

15. An author has signed a contract in which the publisher promises to pay her €10,000 plus 20 per cent of gross receipts from the sale of her book. *True or false*: If both the publisher and the author care only about their own financial return from the project, then the author will prefer a higher book price than will the publisher.

16. A film director has signed a contract in which the production studio promises to pay her €1,000,000 plus 5 per cent of the studio's rental revenues from the film, all of whose costs of production and distribution are fixed. *True or false*: If both the director and the studio care only about their own financial return from the project, then the director will prefer a lower film rental price than will the studio.

ANSWERS TO IN-CHAPTER EXERCISES

12.1.

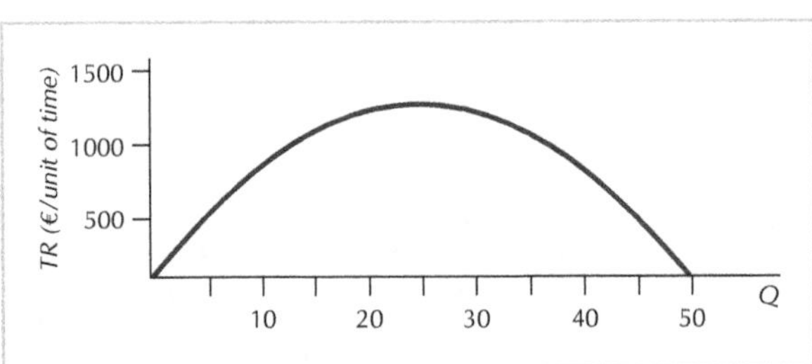

12.2.

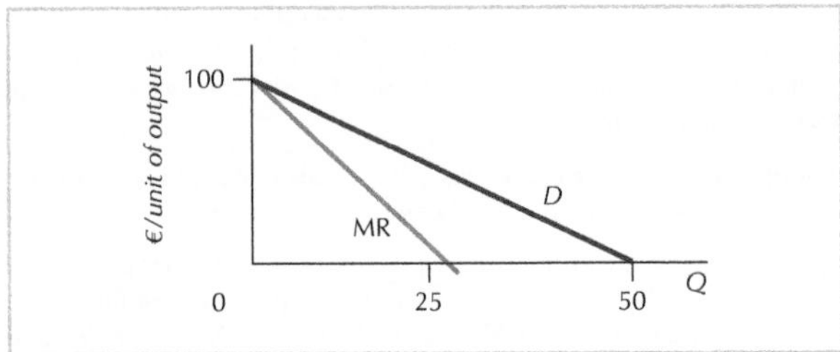

*This problem is most easily solved using the calculus method described in footnote 20.

12.3. MC = 40 = 100 − 4Q, which solves for $Q^* = 15$, $P^* = 100 - 2Q^* = 70$.

12.4. The profit-maximizing level of output for a single-price monopolist occurs where MR = MC. Marginal revenue equals marginal cost at both $Q = 15$ and $Q = 34$, but $Q = 34$ has marginal revenue intersect from above and thus is the maximal one. However, even at $Q = 34$, price does not cover average variable cost ($66 = P < \text{AVC} = 72$). The average variable cost curve lies everywhere above the demand curve (see figure), so the firm can do no better than earn profits equal to negative of the fixed costs. Thus, the optimal quantity is $Q = 0$: the firm should shut down!

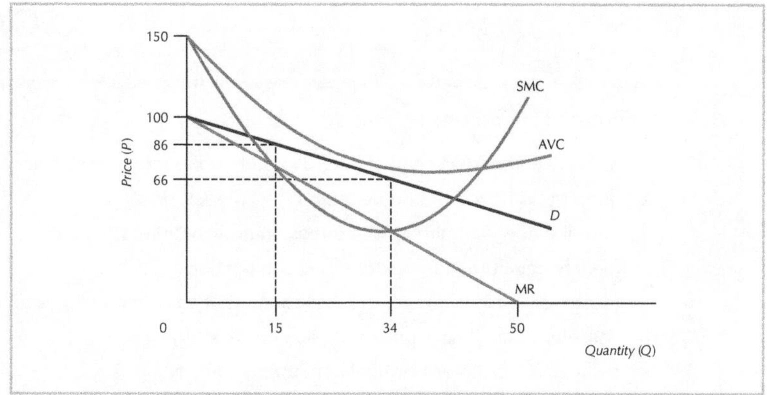

12.5. $\text{MR}_1 = 10 - 2Q_1$ (left panel), and $\text{MR}_2 = 20 - 2Q_2$ (centre panel), so the horizontal summation of the MR curves is given by ΣMR (right panel). The profit-maximizing quantity is 13, 4 of which should be sold in market 1, the remaining 9 in market 2. The profit-maximizing prices are $P_1^* = 6$ and $P_2^* = 11$.

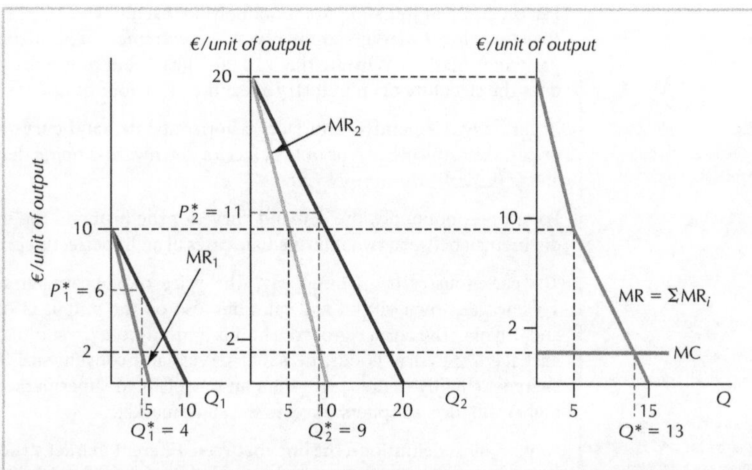

CHAPTER 9

Market structure and imperfect competition

Learning Outcomes

By the end of this chapter, you should be able to:

1 recognize imperfect competition, oligopoly and monopolistic competition
2 understand how cost and demand affect market structure
3 describe how globalization changes domestic market structure
4 identify equilibrium in monopolistic competition
5 recognize the tension between collusion and competition in a cartel
6 describe game theory and strategic behaviour
7 define the concepts of commitment and credibility
8 analyse reaction functions and Nash equilibrium
9 describe Cournot and Bertrand competition
10 understand the Stackelberg leadership
11 recognize why there is no market power in a contestable market
12 define innocent and strategic entry barriers

Perfect competition and pure monopoly are useful benchmarks of the extremes of market structure. Most markets are between the extremes. What determines the structure of a particular market? Why are there 10 000 florists but only a few chemical producers? How does the structure of an industry affect the behaviour of its constituent firms?

An imperfectly competitive firm faces a downward-sloping demand curve. Its output price reflects the quantity of goods it makes and sells.

An oligopoly is an industry with few producers, each recognizing their interdependence.

An industry with monopolistic competition has many sellers of products that are close substitutes for one another. Each firm has only a limited ability to affect its output price.

A perfectly competitive firm faces a horizontal demand curve at the market price. It is a price-taker. Any other type of firm faces a downward-sloping demand curve for its product and is **imperfectly competitive**.

For a pure monopoly, the demand curve for the firm and the industry coincide. We now distinguish between two intermediate cases of an imperfectly competitive market structure.

The car industry is an **oligopoly**. The price of Volkswagen cars depends not only on Volkswagen's own output and sales but also on the output of other car makers like Ford and Toyota. The corner grocer's shop is a **monopolistic competitor**. Its output is a subtle package of physical goods, personal service and convenience for local customers. It can charge a slightly higher price than an out-of-town supermarket. But, if its prices are too high, even local shoppers travel to the supermarket.

As with most definitions, the lines between different market structures can get blurred. One reason is ambiguity about the relevant definition of the market. Is Eurostar a monopoly in cross-channel trains or an oligopolist in cross-channel travel? Similarly, when a country trades in a competitive world market, even the sole domestic producer may have little influence on market price. We can never fully remove these ambiguities, but Table 9.1 shows some things to bear in mind as we proceed through this chapter. The table includes the ease with which new firms can enter the industry, which affects the ability of existing firms to maintain high prices and supernormal profits in the long run.

Table 9.1 Market structure

Competition	Number of firms	Ability to affect price	Entry barriers	Example
Perfect	Lots	Nil	None	Fruit stall
Imperfect: Monopolistic	Many	Little	Small	Corner shop
Oligopoly	Few	Medium	Bigger	Cars
Monopoly	One	Large	Huge	Post Office

9.1 Why market structures differ

Some industries are legal monopolies, the sole licensed producers. Patent laws may confer temporary monopoly on producers of a new process. Ownership of a raw material may confer monopoly status on a single firm. We now develop a general theory of how demand and cost interact to determine the likely structure of each industry.

The car industry is not an oligopoly one day but perfectly competitive the next. Long-run influences determine market structures.

Figure 9.1 shows the demand curve *DD* for the output of an industry in the long run. Suppose all firms and potential entrants face the average cost curve LAC_1. At the price P_1, free entry and exit means that each firm produces q_1. With the demand curve *DD*, industry output is Q_1. The number of firms in the industry is $N_1 = (Q_1/q_1)$. If at q_1, the minimum average cost output on LAC_1 is small relative to *DD*, N_1 will be large. Each firm has a tiny effect on industry supply and market price. We have found a perfectly competitive industry.

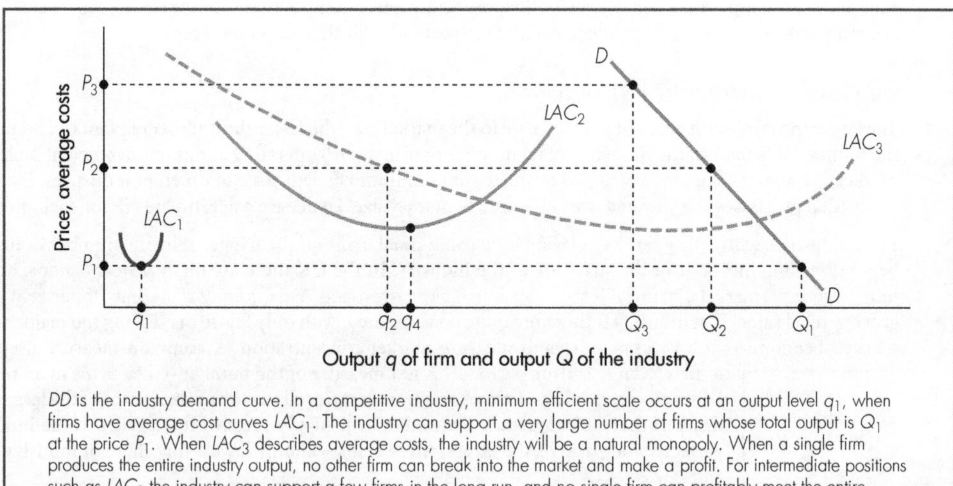

DD is the industry demand curve. In a competitive industry, minimum efficient scale occurs at an output level q_1, when firms have average cost curves LAC_1. The industry can support a very large number of firms whose total output is Q_1 at the price P_1. When LAC_3 describes average costs, the industry will be a natural monopoly. When a single firm produces the entire industry output, no other firm can break into the market and make a profit. For intermediate positions such as LAC_2 the industry can support a few firms in the long run, and no single firm can profitably meet the entire demand. The industry will be an oligopoly.

Figure 9.1 **Demand, costs and market structure**

Next, suppose that each firm has the cost curve LAC_3. Scale economies are vast relative to the market size. At the lowest point on LAC_3, output is big relative to the demand curve DD. Suppose initially two firms each make q_2. Industry output is Q_2. The market clears at P_2 and both firms break even. If one firm expands a bit, its average costs fall. Its higher output also bids the price down. With lower average costs, that firm survives but the other firm loses money. The firm that expands undercuts its competitor and drives it out of business.

A natural monopoly enjoys such scale economies that it has no fear of entry by others.

This industry is a **natural monopoly**. Suppose Q_3 is the output at which its marginal cost and marginal revenue coincide. The price is P_3 and the natural monopoly makes supernormal profits. There is no room in the industry for other firms with access to the same LAC_3 curve.

A new entrant needs a big output to get average costs down. Extra output on this scale so depresses the price that both firms make losses. The potential entrant cannot break in.

Finally, we show the LAC_2 curve with more economies of scale than a competitive industry but fewer than a natural monopoly. This industry supports at least two firms enjoying scale economies near the bottom of their LAC_2 curves. It is an oligopoly. Attempts to expand either firm's output beyond q_4 quickly meet decreasing returns to scale and prevent a firm driving competitors out of business.

Minimum efficient scale is the lowest output at which a firm's *LAC* curve stops falling.

The crucial determinant of market structure is **minimum efficient scale** relative to the size of the total market as shown by the demand curve. Table 9.2 summarizes our analysis of the interaction of market size and minimum efficient scale. When the demand curve shifts to the left, an industry previously with many firms may have room for only a few. Similarly, a rise in fixed costs, raising the minimum efficient scale, reduces the number of firms. In the 1950s there were many European aircraft makers. Today, the research and development costs of a major commercial airliner are huge. Apart from the co-operative European venture Airbus Industries, only the American giant Boeing survives.

Table 9.2 Demand, cost and market structure

Minimum efficient scale relative to market size		
Tiny	Intermediate	Large
Perfect competition	Oligopoly	Natural monopoly

Monopolistic competition lies between oligopoly and perfect competition. Monopolistic competitors supply different versions of the same product, such as the particular location of a newsagent.

Evidence on market structure

The larger the minimum efficient scale relative to the market size, the fewer the number of plants – and probably the number of firms – in the industry. What number of plants (*NP*) operating at minimum efficient scale does a market size allow? Chapter 7 discussed estimates of minimum efficient scale in different industries. By looking at the total purchases of a product, we can estimate market size. Hence we can estimate *NP* for each industry.

Even industries with only a few key players have some small firms on the fringe. The total number of firms can be a misleading indicator of the structure of the industry. In the UK there are many grocery shops; however, four large supermarkets, namely Tesco, Sainsbury's, Morrison and Asda, jointly represent 70 per cent of total grocery retail sales. That industry is therefore quite concentrated, with only few firms serving the majority of the market. Economists use various indices to measure market concentration. A common measure used is the **N-firm concentration ratio**.[1] This is a measure of the number of key firms in an industry. For example, the three-firm concentration ratio tells us the market share of the largest three firms. If there are three key firms, they will supply most of the market. If the industry is perfectly competitive, the largest three firms will only have a tiny share of industry output and sales.

The *N*-firm concentration ratio is the market share of the largest *N* firms in the industry.

1 Another common measure for market concentration is the Herfindahl–Hirschman Index (HHI). For a given market this index is calculated as the sum of the square of the market share of each firm in the market. This index varies from 0 (no concentration) to 1 (the market is a monopoly).

It would be nice to look at cross-country evidence to see if market structures always obey our theory. If this is to be an independent check, we really need national data before globalization and European integration became important. Table 9.3 examines evidence for the UK, France and Germany for the mid-1970s.

Table 9.3 Concentration and scale economies

Industry	UK		France		Germany	
	CR	*NP*	*CR*	*NP*	*CR*	*NP*
Refrigerators	65	1	100	2	72	3
Cigarettes	94	3	100	2	94	3
Refineries	79	8	60	7	47	9
Brewing	47	11	63	5	17	16
Fabrics	28	57	23	57	16	52
Shoes	17	165	13	128	20	197

Note: Concentration ratio *CR* is the percentage market share of the three largest firms; number of plants *NP* is market size divided by minimum efficient scale.

Sources: F. M. Scherer et al., *The economics of multiplant operation* (Harvard University Press, 1975); F. M. Scherer, *Industrial market structure and economic performance* (Rand McNally, 1980).

CR is the three-firm concentration ratio; that is, the market share of the top three firms. *NP* is the number of plants at minimum efficient scale that the market size allows. If our theory of market structure is correct, industries with large-scale economies relative to market size, and thus few plants *NP*, should have a large concentration ratio *CR*. Such industries should have few key firms. Conversely, where *NP* is very high, economies of scale are relatively unimportant and the largest three firms should have a much smaller market share. *CR* should be low.

Table 9.3 confirms that this theory of market structure fits these facts. Industries such as refrigerator and cigarette manufacture had room for few plants operating at minimum efficient scale: these industries had high degrees of concentration. The largest three firms controlled almost the whole market. Scale economies still mattered in industries such as brewing and petroleum refining: the top three firms controlled about half the market. Industries such as shoemaking quickly met rising average cost curves, had room for many factories operating at minimum efficient scale and thus were much closer to competitive industries. The top three firms in shoemaking controlled under one-fifth of the market.

Globalization and multinationals

Table 9.3 showed data before the rise of globalization and multinationals. **Globalization** reflects cheaper transport costs, better information technology and a deliberate policy of reducing cross-country barriers in order to get efficiency gains from large scale and specialization. **Multinationals** sell in many countries at the same time. They may, or may not, also produce in many countries.

Globalization is the closer integration of markets across countries.

Multinationals are firms operating in many countries simultaneously.

CASE 9.1

MARKET STRUCTURE OF THE PC INDUSTRY

The first personal computer was introduced in 1981 by the International Business Machines Corporation (IBM). After that, the PC industry grew swiftly over the years and is now a global business. Countries like Taiwan, Singapore and, more recently, China began to emerge as key players in the PC industry.

According to the data for the first quarter of 2013, the market structure of the PC industry is as shown in the table below.

Company	Market share (%)
HP	15.7
Lenovo	15.3
Dell	11.8
Acer Group	8.1
ASUS	5.7
Others	43.4

Source: IDC press release, 10 April 2013.

The Chinese company Lenovo acquired IBM's PC business in 2005 to accelerate its access to the global market. It is now the second-biggest player in the industry. The five biggest manufacturers control around 57 per cent of the total PC market. Even though the majority of the market is controlled by few firms, the PC industry is still very competitive. The two main characteristics of this industry are:

- *Vertical product differentiation:* this refers to goods that are close substitutes but differ in terms of quality.
- *Fast technological change:* the PC life cycle lasts only four months on average.

Technology adoption is what allows firms to vertically differentiate their products and to gain market share.

Multinationals affect the analysis implied by Figure 9.1 and Table 9.3. They can produce on a large scale somewhere in the world, where production is cheapest, enjoy all the benefits of scale economies, but still sell small quantities in many different markets.

This has three effects. First, it reduces entry barriers in a particular country. A foreign multinational entrant need not achieve a large market share, and therefore need not bid down the price a lot, to achieve scale economies. These now arise because of success in selling globally. Second, small domestic firms, previously sheltered by entry barriers, now face greater international competition and may not survive. Third, greater competition by low-cost producers leads *initially* to lower profit margins and lower prices.

However, if there are only a few multinationals, they may drive the higher-cost domestic firms out of business but then collude among themselves to raise prices again. Some of the debate about globalization hinges on which of these two outcomes dominates: the initial price fall or a possible subsequent price increase. We will return to this issue shortly when we analyse collusion.

9.2 Monopolistic competition

In London there are more than 5000 restaurants. Every year new restaurants open and some close down, meaning that barriers to entering and exiting the market are relatively low. Even if there is a large number of sellers and no relevant barriers, the restaurant industry is far from being perfectly competitive. The food produced by different restaurants is not perceived to be identical. The products in that industry are imperfect substitutes. The food offered by a Michelin-starred restaurant is normally perceived as different from the food served at McDonald's. Italian food is not a perfect substitute for Indian food. This means that a restaurant may charge a higher price for its food and still retain some of its customers. This could not happen in a perfectly competitive industry. The restaurant industry is an example of a monopolistically competitive industry.

The theory of monopolistic competition envisages a large number of quite small firms so that each firm can neglect the possibility that its own decisions provoke any adjustment in other firms' behaviour. There is free entry to and exit from the industry in the long run. In these respects, the industry resembles *perfect* competition. What distinguishes *monopolistic* competition is that each firm faces a *downward*-sloping demand curve.

Monopolistic competition describes an industry in which each firm can influence its market share to some extent by changing its price relative to that of its competitors. Its demand curve is not horizontal because different firms' products are only limited substitutes, as in the location of local shops. A lower price attracts some customers from another shop but each shop always has some local customers for whom convenience is more important than a few pence off the price of a jar of coffee.

Monopolistically competitive industries exhibit *product differentiation*. Firms in a monopolistically competitive market produce goods that are perceived by customers as imperfect substitutes. Corner grocers differentiate by location, hairdressers by customer loyalty. The special feature of a particular restaurant or hairdresser lets it charge a slightly different price from other firms in the industry without losing all its customers.

Monopolistic competition requires not merely product differentiation but also limited opportunities for economies of scale. Firms are small. With lots of producers, each can neglect its interdependence with any particular rival. Many examples of monopolistic competition are service industries where economies of scale are small.

The industry demand curve shows the total output demanded at each price if all firms in the industry charge that price. The market share of each firm depends on the price it charges and on the number of firms in the industry. For a given number of firms, a shift in the industry demand curve shifts the demand curve for the output of each firm. For a given industry demand curve, having more (fewer) firms in the industry shifts the demand curve of each firm to the left (right) as its market share falls (rises). But each firm faces a downward-sloping demand curve. This implies that firms in monopolistic competition have market power and they are price-setters. For a given industry demand curve, number of firms and price charged by all other firms, a particular firm can raise its market share a bit by charging a lower price.

CONCEPT 9.1

IT'S NOT WHAT IT LOOKS LIKE

An investor seeking to hold assets in a mutual fund is a consumer with many choices: in 2001, there were 8307 US mutual funds in operation. A mutual fund investor's choice set has also been growing robustly over time: while there were 834 mutual funds in operation in 1980, this nearly quadrupled to 3100 by 1990, and almost tripled again by 2001. So it appears that the mutual fund market in the US is a market with many firms, most of whose mutual funds are pretty homogeneous, and there is reasonably free entry. Is the market for mutual funds a competitive market?

The answer appears to be no. The fees that investors pay to hold assets in funds are really dispersed, meaning they differ even for mutual funds that are almost homogeneous in their performance. Why should prices be different for goods that are almost homogeneous? The reason is that there are other elements, apart from pure performance of the funds, which can affect investor choice. For example, 60 per cent of investors reported consulting a financial adviser before purchase, implying that the ability of the financial adviser is an important element in investor choice. Funds can have divergent taxable distribution rates for a given return pattern; clearly, investors prefer less tax exposure, all else being equal.

All those facts can explain why products that may appear homogeneous in their physical characteristics can still have some sort of product differentiation that can explain their different prices.

Source: A. Hortaçsu and C. Syverson, *'Product differentiation, search costs and competition in the mutual fund industry: A case study of S&P index funds'*, NBER working paper 9728, 2003.

Figure 9.2 shows a firm's supply decision. Given its demand curve *DD* and marginal revenue curve *MR*, the firm makes Q_0 at a price P_0, making short-run profits $Q_0(P_0 - AC_0)$. In the long run, these profits attract new entrants, diluting the market share of each firm in the industry, shifting their demand curves to the left. Entry stops when each firm's demand curve shifts so far left that price equals average cost and firms just break even. In Figure 9.2 this occurs when demand is DD'. The firm makes Q_1 at a price P_1 in the **tangency equilibrium** at *F*.

> In monopolistic competition, in the long-run tangency equilibrium each firm's demand curve just touches its *AC* curve at the output level at which *MC* equals *MR*. Each firm maximizes profits but just breaks even. There is no more entry or exit.

Note two things about the firm's long-run equilibrium at *F*. First, the firm is *not* producing at minimum average cost. It has excess capacity. It could reduce average costs by further expansion. However, its marginal revenue would be so low that this is unprofitable. Second, the firm has some monopoly power because of the special feature of its particular brand or location. Price exceeds marginal cost.

This explains why firms are usually eager for new customers prepared to buy additional output at the *existing* price. We are a race of eager sellers and coy buyers. It is purchasing

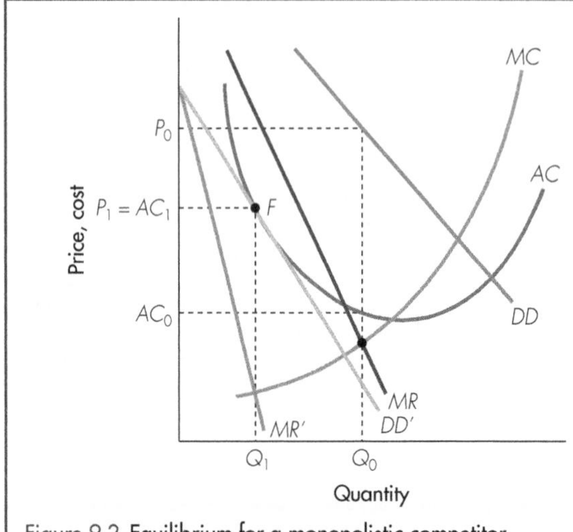

In the short run the monopolistic competitor faces the demand curve DD and sets MC equal to MR to produce Q_0 at a price P_0. Profits are $Q_0 \times (P_0 - AC_0)$. Profits attract new entrants and shift each firm's demand curve to the left. When the demand curve reaches DD' we reach the long-run tangency equilibrium at F. The firm sets MC equal to MR' to produce Q_1 at which P_1 equals AC_1. Firms are breaking even and there is no further entry.

Figure 9.2 **Equilibrium for a monopolistic competitor**

agents who get Christmas presents from sales reps, not the other way round. In contrast, a perfectly competitive firm does not care if another buyer shows up at the existing price. With price equal to marginal cost, the firm is already selling as much as it wants to sell.

9.3 Oligopoly and interdependence

Under perfect competition or monopolistic competition, there are many firms in the industry. Each firm can ignore the effect of its own actions on rival firms. However, the key to an oligopolistic industry is the need for each firm to consider how its own actions affect the decisions of its relatively few competitors. Each firm has to guess how its rivals will react. Before discussing what constitutes a smart guess, we introduce the basic tension between competition and collusion when firms know that they are interdependent. Initially, for simplicity, we neglect the possibility of entry and focus on existing firms.

The profits from collusion

Collusion is an explicit or implicit agreement to avoid competition.

As sole decision maker in the industry, a monopolist would choose industry output to maximize total profits. Hence, the few producers in an industry can maximize their total profit by setting their total output as if they were monopolists.

Figure 9.3 shows an industry where each firm, and the whole industry, has constant average and marginal costs at the level P_C. Chapter 8 showed that a competitive industry produces Q_C at a price P_C but a multi-plant monopolist maximizes profits by making Q_M at a price P_M. If the oligopolists collude to produce Q_M, they act as a *collusive monopolist*. Having decided industry output, the firms agree how to share total output and profits among themselves.

However, it is hard to stop firms cheating on the collective agreement. In Figure 9.3 joint profit is maximized at a total output Q_M and price P_M. Yet each firm can expand output at a marginal cost P_C. Any firm can expand output, selling at a little below the agreed price P_M, and make extra profit since its marginal revenue exceeds its marginal cost. This firm gains at the expense of its collusive partners. Industry output is higher than the best output Q_M, so total profits fall and other firms suffer.

Oligopolists are torn between the desire to collude, in order to maximize joint profits, and the desire to compete, in order to raise market share and profits at the expense of rivals. Yet if all firms compete, joint profits are low and no firm does very well. Therein lies the dilemma.

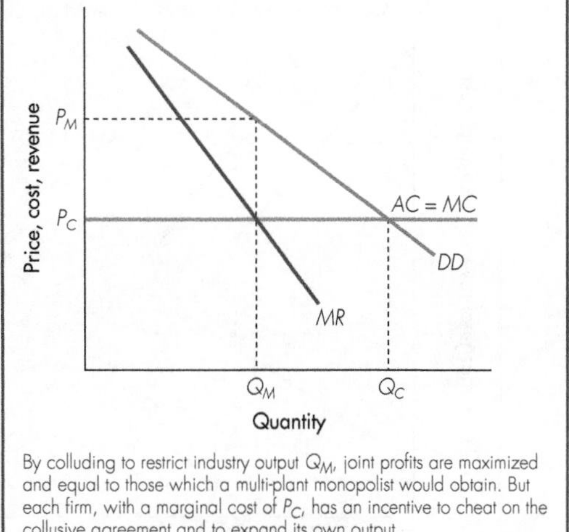

By colluding to restrict industry output Q_M, joint profits are maximized and equal to those which a multi-plant monopolist would obtain. But each firm, with a marginal cost of P_C, has an incentive to cheat on the collusive agreement and to expand its own output.

Figure 9.3 **Collusion versus competition**

Cartels

Collusion between firms is easiest if formal agreements are legal. Such arrangements, called *cartels*, were common in the late nineteenth century, agreeing market shares and prices in many industries. Cartels are now outlawed in Europe, the US and many other countries. There are big penalties for being caught, but informal agreements and secret deals are sometimes discovered even today.

Cartels across continents are harder to outlaw. The most famous cartel is OPEC, the Organization of Petroleum Exporting Countries. Its members meet regularly to set price and output. Initially, OPEC succeeded in organizing quantity reductions to force up the price of oil. Real OPEC revenues rose 500 per cent between 1973 and 1980. Yet many economists predicted that OPEC, like most cartels, would quickly collapse. Usually, the incentive to cheat is too strong to resist and once somebody breaks ranks others tend to follow. One reason that OPEC was successful for so long was the willingness of Saudi Arabia, the largest oil producer, to restrict its output further when smaller members insisted on expansion.

By 1986 Saudi Arabia was no longer prepared to play by these rules and refused to prop up the price any longer. The oil price collapsed from just under $30 to $9 a barrel. During 1987–98, apart from a brief period during the First Gulf War, oil prices fluctuated between $8 and $20 a barrel. Only after 1998 did OPEC recover the cohesion it displayed during 1973–85. The Second Gulf War and continuing uncertainty in the Middle East has continued to restrict supply in any case, also underpinning the high oil prices since 2003.

The kinked demand curve

Collusion is much harder if there are many firms in the industry, if the product is not standardized and if demand and cost conditions are changing rapidly. In the absence of collusion, each firm's demand curve depends on how competitors react. Firms must guess how their rivals will behave.

Suppose that each firm believes that its own price cut will be matched by all other firms in the industry, but that a rise in its own price will not induce a price response from competitors. Figure 9.4 shows the demand curve *DD* that each firm then believes it faces. At the current price P_0, the firm makes Q_0. Suppose the firm raises the price. If competitors do not follow, the firm loses some of its customers, who will now buy from the cheaper competitors. The firm loses market share to other firms. The firm's demand curve is elastic above *A* at prices above the current price P_0. However, if each firm believes that if it cuts prices this action will be matched by other firms, market shares are unchanged. Lower prices then induce extra sales rises only because the whole industry moves down the market demand curve as prices fall. The demand curve *DD* is much less elastic for price cuts from the initial price P_0. The demand faced by each firm has a kink at point *A*, reflecting the asymmetric effects of a price change.

In Figure 9.4 we have to draw marginal revenue *MR* for each of the separate sections of the kinked demand curve. The firm jumps discontinuously from one part of *MR* to the other when it reaches the output Q_0.

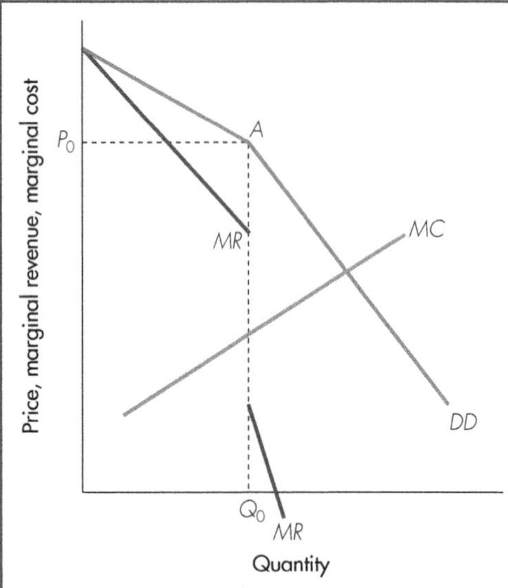

An oligopolist believes rivals will match price cuts but not price rises. The oligopolist's demand curve is kinked at *A*. Price rises lead to a large loss of market share, but price cuts increase quantity only by increasing industry sales. Marginal revenue is discontinuous at Q_0. The oligopolist produces Q_0, the output at which *MC* crosses the *MR* schedule.

Figure 9.4 **The kinked demand curve**

Below Q_0, the elastic part of the demand curve is relevant, and marginal revenue is high since additional output does not depress the price much for existing sales. At the output Q_0, the firm hits the inelastic portion of its kinked demand curve and marginal revenue becomes much lower: now that demand is less elastic, further output increases require much lower prices to sell the extra output, hitting revenue from existing sales. Q_0 is the profit-maximizing output for the firm, given its belief about how competitors respond.

Suppose the *MC* curve of a single firm shifts up or down by a small amount. Since the *MR* curve has a discontinuous vertical segment at Q_0, it remains optimal to make Q_0 and charge the price P_0. In contrast, a monopolist facing a continuously downward-sloping *MR* curve would adjust quantity and price when the *MC* curve shifted. The kinked demand curve model may explain the empirical finding that firms do not always adjust prices when costs change.

It does not explain what determines the initial price P_0. One interpretation is that it is the collusive monopoly price. Each firm believes that an attempt to undercut its rivals will provoke them to co-operate among themselves and retaliate in full. However, its rivals will be happy for it to charge a higher price and see it lose market share.

If we interpret P_0 as the collusive monopoly price, we can contrast the effect of a cost change for a single firm and a cost change for all firms. The latter shifts the marginal cost curve up for the entire industry, raising the collusive monopoly price. Each firm's kinked demand curve shifts up since the monopoly price P_0 has risen. Hence, we can reconcile the stickiness of a firm's price with respect to changes in its own costs alone, and the speed with which the entire industry marks up prices when all firms' costs increase. Examples of the latter are higher taxes on the industry's product or a union wage increase across the whole industry.

9.4 Game theory and interdependent decisions

A good poker player sometimes bluffs. You can win with a bad hand if your opponents misread it for a good hand. Similarly, by having bluffed in the past and been caught, you may persuade opponents to bet a lot when you have a terrific hand.

A game is a situation in which intelligent decisions are necessarily interdependent.

Like poker players, oligopolists try to anticipate their rivals' moves to determine their own best action. To study interdependent decision making, we use *game theory*. The *players* in the **game** try to maximize their own *payoffs*. In an oligopoly, the firms are the players and their payoffs are their profits in the long run. Each player must choose a strategy. Being a pickpocket is a strategy. Lifting a particular wallet is a move.

A strategy is a game plan describing how a player acts, or moves, in each possible situation.

As usual, we are interested in equilibrium. In most games, each player's best **strategy** depends on the strategies chosen by other players. It is silly to be a pickpocket when the police have CCTV cameras or to play four centre backs when the opponents have no proven goal-scorers.

An equilibrium in a game is a situation where each player plays the best strategy given the strategy of the others. In this case, no player would like to change her chosen strategy. This definition of equilibrium, and its application to game theory, was invented by a Princeton University mathematician, **John Nash.**[2]

In Nash equilibrium, each player chooses the best strategy, *given* the strategies being followed by other players.

Dominant strategies

Sometimes (but not usually) a player's best strategy is independent of those chosen by others. We begin with an example in which each player has a **dominant strategy**.

A dominant strategy is a player's best strategy *whatever* the strategies adopted by rivals.

Figure 9.5 shows a game[3] between the only two members of a cartel. Each firm can select a high-output or low-output strategy. In each box of Figure 9.5 the green number shows firm A's profits and the purple number firm B's profits for that output combination.

When both have high output, industry output is high, the price is low and each firm makes a small profit of 1. When each has low output, the outcome resembles collusive monopoly. Prices are high and each firm does better, making a profit of 2. Each firm does best (a profit of 3) when it alone has high output: the other firm's low output helps hold down industry output and keep up the price. In this situation we assume the low-output firm makes a profit of 0.

		Firm B output: High		Firm B output: Low	
Firm A output	High	1	1	3	0
	Low	0	3	2	2

The green and purple numbers in each box indicate profits to firms A and B, respectively. Whether B pursues high or low output, A makes more profit going high; so does B, whichever strategy A adopts. In equilibrium both go high. Yet both would make greater profits if both went low!

Figure 9.5 The Prisoner's Dilemma game

Now we can see how the game will unfold. Consider firm A's decision. It first thinks what to do if firm B has a high-output strategy. Firm A will thus be in one of the two left-hand boxes of Figure 9.5. Firm A gets a profit of 1 by choosing high but a profit of 0 by choosing low. If firm A thinks firm B will choose high output, firm A prefers high output itself.

But firm A must also think what to do if firm B chooses a low-output strategy. This puts firm A in one of the two right-hand boxes. Firm A *still* prefers high output for itself, which yields a profit of 3 whereas low output yields a profit of only 2. Firm A has a dominant strategy. Whichever strategy B adopts, A does better to choose a high-output strategy.

Firm B also has a dominant strategy to choose high output. If firm B anticipates that firm A will go high, facing a choice of the two boxes in the top row, firm B prefers to go high. If B thinks A will go low, B faces a choice from the two boxes in the bottom row of Figure 9.5, but B still wants to go high. Firm B does better to go high whichever strategy A selects. Both firm A and firm B have a dominant strategy to go high. Equilibrium is the top left-hand box. Each firm gets a profit of 1.

Yet both firms would do better, getting a profit of 2, if they colluded to form a cartel and both produced low – the bottom right-hand box. But neither can risk going low. Suppose firm A goes low. Firm B, comparing the two boxes in the bottom row, will then go high, preferring a profit of 3 to a profit of 2. And firm A will be in trouble; earning a profit of 0 in that event. Firm A can figure all this out in advance, which is why its dominant strategy is to go high.

This shows vividly the tension between collusion and competition. In this example, it appears that the output-restricting cartel will never be formed, since each player can already foresee the overwhelming incentive for the other to cheat on such an arrangement. How, then, can cartels ever be sustained? One possibility is that there exist binding **commitments**.

A commitment is an arrangement, entered into voluntarily, that restricts future actions.

2 Nash, who battled schizophrenia, won the Nobel Prize in Economics for his work on game theory. A film about his life, *A Beautiful Mind* (dir. Ron Howard), was released in 2001 and starred Russell Crowe.

3 The game, called the Prisoner's Dilemma, was first used to analyse the choice facing two people arrested and in different cells, each of whom could plead guilty or not guilty to the only crime that had been committed. Each prisoner would plead innocent if only she knew the other would plead guilty. For more information, go to www.mcgraw-hill.co.uk/textbooks/begg where there is a video fully explaining the Prisoner's Dilemma.

If both players in Figure 9.5 could simultaneously sign an enforceable contract to produce low output, they could achieve the co-operative outcome in the bottom right-hand box, each earning profits of 2. This beats the top left-hand box, which shows the Nash equilibrium of the game when collusion cannot be enforced. Without a binding commitment, neither player can go low because then the other player goes high. Binding commitments, by removing this temptation, let both players go low. Both players gain.

This idea of commitment is important and we shall encounter it many times. Just think of all the human activities that are the subject of legal contracts, a simple commitment simultaneously undertaken by two parties or players.

Although this insight is powerful, its application to oligopoly requires care. Cartels within a country are usually illegal and OPEC is not held together by a contract enforceable in international law. Is there a less formal way in which oligopolists can avoid cheating on the collusive low-output solution to the game? If the game is played only once, this is difficult.

Repeated games

In the real world, the game described above is repeated many times: firms choose output levels day after day. Suppose two players try to collude on low output: each announces a *punishment strategy*. If firm A ever cheats on the low-output agreement, firm B says that it will subsequently react by raising its output. Firm A makes a similar promise.

Suppose the agreement has been in force for some time and both firms have stuck to their low-output deal. Firm A assumes that firm B will go low as usual. Figure 9.5 shows that firm A makes a *temporary* gain today if it cheats and goes high. Instead of staying in the bottom right-hand box with a profit of 2, it can move to the top right-hand box and make 3. However, from tomorrow onwards, firm B will also go high and firm A can then do no better than continue to go high too, making a profit of 1 for ever more. But if A refuses to cheat today, it can continue to stay in the bottom right-hand box and make 2 for ever. In cheating, A swaps a temporary gain for a permanent reduction in future profits. Thus, punishment strategies can sustain an explicit cartel or implicit collusion even if no formal commitment exists.

It is all very well to promise punishment if the other player cheats. But this will affect the other player's behaviour only if the **threat is credible**.

A credible threat is one that, after the fact, is still optimal to carry out.

In the preceding example, once firm A has cheated and gone high, it is then in firm B's interest to go high anyway. Hence a threat to go high if A ever cheats is a credible threat.

These insights shed light on the actual behaviour of OPEC in 1986, when Saudi Arabia dramatically raised its output, leading to a collapse of oil prices. In the 1980s, other members of OPEC had gradually cheated on the low-output agreement, trusting that Saudi Arabia would still produce low to sustain a high price and the cartel's prestige. They hoped Saudi threats to adopt a punishment strategy were empty threats. They were wrong. Figure 9.5 shows that, once the others went high, Saudi Arabia had to go high too.

9.5 Reaction functions

In the previous example, in a one-off game each player had a dominant strategy, to produce high output whatever its rival did. This led to a poor outcome for both players because they were not co-operating despite being interdependent. When the game is repeated, commitments and punishment strategies help players co-operate to find an outcome that is better for both of them.

In punishing a rival, a player's actions change in response to bad behaviour by the rival. Dominant strategies are rare. More usually, each player's best action depends on the actual or expected actions of other players. How a player reacts depends on what it assumes about its rivals' behaviour. For simplicity we analyse *duopoly*, in which there are only two players.

Cournot behaviour

In 1838 French economist, Augustin Cournot, analysed a simple model of duopoly. Imagine a duopoly in which both firms produce identical products and have the same constant marginal costs *MC*. Figure 9.6 draws the decision problem for firm A. If firm A assumes that firm B produces 0, firm A gets the whole industry demand curve D_0. This shows what output firm A can sell given the prices that it charges. From this, firm A calculates the marginal revenue MR_0, and produces Q_0 to equate its marginal cost and marginal revenue.

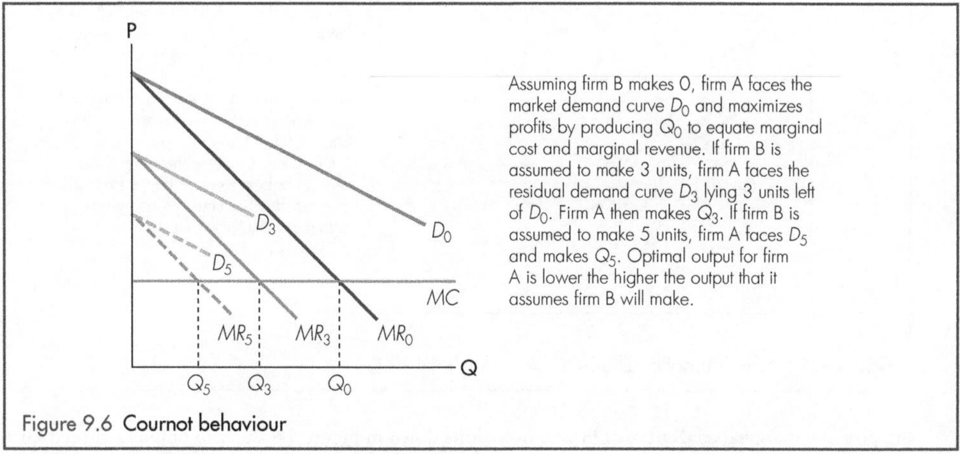

Assuming firm B makes 0, firm A faces the market demand curve D_0 and maximizes profits by producing Q_0 to equate marginal cost and marginal revenue. If firm B is assumed to make 3 units, firm A faces the residual demand curve D_3 lying 3 units left of D_0. Firm A then makes Q_3. If firm B is assumed to make 5 units, firm A faces D_5 and makes Q_5. Optimal output for firm A is lower the higher the output that it assumes firm B will make.

Figure 9.6 **Cournot behaviour**

If, instead, firm A assumes that firm B makes 3 units, firm A faces a demand curve D_3 obtained by shifting the market demand D_0 to the left by 3 units. Firm B gets 3 units and the residual demand is available for firm A. For this demand curve, D_3, firm A computes the marginal revenue curve MR_3 and chooses output Q_3 to equate marginal cost and marginal revenue.

Similarly, if firm A expects firm B to make 5 units, firm A shifts D_0 to the left by 5 units to get D_5, and produces Q_5 in order to equate marginal cost and its marginal revenue MR_5. The larger the output that firm 2 is expected to make and sell, the smaller the optimal output of firm A. Q_5 is smaller than Q_3, which is smaller than Q_0.

Repeating this exercise for every possible belief that firm A has about the output of firm B yields the **reaction function** of firm A.

A firm's reaction function shows how its optimal output varies with each possible action by its rival.

In the Cournot model, each firm treats the *output* of the other firm as given.

In the **Cournot model**, a rival's action is its output choice. Figure 9.7 shows the two outputs Q^A and Q^B. From Figure 9.6 firm A makes less the more it thinks that firm B will make. In Figure 9.7 firm A's optimal output choice is the reaction function R^A. If firm B is expected to produce 1 unit less, firm A chooses to raise output by less than 1 unit. This ensures total output falls, thus raising the price. Because this lets firm A earn more on its previous output units, it is not worth raising its output by as much as it expects the output of B to fall. Equivalently, in Figure 9.6 firm A's demand curve shifts more than its marginal revenue curve; hence its rise in output is smaller than the conjectured fall in the output of firm B.

In the duopoly, both firms are the same since they have the same marginal cost and produce the same good. Hence firm B faces a similar problem. It makes guesses about the output of firm A, calculates the residual demand curve for firm B, and chooses its best output. Figure 9.7 shows the reaction function R^B for firm B, which also makes less the more that it assumes its rival will produce.

Along each reaction function, each firm makes its best response to the assumed output of the other firm. Only in equilibrium is it optimal for the other firm actually to behave in the way that has been assumed. In Nash equilibrium, neither firm wishes to alter its behaviour even after its conjecture about the other firm's output is then confirmed.

Since both firms face the same industry demand curve, their reaction functions are symmetric if they also face the same marginal cost curves in Figure 9.6. The two firms then produce the same output Q^*, as shown in Figure 9.7. If costs differed, we could still construct (different) reaction functions and their intersection would no longer imply equal market shares.

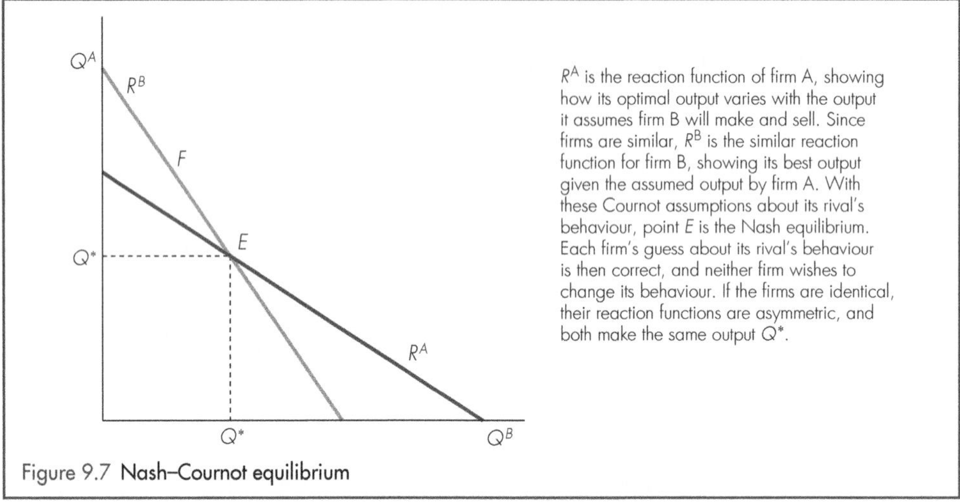

R^A is the reaction function of firm A, showing how its optimal output varies with the output it assumes firm B will make and sell. Since firms are similar, R^B is the similar reaction function for firm B, showing its best output given the assumed output by firm A. With these Cournot assumptions about its rival's behaviour, point *E* is the Nash equilibrium. Each firm's guess about its rival's behaviour is then correct, and neither firm wishes to change its behaviour. If the firms are identical, their reaction functions are asymmetric, and both make the same output Q^*.

Figure 9.7 **Nash–Cournot equilibrium**

Suppose the marginal cost curve of firm A now shifts down in Figure 9.6. At each output assumed for firm B, firm A now makes more. It moves further down any *MR* schedule before meeting *MC*. Hence, in Figure 9.7 the reaction function R^A shifts up, showing firm A makes more output Q^A at any assumed output Q^B of its rival. The new intersection of the reaction functions, say at point *F*, shows what happens to Nash equilibrium in the Cournot model.

It is no surprise that the output of firm A rises. Why does the output of firm B fall? With lower marginal costs, firm A is optimally making more. Unless firm B cuts its output, the price will fall a lot. Firm B prefers to cut output a little, in order to prop up the price a bit, preventing a big revenue loss on its existing units.

As in our discussion of the Prisoner's Dilemma game in Section 9.4, the Nash–Cournot equilibrium does not maximize the joint payoffs of the two players. They fail to achieve the total output that maximizes joint profits. By treating the output of the rival as given, each firm expands too much. Higher output bids down prices for everybody. In neglecting the fact that its own expansion hurts its rival, each firm's output is too high.

Each firm's behaviour is correct given its assumption that its rival's output is fixed. But expansion by one firm induces the rival to alter its behaviour. A joint monopolist would take that into account and make more total profit.

This is considered in Figure 9.8. Suppose there are two identical firms producing cars. The firms have two possible strategies: co-operate and form a cartel or do not co-operate and compete in quantities. The game is played simultaneously and only once, so it is a one-shot game. If they co-operate (collude), they can set the monopoly price and both obtain half of the monopoly profits. If they compete, they both obtain the Cournot profits, which are lower than in the case of collusion. If a firm is co-operating while the rival deviates from the collusive agreement, the firm deviating steals most of the market and obtains high profits. The other firm receives low profits.

		Firm B	
		Co-operate	Not co-operate
Firm A	Co-operate	10, 10	2, 15
	Not co-operate	15, 2	5, 5

Figure 9.8 **Cournot competition and the Prisoner's Dilemma**

From Figure 9.8 we can see that firm A has a dominant strategy (to not co-operate), since that strategy, independently of what the rival is doing, will provide a payoff of 15 or 5 (co-operating will give firm A payoffs of 10 or 2). For firm B, we have a dominant strategy as well. Firm B will always choose not to co-operate. The only Nash equilibrium of the game is for both firms not to co-operate. At that equilibrium, the firms will get profits of 5, lower than in the case of both co-operating.

In this case, firms do not co-operate because the incentive to deviate from the collusive agreement is large. By recognizing that, both firms will simply not co-operate and we are back to the Prisoner's Dilemma case.

MATHS 9.1

DERIVING THE REACTION FUNCTIONS IN A COURNOT DUOPOLY

Consider a market in which there are two firms, A and B, producing the same good and competing on quantities. The inverse market demand is given by $P = a - bQ$, where $Q = Q_A + Q_B$ is the total quantity produced in the market and is simply the sum of what is produced by firm A and firm B. Assume that the cost functions of the two firms are the same, meaning that the two firms are equal (the case of an unequal cost function can be handled easily too).

The cost function of firm A is $TC_A = cQ_A$, while for firm B it is $TC_B = cQ_B$, where $c > 0$ is the marginal cost.

The reaction function (or best response) of firm A tells us how the output produced by firm A depends on the output produced by firm B. The reaction function for firm B is defined in a similar way.

Each firm maximizes profits. This means that each firm chooses a level of output such that the marginal revenue of selling that output is equal to the marginal cost of producing it. The total revenue for firm A is given by $TR_A = P \times Q_A$. Using the inverse demand for substituting for P, we get $TR_A = [a - b(Q_A + Q_B)] \times Q_A = aQ_A - bQ_A^2 - bQ_AQ_B$. As we can see, the total revenue of firm A now depends on the output chosen by firm B as well (Q_B). For firm B, using a similar argument, the total revenue is $TR_B = aQ_B - bQ_B^2 - bQ_BQ_A$.

The marginal revenue functions for the two firms are:

$$\boldsymbol{MR_A \equiv \frac{\partial TR_A}{\partial Q_A} = a - 2bQ_A - bQ_B \quad \text{and} \quad MR_B \equiv \frac{\partial TR_B}{\partial Q_B} = a - 2bQ_B - bQ_A}$$

The marginal costs of the firms are the same:

$$MC_A \equiv \frac{dTC_A}{dQ_A} = c \quad \text{and} \quad MC_B \equiv \frac{dTC_B}{dQ_B} = c$$

The reaction function of each firm is found for the profit-maximization conditions:

$$MR_A = MC_A \quad \text{and} \quad MR_B = MC_B$$

Using our data to express those two conditions, we have:

$$a - 2bQ_A - bQ_B = c \quad \text{and} \quad a - 2bQ_B - bQ_A = c$$

From those two conditions we can find the reaction functions of each firm. For firm A, the reaction function is:

$$Q_A = \frac{a - c}{2b} - \frac{Q_B}{2} \tag{1}$$

For firm B, we have:

$$Q_B = \frac{a - c}{2b} - \frac{Q_A}{2} \tag{2}$$

Notice that the reaction function of each firm depends negatively on the output produced by the rival. If firm B increases its output level, the best response by firm A is to reduce its output level. Reaction function (1) tells us the output that maximizes the profits of firm A, given the output chosen by firm B.

The Nash equilibrium of the Cournot model is where the two reaction functions above are mutually consistent, meaning they cross.

Therefore, we just need to solve a system of two equations in two variables Q_A, Q_B.

By solving the system of equations (1) and (2), we have:

$$Q_A = \frac{a - c}{3b} \quad \text{and} \quad Q_B = \frac{a - c}{3b}$$

Since the two firms are identical by assumption, they must produce the same level of output. The total output produced in the market is therefore: $Q_A + Q_B = 2[(a - c)/3b]$. The equilibrium price is found through the inverse demand function:

$$P = \frac{a + 2c}{3}$$

Bertrand behaviour

To show how the assumption about rivals' behaviour affects reaction functions and hence Nash equilibrium, consider a different model suggested by another French economist, Joseph Bertrand.

Each firm produces the same good. In contrast to Cournot competition, each firm now decides a price (and hence an output) reflecting the price it expects its rival to set. We could go through a similar analysis to the Cournot model, find reaction curves showing how the *price* set by each firm depends on the *price* set by its rival, and hence find the Nash equilibrium in prices for the **Bertrand model**. Knowing the equilibrium price, we could work out equilibrium quantity. If the firms are identical, again they divide the market equally. However, in the Bertrand model, it is easy to see what the Nash equilibrium must be. It is the perfectly competitive outcome: price equals marginal cost. How do we know?

In the Bertrand model of oligopoly, each firm treats the *prices* of rivals as given.

Suppose firm B sets a price above its marginal cost. Firm A can grab the whole market by setting a price a little below that of firm B. Since firm B can anticipate this, it must set a lower price. This argument keeps working until, in Nash equilibrium, both firms price at marginal cost and split the market between them. There is then no incentive to alter behaviour.

Comparing Bertrand and Cournot

Under Bertrand behaviour, Nash equilibrium entails price equal to marginal cost, so industry output is the same as in a perfectly competitive market. Under Cournot behaviour, Nash equilibrium entails lower industry output and a higher price than under Bertrand behaviour. Under Cournot behaviour each firm makes positive profits. But the firms do not co-operate. A joint monopolist would make more profit by co-ordinating output decisions. Industry output would be even lower and the price even higher.

Thus, Nash equilibrium depends on the *particular* assumption each firm makes about its rival's behaviour. Generally, economists prefer the Cournot model. In practice, few oligopolies behave like a perfectly competitive industry, as the Bertrand model predicts.

Moreover, since prices can be changed rapidly, treating a rival's *price* as fixed does not seem plausible. In contrast, we can interpret the Cournot model as saying that firms first choose *output capacity* and then set price. Since capacity takes time to alter, this makes more sense.

CONCEPT 9.2

MERGERS AND COMPETITION POLICY

Two firms can unite in two different ways: via a takeover bid or a merger. When a firm makes a takeover bid, managers of the 'victim' firm usually resist since they are likely to lose their jobs, but the shareholders will accept if the offer is sufficiently attractive.

From now on we use mergers as shorthand for both forms of union. Mergers can be distinguished in the following way: a *horizontal merger* is the union of two firms at the same production stage in the same industry. A *vertical merger* is the union of two firms at different production stages in the same industry. In a *conglomerate merger*, the production activities of the two firms are unrelated.

Are mergers in the public interest, or do they just create private monopolies?

On the one hand, a merger reduces the number of competitors in a market. Consider a market with six main competitors. If two of them merge, the number of competitors is reduced to five. This reduction in competition is beneficial for all the remaining firms in the market, but it may be detrimental for consumers. Less competition may result in higher prices. The merger of two large firms gives them market power from a large market share. The merged company is likely to restrict output and increase prices – a deadweight burden for society as a whole.

On the other hand, two firms may merge for efficiency reasons. The new firm may be more efficient than the two separate firms; there may be gains to co-ordination and planning and in managerial and financial aspects. If companies achieve any of these benefits, they will increase productivity and lower costs. Competition policy related to mergers must compare the gains (potential cost reduction) with the costs (larger market power).

The table below shows annual averages of takeovers and mergers involving UK firms. It shows dramatic merger booms in the late 1980s and late 1990s, which coincided with high stock market values, which raised the value of both firms involved in the merger.

The proliferation of large companies through merger would not have been possible if there had been a tough anti-merger policy.

There are currently two grounds for referring a prospective merger to an investigation by the Competition Commission: (1) that the merger will promote a new monopoly as defined by the 25 per cent market share used in deciding references for existing monopoly positions; or (2) that the company taken over has an annual UK turnover of at least £70 million.

UK takeovers and mergers, 1986–2012 (annual averages)

	Number	Value (1998 £bn)
1986–89	1300	43
1990–98	585	20
1999–00	540	61
2001–06	600	30
2007–12	650	47

Sources: British Business Trends, 1989; *Business Trends,* 1997; ONS.

Since the merger legislation was introduced in 1965, only 4 per cent of all merger proposals have been referred to the Competition Commission. For much of the period, government policy has been to consent to, or actively encourage, mergers. In believing that the benefits would outweigh the costs, UK merger policy reflected two assumptions. The first was that the cost savings from economies of scale and more intensive use of scarce management talent could be quite large. The second was that the UK was part of an increasingly competitive world market so that the monopoly power of the merged firms, and the corresponding social cost of the deadweight burden, would be small. Large as they were, the merged firms were small in relation to European or world markets, and would face relatively elastic demand curves, giving little scope to raise price above marginal cost.

Finally, as with competition policy, EU legislation takes precedence where this is appropriate. It is not appropriate in assessing whether a merger of two UK supermarkets should be allowed, since this predominantly affects only UK consumers. However, the European Commission will investigate mergers involving enterprises with an aggregate worldwide annual turnover of over €5 billion and where the aggregate EU-wide turnover of each of the enterprises exceeds €250 million.

First-mover advantage and the Stackelberg model

So far we have assumed that the two duopolists make decisions simultaneously. Suppose one firm can choose output before the other. This means that we move from a simultaneous game to a sequential game structure. Does it help to move first?

To anticipate how firm B behaves once the output of firm A is fixed, firm A examines the reaction function of firm B as derived in Figures 9.6 and 9.7. In setting output, firm A then takes account of how its own output decisions *affect* output by firm B.

Firm A thus has a different reaction function. Figure 9.7 showed the Cournot reaction function R^A, treating Q^B as chosen independently of Q^A. Now firm A uses the reaction function *RB* to deduce that a higher output Q^A induces a *lower* output Q^B. Hence, firm A expects its own output expansion to bid the price down *less* than under Cournot behaviour. Its marginal revenue schedule is higher up. Firm A knows that firm B will help prop up the price by cutting Q^B in response to a rise in Q^A.

In the Stackelberg model, firm B can observe the output already fixed by firm A. In choosing output, firm A must thus anticipate the subsequent reaction of firm B.

A first-mover advantage means that the player moving first achieves higher payoffs than when decisions are simultaneous.

Facing a higher *MR* schedule as a **Stackelberg** leader than under Cournot behaviour, firm A produces more than under Cournot behaviour. Firm B makes less because it must react to the fact that a high output Q^A is already a done deal. Firm A ends up with higher output and profits than under Cournot behaviour but firm B has lower output and lower profit. Firm A has a **first-mover advantage**.

Moving first acts like a commitment that prevents your subsequent manipulation by the other player. Once firm A has built a large output capacity, firm B has to live with the reality that firm A will produce large output. The best response of firm B is then low output. Propping up the output price helps firm A. Being smart, firm A had already figured all that out.

In some industries, firms are fairly symmetric and Cournot behaviour is a good description of how these oligopolists behave. Other industries have a dominant firm, perhaps because of a technical edge or privileged location. That firm may be able to act as a Stackelberg leader and anticipate how its smaller rivals will then react.

MATHS 9.2

THE STACKELBERG MODEL

Consider a market in which operate two firms, A and B. Firm A is the leader while firm B is the follower.

The market inverse demand function is $P = a - b(Q_A + Q_B)$. Assume that the total cost of firm A is $TC_A = c_A Q_A$, while for firm B it is $TC_B = c_B Q_B$. The marginal cost of firm A is therefore c_A and for firm B is c_B.

The follower (firm B) takes the output produced by the leader (firm A) as given. Let's look at the behaviour of the follower first. The total revenue function of firm B is $TR_B = aQ_B - bQ_AQ_B - bQ_B^2$. The marginal revenue of the follower is $MR_B = a - bQ_A - 2bQ_B$. The reaction function of the follower comes from the profit-maximizing condition of firm B, $MR_B = MC_B$. Using our data, that condition implies $a - bQ_A - 2bQ_B = c_B$. Solve for Q_B:

$$Q_B = \frac{a - c_B}{2b} - \frac{Q_A}{2} \quad (1)$$

This is the reaction function of firm B. Firm A is the leader and takes into account that the follower has the reaction function given by (1).

The total revenue function of the leader is therefore:

$$TR_A = \left[a - b\left(Q_A + \frac{a - c_B}{2b} - \frac{Q_A}{2}\right)\right] \times Q_A \qquad (2)$$

The term in the square brackets is just the inverse demand (and so the price) once we take into account the reaction function of the follower. Equation (2) becomes:

$$TR_A = aQ_A - bQ_A^2 - \frac{a - c_B}{2}Q_A + \frac{b}{2}Q_A^2$$

The marginal revenue of the leader is therefore:

$$\boldsymbol{MR_A \equiv \frac{\partial TR_A}{\partial Q_A} = a - 2bQ_A + bQ_A \frac{a - c}{2}}$$

The output that maximizes the profits of firm A comes from the condition $MR_A = MC_A$, that is: $a - 2bQ_A + bQ_A - (a - c_B)/2 = c_A$. Solve for Q_A:

$$Q_A = \frac{a + c_B - 2c_A}{2b}$$

Once we know the optimal choice for the leader, we can go back to the reaction function of the follower and substitute for the Q_A we just found:

$$Q_B = \frac{a - c_B}{2b} - \left(\frac{a + c_B - 2c_A}{4b}\right)$$

Simplifying that equation we obtain:

$$Q_B = \frac{a - 3c_B + 2c_A}{4b}$$

9.6 Entry and potential competition

So far we have discussed imperfect competition between existing firms. To complete our understanding of such markets, we must also think about the effect of potential competition from new entrants to the industry on the behaviour of existing or incumbent firms. Three cases must be distinguished: where entry is completely easy, where it is difficult by accident and where it is difficult by design.

Contestable markets

Free entry to, and exit from, the industry is a key feature of perfect competition, a market structure in which each firm is tiny relative to the industry. Suppose, however, that we observe an industry with few incumbent firms. Before assuming that our previous analysis of oligopoly is needed, we must think hard about entry and exit. The industry may be a **contestable market**.

A contestable market has free entry and free exit.

By free entry, we mean that all firms, including both incumbents and potential entrants, have access to the same technology and hence have the same cost curves. By free exit, we mean that there are no *sunk* or irrecoverable costs: on leaving the industry, a firm can fully recoup its previous investment expenditure, including money spent on building up knowledge and goodwill.

A contestable market allows *hit-and-run* entry. If the incumbent firms, however few, do not behave as if they were a perfectly competitive industry ($p = MC =$ minimum LAC), an entrant can step in, undercut them and make a temporary profit before quitting again.

As globalization proceeds, we should remember that foreign suppliers are important potential entrants. This can take two forms. First, if monopoly profits are too high in the domestic market, competition from imports may augment supply, bidding down prices and profits in the domestic market. In the extreme case, in which imports surge whenever domestic prices rise above the world price, we are back in the competitive world analysed in Chapter 8.

Globalization also raises the likelihood that foreign firms will set up production facilities in the home market, a tangible form of entry. By raising the supply of potential entrants, globalization increases the relevance of contestable markets as a description of market structure. Moreover, we normally think of an entrant as having to start from scratch. When an existing foreign firm enters the domestic market, its production and marketing expertise may already be highly developed.

Globalization may be a two-edged sword. On the one hand, it raises the size of the relevant market and makes entry easier. On the other hand, by allowing multinationals to become vast by operating in many countries simultaneously, globalization may encourage the formation of large firms that then have substantial market power wherever they operate. Coke and Pepsi are slugging it out for global dominance and Virgin Cola provides only limited competition, even in the UK.

The theory of contestable markets remains controversial. There are many industries in which sunk costs are hard to recover or where the initial expertise may take an entrant some time to acquire, placing it at a temporary disadvantage against incumbent firms. Nor, as we shall shortly see, is it safe to assume that incumbents will not change their behaviour when threatened by entry. But the theory does vividly illustrate that market structure and incumbent behaviour cannot be deduced simply by counting the number of firms in the industry.

In the previous chapter, we were careful to stress that a monopolist is a sole producer *who can completely discount fear of entry*. We now refine the classification in Table 9.1 by discussing entry in more detail.

Innocent entry barriers

Our discussion of entry barriers distinguishes those that occur anyway and those that are deliberately erected by incumbent firms.

The American economist, Joe Bain, identified three types of entry barrier: product differentiation, absolute cost advantages and scale economies. The first of these is not an **innocent barrier**, as we shall shortly explain. Absolute cost advantages, where incumbent firms have lower cost curves than those that entrants will face, may be innocent. If it takes time to learn the business, incumbents will face lower costs, at least in the short run. If they are smart, they may already have located in the most advantageous site. In contrast, if incumbents have undertaken investment or R&D specifically with a view to deterring entrants, this is not an innocent barrier. We take up this issue shortly.

An innocent entry barrier is one not deliberately erected by incumbent firms.

Figure 9.1 showed the role of scale economies as an innocent entry barrier. If minimum efficient scale is large relative to the industry demand curve, an entrant cannot get into the industry without considerably depressing the market price, and it may prove simply impossible to break in at a profit.

The greater such innocent entry barriers, the more appropriate it is to neglect potential competition from entrants. The oligopoly game then comes down to competition between incumbent firms along the lines we discussed in the previous section. Where innocent entry barriers are low, one of two things may happen. Either incumbent firms accept this situation, in which case competition from potential entrants will prevent incumbent firms from exercising much market power – the outcome will be closer to that of perfect competition – or else incumbent firms will try to design some entry barriers of their own.

9.7 Strategic entry deterrence

A *strategy* is a game plan where decision making is interdependent. The word 'strategic' is used in everyday language but it has a precise meaning in economics.

In Figure 9.9 a single incumbent firm plays a game against a potential entrant. The entrant can come in or stay out. If the entrant comes in, the incumbent can opt for the easy life, accept the new rival and agree to share the market – or it can fight. Each party undertakes a series of **strategic moves**. Fighting entry means producing at least as much as before, and perhaps considerably more than before, so that the industry price collapses. In this *price war*, sometimes called *predatory pricing* by the incumbent, both firms do badly and make losses. The top row of boxes in Figure 9.9 shows the profits to the incumbent (in blue) and the entrant (in orange) in each of the three possible outcomes.

> A **strategic move** is one that influences the other person's choice, in a manner favourable to oneself, by affecting the other person's expectations of how one will behave.

If the incumbent is unchallenged it does very well, making profits of 5. The entrant of course makes nothing. If they share the market, both make small profits of 1. In a price war, both make losses. How should the game go?

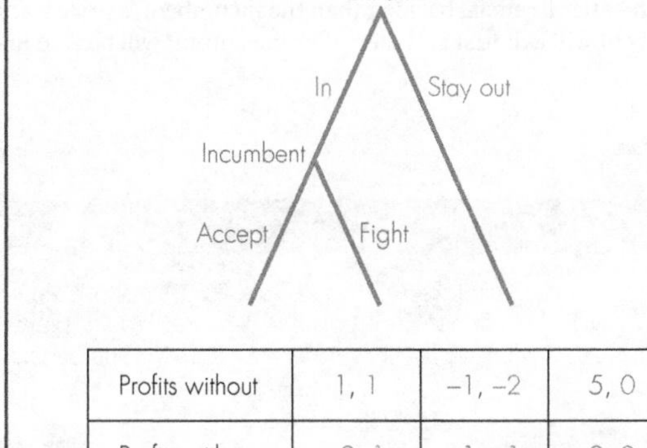

Profits without	1, 1	−1, −2	5, 0
Profits with	−2, 1	−1, −1	2, 0

In the absence of deterrence, if the entrant enters, the incumbent does better to accept entry than to fight. The entrant knows this and enters. Equilibrium is the top left-hand box, and both firms make a profit of 1. But if the incumbent pre-commits an expenditure of 3 which is recouped only if there is a fight, the incumbent resists entry, the entrant stays out and equilibrium is the bottom right-hand box. The incumbent does better, making a profit of 2.

Figure 9.9 **Strategic entry deterrence**

Suppose the entrant comes in. Comparing the left and middle boxes of the top row, the incumbent does better to cave in than to fight. The entrant can figure this out. Any threat by the incumbent to resist entry is not a credible threat – when it comes to the crunch, it will be better to cave in. Much as the incumbent would like the entrant to stay out, in which case the incumbent would make profits of 5, the equilibrium of the game is that the entrant will come in and the incumbent will not resist. Both make profits of 1, the top left-hand box.

The incumbent, however, may have got its act together before the potential entrant appears on the scene. It may be able to invent a binding pre-commitment, forcing itself to resist entry and thereby scare off a future challenge. The incumbent would be ecstatic if a Martian appeared and guaranteed to shoot the incumbent's directors if they ever allowed an entry to be unchallenged. Entrants would expect a fight, would anticipate a loss of 1, and would stay out, leaving the incumbent with a permanent profit of 5.

In the absence of Martians, the incumbent can achieve the same effect by economic means. Suppose the incumbent invests in expensive spare capacity that is unused at low output. The incumbent has low output in the absence of entry or if an entrant is accommodated without a fight. Suppose in these situations the incumbent loses 3 by carrying this excess capacity. The second row of boxes in Figure 9.9 reduces the incumbent's profits by

3 in these two outcomes. In a price war, however, the incumbent's output is high and the spare capacity is no longer wasted; hence we do not need to reduce the incumbent's profit in the middle column of boxes in Figure 9.9. Now consider the game again.

If the entrant comes in, the incumbent loses 2 by caving in but only 1 by fighting. Hence entry is resisted. Foreseeing this, the entrant does not enter, since the entrant loses money in a price war. Hence the equilibrium of the game is the bottom right-hand box and no entry takes place. **Strategic entry deterrence** has been successful. It has also been profitable. Even allowing for the cost of 3 of carrying the spare capacity, the incumbent still makes a profit of 2, which is better than the profit of 1 in the top left-hand box when no deterrence was attempted and the entrant came in.

Strategic entry deterrence is behaviour by incumbent firms to make entry less likely.

Does deterrence always work? No. Suppose in Figure 9.9 we change the right-hand column. In the top row the incumbent gets a profit of 3 if no entry occurs. Without the pre-commitment, the equilibrium is the top left-hand box, as before. But if the incumbent has to spend 3 on a spare capacity pre-commitment, it now makes a profit of 0 in the bottom right-hand box when entry is deterred. The entrant is still deterred but the incumbent would have done better not to invest in spare capacity and to let the entrant in.

This model suggests that price wars should never happen. If the incumbent really is going to fight, then the entrant should not have entered. This of course requires the entrant to know accurately the profits of the incumbent in the different boxes and therefore correctly predict its behaviour. In the real world, entrants sometimes get it wrong. Moreover, if the entrant has much better financial backing than the incumbent, a price war may be a good investment for the entrant. The incumbent will exit first and thereafter the entrant will be able to cash in and get its losses back with interest.

CASE 9.2

BARRIERS AT THE CHECKOUT

In 2004 the Morrisons supermarket chain finally completed its takeover of rival Safeway. At a stroke, Morrisons was catapulted from the supermarket minnow, with a 6 per cent market share, to a big league player with 17 per cent of the UK market, only marginally less than Sainsbury's, onetime leader of the supermarket industry.

The takeover of Safeway was contested, with Tesco, Asda and Sainsbury's all mounting rival bids to Morrisons'. At one stage, Philip Green, the owner of high-street retailer British Home Stores (Bhs), also registered an interest in Safeway. Safeway was such an attractive target because it provided the last chance to enter the supermarket industry. Without access to land, and facing difficulty getting planning permission for new supermarkets, the only entry mode was a takeover. With Safeway now in the hands of Morrisons, and the industry consolidated into large players, the next takeover will be even more difficult.

Morrisons supermarket in Newport, Isle of Wight. © Editor5807

Is spare capacity the only pre-commitment available to incumbents? Pre-commitments must be irreversible, otherwise they are an empty threat, and they must increase the chances that the incumbent will fight. Anything with the character of fixed and sunk costs may work: fixed costs artificially increase scale economies and make the incumbent keener on high output, and sunk costs cannot be reversed. Advertising to invest in goodwill and brand loyalty is a good example. So is product proliferation. If the incumbent has only one brand, an entrant may hope to break in with a different brand. But if the incumbent has a complete range of brands or models, an entrant will have to compete across the whole product range.

9.8 Summing up

Few industries in the real world are like the textbook extremes of perfect competition and pure monopoly. Most are imperfectly competitive. This chapter introduced you to types of imperfect competition. Game theory in general, and concepts such as commitment, credibility and deterrence, allow economists to analyse many of the practical concerns of big business.

What have we learned? First, market structure and the behaviour of incumbent firms are determined *simultaneously*. Economists used to start with a market structure, determined by the extent of scale economies relative to the industry demand curve, then deduce how the incumbent firms would behave (monopoly, oligopoly, perfect competition), then check out these predictions against performance indicators, such as the extent to which prices exceeded marginal cost. Now we realize that strategic behaviour by incumbent firms can affect entry, and hence market structure, except where entry is almost trivially easy.

Second, and related, we have learned the importance of *potential* competition, which may come from domestic firms considering entry or from imports from abroad. The number of firms observed in the industry today conveys little information about the extent of the market power they truly exercise. If entry is easy, even a single incumbent or apparent monopolist may find it unprofitable to depart significantly from perfectly competitive behaviour.

Finally, we have seen how many business practices of the real world – price wars, advertising, brand proliferation, excess capacity or excessive research and development – can be understood as strategic competition in which, to be effective, threats must be made credible by prior commitments.

Summary

- **Imperfect competition** exists when individual firms believe they face downward-sloping demand curves. The most important forms are monopolistic competition, oligopoly and pure monopoly.
- **Pure monopoly** status can be conferred by legislation, as when an industry is nationalized or a temporary patent is awarded. When **minimum efficient scale** is very large relative to the industry demand curve, this innocent entry barrier may be sufficiently high to produce a natural monopoly in which all threat of entry can be ignored.
- At the opposite extreme, entry and exit may be costless. The market is **contestable**, and incumbent firms must mimic perfectly competitive behaviour to avoid being flooded by entrants. With an intermediate size of entry barrier, the industry may be an oligopoly.
- **Monopolistic competitors** face free entry to and exit from the industry but are individually small and make similar though not identical products. Each has limited monopoly power in its special brand. In long-run equilibrium, price equals average cost but exceeds marginal revenue and marginal cost at the tangency equilibrium.
- **Oligopolists** face tension between collusion to maximize joint profits and competition for a larger share of smaller joint profits. **Collusion** may be formal, as in a cartel, or informal. Without **credible threats** of punishment by its partners, each firm faces a temptation to cheat.
- **Game theory** analyses interdependent decisions in which each player chooses a strategy. In the Prisoner's Dilemma game, each firm has a dominant strategy. With binding commitments, both players could do better by guaranteeing not to cheat on the collusive solution.
- A **reaction function** shows one player's best response to the actions of other players. In **Nash equilibrium** reaction functions intersect. No player then wishes to change her decision.

- In **Cournot behaviour** each firm treats the output of its rival as given. In **Bertrand behaviour** each firm treats the price of its rival as given. Nash–Bertrand equilibrium entails pricing at marginal cost. Nash–Cournot equilibrium entails lower output, higher prices and profits. However, firms still fail to maximize joint profits because each neglects the fact that its output expansion hurts its rivals.
- A firm with a **first-mover advantage** acts as a **Stackelberg leader**. By deducing the subsequent reaction of its rival, it produces higher output, knowing the rival will then have to produce lower output. Moving first is a useful commitment.
- **Innocent entry barriers** are made by nature, and arise from scale economies or absolute cost advantages of incumbent firms. **Strategic entry barriers** are made in boardrooms and arise from credible commitments to resist entry if challenged. Only in certain circumstances is strategic entry deterrence profitable for incumbents.

Review questions

EASY

1 'Since a firm's optimal behaviour depends on how it believes that its rival(s) will react, there are as many output decisions, and hence equilibriums, as there are guesses about what rivals will do.' How do economists try to narrow down the assumptions that firms make about their rivals?

2 Many of the interesting games are games against the government. Think of a European airline, until recently state-owned, now private but losing money under the pressure of high oil prices and the growth of low-cost airlines. Believing that the government will bail it out if the worse comes to the worst, the airline has no incentive to take today the tough measures needed to make its business profitable. How can the government signal that it will not bail out the airline, forcing the airline to improve or go bust?

3 A good-natured parent knows that children sometimes need punishing but also knows that, when it comes to the crunch, the child will be let off with a warning. Can the parent undertake any pre-commitment to make the threat of punishment credible?

4 Think of five adverts on television. Is their function primarily informative or the erection of entry barriers to the industry?

5 **Common fallacies** Why are these statements wrong? (a) Competitive firms should get together to restrict output and drive up the price. (b) Firms would not advertise unless they expected advertising to increase sales. (c) A firm in a monopolistically competitive market faces a horizontal demand curve for its product.

MEDIUM

6 The table below shows the three-firm *CR* (concentration ratio) and the *NP* (market size divided by minimum efficient scale) for various industries in the UK, France and Germany in the mid-1970s. Refer to the table and answer the following questions:

Concentration and scale economies

	UK		France		Germany	
Industry	*CR*	*NP*	*CR*	*NP*	*CR*	*NP*
Refrigerators	65	1	100	2	72	3
Cigarettes	94	3	100	2	94	3
Refineries	79	8	60	7	47	9
Brewing	47	11	63	5	17	16
Fabrics	28	57	23	57	16	52
Shoes	17	165	13	128	20	197

(a) True or false: In the fabric industry in Germany, the top three firms accounted for more than half of the market share.

(b) True or false: In the shoe industry in the UK, France and Germany, economies of scale were relatively unimportant.

(c) What can you conclude about the structure of the refrigerator and petroleum industries in the mid-1970s?

(d) In the cigarette and petroleum industries, were there many firms that operated at minimum efficient scale? Explain your answer.

7 An industry faces the demand curve:

Q	1	2	3	4	5	6	7	8	9	10
P	10	9	8	7	6	5	4	3	2	1

(a) Suppose it is a monopoly whose constant $MC = 3$: what price and output are chosen?

(b) Now suppose there are two firms, each with $MC = AC = 3$: what price and output maximize joint profits if they collude?

(c) Why might each firm be tempted to cheat if it can avoid retaliation by the other?

8 With the above industry demand curve, two firms, A and Z, begin with half the market each when charging the monopoly price. Marginal cost is constant at $MC =$ £3.

Now, Z decides to cheat and believes A will stick to its old output level. (a) The following table shows the industry demand curve that Z thinks it faces. Compute the total revenue and marginal revenue and complete the table. (b) What price and output would Z then choose?

Q	1	2	3	4	5	6	7
P	8	7	6	5	4	3	2

MEDIUM

9 Consider two firms, A and B. They have two possible strategies, pricing low or pricing high. The profits that each firm makes from those strategies are reported below:

		Firm B	
		P high	*P* low
Firm A	*P* high	3,3	1,6
	P low	6,1	5,5

What is meant by a Nash equilibrium? Find the Nash equilibrium for the strategies in the grid above.

10 Consider a market with two firms, 1 and 2, producing a homogeneous good. The market demand is $P = 100 - 3(Q_1 + Q_2)$, where Q_1 is the quantity produced by firm 1 and Q_2 is the quantity produced by firm 2. The total cost for firm 1 is $TC_1 = 40Q_1$, while the total cost for firm 2 is $TC_2 = 40Q_2$. Each firm behaves like a competitive firm.

(a) What is the equilibrium quantity in the market?

(b) Suppose both firms exhibit Cournot behaviour. Given that their reaction functions are $Q_1 = 20 - 2Q_2$ and $Q_2 = 20 - 2Q_1$, how would their output change compared to (a)?

11 Vehicle repairers sometimes suggest that mechanics should be licensed so that repairs are done only by qualified people. Some economists argue that customers can always ask whether a mechanic was trained at a reputable institution without needing to see any licence. (a) Evaluate the arguments for and against licensing car mechanics. (b) How would licensing affect the market for mechanics? (c) Are the arguments the same for licensing doctors?

12 **Essay question** 'Globalization, by increasing the size of the market, reduces market power of individual firms and the need to address strategic interactions.' 'Globalization makes mergers more attractive and thus enhances worries about market power.' Is either of these views correct? Or are both correct?

13 Two identical firms, 1 and 2, compete on quantities. The reaction function of firm 1 is $Q_1 = 15 - \frac{1}{2}Q_2$, while for firm 2 we have $Q_2 = 15 - \frac{1}{2}Q_1$. In the table below we have the total quantity produced in the market:

$Q_1 + Q_2$	2	6	10	14	18	22	26	30	34

Using the fact that both firms must produce the same quantity, plot the reaction functions of the two firms in a graph. How is the equilibrium quantity determined?

HARD

14 Consider a market with two firms, 1 and 2 producing a homogeneous good. The market demand is $P = 130 - 2(Q_1 - Q_2)$, where Q_1 is the quantity produced by firm 1 and Q_2 is the quantity produced by firm 2. The total cost for firm 1 is $TC_1 = 10Q_1$, while the total cost for firm 2 is $TC_2 = 10Q_2$. Each firm chooses the quantity to best maximize profits.

(a) From the condition $MR_1 = MC_1$, find the reaction function of firm 1, and from $MR_2 = MC_2$, find the reaction function of firm 2.

(b) Find the equilibrium quantity produced by each firm by solving the system of the two reaction functions you found in (a). Sketch your solution graphically.

(c) Find the equilibrium price and then find the profit of each firm.

For solutions to these questions, contact your lecturer.

CHAPTER 13

Welfare economics

Learning Outcomes

By the end of this chapter, you should be able to:

1 understand what we mean by welfare economics
2 describe horizontal and vertical equity
3 understand the concept of Pareto efficiency
4 recognize how the 'invisible hand' may achieve efficiency
5 define the concept of market failure
6 recognize why partial removal of distortions may be harmful
7 identify the problem of externalities and possible solutions
8 understand how monopoly power causes market failure
9 analyse distortions from pollution and congestion
10 understand why missing markets create distortions
11 analyse the economics of climate change

In this chapter we analyse the concepts of efficiency and equity (fairness), and examine reasons for market failure.

Chapter 1 noted that markets are not the only way society can resolve what, how and for whom to produce. Communist economies relied heavily on central direction or command. Are markets a good way to allocate scarce resources? What is a 'good' way? Is it fair that some people earn much more than others in a market economy? These are not positive issues about how the economy works but normative issues about how well it works. They are normative because the assessment depends on the value judgements adopted by the assessor.

Left - and right-wing parties disagree about how well a market economy works. The right believes the market fosters choice, incentives and efficiency. The left emphasizes the market's failings and the need for government intervention. What lies behind the disagreement? Two themes recur in the analysis of **welfare economics**. The first is *allocative efficiency*. Is the economy getting the most out of its scarce resources or are they being squandered? The second is *equity*. How fair is the *distribution* of goods and services among different members of society?

Welfare economics deals with normative issues. It does not describe how the economy works but assesses how well it works.

Horizontal equity is the identical treatment of identical people.

Vertical equity is the different treatment of different people in order to reduce the consequences of these innate differences.

13.1 Equity and efficiency

Whether or not either concepts of equity – horizontal or vertical – are desirable is a pure value judgement. **Horizontal equity** rules out discrimination between people whose economic characteristics and performance are identical. **Vertical equity** is the Robin Hood principle of taking from the rich to give to the poor.

Many people agree that horizontal equity is a good thing. In contrast, the extent to which resources should be redistributed from the 'haves' to the 'have-nots' to increase vertical equity is an issue on which people disagree.

Efficient resource allocation

A resource allocation is a complete description of who does what and who gets what.

Suppose that **allocations** are made by a dictator. Feasible allocations depend on the technology and resources available to the economy. The ultimate worth of any allocation depends on consumer tastes – how people value what they are given.

Figure 13.1 shows an economy with only two people, David and Susie. The initial allocation at A gives David a quantity of goods Q_D and Susie a quantity Q_S. Are society's resources being wasted? By reorganizing things, suppose society can produce at B, to the north-east of A. If David and Susie assess utility by the quantity of goods they get themselves, and if they would each rather have more goods than less, B is a better allocation than A. Both David and Susie get more. It is inefficient to produce at A if production at B is possible. Similarly, a move from A to C makes both David and Susie worse off. If it is possible to be at A, it is inefficient to be at C.

Figure 13.1 **Allocating goods to two people**

What about a move from A to E or F? One person gains; the other person loses. Whether this change is desirable depends on how we value David's utility relative to Susie's. If we think David's utility is very important we might prefer F to A, even though Susie's utility is reduced.

Since different people will make different value judgements, there is no unambiguous answer to the question of whether a move from A to D, E or F is desirable. It depends on who makes the assessment.

For a given set of consumer tastes, resources and technology, an allocation is Pareto-efficient if there is no other feasible allocation that makes some people better off and nobody worse off.

To try to separate the discussion of equity from the discussion of efficiency, modern welfare economics uses the idea of **Pareto efficiency**, named after the economist Vilfredo Pareto.

In Figure 13.1 a move from A to B or A to G is a *Pareto gain*. Susie is better off; David is no worse off. If B or G is feasible, A is *Pareto-inefficient*. A free lunch is available.

A move from A to D makes David better off but Susie worse off. The Pareto criterion has nothing to say about this change. To evaluate it, we need a judgement about the relative values of David's and Susie's utility. The Pareto principle is of limited use in comparing allocations on efficiency grounds. It only allows us to evaluate moves to the north-east or the south-west in Figure 13.1. Yet it is the most we can say about efficiency without making value judgements about equity.

Figure 13.2 takes the argument a stage further. By reorganizing production, we can make the economy produce anywhere inside or on the frontier *AB*. From inside the frontier, a Pareto gain can be achieved by moving to the north-east on to the frontier. Any point inside the frontier is Pareto-inefficient. One person can be made better off without making the other worse off. But *all* points on the frontier are Pareto-efficient. One person can get more only by giving the other person less. Since no Pareto gain is possible, every point on the frontier is Pareto-efficient.

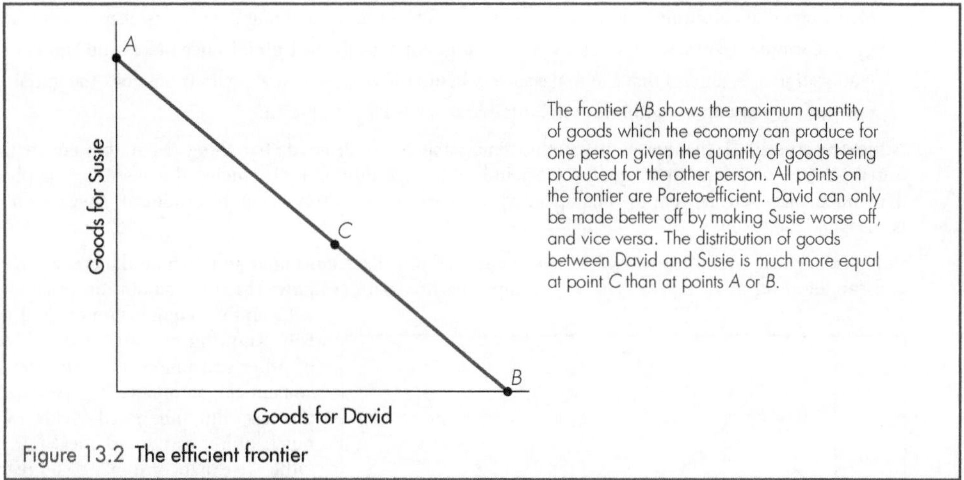

Figure 13.2 The efficient frontier

Thus society should never choose an inefficient allocation inside the frontier. Which of the efficient points on the frontier is most desirable will depend on the value judgement of the relative values of David's and Susie's utility, a judgement about equity.

13.2 Perfect competition and Pareto efficiency

Will a free market economy find a Pareto-efficient allocation, or must it be guided there by government intervention?

Competitive equilibrium in free markets

Suppose there are many producers and many consumers, but only two goods: meals and films. Each market is a free, unregulated market and is perfectly competitive. In equilibrium, suppose the price of meals is £5 and the price of films is £10. Labour is the only factor of production and workers can move freely between industries. We now work through seven steps:

1 The last film yields consumers £10 worth of extra utility. If it yielded less (more) extra utility than its £10 purchase price, the last consumer would buy fewer (more) films. Similarly, the last meal must yield consumers £5 worth of extra utility. Hence consumers could swap 2 meals (£10 worth of utility) for 1 film (£10 worth of utility) without changing their utility.

2 Since each firm sets price equal to marginal cost *MC*, the *MC* of the last meal is £5 and the *MC* of the last film is £10.

3 Labour earns the same wage rate in both industries in competitive equilibrium. Otherwise, workers would move to the industry offering higher wages.

4 The *MC* of output in either industry is the wage divided by the marginal physical product of labour *MPL*. Higher wages raise marginal cost, but a higher *MPL* means fewer extra workers are needed to make an extra unit of output.

5 Wages are equal in the two industries but the marginal cost of meals (£5) is half the marginal cost of films (£10). Hence, the *MPL* is twice as high in the meals industry as in the film industry.

6 Hence reducing film output by 1 unit, transferring the labour thus freed to the meals industry, raises output of meals by 2 units. The *MPL* is twice as high in meals as in films. Feasible resource allocation between the two industries allows society to swap 2 meals for 1 film.

7 Step 1 says that consumers can swap 2 meals for 1 film without changing their utility. Step 6 says that, by reallocating resources, producers swap an output of 2 meals for 1 film. Hence there is no feasible reallocation of resources that can make society better off. Since no Pareto gain is possible, the initial position – competitive equilibrium in both markets – is Pareto-efficient.

Notice the crucial role that prices play in this remarkable result. Prices do two things. First, they ensure that the initial position of competitive equilibrium is indeed an *equilibrium*. By balancing the quantities supplied and demanded, prices ensure that the final quantity of goods being consumed can be produced. They ensure that it is a feasible allocation.

But in *competitive* equilibrium prices perform a second role. Each consumer and each producer is a price-taker and cannot affect market prices. In our example, each consumer knows that the equilibrium price of meals is £5 and the equilibrium price of films is £10. Knowing nothing about the actions of other consumers and producers, each consumer automatically ensures that the last film purchased yields twice as much utility as the last meal purchased. Otherwise that consumer could rearrange purchases out of a given income to increase her utility.

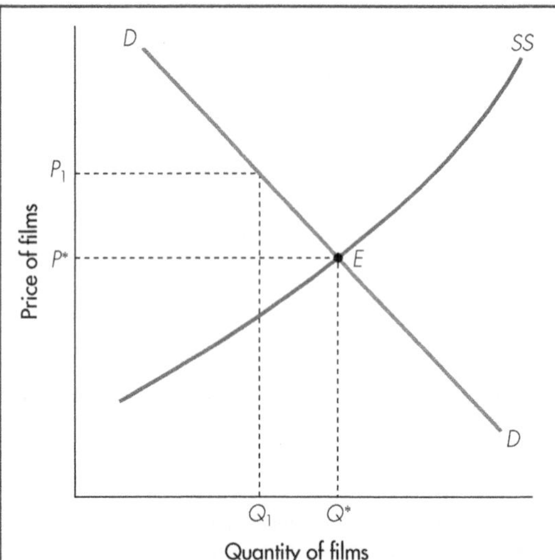

At any output such as Q_1 the last film must yield consumers P_1 pounds worth of extra utility; otherwise they would not demand Q_1. The supply curve *SS* for the competitive film industry is also the marginal cost of films. If the meals industry is in competitive equilibrium, the price of a meal is also the value of its marginal utility to consumers. Thus the marginal cost of a film is not only its opportunity cost in meals but also the value of the marginal utility consumers would have derived from those meals. Hence at any film output below Q^* the marginal utility of films exceeds the marginal utility of meals sacrificed to produce an extra film. Above Q^* the marginal utility of films is less than the marginal utility of meals sacrificed. The equilibrium point *E* for films and the corresponding equilibrium point in the market for meals thus ensure that resources are efficiently allocated between the two industries. No reallocation could make all consumers better off.

Figure 13.3 **Competitive equilibrium and Pareto efficiency**

Thus by her individual actions facing given prices, each consumer arranges that 1 film could be swapped for 2 meals with no change in utility. Similarly, every producer, merely by setting its own marginal cost equal to the price of its output, ensures that the marginal cost of films is twice the marginal cost of meals. Thus it takes society twice as many resources to make an extra film as it does to make an extra meal. By rearranging production, transferring labour between industries, society can swap 2 meals for 1 film, exactly the trade-off that leaves consumer utility unaffected.

Thus, as if by an 'invisible hand', prices are guiding individual consumers and producers, each pursuing only self-interest, to an allocation of the economy's resources that is Pareto-efficient. Nobody can be made better off without someone else becoming worse off.

Figure 13.3 makes the same point. *DD* is the market demand curve for one of the goods, say films. At a price P_1, a quantity of films Q_1 is demanded. The last film demanded yields consumers P_1 pounds' worth of utility; otherwise they would buy a different quantity. Hence *DD* shows also the marginal utility of the last unit of films that consumers purchase. When Q_1 films are purchased, the last film yields exactly P_1 pounds' worth of extra utility to consumers.

In a competitive industry, the supply curve for films *SS* is also the marginal cost of films. The variable factor, labour, is paid its marginal value product in each industry. Labour mobility ensures wage rates are equal in the two industries. Hence the marginal cost of making the last film is the value of the meals sacrificed by using the last worker to make films not meals.

Prices ensure that both industries are in equilibrium. Figure 13.3 shows that, in equilibrium at *E*, the marginal utility of the last film equals its marginal cost. But the marginal cost of the last film is the value of meals sacrificed; the price of meals multiplied by the meals forgone by using labour to make that last film. However, the meals industry is also in equilibrium. An equivalent diagram for the meals industry shows that the equilibrium price of meals is also the marginal utility of the last meal purchased. Hence the value of meals sacrificed to make the last film is also the marginal utility of the last meal multiplied by the number of meals sacrificed.

Thus, provided the *meals* industry is in competitive equilibrium, the marginal cost curve for the *film* industry is the extra pounds' worth of utility sacrificed by using scarce resources to make another film instead of extra meals. It is the opportunity cost in utility terms of the resources being used in the film industry. And equilibrium in the film industry, by equating the marginal utility of films to the marginal utility of the meals sacrificed to make the last film, guarantees that society's resources are allocated efficiently.

At any output of films below the equilibrium quantity Q^*, the marginal consumer benefit of another film exceeds the marginal consumer valuation of the meals that would have to be sacrificed to produce that extra film. At any output of films above Q^*, society is devoting too many resources to the film industry. The marginal value of the last film is less than the marginal value of the meals that could have been produced by transferring resources to the meals industry. Competitive equilibrium ensures that there is no resource transfer between industries that would make all consumers better off.

CONCEPT 13.1

GENERAL VS PARTIAL EQUILIBRIUM: AN EXAMPLE FROM SCHOOL POLICY

In discussing the efficiency properties of a competitive equilibrium we have implicitly followed a *general equilibrium* approach. By that, we mean a situation whereby multiple markets are simultaneously in equilibrium. For example, in the analysis in Section 13.2 we have considered two markets for final goods (films and meals) and one market for inputs (the labour market). In general equilibrium we analyse how different markets are linked to and interact with each other.

This is a different approach from the one we have used in previous chapters, where we have focused mainly on what happens in a single market. When we analyse just a single market, without looking at any interaction with other markets in the economy (remember the expression 'other things equal' that we have used widely in previous chapters), we adopt a *partial equilibrium* approach.

Whatever approach is more suitable in analysing a particular case depends on the objective of the analysis itself. In many cases, a partial equilibrium analysis of a particular market is fine if the objective is to understand that particular market only.

When we are interested in analysing how different markets are linked together, a general equilibrium approach is preferred. The differences between a partial equilibrium and a general equilibrium approach are more evident when we evaluate government policies. Here is an example on school policy.

Heckman[1] et al. (1998) studied the partial and general equilibrium effects of a particular school policy: a \$500 tuition subsidy to college students. The partial equilibrium effect will focus on the effect that such a ►

1 James J. Heckman shared the Nobel Prize in Economics in 2000 with Daniel McFadden.

policy has on the college students, everything else constant. They found that a $500 tuition subsidy leads to an increase of 5.3 per cent in college attendance. This is quite intuitive; with such a subsidy college fees become less expensive and more students can go to college.

However, this is the partial equilibrium effect only.

To get the general equilibrium we need to understand how the effect of the policy is linked to other markets. In particular, Heckman et al. focused on the labour market for college graduates. Now there are two markets linked together: the market for colleges and the labour market for college graduates.

They found that, once we take into account the link between the two markets, the result of the policy is an increase in college students of only 0.49 per cent. Why is that?

In response to the tuition subsidy more people go to college. This makes high school graduates more scarce in the labour market and college graduates more common. As a result, wages of college graduates will fall (higher labour supply of college graduates in the labour market), while wages of high school graduates will increase. Rational students will anticipate this effect and so the result of the policy will be mitigated.

Source: J. Heckman, L. Lochner and C. Taber, 'General equilibrium treatment effects: A study of tuition policy', *American Economic Review* 88, no. 2 (1998): 381–386. © 1998 James J. Heckman, Lance Lochner and Christopher Taber.

Equity and efficiency

We showed that under certain conditions – that is, when all markets are perfectly competitive – an economy can attain a particular Pareto-efficient allocation. This result is known as the *first theorem of welfare economics.* The previous section showed however that there are many possible Pareto-efficient allocations, each with a different distribution of utility between different members of society. What determines each one?

People have different innate abilities, human capital and wealth. These differences mean people earn different incomes in a market economy. They also affect the pattern of consumer demand. Brazil, with a very unequal distribution of income and wealth, has a high demand for luxuries such as servants. In more egalitarian Denmark, nobody can afford servants.

Different inheritances of ability, capital and wealth thus imply different demand curves and determine different equilibrium prices and quantities. In principle, by varying the distribution of initial income-earning potential, we could make the economy pick out each possible Pareto-efficient allocation as its competitive equilibrium. This result is known as the *second theorem of welfare economics.*

The second welfare theorem implies that a government can have a role in determining which efficient allocation is decided by the market. The government is elected to express the value judgements of the majority. If the market gets the economy to the Pareto-efficient frontier, the government can make the value judgement about which point on this frontier the economy should attain. Different efficient allocations correspond to different initial distributions of income-earning potential in a competitive economy. The government could redistribute income and wealth through taxation and welfare benefits in such a way that the market will then attain a particular efficient allocation.

This seems a powerful case for the free enterprise ideal. The government should let markets get on with the job of allocating resources efficiently. We do not need regulations, investigatory bodies or state-run enterprises. The government can redistribute income without impairing the efficient functioning of a free market economy. The right-wing case can be backed up by rigorous economic arguments.

However, the left-wing case can also be made. *Under certain conditions* free markets lead to a Pareto-efficient allocation. The right believes that those conditions tend to hold in reality and, even if they don't, that situation does not seriously challenge the case for a free market economy. The left believes that the fact that those conditions may not hold in reality is so serious that substantial government intervention is necessary to *improve* the way the economy works.

CONCEPT 13.2

EQUITY VS EFFICIENCY IN TRADING: THE EDGEWORTH BOX

Here we show how free trading between agents can be Pareto efficient.

Suppose an economy has two agents, John and Liz. There are two goods in this economy, chocolate bars and DVDs. Each agent is born with an amount of both goods. Suppose Liz is born with 70 chocolate bars and 10 DVDs. This is called Liz's *endowment*. John instead has an initial endowment of 30 chocolate bars and 40 DVDs. The total available amount of chocolate bars is therefore 100 (= 70 + 30) and we have 50 DVDs available. There is no production activity. John and Liz must decide between consuming their initial endowment or trading with each other.

Even though this example is very simplistic and stylized, we can still use it to gather general insights on how trading can achieve a Pareto-efficient allocation of goods and how equitable can be that allocation.

To analyse this simple economy, we use a graphical device known as the Edgeworth box (named after the British economist, Francis Ysidro Edgeworth). This is shown in the figure below.

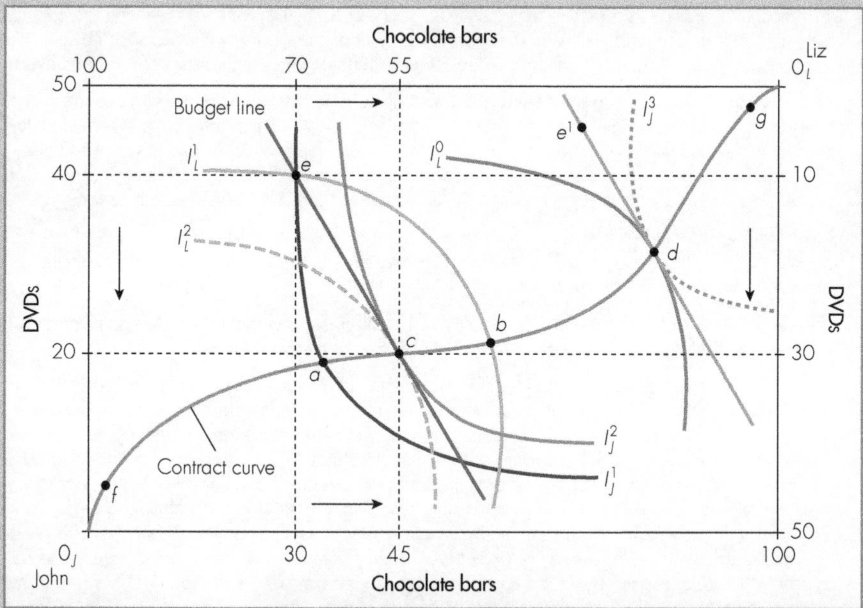

To construct the Edgeworth box, we take two graphs (such as that in Figure 5.3), one for each agent, and we rotate one of the graphs and put it on top of the other to form a box. The length and height of the Edgeworth box are given by the total amount of goods available in the economy. In our case, the length is given by 100 chocolate bars and the height by 50 DVDs. Every point inside the box denotes a particular allocation of goods between the two individuals. Point e represents the initial endowments of Liz and John. At that point, Liz has 70 chocolate bars and 10 DVDs while John has 30 chocolate bars and 40 DVDs.

For both individuals, we draw standard indifference curves representing their preferences for chocolate bars and DVDs. The origin of the graph representing John's indifference curves is the bottom-left corner. His indifference curves have the usual shape. In the graph we plot three of them, I_J^1, I_J^2 and I_J^3. Indifference curves further away from the origin denote higher utility. Therefore John's utility increases as we move from the bottom-left corner towards the top-right corner. For Liz's indifference curves, the opposite is true. Liz's utility increases as we move from the top-right of the box towards the bottom-left. We display three possible indifference curves for Liz, I_L^1, I_L^2 and I_L^3.

Finally, we assume that there is a third agent, Robert. He does not have any goods and he does not trade. He does just one thing: he shouts *relative prices* to John and Liz. For example, making p the price of chocolate bars and q the price of DVDs, he can shout $p/q = 2$ or $p/q = 0.5$, and so on. Robert is called an *auctioneer*. John and Liz take those prices as given and every time they hear a relative price, they decide how much of both goods to trade with each other. Trade occurs only if it is mutually beneficial.

Of course, John and Liz can keep and consume their initial endowment, meaning they do not need to engage in trading. The question is: if they trade, can they achieve a better allocation compared to their initial endowment?

By looking at the Edgeworth box, we can see that the initial allocation is point e. That point lies on Liz's indifference curve I_L^1 and on John's indifference curve I_J^1. They both benefit from trading. They can trade with each other to reach any allocation on the curve connecting points a and b. Any such allocation is a *Pareto gain* compared to their initial endowment allocation. Which allocation between a and b will be chosen? This depends on the relative prices shouted by Robert. In the box we depict a budget line. This represents a line with a slope given by the negative of the relative price of chocolate bars and DVDs; that is, $-p/q$. If the relative price shouted by Robert is the one that gives rise to the budget line depicted in the box, then the chosen allocation is point c, whereby John trades 20 DVDs with Liz in exchange for 15 chocolate bars. At point c, John ends up with 20 DVDs and 45 chocolate bars, while Liz ends up with 30 DVDs and 55 chocolate bars. Once allocation c is reached, no further gain from trading can be achieved.

At allocation c, we have that Liz's marginal rate of substitution (MRS_L) is equal to John's marginal rate of substitution (MRS_J). Liz's indifference curve I_L^2 is tangent to John's indifference curve I_J^2 and they are both tangent to the budget line. Therefore at point c we have $MRS_L = MRS_J = p/q$ in absolute values. Allocation c is Pareto-efficient. There is no way to modify the allocation of goods between the two agents without decreasing the utility of at least one of them. Allocation c represents a *first-best* allocation.

Notice the important result here: there is a relative price level that sustains a Pareto-efficient allocation of goods. This is the message of the first welfare theorem. Competitive markets, through the price system, allocate resources in the most efficient way.

The set of all feasible Pareto-efficient allocations is called the *contract curve*. At each point on the contract curve it must be true that the marginal rate of substitution of the two agents is equal.

Let's now turn to the issue of equity. Any allocation on the contract curve is Pareto-efficient. But allocations such as f or g imply that one of the agents obtains almost all goods while the other gets almost nothing. They are not very equitable. The chosen allocation on the contract curve depends on the initial endowment. Suppose the initial endowment is point e^1. John is born wealthier than Liz. By trading, Liz and John can now reach allocation d on the contract curve. Suppose that Robert now plays another role, that of a *government*. Robert feels that allocation d is not equitable because it results in John having most of both goods. He would prefer John and Liz to share a more even number of both goods as a result of their trading, like in allocation c. He can do the following: before trading takes place he imposes *lump sum* taxes and transfers to Liz and John.[2] In particular, he taxes John by taking some of his chocolate bars and some of his DVDs and transfers them to Liz. If he does a good job, he changes the initial endowments of John and Liz from e^1 to e. Then he lets John and Liz trade so that they can achieve allocation c.

This result shows that, by properly redistributing the initial endowments of the agents, we may sustain a Pareto-efficient allocation of resources. This is the main message of the second welfare theorem.

13.3 Distortions and the second-best

Competitive equilibrium is efficient because the independent actions of producers setting marginal cost equal to price, and consumers setting marginal benefits equal to price, ensure that the marginal cost of producing a good just equals its marginal benefit to consumers.

2 Lump sum taxes are fixed amounts that do not change with changes in the entity taxed. They are an example of non-distortionary taxes.

Taxation as a distortion

To finance subsidies to the poor, a government must tax the incomes of rich people or the goods rich people buy. Suppose everyone buys meals, but only the rich can afford to go to the cinema. A subsidy for the poor can be financed by a tax on films.

In Section 4.9 we showed that the introduction of a tax in a market has the effect of creating a wedge between the price paid by the consumers and the price received by the suppliers. Figure 13.4 shows the effects of introducing a tax on the market for films. The pre-tax price of films paid by consumers (P_1) exceeds the post-tax price received by makers of films (P_2). The difference between the two prices is the tax on each film. Consumers equate the tax-inclusive price to the value of the marginal benefit they receive from the last film, but suppliers equate the marginal cost of films to the lower net-of-tax price of films.

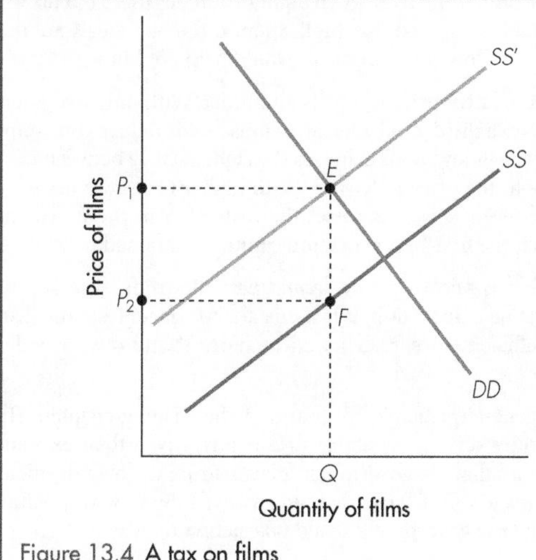

DD shows the demand for films and the marginal benefit of the last film to consumers. *SS* shows the quantity of films supplied at each price received by producers and is also the marginal social cost of producing films. Suppose each unit of films bears a tax equal to the vertical distance *EF*. To show the tax-inclusive price required to induce producers to produce each output, we must draw the new supply curve *SS'* that is a constant vertical distance *EF* above *SS*. The equilibrium quantity of films is *Q*. Consumers pay a price P_1, producers receive a price P_2 and the tax per film is the distance *EF*. At the equilibrium quantity *Q* the marginal benefit is P_1 but the marginal social cost is P_2. Society would make a net gain by producing more films. Hence the equilibrium quantity.

Figure 13.4 **A tax on films**

Because of the tax the price system no longer equates the marginal cost of making films with the marginal benefit of consuming films. The marginal benefit of another film exceeds its marginal cost. The tax on films induces too few films compared to what society would like.

Earlier, we showed that the marginal cost of a film equals the value of the extra meals that society could have had instead. When films are taxed, the marginal benefit of another film exceeds its marginal cost, and hence exceeds the marginal benefit of the extra meals that society could have had by using resources differently. By transferring labour from meals into films, society could make some people better off without making anyone else worse off.

A similar argument holds for any other commodity we tax. A tax causes a discrepancy between the price the purchaser pays and the price the seller receives. The 'invisible hand' no longer equates marginal benefits of resources in different uses.

The choice between efficiency and equity is now clear. If the economy is perfectly competitive, and if the government is happy with the current income distribution, competitive free market equilibrium is efficient and the income distribution desirable.

A distortion exists if society's marginal cost of producing a good does not equal society's marginal benefit from consuming that good.

However if, as a pure value judgement, the government dislikes this income distribution, it has to tax some people to provide subsidies for others. Yet the very act of raising taxes introduces a **distortion**. The resulting equilibrium has a more desirable distribution but is less efficient. Governments may have to make trade-offs between efficiency and equity.

One explanation for differing political attitudes to the market economy is a difference in value judgements about equity. Later, we will see that there may also be disagreements in positive economics. We consider other distortions in the next section. Before leaving our tax example, there is one final point to make.

The second-best

The first-best allocation has no distortions and is fully efficient.

When there is no distortion in the market for *meals*, a tax on *films* leads to an inefficient allocation. If we could abolish the tax on films, neither industry would be distorted and we get the **first-best allocation**.

Suppose, however, that we cannot get rid of the tax on films. The government needs tax revenue to pay for national defence or its EU budget contribution. Given an unavoidable tax on films, at least it should not tax meals as well.

This plausible view is in fact *quite wrong*. Suppose both industries are in equilibrium but there is a tax on films. Above, we saw that too few films are produced and consumed. By implication, too many meals are therefore produced and consumed. Given an inevitable tax on films, a tax on meals would help not hinder.

A suitable tax on meals could restore the original relative price of meals and films. With only two goods, this would restore the first-best. However, there is always a third good – leisure. Households reduce consumption of leisure in order to supply labour for work. Taxing meals and films achieves the right balance between meals and films, but makes the price of both wrong relative to the price of leisure. With higher taxes, the net wage falls, changing the implicit price of leisure. Therefore, even if we can offset the distortion in the film market by introducing an appropriate tax in the meal market, the first-best allocation cannot be attained.

The second-best is the most efficient outcome that can be achieved conditional on being unable to remove some distortions.

However we can achieve what is known as the *second-best* allocation. The **second-best** theory says that, if there must be a distortion, it is a mistake to concentrate the distortion in one market. It is more efficient to spread its effect more thinly over a wide range of markets.

Several applications of this general principle are found in the ensuing chapters. The real world in which we live provides several inevitable distortions. Given their existence, the argument of this section implies that the government may *increase* the overall efficiency of the whole economy by introducing *new* distortions to offset those that already exist. By now you will want to know the source of these inevitable distortions that the government could take action to offset.

13.4 Market failure

In the absence of any distortions, competitive equilibrium is efficient. We use the term *market failure* to cover all the circumstances in which market equilibrium is inefficient. Distortions then prevent the 'invisible hand' from allocating resources efficiently. We now list the possible sources of distortions that lead to market failure.

Imperfect competition

Only perfect competition makes firms equate marginal cost to price and thus to marginal consumer benefit. Under imperfect competition, producers set a price above the marginal cost. Since consumers equate price to marginal benefit, marginal benefit exceeds marginal cost in imperfectly competitive industries. Such industries produce too little compared to the efficient level. Increasing the level of competition in an imperfectly competitive market would result in higher output produced. This would add more to consumer benefit than to production costs (or the opportunity cost) of the resources used.

Equity, taxation and public goods

Redistributive taxation induces allocative distortions by driving a wedge between the price the consumer pays and the price the producer receives. So far, when discussing the goods produced in the market, we have considered private goods. Private goods are those that can be consumed only by the buyer. For example, if you buy a can of Coke, you pay for it and you drink it. Other consumers cannot drink the same can of Coke. In contrast to private goods, public goods are those that, if consumed by one person, can be consumed by others in exactly the same quantity. National defence is an example. Since you get the same quantity of national defence as everyone else, *whether or not you pay for it*, you never buy national defence in a private market. Therefore, in the case of public goods, we have goods that society would like to consume but the private market mechanism cannot provide (or will under-provide). Taxes and public goods are analysed in detail in Chapter 14.

Externalities

Externalities arise when one person's actions have direct costs or benefits for other people, but the individual does not take these into account. Externalities are things like pollution, noise and congestion. Much of the rest of this chapter examines this distortion. The problem arises because there is no market for things like noise. Hence markets and prices cannot ensure that the marginal benefit you get from making a noise equals the marginal cost of that noise to other people.

Asymmetric information

In Chapter 12 we saw how moral hazard and adverse selection inhibit the setting-up of insurance markets to deal with risk. The fact that there exists imperfect information in certain markets may lead to a failure in such markets.

Under asymmetric information, one party in a market transaction has more information than the other party. For example, a seller may know the true quality of the good she is selling while the buyer does not.

Suppose that buyers want to buy used cars. There are various sellers in the market, some selling high-quality used cars, some selling low-quality used cars. If the buyers cannot tell the difference between low and high quality, they will probably be unwilling to pay much for a used car (they always face the possibility of getting a low-quality used car). As a result, the sellers with high-quality used cars may end up selling them at a price that is lower than their value, meaning it is unprofitable for those sellers to stay in the market. In practice, under asymmetric information, the existence of the low-quality product drives the high-quality product out of the market. This is a market failure since the market for the high-quality product is eliminated even if the buyers value it at more than the cost of producing it. To mitigate the effects of asymmetric information, sellers can use warranties. By issuing longer warranties, sellers can signal that their cars are high quality. The case of used cars is known as the market for 'lemons' (whereby lemons means low-quality used cars) – a typical example of adverse selection.

13.5 Externalities

Externalities arise when someone engages in production or consumption activities that affect others but none pay or receive compensation for those effects.

> An externality is a cost or benefit related to the production or consumption of some good that is imposed on others in a way other than by charging prices.

A chemical firm discharges waste into a lake, polluting the water. It affects the production of anglers (fewer fish, harder to catch) or the consumption of swimmers (dirty water). Without a 'market' for pollution, the firm can pollute the lake without cost. It ignores the cost that pollution imposed on anglers and swimmers. This is an example of a negative production externality.

Conversely, by painting your house you make the whole street look nicer and give consumption benefits to your neighbour. However, in deciding how much to paint you do not take into account the benefits you provide for your neighbour. This is an example of a positive consumption externality.

Externalities are side effects of production and consumption. They have economic value (positive or negative) but there is no market for them. When an externality is present in a market there will be a divergence between the individual's private marginal costs and benefits and society's marginal costs and benefits.

In a competitive market without externalities and distortions, the marginal private benefits coincide with the social marginal benefits and the marginal private costs coincide with the marginal social costs. Therefore, in a competitive equilibrium an efficient allocation implies that marginal social benefits equal marginal social costs. When an externality is present, this result does not hold and an inefficient market allocation is created.

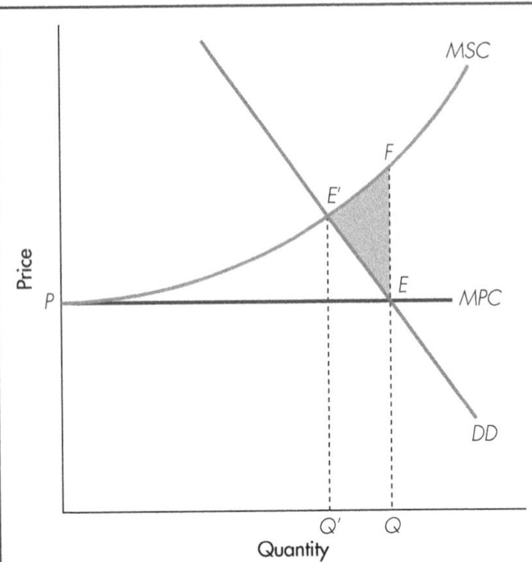

Competitive equilibrium occurs at *E*. The market clears at a price *P*, which producers equate to marginal private cost *MPC*. But pollution causes a production externality which makes the marginal social cost *MSC* exceed the marginal private cost. The socially efficient output is at *E'*, where marginal social cost and marginal social benefit are equal. The demand curve *DD* measures the marginal social benefit because consumers equate the value of the marginal utility of the last unit to the price. By inducing an output *Q* in excess of the efficient output *Q'* free market equilibrium leads to a social cost equal to the area *E'FE*. This shows the excess of social cost over social benefit in moving from *Q'* to *Q*.

Figure 13.5 **The social cost of a negative production externality**

Divergences between private and social costs and benefits

Suppose a chemical firm pollutes a river, the quantity of pollution rising with output. Downstream, companies use river water as an input in making sauce for baked beans. The production of chemicals creates a negative externality for the downstream companies.

Figure 13.5 shows the marginal private cost *MPC* of producing chemicals. For simplicity, we treat *MPC* as constant.[3] It also shows the marginal *social cost MSC* of chemical production. At any output, the divergence between marginal private cost and marginal social cost is the marginal *production externality*.

A production externality makes private and social marginal costs diverge. The demand curve *DD* shows how much consumers will pay for the output of the chemical producer. If that firm is a price-taker, equilibrium is at *E* and the chemical producer's output is *Q*, at which the marginal private cost equals the price of the firm's output.

At this output *Q*, the marginal social cost *MSC* exceeds the marginal social benefit of chemicals, given by the height of the demand curve *DD*. The market for chemicals ignores the production externality inflicted on other firms. At *Q*, the marginal social benefit of the last output unit is less than the marginal social cost inclusive of the production externality. Output *Q* is inefficient. By reducing the output of chemicals, society saves more in social cost than it loses in social benefit. Society could make some people better off without making anyone worse off.

The efficient output is *Q'*, at which the marginal social benefit equals the marginal social cost. *E'* is the efficient point. How much does society lose by producing at the free market equilibrium *E* and not the efficient point *E'*? The vertical distance between the marginal social cost *MSC* and the marginal social benefit shows the marginal social loss of producing the last output unit. By over-expanding from *Q'* to *Q*, society loses the area *E'FE* in Figure 13.5. This is the social cost of the market failure caused by the production externality of pollution.[4]

Production externalities make social and private marginal costs diverge. *A consumption externality makes private and social marginal benefits diverge.* Figure 13.6 shows a positive consumption externality. Planting roses in your front garden also makes your neighbours happy.

With no production externality, *MPC* is both the private and social marginal cost of planting roses. It is the cost of the plants and the opportunity cost of your time. *DD* is the marginal private benefit. Comparing your own costs and benefits, you plant a quantity *Q* of roses.

3 The results of the analysis will not change if we consider a positively sloped *MPC* curve. What matters is that marginal private costs lie below the marginal social costs.

4 Conversely, a farmer who spends money on pest control reduces pests on nearby farms. If production externalities are beneficial, the marginal social cost is below the marginal private cost. Suppose we swap the labels *MSC* and *MPC* in Figure 13.5. Free market equilibrium is at *E'* but *E* is now the efficient allocation.

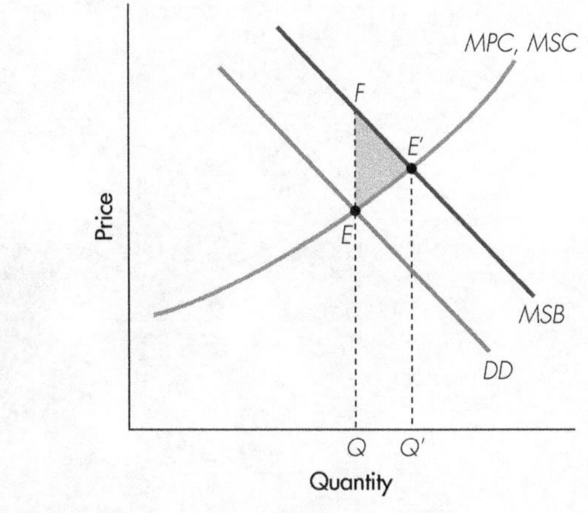

With no production externality, marginal private cost and marginal social cost coincide. *DD* measures the marginal private benefit, and the market equilibrium occurs at *E*. The beneficial consumption externality makes marginal social benefit *MSB* exceed marginal private benefit. *E'* is the socially efficient point. By producing *Q* instead of the efficient output *Q'*, free market equilibrium wastes the area *EFE'*.

Figure 13.6 **A beneficial consumption externality**

But you ignore the consumption benefit to your neighbours. The marginal social benefit *MSB* exceeds your marginal private benefit. The free market equilibrium is at *E*, but the efficient output is *Q'* since marginal social benefit and marginal social cost are equated at *E'*.

Society could gain the area *EFE'*, the excess of social benefits over social costs, by increasing the quantity of roses from *Q* to *Q'*. This triangle measures the social cost of the market failure that makes equilibrium output too low.

From our analysis we can draw a general conclusion: free markets will lead to over-production (*under-production*) of goods with negative (*positive*) externalities.

CASE 13.1

EXTERNALITIES AND THE LONDON 2012 OLYMPIC GAMES

The summer Olympic Games is among the most important sporting events in the world. Moreover, such events provide the possibility for environmental and economic improvements in the host city. In 2012 London hosted the Olympic Games.

There are many costs involved in preparing for such a massive sporting event and there are also many benefits accruing from it. Some of those costs and benefits can be easily measured in monetary terms. For example, according to recent estimates the construction of the venues for the London Olympic Games contributed £5.8 billion to UK GDP in 2012. The boost in tourism was estimated to contribute £2 billion to GDP. We can measure such a benefit because we have a market for tourism. However, many other benefits and costs associated with the Olympic Games are intangible.

By intangible, we mean costs and benefits that will impact the well-being of many people but that will not in general have market prices. In other words, intangible benefits are positive externalities and intangible costs are negative externalities. The Olympic Games is a source of externalities.

For example, hosting the Olympic Games normally boosts the national pride of the hosting country. This can be seen as a positive externality (a sort of 'feelgood' effect) but there is no market for national pride. Another possible positive externality that may be produced is related to environmental improvements through creation of new green spaces and recreational areas. The Olympic Games will probably create a sport and cultural legacy in the UK. This will enhance and accelerate investment in sporting facilities not only within the Olympic zone (and the areas immediately surrounding it) but also in other parts of the UK. It may contribute to increased participation in sport, and this will be expected to promote healthy living.

Cultural and social events may also improve during and after the Olympic Games.

Obviously there are also negative externalities. In some parts of London traffic congestion was a big problem during the Games. Construction of the Olympic site caused disruption for local residents. As a result of building all the facilities, pollution may have increased in the Olympic zone.

All those intangible benefits and costs are difficult to measure in monetary terms. In 2005 the UK Department for Culture, Media and Sport commissioned PricewaterhouseCoopers to study the possible costs and benefits of the London 2012 Games. An interesting finding of that study is the estimated willingness of London households to pay for the intangible benefits of the Olympic Games. On average, London households are willing to pay £22 each per annum for ten years in order to host the Olympic Games. Therefore, there is a positive valuation of the intangible benefits that London 2012 can bring to Londoners.

Wenlock and Mandeville, the London 2012 Mascots. © Richard Allen/Alamy

Sources: PricewaterhouseCoopers, *Olympic Games impact study: Final report*, December 2005; Oxford Economics.'The economic impact of London 2012', July 2012.

Property rights and externalities

Your neighbour's tree obscures your light – a negative consumption externality. If the law says that you must be compensated for any damage suffered, your neighbour has to pay up or cut back the tree.

She likes the tree and wants to know how much it would take to compensate you to leave it at its current size. Figure 13.7 shows the marginal benefit MB that she gets from the last inch of tree and the marginal cost MC to you of that last inch. At the tree's current size S_1, the total cost to you is the area $OABS_1$. This is the marginal cost OA of the first inch, plus the marginal cost of the second inch, and so on to the existing size S_1. The area $OABS_1$ is what you need in compensation if the tree size is S_1.

Your neighbour is about to pay up when her daughter, an economics student, points out that, at size S_1, the marginal benefit of the last inch to her is less than the marginal cost to you, the amount you must be compensated for that last inch of the tree. It is not worth her mother having a tree this big. Nor, she points out, is it worth cutting the tree down altogether. The first inch yields a higher marginal benefit to her than the amount that you need in compensation to offset your marginal cost of that first inch. A tiny tree has little effect on your light.

At the efficient tree size S^*, the marginal benefit to your neighbour equals the marginal cost to you. Above S^*, she cuts back the tree, since the marginal cost (and compensation) exceeds her marginal benefit. Below S^*, she increases the tree size, and pays you marginal compensation that is less than her marginal benefit. At the efficient size S^*, your total cost is the area $OAES^*$. This is the compensation you are paid.

Since a larger tree benefits one party but hurts the other, *the efficient tree size, and therefore the efficient quantity of the externality, is not zero*. It is where the marginal benefit equals the marginal cost.

Property rights are the power of residual control, including the right to be compensated for externalities.

Property rights affect who compensates whom, a distributional implication. Suppose there is no law requiring compensation. Instead of letting her tree grow to S_1, inflicting a huge cost on you, you bribe your neighbour to cut it back. You compensate her for the loss of her marginal benefit. You would pay to have the tree cut back as far as S^* but no further. Beyond

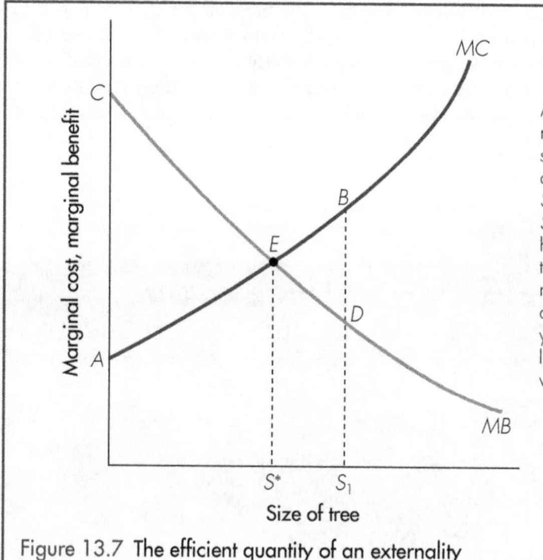

MB and *MC* measure the marginal benefit to your neighbour and marginal cost to you of a tree of size *S*. The efficient size is *S**, where the marginal cost and benefit are equal. Beginning from a size S_1, you might bribe your neighbour the value S^*EDS_1, to cut back to *S**. Below *S** you would have to pay more than it is worth to you to have the tree cut back further. Alternatively, your neighbour might pay you the value *OAES** to have a tree of size *S**. Property rights, in this case whether you are legally entitled to compensation for loss of light to your garden, determine who compensates whom but not the outcome *S** of the bargain.

Figure 13.7 **The efficient quantity of an externality**

that size, you pay more in compensation for loss of marginal benefit than you save yourself in lower cost of the externality. So you pay a *total* of S^*EDS_1 to compensate for the loss of benefit in cutting the tree back from S_1 to S^*. Who has the property rights determines who pays whom, but does not affect the efficient quantity that the bargain determines. It is always worth reaching the point at which the marginal benefit to one of you equals the marginal cost to the other.

Property rights have a distributional implication – who compensates whom – but also achieve the efficient allocation. They set up the 'missing market' for the externality. The market ensures that the price equals the marginal benefit and the marginal cost, and hence equates the two.

Economists say that property rights 'internalize' the externality. The relationship between property rights, efficiency and externalities is known as the *Coase theorem.*[5]

This theorem says that, when there are no transaction costs and trading externalities is possible, then the trading mechanism will lead to an efficient outcome independent of the initial allocation of the property rights. For example, consider two firms: one is polluting and doing so negatively affects the other firm. In this case, it does not matter if we assign the right to pollute to the polluting firm or, alternatively, the right not to be polluted to the other firm. Once the property rights are assigned, the externality will be internalized.

The basic idea behind the Coase theorem is: if people must pay for it they will take its effects into account in making private decisions and there will no longer be market failure. Why, then, do externalities, like congestion and pollution, remain a problem? Why don't private individuals establish the missing market through a system of bribes or compensation?

There are two reasons why it is hard to set up this market. The first is the cost of organizing the market. A factory chimney dumps smoke on a thousand gardens nearby, but it is costly to collect £1 from each household to bribe the factory to cut back to the efficient amount. Second, there is a **free-rider** problem.[6]

A free-rider, unable to be excluded from consuming a good, has no incentive to buy it.

Someone knocks on your door and says: 'I'm collecting money from people who mind the factory smoke falling on their gardens. The money will be used to bribe the factory to cut back. Do

5 From Ronald Harry Coase, Nobel Prize winner in Economics in 1991, who first pointed out the relationship between property rights and efficiency in the presence of externalities.

6 The free-rider problem is an important issue in the provision of public goods. This will be discussed in Chapter 14.

you wish to contribute? I am going round 1000 houses nearby.' Whether you mind or not, you probably say: 'I don't mind, and won't contribute.' If everybody else pays, the factory will cut back and you cannot be prevented from getting the benefits. The smoke will not fall exclusively on your garden just because you alone did not pay. Regardless of what other people contribute, your dominant strategy is to be a free-rider. Everyone else reasons similarly; hence no one pays, even though you are all better off paying and getting the smoke cut back.

MATHS 13.1

INTERNALIZING A NEGATIVE EXTERNALITY USING PROPERTY RIGHTS

Consider a firm that is polluting a lake in order to produce. This is called firm A. There is another firm, B, which uses the fish in the lake. All markets for outputs are competitive. The total cost function of the polluting firm (firm A) is:

$$TC_A = TC_A(Q_A, P_A)$$

That is a function of the quantity produced (Q_A) and the level of pollution (P_A).

We assume that the total cost of firm A is increasing with the output produced:

$$\frac{\partial TC_A}{\partial Q_A} > 0$$

This means that if we increase by a small amount (∂Q_A) the quantity produced, the total cost increases. We assume that the total cost of firm A is decreasing with the pollution level $\partial TC_A/\partial P_A \leq 0$.

More pollution implies lower costs for the firm. Think about the case in which, to pollute less, the firm must invest in an expensive cleaner technology. If p is the market price of output for firm A, then the profit function of that firm is $\pi_A = pQ_A - TC_A(Q_A, P_A)$.

Firm A chooses the optimal quantity to produce (Q_A) at which the marginal revenue is equal to the marginal cost of producing that quantity: $p = \partial TC_A/\partial Q_A$.

Similarly, the optimal quantity of pollution that maximizes profits is where marginal revenue of pollution (in this case, zero) is equal to the marginal cost of pollution:

$$-\frac{\partial TC_A}{\partial P_A} = 0$$

The firm chooses a level of pollution such that the cost of an extra unit of pollution is zero. Since the higher is pollution, the lower is the total cost of the firm, we should expect that the level of pollution that solves that condition to be quite high.

Firm B has the total cost function $TC_B = TC_B(Q_B, P_A)$, with the properties $\partial TC_B/\partial Q_B > 0$ and $\partial TC_B/\partial P_A > 0$.

This means that the total cost of firm B increases with output produced and with the pollution made by firm A. The externality problem is the following: firm A, in deciding how much to pollute, does not take into account the effects that its decision has on firm B. Make f the market price of fish for firm B. The profit of firm B is then given by $\pi_B = fQ_B - TC_B(Q_B, P_A)$.

Suppose we give the right to pollute to firm A. Firm A can sell its right to firm B. The profit function of firm A becomes $\pi_A = pQ_A - TC_A(Q_A, P_A) + qP_A$, where q is now the price that firm A can get by selling its right to pollute to firm B. For firm B, the profit function is now $\pi_B = fQ_B - TC_B(Q_B, P_A) - qP_A$. For firm A, the optimal level of pollution that maximizes profits is given by the condition:

$$-\frac{\partial TC_A}{\partial P_A} + q = 0 \Rightarrow \frac{\partial TC_A}{\partial P_A} = q \quad (1)$$

That condition simply says marginal cost is equal to marginal revenue from polluting (now equal to q).

For firm B, the quantity of pollution that maximizes its profit is given by the condition:

$$-\frac{\partial TC_B}{\partial P_B} - q = 0 \Rightarrow \frac{\partial TC_A}{\partial P_A} = q \quad (2)$$

Equations (1) and (2) imply that the price q should satisfy the following: $-\partial TC_A/\partial P_A = \partial TC_B/\partial P_A$.

In deciding the optimal level of P_A, firm A now takes into account the effect that its decision has on firm B. In particular, it must set a level of pollution such that the marginal private cost of polluting $(-\partial TC_A/\partial P_A)$ is equal to the marginal social cost of polluting $(-\partial TC_B/\partial P_A)$. So, by assigning the property rights we can obtain the efficient level of pollution. You can try to work out the case in which firm B has the right not to be polluted and can sell this right to firm A; does the result above still hold?

13.6 Environmental issues and the economics of climate change

When there is no implicit market for pollution, pollutants are overproduced. Private producers ignore the costs they impose on others. In equilibrium, social marginal cost exceeds social marginal benefit.

The most topical environmental externality we are currently facing is global warming, or climate change; that is, the rise in global temperature due to human activity. In particular, global warming is an externality in two main dimensions:

1 *An intergenerational dimension*: what humans are currently doing will affect future generations not yet born.
2 *An international dimension*: what a country does in terms of emissions will affect other countries.

In the case of a negative externality the government can induce private producers to take account of the costs inflicted on others by charging them (through taxes) for the divergence between marginal private and social costs.

Pollution taxes, especially for water pollution, are used in many countries. But most policy takes a different approach: imposing pollution standards to regulate the quantities of pollution allowed. For example, since the Clean Air Act 1956, UK governments have designated clean air zones in which certain pollutants, notably smoke caused by burning coal, are illegal. Table 13.1 shows a big fall in smoke pollution in the UK over time as a result of this policy.

Table 13.1 Smoke emission, UK (million tonnes per annum)

1958	1974	2003
2.0	0.8	0.1

Sources: Digest of Environmental Protection and Water Statistics; ONS, *Social Trends*.

For global warming, given its international dimension, things are more complicated because an effective policy should be agreed on and implemented by a coalition of governments.

Prices vs quantities

If free markets tend to over-pollute, society can cut pollution either by regulating the quantity of pollution or by using the price system to discourage such activities by taxing them. Is it more sensible to intervene through the tax system than to regulate quantities directly?

Many economists prefer taxes to quantity restrictions. If each firm is charged the same price or tax for a marginal unit of pollution, each firm equates the marginal cost of reducing pollution to the price of pollution. Any allocation in which different firms have different marginal costs of reducing pollution is inefficient. If firms with low marginal reduction costs contract further and firms with high marginal reduction costs contract less, lower pollution is achieved at less cost.

The main problem with using just taxes is uncertainty about the outcome. Suppose pollution beyond a critical level has disastrous consequences, for example irreversibly damaging the ozone layer. By regulating the quantity directly, society can ensure a disaster is avoided. Indirect control, through taxes or charges, runs the risk that the government does its sums wrong and sets the tax too low. Pollution is then higher than intended, and may be disastrous.

Regulating the total quantity of pollution, with spot checks on compliance by individual producers, is a simple policy that avoids the worst outcomes. However, by ignoring differences in the marginal cost of reducing pollution across different polluters, it does not reduce pollution in a way that is cost-minimizing to society.

Lessons from the United States

The US has gone furthest in trying to use property rights and the price mechanism to cut back pollution efficiently. The US Clean Air Acts established an environmental policy that includes an *emissions trading programme* and *bubble policy*.

The Acts lay down a minimum standard for air quality, and impose pollution emission controls on particular polluters. Any polluter emitting less than their specified amount gets an *emission reduction credit* (ERC), which can be sold to another polluter wanting to exceed its allocated pollution limit. Thus, the total quantity of pollution is regulated, but firms that can cheaply reduce pollution have an incentive to do so, and sell off the ERC to firms for which pollution reduction is more expensive. We get closer to the efficient solution in which the marginal cost of pollution reduction is equalized across firms.

When a firm has many factories, the bubble policy applies pollution controls to the firm as a whole. The firm can cut back most at the plants in which pollution reduction is cheapest.

Thus, the US policy combines 'control over quantities' for aggregate pollution, where the risks and uncertainties are greatest, with 'control through the price system' for allocating efficiently the way these overall targets are achieved.

The economics of climate change

There is increasing evidence that global temperatures are rising. The science of climate change means that we are also likely to see greater fluctuations in climate as well. Hence, extreme events will become much more frequent. Large parts of Bangladesh may disappear under water for ever; and English villages, from Yorkshire to Cornwall, have already experienced flash flooding. Conversely, regions of the world that are currently temperate may become arid and uninhabitable. Figure 13.8 shows the dramatic change in global temperatures in recent years.

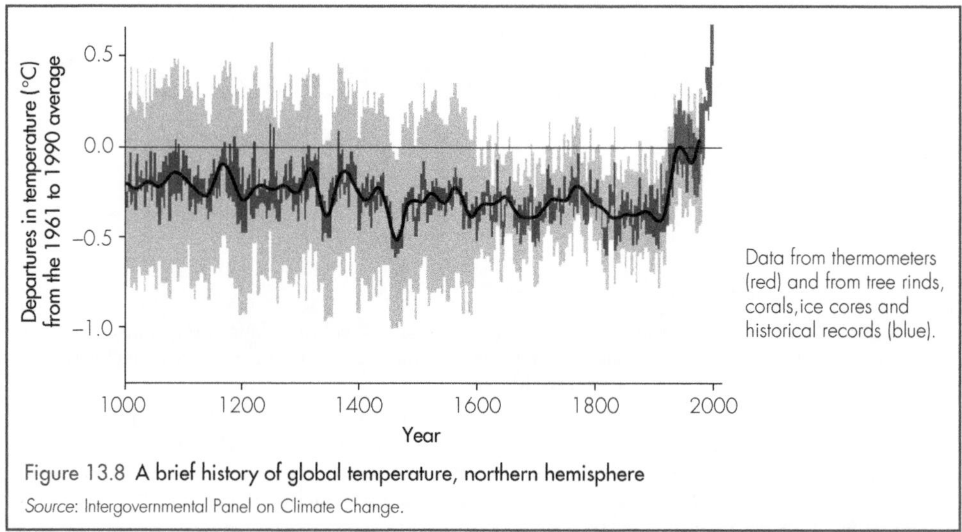

Figure 13.8 **A brief history of global temperature, northern hemisphere**

Source: Intergovernmental Panel on Climate Change.

The science of climate change

The earth's climate is affected by many things, from solar radiation to the consequences of human behaviour. The ebb and flow of previous ice ages reminds us that human behaviour is not the only cause of climate change. Even so, there is increasing evidence that we must look to ourselves as a major cause of recent global warming.

In the same period in which we experienced an increase in global temperature, there was a significant increase in global CO_2 emissions due to human activity. This is shown in Figure 13.9.

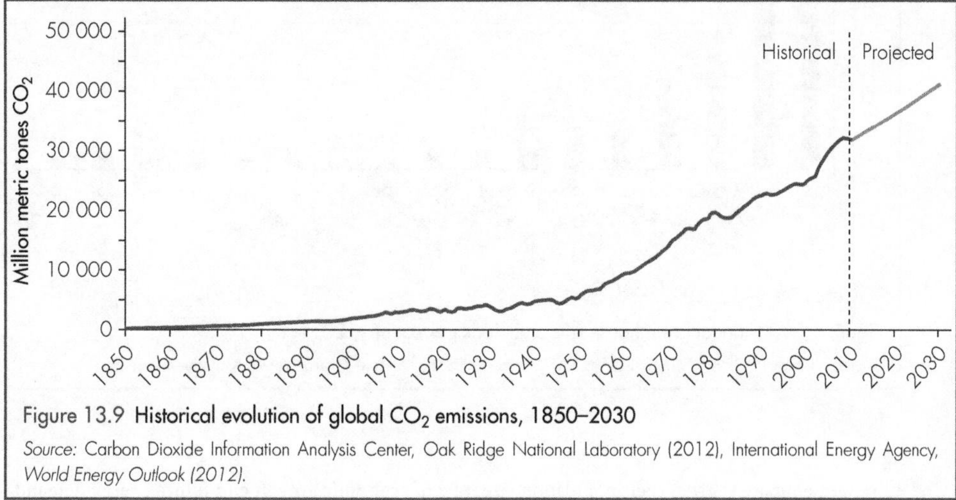

Figure 13.9 Historical evolution of global CO_2 emissions, 1850–2030

Source: Carbon Dioxide Information Analysis Center, Oak Ridge National Laboratory (2012), International Energy Agency, *World Energy Outlook (2012).*

Greenhouse gases – including carbon dioxide and methane – shield the earth from solar radiation, but also trap the heat underneath. Without them, all heat would escape and we would freeze to death. But we need just the right amount. Too much greenhouse gas and the earth overheats, causing global warming.

The recent build-up of greenhouse gases reflects large emissions of carbon dioxide from households, power stations and transport. This may cause ice to melt and water to expand, causing sea levels to rise. A catastrophic eventual consequence would be melting of permafrost in Siberia, releasing such volumes of methane that a large rise in temperature would then be inevitable, perhaps threatening human survival.

Carbon, a key constituent of all greenhouse gases, is a useful common denominator. Slowing, let alone reversing, global warming requires the emission of much less carbon.

Figure 13.10 shows greenhouse gas emissions per country in 2011 (CO_2 is an important greenhouse gas but it is not the only one). As we can see, China is the country that produces the largest amount of greenhouse gases, followed by the US and then the European Union as a whole.

The Kyoto Protocol

In 1997 a group of countries signed an amendment to the UN International Treaty on Climate Change, committing themselves to cut greenhouse gas emissions. By 2006, 169 countries (though not the US) had signed. In December 2012 an agreement was reached to extend the treaty to 2020.

Developed countries accept the obligation to reduce emissions by 2012 to 5 per cent below the level of their emissions in 1990. Developing countries have not yet made a commitment but can take part in the Clean Development Mechanism. Thus, China and India ratified the protocol but are not yet bound by the commitment

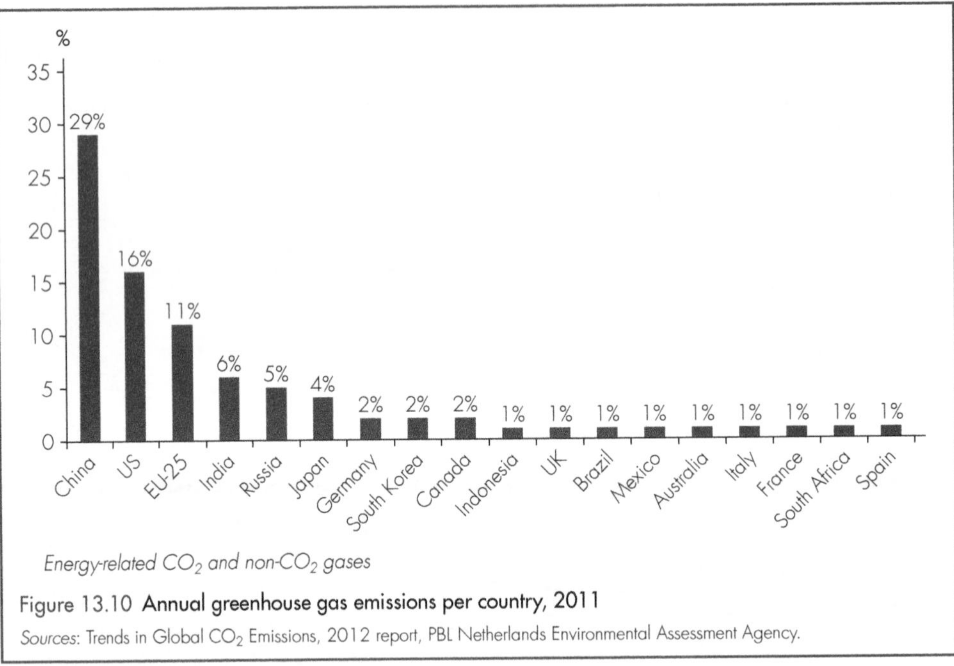

Figure 13.10 **Annual greenhouse gas emissions per country, 2011**

Sources: Trends in Global CO_2 Emissions, 2012 report, PBL Netherlands Environmental Assessment Agency.

to reduce emissions: given their population size, rate of economic growth and future energy demands, China and India will have a huge impact on what happens with greenhouse gases.

Within the EU's overall targets, individual members can buy and sell obligations within the EU Emissions Trading Scheme (which resembles the US pollution scheme discussed earlier). The Clean Development Mechanism allows India or China to invest in emissions reduction, such as by building a cleaner power station, and sell the emissions credit to a UK or German company so that Europe then meets its overall emissions obligations.

Thus the projected total cutbacks can be achieved efficiently – those most easily able to reduce emissions cheaply do so; those for whom emissions reduction is expensive can instead purchase a credit from someone else better placed to cut back emissions cheaply.

If you think about it, this is an application of the property rights argument we have previously discussed.

Cost–benefit analysis

Even if we accept the science, what should we do, and how quickly? This gets to the core of the what, how and for whom questions of Chapter 1. The for whom question is particularly acute. How much pain should the current generation take in order to make life nicer for future generations? Can we expect China and India to slow their economic development to make life nicer for citizens in Europe and the US, who begin with many more economic advantages?

The Kyoto targets are modest, and as yet fail to include the key economies of the US, China and India, on whom much will actually depend. Kyoto supporters see these targets as the thin end of the wedge, creating a political dynamic that will create tougher targets soon; which is precisely why they are opposed by those who would potentially lose out.

In 2006 the UK government published a report on the economics of climate change written by Sir Nicholas Stern, a London School of Economics professor, and ex-Chief Economist of both the World Bank and the

European Bank for Reconstruction and Development. The Stern Review (details of which are available at www.hm-treasury.gov.uk) concluded that 1 per cent of global GDP must be invested from now on if we are to head off the worst effects of climate change; and that failure to act now risks a future cost of up to 20 per cent of global GDP.

Many of the world's leading economists – including economics Nobel Prize winners Sir James Mirrlees, Amartya Sen, Joe Stiglitz and Bob Solow, and Professor Jeffrey Sachs, Director of the Earth Institute at Columbia University in New York – have come out strongly in support of the Stern Review. The principal point of subsequent debate has been the appropriate interest rate at which to discount future costs and benefits, a topic we discuss in Activity 13.1. The decision about how much to discount the welfare of future generations affects the present value of the benefits of tackling climate change today, and hence both the optimal pace of action and estimates of the cost of inaction. Although the quantitative conclusions change, the qualitative conclusions do not.

ACTIVITY 13.1

STERN VIEW OF DISCOUNT RATES

Figure 13.8 showed a 1000-year history of temperatures on the planet. Suppose we could all agree on the science of global warming. This would allow statements of the form, 'If we continue producing emissions at the current rate, global temperatures will rise according to the following profile, with the following consequences in terms of flooding, volatile weather, drought, and so on.'

Suppose too that there was only one country in the world, so we did not have to worry about whether the US or India participated in trying to slow down climate change. The central issue then would be, 'how much pain should we inflict on today's generation in order to mitigate the problem for future generations?'

The lower the discount rate we use in this calculation, the greater the present value of the benefits of helping future generations; the higher the discount rate we use, the less today we care about helping future generations. The Stern Review's recommendation, that we should take urgent action to substantially reduce emissions, follows inexorably from its analysis provided we agree with its assumption that we should not discount the welfare of future generations in making this policy decision today.

Others, such as Professor William Nordhaus of Yale University, have argued that today's decision makers should discount the welfare of future generations – not least because they are still likely to be richer than us and have better options than we face – in which case, the optimal policy response to climate change is a slower mitigation of emissions today, albeit then requiring that future generations will have to take much more drastic action.

The discount rate is not an academic abstraction. It affects key valuations and decisions, whether in the stock market or in the politics of controlling global warming.

Questions

(a) If we wish to weight equally the utility of current and future generations, what discount rate should we apply to future utility?

(b) Still weighting utility equally, suppose future generations are richer than us and we believe in the principle of diminishing marginal utility of consumption. Will a unit of consumption be worth more today when we are poor or more tomorrow when we are rich?

(c) Suppose, by sacrificing consumption today, we invest in physical capital that would make future generations richer. Say, on average, this investment has a rate of return of 5 per cent a year in real terms. What return would an environmental investment (for example, preventing climate change) have to yield in order for future generations to be pleased with the decisions we made today?

To check your answers to these questions, go to page 678.

13.7 Other missing markets: time and risk

The previous two sections were devoted to a single idea. When externalities exist, free market equilibrium is inefficient because the externality itself does not have a market or a price. People take no account of the costs and benefits their actions inflict on others. Without a market for externalities, the price system cannot bring marginal costs and marginal benefits of these externalities into line. We now discuss other 'missing markets' – those for time and for risk.

The present and the future are linked. People save, or refrain from consumption, today in order to consume more tomorrow. Firms invest, reducing current output by devoting resources to training or building, in order to produce more tomorrow. How should society make plans today for the quantities of goods produced and consumed in the future? Ideally, everyone makes plans such that the social marginal cost of goods in the future just equals their social marginal benefit.

Chapter 12 discussed a *forward market*, in which buyers and sellers make contracts today for goods delivered in the future at a price agreed today. Suppose there is a forward market for copper in 2020. Consumers equate the marginal benefit of copper in 2020 to the forward price, which producers equate to the marginal cost of producing copper for 2020. With a complete set of forward markets for all commodities for all future dates, producers and consumers today make consistent plans for future production and consumption of all goods, and the social marginal benefit of every future good equals its social marginal cost.

Chapter 12 explained why few forward markets exist. You can trade gold but not cars or washing machines. Since nobody knows the characteristics of next year's model of car or washing machine, we cannot write legally binding contracts to be easily enforced when the goods are delivered. Without these forward markets, the price system cannot equate the marginal cost and marginal benefits of planned future goods.

There are also few *contingent* or insurance markets for dealing with risk. People usually dislike risk. It reduces their utility. Does society undertake the efficient amount of risky activities?

A complete set of insurance markets lets risk be transferred from those who dislike risk to those who will bear risk at a price. The equilibrium price equates social marginal costs and benefits of risky activities. However, adverse selection and moral hazard inhibit the organization of private insurance markets. If some risky activities are uninsurable at any price, the price system cannot guide society to equate social marginal costs and benefits.

Future goods and risky goods are examples of commodities with missing markets. Like externalities, these are market failures. Free market equilibrium is generally efficient. And the theory of the second-best tells us that, when some markets are distorted, we probably do not want other markets to be completely distortion free.

13.8 Quality, health and safety

Information is incomplete because gathering information is costly. This leads to inefficiency. Consider a firm using benzene in its production process. A worker unaware that exposure to benzene may cause cancer may work for a lower wage than if this information is widely available. The firm's production cost understates the true social cost and the good is overproduced. Governments regulate health, safety and quality standards because they recognize the danger of market failure.

UK examples include the Health and Safety at Work Acts, legislation to control food and drugs production, the Fair Trading Act governing consumer protection, and various traffic and motoring regulations. Such legislation aims to encourage the provision of information that lets individuals more accurately judge costs and benefits, and aims to set and enforce standards designed to reduce the risk of injury or death.

Providing information

Figure 13.11 shows the supply curve *SS* for a drug that is potentially harmful. *DD* is the demand curve if consumers do not know the danger. In equilibrium at *E*, the quantity *Q* is produced and consumed. With full information about the dangers, people would buy less of the drug. The demand curve *DD'* shows the marginal consumer benefit with full information. The new equilibrium at *E'* avoids the deadweight burden *E'EF* from overproduction of the drug.

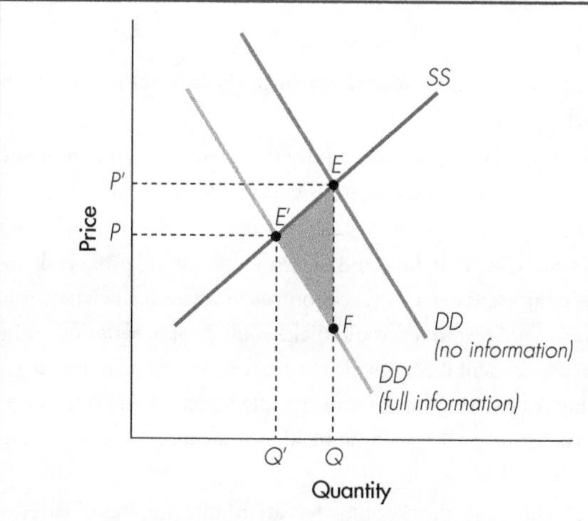

Consumers cannot individually discover the safety risks associated with a particular good. Free market equilibrium occurs at *E*. A government agency now provides information about the product. As a result, the demand curve shifts down and the new equilibrium is at E′, where the true or full information value of an extra unit of the good equals its marginal social cost. Providing information prevents a welfare cost *E′EF* that arises when uninformed consumers use the wrong marginal valuation of the benefits of the good.

Figure 13.11 **Information and unsafe goods**

If information were free to collect, everyone would know the true risks. From the social gain *E′EF*, we should subtract the resources needed to discover this information. Free market equilibrium is at *E* because it is not worth each individual checking up privately on each drug on the market. It makes sense for society to have a single regulatory body to check drugs, and a law whose enforcement entitles individuals to assume that drugs have been checked out as safe. Certification of safety or quality need not be carried out by the government. Sotheby's certify Rembrandts and the AA will check out a used car for you.

Two factors inhibit the use of private certification in many areas of health and safety. First, the public perceives a conflict between the profit motive and the incentive to tell the truth. Public officials may be less easily swayed. Second, a private certification agency might have to decide standards. What margin of error should be built into safety regulations? How safe must a drug be to get a certificate? These are issues of public policy. They involve externalities and have distributional implications. Even if society uses private agencies to *monitor* regulations, it usually sets the standards itself.

Imposing standards

The public interest is important when little is known about a product and where the consequences of any error may be catastrophic. Few believe that safety standards for nuclear power stations can be adequately determined by the private sector.

In imposing standards, governments raise the private cost of production by preventing firms from adopting the cost-minimizing techniques they otherwise would use. Sometimes the government has better information than the private sector. Sometimes standards compensate for externalities neglected by the private firm. Sometimes standards reflect a pure value judgement based on distributional considerations. One contentious area is the value of human life itself.

Politicians often claim that human life is beyond economic calculation and must be given absolute priority at any cost. An economist will make two points in reply. First, it is *impossible* to implement such an objective. It is too costly in resources to try to eliminate *all* risks of premature death. Sensibly, we do not go this far. Second, in occupational and recreational choices, for example driving racing cars or going climbing, people take risks. Society must ask how much more risk-averse it should be than the people it is trying to protect.

Beyond some point, the marginal social cost of further risk reduction exceeds the marginal social benefit. It takes a huge effort to make the world just a little safer, and the resources might have been used elsewhere to greater effect. Zero risk does not make economic sense. We need to know the costs of making the world a little safer, and we need to encourage society to decide how much it values the benefits. Not accounting for those costs and benefits may lead societies to choose inefficient allocations.

Summary

- **Welfare economics** deals with normative issues or value judgements. Its purpose is not to describe how the economy works but to assess how well it works.
- **Horizontal equity** is the equal treatment of equals, and **vertical equity** the unequal treatment of unequals. Equity is concerned with the distribution of welfare across people. The desirable degree of equity is a pure value judgement.
- A **resource allocation** is a complete description of what, how and for whom goods are produced. To separate as far as possible the concepts of equity and efficiency, economists use Pareto efficiency. An allocation is **Pareto-efficient** if no reallocation of resources would make some people better off without making others worse off. If an allocation is inefficient it is possible to achieve a Pareto gain, making some people better off and none worse off. Many reallocations make some people better off and others worse off. We cannot say whether such changes are good or bad without making value judgements to compare different people's welfare.
- For a given level of resources and a given technology, the economy has an infinite number of Pareto-efficient allocations that differ in the distribution of welfare across people. For example, every allocation that gives all output to one individual is Pareto-efficient. But there are many more allocations that are inefficient.
- Under strict conditions, competitive equilibrium is Pareto-efficient. Different initial distributions of human and physical capital across people generate different competitive equilibria corresponding to each possible Pareto-efficient allocation. When price-taking producers and consumers face the same prices, marginal costs and marginal benefits are equated to prices (by the individual actions of producers and consumers).
- Governments face a conflict between equity and efficiency. Redistributive taxation drives a wedge between prices paid by consumers (to which marginal benefits are equated) and prices received by producers (to which marginal costs are equated). Free market equilibrium will not equate marginal cost and marginal benefit and there will be inefficiency.
- **Distortions** occur whenever free market equilibrium does not equate **marginal social cost** and **marginal social benefit**. Distortions lead to inefficiency or **market failure**. Apart from taxes, there are three other important sources of distortion: imperfect competition (failure to set price equal to marginal cost), externalities (divergence between private and social costs or benefits), and other missing markets in connection with future goods, risky goods or other informational problems.
- When only one market is distorted the **first-best** solution is to remove the distortion, thus achieving full efficiency. The first-best criterion relates only to efficiency. Governments caring sufficiently about redistribution might still prefer inefficient allocations with more vertical equity. However, when a distortion cannot be removed from one market, it is not generally efficient to ensure that all other markets are distortion-free. The theory of the **second-best** says that it is more efficient to spread inevitable distortions thinly over many markets than to concentrate their effects in a few markets.
- **Production externalities** occur when actions by one producer directly affect the production costs of another producer, as when one firm pollutes another's water supply. **Consumption externalities** mean one person's decisions affect another consumer's utility directly, as when a garden gives pleasure to neighbours.

- Externalities lead to divergence between private and social costs or benefits because there is no implicit market for the externality itself. When only a few people are involved, a system of **property rights** may establish the missing market. The direction of compensation will depend on who has the property rights. Either way, it achieves the efficient quantity of the externality at which marginal cost and marginal benefit are equated. The efficient solution is rarely a zero quantity of the externality. **Transaction costs** and the **free-rider problem** may prevent implicit markets being established. Equilibrium will then be inefficient.
- When externalities lead to market failure, the government could set up the missing market by pricing the externality through taxes or subsidies. If it were straightforward to assess the efficient quantity of the externality and hence the correct tax or subsidy, such taxes or subsidies would allow the market to achieve an efficient resource allocation.
- In practice, governments often regulate externalities such as **pollution** or **congestion** by imposing standards that affect quantities directly rather than by using the tax system to affect production and consumption indirectly. Overall quantity standards may fail to equate the marginal cost of pollution reduction across different polluters, in which case the allocation will not be efficient. However, simple standards may use up fewer resources in monitoring and enforcement and may prevent disastrous outcomes when there is uncertainty.
- **Global warming** represents a negative environmental externality that is believed to be caused by human activity and is posing a serious threat to the global economy. As an externality, it has two main dimensions: an intergenerational dimension and an international dimension. To assess the possible effects of global warming on our economies, we employ cost–benefit analysis.
- **Moral hazard**, **adverse selection** and **other informational problems** prevent the development of a complete set of **forward markets** and **contingent markets**. Without these markets, the price system cannot equate social marginal costs and benefits for future goods or risky activities.
- **Incomplete information** may lead to inefficient private choices. Health, quality and safety regulations are designed both to provide information and to express society's value judgements about intangibles, such as life itself. By avoiding explicit consideration of social costs and benefits, government policy may be inconsistent in its implicit valuation of health or safety in different activities under regulation.

Review questions

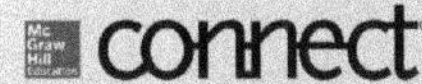

EASY

1 An economy has 10 units of goods to share out between 2 people. $[x, y]$ means that the first person gets a quantity x, the second person a quantity y. For each of the allocations (a) to (e), say whether they are (i) efficient and (ii) equitable: (a) [10, 0], (b) [7, 2], (c) [5, 5], (d) [3, 6], (e) [0, 10]. What does 'equitable' mean? Would you prefer allocation (d) to allocation (e)?

2 John and Jennifer need to decide how to divide a chocolate cake of size one. Putting the quantity of the cake that John can get on the vertical axis and the quantity of the cake that Jennifer can get on the horizontal axis, plot the Pareto frontier of this cake allocation problem. What does a point below the Pareto frontier represent? Is an allocation where John gets the entire cake and Jennifer nothing Pareto-efficient?

3 In deciding to drive a car in the rush hour, you think about the cost of petrol and the time of the journey. Do you slow other people down by driving? Is this an externality? Will too many or too few people drive cars in the rush hour? Should commuter parking in cities be restricted?

EASY

4 **Common fallacies** Why are these statements wrong? (a) Society should ban all toxic discharges. (b) Anything governments can do, the market can do better. (c) Anything the market can do, the government can do better.

5 In 1885, 200 people died when the steam boiler exploded on a Mississippi river boat. Jeremiah Allen and three friends formed a private company offering to insure any boiler that they had inspected for safety. Boiler inspections caught on, and explosion rates plummeted. Would Jeremiah Allen's company have been successful in reducing explosion rates if it had certified boilers but not insured them as well? Explain.

MEDIUM

6 The price of meals is £1 and the price of films is £5. There is perfect competition in the market and no externalities exist. Labour is the variable factor of production and workers can move freely between industries. What can we say about (a) the relative benefit to consumers of a marginal film and a marginal meal, (b) the relative marginal production costs of films and meals, and (c) the relative marginal product of variable factors in the film and meal industries? Why is this equilibrium efficient?

7 A government needs to raise £10 billion from taxes. It knows that taxes create deadweight losses, and it taxes a number of activities and products. For the most efficient outcome possible, should the tax rate on each of the following be low or high: (a) alcohol, (b) branded clothing, (c) caviar, (d) tobacco?

8 A honey firm is located next to an apple field owned by a farmer. The bees go into the apple field and help to make all the trees more productive. This in turn reduces the costs of the farmer. We have a positive externality. The total cost of the honey firm is $TC_H = H^2$, where H is the amount of honey. For the farmer the total cost is $TC_A = A^2 - H$, where A is the amount of apples. Assume that the price of honey is fixed at £2, while the price of an apple is fixed at £4. Write down the profit functions for the honey firm and for the farmer. What is the profit-maximizing level of honey produced by the honey firm? What is the profit-maximizing level of apples produced? Find the profits earned by the honey firm and the farmer.

9 Now suppose that the honey firm and the farmer in Question 8 merge to become a single firm that produces honey and apples. The total cost faced by the merged firm is $TC_M = H^2 + A^2 - H$. The prices of the two goods are the same as in Question 8. Write down the profit function of the merged firm. Find the profit-maximizing levels of honey and apples produced. What is the total profit obtained by the merged firm? Compare your answer with your results in Question 8. Is the externality internalized?

10 Much of the economics of efficiency is about ensuring that we equate the marginal cost of producing the last unit with the marginal benefit of that unit to the last consumer. Suppose the marginal cost of preventing the planet from overheating is £10 000 billion. How would you attempt to assess the marginal benefit?

11 (a) Why might society ban drugs that neither help nor harm the diseases they are claimed to cure? (b) If regulatory bodies are blamed for bad things that happen despite regulations (a train crash) but not blamed for preventing good things through too much regulation (rapid availability of a safe and useful drug), will regulatory bodies over-regulate activities under their scrutiny?

HARD

12 Suppose Jack has 30 apples and 20 oranges and Lisa has 20 apples and 80 oranges. So, there are 100 oranges and 50 apples in total. There is no production activity. Jack and Lisa must decide between consuming their initial endowment of the two goods or trading with each other. Given below is the Edgeworth box showing Jack's and Lisa's allocation of resources. Jack's indifference curves are I^0J, I^1J, I^2J, I^3J and Lisa's indifference curves are I^0L, I^1L, I^2L, I^3L.

(a) Identify the Pareto-efficient allocation of the two goods between Jack and Lisa.

(b) Now suppose the initial endowment is at point e^1. Explain how government intervention can bring about changes in the allocation such that it is not only Pareto-efficient but also equitable.

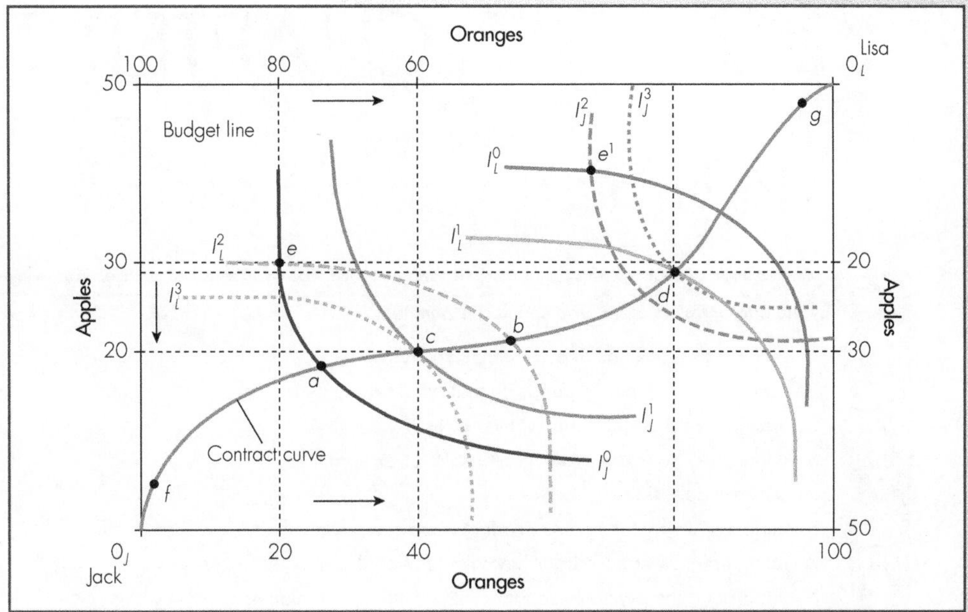

13 **Essay question** Why do politicians pretend that trains can be made perfectly safe and hospitals can supply all the health care that we know how to supply, when it is perfectly obvious that we do not have the resources to do these things and that it would be highly wasteful to try? HARD

14 A firm producing plastic bags is polluting the air in a neighbourhood. In the following table, the marginal private costs (*MPC*) of the firm for different quantities of plastic bags are reported, together with the price of plastic bags.

Q	MPC (£)	Selling price
1	11	28
2	12	26
3	13	24
4	14	22
5	15	20
6	16	18
7	17	16
8	18	14
9	19	12

Polluting the air creates an externality. We know that the value of the externality is £10 for each quantity level. In a graph with *Q* on the horizontal axis, plot the marginal social cost (*MPC*) and the demand. Show the equilibrium in the market. Why is the equilibrium inefficient?

CHAPTER 14

Government spending and revenue

Learning Outcomes

By the end of this chapter, you should be able to:

1. define different kinds of government spending
2. understand why public goods cannot be provided by a market
3. identify average and marginal tax rates
4. understand how taxes can compensate for externalities
5. define supply-side economics
6. understand why tax revenue cannot be raised without limit
7. recognise how cross-border flows limit national economic sovereignty
8. understand the political economy within which governments set policy

The scale of government rose steadily until the 1970s. Then many people felt it had become too big, using resources better employed in the private sector. High taxes were thought to be stifling private enterprise. Electorates in many countries turned to the political leaders who promised to reduce the scale of government.

Now the pendulum is swinging back. After the financial crisis of 2007–08, many developed economies faced a recession. The electorate sees a reduction in public spending as counterproductive, even in countries with a high burden of public debt.

For historical perspective, Table 14.1 shows how government grew everywhere in the last century.

Table 14.1 Government spending (% of GDP)

	1880	1960	2012
Japan	11	18	33.8
US	8	28	35.0
Germany	10	32	45.0
UK	10	32	48.5
France	15	35	56.6
Sweden	6	31	52.0

Sources: EUROSTAT; www.bea.gov; *CIA World Factbook*.

Most government spending is financed by tax revenue. However, just as you may overspend your student income by borrowing now and repaying later, the government need not balance its spending and revenue in any particular period. When the difference between total revenues and total spending is negative, we then have a budget deficit. When that difference is positive, the government is running a **budget surplus**. Table 14.2 shows that, by 2012, the US and the UK had budget deficits higher than in France while Germany had a budget surplus.

The budget surplus (deficit) is the excess (shortfall) of government's spending over its revenue.

After this broad background, we now examine microeconomic issues. First, we distinguish between **marginal and average tax rates.**

The marginal tax rate is the fraction of the last pound of income paid in tax.

The average tax rate is the fraction of total income paid in tax.

In a *progressive* tax structure, the average tax rate rises with an individual's income. The government takes proportionately more from the rich than from the poor. In a *regressive* tax structure, the average tax rate falls as income level rises, taking proportionately less from the rich.

Table 14.3 shows that the UK, like most countries, has a progressive income tax structure. Figure 14.1 explains why. We plot pre-tax income on the horizontal axis and post-tax income on the vertical axis. The line *OG*, with a slope of 45 degrees, implies no taxes. A pre-tax income *OA* on the horizontal axis matches the same post-tax income *OA* on the vertical axis. Now suppose there is an income tax, but the first *OA* of income is untaxed. If the marginal tax rate on taxable income is constant, individuals face a schedule *OBCD*, keeping a constant fraction of each pound of pre-tax income above *OA*. The higher the marginal tax rate, the flatter is *BC*.

Table 14.2 Government activity in 2012 (% of GDP)

	UK	US	France	Germany
Spending	48.5	35.0	56.6	45.0
Total revenue	42.2	27.5	51.7	45.2
Budget deficit	−6.3	−7.5	−4.9	0.2

Sources: EUROSTAT; www.bea.gov.

To calculate the average tax rate at a point such as *D*, we join up *OD*. The flatter the slope of this line, the higher is the average tax rate. Even with a constant marginal tax rate, and a constant slope along *BC*, the initial tax allowance makes the tax structure progressive. The higher an individual's gross income, the smaller is the tax allowance as a percentage of gross income, so the larger is the fraction of total income on which tax is paid.

But Table 14.3 shows that *marginal* tax rates may also rise with income. As individuals move into higher tax bands they pay higher marginal tax rates, moving on to even flatter portions of the tax schedule. The average tax rate now rises sharply with income.

Table 14.3 shows that UK marginal tax rates have fallen a lot in the past two decades, especially for the very rich. A millionaire paying an 83 per cent tax rate on all taxable income except the first £70 000 in 1978 paid only 40 per cent in 2008/09.

Table 14.3 UK income tax rates, 1978–2008

Taxable income (2004 £000s)	Marginal tax rate (%)	
	1978/79	2008/09
2020	34	20
5000	34	20
10 000	34	20
20 000	45	20
31 400	50	20
40 000	70	40
70 000	83	40

Note: Taxable income after deducting allowances. In 2008/09 a single person's allowance was almost £5500.

Sources: HMSO, *Financial Statement and Budget Report*; ONS, *Budget 2007*.

The UK was not alone in cutting tax rates. There was a worldwide move to cut tax rates, especially for the very rich. In part, this reflected the belief that tax rates were previously so high that distortions had been large.

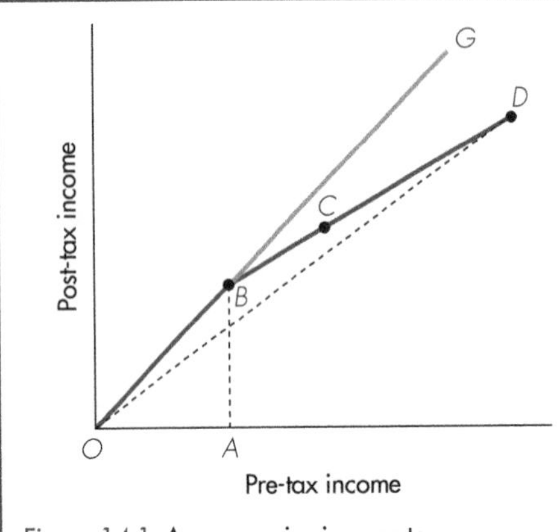

The 45° line *OG* shows zero taxes or transfers so that pre-tax and post-tax income coincide. With an allowance *OA*, then a constant marginal tax rate *t*, the post-tax income schedule is *OBCD*. The slope depends only on the marginal tax rate [on *BCD* it is $(1 - t)$]. The average tax rate at any point *D* is the slope of *OD*. A tax is progressive if the average tax rate rises with pre-tax income.

Figure 14.1 **A progressive income tax**

However, it also reflected increasing competition between governments to attract mobile resources (physical and human capital) to their country. At the end of the chapter we discuss how cross-border mobility undermines national sovereignty.

14.1 Taxation and government spending

Government spending, and the taxes that finance it, are now about 45 per cent of national output. Figure 14.2 shows the composition of government spending and revenue in 2011/12. Total expenditure in 2011/12 was around £710 billion, while revenues were around £589 billion.

A transfer payment requires no good or service in return during the period in which it is paid.

Direct taxes are taxes on income and wealth.

Indirect taxes are taxes on spending and output.

More than a third of total government spending went on **transfer payments** such as social protection of pensions, jobseeker's allowance (formerly unemployment benefit) and debt interest. Of the remaining spending directly on goods and services, the most important spending categories are health, defence and education. Figure 14.2 also shows how this government spending is financed. The most important **direct taxes** are income tax, and corporation tax on company profits.

The most important **indirect taxes** are value added tax (VAT) and customs duties. Note that, since state provision of retirement pensions is included on the expenditure side as a transfer payment, pension contributions under the national insurance scheme are included on the revenue side.

A public good is a good for which individuals cannot be excluded from using it and the use by an individual does not reduce availability to others.

A private good, if consumed by one person, cannot be consumed by others.

14.2 The government in the market economy

How do we justify government spending in a market economy?

Public goods

In Chapter 13 we introduced the idea of **public good** as market failure. Here, we discuss this issue in more detail.

Ice cream is a **private good**. If you eat an ice cream nobody else can eat that particular ice cream. For any given supply, your consumption reduces the quantity available for others to consume. Most goods are private goods.

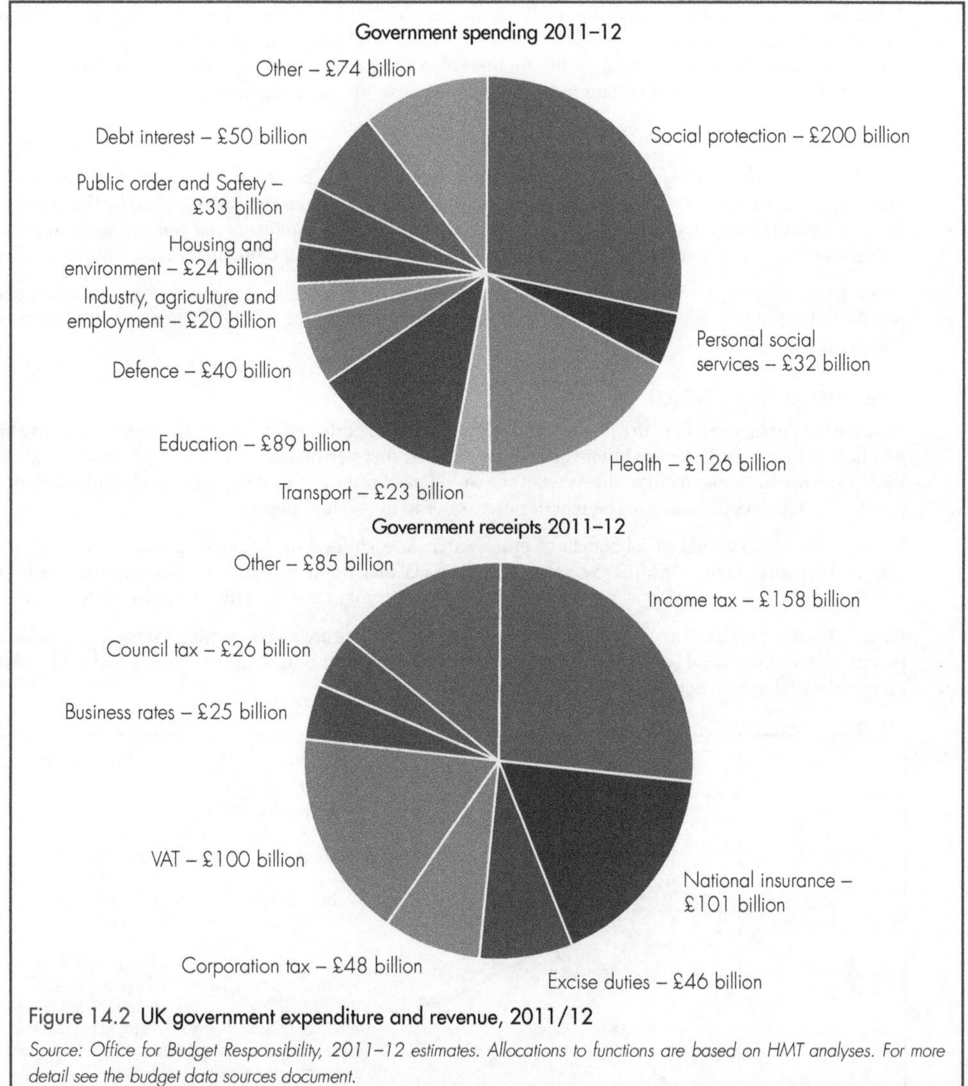

Figure 14.2 UK government expenditure and revenue, 2011/12

Source: Office for Budget Responsibility, 2011–12 estimates. Allocations to functions are based on HMT analyses. For more detail see the budget data sources document.

Source: Office for Budget Responsibility, 2011–12 estimates. Other receipts include capital taxes, stamp duties, vehicle excise duties and some other tax receipts – for example, interest and dividends. Figures may not sum due to rounding.

Clean air and defence are examples of public goods. If the air is pollution-free, your consumption of it does not interfere with our consumption of it. If the navy is patrolling coastal waters, your consumption of national defence does not affect our quantity of national defence. We all consume the same quantity; namely, the quantity is supplied in the aggregate. We may get different amounts of utility if our tastes differ, but we all consume the same quantity.

The key aspects of public goods are:

1 They are *non-rivalrous*: it is technically possible for one person to consume without reducing the amount available for others.
2 They are *non-excludable*: it is impossible to exclude anyone from consumption except at a prohibitive cost.

A football match can be watched by many people, especially if it is on TV, without reducing the quantity consumed by other viewers; but *exclusion* is possible. The ground holds only so many, and some Premier League clubs now charge to watch their games live on their own TV stations. The interesting issues arise when, as with national defence, exclusion of certain individuals from consumption is impossible.

Free-riders

Chapter 13 introduced the *free-rider problem* when discussing why bribes and compensation for externalities might not occur. Public goods are wide open to the free-rider problem if they are supplied by the private sector. Since you get the same quantity of national defence as everyone else, *whether or not you pay for it*, you never buy national defence in a private market. Nor does anyone else. No defence is demanded, even though we all want it.

Public goods are like a strong externality. If you buy defence, everyone else also gets the benefits. Since marginal private and social benefits diverge, private markets will not produce the socially efficient quantity. Government intervention is needed.

The marginal social benefit

Suppose the public good is a pure public water supply. The more infected the water, the more people are likely to get cholera. Figure 14.3 supposes there are two people. The first person's demand curve for water purity is D_1D_1. Each point on the demand curve shows what she would pay for the last unit of purer water; that is, her marginal benefit. D_2D_2 shows the marginal benefit of purer water to the second person.

Curve *DD* is the marginal social benefit of purer water. At each level of the public good, we *vertically* sum the marginal benefit of each individual to get the marginal social benefit. At the output Q, the marginal social benefit is $P = P_1 + P_2$. We sum vertically at *a given quantity* because everyone consumes the same quantity of a public good.

Figure 14.3 also shows the marginal cost of the public good. If there are no production externalities, the marginal private cost and marginal social cost coincide. The socially efficient output of the public good is Q^*, where the marginal social benefit equals the marginal social cost.

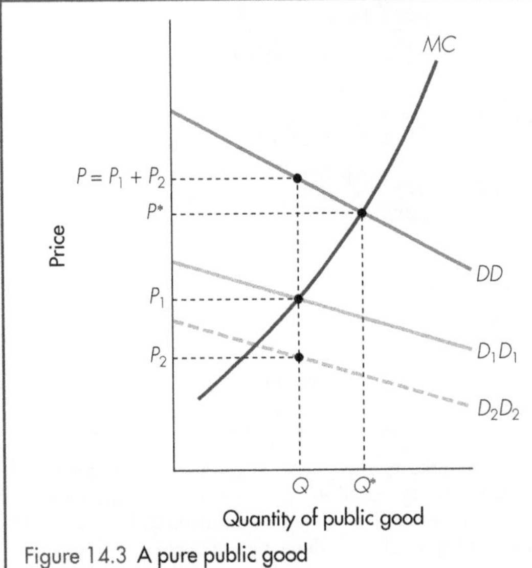

D_1D_1 and D_2D_2 are the separate demand curves of two individuals and show the marginal private benefit of the last unit of the public good to each individual. What is the social marginal benefit of the last unit to the group as a whole? Since both individuals consume whatever quantity of the good is produced, we must add up *vertically* the price each is prepared to pay for the last unit. At the output Q the marginal social benefit is thus $P_1 + P_2$. The curve *DD* showed the marginal social benefit and is obtained by vertically adding the demand curves of the two individuals. If *MC* is the private and social marginal cost of producing the public good, the socially efficient output is Q^*, at which social marginal cost and social marginal benefit are equal.

Figure 14.3 **A pure public good**

What happens if the good is privately produced and marketed? Person 1 might pay P_1 to have a quantity Q produced by a competitive supplier pricing at marginal cost. At the output Q, the price P_1 just equals the marginal private benefit that person 1 gets from the last unit of the public good. Person 2 will not pay to have the output of the public good increased beyond Q. Person 2 cannot be excluded from consuming the output Q that person 1 has commissioned. At the output Q, person 2's marginal private benefit is only P_2, less than the current price P_1. Person 2 will not pay the higher price needed to induce a competitive supplier to expand output beyond Q. Person 2 free-rides on person 1's purchase of Q. This quantity privately produced and consumed in a competitive market is below the efficient quantity Q^*.

Revelation of preferences

If it knows the marginal social benefit curve *DD*, the government can decide the efficient output of the public good. How does the government discover the individual demand curves that must be vertically added to get *DD*? If people's payments for the good are related to their individual demand curves, everyone will lie. People will understate how much they value the good in order to reduce their own payments, just as in a private market. Conversely, we are all for safer streets if we do not have to contribute to the cost.

In practice, democracies try to resolve this problem through election of governments. Politics lets society get closer to the efficient answer than the market can. Different parties offer different quantities of public goods, together with statements on how they will be financed by taxes. By asking 'How much would you like, given that everyone is charged for the cost of providing public goods?' society comes closer to providing the efficient quantities of public goods. However, with only a few parties competing in an election and many policies on which they offer a position, this remains a crude way to decide the quantities of public goods provided.

Government production

The output of public goods must be *decided* by the government, not the market. This need not mean government must produce the goods itself. Public goods need not be produced by the public sector.

National defence is a public good largely produced in the public or government sector. We have few private armies. Street-sweeping, though a public good, can be subcontracted to private producers, even if local government determines its quantity and pays for it out of local tax revenue. Conversely, state hospitals involve public sector production of private goods. One person's hip replacement operation prevents the busy surgeon from operating on someone else.

In the next chapter we examine why the public sector may wish to produce private goods. Whether public goods need to be produced by the public sector depends not on their consumption characteristics, on which our definition of public good relies, but on their production characteristics. There is nothing special about street-sweeping. In contrast, armies rely on discipline and secrecy. Generals and admirals may believe, and society may agree, that offences against these regulations should receive unusual penalties not generally sanctioned in private firms. Few people believe that insubordination is an important offence for street-sweepers.

CASE 14.1

THE PARADOX OF OPEN SOURCE SOFTWARE

Open source software, developed by volunteers, represents a case of a public good that is somehow paradoxical. It is a public good since the 'source code' used to generate the programs is freely available – hence 'open source'.

According to the theory of public goods, without government intervention, a public good will not be provided at the efficient level. However, open source software is now quite popular. Why have private agents, without property rights over the source code, invested effort in developing a public good subject to free-riding?

A possible answer may be that such agents are moved by reputation building and career concerns. A software programmer who is able to prove his skills by programming open source code may have a chance to be employed by important software companies. Therefore, according to this view, private agents have an incentive to provide effort in developing open source software since this will signal their quality as a programmer.

Another possible answer is that open source software is not an alternative to proprietary software (like Microsoft, which has the property rights for its software), but instead can be viewed as a complement.

Proprietary provision fails to effectively meet the needs of many customers in markets where customers have highly disparate needs and products are complex. Open source software and proprietary provision of pre-packaged software can both exist in a market, recognizing that they mainly serve different groups of customers. Open source will be used most by firms that have their own development capability and which have complex, specialized needs; pre-packaged software will be used by firms with simpler needs and those which lack development capabilities.

Source: J. Bessen, 'Open source software: Free provision of complex public goods', working paper, Boston University School of Law and Research on Innovation, 2005.

Transfer payments and income redistribution

Government spending on transfer payments is primarily concerned with *equity* and *income redistribution.* By spending money on the unemployed, the old and the poor, the government alters the distribution of income and welfare that a free market economy would otherwise have produced: there is a minimum standard of living below which no citizen should fall. The specification of this standard is a pure value judgement.

To finance this spending, the government taxes those who can afford to pay. Taken as a whole, the tax and transfer system takes money from the rich and gives it to the poor. The poor get cash transfers but also enjoy the consumption of public goods paid for by income taxes raised from the rich. Figure 14.4 shows the effects of government intervention during 2009/10. The net taxes paid by the richest 10 per cent of the population amount for almost half of their disposable income. In contrast, the poorest 10 per cent of the population benefited from changes to the tax and benefit by an amount almost equal to half of their disposable income.

The desirable amount of redistribution is a value judgement on which people and parties will disagree. There is also the trade-off between efficiency and equity. To redistribute more the government has to raise tax rates, driving a larger wedge between the price paid by the purchaser and the price received by the seller. Since the price system achieves efficiency by inducing each individual to equate marginal cost or marginal benefit to the price received or paid, and hence to one another, taxes are generally distortionary and reduce efficiency.

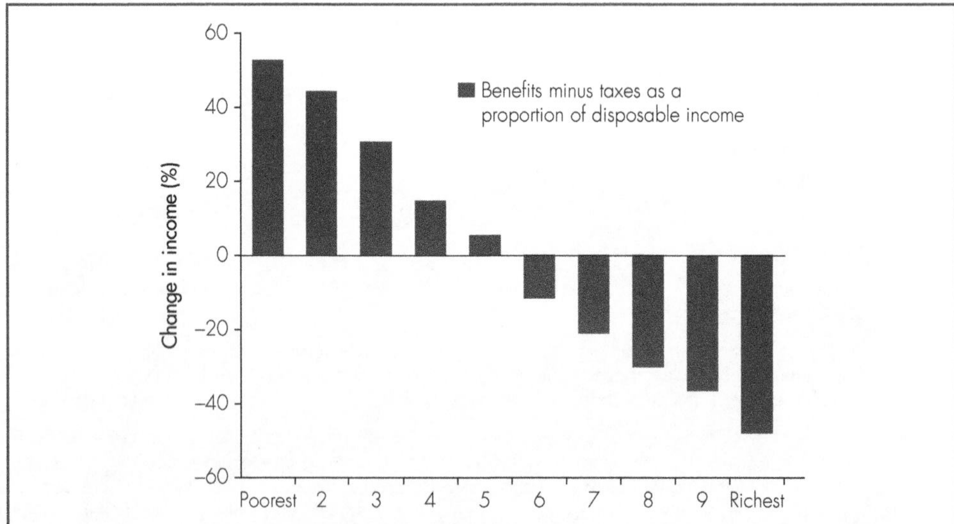

Figure 14.4 **Distributional impact of the UK tax and benefits in 2009–2010 (% of initial disposable income)**

Source: Redistribution, Work Incentives and Thirty Years of UK Tax and Benefit Reform working paper by Stuart Adam and James Browne, © Institute for Fiscal Studies, 2010, http://www.ifs.org.uk/wps/wp1024.pdf

Merit and demerit goods

Merit goods are goods that societies should consume regardless of whether an individual wants them. Those goods are provided by governments despite the fact that they can be consumed and bought individually in the market. The reason is that, if we leave to the private market the burden of providing merit goods, those goods will be underprovided. Merit goods include education and health.

> Merit (demerit) goods are goods that society thinks everyone should have (not have) regardless of whether an individual wants them.

On the other hand, there are also **demerit goods**. Demerit goods include cigarettes and heroin. Since society places a different value on these goods from the value placed on them by the individual, individual choice in a free market leads to a different allocation from the one that society wishes.

There are two reasons for providing merit goods. The first is externalities. Indeed, merit goods generate positive externalities. If more education raises the productivity not merely of an individual worker but also of the workers with whom he co-operates, he ignores this production externality when choosing how much education to acquire. If people demand too little education, society should encourage the provision of education.

Conversely, if people ignore the burden on state hospitals when deciding to smoke and damage their health, society may regard smoking as a demerit to be discouraged. Taxing cigarettes may offset externalities that individuals fail to take into account.

The second reason for providing merit goods is that a society may believe that individuals no longer act in their own best interests and so it has to decide on their behalf. Addiction to drugs, tobacco or gambling are examples. Economists rarely subscribe to paternalism. The function of government intervention is less to tell people what they ought to like than to allow them better to gain what they already like. However, the government sometimes has more information or is in a better position to take a decision. Many people hate going to school, but later are glad they did. The government may spend money on compulsory education or compulsory vaccination because it recognizes that otherwise individuals act in a way they will subsequently regret.

14.3 The principles of taxation

This section is in three parts. First, we consider different taxes through which the government can raise revenue. Then we consider equity implications of taxation. Finally, we examine efficiency implications of taxation.

Types of taxes

Governments can collect tax revenue only if they monitor and enforce the activities being taxed. Before sophisticated records of income or sales, governments raised most of their revenue from customs duties and road tolls, places where transactions were easily monitored. Income tax in peacetime was not introduced in the UK until the 1840s, and VAT not until the 1970s.

How to tax fairly

The last chapter gave two notions of equity: *horizontal equity*, or the equal treatment of equals, and *vertical equity*, the redistribution from the 'haves' to the 'have-nots'.

Progressive taxes reflect the principle of *ability to pay*. The principle of ability to pay reflects a concern about vertical equity. Thus, car users should be taxed to finance public roads. However, the **benefits principle** often conflicts with the principle of ability to pay. If those most vulnerable to unemployment pay the highest contributions to a government unemployment insurance scheme, it is hard to redistribute income or welfare. If the main objective is vertical equity, ability to pay must take precedence.

> The benefits principle is that people getting most benefit from public spending should pay most for it.

Two factors make the entire tax and benefit structure more progressive than an examination of income tax alone would suggest. First, transfer payments actually give money to the poor. The old receive pensions, the unemployed receive unemployment benefit and, as a final safety net, anyone whose income falls below a certain minimum is entitled to supplementary benefit. Second, the state provides public goods that can be consumed by the poor, even if they have not paid any taxes to finance these goods.

However, the system of tax, transfer and spending has some *regressive* elements that take proportionately more from the poor. Beer and tobacco taxes are huge earners for the government. Yet the poor spend a much higher proportion of their income on these goods than do the rich. Regressive taxes inhibit redistribution from the rich to the poor.

Tax incidence is the final tax burden once we allow for all induced effects of a tax.

Tax incidence

The ultimate effect of a tax can be very different from its initial effect. Figure 14.5 shows the market for labour. *DD* is the demand curve and *SS* the supply curve. Without an income tax (a tax on wages), labour market equilibrium is at *E*.

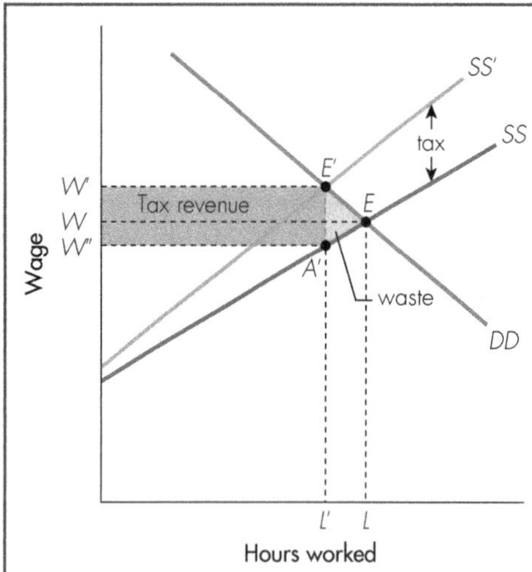

With no tax, equilibrium is at *E* and the wage is *W*. A wage tax raises the gross wage paid by firms above the net wage received by workers. Measuring gross wages on the vertical axis, the demand curve *DD* is unaltered by the imposition of the tax. Firms demand labour to equate the gross wage to the marginal value product of labour. *SS* continues to show labour supply, but as a function of the net wage. To get labour supply in terms of the gross wage we draw the new supply curve *SS'*. *SS'* lies vertically above *SS* by a distance reflecting the tax on earnings from the last hour worked. The new equilibrium is at *E'*. The hourly wage paid by firms is *W'* but the net wage received by workers is *W''*. The vertical distance *A'E'* shows the tax rate. Whether the government collects the tax from firms or from workers, the incidence of the tax is the same. It falls partly on firms, who pay a higher gross wage *W'* and partly on workers, who receive the lower net wage *W''*. The area of pure waste *A'E'E* is discussed in the text.

Figure 14.5 **A tax on wages**

Now the government imposes an income tax. If we measure the gross wage on the vertical axis, the demand curve *DD* is unaltered. Firms' demand for labour depends on the gross wage that they pay. Workers' preferences are unchanged, but it is the wage net-of-tax that workers compare with the marginal value of their leisure in deciding how much labour to supply. *SS* continues to show labour supply in terms of the net-of-tax wage, but we must draw in the higher schedule *SS'* to show the supply of labour in terms of the gross or *tax-inclusive* wage. The vertical distance between *SS'* and *SS* is the tax on earnings from the last hour's work.

DD and *SS'* show the behaviour of firms and workers at any gross wage. At the new equilibrium *E'*, the gross wage is *W'* and firms demand *L'* workers. The vertical distance between *A'* and *E'* is the tax paid on the last hour of work. The net-of-tax wage is W^2, at which workers supply *L'* hours.

The tax on wages has raised the pre-tax wage to *W'*, but lowered the after-tax wage to W^2. It has raised the wage that firms pay but lowered the take-home wage for workers. The incidence of the tax falls on *both* firms and workers.

Figure 14.6 shows the extreme case in which supply is completely inelastic. With no tax, equilibrium is at *E* and the wage is *W*. Since the vertical supply curve *SS* means that a fixed quantity of hours *L* is supplied whatever the after-tax wage, a tax on wages leads to a new equilibrium at *A'*. Only if the gross wage is unchanged will firms demand the quantity *L* that is supplied. Hence the entire incidence falls on the workers.

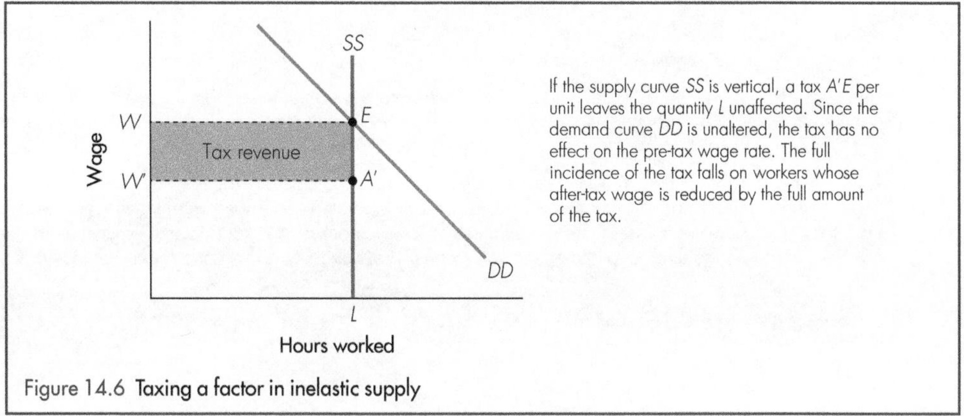

Figure 14.6 **Taxing a factor in inelastic supply**

We can draw one very general conclusion. The more inelastic the supply curve and the more elastic the demand curve, the more the final incidence will fall on the seller rather than on the purchaser.

To check you have grasped the idea of incidence, draw for yourself a market with an elastic supply curve and an inelastic demand curve. Show that the incidence of a tax will now fall mainly on the purchaser.[1]

Taxation, efficiency and waste

Taxes have efficiency effects as well as equity effects. We can use Figure 14.5 again. Before the tax is imposed, labour market equilibrium is at *E*. The wage *W* measures both the marginal social benefit of the last hour of work and its marginal social cost. The demand curve *DD* tells us the marginal benefit of the extra goods produced. The supply curve *SS* tells us the marginal value of the leisure being sacrificed in order to work another hour; that is, the marginal social cost of extra work. At *E*, marginal social costs and benefits are equal, which is socially efficient.

When the tax is imposed, the new equilibrium is at E'. The tax $A'E'$ increases the wage to firms to W' but reduces the after-tax wage for workers to W^2. But there is an additional tax burden or deadweight loss that is pure waste. It is the triangle $A'E'E$. By reducing the quantity of hours from L to L', the tax drives a wedge between marginal benefit, the height of the demand curve *DD*, and marginal social cost, the height of the supply curve *SS*. This distortion makes free market equilibrium inefficient.

CASE 14.2

DO YOU MIND IF I SMOKE? THE SMOKING BAN IN THE UK

The smoking ban that took effect in the UK in 2006/07 is an example of a government policy to tackle a negative externality. The ban makes it illegal to smoke in all enclosed public venues and workplaces in the UK.

Smoking is a negative externality since smokers pollute the air for other people but ignore this in deciding how much to smoke. Doing so has negative effects on passive smokers. Doctors estimate that second-hand smoke kills more than 600 people a year.

Moreover, it has negative effects on society as a whole. By smoking, smokers have a greater likelihood of suffering from smoking-related diseases and so they are likely to need health care in the future. This will affect

1 Does a tax always shift the supply curve? Yes, if we measure the gross price on the vertical axis. If we measure the net-of-tax price on the vertical axis, the tax shifts not the supply curve but the demand curve. In Figures 14.5 and 14.6, in terms of the net wage the demand curve shifts down until it passes through A'. The distance between A' and E still measures the tax and we reach exactly the same conclusions as before.

health care expenditure in the country. Since the public health care system is financed also by non-smokers, smoking will have a negative effect on non-smokers as well.

Finally, smoking is viewed as a demerit good and therefore governments should do something to discourage people from smoking. The smoking ban, together with heavy taxation on cigarettes, aims to reduce the number of smokers so that the negative externality created by smoking will decrease.

After the introduction of the smoking ban, cigarette sales decreased by 7 per cent. By looking at markets linked to the cigarette market, we can also gain a better idea of the general equilibrium effect of the smoking ban. In particular, we can look at the sales figures for public houses. Market research organization Nielsen estimated that beer sales in England and Wales could drop by 200 million pints each year as a result of the ban.

Source: adapted from http://news.bbc.co.uk/1/hi/uk/6258034.stm. © bbc.co.uk/news.

Must taxes distort?

Government needs tax revenue to pay for public goods and make transfer payments. Figure 14.6 shows what happens when a tax is levied but supply is completely inelastic. There is no change in equilibrium quantity. Hence there is no distortionary triangle. The equilibrium quantity remains the efficient quantity.

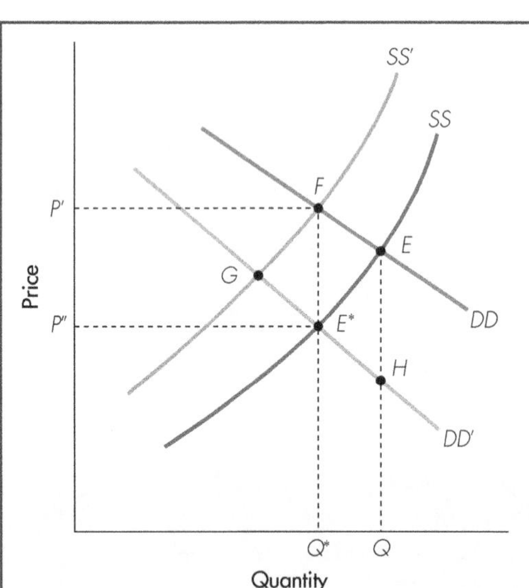

Given private demand *DD* and supply *SS*, free market equilibrium is at *E* with a quantity *Q*. With a negative consumption externality, the social marginal benefit is *DD'* lying below *DD*. *E** is the socially efficient point at which output is *Q**. At this output the marginal externality is *E*F*. By levying a tax of exactly *E*F* per unit, the government can shift the private supply curve from *SS* to *SS'*, leading to a new equilibrium at *F* at which the socially efficient quantity *Q** is produced and the deadweight burden of the externality *E*HE* is eliminated.

Figure 14.7 **Taxes to offset externalities**

We can make this into a general principle. When either the supply or the demand curve for a good or service is very inelastic, a tax leads to a small change in equilibrium quantity. Hence the deadweight loss is small. Given that the government must raise some tax revenues, waste is smallest when the goods that are most inelastic in supply or demand are taxed most heavily.

In the UK tax system, the most heavily taxed commodities are alcohol, fuel and tobacco. Alcohol, fuel and tobacco have inelastic demand.

So far, we have discussed the taxes that do least harm to efficiency. Sometimes taxes improve efficiency and reduce waste. The most important example is when externalities exist.

Cigarette smokers pollute the air for other people but ignore this in deciding how much to smoke. They cause a harmful consumption externality, as discussed in Case 14.2. Figure 14.7 shows the supply curve *SS* of cigarette producers. With no production externalities, *SS* is also the marginal social cost curve. *DD* is the private demand curve; that is, the marginal benefit of cigarettes to smokers. Because of the harmful consumption externality, the marginal social benefit *DD'* lies below *DD*.

With no tax, equilibrium is at *E*, but there are too many cigarettes. The efficient quantity is *Q**, which equates marginal social cost and marginal social benefit. Suppose the government levies a tax, equal to the vertical distance E^*F, on each packet of cigarettes. With the tax-inclusive price on the vertical axis, the demand curve DD is unaffected, but the supply curve shifts up to SS'. Each point on SS' then allows producers to receive the corresponding net-of-tax price on SS.

The tax shifts equilibrium to F. The efficient quantity Q^* is produced and consumed. Consumers pay P' and producers get P' after tax is paid at the rate E^*F per packet.

The tax rate E^*F guides the free market to the efficient allocation. A lower tax rate (including zero) leads to too much consumption and production of cigarettes. A higher tax rate than E^*F moves consumers too far up their demand curve, causing too little consumption and production.

A tax rate E^*F leads to the efficient quantity because this is the size of the marginal externality when the efficient quantity Q^* is produced. A tax at this rate makes consumers behave as if they took account of the externality, though they think only about the tax-inclusive price.

When externalities induce distortions, the government can improve efficiency by levying taxes. The fact that alcohol and tobacco have harmful externalities is another reason to tax them heavily.

MATHS 14.1

USING A TAX TO INTERNALIZE THE NEGATIVE EXTERNALITY

Consider the same example as in Maths 13.1 and two firms, A and B. Firm A pollutes the lake used by firm B for fishing. Here, we briefly report the main features of the two firms. The cost function of firm A is $TC_A = TC_A(Q_A, P_A)$, where Q_A is the quantity produced by A and P_A is the level of pollution of firm A. The cost function of firm A has the following properties:

- It increases with the output produced: $\partial TC_A/\partial Q_A > 0$
- It decreases with the level of pollution: $\partial TC_A/\partial P_A$ £ 0

Firm B has the total cost function $TC_B = TC_B(Q_B, P_A)$, with the following properties:

$$\partial TC_B/\partial Q_B > 0 \quad \text{and} \quad \partial TC_B/\partial P_A > 0$$

If property rights are not assigned and with no government intervention, the optimal level of pollution chosen by firm A satisfies the condition:

$$-(\partial TC_A/\partial P_A) = 0$$

that is, marginal cost of pollution equals marginal revenue of pollution (zero in this case).

Firm A is polluting more than it should, so we can tax firm A in such a way that the socially efficient level of pollution is reached. Those kinds of taxes are also called Pigouvian taxes.

When firm A has to pay a tax for its polluting activity, the profit function of firm A becomes:

$$\pi_A = pQ_A - TC_A(Q_A, P_A) - tP_A$$

where t is the tax rate and p is the market price for the output of firm A. Now the optimal level of pollution (the one that maximizes firm A's profits) is:

$$-(\partial TC_A/\partial P_A) - t = 0 \Rightarrow -(\partial TC_A/\partial P_A) - t$$

The tax simply increases the marginal cost of polluting. Now the level of pollution that maximizes the profits is lower than before since $-\partial TC_A/\partial P_A$ must be equal to t, that is, greater than zero.

What tax level provides the efficient solution for the externality?

If we set $t = \partial TC_B/\partial P_A$, we obtain the efficient solution. Why? Because by setting $t = \partial TC_B/\partial P_A$, firm A now chooses a level of pollution that satisfies $-\partial TC_A/\partial P_A = \partial TC_B/\partial P_A$. In deciding the optimal level of P_A, firm A now takes into account the effect that its decision has on firm B. In practice, in order to obtain the efficient solution we need to set the tax (paid by the polluting firm) equal to the marginal social cost of pollution. This kind of tax is known as *Pigouvian tax*.

14.4 Taxation and supply-side economics

Supply-side economics analyses how taxes and other incentives affect national output when the economy is at full capacity.

Suppose the government cuts spending and tax rates. What are the effects? First, by spending less on goods and services, the government frees some resources for use by the private sector. If the private sector is more productive than the public sector, the transfer of resources may directly raise output. Whether the private sector actually uses resources more productively than the government is unclear. It seems to do many things better but some things worse.

What about the effects of lower tax rates? Figure 14.7 suggests that tax distortions cause inefficiency. Lower taxes mean a lower deadweight burden. The size of this gain depends on supply and demand elasticity. If either elasticity is small, the social gain is low.

For example, Chapter 10 argued that labour supply is fairly inelastic for those in employment, but a bit more elastic for those thinking of joining the labour force. Cutting income tax rates *will* increase labour supply, but perhaps by less than many advocates of tax cuts believe.

The Laffer curve

The Laffer curve shows how much tax revenue is raised at each possible tax rate.

We now discuss the relationship between tax rates and tax revenues. Professor Laffer was an adviser to US President Ronald Reagan.

Figure 14.8 shows that with a zero tax rate the government gets zero revenue. At the opposite extreme, with a 100 per cent income tax rate, there is no point working and again tax revenue is zero. Beginning from a zero rate, a small increase in the tax rate yields some tax revenue. Initially tax revenue rises with the tax rate, but beyond the tax rate t^* (the tax rate at which tax revenues are maximized) higher taxes have major disincentive effects on work effort, and revenue falls.

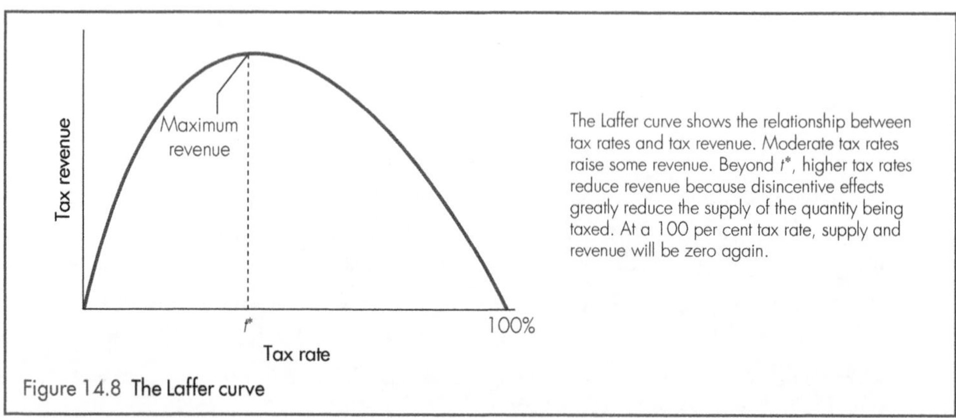

The Laffer curve shows the relationship between tax rates and tax revenue. Moderate tax rates raise some revenue. Beyond t^*, higher tax rates reduce revenue because disincentive effects greatly reduce the supply of the quantity being taxed. At a 100 per cent tax rate, supply and revenue will be zero again.

Figure 14.8 **The Laffer curve**

Professor Laffer's idea was that 'big government–big tax' countries were at tax rates above t^*. If so, tax cuts were the miracle cure. The government would get *more* revenue by cutting taxes. By reducing the tax distortion and increasing the amount of work *a lot*, lower tax rates would be more than offset by higher incomes to tax.

The shape of the Laffer curve is not in dispute. However, many economists disputed the view that *in fact* tax rates were above t^*. Most economists' reading of the empirical evidence is that our economies were always to the left of t^*. Cutting income tax rates may eliminate some of the deadweight burden of distortionary taxation, but governments should probably expect their tax revenue to fall if tax rates are cut. Governments wishing to avoid borrowing need to cut their spending if they wish to cut the tax rate.

14.5 Local government

So much for central government. What about local government? Local government spends on things from sweeping the streets to providing schooling. This is financed both by local taxes and by money from central government financed by national taxes. Local government is also responsible for some types of regulation, for example land use or *zoning* laws.

Economic principles

Why don't we make central government responsible for everything? First, diversity matters. People are different and do not want to be treated the same. Civic pride is necessarily local. Second, people feel that central government is remote from their particular needs. Even if central government paid attention to local considerations, it would find it hard to do so efficiently.

We examine two important models of local government. The *Tiebout model*[2] emphasizes diversity. Some people want high spending, good public services and high local taxes; others want low local taxes even if this means poor public services. The Tiebout model is sometimes called the *invisible foot*: people cluster in the area providing the package of spending and taxes they want. The 'invisible foot' allocates resources efficiently via competition *between* local governments.

The 'invisible foot' is a crude incentive structure. First, it is hard to move between local authorities. You may lose your place in the queue for housing provided by that local authority. Second, if much of local authority revenue comes from central government, the levels of spending and taxes may be insensitive to the wishes of local residents.

Even if the 'invisible foot' led to efficiency, it might also lead to inequity. The rich are likely to cluster together in suburbs. Then they pass zoning laws specifying a minimum size for a house and its garden. The poor cannot move into that area. By forming an exclusive club, the rich ensure that their taxes do not go to supporting the poor. The poor get stuck with one another in inner-city areas whose governments face the biggest social needs but have the smallest local tax base.

The Tiebout model assumes that residents consume the public services provided by their own local authority. When each unit of local government has responsibility for a small geographical area, this may be a bad assumption. If a city supplies free art galleries, financed by taxes on city residents, the rich still come in from the suburbs to use these facilities. Conversely, urban trendies spend their Sundays enjoying countryside facilities supported by rural taxes. In both cases, provision of public services in one area confers a beneficial externality on nearby areas.

Economic theory suggests an answer to this problem. Widen the geographical area of each local government until it includes most of the people who use the public services it provides. It may make sense to have an integrated commuter rail service and inner-city subway, and to subsidize it to prevent people driving through congested streets. However, only a local government embracing both the suburbs and the inner city is likely to get close to the efficient policy.

The Tiebout model favours a lot of small local government jurisdictions to maximize choice and competition between areas. However, the presence of externalities across areas suggests larger jurisdictions to 'internalize' externalities that would otherwise occur. The right answer may involve a bit of both.

14.6 Economic sovereignty

Economic sovereignty is the power of national governments to make decisions independently of those made by other governments.

Nowadays, no country is an economic island, cut off from the rest of the world. We examine the world economy in Part Five, but some issues cannot be postponed until then. In a democratic country insulated from the rest of the world, the government is sovereign: while it retains democratic support and observes existing laws, it has the final say in policy design. Sometimes central government chooses to delegate powers to local government.

2 C. Tiebout, 'A pure theory of local expenditures', *Journal of Political Economy* 64, no. 5 (1956): 416–424.

What this account ignores is the existence of other countries. How do interactions with the rest of the world affect the sovereignty of national governments?

Even in a quarantined economy, governments cannot do anything they like. Within market economies they have to work within the forces of supply and demand. For example, in Section 14.3 we argued that it is generally more efficient to have high tax rates on things for which the demand or supply is inelastic. High tax rates on things with elastic supply and demand induce large distortions since equilibrium quantity is very sensitive to the price. We now apply this insight to economies open to interactions with the rest of the world.

International capital is now highly mobile across countries. Suppose the UK government tries to levy a large tax on capital in Britain. Lots of capital will quickly move elsewhere to escape the high taxes. The *tax base*, in this example the quantity of capital available for taxing in Britain, quickly shrinks. So the high tax *rates* may raise little tax *revenue*. In contrast, since people are much less mobile than capital across national boundaries, the tax base for taxing workers' incomes in Britain is much less sensitive to tax rates than the tax base for capital taxes.

Even people are more mobile across national boundaries than they were a few decades ago. Communication is easier and transport costs are lower. Migration affects not just taxation but government spending as well. Suppose a country wishes to implement a generous welfare state. As a closed economy, all it has to worry about is how much of its tax base disappears from work into leisure. If welfare is too generous, people may not work enough. As an open economy, it also has to consider whether more generous welfare provision will lead to more migration into the country as foreigners take advantage, legally or illegally, of the generous welfare provision.

Closer economic integration with other countries – through trade in goods and movement of factors of production – effectively undermines the sovereignty of nation states. If the tax rate was 80 per cent in Liverpool but 20 per cent in Manchester, one would expect big movements of capital and people from Liverpool to Manchester. The tax base in Liverpool would evaporate. The local government of Liverpool has limited local sovereignty because it is effectively in competition with Manchester.

The economic sovereignty of nation states, their freedom to do what they want, is steadily being constrained by competition from foreign countries. More than one in ten cans of beer now consumed in England was bought by British households in France, hopping across the Channel to take advantage of lower alcohol taxes in France. UK Chancellors of the Exchequer, caught between the pressure to raise revenue and support jobs in the UK drinks industry, have been cutting the real value of UK alcohol taxes. They have already lost the sovereignty to set tax rates at the high levels that they would have liked.

National sovereignty is undermined not just by competition between countries for tax bases but also by two other forces. The first is other cross-country spillovers such as acid rain, greenhouse gases or the threat of pollution from a nuclear accident. Banning nuclear power generation in southern England has limited value if northern France is studded with nuclear power stations.

The second is the scope for redistribution. Economics is about equity as well as efficiency. In an important sense, the right jurisdiction for government is the area within which citizens feel sufficient identity with one another that the rich are prepared to pay for the poor, and the fortunate are prepared to assist the unlucky. European nation states have long histories and strong national identities. But these are not always set in stone. Countries such as Belgium, Italy, Spain and the UK have faced strong internal pressures to allow parts of their country to secede. In the opposite direction, some Europeans now feel as much a citizen of Europe as of their own particular nation.

Nation states are not yet obsolete. But they are coming under pressure. Further developments in technology will increase the transnational scope of economic interactions and cultural identity. The proliferation of ecommerce and the Internet will only accelerate this process.

14.7 Political economy: how governments decide

Political economy is the study of how governments make decisions.

Firms are in business to make profits for their owners. Individuals buy affordable combinations of goods that yield them most satisfaction. These simple assumptions let economists explain most consumer and business decision making. What about government decision making?

Government is the most important single player in the economy. It is important to develop theories of how governments behave. There is no point analysing the consequences of a policy that a sane government will never implement.

Voters elect governments to set spending and taxing, pass new laws and establish new regulations. The electorate chooses among alternative policy *packages* offered by competing parties, but is rarely allowed a referendum on each issue.

The government does not simply do the bidding of society. Government has its own agenda, which may be to promote what it thinks is good for the public or simply to get re-elected.

The median voter

The **median voter** on an issue is the person whose preferences are such that half the population's preferences on the issue lie on one side and half the population's preferences lie on the other side.

If everyone was identical and of one mind, public decision making would be trivial. Through the political process, society tries to reconcile different views and different interests.

Figure 14.9 shows 17 different voters and how much each wants the government to spend on the police. A dot shows each voter's preferred amount. Assume that a voter whose ideal amount is £250 will think that £300 is better than £400 if these are the only choices on offer, and will prefer £200 to £100. Each person has *single-peaked* preferences, being happier with an outcome the closer it is to his peak or preferred level.

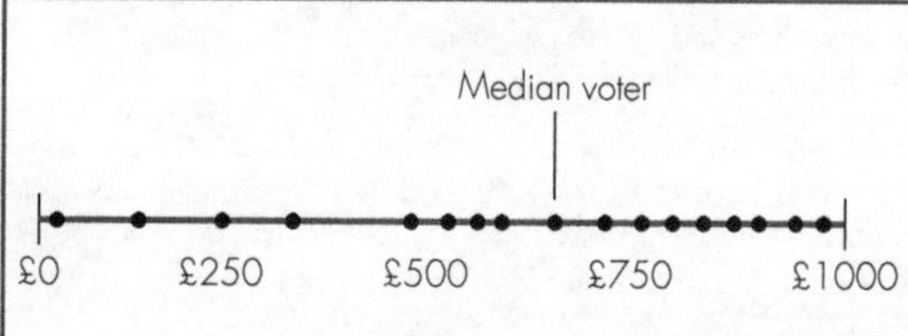

Each dot represents the preferred expenditure of each of 17 voters. The outcome under majority voting will be the level preferred by the median voter. Everybody to the left will prefer the median voter's position to any higher spending level. Everybody to the right will prefer it to any lower spending level. The median voter's position is the only position that cannot be outvoted against some alternative. Hence it will be chosen.

Figure 14.9 **The median voter**

There is a vote on how much to spend on the public good called police. A proposal to spend £0 is defeated by 16 votes to 1. Only the voter who is the left-hand dot in Figure 14.9 votes for £0 rather than £100. From either extreme, as we move to the centre more people vote for a particular proposal. With 17 voters, the median voter is the person who wants to spend the ninth-highest amount on the police. Eight voters want to spend more; eight want to spend less.

Any proposal for higher spending than the median voter's preferred amount can be defeated. The median voter, plus the eight voters below him, all vote against. But any proposal for lower spending is also defeated. The median voter, and the eight voters above him, all vote against. Hence, the median voter gets his way by majority voting.

Log-rolling is a vote for another person's preferred outcome on one issue in order to exchange for their vote your preferred outcome on another issue.

Log-rolling

So far we have assumed each issue is voted on independently. Making decisions through legislative compromises is much more complicated when votes can be traded between different issues. Groups of politicians form parties or coalitions within which some vote trading can take place.

For two issues, A and B, and three politicians, Tom, Dick and Harry, Table 14.4 shows the value of each outcome to each politician. Suppose each person votes for a proposal only if the outcome is positive. Tom votes against A and B, Dick votes against A but for B, and Harry votes for A but against B. Both issues are defeated on a majority vote.

Table 14.4 Log-rolling

Politician	Issue A	Issue B
Tom	−4	−1
Dick	−3	4
Harry	6	−1

ACTIVITY 14.1

HUNTING THE MEDIAN VOTER

After Labour lost the 1979 general election it moved to the left. This pleased party activists but took the party too far away from the preferences of the median voter. The Conservatives were in power for the next 17 years. After heavy defeat in 1983, successive Labour leaders slowly moved the party back to the middle ground that the median voter inhabits. Labour focus groups interviewed people directly to clarify the median voter's view on different issues. The result? Labour victories in 1997, 2001 and 2005.

Did Labour abandon its principles to win and keep office? It gave up old traditions of high welfare spending and high, visible taxes. But, when Gordon Brown was the Chancellor of the Exchequer, he helped the poor substantially without frightening the middle classes. As a result of his budgets, the post-tax income of the poorest 20 per cent of people rose by over 10 per cent (see Figure 14.4 again).

How did he do it? Not by raising income tax or VAT. Some of it was financed by stealth taxes, such as the tax treatment of pension funds, which the median voter did not initially notice or understand. Some was financed by making transfer payments more selective. Instead of a universal benefit, scarce resources were concentrated only on those who really needed them. Some of it was financed by economic growth: as incomes grew, given tax rates yielded more tax revenue, which was given mainly to the poor.

Unusually, Labour did not take credit for the extent to which it helped the poor. This kept the median voter sweet (the middle classes were not told repeatedly how they were paying too much to support the poor), but upset some traditional Labour supporters (who probably still voted Labour anyway).

The electoral success of the Labour Party partly ended in May 2010, when the Conservatives won the majority of seats (not the necessary number to have an overall majority though) at the general election and a coalition government between the Conservatives and the Liberal Democrats was formed. Did the median voter change his mind?

Questions

(a) In a country with two parties, suppose both end up with almost identical policies in the centre ground. What does this tell you about (i) the ideology of the party leaders, and (ii) the extent to which party activists trade off the desire for power and their political beliefs?

(b) Suppose we could order voters from left to right with equal numbers of voters holding each possible opinion. If everyone votes for the party nearest their own beliefs, where should the two parties locate to maximize their vote?

David Cameron (Conservative), Nick Clegg (Liberal Democrat) and Gordon Brown (Labour) in a live televized debate in May 2010 in the lead-up to the UK general election.
© Gareth Fuller/PA Archive/Press Association Images

(c) Now, however, suppose that people abstain if the party is not close to the voters' ideal positions. Does this change the optimal positioning of party manifestos?

To check your answers to these questions, go to page 679.

Now suppose Dick and Harry vote together. They vote for A, which Harry really wants, and for B, which Dick really wants. Dick gains 4 since B passes, and loses only 3 when A passes. Harry gains 6 when A passes and loses only 1 when B passes. By forming a coalition that allows them to express the intensity of their preferences, they do better than under independent majority voting, when neither A nor B would have passed.

Many decisions in the European Union reflect log-rolling. Individual countries get favourable decisions on issues they really mind about, but are expected to repay the favour on other issues.

Commitment and credibility

Chapter 9 introduced **credibility** and **commitment** in the context of games between firms. Similar ideas apply to the political economy of policy design. Because expectations about the future affect current decisions, politicians are tempted to make optimistic promises about the future in the hope of influencing people today.

A credible promise about future action is one that is optimal to carry out when the future arrives.

A commitment is a current device to restrict future room for manoeuvre to make promises more credible today.

Our discussion of strategic entry deterrence in Chapter 9 gives you all the clues you need to think about political credibility. Project your imagination into the future and consider how politicians will then want to behave. Use this insight to form smart guesses today about which promises are credible and which are not.

For example, most post-war Labour governments were big spenders, which required high taxation. When out of office, Labour promises of low spending and low taxes when next in government were not very credible. Gordon Brown's Code for Fiscal Stability was an attempt to enhance Labour's credibility by openly and repeatedly committing to a tough policy that would then be politically costly to abandon. With so much political capital invested in prudence and the Code for Fiscal Stability, the government would look very stupid if it subsequently abandoned it.

Recently, many countries have adopted a commitment that has been very successful. They have made the central bank operationally independent of government control, as Labour did with the Bank of England in 1997. The government chooses the aim of monetary policy – to keep inflation low – but the Bank alone now decides what interest rates are needed to achieve this. By keeping the government's hands off interest rates, central bank independence removes the temptation for the government to overheat the economy in pursuit of a pre-election boom.

Policy co-ordination

Policy co-ordination is the decision to set policies jointly when two interdependent areas have big cross-border spillovers.

Chapter 9 contained another useful insight for modern political economy. In discussing games between oligopolists, we showed that collectively they make more profit acting as a joint monopolist than by acting without co-ordination. In the language you later learned in Chapter 13, when actions are interdependent and externalities matter, the efficient solution needs to take these spillovers fully into account. Internalizing externalities means stopping free-riding.

The more interdependent different nation states become, the more it may be necessary to co-ordinate national policies rather than formulate them in isolation. Global warming is one example, but many forms of regulation and taxation fall under this heading.

French tax rates on alcohol are so much lower than UK rates that UK Chancellors can no longer set UK alcohol taxes as high as they would like. The UK would like continental tax rates on alcohol to be higher. Conversely, continental Europeans complain about low levels of worker protection in the UK and the competitive edge this may give UK firms.

Pressure for closer policy co-ordination is likely to increase as globalization continues.

Summary

- Government revenues come mainly from **direct taxes** on personal incomes and company profits, **indirect taxes** on purchases of goods and services, and **contributions** to state-run social security schemes. Government spending comprises **government purchases** of goods and services and **transfer payments**.
- Governments intervene in a market economy in pursuit of distributional equity and allocative efficiency. A **progressive tax-and-transfer system** takes most from the rich and gives most to the poor. The UK system

is mildly progressive. The less well off receive transfer payments and the rich pay the highest tax rates. Although some necessities, notably food, are exempt from VAT, other goods intensively consumed by the poor, notably cigarettes and alcohol, are heavily taxed.

- **Externalities** are cases of market failure where intervention may improve efficiency. By taxing or subsidizing goods that involve externalities, the government can induce the private sector to behave as if it takes account of the externality, eliminating the **deadweight burden** arising from the misallocation induced by the externality distortion.
- A **public good** is a good for which one person's consumption does not reduce the quantity available for consumption by others. Together with the impossibility of effectively excluding people from consuming it, this implies all individuals consume the same quantity, but they may get different utility if their tastes differ.
- A free market will undersupply a public good because of the **free-rider problem**. Individuals need not offer to pay for a good that they can consume if others pay for it. The socially **efficient** quantity of a public good equates the marginal social cost of production to the sum of the marginal private benefits over all people at this output level. Individual demand curves are vertically added to get the social demand or marginal benefit curves.
- Except for taxes to offset externalities, taxes are **distortionary**. A **wedge** between the sale price and purchase price prevents the price system equating marginal costs and marginal benefits. The size of the **deadweight burden** is higher, the higher is the marginal tax rate and the size of the wedge, but also depends on supply and demand elasticities for the taxed commodity or activity. The more inelastic are supply and demand, the less the tax changes equilibrium quantity and the smaller is the deadweight burden.
- **Tax incidence** describes who ultimately pays the tax. The more inelastic is demand relative to supply, the more incidence falls on buyers not sellers.
- Rising tax rates initially increase tax revenue but eventually lead to such large falls in the equilibrium quantity of the taxed commodity or activity that revenue falls. Cutting tax rates will usually reduce the deadweight tax burden but might increase revenue if taxes were initially very high. Few economies are in this position. Lower tax rates usually reduce tax revenue.
- The **economic sovereignty** of nation states is reduced by cross-border mobility of goods, capital, workers and shoppers. Policy co-ordination may increase efficiency by making decisions reflecting previously neglected policy spillovers.
- **Political economy** examines political equilibrium and incentives to adopt particular policies.
- When all those voting have single-peaked preferences, majority voting achieves what the **median voter** wants.

Review questions

EASY

1 Which of the following are public goods: (a) the fire brigade, (b) clean streets, (c) refuse collection, (d) cable television, (e) social tolerance, (f) the postal service?

2 How would you apply the principles of horizontal and vertical equity in deciding how much to tax two people, each capable of doing the same work, but one of whom chooses to devote more time to sunbathing and therefore has a lower income?

3 Classify the following taxes as progressive or regressive: (a) a higher tax on luxury goods than on necessities, (b) taxes in proportion to the value of owner-occupied houses, (c) a tax on beer, (d) a tax on champagne.

4 There is a flat-rate 30 per cent income tax on all income over £2000. Calculate the average tax rate (tax paid divided by income) at income levels of £5000, £10 000 and £50 000. Is the tax progressive? Is it more or less progressive if the exemption is raised from £2000 to £5000?

5 **Common fallacies** Why are these statements wrong? (a) If the government spends all its revenue, taxes are not a burden on society as a whole. (b) Taxes always distort markets. (c) Political economy is just an excuse to waffle, and cannot be made rigorous.

EASY

6 The lake of Mangrovia is polluted by a firm. A clean lake is considered a public good by the local community. Two residents, Sam and Ronald, are interested in reducing the level of pollution in the lake. The following table shows the marginal benefits (or marginal willingness to pay) of the two residents for each unit of pollution reduction:

Units of pollution reduced	MB Sam	MB Ronald
1	£30	£12
2	£20	£9
3	£15	£4
4	£5	£2

Suppose that the cost of reducing pollution is constant at £19. How much pollution would you expect to be reduced? What is the efficient amount of pollution reduction?

7 A firm that produces steel is polluting the air. Assume that the marginal cost of producing steel is constant at £4. The inverse market demand for steel is $P = 44 - 2Q$, where P is the price of steel and Q is the quantity of steel. The air pollution associated with steel production is creating an externality given by £$\frac{1}{2}Q$. Assuming that the market for steel is competitive, what is the profit-maximizing level of steel when only marginal private costs are taken into account? The marginal social costs are given by the sum of the marginal private costs plus the externality. What is the social level of steel output? Show your solution graphically. What is the social loss associated with the externality? How can we solve this externality problem using taxation?

MEDIUM

8 Why does society try to ensure that every child receives an education? Discuss the different ways this could be done and give reasons for preferring one method of providing such an education.

9 Hypothecation is the promise to use tax revenue from a product to achieve benefits for the group who bear the tax, for example using the London congestion charge to improve London's public transport or using tobacco taxes to build health centres for smokers. (a) Why are politicians attracted by hypothecation and (b) why are economists not attracted by hypothecation?

10 Suppose the local government of a city levies high taxes on its residents and does not provide them with enough public goods. What would the unsatisfied residents do according to the Tiebout model? What are the implications of the model on the city?

11 Tom, Dick and Harry vote for issues A and B. Their votes are given in the table below. According to the simple majority rule, which issue will pass? Is there a chance of log-rolling among the voters? If there is, which issue will pass?

Politician	Issue A	Issue B
Tom	−4	−1
Dick	−3	4
Harry	6	−1

12 The market demand for milk is $Q^D = 60 - 4p$, while the market supply is $Q^S = p + p$, where p is the milk's price. Suppose that the government imposes a specific tax $t = 5$ on the suppliers of milk. Find the equilibrium in the milk market. Show your solution graphically. Calculate the total revenues generated by the tax.

What proportion of the tax revenue is paid by consumers? What proportion is paid by the suppliers? Explain graphically how those proportions may depend on the elasticity of demand.

HARD

13 (a) Suppose labour supply is completely inelastic. Show why there is no deadweight burden if wages are taxed. Who bears the incidence of the tax? (b) Now suppose labour supply is quite elastic. Show the area that is the deadweight burden of the tax. How much of the tax is ultimately borne by firms and how much by workers? (c) Refer to the graphs given below. In graph (i) the labour demand is elastic; in graph (ii) the labour demand is inelastic. In which graph does the tax burden fall to a greater extent on firms?

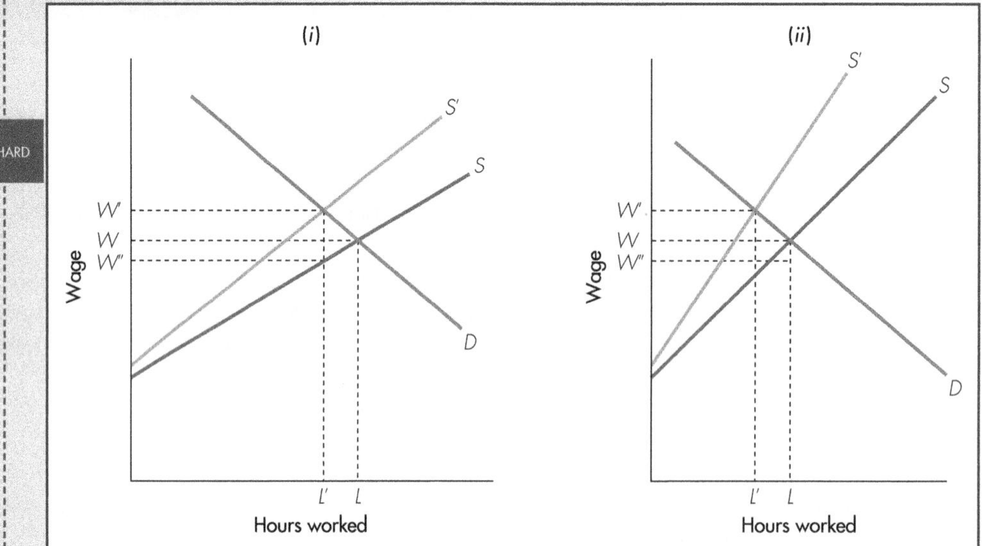

14 **Essay question** Imagine a new UK government, to the surprise of everyone, announces that income tax rates will rise by 15 percentage points in order to provide decent schools and hospitals. Describe the good and bad consequences. How did you decide what you meant by good and bad?

For solutions to these questions, contact your lecturer.

PART TWO: PRINCIPLES OF MACROECONOMICS

Macroeconomics

Part Four studies the economy as an interrelated system. Output is demanded by firms, by households, by the government and by foreigners. Since interest rates and bank lending affect the demand for output, the financial sector interacts with the real economy. Price and wage adjustments help restore output to full capacity, but monetary policy and fiscal policy also play a role. Together, all this affects inflation and unemployment. Economies are increasingly open to foreign trade and foreign capital. The balance of payments records transactions with foreigners. The dynamics of the national economy also depend on the exchange rate policy pursued. By the end of Part Four, we can explain business cycles around full capacity and long-run growth in full capacity output.

Chapter 15 introduces the macroeconomy. Chapters 16–17 develop a basic model of output determination in the short run. Chapters 18–19 describe money, banking and how interest rates are set. Chapter 20 examines monetary and fiscal policy. Chapter 21 introduces aggregate supply and price adjustment. Chapters 22–23 look at inflation and unemployment.

The final two chapters of Part Four pull together our discussion of macroeconomics. Chapter 27 examines short-run business cycles and competing schools of economic thought about how the macroeconomy works. Chapter 28 discusses supply-side economics and the economics of long-run growth.

Contents

Understanding the financial crisis – a roadmap

Mastering macroeconomics will allow you a much deeper understanding of the financial crash and its lingering consequences. Listed below are sections dedicated to analysis of the crisis.

Chapter 16 Case 16.2 contrasts the current crisis with the depression of the 1930s. Case 16.3 examines how the crash has had long-term effects on investment in new capital. Case 16.4 explores how households and firms have reacted to the crash by tightening their belts and increasing saving.

Chapter 17 Case 17.1 discusses how Japan is only just recovering, two decades after a financial crash, and draws lessons for Western economies. Case 17.2 introduces cyclical fluctuations in budget deficits, and therefore asks how much high deficits are the *consequences* of slow output growth since the crash. Section 17.5 contains an extensive discussion of the economics of budget deficits and government debt.

Chapter 18 Concept 18.2 examines the collapse of the bank deposit multiplier, and contraction of bank lending. Case 18.1 provides an extensive discussion of the sub-prime crisis and its aftermath, documenting the chronology of the crisis and showing its effects on house prices and wealth.

Chapter 19 Case 19.1 discusses reforms that might reduce the risk of future banking crises. Concept 19.1 explains quantitative easing. Activity 19.1 explores how transmission lags in monetary policy were exacerbated by the crisis.

Chapter 20 Case 20.1 analyses Eurozone countries that developed acute debt and deficit problems after the crisis. Activity 20.1 explores how the mix of monetary and fiscal policy was altered once interest rates could not be reduced further.

Chapter 21 Activity 21.1 discusses output gaps in European countries during the last 15 years, showing the dramatic output falls and slow recovery falls after the crisis.

Chapter 22 Case 22.1 analyses why acute crises can give rise to deflation, and explains why this problem is difficult to solve.

Chapter 23 Concept 23.2 introduces hysteresis, the case in which recession today can permanently reduce future supply.

Chapter 27 Section 27.4 discusses supply-side effects of the financial crash.

CHAPTER 15

Introduction to macroeconomics

Learning Outcomes

By the end of this chapter, you should be able to:

1. view macroeconomics as the study of the whole economy
2. discuss the scope of macroeconomic analysis
3. show how the national accounts measure macroeconomic variables
4. explain the circular flow between households and firms
5. appreciate why leakages always equal injections
6. analyse comprehensive measures of national income and output
7. discuss whether national output contributes to national happiness

We now turn to the big economic issues, such as unemployment, inflation, economic growth and financial crashes. Macroeconomics sacrifices details to study the big picture.

The distinction between microeconomics and **macroeconomics** is more than the difference between economics in the small and economics in the large. The purpose of the analysis is also different.

> Macroeconomics is the study of the economy as a system.

A model deliberately simplifies in order to focus on the key elements of a problem and think about them clearly. We could study the whole economy by piecing together a microeconomic analysis of every market, but it would be hard to keep track of all the economic forces at work. Our brains do not have a big enough Intel chip to make sense of it.

Microeconomics and macroeconomics take different approaches to keep the analysis manageable. Microeconomics stresses a detailed understanding of particular markets. To achieve this detail, many interactions with other markets are suppressed. In saying a tax on cars reduces the equilibrium quantity of cars, we ignore what the government does with the tax revenue. If government debt is reduced, interest rates may fall, making households more willing to borrow to buy new cars.

Microeconomics is like looking at a horse race through a pair of binoculars. It is great for details, but sometimes we get a clearer picture of the whole race by using the naked eye. Because macroeconomics studies the interaction of different parts of the economy, it uses a different simplification to keep the analysis manageable. Macroeconomics simplifies the building blocks in order to focus on how they fit together and influence one another.

Macroeconomics stresses broad aggregates, such as the total demand for goods by households or total spending on machinery and building by firms. Like watching a horse race with the naked eye, individual details are more blurred but our full attention is on the big picture. We are more likely to notice the horse sneaking up on the rails.

The scope of macroeconomics is therefore to understand the interrelationship of the big issues that affect the economy – growth, inflation, unemployment, fluctuations and crises.

15.1 The scope of macroeconomics: the big issues

Real gross domestic product (GDP) measures the output of goods and services produced by an economy.

The business cycle refers to swings in GDP around an economy's trend rate of output growth.

Economic growth is a rise in real GDP.

The labour force is the number of people at work or looking for work.

The unemployment rate is the fraction of the labour force without a job.

The inflation rate is the percentage annual increase in the average price of goods and services.

What determines the total output of a country, which we call its real **GDP**? Why was there a long boom in output and house prices before 2007 but then the worst post-war crash in asset prices and output levels? Are there inevitably **business cycles**, or can output grow smoothly over time? Why do some countries **grow** faster than others over sustained periods? Will growth go on forever? After centuries asleep, why did the Chinese and Indian economic giants finally awaken?

We care not just about the output of goods and services, but also the market for **labour**. Why did unemployment rise in the 1970s but fall substantially thereafter? How much **unemployment** was caused by the financial crisis? Do workers price themselves out of jobs by greedy wage claims? Does technical progress destroy jobs? Can the government create more jobs? These are questions we need to answer in Part Four.

A third big theme is **inflation**. The price level is a weighted average of the prices of goods and services. Inflation is a rise in the price level. What causes inflation? Money growth, oil price rises or a budget deficit? Have we learned how to defeat inflation? Could a boom in China cause inflation in Europe? Will the vast money creation deliberately undertaken since 2009 to mitigate the recession lead to subsequent inflation? With prices actually falling in some countries because of the severity of the recession, could economies experience a death spiral of falling prices?

A fourth big theme is boom and bust. Why can't we arrange for economic growth to be smooth? What caused the spectacular crash of 2007–09? Can we prevent another one? Can we even escape the previous one? How does the overhang of inherited debt now affect the choices of households, firms and governments?

Gross debt is total liabilities owed to creditors. Net debt is total liabilities minus total assets that could be sold in order to raise money to pay creditors.

Which debt measure is being used makes a difference. By 2012 Japan's government **gross debt** was 220 per cent of its national output, but its **net debt** was only 140 per cent. You will see references to both in the media, and need to be clear which is being used. Typically, government net debt subtracts from gross debt only that part of assets that could be sold fairly easily. Japan would find it hard to sell its nuclear power stations.

Almost every day, the media discusses inflation, unemployment, economic growth, output fluctuations and debt. These issues help determine elections, and make people interested in macroeconomics.

15.2 Some facts and economic history

We begin with some facts. Table 15.1 puts recent performance in perspective, showing data since 1960 for annual averages for economic growth, unemployment and inflation.

The 1960s was a golden age of low unemployment, rapid growth and low inflation in advanced economies. In the early 1970s, with the world economy booming, OPEC quadrupled the price of oil. The rest of the 1970s saw high inflation, low growth and rising unemployment. After another oil price hike in 1979–80, the 1980s were another tough period. By the 1990s, inflation was coming down in most countries, and unemployment was falling in the UK and the US, though not in continental Europe.

The long period of economic success during 1990–2008 – steady growth, low unemployment and low inflation – made people confident that successful economic policies had finally been discovered. Confidence bred overconfidence, large borrowing, spiralling house prices and rash lending by banks. In 2008 the financial crash finally came, leading governments to step in to rescue failing private banks, but at the cost of a sharp rise in government debt. Table 15.1 shows that, as a result of the crisis, economic growth stalled and unemployment rates were sharply higher.

The largest emerging economies were often slow to get going, in many cases shackled by extensive government regulation and planning. Deregulation in the 1980s and 1990s had a dramatic effect. The BRICs – Brazil,

Table 15.1 The big picture, 1960–2013 (annual averages, %)

	1960s	1970s	1980s	1990s	2000–07	2008–13
Real GDP growth						
UK	2.9	2.4	2.4	2.1	3.1	−0.1
US	4.3	3.3	3.1	3.1	2.6	1.0
EU	5.8	3.8	2.3	2.2	2.1	0.0
China	3.0	7.4	9.8	10.0	10.8	8.9
Unemployment						
UK	2.2	4.5	10.2	8.1	5.2	8.3
US	4.1	6.1	7.3	5.8	4.9	8.2
EU	2.5	4.0	9.3	10.5	8.3	9.8
China	–	–	2.6	2.8	3.9	4.0
Inflation						
UK	3.8	12.6	7.4	3.7	1.5	3.1
US	2.4	7.1	5.6	3.0	2.7	2.4
EU	3.7	9.5	6.5	2.9	2.3	2.1
China	–	–	7.5	7.8	1.5	3.2

Sources: OECD; IMF.

Russia, India and China – took off. Table 15.1 shows the dramatic rise of China, which is now approaching 40 years of 10 per cent annual real growth. Although the BRICs are growing quickly, they begin from such low levels that income per person is still well below that enjoyed in advanced economies.

Figure 15.1 takes a longer look at UK inflation, which soared in the 1970s. The Thatcher government reduced inflation after 1980, but lost control in the late 1980s when it let the economy grow too rapidly, leading to more inflation. Subsequent governments gradually got the UK back on an even keel, not least by giving the Bank of England much more independence in decisions on monetary policy.

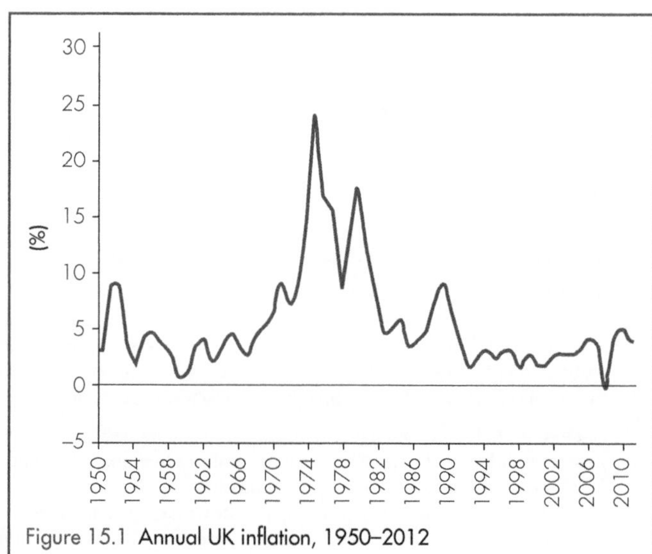

Figure 15.1 Annual UK inflation, 1950–2012

Source: ONS.

Table 15.2 Government net debt (% of GDP)

	2007	2013
Italy	87	96
Greece	83	141
Japan	81	142
US	48	88
Germany	43	56
France	36	68
UK	28	78
Spain	18	57
Ireland	0	87

Source: Based on data from Economic Outlook Statistical Annex, © OECD, 2013, http://www.oecd.org/eco/economicoutlook.htm, accessed on 18/06/2013.

The financial crisis temporarily reduced inflationary pressures after 2008. Despite ongoing stagnation of output growth, the UK has subsequently imported inflation (higher food and energy prices that are being bid up in the world economy by countries such as China, which continue to grow strongly).

Table 15.2 shows the impact of the financial crisis on government debt. We examine debt relative to GDP, since the latter gives an idea of the likely tax revenues that can be used to pay interest on the debt. A rise in the debt/GDP ratio means that a country faces a greater debt burden. We show data for 2007 just before the crisis, and for 2013.

Table 15.2 shows that different countries entered the financial crisis with very different levels of government debt. Italy, Greece and Japan were already very indebted; the UK, Spain and Ireland had low debt levels prior to the crisis.

Government finances deteriorated, both because governments had to bail out private banks (the alternative would have been even worse) and because, as economies stagnated, governments got less tax revenue and had to spend more on welfare benefits. Both effects increased government debt. Countries, such as the UK, with a large financial sector experienced a large increase in government debt. Financial markets now worry that countries, such as Greece, with the largest debts will not be able to meet the interest payments on them. By the end of Part Four, we need to explain what options such countries now have.

15.3 The circular flow

The circular flow shows how both real resources and financial payments flow between firms and households.

The economy comprises millions of individual economic units: households, firms and the departments of central and local government. Together, their individual decisions determine the economy's total spending, income and output.

Initially, we ignore the government and other countries, leaving just firms and households. Table 15.3 shows transactions between these two sectors. Households own the factors of production (inputs to production). Households rent labour to firms in exchange for wages. Households are also the ultimate owners of firms and get their profits. Capital and land, even if held by firms, are ultimately owned by households.

Households supply inputs to firms, which use these to make output. The second row of Table 15.3 shows the corresponding payments. Households earn incomes (wages, rents, profits), which are payments by firms for using these inputs. The third row shows that households spend their incomes buying the output of firms, giving firms the money to pay for renting production inputs.

Table 15.3 Transactions by households and firms

Households	Firms
Supply inputs to firms	Use inputs to make output
Receive incomes from firms	Rent inputs from households
Buy output of firms	Sell output to households

This suggests, correctly, that there are three equivalent ways in which to measure the total economic activity in an economy: (a) the value of all goods and services produced, (b) the total value of earnings arising from the factor services supplied or (c) the total value of spending on goods and services. All payments are the counterparts of real resources. For the moment, we assume all payments are spent buying real resources. We get the same estimate of total economic activity whether we use the value of production, the level of factor incomes or total expenditure on goods and services.

Household income equals household spending if all income is spent. The value of output equals total spending on goods and services if all goods are sold. The value of output also equals the value of household incomes. Since profits are residually defined – the value of sales minus the rental of inputs – and since profits accrue to the households that own firms, household incomes (from renting out inputs or from profits) equal the value of output.

Our model is still very simple. What happens if firms do not sell all their output? What happens if firms sell output not to households but to other firms? What happens if households do not spend all their incomes? The next section answers these questions. Our conclusion will be unchanged: the level of economic activity can be measured by valuing total spending, total output or total earnings. All three methods give the same answer.

Our framework still omits key features of the real world: saving and investment, government spending and taxes, transactions between firms and with the rest of the world. These are all easily remedied, later in the chapter, to create a comprehensive system of national accounts.

15.4 National income accounting

Measuring national income and output

Gross domestic product (GDP) measures the value of output produced in a country, no matter whose citizens contribute to this production. **Gross national product (GNP)**, sometimes called **gross national income**, measures the value of the income that its citizens earn, from whatever countries this income is derived.

Gross national product (GNP), also called gross national income (GNI), is the total income of a country.

Thus, a German working in a bank in London contributes to UK GDP because that is the location at which the inputs were supplied and output produced. However, if the German then sends some of this income back to relatives in Germany, this act adds to German GNP (but not to UK GNP). Similarly, Irish foreign investments in the UK contribute to UK output and GDP, but the income derived will ultimately add to Irish GNP rather than UK GNP. Thus, GNP measures the total worldwide income of citizens of a country; GDP measures the output produced within a country, no matter which citizens produce it.

Initially we discuss a *closed economy*, not linked to the rest of the world, in which output and income are the same. First, we extend the simple circular flow between firms and households shown in Table 15.3. Transactions do not take place exclusively between a single firm and a single household. Firms hire labour services from households but buy raw materials and machinery from *other* firms. To avoid double counting, we use **value added**.

Value added is gross output minus the value of input goods used up in making that output. Closely related is the distinction between final goods and intermediate goods. Ice cream is a **final good** consumed by its ultimate user. Steel is an **intermediate good**, made by one firm but then used as an input by another firm. Capital goods are final goods because they are *not* used up in subsequent production. They do not fully depreciate during the production period under study.

Value added is the increase in the value of goods as a result of the production process.

Final goods are purchased by the ultimate user, either households buying consumer goods or firms buying capital goods such as machinery.

Intermediate goods are partly finished goods that form inputs to a subsequent production process that then uses them up.

An example will clarify these concepts. Suppose there are four firms in the economy: a steel maker, a producer of capital goods (machines) for the car industry, a tyre maker and a car producer who sells to the final user, households. Table 15.4 calculates GDP for this simple economy.

Table 15.4 Calculating GDP

(1) Good	(2) Seller	(3) Buyer	(4) Transaction value	(5) Value added	(6) Spending on final goods	(7) Household earnings
Steel	Steel maker	Machine maker	£1000	£1000	–	£1000
Steel	Steel maker	Car maker	£3000	£3000	–	£3000
Machine	Machine maker	Car maker	£2000	£1000	£2000	£1000
Cars	Car maker	Households	£5000	£2000	£5000	£2000
Total transactions			**£11 000**			
GDP				£7000	£7000	£7000

The steel firm makes £4000 worth of steel, one-quarter sold to the machine maker and three-quarters sold to the car maker. All £4000 is value added or net output of the steel firm, paid out as household income (wages, rents, residual profits). Hence, the first two rows of the last column also add up to £4000. Firms have spent £4000 buying this steel output, but it is not expenditure on final goods. Steel is an intermediate good, used up in later stages of the production process.

The machine maker buys £1000 of steel input, converting it into a machine sold to the car maker for £2000. The value added by the machine maker is £2000 minus £1000 spent on steel input. Net revenue of £1000 accrues directly to households as income or profit. Since the car firm intends to keep the machine in the future, the full value of £2000 is shown under 'final expenditure' during the period.

The car producer spends £3000 on steel, used up during the period in which cars are made. We subtract £3000 from the car output of £5000 to get the value added of the car maker. Value added and household income are £2000.

Finally, the car producer sells the car for £5000 to the final consumer – households. Only then does the car become a final good. Its full price of £5000 is final expenditure.

Table 15.4 shows that the gross value of all the transactions is £11 000. This overstates the value of the goods the economy has actually produced. The £3000 that the steel producer earned by selling steel to the car producer is already included in the final value of car output. National output cannot count this twice.

Column (5) shows the value added at each stage in the production process; £7000 is the true net output of the economy. Since each firm pays the corresponding net revenue to households either as direct factor payments or indirectly as profits, household earnings are £7000 in the last column of the table. If we add up payments made to households as income and profits, we get the same measure of GDP.

Table 15.4 confirms that we also get the same answer if we measure spending on *final* goods and services. In this case, final users are households buying cars and the car producer buying the (everlasting) machinery used to make cars.

Investment and saving

If total output and household incomes are each £7000, but households spend only £5000 on cars, what do they do with the rest of their incomes? And who does the rest of the spending? To resolve these issues, we need **investment** and **saving**.

Investment is the purchase of new capital goods by firms.

Saving is the part of income not spent buying goods and services.

Households spend £5000 on cars. Their income is £7000, so they save £2000. The car maker spends £2000 on investment, buying new machinery. Figure 15.2 shows what happens to the circular flow. The bottom half of the figure shows that incomes and factor services are each £7000. But £2000 leaks out from the circular flow when households save. Only £5000 finds its way back to firms as household spending on cars.

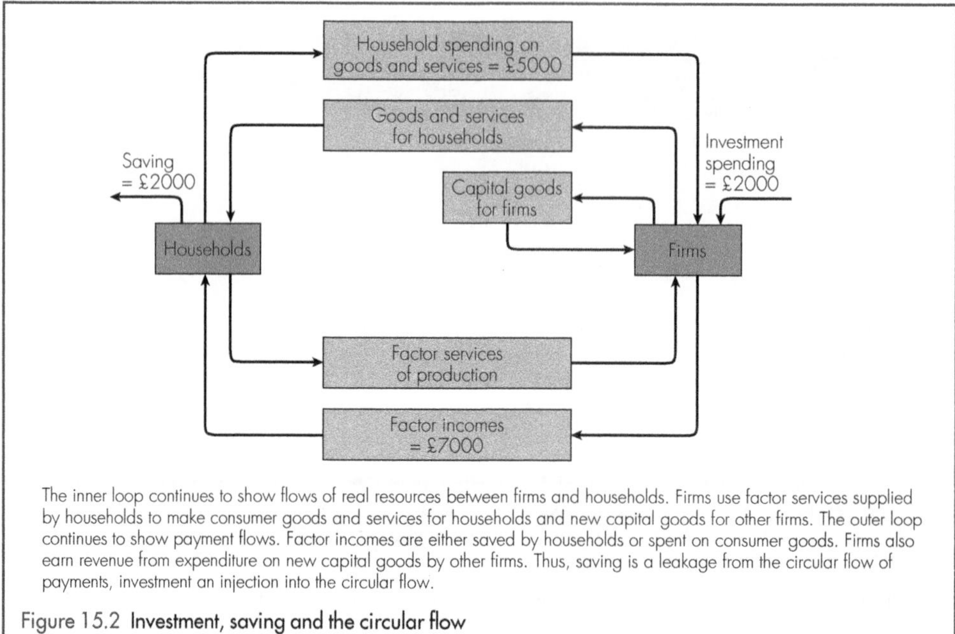

The inner loop continues to show flows of real resources between firms and households. Firms use factor services supplied by households to make consumer goods and services for households and new capital goods for other firms. The outer loop continues to show payment flows. Factor incomes are either saved by households or spent on consumer goods. Firms also earn revenue from expenditure on new capital goods by other firms. Thus, saving is a leakage from the circular flow of payments, investment an injection into the circular flow.

Figure 15.2 **Investment, saving and the circular flow**

The top half of the figure shows that £5000 is both the value of output of consumer goods and of household spending on these goods. Since GDP is £7000, the other £2000 comes from spending by firms themselves. It is the £2000 of investment expenditure made by the car producer buying machinery for car production.

On the inner loop, firms make an output of £5000 for consumption by households and an output of £2000 of capital goods for investment by firms. On the outer loop, which relates to money payments, saving is a **leakage** of £2000 from the circular flow and investment spending is an **injection** of £2000 to the circular flow.

A leakage from the circular flow is money not recycled from households to firms.

An injection is money that flows to firms without being recycled through households.

Is it coincidental that household savings of £2000 exactly equal investment expenditure of £2000 by firms? If not, how is the money saved by households transferred to firms to allow them to pay for investment spending?

Suppose Y denotes GDP, which also equals the value of household incomes, C denotes household spending on consumption and S denotes saving. By definition, saving is unspent income, so $Y \equiv C + S$, where the symbol $\equiv$ means 'is identically equal to, as a matter of definition'. Since one definition of GDP is the sum of final expenditure, $Y \equiv C + I$. Putting these two definitions together,

$$S \equiv I$$

since both are identical to $(Y - C)$.

It is no accident that saving and investment are each £2000 in our example. Saving and investment are always equal, in the absence of government and foreign sectors.

It is initially hard to grasp the difference between an equals sign and an identity sign. The latter means always equal, no matter what the values of the other variables. The equals sign means that some particular values of the variables (output, consumption, and so on) are needed in order to ensure the equality of the two sides of the equation.

Look again at the outer loop of Figure 15.2. All household spending in the top half of the figure returns to households as income in the bottom half of the figure. Investment spending by firms is matched by an income flow to households in excess of their consumer spending. Since saving is *defined* as the excess of income over consumption, investment and savings must always be equal.

These accounting identities follow from our definitions of investment, saving and income. *Actual* saving must equal *actual* investment. This need not mean *desired* saving equals *desired* investment. To study that, we need models of desired saving and investment, a task we begin in the next chapter.[1] In a market economy, financial institutions and financial markets channel household saving to the firms that wish to borrow to invest in new capital goods.

What happens if firms cannot sell all the output that they produce? Surely this creates a gap between the output and expenditure measures of GDP? Producers then add to their **inventories** or **stocks** of finished goods awaiting sale to consumers in the next period.

Inventories or stocks are goods currently held by a firm for future production or sale.

Stocks are sometimes called *working capital.* Not used up in production and sale during the current period, stocks are classified as capital goods. Adding to stocks is investment in working capital. When stocks are depleted, we treat this as negative investment, or disinvestment. This keeps the national accounts straight. Any unsold output is treated as temporary investment in inventories. Depletion of inventories in subsequent periods will then be treated as negative investment during the periods in which it occurs.

The domestic government and foreign countries

Firms and households are not the only sectors in the economy. We now recognize the existence of governments and of foreign countries.

Governments raise revenue both through direct taxes on income (wages, rents, interest and profits) and through indirect taxes or expenditures taxes (VAT, petrol duties and cigarette taxes). Taxes finance two kinds of expenditure. Government spending on goods and services G is purchases by the government of physical goods and services. It includes the wages of civil servants and soldiers, the purchase of computers, tanks and military aircraft, and investment in roads and hospitals.

Governments also spend money on **transfer payments** or benefits, B. These include pensions, unemployment benefit and subsidies to firms.

Transfer payments are monetary payments that require no goods or services in return.

Transfer payments do not affect national income or national output. They are not included in GDP. There is no corresponding net physical output. Taxes and transfer payments merely redistribute existing income and spending power away from people being taxed and towards people being subsidized. In contrast, spending G on goods and services produces net output, and gives rise to factor earnings in the firms supplying this output and also to additional spending power of the households receiving this income. Hence government spending G on goods and services is part of GDP. It is final expenditure since government is now an additional end user of the output.

National income accounts aim to provide a logically coherent set of definitions and measures of national output. However, taxes drive a wedge between the price the purchaser pays and the price the seller receives. We can choose to value national output either at **market prices** inclusive of indirect taxes on goods and services (the price consumers pay), or at the prices received by producers after indirect taxes have been paid.

GDP at market prices measures domestic output inclusive of indirect taxes on goods and services.

So far we have studied a closed economy not transacting with the rest of the world. We now examine an *open economy* that deals with other countries.

Households, firms and the government may buy imports Z that are not part of domestic output and do not give rise to domestic factor incomes. These goods are not in the output measure of GDP, the *value added* by domestic producers. However, imports show up in final expenditure. There are two solutions to this problem.

1 It helps to draw parallels with microeconomics. The demand curve shows desired purchases at any price; the supply curve shows the desired sales at any price. In equilibrium, desired purchases equal desired sales. When the price is too high, there is excess supply and some desired sales are frustrated. But since every transaction has a buyer and a seller, actual purchases equal actual sales whether or not the market is in equilibrium.

MATHS 15.1

THE CIRCULAR FLOW REVISITED

If Y is GDP at basic prices, the economy's value added or net output is goods and services for domestic consumption, investment, government spending and net exports minus indirect taxes:

$$Y \equiv \textit{GDP at basic prices} \equiv C + I + G + NX - T_e$$

Household incomes at basic prices are supplemented by welfare benefits B less direct taxes T_d. This gives us *personal disposable income* ($Y + B - T_d$) available for households to spend. Suppose for the moment that saving is done only by households. Disposable income must be spent on consumption or saving:

$$Y + B - T_d \equiv C + S$$

The figure below shows the extended picture of the circular flow.

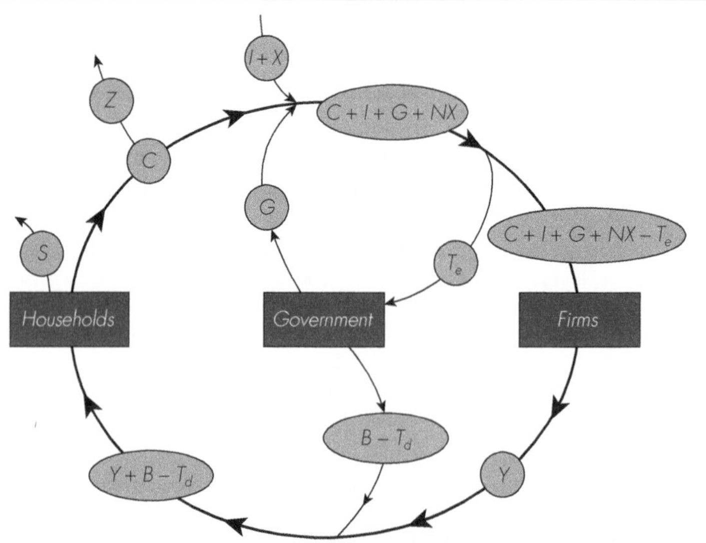

The figure extends the circular flow between households and firms to include the government and foreign sectors. Firms make factor payments Y to households. Disposable income $Y + B - T_d$ also includes transfer payments B less direct taxes T_d. Disposable income goes on saving S or consumption C. This spending is augmented by injections of government spending G on goods and services and by investment spending I and by exports X, but is reduced by the additional leakage Z into imports. From $C + I + G + NX$ or GDP at market prices, we must subtract the leakage of indirect taxes T_e to get GDP at basic prices Y which firms pay out to households.

Round the top loop of the figure, consumption C at market prices is supplemented by injections of investment spending I, net exports NX and government spending G. From this GDP at market prices, we subtract indirect taxes T_e to get GDP at basic prices.

Since total leakages are *always* equal to total injections, this implies

$$S + NT + Z \equiv I + G + X$$

where net taxes NT are direct and indirect taxes minus welfare benefits. Investment, government spending and exports are all injections to the circular flow that do not originate from households. Conversely, household spending leaks out, directly or indirectly, through saving, taxes (net of benefits) and imports: only the remaining spending flows back to domestic firms and round again as household incomes. If there is no government or foreign sector, this becomes $S \equiv I$, as we had before. More generally,

$$(S - I) + (NT - G) \equiv (X - Z)$$

Exports minus imports measure the country's net external surplus achieved by exporting more than it imports. This external surplus allows some domestic combination of a private sector surplus (saving minus investment) or a government surplus (net taxes minus government spending).

Exports (X) are domestically produced but sold abroad.

Imports (Z) are produced abroad but purchased for use in the domestic economy.

We could subtract the import component separately from C, I, G and X and measure only final expenditure on the domestically made bit of consumption, investment, government spending and exports. But it is easier to continue to measure total final expenditure on C, I, G and **exports** (X) and then to subtract from this total expenditure on **imports** (Z). It comes to exactly the same thing.

In the previous section, we saw that our definitions should imply that total income, expenditure and output measures of total activity should coincide. We now explain how this works once we introduce the government and foreign sectors as well. The complete system of national accounts is summarized in Figure 15.3.

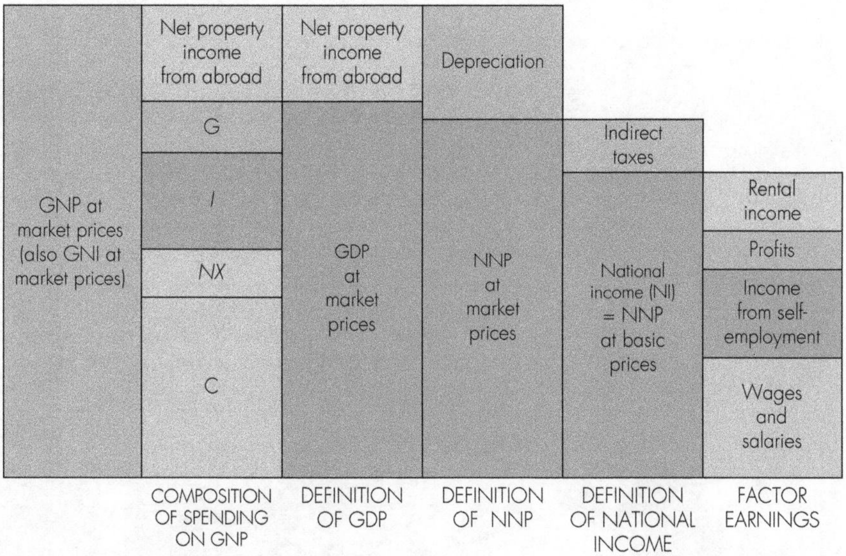

GNP at market prices (also GNI at market prices)

Net property income from abroad | G | I | NX | C

Net property income from abroad | GDP at market prices

Depreciation | NNP at market prices

Indirect taxes | National income (NI) = NNP at basic prices

Rental income | Profits | Income from self-employment | Wages and salaries

COMPOSITION OF SPENDING ON GNP | DEFINITION OF GDP | DEFINITION OF NNP | DEFINITION OF NATIONAL INCOME | FACTOR EARNINGS

Figure 15.3 **Summarizing the national accounts**

We begin on the left with gross national product (or gross national income – same thing) at market prices. The second column is the expenditure measure of GNP, which comprises spending by households on consumption, spending by firms on investment, spending by government goods and services (which we could think of as government contributions to consumption and investment), net exports (the excess of exports over imports) and, finally, net international transfers from abroad.

This last item is sometimes called *net international property income*, since most transfers arise from the return on assets held abroad (minus the return paid by us to foreigners holding assets in our country). International transfer payments also include outflows in aid by the UK when an earthquake hits Haiti, and inflows from remittances of cash to UK workers temporarily working abroad.

The third column takes us from GNP to GDP; that is, gross output during the period. Whereas net international transfer payments add to our income, they do not add to our physical output of goods and services. Hence, Figure 15.3 deducts these from GNP to get to GDP.

The fourth column shows the difference between gross and net output. Net means deducting depreciation of physical capital – buildings and machinery wear out or become obsolete. Statisticians make some fairly heroic guesses sometimes about how much depreciation is going on. So far, our national accounts leave out depreciation of environmental capital. One day, if global warming continues, it will become essential to make explicit estimates for depreciation of our environmental capital.

The fifth column shows the role of indirect taxes. Measurements at market prices include indirect taxes in the statistics; this reflects prices paid by consumers. Measurements at **basic prices** remove the effects of indirect taxes to reflect the prices received by producers.

GDP at basic prices measures domestic output exclusive of indirect taxes on goods and services.

The final column shows the net incomes that accrue to the inputs (factors of production) used in making output. Total factor incomes arise from the supply of labour to earn wages and salaries, self-employed work, the supply of land to earn rent or the supply of capital to earn profits.

Understanding Figure 15.3 is a key step in mastering the definitions, confirming that they make sense, and checking that we have not left anything out.

CASE 15.1

PROBLEMS IN MEASURING GDP

When things are traded in a market, or embedded in government tax statistics, they are relatively easy to measure. Many of our measurement difficulties arise precisely because some of the most valuable things are not easily measurable. GDP easily captures the output of washing machines, but not of happiness, health or environmental depreciation. Since we do not buy and sell clean air or moderate temperatures in a marketplace, governments are not automatically collecting statistics for use in national accounts data.

The United Nations Human Development Index systematically tries to measure three broad dimensions of economic development – health, education and material standard of living – and produces annual statistics for all UN member countries. The map below shows the geographic range of outcomes – no prizes for guessing which colours represent prosperity and which represent poverty as measured by the Human Development Index.

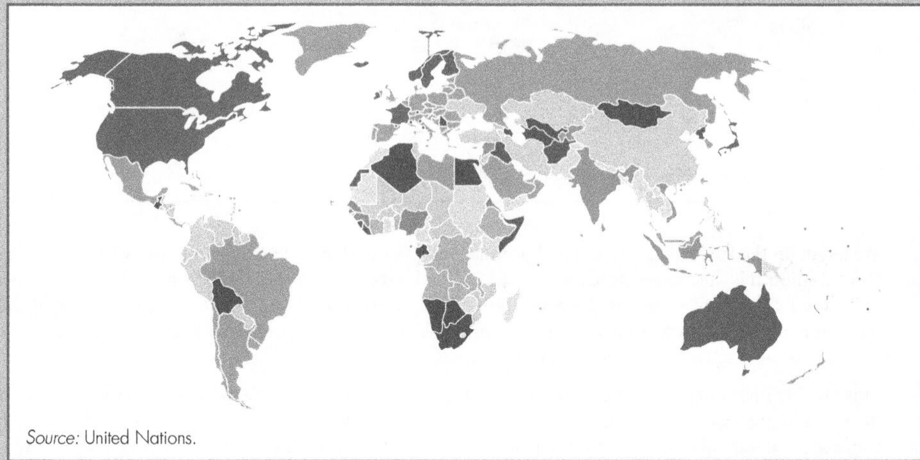

Source: United Nations.

Health is crudely captured by life expectancy at birth, education by the proportion of the children enrolled at school and by the proportion of adults who can read, and material standard of living by per capita GDP.

Some of these indicators are more stable than others. For example, before the financial crash, Iceland came top in the world in the UN measure, and Sierra Leone bottom. But Iceland's banks experienced the biggest crash of all, and the Icelandic economy got into serious trouble. This did not immediately affect its adult literacy or the life expectancy of its population, but these will gradually suffer unless economic prosperity can be restored.

Like sausages, economic statistics simply reflect what you put into them. If you care about democracy, equality or environmental sustainability, don't get hung up merely because your country is not doing well on the particular things that GDP does measure.

People who visit France quickly learn that the French have a good quality of life, better than you would expect simply by looking at their GDP. They enjoy a nice climate, long lunches, access to Mediterranean beaches and little congestion since they have plenty of land in relation to their population. They also retire at a relatively young age and, having long life expectancy, spend plenty of happy years in retirement. Their GDP statistics are measuring production of Renault and Peugeot, and of luxuries from Louis Vuitton and Hermès, but omit plentiful leisure, lack of stress and little congestion.

Similarly, the output of the police, civil service and teachers in free state schools is not charged for in the market and hence not automatically valued by the market. How do we measure the output of the police? Typically, national income statisticians measure the inputs (the wage bill of police forces, rent of police stations, the cost of using police cars and police computers). This is a large step in the right direction but it is far from perfect. If society becomes more unlawful, we end up choosing to have more police to counter crime. So GDP rises because we are spending more on the police force. But in reality, people are feeling less happy with the greater prevalence of crime, and resent having to 'waste' more resources on additional policing in order to counter the crime wave. Conversely, when we cut back the size of the army, GDP falls since less is being spent on the military, but we are actually receiving less defence as a consequence.

Think of all this as a health warning on GNP and GDP statistics. They measure what they measure. Unless and until electorates want to spend a lot more money collecting more comprehensive statistics, GNP and GDP will use data already being collected annually for other purposes such as taxation.

Measuring UK GDP in 2011

We now know that there are three equivalent ways in which to measure GDP, using income, output and expenditure. How does this work out in practice? Can the statisticians reconcile the different estimates? Table 15.5 shows the answer.

The first two columns show the income measure of UK GDP. The largest component is wages and salaries, then operating surpluses and, finally, other incomes. Adding these factor incomes, we get £1327 000 million, what nowadays we call £1327 billion as the measure of GDP (or gross value added, GVA) at basic prices. Adding on indirect taxes takes us to £1522 billion. A small statistical discrepancy in the income approach reduces this to a final estimate of £1519 billion at market prices.

The middle two columns reach the same answer, using the expenditure approach. Consumption spending by households is the largest component (£977 billion); then we add private investment *I*, the two parts of government spending on goods and services – that related to purchase of consumption goods and services and that to investment goods – and net exports to reach a total of £1517 billion. A small statistical discrepancy of £2 billion reconciles this with the estimate of GDP obtained from the income method.

The final two columns repeat the exercise, starting from estimates of value added in each industry. Nowadays, agriculture, forestry and fisheries are a tiny part of the economy. Even manufacturing is only about 10 per cent of GDP. Total production of goods, plus the output of agriculture, forestry and fisheries, still comes only to £162 billion – that is, about 11 per cent of total GDP. Construction accounts for another £103 billion, but the vast majority – £1170 billion, or 77 cent of GDP – is made up of services, everything from wholesale and retail distribution, transport and communications, financial services, government services and other privately

Table 15.5 UK GDP, 2011, at market prices (£ billion, at 2009 prices)

Income method	£ bn	Expenditure method	£ bn	Output method	£bn
Wages and salaries	814	Household consumption C	977	Agriculture, forestry, fisheries	9
Operating surpluses (profit, rent, interest of private and public firms)	329	Government consumption G_c	337	Manufacturing	159
Other incomes	184	Private investment I + government investment G_I	227	Other production (mining, energy, water)	78
GDP at basic prices	**1327**	Exports	493	Construction	103
Net indirect taxes	195	Less imports	−517	Services, of which:	1170
				Distribution, catering	213
				Transport, communications	161
Subtotal	1522	Subtotal	1517	Business/financial services	442
Statistical discrepancy	−3	Statistical discrepancy	+ 2	Govt and other services	354
GDP at market prices	**1519**	**GDP at market prices**	**1519**	**GDP at market prices**	**1519**

supplied services. Adding the entire production of goods and services, we get £1519 billion as the output measure of GDP. All three measures lead essentially to the same answer. Were everything perfectly measured, the three measures would be identical even without any statistical adjustment.

15.5 What GDP measures

A firm's accounts show how the company is doing. Our national income accounts let us assess how the economy is doing. Just as a firm's accounts may conceal as much as they reveal, we must interpret the national income accounts with care.

We focus on GDP as a measure of economic performance. Since depreciation is rather difficult to measure, and consequently may be treated differently in different countries or during different time periods, using GDP avoids the need to argue about depreciation.

In this section we make three points. First, we recall the distinction between nominal and real variables. Second, we show how per capita GDP can provide a more accurate picture of the standard of living of an average person in an economy. Finally, we discuss the incompleteness of GDP as a measure of the activities that provide economic welfare to members of society.

> Nominal GDP measures GDP at the prices prevailing when output was produced
>
> Real GDP, or GDP at constant prices, adjusts for inflation, measuring GDP in different years at the prices prevailing at a particular date, known as the *base year*.

Nominal and real GDP

Since it is physical quantities of output that yield people utility or happiness, it can be misleading to judge the economy's performance by looking at **nominal GDP**.

Table 15.6 presents a simple hypothetical example of a whole economy. Nominal GDP rises from £600 to £1470 between 1980 and 2013. If we take 1980 as the base year, we can measure **real GDP** in 2008 by valuing output quantities in 2013 using 1980 prices. Real GDP rises only from £600 to £860. This rise of 43 per cent in real GDP gives a truer picture of the extra quantity of goods made by the economy as a whole.

CASE 15.2

TAX EVASION, CRIME AND UNDER-REPORTING OF GDP

Gangster Al Capone, never charged with murder, was eventually convicted of tax evasion. Taxes are evaded by smugglers and drug dealers but also by gardeners, plumbers and everyone else doing things 'for cash'. Since GDP data are based on tax statistics, the 'hidden' economy is unreported and official statistics understate the true value of GDP. This undeclared economic activity is sometimes called the shadow or hidden economy.

Economists have various ways to estimate its size. One way is to count large-denomination banknotes in circulation. People with fistfuls of £50 notes are often engaged in tax evasion. When the euro was first launched, the decision to make the most valuable note €500 (more valuable than the $100 bill) led to fierce discussion as to whether the euro would replace the dollar as the preferred currency of crooks. In 2010 British bank wholesalers withdrew it from circulation in the UK, but they still circulate in the Eurozone, where they acquired the nickname 'Bin Ladens' because everyone knew they existed but they were rarely seen.

top: © Aidart. bottom: © AcePixure

Another way is to guess people's income by studying what they spend. Maria Lacko exploited the stable relationship between household use of electricity and its main determinants – income and weather temperature – to estimate incomes from data on electricity consumption and temperature. She confirmed two popular views. The hidden economy is large both in former communist economies, where the new private sector is as yet unrecorded, and in several Mediterranean countries with a history of poor tax collection. She found that the size of the hidden economy might be around 20–30 per cent of reported GDP in the countries of Eastern Europe and the Mediterranean, but probably only 5–10 per cent of the size of GDP in the US and the UK. Measured properly, GDP would therefore be larger. Another way to estimate the hidden economy is to conduct surveys and offer people immunity if they tell the truth.

The broad thrust of these estimates has been confirmed in recent work by Friedrich Schneider, cited in 2012 by the EU Commission.

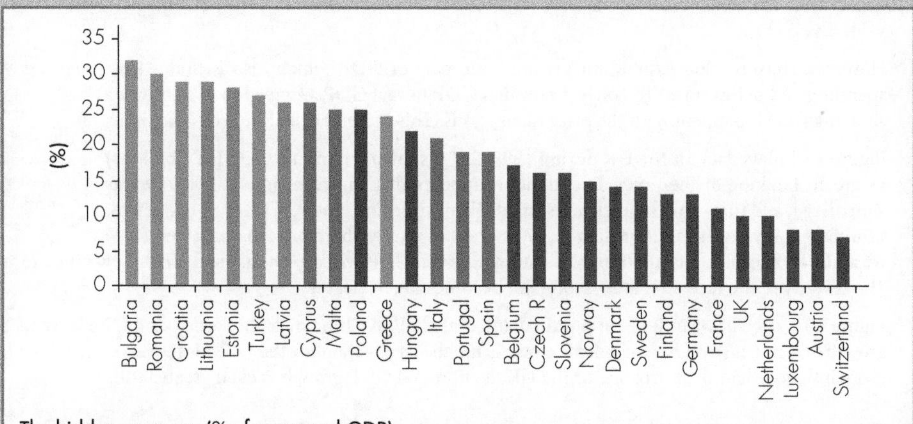

The hidden economy (% of measured GDP)

Source: F. Schneider, *The size and development of the shadow economy from 2003–2012* (EU Commission, 2011).

The hidden economy ranges from 7–8 per cent of GDP in law-abiding Switzerland and Austria to around 30 per cent in many of the Balkan countries (shown in green). Tax evasion and under-reporting of GDP is also prevalent in the Baltic states (shown in orange).

Why does a country have a large shadow economy? Partly, the answer lies in culture and history. Balkan states, ruled by the Ottoman Empire for 400 years, got used to evading central government; in contrast, Switzerland, with its recurring referenda consulting citizens on many policy issues, has much greater buy-in to government policy.

Economic arguments also play a role. When tax rates get too high, citizens become increasingly preoccupied with tax avoidance (legal) or tax evasion (illegal). How high tax rates have to be before inducing such antisocial behaviour is still a matter of controversy.

Table 15.6 Nominal and real GDP

		1980	2013
Quantity	Apples	100	150
	Chickens	100	140
Price £s	Apples	2	4
	Chickens	4	6
Value in 2013 £s	Apples	200	600
	Chickens	400	840
	Nominal GDP	600	1440
Value in 1980 £s	Apples	200	300
	Chickens	400	560
	Real GDP	600	860

The GDP deflator

Chapter 2 introduced the consumer price index (CPI), an index of the average price of goods purchased by consumers. The most common measure of the inflation rate in the UK is the percentage rise in the CPI over its value a year earlier.

However, consumption expenditure is only one part of GDP, which also includes investment, government spending and net exports. To convert nominal GDP to real GDP, we need to use an index showing what is happening to the price of all goods. This index is called the **GDP deflator**.

The GDP deflator is the ratio of nominal GDP to real GDP expressed as an index.

Figure 15.4 plots data for the UK during 1998–2011, showing nominal GDP (in £ billions) in green. Looking at the green line alone, it appears that the recession of 2008/09 was short-lived, and that growth quickly resumed. The purple line plots UK GDP in real terms, valuing it always at the prices ruling in 2009. The two curves therefore cross in 2009. Once we allow for the effect of inflation in boosting nominal GDP, we can see that real GDP grew much more slowly. The severity of the recession after 2008 then becomes much clearer.

Figure 15.4 also shows indexes of nominal and real GDP in China over the same period. Because its real GDP growth was much stronger, the purple curve is much steeper than for the UK. Moreover, since China has much more inflation than the Eurozone or the UK, its nominal GDP growth is even greater still.

Per capita real GDP

Real GDP measures the real output of an economy. Its annual percentage increase tells us how fast an economy is growing. Table 15.7 shows average annual growth rates of real GD during 2000–2010 for a range of countries.

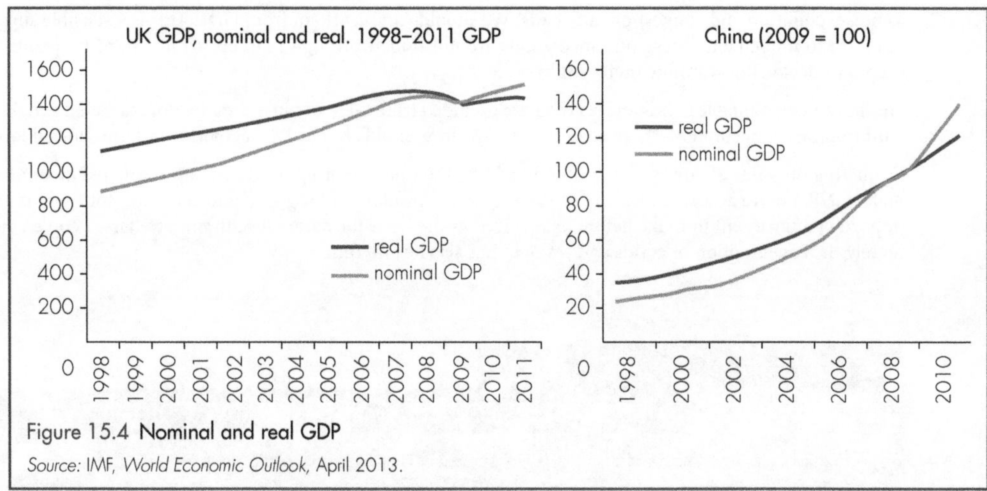

Figure 15.4 **Nominal and real GDP**

Source: IMF, *World Economic Outlook*, April 2013.

It also shows average annual population growth during the period. The difference between these two columns shows us the average annual growth of output per person.

Chinese real GDP grew on average by 10.8 per cent a year. Because of its one child per family policy, its population hardly grew. Hence it achieved a stunning 10.2 per cent a year increase in **per capita** output, allowing its living standards to grow rapidly. Although Ethiopian GDP grew by 8.8 per cent annually, its population was also growing strongly. Output per person grew by 6.2 per cent. In the UK and Switzerland, annual GDP growth was less than 2 per cent, implying annual growth rates of around 1 per cent in per capital GDP. In the Palestine areas of the West Bank and Gaza, not only did real GDP fall over the period, rapid population growth of 3.2 per cent a year meant that per capita GDP was falling by 3.7 per cent a year during 2000–2010.

Per capita real GDP is real GDP divided by total population. It is real GDP per head.

Table 15.7 Annual growth of real GDP and per capital real GDP, 2000–12 (% per annum)

	Real GDP	Population	Per capita real GDP
China	10.8	0.6	10.2
Ethiopia	8.8	2.6	6.2
Switzerland	1.9	0.8	1.1
UK	1.6	0.6	1.0
West Bank/Gaza	−0.9	3.2	−3.7

Whether we are interested in GDP or per capita GDP depends on the question we want to answer. For example, total GDP will give an indication of a country's economic size and power, whereas per capita GDP is more informative about productivity and likely living standards of the representative person. Of course, individuals do not always follow the average. The more the dispersion changes over time, the less reliable the average or per capita statistics are in thinking about what is happening to particular people.

A comprehensive measure of GDP

Because we use GDP to measure the output of the economy, the coverage of GDP should be as comprehensive as possible. In practice, we encounter two problems in including all production in GDP. First, some outputs, such as noise, pollution and congestion, are 'bads'. We should *subtract* them from GDP. This is a sensible suggestion but hard to implement. These nuisance goods are not traded through markets, so it is hard to quantify their output or decide how to value their cost to society.

Similarly, many valuable goods and services are excluded from GDP because they are not marketed and therefore hard to measure accurately. These activities include household chores, DIY activities and unreported jobs.

Deducting the value of nuisance outputs and adding the value of unreported and non-marketed incomes would make GNP a more accurate measure of the economy's production of goods and services. But there is another important adjustment to make before using GNP as the basis for national economic welfare. People enjoy not merely the consumption of goods and services but also leisure time.

ACTIVITY 15.1

SUSTAINABILITY, POLLUTION AND NEGATIVE GDP GROWTH

The first table below shows data on the successful industrialization of Asian economies. The Asian tigers comprise small countries in East Asia that abandoned protectionism in the 1960s and began half a century of rapid export-led industrialization.

Global manufacturing success of the Asian tigers

	Per capita real GDP annual growth (%), 1965–2012	Manufactured exports (% of total exports)	
		1965	2012
Indonesia	6	2	41
Malaysia	5	6	70
Singapore	7	34	74
South Korea	6.5	59	90
Thailand	6	4	75

Source: World Bank, *World Development Report* (various issues).

In the 1990s a second wave of countries embraced globalization, exports and significant deregulation. The most important of these – because of their size, their success has had a huge impact on the world economy – are now known as the BRICs (Brazil, Russia, India and China).

BRICs economic success

	GDP growth Annual average (%) 2000–12	Per capita GDP growth Annual average (%) 2000–12	Share of manufactures in total exports (%)	
			1980	2012
Brazil	3.5	3.5	39	39
Russia	5	5	–	17
India	8	3	59	67
China	10	10	48	94

Although China, and to a lesser extent India, industrialized in a manner similar to the Asian tigers, Russia is essentially an energy exporter and Brazil's growth (like Australia's) has largely reflected exports of raw materials to booming Asian manufacturers.

Whatever the differences between countries, the central point is that emerging markets are booming, industrializing quickly (even in raw material extraction) and developing large urban populations of sophisticated consumers.

From earlier industrial revolutions in Europe, the US and Japan, we know that this phase of economic development usually entails considerable pollution – the dark satanic mills of England, or the pall that used to hang over New York and Chicago. Environmental quality is a luxury of much greater concern to countries already secure in reasonable standards of material welfare. Rich and educated Europe now places much greater weight on the green agenda.

A study by the Asian Development Bank noted that Asian emissions of greenhouse gases will treble in the next 25 years. Asia will overtake Western economies as the world's biggest source of greenhouse gas pollutants. China is currently building a new coal-fired power station every two weeks, and India's microcar – the Tata Nano – will make motoring affordable to tens of millions of new drivers every year. As populations move from villages to the cities, demand for heat and power increases steadily.

Environmental degradation means that almost 40 per cent of Asia's population now lives in areas prone to drought and erosion. With the Asian population set to triple in the next 20 years, and half these people living in cities, air pollution will reach new records. Nor is access to clean water much better.

If national accounts kept a proper account of environmental depreciation – a cost subtracted from gross output when measuring the true net output of an economy – many Asian countries would have less impressive growth records. We might even have to call them Asian snails instead of tigers. Their success in making consumer electronics is offset by extensive pollution and urban congestion. Ask anyone who recently visited Bangkok.

Questions

(a) How does depreciation of ordinary machinery and buildings enter calculations of GDP or national income?

(b) What national accounts measure properly reflects depreciation of physical capital?

(c) How are conventional estimates of depreciation made?

(d) What would be entailed in following the same procedures for environmental capital?

(e) How would environmental capital for the whole planet affect national accounts?

To check your answers to these questions, see page 679.

Suppose Leisurians value leisure more highly than Industrians. Industrians will therefore choose to work more than Leisurians, and therefore will also produce more goods and services. Industria has a higher measured GDP. It is silly to say this proves that Leisurians have lower welfare. By choosing to work less, they reveal that the extra leisure is worth at least as much as the extra goods and services they could have made by working more. Ideally, we should be measuring the output of leisure as well as of goods and services.

Because it is difficult and expensive to collect regular measurements on non-marketed and unreported goods and bads, and to make regular assessments of the implicit value of leisure, real GDP inevitably remains the commonest measure of economic activity. Far from ideal, it is the best measure available on a regular basis.

15.6 International comparisons

International agencies prefer to compare like with like, which means eliminating measures that are sensitive to large differences in national practices. No country invests much of its resources in collecting accurate data for depreciation. Hence international statistics focus on gross measures rather than net measures, since the latter would entail making allowances for depreciation, which vary from country to country.

Similarly, it is generally felt that GDP data are more reliable than GNP data, since the latter includes estimates of property income earned abroad. One reason why people hold assets abroad is to avoid declaring the income to national tax authorities. Assessing capital gains (which are really income) on foreign assets is also problematic. Hence, most international comparisons are based on GDP. We have a more reliable idea of gross output than of gross income.

The new economics of happiness

Suppose we wanted to go beyond imperfect measures of material goods and services. How might we proceed? The new economics of happiness tries to ask people directly how happy they feel and then correlates this with various measures of their economic, social and psychological environment.

Simple economics might suggest that the average happiness of a citizen of a particular country should be correlated with per capita GDP in that country. There is quite a lot of empirical support for this correlation if we are talking about fairly poor countries – a higher standard of living makes a big difference. However, research by Richard Easterlin discovered that, beyond some threshold of material well-being, additional levels of material goods and services lead to surprisingly small additions to subjective happiness. Once basic needs have been met, people appear to derive more happiness from being *relatively* better off than other citizens. Nor is material standard of living the only relevant determinant – people report greater happiness if they are in a stable relationship with a partner, have a reasonable amount of freedom and political control over their lives, have plenty of leisure, enjoy good health and live in a society free from conflict and warfare.

The Satisfaction with Life index, based on survey data, allows the construction of a global happiness map. In Figure 15.5, purple denotes the happiest countries, and red the least-happy countries. There is obviously quite a strong correlation with per capita GDP – North America, Europe, Australia and New Zealand and Saudi Arabia all score highly, whereas Africa fares poorly. However, Russia is less happy than its per capita GDP would imply, whereas Mexicans appear as happy as Europeans, despite making and earning considerably less.

Amongst individual countries, Denmark, Switzerland and Austria topped the ranking, whereas Burundi, Zimbabwe and the Democratic Republic of the Congo came bottom. To keep track of the latest version of this index, use your favourite Internet search engine to look for the Economist Quality of Life index.

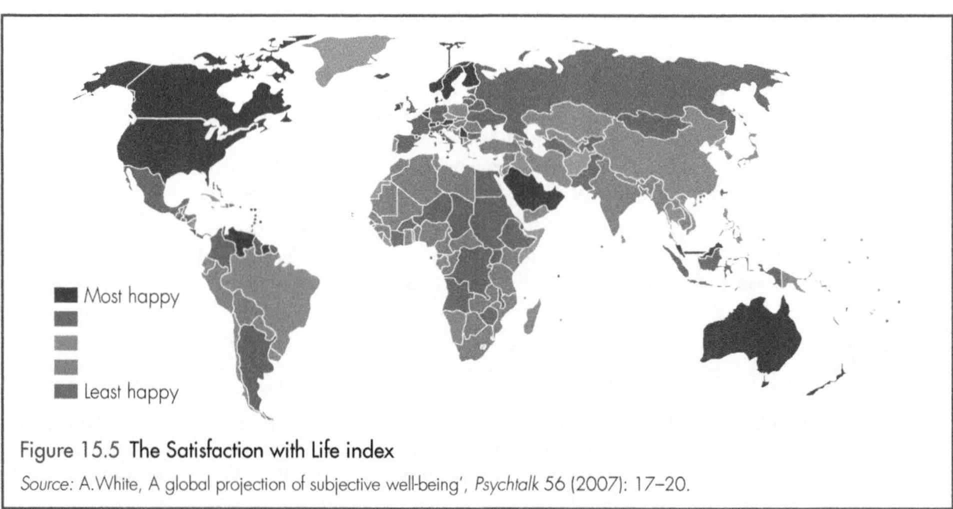

Figure 15.5 **The Satisfaction with Life index**

Source: A.White, A global projection of subjective well-being', *Psychtalk* 56 (2007): 17–20.

Summary

- **Macroeconomics** examines the economy as a whole.
- Macroeconomics sacrifices individual detail to focus on the interaction of broad sectors of the economy. Households supply production inputs to firms that use them to make output. Firms pay factor incomes to households, who buy the output from firms. This is the **circular flow**.
- **Gross domestic product (GDP)** is the value of net output of the factors of production located in the domestic economy. It can be measured in three equivalent ways: value added in production, factor incomes including profits or final expenditure.
- **Leakages** from the circular flow are those parts of payment by firms to households that do not automatically return to firms as spending by households on the output of firms. Leakages are saving, taxes net of subsidies and imports. **Injections** are sources of revenue to firms that do not arise from household spending. Investment expenditure by firms, spending on goods and services by the government and exports are injections. By definition, total leakages equal total injections.
- **GDP at market prices** values domestic output at prices inclusive of indirect taxes. **GDP at basic prices** measures domestic output at prices exclusive of indirect taxes. **Gross national product (GNP)**, also called gross national income (GNI), adjusts GDP for net property income from abroad.
- **National income** is net national product (NNP) at basic prices. NNP is GNP minus the **depreciation** of the capital stock during the period. In practice, many assessments of economic performance are based on GNP since it is hard to measure depreciation accurately.
- **Nominal GDP** measures output at current prices. **Real GDP** measures output at constant prices. It adjusts nominal GDP for changes in the **GDP deflator** as a result of inflation.
- **Per capita real GDP** divides real GDP by the population. It is a more reliable indicator of average output per person in an economy.
- Real GDP and per capita real GDP are crude measures of national and individual welfare. They ignore non-market activities, bads such as pollution, valuable activities such as work in the home, and production unreported by tax evaders. Nor do they measure the value of leisure.
- Because it is expensive, and sometimes impossible, to make regular and accurate measurements of all these activities, in practice GDP is the most widely used measure of national performance.
- By using data based on surveys of how happy people feel, it is possible to explore how reliable per capita GDP is as a measure of national happiness. There is a strong relationship, especially before an acceptable living standard has been reached, but happiness also depends on environmental factors (security, access, freedom) and other personal factors (health, success of relationships).

Review questions

EASY

1 Car firms buy raw materials (steel), intermediate goods (windscreens, tyres) and labour to make cars. Windscreen and tyre companies hire workers and also buy raw materials from other industries. What is the value added of the car industry (the three firms shown below)?

Producer of	Output	Intermediate goods used	Raw materials used	Labour input
Cars	1000	250	100	100
Windscreens	150		10	50
Tyres	100		10	30

2 GNP at market prices is £300 billion. Depreciation is £30 billion; indirect taxes £20 billion. (a) What is the national income? (b) Why does depreciation cause a discrepancy between GNP and national income? (c) Why do indirect taxes enter the calculation?

3 Which of the following statements is correct? (a) Increasing the staff of the police force in response to higher crime raises national income because government spending is higher. (b) Increasing the staff of the police force reduces national income because society wastes resources tackling crime. (c) There is no effect on national income because the benefit of more police is offset by the cost of more crime.

4 Given the data below: (a) What is 2010 GNP in 2009 prices? (b) What is the growth rate of real GNP from 2009 to 2010? (c) What is the inflation rate?

EASY

Year	Nominal GDP (£)	Income elasticity
2009	2000	100
2010	2400	110

5 **Common fallacies** Why are these statements wrong? (a) Unemployment benefit props up national income in years when employment is low. (b) A high per capita real GNP is always a good thing. (c) In 2010, *Crummy Movie* earned £1 billion more at the box office than *Gone with the Wind* earned 50 years ago. *Crummy Movie* is definitely a bigger box office success.

6 Suppose a country is unable to borrow from abroad and must always equate the value of its exports and imports. If the private sector is saving a lot more than it is investing, is the government in surplus or deficit? Why?

7 It is the year 2060. Nation states have been abolished and there is a world government whose spending is entirely financed by income tax. How does the diagram below have to be amended?

MEDIUM

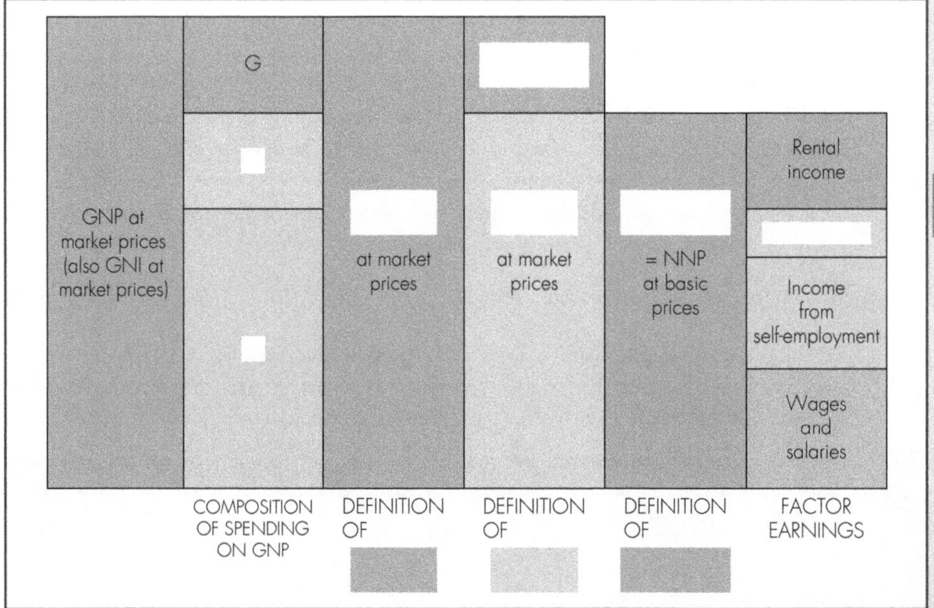

8 Suppose the injections to the circular flow (investment I, government spending G and exports X) do not depend on the current level of national output Y. In contrast, suppose leakages increase as output increases. (a) Suppose saving $S = 0.1Y$. If total injections equal 10, what is the equilibrium level of output? (Assume a circular flow model without government and foreign sectors.) (b) Now suppose imports $Z = 0.4Y$ and taxes $T = 0.5Y$. If $G = £40$, is the government budget ($G - T$) in surplus or deficit?

MEDIUM

9 GNP = £2000, $C = £1700$, $G = £50$ and $NX = £40$. (a) What is investment I? (b) If exports are 350, what are imports? (c) If depreciation = £130, what is national income? (d) In this example, net exports are positive. Could they be negative?

10 Should these be in a comprehensive measure of GNP? (a) Time spent by students in lectures. (b) The income of muggers. (c) The wage paid to traffic wardens. (d) Dropping litter.

11 The price of a new television has remained roughly constant for the last 30 years. What does this show?

HARD

12 Suppose the government publishes world economic accounts that estimate not merely depreciation of the stock of physical capital but also the stock of environmental capital. (a) Complete the composition of world income and output in the diagram given below. (b) If pollution and climate change are causing adverse effects, how does your new diagram on world income and output differ from the diagram given below? (c) Suppose environmental depreciation was initially $500 billion and the world government spends $100 billion on pollution control with the consequence that environmental depreciation is now only $300 billion. How must the diagram below be amended?

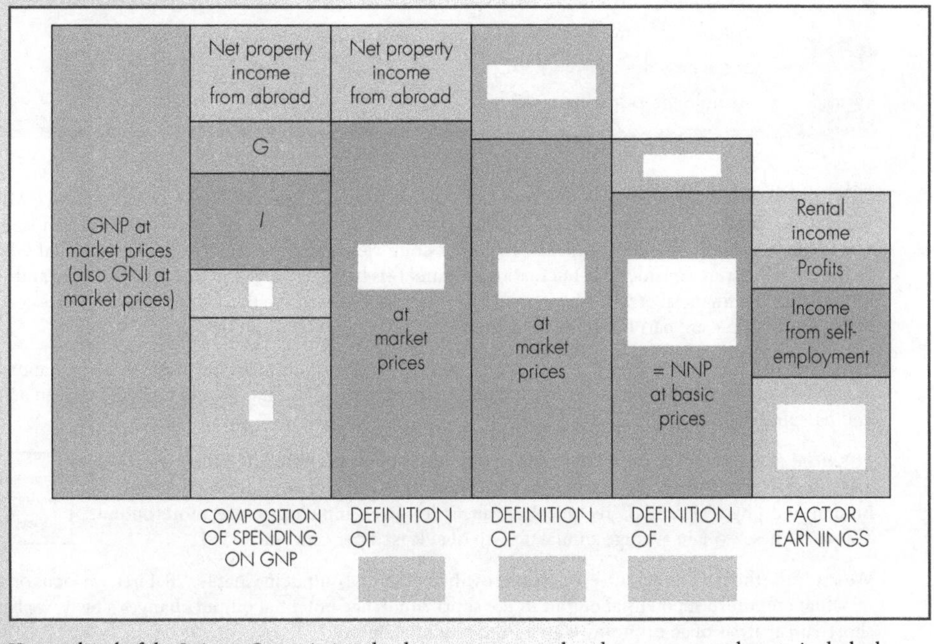

13 You are head of the Leisure Commission that has to recommend to the government how to include the value of leisure in GDP. How do you come up with an estimate?

14 **Essay question** 'Economists are preoccupied with what they can measure. GDP is so misleading an indicator of welfare that it is almost pointless to gather statistics about it, either for international comparison across countries or to assess how well particular governments are doing.' How useful is GDP? Could we easily have a better indicator?

For solutions to these questions, contact your lecturer.

CHAPTER 16

Output and aggregate demand

Learning Outcomes

By the end of this chapter, you should be able to:

1. contrast actual output and potential output
2. explain why output is demand determined in the short run
3. define short-run equilibrium output
4. analyse consumption and investment demand
5. show how aggregate demand determines short-run equilibrium output
6. explain inflationary and deflationary gaps
7. define the marginal propensity to consume *c*
8. calculate the multiplier
9. show how the marginal propensity to consume affects the multiplier
10. explain the paradox of thrift

GDP growth is seldom smooth. Using data from the very helpful International Monetary Fund (IMF) website, Figure 16.1 shows annual real GDP growth for the UK, Ireland, Sweden and the Netherlands since 1981. On average, Ireland grew most quickly, the other countries averaging about 2 per cent annual GDP growth. However, there were considerable fluctuations around this trend, even before the sharp collapse and recovery of output after the financial crash. Words used by economists to describe these fluctuations – recession, recovery, boom and slump – are part of everyday language.

Why does real GDP fluctuate? To construct a simple model, we ignore discrepancies between national income, real GNP and real GDP. We use income and output interchangeably. First, we distinguish between *actual* output and *potential* output.

Potential output tends to grow over time as the supply of inputs grows. Population growth adds to the labour force. Investment in education, training and new machinery adds to human and physical capital. Technical advances let given inputs produce more output. Together, these explain average annual growth of at least 2 per cent since 1981.

Potential output is the economy's output when inputs are fully employed.

We study the theory of long-run economic growth in potential output in Chapter 28. First, we focus on deviations of actual output from potential output in the short run. Since potential output changes slowly, we begin with a short-run analysis of an economy with a fixed potential output.

Potential output is not the maximum an economy can conceivably make. With a gun to our heads, we could all make more. Rather, it is the output when every market in the economy is in long-run equilibrium. Every worker wanting to work at the equilibrium wage can find a job, and every machine that can profitably be used at the equilibrium rental for capital is in use. Potential output includes an allowance for 'equilibrium unemployment'. Some people do not want to work at the equilibrium wage rate. Moreover, in a constantly changing economy, some people are temporarily between jobs. Today, UK potential output probably entails an unemployment rate of about 5 per cent, yet recent actual unemployment has exceeded 8 per cent.

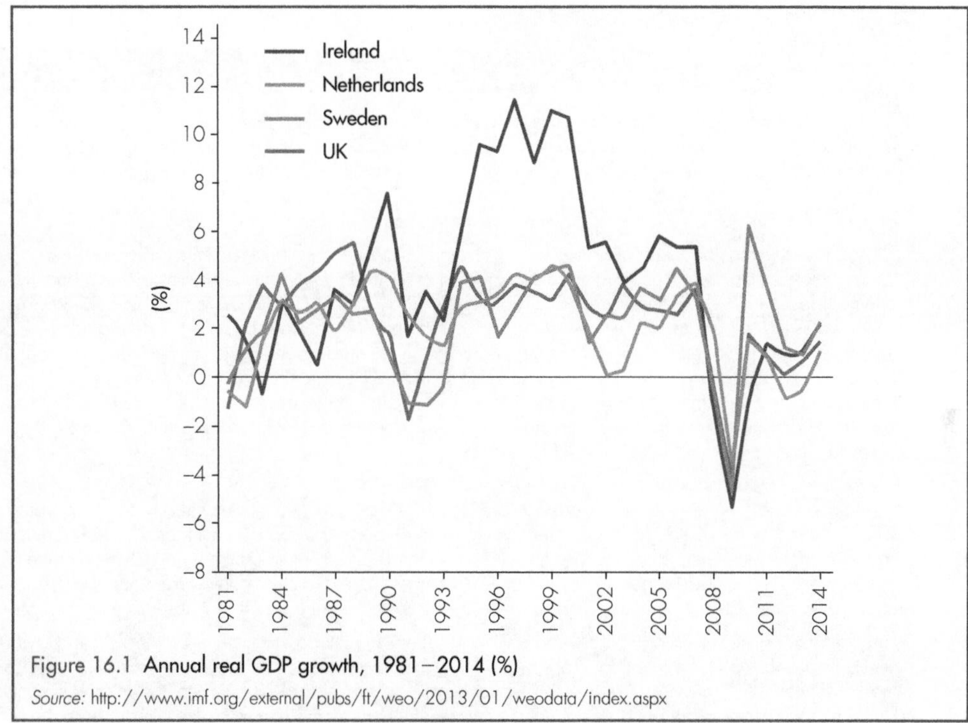

Figure 16.1 Annual real GDP growth, 1981–2014 (%)

Source: http://www.imf.org/external/pubs/ft/weo/2013/01/weodata/index.aspx

Suppose actual output falls below potential output. Workers are unemployed and firms have idle machines or spare capacity. A key issue in macroeconomics is how quickly output returns to potential output. In microeconomics, studying one market in isolation, we assumed excess supply would quickly bid the price down, eliminating excess supply to restore equilibrium. In macroeconomics, this cannot be taken for granted. Disturbances in one part of the economy induce changes elsewhere that may feed back again, exacerbating the original disturbance.

We cannot examine this issue by *assuming* that the economy is always at potential output, for then a problem could never arise. We must build a model in which departures from potential output are possible, examine the market forces then set in motion and decide how successfully market forces restore output to potential output. Because we want initially to focus on the possibility of additional unemployment, we start by considering a world in which there might be idle capacity and too little demand.

Trade is voluntary: actual exchange is always the smaller of supply and demand. Output is demand-determined if there is excess supply. Wages and prices have yet to adjust to restore long-run equilibrium. Until then, output depends only on aggregate demand.

Conversely, if excess demand exists, as under rationing in the former USSR, output is supply-determined.

Thus our initial model has two crucial properties. First, all prices and wages are fixed at a given level. Second, at these prices and wage levels, there are workers without a job who would like to work, and firms with spare capacity they could profitably use. The economy has spare resources. It is then unnecessary to analyse the supply side of the economy in detail. Any rise in demand is happily met by firms and workers until potential output is reached.

Below potential output, firms happily supply whatever output is demanded. Total output is **demand-determined**. (Conversely, if excess demand exists, as under rationing in the former USSR, output is **supply-determined**.)

Later, we relax the assumption that prices and wages are fixed. Not only do we want to study inflation, we also want to examine how quickly market forces, acting through changes in prices and wages, can eliminate unemployment and spare capacity. But first we must learn to walk. We defer analysis of price and wage adjustment until Chapter 21.

CASE 16.1

A BRIEF HISTORY OF MACROECONOMICS

Two of the most fundamental questions in macroeconomics are whether, and if so how quickly, we can rely on markets to restore actual output to potential output. If this happens reliably and quickly, output is usually near potential output; most economic analysis and economic policy should then focus on how potential output increases over time. However, if actual output can deviate from potential output for long periods and by large amounts, we must focus much more on what determines actual output.

Classical economists of the eighteenth and nineteenth centuries were market optimists, believing that market forces restore actual output to potential output quite quickly. The supply of potential output then became the principal focus of study. French economist Jean-Baptiste Say (1767–1832) gave his name to 'Say's Law', which states that supply creates its own demand. If goods and services are being produced, and the income thereby derived is passed on to the owners of the factors of production, the latter then have the spending power to purchase the original output. Nineteenth-century UK economists in the classical tradition include James Mill, his son John Stuart Mill, and David Ricardo. Classical economists still had some explaining to do – for example, why was there a Great Depression during 1873–79 in many leading economies? Had potential output really fallen by that much that quickly?

Nevertheless, classical economics largely persisted until the 1920s. After the First World War, European economies were struggling to regain pre-war prosperity. At the time, they all belonged to the gold standard, which in effect was a fixed exchange rate system. Within this system, countries such as the UK had become seriously uncompetitive as a result of wartime inflation. The 1926 General Strike in the UK was the result of austerity designed to push wages down to restore UK competitiveness, a close analogy of modern Greek misery as it tries to reduce its budget deficit and increase its competitiveness in order to survive within the Eurozone.

Less ravaged by the war and unburdened by wartime debts, the US boomed in the late 1920s, in ways very similar to the run-up to the financial crash of 2008: an asset price bubble in the stock market and housing market, excessive borrowing and injudicious lending. The crash of 1929 tipped the locomotive of the world economy into its own protracted recession. The 1930s became known as the Great Depression. The explanation offered by classical economics became less and less convincing.

The intellectual revolution was led by UK economist John Maynard Keynes, culminating in his *General Theory of Employment, Interest and Money* (1936). Keynes used the model to explain high unemployment and low output in the Great Depression of the 1930s. Discarding classical assumptions, Keynes argued that market forces – the adjustment of wages and prices in response to booms and slumps – were too slow and too ineffective to prevent serious and prolonged departures of demand and output from potential output.

© ClassicStock | Alamy

Many young economists soon became *Keynesians*, advocating government intervention to manage demand and output, keeping them close to potential output. This approach dominated economic policy and intellectual thinking in the 1950s and 1960s, when governments were proud of their expertise in keeping output growth smooth and unemployment low.

However, the magic began to wear off by the late 1960s. Inflation was steadily rising and the normal level of unemployment was creeping up, even when governments boosted demand. Indeed, the pursuit of 'artificially low' unemployment, and failure to recognize that the underlying sustainable level of unemployment had increased, was a principal cause of the rising inflation.

Monetarists, led by Chicago economist Professor Milton Friedman, argued that we could at least take care of inflation, by pursuing a prudent rate of money growth. In essence, this meant abandoning the attempt to micromanage demand and output and relying to a greater degree on market forces again to restore output slowly to potential output. Friedman famously argued that the lags in macroeconomic policy were 'long and variable'. Even well-meaning interventions took an unpredictable time to take effect, by which time the economy might have sorted itself through market forces. Active macroeconomic policy risked blowing the economy off course just as it was recovering unaided.

The monetarist revival also reminded everyone that incentives and 'supply-side policies' matter – whatever the path of actual output, we still want a good evolution of potential output and the corresponding level of normal or 'equilibrium' unemployment.

Following the sharp rise in oil prices achieved by OPEC, in the 1970s output stagnated, unemployment rose and inflation was initially obdurately high. Some economists discarded Keynesian economics completely. Not only did they deny the effectiveness of government policy to stabilize output, they argued that stabilizing output might not even be desirable. This prompted a fightback by *New Keynesians*, who believe that the central messages of Keynes, right all along, can be understood better by using modern microeconomics to explain the market failures that justify Keynesian intervention to assist the effective operation of markets.

After the mid-1990s, there appeared to be considerable convergence in ideas about macroeconomics. Central banks were made independent from government interference and asked to stabilize national economies, particularly their inflation rates. Central banks appeared to combine responsible underlying monetary growth with active fine-tuning of interest rates to keep output close to potential output. This appeared to confirm (a) that, properly managed and without political interference, demand management could succeed; and (b) that active demand management could be combined with long-run inflation control. For nearly two decades, this appeared to work well.

Perhaps it all worked too well. In stabilizing economies, central banks eliminated a lot of risk for the private sector. In a climate of safety, the private sector felt able to take huge 'risks' precisely because it did not think they were risky. Households borrowed too much and speculated on property, banks borrowed too much and invested in more and more dubious assets in pursuit of ever-higher returns. The central banks were so focused on macroeconomic stability of inflation and GDP that nobody blew the whistle on increasingly dangerous private sector behaviour. The result was the crash of 2008.

Clawing our way out of this large hole is proving extremely difficult and slow. As asset prices collapsed, banks and their borrowers approached bankruptcy. Sensibly, governments stepped in to prevent the crisis spiralling, but at the cost of transferring the debts to the governments themselves. This has severely constrained future policy. With everyone fearful, few now wish to spend. Without their demand, firms are reluctant to supply.

Mastering modern macroeconomics will take us to great heights and shed light on these issues. But we need to climb slowly, and to begin at the foothills.

Chapter 15 introduced the circular flow of income and payments between households and firms. Households buy the output of firms. Firms' revenue is ultimately returned to households. We now build a simple model of this interaction of households and firms. Then, in Chapter 17, we continue the analysis after adding the government and the foreign sector.

16.1 Components of aggregate demand

Without a government or a foreign sector, there are two sources of demand: consumption demand by households and investment demand by firms. Aggregate demand *AD* is the sum of consumption demand *C* and investment demand *I*. Consumption demand and investment demand are chosen by different economic groups and depend on different things.

Consumption demand

Personal disposable income is the income households receive from firms, plus transfers received from government, minus taxes paid to government. It is the net income households can spend or save.

Households buy goods and services from cars to cinema tickets. These consumption purchases account for most of **personal disposable income**.

With no government, disposable income is simply the income received from firms. Given its disposable income, each household plans how much to spend and to save. Deciding one, decides the other. One family may save to buy a bigger house; another may spend more than its income, or 'dissave', taking the round-the-world trip it always wanted.

Many things affect consumption and saving decisions. We examine these in detail in Chapter 20. To get started, one simplification takes us a long way. We assume that, in the aggregate, households' consumption demand rises with aggregate personal disposable income.

Figure 16.2 shows real consumption and real GDP, both corrected for inflation, during 1948–2011. The figure confirms that the basic relation between income and consumption is strong and stable over time. Each extra £1 of GDP was accompanied by around £0.7 extra consumption.

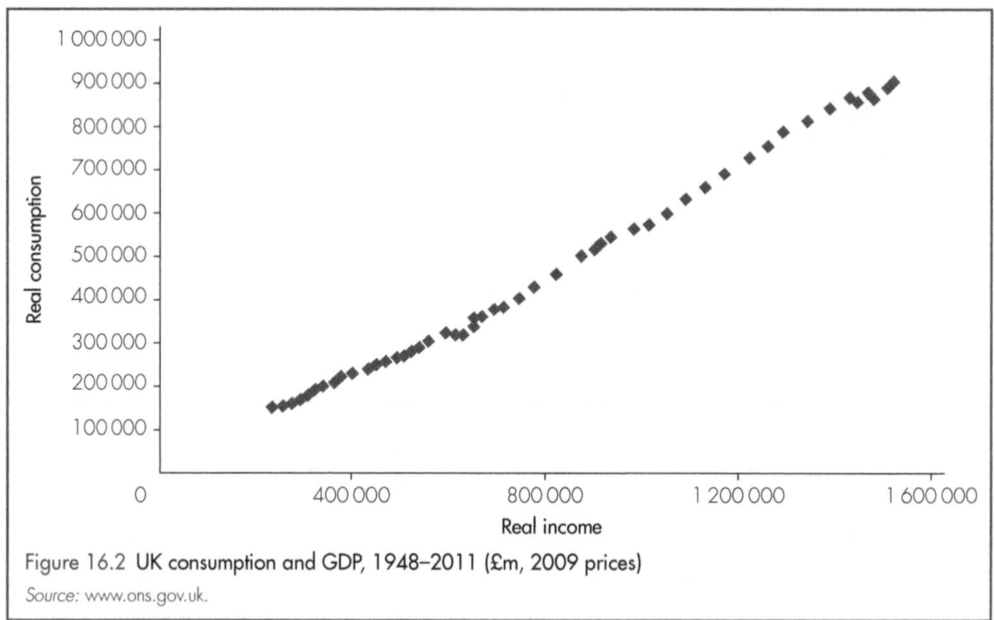

Figure 16.2 UK consumption and GDP, 1948–2011 (£m, 2009 prices)

Source: www.ons.gov.uk.

The consumption function

This positive relation between income and consumption demand is shown in Figure 16.3 and is called the **consumption function**.

The consumption function shows aggregate consumption demand at each level of income.

The consumption function tells us how to go from income Y to consumption demand C. If A is a positive constant, and c is a positive fraction between 0 and 1, then

$$C = A + cY$$

Our bare-bones model has no government, no transfer payments and no taxes. The consumption function is a straight line. A straight line is completely described by its intercept – the height at which it crosses the vertical axis – and its slope – the amount it rises for each unit we move horizontally to the right.

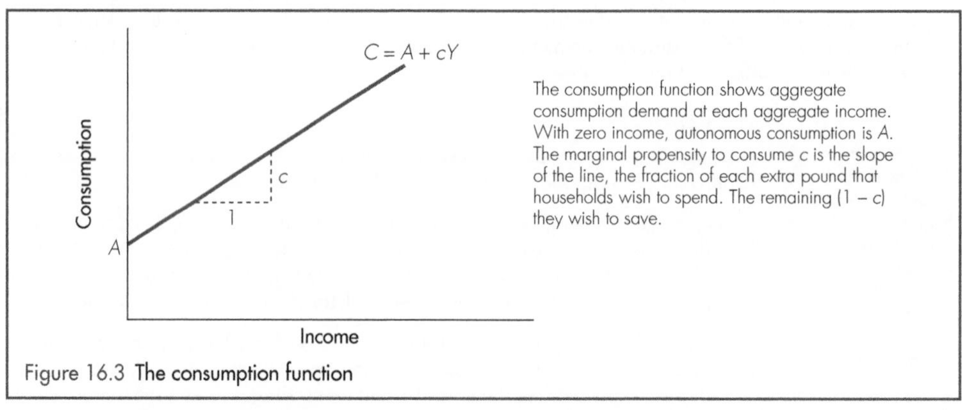

The consumption function shows aggregate consumption demand at each aggregate income. With zero income, autonomous consumption is A. The marginal propensity to consume c is the slope of the line, the fraction of each extra pound that households wish to spend. The remaining $(1 - c)$ they wish to save.

Figure 16.3 The consumption function

The intercept is A. We call this *autonomous* consumption demand. Since our basic model is that income determines consumption demand, autonomous means those determinants of consumption demand other than income. Households wish to consume A even if income Y is zero.[1]

We might think of autonomous demand as reflecting the minimum consumption needed for survival, but the reality is more subtle. Autonomous consumption demand can change in response to changes in other economic variables, for example expectations about *future* incomes. Students expecting prosperous futures may spend more than is justified by their current incomes alone! The key point for our current analysis is that autonomous consumption demand does not depend upon current income.

Marginal propensity to consume is the fraction of each extra pound of disposable income that households wish to consume.

The slope of the consumption function is the **marginal propensity to consume.**

Different people may exhibit different marginal propensities to consume. Poor people, with many unmet needs, are likely to spend immediately any extra income that they receive. For them, c is close to 1. Billionaires may already be consuming everything they could possibly want. For them, any extra income is largely unspent: c is close to 0. In macroeconomics, we are interested in aggregate behaviour, so the *MPC* will be less than 1 but well above 0.

In Figure 16.3 the marginal propensity to consume *MPC* is c. If income rises by £1, desired consumption rises by £c. In Figure 16.2, c was around 0.6. Different people may behave differently. When poor people get extra income, they tend to consume almost all the extra. When a billionaire gets extra income, his consumption demand may be unchanged. The aggregate consumption function reflects average behaviour for the population as a whole.

The saving function shows desired saving at each income level.

Saving is income not consumed. When income Y is zero, saving is $-A$. Households are dissaving, or running down their assets. Since a fraction c of each pound of extra income is consumed, a fraction $(1 - c)$ of each extra pound of income is saved. The marginal propensity to save *MPS* is $(1 - c)$. Since an extra pound of income leads either to extra desired consumption or to extra desired saving, $MPC + MPS \equiv 1$. The three-line identity symbol means that *MPC* plus *MPS* necessarily equals 1 as a matter of definition. Figure 16.4 shows the **saving function** corresponding to the consumption function in Figure 16.3.

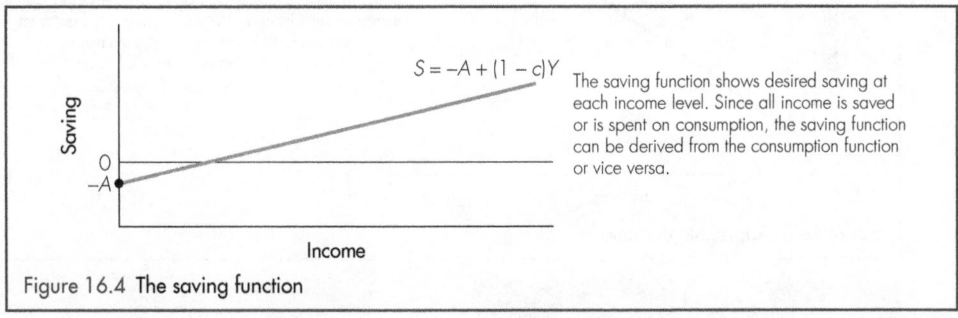

The saving function shows desired saving at each income level. Since all income is saved or is spent on consumption, the saving function can be derived from the consumption function or vice versa.

Figure 16.4 **The saving function**

Since saving is defined as the part of income unspent, $Y \equiv C + S$, the three-line symbol promising us that this is always true as a matter of definition. We can replace C by the consumption function to deduce the relation between desired saving and income, the saving function shown in Figure 16.4.

At an income of zero, autonomous consumption is A. With income Y at zero, desired saving must therefore be $-A$. Since each unit increase in income leads to an extra c of desired consumption, it must also lead to an extra $(1 - c)$ of desired saving. Whatever is not consumed must be saved. Hence the saving function is as shown in Figure 16.4. Planned saving is the part of income not planned to be spent on consumption.

Sometimes we will refer to the *saving rate* S/Y, which is simply the fraction of income saved.

1 A is the minimum consumption needed for survival. How do households finance it when their incomes are zero? In the short run they dissave and run down their assets. But they cannot do so for ever. The consumption function may differ in the short run and the long run, an idea we discuss in Chapter 20.

Investment spending

Income is the key determinant of household consumption or spending plans as described by the consumption function. What about the factors determining the investment decision by firms; that is, their planned spending on new capital goods in the form of factories, machinery and buildings?

Firms' **investment demand** depends chiefly on firms' current guesses about how fast the demand for their output will increase. Sometimes output is high and rising, sometimes it is high and falling. Since there is no close connection between the current *level* of income and firms' guesses about how the demand for their output is going to *change*, we make the simple assumption that investment demand is autonomous. Desired investment I is constant, independent of current output and income. In Chapter 20 we discuss investment demand in more detail.

Investment demand is firms' desired or planned additions to physical capital (factories and machines) and to inventories.

16.2 Aggregate demand

In our simple model, **aggregate demand** is simply households' consumption demand C plus firms' investment demand I.

Aggregate demand is the amount firms and households plan to spend at each level of income.

Figure 16.5 shows the aggregate demand schedule. To the previous consumption function it adds a constant amount I for desired investment. Each extra unit of income adds c to consumption demand but nothing to investment demand: aggregate demand rises by c. The AD schedule is parallel to the consumption function. The slope of both is the marginal propensity to consume.

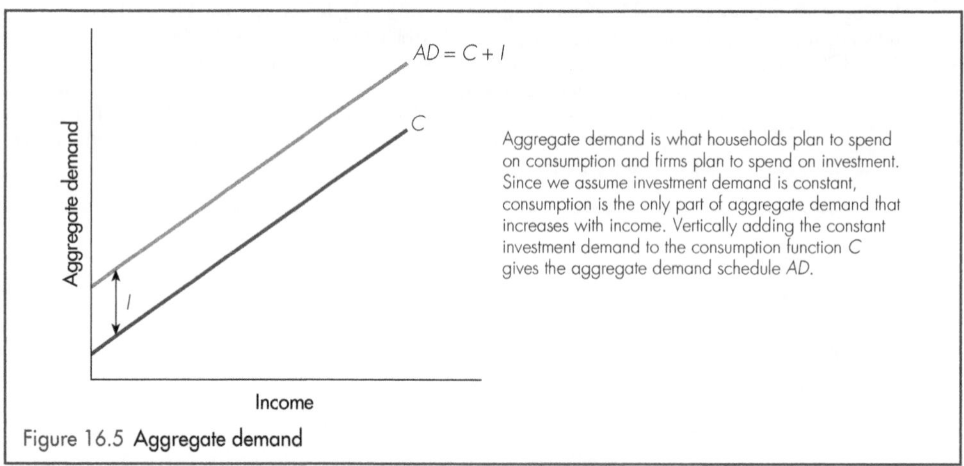

Aggregate demand is what households plan to spend on consumption and firms plan to spend on investment. Since we assume investment demand is constant, consumption is the only part of aggregate demand that increases with income. Vertically adding the constant investment demand to the consumption function C gives the aggregate demand schedule AD.

Figure 16.5 **Aggregate demand**

CONCEPT 16.1

EXOGENOUS AND ENDOGENOUS VARIABLES

A model is like a sausage machine. Our economic theory is the design of how the machine works, which is deduced from our assumptions about how people behave. Even once it has been built, a sausage machine still needs inputs – raw meat, breadcrumbs, spices and the butcher's secret ingredients – in order to deliver an output of sausages. In the same way, our economic models require inputs of some economic variables in order then to deliver implications for how other variables will behave.

In our simple model of aggregate demand, the levels of both investment and autonomous consumption are **exogenous**, or given from outside the model. Conditional on these inputs to the model, the model then determines the **endogenous variables**: consumption demand, and thus total aggregate demand.

Exogenous variables are those fed into the model as inputs.

Endogenous variables are those which the model then delivers as outputs, conditional on the values of the exogenous inputs.

16.3 Equilibrium output

Wages and prices are *fixed*, and output is demand determined. If aggregate demand falls below potential output, firms cannot sell as much as they would like. There is *involuntary* excess capacity. Workers cannot work as much as they would like. There is *involuntary* unemployment.

When prices and wages are fixed, at short-run equilibrium output aggregate demand or planned spending equals the output actually produced.

To define **short-run equilibrium** we cannot use the definition used in microeconomics, the output at which both suppliers and demanders are happy with the quantity bought and sold. We wish to study a situation in which firms and workers would like to supply more goods and more labour. Suppliers are frustrated. At least we can require that demanders are happy.

Thus, spending plans are not frustrated by a shortage of goods. Nor do firms make more output than they can sell. In short-run equilibrium, actual output equals the output demanded by households as consumption and by firms as investment.

Figure 16.6 shows income on the horizontal axis and planned spending on the vertical axis. It also includes the 45-degree line, along which quantities on the horizontal and vertical axes are equal.

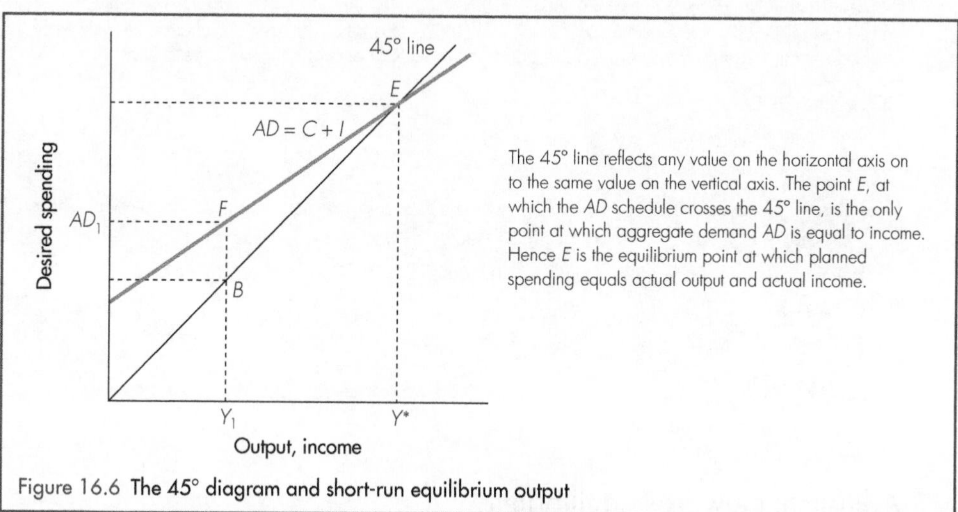

Figure 16.6 **The 45° diagram and short-run equilibrium output**

We draw in orange the aggregate demand schedule from Figure 16.5. This crosses the 45-degree line at *E*. On the 45-degree line, the value of output (and income) on the horizontal axis equals the value of spending on the vertical axis. Since *E* is the *only* point on the *AD* schedule also on the 45-degree line, it is the only point at which output and desired spending are equal.

Hence Figure 16.6 shows equilibrium output at *E*. Firms produce Y^*. That output is equal to income. At an income Y^*, the *AD* schedule tells us the demand for goods is also Y^*. At *E*, planned spending is exactly equal to the output produced.

At any other output, output is not equal to aggregate demand. Suppose output and income are only Y_1. Aggregate demand exceeds actual output. There is excess demand. Spending plans cannot be realized at this output level.

Figure 16.6 shows that, for all outputs below the equilibrium output Y^*, aggregate demand *AD* exceeds income and output. The *AD* schedule lies *above* the 45-degree line along which spending and output are equal. Conversely, at all outputs above the equilibrium output Y^*, aggregate demand is less than income and output.

ACTIVITY 16.1

THE *AD* SCHEDULE: MOVING ALONG IT OR SHIFTING IT?

The aggregate demand *AD* schedule is a straight line whose position depends on its intercept and its slope. The intercept, the height of the schedule when income is zero, reflects autonomous demand: the autonomous part of consumption demand and all of investment demand. The slope of the schedule is the *MPC*. Changes in income induce movements *along* a given *AD* schedule.

Autonomous demand is influenced by many things that we study in Chapter 20. It is not fixed for ever. But it *is* independent of income. The *AD* schedule separates out the change in demand directly induced by changes in income. All other sources of changes in aggregate demand are shown as *shifts* in the *AD* schedule. If firms get more optimistic about future demand and invest more, autonomous demand rises. The new *AD* schedule is parallel to, but higher than, the old *AD* schedule. The entire schedule has shifted upwards.

Mathematically, since aggregate demand is $AD = (A + I) + cY$, the level of autonomous demand $(A + I)$ shows the height of the aggregate demand schedule when income is zero. Hence, changes in the autonomous components of consumption or investment change the height of the schedule, leading to a parallel shift. The slope of the schedule – how aggregate demand changes as income changes – is the marginal propensity to consume c. Movements in income Y lead to movements along a schedule of given height (since neither A nor I has changed). Finally, a change in the marginal propensity to consume c changes the slope of the *AD* schedule, causing it to rotate around the point on the vertical axis at which income is zero.

Questions

In each case, decide whether the *AD* schedule is shifting or whether the economy is moving along a given *AD* schedule:

(a) As the Eurozone crisis continued, there was a wave of pessimism among UK consumers, who decided to save a lot more in order to pay off the debts they had previously accumulated.

(b) UK consumer spending has risen because households are having a good year and enjoying high incomes.

(c) The 2012 Olympic Games in London caused an investment boom in UK construction.

To check your answers to these questions, go to page 679.

Adjustment towards equilibrium

In Figure 16.6, suppose that the economy begins with an output of Y_1, below equilibrium output Y^*. Aggregate demand AD_1 exceeds output Y_1. If firms have inventories from the past, they can sell more than they have produced by running down stocks for a while. Note that this destocking is *unplanned*; planned changes of stocks are already included in the total investment demand I.

If firms cannot meet aggregate demand by unplanned destocking, they must turn away customers. Either response – unplanned destocking or turning away customers – is a signal to firms to raise output above Y_1. Similarly, at *any* output below Y^*, aggregate demand exceeds output and firms get signals to raise output.

Conversely, if output is initially above its equilibrium level, Figure 16.6 shows that output will then exceed aggregate demand. Firms cannot sell all their output, make *unplanned* additions to inventories and respond by cutting output.

Hence, when output is below its equilibrium level, firms raise output. When output is above its equilibrium level, firms reduce output. At the equilibrium output Y^*, firms sell all their output and make no unplanned changes to their stocks. There is no incentive to change output.

In this example, short-run equilibrium output is Y^*. Firms sell all the goods they produce, and households and firms buy all the goods they want. But nothing guarantees Y^* is the level of potential output.

The economy can end up at a short-run equilibrium output below potential output, with no forces then present to move output to potential output. At the given level of prices and wages, a lack of aggregate demand will prevent expansion of output above its short-run equilibrium level.

CASE 16.2

THE LITTLE DEPRESSION AND THE GREAT DEPRESSION

Economic historians teach their students about the Great Depression of the 1870s. Nowadays, they often call it the Long Depression, to distinguish it from the depression of the1930s, which we have all come to call the Great Depression. However, at least in Europe, we may have to start calling the 1930s the Little Depression to distinguish it from the Great Depression that began in 2008.

We are all familiar with the terms of the business cycle – boom and bust, growth and recession, forwards and backwards. Does depression just mean recession or does it mean something else? A recession denotes two consecutive quarters of negative GDP growth; a depression is a protracted period in which output is significantly below potential output.

Thus, a depression is initially a deep recession, from which output then fails to recover in the normal way. The following chart is worth a thousand words. Constructed by the London-based National Institute for Economic and Social Research, it compares five UK recessions since 1930, plotting along the horizontal axis the number of elapsed months from the previous output peak, and on the vertical axis the cumulative change in GDP since the original start of the recession. Thus, a country exits recession once the curve's slope turns up (output is no longer falling), but output does not return to its previous level until the curve climbs back to 0 per cent.

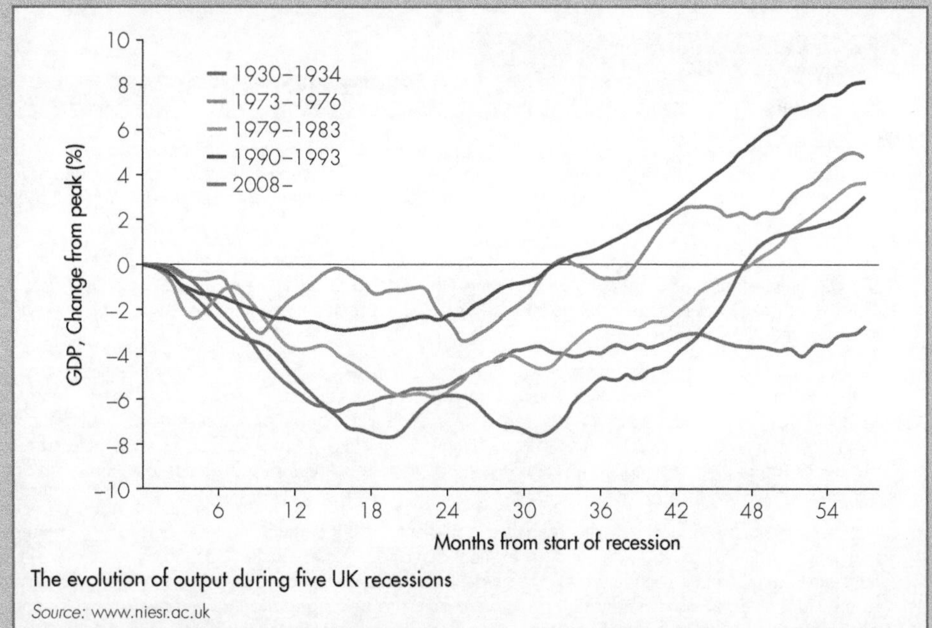

The evolution of output during five UK recessions

Source: www.niesr.ac.uk

Since all the curves begin at 0 per cent on the left-hand side, we discuss the curves according to their height at the right-hand side. The purple curve shows the recession of 1990–93 when the UK pegged its exchange rate and interest rate to European countries at a time that just happened to include German unification. German interest rates were sky high to prevent inflation exploding in Germany, and the UK could not live with these high interest rates. On 'Black Wednesday' in September 1992, the UK abandoned the experiment, allowed its exchange rate to fall and slashed interest rates – economic recovery soon followed. Although output growth was quickly restored, it was not until three years (36 months) after the start of the crisis that output climbed back to its original level.

The orange curve depicts the recession after 1974 caused by a huge jump in oil prices after OPEC first became effective. Again, output was growing steadily within 24 months of the onset of the crisis, and had got back to its original level within around 36 months. Similarly, the green curve shows the sharp recession, but quick recovery, after Mrs Thatcher took office in 1979 and squeezed the economy to defeat inflation. Again, output was growing within 24 months, though it took 48 months to get back to the initial level of output.

The purple, orange and green curves all depict fairly conventional recession and recovery. The red curve depicts the Little Depression of the 1930s. It displayed the deepest fall in output, twice down nearly 8 per cent from its initial level, and was clearly a 'double dip' since the initial recovery after 18 months was not sustained, leading to a new dip after 24 months. Even so, recovery took hold after 32 months and never looked back thereafter.

Finally, we come to the Great Depression since 2008 shown by the turquoise curve. Despite the enormity of the adverse shock – and the fact that it hit all major economies simultaneously – UK output initially fell by less than in the 1930s, in part because governments, led by the US and the UK, engaged in emergency expansionary measures to stave off the worst of the crisis. However, 48 months into the crisis, the turquoise curve is the *only* one still below its original level at the start, and as yet with no clear signs of getting back to its initial position. A third, or triple, dip is still a real possibility.

Thus, if we scale depressions by the length of time for which output is depressed, the most recent experience is not just the worst 'since the 1930s', it is already much worse 'than the 1930s'.

CASE 16.3

HOW DID THE CRASH AFFECT INVESTMENT?

Our simple model of aggregate demand assumes that output is the principal driver of consumption demand but does not directly affect investment demand. This does not mean that investment demand is always constant; merely that it is not well explained by changes in income. In later chapters we return to the question of what does affect investment demand.

Even at this early stage, it is a good idea to check our theory is proceeding along the right lines. How did consumption and investment respond during the crash of 2009? The figure below shows data during 2006–12. It shows annual percentage changes in output, consumer spending and investment, and compares the Eurozone, the US and the UK.

In each figure below, the first three bars show changes in real output, the middle three show changes in real consumption, and the final three show changes in real investment. In the Eurozone, the US and the UK, output *Y* was growing by at least 2 per cent a year during 2006–07 prior to the crash, then fell to around −2 per cent a year during 2008–09, before resuming slow growth after 2010. As we would expect from our discussion of the consumption function, these changes in output induced similar, but smaller, changes in consumption demand.

However, the behaviour of investment was very different. First, it certainly was not constant – it changed by much more than consumption demand. Investment demand is more volatile. Second, when the crash came, firms slashed investment spending by large amounts, and not merely because current income and output had fallen. Firms foresaw that the next few years were going to be tough, and that there would be little need for additional capital goods since production levels were not going to grow rapidly.

Thus, the figures support the basic idea of the consumption function – a close relation between current output and current consumption demand – but denies any similar relationship will work between output and investment demand. For now, we assume that investment is part of autonomous demand, independent of the level of output. Other things equal, investment is constant. But other things are not always equal, and actual investment can be highly volatile. We return to models of investment demand in later chapters.

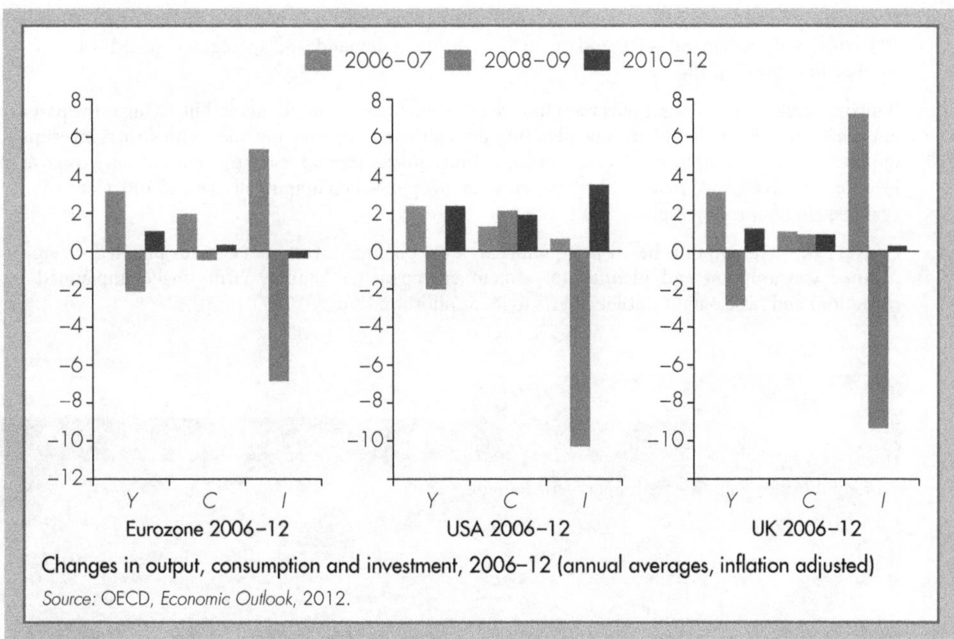

Changes in output, consumption and investment, 2006–12 (annual averages, inflation adjusted)

Source: OECD, *Economic Outlook*, 2012.

16.4 Planned saving equals planned investment

Equilibrium output equals the demand from investment and consumption: $Y = C + I$. This is not a definition, but holds only when output and income are at the right level to achieve equilibrium output. However, planned saving S is defined as the part of income Y not devoted to planned consumption C. Thus, $Y \equiv C + S$. Together with $Y = C + I$, this implies that in equilibrium, but only in equilibrium, planned investment equals planned saving

$$I = S$$

In modern economies, firms make investment decisions, and the managers of these firms are not the same decision units as the households making saving and consumption plans. But household plans depend on their income. Since planned saving depends on income but planned investment does not, equilibrium income adjusts to make households plan to save as much as firms are planning to invest. Figure 16.7 illustrates.

Planned investment I is autonomous, and so a horizontal line since its magnitude is independent of the level of income. Planned saving increases with income and output, since the marginal propensity to save exceeds zero. Hence, equilibrium output must be Y^*, the only output at which planned investment equals planned saving.

Suppose investment demand is 30 and the saving function is $S = -10 + 0.4Y$. Hence, equilibrium output Y is 100. At this Y, planned saving is $[-10 + 40] = 30$. Hence 30 is both planned saving and planned investment.

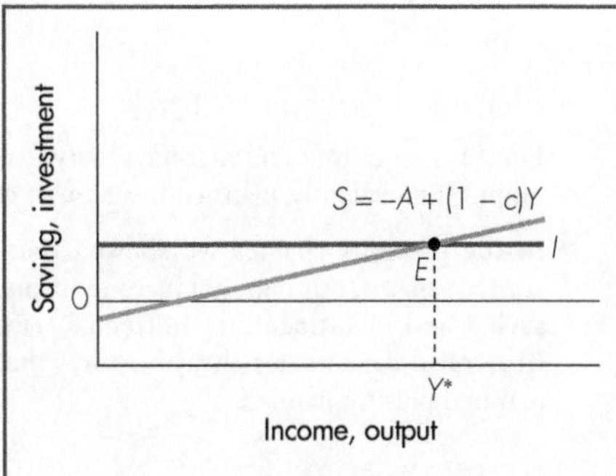

At equilibrium output Y^*, planned investment I equals planned saving $S = -A + (1 - c)Y$. Hence equilibrium output $Y^* = [A + I]/[1 - c]$.

Figure 16.7 At equilibrium output, planned I equals planned S

If the saving function is $S = -10 + 0.4Y$, the consumption function must be $C = 10 + 0.6Y$. At an income of 100, consumption demand is 70. Add on 30 for investment demand, and aggregate demand is 100, just equal to equilibrium output of 100.

If income exceeds 100, households want to save more than firms want to invest. But saving is the part of income not consumed. Households are not planning enough consumption, together with firms' investment plans, to purchase all the output produced. Unplanned inventories pile up and firms cut output. Lower output and income reduces planned saving, which depends on income. When output falls back to 100, planned investment again equals planned saving.

Conversely, when output is below its equilibrium level, planned investment exceeds planned saving. Together, planned consumption and planned investment exceed actual output. Firms make unplanned inventory reductions and raise output until it reverts to its equilibrium level of 100.

MATHS 16.1

AUTONOMOUS DEMAND AND EQUILIBRIUM OUTPUT

In equilibrium, output equals aggregate demand, Hence

$$Y = AD = C + I = [A + cY] + I = [A + I] + cY$$

Hence, in equilibrium

$$Y^* = [A + I]/(1 - c) \qquad (1)$$

Notice that this implies that a unit increase in either A or I then leads to an increase of $[1/(1 - c)]$ in equilibrium output Y^*. Since c is a positive fraction, $[1/(1 - c)]$ is greater than 1. So a unit increase in either autonomous consumption demand or investment demand leads to a larger increase in equilibrium output because a further increase in consumption demand is then induced. We explain below why this is called the *multiplier*.

Desired saving is $S = Y - C = Y - [A + cY] = -A + (1 - c)Y$, the saving function corresponding to the consumption function $C = A + cY$. In equilibrium, equation (1) implies

$$I = Y^*(1 - c) - A \qquad (2)$$

But the right-hand side of equation (2) is simply desired saving in equilibrium when output is Y^*. Hence in equilibrium $I = S$. Planned investment equals planned leakages.

Planned versus actual

Equilibrium output and income satisfy two equivalent conditions. Aggregate demand must equal income and output. Equivalently, planned investment must equal planned saving.

In the previous chapter we showed that *actual* investment is *always* equal to *actual* saving, purely as a consequence of our national income accounting definitions. When the economy is not in equilibrium, planned saving and investment are not equal. However, unplanned investment in stocks and/or unplanned saving (frustrated consumers) always ensures that actual investment, planned plus unplanned, equals actual saving, planned plus unplanned.

16.5 A fall in aggregate demand

The *slope* of the *AD* schedule depends only on the marginal propensity to consume (*MPC*). For a given *MPC*, the level of autonomous spending $[A + I]$ determines the *height* of the *AD* schedule. Autonomous spending is spending unrelated to income.

Changes in autonomous spending lead to parallel shifts in the *AD* schedule. Investment demand depends chiefly on current guesses by firms about future demand for their output. Beliefs about this future demand can fluctuate significantly, influenced by current pessimism or optimism about the future. Similarly, a fall in consumer confidence reduces autonomous consumption demand.

Suppose firms get pessimistic about future demand for their output. Planned investment falls. If autonomous consumption is unaffected, the aggregate demand schedule *AD* is now lower at each income than before. Figure 16.8 shows this downward shift from *AD* to *AD'*.

Before we go into the details, think about what is likely to happen to output. It will fall, but how much? When investment demand falls, firms cut output. Households have lower incomes and cut consumption. Firms cut output again, further reducing household incomes. Consumption demand falls further. What brings the process of falling output and income to an end?

Figure 16.8 shows that a given downward shift of the *AD* schedule reduces equilibrium output by a *finite* amount, but by an amount larger than the vertical fall in the *AD* schedule. This is because the *AD* schedule has a slope flatter than the 45-degree line: its slope, the marginal propensity to consume, is always smaller than unity.

Equilibrium moves from *E* to *E'*. Equilibrium output falls *more* than the original cut in investment demand, but does not fall all the way to zero.

Table 16.1 explains. Since many students find arithmetic easier than algebra, we illustrate for the particular values $[A = 10]$ for autonomous consumption demand and $[c = 0.6]$ for the marginal propensity to consume. Thus the consumption function is $C = 10 + 0.6Y$.

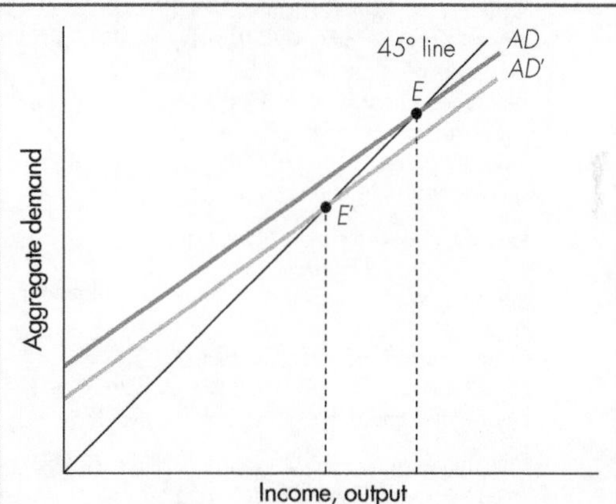

When investment demand falls, the aggregate demand schedule shifts down from *AD* to *AD'* and equilibrium output falls by a larger amount.

Figure 16.8 A fall in investment demand

Table 16.1 Adjustment to a shift in investment demand

	Y	I	$C = 10 + 0.6Y$	$AD = C + I$	$Y - AD$	Unplanned stocks	Output
Step 1	100	30	70	100	0	Zero	Constant
Step 2	100	20	70	90	10	Rising	Falling
Step 3	90	20	64	84	6	Rising	Falling
Step 4	84	20	60.4	80.4	3.6	Rising	Falling
New equilibrium	75	20	55	75	0	Zero	Constant

If original investment demand is 30, the first row of Table 16.1 shows that the original equilibrium output is 100, since consumption demand is then $[10 + 60]$ and investment demand is 30. Thus aggregate demand just equals actual output.

In step 2, investment demand falls to 20. Firms did not expect demand to change, and still produced 100. Output exceeds aggregate demand by 10. Firms add this 10 to unplanned inventories, then cut output to get rid of these again.

CONCEPT 16.2

INFLATIONARY AND DEFLATIONARY GAPS

We now make explicit the extent to which short-run equilibrium output deviates from potential output. First, we need some terminology. Nowadays, we use inflation and deflation to refer to rises and falls in the price level. Earlier economists assumed that these were largely caused by output levels that were above or below potential output. We now know that this is one cause, but not the only cause, of price changes, as we discuss in later chapters.

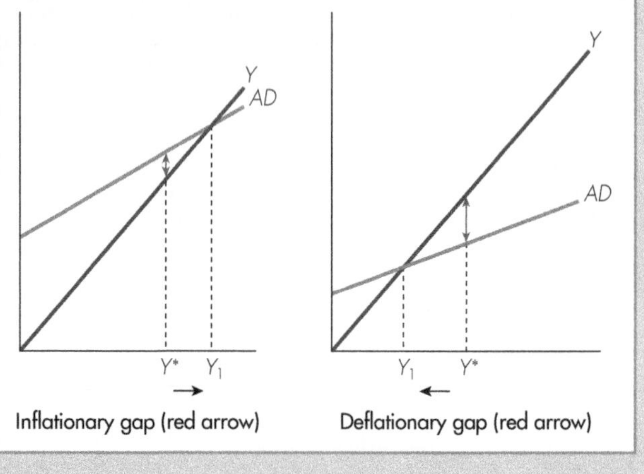

Inflationary gap (red arrow)

Deflationary gap (red arrow)

Even so, some of the old terminology survives. The **inflationary gap** is a measure of the extent to which aggregate demand exceeds the level needed to ensure output equals potential output, and the **deflationary gap** is a measure of the extent to which aggregate demand falls short of the level required to achieve potential output.

> The inflationary gap measures the excess of aggregate demand over output when output is at potential output.
>
> The deflationary gap measures the shortfall of aggregate demand over output when output is at potential output.
>
> The output gap measures the discrepancy between output and potential output.

Both figures above show aggregate demand *AD* and the 45-degree line along which demand equals output *Y*. In the left-hand diagram, aggregate demand exceeds that at which equilibrium output Y_1 and potential output Y^* would coincide. We can measure this excess either in the vertical direction or in the horizontal direction.

Thus, in the left-hand figure, the inflationary gap corresponds to the vertical distance shown in red. Conversely, in the right-hand figure, aggregate demand is insufficient to allow equilibrium output Y_1 and potential output Y^* to coincide.

Thus, in the right-hand figure, the deflationary gap corresponds to the vertical distance shown in red.

We could instead measure these excesses and shortfalls in the horizontal direction rather than the vertical direction.

Thus, in the left-hand figure, the **output gap** is the positive amount shown by the black arrow, the distance between Y_1 and Y^*. In the right-hand figure, the output gap is the negative distance shown by the black arrow, the amount by which Y_1 falls short of Y^*.

Modern economics tends to use output gaps rather than inflationary and deflationary gaps to describe the strength of aggregate demand. We will show empirical estimates of output gaps in later chapters.

Step 3 shows firms making 90, the level of demand in step 2. But when firms cut output, income falls. Step 3 shows consumption demand falls from 70 to 64. Since the *MPC* is 0.6, a cut in income by 10 has caused a fall in consumption demand by 6. The induced fall in consumption demand means that output of 90 still exceeds aggregate demand, which is now 84. Again inventories pile up unexpectedly, and again firms respond by cutting output.

At step 4, firms make enough to meet demand at step 3. Output is 84, but again this induces a further cut in consumption demand. Output still exceeds aggregate demand. The process keeps going, through many steps, until it reaches the new equilibrium, an output of 75. Output and income have fallen by 25, consumption demand has fallen by 15 and investment demand has fallen by 10. Aggregate demand again equals output.

How long it takes for the economy to reach the new equilibrium depends on how well firms figure out what is going on. If they keep setting output targets to meet the level of demand in the previous period, it takes a long time to adjust. Smart firms may spot that, period after period, they are overproducing and adding to unwanted inventories. They anticipate that demand is still falling and cut back output more quickly than Table 16.1 suggests.

Why does a fall of 10 in investment demand cause a fall of 25 in equilibrium output? Lower investment demand induces a cut in output and income that then induces an extra cut in consumption demand. Total demand falls by more than the original fall in investment demand, but the process does not spiral out of control. Equilibrium output is 75.

The multiplier is the ratio of the change in equilibrium output to the change in autonomous spending that caused the change.

In our example, the initial change in autonomous investment demand is 10 and the final change in equilibrium output is 25. The **multiplier** is 2.5. That is why, in Figure 16.7, a small downward shift in the *AD* schedule leads to a much larger fall in equilibrium income and output.

16.6 The multiplier

The multiplier tells us how much output changes after a shift in aggregate demand. The multiplier exceeds 1 because a change in autonomous demand sets off further changes in consumption demand. The size of the multiplier depends on the marginal propensity to consume. The initial effect of a unit fall in investment demand is to cut output and income by a unit. If the *MPC* is large, this fall in income leads to a large fall in consumption and the multiplier is big. If the *MPC* is small, a given change in investment demand and output induces small changes in consumption demand and the multiplier is small.

Table 16.2 examines a one-unit increase in investment demand. In step 2, firms raise output by 1 unit. Consumption rises by 0.6, the marginal propensity to consume times the one-unit change in income and output. At step 3, firms raise output by 0.6 to meet the increased consumption demand in step 2. In turn, consumption demand is increased by 0.36 (the *MPC* 0.9 multiplied by the 0.9 increase in income) leading in step 4 to a rise in output of 0.36. Consumption rises again and the process continues.

Table 16.2 Calculating the multiplier when the *MPC* equals 0.6

Change in	Step 1	Step 2	Step 3	Step 4	Step 5	*	*	*
I	1	0	0	0	0	*	*	*
Y	0	1	0.6	$(0.6)^2$	$(0.6)^3$	*	*	*
C	0	0.6	$(0.6)^2$	$(0.6)^2$	$(0.6)^3$	*	*	*

To find the multiplier, we add all the increases in output from each step in the table and keep going:

$$\text{Multiplier} = 1 + (0.6) + (0.6)^2 + (0.6)^3 + (0.6)^4 + (0.6)^5 + \ldots$$

The dots at the end mean that we keep adding terms such as $(0.9),^6$ and so on. The right-hand side of this equation is called a geometric series. Each term is (0.9) times the previous term. Fortunately, mathematicians have shown that there is a general formula for the sum of all the terms in such a series:

$$\text{Multiplier} = 1/(1 - 0.6) = 1/0.4 = 2.5$$

The formula applies whatever the (constant) value of *c*, the marginal propensity to consume:

$$\text{Multiplier} = 1 + c + c^2 + c^3 + c^4 + c^5 + \ldots = 1/(1 - c)$$

For the particular value of $c = 0.6$, the multiplier is $1/(0.4) = 2.5$. Hence a cut in investment demand by 10 causes a fall in equilibrium output by 25, as we know from Table 16.1. For those of you who 'did the maths' above, equilibrium output is simply autonomous demand multiplied by the multiplier!

As an example, suppose $c = ½$. The multiplier is then $1/2 + 1/4 + 1/8 + 1/16 + \ldots$ you can probably guess that this is eventually going to cumulate to 2, which is exactly what the general formula promises us.

The marginal propensity to consume tells how much of each extra unit of income is spent on consumption. Thus c is a number between zero and unity. The higher is c, the lower is $(1 - c)$. Dividing 1 by a smaller number leads to a larger answer. The general formula for the multiplier confirms that a larger c implies a larger multiplier.

The multiplier and the *MPS*

Any part of an extra unit of income not spent must be saved. Hence $1 \equiv c + s$, where s is the marginal propensity to save.

Hence we can also think of the multiplier as $1/s$. The higher the **marginal propensity to save**, the more of each extra unit of income leaks out of the circular flow into savings and the less goes back round the circular flow to generate further increases in aggregate demand, output and income. Since the marginal propensity to save is a positive fraction, the multiplier exceeds unity, as we already know.

The marginal propensity to save is the fraction of each extra unit of income that households wish to save.

In the next chapter, we will see that, after introducing the government and foreign sectors, it remains true that the multiplier equals $1/mpl$ where mpl is the marginal propensity to leak out of the circular flow. Here, saving is the only leakage. Whatever the leakages, a 1-unit increase in injections (automonous demand), from whatever source, must eventually induce a 1-unit increase in desired leakages to restore equilibrium. Once we know the marginal propensity to leak, we know how much output has to rise to create a 1-unit increase in leakages. In this chapter, the only leakage is through saving, so the multiplier is $1/s$

1 = Assumed rise in autonomous demand

= Rise in planned injections

= Rise in planned leakages once equilibrium restored

= (Rise in output, ΔY) × (marginal propensity to save, s)

Hence, $1 = \Delta Y \times s$, so $\Delta Y = 1/s$.

16.7 The paradox of thrift

The previous section analysed a change in equilibrium output caused by a change in autonomous investment demand. We now examine the consequences of a change in the autonomous part of planned consumption and saving.

We could use the 45-degree diagram to show how aggregate demand shifts and causes a change in equilibrium output. Suppose households increase autonomous consumption demand by 10. There is a parallel upward shift in the consumption function, and hence also in the aggregate demand schedule *AD*. A higher aggregate demand schedule must intersect the 45-degree line at a higher level of output. Hence, equilibrium output increases.

But what happens to planned saving? Households wish to consume more (save less) at each level of income, but now face a higher equilibrium income. They save a lower fraction of a higher income. Does saving rise or fall? In equilibrium, planned saving *always* equals planned investment, and the latter is unaltered. Hence planned saving cannot change. Equilibrium income must therefore have risen just enough to offset the desire to save a lower fraction of any particular income level, leaving overall planned saving unaltered once the new equilibrium is reached.

This chain of reasoning may seem quite complicated. Fortunately, it can be grasped much more directly, using Figure 16.9, which focuses on the equality of planned saving and planned investment in equilibrium. A decline in thriftiness – a fall in the desire to save – shifts the planned saving schedule from S to S'. Planned investment is unaffected. Hence equilibrium income must rise from Y^* to Y^{**} to maintain the equality of planned saving and planned investment.

A change in the amount households wish to save at each income leads to a change in equilibrium income, but *no change* in equilibrium saving, which must still equal planned investment. This is the paradox of thrift.

The **paradox of thrift** helps us to understand an old debate about the virtues of saving and spending. Does society benefit from thriftiness and a high level of desired saving at each income level? The answer depends on whether or not the economy is at full employment.

When aggregate demand is low and the economy has spare resources, the paradox of thrift shows that a *reduction* in the desire to save (higher desire to consume) will increase aggregate demand and the equilibrium output level. Society benefits from higher output and employment. Since investment demand is autonomous, a change in the desire to save has no effect on the desired level of investment.

Applying the same argument in reverse, during the crash of 2008 politicians were worried that the panic might lead to too great a desire to save. At a time when aggregate demand had already fallen, equilibrium output had fallen even with a constant propensity to save: any additional desired saving would reduce equilibrium output even further. Case 16.4 discusses the saving rate in more detail.

In contrast, think what happens in the long run once the economy has time to return to the level of potential output (see Chapter 21). If output equals potential output, an *increase* in the desire to save will increase saving, and reduce consumption, at potential output. Other adjustments may then induce investment demand to rise to restore aggregate demand to its full-employment level. The next few chapters explain why. Hence, in the long run, society may benefit from an *increase* in the desire to save. Investment will rise and the economy's capital stock and potential output may grow more quickly.

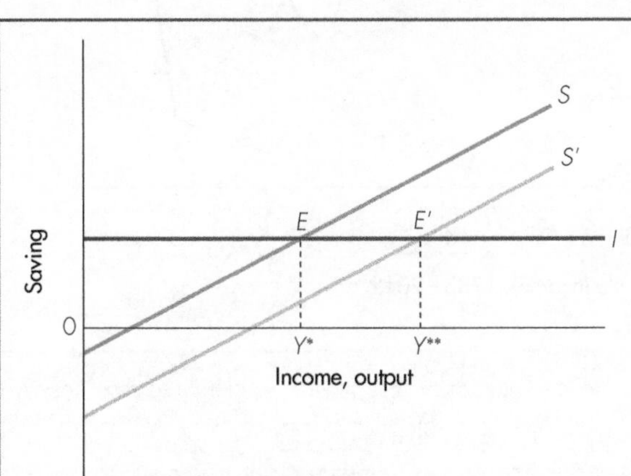

In equilibrium planned saving equals planned investment. A fall in the desire to save induces a rise in equilibrium output to keep planned saving equal to planned investment.

Figure 16.9 **The paradox of thrift**

In this chapter we have focused on the short run before prices and wages have time to adjust. Saving and investment decisions are made by different people. There is no automatic mechanism to translate higher saving into a corresponding rise in investment demand. Since planned saving depends on the level of income, income adjusts to equate planned saving and planned investment.

CASE 16.4

HOW STABLE IS THE SAVING RATE?

The saving rate S/Y is the fraction of income that is saved. In the Thatcher boom of the late 1980s, heady optimism and easy access to credit made UK consumers spend a lot. Personal saving collapsed as people bought champagne, sports cars and houses. The boom didn't last. As inflation rose, the government raised interest rates to slow down the economy. House prices fell. People's mortgage debt was larger than the value of their houses. To pay off this 'negative equity', households raised saving sharply in the early 1990s.

During 1992–2008, UK households were borrowing again. Low interest rates fuelled a spending boom and a protracted rise in house prices. People saved less and borrowed more in order to spend. TV shows such as *The Property Ladder* and *Location, Location, Location* showed people how to renovate houses for subsequent letting or sale. In a rising market, people made money on buying and selling houses whether or not they were actually any good at redeveloping them.

The chart shows household saving, as a percentage of household disposable income. It shows the saving rate fell sharply in the spending boom of the late 1980s, rose in the recession of the early 1990s, then fell steadily during the sustained boom of 1992–2008. By 2008, UK households were saving less than 2 per cent of their disposable income. With steady economic growth assured, people thought it made sense to borrow rather than save. The good times had arrived.

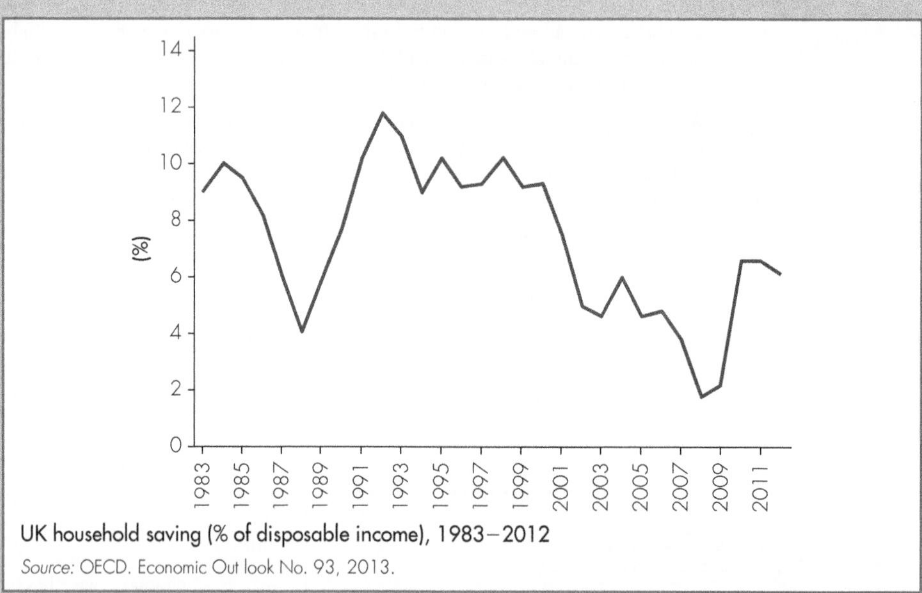

UK household saving (% of disposable income), 1983–2012

Source: OECD. Economic Out look No. 93, 2013.

What do you think happened as a result of the financial crash in 2008? People got scared. Property prices began to fall and borrowing for house purchase no longer seemed a good idea. Banks became terrified their customers could not repay, so the supply of new lending from banks dried up completely. Credit card debt suddenly seemed expensive. And people who foresaw a deep recession began to cut out unnecessary expenditure. They chose to save a larger fraction of their income.

The saving rate rose very sharply in 2009, as the chart confirms. The saving rate is likely to stay high until (a) households feel they have paid off a reasonable amount of their large inherited debts and (b) confidence in future growth of income and employment returns.

Clearly, then, the saving rate can fluctuate a lot. Although in this chapter we assume a constant marginal propensity to save, Chapter 20 discusses more sophisticated theories of consumption and saving that help us understand why the saving rate fluctuates.

One final remark. Does it matter whether households borrow in order to buy a foreign holiday or to buy a house for subsequent rental to others? In the former case, no asset is purchased for the future; in the latter case, the household acquires an asset that will give rise to future incomes. Simply measuring today's income and today's spending gives a misleading picture of the long-run economic position of the household. We return to this issue in Chapter 19.

16.8 The role of confidence

Shifts in autonomous demand – whether autonomous consumption demand or autonomous investment demand – are often caused by changes in confidence; that is, swings in optimism or pessimism about the future. Our simple model assumes these are independent of current income and output.

This does not mean that they are not important, and not subject to influence by policy and politicians. Rather than spend taxpayers' money trying to boost aggregate demand through a subsidized car scrappage scheme, most governments would rather talk up demand if only they could.

Like the boy who cried wolf once too often, governments who mislead the public soon become distrusted, and their warm words are then ignored. However, if governments can provide a clear and credible account of why the future may be rosier than the present, they may indeed be able to stimulate aggregate demand through increasing confidence and thereby inducing households and firms to spend more. Conversely, when they announce bad news that had not previously been foreseen, then at any particular level of current output firms and households will reduce their demand, and aggregate demand will fall.

CONCEPT 16.3

SAVING OR SAVINGS?

What is the difference between saving and savings? Can we use them interchangeably? Should we talk about the savings rate or the saving rate?

To get things right, we need to return to the distinction between stocks and flows. A stock can be measured at a point in time, whereas a flow needs a time dimension and the size of the flow vanishes as the time interval becomes shorter and shorter. The volume of water in a basin is a stock, still existing if we take a picture with a high-speed camera. The inflow from the tap or outflow down the plughole are flows – if we contemplate a short enough nano-second, essentially there is no time for water to flow in or out.

So far, our national accounts have been about flows: the flow of output per year, the flow of consumption spending or investment spending during that period. If we think about a month, rather than a year, we get a different numerical answer for the size of GDP or consumption. Corresponding to these flows, in principal there are a set of stock accounts. For the country, this is the stock of national assets, the stock of national liabilities, and hence net national wealth. Similarly, we can think about the assets and liabilities of households or of firms.

Saving is the flow of income not spent within a period. It is always a flow concept. *Savings* is the stock of assets accumulated as a result of the past flows of saving decisions.

That is why it is correct to talk about the saving rate, but wrong to talk about the savings rate. If we want to examine how much of the flow of disposable income is not spent, we need to use the flow measure, *saving*, not the stock measure, *savings*.

Summary

- **Aggregate demand** is planned spending on goods (and services). The *AD* schedule shows aggregate demand at each level of income and output.
- This chapter neglects planned spending by foreigners and by the government and studies **consumption demand** by households and **investment demand** by firms (desired additions to physical capital and to inventories). We treat investment demand as constant.
- Consumption demand is closely, though not perfectly, related to **personal disposable income**. Without taxes or transfers, personal disposable income and total income coincide.
- **Autonomous consumption** is desired consumption at zero income. The **marginal propensity to consume (*MPC*)** is the fraction by which planned consumption rises when income rises by a pound. The **marginal propensity to save (*MPS*)** is the fraction of an extra pound of income that is saved. Since income is consumed or saved, $MPC + MPS = 1$.

- For given prices and wages, the goods market is in equilibrium when output equals planned spending or aggregate demand. Equivalently, in equilibrium, planned saving equals planned investment. **Goods market equilibrium** does not mean output equals potential output. It means planned spending equals actual spending and actual output.
- The **equilibrium output is demand-determined** because we assume that prices and wages are fixed at a level that implies an excess supply of goods and labour. Firms and workers are happy to supply whatever output and employment is demanded.
- When aggregate demand exceeds actual output there is either unplanned disinvestment (inventory reductions) or unplanned saving (frustrated customers). Actual investment always equals actual saving, as a matter of definition. Unplanned inventory reductions or frustrated customers act as a signal to firms to raise output when aggregate demand exceeds actual output. Similarly, unplanned additions to stocks occur when aggregate demand is below output.
- A rise in planned investment increases equilibrium output by a larger amount. The initial increase in income to meet investment demand leads to further increases in consumption demand.
- The **multiplier** is the ratio of the change in output to the change in autonomous demand that caused it. In the simple model of this chapter, the multiplier is $1/[(1 - MPC)]$ or $1/MPS$. The multiplier exceeds 1 because MPC and MPS are positive fractions.
- The **paradox of thrift** shows that a reduced desire to save leads to an increase in output but no change in the equilibrium level of planned saving, which must still equal planned investment.

Review questions

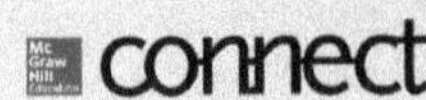

1 (a) Find equilibrium income when investment demand is 400 and $C = 0.8Y$. (b) Would output be higher or lower if the consumption function were $C = 100 + 0.7Y$?

2 Which of the following statements is correct? (a) Any tax is a tax on jobs because it reduces aggregate demand. (b) Provided the government spends the tax revenue, the impact of higher spending outweighs the adverse demand effect of higher taxes. (c) Autonomous consumption demand is directly related to consumer confidence. (d) All the above statements could be true, depending on the other things assumed equal.

EASY

3 Suppose firms are initially surprised by changes in demand. (a) When demand falls, what is the initial effect on stocks of unsold goods held by firms? (b) What do firms plan to do to stocks as soon as they have time to adjust production? Does this reduce or increase the initial fall in demand? (c) Once stocks have been adjusted, what then happens to production and output?

4 Could the multiplier ever be less than 1?

5 **Common fallacies** Why are these statements wrong? (a) If people were prepared to save more, investment would increase and we could get the economy moving again. (b) Lower output leads to lower spending and yet lower output. The economy could spiral downwards forever.

6 Assume that an economy is in equilibrium. Planned investment is £100. The MPC is 0.6. Suppose investment rises by £30. (a) What happens to the equilibrium output?

Now suppose people decide to save a higher proportion of their income: the consumption function changes from $C = 0.8Y$ to $C = 0.5Y$. (b) What happens to equilibrium income (planned investment being £100)? (c) What happens to the equilibrium proportion of income saved? Explain.

MEDIUM

7 Assume that the economy is in equilibrium. The *MPC* is 0.6. Suppose investment demand rises by £30. (a) By how much does the equilibrium output increase? (b) How much of that increase is extra consumption demand? Draw the corresponding diagram using planned investment and planned saving assuming that the initial output is 100.

8 Suppose the consumption function is $C = 0.75Y$ and planned investment is 40. (a) Draw a diagram showing the aggregate demand schedule. (b) If actual output is 100, what unplanned actions will occur? (c) What is the equilibrium output? (d) Do you get the same answer using planned saving equals planned investment?

9 The diagram below shows the aggregate demand and output of an economy. Along the 45-degree line Y, demand equals output. Is there an inflationary gap or a deflationary gap if the answer is 250?

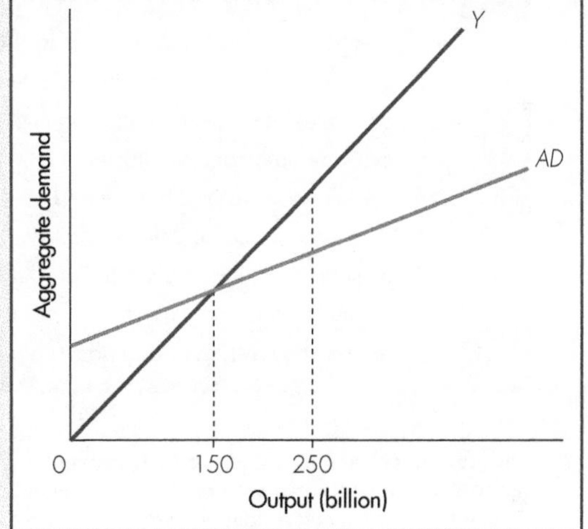

10 Suppose confidence depends a little on the current level of output, and the model therefore becomes

$I = aY + I^*$

$C = [A] + cY = [A^* + BY] + cY$

where I^* and A^* remain autonomous and independent of output, but a and b reflect the dependence of confidence on the current level of output. (a) What is the new value of the multiplier? (b) Is this higher or lower than before? (c) Is equilibrium output higher or lower than before?

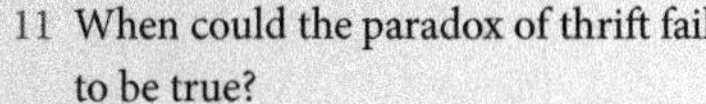

11 When could the paradox of thrift fail to be true?

12 **Essay question** 'The remarkably strong relationship between consumption and income confirms that most people want to spend most of their income as soon as they can. We are all material girls and boys at heart.' Is the inference justified?

13 Planned investment is 100. Initially, the consumption function is $C = 100 + 0.8Y$. There are three ways in which greater pessimism about the future might affect behaviour: (a) planned investment falls from 100 to 50, (b) autonomous consumption falls from 100 to 50, (c) the marginal propensity to consume falls from 0.8 to 0.7 as people save more of each unit of additional income. Draw a graph of each change and its effect on short-run equilibrium output.

14 Suppose your economy is going through a recession. Individuals desire to save more and spend less. How does the paradox of thrift explain the consequences of increased savings in your economy?

CHAPTER 17

Fiscal policy and foreign trade

Learning Outcomes

By the end of this chapter, you should be able to:

1. analyse how fiscal policy affects aggregate demand
2. discuss equilibrium output in this extended model
3. calculate the balanced budget multiplier
4. evaluate automatic stabilizers
5. explain the structural budget and the inflation-adjusted budget
6. discuss how budget deficits add to national debt
7. evaluate the limits to discretionary fiscal policy
8. define imports and exports
9. analyse how foreign trade affects equilibrium output

The previous chapter discussed aggregate demand in a model with only firms and households. Now we need to reintroduce the other two sectors, the government and countries overseas. This chapter examines aggregate demand and output determination in this expanded model.

17.1 The scope of government activity

In most European countries, the government directly buys about a fifth of national output and spends about the same again on transfer payments. This spending is financed mainly by taxes, though some is financed by borrowing. What is the macroeconomic impact of government **fiscal policy**? Why did governments conclude that a massive fiscal response was required when confronted with the financial crash of 2008? Has the extra government debt then incurred constrained the subsequent use of fiscal policy to boost demand and economic recovery?

We first show how fiscal policy affects aggregate demand and equilibrium output. Then we study three fiscal issues. We analyse opportunities and limitations in using fiscal policy to **stabilize output**.

We then examine the significance of the government's **budget deficit**. When the government runs a deficit, it spends more than it earns. How can the government keep spending more than it receives? We examine the size of the deficit, and ask how much it matters.

A government deficit is financed mainly by borrowing from the public by selling bonds, which are promises to pay specified amounts of interest payments at future dates in exchange for cash up front. This borrowing adds to **national debt** to the public.[1] During 2009 governments around the world had huge budget deficits as they bailed out their banking

Fiscal policy is government policy on spending and taxes. It affects the size of government deficits and thus government debt.

Stabilization policy is government action to keep aggregate demand and actual output close to potential output.

The budget deficit is the excess of government spending over government receipts during a particular period.

The national debt is the stock of government debt outstanding.

1 Government is responsible not merely for its own deficits but also for any losses made by state-owned firms. The public sector net cash requirement (PSNCR) is the *government deficit plus net losses of these firms.*

systems and spent money on car scrappage schemes to try to prevent the car industries imploding. Just as for an individual, when a government spends more than it earns it adds to its debts.

Most of this chapter is about the government's role in aggregate demand, but to complete our model of output determination, we must also add foreign trade. Exports X and imports Z are each about 15 per cent of GDP in a large country such as the United States (which mainly trades with itself), but can reach up to 75 per cent of GDP in a small open economy such as Belgium or the Netherlands. In middle-sized countries such as the UK, France and Germany, exports and imports are around 30 per cent of GDP. Thus, the effects of foreign trade are too important to ignore.[2] Exports add to aggregate demand for domestic output, but imports reduce aggregate demand for domestic output by diverting desired spending to foreign output.

17.2 Government and aggregate demand

Government spending G on goods and services adds directly to aggregate demand. The government also withdraws money from the circular flow through indirect taxes T^e on expenditure and direct taxes T^d on factor incomes, less transfer benefits B that augment factor incomes. However, transfer payments affect aggregate demand only by affecting other components such as consumption or investment demand.

Since it is a pain to keep distinguishing between market prices and basic prices, we assume all taxes are direct taxes. With no indirect taxes, measurements at market prices and at basic prices coincide. Initially, we still ignore foreign trade.

Aggregate demand AD is consumption demand C, investment demand I and government demand G for goods and services. Transfer payments affect aggregate demand only by affecting C or I. It would be double-counting to include transfer payments directly in aggregate demand. Thus $AD = C + I + G$.

In the short run, we assume G is fixed, or at least independent of income. Its size reflects how many hospitals the government wants to build and how many teachers it wants to hire. We now have three autonomous components of aggregate demand independent of current income and output: autonomous consumption demand, investment demand I and government demand G.

> Net taxes are taxes minus transfer benefits.
>
> Disposable income is gross income minus taxes plus benefits; that is, the net income available to spend or save.

The government also levies taxes and pays out transfer benefits. **Net taxes** NT are taxes minus transfer benefits. Net taxes reduce personal disposable income – the amount available for spending or saving by households – relative to national income and output. If YD is **disposable income**, Y national income and t the *net tax rate* (assumed to be a constant proportion of income), then disposable income $YD = (1 - t)Y$.

If taxes, net of transfer benefits, are 20 per cent of national income, the net tax rate t is 0.2. If national income rises by £1, net tax revenue rises by 20 pence, and household disposable income rises by 80 pence.

Suppose households wish to consume 90 per cent of their *disposable* income. Since disposable income is only 80 per cent of national income, the marginal propensity to consume out of national income is only 0.72. More generally, if the marginal propensity to consume out of disposable income is c, the marginal propensity to consume out of national income c' is reduced to $c(1 - t)$.

The larger the net tax rate, the smaller is c' and the flatter is the slope of the consumption function, when plotted against national income and output. Figure 17.1 illustrates.

The effect of net taxes on output

Suppose initially that government spending is zero. Figure 17.2 illustrates. A rise in the net tax rate from zero to 0.2 made the consumption function pivot downwards from CC to CC' in Figure 17.1. Adding on the constant investment demand I to that consumption function, we obtain aggregate demand. Hence, a rise in the net tax rate rotates the consumption function from CC to CC' in Figure 17.1 and rotates aggregate demand from AD to AD' in Figure 17.2. Aggregate demand equals actual output at a lower output level than before, at E' not E. Equilibrium income and output are lower.

2 In contrast, net property income is 1 per cent of GNP. We continue to treat GNP and GDP as equivalent.

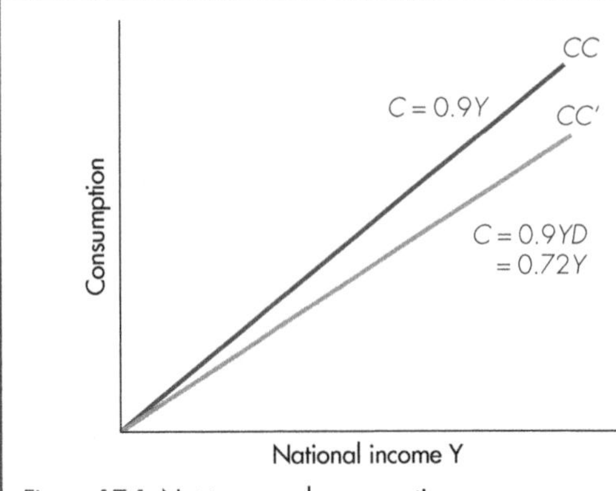

In the absence of taxation, national income Y and disposable income YD are the same. The consumption function CC' shows how much house holds wish to consume at each level of national income. With a proportional net tax rate of 0.2, households still consume 90p of each pound of disposable income. Since YD is now only $0.8Y$, households consume only $0.9 \times 0.8 = 0.72$ of each extra unit of national income. Relating consumption to national income, the effect of net taxes is to rotate the consumption function downwards from CC to CC'.

Figure 17.1 **Net taxes and consumption**

Raising the net tax rate reduces equilibrium output. Conversely, if aggregate demand and equilibrium output are below potential output, lower tax rates or higher transfer benefits will raise aggregate demand and hence equilibrium output.

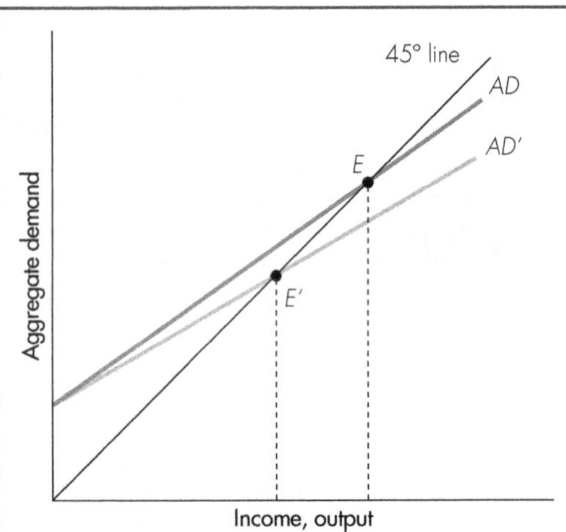

An increase in the income tax rate or a reduction in rate of unemployment benefit will increase the net tax rate t. The consumption function rotates from CC to CC' in Figure 17.1. With constant investment demand, the aggregate demand schedule rotates from AD to AD' in Figure 17.2. The equilibrium level of output falls and the equilibrium point moves from E to E'.

Figure 17.2 **A higher net tax rate**

The effect of government spending on output

Now forget taxes and think government spending. Suppose the net tax rate is zero. National income and disposable income once again coincide. Figure 17.3 shows that a higher level of autonomous government spending has an effect similar to that of higher autonomous investment demand studied in Chapter 16. With a marginal propensity to consume of 0.9, the multiplier is again $1/(1 - c) = 10$. A rise in government spending G induces a rise in equilibrium output by 10 times that amount. In Figure 17.3 equilibrium moves from E to E' as aggregate demand shifts from AD to AD'.

The combined effects of government spending and taxation

Suppose an economy begins with equilibrium output of 1000 but no government. Assume demand from autonomous consumption and investment is 100. With a marginal propensity to consume out of disposable income of 0.9, a disposable income of 1000 induces consumption demand of 900. Aggregate demand is $(900 + 100) = 1000$, which is also actual output.

Now add autonomous demand of 200 from the government, taking total autonomous demand to 300. Also introduce a net tax rate of 0.2. The marginal propensity to consume out of national income falls from 0.9 to 0.72, and the multiplier becomes $1/(1 - 0.72) = 1/0.28 = 3.57$. Multiplying autonomous demand of 300 by 3.57 yields equilibrium output of 1071, above the original equilibrium output of 1000. Figure 17.4 illustrates.

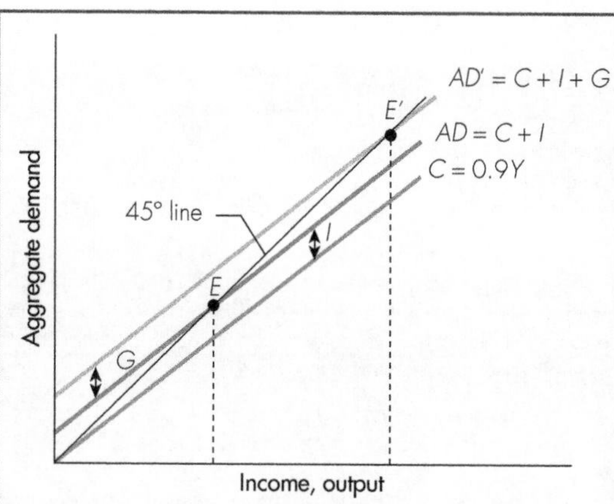

Beginning from equilibrium at *E*, *AD* shifts up to *AD'*. The new equilibrium is *E'* and equilibrium output rises by 10 times the rise in *G*.

Figure 17.3 Government spending and equilibrium output

The balanced budget multiplier

The economy began at an equilibrium output of 1000. With a proportional tax rate of 20 per cent, initial tax revenue was 200, precisely the amount of government spending.

This balanced increase in government spending and taxes did not leave demand and output unaltered. Figure 17.4 shows equilibrium output is larger. The new 200 of government spending raises aggregate demand by 200. The tax increase cuts disposable income by 200, but with $c = 0.9$ lower disposable income reduces consumption demand by only 180.

The initial net effect of the tax and spending package raises aggregate demand by 20. Output rises, inducing further rises in consumption demand. When the new equilibrium is reached, output has increased by 71, from 1000 to 1071. This is the famous **balanced budget multiplier**, which gives the government a fiscal tool to boost aggregate demand without adding to the deficit or debt.

The balanced budget multiplier says that a rise in government spending plus an equal rise in taxes leads to higher output.

To use this tool, however, the government has to have the political courage to raise tax revenue in line with higher expenditure. Sometimes governments are unable or unwilling to do this.

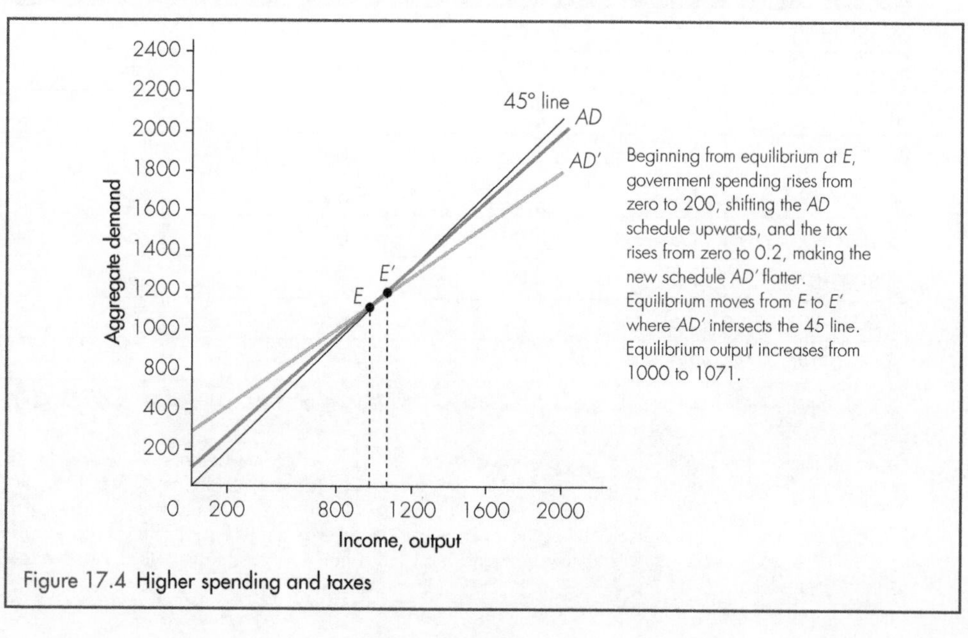

Beginning from equilibrium at *E*, government spending rises from zero to 200, shifting the *AD* schedule upwards, and the tax rises from zero to 0.2, making the new schedule *AD'* flatter. Equilibrium moves from *E* to *E'* where *AD'* intersects the 45 line. Equilibrium output increases from 1000 to 1071.

Figure 17.4 Higher spending and taxes

CASE 17.1

FISCAL POLICY, AUSTERITY AND DEBT: LESSONS FROM JAPAN

For the last 20 years, this textbook has used the Japanese example both to illustrate what hypothetically might happen to Western economies if they got into a macroeconomic mess, and to draw lessons for what policy options were available. Since 2009, Western economies have been in that mess themselves. The Japanese example is more relevant than ever.

After three decades of post-war success, Japanese economic growth came to an abrupt end in the 1990s. A crash in property prices made banks bankrupt. Instead of admitting this and sorting it out, policy makers ignored the problem. Consumers lost confidence, and output fell. To restore confidence, Japan had big fiscal expansions to boost demand. Why did Japanese output not recover in the 1990s?

Facing fiscal expansion in a severe recession, Japanese households and firms decided aggressively expansionary government policy was being undertaken only because the government knew things were even worse than the private sector had previously thought. The private sector took on board this new information and became even more pessimistic. The autonomous parts of consumption and investment demand fell sufficiently to offset the fiscal expansion injected by the government; and this fall in autonomous demand was therefore caused by the expansionary policy itself. Fiscal expansion failed to boost output by much. In macroeconomics the induced effects can outweigh the direct effect. Not until 2010 did sustainable growth appear to return.

After further bouts of fiscal stimulus, by 2013 Japan's government net debt had reached nearly 140 per cent of GDP, the highest among developed economies. Worries about how this debt will be financed in the future also undermine the confidence of households and firms, further reducing consumption and investment demand. The table below illustrates Japan's economic misery during this period.

Japan's macroeconomic misery 1993–2012

	Annual GDP growth (%)	Interest rate (%)	Budget deficit (% of GDP)	Government net debt (% of GDP)
1991–92	2.5	6.5	−1.5	13
1993–94	0.5	2.5	3.0	19
1994–95	1.5	1.5	3.0	23
1995–96	2.5	2.5	5.0	28
1997–99	−1.0	0.5	7.5	34
2000–02	1.0	0	6.0	67
2003–07	1.5	0	4.5	81
2008–09	−3.5	0	5.0	100
2010–12	2.0	0	9.5	134

Source: Based on data from Economic Outlook Statistical Annex, various issues © OECD, accessed on 18/06/2013.

Cutting interest rates to near zero levels probably prevented the outcome being even worse, but alone it was insufficient to restore healthy growth. Japan's government deficits ranged from 3 to 9.5 per cent during the 20-year period from 1993–2012 as it attempted fiscal stimulus to boost aggregate demand. Again, this may have prevented something even worse, but it was certainly not sufficient to resolve the crisis; other components of autonomous demand fell. And it has now left Japan with a massive level of government debt.

Lessons for Western economies

The Japanese example thus contains three important lessons. First, when confidence collapses, even fiscal policy may not be able to boost aggregate demand. This means that governments should do all they can to prevent confidence ever collapsing to this extent. In retrospect, Western banks were too loosely regulated during the long boom before 2007. Governments had failed to discharge their responsibility to create a stable financial environment.

Second, cleaning up the banks is an important priority. The Japanese government's unwillingness to lose face by admitting the extent of the problem in its banking system meant that suspicion and lack of confidence persisted longer than was necessary. When global financial meltdown began in 2008/09, Western governments thought they had learned this lesson, and tried hard to fix the banks. Did they succeed?

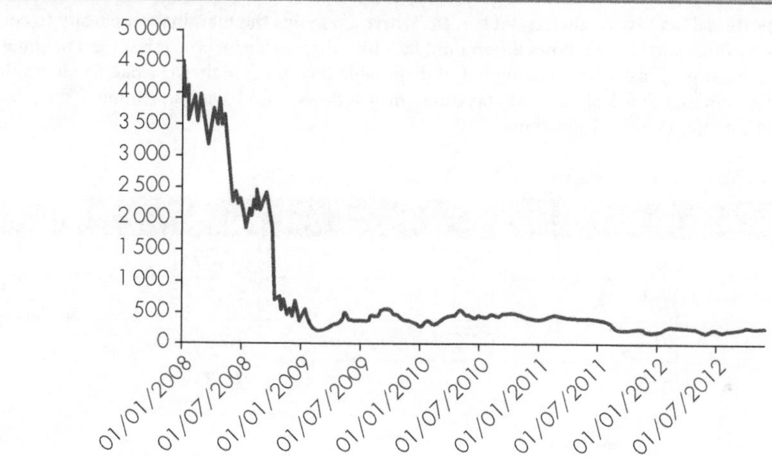

RBS share price 2008–12

Source: www.finance.yahoo.co.uk.

Note: In 2012, RBS exchanged 10 old shares for 1 new share. Each 10 shares at 20 pence became 1 share worth 200 pence. There was no change in the value of holdings, merely a 10-fold jump in the price. The chart above expresses all historical prices as if for new shares, eliminating this artificial jump in the share price in 2012.

By early 2010, many of the banks seemed to be slowly recovering. The chart shows the share price of Royal Bank of Scotland. In 2009, the government took an 84 per cent stake in order to avert its collapse. Its share price, having fallen from 4000 pence to 100 pence, then seemed to stabilize around the 200–300 pence range. The price needs to climb above 500 before the UK government can sell its shares and break even on the original purchase price.

There has been a big difference between the US–UK approach and the approach within the Eurozone. The US was the most aggressive in recapitalizing its banks at the time of the crisis, injecting substantial government funds to restore quickly the solvency of private banks. The UK also undertook major steps to help its banks. In continental Europe, there was generally less injection of public funds to the private banks, leaving some economists worried that Eurozone banks remain fragile and at risk if any new crisis should erupt.

In all countries, improved private sector solvency came at the price of reduced government solvency. Since economies were in recession, government did not raise taxes to pay for the banking bailouts and fiscal stimuli – this would have made recession worse – but rather borrowed money and ran larger budget deficits themselves. Whether governments can cope with high debt burden is a subject to which we return.

This leads to the third lesson from the Japanese experience. If pressing the fiscal accelerator is difficult once the government is heavily indebted, at least the monetary accelerator must be flat on the floor. Japanese monetary policy eventually cut interest rates to zero. Having learned from this experience, central banks in the US, the UK and the Eurozone were quick to slash interest rates to very low levels in 2009 when aggregate demand and output began to plummet. Interest rates have remained low ever since.

The multiplier revisited

The multiplier relates changes in autonomous demand to changes in equilibrium income and output. The formula in Chapter 16 still applies, provided we use c', the marginal propensity to consume out of gross income, not out of disposable income.

$$\text{Multiplier} = 1/(1 - c')$$

With proportional net taxes t, then $c' = (1 - t)c$, where c remains the marginal propensity to consume out of disposable income, and $(1 - t)$ shows the amount by which disposable income is less than national income. For a given marginal propensity to consume out of disposable income, a higher tax rate t reduces the multiplier. The more the circular flow leaks out into taxation, the less flows round again to stimulate further expansion of output and income. Table 17.1 illustrates.

Table 17.1 Values of the multiplier

C	T	$c' = c(1 - t)$	Multiplier $= 1/(1 - c') = 1/[s(1 - t) + t]$
0.9	0	0.90	10.00
0.9	0.2	0.72	3.57
0.7	0	0.70	3.33
0.7	0.2	0.56	2.27
0.7	0.4	0.42	1.72

In Chapter 16, without government the multiplier was simply $1/(1 - c)$ or $1/s$. With a larger marginal propensity to save, there was a larger leakage from the circular flow between firms and households, and the multiplier was correspondingly smaller. Table 17.1 merely extends this insight. Now leakages arise both from saving and from net taxes. When both are large, the multiplier is small. The bottom row of the table has a much smaller multiplier than the top row.

Since $1 - s = c$, Table 17.1 also points out that the denominator of the multiplier $[1 - c(1 - t)]$ is just $s + ct$, which can also be written as $s(1 - t) + t$. From the circular flow, leakages occur through taxation and through saving out of disposable income. The denominator of the multiplier continues to reflect the 'marginal propensity to leak', as promised in Chapter 16.

Even Table 17.1 overstates the value of the multiplier in practice. If there was such a large benefit to fiscal expansion, governments would be more willing to boost fiscal policy in order to expand output. By the end of the chapter, you will understand how leakages from imports further reduce the value of the multiplier.

17.3 The government budget

The government **budget** describes what goods and services the government will buy during the coming year, what transfer payments it will make and how it will pay for them. Most of its spending is financed by taxes. When spending exceeds taxes, there is a budget deficit. When taxes exceed spending, there is a budget surplus. Continuing to use G for government spending on goods and services, and NT for net taxes or taxes minus transfer payments,

> A budget is the spending and revenue plan of an individual, a firm or a government.

$$\text{Government budget deficit} = G - NT$$

Figure 17.5 shows government purchases G and net taxes tY in relation to national income. We assume G is fixed at 200. With a proportional net tax rate of 0.2, net taxes are $0.2Y$. At outputs below 1000, the government budget is in deficit; at an output of 1000, the budget is balanced; and at higher outputs, the budget is in surplus.

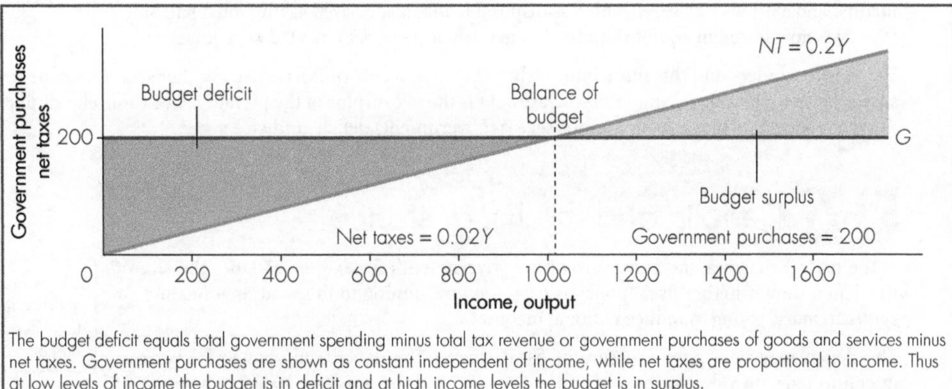

The budget deficit equals total government spending minus total tax revenue or government purchases of goods and services minus net taxes. Government purchases are shown as constant independent of income, while net taxes are proportional to income. Thus at low levels of income the budget is in deficit and at high income levels the budget is in surplus.

Figure 17.5 **The government budget**

The budget surplus or deficit is determined by three things: the tax rate t, the level of government spending G and the level of output Y. With a given tax rate, an increase in G will raise output and hence tax revenue. Could the budget deficit be *reduced* by higher spending? We now show that this is impossible.

Investment, saving and the budget

By definition, actual leakages from the circular flow always equal actual injections to the circular flow. Payments cannot vanish into thin air. Our model now has two leakages – saving by households and net taxes paid to the government – and two injections – investment spending by firms and government spending on goods and services. Thus *actual* saving plus *actual* net taxes always equal *actual* government spending plus *actual* investment spending.

In the last chapter we saw that, when the economy is not at equilibrium income, actual saving and investment differ from *desired* or *planned* saving and investment. Firms make unplanned changes in inventories and households may be forced to make unplanned saving if demand exceeds the output actually available.

The economy is in equilibrium when all quantities demanded or *desired* are equal to *actual* quantities. In equilibrium, planned saving S plus planned net taxes NT must equal planned government purchases G plus planned investment I. Planned leakages equal planned injections:

$$S + NT = G + I$$

Without the government, this reduces to the equilibrium condition of Chapter 16: planned saving equals planned investment. Notice that the above equation implies that in equilibrium desired saving minus desired investment equals the government's desired budget deficit:

$$S - I = G - NT$$

A rise in planned government spending G must *raise* the budget deficit. For a given tax rate, a rise in G increases aggregate demand and equilibrium income. Disposable income must rise. Households increase both desired consumption and desired saving.

Since desired investment I is independent of income, this rise in desired saving must increase $(S - I)$ and thus raise $(G - NT)$. This proves that the equilibrium budget deficit rises if government spending increases but the net tax rate is unaltered.

Higher government spending on goods and services increases equilibrium output. With a given tax rate, tax revenue rises but the budget deficit increases (or the budget surplus falls).

For given government spending G, a higher net tax rate reduces both equilibrium output and the budget deficit.

We can analyse a tax increase in a similar way. A rise in the tax rate reduces aggregate demand and equilibrium income. Disposable income falls, both because of lower national income and a **higher tax rate**. With less disposable income, desired saving must fall. Since $(S - I)$ is now lower, in equilibrium the budget deficit $(G - NT)$ must also be lower.

We can also understand this more intuitively. When one sector runs a deficit, another sector must be running a surplus to compensate. Saving minus investment is the net surplus of the private sector (households plus firms). A private sector surplus equals a public sector (government) deficit, and vice versa.

17.4 Deficits and the fiscal stance

Is the budget deficit a good measure of the government's **fiscal stance**? Does the size of the deficit show whether fiscal policy is *expansionary*, aiming to raise national income, or *contractionary*, trying to reduce national income?

The fiscal stance shows the intended effect of fiscal policy on demand and output.

The deficit may be a poor measure of fiscal stance. The deficit can change for reasons unconnected with a change in fiscal policy. Even if G and t are unaltered, a fall in investment demand reduces output and income, and hence net tax revenue, raising the budget deficit.

For given levels of government spending and tax rates, the budget has larger deficits in recessions, when income is low, than in booms, when income is high. Suppose aggregate demand suddenly falls. The budget will go into deficit. Someone looking at the deficit might conclude that fiscal policy was expansionary and that there was no need to expand fiscal policy further. That might be wrong. The deficit may exist because of the recession.

The structural budget

To indicate the fiscal stance, we calculate the **structural budget**, sometimes known as the *underlying* or *cyclically adjusted* budget. From actual government spending, we subtract not actual net taxes tY but the taxes tY^* that would apply, at the current net tax rate t, if output was hypothetically at potential output Y^*.

The structural budget shows what the budget will be if output is at potential output.

The cyclically adjusted budget $(G - tY^*)$ is affected by proactive fiscal decisions – changes in government spending G or in net tax rate t, but is insulated from fluctuations in actual tax revenue caused by cyclical deviations of output from potential output. Throughout the recent recession, tax revenue has been disappointingly small. One reason has been that the recovery of output has been slower than hoped and expected. Hence, there has been less tax revenue and more spending on welfare benefits to support citizens in economic distress.

The structural budget depends on the level of potential output Y^*. If a deep recession has permanent effects on potential output itself – for example, firms scrap factories that are then lost forever – the government will have permanently less tax revenue and a permanently larger budget deficit unless other spending is cut or the tax rate increased.

CASE 17.2

CYCLICAL OUTPUT FLUCTUATIONS AND THE GOVERNMENT BUDGET

The table below shows estimates by the UK Treasury for 2000–15, for fiscal years (April to April). All data are percentages of that period's GDP. The *current budget* includes net tax revenue and government spending on consumption (teachers, nurses, soldiers) but not government investment projects (road building, school building). The total budget deficit, or *net borrowing*, includes government investment expenditure as well as current expenditure on government consumption. By estimating potential output, we can compute

The output gap is the percentage deviation of actual output from potential output.

cyclically adjusted net tax revenue. The discrepancy between the actual budget and the cyclically adjusted budget is caused only by the output gap.

The table shows actual and cyclically adjusted budget deficits of the UK government during 2000–15, both for the total budget and for the current budget – that is, government consumption plus benefit payments less taxes – but excluding government investment. A negative number denotes a budget surplus. It also shows the output gap during the period. A positive number means that output temporarily exceeded potential output; a negative number implies that output was less than potential output.

Budget deficits and the output gap

	Budget deficit (% of GDP)		Cyclically adjusted budget deficit (% of GDP)		Output gap (% of GDP)
	Total	Current	Total	Current	
2000/01	−4	−2.3	1.1	−1.6	1.2
2001/02	0.1	−1.1	0.2	−0.9	−0.1
2002/03	2.4	1.1	1.9	0.6	−0.8
2003/04	2.9	1.5	2.6	1.2	−0.3
2004/05	3.4	1.7	3.1	1.4	−0.3
2005/06	3	1.1	2.8	0.9	−0.2
2006/07	2.5	0.5	2.3	0.4	0.1
2007/08	2.6	0.5	2.6	0.6	0.5
2008/09	6.9	3.6	6.4	3.1	−1.0
2009/10	11.3	7.9	8.9	5.3	−4.2
2010/11	9.6	7	7	4.4	−2.9
2011/12	8	6.2	6.4	4.6	−2.6
2012/13	5.8	6	4	4.2	−2.7
2013/14	5.9	4.5	4.1	2.7	−2.4
2014/15	4.3	3	2.9	1.5	−1.9

The budget deficit rose sharply after the financial crash, peaking in 2009/10. Was this because the recession deprived the government of net tax revenue – less from income tax, VAT and excise duties; more on welfare benefits – or because the government deliberately raised government spending and cut tax rates in order to avert a deeper recession? The table helps us answer this question.

The actual deficit in 2009/10 was 11.3 per cent of GDP, compared with only 2.6 per cent a couple of years earlier. The output gap in 2009/10 was −4.2 per cent, the amount by which actual output was below potential output at the bottom of the recession. The cyclically adjusted total deficit in that year was 8.9 per cent compared with 2.6 per cent a couple of years earlier. What does this imply?

First, the recession deprived the government of net tax revenue equal to 2.4 per cent of GDP – the difference between 11.3 and 8.9 per cent. The recession had a big effect on government finances, but it was only part of the story. Since the cyclically adjusted budget deficit rose from 2.6 per cent to 8.9 per cent in two years, deliberate new policy actions by the government (higher spending, higher subsidies, lower tax rates) accounted for a rise of 6.3 per cent in the government budget. The effect of deliberate fiscal expansion was more than twice as important as the effect of lower output in causing the actual budget deficit to rise.

The chart below shows more generally the systematic effect of fluctuations in the output gap (shown in green) on the difference between the actual deficit and the cyclically adjusted deficit. This time we focus on the current budget deficit, excluding government investment. The purple columns show the excess of the current budget deficit over its cyclically adjusted measure. The purple columns are about 70 per cent of the height of the green columns. Hence a 1 per cent cyclical fall in output is roughly associated with a 0.7 per cent rise in the current budget deficit (relative to the cyclically adjusted measure), caused by a fall in net tax receipts.

How much the business cycle affects government revenue varies from country to country. For example, at the onset of the financial crash, the US and UK governments both suffered large falls in tax revenue. The fall in Germany was much smaller. The explanation ought to depend on the marginal rate of net taxes – how net tax revenue varies with output and income.

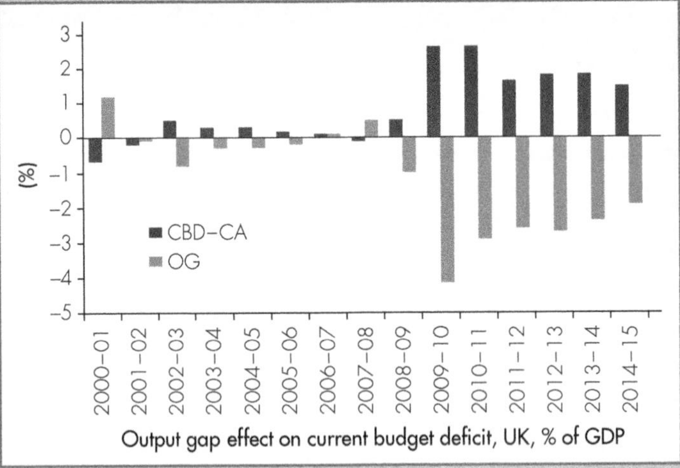

Output gap effect on current budget deficit, UK, % of GDP

Despite its low-tax rhetoric, the US has a surprisingly 'progressive' tax structure that relies heavily on taxing the rich. Germany and most European countries raise most of their revenues through 'regressive' consumption and energy taxes – petrol, alcohol, cigarettes, VAT – bearing mainly on the poor and the middle class. Hence, US tax revenue suffers much more in severe recessions, especially if these hit wealthy citizens, such as bankers and stock market investors. Britain's system lies somewhere in-between, with more reliance on highly redistributive income and capital tax than Germany but also a much bigger yield than in the US from less progressive taxes on energy and from VAT.

Inflation-adjusted deficits

A second reason why actual government deficits may be a poor measure of fiscal stance is the distinction between real and nominal interest rates. The budget deficit treats all nominal interest paid by the government on the national debt as government expenditure on transfer payments. It makes more sense to count only the *real* interest rate multiplied by the outstanding government debt.

The inflation-adjusted budget uses real not nominal interest rates to calculate government spending on debt interest.

Suppose inflation is 10 per cent, nominal interest rates are 12 per cent and real interest rates are 2 per cent. From the government's viewpoint, the interest burden is only really 2 per cent on each £1 of debt outstanding. Although nominal interest rates are 12 per cent, inflation will inflate future nominal tax revenue at 10 per cent a year, providing most of the revenue needed to pay the high nominal interest rates. The real cost of borrowing is only 2 per cent.

Consider what happens when interest rates are 1 per cent (the central bank, worried about recession, has reduced interest rates to a low level) and inflation is 3 per cent (booming China and India keep bidding up the prices of energy and food). The real interest rate is now *minus* 2 per cent. Borrowing now *hurts* the creditor (who gets insufficient interest to cover even inflation) and therefore *helps* the borrower (who by next year will enjoy more than enough inflated tax revenues with which to pay the modest interest charge on the debt).

It is very rare to see estimates of the inflation-adjusted budget. Inflation is therefore governments' secret weapon – it reduces the real burden of the debt unless nominal interest rates exceed the rate of inflation.

17.5 Automatic stabilizers and discretionary fiscal policy

Automatic stabilizers reduce the multiplier and thus output response to demand shocks.

Table 17.1 showed that a higher net tax rate *t* reduces the multiplier. A high net tax rate is therefore a good automatic stabilizer. Income tax, VAT and unemployment benefit are important **automatic stabilizers**, dampening the output response to changes in autonomous aggregate demand. Automatic stabilizers have a great advantage: nobody has to decide to make any policy decisions. By reducing the responsiveness of the economy to shocks, automatic stabilizers reduce output fluctuations.

All leakages are automatic stabilizers. A higher saving rate (hence a lower marginal propensity to consume) reduces the multiplier. A higher tax rate reduces the multiplier. Later in the chapter, we shall see that a high marginal propensity to import also dampens output fluctuations.

Discretionary fiscal policy is decisions about tax rates and levels of government spending.

Although automatic fiscal stabilizers are always at work, governments also use **discretionary fiscal policies** to change spending levels or tax rates to stabilize aggregate demand. When other components of aggregate demand are abnormally low, the government can boost demand by cutting taxes, raising spending, or both. When other components of aggregate demand are abnormally high, the government raises taxes or cuts spending.

By now you should be asking two questions. First, why can fiscal policy not stabilize aggregate demand completely? Surely, by maintaining aggregate demand at its full-employment level, the government could eliminate booms and slumps altogether? Second, why are governments reluctant to expand fiscal policy and aggregate demand to a level that would completely eliminate unemployment? Concept 17.1 provides some of the answers.

CONCEPT 17.1

THE LIMITS TO FISCAL POLICY

Why can demand shocks not be fully offset by fiscal policy?

1 *Time lags* It takes time to spot that aggregate demand has changed. It may take six months to get reliable statistics on output. Then it takes time to change fiscal policy. Long-term spending plans on hospitals or defence cannot be changed overnight. And once the policy is changed, it takes time to work through the steps of the multiplier process to have its full effect. Where possible, modern economies rely on interest rate changes, not fiscal changes, to make short-term adjustments to aggregate demand.

2 *Uncertainty* The government faces two problems. First, it is unsure of key magnitudes such as the multiplier. It only has estimates from past data. Mistaken estimates induce incorrect decisions about the extent of the fiscal change needed. Second, since fiscal policy takes time to work, the government has to forecast the level that demand will reach by the time fiscal policy has its full effects. If investment is low today but about to rise sharply, a fiscal expansion may not be needed. Mistakes in forecasting nongovernment sources of demand, such as investment, lead to incorrect decisions about the fiscal changes currently required.

3 *Induced effects on autonomous demand* Our model treats investment demand and the autonomous consumption demand as given. This is only a simplification. Changes in fiscal policy may lead to offsetting changes in other components of autonomous demand, as they did in Japan. These induced effects may

offset the direct effect of fiscal stimulus if fiscal expansion causes a collapse of confidence because of worries about government debt. If estimates of these induced effects are wrong, fiscal changes have unexpected effects. To study this issue, we extend our model of aggregate demand in Chapter 20.

Why not expand fiscal policy when unemployment is high?

1 *The budget deficit* When output is low and unemployment high, the budget deficit may be large. Fiscal expansion makes it larger. The government may worry about the size of the deficit itself or worry that a large deficit will lead to inflation.

2 *Maybe we are at full employment!* Our simple model assumes there are spare resources. Output is demand-determined. Fiscal expansion raises demand and output. But we could be at potential output. People are unemployed, and machines idle, only because they do not wish to supply at the going wages or rentals. If so, there are no spare resources to be mopped up raising aggregate demand. If high unemployment and low output reflect not low demand but low supply, fiscal expansion is pointless.

17.6 The national debt and the deficit

Occasionally, governments run a budget surplus. Historically, this is rare. Most governments have budget deficits. The flow of deficits is what adds to the stock of debt. Figure 17.6 shows the history of the UK national debt since the foundation of the Bank of England in 1694.

This figure should be compulsory viewing for all those arguing that today's government debt is 'too high'. For example, the Maastricht Treaty set a ceiling of 60 per cent for the debt/GDP ratio of each member state in the Eurozone. Greece and Japan are thought to be in terrible trouble because their debt GDP ratios are nearly 150 per cent, yet the UK has reached much higher levels on three occasions – 1815, 1918 and 1945. The Brits borrowed in wartime, and paid it off in peacetime.

The 260 per cent debt/GDP ratio of 1815 was the prelude to the biggest boom in British history, nearly a century in which Britain was the undisputed economic powerhouse of the world. Why was Britain not crippled with the burden of the debt?

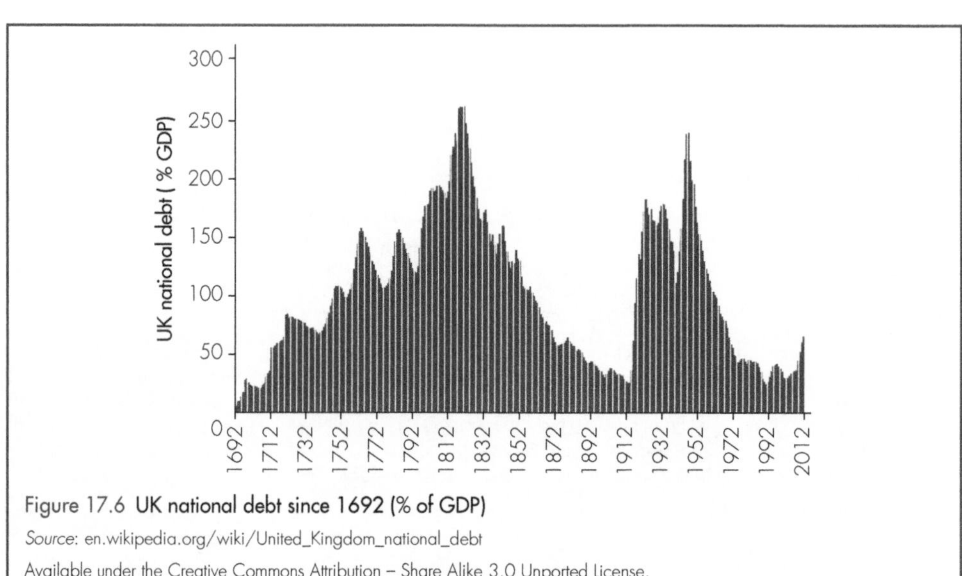

Figure 17.6 **UK national debt since 1692 (% of GDP)**

Source: en.wikipedia.org/wiki/United_Kingdom_national_debt

We measure debt *relative to GDP* because the latter is a proxy for the likely tax revenue that can be raised at 'reasonable' tax rates. Nominal debt rises when there is a budget deficit, but nominal GDP rises because of both real output growth and inflation. Hence, isolating the effect of the inherited debt, the debt burden's effect on this year's debt/GDP ratio is given by

$$(r - \pi - g)\ D/pY$$

where D is nominal debt, p the price level, Y real output, r the nominal interest rate, g the growth rate of real output and π the inflation rate. The debt only hurts if the interest rate r exceeds the rate of nominal income growth $(\pi + g)$. The latter shows how quickly the denominator of the debt/GDP ratio is growing; the former shows how interest on inherited debt is increasing the numerator of the debt/GDP ratio.

Since both output growth g and inflation π are normally positive, some steady increase in debt is sustainable without jeopardizing the debt/GDP ratio. Only when interest rates are higher than the rate of nominal income growth does inherited debt create sustainability problems.

This explains what happened to the UK in the nineteenth century. Strong growth and low interest rates made the debt burden negative. The UK added so much to GDP that the debt/GDP ratio steadily fell. The UK 'grew its way out of the problem'. Today, Greece, Ireland, Spain and Portugal would love the opportunity to do the same. However, in a global financial market, overseas lenders may panic when they see a country with a high debt/GDP ratio, and therefore raise substantially the interest rate that they charge governments with high debts.

This suggests, correctly, that there may be two possible outcomes, each a self-fulfilling prophecy. First, lenders lose confidence, charge high interest rates, prevent sustainable growth and force the country into a tough choice between a long period of austerity – running budget surpluses despite having low output and low tax revenue. Second, lenders may have faith, keep interest rates low and allow sustainable growth to reduce the debt/GDP ratio. One role of international institutions such as the IMF is to try to engineer the second solution.

Real output growth is one way to solve the problem of an inherited debt burden. A second solution is to print money and create inflation. Rapid inflation benefits the budget in three ways. First, it directly increases nominal GDP and the denominator of the debt/GDP ratio. Future nominal tax revenue increases. Provided interest rates don't rise by as much as inflation, the real interest rate on the debt is reduced. Second, this applies automatically to that part of the debt that is cash, which has a zero interest rate that cannot rise with higher inflation. So inflation erodes the real value of that part of the debt that is cash rather than bonds. Third, the government cheats. Some taxes are not properly inflation indexed, so that higher inflation actually raises real tax rates. For example, income tax thresholds may not be fully raised in line with inflation, and income tax may apply to nominal interest rates not just to the component that is the real interest rate.

Looking back at Figure 17.6, one reason that the national debt fell in the 1970s, despite little real economic growth, was that double digit inflation eroded the value of nominal debts.

The final way in which a sustainable debt/GDP ratio may be re-established is simply to default on the debt. Creditors hate it, but the day after a large default the government may well be highly solvent and a safer investment from now on than lending to other governments that continue to struggle with high levels of inherited debt. In practice, lenders are likely to be reluctant to lend to a defaulting government for many years thereafter. They are worried the government might default again, and they wish to send a message to other governments that default is a costly option that will freeze the country out of international financial markets for a long time.

A 'sustainable' level of debt depends on the beliefs of lenders, and on their perceptions of the likely behaviour of future governments in the indebted country. What debt level lenders will willingly finance is a matter of politics and psychology as well as economics. In their survey of previous financial crashes and debt crises, Professors Ken Rogoff and Carmen Reinhart conclude that, in practice, the warning bells start sounding when a country's debt/GDP ratio reaches 90 per cent and/or creditors start charging at least 6 per cent for new loans.[3]

Figure 17.7 shows the evolution of debt/GDP ratios in a range of countries – the UK, the US, Japan (J), Spain (E) and Germany (D). In 1993, in the green columns, all these countries had debt/GDP ratios below 60 per cent.

3 Ken Rogoff and Carmen Reinhart, *This time is different: 8 decades of financial folly* (Princeton University Press, 2011).

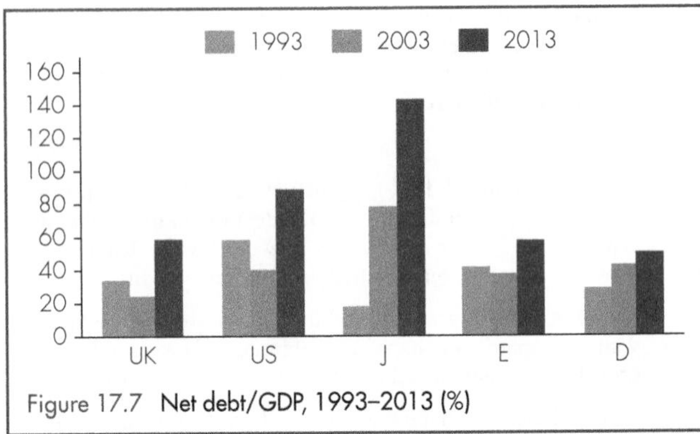

Figure 17.7 **Net debt/GDP, 1993–2013 (%)**

Debt was not much of a problem. By 2003, in the orange columns, the big change was the increase in Japan's government net debt to 78 per cent. After its financial crash in 2003, the government had lost tax revenue due to the subsequent recession, but also had tried to stimulate the economy with a range of discretionary changes to loosen the cyclically adjusted budget.

By 2013, in the purple columns, debt had increased everywhere. Interestingly, in the US it was much higher than in Spain, yet it was Spain that was experiencing the debt crisis. Investors knew, as a last resort, that the UK and the US could create inflation to ease their budgetary problems. Spain, like other Eurozone countries, was bound by the common monetary policy. The European Central Bank could not create inflation for Spain but keep prices stable for Germany.

This completes our introduction to fiscal policy, aggregate demand and the economy. We now extend our model of income determination to include the sector we have so far neglected – foreign trade with the rest of the world.

ACTIVITY 17.1

FISCAL STABILITY, RESPONSIBILITY AND AGGREGATE DEMAND

In 1993, US President Bill Clinton pushed a major tax increase through Congress, yet in subsequent years the US economy recovered from its recession of the early 1990s. Aggregate demand increased. Fiscal conservatives use this as an example of how responsible fiscal policies may actually boost demand, output and employment. We therefore need to explore two issues. First, is this what actually happened in the United States? Second, can it be reconciled with our theoretical model?

The table below shows annual growth of US real GDP, and the level of tax revenue as a percentage of GDP. The US suffered a growth slowdown in 1990 and a small recession in 1991. By 1992 the economy was growing strongly again. With the economy growing, tax revenue should be increasing in absolute terms after 2002. However, with a marginal tax rate of less than 1, tax revenue should grow more slowly than output if tax rates are constant. The *rising* ratio of tax revenue to GDP is indeed evidence of fiscal tightening.

However, the tax rises of 1993 did not initiate output recovery, which began earlier, and it is difficult to know what output growth would subsequently have been if the tax rises had not taken place. So, empirically, the case for a 'perverse expansion' caused by a tighter fiscal policy is at best unproven.

US	1999	2000	2001	2002	2003	2004	2005
Real GDP growth (% per annum)	4.2	1.8	−0.5	3.1	2.7	4.0	2.7
Tax revenue (% of GDP)	29.5	29.3	29.2	28.9	29.2	29.4	29.8

Source: Based on data from Economic Outlook Statistical Annex, © OECD, 2013, http://www.oecd.org/eco/economicoutlook.htm, accessed on 18/06/2013.

If the example is not empirical proof, what about theoretical arguments. How could a fiscal contraction lead to an output expansion? Implicitly this is a question about which of our model's assumptions might need to be changed.

Consider the effect on confidence and autonomous aggregate demand. If households and firms believe that the government budget is unsustainable, they worry about a future fiscal crisis. Fearing uncertainty, households cut back on consumption demand and firms postpone investment decisions. In these circumstances, measures to solve the government's budget problem by increasing taxes or cutting its spending – both of which impact adversely on aggregate demand – could *theoretically* cause a boost to autonomous consumption and investment demand that is large enough to outweigh the contractionary effects of tighter fiscal policy. Usually, this is unlikely. In an acute financial and fiscal crisis, resolving the crisis may indeed generate stability and growth.

A second, related channel is via interest rates. We begin the study of money and interest rates in the next chapter. A country with an unsustainable budget deficit will pay very high interest rates on its debt for two reasons. First, lenders are worried about outright default. Second, the government may deliberately create inflation to erode the real value of debts that are not index-linked. Lenders need to be compensated for both risks.

Very high interest rates reduce consumption demand (households struggle to pay mortgages, house prices may well have collapsed, debt in general is expensive) and investment demand (firms see fewer opportunities to make returns on investment that exceed the high cost of borrowing). Reducing the budget deficit may lead to a sharp reduction in interest rates, boosting autonomous consumption and investment demand enough to offset the contractionary effect of tighter fiscal policy. As with confidence, this channel enters our simple model by altering the level of autonomous aggregate demand; that is, that part of demand not directly associated with current levels of income and output.

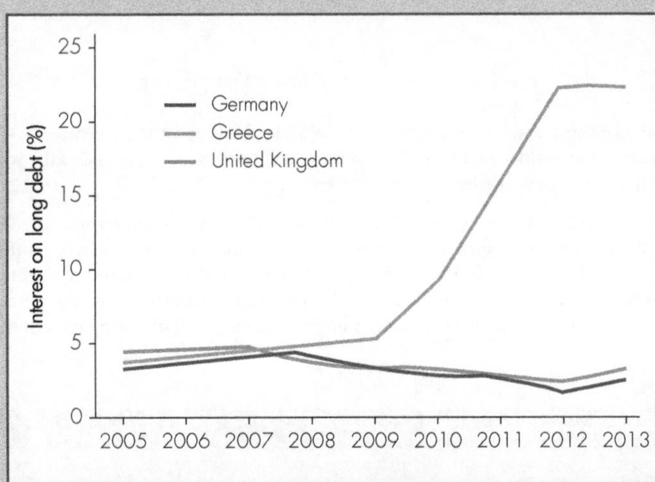

The chart shows long-term interest rates in the UK, Germany and Greece. The chart makes two points. First, despite being badly affected by the financial crash because of its large financial sector, the UK government enjoyed the same credibility as Germany. Second, investors completely lost confidence in Greece, which faced interest rates of 22 per cent a year, making fiscal policy unsustainable.

This shows the key role played by expectations about the future. If firms, households and market participants believe the future will be satisfactory, they act today in ways more likely to bring that outcome about; if firms and households believe the future will be unsatisfactory, then today they act in order to defend against the bad things they then expect to happen.

How can a government seek to enhance its credibility? It can announce and publicize promises of responsibility that raise the political costs of then backtracking. For example, a *Code for Fiscal Stability* might commit the government to balancing the current budget over the lifetime of the business cycle, borrowing money only for government investment (infrastructure, and so on) that raises future output and future tax revenue. This is sometimes called the *golden rule* of fiscal responsibility, though it is merely one aspect, since it ignores the effect of inflation and economic growth on the debt/GDP ratio.

Fiscal positions – not just in Mediterranean countries but in countries such as the UK, France and the US – were clearly unsustainable by 2011 after the emergency response to the crash. The issue was and remains *how quickly* the adjustment then has to be made. Eventually, the debt/GDP ratio must stop rising, and ideally be reduced again, which requires that large budget deficits be curtailed. However, too much austerity can be counterproductive if it shrinks tax revenue and makes the budget deficit even harder to close.

Questions

(a) Why is it important to assess the fiscal position in the medium run and not merely at a point in time?

(b) If the government can choose the definition of the cycle's length in order to suit its own purposes, why is there a gain from a report by an independent group of fiscal experts in the same way as the Bank of England publishes an independent *Inflation Report* on monetary policy?

(c) How would you expect financial markets to react if they thought that the government was being misleading in respect of its assessment of whether long-run solvency is gradually being achieved?

(d) Why does the *golden rule* apply to current expenditure by the government but exclude spending on physical investment?

(e) Suppose a new government promised to eliminate the large budget deficit within a year to 'put the economy on a sounder footing'. (i) Describe some steps it would have to take on spending and taxes. What effect would this have on: (ii) national output; (iii) tax revenue; (iv) the deficit itself; (v) autonomous investment?

To check your answers to these questions, go to page 679.

17.7 Foreign trade and income determination

Thus far, we have analysed an economy with three sectors – households, firms and the government. We know from our discussion of the national accounts in Chapter 15 that there is a fourth sector, the rest of the world. We now examine output determination once we include the foreign sector.

Exports X are goods and services made at home but sold abroad. Imports Z are goods and services made abroad but bought by domestic residents. Table 17.2 shows UK exports, imports and net exports. Two points should be noted. First, net exports are small relative to GDP, which implies that exports and imports are about equal in size. The UK has fairly balanced trade with the rest of the world. Second, economies are becoming more open as globalization occurs. Both exports and imports have become a larger fraction of GDP during the last 60 years.

Table 17.2 UK foreign trade, 1950–2011 (% of GDP)

	Exports	Imports	Net exports
1950	23	23	0
1970	22	21	1
2011	32	33	−1

Sources: ONS, *Economic Trends*; www.statistics.gov.uk.

Figure 17.8 confirms that this trend applies across a range of countries. The largest economies, the US and Japan, have a considerable amount of internal trade – enjoying a large domestic market, their producers can specialize and achieve scale economies without the need to export. Large economies are less open to foreign trade. This is not a statement about government policy, merely about the consequences of size itself.

Small economies, such as Ireland and the Netherlands, need to export most of their GDP in order to attain the scale needed to compete in international markets. Their export revenue is used to buy a large quantity of imports. Figure 17.8 shows that imports (and, by implication, exports) account for around 75 per cent of GDP in Ireland and the Netherlands. Larger European countries, such as the UK and France, lie somewhere between these small open economies and the large, quite closed economies. International trade accounts for just over 30 per cent of GDP in France and the UK.

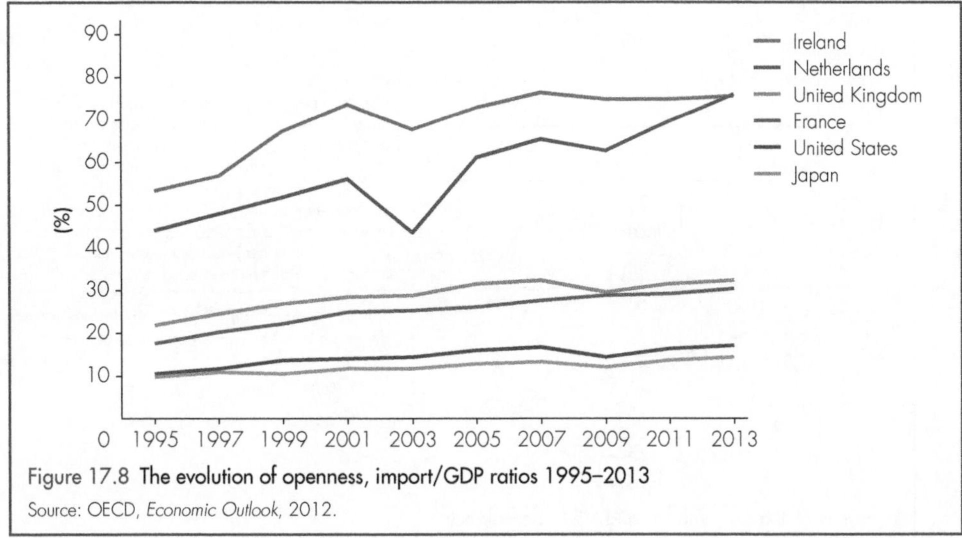

Figure 17.8 **The evolution of openness, import/GDP ratios 1995–2013**

Source: OECD, *Economic Outlook*, 2012.

We now explore the consequences of international trade for aggregate demand and output determination. Keep in mind that the importance of the foreign sector for aggregate demand depends a lot on the economy's size, and hence openness.

Net exports $X - Z$ add to income and output. Hence, the equilibrium condition for the goods market must now be expanded to

$$Y = AD = C + I + G + X - Z$$

What determines desired exports and imports? Export demand depends mainly on what is happening abroad. If foreign income and foreign demand are largely unrelated to domestic output, we can treat the demand for exports as autonomous. It does not depend on the level of domestic demand.

The marginal propensity to import z is the fraction of each extra pound of national income that domestic residents wish to spend on extra imports.

The trade balance is the value of net exports. If this is positive, the economy has a trade surplus. If imports exceed exports, the economy has a trade deficit.

Demand for imports rises when domestic income and output rise. Figure 17.9 shows the demand for exports, imports and net exports, as domestic income changes. The export demand schedule is horizontal. Export demand is independent of domestic income. Desired imports are zero when income is zero but rises as income rises. The slope of the import demand schedule is the **marginal propensity to import**.

The import demand schedule in Figure 17.9 assumes a value of 0.2 for the marginal propensity to import. Each additional pound of national income adds 20 pence to desired imports. This might be true for a very large economy. In small open economies, the marginal propensity to import z is much higher than 0.2. Any increase in national income leads to a large increase in the demand for imports.

At each output, the gap between export demand and import demand is the demand for net exports. At low output, net exports are positive. There is a **trade surplus** with the rest of the world. At high output, there is a **trade deficit** and net exports are negative. By raising import demand while leaving export demand unchanged, higher output worsens the **trade balance**.

Net exports and equilibrium income

Figure 17.10 shows how equilibrium income is determined. We start from the aggregate demand schedule $C + I + G$, described earlier in the chapter, then add net export demand NX, which is simply export demand minus import demand. At low output, net export demand is positive. Aggregate demand $C + I + G + X - Z$ will then exceed $C + I + G$. As output rises, import demand rises, export demand is constant, so desired *net* exports fall.

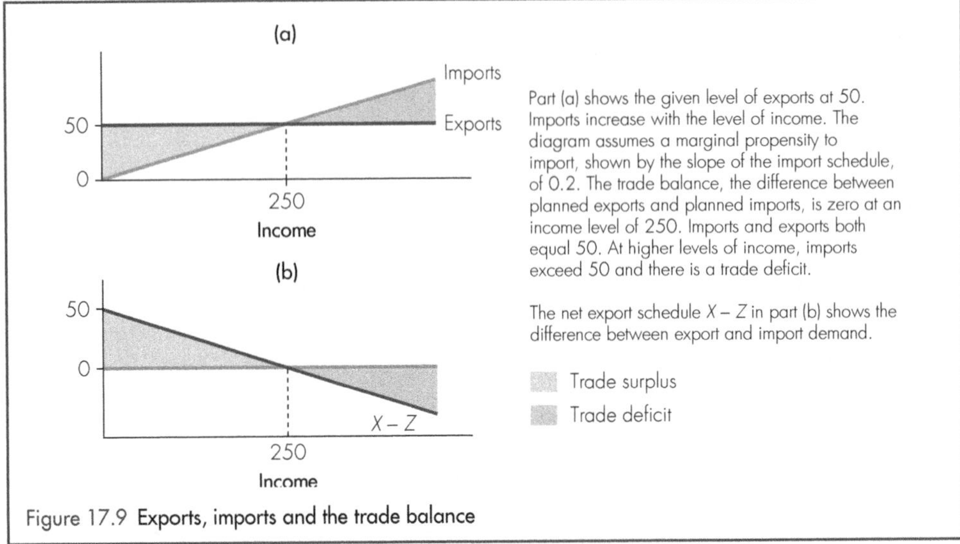

Figure 17.9 **Exports, imports and the trade balance**

At the output of 250, Figure 17.9 told us that net export demand is zero. Figure 17.10 shows the new aggregate demand schedule AD crossing $C + I + G$ at an output of 250. Beyond this output, net export demand is negative and the aggregate demand schedule is below $C + I + G$.

At a zero income, Figure 17.10 shows autonomous demand $I + G + X$. Suppose the marginal propensity to consume out of national income MPC is still 0.72. The $C + I + G$ schedule has a slope of 0.72, but the aggregate demand schedule AD is flatter. Each extra pound of national income adds 72 pence to consumption demand but also adds 20 pence to desired imports, since $MPZ = 0.2$. Thus, each extra pound of national income adds only 52 pence to aggregate demand for domestic output. The AD schedule has a slope of 0.52.

In Figure 17.10 equilibrium is at E, where aggregate demand equals domestic income and output. Planned spending, actual incomes and domestic output coincide at Y^*. Knowing this, we can deduce the levels of tax revenue and of imports, and hence compute the budget deficit (or surplus), and the trade deficit (or surplus). Neither is automatically zero merely because the economy is at equilibrium output.

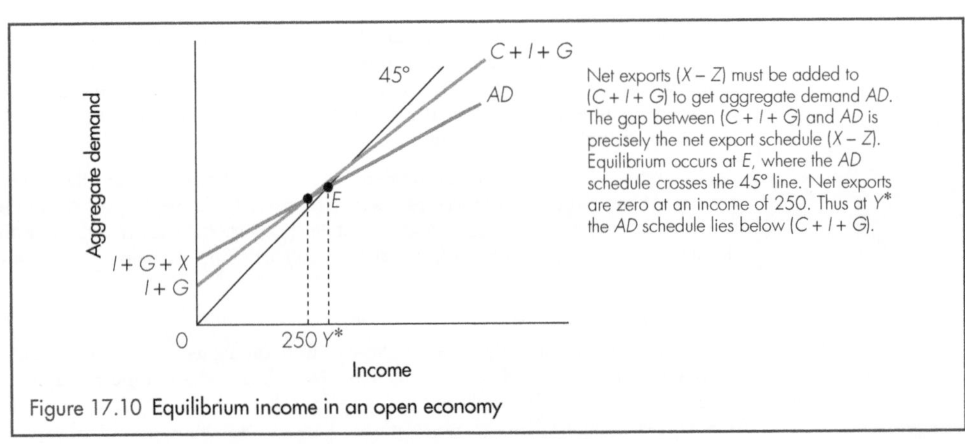

Figure 17.10 **Equilibrium income in an open economy**

The multiplier in an open economy

Each extra unit of national income raises consumption demand for *domestically produced goods* not by c', the induced additional consumption demand, but only by $(c' - z)$. Some of the extra demand now leaks out into imports without adding to the demand for domestic output. The multiplier is lower because there are leakages not only through saving and taxes but also through imports. In an open economy, the multiplier becomes $1/[1 - (c' - z)]$, which is just

$$1/[1 - c' + z]$$

or in full

$$1/[t + s(1 - t) + z]$$

As in our previous discussions of the multiplier, it is possible to interpret the denominator as the marginal propensity to leak through all channels – these now occur through taxes, through saving out of disposable income and through imports.

Table 17.3 shows what a difference the inclusion of foreign trade can make to the size of the multiplier. It shows different assumptions about the number of sectors and different assumptions about the marginal propensities.

Table 17.3 How different parameters affect the multiplier

c	t	$c' = c(1 - t) = t + s(1 - t)$	z	Multiplier $1/[1 - c' + z] = 1/[t + s(1 - t) + z]$	Sectors
0.9	0	0.90	0	10.00	Only firms (F) and households (H)
0.9	0.2	0.72	0	3.57	F, H and government (G)
0.9	0.2	0.72	0.4	1.48	F, H, G and foreign (Fo)
0.7	0	0.70	0	3.33	Only F and H
0.7	0.2	0.56	0	2.27	F, H and G
0.7	0.5	0.35	0.5	0.87	F, H, G and Fo

Without government or foreign sectors, it is easy to get the idea that the multiplier is very large, and aggregate demand very sensitive to changes in autonomous demand. Thus, when $c = 0.9$, the multiplier is 10, and even with $c = 0.7$, the multiplier is 3.33. However, leakages not just through saving but also net taxes reduce the multiplier substantially.

Once we also add imports, and note that the marginal propensity to import can be large in a small open economy, the value of the multiplier is reduced yet further. The final row shows that the multiplier could easily be *less* than 1 (a *divider* rather than a *multiplier*!) if the government and foreign sectors are large enough. The multiplier is still positive – boosts to autonomous demand *do* increase equilibrium output – but by less than you might have supposed. Low multipliers are one reason why proponents of fiscal austerity argue that the output effects will not be too bad.

This matters for economic policy design. A relatively closed economy, such as the US, can engage in fiscal stimulus knowing that (a) the multiplier is a decent size and (b) that only a limited amount of the benefit of the stimulus will leak out into imports. However, in a small open economy, such as Ireland or the Netherlands, most of the effect of fiscal stimulus leaks abroad. Higher domestic autonomous demand still boosts domestic output, but by only a small amount.

Small economies with large governments thus face powerful automatic stabilizers. Whatever shocks occur to autonomous demand are heavily dampened by subsequent leakages to imports and taxation. Larger economies with small governments face fewer leakages and hence, other things equal, shocks to autonomous demand lead to larger output fluctuations.

Higher export demand

A rise in export demand leads to a parallel upward shift in the aggregate demand schedule *AD*. Equilibrium income must increase. A higher *AD* schedule crosses the 45-degree line at a higher level of income. With a higher income, desired imports rise. The analysis of what happens to net exports is very similar to our analysis of the effect of an increase in government spending on the budget deficit.

As a matter of national income accounting, total leakages from the circular flow always equal total injections to the circular flow. And in equilibrium, desired spending must coincide with actual income and spending on domestic goods. Hence the amended equilibrium condition for an open economy is

$$I + G + X = S + NT + Z$$

Desired saving out of disposable income, plus net taxes, plus desired imports, equals desired investment, plus desired government spending, plus desired exports. Higher export demand X raises equilibrium domestic income and output. Because income rises, this raises desired saving, net tax revenue and desired imports. Since S, NT and Z all rise when X rises, the rise in desired imports must be smaller than the rise in desired exports. For example, if export demand rises by 100, desired saving may rise by 20 and net tax revenue by 40, so desired imports can only rise by 40. Net export demand increases. The domestic country's trade balance with the rest of the world improves.

Imports and employment

Do imports steal jobs from the domestic economy? In equilibrium, final demand $C + I + G + X$ is met from domestic output Y and imports Z. By reducing imports, we can create extra output and employment at home. This view is correct, but also dangerous. It is correct because higher consumer spending on domestic rather than foreign goods *will* increase aggregate demand for domestic goods and so raise domestic output and employment.

Figure 17.11 shows planned injections and planned leakages, which are equal in equilibrium at point *A*, at which output is *Y*. If the government takes action to reduce the propensity to import, shifting the schedule down from *Z to Z'*, the new equilibrium is at point *B*, at which output is now *Y'*. With fewer leakages at any output level, it takes higher output and income to generate sufficient planned leakages to equal the unchanged level of planned investment.

There are many ways to restrict import spending at each level of output. In later chapters, we analyse how foreign trade is affected both by the exchange rate and by import tariffs or quotas.

The view that import restrictions help domestic output and employment is dangerous because it ignores the possibility of retaliation by other countries. By reducing our imports, we cut the exports of others. If they retaliate by doing the same thing, the demand for our exports will fall. In the end, nobody gains employment but world trade disappears. If the whole world is in recession, what is needed is a worldwide expansion of fiscal policies, not a collective, and ultimately futile, attempt to steal employment from other countries.

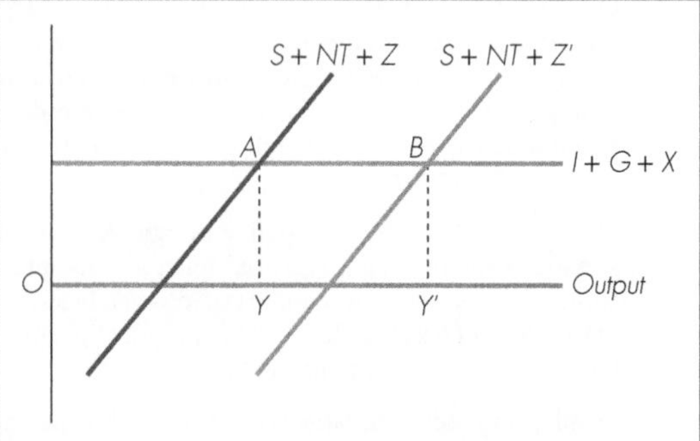

Figure 17.11 **A lower import propensity increases equilibrium output**

Figure 17.11 can of course also be used to illustrate the effect of a fall in export demand, which we discussed earlier. With lower planned injections, but an unchanged planned leakage schedule, equilibrium output must fall.

If you have been paying close attention, you will have noticed that, in analysing changes in equilibrium output, we sometimes use the diagram with aggregate demand and the 45-degree line, but sometimes use the diagram with planned leakages and planned injections. The two diagrams yield the same answer; which one we use is purely a matter of convenience. Sometimes, the answer is more immediately apparent in one diagram than the other. It is therefore a matter of trial and error which yields the answer more directly and conveniently. However, since it is the same economy being examined, the two diagrams always lead to the same conclusion. If you get a different answer, you made a mistake.

MATHS 17.1

EQUILIBRIUM OUTPUT REVISITED

Short-run equilibrium is given by

$$Y = C + I + G + X - Z$$

where $C = A + c(1 - t)Y$ and $Z = zY$. Hence, $Y = [A + G + X + I] + c(1 - t)Y - zY$, which implies

$$Y = [A + I + G + X] \,/\, [1 - c(1 - t) + z] \quad (1)$$

Equilibrium output is the product of autonomous spending – autonomous consumption demand A, plus injections from investment, government spending and exports – and the multiplier $\{1/[1 - c(1 - t) + z]\}$. Because of leakages into saving, taxes and imports, the multiplier may be quite small. In a very small open economy, the marginal propensity to import z will be much higher than in a large closed economy such as the US. Hence the multiplier will be lower in Belgium than in the US. In principle, if the tax rate and marginal propensity to import are large enough, the multiplier could be less than 1. Raising injections by £1 would then raise equilibrium income by less than £1.

Imagine a country such as the US that is large relative to the world economy. It might now need to recognize that US exports depend on how well the world is doing, which in turn is affected by how much the US imports from the rest of the world, and hence on the level of US output itself. Such interdependence would imply that $X = X^* + fY$, where X^* is autonomous export demand and the positive fraction f measures how much an increase in US output increases exports from the rest of the world, stimulates that economy and thereby increases their import demand for US exports.

The amended level of equilibrium output, and the product of the corresponding levels of autonomous demand and the new multiplier, would then be

$$Y = [A + I + G + X^*]/[1 - f - c(1 - t) + z]$$

CASE 17.3

GLOBALIZATION AND INTERNATIONAL TRADE

As the global economy becomes more interconnected, to which countries does the UK now export? The figure below provides a snapshot for 2011. The numbers in purple show the value of exports to particular countries and the green (orange) circles show how much higher (lower) this was than in the previous year. £31.7 billion of UK exports still go to the US, but this amount is growing only slowly over time, up just 2.7 per cent from the year before. The Eurozone is now a much more important trading partner, with Germany accounting for £27.5 billion of UK exports, France £18.9 billion and the Netherlands and Belgium together £31.7 billion. When it comes to international trade, countries trade especially strongly with their nearest neighbours. Although trade with emerging market economies is growing much more rapidly, it begins from a much smaller baseline. Hence, in 2011, UK trade with China accounted for only £7 billion of UK exports, and exports to India only £4.6 billion.

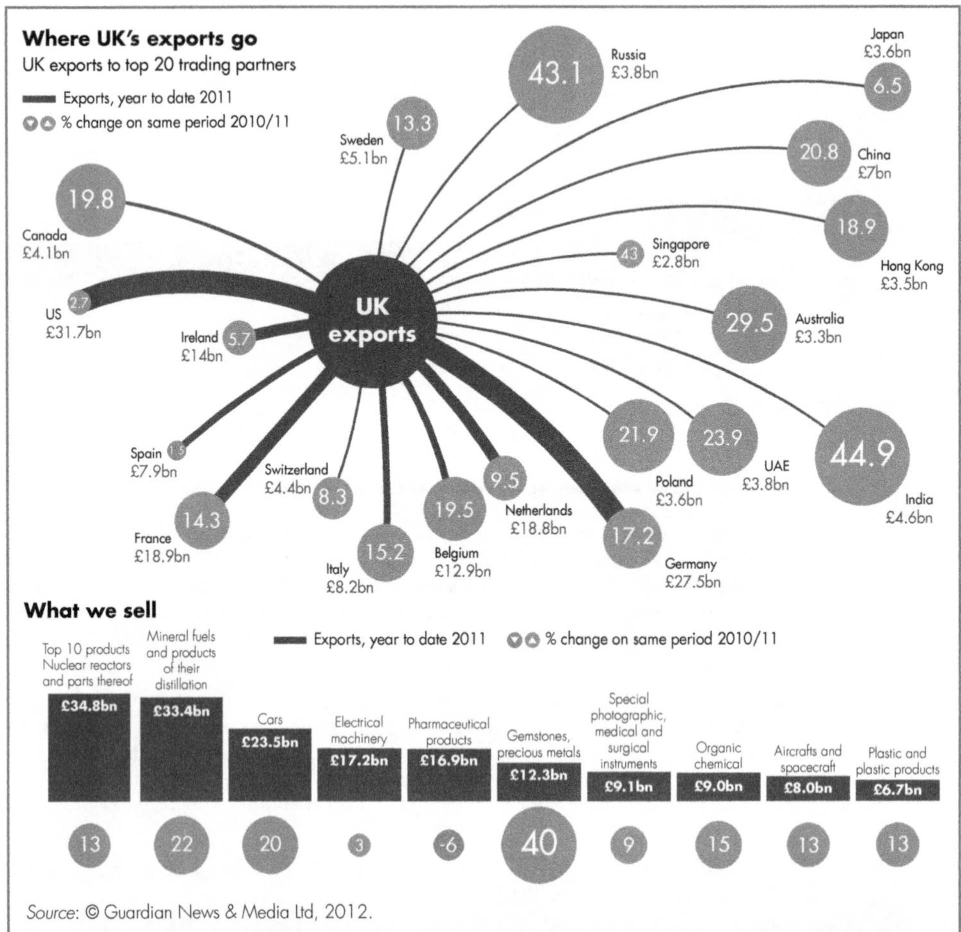

Source: © Guardian News & Media Ltd, 2012.

In macroeconomic terms, this means that UK aggregate demand depends most strongly on exports to the Eurozone and hence on how well these countries are doing economically. When the Eurozone expands, it imports more goods from everyone, including the UK; when it contracts, it demands fewer imports and hence UK exports are likely to suffer. Next most important for UK exporting is the economic performance of the US.

UK aggregate demand depends less directly on what is happening in China, but of course there are also indirect effects. If Chinese economic growth slows, not only does this mean fewer Chinese imports from the UK but also fewer imports from other countries such as the US and from the Eurozone. Lower exports to China from the US and the Eurozone lead to lower aggregate demand, as a result of which their demand for imports falls. Hence the UK loses out directly because it exports less to China, but also indirectly because it exports less to the US and the Eurozone. The more interconnected the world, the harder it is to keep track of all these indirect linkages.

We can think about UK imports in exactly the same way. Data from HM Revenue and Customs show that, in 2011, the UK imported £41 billion worth of goods and services from Germany, £25 billion from the US and £24 billion from China. As with exports, the UK's biggest trading bloc for imports is the Eurozone as a whole. Notice that China features much more strongly in UK imports than it does in UK exports. A UK recession will therefore directly reduce aggregate demand most in the Eurozone, the US and China. The full effect will also depend on all the indirect effects, such as the consequence of lower aggregate demand in the Eurozone then feeding back on its import demand from other countries, which in turn will experience lower demand for their exports.

Summary

- The government buys goods and services, and levies taxes (net of transfer benefits) that reduce disposable income below national income and output.
- **Net taxes**, if related to income levels, lower the marginal propensity to consume out of national income. Households get only part of each extra pound of national income to use as disposable income.
- **Higher government spending on goods and services** raises aggregate demand and equilibrium output. A **higher tax rate** reduces aggregate demand and equilibrium output.
- An equal initial increase in government spending and taxes raises aggregate demand and output. This is the **balanced budget multiplier**.
- The **government budget** is in deficit (surplus) if spending is larger (smaller) than tax revenue. Higher government spending raises the budget deficit. A higher tax rate reduces it.
- In equilibrium in a closed economy, desired saving and taxes equal desired investment and government spending. An excess of desired saving over desired investment must be offset by an excess of government purchases over net tax revenue.
- The budget deficit is a poor indicator of **fiscal stance**. Recessions make the budget go into deficit; booms generate a budget surplus. The **structural budget** calculates whether the budget would be in surplus or deficit if output were at potential output. It is also important to **inflation-adjust** the deficit.
- **Automatic stabilizers** reduce fluctuations in GDP by reducing the multiplier. Leakages act as automatic stabilizers.
- The government may also use **active or discretionary fiscal policy** to try to stabilize output. In practice, active fiscal policy cannot stabilize output perfectly.
- Budget deficits add to the **national debt**. If the debt is mainly owed to citizens of the country, interest payments are merely a transfer within the economy. However, the national debt may be a burden if the government is unable or unwilling to raise taxes to meet high interest payments on a large national debt.
- Deficits are not necessarily bad. Particularly in a recession, a move to cut the deficit may lead output further away from potential output. But huge deficits can create a vicious cycle of extra borrowing, extra interest payments and yet more borrowing.
- In an open economy, **exports** are a source of demand for domestic goods but **imports** are a leakage since they are a demand for goods made abroad.
- Exports are determined mainly by conditions abroad and can be viewed as autonomous demand unrelated to domestic income. Imports are assumed to rise with domestic income. The **marginal propensity to import** *MPZ* tells us the fraction of each extra pound of national income that goes on extra demand for imports.
- Leakages to imports reduce the value of the **multiplier** to $1/[1 - c' + z]$.
- Higher export demand raises domestic output and income. A higher marginal propensity to import reduces domestic output and income.
- The **trade surplus**, exports minus imports, is larger the lower is output. Higher export demand raises the trade surplus; a higher marginal propensity to import reduces it.
- In equilibrium, desired leakages $S + NT + Z$ must equal desired injections $G + I + X$. Thus any surplus $S - I$ desired by the private sector must be offset by the sum of the government deficit $(G - NT)$ and the desired trade surplus $(X - Z)$.

Review questions

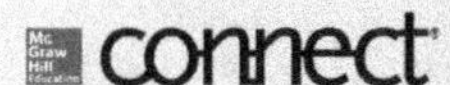

1 In equilibrium, desired saving equals desired investment. Is the statement true or false? Explain.

2 Why does the government raise taxes when it could borrow to cover its spending?

3 The EU's trading partners are in recession. (a) What happens to the EU's trade balance? (b) What happens to equilibrium EU output? Explain.

4 **Common fallacies** Why are these statements wrong? (a) The Chancellor raised taxes and spending by equal amounts. It will be a neutral budget for output. (b) Government policy should balance exports and imports but ensure that the government and private sector spend less than they earn.

5 Which of the following statements is correct? The trade surplus equals (a) the government surplus plus the private sector surplus, (b) the government deficit plus the private sector surplus or (c) the government deficit plus the private sector deficit.

EASY

6 Equilibrium output in a closed economy is £1000, consumption is £800 and investment is £80. (a) Deduce *G*. (b) Investment rises by £50. The marginal propensity to consume out of national income is 0.8. What are the new equilibrium levels of *Y*, *C*, *I* and *G*? (c) Suppose instead that *G* had risen by £50. What would be the new equilibrium levels of *Y*, *C*, *I* and *G*? (d) If potential output is £1200, to what must *G* rise to make output equal potential output?

7 The government spends £6 billion on rail track. The income tax rate is 0.25 and the *MPC* out of disposable income is 0.8. (a) What is the effect on equilibrium income and output? (b) Assuming that the government budget is in deficit, does the budget deficit rise or fall? Why?

8 In 2010, the new UK government wanted to reduce the size of the enormous budget deficit, but also pointed out that the structural budget deficit was significantly smaller than the actual deficit. (a) What does this mean? (b) Why does it matter? (c) Why does this make the subsequent growth of the UK economy so important?

9 If Y^{**} is the level of long-run equilibrium output of an open, mixed economy, and if short-run equilibrium output Y^* is given by the model in this chapter, deduce the relationship between the marginal tax rate t, the discrepancy between the actual budget and the structural budget, and the power of the automatic stabilizers.

10 Is the ratio of government debt to GDP a useful indicator of a government's indebtedness? When could it be misleading?

11 What values of the marginal propensity to save s, the marginal tax rate t and the marginal propensity to import z would be consistent with a multiplier as low as 0.67?

MEDIUM

12 **Essay question** 'By 2007, the UK had had over 50 consecutive quarters of steady growth. This period coincided with the period in which it was decided to make the Bank of England responsible for macroeconomic stabilization. Because interest rates can be changed easily and quickly, whereas tax rates and spending programmes cannot, this example confirms the superiority of monetary policy over fiscal policy in demand management.' Is this broadly correct? Can you think of examples in which fiscal policy would still be crucial? Did events after 2007 help you answer this question?

13 Suppose the marginal propensity to consume out of disposable income is 0.8, the marginal tax rate is 0.5 and the marginal propensity to import is 0.8. Draw a diagram showing the 45-degree line and the aggregate demand schedule. (a) How does this diagram differ from those earlier in the chapter? (b) What is the size of the multiplier? (c) Illustrate graphically the effect of a shift in aggregate demand.

HARD

HARD

14 Suppose the marginal propensity to consume out of disposable income is 0.8, the marginal tax rate is 0.5 and the marginal propensity to import is 0.8. Draw a diagram showing the 45-degree line and the aggregate demand schedule using the diagram in which planned injections equal planned leakages. (a) How does this diagram differ from those earlier in the chapter? (b) What is the size of the multiplier? (c) Illustrate graphically the effect of a shift in aggregate demand using the diagram in which planned injections equal planned leakages.

For solutions to these questions, contact your lecturer.

CHAPTER 18

Money and banking

Learning Outcomes

By the end of this chapter, you should be able to:

1. explain the medium of exchange as the key attribute of money
2. understand other functions of money
3. describe how banks create money
4. differentiate between liquidity crisis and solvency crisis
5. understand narrow and broad money
6. explain the money multiplier and bank deposit multiplier
7. recognize different measures of money
8. identify motives for holding money
9. understand how money demand depends on output, prices and interest rates

Money is a symbol of success, a source of crime and it makes the world go round.

> Money is any generally accepted means of payment for delivery of goods or settlement of debt.

Dogs' teeth in the Admiralty Islands, sea shells in parts of Africa, gold in the nineteenth century: all are examples of money. What matters is not the commodity used but the social convention that it is accepted *without question* as a means of payment. We now explain how society uses money to economize on scarce resources used in the transacting process.

18.1 Money and its functions

Although the crucial feature of money is its acceptance as the means of payment or **medium of exchange**, money also has three other functions: a unit of account, a store of value and a standard of deferred payment.

> The medium of exchange is something accepted as payment only to be subsequently reused to pay for something else.

The medium of exchange

Money is used in almost half of all exchanges. Workers exchange labour services for money. People buy or sell goods for money. We accept money not to consume it directly but to use it subsequently to buy things we do wish to consume. Money is the medium through which people exchange goods and services.[1]

To see that society benefits from a medium of exchange, imagine a **barter economy**, in which the seller and the buyer *each* must want something the other has to offer. Each person is simultaneously a seller and a buyer. To see a film, you must swap a good or service that the cinema manager wants. There has to be a *double coincidence of wants.*

> A barter economy has no medium of exchange. Goods are swapped for other goods.

1 For an interesting account of cigarettes as money in prisoner-of-war camps, see R. A. Radford, 'The economic organisation of a POW camp', *Economica* 48 (1945): 189–201, which was introduced in Activity 1.1.

Trading is very expensive in a barter economy. People spend a lot of time and effort finding others with whom to make mutually satisfactory swaps. Time and effort are scarce resources. A barter economy is wasteful. The use of money – any commodity *generally* accepted in payment for goods, services and debts – makes trading simpler and more efficient. By economizing on time and effort spent in trading, society can use these resources to produce extra goods or leisure, making everyone better off.

Other functions of money

The unit of account is the unit in which prices are quoted and accounts kept.

Money is a store of value that can be used to make future purchases.

In Britain prices are quoted in pounds sterling; in Germany, in euros. It is convenient to use the same units for the medium of exchange and **unit of account**. However, there are exceptions. During the German hyperinflation of 1922–23, when prices in marks changed very quickly, German shopkeepers found it more convenient to use dollars as the unit of account. Prices were quoted in dollars but payment was made in marks, the German medium of exchange. In 2009 Zimbabwe had to legalize the use of foreign currency as money because its domestic currency was almost worthless after years of hyperinflation.

To be accepted in exchange, money *has* to **store value**. Nobody will accept money in payment for goods supplied today if the money is worthless when they try to buy goods with it later. But money is not the only, nor necessarily the best, store of value. Houses, stamp collections and interest-bearing bank accounts all serve as stores of value. Since money pays no interest and its real purchasing power is eroded by inflation, there are better ways to store value.

Finally, money is a *standard of deferred payment* or unit of account over time. When you borrow, the amount to be repaid next year is measured in pounds. However, the key feature of money is its use as a medium of exchange. For this, it must act as a store of value as well. And it is usually, though not invariably, convenient to make money the unit of account and standard of deferred payment as well.

Different kinds of money

In prisoner-of-war camps, cigarettes were money. In the nineteenth century money was mainly gold and silver coins. These are examples of *commodity money*, ordinary goods with industrial uses (gold) and consumption uses (cigarettes), which also serve as a medium of exchange. To use a commodity money, society must either cut back on other uses of that commodity or devote scarce resources to additional production of the commodity. There are cheaper ways for society to make money.

A £10 note is worth far more as money than as a 7.5 × 14 cm piece of high-quality paper. Similarly, the monetary value of most coins exceeds what you would get by melting them down and selling off the metal. By collectively agreeing to use token money, society economizes on the scarce resources required to produce a medium of exchange. Since the manufacturing cost is tiny, why doesn't everyone make £10 notes? The survival of **token money** requires a restriction on the right to supply it. Private production is illegal.[2] Token money is sometimes called *fiat* money – from the Latin word for 'let it be done' – because its value arises only because of the existence of a government law or regulation.

A token (or fiat) money is a means of payment whose value or purchasing power as money greatly exceeds its cost of production or value in uses other than as money.

An IOU money is a medium of exchange based on the debt of a private firm or individual.

Society enforces the use of token money by making it *legal tender*. By law, it must be accepted as a means of payment. However, when prices rise very quickly, domestic token money is a poor store of value. People are reluctant to accept it as a medium of exchange. Shops and firms give discounts to people paying in gold or in foreign currency.

In modern economies, token money is supplemented by **IOU money**, principally bank deposits, which are debts of private banks. When you have a bank deposit, the bank owes you money. The bank is obliged to pay your cheque. Bank deposits are a medium of exchange because they are generally accepted as payment.

2 The existence of forgers confirms society is economizing on scarce resources by producing money whose value as a medium of exchange exceeds its production cost.

CONCEPT 18.1

BARTER ECONOMY VS MONETARY ECONOMY

Life without money

> Some years since, Mademoiselle Zelie, a singer, gave a concert in the Society Islands in exchange for a third part of the receipts. When counted, her share was found to consist of 3 pigs, 23 turkeys, 44 chickens, 5000 cocoa nuts, besides considerable quantities of bananas, lemons and oranges [. . .] as Mademoiselle could not consume any considerable portion of the receipts herself it became necessary in the meantime to feed the pigs and poultry with the fruit.
>
> (W. S. Jevons, 1898)

This vivid example shows just how costly a barter economy can be. The direct exchange of goods and services for other goods and services either leaves one party with a load of stuff in which they have little interest – in which case they then have to go to the further effort of bartering this in turn for something more useful – or else restricts barter opportunities to the rare cases in which there is a 'double coincidence of wants', such that not only does person A want what person B is offering but also person B wants what person A is offering.

The great benefit of a monetary economy is that the medium of exchange can be confidently accepted in the knowledge that it can easily be reused for another transaction. The example below documents the first European to discover paper money. But Europeans did not invent it. As in many other things, the Chinese got there first.

Marco Polo discovers paper money

> In this city of Kanbula [Beijing] is the mint of the Great Khan, who may truly be said to possess the secret of the alchemists, as he has the art of producing money. [. . .]
>
> He causes the bark to be stripped from mulberry trees [. . .] made into paper [. . .] cut into pieces of money of different sizes. The act of counterfeiting is punished as a capital offence. This paper currency is circulated in every part of the Great Khan's domain. All his subjects receive it without hesitation because, wherever their business may call them, they can dispose of it again in the purchase of merchandise they may require.
>
> (*The Travels of Marco Polo*, Book II)

Source: World Bank, *World Development Report*, 1989.

18.2 Modern banking

When you deposit your coat in the theatre cloakroom, you do not expect it to be rented out during the performance. Banks lend out most of the monetary coats in their monetary cloakroom. A theatre would have to get your particular coat back on time, which might be tricky. A bank finds it easier because one piece of money looks just like another.

Unlike other financial institutions, such as pension funds and insurance companies, the key aspect of banks is that some of their liabilities are used as the medium of exchange: cheques allow their deposits to be used as money.

At any time, some people are writing cheques on a Barclays account to pay for goods purchased from a shop that banks with Lloyds; others are writing cheques on Lloyds' accounts to finance purchases from shops banking with Barclays. The *clearing system* is the process of interbank settlement of the net flows required between banks as a result. Thus the system of clearing cheques represents another way in which society reduces the cost of making transactions.[3]

3 Society continues to find new ways to save scarce resources in producing and using a medium of exchange. Many people use credit cards. Some supermarket tills directly debit customers' bank accounts. And shopping via the TV, telephone and Internet is growing rapidly.

Liquidity is the cheapness, speed and certainty with which asset values can be converted back into money.

Bank reserves are the money that a bank has available to meet possible withdrawals by depositors.

The money in sight deposits can be withdrawn 'on sight' without prior notice.

Time deposits, paying higher interest rates, require the depositor to give notice before withdrawing money.

Private commercial banks have assets and liabilities. Their assets are mainly loans to firms and households, and purchases of financial securities such as bills and bonds issued by governments and firms. Because many securities are very **liquid**, banks can lend short term and still get their money back in time if depositors withdraw their money.

In contrast, many loans to firms and households are quite illiquid. The bank cannot easily get its money back in a hurry. Modern banks thought they could get by with very few **cash reserves** in the vault because they thought they had sufficient liquid assets that would fulfil the same function: in an emergency they could be sold easily, quickly and for a predictable price.

Liabilities of commercial banks include sight and time deposits. Chequing accounts are **sight deposits**. **Time deposits**, which include some savings accounts, pay higher interest rates because banks have time to organize the sale of some of their high-interest assets in order to have the cash available to meet withdrawals. Certificates of deposit (CDs) are large 'wholesale' time deposits – one-off deals with particular clients for a specified period, paying more generous interest rates. The other liabilities of banks are various 'money market instruments': various types of short-term and highly liquid borrowing by banks.

The business of banking

A bank makes profits by lending and borrowing. To get money in, the bank offers attractive interest rates to depositors, and offers higher interest rates on time deposits than sight deposits since the latter are subject to the possibility of immediate and unpredictable withdrawal.

Banks have to find profitable ways to lend what has been borrowed. In sterling, most is lent as advances of overdrafts to households and firms, usually at high interest rates. Some is used to buy securities, such as long-term government bonds. Some is more prudently invested in liquid assets. Although these pay a lower interest rate, the bank can get its money back quickly if people withdraw a lot of money from their sight deposits. And some money is held as cash, the most liquid asset of all.

A bank uses its specialist expertise to acquire a diversified portfolio of investments. Without the existence of the bank, depositors would have neither the time nor the expertise to decide which of these loans or investments to make. Prior to the financial crisis, modern banks often held reserves as low as 2 per cent of the sight deposits that could be withdrawn at any time. This shows the importance of the other liquid assets in which banks had invested. At very short notice, banks could cash in liquid assets easily and for a predictable amount. The skill in running a bank entails being able to judge how much must be held in liquid assets, including cash, and how much can be lent out in less liquid forms that earn higher interest rates.

Commercial banks are financial intermediaries licensed to make loans and issue deposits, including deposits against which cheques can be written.

A financial intermediary specializes in bringing lenders and borrowers together.

A **commercial bank** borrows money from the public, crediting them with a deposit. The deposit is a liability of the bank. It is money owed to depositors. In turn, the bank lends money to firms, households or governments wishing to borrow. Banks are not the only **financial intermediaries**. Insurance companies, pension funds and building societies also take in money in order to re-lend it. The crucial feature of banks is that some of their liabilities are used as a means of payment, and are thus part of the money stock.[4]

18.3 How banks create money

The reserve ratio is the ratio of reserves to bank deposits.

To simplify the arithmetic, assume banks use a **reserve ratio** of 10 per cent. Suppose, initially, the non-bank private sector has wealth of £1000 held in cash, which is a private sector asset but a liability of the government, who issued it, but not a liability of the private banks. The first row of Table 18.1 shows this cash as an asset of the non-bank private sector.

4 In fact, building societies now issue cheque books to their depositors, which is why building societies are now included in monetary statistics.

Table 18.1 Money creation by the banking system

	Banks		Non-bank private sector	
	Assets	Liabilities	Monetary assets	Liabilities
Initial	Cash 0 Loans 0	Deposits 0	Cash 1000	Loans from banks 0
Intermediate	Cash 1000	Deposits 1000	Cash 0 Deposits 1000	Loans from banks 0
Final	Cash 1000 Loans 9000	Deposits 10 000	Cash 0 Deposits 10 000	Loans from banks 9000

Now people pay this £1000 of cash into the banks by opening bank deposits. Banks have assets of £1000 cash, and liabilities of £1000 of deposits – money owed to depositors. If banks were like cloakrooms, that would be the end of the story. Table 18.1 would end in row 2.

However, banks do not need all deposits to be fully covered by cash reserves. Suppose banks create £9000 of overdrafts. This is a simultaneous loan of £9000, an asset in banks' balance sheets and the granting to customers of £9000 of deposits, against which customers can write cheques. The deposits of £9000 are a liability on banks' balance sheets. Now the banks have £10 000 total deposits – the original £1000 when cash was paid in, plus the new £9000 as counterpart to the overdraft – and £10 000 of total assets, comprising £9000 in loans and £1000 cash in the vaults. The reserve ratio is still 10 per cent in row three of Table 18.1.

It does not even matter whether the 10 per cent reserve ratio is imposed by law or is merely profit-maximizing, smart behaviour by banks that balances risk and reward. The risk is the possibility of being caught short of cash; the reward is the **interest rate spread**.

How did banks create money? Originally, there was £1000 of cash in circulation. That was the **money supply**. When paid into bank vaults, it went out of general circulation as the medium of exchange. But the public acquired £1000 of bank deposits against which cheques may be written. The money supply was still £1000. Then banks created overdrafts *not* fully backed by cash reserves. Now the public had £10 000 of deposits against which to write cheques. The money supply rose from £1000 to £10 000. Banks created money.

The interest rate spread is the excess of the loan interest rate over the deposit interest rate.

The money supply is the value of the stock of the medium of exchange in circulation.

ACTIVITY 18.1

A BEGINNER'S GUIDE TO FINANCIAL MARKETS

Financial asset A piece of paper entitling the owner to a specified stream of income for a specified period. Firms and governments raise money by selling financial assets. Buyers work out how much to bid for them by calculating the present value of the promised stream of payments. Assets are frequently retraded before the date at which the original issuer is committed to repurchase the piece of paper for a specified price.

Cash Notes and coins, paying zero interest. It is the most liquid asset.

Bills Short-term financial assets paying no interest directly but with a known date of repurchase by the original borrower at a known price. Consider a three-month UK Treasury bill. In April the government sells a piece of paper, promising to repurchase it for £100 in July. If people bid £98.50 in April, they will make

1.5 per cent in three months by holding the bill until July, when it is worth £100. As July gets nearer, the price at which the bill is retraded climbs towards £100. Buying it from someone else in June for £99.50 and reselling to the government in July for £100 still yields 0.5 per cent in a month, or over 6 per cent a year at compound interest. Treasury bills are easily bought and sold. Their price can only fluctuate over a small range (say, between £98 and £99 in May when they expire in July), so they are highly liquid. People can get their money out easily, cheaply and predictably. Bills issued by companies rather than government are known as *corporate bills*.

Bonds Longer-term financial assets, which again can be issued by companies or by governments as a means of longer-term borrowing. Long-term UK government bonds are known as gilts because their safety is gilt-edged. Look under GILTS – UK CASH MARKET in the second section of the *Financial Times*. You will find a bond listed as Tr 5pc '25, which means that in the year 2025, the UK government will buy back this bond for £100 (the usual repurchase price). Until then, the bondholder gets interest payments of £5 a year (5 per cent of the repurchase price). Bonds are less liquid than bills, not because they are hard to sell, but because the price for which they could be sold, and the cash this will generate, is less certain in the meantime. To see why, we study the most extreme kind of bond.

Perpetuities Bonds never repurchased by the original issuer, who pays interest for ever. These are sometimes called Consols in the UK, because in 1752 the Chancellor and Prime Minister, Sir Henry Pelham, repurchased all the various debts outstanding and financed doing so by issuing one new consolidated bond. Nowadays, 'Consols 2.5%' pay £2.50 a year for ever. Most were issued when interest rates were low, around 2.5 per cent. People originally would have bid around £100 for this Consol. Suppose interest rates on other assets rise to 10 per cent. Consols are retraded between people at around £25 each so that new purchasers of these old bonds get about 10 per cent on their financial investment. The person holding a bond makes a capital loss when other interest rates rise and the price of the bond falls. Moreover, since the price of Consols, once £100, could fall to £25 if interest rates rise a lot, Consol prices are much more volatile than the price of Treasury bills. The longer the remaining life of a bond, the more its current price can move around as existing bondholders try to sell on to new buyers at a rate of return in line with other assets today. Bonds can easily be bought and sold, but are not very liquid. You do not know how much you would get if you had to sell out in six months' time.

Company shares (equities) Entitlements to dividends, that part of firms' profits paid out to shareholders rather than retained to buy new machinery and buildings. In good years, dividends are high; in bad years dividends may be zero. Hence a risky asset that is not very liquid. Share prices are volatile. Firms could even go bust, making the shares worthless.

Derivatives Contracts that refer to bets on the value of underlying financial securities. For example, a European aircraft manufacturer might have equities that trade for €300 per share. Somebody might offer to sell a contract paying €50 in three months' time if, but only if, the equity price has risen to at least €350 by that date. The seller of this contract is not very optimistic about the future of the share price. If you think the underlying share price is going to rise beyond €350, you might be happy to buy the derivative contract at a cheap price today. Some derivatives are bets on prices rising; others are bets on price falling.

Securitization The practice of aggregating collections of individual contracts (such as individual mortgages) into bundles of contracts that are then sold and bought by institutions far removed from the original deal. In theory, securitization was meant to spread the risk of an individual contract going wrong, thereby reducing risk in total. In practice, many of the buyers of these securities understood little about them and were amazed when the contracts all became worthless together. The most famous example was the securitization of US sub-prime mortgages – dubious loans to poor people who were often duped into taking out mortgages whose repayments they would later be unable to afford. Suddenly, many institutions around the world found themselves holding 'assets' that were revealed to be worth almost nothing, setting up a tsunami of insolvency.

The chart below shows the huge growth of securitization, and corresponding fall in old-fashioned bank loans, in the US in the run-up to the financial crash.

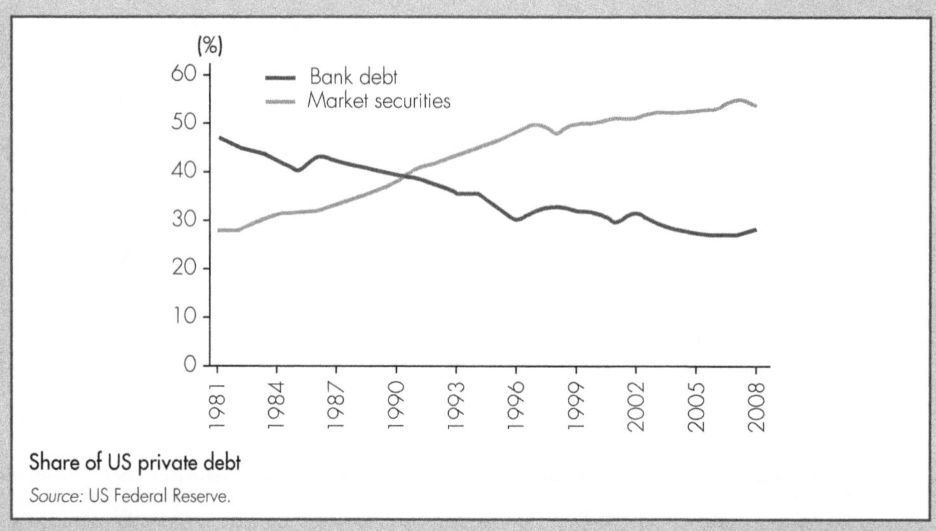

Share of US private debt

Source: US Federal Reserve.

Questions

(a) If cash pays no interest, why does anyone hold it?

(b) Since firms could use bills and bonds to raise finance, what advantages do they see in raising money through issuing equities?

(c) If it is good for firms to issue equities, can it simultaneously be good for investors?

(d) While the Treasury is closed and the prime minister is on holiday, the Bank of England announces it has made a loan to a regional bank whose depositors were panicking. Did the Bank of England think this was a liquidity crisis or a solvency crisis? Explain your answer.

To check your answers to these questions, go to page 679.

18.4 The traditional theory of money supply

We begin the traditional account of the role of banks in the money supply. The *central bank* – the Bank of England in the UK, the ECB in the Eurozone, the Federal Reserve in the US – controls the issue of token money in a modern economy. Private creation of token money must be outlawed when its value as a medium of exchange exceeds the direct cost of its production.

People hold cash for many reasons. It makes transactions easier and cheaper. Moreover, some people do not trust banks; they keep their savings under the bed. Remarkably, only three-quarters of British households have chequing accounts. Some people hold cash in order to make illegal or tax-evading transactions in the 'black economy'. In a modern economy most of the broad measure of money is in bank deposits.

Suppose, as was the case a few years ago, UK banks hold cash reserves equal to 1 per cent of their total deposits, and the private sector holds cash in circulation equal to 3 per cent of the value of sight deposits. Maths 18.1 shows that this implies a **money multiplier** of 26. Each £100 rise in the monetary base increases the money supply by £2600.

The money multiplier is the ratio of broad money to the monetary base.

MATHS 18.1

THE MONEY MULTIPLIER

Suppose banks wish to hold cash reserves R equal to some fraction c_b of deposits D, and that the private sector holds cash in circulation C equal to a fraction c_p of deposits D:

$$R = c_bD \qquad \text{and} \qquad C = c_pD$$

The monetary base H is either in circulation or in bank vaults:

$$H = C + R = (c_p + c_b)D$$

Finally, the money supply is circulating currency C plus deposits D:

$$M = C + D = (c_p + 1)D$$

These last two equations give us the money multiplier, the ratio of M to H:

$$M/H = (c_p + 1)/(c_p + c_b) > 1$$

If the public hold cash to the value of 2 per cent of their deposits, $c_p = 0.02$, and if banks hold reserves equal to 2 per cent of deposits, $c_b = 0.02$. Hence the money multiplier is

$$M/H = 1.02/(0.04) = 25.5$$

The bank deposit multiplier is the ratio of broad money to bank reserves.

the ratio of broad money to the monetary base. The ratio M/R, dividing broad money only by bank reserves but not by cash held outside the banks, is called the **bank deposit multiplier**:

$$M/R = (c_p + 1)/(c_b) = 1.02/0.02 = 51$$

Notice that, if banks now become cautious about lending and raise their reserve ratio c_b to 10 per cent of deposits, then

Money multiplier $= M/H = 1.02/0.12 = 8.5$

Bank deposit multiplier $= M/R = 1.02/0.10 = 10.2$

so the values of both the money multiplier and bank deposit multiplier are considerably smaller. If the government wishes to maintain the previous level of broad money M, it will need to inject considerably more narrow money than previously.

For now, it is important to remember that a fall in either the banks' desired cash reserve ratio or the private sector's desired ratio of cash to bank deposits raises the money multiplier (and the bank deposit multiplier). For a given monetary base, the money supply rises.

What determines the cash reserve ratio desired by banks? The higher the interest rate spread, the more banks wish to lend and the more they risk a low ratio of cash reserves to deposits. Conversely, the more unpredictable are withdrawals from deposits, or the fewer lending opportunities banks have in very liquid loans, the higher cash reserves they have to maintain for any level of deposits.

The public's desired ratio of cash to deposits partly reflects institutional factors, for example whether firms pay wages by cheque or by cash. It also depends on the incentive to hold cash to make untraceable payments to evade taxes. And credit cards reduce the use of cash. Credit cards are a temporary means of payment; that is, a *money substitute* not money itself. A signed credit card slip cannot be used for *further* purchases. Soon, you have to settle your account using money. Nevertheless, since credit cards allow people to carry less cash in their pocket, their increasing use reduces the desired ratio of cash to bank deposits.

Figure 18.1 summarizes the traditional account of the **monetary base** and the money supply. The monetary base, or stock of high-powered money, is held either as cash reserves by the banks or as cash in circulation. Since bank deposits are a multiple of banks' cash reserves, the money multiplier exceeds unity. The money multiplier is larger (a) the lower the non-bank public's desired ratio of cash to bank deposits, giving the banks more cash with which to create a multiplied deposit expansion, and (b) the lower is the banks' desired ratio of cash to deposits, leading them to create more deposits for any given cash reserves.

The monetary base, or narrow money, is the quantity of notes and coins in private circulation plus the quantity of reserves held by commercial banks.

How does the central bank change the level of the monetary base? It is the monopoly supplier of cash, but it does not get it into circulation by dropping it from a helicopter. Rather, it buys financial assets in exchange for cash that it has itself created, or it sells financial assets in exchange for cash which it then retires from use. We discuss this process more fully in the next chapter.

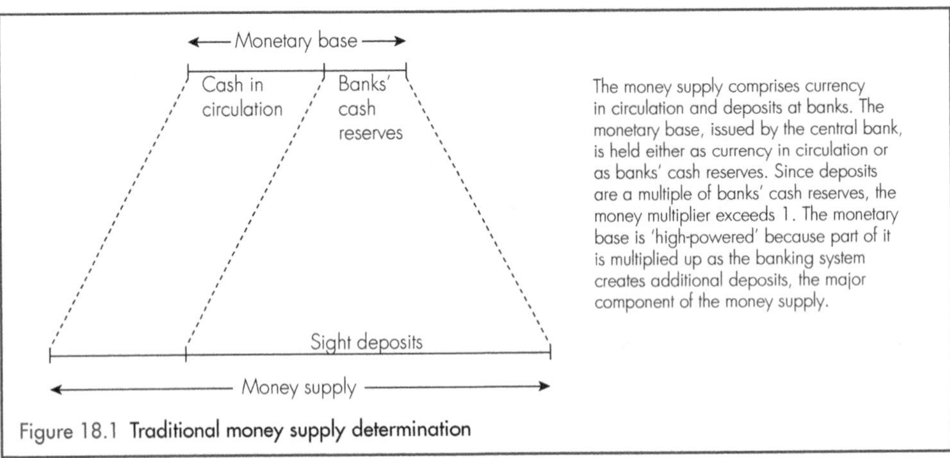

Figure 18.1 **Traditional money supply determination**

CONCEPT 18.2

THE COLLAPSE OF BANK LENDING

The bank deposit multiplier

The money multiplier is $M/(R + C_p)$, the broad money supply M divided by banks' reserves R and cash held by the public C_p. Prior to the financial crisis, it had a value of around 26. The bank deposit multiplier M/R is several times larger, since the denominator is smaller. The figure shows that, just before the crisis, the bank deposit multiplier was around 90. Banks had £90 of deposits for every £1 in reserves.

However, the more bank lending dried up during the credit crunch, the smaller the bank deposit multiplier became. For any given level of reserves, **broad money** was much smaller. The figure shows that the bank deposit multiplier fell from 90 to around 14 in 2010 and to below 10 by 2012.

Broad money includes all assets fulfilling the functions of money, and is principally bank deposits.

This has two implications. First, the theory of monetary control, which we discuss in Chapter 19, cannot assume that financial multipliers are stable over time: they are very sensitive to the level of confidence in banks and the extent of risk-taking they feel able to undertake.

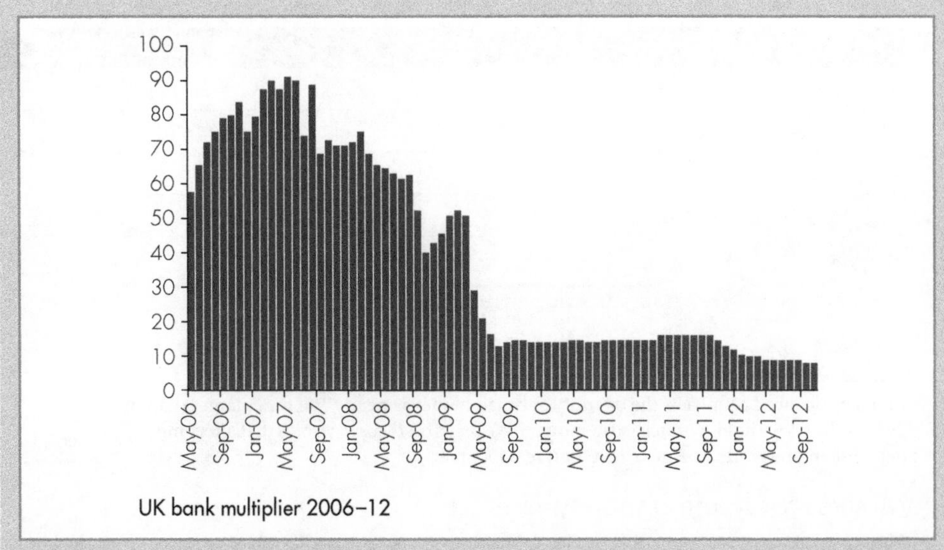

UK bank multiplier 2006–12

Second, without some additional change in behaviour by the Bank of England, the collapse of the bank deposit multiplier threatened to lead to a corresponding collapse of broad money. The attempt to prevent this, known as quantitative easing, is discussed in Chapter 19.

Measures of money

Money is the medium of exchange available to make transactions. Hence, the money supply is cash in circulation outside banks, plus bank deposits. It sounds simple, but is not. Two issues arise: which bank deposits, and why only bank deposits?

We can think of a spectrum of liquidity. Cash, by definition, is completely liquid. Sight deposits (chequing accounts) are almost as liquid. Time deposits (savings accounts) used to be less liquid, but now many banks offer automatic transfer between savings and chequing accounts when the latter run low. Savings deposits are almost as liquid as chequing accounts.

UK statistics distinguish between *retail* and *wholesale* deposits. Retail deposits are made in high-street branches at the advertised rate of interest. Wholesale deposits, big one-off deals between a corporate depositor and a bank at a negotiated interest rate, are also quite liquid.

Everyone used to be clear about what a bank was, and hence whose deposits counted towards the money supply. Financial deregulation blurred this distinction in the UK and the US, and is now doing so in continental Europe. Before 1980, UK banks did not lend for house purchase, and cheques on building society deposits could not be used at the supermarket checkout. Now 'banks' compete vigorously for mortgages, supermarket chains are in the banking business and building society cheques are widely accepted as a means of payment. There is no longer a reason to exclude building society deposits from measures of the money supply. Since January 2010, UK monetary statistics do not even distinguish between banks and building societies.

Table 18.2 shows the components of broad money in the UK in 2009. Notes and coins in circulation outside the Bank of England are the most liquid form of the medium of exchange. To this we add retail deposits in banks and building societies. Next, we add wholesale deposits. The sum of all these is M4, the most commonly used measure of broad money.

Table 18.2 Narrow and broad money in the UK, October 2012

	£ billion
cash in circulation (outside central bank)	46
+ retail deposits in banks and building societies	1134
+ wholesale deposits	867
= Money supply M4 (broad money)	2047

Source: Bank of England.

18.5 The demand for money

In most advanced countries, the quantity of broad money is nearly 100 times larger than in 1960. Why do we hold so much extra money? We focus on three variables that affect money demand: interest rates, the price level and real income.

The demand for money is a demand for *real* money balances.

Motives for holding money

Money is a stock. It is the quantity of circulating currency and deposits *held* at any given time. Holding money is not the same as *spending* it. We hold money now to spend it later.

Money is the medium of exchange, for which it must also be a store of value. These two functions of money provide the reasons why people wish to hold it. People can hold their wealth in various forms – money, bills, bonds, equities and property. For simplicity, assume that there are only two assets: money, the medium of exchange that pays no interest, and bonds, which we use to stand for all other interest-bearing assets that are not directly a means of payment. As people earn income, they add to their wealth. As they spend, they deplete their wealth. How should people divide their wealth between money and bonds?

The cost of holding money is the interest given up by holding money rather than bonds.

People **hold money** only if there is a benefit to offset this cost. What is that benefit?

The transactions motive

Transacting by barter is costly in time and effort. Holding money economizes on these costs. If all transactions were perfectly synchronized, we could be paid at the same instant as we did our spending. Except at that instant, we need hold no money at all.

The transactions motive for holding money reflects the fact that payments and receipts are *not* synchronized.

Must we hold money between being paid and making subsequent purchases? We could put our income into interest-earning assets, to be resold later when we need money for purchases. However, every time we buy and sell assets there are brokerage and bank charges. And it takes an eagle eye to keep track of cash flow and judge the precise moment at which money is needed and assets must be sold. If small sums are involved, the extra interest does not compensate for the brokerage fees, and the time and effort. It is easier to hold some money.

How much money we need to hold depends on the value of the transactions we later wish to make and the degree of synchronization of our payments and receipts. Money is a nominal variable not a real variable. How much £100 buys depends on the price of goods. If all prices double, our receipts and our payments double in nominal terms. To transact as before we need to hold twice as much money.

We need a given amount of real money, nominal money deflated by the price level, to make a given quantity of transactions. When the price level doubles, other things equal, the demand for nominal money balances doubles, leaving the demand for real money balances unaltered. People want money because of its purchasing power in terms of the goods it will buy.

Real GNP is a good proxy for the total real value of transactions. Thus we assume that the transactions motive for holding real money balances rises with real income.

The transactions motive for holding money also depends on the synchronization of payments and receipts. Suppose, instead of shopping throughout the week, households shop only on the day they get paid. Over the week, national income and total transactions are unaltered, but people now *hold* less money over the week.[5]

A nation's habits for making payments usually change only slowly. In our simplified model we assume that the degree of synchronization is constant over time. Thus we focus on real income as *the* measure of the transactions motive for holding *real* money balances.

Of course, the degree of synchronization is not literally constant over time. For example, compared with having to queue up in a bank to withdraw cash from one's account, the introduction of ATMs (cash machines) made it easier to get cash, even when banks were closed. People therefore held less cash on average in their pocket because they could easily get more. Conversely, bank accounts were even more useful than previously.

The precautionary motive

We live in an uncertain world. Uncertainty about the timing of receipts and payments creates a precautionary motive for holding money.

Suppose you buy a lot of interest-earning bonds and get by with a small amount of money. Walking down the street you see a great bargain in a shop window, but have too little money to close the deal. By the time you cash in some bonds, the bargain is gone, snapped up by someone with ready money.

How can we measure the benefits from holding money for precautionary reasons? The payoff grows with the volume of transactions we undertake and with the degree of uncertainty. If uncertainty is roughly constant over time, the level of transactions determines the benefit of real money held for precautionary reasons. As with the transactions motive, we use real GNP to proxy the level of transactions. Thus, other things equal, the higher is real income, the stronger is the **precautionary motive** for holding money.

In an uncertain world, there is a precautionary motive to hold money. In advance, we decide to hold money to meet contingencies that we cannot yet foresee.

The transactions and precautionary motives are the main reasons to hold the medium of exchange, and are most relevant to the benefits from holding a narrow measure of money. The wider measure, M4, includes higher-interest-earning deposits. The wider the definition of money, the less important are the transactions and precautionary motives that relate to money as a medium of exchange, and the more we must take account of money as a store of value.

The asset motive

Forget the need to transact. Think of someone deciding in which assets to hold wealth. At some distant date, wealth may be spent. In the short run, the aim is a good but safe rate of return.

Some assets, such as company shares, on average pay a high return but are risky. Some years their return is *very* high, in other years it is negative. When share prices fall, shareholders make a capital loss that swamps the dividends they receive. Other assets are less risky, but their average rate of return is correspondingly lower.

The asset motive for holding money reflects dislike of risk. People sacrifice a high average rate of return to obtain a portfolio with a lower but safer return.

How should people divide their portfolios between safe and risky assets? You might like to reread Chapter 13. Since people dislike risk, they will not put all their eggs in one basket. As well as holding some risky assets, they will keep some of their wealth in safe assets.

The **asset motive** for holding money is important when we consider why people hold broad measures of money such as M4.

The demand for money: prices, real income and interest rates

The transactions, precautionary and asset motives suggest that there are benefits to holding money. But there is also a cost, the interest forgone by not holding high-interest-earning assets instead. People hold money up

5 By allowing us to pay all at once when the statement arrives monthly, credit cards have this effect.

to the point at which the marginal benefit of holding another pound just equals its marginal cost. Figure 18.2 illustrates how much money people want to hold.

People want money for its purchasing power over goods. The horizontal axis plots real money holdings; that is, nominal money in current pounds divided by the average price of goods and services. The horizontal line *MC* is the marginal cost of holding money; that is, the interest forgone by not holding bonds. *MC* shifts up if interest rates rise.

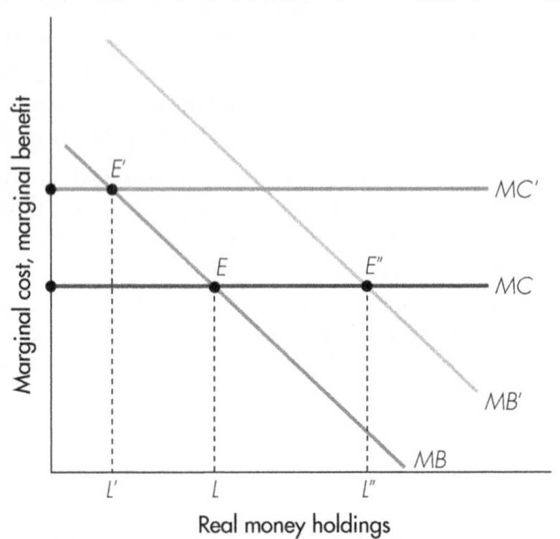

The horizontal axis shows the purchasing power of money in terms of goods. The *MC* schedule shows the interest sacrificed by putting the last pound into money rather than bonds. The *MB* schedule is drawn for a given real income and shows the marginal benefits of the last pound of money. The marginal benefit falls as money holdings increase. The desired point is *E*, at which marginal cost and marginal benefit are equal. An increase in interest rates, a rise in the opportunity cost schedule from *MC* to *MC*′, reduces desired money holdings from *L* to *L*′. An increase in real income increases the marginal benefit of adding to real balances. The *MB* schedule shifts up to *MB*′. Facing the schedule *MC*, a shift from *MB* to *MB*′ increases real money holdings to *L*″.

Figure 18.2 **Desired money holdings**

The *MB* schedule is the marginal benefit of holding money. We draw *MB* for a given real GDP measuring the transactions undertaken. For this level of transactions, it is possible but difficult to get by with low real money holdings. We have to watch purchases and receipts and be quick to invest money as it comes in and ready to sell off bonds just before we make a purchase. Nor do we have much precautionary money. We may be frustrated or inconvenienced if, unexpectedly, we want to make a purchase or settle a debt.

With low real money holdings, the marginal benefit of another pound is high. We can put less effort into timing our transfers between money and bonds, and have more money for unforeseen contingencies. For a given real income and level of transactions, the marginal benefit of the last pound of money holdings declines as we hold more real money. With more real money, we have plenty both for precautionary purposes and for transaction purposes. Life is easier. The marginal benefit of yet more money holding is low.

Given our real income and transactions, desired money holdings are at *E* in Figure 18.2. For any level of real money below *L*, the marginal benefit of another pound exceeds its marginal cost in interest forgone. We should hold more money. Above *L*, the marginal cost exceeds the marginal benefit and we should hold less. The optimal level of money holding is *L*.

To emphasize the effect of prices, real income and interest rates on the quantity of money demanded, we now change each of these variables in turn. If all prices of goods and services double but interest rates and real income are unaltered, neither *MC* nor *MB* shifts. The desired point remains *E* and the desired level of *real* money remains *L*. Since prices have doubled, people hold twice as much nominal money to preserve their real money balances at *L*.

If interest rates on bonds rise, the cost of holding money rises. Figure 18.2 shows this upward shift from *MC* to *MC*′. The desired point is now *E*′ and the desired real money holding falls from *L* to *L*′. Higher interest rates reduce the quantity of real money demanded.[6]

6 The cost of holding money is the differential return between bonds and money. If π is the inflation rate and r the nominal interest rate, the real interest rate is $r - \pi$. In financial terms, the real return on money is $-\pi$, the rate at which the purchasing power of money is eroded by inflation. The differential real return between bonds and money is $(r - \pi) - (-\pi) = r$. The *nominal* interest rate is the opportunity cost of holding money.

Finally, consider a rise in real income. At each level of real money holdings, the marginal benefit of the last pound is higher than before. With more transactions to undertake and a greater need for precautionary balances, a given quantity of real money does not make life as easy as it did when transactions and real income were lower. The benefit of a bit more money is now greater. Hence, when real income rises, in Figure 18.2 we can show this as an upward shift in marginal benefit from *MB* to *MB'*.

At the original interest rate and *MC* schedule, the desired level of money balances is L_0. Thus a rise in real income raises the quantity of real money balances demanded. Table 18.3 summarizes our discussion of the demand for money as a medium of exchange.

Table 18.3 The demand for money

	Effect of rise in		
Quantity demanded	Price level	Real income	Interest rate
Nominal money	Rises in proportion	Rises	Falls
Real money	Unaffected	Rises	Falls

So far we have studied the demand for cash, the narrowest measure of money. Wider definitions of money must also recognize the asset motive for holding money. To explain the demand for M4, we interpret *MC* as the average extra return by putting the last pound into risky assets rather than time deposits, which are safe but yield a lower return. For a given wealth, *MB* is the marginal benefit of time deposits in reducing the risk of the portfolio. If no wealth is invested in time deposits, the portfolio is very risky. A bad year is a disaster. There is a big benefit in having some time deposits. As the quantity of time deposits increases, the danger of a disaster recedes and the marginal benefit of more time deposits falls.

A rise in the average interest differential between risky assets and time deposits shifts the cost of holding broad money from *MC* to *MC'*, reducing the quantity of broad money demanded. Higher wealth shifts the marginal benefit from *MB* to *MB'*. More time deposits are demanded.

Explaining the rise in UK money holdings from 1965 to 2012

Why were nominal money holdings 90 times higher in 2012 than in 1965? We have identified three explanations: prices, real income and nominal interest rates. Table 18.4 shows how these variables changed over the period.

Table 18.4 Holdings of M4, 1965–2012

	1965	2012
Index of:		
Nominal M4	100	9494
Real M4	100	720
Real GDP	100	290
Interest rate (%)	6	1

Sources: Bank of England; OECD.

Although nominal money holdings rose 95-fold, the price level also rose a lot between 1965 and 2012. Table 18.4 shows real money rising more than seven-fold over the period. Real GDP was almost three times its initial level. Higher real output and income raised the quantity of real money demanded. Nominal interest rates fell substantially, which also added to the demand for money.

To sum up, most of the increase in desired holdings of nominal money was merely because prices were higher: it took more nominal money merely to maintain the purchasing power of money holdings. Real economic growth caused an increase in real GDP and in real income: this led to a significant increase in the demand for real money, but cannot explain the whole of that increase. The remaining part is explained by a lower opportunity cost of holding money: as interest rates fell, it was no longer so expensive to allocate wealth to money rather than to other interest-bearing assets.

18.6 Financial crises

Everybody knows what the banks are doing. Usually, people do not mind. But if people believe that a bank has lent too much and will be unable to meet depositors' claims, there will be a *run* on the bank – a **financial panic**. If the bank cannot repay all depositors, you try to get your money out first while the bank can still pay. Since everyone does the same thing, they ensure that the bank is unable to pay. Some of its loans will be too illiquid to get back in time.

A financial panic is a self-fulfilling prophecy. Believing a bank will be unable to pay, people rush to get their money out. But this makes the bank go bankrupt.

Notice that there are two kinds of financial crisis. First, a bank may have made loans that turn out to be worthless. They are no longer valuable assets of the bank. Liabilities now exceed assets and the bank is insolvent. Unless rapidly bailed out by injections of new assets by shareholders or the government, the bank will be declared bankrupt and it will be closed down. In such circumstances, depositors are simply being smart in trying to get their money out before this happens.

However, there may also be self-fulfilling panics even when the bank's assets are fine and the bank is not insolvent. If a depositor believes that other depositors will panic and withdraw money, it makes no sense to be last in the queue – the bank may have trouble selling enough liquid assets quickly enough to meet all the withdrawals, and it may be forced into difficulty by the panic itself.

We call this second case a **crisis of liquidity**, whereas the first case is a true crisis of insolvency. The problem for policy makers is to diagnose which is taking place. If the bank is fundamentally sound, lending it some cash or other liquid assets will allow the panic to subside and confidence to be restored. On the other hand, if the bank is truly insolvent, temporary loans will not help it. Its assets are less than its liabilities and more drastic action is required – donate enough government funds to make it solvent again, force shareholders to do the same or close the bank.

In a liquidity crisis, an institution is temporarily unable to meet immediate requests for payment even though its underlying assets exceed its liabilities.

When the financial crisis first erupted in the UK in 2008, with a panic by depositors of Northern Rock and long queues of people shown on the news, this was initially interpreted as a liquidity crisis that some temporary assistance, or government promises to guarantee depositors' money, could reverse. It soon became apparent that the Rock was in much deeper trouble than that. Its entire solvency was at stake.

Whether it is a liquidity or a **solvency crisis** determines which arm of government might potentially be involved in a solution. The Bank of England can make emergency loans if it expects them to be repaid in full, for there are then no long-term issues for taxpayers. Fixing insolvency, on the other hand, requires permanent injections of taxpayers' money, for which the authority of the Treasury (and ultimately the prime minister) is required. Since crises move quickly once they have begun, co-ordination of the fiscal and monetary authorities is vital if crisis resolution is to be effective.

In a solvency crisis, an institution's assets have become less than its liabilities. It is bankrupt without a rapid new injection of assets from government or shareholders.

CASE 18.1

THE SUB-PRIME CRISIS AND ITS AFTERMATH

Most countries experienced an explosion in house prices circa 2005–06. Inflation appeared to have been conquered, interest rates were low and borrowing did not look too risky. Many of those working in the financial sector – whether in banks or in property – were getting big bonuses based on the volume of lending not the prudence of these loans. There were strong incentives to dream up new products and find new lines of business.

In the US, one of these new products was the sub-prime mortgage, a housing loan to a low-income high-risk person who had previously been unable to borrow in order to buy a house. Most of these mortgages were at variable interest rates: although initially low and 'affordable', they were subsequently raised if either general market interest rates rose or if lots of people started to default and it became necessary to build a larger risk premium into the interest rate. It is unclear how much of this was explained to the low-income people being signed up for first-time mortgages.

US house prices peaked in 2006. As they then fell, lenders got scared and began to raise mortgage interest rates, driving many of the poor to default. Suddenly, these sub-prime mortgages were worth a lot less than had been thought. And the crisis fed upon itself. The more scared people became, the more asset prices fell, validating the initial fears.

If mortgages had simply been issued by a few institutions specializing in loans for house purchase, the damage might have been quarantined. The US government would have had to decide whether to (a) let these particular institutions go bust or (b) inject taxpayers' money to prop them up.

Securitization transformed a local crisis into a global problem. Smart financiers, driven by the prospect of new business and big personal bonuses, had grouped lots of individual sub-prime mortgages into large bundles and sold them on to new buyers in London, Frankfurt and Mumbai. The market was convinced that this trick was a bit like insurance – one poor sub-prime household might go bust, but they would not all go bust together. Holding a large bundle made them safer, just as an insurance company pools the risk of individual burglary by having a large number of clients. This was the alchemy of risk reduction, a recipe for immediate profits and bonuses.

Two things went wrong. First, buyers of securitized mortgages had miscalculated. Unsurprisingly, all sub-prime borrowers got into trouble at the same time, as a result of a fall in house prices, a fall in confidence and a rise in risk perception. Supposedly smart bankers in London, New York and other financial capitals had mispriced the risk: the securitized bundles were riskier than had been thought.

The figure shows US house prices, inflation-adjusted, since 1890. The extent of the house price bubble was unprecedented by 2006, as was the severity of the subsequent crash – it was not until 2012 that US house prices began to turn upwards again.

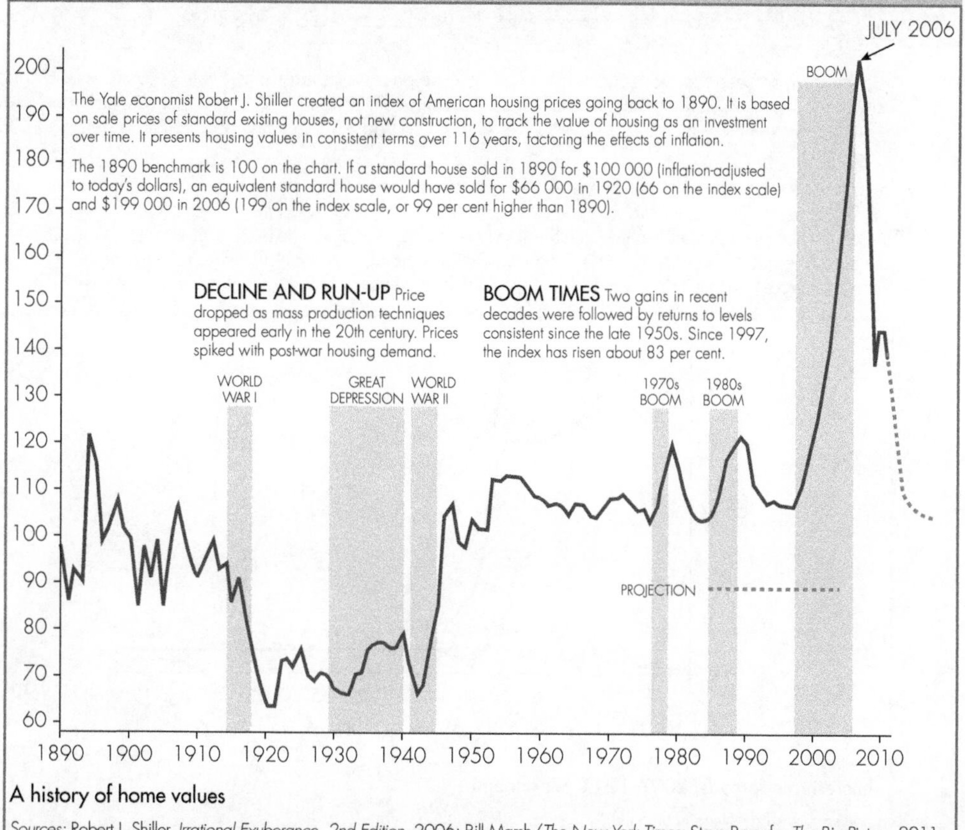

A history of home values

Sources: Robert J. Shiller, *Irrational Exuberance, 2nd Edition*, 2006; Bill Marsh/*The New York Times*; Steve Barry for *The Big Picture*, 2011.

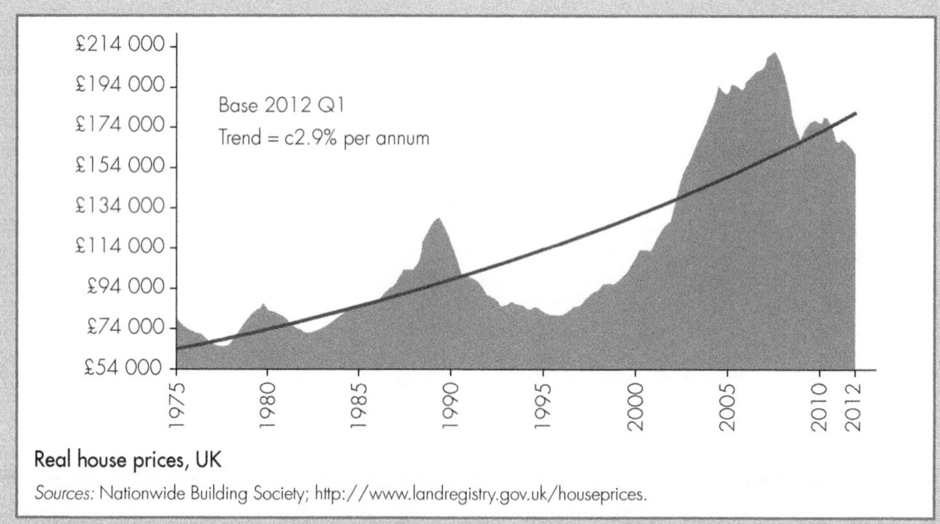

Real house prices, UK

Sources: Nationwide Building Society; http://www.landregistry.gov.uk/houseprices.

The figure above shows real house prices in the UK, which collapsed a couple of years later, in 2008. Again there was a severe correction, though less acute than in the US.

Second, the perfect storm did indeed arise. As US house prices fell sharply, the chain of events was triggered. Banks found their assets worth much less than they had thought. Worse, the boards of the banks had not even realized the extent to which their bonus-hungry employees had exposed them to such large risks.

As the solvency of banks came into question, people became reluctant to lend to banks, and banks themselves became reluctant to lend to anyone else – aware of the potentially fatal hole in their balance sheet, banks prioritized using resources to rebuild their own reserves. The entire, apparently well-oiled, system of liquidity dried up as banks disappeared from the lending business. One way to see how dramatic this was is to examine interest rate spreads; that is, the difference between the interest rate banks were charging for the few scarce loans they were prepared to make and the interest rate at which banks could borrow from the Bank of England.

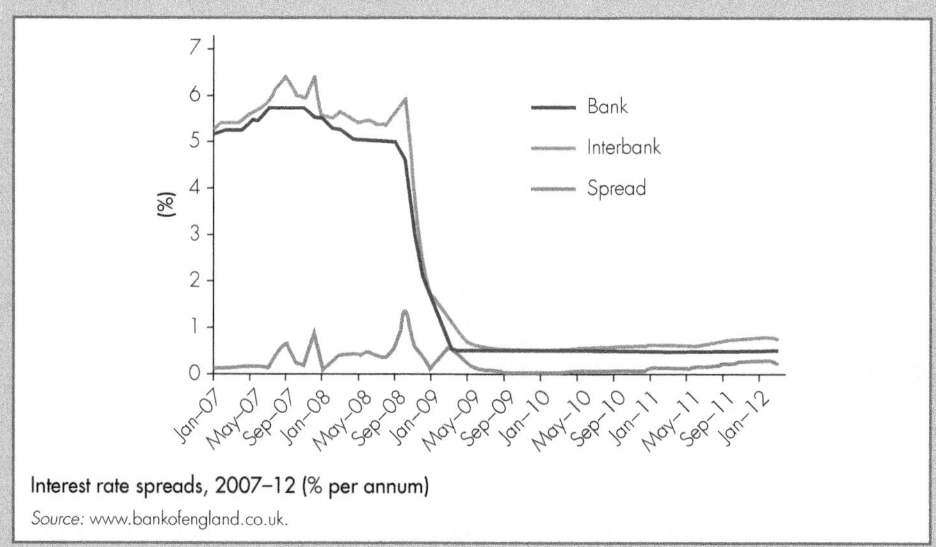

Interest rate spreads, 2007–12 (% per annum)

Source: www.bankofengland.co.uk.

The interest rate spreads figure plots in purple the official bank rate, the interest rate at which commercial banks can borrow from the Bank of England; and in green plots the interbank rate at which banks lend temporary excess funds to one another. In normal times, competition between banks means that the 'profit margin' between the lending rate and the borrowing rate is very small. Banks charging too much are quickly outcompeted by banks prepared to offer a better deal. This spread between the interbank rate at which banks lend and the bank rate at which they can borrow from the Bank of England is shown in orange.

The interest rate spread is a thermometer with which to monitor the health of the banking system. In a healthy system, banks feel confident, competition prevails and spreads are very small. When a crisis breaks out, spreads shoot up, raising the price to ration loans only to the very safest customers. And the volume of bank lending collapses. The figure above shows spreads rising in 2007 and more sharply in 2008–09. Notice that by September 2009 the crisis was largely over, though new concerns (based on possible defaults within the Eurozone) re-emerged in 2011–12.

The chronology of crisis (through UK spectacles)

2006	US house prices start to fall, the sub-prime crisis begins, interest spreads edge up around the world, bank lending slows down, liquidity begins to evaporate.
2007	UK bank Northern Rock hits a liquidity crisis in September 2007 – not yet because its asset values have fallen (UK house prices are still rising) – but because UK credit markets have dried up and the Rock cannot roll over its short-term loans. Borrowing short term to lend long term for housing loans is always a risky business. Crisis temporarily resolved once Bank of England agree to provide liquidity financing to Northern Rock.
2008	***February*** – with UK house prices now having peaked, the market becomes worried not just about Northern Rock's ability to refinance its loans, but also about the value of its underlying assets. A full-blown insolvency crisis. UK government decides to nationalize the Rock. ***March*** – US investment bank Bear Sterns, a pioneer in securitizing mortgage-backed securities, suffers an insolvency crisis. Competitor JPMorgan Chase buys Bear Sterns cheaply. Getting competitors to take over failing banks is often a good way out, since no bankruptcy or severe dislocation ensues. ***September*** – US Treasury has to bail out Freddie Mac and Fannie Mae, the two largest mortgage lenders in the US. – US investment bank giant Lehman Brothers is allowed to go bankrupt without US Treasury managing to arrange a satisfactory bail out, arguably the single event that triggered financial panic around the world, from which no country was immune. ***October*** – Royal Bank of Scotland, which had overextended itself buying Dutch bank ABM AMRO at too high a price after a bidding war with Barclays, faces a solvency crisis, temporarily resolved by UK Treasury taking a 58 per cent stake in RBS.
2009	***January*** – UK government persuades Lloyds bank to buy the potentially insolvent Halifax Bank of Scotland group. Lloyds' shareholders subsequently discover HBOS worth much less than they paid for it. The outcome is good for the system but bad for Lloyds. UK taxpayer raises stake in RBS to 84 per cent to prevent its bankruptcy. Governments around the world gradually admit to the scale of government injections to bail out their banks. Since taxes are not raised to pay for this, the initial consequence is a huge jump in levels of government deficits and government debt.
2010	How much of their 'forced' stakes in private banks will governments eventually recover? If the assets are permanently bad, government funding has restored solvency but cannot be withdrawn. However, if there was an element of liquidity crisis, or if asset prices fell too much in the panic, asset values may recover enough to allow substantial repayments by banks (or privatization of those that were nationalized). In the extreme case, governments may even eventually make some profits.

	Bank behaviour is becoming more cautious – they are reluctant to lend to anyone who is not guaranteed to repay, and they are charging customers high interest rates to make profits to rebuild their own balance sheets. Governments are discussing changes in the regulation of banks to ensure greater control and less risk taking.
2011	Having split Northern Rock into a 'good bank' and a 'bad bank', UK government agrees sale of good bank, and its associated high street branches, to Virgin Money. Still unable to sell RBS. A commission chaired by Sir John Vickers, Oxford economics professor and former chief economist of the Bank of England, recommends tackling the problem of banks being 'too big to fail' and hence holding the government hostage in a crisis. The report stopped short of recommending that 'boring retail banking' and 'casino investment banking' be undertaken in separate companies, entailing the splitting-up of existing banks, but did propose that retail banking and investment banking be separately ring-fenced within the company, and any implicit government guarantee being extended only to the retail banking part intrinsic to protection of the payments system. Private creditors of Greece are strong-armed into 'volunteering' to take a substantial writedown of the value of their loans. Mario Draghi, new governor of the European Central Bank, provides massive medium-term loans to European banks, preventing a lack of liquidity leading to another major crisis. This buys time and is hailed a success. However, European governments continue to dither in providing a fundamental solution to the solvency problems of banks/governments, the two having become inseparable.
2012	The Eurozone crisis rumbles on, all European banks discovering they have more exposure than they thought to a default by governments of peripheral Eurozone countries such as Greece. Even banks with little direct lending to the Greek or Spanish government find they have lent to French or other country banks that in turn have lent extensively to peripheral countries. In July, Mario Draghi promised to do 'whatever it takes' to solve the crisis, and European stock markets boom. UK government agrees in principle to adopt the reforms in the Vickers report and implement them 'by 2019'. Critics argue implementation should be rapid in case there is another crisis; bankers argue that London will be disadvantaged if sweeping restrictions are quickly imposed.

Summary

- **Money** has four functions: a **medium of exchange** or means of payment, a **store of value**, a **unit of account** and a **standard of deferred payment**. Its use as a medium of exchange distinguishes money from other assets.
- In a **barter economy**, trading is costly because there must be a double coincidence of wants. Using a medium of exchange reduces the cost of matching buyers and sellers, letting society devote scarce resources to other things. A **token money** has a higher value as a medium of exchange than in any other use. Because its monetary value greatly exceeds its production cost, token money economizes a lot on the resources needed for transacting.
- Token money is accepted either because people believe it can subsequently be used to make payments or because the government makes it legal tender. The government controls the supply of token money.
- **Banks create money** by making loans and creating deposits that are not fully backed by cash reserves. These deposits add to the medium of exchange. Deciding how many reserves to hold involves a trade-off between interest earnings and the danger of insolvency.

- Modern banks attract deposits by acting as **financial intermediaries**. A national system of clearing cheques, a convenient form of payment, attracts funds into sight deposits. Interest-bearing time deposits attract further funds. In turn, banks lend out money as short-term liquid loans, as longer-term less liquid advances or by purchasing securities.
- Sophisticated financial markets for short-term liquid lending allow modern banks to operate with very low cash reserves relative to deposits. The **money supply** is currency in circulation plus deposits. Most is the latter.
- The **monetary base M0** is currency in circulation plus banks' cash reserves. The **money multiplier**, the ratio of the money supply to the monetary base, is big. The money multiplier is larger (a) the smaller is the desired cash ratio of the banks and (b) the smaller is the private sector's desired ratio of cash in circulation to deposits.
- **Financial deregulation** has allowed building societies into the banking business. **M4** is a broad measure of money and includes deposits at both banks and building societies.
- The **demand for money** is a demand for real money, for its subsequent purchasing power over goods. The demand for **narrow money** balances the transactions and precautionary benefits of holding another pound with the interest sacrificed by not holding interest-bearing assets instead. The quantity of real money demanded falls as the interest rate rises. Higher real income raises real money demand at each interest rate.
- For **wide money** such as M4, the asset motive for holding money also matters. When other interest-bearing assets are risky, people diversify by holding some safe money. With no immediate need to transact, this leads to an asset demand for holding interest-bearing bank deposits. This demand is larger, the larger the total wealth to be invested and the lower the interest differential between deposits and risky assets.

Review questions

1 (a) A person trades in a car when buying another. Is the used car a medium of exchange? Is this a barter transaction? (b) Could you tell by watching someone buying mints (white discs) with coins (bronze discs) which one is money?

2 **Common fallacies** Why are these statements wrong? (a) Since their liabilities equal their assets, banks cannot create anything. (b) The money supply has risen because of tax evasion. Since cash is untraceable, people are putting less in the banks.

3 Saying that banks have become too big to fail means: (a) large banks are safer, (b) large banks are less safe, (c) managers of large banks realize they can take risks because politicians will have to bail them out if things go wrong?

4 Suppose sight deposits = £30, time deposits = £60, banks' cash reserves = £2, currency in circulation = £12, building society deposits = £20. Calculate M0 and M4.

5 Which of these is the correct answer? After the financial crash, bank lending to the private sector slumped because (a) new regulations were introduced, (b) banks were broken up to prevent another crisis, (c) banks thought prospective borrowers were too risky, (d) the value of bank reserves had fallen, (e) only answers a and d, (f) only answers c and d.

MEDIUM

6 Initially gold coins were used as money but people could melt them down and use the gold for industrial purposes. (a) What must have been the relative value of gold in these two uses? (b) Explain the circumstances in which gold could become a token money. (c) Explain the circumstances in which gold could disappear from monetary circulation completely.

7 Suppose banks raise interest rates on time deposits whenever interest rates on bank loans and other assets rise. Does a rise in the general level of interest rates have a big or small effect on the demand for time deposits?

8 How do commercial banks create money?

9 Suppose banks initially wish to hold reserves R equal to 1 per cent of the deposits D that they provide, and that the general public wishes to hold cash C equal to 2 per cent of the deposits that they hold. The monetary base $H = C + R$, and broad money is cash with the public plus bank reserves. What is the value of the money multiplier?

MEDIUM

10 Since credit cards can be used to make payments, why are they not treated as money?

11 Would it make sense to include (a) travellers' cheques, (b) student rail cards or (c) credit cards in measures of the money supply?

12 **Essay question** Lots of institutions accept deposits and reissue them on demand – building societies, Christmas savings clubs and theatre cloakrooms. What is the key feature of banks that distinguishes them from other institutions? Why does this matter?

13 The following diagram shows the downward-sloping demand curve for broad money. (a) Suppose the supply curve is vertical. Show the money market equilibrium. (b) Depict the effect of the financial crash of 2008 on supply of and demand for broad money. (c) Why did monetary policy create substantial quantities of narrow money in these circumstances?

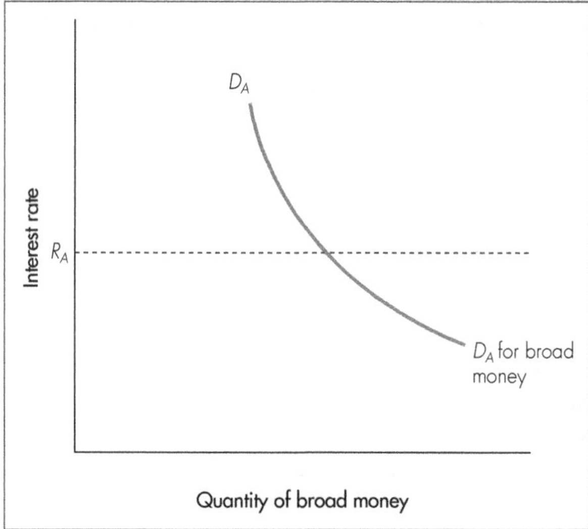

HARD

14 In the diagram in Question 13, what would be the consequence of a sharp increase in confidence about the health of the financial sector? How would monetary policy be likely to respond?

For solutions to these questions, contact your lecturer.

CHAPTER 19

Interest rates and monetary transmission

Learning Outcomes

By the end of this chapter, you should be able to:

1. realise how a central bank can affect the money supply
2. understand quantitative easing
3. describe the central bank's role in financial regulation
4. describe money market equilibrium
5. recognise an intermediate target for monetary policy
6. understand the transmission mechanism of monetary policy
7. describe how a central bank sets interest rates
8. understand how interest rates affect consumption and investment demand

Today, every country of any size has a central bank. Originally private firms in business for profit, central banks came under public control as governments placed more emphasis on monetary policy. Founded in 1694, the Bank of England (www.bankofengland.co.uk) was not nationalized until 1947. The Federal Reserve System, the US central bank, was not set up until 1913. Within the Eurozone, individual central banks survive, but the European Central Bank, established by the 1998 Treaty of Amsterdam, is in charge of the single monetary policy.

A central bank is banker to the government and to the banks. It conducts monetary policy.

This chapter examines the role of the **central bank**, and shows how it influences financial markets. The central bank influences the supply of money. Combining this with the demand for money, examined in the previous chapter, we analyse money market equilibrium. The central bank's monopoly on the supply of cash allows it to control equilibrium interest rates. Finally, we discuss how monetary policy decides what interest rates to set.

19.1 The Bank of England

The Bank of England, usually known simply as the Bank, is the UK central bank. It is divided into Issue and Banking Departments. Its balance sheet is shown in Table 19.1.

Banknotes and coins are liabilities of the Bank. Your £1 coin is a debt of the Bank of England. When commercial banks have reserves at the Bank of England, these are owed by the Bank to the commercial banks, the ultimate owners of these reserves. Cash in circulation, banks' reserves held at the Bank of England and other liabilities of the Bank in total came to £414 billion in November 2012.

What were the corresponding assets? To introduce cash into circulation, the Issue Department engages in open market operations to buy financial securities issued by the government, commercial firms or local authorities. One such asset is bonds; another is a reverse repo, which we explain below. In 2012 the largest class of assets of the Bank was in fact 'other assets', which were largely explained by the programme of 'quantitative easing' described in Concept 19.1. Together, these assets came to £414 billion.

Table 19.1 Bank of England, balance sheet, November 2012

Liabilities	£bn	Assets	£bn
Cash in circulation	57	Reverse repos	11
Banks' reserves	282	Bonds bought	14
Other liabilities	75	Other assets	389
Total liabilities	414	Total assets	414

Source: Data taken from Statistical Interactive Database, © Bank of England, http://www.bankofengland.co.uk/boeapps/iadb/ accessed on 18/06/2013.

Table 19.1 resembles the balance sheet of a commercial bank, with one key difference. *A central bank cannot go bankrupt.* You take £50 to the Bank and cash it in for £50. The Bank gives you £50 in cash. It can always create new cash. Hence, it can never run out of money.

A **repo** is a *sale and repurchase agreement*. A bank sells you a bond, simultaneously agreeing to buy it back at a specified price on a particular future date. You have made the bank a short-term loan secured or 'backed' by the long-term bond temporarily in your ownership. Thus repos use the outstanding stock of *long-term* assets as backing for new and secured *short-term* loans.

A repo is the sale of an asset with a simultaneous agreement to repurchase later.

A reverse repo is a purchase with a simultaneous agreement to resell later.

One party's repo is the other party's **reverse repo**. Suppose you get a short-term loan from the bank by initially selling bonds to the bank, plus an agreement for you to repurchase the bonds at a specified date in the near future at a price agreed now. Reverse repos are effectively secured temporary fixed-term loans by the Bank. That is why they appear on the asset side of its balance sheet.

Repos and reverse repos are very like other short-term lending and borrowing. The Bank of England used to alter cash in circulation by buying or selling Treasury bills. Now it follows other central banks in using the repo market to conduct these 'open market operations' in order to alter cash in circulation.

Similarly, Table 19.2 shows the balance sheet of the *Eurosystem*, which comprises the European Central Bank and the 17 central banks of Eurozone member states.

Table 19.2 Eurosystem balance sheet, March 2012

Liabilities	€bn	Assets	€bn
Cash in circulation	871	Gold	423
Banks' reserves	1149	Loan to Eurobanks	1130
Other liabilities	75	Financial securities	632
		Other assets	838
Total liabilities	3023	**Total assets**	3023

Source: Data taken from European Central Bank, 'Consolidated finalcial statement of the Eurosystem as at 2 March 2012', www.ecb.int/press/pr/wfs/2012/html/fs120306.en.html.

19.2 Traditional means of monetary control

The **money supply** (M4) is partly a liability of the Bank (currency in private circulation) and partly a liability of banks (bank deposits). Henceforth, we talk of 'banks' without distinguishing between banks and building societies.

The money supply is currency in circulation *outside* the banking system, plus deposits of commercial banks and building societies.

The central bank can therefore affect broad money M4 either by affecting the cash in circulation or by affecting the number of deposits for any given amount of cash in circulation. We begin with policies that affect the latter.

Reserve requirements

Banks can hold more than the required cash reserves but not less. If their reserves fall below the required amount, they must immediately borrow cash, usually from the central bank, to restore their **required reserve ratio.**

A required reserve ratio is a minimum ratio of cash reserves to deposits that banks are required to hold.

Suppose banks have £1 billion in cash and, for commercial purposes, want cash reserves equal to 5 per cent of deposits. Deposits are 20 times cash reserves. Banks create £20 billion of deposits against their £1 billion cash reserves. However, if there is a reserve requirement of 10 per cent, banks only create £10 billion deposits against cash reserves of £1 billion. The money supply falls from £20 billion to £10 billion.

When the central bank imposes a higher reserve requirement than the reserve ratio that prudent banks would anyway have maintained, the effect is fewer bank deposits and a lower money supply for any amount of cash in circulation. Raising the reserve requirement reduces the money supply.

The discount rate

The discount rate is the interest rate that the Bank charges when banks want to borrow cash.

Suppose banks think the *minimum* safe ratio of cash to deposits is 10 per cent. It does not matter whether this figure is a commercial judgement or a requirement imposed by the Bank. Banks may also hold extra cash. If their cash reserves are 12 per cent of deposits, how far dare they let their cash fall towards the 10 per cent minimum?

Banks balance the interest rate on extra lending against the cost incurred if withdrawals push their cash reserves below the critical 10 per cent. If the central bank lends to banks at market interest rates, there is no penalty incurred from being caught short and having to borrow from the central bank. Banks lend as much as they can and their cash reserves fall to the minimum required.

Suppose the Bank only lends to banks at an interest rate above market interest rates. Now commercial banks will not drive down their reserves to the minimum permitted. They hold extra cash as a cushion, to avoid possibly having to borrow from the central bank at penalty rates.

By setting the discount rate above general interest rates, the Bank can induce banks voluntarily to hold extra cash reserves. Bank deposits are a lower multiple of banks' cash reserves, and the money supply is lower for any given level of cash in circulation. Variations in the discount rate can change the money supply.

Open market operations

Whereas the previous two methods of monetary control alter the amount of deposits created for any given amount of cash in circulation, open market operations alter the amount of cash in circulation. Since this then affects the amount of deposits that banks wish to create, open market operations alter the money supply both directly (via the effect on cash in circulation) and indirectly (via the induced effect on the number of deposits created).

An open market operation occurs when the central bank alters the monetary base by buying or selling financial securities in the open market.

The Bank prints £1 million of new banknotes and buys bonds on the **open market**. There are £1 million fewer bonds in private hands but £1 million more in cash. Some of the extra cash is held in private circulation but most is deposited with the banks, which then expand deposit lending against their higher cash reserves. Conversely, if the Bank sells £1 million of bonds from its existing holdings, the monetary base falls by £1 million. Banks lose cash reserves, have to reduce deposit lending and the money supply falls.

Open market operations are nowadays the principal channel by which the central bank affects the money supply. Having discussed the central bank's role in monetary control, we turn next to its role in financial stability.

19.3 Lender of last resort

Modern fractional reserve banking lets society produce the medium of exchange with tiny inputs of scarce physical resources. But the efficient production of the medium of exchange yields a system of fractional reserve banking vulnerable to financial panics. Since banks have too few reserves to meet a withdrawal of all their deposits, a hint of big withdrawals may become a self-fulfilling prophecy as people scramble to get their money out before the banks go bust.

In Chapter 18 we described how the central bank can create and lend cash to banks to stave off a liquidity crisis. This requires a guarantee that banks can get cash if they really need it. The central bank is the only institution that can manufacture cash in unlimited amounts. The threat of financial panics is greatly diminished if it is known that the central bank will act as **lender of last resort**. As lender of last resort, the Bank can maintain confidence in the banking system, provided the underlying solvency of banks is not threatened. What went wrong during the financial crisis was that some banks acquired assets that turned out to be worthless, and became insolvent. Last resort lending could not save them since it made no difference to their underlying solvency.

The lender of last resort lends to banks when financial panic threatens the financial system.

Prudential regulation

The prospect of insolvency raises two issues: how to respond to a particular insolvency crisis, and how to prevent such a crisis arising in the first place.

Generally, it is the shareholders of the particular bank that bear the cost of its poor performance. To try to make sure that shareholders have sufficient funds for this purpose, financial regulations require banks to meet **capital adequacy ratios**.[1]

A capital adequacy ratio is a required minimum value of bank capital relative to its outstanding loans and investments.

Banks face the liquidity risk that depositors may withdraw money before banks can sell their less liquid assets, and the solvency risk that a downward revaluation of the value of their assets may leave assets worth less than their liabilities. Bank reserves help protect against liquidity risk. Bank capital helps protect against solvency risk. Bank capital is supplied originally by shareholders or represents bank profits ploughed back into the business.

A crisis depletes this capital reserve and thereby reduces the share price of the bank. *Shareholders* suffer, but *depositors* are protected if the bank still has adequate bank reserves to meet the prospect of future withdrawals. Depositors may also have an explicit or implicit guarantee from the government.

If a bank makes larger losses, it may go bankrupt. Losses incurred by rogue trader Nick Leeson brought down Barings Bank in the 1990s. Typically, governments then compensate depositors but not shareholders. Barings was actually sold to Dutch bank ING for a notional amount and deposits were honoured in full. The knowledge that depositors are unlikely to suffer helps prevent unjustified financial panics. The knowledge that shareholders *are* likely to suffer helps keep management on its toes.

Three things went wrong in the perfect storm of 2008/09. First, the magnitude of the initial shock was very large. Greedy banks had borrowed billions to speculate on securitized products whose true risk characteristics they did not properly understand, and which subsequently proved a very bad investment.

Second, capital adequacy regulations had been poorly designed. What was adequate financial backing by shareholders in good times turned out to be grossly inadequate capital reserves in a big crisis. This has led to calls for future capital adequacy requirements to be variable – less onerous when economies are doing well, but increasingly demanding as risks of crises get larger. As the sub-prime crisis got off the ground in 2006, variable capital adequacy requirements would have required banks around the world to retain more profits or ask shareholders for new funds in order to build up capital reserves.

The third lesson is that many banks had become 'too big to fail'. In a capitalist economy, you might have expected insolvent banks to be made bankrupt in the same way as a defunct car company or steel producer. However, as the US discovered when it allowed Lehman Brothers to go bust, if the bank is large enough it causes massive ripples throughout the financial system. Sometimes, the government concludes that injecting taxpayers' money into keeping the bank going is the lesser of two evils, and preferable to letting the bank go under.

This, of course, is what happened in many Western economies in 2008. Nor were governments prepared instantly to raise taxes to pay for this huge spike in their spending on bank bailouts. Instead, they borrowed money and acquired debt; as a result they now owe huge amounts that will take years to pay back.

1 Financial regulation is sometimes the responsibility of the central bank, but sometimes the responsibility of a separate financial regulator. In the UK, responsibility was transferred from the Bank of England to the Financial Services Agency in 1997.

How do we minimize the chances of such an awful dilemma arising in the future? Case 19.1 discusses possible solutions.

CASE 19.1

PREVENTING A FUTURE BANKING CRISIS?

In our discussion of microeconomics in Part Two, we examined two important ideas: moral hazard and imperfect commitment. *Moral hazard* arises when the adoption of a set of rules that would be ideal under perfect information then fosters unwelcome behaviour because it is too costly subsequently to monitor individual behaviour. For example, insurance reduces the cost of bearing risk, which is a good thing. However, fully insured people may no longer bother to act prudently to avoid risk, which is the consequence of moral hazard. It is too costly to verify which individuals had acted prudently and which had not. We generally solve this problem with a compromise: we offer partial but not full insurance so that individuals still have an incentive to act prudently.

Bank of England governor, Mervyn King, has repeatedly drawn attention to the moral hazard problems in bailing out banks. Even if bank bailouts are helpful in preventing a crisis from escalating today, the signal that future bailouts are also likely may increase behaviour that makes future crises more likely. If all bankers know they are going to be bailed out, they might as well take big risks. When these come off, the banks do well and bankers' bonuses are high; when the risks prove disastrous, the government steps in. This is a one-way bet for bankers.

Imperfect commitment is also a problem. Most governments say they will be tough in the future – thereby scaring bankers into more prudent behaviour today – but if bankers can deduce that governments always cave in when it comes to the crunch, tough words today are empty threats that the bankers can ignore.

Either we live with the reality that bailouts are likely, because the financial tsunami caused by allowing Lehman Brothers to go bankrupt can never be repeated, or we have to find a structural solution that prevents such problems recurring in the future.

The first possibility is the separation of *retail banking* – the relatively boring business of taking deposits from the general public and making loans of a traditional nature, a key aspect of which is that these banks are banned from speculating with their own capital – and *investment banking*, in which banks may gamble extensively with their own funds in derivatives and other volatile and fancy products. This distinction is sometimes called that between *narrow* banks and *broad* banks.

We have seen all this before. In response to the Wall Street crash of 1929, after a previous episode of banking irresponsibility, the US passed the Glass–Steagall Act, which prevented retail banks undertaking risky investment banking activities. The intention was to ensure that neither the real economy nor government finances would again be endangered by casino banking. If investment banks got into trouble, they could be allowed to fail and repercussions for the rest of us would be much smaller. In turn, this made it more credible that they would indeed be allowed to fail if necessary.

For 70 years this approach was largely a success. Yet as the financial sector became increasingly competitive internationally, institutions facing legal restrictions on their behaviour pressed to be allowed to join the lucrative investment banking business which had prospered during decades of stability and growth. The UK began liberalizing its financial sector in 1986, the so-called Big Bang that paved the way for building societies to behave like banks, and for banks to behave like investment banks. Gradually, other European countries were also forced to liberalize in order to get a share of the lucrative investment banking business. The US repealed the Glass–Steagall Act in 1999.

The first solution affects the permitted structure of banks; a second possible solution limits the types of activity that deposit-taking retail banks can undertake. In 2010 the US adopted the Volcker Rule, prohibiting retail deposit banks from speculating with their own capital. In the UK, the Vickers Commission recommended in 2011 not a complete separation into retail and investment banks but a clear separation of these activities within each bank. Retail activities could still rely on government support in a crisis. Investment activities would be the responsibility of the bank's shareholders and allowed to fail if necessary. The UK has committed to implement this proposal by 2019, leaving a long intervening period in which its banks will still be considered vulnerable.

A third solution is to let all banks undertake all types of transaction, but to place an absolute limit on the size of banks eligible for deposit guarantees and fiscal bailouts. If the problem is that some banks became 'too big to fail' – governments then being forced to rescue them – the solution is to keep banks sufficiently small that it is credible that their failure would not trigger automatic bailout by government.

> It is impossible for regulators to prevent business failure, and undesirable to pursue that objective. The essential dynamic of the market economy is that good businesses succeed and bad ones do not. There is a sense in which the bankruptcy of Lehman was a triumph of capitalism, not a failure. It was badly run, it employed greedy and overpaid individuals, and the services it provided were of marginal social value at best. It took risks that did not come off and went bust. That is how the market economy works.
>
> The problem now is how to have greater stability while extricating ourselves from the 'too big to fail' commitment, and taking a realistic view of the limits of regulation. 'Too big to fail' exposes taxpayers to unlimited, uncontrolled liabilities. The moral hazard problem is not just that risk-taking within institutions that are too big to fail is encouraged but that private risk-monitoring of those institutions is discouraged.
>
> John Kay, 'Too big to fail is too dumb an idea to keep', *Financial Times*, 27 October 2009.

A fourth possibility is to rely on stronger prudential supervision by regulatory agencies, particularly by enforcing tougher capital adequacy ratios. If banks have larger reserves, failure of private banks is less likely. Banks are forced to set aside large reserves that earn little return but are available as shareholder capital with which to meet future crises.

One problem is the need to co-ordinate regulation across different regulators. When RBS took excessive risks, should this have been a concern for the Financial Services Authority (the UK body charged with supervising financial institutions), the Bank of England (the potential lender of last resort in a liquidity crisis) or the Treasury (the government department potentially responsible for injecting taxpayers' money in a solvency crisis)?

This problem is particularly acute within the Eurozone. When a bank operates across many countries, whose taxpayers pay if the bank fails? This dilemma has led to demands for a *banking union* within the Eurozone, common regulations and clear criteria about what happens in the event of failure. As is so often the case, the economics is easier than the politics. Politicians find it hard to convince national voters to 'give up' national sovereignty, even if pooling sovereignty might lead to a much more effective outcome.

Thus, it may be easier to obtain a one-off agreement for a long-term structural solution, as in Glass–Seagall, than to co-ordinate different agencies on a daily basis to evaluate ongoing performance.

Moreover, much of this risky financial business is globally footloose. If some financial centres regulate more than others, private business may tend to migrate to the least-intrusive location. Competition *between* financial centres was and remains part of the problem. London might have regulated earlier if it had been less frightened of losing business to Frankfurt and New York. This suggests that any reforms that will make an enduring difference may have to be negotiated at the level of the top ten global countries, not merely a country at a time.

Basel III Accord

The third Basel Accord is a global, voluntary, regulatory standard on bank capital adequacy, stress testing and market liquidity risk. During 2014–19, tougher capital requirements for banks will gradually be phased in. During 2013–17, measures of risk will be tracked for individual banks, and passing these tests will become mandatory by 2018. During 2015–18, minimum liquidity requirements will steadily be phased in. All major countries are expected to endorse Basel III. Its provisions mark a considerable step away from the idea that banks need little regulation.

19.4 Equilibrium in financial markets

Having discussed the role of the central bank in financial crises, we now revert to its more normal role.

The traditional account of central banking views the central bank as controlling the *nominal* money supply (it has monopoly power to supply narrow money; that is, cash plus banks' reserves at the central bank). If, but only if, the money multiplier is stable, this allows it to control the nominal supply of broad money by setting the quantity of narrow money.

When we simplify by assuming that the price of goods is fixed, the central bank also controls the *real* money supply. In later chapters, we allow the price level to change. Changes in nominal money tend to lead to changes in prices. The central bank can still control the **real money supply** M/P in the short run – it can change M faster than prices P respond – but, in the long run, other forces determine real money M/P. For the moment, we treat the price level as fixed.

The real money supply L is the nominal money supply M divided by the price level P.

In the previous chapter, we argued that the quantity of real money demanded rises when real income rises, but falls when the nominal interest rate rises.

Money market equilibrium

In money market equilibrium the quantity of real balances demanded and supplied is equal.

Figure 19.1 shows the demand curve LL for real money balances for a given real income. The higher the interest rate and the cost of holding money, the less real money is demanded. With a given price level, the central bank controls the quantity of nominal money and real money. The supply curve is vertical at this quantity of real money L_0. Equilibrium is at E. At the interest rate r_0, the real money people wish to hold just equals the outstanding stock L_0.

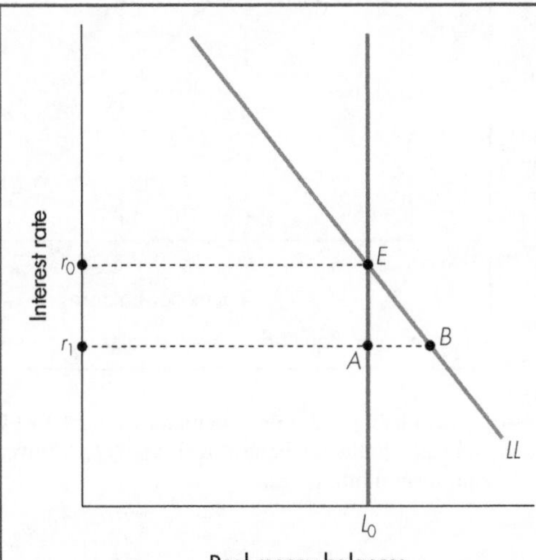

The demand schedule LL is drawn for a given level of real income. The higher the opportunity cost of holding money, the lower the real balances demanded. The real money supply schedule is vertical at L_0. The equilibrium point is E and the equilibrium interest rate r_0. At a lower interest rate r_1 there is excess demand for money AB. There must be a corresponding excess supply of bonds. This reduces bond prices and increases the return on bonds, driving the interest rate up to its equilibrium level at which both markets clear.

Figure 19.1 **Money market equilibrium**

Suppose the interest rate is r_1, below the equilibrium level r_0. There is excess demand for money AB in Figure 19.1. How does this excess demand for money bid the interest rate up from r_1 to r_0 to restore equilibrium? The answer is rather subtle. Strictly speaking, there is no market for money. Money is the medium of exchange for payments and receipts in *other* markets. A market for money would exchange pounds for pounds.

The other market relevant to Figure 19.1 is the market for bonds. Since the interest rate is the cost of holding money, people who do not hold money hold bonds. What happens explicitly in the market for bonds determines what is happening in the implicit market for money in Figure 19.1.

Real wealth W is the existing supply of real money L_0 and real bonds B_0. People divide their wealth W between desired real bond holdings BD and desired real money holdings LD. Hence

$$B_0 - B_D = L_D - L_0$$

An excess demand for money must be exactly matched by an excess supply of bonds. Otherwise people are planning to hold more wealth than they actually possess.

In Figure 19.1, any excess demand for money at the interest rate r_1 bids up the interest rate to its equilibrium level r_0. With excess demand for money, there is an excess supply of bonds. To make

3 A bond is a promise to pay a given stream of interest payments over a given time period. The bond price is the present value of this stream of payments. The higher the interest rate at which the stream is discounted, the lower the price of a bond. With an excess supply of bonds, bond prices fall and the interest rate or rate of return on bonds rises.

people want more bonds, suppliers of bonds offer a higher interest rate.[3] People switch from money to bonds. The higher interest rate reduces both the excess supply of bonds and the excess demand for money. At the interest rate r_0, money supply equals money demand. Bond supply equals bond demand. Both markets are in equilibrium. People wish to divide their wealth in precisely the ratio of the relative supplies of money and bonds.

From now on, we examine the implicit market for money. However, any statement about the money market is also a statement about the bond market.

Changes in equilibrium

A shift in either money supply or money demand changes equilibrium in the money market (and the bond market). These shifts are examined in Figure 19.2.

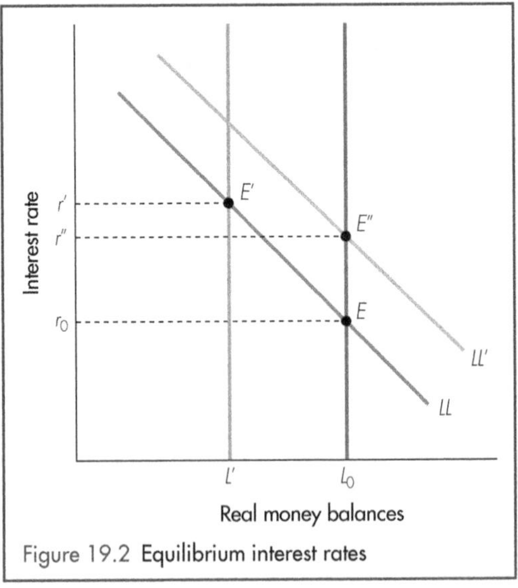

Figure 19.2 Equilibrium interest rates

A fall in the money supply

Suppose the central bank lowers the money supply. For a fixed price level, lower nominal money reduces the real money supply. Figure 19.2 shows this leftward shift in the supply curve. Real money falls from L_0 to L'. The equilibrium interest rate rises from r_0 to r'. A higher interest rate reduces the demand for real money in line with the lower quantity supplied. Hence a lower real money supply raises the equilibrium interest rate. Conversely, a rise in the real money supply reduces the equilibrium interest rate.

A rise in real income

Figure 19.2 shows real money demand LL for a given real income. A rise in real income increases

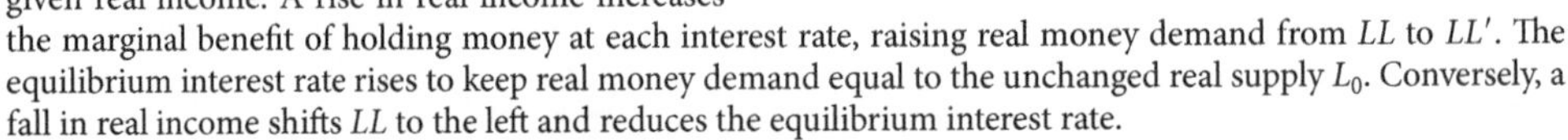

the marginal benefit of holding money at each interest rate, raising real money demand from LL to LL'. The equilibrium interest rate rises to keep real money demand equal to the unchanged real supply L_0. Conversely, a fall in real income shifts LL to the left and reduces the equilibrium interest rate.

More competition in banking

Figure 19.2 also draws money demand LL for a given interest rate paid on bank deposits. Holding this rate constant, a rise in bond interest rates r raises the cost of holding money and reduces the quantity of money demanded. This implies the economy moves up a given demand curve LL.

However, more competition between banks, reflected in permanently higher interest rates paid on bank deposits, reduces the cost of holding money at each level of r. By raising money demand at each interest rate r, this shifts the demand for money up from LL to LL'. For a given money supply, this equilibrium interest rate on bonds is higher.

To sum up, a higher real money supply reduces the equilibrium interest rate, raising real money demand in line with the higher real money supply. Conversely, higher real income, which tends to raise real money demand, must lead to a rise in the equilibrium interest rate, which tends to reduce real money demand. Only then does real money demand remain equal to the unchanged supply. An increase in banking competition has similar effects to a rise in real income.

If attempts to regulate banks more closely, in order to reduce the risk of future financial crises, have the effect of *reducing* the competition between banks, then we can use the above analysis in reverse. The cost of holding money will increase, and the demand for money will shift downwards.

MATHS 19.1

SHIFTS IN MONEY DEMAND

Suppose the supply of real money is LS and that demand for real money is given by

$$LD = \alpha + \beta Y - \gamma(r - r_d) \qquad \alpha > 0,\ \beta > 0, \gamma > 0$$

so that money demand rises with the level of income Y, but falls with the opportunity cost of holding money $(r - r_d)$, the difference between the interest rate r that could be earned by investing wealth elsewhere and the lower interest rate r_d that can be earned on bank deposits (often this is zero). In money market equilibrium, $LS = LD$. Changes in income and output Y move us along a *given* money demand curve, but changes in autonomous money demand α or in the cost of holding money $(r - r_d)$ lead to a shift in money demand.

For given levels of LS, Y and r_d, there is only one level of r that ensures

$$LS = LD = \alpha + \beta Y - \gamma(r - r_d)$$

An exogenous increase in money supply LS requires a fall in r to increase money demand in line with the new higher money supply. An exogenous increase in r_d, by reducing the opportunity cost of holding money, increases money demand. Yet, if money supply is unaltered, in equilibrium money demand cannot be allowed to increase. This is achieved by an increase in the interest rate r on other assets, to restore the cost of holding money $(r - r_d)$ to its original level. In this case, the increase in bank deposit rates is matched by an increase in the interest rate on other assets.

In all these examples, we can think of interest rates as adjusting almost instantaneously; that is, much more quickly than output and income adjust. It is therefore interest rate adjustments that ensure almost continuous equilibrium in the market for money.

19.5 Monetary control

The central bank can control the money supply by using open market operations to affect cash in circulation, or by using reserve requirements and the discount rate to affect the incentive of banks to create deposits, thereby affecting the money multiplier. This is easy in theory, but not so in practice.

It is hard for the Bank to control cash, because it is also lender of last resort. When the banks wish to increase lending and deposits they can *always* get extra cash from the Bank.

Nor, for any given quantity of cash, are deposits easily manipulated. To affect them, reserve requirements must force banks to hold reserves they would not otherwise have held. This is a tax on banks, stopping them conducting profitable business. Modern banks operating in global markets find ways around these controls. UK banks do business with UK borrowers using financial markets in Frankfurt or New York, and London is disadvantaged as a global financial centre.

Although the European Central Bank still retains minimum reserve ratios, the UK has given up required reserve ratios on banks for the purpose of monetary control. Since 2006, the Bank rewards banks for announcing their reserves at the Bank and sticking to them within the month. In essence, this allows the Bank to forecast the largest part of bank reserves. However, to translate this into a forecast for broad money, the Bank then has to forecast the size of the bank deposit multiplier. Concept 18.2 showed how volatile this can be, especially in a crisis when it really matters.

Hence precise control of broad money is difficult if viewed as the process of controlling narrow money or the money multiplier. Most central banks no longer try. Instead, they focus on broad money directly, and set interest rates to affect the demand for money, then passively supply whatever narrow money is necessary to bring broad money supply in line with this broad money demand. The TV news reports central bank decisions on interest rates, not its decisions on the money supply.

Control through interest rates

Figure 19.3 shows again the market for money. We draw the money demand schedule *LL* for a given level of real income. If the central bank can control the money supply, then, for a given level of goods prices, it can fix the real money supply at L_0. The equilibrium interest rate is r_0. Instead, the central bank can fix the interest rate at r_0 and supply the money needed to clear the market at this interest rate. In equilibrium, the central bank supplies L_0.

The central bank can fix the money supply and accept the equilibrium interest rate implied by the money demand equation, or it can fix the interest rate and accept the equilibrium money supply implied by money demand. Central banks now do the latter.

Uncertainty about the exact size of the money multiplier or bank deposit multiplier is now unimportant. When the interest rate starts to fall below the level r_0, either because of too little demand for money or too much supply, the Bank reduces the monetary base, through an open market operation, until the interest rate is again r_0. Conversely, when the interest rate exceeds r_0, the Bank simply increases the monetary base until the interest rate falls to r_0.

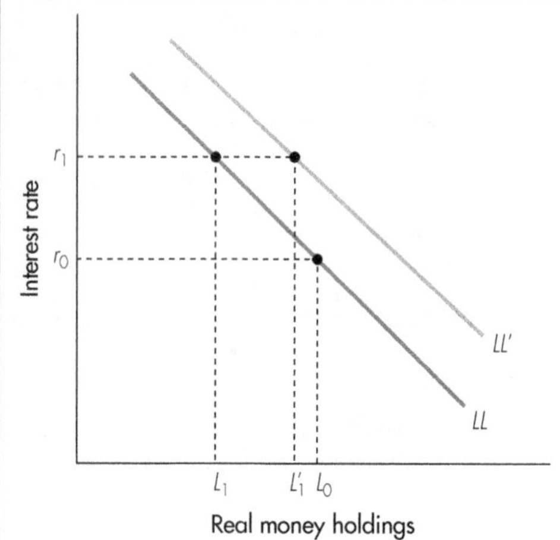

The money demand schedule *LL* is drawn for a given level of real income. If the Bank can fix the real money supply at L_0 the equilibrium interest rate will be r_0. Alternatively, if the Bank sets the interest rate r_0 and provides whatever money is demanded, the money supply will again be L_0. To control the money supply by using interest rates, the Bank must know the position of the demand schedule. Fixing an interest rate r_1, the resulting money supply will be L_1 if the demand schedule is *LL* but will be L'_1 if the demand schedule is *LL'*.

Figure 19.3 **Interest rates and monetary control**

CONCEPT 19.1

QUANTITATIVE EASING

Banks responded to the financial crisis by prioritizing the rebuilding of their solvency. There were four aspects to this response: (a) holding a much higher percentage of their assets in ultra-safe bank reserves and other very liquid assets; (b) avoiding any new lending that was thought to be risky; (c) raising profit margins throughout the industry in order to build up capital reserves; and, where possible, (d) issuing new shares in order to attract additional capital from shareholders. Here we focus on the implications of (a) and (b).

Quantitative easing is the creation of plentiful bank reserves to offset a lower bank deposit multiplier, preventing large falls in bank lending and broad money.

In the charts below, we show again the collapse of the bank deposit multiplier – the ratio of broad money to bank reserves – which fell from 90 in mid-2007 to just 7 by 2012. If reserves had remained constant, broad money would have fallen to a thirteenth of its previous level! The complete drying up of bank lending – to each other and to private firms – transmitted a huge shock to the real economy. House prices fell since new mortgages were hard to get, industrial production fell as firms struggled to finance work-in-progress until it could be sold, and increasing numbers of bankruptcies were reported.

The Treasury tried to help, by making it a condition of government support for banks such as RBS that they continued to lend to the private sector at the same level as in previous years. Unsurprisingly, the banks said they would but then failed to do so; there was little that the government could do.

UK and US central banks have usually been run by professional bankers, not world-class economics professors. At the time of the crisis, the governor of the Bank of England happened to be Mervyn King, former professor at the London School of Economics, and the governor of the US Federal Reserve was Ben Bernanke, former economics professor at Princeton University. They understood the problem and adopted a bold solution: quantitative easing (QE).

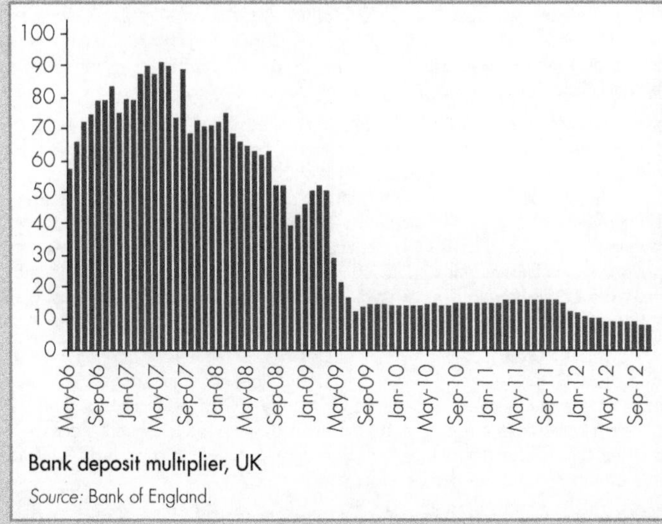

Bank deposit multiplier, UK

Source: Bank of England.

The first broad money and nominal GDP figure shows the evolution of the reserves of the UK banks and of the M4 measure of broad money, in each case using an index that sets the May 2006 level equal to 100. The QE programme began in the UK in 2009 and was extended in subsequent years. A similar programme was conducted in the US.

The reserves of UK banks rose six-fold between May 2008 and July 2009 as the Bank of England took action. The consequence was achieving steady growth in broad money – notice from the second broad money figure that there was no spike in broad money growth. Broad money was nevertheless 60 per cent higher at the end of 2010 than it had been in mid-2006. This raises three obvious questions. (a) How did the Bank achieve quantitative easing? (b) Why did it want broad money to grow by 50 per cent when real output was stagnating? (c) Is inflation just around the corner?

To accomplish QE, the Bank announced that it would buy 'safe' bonds from private firms or government, in quantities that made this the mother of all open market operations. This put narrow money into the system. The charts show that most of this injection of narrow money, having circulated around the system a few times, ended up being held by banks as reserves at the Bank of England. Banks were still afraid of lending

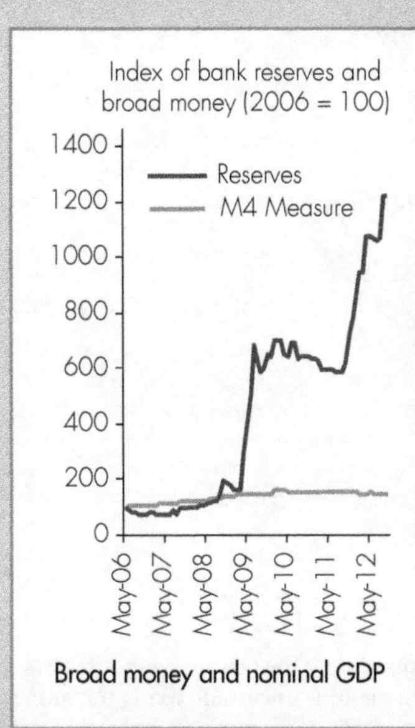

Broad money and nominal GDP

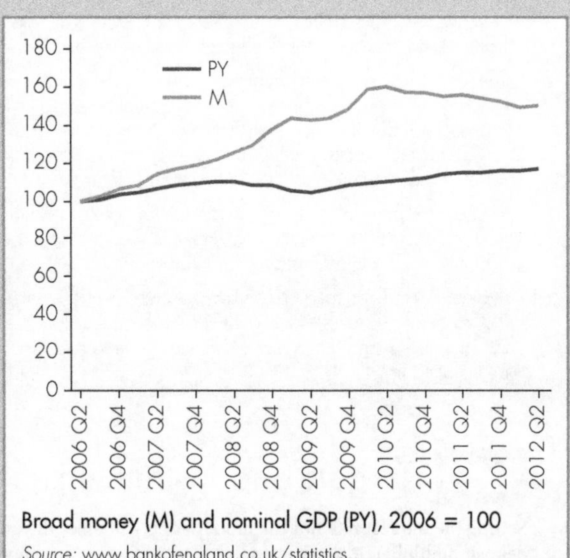

Broad money (M) and nominal GDP (PY), 2006 = 100

Source: www.bankofengland.co.uk/statistics.

very much. But overall lending did increase. From May 2008 to July 2009, banks' reserves increased from £27 billion to £152 billion, whereas broad money increased from £1737 billion to £2001 billion – so the £264 billion increase in broad money was caused not only by the £125 billion in bank reserves. As banks felt a little safer, they lent a little more, thereby raising bank deposits.

The Bank of England's own research suggests that UK quantitative easing reduced the interest rate on long assets by up to 1 percentage point. Is this success or failure? The real interest rate matters for long-run decisions on investment by firms and consumption by households. Suppose nominal interest rates are 5 per cent and inflation is 3 per cent; the real interest rate is thus 2 per cent. If QE reduces the long nominal interest rate by 1 per cent, the real interest rate is now only 1 per cent, half its former level. This is a material cut in the real cost of borrowing. For firms and households that are optimistic about the future, it may stimulate additional spending. However, for pessimistic firms and households, expecting low demand in the immediate future, there is little need for extra capital equipment or consumer durables, however cheap it is to borrow. QE may be a useful boost to aggregate demand, but alone it cannot restore demand to previous levels.

Why was broad money allowed to grow so much despite the fact that the real economy was going backwards? The Bank of England was doing everything it could to stimulate economic recovery. Interest rates were reduced to near zero, which in itself raised the demand for money, which the Bank was then happy to see supplied. Thus, the main explanation of the rise in broad money is a sharp reduction in the cost of holding money. The second broad money figure shows that increases in real output and the price level, and hence in nominal GDP, played little role in increasing the demand for broad money.

Although we defer our discussion of inflation until Chapter 22, we are already in a position to sketch an answer to our third question. If the economy is at full capacity, one might expect a 50 per cent increase in the broad money supply, and the interest rate reductions that presumably accompanied this, to cause a large rise in aggregate demand, well above the economy's capacity to supply – a recipe for a surge in inflation.

However, when the economy is facing its sharpest output downturn since the Great Depression, private firms and households are in no mood to spend. The immediate task is to raise aggregate demand back to acceptable levels. If and when that is accomplished, confidence will return. The proper task for the central bank is then to reverse the quantitative easing, reduce the money supply to more normal levels, and raise interest rates to the levels then required to prevent recovery spilling over into excess demand.

If it is technically possible to inject so much narrow money in such a short time, it is technically possible to do the reverse – the Bank sells the bonds it has recently acquired and receives narrow money in exchange, which is then 'retired' from circulation. Narrow money falls, and broad money falls even more as the normal bank deposit multiplier takes effect.

The key issue concerning financial markets is how the Treasury will then cope. During quantitative easing, it has been a simple matter to sell government debt to cover the budget deficit – if necessary, the Bank of England will buy it. Once the Bank is no longer a buyer but now an active seller of government debt, many private buyers must be found. This could cause a collapse in bond prices or, equivalently, a rise in the interest rates the government must pay to finance its debt.

If it became politically impossible for central banks to withdraw narrow money as confidence and the money multiplier increased, then the consequence would indeed be a surge in the broad money supply at that point, and this would almost certainly be inflationary.

In deciding to undertake QE on such a scale, central banks decided that these possible future outcomes were the lesser of two evils – without QE, the severe cutback in bank lending would have crippled the private sector in the immediate present. We shall have to see whether, at some future date, unwinding QE is as easy as initiating it.

19.6 Targets and instruments of monetary policy

Setting the interest rate not the money supply finesses the question of how the central bank forecasts the bank deposit multiplier. It also has a second advantage. When money demand is uncertain, fixing the money supply makes the interest rate uncertain; whereas fixing the interest rate makes the money supply uncertain. If the *effects* of monetary policy on the rest of the economy operate mainly via the interest rate, it is better to view monetary policy as the choice of interest rates not the money supply. In normal times, this is usually the case. However, if credit is in effect rationed because the banks are too scared to lend, the interest rate is not the whole story. Since we do not live in a permanent crisis – otherwise we would not call it a crisis – we revert to the discussion of monetary policy when the weather is less stormy.

Two other concepts guide our discussion of monetary policy in later chapters. One is the *ultimate objective* of monetary policy. Possible objectives could include price stability, output stabilization, influencing the exchange rate and reducing swings in house prices.

To pursue its ultimate objective, what information does a central bank use at its frequent meetings to decide interest rates? It gets up-to-date forecasts of many variables. Sometimes, it concentrates on one or two key indicators.

The **monetary instrument** is the variable over which the central bank makes day-to-day choices.

An **intermediate target** is a key indicator used to guide interest rate decisions.

Interest rates are the **instrument** about which policy decisions are made, but interest rates are chosen to try to keep the **intermediate target** on track.

This shows how interest rates should adjust to the state of the economy. New data on the money supply (largely bank deposits) come out faster than new data on the price level or output. In the heyday of monetarism, central banks changed interest rates to try to meet medium-run targets for the path of nominal growth. In terms of Figure 19.3, it was as if they were fixing the money supply, not interest rates.

Throughout the world, in the past two decades there have been two key changes in the design of monetary policy. First, central banks have been told that their ultimate objectives should concentrate more on price stability.

Second, money has become less important as an intermediate target. The financial revolution reduced its reliability as a leading indicator of future inflation. When structural changes in the financial sector are causing changes in money demand, it is hard to predict how much money will be held and how much will be spent. Increasingly, central banks use *inflation targets* as the intermediate target to which interest rate policy responds.

MATHS 19.2

QUANTITATIVE EASING REVISITED

Suppose money demand is given by

$$M = aY - br \qquad a > 0, b > 0 \qquad (1)$$

where r is the nominal interest rate. Money demand is higher if income is higher (greater benefit to holding money), but lower if interest rates are higher (higher cost of holding money). Broad money is related to bank reserves R via the bank deposit multiplier m:

$$M = mR \qquad m > 0 \qquad (2)$$

Aggregate demand AD increases with autonomous demand A but is reduced by higher interest rates:

$$AD = A - hr \qquad A > 0, h > 0 \qquad (3)$$

Consider a fall in autonomous demand from A to λA, where $0 < \lambda < 1$. Simultaneously, banks get scared and the bank deposit multiplier falls from m to pm, where $0 < p < 1$. By how much does the central bank need to increase bank reserves R in order to maintain aggregate demand for output at its original level? Originally,

$$mR = M = aY - br \qquad (4)$$

However, $r = (A - AD)/h = (A - Y)/h$, once short-run equilibrium equates output and aggregate demand, hence substituting this value of r into equation (4):

$$R = [aY - b(A - Y)/h]/m = [(ah + b)Y - bA]/hm \qquad (5)$$

For a given level of autonomous demand A, aggregate demand and output can be higher only if interest rates are lower, which requires a larger money supply, for which a larger quantity of narrow money is necessary if there is a fixed ratio of broad money to narrow money. Conversely, if autonomous demand A

is higher, output and aggregate demand can remain fixed only if interest rates increase to offset the rise in autonomous demand, for which a reduction in the money supply is necessary. Hence, with a fixed bank deposit multiplier, reserves must be lower.

When the deposit multiplier falls from m to ρm, this effect alone induces the central bank to increase R in order to maintain output at its former level. The new level of reserves would be $R/\rho > R$, since $\rho < 1$. Additionally, the fall in autonomous demand from A to λA raises the level of reserves that the central bank must supply if output and aggregate demand are not to fall. Quantitative easing is the central bank response to twin problems, with the same cause: lower aggregate demand and a lower bank deposit multiplier.

19.7 The transmission mechanism

The central bank sets interest rates. How do interest rates affect the real economy?

In a closed economy, monetary policy affects consumption and investment demand by affecting real interest rates.[4] The central bank chooses the nominal interest rate. If prices are fixed, this is also the real interest rate. Once we allow prices to vary, monetary policy needs to anticipate what inflation will be. Since the real interest rate is simply the nominal interest rate minus the inflation rate, monetary policy then sets the nominal interest rate to get the desired real interest rate.

The transmission mechanism of monetary policy is the channel through which it affects output and employment.

Consumption demand revisited

Chapter 16 used a very simple consumption function, an upward-sloping straight line relating aggregate consumption to the disposable income of households. The slope of this line, the marginal propensity to consume, showed the fraction of each extra pound of disposable income that households wished to spend, not save.

The height of the consumption function showed autonomous consumption demand; that is, the part unrelated to personal disposable income. Changes in disposable income moved households *along* the consumption function. Changes in autonomous demand *shifted* the consumption function. How can monetary policy affect autonomous consumption demand?

Household wealth

Suppose real **wealth** rises because of a stock market boom. Households spend some of their extra wealth on a new car. At each level of disposable income, consumption demand is higher. The entire consumption function shifts up when household wealth increases.

The wealth effect is the shift in the consumption function when household wealth changes.

Money and interest rates affect household wealth, and thus consumption and aggregate demand, in two ways. First, since money is a component of household wealth, a higher real money supply adds directly to household wealth. Second, interest rates affect household wealth indirectly. The price of company shares and long-term government bonds is the present value of the expected stream of dividend earnings or promised coupon payments. When interest rates fall, future earnings, now discounted at a lower interest rate, are worth more today. Lower interest rates make the price of bonds and corporate shares rise and make households wealthier.[5]

Durables and consumer credit

When spending exceeds disposable income, net wealth falls. People sell off assets or borrow money to finance their dissaving. A lot of borrowing is to finance purchases of *consumer durables*; that is, household capital goods such as televisions, furniture and cars. Splashing out on a new car can cost a whole year's income.

4 In Chapter 29 we show that, in an open economy, there is also a strong relationship between interest rates, the exchange rate and competitiveness. Monetary transmission then includes effects on export and import demand.

5 When interest rates are 10 per cent, a bond paying £2.50 for ever is worth £25. New buyers get about 10 per cent a year on their investment. If interest rates fall to 5 per cent, bond prices rise to £50. New buyers still get an annual return in line with interest rates on other assets. A similar argument applies to company shares.

Two aspects of consumer credit or borrowing possibilities affect consumption spending. First, there is the quantity of credit on offer. If banks or retailers make more credit available to customers, people are more likely to buy the car or dream kitchen they have always wanted. An increase in the supply of consumer credit shifts the consumption function upwards. People spend more at any level of disposable income. Second, the cost of credit matters. The higher the interest rate, the lower the quantity that households can borrow while still being able to make repayments out of their future disposable incomes.

Money and interest rates thus affect consumer spending by affecting both the quantity of consumer credit and the interest rates charged on it. An increase in the monetary base increases the cash reserves of the banking system and allows it to extend more consumer credit in the form of overdrafts. And by reducing the cost of consumer credit, lower interest rates allow households to take out bigger loans while still being able to meet the interest and repayments.

Those two forces – wealth effects and changes in consumer credit – explain most of the shifts in the consumption function. They are part of the *transmission mechanism* through which monetary policy affects output and employment. Operating through wealth effects or the supply and cost of consumer credit, changes in the money supply and in interest rates shift the consumption function and the aggregate demand schedule, thus affecting equilibrium income and output.

Two closely related theories of the consumption function reinterpret these phenomena and make some of their subtleties more explicit.

The permanent income hypothesis

Developed by Professor Milton Friedman, this hypothesis assumes that people's incomes fluctuate but that people dislike fluctuating consumption. Because of diminishing marginal utility, a few extra bottles of champagne in the good years does not compensate for hunger in the bad years. Rather than allow fluctuations in income to induce fluctuations in consumption, people smooth out fluctuations in consumption. People go without champagne to avoid being hungry.

What determines the consumption people can afford on average? Friedman coined the term **permanent income** to describe people's average income in the long run, and argued that consumption depends not on current disposable income but on permanent income.

The permanent income hypothesis says that consumption reflects long-run or permanent income.

Suppose people think current income is unusually high. This temporarily high income makes little difference to their permanent income or the consumption they can afford in the long run. Since permanent income has hardly risen, they hardly increase current consumption.

They save most of their temporary extra income and put money aside to see them through the years when income is unusually low. Only if people believe that a rise in today's income will be sustained as higher future incomes will their permanent income rise significantly. Only then is a large rise in current income matched by a large rise in current consumption.

The life-cycle hypothesis

The life-cycle hypothesis asserts that people make a lifetime consumption plan (including bequests to their children) just affordable out of lifetime income (plus any initial wealth inherited).

Developed by Professors Franco Modigliani and Albert Ando, this theory takes a long-run approach like the permanent income hypothesis, but recognizes that changing tastes over a lifetime may undermine complete consumption smoothing.

Each individual household need not plan a constant consumption level over its lifetime. There may be years of heavy expenditure (a round-the-world cruise, sending the children to private school) and other years when spending is a bit less. However, such individual discrepancies tend to cancel out in the aggregate. Like the permanent income hypothesis, the life-cycle hypothesis suggests that it is average long-run income that determines the total demand for consumer spending.

Figure 19.4 shows a household's actual income over its lifetime. Income rises with career seniority until retirement, then drops to the lower level provided by a pension. The household's permanent income is *OD*. Technically, this is the constant annual income with the same present value as the present value of the actual stream of income. If the household consumed exactly its permanent income, it would consume *OD* each year and die penniless. The two areas labelled *A* show when the household would be spending more than its current income and the area *B* shows when the household would be saving.

The household spends its income over its lifetime, but area *B* is not the sum of the two areas *A* because of compound interest. In the early years of low income, the household borrows. The area *B* shows how much the household has to save to pay back the initial borrowing *with interest* and accumulate sufficient wealth to see it through the final years when it is again dissaving.

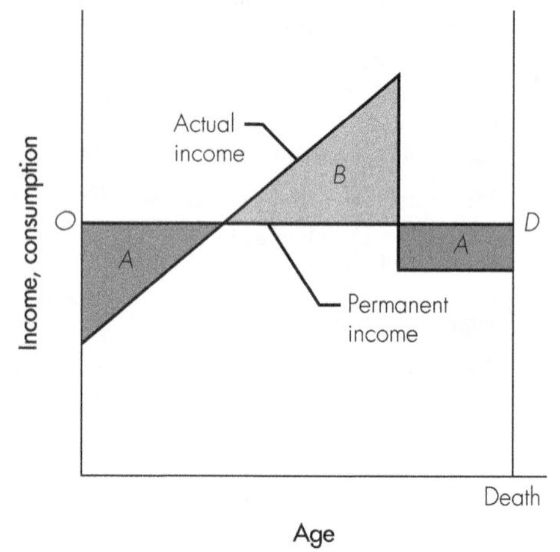

Actual disposable income rises over a household's lifetime until retirement, then falls to the pension level. Permanent income is the constant income level *OD* with the same present value as actual income. Suppose consumption equals permanent income. The two areas *A* show total dissaving and the area *B*, total saving. In the absence of inherited wealth and bequests, *B* must be large enough to repay borrowing with interest and also build up enough wealth to supplement actual income during retirement.

Figure 19.4 **Consumption and the life-cycle**

Now let's think again about wealth effects and consumer credit. With more initial wealth, a household can spend more in every year of its lifetime without going broke. We can shift the permanent income line in Figure 19.4 upwards and consumption will rise. Although area *B* is now smaller and the areas *A* are now larger, the household can use its extra wealth to meet this shortfall between the years of saving (the area *B*) and the years of dissaving (the two areas *A*).

Again, we conclude that higher wealth leads to more consumption at any current disposable income, but we pick up something we missed earlier. If households believe their *future* income will be higher than previously imagined, this also raises their permanent income. Households can spend more each year and still expect to balance their lifetime budget. They raise *current* consumption as soon as they raise their estimates of future incomes. The present value of future income plays a role very similar to wealth. It is money to be shared out in consumption over the lifetime. Friedman called it 'human wealth', to distinguish it from financial and physical assets. Rises in expected future incomes have wealth effects. They shift up the simple consumption function relating *current* consumption to *current* disposable income.

What about consumer credit? A rise in interest rates reduces the present value of future incomes and makes households worse off. In Figure 19.4, households must enlarge area *B* to meet the extra interest costs of paying back money borrowed in area *A* early in the lifetime. We must shift the permanent income line downwards. A rise in interest rates reduces current consumption not merely by reducing the market value of financial assets, but also by reducing the present value of future *labour* income. By reducing human wealth, it shifts the consumption function downwards.

From short-term interest rates to long-term interest rates

The market for money determines **short-term interest** rates, for loans of duration ranging from a day to a month. However, long-term investment decisions about building a factory that will last for 20 years need to consider **long-term interest rates** over a similar duration.

Short-term interest rates apply to loans of very short maturity.

Long-term interest rates apply to long-term loans during which the interest rate is usually fixed.

Sometimes, a 20-year loan will be at variable interest rates, as with a UK mortgage. In such a contract, the lender commits to lend for the long duration but varies the interest rate during the loan, in line with what is happening to short-term loans in the money market. Most other long-term loans (including mortgages in most continental European countries) entail a fixed rate of interest over the entire life of the contract.

Since firms could in principle finance long-term investment by a succession of short-term loans, there ought to be a close relation between the long-term interest rate today and the sequence of expected short-term interest rates over the same period.

Either way, the effect of interest rates on investment demand for long-term capital assets should not depend solely on today's short-term interest rate but on the average of expected short-term interest rates during the life of the loan, plus a little extra for risk to compensate being locked into the long-term loan.

Governments therefore affect long-term decisions – for investment by firms and for some important longer-term spending by households – by affecting beliefs about current and future short-term interest rates. If changing the current interest rate has little effect on the long-term interest rate, then the transmission mechanism from monetary policy to aggregate demand will at best be weak.

ACTIVITY 19.1

TRANSMISSION LAG

In the UK, people rarely get access to fixed-rate mortgages for the entire life of the loan, but are sometimes offered interest rates fixed for the first two years. During this initial period, changes in short-term interest rates have little effect on such households, since the interest rate they care about most is fixed. However, as this initial period expires, households then have to face whatever the new level of interest rate has become.

Thus, UK households cannot fix their mortgage interest rate for an extended period. Taking a 20-year view, they basically have a variable-rate mortgage, with successive small steps in which the interest rate may be temporarily fixed.

In fact, the UK is quite unusual in having such a high proportion of variable-rate mortgages – many continental European countries fix the mortgage interest rate for 20 years or whatever the duration of the mortgage loan. This has important consequences for the transmission mechanism of monetary policy. When most households are immune to the mortgage impact of interest rate changes, then, other things equal, the central bank has to move the interest rate by more in order to have the same effect on aggregate demand. If interest rates do not work through existing mortgages, they have to work more on other determinants of aggregate demand. Conversely, since the UK is so exposed to the effect of interest rate changes in the short run, the Bank of England has a more powerful weapon with which to manage aggregate demand. Since the weapon works more effectively, it requires smaller interest rate changes to achieve the same effect.

This is one of many reasons why changes in interest rates may take several years to have their full effect on aggregate demand. Overnight, people are locked into old contracts that shield them for a while from the effect of the new interest rate. Even after they feel its effect, it may take time to assess how painful it is and to look for alternative ways to behave.

In the US, Ben Bernanke, president of the US central bank, recognized in 2012 that, with US interest rates already near zero, monetary policy had lost its power to boost aggregate demand through yet lower short-term interest rates in 2012. However, he understood the relationship between long-term interest rates and short-term interest rates. So he promised that the US central bank would keep interest rates near zero for several years to come. The purpose of this promise was not to change the short-term interest rate in 2012, but to reduce the long-term interest rate – relevant to aggregate demand – by changing beliefs about the short-term interest rates in the future that should be averaged to get the *long-term* interest rate in 2012.

Bernanke adopted other unconventional means to overcome the breakdown of the normal transmission mechanism of monetary policy. In Operation Twist, the US Federal Reserve bought massive quantities of long-term government bonds, inducing higher prices and lower interest rates on long bonds, financing these purchases not by printing money but by selling off the Fed's holdings of short bonds.

Bernanke also pursued quantitative easing – the purchase of large quantities of bonds by printing money – for the purpose of getting long-term interest rates down in order to boost aggregate demand. As in the UK, it is acknowledged that this policy should be unwound – selling bonds and removing cash from the market – once recovery is sustainably established.

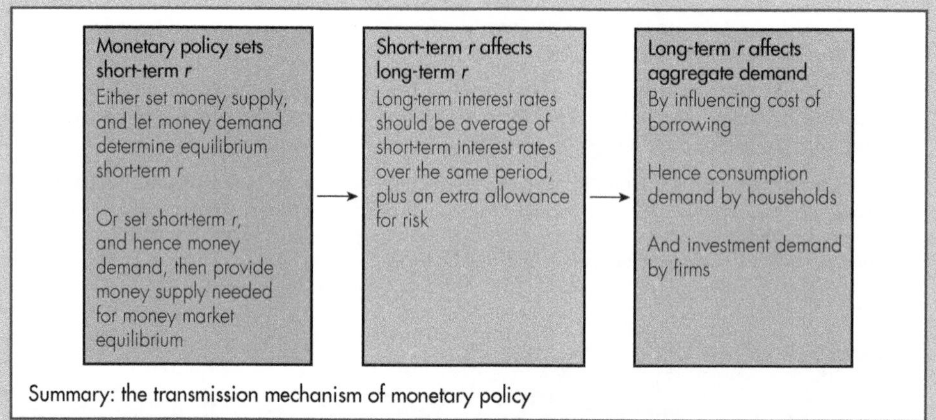

Summary: the transmission mechanism of monetary policy

In the Eurozone, Central Bank President Mario Draghi became worried about a different transmission failure. Although all Eurozone countries face the same short-term interest rate – the one set by the European Central Bank (ECB) – different member states faced very different long-term interest rates. In countries like Germany, long-term interest rates were low, foreseeing a long period of low short-term interest rates.

However, in Greece, Spain, Portugal, Italy and Ireland, long-term interest rates had become huge because of the fear of default on long-term government bonds. Draghi argued that this was preventing the 'normal transmission mechanism of monetary policy' in these countries. He promised that the ECB would buy these long-term bonds – in whatever quantities needed – to restore more normal relationships between short- and long-term interest rates, thereby allowing monetary policy to start working again.

Critics argued this was simply covert support for the budget deficits in these countries. Supporters argued that Draghi had saved the Eurozone by preventing peripheral countries being forced into bankruptcy by self-fulfilling prophecies that made the interest burden of their debt unsustainable. The figure below summarizes our discussion of the transmission mechanism of monetary policy.

Questions

(a) Suppose we are creatures of habit – calculating optimal behaviour takes time and effort so we recalculate only rarely, when it has become obvious to us that circumstances have changed substantially and previous behaviour cannot possibly be optimal. Could this explain a delay in the transmission mechanism of monetary policy even if there are no long-term contracts in force? Give an example.

(b) Would this justify a transmission lag in responses to fiscal policy too?

(c) Suppose interest rates can be changed frequently whereas fiscal policy changes are infrequent. Would this help explain why people are slower to respond to monetary changes than fiscal changes?

(d) Milton Friedman argued that the lags in monetary policy are 'long and variable'. Using the figure above, outline the various points in the transmission mechanism at which this could apply.

To check your answers to these questions, go to page 680.

Finally, what about a rise in the quantity of consumer credit on offer? Figure 19.4 assumes that people spend more than their incomes early in life. Students run up overdrafts knowing that, as rich economists, they can pay them back later. What if nobody will lend? People without wealth are restricted by their actual incomes, although people with wealth can lend to themselves by running down their wealth. Hence a rise in the availability of consumer credit lets people dissave in the early years. Total consumption rises. More students run up overdrafts and buy cars.

Conversely, in the aftermath of a financial crash, banks are preoccupied with restoring their own solvency. They may be very reluctant to lend to any borrower who looks at all risky. In such circumstances, the supply of credit can contract sharply, forcing households to reduce their spending.

Having discussed how monetary policy affects consumption demand, we conclude our examination of monetary transmission by analysing how interest rates affect investment demand.

Investment demand

In earlier chapters we treated investment demand as autonomous, or independent of current income and output. We now begin to analyse what determines investment demand. Here we focus on interest rates.

Total investment spending is investment in fixed capital and investment in working capital. Fixed capital includes factories, houses, plant and machinery. The share of investment in GDP fluctuates between 10 and 20 per cent.[6] Although the total change in inventories is quite small, this component of total investment is volatile and contributes significantly to changes in the total level of investment.

In a closed economy, aggregate demand is $C + I + G$. Public investment is part of G. We still treat government demand as part of fiscal policy. Thus we assume that G is fixed at a level set by the government. In this section we focus on private investment demand I.

Investment in fixed capital

Firms add to plant and equipment because they foresee profitable opportunities to expand output or because they can reduce costs by using more capital-intensive production methods. BT needs new equipment because it is developing new products for data transmission. Nissan needs new assembly lines to substitute robots for workers in car production.

The firm weighs the benefits from new capital – the rise in profits – against the cost of investment. The benefit occurs in the future, but the costs are incurred when the plant is built or the machine bought. The firm compares the value of extra future profits with the current cost of the investment.

Will the investment yield enough extra profit to pay back *with interest* the loan used to finance the original investment? Equivalently, if the project is funded out of existing profits, will the new investment yield a return at least as great as the return that could have been earned by lending the money instead? The higher the interest rate, the larger must be the return on a new investment to match the opportunity cost of the funds tied up.

At any moment, there are many investment projects a firm *could* undertake. The firm ranks these projects, from the most profitable to the least profitable. At a high interest rate, only a few projects earn enough to cover the opportunity cost of the funds employed. As the interest rate falls, more and more projects earn a return at least matching the opportunity cost of the funds used to undertake the investment. The firm invests more.

The investment demand schedule shows the desired investment at each interest rate.

Figure 19.5 plots the **investment demand schedule** ***II*** relating interest rates and investment demand.

If the interest rate rises from r_0 to r_1, fewer investment projects cover the opportunity cost of the funds tied up, and desired investment falls from I_0 to I_1. The height of the schedule II reflects the cost of new capital and the stream of profits to which it gives rise. For a given stream of expected future profits, a higher price of new capital goods reduces the return on the money tied up in investment. Fewer projects match the opportunity cost of any particular interest rate. Since desired investment is then lower at any interest rate, a rise in the cost of new capital goods shifts the investment demand schedule II downwards.

Similarly, pessimism about future output demand reduces estimates of the stream of profits earned on possible investment projects. The return on each project falls. At each interest rate, fewer projects match the opportunity cost of the funds. Desired investment falls at any interest rate. Lower expected future demand shifts the investment demand schedule downwards.[7]

6 These numbers refer to gross investment: the production of new capital goods that contribute to aggregate demand. Since the capital stock is depreciating, or wearing out, some gross investment is needed merely to keep the existing capital stock from falling.

7 We can make the same points another way. Given the stream of future profits and the interest rate, a firm does all projects for which the present value of operating profits exceeds the initial price of the capital goods. A higher interest rate cuts the present value of profits. Some projects no longer cover the initial cost of capital goods. Higher interest rates reduce desired investment. Similarly, a lower expected future profit stream, or higher purchase price of capital goods, cuts the present value of operating profits relative to the initial cost, reducing investment demand.

The investment demand schedule *II* can be used to analyse both business investment in plant and machinery and residential investment in housing. What about the slope of the schedule? There is a big difference between a machine that wears out in three years and a house or a factory lasting 50 years. The longer the economic life of the capital good, the larger the fraction of its total returns earned in the distant future, and the more the original cost of the goods accumulates at compound interest before the money is repaid.

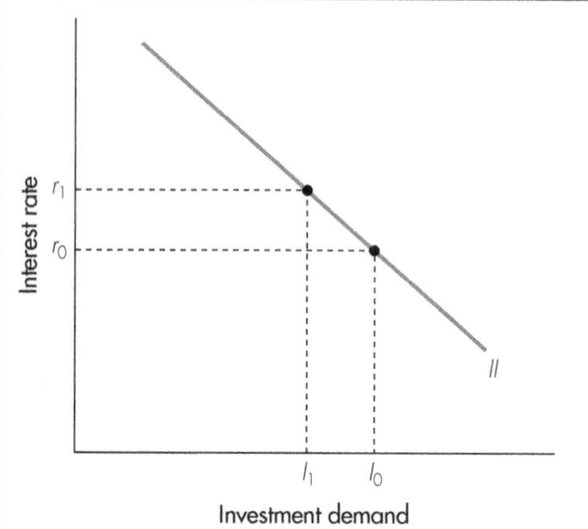

For a given price of capital goods and given expectations about the profit stream to which new investments give rise, a higher interest rate reduces the number of projects that can provide a return matching the opportunity cost of the funds used. As interest rates rise from r_0 to r_1, desired investment falls from I_0 to I_1.

Figure 19.5 **The investment demand schedule**

Hence a change in short-term interest rates today has two effects. First, it affects the long-term interest rates relevant to the life of a loan to finance a long-term capital good. Second, for a given change in long-term interest rates, the investment demand schedule is flatter, and the monetary transmission mechanism more powerful, for long-lived houses and factories than for short-term machinery.[8] A change in interest rates has more effect on long-term projects.

This conclusion has to be qualified with the caveat that a temporary change in short-term interest rates, achieved through monetary policy, may have little effect on long-term interest rates if it is believed today that future short-term interest rates will be largely unaffected. However, a change in short-term interest rates that is believed today to be permanent will have a powerful effect on long-term rates and hence on long-term investment.

Inventory investment

There are three reasons why firms desire stocks of raw materials, partly finished goods and finished goods awaiting sale. First, the firm may be betting on price changes. Sometimes, firms hold large stocks of oil, believing it cheaper to buy now rather than later. Similarly, firms may hold finished goods off the market hoping to get a better price later.

Second, many production processes take time. A ship cannot be built in a month, or even a year. Some stocks are simply the throughput of inputs on their way to becoming outputs.

Third, stocks help smooth costly adjustments in output. If output demand rises suddenly, plant capacity cannot be changed overnight. A firm has to pay big overtime payments to meet the upsurge in orders. It is cheaper to carry some stocks, available to meet a sudden rise in demand. Similarly, in a temporary downturn, it is cheaper to maintain output and pile up stocks of unsold goods than to incur expensive redundancy payments to cut the workforce and reduce production.

CONCEPT 19.2 THE CREDIT CHANNEL OF MONETARY POLICY

Recent research emphasizes that interest rates are not the only channel through which monetary policy affects consumption and investment, and hence aggregate demand.

A lender usually asks for collateral – assets available for sale if you fail to repay the loan. Collateral is how lenders cope with moral hazard and adverse selection: borrowers who know more about their ability and willingness to repay than lenders know.

The credit channel affects the value of collateral for loans, and thus the supply of credit.

8 Equivalently, a 1 per cent rise in the interest rate has a small effect on the present value of earnings over a three-year period but a large effect on the present value of earnings over the next 50 years. Note that this is the same argument as we used in Chapter 17, in saying that a change in interest rates would have little effect on the price (present value of promised payments) of a short-term bond but a large effect on the price of a long-term bond.

Suppose the price of goods falls, raising the real value of nominal assets. People have more collateral to offer lenders, who lend more than before at any particular interest rate. The supply of credit rises, and aggregate demand for goods increases.

There are really two credit channels, since there are two reasons for changes in the value of collateral. First, changes in goods prices change the real value of nominal assets. Second, and quite distinct, when monetary policy changes the interest rate, this affects the present value of future income from assets and the market value of collateral assets themselves.

This theoretical reasoning is supported by evidence from quantitative easing. Its purpose was not simply to raise the broad money supply to support the desired low level of interest rates. It was also believed that credit rationing by lenders was curtailing private spending. Injecting more money provided additional liquidity to people who would otherwise have been credit-rationed, and the consequent spending helped bid up house prices and share prices on the stock market. In turn, this improved private sector collateral and made banks more willing to lend, causing a second-round beneficial effect.

In this extreme example, raising the money supply has beneficial effects despite the fact that interest rates have already fallen as low as they can go.

John Maynard Keynes thought monetary policy became powerless once interest rates had been driven down to zero, what he called the *liquidity trap*. Great man that he was, he did not get everything right. Nowadays, we know about the credit channel, and quantitative easing is proof that it can work.

These are benefits of holding inventories. The cost is that, by retaining unsold goods or buying goods not yet inputs to production, a firm ties up money that could have earned interest. The cost of holding inventories is the interest forgone, plus any storage charges for holding stocks.

Thus the investment demand schedule *II* for fixed capital in Figure 19.5 also applies to increases in working capital, or inventories. Other things equal, a higher interest rate reduces desired stockbuilding, an upward move *along* the investment demand schedule. This is part of the monetary transmission mechanism. But a rise in potential speculative profits, or fall in storage costs for inventories, *shifts* the schedule *II* up and raises inventory investment at any interest rate. Not all changes in investment demand are caused by monetary policy.

Summary

- The Bank of England, the UK **central bank**, is banker to the banks. Because it can print money it can never go bust. It acts as **lender of last resort** to the banks.
- The Bank conducts the government's monetary policy. It affects the monetary base through **open market operations**, buying and selling government securities. It can also affect the money multiplier by imposing **reserve requirements** on the banks, or by setting the **discount rate** for loans to banks at a penalty level that encourages banks to hold excess reserves.
- There is no explicit market in money. Because people plan to hold the total supply of assets that they own, any excess supply of bonds is matched by an excess demand for money. Interest rates adjust to clear the market for bonds. In so doing, they clear the money market.
- A rise in the real money supply reduces the equilibrium interest rate. For a given real money supply, a rise in real income raises the equilibrium interest rate.
- In practice, the Bank cannot control the money supply exactly. Imposing artificial regulations drives banking business into unregulated channels. **Monetary base control** is difficult since the Bank acts as lender of last resort, supplying cash when banks need it.

- Thus the Bank sets the interest rate not money supply. The demand for money at this interest rate determines the quantity of money supplied. **Interest rates are the instrument of monetary policy.**
- Interest rates take time to affect the economy. **Intermediate targets** are used as leading indicators when setting the interest rate.
- **Quantitative easing** is the creation of substantial quantities of bank reserves in order to offset a fall in the bank deposit multiplier and prevent large falls in bank lending and broad money.
- A higher interest rate reduces household wealth and makes borrowing dearer. Together, these effects reduce autonomous consumption demand and shift the consumption function downwards.
- **Consumption demand** reflects long-run disposable income and a desire to smooth out short-run fluctuations in consumption. Higher interest rates reduce consumption demand by reducing the present value of expected future labour income.
- Given the cost of new capital goods and expected stream of future profits, a higher interest rate reduces **investment demand**, a movement down a given investment demand schedule *II*. Higher expected future profits, or cheaper capital goods, shift the *II* schedule upwards.
- Long-term interest rates are an average of the sequence of short-term interest rates expected to prevail during the life of the long loan contract, plus an extra allowance for risk.
- The effect of change in short-term interest rates on consumption and investment demand, often operating through an induced change in the long-term interest rate, is the **transmission mechanism** of monetary policy.

Review questions

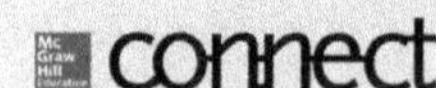

EASY

1. The Bank of England sells £1 million of securities to Mr Jones who banks with Barclays. The Bank of England requires other commercial banks to hold 100 per cent cash reserves against deposits. What is the money multiplier?
2. Which of these statements is correct? The purpose of quantitative easing is: (a) to create money in order to create inflation and reduce the real value of government debt; (b) to force banks to create deposits despite having inadequate bank reserves; (c) to make the central bank the purchaser of last resort for government bond issues; (d) to prevent a collapse of broad money when banks are unable or unwilling to lend.
3. What are the desirable properties of a good leading indicator for interest rate decisions?
4. What happens to the consumption function if the banks decide to offer credit cards on easier terms and conditions? Why?
5. **Common fallacies** Why are these statements wrong? (a) By abolishing reserve requirements, the central bank gave up any attempt to control the money supply. (b) When real interest rates are negative, people are being paid to hold cash. (c) Consumers are said to behave irrationally if their spending is up when their disposable income is lower.

MEDIUM

6. The Bank of England sells £1 million of securities to Mr Jones who banks with Barclays. (a) If Mr Jones pays by cheque, show the effect on the balance sheets of the Bank of England and Barclays. (b) What happens to the money supply? (c) Is the answer the same if Mr Jones pays in cash?
7. Using a diagram like Figure 19.1: (a) illustrate the initial effects of a recovery in confidence after a financial crash. (b) Did you expect a larger effect on money supply or money demand? (c) How will monetary policy then respond?

8 Suppose banks begin lending again as confidence is restored. (a) If monetary policy takes no action, what will be the likely outcome? (b) What action by the central bank would then be appropriate?

9 Why might it take up to two years for a change in interest rates fully to affect aggregate demand? What does this imply about decisions to set interest rates?

MEDIUM

10 If the permanent income hypothesis is correct, we should expect to see a lower marginal propensity to consume in the short run than in the long run. Why?

11 Why do higher interest rates reduce investment demand? Be sure to discuss all the different ways in which firms might finance their investment projects.

12 Consider a simplified version of the model in Maths 19.2, in which money demand, the deposit multiplier and aggregate demand are, respectively:

$M = Y - r$ $M = mR$ $Y = 100 - r$

(a) If output is 90, find the interest rate and the level of bank reserves and the level of bank reserves. (b) Suppose, autonomous aggregate demand falls from 100 to 95, and the deposit multiplier falls from m to $m/2$. How much must reserves increase to preserve the initial level of output? (c) What is the maximum fall in autonomous aggregate demand that can be offset by quantitative easing?

HARD

13 **Essay question** Why do modern central banks think of monetary policy as choosing the interest rate rather than the money supply?

14 You live for five periods, during which, respectively, you earn 100, 200, 300, 200 and 100. (a) Draw a diagram of your lifecycle income. (b) If the interest rate is zero, and there is no inflation, what is your permanent income? (c) Using your diagram, or otherwise, identify your saving or dissaving in each period of your life. (d) If the real interest rate is positive instead of zero, what effect does this have on your initial estimate of your permanent income? Illustrate in your diagram.

For solutions to these questions, contact your lecturer.

CHAPTER 20

Monetary and fiscal policy

Learning Outcomes

By the end of this chapter, you should be able to:

1. describe different forms of monetary policy
2. recognise a monetary target
3. understand the *IS* and *LM* schedules
4. understand equilibrium in both the output and money markets
5. describe the effect of a fiscal expansion
6. describe the effect of a monetary expansion
7. understand the mix of monetary and fiscal policy
8. realise how expected future taxes affect current demand

Chapters 16 and 17 introduced a simple model of income determination, and studied how fiscal policy affects aggregate demand and equilibrium output. Chapters 18 and 19 examined the demand for money, the supply of money and the determination of interest rates. Interest rates connect the present and the future, affecting spending decisions of both households and firms. We analysed the transmission mechanism by which monetary policy affects aggregate demand.

We now examine the interaction of the markets for goods and for money. Interest rates affect the demand for goods and the level of income and output, but income and output affect the demand for money and the interest rates set by the central bank.

We need to think about both markets at once. In so doing, we explain how equilibrium income and interest rates are simultaneously determined. In this richer model, we study changes in monetary and fiscal policy. Finally, we discuss how the mix of monetary and fiscal policy affects the composition as well as the level of equilibrium output.

This is the last chapter in which we retain the simplifying assumption that prices are fixed. The interest rate is the key variable connecting the markets for money and output. In the next chapter, we allow prices to change, and introduce aggregate supply for the first time.

20.1 Monetary policy

Economists distinguish between rules and discretion. A smoker decides from minute to minute whether to have a cigarette. Once we understand her preferences, the price of cigarettes, her income and the attitude of her friends, we can model her behaviour and predict how she will behave, even though she has discretion or freedom to decide how much to smoke.

A rule is a commitment describing how behaviour changes as circumstances change. Discretion means free choice without restrictions imposed by prior commitments.

A particular monetary policy is a relationship between the state of the economy and the interest rate chosen by the central bank.

A **rule** is a commitment on how to behave, for example to smoke no more than ten cigarettes a day. This rule is credible only if we understand what prevents the smoker having the eleventh cigarette when she desperately wants one. Losing her friends if she smokes more than ten might be a commitment mechanism to enforce the rule. A rule constrains her **discretion**, limits her freedom and precludes the choice she would otherwise have made.

What do we mean by a given **monetary policy**? This has two aspects. First, to what variable does it refer – the interest rate or the money supply? For the reasons given in the previous two chapters, we prefer to focus on the interest rate.

Second, does a given policy mean the choice of a particular interest rate? Changing the interest rate would then be a change in policy. This is simple, but we can do better. We can usually model *why* that interest rate was chosen: the relationship between the chosen interest rate and other economic variables.

Interest rates change either because economic circumstances change (within a *given* monetary policy) or because the central bank switches to a different preferred relationship between interest rates and the state of the economy (a *change* in monetary policy).

In the heyday of monetarism, central banks used to adjust interest rates to stop the money supply deviating from a given target path of monetary growth. Most central banks have abandoned this policy, preferring to target the inflation rate itself.

Following a monetary target, the central banks adjust interest rates to maintain the quantity of money demanded in line with the target path for money supply.

Inflation targeting makes no sense in a model in which we still assume prices are fixed. We introduce inflation targeting in Chapter 21. In this chapter, we assume instead that the central bank pursues a **monetary target**. This is a good way to introduce many key ideas, and is useful in understanding how monetary policy was set in the 1980s before inflation targeting became popular.

We now combine our analysis of the goods market and money market to examine interest rates and output simultaneously. Chapters 16 and 17 analysed short-run equilibrium output using a diagram plotting income against demand. Since we now wish to keep track of interest rates explicitly, we need a new diagram.

20.2 The *IS–LM* model

We consider *combinations* of income and interest rates that lead to equilibrium in each of the two markets – output and money – and thus determine the unique combination of income and interest rates yielding equilibrium in both markets at the same time.

The *IS* schedule shows combinations of income and interest rates at which aggregate demand equals actual output.

The *IS* schedule: goods market equilibrium

The goods market is in equilibrium when aggregate demand equals actual income. Hence, as shorthand, the combinations of interest rates and income compatible with short-run equilibrium in the goods market is called the *IS* schedule.[1]

Figure 20.1 shows the *IS* schedule. It is drawn for a given level of present and future government spending, a given level of present and future taxes and given present beliefs about future output

1 The name *IS* schedule derives from the fact that, in the simplest model without either a government or a foreign sector, equilibrium income is where planned investment *I* equals planned saving *S*. However, the *IS* schedule – the combinations of income and interest rates consistent with equilibrium income – can be constructed for models including the government and foreign sector as well.

and income. Holding these constant, lower interest rates increase both investment and consumption demand. At an interest rate r_1, aggregate demand and short-run equilibrium output Y_1 are higher than their level Y_0 when the interest rate is r_0.

Changes in interest rates move the goods market along a given *IS* curve. Anything else that affects aggregate demand is shown as a shift in the *IS* schedule.

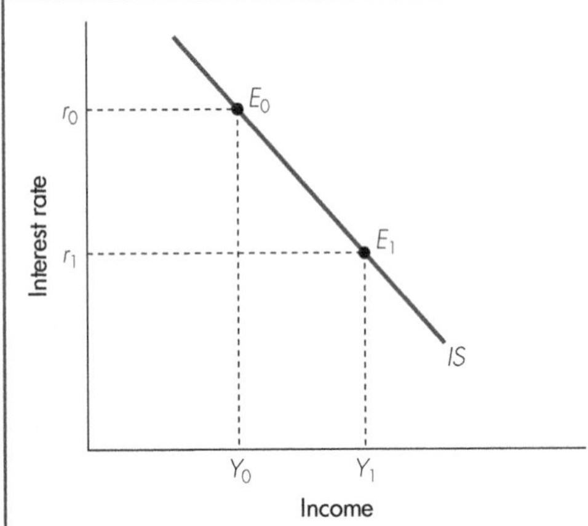

The *IS* schedule shows how a change in interest rates affects aggregate demand and short-run equilibrium output. A lower interest rate boosts demand and output. Anything else affecting aggregate demand shifts the *IS* schedule.

Figure 20.1 **The *IS* schedule**

The slope of the *IS* schedule

The *IS* schedule slopes down. Lower interest rates boost aggregate demand and output. The *slope* of the *IS* schedule reflects the sensitivity of aggregate demand to interest rates. If demand is very sensitive to interest rates, the *IS* schedule is flat. A small change in interest rates causes a large change in aggregate demand for output. Conversely, if output demand is insensitive to interest rates, the *IS* schedule is steep. Changes in interest rates have only a small effect on aggregate demand for output.

Although, for simplicity, we often show the *IS* schedule as a *straight* line, it may in fact get steeper as we move downwards along it – there are probably diminishing returns to the effect of lower interest rates in boosting aggregate demand. We therefore sometimes refer to it as the *IS* curve, and never refer to it as the *IS* line.

Shifts in the *IS* schedule

Movements along the *IS* schedule show how interest rates affect aggregate demand and equilibrium output. Other changes in aggregate demand shift the *IS* schedule. For a *given* interest rate, more optimism about future profits raises investment demand. Higher expected future incomes raise consumption demand. Higher government spending adds directly to aggregate demand. Any of these, by raising aggregate demand at a given interest rate, raises equilibrium output at any interest rate – an *upward shift* in the *IS* schedule.

Conversely, greater pessimism among firms or households, a cut in government spending or higher tax rates cause a downward shift in the *IS* schedule.

CASE 20.1

FISCALLY CHALLENGED EUROZONE COUNTRIES

Since 2009 financial markets have been concerned about the fiscal solvency of a number of countries. Within the Eurozone , and setting aside the case of tiny Cyprus, attention has largely focused on Portugal, Italy, Greece and Spain – which had four characteristics: high government debt, high budget deficits, lack of international competitiveness and membership of the Eurozone. Their fiscal problems became the first real crisis of the Eurozone.

Despite sharing a common currency, interest yields on their bonds were many percentage points higher than interest yields on German bonds, and their subsequent bond issues were expensive for their governments and taxpayers.

Optimists, such as Nobel Laureate Professor Joseph Stiglitz, argued that both interest rates and budget deficit indicators were misleading. If the crisis could be solved, risk premia embedded in their interest rates would evaporate as quickly as they had arisen. Budget deficits were also misleading because, as we saw in Chapter 17, the size of the budget deficit fluctuates with the level of output – in a slump tax revenue falls but, as output recovery occurs, tax revenue automatically rises again. Focusing on budget deficit data at the bottom of the slump gives a misleading impression of how bad the fiscal situation has become. Stiglitz therefore argued that Germany and France could help fiscally challenged members at little risk to themselves.

If the speculators could be defeated, the situation would correct itself without a need for default. In 2012, ECB President Mario Draghi undertook to purchase debts of these countries, justifying it by the need to fix the *transmission mechanism* of monetary policy within the Eurozone, whereby low ECB interest rates were supposed to feed through to low interest rates throughout the Eurozone. Many saw the move as a direct attempt to help the solvency of fiscally challenged countries, even though this was outside the remit of the ECB.

A fall in long-term interest rates has two effects on the *IS* schedule in such countries. First, it would move such countries down a given *IS* schedule, the direct effect of lower interest rates relevant for consumption and investment demand. Second, by easing the government's budget problems, it allows the government to have higher spending and/or lower tax rates than it would have had if it had continued to face higher borrowing costs. This fiscal expansion (relative to what might have been) leads to an *IS* schedule that is higher than it would have been in the presence of higher interest rates.

How large could such an effect be? The *primary* budget deficit shows the budget deficit *excluding* the interest payments on the debt. We can think of this as (a) an exact indicator of what would happen to the budget deficit if a country defaulted completely on its debt interest payments or (b) as a rough indicator of what would happen to its deficit if interest rates fell from high penal levels to much lower levels. The Organization for Economic Cooperation and Development (OECD) makes estimates of the 'underlying primary deficit', not merely excluding interest payments but also using the hypothetical tax revenue that would accrue if output had been at 'normal' rather than 'actual' levels.

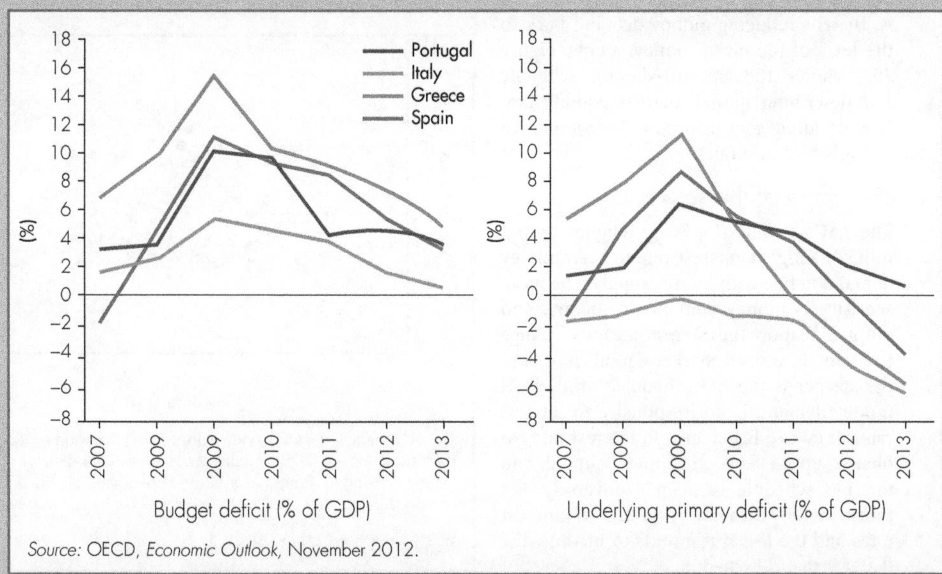

Source: OECD, *Economic Outlook*, November 2012.

The underlying primary deficit thus shows the state of the budget deficit once we strip out both debt problems and cyclical recession. It indicates how far off track the budget is in the long run. The charts show both the actual budget deficits of Portugal, Italy, Greece and Spain, and their underlying primary deficits.

The left-hand charts show all four countries gradually bringing their budget deficits under control after 2009, achieved by very austere fiscal policies that led to downward shifts in their *IS* curves, causing falls in output and higher unemployment. The right-hand chart shows the considerable progress that has been made with the underlying primary budgets, which are now in surplus or close to being in surplus. Inherited debts, penal interest rates and ongoing recessions are the cause of continuing problems. If these could be addressed somehow, fiscal policies themselves would not then be irresponsible or unsustainable.

Clearly, debtors should generally expect, and be expected, to repay their loans with interest. Sometimes, however, debtors are victims of circumstances not of their own making. Greece apart, none of the others had unsustainable policies when the crisis first occurred, and irresponsible behaviour in the US was the proximate cause of the crisis (albeit that property booms and irresponsible lending also occurred in most of Europe).

As the IMF and Eurozone ponder how much assistance now to offer countries in trouble, they need to consider two things. First, how much of the current predicament is a self-fulfilling crisis that could be resolved by long-term loans to allow struggling countries to enjoy lower interest rates, consequently loosen fiscal policy a little and shift *IS* schedules upwards? Second, how bad a precedent would be created by bailing out debtors in trouble, thereby undermining future incentives for prudent government behaviour?

The *LM* schedule: money market equilibrium

Pursuing a monetary target, the central bank endeavours to fix the money supply itself. In Figure 20.2, along the **LM schedule**, the demand for money (or liquidity *L*) equals the given supply of money (*M*, hence the shorthand *LM*).

> The *LM* schedule shows combinations of interest rates and income that lead to money market equilibrium when the central bank pursues a given target for the nominal money supply.

The quantity of money demanded rises with level of output *Y* but falls with the level of the interest rate *r*. In money market equilibrium, money demand equals the given money supply. Hence if output rises from Y_0 to Y_1 – tending to raise the quantity of money demanded – money market equilibrium is restored only if interest rates rise from r_0 to r_1, thereby reducing money demand back to the level of the given money supply. Figure 20.2 shows the upward-sloping schedule *LM* describing money market equilibrium. Higher output and income are accompanied by higher interest rates.

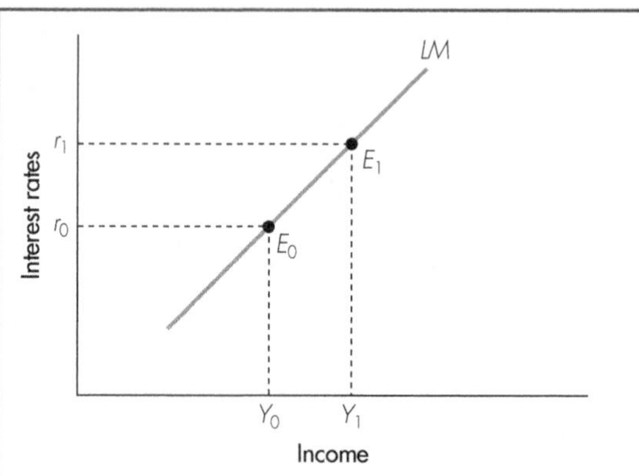

The *LM* schedule depicts money market equilibrium and is drawn for a given money supply. Higher income raises the quantity of money demanded. Only if interest rates are higher can the quantity of money demanded continue to equal the unchanged money supply.

Figure 20.2 **The LM schedule**

The slope of the schedule

The *LM* schedule slopes up. Higher output induces a higher interest rate to keep money demand in line with money supply. The more sensitive is money demand to income and output, the more the interest rate must change to maintain money market equilibrium, and the steeper is the *LM* schedule. Similarly, if money demand is not responsive to interest rates, it takes a big change in interest rates to offset output effects on money demand, and the *LM* schedule is steep. Conversely, the more money demand responds to interest rates and the less it responds to income, the flatter is the *LM* schedule.

As with the *IS* schedule, the *LM* schedule is almost certainly *not* a straight line. In particular, interests cannot fall below zero, so the *LM* schedule can never cross the horizontal axis. Again, we sometimes call it the *LM* curve, but never the *LM* line.

Shifts in the *LM* schedule

Movements along the schedule indicate interest rate changes to implement the *existing* policy as output changes. Shifts in the schedule reflect a *change* in monetary policy.

We draw an *LM* schedule for a *given* nominal money target. A rise in the target money supply means that money demand must also be increased to maintain money market equilibrium. This implies a rightward *shift* in the *LM* schedule. Output is higher, or interest rates lower, raising money demand in line with the rise in real money supply.

Conversely, a lower monetary target shifts the *LM* schedule to the left. Since money demand must also be reduced to preserve money market equilibrium, a higher interest rate is required at each income level. To sum up, moving along the *LM* schedule, higher interest rates need higher income to keep real money demand equal to the fixed supply. A higher (lower) target for money supply shifts the *LM* schedule to the right (left).

CONCEPT 20.1

A MODERN INTERPRETATION OF THE *LM* SCHEDULE

The *LM* schedule shows the relationship between interest rates and output implied by the monetary policy in force. Such a policy might be the pursuit of a fixed target for the quantity of money supplied.

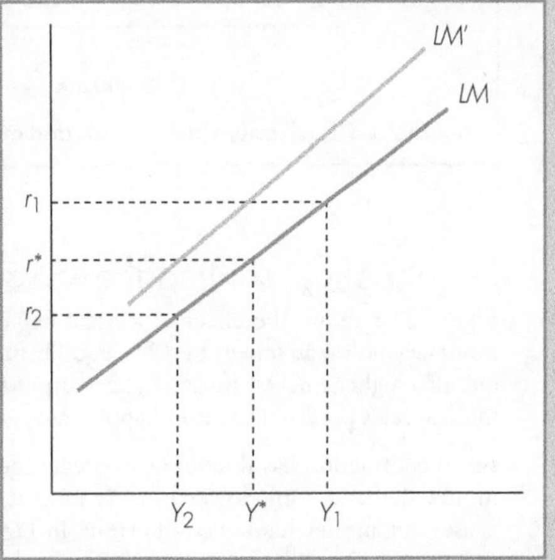

We could instead interpret the *LM* schedule as a monetary policy in which the central bank deliberately sets higher interest rates when output is higher. This is consistent with a desire to stabilize output around its full capacity level. The steeper the *LM* schedule, the more aggressively the central bank 'leans into the wind' in order to offset deviations of output from full capacity. When aggregate demand falls and output is below potential output Y^*, the central bank reduces interest rates to r_2, helping to mitigate the fall in aggregate demand and ensure output falls only to Y_2. Conversely, when aggregate demand is higher than potential output, the central bank raises interest rates to r_1, thereby restricting the increase in demand and output to Y_1.

What is happening to the quantity of money supplied? The central bank is passively supplying whatever money is necessary to achieve money market equilibrium at the interest rate that the central bank wishes, given the level of output that is being produced. If the resulting money demand is large, the central bank simply ensures that the money supply is larger.

A steeper schedule means that interest rates are adjusted more, thereby achieving even greater stabilization of output, a flatter *LM* schedule means interest rates are adjusted less to stabilize output. A vertical *LM* schedule would stabilize output completely.

As well as the *slope* of the *LM* schedule, we also have to think about *shifts* in the schedule. An upward shift in the *LM* schedule, from *LM* to *LM'*, reflects a tighter monetary policy. At any output level, interest rates are higher under the new policy than under the previous one. For example, at output Y^*, the interest rate is now r_1 instead of r^*. The new monetary policy is more restrictive than the old one.

20.3 The *IS–LM* model in action

Figure 20.3 shows both the *IS* schedule, depicting combinations of income and interest rates consistent with goods market equilibrium, and the *LM* schedule, depicting combinations of interest rates and income consistent with money market equilibrium when the central bank's monetary policy rule is to pursue a fixed money supply target. Equilibrium in both the money market and the output market is at point *E*, with an interest rate r^* and income level Y^*.

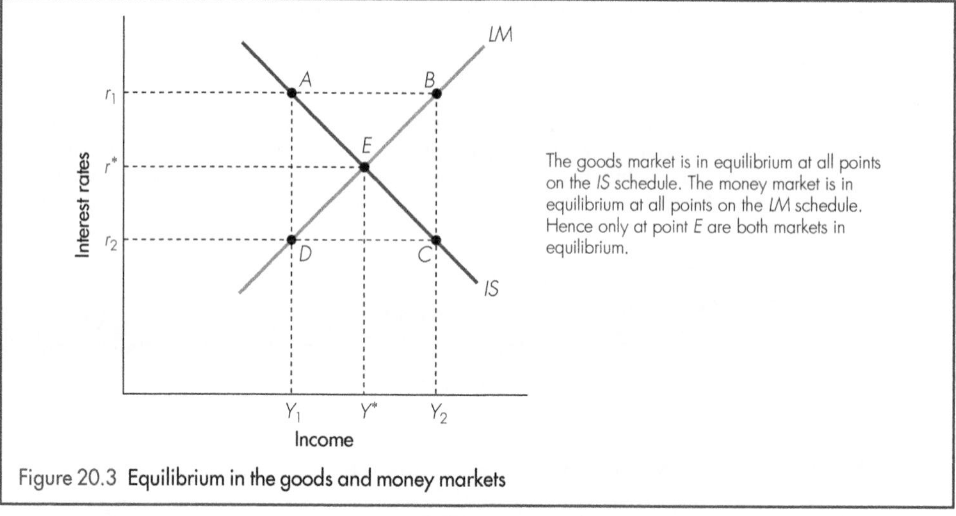

The goods market is in equilibrium at all points on the *IS* schedule. The money market is in equilibrium at all points on the *LM* schedule. Hence only at point *E* are both markets in equilibrium.

Figure 20.3 **Equilibrium in the goods and money markets**

Fiscal policy: shifting the *IS* schedule

Figure 20.4 shows the effect of a fiscal expansion that shifts the *IS* schedule from IS_0 to IS_1. If unchanged monetary policy is shown by LM_0, equilibrium moves from E to E_1. Fiscal expansion leads to higher income but also higher interest rates. Higher output tends to increase the quantity of money demanded. Only higher interest rates prevent this from happening.

Fiscal contraction has the opposite effect. The *IS* schedule shifts to the left and output falls, tending to reduce money demand. Only lower interest rates restore money demand to the unchanged level of money supply, preserving money market equilibrium. In Figure 20.4, this is a move from E_1 to E when the *IS* schedule shifts down from IS_1 to IS_0.

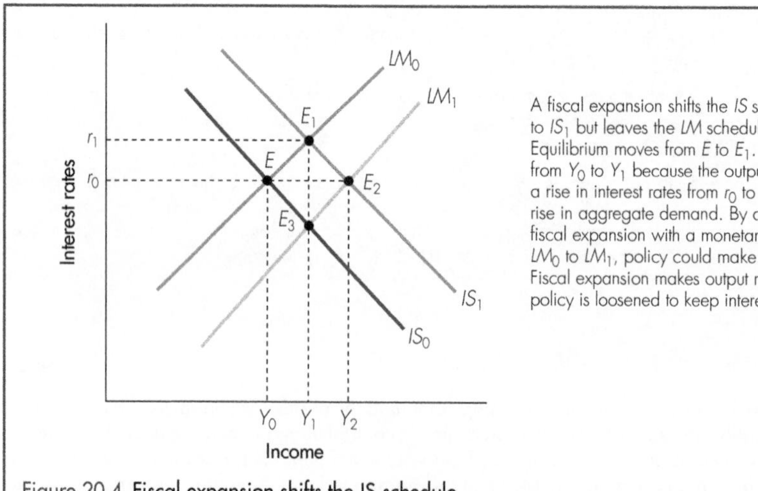

A fiscal expansion shifts the *IS* schedule from IS_0 to IS_1 but leaves the *LM* schedule unaltered at LM_0. Equilibrium moves from E to E_1. Output rises only from Y_0 to Y_1 because the output expansion induces a rise in interest rates from r_0 to r_1 that dampens the rise in aggregate demand. By accompanying the fiscal expansion with a monetary expansion from LM_0 to LM_1, policy could make output rise to Y_2. Fiscal expansion makes output rise more if monetary policy is loosened to keep interest rates unaltered.

Figure 20.4 **Fiscal expansion shifts the IS schedule**

A fiscal stimulus to aggregate demand crowds out in the Keynesian model some private spending. Higher output induces higher interest rates that dampen the expansionary effect on aggregate demand.

Figure 20.4 makes three other points. First, **crowding out in the Keynesian model** is complete – extra government spending G leads to an equivalent reduction in consumption and investment ($C + I$), leaving output unaltered – only if the LM schedule is vertical. Then, an upward shift in the IS schedule raises interest rates but not income.

In practice, the LM schedule is never completely vertical, which would occur only if it took an *infinite* rise in interest rates to offset the effect of slightly higher output on money demand. Since the LM schedule normally has a positive slope, fiscal expansion raises demand and output despite some induced rise in interest rates.

Second, fiscal policy is not the only possible autonomous change in aggregate demand. An increase in export demand would also shift the IS schedule to the right, again inducing higher output and higher interest rates. Movements *along* the IS schedule show the effect of interest rates. All other shifts in aggregate demand imply *shifts* in the IS schedule.

Third, Figure 20.4 shows what happens if fiscal expansion is *accompanied* by a looser monetary policy. Fiscal expansion shifts IS to the right, but monetary expansion – a higher money supply target – shifts LM to the right. It is possible to loosen monetary policy just enough to keep interest rates at their original level when income expands. Fiscal expansion then leads to a new equilibrium at E_2, with interest rates unchanged at r_0. Hence, the output effect of a fiscal expansion depends on the monetary policy in force. The more that monetary policy prevents a rise in interest rates, the more the fiscal expansion will lead to higher output.

CONCEPT 20.2

A HORIZONTAL *LM* SCHEDULE

If monetary policy is always adjusted to keep interest rates constant, we may as well view the *LM* schedule as horizontal at the target interest rate, as shown in the figure below. Suppose a fiscal expansion shifts the *IS* schedule from *IS* to *IS'*. If the central bank loosens monetary policy from *LM* to *LM'*, it can maintain interest rates at the original level despite the increase in output and money demand – it has simply increased money supply to match. The money supply is passively adjusted to whatever level of money is demanded at that interest rate. Shifts in the *IS* schedule no longer lead to crowding out because the money supply is adjusted to prevent interest rates from changing. Instead of depicting monetary policy as a whole potential set of parallel *LM* schedules, it is easier just to summarize it by the horizontal line at height r^*. Whatever happens to the *IS* schedule, monetary policy will then be adjusted to maintain the interest rate at a constant level.

A horizontal *LM* schedule implies the money supply is adjusted to keep interest rates constant.

In Chapter 24 we show that defending a fixed exchange rate may require a constant interest rate and hence a horizontal *LM* schedule. Hence, small countries within the Eurozone may face a horizontal *LM* schedule. The European Central Bank (ECB) sets an interest rate for the whole Eurozone, and countries such as Belgium and the Netherlands have to take this interest rate as given. Germany is a little luckier – as the largest country within the Eurozone, German economic conditions tend to affect the ECB's decisions regarding the interest rate within it. Most of the time, euro interest rates are higher when German output is higher; Germany enjoys an *LM* curve that slopes upwards. Upward-sloping *LM* curves mean that monetary policy is acting to stabilize output fluctuations by raising interest rates when that country's output is higher.

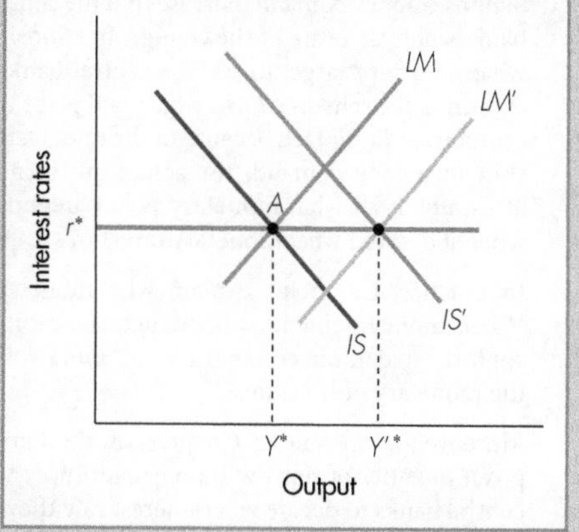

Monetary expansion: shifting the *LM* schedule

Similarly, beginning from *E* in Figure 20.4, an increase in the target money supply shifts the *LM* schedule from LM_0 to LM_1: for any income, it requires lower interest rates to help raise money demand in line with the new higher money supply. Lower interest rates also boost income, which also helps raise money demand. Equilibrium moves from *E* to E_3. Conversely, a reduction in the target money supply shifts the *LM* schedule to the left, leading to higher interest rates but lower output.

20.4 Shocks to money demand

In the last three decades, competition between banks has increased dramatically, raising interest rates paid on deposits. Since the opportunity cost of holding money in a bank deposit is only the differential between the deposit interest rate and the higher interest rate available on other financial assets, changes in banking competition change the opportunity cost of holding money *at any market interest rate* r. Conversely, since the financial crash, banks have been desperate to increase profit margins in order to rebuild capital reserves. The spread between deposit interest rates and market interest rates has widened sharply.

We draw an *LM* schedule for a given nominal money target. Greater banking competition raises money demand at every combination of output and interest rates. To keep money demand in line with the unchanged supply, either output must fall or interest rates must rise. The *LM* schedule *shifts* left. Conversely, if spreads widen and the opportunity cost of holding money increases, the *LM* schedule shifts to the right.

Figure 20.4 showed how changes in money *supply* shift the *LM* schedule under monetary targeting. We have now discovered that changes in money *demand*, other than those caused by changes in output and interest rates, also shift the *LM* schedule under monetary targeting.

In Figure 20.5, LM_1 corresponds to 'low' money demand and LM_2 to 'high' money demand. Suppose money demand increases but the central bank is not yet aware of the change. In choosing what monetary target to set, the central bank is expecting the schedule LM_1, which will place the economy at E_1. In fact, because of the undetected shift in money demand, the actual out-turn is at E_2, not at all what monetary policy intended when it decided what monetary target to set.

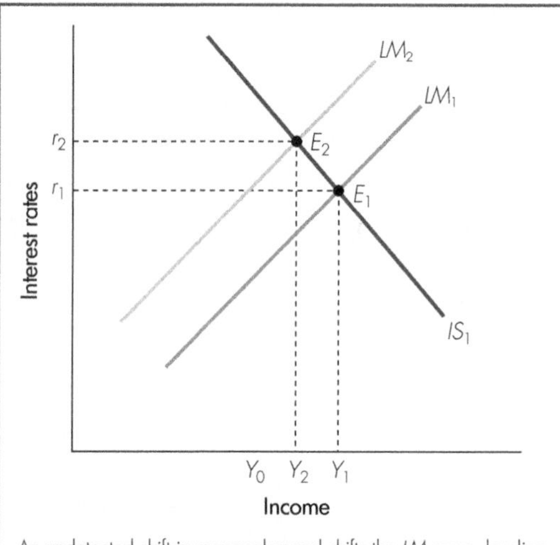

An undetected shift in money demand shifts the *LM* curve, leading to a different equilibrium from that which the central bank intended when deciding what level of the money supply to target.

Figure 20.5 **An unexpected rise in money demand**

In practice, this helps explain why monetary targets were gradually abandoned by many central banks. When money demand was predictable, monetary targets worked fine. As the financial sector became more sophisticated, more competitive and more volatile, monetary targets were gradually abandoned as the basis for the monetary policy rule.

Moreover, as we saw in Chapter 18, the bank deposit multiplier can be highly unstable. This means that a given quantity of narrow money can imply very different quantities of broad money. It is much simpler for central banks to decide what interest rate they wish to set, and then passively supply whatever narrow money is necessary to get whatever quantity of broad money is needed for money market equilibrium at that interest rate.

MATHS 20.1

THE MONETARY FISCAL MIX

Consider the model:

$$Y = A - br \quad IS \text{ schedule} \quad A, b > 0 \quad (1a)$$

$$Y = D + er \quad LM \text{ schedule} \quad e > 0, 0 < D < A \quad (1b)$$

Hence, $Y = A - br = D + er$, so in short-run equilibrium:

$$r = (A - D)/(b + e) \qquad Y = (Ae + bD)/(b + e) \quad (2)$$

Thus, for example, a rise in autonomous aggregate demand will lead to an increase in short-run equilibrium output and interest rates.

To understand the *LM* schedule in more detail, we can use the money market equations:

$$M = fY - hr \quad \text{Money demand} \quad f, h > 0$$

$$M = mR \quad \text{Deposit multiplier} \quad m > 0$$

Hence,

$$Y = [mR + hr]/f = [mR/f] + (h/f)r \quad (3)$$

Comparing this with equation (1b), we can see that the constant D in the *LM* schedule, which determines how far to the right the *LM* schedule lies, is just $[mR/f]$ and will increase if the central bank supplies more reserves R, if banks raise the deposit multiplier m, or if money demand becomes more sensitive to income via the parameter f. Moreover, the slope of the schedule, which depends on e in equation (1b), simply depends on the parameters h and f.

20.5 The policy mix

Fiscal policy is government decisions about tax rates and spending levels. Changes in fiscal policy shift the *IS* schedule. Changes in monetary policy shift the *LM* schedule.

We now explore consequences of different *IS* and *LM* schedules (different monetary and fiscal policies). Budget deficits can be financed by printing money or by borrowing. In the latter case, there is no short-run connection between monetary and fiscal policy provided the government is solvent and can borrow any reasonable amount that it wishes. The government can then pursue independent monetary and fiscal policies.

Although both fiscal and monetary policy can alter aggregate demand, the two policies are not interchangeable. They affect aggregate demand through different routes and have different implications for the *composition* of aggregate demand.

Figure 20.6 shows the mix of monetary and fiscal policy. There are two ways to stabilize income at Y^*. First, there is expansionary or *easy* fiscal policy (high government spending or low tax rates). This leads to a high *IS* schedule, IS_1. To keep income in check with such an expansionary fiscal policy, *tight* monetary policy is needed. With a low money supply target, the schedule LM_1 is far to the left.

Equilibrium at E_1 achieves an output Y^* but also a high interest rate r_1. With high government spending, private demand must be kept in check. The mix of easy fiscal policy and tight monetary policy implies government spending G is a big share of national income Y^* but private spending $(C + I)$ a small share.

Alternatively, the government can adopt a tight fiscal policy (a low IS_0 schedule) and an easy monetary policy (LM_0 far to the right). The target income Y^* is now attained with a lower interest rate r_2 at the equilibrium E_2. With easy monetary policy and tight fiscal policy, the share of private expenditure $(C + I)$ is higher, and the share of government expenditure is lower, than at E_1. With lower interest rates, there is less crowding out of private expenditure.

Of course, easy monetary policy *and* easy fiscal policy together are highly expansionary. With the schedules IS_1 and LM_0 the equilibrium in Figure 20.6 is at E_4. Income is well above Y^*. Conversely, with tight monetary policy and tight fiscal policy, and schedules LM_1 and IS_0, equilibrium is at E_3, with income well below Y^*.

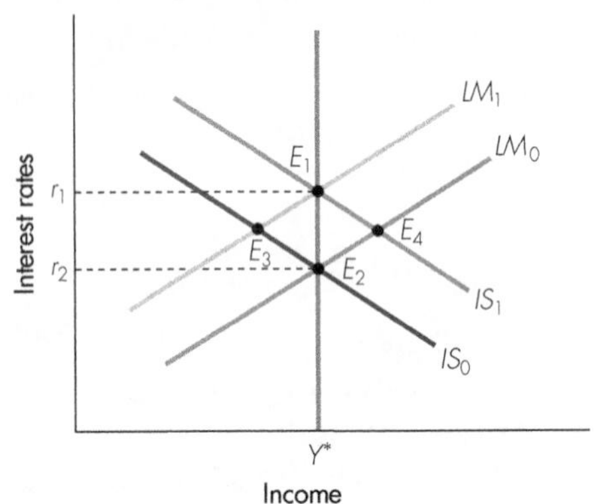

The target income Y can be attained by easy fiscal policy and tight monetary policy. Equilibrium at E_1, the intersection of LM_1 and IS_1, implies high interest rates r_1 and a low share of private sector investment and consumption in GNP. Alternatively, with easy monetary policy and tight fiscal policy, equilibrium at E_2, the intersection of LM_0 and IS_0, still attains the target income but at lower interest rates r_2. The share of private sector investment and consumption in GNP will be higher than at E_1.

Figure 20.6 **The policy mix**

What should determine the mix of fiscal and monetary policy? In the long run, the government may care not just about keeping output close to potential output, but also about raising potential output. High investment increases the capital stock more quickly, giving workers more equipment with which to work and raising their productivity. Governments interested in long-run growth may choose a tight fiscal policy and an easy monetary policy. Conversely, if governments are politically weak and unable to resist demands for high government spending to pay off various factions, fiscal policy will be loose and a tight monetary policy is needed to keep aggregate demand in line with potential output.

Solvency concerns also affect the feasible monetary–fiscal mix. When financial markets panic about the solvency of particular governments, further bond-financed fiscal expansion may not be possible. Nobody will buy the bonds. The more difficult it is to meet aims through one policy, the more desirable it is for the other policy to do the work. The problem for Eurozone countries such as Greece was that, as members of the Eurozone, they had surrendered the ability to use an independent monetary policy to target their needs alone.

One final point about the monetary–fiscal mix: changing fiscal policy takes time whereas monetary policy can be changed very quickly.

ACTIVITY 20.1

MONETARY OR FISCAL POLICY?

Concept 17.1 noted some reasons why fiscal policy may not be ideal for short-run management of aggregate demand. Some of these reasons – for example, problems in diagnosing where the economy is and forecasting where it might go if policy is left unchanged – apply just as much to monetary policy as to fiscal policy. However, two problems are often thought to make fiscal policy less suitable for short-run variation.

First, fiscal policy is difficult to change quickly. Rapid changes in hospital building or in tax rates are more costly than rapid changes in interest rates. Financial markets are accustomed to asset prices changing quickly. Second, it is politically easy to loosen fiscal policy but politically much more difficult to tighten it again later. For this reason, the most important source of short-term movements in fiscal policy is the operation of automatic stabilizers. Since tax rates are not changing, no visible decisions are being made to which voters could object. Yet tax revenue is varying with output.

It used also to be politically difficult to tighten monetary policy. For example, people (voters!) who have borrowed to buy a house get upset when interest rates rise sharply. The main reason that most countries have made their central banks independent of political control in decisions about interest rates is precisely to take the politics out of monetary policy. Nowadays, interest rates can and do change rapidly, in both directions, though usually by very small amounts. The chart shows UK data from 1997, when the Bank of England formally became independent, until 2012.

▶

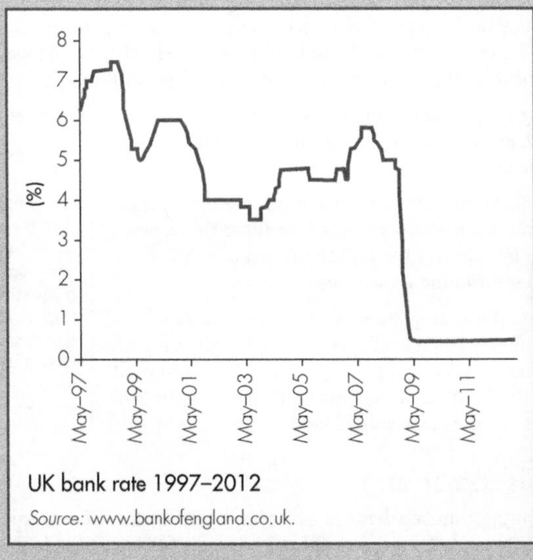

UK bank rate 1997–2012

Source: www.bankofengland.co.uk.

The figure confirms how aggressively interest rates were reduced in 2008/09 once the magnitude of the financial crisis became apparent.

What does this imply about the monetary–fiscal mix? The budget deficit was already high by 2009 because of the need to bail out banks. Further fiscal expansion threatened to create unsustainable levels of government debt that would have been difficult to repay. In these circumstances, monetary policy had to provide as much stimulus as possible, both because a large stimulus was needed and because fiscal policy was already overstretched.

By March 2009 the Bank of England's official rate had been cut to 0.5 per cent and could hardly go much lower. It remained there for the next three years. As we saw in Chapter 19, the Bank then embarked on a programme of quantitative easing, partly to offset the collapse of the bank deposit multiplier and partly in the hope of providing additional stimulus by bidding down the prices of long bonds, thereby reducing long-term interest rates.

Questions

(a) During which periods since 1997 was the Bank of England most worried about inflation? Why do you think this?

(b) Were interest rates changed in response to inflation at the time or to the prospect of inflation a year or two subsequently? Why do you think this?

(c) Should the Bank worry about changing its mind, raising interest rates but sometimes lowering them shortly afterwards if necessary, or should it act more slowly so that it rarely has to reverse its recent decisions?

(d) Suppose an output slump leads to a period of negative inflation. What is the lowest possible nominal interest rate? What would then happen to real interest rates?

To check your answers to these questions, go to page 680.

20.6 The effect of future taxes

Chapter 19 argued that consumption demand reflects both *current* disposable income and expected *future* disposable income. Two hundred years ago, the English economist David Ricardo noticed a striking implication. Suppose the path of government purchases G is fixed over time. What path of taxes over time finances this spending?

The government can lend and borrow. In some years, its spending may exceed taxes; in other years, taxes must then exceed spending.

Government solvency requires that the present value of current and future tax revenue equals the present value of current and future spending plus any initial net debts.

For a given planned path of spending, and a suitable planned path of tax revenue, the government cuts taxes this year, and pays for it by borrowing – hence achieving **government solvency**. It sells bonds. The tax cut is a fiscal expansion that boosts aggregate demand. Right?

If the tax cut is £1 billion, this is also the value of bonds issued to finance it. The market value of bonds is the present value of future income to bondholders. By assumption, the path of government spending is fixed. Hence, interest payments to bondholders must be financed by higher taxes in the future.

£1 billion is the value of the tax cut, *and* the value of the new bonds, *and* the present value of the extra future taxes. The private sector gets a handout today (a tax cut) offset by a future penalty (higher taxes) of identical present value. The private sector is neither richer nor poorer. Its desired spending should not change. Today's tax cut has no effect on aggregate demand because it is matched by the *prospect* of higher future taxes.

Equivalently, the fall in government saving (larger deficit today) is exactly offset by a rise in private saving: private spending is unaltered, and larger disposable incomes (because of the tax cut) go entirely in extra saving (to pay for the future taxes).

Some people getting tax cuts today will die before future taxes arrive. But suppose these people have children and care about them. After a tax cut today, parents save more to bequeath extra money to their children, or grandchildren, to pay the higher future taxes. The extra disposable income is saved to raise the bequest for future generations.

Ricardian equivalence does not deny that road-building, financed by higher taxes, affects aggregate demand. Government spending always has real effects. Rather, for a *given* path of real government spending, it may not matter *when* people pay for it. Ricardo himself thought the equivalence hypothesis would not hold in the real world. Economists are still arguing about the extent to which **Ricardian equivalence** should hold.

Ricardian equivalence says that it does not matter *when* a government finances a given long-run spending programme. Tax cuts today do not affect private spending if, in present value terms, future taxes have to rise to match.

Why Ricardian equivalence is too strong

There are three reasons why the tax cuts today *do* stimulate demand a bit even if future taxes are correspondingly higher. First, people without children get the benefit of tax cuts without paying the full burden of higher future taxes in the distant future. They spend more at once.

Second, by reducing marginal tax rates and distortions, tax cuts may increase potential output and raise income. Expecting higher incomes, people spend more immediately.

Third, solvent governments can borrow at a low interest rate. Ricardian equivalence holds only if we can all borrow as easily as the government. If only! Households and firms are individually riskier than governments. Private people have no residual power to tax or print money when things go wrong. Hence, lenders charge private borrowers a higher rate of interest, and may refuse to lend at all.

Now do the sums again. £1 billion is the value of the tax cut, the extra government bonds and the present value of extra tax payments *discounted at the interest rate faced by the government*. We face a higher interest rate when we try to borrow. *As viewed by us, the present value of our extra future taxes is less than £1 billion because we discount at a higher interest rate.*

The tax cut is a fiscal expansion because in effect the government borrows on the good terms it enjoys, then lends to us at better terms than the capital market. It gives us a loan, tax cuts today, which we repay later in higher taxes. But we are charged the government's low interest rate for our loan. We are better off and spend more. Aggregate demand increases.

Theory and evidence suggest that complete Ricardian equivalence is too extreme to fit the real world. Tax cuts do boost aggregate demand today (though higher future taxes will reduce demand at some future date). Ricardian equivalence is not completely right, but not completely wrong. Expectations of future conditions affect current behaviour. Private saving rises a bit when public saving falls. The private sector does substitute between present and future, despite obstacles to doing this easily. These obstacles make consumption demand more sensitive to current disposable income than it would be if borrowing were easy and only permanent income mattered.

Current demand by firms and households depends both on current fiscal policy and expected future fiscal policy. Since one does not fully offset the other, for simplicity we can look at current fiscal policy in isolation. We need to remember only that some of its quantitative effects will be smaller if people expect fiscal policy to have to be reversed at some future date.

If Ricardian equivalence held exactly, government efforts to prop up aggregate demand in the aftermath of a financial crisis by running budget deficits would have been a waste of time. But understanding the trade-off between the present and the future allows three insights into the events since 2008:

1 It was precisely in 2009 that banks were most scared to lend and the private sector had so much difficulty borrowing. People who cannot borrow at all have to use an infinite discount rate in discounting the future.

These are the circumstances in which bond-financed tax cuts are most powerful. They increase private sector liquidity at the critical time. The government can borrow on better terms than its individual citizens can.

2 Conversely, as governments get closer to the limits of what they can easily borrow and guarantee to repay, the differential between private sector and government creditworthiness narrows. At some future point, deficit-financed tax cuts (or other subsidies to the private sector) lose most of their power.

3 Two specific measures adopted in 2009 – a temporary VAT cut and a temporary subsidy to scrappage of old cars –worked not by increasing the permanent income of households but by persuading them to bring forward spending from the future to the present. This is great when the measures are first introduced (and helped explain positive UK output growth by the fourth quarter of 2009), but then leads to a corresponding fall in demand when we get to the future from which the spending has been brought forward. All that has occurred is a retiming of spending, not an increase in the entire path of spending.

Governments wish to bring spending forward because of the effect on confidence. If this can be established, by ending the downward spiral, growth may become strong enough to cope with the future lack of spending for a while. Given that most European economies were back in recession by 2012, the temporary restoration of confidence did not then set their economies on sustainable growth paths. Once growth became fragile, confidence soon evaporated again.

20.7 Demand management revisited

Demand management uses monetary and fiscal policy to stabilize output near potential output.

In the last five chapters we have studied how aggregate demand determines output and employment. Fiscal and monetary policy can manage aggregate demand, aiming to keep the economy close to its full-employment level. In periods of recession, when aggregate demand is insufficient, monetary and fiscal expansion can boost demand, output and employment.

Thus far, we have treated the price level as given. If the price level can change, boosting demand may lead not to higher output but to higher prices. In the next chapter, we begin the study of prices and inflation. In so doing, we introduce aggregate supply, and hence the balance between aggregate supply and aggregate demand.

However, you have now completed the first stage of macroeconomics, learning how to analyse the demand side of the economy. Even after mastering the analysis of supply, adjustment and price behaviour, the demand analysis of the last few chapters remains a key part of the story, especially in the short run.

Summary

- A **given fiscal policy** means a given path of government spending and tax rates. A **given monetary policy** must specify the implicit **monetary policy rule** by which interest rates are set. In this chapter, we assume that is to achieve a given **money supply target**.
- The *IS* **schedule** shows combinations of interest rates and output compatible with short-run equilibrium output in the goods market. Lower interest rates boost demand and output. Other causes of shifts in demand are shown as shifts in the *IS* schedule.
- The *LM* **schedule** shows combinations of interest rates and output compatible with money market equilibrium when the central bank pursues a money supply target. Higher output is associated with higher interest rates to maintain the equality of money supply and money demand.
- The intersection of *IS* and *LM* schedules shows simultaneous equilibrium in both goods and money markets, jointly determining output and interest rates.

- With a given monetary policy, a **fiscal expansion** increases output, money demand and interest rates, thus **crowding out** or partially displacing private consumption and investment demand.
- For a given fiscal policy, a **monetary expansion** leads to lower interest rates and higher output.
- The **mix of monetary and fiscal policy** affects the equilibrium interest rate as well as the level of output.
- **Ricardian equivalence** says that, for a given present value of government spending, the private sector does not care *when* this is financed by taxes, since the total present value of taxes is the same. A tax cut today has no effect on aggregate demand since people anticipate higher future taxes to finance the extra debt interest.
- Ricardian equivalence is true only under extreme assumptions not generally true in practice. Tax cuts today do have some effect today. This effect is dampened by the knowledge that, unless government spending is also cut, future taxes will have to rise.
- **Demand management** helps stabilize output. Fiscal policy may be difficult to adjust quickly, and may be difficult politically to reverse later: much of its impact on aggregate demand thus arises through **automatic stabilizers** with an unchanged fiscal policy.

Review questions

EASY

1 A small country that has adopted the euro must accept the single interest rate set for the whole of Euroland. Draw the *LM* schedule relating the interest rate to that country's national output. Why would this schedule ever shift?

2 Which of the following is correct? Other things equal, high output and high interest rates imply: (a) loose monetary policy and loose fiscal policy, (b) tight fiscal policy and tight monetary policy, (c) tight fiscal policy and loose monetary policy, (d) none of the above.

3 Why do people usually save a 'one-off income tax rebate'?

4 Suppose a government lived for ever and never broke its promises. Facing a large budget deficit and large government debt today, should the bond market be confident that any level of initial debt will be repaid provided the government pledges to do so sometime in the future?

5 **Common fallacies** Why are the following statements wrong? (a) If tax rates never change, fiscal policy cannot stabilize output. (b) Higher government spending makes interest rates rise, which could cut aggregate demand by more than the rise in government spending. (c) Future policy cannot affect present behaviour.

MEDIUM

6 Suppose mortgage lenders issued 20-year loans at fixed interest rates.
 (a) How would short-term changes in interest rates impact households with a mortgage?
 (b) Would the Bank of England have to change interest rates by more or by less to have the same effect on aggregate demand at present?

7 Suppose the European Central Bank has a monetary policy rule that relates Euroland's interest rate to total output in Euroland. If a small Euroland country's output is perfectly correlated with the output of all Euroland, draw the *LM* schedule (a) for Euroland and (b) for the small member country.

8 In 2010, having accumulated substantial government debt owed by foreigners and having a large budget deficit, Greece lost the confidence of its international creditors and was given a loan on condition that it embarked on substantial fiscal tightening.
 (a) Illustrate these changes, using the *IS–LM* diagram, recognizing that Greece is a Eurozone member. (b) Suppose Greece left the Eurozone; what, if anything, would be different?

9 For each of these shocks, say whether it shifts the *IS* schedule or the *LM* schedule, and in which direction: (a) an expected future fiscal expansion, (b) a higher money supply target, (c) a rise in money demand causing higher interest rates being paid by banks on bank deposits.

MEDIUM

10 Suppose monetary policy raises nominal interest rates by 0.8 every time inflation rises by 1. (a) How do you expect the central bank gets on in stabilizing inflation around a low level? (b) Suppose inflation is nevertheless low and stable: how might you explain this outcome?

11 The diagram below shows the working of the *IS–LM* model where a mix of monetary and fiscal policy is used to stabilize income at Y^*.

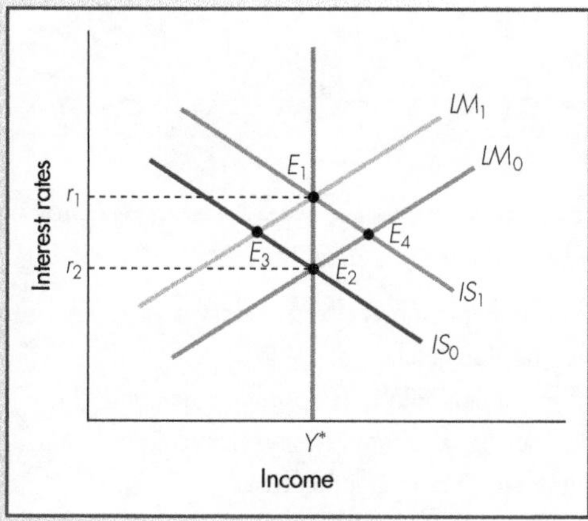

If the government adopts a tight monetary policy and an easy fiscal policy, how can income be stabilized at Y^*? How can income be stabilized with an easy monetary policy and a tight fiscal policy? Can income be stabilized at Y^* if the government adopted a tight monetary policy and tight fiscal policy?

HARD

12 **Essay question** 'If households can lend and borrow easily, their consumption and saving decisions simply offset anticipated future tax changes. The principal power of taxation policy to influence aggregate demand arises because households in practice face difficulties borrowing what would be required to implement Ricardian equivalence.' Discuss.

13 Use the *IS–LM* diagram to depict (a) the start of a financial crash in which confidence evaporates in the private sector and the banking system and (b) a subsequent policy of quantitative easing.

14 Imagine a world of only two periods and zero interest rates. A consumer's income is 100 in each period, taxes are 50 each period, permanent disposable income is therefore 50, and consumption is 50 per period (since the world ends after period 2). The government now offers a tax cut of 10 in period 1, financed by government borrowing that will be repaid in period 2. (a) Since interest rates are zero, by how much must the government raise taxes in period 2 in order to pay off its loan in full? (b) What is the consumer's disposable income now in each period? (c) Since the interest rate is zero, what is permanent disposable income? (d) What is the effect on consumption decisions? (e) If the government pays zero interest on loans, but the consumer pays 10 per cent interest, how is permanent income affected? (f) What is now the effect of the temporary tax cut?

For solutions to these questions, contact your lecturer.

CHAPTER 21

Aggregate supply, prices and adjustment to shocks

Learning Outcomes

By the end of this chapter, you should be able to:

1 understand inflation targets for monetary policy
2 recognise the *ii* schedule
3 describe how inflation affects aggregate demand
4 understand aggregate supply in the classical model
5 analyse the equilibrium inflation rate
6 understand complete crowding out in the classical model
7 recognise why wage adjustment may be slow
8 analyse short-run aggregate supply
9 understand temporary and permanent supply shocks
10 describe how monetary policy reacts to demand and supply shocks
11 recognise flexible inflation targets
12 identify a Taylor rule

Keynesian models suggest that higher aggregate demand always raises output. However, with finite resources, the economy cannot expand output indefinitely. We now introduce aggregate supply – firms' willingness and ability to produce – and show how demand and supply together determine output. Aggregate demand reflects the interaction of the markets for goods and money. Aggregate supply reflects the interaction of the markets for goods and labour.

Introducing supply means that we abandon the simplifying assumption that output is determined by demand alone. With both supply and demand, we can also explain what determined prices. We no longer need to assume that prices are given. And since inflation is simply the growth of prices from period to period, a model of prices is also a model of inflation. This allows us to represent monetary policy as inflation targeting, the policy rule actually followed by most central banks today.

To get started, we swap the Keynesian extreme, with fixed wages and prices, for the opposite extreme, full wage and price flexibility. In the **classical model**, the economy is *always* at full capacity. Any deviation of output from full capacity causes instant price and wage changes to restore output to potential output. In the classical model, monetary and fiscal policies affect prices but not output.

The classical model of macroeconomics assumes wages and prices are completely flexible.

In the short run, until prices and wages adjust, the Keynesian model is relevant. In the long run, once all prices and wages have adjusted, the classical model is relevant. We study the transition from the Keynesian short run to the classical long run.

21.1 Inflation and aggregate demand

Inflation is the growth rate of the price level of aggregate output.

If a central bank behaves predictably, its behaviour can be modelled. Many central banks used to set interest rates to achieve a desired path for nominal money. Knowing the money demand schedule – the relation between interest rates, income and desired money holdings – the central bank forecast income, and chose interest rates to ensure that the quantity of money demanded equalled that it wished to supply.

Money demand became increasingly volatile and unpredictable because of financial innovation and changing competition between banks. Both affected the interest rates paid on bank deposits, and hence the opportunity cost of holding money. If central banks could not predict money demand, they did not know at what level to set interest rates in order to achieve desired money supply.

Monetary targeting was first abandoned in the countries experiencing the greatest financial innovation and banking competition: the US and the UK. Germany, initially more cautious about financial deregulation, retained monetary targeting for longer. Today, most central banks pursue an **inflation target**. Because of its strong German heritage, the European Central Bank pays attention both to inflation and monetary targets, a slightly uneasy compromise.

With an inflation target, the central bank adjusts interest rates to try to keep inflation close to the target inflation rate.

Target annual inflation π^* varies from country to country, but is usually around 2 per cent. Why not target zero inflation? Policy makers are keen to avoid *deflation* (negative inflation). Even if the nominal interest rate r is reduced to zero, the real interest rate i, which is simply $(r - \pi)$, can be large if inflation π is large but negative. High real interest rates cause further contraction, make inflation more negative still, thus making real interest rates even higher. If nominal interest rates have already been reduced to zero, monetary policy can do little to combat shrinking aggregate demand.

To avoid this black hole, a positive inflation target leaves a margin of error. If an unforeseen shock reduces inflation, there is still time for the central bank to boost the economy before it gets too close to a deflationary spiral.

Figure 21.1 shows how monetary policy works when interest rates are set to achieve an inflation target. If inflation is high, the central bank ensures that real interest rates are high, reducing aggregate demand, and putting downward pressure on inflation.

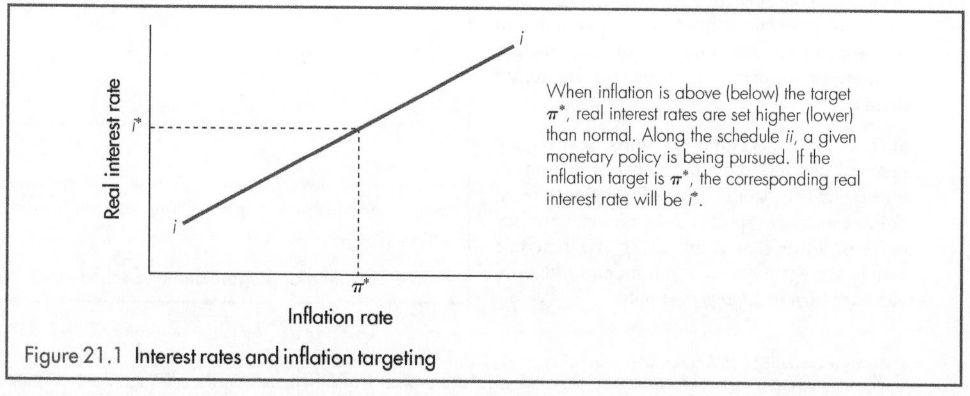

Figure 21.1 Interest rates and inflation targeting

Under inflation targeting, the *ii* schedule shows that, at higher inflation rates, the central bank will wish to have higher real interest rates.

With a vertical ***ii* schedule**, inflation would be completely stabilized at its target rate π^*. If inflation started to rise, real interest rates would be raised as much as necessary to restore inflation to its target level. Conversely, if inflation started to fall, real interest rates would be reduced to the level needed to restore the inflation to target.

Such a monetary policy would be too aggressive. Later in the chapter we show why some of its side effects would be undesirable. The *ii* schedule in Figure 21.1 shows more moderate intervention. When inflation is too high, the central bank raises real interest rates a bit; when inflation is too low, real interest rates are reduced a bit.

Although the central bank is interested in the real interest rate, which affects aggregate demand, the central bank does not directly control the price of output or the inflation rate. Hence, to achieve the *ii* schedule of Figure 21.1, the central bank first forecasts inflation, then sets a **nominal interest rate** *r* to achieve the desired **real interest rate** *i* (which is just $r - \pi$).

The central bank sets the nominal interest rate *r* not the real interest rate *i*.

An implication of Figure 21.1 is that higher inflation leads to a *larger* rise in the nominal interest rate, so that the real interest rate is higher when inflation is higher.[1]

The aggregate demand schedule *AD* shows how inflation affects aggregate demand when the interest rate is set in pursuit of an inflation target.

A particular *ii* schedule is a particular monetary policy. Moving along the schedule, the central bank adjusts interest rates to inflation according to the policy rule already adopted. The policy is not changing. *Changes* in monetary policy are shown by *shifts* in the schedule. A looser monetary policy means a downward shift in the *ii* schedule; that is, a lower interest rate at each possible inflation rate. A tighter monetary policy shifts the *ii* schedule upwards; that is, a higher interest rate at each possible inflation rate.

If π^* is the inflation target, the chosen height of the *ii* schedule determines the corresponding real interest rate i^* when the inflation target is being met. A tighter monetary policy (higher *ii* schedule) means accepting a higher real interest rate i^* at the given inflation target π^*, or a lower inflation target at the same real interest rate i^*.

Figure 21.2 shows the level of aggregate demand for output when interest rates obey the *ii* schedule implied by inflation targeting. Movements *along* the **aggregate demand schedule** *AD* show how inflation makes the central bank alter real interest rates and thus aggregate demand.[2] The *AD* schedule is flat when (a) interest rate decisions react a lot to inflation and (b) interest rates have a big effect on aggregate demand. The *AD* is steep when (a) interest rate decisions do not respond much to inflation and (b) changes in interest rates have a small effect on aggregate demand.

Shifts in *AD* reflect all other shifts in aggregate demand *not* caused by the effect of inflation on interest rate decisions. Thus, *AD* shifts up if fiscal policy eases, net exports rise or monetary policy eases (a lower *ii* schedule). The *AD* schedule relates aggregate demand, output and inflation. Next, we turn to aggregate supply.

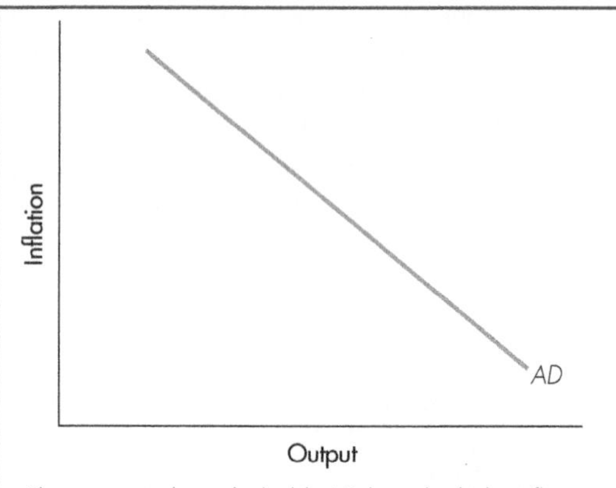

The aggregate demand schedule *AD* shows that higher inflation reduces aggregate demand by inducing the central bank to raise real interest rates.

Figure 21.2 The aggregate demand schedule

1 Across countries, higher inflation is often matched by equally higher nominal interest rates, leaving real interest rates roughly constant. This reflects the relative constancy of i^* in the long run. For short-run data for a single country, nominal interest rates vary more than inflation, reflecting the central bank behaviour embodied in Figure 21.1. Recognizing that interest rates must rise sharply when inflation increases has been a key breakthrough of monetary policy design in the last two decades.

2 A similar *AD* schedule exists if, instead, the central bank pursues a money supply target. For a given path of nominal money *M*, higher inflation, by raising prices more, reduces the real money supply *M/P* by more. With lower real money supply, interest rates rise to reduce real money demand and maintain money market equilibrium. Higher real interest rates reduce aggregate demand, just as in Figure 21.2. Under a monetary target, interest rates rise because inflation has reduced the real money supply. Under inflation targeting, interest rates rise in direct response to inflation itself, and the real money supply is then reduced to make this an equilibrium. Either way, higher inflation induces higher real interest rates and lower aggregate demand.

CONCEPT 21.1

AGGREGATE DEMAND, THE *IS* SCHEDULE AND THE *II* SCHEDULE

By now, any sensible person is asking two questions. First, why are there so many ways in which to model aggregate demand? Second, how do these different approaches fit together? The figure provides the answers.

We measure output on the horizontal axis in the right-hand panels – a movement to the right denotes higher output and aggregate demand. We measure nominal interest rates in the upward vertical direction – higher up denotes a higher nominal interest rate. We measure inflation in the horizontal direction in the left-hand panel – a movement further to the left denotes higher inflation. We also measure inflation in the bottom panel – a movement further down denotes higher inflation. The 45-degree line ensures that whatever inflation rate we measure in the horizontal direction is the same as the inflation rate we measure in the vertical direction.

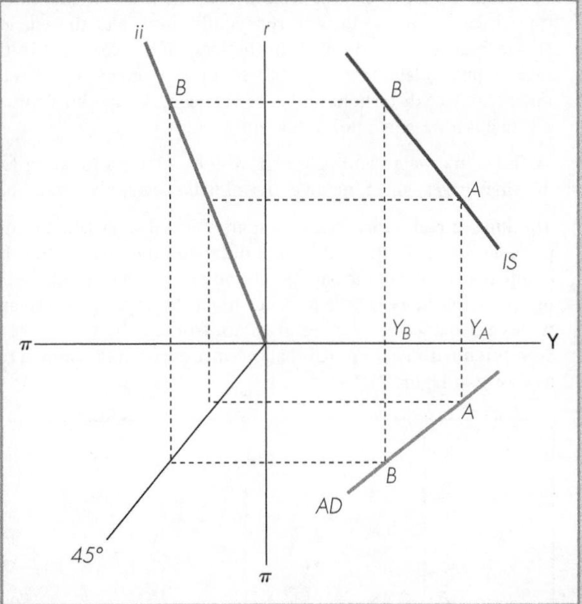

Begin in the top right-hand panel, which relates aggregate demand to nominal interest rates. The *IS* schedule shows, other things equal, how lower interest rates boost aggregate demand as we move along the *IS* schedule. Any other change, such as a fiscal expansion, would be shown as an upward shift in the *IS* schedule.

The top left-land panel relates nominal interest rates to inflation. The *ii* schedule describes the given monetary policy in force. As drawn, any particular increase in inflation leads to a larger increase in nominal interest rates – the central bank ensures that real interest rates rise when inflation rises in order to keep inflation under control.

Thus, if we begin at point *A* in the top right-hand panel, we can deduce the associated nominal interest rate on the vertical axis, and, for the given monetary policy, the associated inflation rate on the horizontal axis. Using the 45-degree line, we convert this to the same inflation rate on the vertical axis. Hence we derive point *A* in the bottom right-hand panel. This shows the implied inflation rate when output and aggregate demand are Y_A.

Similarly, if we begin at point *B* in the top right-hand panel, we can again infer the corresponding levels of nominal interest rates and inflation, leading to point *B* in the bottom right-hand panel. Repeating this for each of the points on the *IS* schedule in the top right-hand panel, we trace out the aggregate demand schedule *AD* in the bottom right-hand panel; that is, the entire relationship between output demand and inflation.

Movements along the *AD* schedule show how demand, interest rates and inflation rates move together. What would shift the aggregate demand schedule? The 45-degree line cannot change, so the answer has to be a shift in the *ii* schedule (a change in monetary policy) or a shift in the *IS* schedule (autonomous demand changes caused by shifts in consumer demand, investment demand, government demand or export demand – everything except the effect of changes in interest rates).

To do everything properly, we could carry the entire toolkit of the above figure around. But it is quite a heavy toolbox. Often, we can get by using part of the analysis – just the *ii* schedule, just the *AD* schedule or just the *IS* schedule. However, if you ever find yourself struggling to understand the full picture, it is to the diagram above that you should eventually return. It will not let you down.

21.2 Aggregate supply

When prices and wages are completely flexible, output is always at **potential output**.

Potential output depends on the level of technology, the quantities of available inputs (labour, capital, land, energy) in long-run equilibrium, and the efficiency with which resources and technology are exploited. In the long run, investment in physical and human capital raises inputs of labour and capital, technical progress improves technology, and supply-side policies reduce distortions and raise efficiency. In the short run, we treat potential output as given; it is **long-run equilibrium output**.

With flexible wages and prices, how does a rise in inflation (and hence faster growth of nominal wages) affect the incentive of firms to supply goods and services?

Thinking in real terms, firms compare the real wage (the nominal wage W divided by the price level P) with the real benefit of labour, the extra output it makes. Similarly, workers compare real take-home pay (purchasing power over goods and services) with the disutility of sacrificing more leisure in order to work longer. If wages and prices both double, real wages are unaffected. Neither firms nor workers should change their behaviour. **Aggregate supply** is unaffected by pure inflation since everything nominal rises by the same proportion, as shown in Figure 21.3.

The aggregate supply schedule shows the output that firms wish to supply at each inflation rate.

At potential output all inputs are fully employed.

Long-run equilibrium output occurs when physical production inputs are fully employed. This output level is independent of inflation.

In the classical model, the aggregate supply schedule is vertical at potential output.

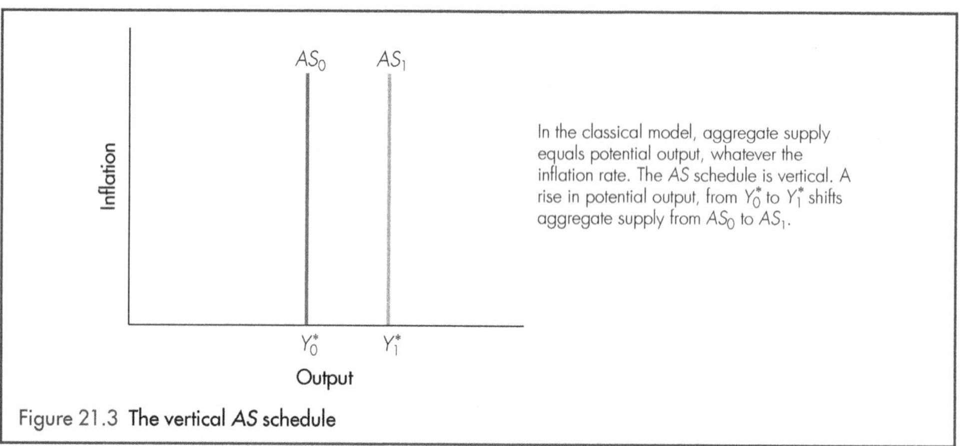

Figure 21.3 **The vertical *AS* schedule**

Wage and price flexibility ensures all nominal variables rise together. Without **money illusion**, people see through nominal changes: real variables are unaltered. In the classical model, real things determine real things, and nominal things determine other nominal things. Better technology, more capital or greater labour supply raise potential output, shifting the vertical supply curve from AS_0 to AS_1 in Figure 21.3. However, for any given level of potential output, lower inflation does *not* reduce the real output that firms wish to supply.

Money illusion exists if behaviour responds to changes in nominal variables rather than real variables.

21.3 Equilibrium inflation

For the classical model, Figure 21.4 shows the aggregate demand schedule AD_0 and the vertical aggregate supply schedule AS_0. Output is at potential output and inflation is π_0^*. At point A, there is equilibrium in all markets: for output, money and labour.

The labour market is in equilibrium anywhere on the AS_0 schedule, since the economy is at potential output and full employment. A is also on the aggregate demand schedule along which interest rates are adjusted in line with monetary policy and the aggregate demand for goods equals the actual output of goods.

The equilibrium inflation rate π_0^* reflects the positions of the *AS* and *AD* schedules. Potential output Y_0^* reflects technology, efficiency and available input supplies. The macroeconomic demand schedule depends on the *IS* schedule, showing how interest rates affect aggregate demand, and on the *ii* schedule of Figure 21.1, showing how interest rates respond to deviations of inflation from its target level.

To ensure that equilibrium inflation π_0^* coincides with the inflation target π^*, the central bank chooses the correct height of the *ii* schedule in Figure 21.1, thereby ensuring the *AD* schedule has the correct height to make equilibrium inflation π_0^* coincide with the target inflation rate π^*. If π_0^* is too low, the central bank loosens monetary policy, shifting the *ii* schedule down and the *AD* schedule up. If π_0^* exceeds the inflation target, a tighter monetary policy shifts the *ii* schedule up and the *AD* schedule down.

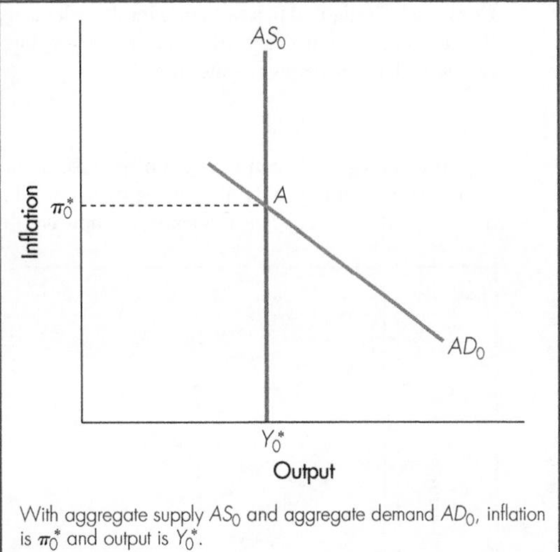

With aggregate supply AS_0 and aggregate demand AD_0, inflation is π_0^* and output is Y_0^*.

Figure 21.4 Equilibrium inflation

A supply shock

Supply shocks may be beneficial, such as technical progress, or may be adverse, such as higher real oil prices or loss of capacity after an earthquake. Suppose potential output rises. In Figure 21.5 the *AS* schedule shifts to the right, from AS_0 to AS_1. For a *given AD* schedule, equilibrium inflation falls to π_2^*, with equilibrium at *D*.

Monetary policy accommodates a permanent supply change by altering the real interest rate (shift in the *ii* schedule) to induce a similar change in aggregate demand.

However, the central bank still wants a long-run equilibrium inflation rate π_0^*. Hence, in response to the supply shock, the central bank loosens **monetary policy**, shifting the *ii* schedule downwards and the *AD* schedule upwards. Lower real interest rates boost aggregate demand in line with higher potential output Y_1^*. The new equilibrium is at *C*, not *D*. With unchanged inflation, the lower real interest rate also implies a lower nominal interest rate.

Lower interest rates raise the demand for money. To restore money market equilibrium, the central bank must then supply more money.

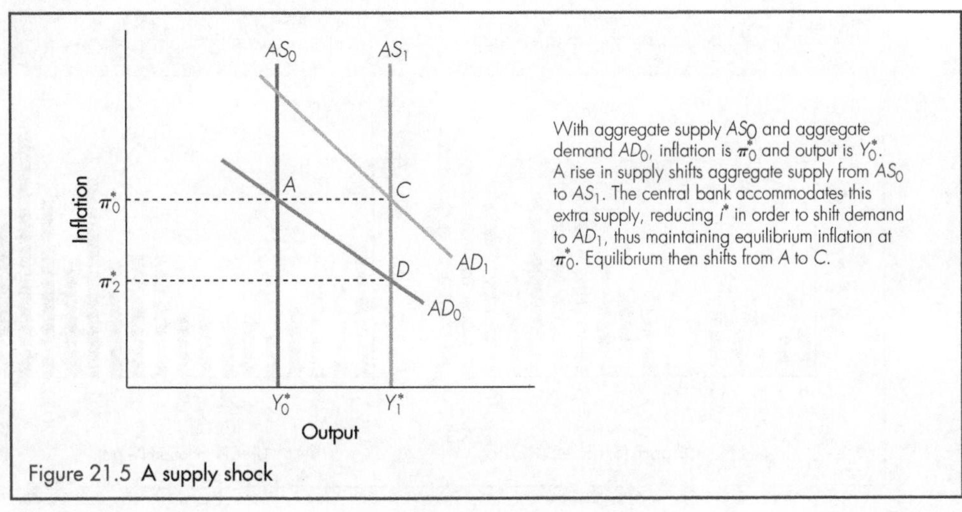

With aggregate supply AS_0 and aggregate demand AD_0, inflation is π_0^* and output is Y_0^*. A rise in supply shifts aggregate supply from AS_0 to AS_1. The central bank accommodates this extra supply, reducing i^* in order to shift demand to AD_1, thus maintaining equilibrium inflation at π_0^*. Equilibrium then shifts from *A* to *C*.

Figure 21.5 A supply shock

Conversely, if high oil prices permanently reduce aggregate supply, this shifts AS_1 to AS_0. Beginning at point *C*, the central bank must then tighten monetary policy so that higher real interest rates reduce aggregate demand in line with the lower aggregate supply.

A demand shock

Suppose aggregate demand shifts up because of easier fiscal policy or greater private sector optimism about future incomes and profits. Beginning from equilibrium at *A* in Figure 21.6, but keeping supply fixed at AS_0, a demand shift from AD_0 to AD_1 leads to a new equilibrium at *B*.

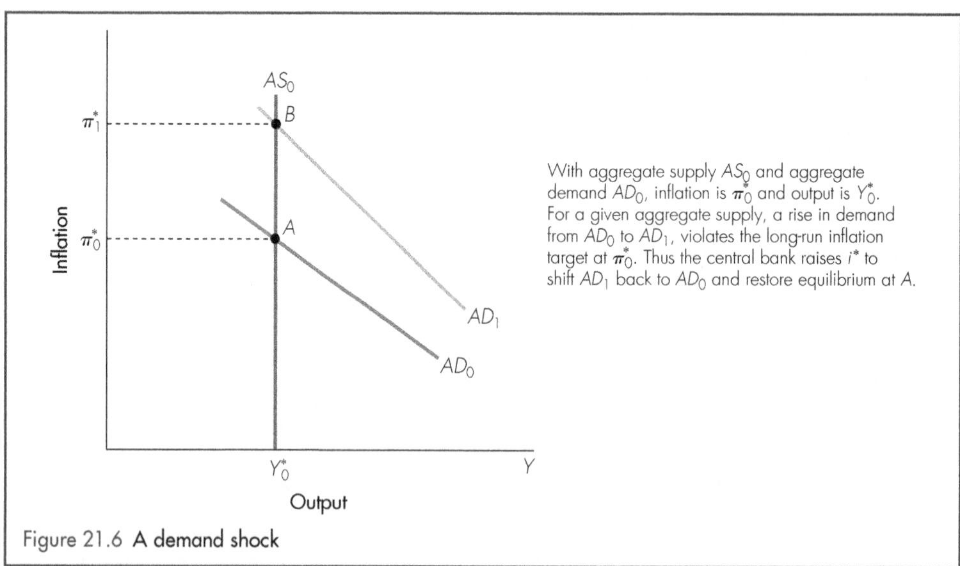

Figure 21.6 **A demand shock**

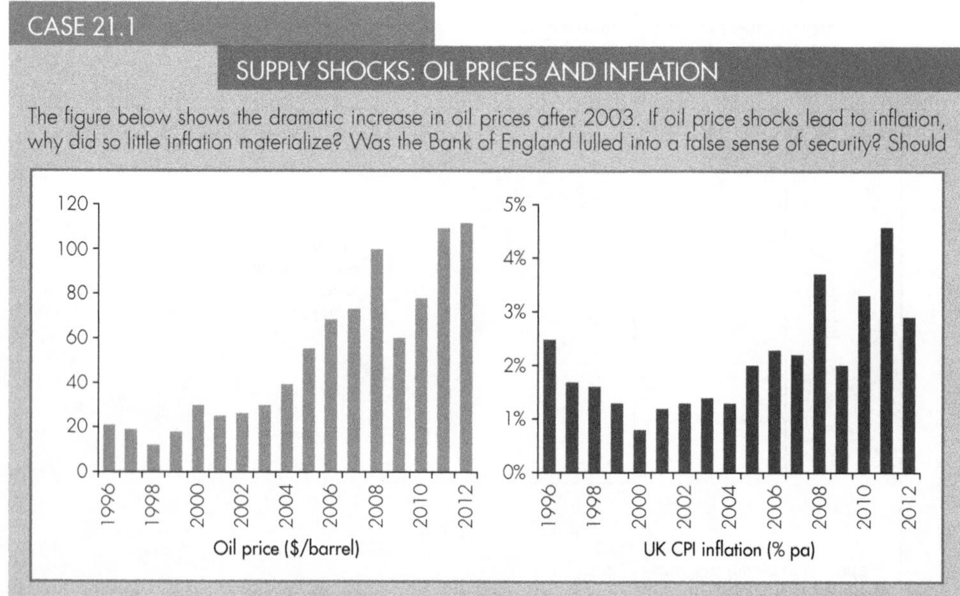

CASE 21.1

SUPPLY SHOCKS: OIL PRICES AND INFLATION

The figure below shows the dramatic increase in oil prices after 2003. If oil price shocks lead to inflation, why did so little inflation materialize? Was the Bank of England lulled into a false sense of security? Should we be surprised that, by April 2007, the Bank had to justify why it had allowed UK inflation to exceed the target range to which it is committed? Was it only the financial crash that spared the Bank further embarrassment?

The early years of inflation targeting were a benevolent environment for monetary policy. Globalization was flooding the West with cheap imports from China – helping to keep prices down – and trade unions in Europe and the US were aware that they could make domestic firms uncompetitive by pressing too hard for wage increases.

This same globalization put upward pressure not just on oil but on other commodity prices. Once China and India, the world's two most-populous economies, were growing at 8–10 per cent a year, their demands for raw materials were substantial: demand grew faster than supply could keep up, so commodity prices increased.

The tripling of oil prices during 2003–07 was potentially as dramatic a supply shock as the world had experienced when OPEC first flexed its muscles in 1973. Yet the effects were very different. In the 1970s, oil price rises led to a decade of high inflation and output stagnation. In the 2000s, economies continued to boom until the financial crash, and inflation remained muted.

Why was the impact of higher oil prices so modest? First, the increase took place steadily rather than in a step jump. Having longer to adjust, purchasers of oil had more time to switch to alternative energy sources. Second, the pressure of globalization encouraged importing countries to absorb the oil price increase rather than attempt to pass it on in higher prices. Workers accepted reductions in real wages, and firms accepted a reduction in profit margins.

Central banks argued that inflation targeting had affected the outcome in a helpful way. Firms and workers understood that attempts to pass on higher energy costs into higher wages and output prices would simply induce the central bank to raise interest rates dramatically causing a recession that would be more painful than absorbing the oil price rise. By anchoring inflation expectations, monetary policy encouraged adjustment in real wages and real profit margins.

Even so, by 2008, inflation was clearly increasing sharply. We will never know what would have happened in the absence of the financial crash. Presumably world commodity prices would have remained high, and central banks would have had to raise interest rates, possibly quite a bit, to get inflation back on track.

The financial crash imposed a sharp fall in aggregate demand, and initiated rapid contraction. World demand and world commodity prices fell for a bit. But by 2009, China had returned to 10 per cent growth, and the price of oil and other commodities began rising again. Significant growth rates were being seen in many emerging markets. Upward pressure on world commodity prices was more intense than ever.

Despite the post-crash austerity experienced in Europe, Japan and even the US, these countries continued to face rising import prices, creating an acute dilemma for monetary policy: raise interest rates to choke off imported inflation, or leave interest rates low to support the real economy at a time when fiscally challenged governments had few other tools with which to stave off outright depression.

Central banks in Europe, the US and Japan opted to keep interest rates low even if this meant deviating from the inflation target for a while. The right-hand chart shows that UK inflation tumbled in 2009 in the post-crash austerity. However, UK inflation picked up again in 2010 because of tax rises and exchange rate depreciation.

The Bank of England announced in advance that it would regard the inevitable rise in UK inflation during 2010 as temporary, and would not expect to raise interest rates immediately to stave this off. Given the fragility of the economy, it preferred to keep interest rates low for a little longer. In contrast, the ECB temporarily raised interest rates in 2011 to combat the rising inflation faced in the Eurozone, preferring to prioritize low inflation over output recovery.

This episode illustrates the differing degrees of flexibility with which a credible central bank can pursue inflation targeting. The more people believe that the central bank will keep a grip on inflation in the long run, the less people will care about blips in the short run.

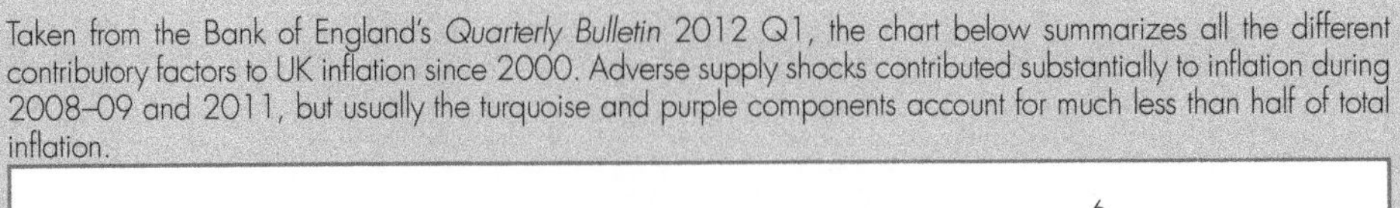
Taken from the Bank of England's *Quarterly Bulletin* 2012 Q1, the chart below summarizes all the different contributory factors to UK inflation since 2000. Adverse supply shocks contributed substantially to inflation during 2008–09 and 2011, but usually the turquoise and purple components account for much less than half of total inflation.

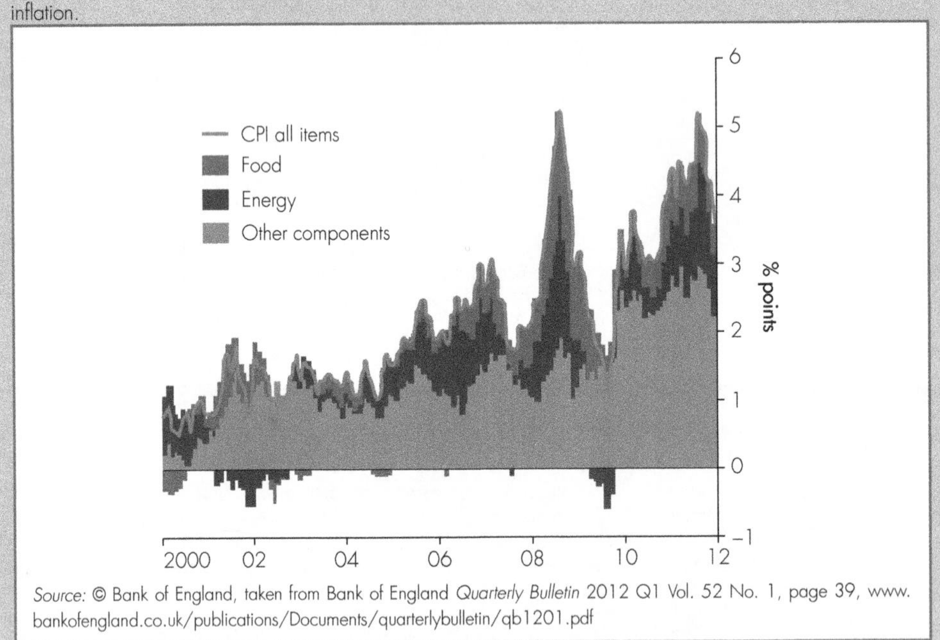

Source: © Bank of England, taken from Bank of England *Quarterly Bulletin* 2012 Q1 Vol. 52 No. 1, page 39, www.bankofengland.co.uk/publications/Documents/quarterlybulletin/qb1201.pdf

The central bank can continue to hit its inflation target π_0^* only by tightening monetary policy to offset the demand shock. In full equilibrium, with unchanged supply AS_0, aggregate demand must not change. By raising real interest rates, the central bank can reduce aggregate demand again. The central bank thus tightens monetary policy (an upward shift in the *ii* schedule) until the demand shock is fully offset and AD_1 has shifted down to AD_0 again. Equilibrium remains at *A* and the inflation target π_0^* is still achieved.

The original rise in demand could have come from the private or the public sector. If from higher private demand, the higher real interest rate simply reduces private demand back to its original level. If from higher government spending, the central bank raises interest rates until private spending falls by as much as government spending increased.

Note the distinction between partial crowding out in the Keynesian model and complete **crowding out in the classical model**. In the Keynesian model, output was demand-determined in the short run. Higher *output* induced the central bank to raise interest rates, which partly offset the expansionary effect of higher government spending. In the classical model, aggregate supply is the binding constraint. Output does not change. When higher government expenditure raises aggregate demand, higher interest rates must reduce consumption and investment to leave aggregate demand unaltered.

In the classical model with a vertical *AS* schedule, a rise in government spending crowds out an equal amount of private spending. Aggregate demand remains equal to potential output.

We may draw a second conclusion from Figure 21.6. Suppose monetary policy changes because the inflation target is raised from π_0^* to π_1^*. With a higher target inflation rate, the central bank no longer needs such high real interest rates at any particular level of inflation. Real interest rates fall and the aggregate demand schedule shifts up from AD_0 to AD_1. With an unchanged *AS* schedule, equilibrium moves from *A* to *B*.

In the classical model, faster nominal money growth is accompanied by higher inflation but leaves real output constant at potential output.

In the new equilibrium, inflation is higher but real output is unaltered. Since it is a full equilibrium, all real variables are then constant. One of these variables is the real money stock M/P. Since prices grow at the rate π_1^*, the nominal money supply must also grow at this rate.

The idea that **nominal money growth** is associated with inflation, but not growth of output or employment, is the central tenet of *monetarists*. Figure 21.6 shows this is correct in the classical model with full wage and price flexibility and no money illusion.

How long does all this take?

The classical model studies the economy once all variables have fully adjusted. Instead of thinking of adjustment as instant, we can view the classical model as applying to a long enough time for slower adjustment to be completed. This means not just wage and price adjustment, but also time for the central bank to work out what is going on and amend monetary policy if necessary, and time for these interest rate changes to have their full effect on private behaviour. Suppose the economy faces a fall in aggregate demand. What happens next?

The classical model

With aggregate supply unaffected, a fall in aggregate demand leads to lower inflation, to which the central bank immediately responds by easing monetary policy, reducing the real interest rate, boosting private sector demand and thus restoring aggregate demand to the unchanged level of potential output.[3]

The Keynesian model

Before wage and price adjustment is possible, there is no change in inflation to which the central bank can respond. The initial effect of lower aggregate demand is simply a fall in output. The rest of this chapter studies the adjustment process by which the economy gradually makes the transition from the Keynesian short run to the classical long run. To do so, we introduce the short-run aggregate supply curve.

21.4 The labour market and wage behaviour

Downward shocks cause recessions lasting years not weeks. Why don't changes in prices react faster, allowing changes that restore potential output? Firms relate prices to costs. Wages are the largest part of costs. Sluggish wage adjustment to departures from full employment is the main cause of slow adjustment of prices.

For both firms and workers, a job is often a long-term commitment. For the firm, it is costly to hire and fire workers. Firing entails a redundancy payment and the loss of the expertise the worker had built up on the job. Hiring entails advertising, interviewing and training a new worker in the special features of that firm. Firms are reluctant to hire and fire workers just because of short-term fluctuations in demand.

For the worker, seeking a new job takes time and effort, and throws away experience, seniority and the high wages justified by the high productivity that comes from having mastered a particular job in a particular firm. Like firms, workers care about long-term arrangements. Firms and workers reach an understanding about pay and conditions *in the medium term*, including how to handle fluctuations in the firm's output in the short run.

A firm and its workers have explicit contracts, or implicit agreements, specifying working conditions. These include normal hours, overtime requirements, regular wages and pay schedules for overtime work. The firm then sets the number of hours, within the limits of these conditions, depending on how much output it wishes to make in that week.

3 A similar analysis applies under monetary targeting. Suppose this is 2 per cent annual growth in nominal money. Long-run inflation will also be 2 per cent. A fall in aggregate demand bids down wage and price growth *below what they would have been*. With inflation below 2 per cent but an unchanged nominal money growth of 2 per cent, the real money supply expands. This causes a fall in real interest rates and boosts aggregate demand back to potential output. Thereafter, money and prices both grow at 2 per cent. The real money supply is permanently higher and real interest rates permanently lower.

When demand falls, the firm initially reduces hours of work. Overtime ends and factories close early. If demand does not recover, or declines further, firms start firing workers. Conversely, in a boom a firm makes its existing workforce work overtime. Then it seeks temporary workers to supplement the existing labour force. Only when the firm is sure that higher sales will be sustained does it hire extra permanent workers.

Wage adjustment

Wages are not set in a daily auction in which the equilibrium wage clears the market for labour. Firms and workers both gain from long-term understandings. This mutual commitment partly insulates a firm and its workforce from temporary conditions in the labour market.

Nor can a firm and its workforce spend every day haggling. Bargaining is costly, using up valuable time that could be used to produce output. Bargaining costs mean wages change only at discrete intervals. Immediate wage adjustment to shocks is ruled out. At best, firms must wait until the next scheduled date for a revision in the wage structure. In practice, complete wage adjustment is unlikely to take place even then. Chapter 10 discussed other reasons why involuntary unemployment is not instantly eliminated by wage adjustment.

Recap

In the short run (first few months), changes in labour input are largely changes in hours. In the medium run (up to two years), as changes in labour demand persist, the firm begins to alter its permanent workforce. In the long run (perhaps four to six years), adjustment is complete.

In the short run, trends in wages are largely given. The firm can affect earnings, as distinct from negotiated wage rates, because fluctuations in overtime and short time affect average hourly earnings. This flexibility is limited. In the medium run, the firm begins to adjust the path of wages. In the long run, the process is complete and the economy is back at potential output.

Now think about the market for output. By distinguishing between supply in the short and long run, our model of output reflects *both* supply and demand, even in the short run. Nevertheless, its short-run behaviour is like the simple Keynesian case in which output is demand-determined. Its long-run behaviour is fully classical.

21.5 Short-run aggregate supply

In Figure 21.7 the economy is at potential output at *A*. In the short run, the firm inherits a given rate of nominal wage growth (not shown in the figure). Previous wage negotiations anticipated remaining in long-run equilibrium at *A* with inflation π_0. By keeping up with inflation, nominal wage growth is expected to maintain the correct real wage for labour market equilibrium.

If inflation exceeds the expected inflation rate π_0, this helps firms by raising their output prices. The real wage is lower than expected. If this had been foreseen when wages were negotiated, the inherited nominal wage would have been higher; but it was not

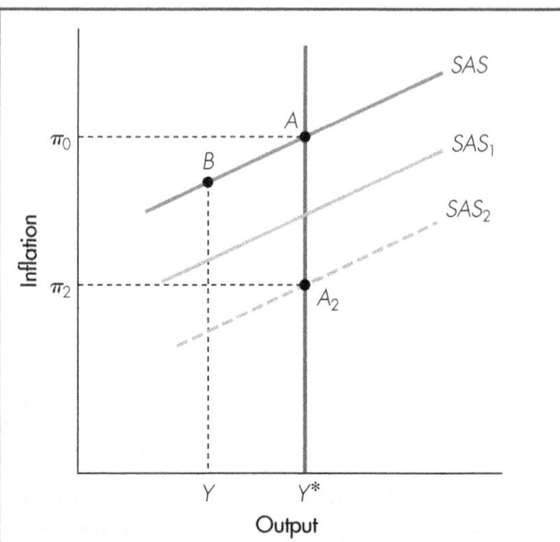

Firms raise prices when wage costs rise. Each short-run aggregate supply schedule reflects a different rate of inherited nominal wage growth. For any given rate, higher inflation moves firms up a given short-run supply schedule. A persisting boom or slump gradually bids nominal wage growth up or down, shifting short-run aggregate supply schedules. When these shift enough to restore to the inflation rate at which *AD* and *AS* intersect, potential output is restored.

Figure 21.7 **Short-run aggregate supply**

foreseen. Firms take advantage of their good luck by supplying a lot more output. They can afford to pay overtime to ensure that the workforce co-operates, and may also take on temporary extra staff.

The short-run supply curve (*SAS*) shows how desired output varies with inflation, for a given inherited growth of nominal wages.

Conversely, if inflation is below π_0, the real wage is now higher than anticipated when the nominal wage was agreed. Since labour is now costly, firms cut back output a lot. They move from *A* to *B* in Figure 21.7. Firms move along the **short-run supply curve (*SAS*)** in the short run.

If demand and output remain low, the growth rate of negotiated nominal wages gradually falls. With lower wage growth, firms do not need to raise output prices so quickly. The short-run aggregate supply schedule shifts down from *SAS* to SAS_1 in Figure 21.7. Lower inflation moves the economy down its aggregate demand schedule, increasing the demand for goods. If full employment and potential output are still not restored, negotiated wage growth falls again, leading to a short-run aggregate supply schedule such as SAS_2.

These short-run aggregate supply schedules give a realistic picture of adjustment to demand shocks. Because the short-run aggregate supply schedule is flat, a shift in aggregate demand leads mainly to changes in output not prices in the short run. This is the Keynesian feature. But deviations from full employment gradually change wage growth and short-run aggregate supply.

The economy gradually works its way back to potential output. That is the classical feature. We now describe adjustment in more detail.

21.6 The adjustment process

We now combine the aggregate demand schedule with the short-run aggregate supply schedule to show how demand or supply shocks set up an adjustment process. In so doing, we now assume that the goods market clears, even in the short run. Short-run aggregate supply gradually changes over time as wage growth adjusts to the rate that restores full employment and potential output, placing firms eventually on their long-run aggregate supply schedule.

Output is no longer demand-determined when aggregate demand lies below the level of potential output. In the short run, firms are also on their short-run supply schedules producing what they wish, *given the inherited nominal wages.*

However, sluggish wage adjustment prevents immediate restoration of full employment. When aggregate demand for goods falls, firms reduce output and employment. Since wages do not fall at once, there is involuntary unemployment. *Employment* is demand-determined in the short run.

Figure 21.8 shows a downward shift in the aggregate demand schedule from *AD* to *AD'* because monetary policy is tightened (a higher *ii* schedule in Figure 21.1). In the long run, aggregate demand must return to potential output, and the economy will end up at E_3. Hence, the tighter monetary policy can be viewed as a cut in the target inflation rate from π^* to π_3^*.

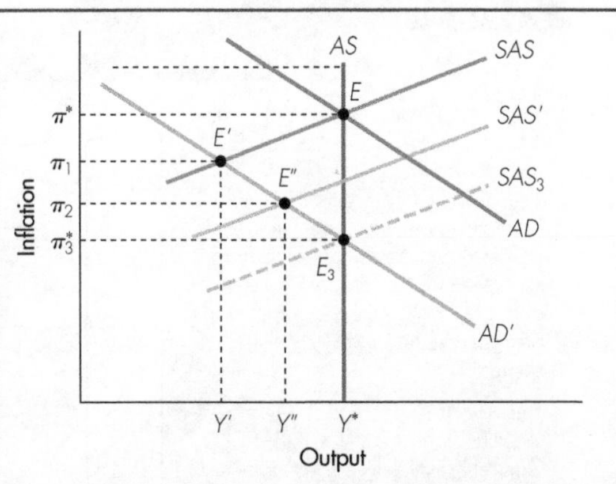

Beginning at *E*, a lower inflation target shifts *AD* to *AD'*. Given inherited wage growth, the new equilibrium is at *E'*. Output falls from Y^* to Y', and actual inflation is only π_1. Since wages have risen faster than prices despite the fall in output, unemployment rises. In the next wage settlement, nominal wage growth slows, and the short-run supply schedule becomes *SAS'*. Equilibrium is now at *E"*, and output recovers to *Y"*. Once wage growth slows enough to make SAS_3 the supply curve, long-run equilibrium is re-established at E_3.

Figure 21.8 A lower inflation target

When monetary policy is tightened, interest rates initially rise since actual inflation at E is now above target. Aggregate demand shifts down to AD'. In the classical model, there is an instant adjustment of prices and wages to keep the economy at full employment and potential output. Equilibrium inflation immediately falls to π_3^* and the new equilibrium is at E_3. Output remains at potential output Y^*.

These classical results are valid only in the long run. When adjustment of wages and prices is slow, the economy faces the short-run aggregate supply schedule *SAS*, reflecting the nominal wages recently agreed.

In the short run, the downward shift in AD causes a move from E to E'. Since firms cannot cut costs much, they reduce output to Y'. At E' the goods market clears at the intersection of the aggregate demand schedule AD' and the supply schedule *SAS*. Inflation has fallen a little because of lower demand, but output has fallen a lot. With lower inflation than the expectation built into nominal wage agreements, *real wages have risen*, despite the fall in output. Once firms can adjust employment, some workers are fired and unemployment rises.

In the medium run, this starts to reduce wage growth. With inherited wages lower than they would have been, firms move on to a lower short-run aggregate supply schedule SAS'. The goods market now clears at E''. Output and employment recover a bit, but some unemployment persists. Since inflation has fallen, the central bank is less worried about the amount by which inflation exceeds its new target and cuts real interest rates, moving the economy down AD' to E''.

In the long run, adjustment is complete. Wage growth and inflation fall to π_3^*. The short-run aggregate supply schedule is SAS_3 in Figure 21.8. The economy is in full equilibrium at E_3, on AS, SAS_3 and AD'. Output is Y^* and the labour market is back at full employment.

The real world lies between the extreme simplifications of the simple Keynesian model and classical models. In practice, prices and wages are neither fully flexible nor fully fixed. A tougher inflation target has real effects in the short run, since output and employment are reduced. But after wages and prices adjust fully, output and employment return to normal. Inflation is permanently lower thereafter.

ACTIVITY 21.1

OUTPUT GAPS, 1998–2013

The output gap $(Y - Y^*)$ is the percentage deviation of actual output Y from potential output Y^*. Each year the OECD *Economic Outlook* estimates potential output for all its member countries. The diagram shows estimates for the UK, the US and Germany. Positive output gaps are booms; negative gaps indicate slumps.

The diagram shows the relative stability of the period 1998–2006. Central banks were successfully managing aggregate demand to keep it close to full capacity.

The diagram also shows that all four countries were overheating in 2007/08. Aggregate demand was higher than potential output, and in the UK, Greece and Germany had increased sharply since 2005.

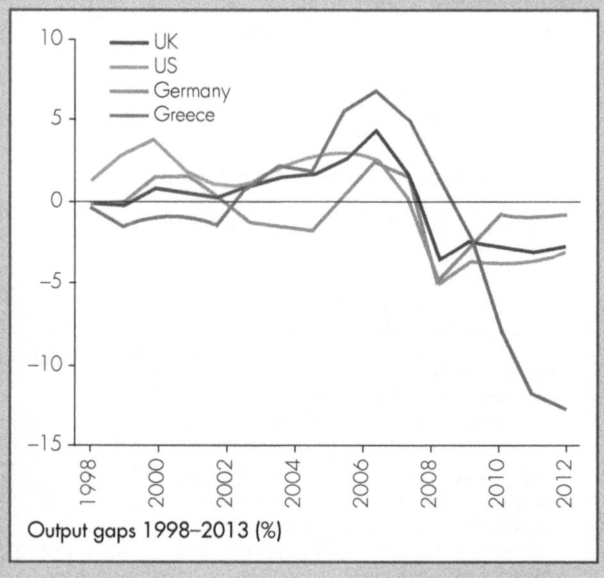

Output gaps 1998–2013 (%)

Greece was experiencing a boom that was completely unsustainable, with demand almost 6 per cent in excess of potential output.

When the financial crisis hit, some economists thought that Germany would be relatively well insulated, since its regulation of banks had been more stringent than in the UK and the US. Yet, the diagram shows that Germany experienced nearly as dramatic a slump in aggregate demand as its Anglo-Saxon competitors. Sub-prime mortgages had found their way even into Stuttgart and Frankfurt. Even China did not escape. When aggregate demand in China fell in 2009, German exports were hard hit. Thus different countries experienced the crash through different channels. The crisis originated in the US, and UK banks were then very exposed. Germany suffered both because all export markets suffered, and because its banks were exposed to banks in other countries that themselves had behaved less prudently.

Nowhere was the turnaround more acute than in Greece. Over the six-year period from 2007 to 2013, aggregate demand for Greek output fell by more than 20 per cent. In part, this reflected the same world recession and banking crises experienced by other countries, but it was exacerbated by the need to seek several bailouts from foreign governments, whose terms for emergency assistance included additional fiscal austerity in Greece.

Greece aside, the diagram shows that the upturn is slowly starting to take effect. It also confirms that for the next few years all major economies will have substantial spare capacity – the underlying assumption of the Keynesian perspective.

Finally, the diagram helps identify periods in which simple Keynesian analysis cannot be the whole story. Once the output gap has been eliminated, as during the period around 2000, there is no spare capacity remaining, and the classical model is increasingly relevant.

Questions

There are two ways in which you might try to calculate potential output, and hence the output gap: (i) statistically, by fitting trend lines through previous business cycles or (ii) economically, by trying to get an idea of the balance of aggregate supply and aggregate demand.

(a) If you wanted a quick procedure capable of being replicated across many countries, which of the two would you be inclined to choose?

(b) How might you build up an idea of an empirical economic model of the balance between actual output and potential output?

(c) A central bank reduces interest rates but is disappointed to find that this quickly generates higher inflation not higher output. What can you infer about the initial level of the output gap? Why?

To check your answers to these questions, go to page 680.

21.7 Sluggish adjustment to shocks

A permanent supply shock

Suppose a change in attitudes towards women working leads to an increase in labour supply. Potential output rises. In the long run, aggregate demand must rise in line with aggregate supply. Lower real interest rates allow higher aggregate demand at the unchanged inflation target π^*. Provided monetary policy is loosened, the rightward shift in AD can match the rightward shift in aggregate supply. By accommodating the extra supply with looser monetary policy, the inflation rate remains π^*, and the economy moves directly to the new long-run equilibrium, from E_0 to E_1 in Figure 21.9.

A permanent supply shock changes the level of potential output.

Because of lags in diagnosing the shock, and in the response of consumption and investment demand to lower interest rates, Figure 21.9 exaggerates the ease of adjustment to a **permanent supply shock**. In practice, output may not jump all the way to the new level of potential output.

If the aggregate demand schedule does not fully and immediately shift to AD_1, output is below Y_1^*. This reduces inflation and the central bank responds with lower interest rates. Over time, the aggregate demand schedule will drift to the right until it reaches AD_1 in Figure 21.9.

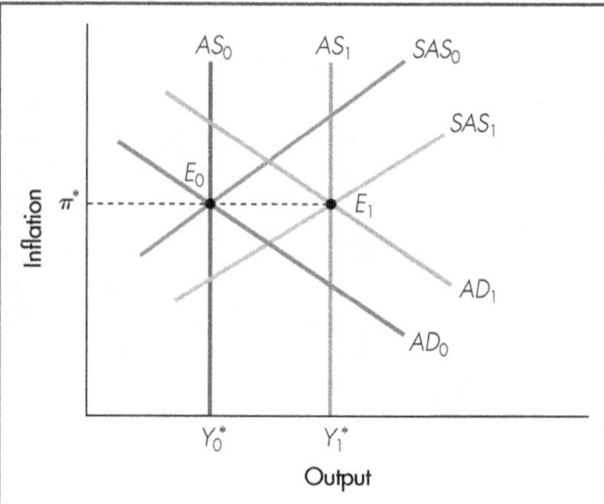

A permanent rise in supply shifts AS_0 and SAS_0 to AS_1 and SAS_1. By permanently reducing interest rates, the central bank shifts AD_0 to AD_1, meeting its inflation target π^* in the new equilibrium at E_1. If the central bank acts quickly, no further shifts in SAS_1 are required.

Figure 21.9 **A permanent supply increase**

A temporary supply shock

A **temporary supply shock** leaves potential output unaffected in the long run. With the vertical *AS* schedule unaltered, the short-run supply curve must shift. Although the *SAS* schedule is *mainly* influenced by inherited nominal wages, it is *also* affected by other input prices. Suppose a temporary oil price rise makes firms charge higher prices at any output level. Figure 21.10 shows a shift upwards in short-run supply, from *SAS* to *SAS'*. The new short-run equilibrium is at *E'*. Inflation rises but output and employment fall because the central bank raises real interest rates in response to higher inflation.

If the central bank maintains its inflation target π^*, lower output and employment at *E'* gradually reduce inflation and nominal wage growth, shifting *SAS'* gradually back to *SAS*. The economy slowly moves down the *AD* schedule back to the original equilibrium at *E*.

A temporary supply shock shifts the short-run aggregate supply schedule, but leaves potential output unaltered.

A different outcome is possible. When the higher oil price shifts *SAS* to *SAS'*, it is possible to *avoid* the period of low output as the economy moves along *AD* from *E'* back to *E*. A *change* in monetary policy can *shift AD* up enough to pass through *E'*. Output can quickly

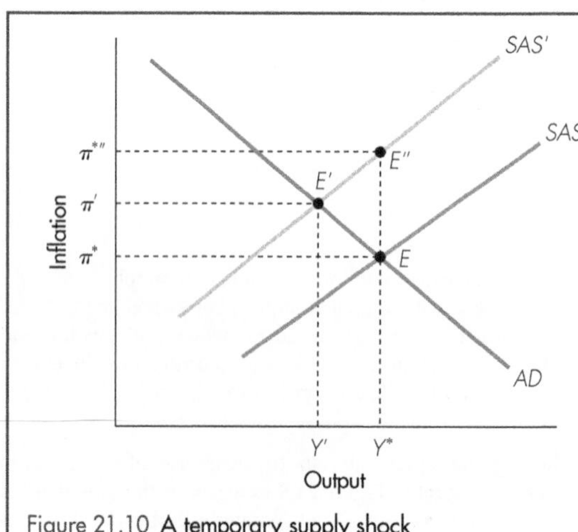

Higher oil prices force firms to raise prices. In the short run, *SAS* shifts up to *SAS'*, and equilibrium shifts from *E* to *E'*. Higher inflation reduces aggregate demand since the central bank raises real interest rates. Once the temporary supply shock disappears, *SAS'* gradually falls back to *SAS*, and equilibrium is eventually restored at *E*.

Figure 21.10 **A temporary supply shock**

return to potential output, but only because the inflation target[4] has been loosened from π^* to $\pi^{*\prime\prime}$. The new long-run new equilibrium is then at E''.

> Monetary policy accommodates a temporary supply shock when monetary policy is altered to help stabilize output. The consequence, however, is higher inflation.

A central bank caring a lot about output stability may **accommodate short-run supply shocks**, even if this means higher inflation. A central bank caring more about its inflation target than about output stability will not accommodate temporary supply shocks.

It matters a lot whether the supply shock is temporary or permanent. If potential output is *permanently* affected, aggregate demand *must* eventually rise to match. Once a supply side shock is diagnosed as permanent, it should be accommodated.

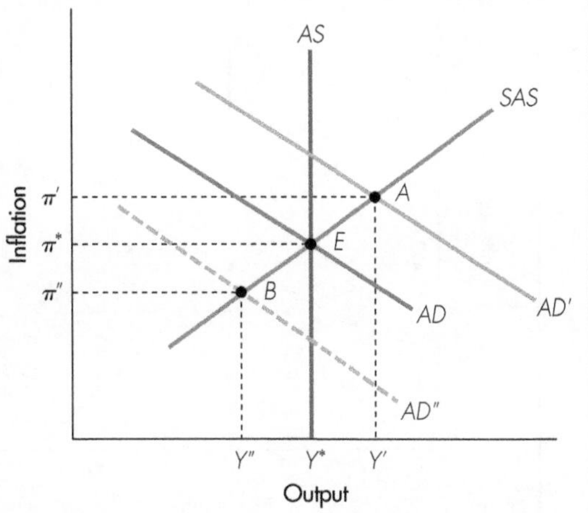

Demand fluctuates between AD' and AD'', causing fluctuations in output and inflation. If the central bank can react quickly, it can offset demand shocks by changing i^* to shift demand back to AD. Stabilizing inflation at π^* has the effect of stabilizing output at Y^*.

Figure 21.11 **Demand shocks**

Demand shocks

Figure 21.11 explores demand shocks *not* caused by monetary policy. If demand is high, facing AD' the economy moves along its short-run supply curve to point A. If demand is low, facing AD'' the economy moves along the SAS curve to point B.

Suppose the central bank diagnoses that an expansionary demand shock has occurred. It can tighten monetary policy and shift AD' back down to AD again. Similarly, it can loosen monetary policy in response to low aggregate demand AD'', restoring AD again. The economy remains at E. Both inflation *and* output are stabilized.

It is easy for the central bank to tell where inflation is relative to its target rate. It is harder to estimate the level of potential output, which can change over time. This is part of the modern case for using inflation targeting as the intermediate target of monetary policy. When all shocks are **demand shocks**, it works perfectly.

> When all shocks are demand shocks, stabilizing inflation also stabilizes output, even in a Keynesian model.

Suppose, instead, that all shocks are supply shocks. Figure 21.12 shows the long-run supply curve AS, vertical at potential output Y^*, and a set of short-run supply curves whose average level is SAS but which fluctuate between SAS' and SAS''.

On average, output is Y^* and inflation is π^*. If interest rates are varied very aggressively to stabilize inflation in the face of supply shocks, the AD schedule is effectively horizontal at π^*. Inflation is stabilized, but output fluctuates between Y' and Y'' when supply fluctuates between SAS' and SAS''. Unlike the case of demand shocks, it is no longer possible to stabilize output *and* inflation.

Similarly, it is possible to stabilize output completely but only at the cost of allowing big fluctuations in inflation. The AD schedule is then vertical at potential output. A rise in short-run supply to SAS' induces a big rise in interest rates to reduce aggregate demand to Y^* again. With high supply but low demand, inflation is temporarily low (relative to inherited wage growth) and firms wish to supply only Y^*. When supply shrinks temporarily to SAS'', firms supply output Y^* only if inflation is high (relative to inherited wage growth), which needs a low interest rate to boost demand.

4 Looser monetary policy shifts the *ii* schedule to the right in Figure 21.1. However, once long-run equilibrium is restored, i^* must be unaltered: since aggregate supply is eventually unaltered, aggregate demand cannot eventually change. The only way for the central bank to loosen monetary policy without changing i^* is to accept a higher inflation target π^*.

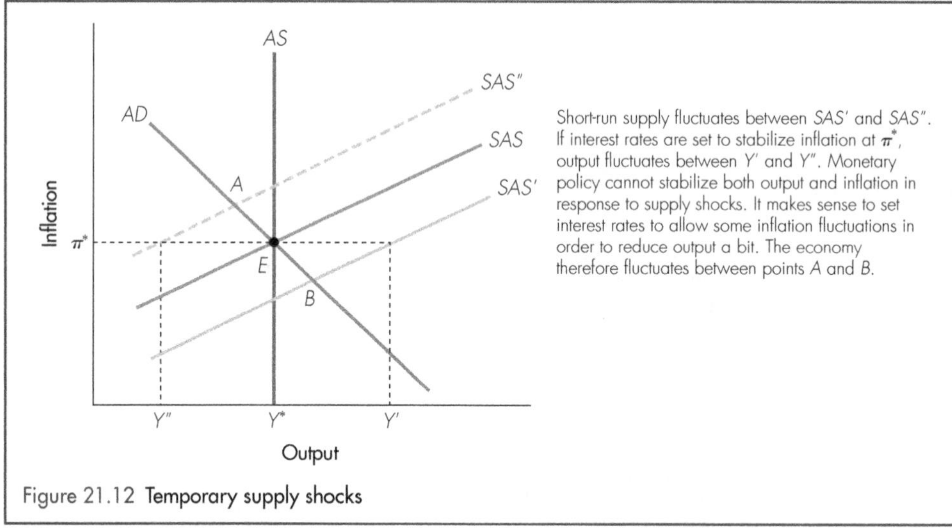

Short-run supply fluctuates between *SAS′* and *SAS″*. If interest rates are set to stabilize inflation at π^*, output fluctuates between *Y′* and *Y″*. Monetary policy cannot stabilize both output and inflation in response to supply shocks. It makes sense to set interest rates to allow some inflation fluctuations in order to reduce output a bit. The economy therefore fluctuates between points *A* and *B*.

Figure 21.12 **Temporary supply shocks**

21.8 Trade-offs in monetary objectives

Facing supply shocks, Figure 21.12 implies that it is a bad idea either to stabilize inflation at π^* (which induces big fluctuations in output) or to stabilize output at Y^* (which induces big fluctuations in inflation). The aggregate demand schedule *AD* in Figure 21.12 is a particular compromise in the way interest rates are set.[5]

Any *AD* schedule through point *E* achieves, on average, the targets π^* and Y^*. The particular schedule *AD* in Figure 21.12 makes the economy fluctuate between *A* (when supply is *SAS″*) and *B* (when supply is *SAS′*). This achieves acceptable fluctuations in both output and inflation. A steeper *AD* schedule, still through *A*, induces lower output fluctuations but larger inflation fluctuations. A flatter schedule has the opposite effect. The steepness of the schedule reflects the relative weight the central bank places on stabilizing inflation and output.

This trade-off does not arise for demand shocks. Figure 21.11 showed that, by fully offsetting demand shocks, the central bank stabilizes both output and prices. In reality, the central bank faces both supply and demand shocks, and cannot always diagnose which is which. It must choose a monetary policy that gives reasonable answers under both kinds of shock.

There is no conflict between output stability and inflation stability when shocks are demand shocks. It makes sense to try to hit the target as quickly as possible. Similarly, a permanent supply shock requires a permanent change in demand, which there is little reason to postpone. However, facing a *temporary supply shock*, Figure 21.12 showed that it makes sense temporarily to allow inflation to deviate from its target in order to mitigate the shock to output.

The *ii* schedule in Figure 21.12 reflects the average behaviour of the central bank under flexible inflation targeting. Deviations of inflation from target are not all immediately eliminated, but they are eventually eliminated by the policy of raising (lowering) real interest rates whenever inflation is too high (low). Temporary deviations of inflation from target are the price to be paid for ensuring that output fluctuations are not too large. The key to successful **flexible inflation targeting** is that any deviation of inflation from target should be *temporary*.

Flexible inflation targeting commits a central bank to hit inflation targets in the medium run, but gives it some discretion about *how quickly* to hit its inflation target.

5 And this finally explains why in Figure 21.1 the central bank does not simply choose a vertical *ii* schedule at the target inflation rate. When adjustment is sluggish and supply shocks occur, this would imply big swings in output.

CONCEPT 21.2

A TAYLOR RULE FOR MONETARY POLICY

Stanford professor John Taylor suggested that a neat way to describe flexible inflation targeting is to say that interest rates respond to deviations of both inflation and output from their target long-run equilibrium levels. Inflation above target, or output above target, is a signal to raise interest rates; inflation below target or output below target is a signal to reduce interest rates. We can think of the Taylor rule as applying to either nominal or real interest rates. However, a key insight of the Taylor rule is that, if inflation rises by 1 per cent, nominal interest rates must be increased by more than 1 per cent to ensure that real interest rates rise when inflation is higher. In the short run, the central bank – which must deal with a world in which both supply and demand shocks occur, and may not immediately be able to diagnose which – sets higher real interest rates if inflation exceeds the target and/or if real output exceeds potential output. Taylor showed that this formula provides a good empirical description of the behaviour of all major central banks.

In terms of rules versus discretion, this behaviour is not imposed on the central bank. It is largely the result of its discretionary behaviour, so it is a rule only in the sense of being a stable empirical relationship. But it does not reflect complete discretion. The target inflation rate itself is usually delegated by the government, not freely chosen by the central bank. For example, in the UK the government reserves the right to alter the inflation target during a crisis.

The Taylor rule also provides a way to indicate how rare and extreme an event the financial crash has been. For example, Princeton professor Paul Krugman, himself a Nobel Prize winner, took empirical estimates of the Taylor rule for the US and calculated that, at the height of the recession in 2009, 'normal' behaviour of the US central bank, given observed levels of inflation and output, would have implied a nominal interest rate of *minus* 5.6 per cent.[6] Central banks would ideally liked to have cut interest rates way below zero if following their normal behaviour. The fact that they could not drive nominal interest rates below zero was really getting in the way of normal monetary policy.

This had two implications. First, fiscal policy was going to be asked to do 'too much' because monetary policy could not do enough. Second, quantitative easing was adopted not merely because of the need to offset the collapse of the bank deposit multiplier but also in the hope that the credit channel of monetary policy could help boost aggregate demand at a time when further interest rate cuts were not possible.

Taylor rule or nominal GDP target?

A Taylor rule allows the central bank to respond to changes in both real income and the price level. A special case of the Taylor rule is when the central bank sets a target for the path of nominal GDP. Since nominal GDP is simply $P \times Y$, the price level multiplied by real output, a nominal income target is a Taylor rule in which prices and real output have *equal* weights in determining the central bank's response to deviations from target. A Taylor rule is more general since there is no requirement to place the same priority on inflation deviations and on real output deviations from target. In 2012, shortly after being confirmed as the next governor of the Bank of England, Mark Carney raised the possibility that the Bank of England should examine nominal GDP as a target for interest rate setting.

MATHS 21.1

THE FORMULA FOR THE TAYLOR RULE

In the long run, the real interest rate is i^*, inflation is π^* and real output is Y^*. Formally, the Taylor rule implies that real interest i obeys

$$i - i^* = a(\pi - \pi^*) + b(Y - Y^*) \qquad a > 0, b > 0 \qquad (1)$$

The nominal interest rate r is simply the real interest rate i plus the inflation rate π,

$$r - r^* = (1 + a)(\pi - \pi^*) + b(Y - Y^*) \qquad a > 0, b > 0 \qquad (2)$$

6 Paul Krugman's *New York Times* column of 10 October 2009 is reproduced on his blog at http://krugman.blogs.nytimes.com.

where $r^* = i^* + \pi^*$

Hence, the long-run target for nominal interest rates depends both on the long-run inflation target and on the desired level of real interest rates in the long run, which may depend, among other things, on the monetary–fiscal mix.

Thus, we can think of the Taylor rule as applying to either nominal or real interest rates, with the key requirement that the nominal interest version in equation (2) insists that any increase in inflation leads to a larger increase in nominal interest rates – by $(1 + a)$ times – in order to ensure that real interest rates move in the right direction to stabilize inflation. The absolute size of the parameters a and b tells us how aggressively monetary policy attempts to stabilize inflation and output. The relative size of the parameters tells us the relative importance of inflation and output to policy makers in the short run.

Many economists have noted that deviations of output from target are an important indicator of future inflation. Hence it is also possible to interpret the empirical success of the Taylor rule as implying central bank concern for current and future inflation, rather than for current output and current inflation.

Finally, as noted in Concept 21.2, empirical estimates of Taylor rules using data for the previous decade would have led to choices of nominal interest rates that were negative, which is not possible in practice. With no danger of inflation and output well below target, central banks would have loved to set negative interest rates if only they could. This led IMF chief economist Olivier Blanchard to note that a temporarily *higher* inflation target might have been one way in which real interest rates could become more negative. Suppose, for example, inflation was 4 per cent and nominal interest rates were still close to zero. Real interest rates would then have been −4 per cent, a powerful stimulus to aggregate demand. Mathematically, the Blanchard proposal achieves the appropriately negative left-hand side of equation (2) not by reducing r below zero but by raising π^* and hence r^* above previous levels. Most central banks were unenthusiastic about this proposal: whatever its short-run attraction, they feared it would then be hard to restore belief in a low inflation target again after the crisis was over.

Summary

- The **classical model** of macroeconomics assumes full flexibility of wages and prices and no money illusion.
- The *ii* **schedule** shows, under a policy of **inflation targeting**, how the central bank achieves high interest rates when inflation is high and low interest rates when inflation is low. Central banks set nominal not real interest rates, and hence must first forecast inflation in order to calculate what nominal interest rate they wish to set.
- The *ii* schedule shifts to the left, a higher real interest rate at each inflation rate, when monetary policy is tightened, and to the right, a lower real interest rate at each inflation rate, when monetary policy is loosened.
- The **aggregate demand schedule** shows how higher inflation reduces aggregate demand by inducing monetary policy to raise real interest rates.
- The classical model always has full employment. The **aggregate supply schedule** is vertical at **potential output**. **Equilibrium inflation** is at the intersection of the aggregate supply schedule and the aggregate demand schedule. The markets for goods, money and labour are all in equilibrium. Monetary policy is set to make the equilibrium inflation rate coincide with the inflation target.
- In the classical model, fiscal expansion cannot increase output. To continue to hit its inflation target, the central bank must raise real interest rates to restore aggregate demand to the level of potential output.

Higher government spending crowds out an equal amount of private spending, leaving demand and output unaltered.

- Changing the target inflation rate leads to an equivalent change in the growth of wages and nominal money in the classical model, but not to a change in output.
- In practice, wages adjust slowly to shocks since job arrangements are long term. **Wage adjustment** is sluggish not merely because wage bargaining is infrequent, but also because workers prefer their long-term employers to smooth wages.
- Prices reflect mainly labour costs. The **short-run aggregate supply schedule** shows firms' desired output, given the inherited growth of nominal wages. Output is temporarily responsive to inflation, since nominal wages are already determined. As wage adjustment occurs, the short-run supply schedule shifts.
- The **Keynesian model** is a good guide to short-term behaviour but the **classical model** describes behaviour in the long run.
- **Permanent supply shocks** alter potential output. **Temporary supply shocks** merely alter the short-run supply curve for a while.
- If its effects were instant, monetary policy could completely offset **demand shocks**, stabilizing both inflation and output. **Temporary supply shocks** force a trade-off between output stability and inflation stability. The output effect of **permanent supply shocks** cannot be escaped indefinitely.
- **Flexible inflation targeting** implies the central bank need not immediately hit its inflation target, allowing some scope for temporary action to cushion output fluctuations.
- A **Taylor rule** views interest rate decisions as responding to both deviations of output from target and deviations of inflation from target. Except during the financial crash, when interest rates could not be reduced below zero, this fits the data well for most countries over an extended period.

Review questions

1 (a) Define the aggregate demand schedule. (b) How does a fiscal expansion affect the schedule under a flexible inflation target? (c) How would the central bank have to change monetary policy to hit its given inflation target in the long run?

2 **Common fallacies** Why are these statements wrong? (a) Fiscal expansion can increase output for ever. (b) Higher inflation always reduces output.

EASY

3 An economy has the choice of having half its workers make annual wage agreements every January, and the other half make annual wage agreements every July, or instead forcing everyone to make their annual agreement on 1 July. Which system is likely to induce greater wage flexibility during a period of a few months and during a period of several years?

4 How do the following affect the short-run supply schedule, and hence output and inflation in the short run: (a) a higher tax rate; (b) higher labour productivity?

5 Which of the following statements is correct? (a) Inflation targeting implies the central bank can ignore what is happening to output. (b) Inflation targeting implies nominal interest rates will typically rise by more than the rise in inflation. (c) Inflation targeting was immediately abandoned once the financial crash of 2009 occurred.

6 Suppose opportunities for investing in high-tech applications boost aggregate demand in the short run but aggregate supply in the long run. Using *AS* and *AD* schedules, show why output might rise *without* much inflation.

7 OPEC raises the price of oil for a year but then an increase in the supply of oil from Russia bids oil prices back down again. Contrast the evolution of the economy if monetary policy follows: (a) a fixed interest rate or (b) flexible inflation targeting.

8 Distinguish between adjustment in the UK (small open economy, flexible exchange rate) and the US (large economy, international trade a much smaller proportion of its GDP).

MEDIUM

9 Use the Taylor rule $r - r^* = (1 + a)(\pi - \pi^*) + b(Y - Y^*)$ to answer the following questions: (a) What does the long-run target for the nominal interest rate depend on? (b) In the nominal interest version of the Taylor rule, what happens when there is an increase in inflation? (c) What do the absolute and relative sizes of both the parameters a and b respectively tell us?

10 In 2007, the governor of the Bank of England had to write to the Chancellor of the Exchequer to explain why UK inflation had exceeded the target range laid down by the Chancellor. (a) Why were these difficult circumstances? (b) Was the letter proof that the Bank of England was unable to keep inflation in check?

11 'Central banks, by focusing too much on the inflation rate for goods and services, neglected important signals from asset prices that risk-taking had become excessive.' Do you agree? What is this likely to imply in future?

HARD

12 Imagine that the UK adopts the euro, and interest rates are set by the European Central Bank. (a) Are euro interest rates likely to be adjusted to help stabilize either UK inflation or UK output? (b) What automatic mechanisms, if any, can still achieve these outcomes? (c) Would UK fiscal policy be able to help more?

13 Use Figure 21.8 to explore how the collapse of bank lending to companies affects short-run supply curves, and show how the adjustment process subsequently occurs.

14 **Essay question** 'Climate change is essentially a permanent adverse supply shock. Production costs will rise; potential output will fall. If the private sector fails to adjust, then either monetary or fiscal policy will have to reduce aggregate demand to the required lower level.' Discuss.

For solutions to these questions, contact your lecturer.

CHAPTER 22

Inflation, expectations and credibility

Learning Outcomes

By the end of this chapter, you should be able to:

1. explain the quantity theory of money
2. discuss how nominal interest rates reflect inflation
3. analyse seigniorage, the inflation tax and why hyperinflations occur
4. assess when budget deficits cause money growth
5. explain the Phillips curve
6. analyse inflation expectations
7. evaluate the costs of inflation
8. understand central bank independence and inflation control
9. analyse how central banks set interest rates

Sustained inflation is a recent phenomenon. Before 1939, prices rose in some years but fell in others. The UK price level was not substantially higher in 1950 than its level of 1750. Since some years experienced rapid inflation, others must have experienced rapid deflation; that is, a fall in prices. Figure 22.1 confirms this, over an extended period. During this period, the UK was on the gold standard, which anchored money creation to gold reserves. In the long run, money grew slowly, and so did prices. During 1750–1945 falling prices were nearly as likely as rising prices.

Since the Second World War, things have been very different. The world abandoned the gold standard and adopted, first, paper money and, then, electronic money; both could be increased at will by the central bank. There were always economic and political reasons to increase the money supply – and rarely reasons to reduce it. The post-war price level has never fallen: the graph in Figure 22.1 never falls below the horizontal axis after the 1930s. Since 1950 the price level has risen more than 20-fold; that is, more than its rise over the previous three centuries. This story applies in most advanced economies.

> Inflation is a rise in the price level. Pure inflation means that prices of goods and inputs rise at the same rate.

We start with the causes of **inflation**, then examine its effects, which partly depend on whether inflation was anticipated or took people by surprise. We contrast costs that inflation imposes on individuals and costs it imposes on society as a whole. We conclude by considering what the government can do about inflation.

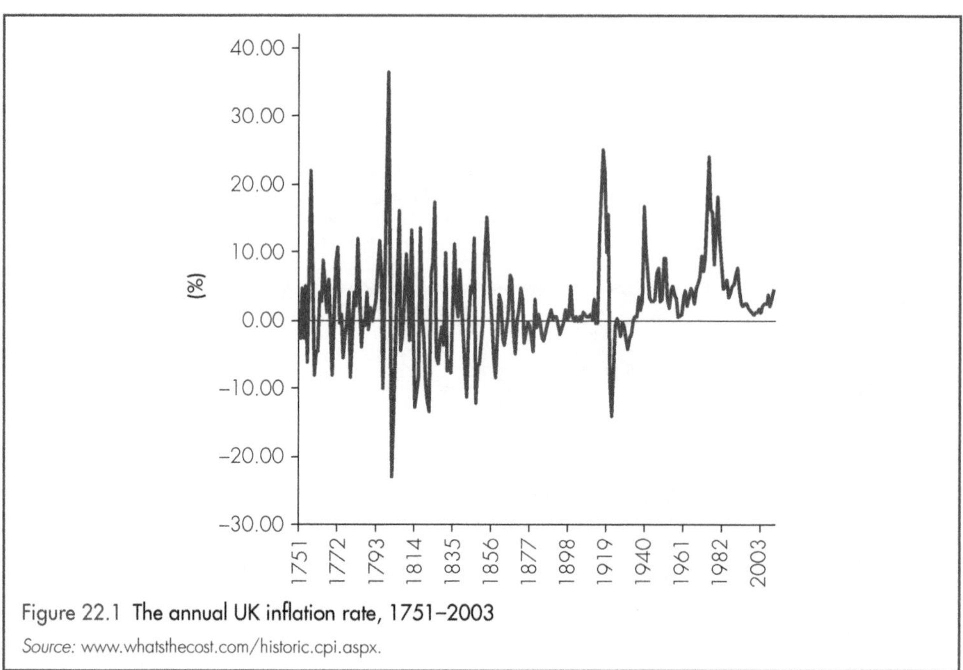

Figure 22.1 **The annual UK inflation rate, 1751–2003**

Source: www.whatsthecost.com/historic.cpi.aspx.

22.1 Money and inflation

What is the link between nominal money and the price level, and hence between money growth and inflation?

People demand money because of its purchasing power over goods. They demand *real* money. Suppose real income is Y and the interest rate is r. The stock of real money demanded rises if (a) Y increases or (b) r falls. Conversely, lower income or a higher interest rate leads to a fall in the stock of real money demanded. If L denotes real money demand, we can summarize as

$$M/P = L(Y, r) \quad (1)$$

the left-hand side being real money supplied, the right-hand side real money demanded, depending on income and interest rates. In money market equilibrium, real money supply and demand are equal. Flexible interest rates maintain continuous money market equilibrium. Equation (1) always holds.

CONCEPT 22.1

THE QUANTITY THEORY OF MONEY: $MV = PY$

The velocity of circulation V is nominal income PY divided by nominal money M. If prices adjust to keep real output at potential output Y^*, assumed constant, M and P must move together, *provided velocity* V *stays constant*. Velocity is the speed at which the stock of money is passed round the economy as people transact. If everyone holds money for less time and passes it on more quickly, the economy needs less money relative to nominal income. How do we assess whether velocity is constant, as the simple quantity theory requires?

The quantity theory equation implies $M/P = Y/V$. The left -hand side is the real money supply. The right-hand side must be real money demand. It rises with real income and

The real money supply M/P is the nominal money supply M divided by the price level P.

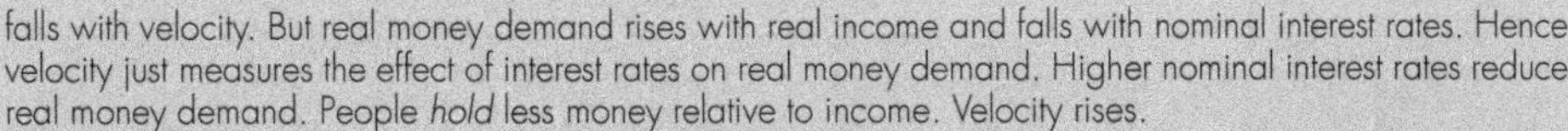

falls with velocity. But real money demand rises with real income and falls with nominal interest rates. Hence velocity just measures the effect of interest rates on real money demand. Higher nominal interest rates reduce real money demand. People *hold* less money relative to income. Velocity rises.

While inflation and nominal interest rates are rising, velocity is rising. But if inflation and nominal interest rates settle down at a particular level, velocity is then constant. Thereafter, the simple quantity theory once more applies.

This assumes prices are fully flexible. In the short run, if prices are sluggish, changes in nominal money change the real money supply. Changes in nominal money are not matched by changes in prices. The quantity theory of money will fail in the short run.

If nominal wages and prices adjust slowly in the short run, higher nominal money supply M leads initially to a higher real money stock M/P since prices P have not yet adjusted. The excess supply of real money bids down interest rates. This boosts the demand for goods. Gradually this bids up goods prices. In the labour market, wages start to rise.

After complete adjustment of wages and prices, a one-off rise in nominal money leads to an equivalent one-off rise in nominal wages and prices. Output, employment, interest rates and real money revert to their original levels. After adjustment is complete, the demand for real money is unchanged. Hence the price level changes in proportion to the original change in the nominal money stock.

The quantity theory of money says that changes in nominal money lead to equivalent changes in the price level (and money wages), with no effect on output and employment.

The theory is over 500 years old and may date from Confucius. The **quantity theory** is espoused by monetarists, who argue that *most* changes in prices reflect changes in the nominal money supply.

The theory must be interpreted with care. If the demand for real money is constant, the supply of real money must be constant: changes in nominal money are matched by equivalent changes in prices. This raises two issues: (a) even if the demand for real money is constant, do changes in nominal money cause changes in prices or vice versa; and (b) is the demand for real money constant?

Money, prices and causation

Suppose the demand for real money is constant over time. Money market equilibrium implies the real money supply M/P is constant. Monetary policy could fix the nominal money supply M, in which case money M determines prices P to get the required level of M/P implied by money demand.

Conversely, monetary policy may choose a target path for the price level P. Changes in this path then cause changes in the nominal money supply to achieve the required real money supply. Equation (1) says prices and money are correlated, but is agnostic on which causes which. That depends on the form of monetary policy pursued. With an intermediate target for nominal money, the causation flows from money to prices. With a target for prices or inflation, the causation flows the other way.

The leading monetarist Professor Milton Friedman always said that inflation is a monetary phenomenon. Sustained price increases, what we call inflation, are possible only if nominal money is also growing. It is always an option to change monetary policy and stop printing money. Sooner or later prices have to stop rising. Take away the oxygen and the fire goes out.

Is real money demand constant?

Real money demand depends on income Y and the cost of holding money (the spread between interest rates on assets and interest earned, if any, while holding money). Countries with sustained income growth will experience a sustained increase in the demand for real money; countries growing more slowly will have slower growth in real money demand.

Second, countries experiencing different degrees of financial competition will face different costs of holding money. Greater banking competition bid up interest paid on bank deposits, boosting money demand. Changing degrees of banking competition will lead to changes in real money demand.

Third, countries with high inflation are likely to face high nominal interest rates, larger spreads and a higher cost of holding money. Since inflation can become very large, this is potentially the most important reason why real money demand may change. We study this effect in the next section.

To sum up, even once equilibrium is restored, real money demand may be steadily changing, requiring a break in the one-for-one link between money and prices. However, *if* real income and interest rates are unaltered, changes in nominal money would eventually be accompanied by equivalent changes in nominal wages and prices.

Inflation

So far we have studied levels. Now we focus on rates of change. The growth in real money demand must equal the growth in real money supply; namely, the excess of nominal money growth over the growth in prices. Hence,

$$\text{Nominal money growth} = \text{real money demand growth} + \text{inflation rate}$$

Since real income and interest rates *usually* change only a few percentage points a year, real money demand usually changes slowly.[1] The essential insight of the quantity theory of money is that real variables usually change slowly.

Large changes in one nominal variable (money) are then accompanied by large changes in other nominal variables (prices, nominal wages) to keep real money (and real wages) at their equilibrium values. This is a useful first look at inflation, but we simplified too much.

22.2 Inflation and interest rates

Figure 22.2 shows interest and inflation rates for 15 countries in 2013. Countries with high inflation have high interest rates. An extra percentage point of inflation is accompanied on average by a nominal interest rate nearly one percentage point higher, a proposition first suggested by Professor Irving Fisher. By definition,

$$\text{Real interest rate} = [\text{nominal interest rate}] - [\text{inflation rate}]$$

The Fisher hypothesis says higher inflation leads to similarly higher nominal interest rates.

The **Fisher hypothesis** says that *real* interest rates do not change much. If they did, there would be large excess supply or demand for loans. Hence, higher inflation is largely offset by higher nominal interest rates to stop the real interest rate changing much. Figure 22.2

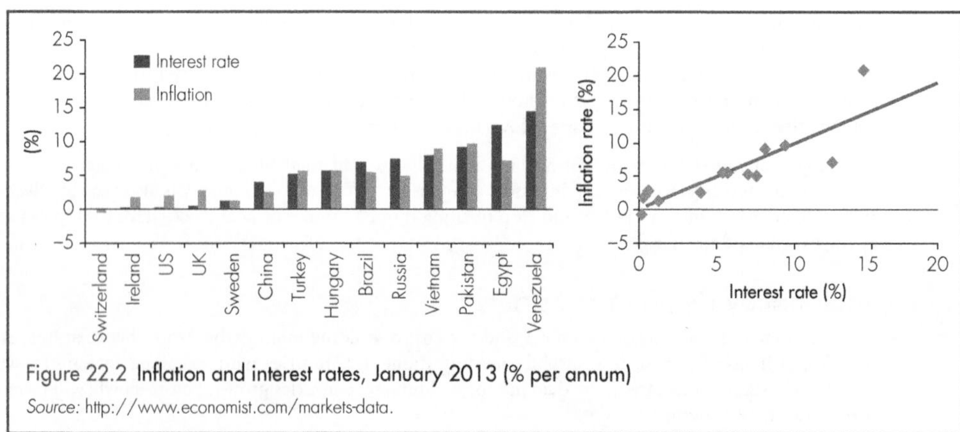

Figure 22.2 **Inflation and interest rates, January 2013 (% per annum)**

Source: http://www.economist.com/markets-data.

1 An exception is the hyperinflation example of the next section.

shows this is a good rule of thumb in reality. Countries, such as Switzerland, with inflation rates close to zero have correspondingly low nominal interest rates. Turkey and Hungary have interest rates around 5 per cent, largely because their inflation rates are at similar levels. In Pakistan, the levels of both are around 9 per cent, and in Venezuela nominal interest rates are nearly 15 per cent, but then inflation is over 20 per cent.

Faster nominal money growth leads both to higher inflation and higher nominal interest rates. Hence a rise in the rate of money growth leads to a rise in nominal interest rates. This reduces the demand for real money, requiring money and prices to grow at *different* rates until the real money supply adjusts to the change in real money demand. To show how this works, we study a spectacular example – the German hyperinflation.

Hyperinflation

Hyperinflation is a period of very high inflation.

Bolivian annual inflation reached 11 000 per cent in 1985, Ukraine's inflation topped 10 000 per cent in 1993, and in 2009 inflation in Zimbabwe may have exceeded a trillion per cent – its central bank had to resort to printing banknotes denominated in 100 trillion Zimbabwean dollars that were still worth only a few US dollars or UK pounds.

The most famous, and most studied, hyperinflation is that in Germany during 1922–23. Germany lost the First World War. The German government had a big deficit, financed by printing money. Table 22.1 shows what happened. The government had to buy faster printing presses. In the later stages of the hyperinflation, they took in old notes, stamped on another zero, and reissued them as larger-denomination notes in the morning.

Table 22.1 The German hyperinflation, 1922–23

	Money	Prices	Real money	Inflation % monthly
January 1922	1	1	1.00	5
January 1923	16	75	0.21	189
July 1923	354	2021	0.18	386
September 1923	227 777	645 946	0.35	2532
October 1923	20 201 256	191 891 890	0.11	29 720

Source: adapted from C. L. Holtfrerish, *Die Deutsche Inflation 1914–23* (Walter de Gruyter, 1980).

If inflation is π and the nominal interest rate is r, the real interest rate is $(r - \pi)$ but the real return on non-interest-bearing cash is $-\pi$, which shows how quickly the real value of cash is being eroded by inflation. The extra real return on holding interest-bearing assets rather than cash is $(r - \pi) - (-\pi) = r$. The *nominal* interest rate measures the *real* cost of holding cash. Nominal interest rates rise with inflation. In the German hyperinflation the cost of holding cash became enormous.

Table 22.1 shows that German prices rose 75-fold in 1922, and more in 1923. People carried money in wheelbarrows to go shopping. By October 1923, real money holdings were only 11 per cent of their level in January 1922. How did people get by with such small holdings of real cash?

People, paid twice a day, shopped in their lunch hour before the real value of their cash depreciated too much. Any cash not immediately spent was quickly deposited in a bank where it could earn interest. People spent a lot of time at the bank.

The flight from cash is the collapse in the demand for real cash when high inflation and high nominal interest rates make it very expensive to hold cash.

What lessons can we draw? First, *rising* inflation and *rising* interest rates significantly reduce the demand for *real* cash. Hyperinflations are a rare example in which a real quantity (real cash) changes quickly and by a lot. Second, and as a result, money and prices can get quite out of line when inflation and nominal interest rates are rising. Table 22.1 shows that prices rose by six times as much as nominal money between January 1922 and July 1923, reducing the real money supply by 82 per cent, in line with the fall in real money demand – a **flight from cash**.

22.3 Inflation, money and deficits

Persistent inflation must be accompanied by continuing nominal money growth. Printing money to finance a large deficit is a source of inflation. Budget deficits may explain why governments have to print money rapidly. Tight *fiscal* policy is needed to fight inflation.

If government debt is low relative to GDP, the government can finance deficits by borrowing. It has enough tax revenue with which to pay interest and repay the debt. For governments with low debt, there may be no relation between their budget deficit and how much money they print. Sometimes they print money; sometimes they issue bonds. We do not expect a close relationship between deficits and money creation in most advanced countries.

Many years of deficits may make government debt large relative to GDP. The government then cannot finance deficits by more borrowing. It has to tighten fiscal policy to shrink the deficit or print money to finance the continuing deficit.

To ensure that the European Central Bank did not face fiscal pressure to print too much money and thus create inflation, members of the Eurozone had to obey the Stability and Growth Pact, which restricts their budget deficits to less than 3 per cent of GDP, except in severe recession. Of course, when severe recession arrived in 2009, budget deficits escalated to 10 per cent and beyond. We never know how binding a commitment will be until a crisis occurs.

Deficits, money growth and real revenue

A hyperinflation is a situation in which fiscal policy is out of control. A government with a persistently high deficit, financed by borrowing, now has so much debt that nobody will lend it any more. Instead, it prints money to finance its deficit.

How much real revenue can the government get by printing banknotes? The government has a monopoly on cash. As a token money, its production cost is tiny relative to its value as money. The government prints money for nothing, then uses it to pay nurses and build roads. Real money demand M/P rises with real income. Long-run growth of real income allows the government some scope to raise M without adding to P. This extra money can be used to finance government spending, and so is as good as tax revenue, without causing inflation. It is called **seigniorage**, and arises from the government monopoly on creating money with a value vastly in excess of its production cost.

Seigniorage is non-inflationary real revenue acquired by the government through its ability to print money.

A second potential source of real revenue is the inflation tax. Suppose real income and output are constant but that a weak government cannot shrink its budget deficit and now has debt so large that nobody will lend to it. It prints money to cover the budget deficit. If ΔM is the amount of new cash created, this finances an amount of real spending $(\Delta M)/P$, which is the same as $(\Delta M/M) \times (M/P)$, the growth rate of cash multiplied by the real demand for cash. The rise in nominal money must feed into prices sooner or later. Suppose the rate of nominal money growth $(\Delta M/M)$ equals the inflation rate π. Thus,

$$\text{Real revenue from inflation} = \pi \times M/P$$

Inflation helps the government by reducing the real value of the non-interest-bearing part of the government debt, namely cash. Think of inflation as the tax rate and real cash as the tax base for the **inflation tax**.

The inflation tax is the effect of inflation in raising real revenue by reducing the real value of the government's nominal debt.

Now for the part that may be new to you. If money growth and inflation rise, does the government get more *real* revenue from the inflation tax? Higher inflation raises nominal interest rates and hence reduces the real demand for cash.

Figure 22.3 shows the answer. At low inflation, real cash demand is high, but the multiple of inflation and real cash demand is small. Similarly, at high inflation, although the inflation tax rate is high, the tax base – real cash demand – is now tiny because nominal interest rates are so high. The multiple of inflation and real cash is again low. Real revenue raised through the inflation tax cannot be increased indefinitely. After a certain point, faster money growth and higher inflation shrink the tax base more than they raise the tax rate.

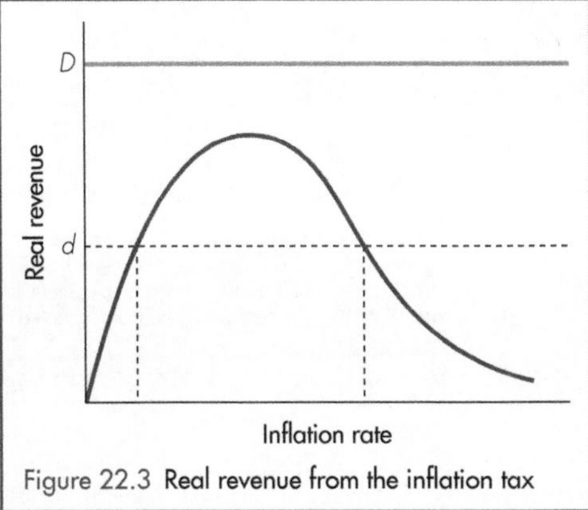

Figure 22.3 Real revenue from the inflation tax

The figure has two implications. First, if the government needs to cover a particular *real* deficit *d* by printing money, there may be two rates of money growth and inflation that do the job. Either is a long-run equilibrium in which inflation is constant.

Second, if for political reasons the government has a real deficit as large as *D*, printing money cannot do the job. The economy explodes into hyperinflation. At high inflation, real cash demand is already low. Raising inflation further causes such a large percentage fall in the tiny demand for real cash that inflation tax revenue falls, the government prints even more cash and the problem gets even worse.

That is how hyperinflation starts. The only solution is to cut the size of the deficit. Often the government does this by defaulting on its debt, which slashes the burden of interest payments.

Notice that the inflation tax applies to cash which has no nominal interest rate to increase in line with inflation. For interest-bearing money, in principle interest rates can rise to protect money holders. Then it is only unforeseen inflation, not incorporated in interest rates, that acts as a tax.

This is one reason we tend to see hyperinflation in more primitive economies, in which cash is very important. In modern European economies, cash is much less important and the potential tax base for the inflation tax is a lot lower.

22.4 Inflation, unemployment and output

One of the most famous relationships in post-war macroeconomics is the Phillips curve.

The Phillips curve

In 1958 Professor Phillips of the London School of Economics found a strong statistical relationship between annual inflation and annual unemployment in the UK. Similar relationships were found in other countries. The Phillips curve is shown in Figure 22.4.

The Phillips curve shows that a higher inflation rate is accompanied by a lower unemployment rate. It suggests we can trade off more inflation for less unemployment or vice versa.

The **Phillips curve** seemed a useful compass for choosing macroeconomic policy. By its choice of fiscal and monetary policy, the government set aggregate demand and hence unemployment. The Phillips curve showed how much inflation then ensued. Higher aggregate demand bid up wages and prices, causing higher inflation but lower unemployment.

The Phillips curve shows the trade-off that people believed they faced in the 1960s. In those days UK unemployment was rarely over 2 per cent of the labour force. But people believed that, if they did the unthinkable and reduced aggregate demand until unemployment rose to 2.5 per cent, inflation would fall to zero.

Since then there have been years when *both* inflation and unemployment were over 10 per cent. Something happened to the Phillips curve. The next two chapters explain why the simple Phillips curve of Figure 22.4 ceased to fit the facts.

Equilibrium unemployment is not zero, for reasons that we explore in Chapter 23. Suppose equilibrium employment and potential output are fixed in the long run, but there is sluggish wage and price adjustment. Chapter 21 discussed the vertical long-run aggregate supply curve and sloping short-run supply curve, relating output and the price level. These ideas are easily translated from inflation and output to inflation and unemployment.

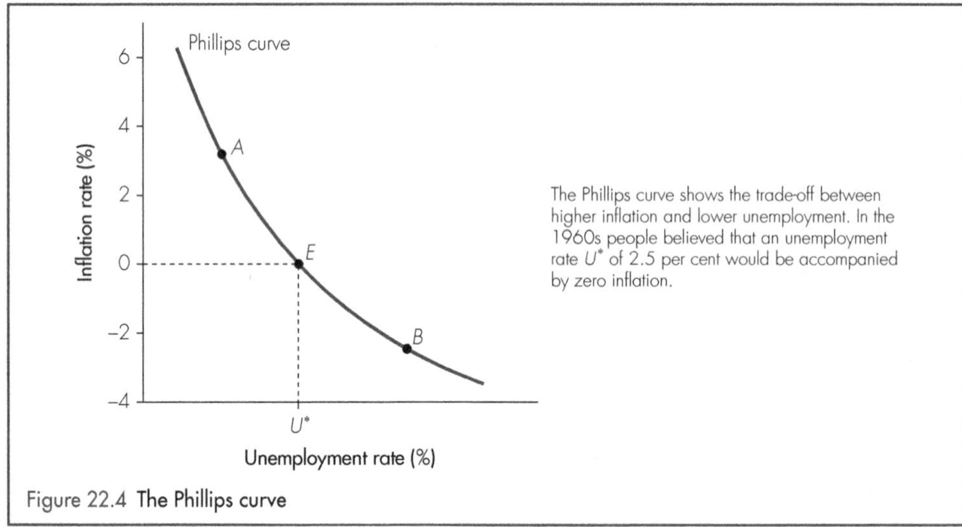

The Phillips curve shows the trade-off between higher inflation and lower unemployment. In the 1960s people believed that an unemployment rate U^* of 2.5 per cent would be accompanied by zero inflation.

Figure 22.4 **The Phillips curve**

The vertical long-run Phillips curve

In long-run equilibrium, the economy is at both potential output and equilibrium unemployment. Sometimes these are referred to as the **natural level of output** and the **natural rate of unemployment**.

The natural level of output and the natural rate of unemployment are the long-run equilibrium levels of output and unemployment levels, respectively.

Both are determined by real things, not nominal things. They depend on the supply of inputs, the level of technology, the level of tax rates, and so on. They do not depend on inflation, provided all prices *P* and nominal wages *W* are rising together. Equilibrium unemployment depends on the real wage *W*/*P*, as we discuss in Chapter 23.

Just as long-run aggregate supply is vertical at potential output – output is unaffected by inflation – so the long-run Phillips curve is vertical at equilibrium unemployment. Equilibrium unemployment is independent of inflation. Plotting inflation and unemployment, Figure 22.5 shows the long-run Phillips curve vertical at equilibrium unemployment U^*.

In long-run equilibrium, inflation is constant. People correctly anticipate inflation, and adjust the growth of nominal wages to keep real wages constant, at the real wage required for long-run equilibrium. Similarly, nominal interest rates are sufficiently high to offset inflation and maintain real interest rates at their equilibrium level. Everyone adjusts to inflation because it can be completely foreseen.

Suppose inflation is 10 per cent a year. This is consistent with many forms of monetary policy. We can think of monetary policy as having either a target of 10 per cent annual money growth, or an inflation target of 10 per cent a year, or as a Taylor rule in which the inflation part aims for 10 per cent annual inflation. In Figure 22.5 long-run equilibrium is at *E*. Inflation is 10 per cent, as everybody expects. Nominal money grows at 10 per cent a year. Unemployment is at its natural rate.

The short-run Phillips curve

Beginning from *E*, suppose something raises aggregate demand. Unemployment falls, inflation rises and the economy is at *A*. Then the central bank raises interest rates to achieve its targets (in whichever form), and the economy slowly moves back down the short-run Phillips curve PC_1 from *A* back to *E* again. Since interest rates take time to affect aggregate demand, this may take one or two years.

Conversely, beginning from *E* a downward demand shock takes the economy to *B* in the short run. The central bank alters interest rates to bring the economy steadily back from *B* to *E*.

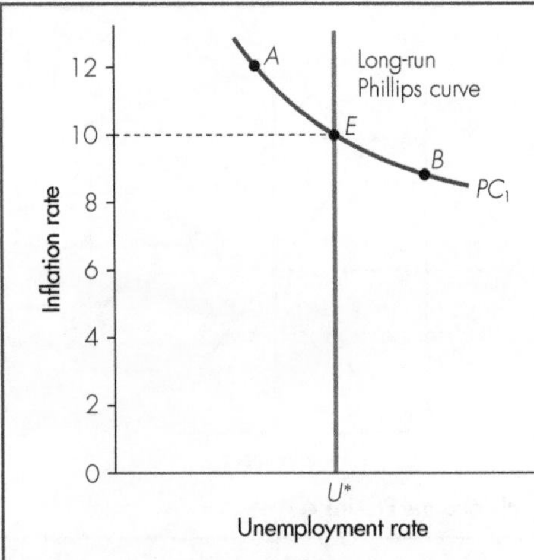

Since people care about real variables not nominal variables, when full adjustment has been completed people will arrange for all nominal variables to keep up with inflation. The vertical long-run Phillips curve shows that eventually the economy gets back to the natural rate of unemployment U^*, whatever the long-run inflation rate. There is no long-run trade-off between inflation and unemployment. The short-run Phillips curve PC_1 shows short-run adjustment as before. The height of the short-run Phillips curve depends on the rate of inflation and nominal money growth in long-run equilibrium, as shown by the position of point E on the long-run Phillips curve.

Figure 22.5 **The long-run Phillips curve**

> The short-run Phillips curve shows that, in the short run, higher unemployment is associated with lower inflation. The height of the short-run Phillips curve reflects expected inflation. In long-run equilibrium at E, expectations are fulfilled.

The **short-run Phillips curve** corresponds to the short-run supply curve for output. Given inherited wages, higher prices make firms supply more output and demand more workers. For any level of last period's prices, higher prices today imply higher inflation today. In Chapter 21, the height of the short-run aggregate supply curve depended on the inherited growth rate of nominal wages. Similarly, the height of the short-run Phillips curve reflects inherited nominal wage growth.

When workers and firms expect high inflation, they agree a large rise in nominal wages. If inflation turns out as expected, real wages are as forecast and the nominal wage growth was justified. If inflation is higher than expected, real wages are lower than planned. Firms supply more output and demand more labour. High inflation (relative to expectations) goes with lower unemployment. The short-run Phillips curve slopes down. Its height reflects the inflation expectations embodied in the inherited wage agreement.

This explains why most economies had high inflation at each unemployment rate in the 1970s and 1980s: the short-run Phillips curve had shifted upwards. Governments were printing money at a faster rate than before. The long-run equilibrium inflation rate was high, and expected to be so.

The point E lay further up the long-run Phillips curve in Figure 22.5. The short-run Phillips curve through this point was much higher than the short-run Phillips curve in the data originally studied by Professor Phillips. The 1970s and 1980s were periods of high inflation. The original Phillips curve data had been for a period of much lower inflation.

Figure 22.6 confirms the complete correspondence between the aggregate supply schedules of the previous chapter and the Phillips curves in this chapter. In the long run, the economy is at potential output Y^* and equilibrium unemployment U^*. Suppose the inherited level of inflation expectations is the level π. The economy then faces the short-run aggregate supply schedule *SAS* in the left-hand panel and the short-run Phillips curve *PC* in the right-hand panel – one implies the other. Initially the economy is at point A in both panels.

A fall in aggregate demand shifts the economy to point A' in both panels – there is less demand, inflation falls, output falls and unemployment rises. Conversely, the short-run effect of a rise in aggregate demand takes the economy to point A'' in both panels.

If inflation expectations are firmly anchored, eventually the economy will return to point A in both panels. However, if having first experienced an increase in aggregate demand and a move to point A'', inflation

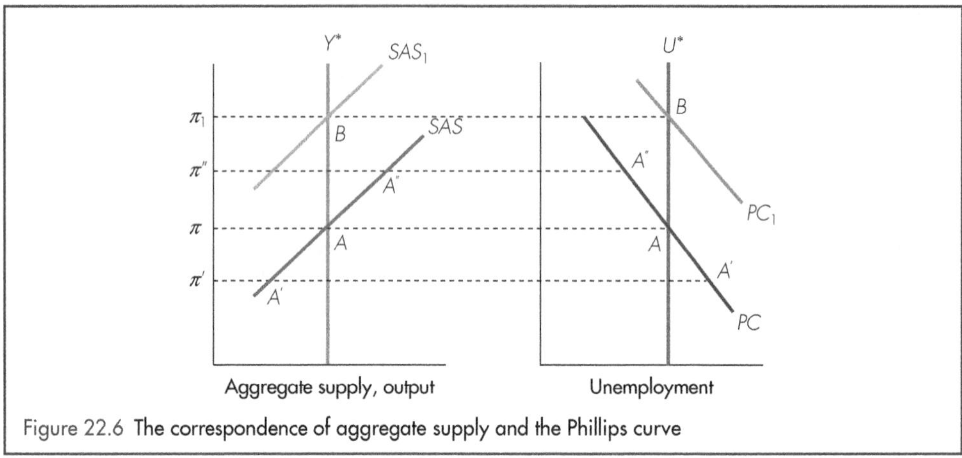

Figure 22.6 The correspondence of aggregate supply and the Phillips curve

expectations then increase permanently from π to π_1, the short-run aggregate supply curve shifts up from *SAS* to SAS_1 and the short-run Phillips curve from *PC* to PC_1.

We could also use Figure 22.6 to explore permanent supply shocks. For example, an increase in work incentives would shift the vertical long-run Phillips curve to the left, reducing equilibrium unemployment. Correspondingly, long-run aggregate supply of output would increase, shifting the vertical long-run aggregate supply curve to the right.

We draw two conclusions. First, it was wrong to interpret the original Phillips curve as a *permanent* trade-off between inflation and unemployment. It was the temporary trade-off, corresponding to a particular short-run aggregate supply schedule, while the economy adjusted to a demand shock.

Second, the speed with which the economy moves back along the Phillips curve depends on two things: the degree of flexibility of nominal wages and hence prices; and the extent to which monetary policy adjusts interest rates to restore demand more quickly. Complete wage flexibility would restore the vertical Phillips curve and the vertical aggregate supply curve. Rapid adjustment of interest rates would offset the demand shock, restoring output, unemployment and inflation to their long-run equilibrium levels.

Extreme monetarists believe that wage flexibility is very high. In the extreme version, it is only the fact that workers make annual wage settlements that prevents the economy always being in long-run equilibrium. Changes in aggregate demand unforeseen when nominal wages were set mean that wages and prices are temporarily at the wrong level. But such mistakes are rectified as soon as wages are renegotiated.

If wage and price adjustment are more sluggish than this, full employment is not immediately restored. However, we know from the previous chapter that monetary policy can completely compensate for a demand shock once it has been diagnosed. Nor is there any conflict between stabilizing inflation and stabilizing output or employment. Such conflicts arise only in response to supply shocks.

We have made considerable progress in understanding the Phillips curve, but there is more still to study. First, we need to analyse changes in long-run inflation expectations, which shift the short-run Phillips curve. Second, we need to examine supply shocks. Temporary supply shocks also shift the short-run Phillips curve. Permanent supply shocks alter equilibrium unemployment and shift the long-run Phillips curve.

Expectations and credibility

Figure 22.7 puts this apparatus to work to discuss what happens when a new government is elected with a commitment to reduce inflation. The economy begins in long-run equilibrium at *E*, facing the short-run Phillips curve PC_1. Nominal money, prices and money wages are all rising at the rate π_1.

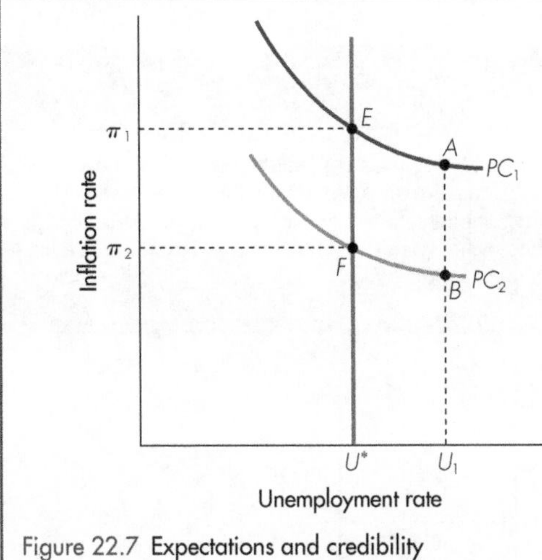

Beginning at E, the target inflation rate is cut from π_1 to π_2. Having expected inflation π_1, nominal wage growth has been too high. Firms cut back output and employment and the economy moves to A. If the new policy is credible, the next wage settlement reflects lower inflation expectations, the short-run Phillips curve shifts to PC_2 and the economy moves from A to B. Thereafter, it slowly adjusts along PC_2 to F.

However, if people doubt that the new tough policy will be sustained, nominal wages may keep growing at π_1. The short-run Phillips curve remains PC_1. Unemployment stays high, and inflation refuses to fall.

Figure 22.7 **Expectations and credibility**

The government wants to reduce inflation to π_2 to reach point F. The day the government is elected it announces a cut in the inflation target from π_1 to π_2.

Overnight, firms inherit nominal wage increases that had anticipated the old inflation rate π_1. They have little scope to reduce inflation. If inflation does fall, real wages are now too high. Firms reduce output and employment. Inflation falls a little and unemployment rises. The economy moves along the short-run Phillips curve PC_1 to A.

What happens next? In the good scenario, workers believe the tighter monetary policy will last. The next wage bargain is based on inflation expectations π_2. The short-run Phillips curve shifts down to PC_2 and the economy moves from A to B. Inflation falls quickly. The economy then moves slowly along PC_2 from B to F.

Now for the bad scenario. When the economy first reaches A, workers do not believe that the tough new monetary policy will last. They think π_1 will remain the inflation rate in the long run. Thinking inflation will remain high, workers do not reduce nominal wage growth. They believe PC_1 not PC_2 will be relevant.

A self-fulfilling prophecy is an expectation that creates the incentive to make it come true.

Suppose workers are wrong. Although nominal wages grow at π_1, the tough policy lasts and actual inflation is below π_1. Real wages rise and unemployment gets worse without much fall in inflation. The worse the slump becomes, the more likely is the government to give in, easing monetary policy to boost aggregate demand again. A belief that the government's nerve will crack can become a **self-fulfilling prophecy**.

The economy stays on PC_1 and the attempt to reduce inflation fails. Gradually the economy moves back along PC_1 to equilibrium at E.

This explains why governments go to such lengths to commit to tight monetary policy. The sooner people accept that long-run inflation will be low, the sooner nominal wage growth will slow. Making central banks independent is an institutional reform designed to increase the credibility of monetary policy by insulating it from short-term political expediency.

Figure 22.7 was used to describe a fall in inflation expectations, but the opposite is also possible. By 2010 many people were wondering whether Western governments would indeed curtail government spending and raise taxes in order to bring budget deficits under control. If future governments are weak, they may resort to money creation instead. We could then envisage a shift upwards in the short-run Phillips curve in Figure 22.7 as inflation expectations increase.

In assessing how likely this is, people will look at the independence of the central banks and whether they are prepared to use this to adhere to the monetary targets they have been set. In principle, central banks should be prepared to raise interest rates if they foresee any systematic increase in inflation above its target level.

CONCEPT 22.2

EXPECTATIONS FORMATION AND THE ACCELERATIONIST HYPOTHESIS

How should economists model inflation expectations? One solution is simply to treat inflation expectations as exogenous or autonomous – given from outside the model. We analyse conditional on a particular assumption, then explore the consequences of changing that assumption. This is simple, but not very satisfactory – if the Phillips curve is telling us about inflation and unemployment, should not the people who populate the model be reacting to the same information when they form expectations?

For many years, economists relied on the assumption of adaptive (or extrapolative) expectations, which assumes that people use the past history of inflation to forecast its future values. If at any time their forecast turns out to be too low (high), they revise upwards (downwards) their inflation expectations for the following period. Eventually, in long-run equilibrium, expectations and actuality have converged.

This expectations assumption gave rise to a clear prediction. If governments could *accelerate* the rate of money creation, steadily increasing its rate, they could manufacture inflation that kept ahead of people's expectations for a *sustained* period. Workers would repeatedly settle for nominal wage growth that did not keep place with inflation, reducing the real wage, and promoting higher employment and output. The figure below illustrates.

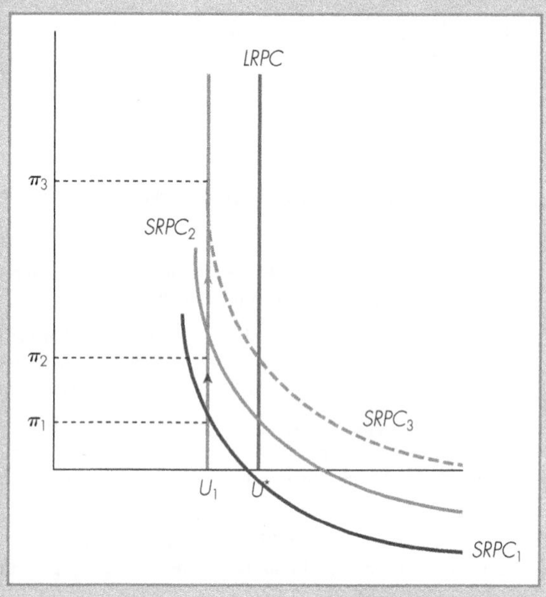

In the long run, the Phillips curve is vertical at the equilibrium unemployment rate U^*. Eventually, the labour market can adjust to any level of sustained inflation.

Initially, suppose expected inflation is zero. The short-run Phillips curve $SRPC_1$ would be compatible with unemployment at U^* if actual inflation turned out to equal the expected inflation rate of zero. However, the government can artificially lower actual unemployment to U_1 by generating inflation π_1. Since this exceeds the zero inflation expectations embodied in wage settlements, it temporarily reduces the value of real wages until the labour market has time to adjust.

Next period, everybody has raised their inflation expectations a bit, and nominal wages increase a bit. The short-run Phillips curve $SRPC_2$ captures the higher inflation expectations. Its intersection with the long-run Phillips curve shows how much inflation is now being expected. However, by boosting the economy even more strongly, the government can achieve an actual inflation rate π_2 that again exceeds expectations and lowers real wages. Again, actual unemployment is reduced to U_1. The next wage settlement recognizes that expectations have twice been too low. The short-run Phillips curve reflects another increase in inflation expectations. A government determined to keep unemployment down could still achieve actual inflation π_3, and again engineer a reduction in real wages that reduces unemployment to U_1.

The conclusion is that, if expectations adjust adaptively in this way, a determined government could reduce unemployment for a sustained period by a sustained sequence of inflation surprises. But as inflation expectations rise, it takes ever higher inflation to keep surprising the labour market.

Conversely, if a new inflation-hating government takes over, it can gradually bash down inflation expectations, and gradually shift the short-run Phillips curve down again. Each time, it will generate *less* inflation than had been expected, inducing a subsequent downward revision in expectations, till eventually $SPRC_1$ can again be reached. During the transition, each episode entails *less* inflation than expected, and hence implies real wages that are higher than intended when nominal wage settlements were reached. Hence, there is a period of abnormally high unemployment while the *SRPC* is gradually being shifted downwards.

The accelerationist hypothesis states that, by accelerating inflation faster than workers' expectations can adjust, the government can depress real wages and achieve abnormally low unemployment for a sustained period.

Adaptive expectations are a model of limited rationality. People get fooled in the short run, but eventually get things right once long-run equilibrium is reached. Some economists think people are smarter than this. The **accelerationist hypothesis** relies on fooling people period after period with the same trick. If people grasp what the government is doing, they will anticipate the additional inflation and the power to surprise will be weakened or eliminated.

Supply shocks

In the long run, other things equal, the Phillips curve is vertical at equilibrium unemployment U^*. But other things are unequal, and U^* is not constant. In terms of Figure 22.6, a rise in equilibrium unemployment shifts the vertical long-run Phillips curve to the right. Changes in equilibrium unemployment reflect **permanent supply shocks.**

A permanent supply shock affects equilibrium unemployment and potential output.

The short-run Phillips curve can shift for two reasons. Inherited nominal wage growth changes if inflation expectations change, as analysed in Figure 22.7. Alternatively, a change in firms' desired supply of output and demand for workers, for a given rate of inherited nominal wage growth, shifts the short-run Phillips curve. Examples include a change in oil prices, regulations or tax rates.

MATHS 22.1

SHORT-RUN AND LONG-RUN PHILLIPS CURVES

Consider the short-run Phillips curve:

$$\pi = \pi^e - b(U - U^*) \qquad b > 0 \qquad (1)$$

where U and U^* are, respectively, actual unemployment and equilibrium unemployment, π is inflation and π^e is expected inflation. When actual and equilibrium unemployment coincide, inflation is determined by the inherited level of inflation expectations, which therefore determines the height of the short-run Phillips curve. When expected inflation is higher, the entire short-run Phillips curve is higher. The parameter b determines the slope of the short-run Phillips curve. The larger is b, the steeper is the short-run curve. Because b is a constant, in this example *SRPC* has a constant negative slope. In the long run, any level of inflation expectations can prevail when U and U^* coincide. All we know is that then actual and expected inflation coincide along the long-run Phillips curve. Any actual inflation rate is compatible eventually with U^*. *LRPC* is vertical.

Suppose people believe the central bank will try to stabilize inflation at 2 per cent, but that this cannot be achieved overnight. People therefore expect:

$$\pi^e = 0.02 - a(U - U^*) \qquad a > 0 \qquad (2)$$

When unemployment exceeds U^*, people expect inflation to be lower than normal; when unemployment is below U^*, people expect a boom to be leading to above normal inflation.

Combining equations (1) and (2):

$$\pi = 0.02 - (a + b)(U - U^*) \qquad (3)$$

In this example, when unemployment has reverted to its long-run equilibrium, inflation is then 2 per cent. In the short run, inflation is affected by deviations of unemployment from equilibrium unemployment not only because this affects wages, prices and inflation, but also because it has a second effect on inflation expectations themselves. Exactly how inflation expectations adjust over time in the real world is a subject of continuing controversy.

We can also examine the relationship between the Phillips curve in this chapter and our discussion of aggregate supply in the previous chapter. If Y^* is the level of potential output, determined in the long run by aggregate supply, and the short-run output gap is $(Y - Y^*)$, then demand-driven cyclical fluctuations in output should lead to corresponding cycles in employment, and hence in unemployment:

$$Y - Y^* = -h(U - U^*) \qquad h > 0 \qquad (4)$$

When output exceeds potential output, unemployment lies below its natural rate. Combining equations (1) and (4):

$$Y = Y^* + (h/b)(\pi - \pi^e) \qquad (5)$$

which we can interpret as the short-run aggregate supply curve of the previous chapter. For a given level of inherited inflation expectations, higher current inflation induces firms to supply additional current output. In the long run, inflation and expected inflation coincide, and current output simply equals potential output.

Figure 22.8 shows an adverse **temporary supply shock**. The short-run Phillips curve shifts up, from PC_1 to PC_2. If monetary policy accommodates the shock, the target inflation rate rises from π_1 to π_2. The economy moves from E to F with no change in output or unemployment, but at the cost of higher inflation. Eventually the shock wears off, since it is temporary, and the economy reverts to E, with another accommodating change in monetary policy.

A temporary supply shock leaves these long-run values unaffected, but shifts the short-run Phillips curve and the short-run aggregate supply schedule for output.

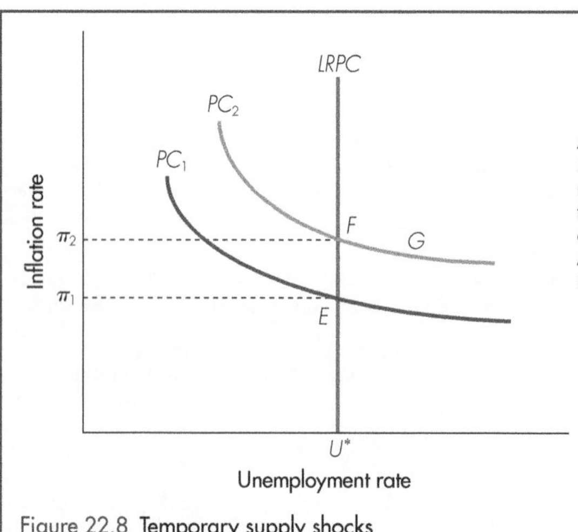

An adverse but temporary supply shock shifts PC_1 to PC_2 without affecting *LRPC*. Beginning from *E* monetary policy can accommodate the shock, moving to *F*. If interest rates are raised to prevent inflation rising as high as π_2, the fall in demand raises unemployment. At *G* the economy experiences stagflation, both high inflation and high unemployment.

Figure 22.8 **Temporary supply shocks**

Stagflation is high inflation and high unemployment, caused by an adverse supply shock.

Alternatively, monetary policy may *not* fully accommodate the supply shock. In Chapter 21, we showed that this would mean higher inflation *and* lower output. Now, the analogue is higher inflation *and* higher unemployment – **stagflation**. To prevent inflation shifting up by as much as the vertical shift up in the short-run Phillips curve, monetary policy makes sure that aggregate demand falls a bit. Hence inflation rises a bit and unemployment rises a bit. The economy moves from *E* to *G* in Figure 22.7. Output stagnates despite higher inflation.

Again, the credibility of policy is crucial. If workers think the government, frightened of high unemployment, will accommodate any shock, large wage rises buy temporarily higher real wages until prices adjust fully. And in the long run, monetary policy is loosened to maintain aggregate demand at full employment, so there is little danger of extra unemployment.

Once a government proves that it will not accommodate shocks, nominal wage growth slows. Workers then fear that higher wages will reduce demand and price workers out of a job.

22.5 The costs of inflation

People dislike inflation, but why is it so bad? Some reasons commonly given are spurious.

Inflation illusion?

People have inflation illusion if they confuse nominal and real changes. People's welfare depends on real variables, not nominal variables.

It is wrong to say that inflation is bad because it makes goods more expensive. If *all* nominal variables rise at the same rate, people have larger nominal incomes and can buy the same physical quantity of goods as before. If people realize that prices have risen but forget that nominal incomes have also risen, they have **inflation illusion**. It is real incomes that tell us how many goods people can afford to buy.

A second mistake is more subtle. Suppose there is a sharp rise in the real price of oil. Oil-importing countries are worse off. Domestic consumption per person has to fall. It can fall in one of two ways.

If workers do not ask for 'cost-of-living' wage increases to cover the higher cost of oil-related products, real wages fall. Nominal wages buy fewer goods. Suppose too that domestic firms absorb higher oil-related fuel costs, not passing on these costs in higher prices. There is no rise in domestic prices or nominal wages. The domestic economy has adjusted to the adverse supply shock without inflation. People are worse off.

Suppose instead that people try to maintain their old standard of living. Workers claim cost-of-living rises to restore their real wages, and firms protect their profit margins by raising prices in line with higher wage and fuel costs. There is a lot of domestic inflation, which the government accommodates by printing extra money. Eventually the economy settles down in its new long-run equilibrium position.

People must still be worse off. The rise in the real oil price has not disappeared. It still takes more domestic exports, using resources no longer available to make output for domestic consumption, to pay for the more expensive oil imports. In the new long-run equilibrium, wages do not quite keep up with higher prices, and prices do not quite keep up with higher costs. The market brings about the required fall in real domestic spending, letting resources go into exports to pay for the more expensive oil imports.

People notice (a) rising prices and (b) lower real incomes, but draw the wrong conclusion. Inflation did not make them worse off, higher oil prices did. Inflation is a symptom of the initial refusal to accept the new reality.

We now turn to better arguments about the cost of inflation. Our discussion has two themes. First, was the inflation fully expected, or were people surprised? Second, do our institutions, including regulations and the tax system, let people adjust fully to inflation once they expect it? The cost of inflation depends on the answer to these two questions.

Complete adaptation and full anticipation

Imagine an economy with annual inflation of 10 per cent for ever. Everybody anticipates it. Nominal wages grow and nominal interest rates incorporate it. Real wages and real interest rates are unaffected. The economy is at full employment. Government policy is fully adjusted. Nominal taxes are changed every year to keep real tax revenue constant. Nominal government spending rises at 10 per cent a year to keep real government spending constant. Share prices rise with inflation to maintain the real value of firms. The tax treatment of interest earnings and capital gains is adjusted to reflect inflation. Pensions and other transfer payments rise every year, in line with expected inflation.

This economy has no inflation illusion. Everyone has adjusted to it. This explains the long-run vertical Phillips curve in the previous section. Is complete adjustment possible?

Nominal interest rates usually rise with inflation to preserve the real rate of interest. But the nominal interest rate is the opportunity cost of holding cash. When inflation is higher, people hold less real cash. Society uses money to economize on the time and effort involved in undertaking transactions. High nominal interest rates make people economize on real money – thus incurring **shoe-leather costs**. Using more resources to transact, we have fewer resources for production and consumption of goods and services.

Shoe-leather costs of inflation are the extra time and effort in transacting when we economize on holding real money.

Menu costs of inflation are the physical resources needed for adjustments to keep real things constant when inflation occurs.

When prices rise, price labels have to be changed. Menus are reprinted to show the higher price of meals. The faster the rate of price change, the more often menus must be reprinted if real prices are to remain constant. Among the **menu costs of inflation** is the effort of doing mental arithmetic. If inflation is zero, it is easy to see that a beer costs the same as it did three months ago. When inflation is 25 per cent a year, it takes more effort to compare the real price of beer today with that of three months ago. People try to think in real terms, but the mental arithmetic involves time and effort.

How big are menu costs? Supermarkets easily change price tags. The cost of changing parking meters, pay telephones and slot machines is larger. In countries with high inflation, pay phones usually take tokens whose price is easily changed without having physically to alter the machines.

Even when inflation is perfectly anticipated and the economy has fully adjusted to it, we cannot avoid shoe-leather and menu costs. These costs are big when inflation is high, but may not be too big when inflation is moderate. However, if we cannot adjust to expected inflation, the costs are then larger.

Fully anticipated inflation when institutions do not adapt

Assume inflation is fully anticipated but institutions prevent people fully adjusting to expected inflation. Inflation now has extra costs.

Taxes

Tax rates may not be fully inflation-adjusted. One problem is **fiscal drag**. Suppose income below £10 000 was untaxed, but you pay income tax at 50 per cent on all income over that amount. Initially, you earn £15 000 and pay income tax of £2500. After ten years of inflation, all wages and prices double but tax brackets and tax rates remain as before. You now earn £30 000. Paying tax at 50 per cent on the £20 000 of taxable income, you pay tax of £10 000. Wages and prices only doubled. Your nominal tax rose from £2500 to £10 000. Fiscal drag raised the real tax burden. The government gained from inflation. You lost.

Fiscal drag is the rise in real tax revenue when inflation raises nominal incomes, pushing people into higher tax brackets in a progressive income tax system.

To be inflation-neutral, nominal tax brackets must rise with inflation. When prices double, the nominal tax exemption must rise, from £10 000 to £20 000. At your new nominal income of £30 000, you pay £5000 tax, exactly twice in nominal terms what you paid before prices increased. In real terms, nothing has changed.

Percentage taxes on value, such as VAT, automatically raise nominal tax revenue in line with the price level. However, *specific* duties, such as £5 on a bottle of whisky, must be raised as the price level rises.

Taxing capital

Income tax on interest income is also affected by inflation. Suppose there is no inflation. Nominal and real interest rates are both 4 per cent. With a 40 per cent tax rate, the after-tax real return on lending is 2.6 per cent.

Now suppose inflation is 11 per cent and nominal interest rates are 15 per cent to keep a pre-tax real interest rate of 4 per cent. Suppose lenders must pay income tax on nominal interest income. The after-tax nominal interest rate is 9 per cent (0.6 × 15). Subtracting 11 per cent inflation, the after-tax *real* interest rate is −2 per cent. This compares with +2.6 per cent when inflation was zero.

Inflation accounting uses fully inflation-adjusted definitions of costs, income and profit.

When inflation was 11 per cent, nominal interest rates were 15 per cent. Eleven per cent of this was not real income, merely a payment to keep up with inflation. Only 4 per cent was the real interest rate providing real income. But income tax applied to all 15 per cent. Higher inflation reduced the real return on lending because the tax system was not properly inflation-adjusted; that is, it did not use **inflation accounting**. The government gained more real tax revenue. You lost.

Capital gains tax is another example. Suppose people pay tax of 40 per cent on any capital gain made when asset prices rise. When inflation is zero, only real gains are taxed. When inflation is 10 per cent, nominal asset prices rise merely to preserve their real value. People pay capital gains tax even though they are not making real capital gains.

Institutional imperfections help explain why inflation has real effects even when inflation is fully anticipated. These effects can be large. Usually, the government is the winner.

Unexpected inflation

Previously, we assumed that inflation was fully anticipated. What if inflation is a surprise?

Redistribution

When prices rise unexpectedly, people with nominal assets lose and people with nominal liabilities gain. Nominal contracts to buy and sell, or lend and borrow, can reflect expected inflation, but cannot reflect surprise inflation.

Expecting inflation of 10 per cent, you lend £100 for a year at 12 per cent, expecting a real interest rate of 2 per cent. Unexpectedly, inflation is 20 per cent. The real interest rate on your loan is [12 − 20] = −8 per cent.

You lose by lending. Conversely, borrowers gain 8 per cent. Their nominal income rises 20 per cent with inflation but they repay at 12 per cent interest. For every borrower, there is a lender. One person's gain is another person's loss. In the aggregate, they cancel out. But unexpected inflation redistributes real income and wealth; in this case, from lenders to borrowers. This may lead to economic dislocation. Some people may have to declare bankruptcy, which then affects other people. We also have to make a value judgement about whether we like the redistribution that is taking place.

One redistribution is between the government and the private sector. *Unexpected* inflation reduces the real value of all outstanding nominal government debt. It is as if the government had taxed us in order to repay this debt.[2]

The old and the young

In practice, many savers are the old. Having paid off their mortgages and built up savings during their working life, they put their wealth into nominal bonds to provide income during retirement. These people lose out from surprise inflation.

Nominal debtors are the young and, mainly, those entering middle age with a large mortgage. They gain when surprise inflation raises house prices and nominal incomes without a matching rise in the nominal sum they owe the bank or building society.

Surprise inflation redistributes from the old to the young. We may judge this redistribution undesirable. With technical progress and productivity growth, each generation is richer than the one before. Redistribution from the old to the young raises intergenerational inequality.

2 Why stress unexpected inflation? Because expected inflation is already built into the terms on which bonds were originally issued. Expected inflation affects nominal interest rates.

Uncertain inflation

Uncertainty about future inflation has two costs. First, it makes planning more complex, raising the real resources society uses to make plans and do business.

Second, people dislike risk. The extra benefits of the champagne years are poor compensation for the years of starvation. People would rather average out these extremes and live comfortably all the time. The psychological costs of worrying about how to cope with the bad years may also be important.

When people make nominal contracts, uncertainty about inflation means uncertainty about the eventual real value of the nominal bargains currently made. This is a true cost of inflation. If a lower average level of inflation also reduces uncertainty about inflation, this may be a reason to aim for low inflation. The institutions that commit the government to low inflation may also reduce the scope for uncertainty about inflation. If so, lower average inflation has a real benefit because it is also more certain.

CASE 22.1

PUBLIC ENEMY NUMBER TWO

For several decades, policy makers convinced themselves that inflation was public enemy number one. Inflation is certainly destructive, for the reasons discussed above. However, when financial crisis erupted, concerns about inflation were temporarily but completely set aside. Saving the banking system was more important, preventing another Great Depression was more important, and getting output on the path to recovery was more important. Several of these judgements reflected a fear that Western economies were about to experience deflation.

Deflation is negative inflation, when the price level is falling.

If inflation is bad, you might be forgiven for thinking that deflation is good. Nothing could be further from the truth. Price stability is good. Low inflation is good. Negative inflation is horrible. Here's why.

Imagine you have borrowed money, and have a nominal debt of £1000. If inflation is foreseen and is 10 per cent, the chances are you had to pay 12 per cent interest in order to provide the lender with a real interest rate of 2 per cent.

Now suppose inflation is −2 per cent. A nominal interest rate of zero will still achieve a real interest rate of 2 per cent. But what happens if inflation is −4 per cent. Nominal interest rates cannot fall below zero, so now the real interest rate is $[(0 - (-4)] = +4$ per cent. This situation cripples the borrower.

Worse yet, if, as a result of this heavy debt burden, borrowers then spend less, reducing aggregate demand, this puts downward pressure on inflation, taking it to, say, −5 per cent, which causes a bigger debt burden still, a further reduction in aggregate demand, further deflation and yet higher real interest rates. This is an economic black hole, a vicious spiral downwards, from which the economy may not easily escape.

Understanding the dangers of deflation, then, makes sense of two things. First, this is why we normally set inflation targets for monetary policy at 2 per cent not 0 per cent. This provides a margin of safety before any dangers of deflation arise. Aiming on average for zero inflation is a bit too close to the edge of the cliff.

Second, the threat of deflation at the height of the financial crisis was one reason why so many governments loosened fiscal policy at that time. They preferred to cope later with the problem of large government debt rather than cope immediately with debt deflation.

As Yale professor, Irving Fisher, put it during the Great Depression:

> In the great booms and depressions [. . .] there were two dominant factors, namely over-indebtedness to start with and deflation following soon after; also that where any of the other factors do become conspicuous, they are often merely effects or symptoms of these two.[3]

▶

3 Irving Fisher, 'Debt-deflation theories of great depressions', *Econometrica* 1, no. 4 (1933): 337–357.

During 2009, quite a few countries did experience deflation.

Country	Inflation (%)
Canada	−1.9
Denmark	−0.5
Ireland	−3.8
Netherlands	−0.3
Norway	−3.3
Slovakia	−0.6

Source: OECD, *Economic Outlook 2012, Statistical Annex.*

Without fiscal expansion, the slashing of interest rates and quantitative easing, we might already be stuck in a downward spiral. The countries above avoided protracted deflation partly by their own efforts, and partly because a sufficient number of their trading partners re-established positive growth by stimulatory policy. The more globalized the world, the more a single country's aggregate demand depends on the actions of its partners as well as itself. The prospect of rising export demand provides a backstop in many situations.

Notice that there are now two different reasons why inflation might arise as a postscript to the financial crash. First, governments might be unwilling or unable to raise sufficient tax revenue to service the interest on their huge debt levels. They might create money to finance budget deficits. Second, and nothing to do with the fiscal argument, governments might prefer a period of slightly higher inflation to overcome the fact that, when prices are stable, real interest rates cannot be negative even when nominal interest rates have fallen to zero. This second argument for inflation aims to make monetary policy more powerful by allowing negative real interest rates, which requires positive inflation when nominal interest rates are close to zero.

After two decades of actual or near deflation, following the property crash in the 1990s, Japan finally elected a government in December 2013 committed to *raising* the inflation target in order to break out of the stagnation and deflation.

22.6 Controlling inflation

Policy makers are reluctant to sanction higher inflation because they have spent the last 30 years bringing inflation down. We now discuss how they did it and what they might have to do again. Essentially, inflation is low if people expect it to be low. Credibility is vital.

Incomes policy

Incomes policy is the direct control of wages and other incomes.

A freeze on wage increases certainly gets inflation down quickly. Historically, it has not been able to keep inflation down. Why were past incomes policies unsuccessful?

Once governments intervene in the labour market, they often cannot resist pursuing other aims at the same time. For example, they try to compress relative wages across different skills in the name of fairness. Such policies alter real wages for particular skills, causing excess supply in some skills and excess demand in others. Market forces eventually break the policy.

At best, incomes policy is a temporary adjustment device. In the long run, low nominal money growth is essential if low inflation is to be maintained. Some incomes policies failed because governments introduced a wage freeze but kept printing money – a guarantee that excess demand for workers would eventually break the policy.

Long-term incomes policies are also hard to administer because equilibrium real wages for particular skills change over time. Freezing the existing wage structure gradually sets up powerful market forces of excess supply and excess demand.

Institutional reform

This approach is concerned not with the temporary costs of first getting inflation down, but with how to *keep* inflation down. Central bank independence is a useful pre-commitment to tight monetary policy and low inflation. Here are some examples drawn from the past 20 years.

The Maastricht Treaty

Signed in 1991, the treaty set out conditions both for entering the Eurozone and after admission to it. The first requirement was to avoid loose fiscal policy: a ceiling of 3 per cent on budget deficits relative to GDP.

High-debt countries were also supposed to initiate actions to bring their debt/GDP levels below 60 per cent to minimize the possibility that member states could get into fiscal difficulties and pressurize the European Central Bank to create money to help them out. Moreover, Eurozone entrants first had to succeed in disinflating to low levels, measured both directly by changes in price indexes and indirectly by nominal interest rates.

Not only did EU governments have to sign up for tight policy in the 1990s and beyond, Eurozone hopefuls had to undertake institutional reform, making their national central banks formally independent. The Maastricht Treaty also made the new European Central Bank independent of government, with a mandate to pursue price stability.

It is easy to make commitments, but harder to stick to them, as those in the Eurozone have discovered in the aftermath of the crisis.

Bank of England independence

In May 1997 the new Chancellor, Gordon Brown, gave the Bank of England 'operational independence' to set interest rates. The Bank aims to achieve an inflation target set by the Chancellor. In an emergency (a very adverse supply shock), the government can temporarily raise the target rather than force the Bank to initiate a drastic recession merely to hit the inflation target quickly. Nevertheless, any change in the target is politically hard except in truly exceptional circumstances. Operational independence is a commitment to policies favouring low inflation.

ACTIVITY 22.1

IS ASIA'S INFLATION UNDER CONTROL?

In early 2010, Asian inflation rose sharply, after a muted period during the financial crash. Unlike Europe and North America, where fears surrounding renewed recession kept the lid on inflation, Asia was experiencing its highest inflation for over a decade.

India, where prices were flat in mid-2009, had wholesale price inflation of almost 10 per cent; in Vietnam it was 8.5 per cent, in South Korea 4.2 per cent and in China around 3 per cent. In Australia, with inflation creeping upwards, the Reserve Bank of Australia became the first central bank to increase interest rates several times after the financial crash. Meanwhile, Europe and the US were still pursuing quantitative easing and keeping interest rates as low as they dared.

Indian inflation was largely driven by food and oil prices, while Australian inflation was driven by demand from China for commodities. But why did these supply shocks occur at this particular time? 'The main driver was the speed and breadth of the recovery, and corresponding aggregate demand generated by most of Asia outside Japan', concluded the *Financial Times*.[4] For emerging Asia as a whole, the level of GDP by early 2010 was 4 per cent above its previous peak in the third quarter of 2008, before the output effects of the financial crash then took their toll.

▶

4 'Asia's inflation genie leaps out of the bottle', *Financial Times*, 18 March 2010.

Did this trend continue? The figure shows that inflation remained stubbornly high in India but generally subsided elsewhere. Economic growth in China and India slowed in 2012, taking some of the heat off demand for raw materials and commodity prices.

Even so, by early 2013 new worries about Asian inflation were emerging. Economist Andy Xie told US broadcaster CNBC:

> Unprecedented monetary easing by central banks (around the world) will push prices higher. India's inflation could rise to 10 per cent, and above 5 per cent in Southeast
>
> Asia. Inflation in China could rise to 4 per cent, twice its current level.[5]

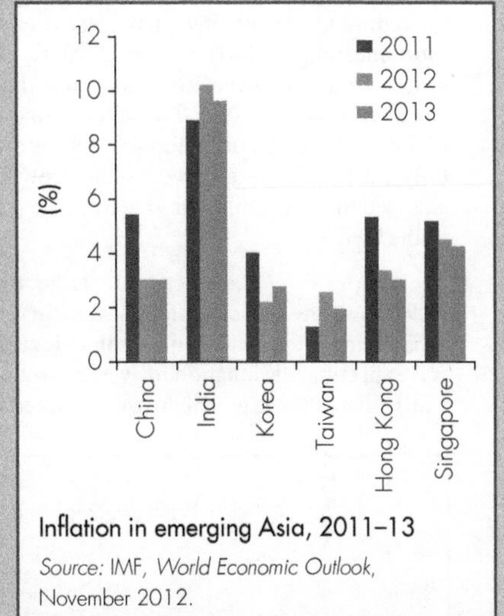

Inflation in emerging Asia, 2011–13

Source: IMF, *World Economic Outlook*, November 2012.

Many emerging markets believe that previous bouts of quantitative easing in stagnating developed economies ended up spilling over into inflation in emerging markets, even though lack of demand in the developed world prevented any resurgence of inflation in the countries actually undertaking the quantitative easing. Supporters of QE respond that the principal purpose of QE was to *prevent* a fall in broad money that would otherwise have occurred when bank deposit multipliers collapsed, rather than to *increase* the supply of broad money.

Questions

(a) If Europe, North America and Japan were still stagnating, what must have been the source of aggregate demand for Asian goods?

(b) How much spare capacity – for output and for labour – is likely now to be left in emerging Asian markets?

(c) What does this imply about the likely course of future monetary policy in these countries?

(d) After two decades of stagnation, Japan remains concerned about deflation. Would you expect Japanese monetary policy now to follow policies in Europe and the US, or those in China and India?

(e) If energy, food and commodities prices rise sharply, what dilemma will then face policy makers in Europe, the US and Japan?

To check your answers to these questions, go to page 681.

22.7 The Monetary Policy Committee

Underlying inflation is the growth of the retail price index (RPI), after omitting the effect of mortgage interest rates on the cost of living (hence the abbreviation RPIX).

Headline inflation is actual inflation, the growth in the RPI.

Since 1997 UK interest rates have been set by the Bank of England's Monetary Policy Committee (MPC), which meets monthly to set interest rates to try to hit the inflation target laid down by the Chancellor. Initially, the target was 2.5 per cent annual inflation, plus or minus 1 per cent. The target applied to **underlying inflation** (which ignores mortgage interest rates) not **headline inflation**.

Why omit mortgage interest from the price level on which monetary policy should focus? Suppose inflation is too high. To reduce aggregate demand, interest rates are raised. But higher interest rates *raise* the RPI by raising the cost of living for homeowners. Moreover, when temporary changes in interest rates are required to get the economy back on track, it may also be more sensible to target the underlying rate of inflation.

5 *Watch out, Asia: Inflation is coming*, 2 January 2013 (www.cnbc.com).

Different countries construct price indexes in slightly different ways. EU countries have each adopted a common procedure for calculating their consumer price index (CPI), making cross-country comparisons of inflation more meaningful. In December 2003, the UK Chancellor, Gordon Brown, instructed the Bank of England to switch from using the RPIX to using the CPI as the basis for inflation targeting. For statistical reasons, **CPI inflation** tends to grow less rapidly than RPIX inflation. At the time of the crossover, UK inflation was 2.9 per cent measured by the growth rate of the RPIX but only 1.3 per cent measured by the growth rate of the CPI. Hence, Gordon Brown also changed the target inflation rate from 2.5 per cent growth in the RPI to 2.0 per cent growth in the CPI.

CPI inflation measures the rate of growth of an index of consumer prices.

The quarterly *Inflation Report* includes the famous **fan chart** for CPI inflation. Figure 22.9 shows the fan chart for November 2012. A darker projected line implies a higher probability of that inflation outcome. Figure 22.9 shows that, in November 2012, the Bank was expecting UK inflation to average around 2 per cent in 2013, and then perhaps increase a little thereafter as global growth resumed more strongly.

A fan chart indicates the probability of different outcomes.

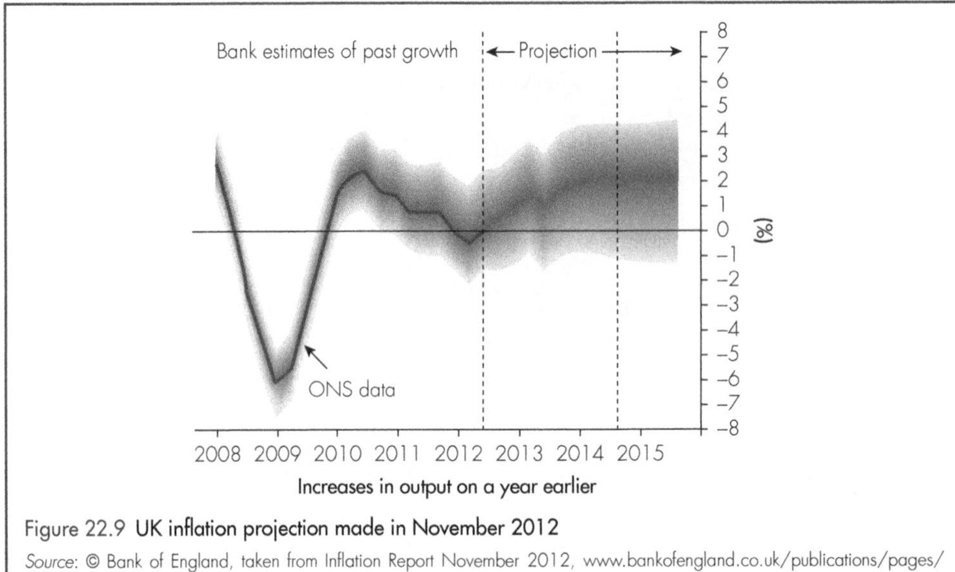

Figure 22.9 **UK inflation projection made in November 2012**

Source: © Bank of England, taken from Inflation Report November 2012, www.bankofengland.co.uk/publications/pages/inflationreport.

The Bank has been criticized for its track record of under-predicting UK inflation, and it is not impossible that this will happen again. If there is a boom in commodity prices (more demand, driven by the Asian boom) and food prices (lower supply, caused by floods, droughts and other implications of climate change), then UK monetary policy will face a very tough choice. Does it raise interest rates to choke off imported inflation, despite a feeble economic recovery, or does it keep interest rates low and allow inflation to exceed the target yet again?

In this section, we discuss three questions. Why was the MPC given a target for inflation? How does it work? How easy was it for the MPC to decide where to set interest rates?

Inflation targets

Without a nominal anchor, nothing ties down the price level or any other nominal variable. Market forces only determine real variables.

Nominal money is a possible nominal anchor and is attractive as an intermediate target because new data on money come out faster than data on prices or output. Monetary targets fell out of favour because large and unpredictable changes in real money demand made it hard to know where to set the nominal money target; more recently, broad money supply has also been unpredictable because of changes in the bank deposit multiplier. When it is hard to predict M/P, it is hard to know where to set M in order to get the desired path of P.

As explained in previous chapters, most modern central banks implicitly follow a Taylor rule but their policy is often portrayed and communicated as a flexible inflation target. This is easily understood by the public, and more easily monitored than a Taylor rule, which could lead to disputes about what the (unobservable) level of potential output really is.[6]

Back to the future

Delays in data availability mean that the MPC has to forecast where the economy is today. Moreover, the interest rate medicine takes up to two years to have its full effect on private behaviour. Hence the MPC has to *forecast* the path of prices at least two years into the future merely to know where to set interest rates *today*!

On occasion, the MPC may raise interest rates even though current inflation is under control. This means that, in the absence of any change in interest rates, the MPC is forecasting that inflation will be too high. It then has to act quickly to keep inflation on track.

Reasonable on inflation, shame about the crash

Despite overshooting its inflation target by small amounts, the MPC successfully maintained UK inflation within a much narrower range than previously accomplished. The Bank was prepared to change interest rates even when this was unpopular. But low levels of inflation led to low nominal interest rates, which encouraged more reckless private sector behaviour. Determining sensible monetary policy was never the entire remit of the Bank of England – it has a *financial stability* wing as well as a *monetary stability* wing – and the Financial Services Authority was explicitly charged with financial regulation. Good monetary policy cannot be held responsible for inadequate financial regulation.

Figure 22.10 shows the history of UK interest rates since 1980. Although the Bank's operational independence to set interest rates was formally granted in 1997, Figure 22.10 shows that the decisive break was in 1992 when sterling left the Exchange Rate Mechanism and changed nominal anchors from a pegged exchange rate to an inflation target. Reinforced by formal independence, since 1997 the MPC has built on its earlier success during 1992–97. The low interest rates since 2008 are clearly an abnormal response, caused by the unique period since the financial crash.

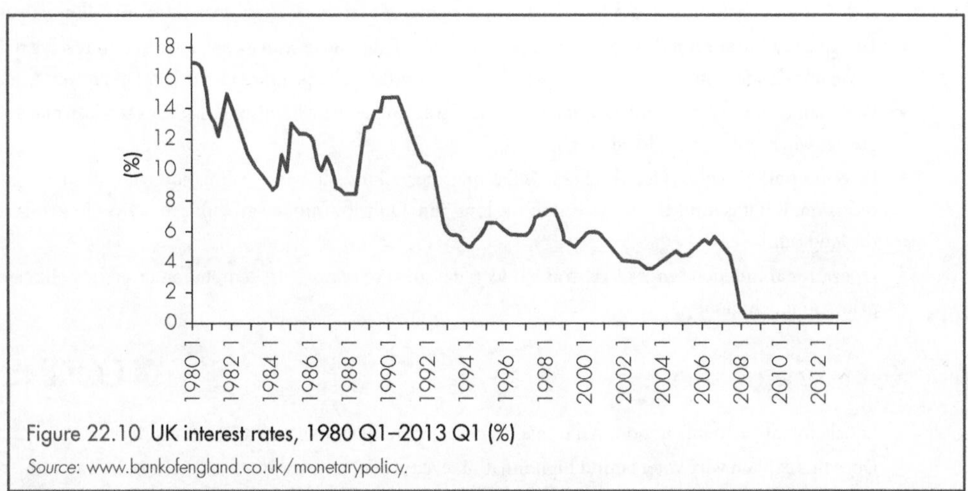

Figure 22.10 **UK interest rates, 1980 Q1–2013 Q1 (%)**

Source: www.bankofengland.co.uk/monetarypolicy.

6 Like central banks deciding where to set interest rates, academic researchers engaged in empirical evaluation of monetary policy have to make estimates of how potential output is evolving. The OECD regularly publishes estimates of output gaps ($Y - Y^*$) for the major countries.

Summary

- The **quantity theory of money** says changes in prices are caused by equivalent changes in the nominal money supply. In practice, prices cannot adjust at once to changes in nominal money, so interest rates or income alter, changing real money demand. Nevertheless, in the long run, changes in prices are usually associated with changes in nominal money.
- The **Fisher hypothesis** is that a 1 per cent rise in inflation leads to a similar rise in nominal interest rates so real interest rates change little. Since the nominal interest rate is the cost of holding money, higher inflation reduces real money demand. The *flight from cash* during hyperinflation is a vivid example.
- For a solvent government, there need be no close relationship between the budget deficit and nominal money growth. In the long run, persistent borrowing to finance large deficits may leave the government so indebted that further borrowing is impossible. It must resort to printing money or take fiscal action to cut the deficit.
- The **long-run Phillips curve** is vertical at equilibrium unemployment. If people foresee inflation and can completely adjust to it, inflation has no real effects.
- The **short-run Phillips curve** is a temporary trade-off between unemployment and inflation in response to demand shocks. Supply shocks shift the Phillips curve. The height of the short-run Phillips curve also depends on underlying money growth and expected inflation. The Phillips curve shifts down if people believe inflation will be lower in the future.
- Temporary supply shocks also shift the short-run Phillips curve. **Stagflation** is high inflation plus high unemployment.
- Some so-called **costs of inflation** reflect inflation illusion or a failure to see inflation as the consequence of a shock that would have reduced real incomes in any case. The true costs of inflation depend on whether it was anticipated and on the extent to which the economy's institutions allow complete inflation-adjustment.
- **Shoe-leather costs** and **menu costs** are unavoidable costs of inflation and are larger the larger the inflation rate. Failure fully to inflation-adjust the tax system may also impose costs, even if inflation is anticipated.
- **Unexpected inflation** redistributes income and wealth from those who have contracted to receive nominal payments (lenders and workers) to those who have contracted to pay them (firms and borrowers).
- Uncertainty about future inflation rates imposes costs on people who dislike risk. Uncertainty may be greater when inflation is already high.
- **Incomes policy** may accelerate a fall in inflation expectations, allowing disinflation without a large recession. But it is unlikely to succeed in the long run. Only low money growth can deliver low inflation in the long run.
- **Operational independence of central banks** is designed to remove the temptation faced by politicians to print too much money.

Review questions

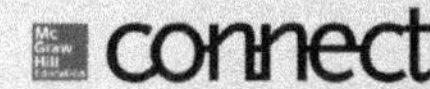

1 Equal annual payments in nominal terms become declining annual payments in real terms. Does this explain why voters mind high inflation even when nominal interest rates rise in line with inflation?

2 Looking at data on inflation and unemployment over ten years, could you tell the difference between supply shocks and demand shocks?

3 **Common fallacies** Why are these statements wrong? (a) Getting inflation down is the only way to cure high unemployment. (b) Inflation stops people from saving. (c) Inflation stops people from investing.

EASY

4 Which of the following statements is correct? (a) The long-run Phillips curve should really have a positive slope because higher inflation makes firms substitute away from workers who are causing the underlying problem. (b) If inflation leads people to economize on some forms of money, this must make the economy less productive and probably raises long-run unemployment. (c) When other things are assumed to be equal, it is a tolerable approximation to view the long-run Phillips curve as vertical.

5 Name three groups which lose out during inflation. Does it matter whether this inflation was anticipated?

6 (a) Explain the following data taken from *The Economist* a few years ago (when some countries still had proper inflation!). (b) Is inflation always a monetary phenomenon?

	Money growth (%)	Inflation (%)
Eurozone	3	2
Japan	12	−3
UK	6	2
Australia	15	3
US	8	2

7 Professor Milton Friedman argued that money was socially useful but essentially free to create. Society should therefore reduce the opportunity cost of holding money to zero, so that people would demand it up to the point at which its marginal benefit was zero. (a) Suppose the real interest rate on other assets is around 3 per cent. Is there any way society could arrange for cash to earn a similar real return? (b) Why don't governments do this?

MEDIUM

8 Your real annual income is constant, and initially is £10 000. You borrow £200 000 for 10 years to buy a house, paying interest annually and repaying the £200 000 in a final payment at the end. (a) List your annual incomings and outgoings in the first and ninth year if inflation is 0 and the nominal interest rate is 2 per cent a year. (b) Repeat the exercise if annual inflation is 100 per cent and the nominal interest rate is 102 per cent. Is the real interest rate the same in both situations?

9 Inflation in Zimbabwe, high for many years, reached hyperinflation levels in the recent past. (a) President Mugabe blamed Western governments for restricting trade and driving up prices. Could a fall in supply have generated sustained high inflation? (b) Why do you think Zimbabwe has such high inflation? (c) Is inflation high enough to raise the maximum possible revenue for the government?

10 Suppose D is real government debt, s the primary budget surplus $T - G$ (that is, excluding interest payments on debt), i the real interest rate, Y real output and g the rate of output growth. The debt burden D/Y rises with debt but falls with output and the ability to repay debt. Let Δ denote the increase in a variable. (a) If $\Delta(D/Y) = (\Delta D/D) - (\Delta Y/Y)$, show that the debt/GDP ratio shrinks only if $s/D > i - g$. (b) Suppose all debt is cash, paying no interest. Show that the above relationship becomes $s/D > (g + \pi)$.

11 Suppose Asia emerges from the financial crisis much more quickly than Europe and North America. As China and India bid up world commodity prices, use a figure resembling Figure 22.8 to illustrate the effect on European unemployment.

HARD

12 Draw a curve to illustrate how the real revenue raised by the government through foreseen inflation varies with the inflation rate. If an economy moves from using a lot of cash to using a lot of electronic money on which market interest rates are paid, illustrate how the curve changes.

13 The diagram below illustrates the short-run and long-run Phillips curves. (a) Why is the long-run Phillips curve vertical in the diagram? (b) What is the rate of unemployment when the expected inflation is zero per cent? (c) Use the diagram to explain how government reduces the unemployment rate as people's inflation expectations keep changing.

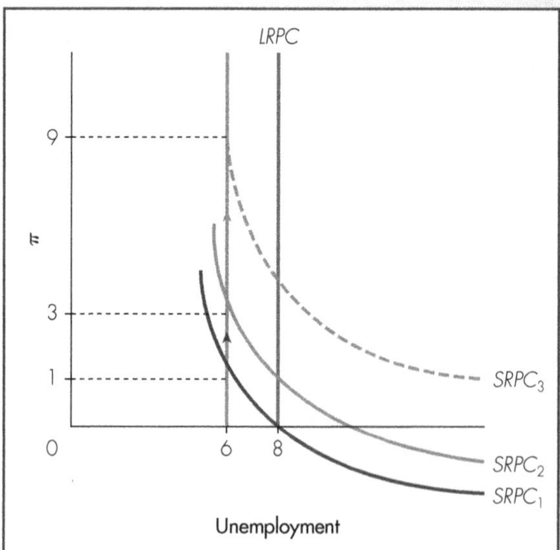

14 **Essay question** Does the huge success of central bank independence in so many countries suggest that other decisions should be removed from government? Your answer should include assessments of the case for (a) an independent health services board, (b) an independent budget deficit commission, and (c) a redistribution commission.

For solutions to these questions, contact your lecturer.

CHAPTER 23

Unemployment

Learning Outcomes

By the end of this chapter, you should be able to:

1. define classical, frictional and structural unemployment
2. distinguish between voluntary and involuntary unemployment
3. discuss measured unemployment, both claimant count and standardized rate
4. analyse determinants of unemployment
5. explain how supply-side policies reduce equilibrium unemployment
6. evaluate private and social costs of unemployment
7. explain hysteresis

In the early 1930s, nearly a quarter of the UK labour force was unemployed, and other countries suffered similarly. Society threw away output by failing to put people to work. For the next 40 years macroeconomic policy tried to manage aggregate demand to avoid a rerun of the 1930s. Figure 23.1 shows that until the 1970s the policy succeeded.

In the 1970s high inflation emerged for reasons discussed in the previous chapter. Governments eventually tightened monetary and fiscal policy to get inflation under control. The mix of tighter demand policies and adverse supply shocks led to a big rise in unemployment in the 1980s.

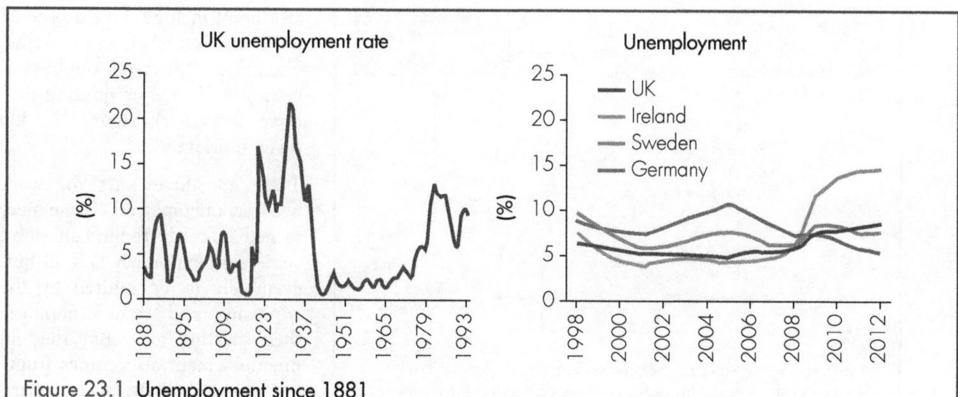

Figure 23.1 Unemployment since 1881

Sources: 'Unemployment statistics from 1881 to the present day,' *Labour Market Trends*, January 1996; OECD, *Economic Outlook, Statistical Annex 2012.*

After the economy adjusted, deficient demand was no longer the cause of high unemployment. Equilibrium unemployment remained high because of adverse changes in supply. Better supply-side policies since the mid-1990s reduced UK unemployment to levels not seen since before the 1970s.

The right-hand panel also shows recent data for Germany, Ireland and Sweden. Although, like the UK, these countries experienced unemployment in the 5–10 per cent range in the years before the financial crash, their subsequent experiences differed. In order to secure a bailout, the Irish government had to adopt drastic austerity which drove Irish unemployment back up to almost 15 per cent, much higher than the level in the UK, Sweden or Germany. By 2013, Spanish unemployment (not shown above) had reached 27 per cent.

23.1 The labour market

Not everyone wants a paid job. Full-time homemakers, voluntary workers, the old and the young, and those with long-term sickness are all excluded from the category of people seeking paid work. The people who want a job are called the **labour force**. The **participation rate** measures how many people of working age want to work.

The labour force comprises people with a job or registered as looking for work at the current wage rate.

The participation rate is the fraction of the population of working age in the labour force.

The unemployment rate is the fraction of the labour force without a job but registered as looking for work.

Some people looking for work do not register as unemployed. They do not appear in official statistics for the registered labour force or the registered unemployed. Yet from an economic viewpoint, such people *are* in the labour force and *are* unemployed. For the moment, our data on the labour force or the unemployed refer only to those registered. The **unemployment rate** measures unemployment relative to the size of the labour force.

Figure 23.1 showed that UK unemployment was high in the inter-war years, especially in the 1930s. By comparison, the post-war unemployment rate was tiny until the late 1970s. In the 1980s it started to get back to pre-war levels, but then fell thereafter. Was this because policy makers learned the secret of demand management or because structural reforms in the labour market reduced equilibrium levels of unemployment? By the end of this chapter, you should have a clearer idea about the answers.

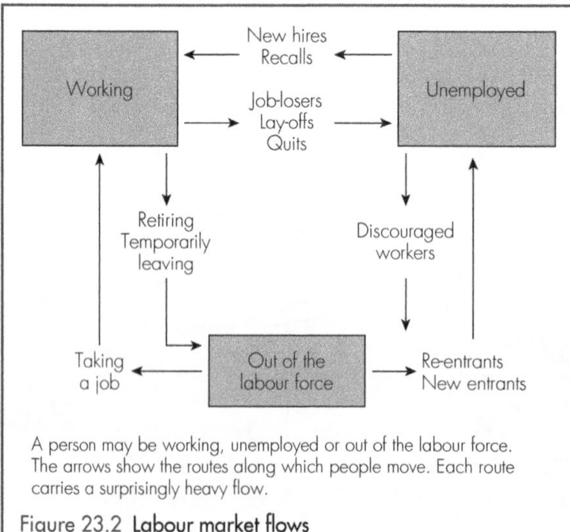

A person may be working, unemployed or out of the labour force. The arrows show the routes along which people move. Each route carries a surprisingly heavy flow.

Figure 23.2 **Labour market flows**

Stocks and flows

Unemployment is a stock concept measured at a point in time. Like a pool of water, its level rises when inflows (the newly unemployed) exceed outflows (people getting new jobs or quitting the labour force altogether). Figure 23.2 illustrates this important idea.

There are three ways for workers to become unemployed. Some people are sacked or made redundant (job-losers); some are temporarily laid off but expect eventually to be rehired by the same company; and some voluntarily quit their existing jobs. But the inflow to unemployment also comes from people not previously in the labour force: school-leavers (new entrants) and people who, having left the labour force, are now returning to look for a job (re-entrants).

Discouraged workers, pessimistic about finding a job, leave the labour force.

People leave the unemployment pool in the opposite direction. Some get jobs. Others give up looking for jobs and leave the labour force completely. Some of this latter group may simply have reached the retirement age at which they get a pension, but many are **discouraged workers.**

Table 23.1 shows that the pool of unemployment is not stagnant. In 2011 Q3, of UK adults between the ages of 16 and 64, there were 2.7 million unemployed, 9.2 million who were inactive (outside the labour market) and 28.3 million in employment. Figure 23.3 shows that there had been considerable two-way flows between each of these categories since the previous quarter 2011 Q2. In fact, in a single quarter, 2.9 million people were moving categories within the labour market, a larger number than the entire stock of unemployment. The labour market is not stagnant.

Table 23.1 Unemployment by duration, October 2012 (million people)

<6 months	6–12 months	12–24 months	24+ months
1.2	0.4	0.4	0.5

Source: ONS, *Labour market statistics*, December 2012.

When unemployment is high, people often have to spend longer in the pool before they find a way out. Table 23.1 gives data on the duration of unemployment. Unemployment is not always a temporary stopover on the way to better things. A higher unemployment rate usually also means that people are spending longer in the pool of unemployment before escaping. Table 23.1 shows the 2.5 million UK unemployed in October 2012, according to the period for which they have already been unemployed.

Even by late 2012, the labour market had not experienced the massive rise in unemployment that the sharp 2009 output contraction would usually have implied. Why did unemployment not increase by even more than it did? Since labour is expensive both to recruit and to dismiss, firms try to ride out a temporary storm by hoarding

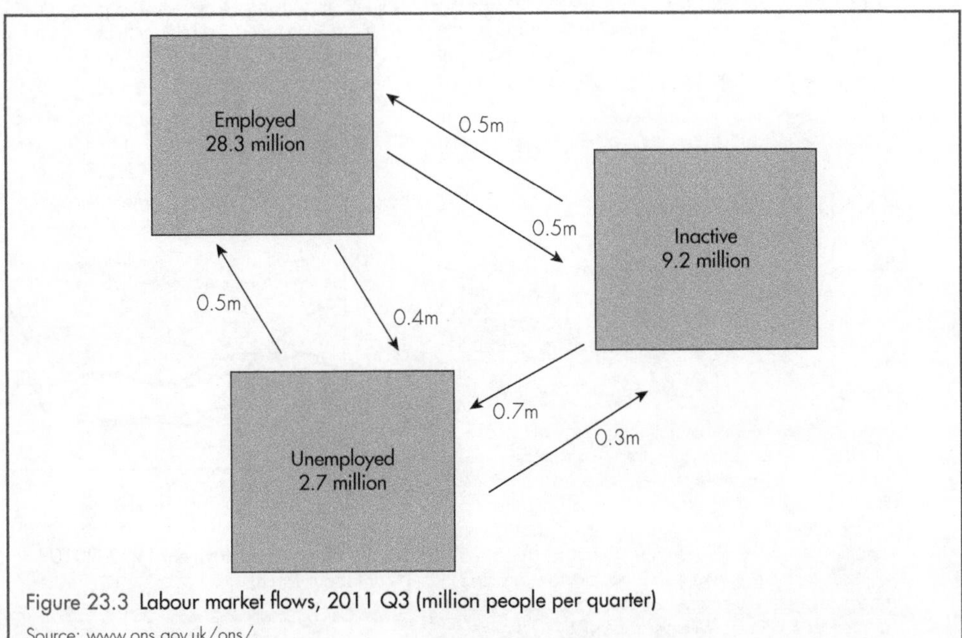

Figure 23.3 Labour market flows, 2011 Q3 (million people per quarter)

Source: www.ons.gov.uk/ons/.

the workers that they have. Once the recession is evidently going to persist for some time, firms then have little choice but to adjust the number of workers in their employment. In Table 23.1 there are relatively few 'long-term' unemployed because the previous decade had been a period of economic growth with strong employment opportunities. The longer the recession persists, the more we expect to see a 'drift to the right' in Table 23.1, with larger numbers out of work for longer periods at a stretch.

It may also be the case that changes in the structure of the labour market, and in technology, have enabled much greater part-time working than would have been the case in previous recessions. Although the demand for labour contracted, some of this was met by working shorter hours rather than by throwing people entirely out of work. The Internet has made self-employment and flexible working from home much easier than before.

CASE 23.1

MEASURING UNEMPLOYMENT

The unemployed are those without a job but willing to work at the prevailing wage rate – the difference between the labour force and those with jobs. Measuring those with jobs is not so controversial, but how do we measure the labour force? How do we know how many people would like to work at the current wage rate?

Claimant unemployment

One convenient short cut is simply to measure the number of people in receipt of unemployment-related benefit. In the UK, this transfer payment from government used to be called unemployment benefit. To diminish any stigma attached, it was renamed jobseeker's allowance.

Over time and across countries, governments differ in the generosity of the eligibility criteria for claiming this benefit. If we use the claimant count as our measure of unemployment, any government attempt to toughen the criteria for eligibility for benefit will appear to have reduced measured unemployment, and international comparisons are hard to interpret because of national differences in eligibility for benefit.

Those ineligible for UK jobseeker's allowance included: (a) those with savings above a certain amount, (b) those unable to work at least 40 hours a week, (c) those aged 16–17, and (d) those unwilling to sign a 'jobseeker's agreement' systematically to seek work. Those whose previous job terminated because of misconduct did not have an automatic right to jobseeker's allowance. Other countries make other stipulations. Those ineligible for unemployment-related benefits are usually eligible for a residual welfare safety net at a less generous level.

Thus, in every country, measured unemployment based on counting claimants for unemployment-related benefit understates 'true unemployment' because some of those declared ineligible are in fact in the labour force, seeking a job, and unemployed.

Standardized unemployment

Fully aware of this issue, international agencies have endeavoured to produce a more comprehensive definition capable of being compared across countries. Accurate measures of unemployment depend on knowing people's intentions. It would be prohibitively expensive to ask every individual and assess whether their answers were truthful.

Standardized measures use surveys of smaller numbers of people and then extrapolate the answers to an estimate for the entire economy, just as opinion poll surveys try to predict election results and crime surveys try to estimate national crime statistics. Surveys are always subject to a margin of error, but the widespread use of standardized unemployment measures suggests that there is a degree of confidence in this approach.

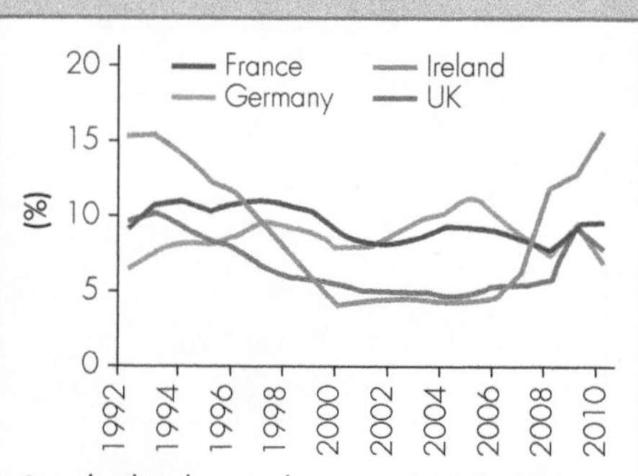

Standardized unemployment 1992–2010 (% of labour force)

Source: OECD, *Economic Outlook*, 2012.

The surveys ask people of working age, but without work, whether they: (a) are available to work within two weeks and actively job-hunting, (b) are waiting to take up a job already offered or (c) have no wish to have a job at current wage rates. Those replying yes to (a) and (b) are included in the standardized measure of unemployment.

The figure shows the evolution of standardized unemployment rates during 1992–2010 reported by the OECD. The year 2008 may yet prove to have been a point of low unemployment – as European economies are driven to fiscal austerity to combat their high levels of government debt, they will be delighted if other sources of aggregate demand increase sufficiently quickly to keep pace with the underlying growth of aggregate supply. By 2012, the UK had already experienced a 'double dip recession' and commentators were starting to discuss the prospect of a 'triple dip'.

The composition of unemployment

Table 23.2 gives a recent breakdown of unemployment by gender and age. Young workers find it much harder to get a job. Unlike established workers with accumulated skills and job experience, young workers have to be trained from scratch. Youth unemployment was over 30 per cent, which considerably exceeds the national average of around 8 per cent.

The unemployment rate is lower for women than for men, perhaps because more women leave the labour force if they do not succeed in getting jobs.

Table 23.2 UK unemployment rates, October 2012 (% of relevant group)

Age	Men	Women
16–17	39	34
18–24	21	15
16–64	8	7

Source: ONS, *Labour Market Statistics*.

23.2 Analysing unemployment

We now develop a theoretical framework in which to analyse unemployment. We can classify unemployment by the source of the problem or by the nature of behaviour in the labour market.

Types of unemployment

Frictional unemployment is the irreducible minimum unemployment in a dynamic society.

Frictional unemployment includes people whose handicaps make them hard to employ. More importantly, it includes people spending short spells in unemployment as they hop between jobs in a dynamic economy.

As the labour force evolves, and the skill needs of employers change with new products, services and technologies, finding more effective matches between what workers can offer and what firms require is a significant part of remaining efficient and sustaining productivity growth. Since perfect matching cannot be achieved instantaneously, it is important to recognize that some unemployment is actually good for the economy if it corresponds to a vigorous search for better job matching. Frictional unemployment is sometimes called search unemployment.

Structural unemployment arises from the mismatch of skills and job opportunities as the pattern of demand and supply changes.

Structural unemployment reflects the time taken to acquire human capital. A skilled steelworker may have worked for 25 years but is made redundant at age 50 when the industry contracts in the face of foreign competition. That worker may have to retrain in a new skill which is more in demand in today's economy. Firms may be reluctant to take on and train older workers who have only a short remaining working life in which to repay the expensive investment. Such workers are victims of structural unemployment.

Structural unemployment implies that the market price for a worker's skill has fallen because of a shift in supply or demand, often caused by new technology or changes in international competition. Faced with a job offer at a low wage, the worker may prefer to retrain in order to earn something closer to the previous wage; if there are few such opportunities, the worker may become unemployed. Even low-skilled, low-paid alternatives may be difficult to find. Many such jobs are now outsourced abroad, and domestic service employers may prefer younger workers with fewer demands.

A third type of unemployment is purely the consequence of a fall in aggregate demand. Until wages and prices have adjusted to their new long-run equilibrium level, a fall in aggregate demand reduces output and employment. Some workers want to work at the going real wage rate but cannot find jobs. Only when demand has returned to its long-run level is **demand-deficient unemployment** eliminated.

Demand-deficient unemployment occurs when output is below full capacity.

Classical unemployment describes the unemployment created when the wage is deliberately maintained above the level at which the labour supply and labour demand schedules intersect.

If wages and prices were perfectly flexible, demand-deficient unemployment would not occur. Since the **classical** model assumes that flexible wages and prices maintain the economy at full employment, classical economists had difficulty explaining high unemployment in the 1930s. Within their paradigm, it had to be attributed either to frictional or structural unemployment. They concluded that the wage was prevented from adjusting to its equilibrium level, caused either by the exercise of trade union power or by minimum wage legislation which enforces a wage in excess of the equilibrium wage rate. Effectively, these had created unnecessary structural unemployment.

The modern analysis of unemployment takes the same types of unemployment but classifies them differently to highlight the behavioural implications and consequences for government policy. Modern analysis stresses the difference between *voluntary* and *involuntary* unemployment.

Equilibrium unemployment

Figure 23.4 shows the labour market. The labour demand schedule *LD* slopes down. Firms demand more workers at a lower real wage because the cost of labour is lower. As in most economic applications, demand curves slope downwards.

The *LF* schedule shows the number of people in the labour force. A higher real wage increases the number of people wishing to work. This is not as obvious as it may at first appear. A higher wage increases the benefit of an hour of work relative to an hour of leisure. The substitution effect leads to a desire to work more and consume less leisure. But there is also an income effect. A higher wage makes people richer, raising the quantity of goods

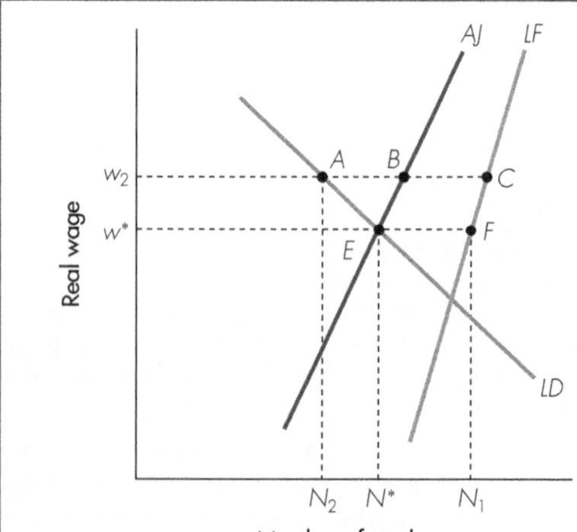

Figure 23.4 **Equilibrium unemployment**

The schedules *LD*, *LF* and *AJ* show, respectively, labour demand, the size of the labour force and the number of workers willing to accept job offers at any real wage. *AJ* lies to the left of *LF* both because some labour force members are between jobs and because optimists are hanging on for an even better job offer. When the labour market clears at *E*, *EF* is the natural rate of unemployment, the people in the labour force not prepared to take job offers at the equilibrium wage w^*. If union power succeeds in maintaining the wage w_2 in the long run, the labour market will be at *A*, and the natural rate of unemployment *AC* now shows the amount of unemployment chosen by the labour force collectively by enforcing the wage w_2.

and leisure demanded. This income effect makes people less interested in working when wages are higher. Figure 23.4 shows what we have learned from considerable empirical research – higher real wages do increase the size of the labour force, but by only a little. The *LF* schedule is pretty steep.

The schedule *AJ* shows how many people accept job offers at each real wage. The schedule is to the left of the *LF* schedule: only people in the labour force can accept a job. Hence, at any horizontal level corresponding to a particular market wage, the *AJ* schedule must lie to the left of the *LF* schedule. How far *AJ* lies to the left of *LF* depends on several things. Some people are inevitably between jobs at any point in time. Also, a particular real wage may tempt some people into the labour force even though they will accept a job offer only if it provides a higher real wage than average.

We draw these schedules for a given level of jobseeker's allowance. When wages are high, jobseekers grab available jobs. The two upward-sloping schedules are close together. When wages are low (relative to unemployment benefit), potential workers are more selective in accepting job offers. People invest in searching longer for an even better job. The two schedules are further apart.

Equilibrium unemployment (also called the *natural rate of unemployment*) is the unemployment rate when the labour market is in equilibrium.

A worker is voluntarily unemployed if, at the given level of wages, she wishes to be in the labour force but does not yet wish to accept a job.

Labour market equilibrium is at *E* in Figure 23.4. *Equilibrium employment* is N^*. The distance *EF* is **equilibrium unemployment**. This unemployment is entirely *voluntary*.

At the equilibrium real wage w^*, N_1 people want to be in the labour force but only N^* accept job offers; the remainder do not yet want to work at the equilibrium real wage.

Equilibrium unemployment includes frictional and structural unemployment. Suppose a skilled welder earned £1000 a week before being made redundant. The issue is not why workers became redundant (the decline of the steel industry), but why these workers will not take a lower wage as a dishwasher to get a job. Their old skills are obsolete. Until new skills are learned, dishwashing may be their only skill valued by the labour market. People not prepared to work at the going wage rate for their skills, but wanting to be in the labour force, are **voluntarily unemployed**.

First time round, it can be difficult to grasp the concept of voluntary unemployment. The key is to remember that, at any instant, we are taking a snapshot of a highly dynamic labour market. Take another look at Figure 23.4. The gross number of people flowing between employment, unemployment and inactivity (being out of the labour force) is larger every quarter than the total stock of unemployment. With so many people in motion, at any particular measurement point they cannot all be recorded as employed or inactive. A voluntarily unemployed worker is interested enough in finding a job to be in the labour force, but has not yet found a job offer that she is prepared to accept. Such workers are still looking and still hoping.

A worker involuntarily unemployed would accept a job offer at the going wage rate.

What about classical unemployment, for example if unions keep wages above their equilibrium level? This is shown in Figure 23.4 as a wage w_2 above w^*. Total unemployment is *AC*. As individuals, *AB* workers want jobs at the wage w_2 but cannot find them. Firms wish to be at point *A*. As individuals, the workers *AB* are **involuntarily unemployed**.

However, through their unions, workers collectively opt for the wage w_2 above the equilibrium wage, thus reducing employment. For workers as a whole, the extra unemployment is voluntary – they could have chosen a different wage and a different employment level, but preferred not to. We include classical unemployment in equilibrium unemployment. If unions maintain the wage w_2, the economy stays at *A* and *AC* is equilibrium unemployment.

CONCEPT 23.1

THE LUMP-OF-LABOUR FALLACY

Those without economics training often think there is a simple solution for reducing unemployment: shorten the working week, so that the same amount of total work is shared between more workers, leaving fewer people unemployed. What's wrong with this argument?

It presumes the demand for labour (hours × people) is fixed, whatever the cost of hiring workers or their benefit in goods produced and revenue earned. In practice, both would be affected by the proposal.

You go to work for seven hours a day, but probably have an hour of dead time (visiting a coffee shop, tidying your desk, being nice to colleagues, talking about sport, texting friends). This is a fixed cost, say an hour of time. There are probably economies of scale to shift length. Shortening the shift length adds to the cost of labour, making firms less competitive. For any given output demand for their product, from which we can derive the labour demand curve, a higher cost of labour makes firms choose to demand fewer workers. Firms move up their downward-sloping demand curve for labour and offer fewer jobs.

Few economists think compulsory reductions in the length of the working week are a promising solution to the problem of high unemployment.

Figure 23.5 illustrates how Keynesian or demand-deficient unemployment may arise. Initially, labour demand is *LD* and the labour market is in equilibrium at *E*, with equilibrium unemployment *EF*. Then labour demand shifts down to *LD′*. Before wages or prices adjust, the real wage is still w^*. At this wage, workers want to be at *E* but firms want to be at *A*. The distance *AE* is demand-deficient unemployment; that is, involuntary unemployment caused by sluggish adjustment of wages and prices. *EF* remains voluntary unemployment.

If labour demand remains *LD′*, eventually real wages fall to w^{**} to restore equilibrium at *G*. However, by reducing interest rates, monetary policy can shift labour demand up to *LD* again and restore equilibrium at *E*. At *A*, output and employment are low. Involuntary unemployment also reduces wage growth and inflation.

Thus, we can divide total unemployment into two parts. The equilibrium or natural rate is the equilibrium unemployment determined by normal labour market turnover, structural mismatch, union power and incentives in the labour market. Keynesian unemployment, also called demand-deficient or cyclical unemployment, is involuntary unemployment in disequilibrium, caused by low aggregate demand and sluggish wage adjustment.

This division helps us think clearly about the policies needed to tackle unemployment. Keynesian unemployment reflects spare capacity and wasted output. By boosting labour demand, policy can mop up this spare capacity and increase output and employment. Wage adjustment could logically accomplish the same outcome, but may take several years to do so. The more sluggish are market forces, the more it makes sense for policy to intervene. Most forms of monetary policy have the consequence that interest rates will adjust to such a situation and help offset the original demand shock. The automatic fiscal stabilizers also act in this direction.

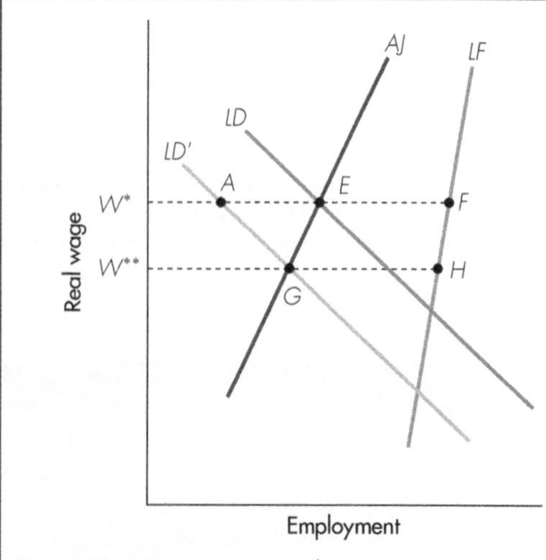

Beginning from equilibrium at *E* labour demand falls from *LD* to *LD′*. Before price and wage adjustment occurs, the economy moves to *A*. *EF* is still voluntary unemployment, but now *AE* is involuntary unemployment, since workers want to be at *E* at a real wage W^*. If labour demand remains *LD′*, eventually real wages fall to W^{**} to restore equilibrium at *G*. By reducing interest rates, monetary policy can shift labour demand up to *LD* and restore equilibrium at *E*. Eliminating spare capacity *AE* allows higher output and employment.

Figure 23.5 **Keynesian unemployment**

In marked contrast, when the economy is already in long-run equilibrium, further demand expansion is pointless. Even though unemployment is not zero, there is no spare capacity. At points *E* or *G* in Figure 23.5, all remaining unemployment is voluntary.

It is true that, beginning from *G*, shifting labour demand up from *LD′* to *LD* achieves a small reduction in equilibrium unemployment. The distance *EF* is smaller than *GH* because the *AJ* and *LF* schedules are not parallel to one another. However the main effect of raising demand is to bid up wages, not to increase output or employment.

Hence, when the economy begins with only voluntary unemployment, reductions in unemployment and increases in output are mainly accomplished not by demand policies but by supply-side policies. These policies either *shift* the supply schedules *AJ* and *LF* or they reduce distortions that prevented the economy getting to points like *E* or *G*.

The next section presents some evidence on the relative magnitude of unemployment responses to demand and supply, and then analyses these supply-side policies in more detail.

23.3 Explaining changes in unemployment

Empirical research aims to decompose causes of unemployment into those that changed equilibrium and those that caused demand-deficient unemployment. Figure 23.6 compares the actual unemployment rate with estimates of the equilibrium unemployment rate from 1956 to 2009. Averaging data within sub-periods reduces the influence of short-term fluctuations.

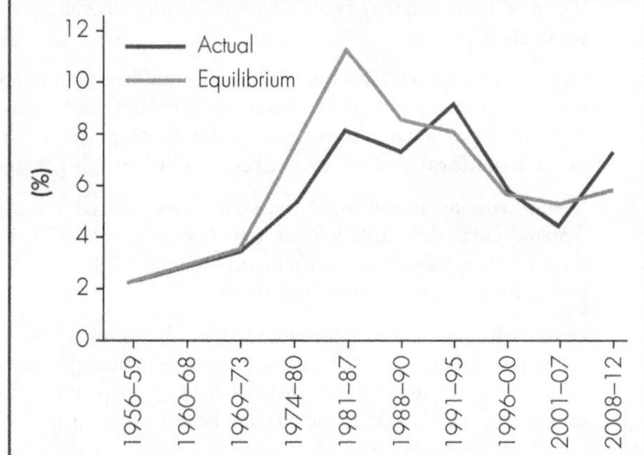

Figure 23.6 UK unemployment, 1956–2012 (% annual average)

Sources: R. Layard, S. Nickell and R. Jackman, *Unemployment* (Oxford University Press, 1991); S. Nickell, 'Inflation and the UK Labour Market', in T. Jenkinson (ed.), *Readings in Macroeconomics* (Oxford University Press 1996); authors' estimates.

Until the 1970s, demand management maintained aggregate demand in line with aggregate supply in the output market. Hence, in the labour market, actual and equilibrium unemployment pretty much coincided. When unemployment then rose during the 1970s, people initially assumed that this must be due to deficient demand.

In retrospect, we know that the diagnosis was wrong – it was really the supply side that was deteriorating. Equilibrium unemployment was increasing steadily as work incentives deteriorated and the economy was hit with adverse supply shocks. Misreading the situation, governments tried boosting demand to eliminate spare capacity. Since they had no spare capacity, instead they stoked up inflation.

When Mrs Thatcher came to power in 1979 the Conservative government reduced aggregate demand to try to tackle inflation, and embarked on supply-side reform to reduce equilibrium unemployment. Figure 23.6 shows that demand-deficient unemployment rose sharply when aggregate demand was first reduced, whereas it took longer to obtain reductions in equilibrium unemployment.

Nevertheless, the rise in equilibrium unemployment was slowly reversed. The government became overconfident in its success, allowing aggregate demand to increase sharply during the 'Lawson boom' of the late 1980s. Figure 23.6 shows that actual unemployment had fallen below equilibrium unemployment as the economy overheated and inflation picked up again.

The 1990s saw the restoration of balance between demand and supply, and the continuing benefits of supply-side reform. By the late 1990s the UK was enjoying a period of low inflation, low unemployment and considerable stability. Figure 23.6 shows that actual and equilibrium unemployment were close together until the financial crash, after which aggregate demand plummeted and a new gap emerged between actual and equilibrium unemployment.

Figure 23.6 confirms three periods in which involuntary unemployment became important – the Thatcher squeeze in the early 1980s, the Major squeeze in the early 1990s and the aftermath of the financial crash of 2008. In the first two examples, sharp reductions in demand were the result of policies to combat inflation.

However, the main message of Figure 23.6 is that longer-term trends in unemployment have been largely caused by supply-side changes and their consequences for equilibrium unemployment.

Supply-side factors

Keynesians believe that the economy can deviate from full employment for quite a long time, certainly for several years. Monetarists believe that the classical full-employment model is relevant much more quickly. Everyone agrees that long-run performance is changed only by affecting the level of full employment and the corresponding level of potential output.

Supply-side economics is the use of microeconomic incentives to alter the level of full employment, the level of potential output and equilibrium unemployment.

Mismatch occurs if the skills that firms demand differ from the skills the labour force possesses.

We now discuss four reasons why equilibrium unemployment rose and then fell during 1970–2010.

First, increasing skill **mismatch** raised equilibrium unemployment after 1970. Recent research emphasizes that the labour market is not very good at processing workers as they step out of one job and hope to step into another. The larger is mismatch, the harder the task is to perform, and the more likely it is that people get stuck in unemployment.

When firms no longer want the skills possessed by the existing workforce, the labour demand curve *LD* shifts leftwards to *LD′* in Figure 23.7, leading to a lower equilibrium real wage, and an increase in equilibrium unemployment from *AB* to *CD*. A rise in mismatch explained some of the rise in unemployment in the 1970s and 1980s.

Conversely, since 1990, government policy has stressed reconnecting the unemployed with the labour market rather than leaving them to languish in long-term unemployment. By offering the unemployed advice on how to get back into work quickly, government policy stopped people becoming stigmatized as unemployable. This raised the demand for their labour, reducing equilibrium unemployment. At a higher real wage, *AJ* and *LF* are closer together.

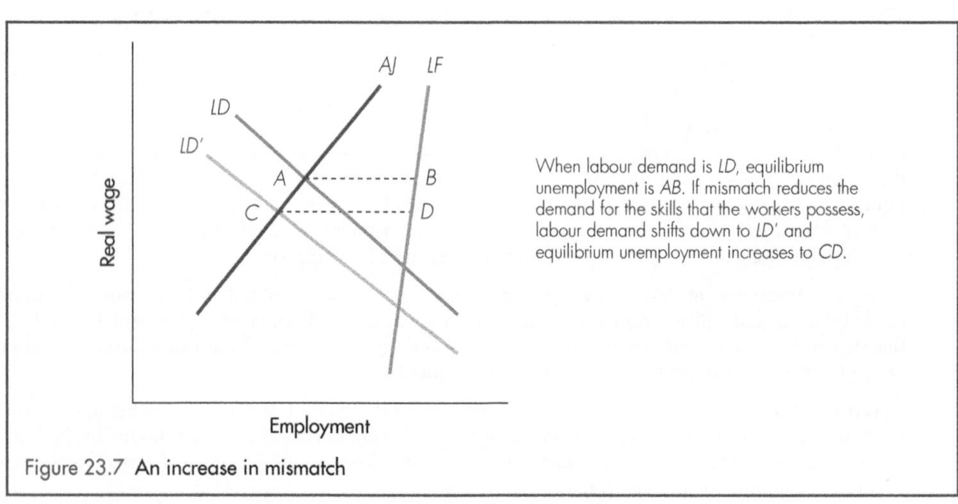

Figure 23.7 An increase in mismatch

The replacement rate is the level of benefits relative to wages in work.

A second potential explanation of a rise in equilibrium unemployment is a rise in the generosity of unemployment benefit relative to wages in work. A higher **replacement rate** may entice more people into the labour force, shifting *LF* to the right. More significantly, it shifts *AJ* to the left. People spend longer in unemployment searching for the right job. For both reasons, equilibrium unemployment increases in Figure 23.8.

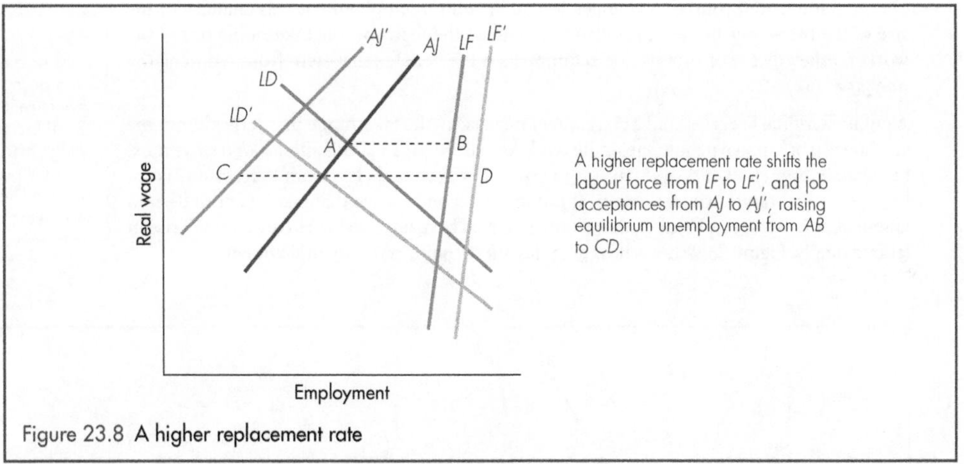

Figure 23.8 A higher replacement rate

Most empirical research concludes that higher benefits caused some of the increase in equilibrium unemployment, though less than sometimes supposed. In practice, UK unemployment benefit (now jobseeker's allowance) did not rise enough to explain the rise in unemployment.

However, benefits policy probably does explain some of the fall in equilibrium unemployment after 1992. First, as in other countries such as the Netherlands, the UK redefined many of its long-term unemployed as sick. People on sickness benefit are no longer measured as unemployed. This improves statistical unemployment, though of course in economic terms it is entirely cosmetic.

Second, Labour's employment policy viewed getting the unemployed back into work as the best form of social policy. People reacquire the work habit and rebuild their confidence. Accordingly, Labour focused on its *Welfare to Work* and *Making Work Pay* – measures intended, respectively, to actively assist the unemployed to look for work and to incentivize them to want to look for work. Measures of these types are sometimes called *active labour market policy.*

Since 2010 the coalition government has begun another reform of welfare policy designed to enhance work incentives further and/or to reduce the fiscal cost of benefits (and thereby the tax rate levied on other workers in order to keep the Treasury solvent). New measures include capping the rate of increase of nominal benefit levels, in effect ensuring a gradual reduction of the real benefit level for those out of work. We discuss these in more detail in Activity 23.1

Trade union power is measured by the ability of unions to co-ordinate lower job acceptances, thereby increasing wages but reducing employment.

A third source of changes in equilibrium unemployment has been changes in **trade union power.**

Rises in union power, especially in the 1970s, had a big effect on equilibrium unemployment. Powerful unions made labour scarce and forced up its price. By shifting the *AJ* curve to the left, unions forced up real wages but increased equilibrium unemployment. Conversely, the fall in union power has shifted the *AJ* schedule right, reducing equilibrium unemployment.

Union power increased in the 1970s partly because sympathetic governments passed legislation enhancing worker protection and partly because many nationalized industries were sheltered state monopolies from which unions could extract potential profits as extra wages for their members. Their power declined after the 1980s, partly because a less sympathetic government reduced the legal protection of unions, privatization removed the Treasury as last-resort funder of union wage claims and globalization increased competition in general. The combination of (a) privatization, (b) globalization, (c) the advent of new technologies, particularly the Internet, which enable more flexible working, and (d) the continuing rise of the service sector and decline of large manufacturing industry has considerably reduced the significance of trade unions over the last 40 years.

The final important source of changes in equilibrium unemployment was changes in the size of the **tax wedge** between the cost of labour to the firm and the take-home pay of the worker. A key theme of supply-side economists is the benefits that stem from reducing the **marginal tax rate**.

The marginal tax rate is the fraction of each extra pound that the government takes in tax. This creates a tax wedge between the price the purchaser pays and the price the seller receives.

A cut in marginal tax rates, and a consequent increase in the take-home pay derived from the last hour's work, make people substitute work for leisure. Against this *substitution effect* must be set an *income effect*. If people pay less in taxes, they have to do less work to reach any given living standard target. Thus, theoretical economics cannot prove that tax cuts raise desired labour supply. Most empirical studies confirm that, at best, tax cuts lead to only a small rise in labour supply. Figure 23.9 shows how tax rates affect equilibrium unemployment.

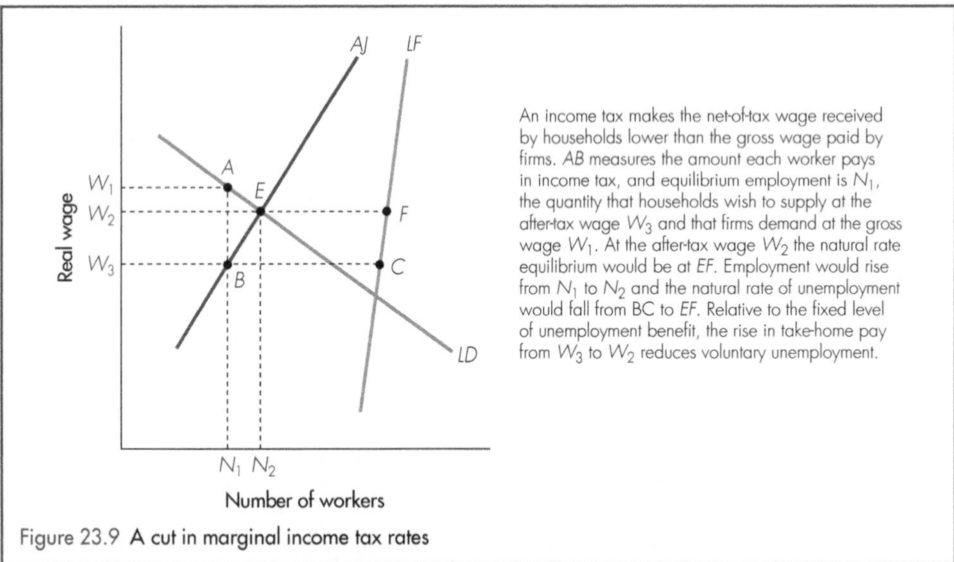

Figure 23.9 A cut in marginal income tax rates

Suppose the marginal tax rate equals the vertical distance *AB*. Equilibrium employment is then N_1. The tax drives a wedge between the gross-of-tax wages paid by firms and the net-of-tax wages received by workers. Firms wish to hire N_1 workers at the gross wage w_1. Subtracting the income tax rate *AB*, N_1 workers want to take job offers at the after-tax wage w_3. Thus N_1 is equilibrium employment, where quantities supplied and demanded are equal. The horizontal distance *BC* shows equilibrium unemployment: the number of workers in the labour force not wishing to work at the going rate of take-home pay.

Suppose taxes are abolished. The gross wage and the take-home pay now coincide, and the new labour market equilibrium is at *E*. Two things happen. First, equilibrium employment rises. Second, although more people join the labour force because take-home pay has risen from w_3 to w_2, equilibrium unemployment falls from *BC* to *EF*. A rise in take-home pay relative to unemployment benefit reduces voluntary unemployment. If lower tax rates reduce equilibrium unemployment, higher tax rates increase equilibrium unemployment.

ACTIVITY 23.1

DOES THE TAX CARROT WORK?

A lower marginal tax rate on income makes people substitute work for leisure. Since working is now better rewarded, people choose to work a bit more. But tax cuts also make workers better off by raising disposable income earned from any particular number of hours of work. This income effect makes people want to consume more leisure, and hence work fewer hours. The combined effect on hours of work is small for those already in work. The income and substitution effects roughly cancel out.

Of more importance is the decision about whether to work at all. Higher take-home pay, for example because of tax cuts, makes more people join the labour force by reducing the significance of the fixed costs of working (commuting, finding cleaners and babysitters, giving up social security).

Over a long period, UK evidence has shown that tax cuts had a tiny effect on labour supply by the primary breadwinner in a household. But in households where both partners consider working, higher take-home pay encourages labour force participation by encouraging the second partner to work, overcoming the fixed costs of going out to work.

The Thatcher programme

The most dramatic natural experiment with which to assess the effectiveness of tax cuts is the programme of the Thatcher government in the 1980s. The real value of personal allowances – how much you can earn before paying income tax – rose by 25 per cent. The basic rate of income tax fell from 33 to 22 per cent and, for top income-earners, from 83 to 40 per cent. Many politicians anticipated a surge in labour supply. Most economists were pessimistic because of the evidence from the past.

The effect of the Thatcher programme was assessed by C. V. Brown in 1988.[1] Brown found that the big rise in tax allowances led to less than 0.5 per cent extra hours of labour supply. The cut in the basic rate of income tax had no detectable effect at all. The massive cut in the marginal tax rate of top earners had a small effect in stimulating extra hours of work by the rich. The evidence from the past stood up well to a big change in tax policy.

New Labour after 1997

During 1997–2001 Chancellor of the Exchequer Gordon Brown quietly raised taxes to help the poor and provide funding for public services. In order not to scare the middle classes, the government kept rather quiet about these tax increases, which were sometimes labelled 'stealth taxes'. Neither theory nor past evidence suggests that these had a large and adverse incentive effect. We know from Figure 23.6 that equilibrium unemployment remained low thereafter.

It remains to be seen whether some sharper adjustments required by the labour market as the economy reacts to the financial crash and its austerity aftermath will lead to a renewed rise in equilibrium unemployment; for example, because the composition of demand in the new economy requires substantially different skills, as would be the case if the UK experienced another shakeout of old manufacturing jobs and the further rise of new service industries. We can be fairly sure that there will be a period of demand-deficient unemployment.

Emigrating non-doms and hedge fund managers

A general lesson of tax policy is that, when things are very elastically supplied or demanded (very price sensitive), tax rates can have large effects on the quantity traded. Conversely, when things are very inelastic in supply or demand (very price insensitive), tax rates have little effect on the quantity traded.

Since most workers are reluctant either to emigrate or to give up working, income tax usually has only a small effect on labour supply. But there are exceptions. Investment bankers, hedge fund managers and the super-rich may sometimes fall into this category. If they have global lifestyles anyway, they may be relatively indifferent as to whether they live in Manhattan, London, Paris or Geneva. If a single country attempts to tax them very differently from other countries, they may move location in order to find a more agreeable tax regime.

1 C. V. Brown, 'The 1988 tax cuts, work incentives and revenue', *Fiscal Studies* 9, no. 4 (1988): 93–107.

Of course, they are likely to threaten to move, whether or not they really will. This may deter a government from trying to tax them more heavily. In 2009 the UK announced both that it was going to raise its top income tax rate from 40 to 50 per cent in 2010, and also proposed eliminating some of the tax breaks enjoyed by rich foreign residents (the so-called non-domiciles or non-doms). In the subsequent outcry, the government backed down on non-doms, but the top marginal income tax rate was increased to 50 per cent as planned.

The Coalition Reforms

In 2013, the coalition government cut this top rate from 50 to 45 per cent in order to mitigate perverse incentive effects. This will provoke a new burst of empirical research to see if any beneficial effects can be detected. If the evidence from the past continues to hold up, such effects will be disappointingly small.

Finally, it should be remembered that it is the combined effect of the tax and benefit systems that determines work incentives. For poorer people, the benefits system is much more important than the tax system. Under New Labour (1997–2010) there was a focus on providing in-work benefits to try to get as many people as possible into the labour force. Given the modern prevalence of part-time working, New Labour decided to make these benefits available only for people working at least 16 hours a week (reckoned to be what a single mother with children could manage). Hence quite a large number of part-time workers clustered around 16 hours a week of part-time work, thereby getting additional welfare support.

Since 2010, UK government policy on welfare has focused on the possibility of a 'universal benefit' that everyone gets, combined with steady loss of benefits as income rises. Effectively, this raises the marginal tax rate of the 'tax plus benefit' system in the income range in which people are losing benefit by working longer.

This system is 'less distortionary' than the previous one, since it provides continuous and smooth incentives rather than big discontinuities at particular levels of work. In principle, that is a good idea. Critics argue that it may nevertheless be counterproductive if its main effect is to remove the incentive for potential part-time workers to work a minimum of 16 hours. Under the new system, they may choose to work less than that.

Questions

(a) Suppose national insurance contributions by firms – which depend on the value of wages paid to workers – are increased by 1 per cent. Draw a diagram to display the effect on equilibrium unemployment. Does this constitute a 'tax on jobs'?

(b) Now suppose that, instead of higher national insurance contributions by firms, the same additional revenue for the Treasury is raised by asking workers to increase the contributions they make to national insurance. How, if at all, does the outcome differ from that in (a)?

(c) Suppose that the revenue raised is spent entirely on additional nurses for the National Health Service. Is the combined effect of the two policies a tax on jobs?

To check your answers to these questions, go to page 681.

Another possible supply-side policy is to cut unemployment benefit. For a given labour force schedule *LF*, fewer people now wish to be unemployed at any real wage. In Figure 23.10, the schedule *AJ*, showing acceptances of job offers, shifts to the right. This raises equilibrium employment (and hence potential output) and reduces equilibrium unemployment.

What about changes in the national insurance contributions paid both by firms and by workers? These are mandatory contributions to state schemes that provide unemployment and health insurance. They act like an income tax, driving a wedge *AB* between the total cost to a firm of hiring another worker and the net take-home pay of a worker. Figure 23.9 implies that a fall in these contributions will raise equilibrium employment and cut equilibrium unemployment.

Supply-side policies can reduce equilibrium unemployment. Where this involves being tough on those already relatively disadvantaged, there is a conflict between efficiency and fairness, and only through the political process can society express its view.

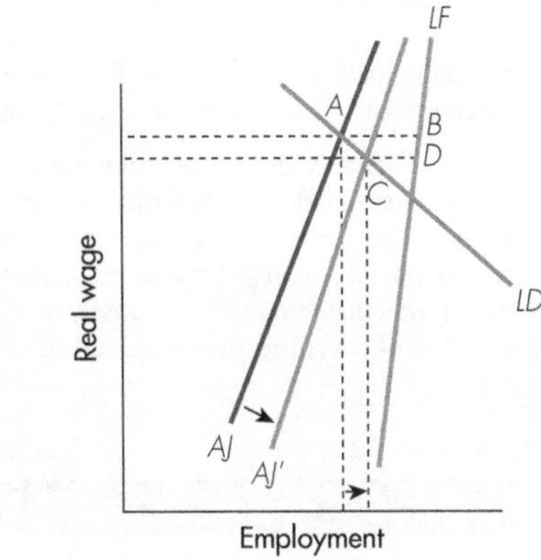

Initially, the job acceptance schedule is *AJ* and equilibrium unemployment is the distance *AB*. A fall in unemployment benefit raises the cost of searching for a better job offer. Job acceptances shift to *AJ'* and equilibrium unemployment falls to the distance *CD*.

Figure 23.10 **A reduction in unemployment benefit**

MATHS 23.1

THE LABOUR MARKET INCIDENCE OF POLICY CHANGES

Suppose the labour force L, job acceptances A and labour demand D obey the equations:

$$L = a + bw \qquad A = (b + c)w \qquad D = e - f(w + t) \qquad a, b, c, e, f > 0\, t > 0 \qquad (1)$$

where a, b, c, e and f are positive constants, and t is the effective tax rate on working. Workers care about take-home pay w, whereas firms care about the gross cost $(w + t)$ of hiring a worker. In labour market equilibrium, job acceptance A equals labour demand D, whence

$$w = (e - ft)/(b + c + f) \qquad A = (e - ft)(b + c)/(b + c + f) \qquad (2)$$

and equilibrium unemployment $(L - A)$, which is simply $(a - cw)$, is given by

$$u^* = \{a(b + c + f) - c(e - ft)\}/(b + c + f) \qquad (3)$$

Does a rise in labour taxes t increase equilibrium unemployment? In the model, the answer is yes – a one-unit increase in t increases u^* by $cf/(b + c + f)$. In terms of figures such as 23.7 and 23.8, once we assume that job acceptances are more sensitive than the labour force to increases in take-home pay, anything that reduces take-home pay widens the gap between those wishing to work and those accepting jobs. Equation (2) above confirms that higher labour taxes reduce the number of job acceptances by reducing the component $(e - ft)$ in take home pay. Check for yourself that labour demand D is reduced by the same amount. This occurs because the gross cost of labour $(w + t)$ increases despite the fall in w, as implied by equation (2):

$$w + t = [e + (b + c)t]/[b + c + f]$$

which unambiguously increases with the tax rate t. In policy terms, the key issue is how much more sensitive to wage increases is the job acceptance schedule in comparison with the labour force schedule. If the two schedules had equal slope $(c = 0)$, then equation (3) implies that the tax rate would have *no effect* on equilibrium unemployment. Intuitively, in terms of the diagrams earlier in the chapter, when the *LF* and *AJ* schedules are parallel, then the changes in the equilibrium quantity of employment, for whatever reason, have no effect on the horizontal gap that corresponds to the equilibrium rate of unemployment. However, the more responsive is the job acceptance schedule (larger c, flatter slope), the more a reduction in equilibrium employment widens the gap between job acceptances and the labour force, raising the equilibrium rate of unemployment.

23.4 Cyclical fluctuations in unemployment

We discuss business cycles in Chapter 27. Cycles may reflect fluctuations in demand or fluctuations in supply. Since supply usually changes slowly, most of the sharp movements in the short run are caused by changes in demand.

Unless a counter-cyclical demand management policy is deliberately and successfully pursued, there may well be a business cycle. If so, there tends to be a cyclical relationship between demand, output, employment and unemployment. On average, boosting aggregate demand by 1 per cent will not raise employment by 1 per cent or reduce unemployment by 1 per cent, even if the economy begins with spare resources. Table 23.3 shows two periods of demand growth and two of demand decline. In practice, booms lead initially to a sharp increase in shift lengths and hours worked; slumps lead to the abolition of overtime, the introduction of short time and a marked decline in hours worked.

Table 23.3 Output, employment and unemployment: evidence from the past

Cumulative change in	79ii–81ii	86ii–88ii	90ii–91ii	92iv–98ii
Real GDP (%)	−7.8	+9.1	−3.4	+16.8
Employment (%)	−6.3	+2.5	−2.9	+6.8
Employed (million)	−1.7	+0.5	−0.7	+1.5
Unemployed (million)	+1.4	−0.9	+0.6	−1.2

Source: ONS, *Economic Trends*.

The table confirms that changes in demand and output lead to smaller changes in employment. For example, when output grew by 16.8 per cent between the fourth quarter of 1992 and the second quarter of 1998, employment rose by only 6.8 per cent. Nor do changes in employment lead to corresponding changes in unemployment. The last two rows of the table show that rapid expansion or contraction of employment leads to significantly smaller changes in unemployment.

One reason is the 'discouraged worker effect'. When unemployment is high and rising, some people who would like to work become pessimistic and stop looking for work. No longer registered as looking for work, they are not recorded in the labour force or the unemployed. Conversely, in a boom, people who had previously given up looking for work rejoin the labour force since there is now a good chance of getting a suitable job. Hence in booms and slumps recorded employment data change by more than recorded unemployment data. After 1997, the Monetary Policy Committee kept the UK economy on a more even keel until the recession of 2009.

CASE 23.2

HOW BAD COULD UNEMPLOYMENT BECOME?

The OECD is a club of the most advanced economic nations in the world – living standards and per capita income count more than absolute size. Newer members include Turkey, Mexico and Hungary. China and India are not yet members despite their vast populations. Currently, the OECD has 32 members.

The 2009 OECD *Employment Outlook* discusses prospects for unemployment and possible policy responses. The evolution of unemployment depends on: (a) the size of the shock, (b) the flexibility of the economy to respond, and (c) the extent of support by government. In the worst previous post-war recession, that of 1973–76, OECD unemployment increased by half. By 2009 the OECD reckoned that unemployment would rise by 80 per cent – from 5.5 to 10 per cent of the labour force – during 2007–10.

This analysis reflected the magnitude of the initial shock. Clearly, this would affect different countries differently. One way in which to assess which economies were most vulnerable is to estimate their capacity to absorb shocks through flexible labour markets that match potential workers and job opportunities more quickly. This is likely to depend on wage flexibility, labour market mobility, attitudes of trade unions and the extent of labour market regulation.

The figure below shows a measure of labour market flexibility based on labour market history during 2000–05. It plots the annual fraction of workers hired in new jobs or leaving existing jobs (by choice or dismissal) during the year. It shows that, in Turkey, Denmark and the US, half of all workers are changing jobs annually. In contrast, the countries with the lowest labour market mobility are Greece, Italy and Austria.

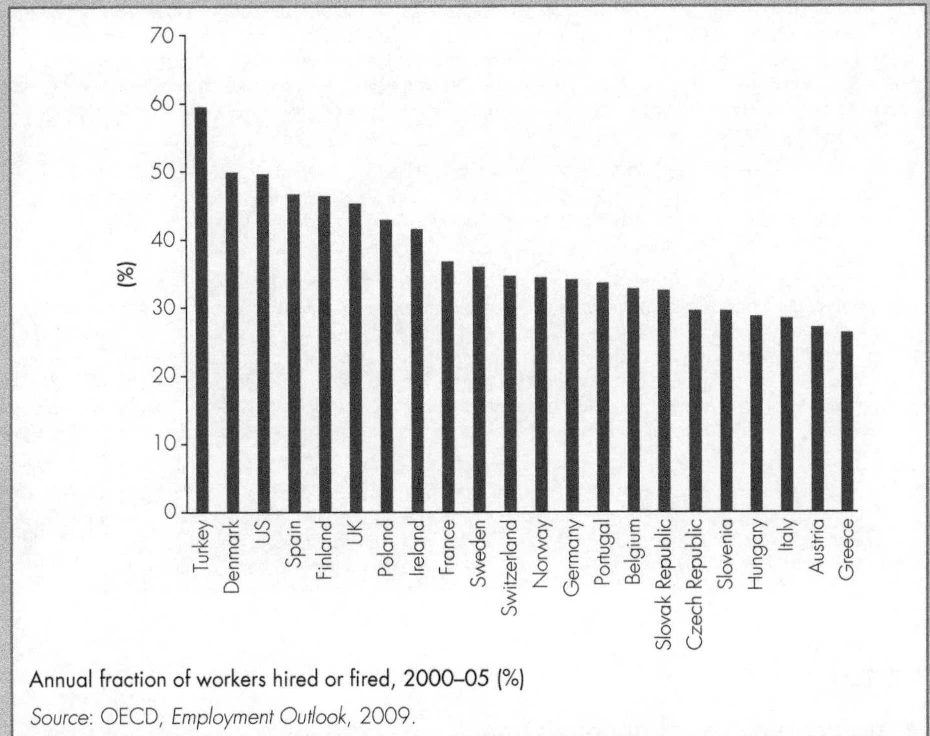

Annual fraction of workers hired or fired, 2000–05 (%)

Source: OECD, *Employment Outlook*, 2009.

Countries with greater job stability are probably slower to experience initial unemployment but, when unemployment does increase, they are also less successful at helping people out of unemployment back into work. Since there is considerable cross-country evidence that those in longer-term unemployment find it ever more difficult to reconnect with the labour market, in the medium run this fiscal burden of unemployment benefits is likely to be greater in countries with less flexible labour markets.

Duration of unemployment	Year 1	Year 2	Year 5
	Replacement rate (%)		
Norway	72	72	72
Belgium	65	63	63
France	67	64	31
UK	28	28	28
Japan	45	3	3
Greece	33	5	1
US	28	0	0

Source: OECD, *Employment Outlook*, 2009.

Governments provide two kinds of support. The first is measurable by the generosity of unemployment benefit, which has two dimensions – the replacement rate (the ratio of benefit to previous wages in work) and the number of years for which benefit is available. The table documents considerable differences across countries.

In Norway and Belgium, with strong traditions of social democracy, unemployment benefit is generous both because it is high relative to wages in work and because it continues for at least five years after a spell of unemployment begins. French unemployment benefit is initially as generous but less so after year two. The UK is considerably less generous in its replacement rate, but entitlement continues undiminished over the five-year period. In countries such as Japan, Greece and the US, unemployment benefit is almost worthless after the first year in unemployment.

The second aspect of state support for the unemployed is active labour market policies that enhance incentives, confidence and the ability of the unemployed to look for jobs. Even if the post-crash recession reflected a sharp fall in demand – for output and then for labour – it is important not to neglect supply-side policies that maintain maximum labour market flexibility.

With the benefit of hindsight, the most puzzling features of the labour market since the financial crash have been (a) the relatively small increase in unemployment and (b) the disappointing performance of labour productivity. For example, UK unemployment was still only 8 per cent in late 2012. The US has also avoided double-digit unemployment and appeared to have resumed steady if modest output growth. Two explanations consistent with facts (a) and (b) are that (i) firms engaged in more labour hoarding in recession than in previous cyclical recessions, and (ii) that many workers who would otherwise have become unemployed took up part-time working or self-employment. The rise of the Internet allowed many people to embark on small businesses in the service sector.

With long-term demographic trends also implying that pension schemes would face greater and greater financial strains, and with governments removing subsidies to pension contributions in an effort to retain fiscal solvency, it is also possible that some older workers simply retired while the going was good, rather than face a period of unemployment when rehiring of older workers was likely to be a tough prospect.

23.5 The cost of unemployment

The private cost of unemployment

It is important to distinguish between voluntary and involuntary unemployment. When individuals are voluntarily unemployed, they reveal that they do better by being unemployed than by immediately taking a job offer at the going wage rate. The private cost of unemployment (the wage forgone by not working) is less than the private benefits of being unemployed. What are these benefits?

The first is transfer payments from government. Workers who have contributed to the national insurance scheme get jobseeker's allowance for the first 12 months after becoming unemployed. Thereafter they get income support, the ultimate backstop in the British welfare state.

There are other benefits, too. First, there is the value of leisure. By refusing a job, some people reveal that the extra leisure is worth more to them than the extra disposable income if they took a job. Second, some people expect to get a better job by being choosy about accepting offers. These future benefits must be set against the current cost: a lower disposable income as a result of being out of work.

When people are involuntarily unemployed, the cost changes. Involuntary unemployment means that people would like to work at the going wage but cannot find a job because there is excess labour supply at the existing wage rate. These people are worse off by being unemployed.

The distinction between voluntary and involuntary unemployment matters because it may affect our value judgement about how much attention to pay to unemployment. When unemployment is involuntary, people are suffering more and the case for helping them is stronger.

The social cost of unemployment

Again we distinguish between voluntary and involuntary unemployment. When unemployment is voluntary, individuals prefer to be unemployed. Does this unemployment also benefit society?

An individual receives transfer payments during unemployment, but these transfers give no corresponding benefit to society as a whole. They may ease the collective conscience in regard to poverty and income inequality, but they are not payments for the supply of any goods or services that other members of society may consume. Since the private benefit exceeds the social benefit, too many people may be voluntarily unemployed.

CONCEPT 23.2

HYSTERESIS AND HIGH UNEMPLOYMENT

Supply and demand curves are supposed to be independent of one another. The labour supply curve or job acceptances schedule *AJ* shows the people willing to work at each real wage whatever the position of the labour demand curve *LD*, and vice versa. But this may be wrong.

In the diagram, the initial equilibrium is at *E*. Something then shifts labour demand down from *LD* to *LD'*. Suppose this causes a permanent fall in labour supply. *JA* shifts to *JA'*. When labour demand reverts to *LD*, the new equilibrium is at *F*, not *E*. The short-run history of the economy has affected its long-run equilibrium.

An economy experiences hysteresis when its long-run equilibrium depends on the path it follows in the short run.

Hysteresis may explain high and persistent unemployment in much of continental Europe. Here are some channels through which it might work.

The insider–outsider distinction

Outsiders are those unemployed without jobs. Only insiders with jobs participate in wage bargaining. At the original equilibrium *E*, the numerous insiders in work ensure that real wages are low enough to preserve their own jobs. When a recession occurs, *LD* shifts to *LD'*. Some insiders get fired and become outsiders. Eventually, as explained in Chapter 21, market forces restore labour demand to *LD*. But now there are fewer insiders than originally. They exploit their scarcity by securing higher wages for themselves rather than encouraging firms to rehire. The economy is trapped in the high-wage, low-employment equilibrium at *F* instead of the low-wage, high-employment equilibrium at *E*. Thereafter, only long-run supply-side measures aimed at breaking down insider power can gradually break the economy out of this low-employment equilibrium.

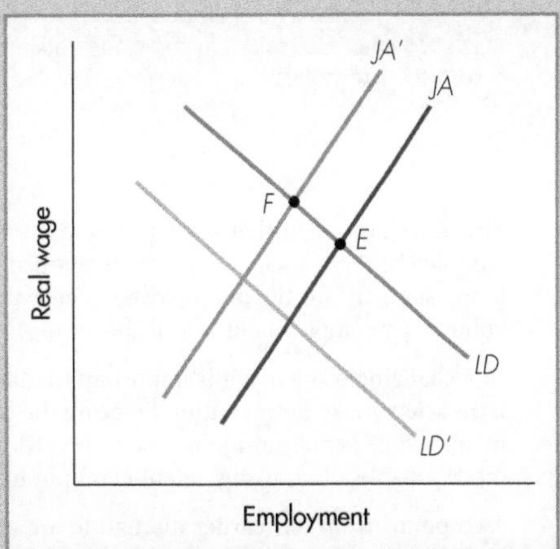

Discouraged workers

Again, the economy begins at *E*. It has a skilled and energetic labour force. A temporary recession leads to unemployment. If the recession is protracted, we see the emergence of long-term unemployed people and a culture in which they stop looking for jobs. Again, when demand picks up, labour supply has been permanently reduced and equilibrium reverts to *F*, not *E*. Only long-term supply-side measures to restore the work culture will succeed.

Search and mismatch

When employment is high at *E*, firms are trying to find scarce workers, and potential workers are searching hard for a job. A recession makes firms advertise fewer vacancies, and workers realize it is a waste of time searching for jobs. When demand picks up again, both firms and workers are accustomed to low levels of search. New jobs are not created.

The capital stock

At *E*, the economy has a lot of capital. Labour productivity is high and firms want lots of workers. During a temporary recession, firms scrap old machines. When demand picks up again, firms have permanently lower capital. The demand for labour, which depends on the marginal product of labour, never rises to its original level. Again, the economy returns to *F*, not *E*.

Policy implications of hysteresis

Hysteresis means that a temporary fall in demand induces permanently lower employment and output, and higher equilibrium unemployment. There are two policy implications. First, once the problem has emerged, it is dangerous to try to break out of it simply by expanding aggregate demand. Before long-run supply can respond, you get major inflation. Supply-side policies, needed to rebuild aggregate supply, take a long time to work.

Second, because the problem is so hard to cure once it occurs, it is vital not to let demand fall in the first place. The payoff to demand management is higher than in an economy with a unique long-run equilibrium where all that is at stake is how quickly the economy reverts to its original point.

These arguments help explain why governments intervened so heavily in 2009–10 to endeavour to offset the worst of the demand effects of the financial crash. They feared that too little action would imply a dramatic fall in aggregate demand from which it would be hard to recover.

Empirical evidence

A useful survey of the evidence that hysteresis exists is provided by Laurence Ball.[2] Examining data for 20 countries, Ball found that large increases in *equilibrium* unemployment occur after a period of disinflation, as the figure above would imply.

This does not mean that society should go to the opposite extreme and eliminate voluntary unemployment completely. First, society is perfectly entitled to adopt the value judgement that it will maintain a reasonable living standard for the unemployed, whatever the cost in resource misallocation. Second, the efficient level of voluntary unemployment is well above zero.

In a changing economy, it is important to match up the right people to the right jobs. Getting this match right lets society make more output. Freezing the existing pattern of employment in a changing economy leads to a mismatch of people and jobs. The flow through the pool of unemployment allows people to be reallocated to more suitable jobs, raising potential output in the long run.

Two points from our earlier discussion are also relevant here. First, even when unemployment is high, flows both into and out of the pool are large relative to the pool itself. Second, people who do not get out of the pool quickly are in danger of stagnating when unemployment is high: the fraction of the unemployed who have been unemployed for over a year was higher in the 1990s than at the end of the 1970s when unemployment was much lower.

Involuntary or Keynesian unemployment has an even higher social cost. Since the economy is producing below capacity, it is literally throwing away output that could have been made by putting these people to work. Moreover, since Keynesian unemployment is involuntary, it may entail more human and psychological suffering than voluntary unemployment. Although hard to quantify, it is also part of the social cost of unemployment.

2 Laurence Ball, 'Hysteresis in unemployment: Old and new evidence', in J. Fuhrer (ed.), *A Phillips curve restrospective* (Federal Reserve Bank of Boston and MIT Press, 2009).

Summary

- People are either **employed**, **unemployed** or out of the **labour force**. The level of unemployment rises when inflows to the pool of the unemployed exceed outflows. Inflows and outflows are large relative to the level of unemployment.
- As unemployment has risen, the average duration of unemployment has increased.
- Women face lower unemployment rates than men. The unemployment rates for old workers and, especially, for young workers are well above the national average.
- **Unemployment** can be classified as **frictional**, **structural**, **classical** or **demand-deficient**. In modern terminology, the first three types are **voluntary unemployment** and the last is **involuntary unemployment**. The **natural rate of unemployment** is the equilibrium level of voluntary unemployment.
- In the long run, sustained rises in unemployment must reflect increases in the natural rate of unemployment. During temporary recessions, **Keynesian unemployment** is also important.
- **Supply-side economics** aims to increase equilibrium employment and potential output, and to reduce the natural rate of unemployment, by operating on incentives at a microeconomic level. Supply-side policies include reducing mismatch, reducing union power, tax cuts, reductions in unemployment benefit, retraining and relocation grants and investment subsidies.
- A 1 per cent increase in output is likely to lead to a much smaller reduction in Keynesian unemployment. Some of the extra output will be met by longer hours. And as unemployment falls, some people, effectively in the labour force but not registered, look for work again.
- **Hysteresis** means that short-run changes can move the economy to a different long-run equilibrium. It may explain why European recessions have raised the natural rate of unemployment substantially.
- People voluntarily unemployed reveal that the private benefits from unemployment exceed the private cost in wages forgone. Society derives no output from transfer payments to support the unemployed. However, society would not benefit by driving unemployment to zero. Some social gains in higher productivity are derived from improved matching of people and jobs that temporary unemployment allows.
- Keynesian unemployment is involuntary and hurts private individuals who would prefer to be employed. Socially it represents wasted output. Society may also care about the human misery inflicted by involuntary unemployment.
- Most European countries took two decades to reverse the high unemployment of the 1980s. Having brought unemployment down, they now face a new period of higher unemployment as budgets are cut back to cope with the fiscal crises caused by trying to offset the effects of the financial crash.

Review questions

1 How is high unemployment explained by (a) a Keynesian and (b) a classical economist?
2 Which of the following statements is correct? The fact that unemployment rose in 2009 in the UK by less than originally predicted shows that: (a) the fall in output and demand was illusory; (b) wages were more flexible than in previous recessions; (c) firms believed that lower output would be very short lived?
3 What is the discouraged worker effect? Suggest two reasons why it occurs.
4 'The average duration of an individual's unemployment rises in a slump. Hence the problem is a higher inflow to the pool of unemployment, not a lower outflow.' Do you agree?
5 Explain why boosting demand sometimes fails to reduce unemployment.

6 'The microchip caused a permanent rise in the level of unemployment.' Did it? What about all previous technical advances?

7 Illustrate on a graph the effect of a labour skill mismatch on the equilibrium level of unemployment in the labour market.

8 'An increase in national insurance contributions by workers reduces the income per hour that workers take home and therefore reduces the incentive to work.' 'An increase in national insurance contributions, by reducing income per hour, forces people to work longer hours to attain their target take-home income.' Is either statement correct? Are both correct? What light does this shed on national insurance contributions as a 'jobs tax'? Draw a diagram to illustrate your answer.

9 Labour supply L, job acceptances J and labour demand D are, respectively, related to the real wage W by:

$$L = 10 + W, J = bW, 0 < b < 1\ D = 50 - dW, d > 0$$

MEDIUM

(a) Find equilibrium unemployment. (b) If there is now an income tax at rate t on wages, what happens to equilibrium unemployment?

10 Suppose the government wants to encourage lone parents to take part-time jobs and thinks 15 hours a week is consistent with children being in a crèche for 3 hours a day, Monday to Friday. Which of the following might achieve the government's aim: (a) an additional lump-sum payment to lone parents, (b) a lower income tax rate for lone parents, or (c) a payment conditional on their taking at least 15 hours of work a week?

11 **Common fallacies** Why are these statements wrong? (a) Unemployment is always a bad thing. (b) So long as there is unemployment, there is pressure on wages to fall. (c) Unemployment arises only because greedy workers are pricing themselves out of a job.

12 Why is teenage unemployment so high?

13 **Essay question** For two decades, unemployment in France has been significantly higher than that in the UK. If you become the president of France, should you: (a) blame the European Central Bank for cautious monetary policy; (b) blame the French Treasury for a fiscal policy that has been too tight; or (c) tackle labour market reform in France? Explain your answer.

HARD

14 Most economists forecast a period of protracted unemployment after 2009 as government takes tough measures for a sustained period to bring the budget deficit and national debt under control. (a) Why might such an evolution involve hysteresis? (b) Draw a diagram to illustrate both the initial increase in unemployment and the subsequent developments when demand eventually expands again.

For solutions to these questions, contact your lecturer.

CHAPTER 27

Business cycles

Learning Outcomes

By the end of this chapter, you should be able to:

1 distinguish between trend growth and economic cycles around this path
2 discuss why business cycles occur
3 analyse why output gaps may fluctuate
4 discuss whether potential output also fluctuates
5 understand the role of dynamic general equilibrium models
6 contrast real business cycle models and New Keynesian analysis
7 assess whether national business cycles are now more correlated
8 apply these principles to UK business cycles
9 summarize key issues dividing the main schools of macroeconomic thought

This chapter discusses cyclical movements in output around its long-run trend. We explore theories of why cycles occur, and use this analysis to discuss the different schools of macroeconomic thought and the reasons why they differ.

For decades, politicians were accused of two policy failings. First, they pursued short-run stimulus too much in the pursuit of electorally popular high employment. The result was high inflation. Second, they could not resist boosting the economy just before elections, causing unnecessary and unhelpful swings in output.

By the late 1990s, many countries had made their central banks operationally independent of government control. This was intended both to control long-run inflation and to reduce electorally motivated cycles in aggregate demand and output. This institutional change was necessary but not sufficient to achieve these aims. Fiscal policy could still be irresponsibly loose, and financial regulation could be dangerously weak.

Until 2007–08, it appeared that central bank independence had succeeded remarkably in delivering low inflation and lower output cycles. Then the financial crash happened. Interest rates were cut sharply and fiscal policy was loosened dramatically, both to bail out the financial system and to avert a catastrophic fall in aggregate demand, whose effects would be more prolonged the more hysteresis was a key feature of the labour market.

Central bank independence had not abolished boom and bust. Since 2009, most Western economies have had a mixture of recession and low growth, despite loose monetary policy and fiscal austerity that was more talked about than yet delivered.

These episodes illustrate many of the issues that we examine in this chapter. First, is there a business cycle? Output fluctuates a lot in the short run, but a cycle does not mean merely temporary departures from trend: it also requires a degree of regularity. Can we see it in the data? Can monetary and fiscal policy insulate economies from business cycles? If so, which should get the credit?

We also look at the international dimension. Can a country display cycles out of phase with those in its trading partners? Is globalization making business cycles more correlated across countries? If so, might a single monetary policy become increasingly appropriate?

27.1 Trend and cycle: statistics or economics?

In practice, aggregate output and productivity do not grow smoothly. In some years they grow very rapidly but in others they actually fall. Actual output fluctuates around this hypothetical **trend path**.

The trend path of output is the smooth path of long-run output once its short-term fluctuations are averaged out.

The business cycle is the short-term fluctuation of total output around its trend path.

Figure 27.1 shows a stylized picture of the business cycle. The purple curve is the steady growth in trend output over time. Actual output follows the green curve. Point *A* represents a *slump*, the bottom of a **business cycle**. At *B*, the economy has entered the *recovery* phase of the cycle. As recovery proceeds, output climbs above its trend path, reaching point *C*, which we call a *boom*. Then the economy enters a period in which output is growing less quickly than trend output, and is possibly even falling. When output is falling for at least two successive quarters, we call this a *recession*. Point *E* shows a *slump*, after which recovery begins and the cycle starts again.

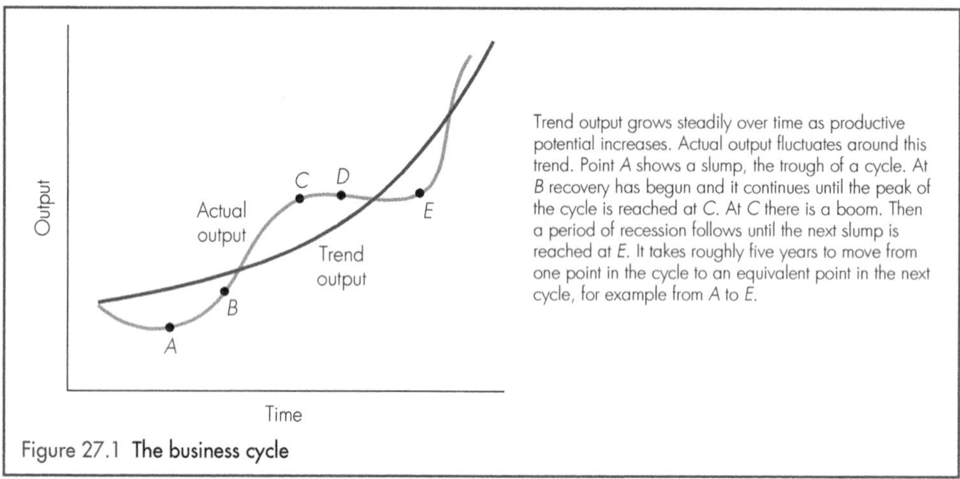

Trend output grows steadily over time as productive potential increases. Actual output fluctuates around this trend. Point *A* shows a slump, the trough of a cycle. At *B* recovery has begun and it continues until the peak of the cycle is reached at *C*. At *C* there is a boom. Then a period of recession follows until the next slump is reached at *E*. It takes roughly five years to move from one point in the cycle to an equivalent point in the next cycle, for example from *A* to *E*.

Figure 27.1 **The business cycle**

Figure 27.2 shows the annual growth of real GDP and of real output per employed worker in the UK during the period 1975–2012. The figure makes four points.

First, growth of output and productivity fluctuates in the short run. Second, although cycles are not perfectly regular, there is evidence of a pattern of slump, recovery, boom and recession, over five–six years. Third, output and output per person are *closely* correlated in the short run. Typically, output fluctuations used to precede fluctuations in productivity by about a year; since the mid-1990s this gap has fallen. Fourth, during 1995–2007 cycles became less pronounced than previously – hence the optimism that boom and bust had been defeated. The output fall of 2009 was then the worst annual fall of the post-war period. The rest of the chapter seeks to explain these facts.

Any series of points may be decomposed statistically into an average trend and fluctuations around that trend. We first assume that potential output grows smoothly. Later we ask whether potential output itself can fluctuate significantly in the short run. Thus, we start by assuming that business cycles reflect fluctuations in the **output gap**.

The output gap is the deviation of actual output from potential output.

Figure 27.2 shows that business cycles are too regular to be a coincidence. What causes cycles? Potential output reflects aggregate supply in the long run. First, we explore aggregate demand shocks as the source of cyclical deviations of actual output from potential output.

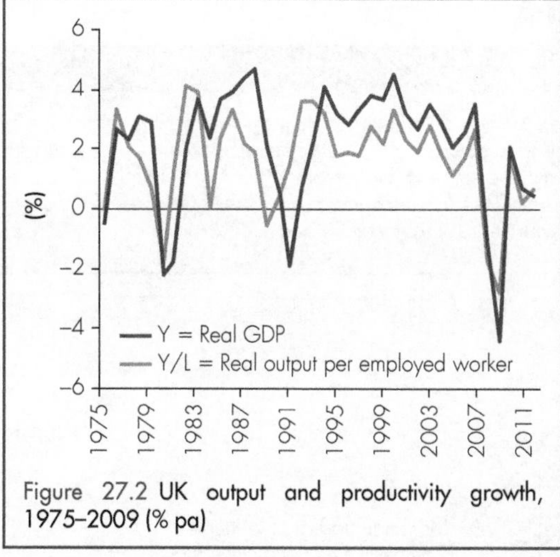

Figure 27.2 UK output and productivity growth, 1975–2009 (% pa)

We know what shifts demand: changes in export demand, in the desire to save, in expected future profits and incomes, and in monetary and fiscal policy.

If demand shocks happen to be cyclical, this causes cycles in actual output. That is not an *explanation* of the business cycle: it does not tell us why demand shocks have this cyclical pattern. One version of this approach does at least claim to be a theory.

Suppose voters, having short memories, are heavily influenced by how the economy is doing immediately prior to the election. Knowing this, the government uses monetary and fiscal policy to manipulate aggregate demand. Policy is tight just after a government is elected, creating a slump and spare capacity. As the next election date approaches, expansionary policy can then create unsustainably rapid growth by eliminating spare capacity. Voters misinterpret this as permanently faster growth of potential output and gratefully re-elect the government.

A political business cycle arises if politicians manipulate the economy for electoral advantage.

This theory provides a reason for fluctuations and suggests why **political business cycles** tend to last about five years – that is about the period between successive elections. The theory probably contains a grain of truth. On the other hand, it supposes that voters are naïve. Voters are not always so short-sighted. In 1997 the Major government lost the election despite fast output growth: voters thought Labour could do even better. In the US, President Obama was re-elected in 2012 despite low growth since 2009.

Recent institutional changes to improve the credibility of policy – particularly central bank independence – reduce the scope for political business cycles. Having discussed political causes of cycles, we now concentrate on economic causes.

27.2 Theories of the business cycle

Fluctuations in export demand might cause cycles. One country's exports are another country's imports, and these imports will fluctuate only if foreign income fluctuates. International trade helps explain how cycles get transmitted from one country to another, but we require a theory of domestic business cycles to initiate the process.

Sluggish adjustment is necessary but not sufficient to generate cycles caused by demand shocks. It is necessary because rapid adjustment would quickly eliminate output gaps and restore output to potential output. It is not sufficient because sluggishness only explains why the return to potential output takes time. An oil tanker moves sluggishly but it does not oscillate its way into port. Cycles require a mechanism by which deviations in one direction then set up forces that cause output to overshoot potential output on its return.

Having ruled out the government, a theory of domestic cycles must be based on consumption or investment spending. Investment spending is the most likely candidate, since it is more likely to take time to assess and adjust. Firms do not rush into major and irreversible investment projects, nor are new factories built overnight.

ACTIVITY 27.1

THE CYCLICAL BEHAVIOUR OF WAGES

In a recession, firms employ fewer workers. A competitive firm would pay workers the real value of their marginal product. Given a diminishing marginal product of labour, cutting back on workers should raise labour's marginal product. Fewer workers have the same capital as before to work with. Real wages should rise in a slump, as the economy moves from point *B* to *A* in the figure below. But in practice, real wages don't rise, they fall. This is the *real-wage puzzle* over the business cycle.

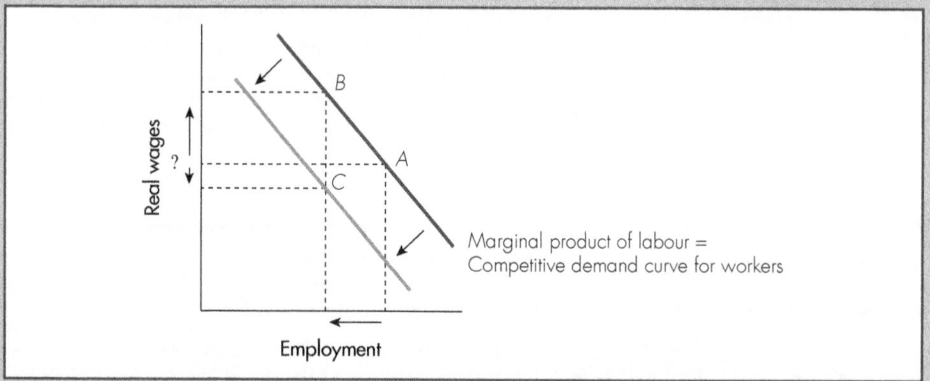

To explain the real-wage puzzle, we have to explain why the demand for labour shifts down so the economy moves in a slump from point *A* to *C* not from *A* to *B*. One answer is that most of the economy faces imperfect competition. When demand for output falls, profit margins are reduced, so the marginal revenue product of labour falls too, reducing the demand for labour. Profit margins are not constant over the business cycle.

Second, at lower output levels, firms may scrap old factories and old machines that were only just sustainable provided output remained high, reducing the total stock, causing a downward shift in labour demand, even under perfect competition in the output markets.

Third, trade union power may be weakened by a recession and the prospect of job cuts, leading to a lower wage settlement. In effect, unions cut wages in order to preserve employment for their members.

Fourth, some of the adjustment to recession may come via less overtime and shorter working weeks. This makes sense if it is cheaper to adjust hours of work than to hire and fire workers. Shorter working hours mean both lower output per worker and lower take-home pay per worker. The cost of firing, and then subsequently rehiring, means that firms may actually hoard labour in a recession, keeping on workers that they don't fully need today in anticipation of better times to come tomorrow.

Nor do recessions originate only from adverse demand shocks in the output market. Suppose there is a temporary adverse supply shock – either a surge in raw materials prices or a temporary reduction in labour productivity. In either case, the demand for labour is reduced, as in the figure above.

Shifts in labour supply may further complicate the analysis. When times are tough and wages low, you don't sacrifice much by taking time off; lifetime earnings can be rebuilt when conditions are easier. So recessions, caused by temporarily low productivity, make firms offer temporarily low wages, and households temporarily reduce their labour supply. We can get low employment *and* low wages.

The next set of figures, taken from the OECD's *Economic Outlook* of November 2009, confirm that this phenomenon is pervasive. Hours worked per worker (bottom panel) fell sharply in 2008, just before employment turned down (middle panel) and unemployment turned up (top panel).

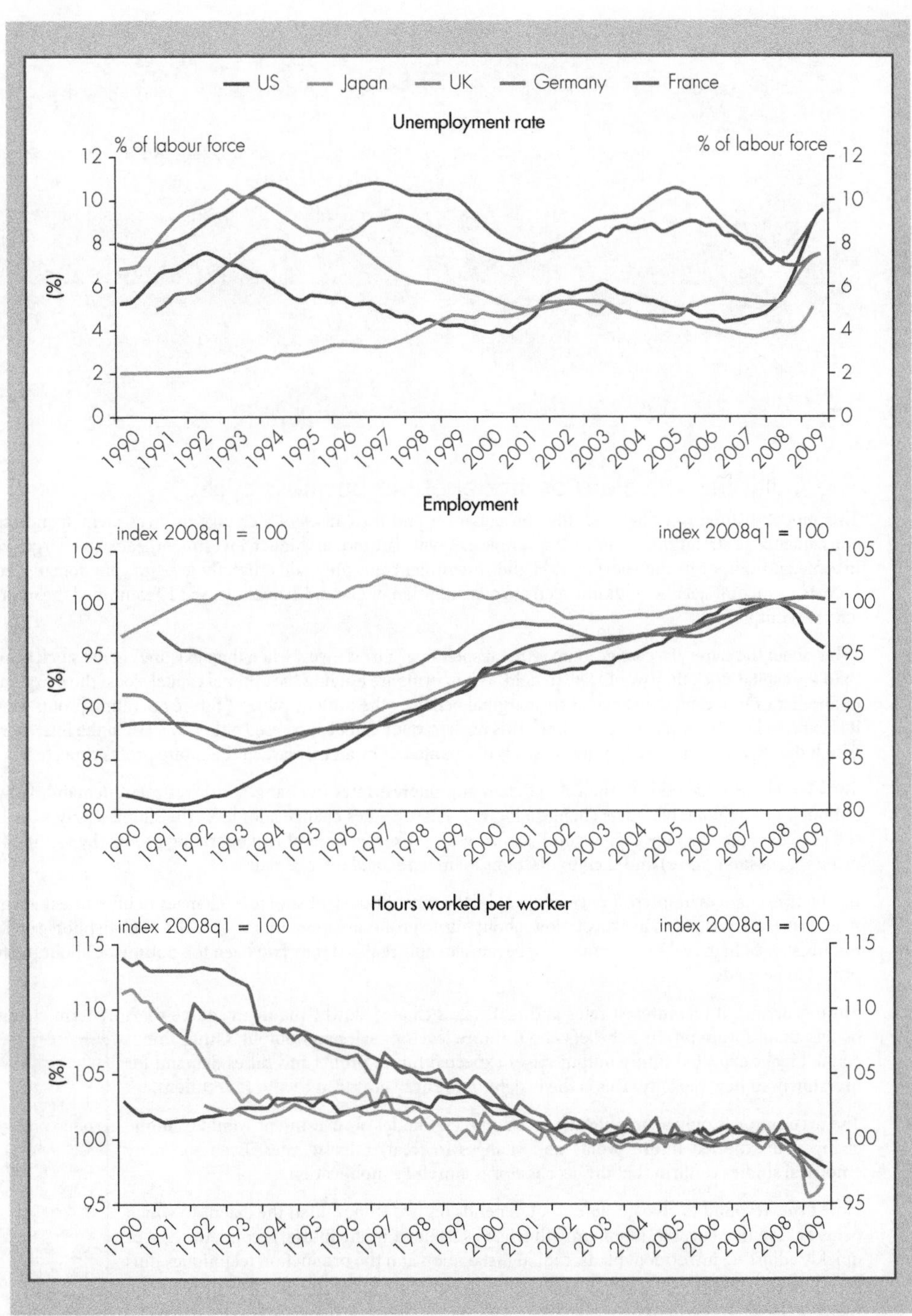
US
Japan
UK
Germany
France
Unemployment rate
% of labour force
% of labour force
(%)
Employment
index 2008q1 = 100
index 2008q1 = 100
(%)
Hours worked per worker
index 2008q1 = 100
index 2008q1 = 100
(%)

Questions

(a) If the labour demand curve does not shift, should lower employment be associated with higher or lower real wages?

(b) In which direction might labour demand curves shift during a recession? What would you then expect the correlation to be between changes in wages and changes in employment?

(c) Would it matter whether the recession was caused by an adverse demand shock or an adverse supply shock?

(d) When it is expensive to hire and fire workers, how are firms likely to react to a recession that is perceived as temporary?

(e) If firms then become pessimistic about the persistence of the recession, what is likely to happen to their demand for labour?

To check your answers to these questions, go to page 682.

The multiplier–accelerator model of the business cycle

This model distinguishes between the consequences and the causes of a change in investment spending. The consequence is straightforward. In the simplest Keynesian model, higher investment leads to a larger rise in income and output in the short run. Higher investment not only adds directly to aggregate demand but, by increasing incomes, it also adds indirectly to consumption demand. Chapters 16 and 17 examined the multiplier effect on output.

What about the cause of a change in investment spending? Firms invest when their existing capital stock is smaller than the capital stock they would like to hold. When firms are holding the optimal capital stock, the marginal cost of another unit of capital just equals its marginal benefit – the present value of future operating profits to which it is expected to give rise over its lifetime. This present value can be increased either by a fall in the interest rate at which the stream of expected future profits is discounted or by an increase in the future profits expected.

Thus far we have focused on the role of changing interest rates in changes in investment demand. However, although nominal interest rates change a lot, real interest rates change a lot less. The simplest way to calculate the present value of a new capital good is to assess the likely stream of *real* operating profits (by valuing future profits at *constant prices*) and then to discount them at the *real* interest rate.

In practice, changes in interest rates may *not* be the most important source of changes in investment spending. Almost certainly, changes in expectations about future profits are more important. The dotcom bubble collapsed not because of high real interest rates but because people realized they had been too optimistic about the future profits to be made.

More generally, if real interest rates and real wages change slowly, the main source of short-term changes in beliefs about future profits is beliefs about future levels of sales and output. Other things equal, higher expected future output raises expected future profits and raises demand for investment in new capacity. This is the insight of the **accelerator model of investment**.

The accelerator model of investment assumes that firms guess future output and profits by extrapolating past output growth. Constant output growth leads to a constant level of investment. It takes *accelerating* output growth to *raise* desired investment.

The accelerator is only a simplification. A complete model of investment would examine changes in expected future profits and changes in (real) interest rates. Even so, many empirical studies confirm that the accelerator is a useful simplification.

How firms respond to changes in output depends on two things: first, the extent to which firms believe that current output growth will be sustained in the future; second, the cost of quickly adjusting investment plans, capital installation and the production techniques thus embodied. The more costly it is to adjust *quickly*, the more firms spread investment over a longer period.

This simple multiplier–accelerator model can lead to a business cycle. In Table 27.1 we make two specific assumptions, although the argument holds much more generally. First, we assume that the value of the multiplier is 2. An extra unit of investment raises income and output by 2 units. Second, we assume that current investment responds to the growth in output *last* period. If last period's income grew by 2 units, we assume that firms raise current investment by 1 unit.

Table 27.1 The multiplier–accelerator model of the business cycle

Period	Change in last period's output $(Y_{t-1} - Y_{t-2})$	Investment I_t	Output Y_t
$t = 1$	0	10	100
$t = 2$	0	10	120
$t = 3$	20	20	140
$t = 4$	20	20	140
$t = 5$	0	10	120
$t = 6$	−20	0	100
$t = 7$	−20	0	100
$t = 8$	0	10	120
$t = 9$	20	20	140

In period 1, the economy is in equilibrium with output $Y_1 = 100$. Since output is constant, last period's output change was zero. Investment $I_1 = 10$, which we can think of as the investment needed to offset depreciation and keep the capital stock intact.

Suppose in period 2 that some component of aggregate demand rises by 20 units. Output increases from 100 to 120. Since we have assumed that a growth of 2 units in the previous period's output leads to a 1-unit increase in current investment, the table shows that in period 3 there is a 10-unit increase in investment in response to the 20-unit output increase during the previous period. Since the assumed value of the multiplier is 2, the 10-unit increase in investment in period 3 leads to a further increase of 20 units in output, which increases from 120 to 140.

In period 4 investment remains at 20 since the output growth in the previous period was 20. Thus output in period 4 remains at 140. But in period 5 investment reverts to its original level of 10, since there was no output growth in the previous period. This fall of 10 units in investment leads to a multiplied fall of 20 units in output in period 5. In turn, this induces a further fall of 10 units of investment in period 6 and a further fall of 20 units in output.

Since the rate of output change is not accelerating, investment in period 7 remains at its period 6 level. Output is stabilized at 100 in period 7. With no output change in the previous period, investment in period 8 returns to 10 units and the multiplier implies that output rises to 120. In period 9 the 20-unit increase in output in the previous period increases investment from 10 to 20 units and the cycle begins all over again.

The multiplier–accelerator model explains business cycles by the dynamic interaction of consumption and investment demand. The insight of the model is that it takes accelerating output growth to increase investment. Once output growth stabilizes, so does investment. In the following period, investment must fall, since output growth has been reduced. The economy moves into a period of recession, but once the rate of output fall stops accelerating, investment starts to pick up again.

This simple model is not the definitive model of a business cycle. If output keeps cycling, surely firms stop extrapolating past output growth to form assessments of future profits? Firms, like economists, recognize that there is a business cycle. The less investment decisions respond to the most recent change in past output, the less pronounced will be the cycle.

MATHS 27.1

THE MULTIPLIER–ACCELERATOR MODEL OF CYCLES

Suppose I denotes current investment, I_{-1} denotes investment in the previous period, Y denotes output and ΔY denotes $(Y - Y_{-1})$, the increase in output between last period and the current period. Output Y is related to current investment I by the multiplier $Y = I/(1 - c)$, where c is the marginal propensity to consume. Investment depends on output growth, so $I = a\,\Delta Y$. Hence,

$$I = a\,\Delta Y = [a/(1 - c)][I - I_{-1}]$$

Hence,

$$I = -\{a/[1 - c - a]\}I_{-1}$$

This equation is of the general form $I = bI_{-1}$. If b is a positive fraction, I is always smaller than the period before and gradually converges on zero. If b exceeds unity, I gets larger and larger for ever. Negative values of b imply I becomes negative every second period, either converging to zero or becoming ever larger. None of this generates things like business cycles.

Cycles emerge, however, with small changes to these formulae. Table 27.1 offers one example. Here is another. Suppose the consumption function depends not on current income but on previous period income so that $C = A + cY_{-1}$ and current investment depends on output growth in the previous period, so that $I = a[Y_{-1} - Y_{-2}]$. Since $Y = C + I$ in this simple economy,

$$Y = A + cY_{-1} + a[Y_{-1} - Y_{-2}] \quad (1)$$

If the economy is in long-run equilibrium, output is constant, the final term is zero, and equilibrium output Y^* is given by $Y^* = A/(1 - c)$. Using y to denote $Y - Y^*$, the deviation of output from its long-run level, we can subtract Y^* from both sides of equation (1) to yield

$$y = cy_{-1} + a[y_{-1} - y_{-2}] \quad (2)$$

Depending on the values of c and a, equation (2) can yield constant cycles, damped cycles that gradually get smaller and smaller or explosive cycles that get larger and larger. When $c = a$, we simply get

$$(y - y_{-1}) = -(y_{-1} - y_{-2})$$

so that positive and negative growth of similar size alternate for ever.

Ceilings and floors

The multiplier–accelerator model can generate cycles even without any physical limits on the extent of fluctuations. Cycles are even more likely when we recognize the limits imposed by supply and demand. Aggregate supply provides a *ceiling* in practice. Although it is possible temporarily to meet high aggregate demand by working overtime and running down stocks of finished goods, output cannot expand indefinitely.

This tends to slow down growth as the economy reaches a boom. Having overstretched itself, the economy has to bounce back off the ceiling and begin a downturn. Conversely, there is a *floor*, below which aggregate demand cannot fall. Gross investment (including replacement investment) cannot be negative unless, for the economy as a whole, machines are unbolted and shipped abroad for sale to foreigners. Falling investment is an important component of a downswing, but investment cannot fall indefinitely, whatever our model of investment behaviour.

Fluctuations in stockbuilding

Having examined investment in fixed capital, we now look at inventory investment in working capital. Firms hold stocks of goods despite the cost; namely, the interest payments on the funds tied up in producing the goods for which no revenue from sales has yet been received. What is the corresponding benefit of holding stocks? If output could be instantly and costlessly varied, it would always be possible to meet sales and demand by varying current production. Holding stocks makes sense because it is expensive to adjust production *quickly*. Output expansion may involve heavy overtime payments and costs of recruiting new workers. Cutting output may involve expensive redundancy payments. Holding stocks allows firms to meet short-term fluctuations in demand without incurring the expense of short-run fluctuations in output.

How do firms respond to a fall in aggregate demand? Since rapid output adjustment is expensive, in the short run firms undertake the adjustments that can be made more cheaply. They reduce hours of overtime and possibly even move on to short-time working. If demand has fallen substantially, this still leaves firms producing a larger output than they can sell. Firms build up stocks of unsold finished output.

If aggregate demand remains low, firms gradually reduce their workforce. Natural wastage occurs (departing workers are not replaced). It also becomes cheaper to sack some workers than to meet the interest payments on holding ever-larger volumes of stock. Once aggregate demand recovers, firms are still holding all the extra stocks built up during recession. Only by increasing output *more slowly* than the increase in aggregate demand can firms eventually sell off these stocks and get back to their long-run equilibrium position.

Costs of employment adjustment explain both the pattern of inventories over the business cycle and the pattern of labour productivity in Figure 27.2. Output per worker rises in a boom and falls in a slump. In other words, output adjusts more quickly than employment. This is what we expect, given the costs of adjusting employment rapidly.

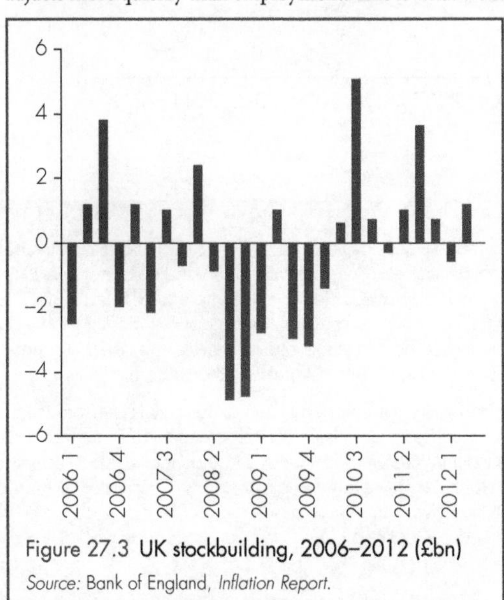

Figure 27.3 UK stockbuilding, 2006–2012 (£bn)

Source: Bank of England, *Inflation Report*.

A fall in demand is met initially by cutting hours and increasing stocks. With a shorter working week, there is a fall in output per worker. Only as the recession intensifies do firms undertake the costlier process of sacking workers and restoring hours to their normal level. Conversely, a boom is the time when output and overtime are high and productivity per worker peaks.

Figure 27.3 confirms this clearly in response to the fall in aggregate demand that began in 2008. During 2006–07, the level of stocks fluctuated from quarter to quarter without any particular trend. In the first quarter of 2008, aggregate demand fell and firms were left with unsold goods. Their stocks rose unexpectedly. Foreseeing that demand would be weak for some time, firms began to cut back production, reducing stocks of work in progress. When production had fallen more than demand, stocks of unsold finished goods also fell. Figure 27.3 shows substantial destocking during the rest of 2008 and early 2009. Once production had fallen more than demand, stocks started to increase again.

Competitiveness

Chapter 24 identified another potential mechanism that could generate cycles. An economy on a fixed exchange rate experiences a downward domestic demand shock. Interest rates, fixed at world levels to peg the exchange rate, cannot be used to restore aggregate demand.

Recession eventually bids down wages and prices, thus raising competitiveness and restoring internal balance by raising the demand for net exports. However this is not external balance, since net exports are now positive. With a current account surplus, the country gets richer, and additional wealth gradually boosts consumption demand. The economy now has a boom, which bids up prices and reduces competitiveness. Long-run equilibrium is restored when the current account falls back to zero.

This is a proper story about cycles. Output gaps induce changes in the price level that restore internal balance only by destroying external balance. This sets off a movement in the opposite direction that gradually reverses all these effects. Adjustment entails necessary overshooting of the final equilibrium.

CASE 27.1

EUROZONE BUSINESS CYCLES

EuroCOIN, the monthly coincident indicator of the Eurozone business cycle, is published by the Centre for Economic Policy Research based in London. The figure shows values of the indicator (in purple) and the quarterly growth rate of Eurozone GDP (in green) during 2003–12.

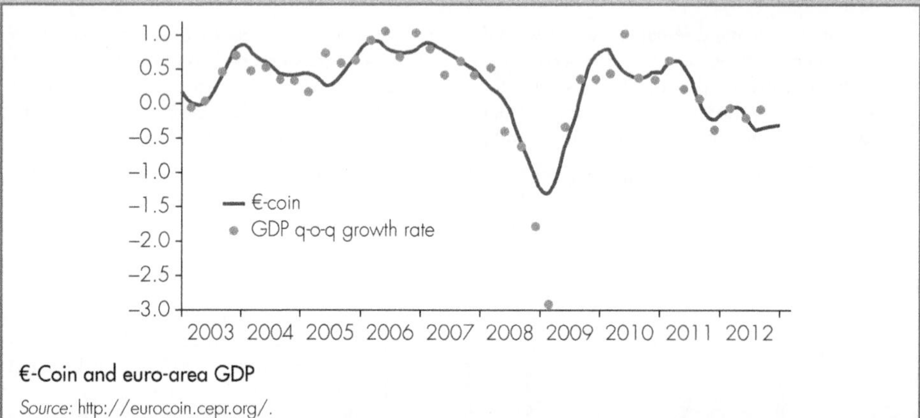

€-Coin and euro-area GDP

Source: http://eurocoin.cepr.org/.

Why not use changes in GDP itself to measure the business cycle? Mainly because initial estimates of GDP are unreliable and the data are often revised a lot as time elapses. The *EuroCOIN* indicator not only estimates the cyclical component of GDP more accurately but is also available monthly, whereas GDP estimates appear only quarterly. By examining past correlations of GDP growth with data that do appear monthly, the indicator provides a more frequent and more reliable picture of the Eurozone business cycle – helpful information for the monthly meetings of the European Central Bank at which interest rate decisions are made.

The figure shows that, like other independent central banks, the European Central Bank had been fairly successful up to 2007 in stabilizing output. There was not much of a business cycle. The monthly *EuroCOIN* indicator shows a slowdown beginning to happen even during 2007 and then rapidly during 2008. The indicator dates early 2009 as the cyclical bottom for output growth, even though the growth indicator did not climb above zero until later in 2009, and did not deliver two successive quarters of positive growth – the official definition of the end of the recession – until the end of 2009. By 2012 the Eurozone was back in recession.

Source: http://www.cepr.org/Data/eurocoin.

27.3 Real business cycles

Real business cycle theories explain cycles as fluctuations in potential output itself.

So far our analysis of business cycles focuses on demand shocks and cyclical movements in output gaps. This is compatible with our earlier analysis of sluggish wage adjustment in the short run. This view of cycles is consistent with a model that is Keynesian in the short run, but classical or monetarist in the long run.

Not all economists share our assessment of how the economy works. In particular, there is an influential school, known as the New Classical economists, whose intellectual leader is the Nobel Laureate Robert Lucas of the University of Chicago. A key assumption of the New Classical school is that all markets clear almost instantaneously. Effectively, output is almost always at its full-employment level.[1]

1 For an accessible introduction to these issues, see the lively exchange between Charles Plosser and Greg Mankiw, 'Real business cycles: A new Keynesian perspective', *Journal of Economic Perspectives* 3, no. 3 (1989): 79–90.

Proponents of the theory argue that macroeconomics should base theories of firms and households in a microeconomic analysis of choice between the present and the future. For example, this approach would view each household as making a plan to supply labour and demand goods both now and in the future in such a way that lifetime spending was financed out of lifetime income plus any initial assets. Such plans would then be aggregated to get total consumption spending and total labour supply. An equivalently complex story would apply to firms and investment.

One implication of this approach is that it is no longer helpful to distinguish between supply and demand. If labour supply and consumption demand are part of the same household decision, things that induce the household to change its consumption demand also induce it to change its labour supply.

For this reason, real business cycle theorists simply discuss what happens to actual output, which reflects both supply and demand and, by assumption, equates the two at potential output. In this view, the economy is then bombarded with shocks (for example, breakthroughs in technology, changes in government policy, changes in oil prices), which alter these complicated plans and give rise to equilibrium behaviour that looks like a business cycle.

Why is this approach called the *real* business cycle approach? In the classical model, nominal money only affects other nominal variables. Output and employment depend only on real variables. Since real business cycle theorists believe in the classical model, they take it for granted that the source of business cycles must be in real shocks. Fancy dynamics can then explain why shocks last and have convoluted effects.

Intertemporal substitution: a key to persistence

Real business cycle theories need to combine rapid market adjustment to equilibrium with sluggish behaviour of aggregate output over the business cycle. Intertemporal substitution means making trade-offs over time, postponing or bringing forward actions in the sophisticated long-run plans of households and firms. This behaviour can cause effects to persist and look like part of a business cycle.

Suppose the productivity genie visits while we are all asleep. When we wake up, our productivity has doubled, but only for a year. We know that by next year our productivity will have returned to normal. We face a temporary productivity shock, a blip in our technology. What should we do?

We are definitely wealthier after the genie's visit. We are pleased it happened. We could simply behave as before, working just as hard and investing just as much. In that case, our extra productivity would make extra output this year, but it is output that we would blow entirely on consumption this year. We would get little extra utility out of the hundredth bottle of champagne, and we would be making no provision for the future. There must be a better way.

We could put in a temporary spurt of extra work while we are super-productive, but in itself that would only exacerbate the problem: even more champagne today, still nothing extra for tomorrow. In fact, because leisure is a luxury and because we are better off than before, we may feel like taking it easy and doing less work.

We need a way of transferring some of our windfall benefit into future consumption. The solution is investment. A sharp rise in the share of output going to investment will provide more capital for the future, thereby allowing higher future consumption even after our productivity bonus has evaporated. Once we get to the future, being then richer than we would have been without the genie, we may in consequence work less hard than we would have done, since leisure is a luxury.

The point of this example is to show that even a temporary shock can have effects that persist well into the future. Persistence occurs both through investment (in human as well as physical capital) and through intertemporal labour substitution – deciding when in one's life to put in the effort.

Real business cycle theories continue to be developed fully. Apart from optimism about the speed of adjustment, they have been criticized on two grounds. First, they are usually theories of persistence not cycles. Shocks have long-drawn-out effects, but rarely are these cyclical. To 'explain' business cycles, so far real business cycle theorists have had to assume a cyclical pattern to the shocks themselves. The theory is therefore incomplete.

Second, and related, since the most widely researched example involves shocks to technology, a cyclical pattern of shocks implies that in some years technical knowledge actually diminishes: we forget how to do things. Not just once, but regularly every few years. This may be a bit hard to swallow.

However, this can be given a more plausible interpretation. In the dotcom bubble of the late 1990s, investors made extravagant projections about future productivity growth and associated profits from the new technologies. By 2000 evidence was accumulating that previous estimates, necessarily guesses in a new situation, were too optimistic. In 2001 investment collapsed, particularly in the US where dotcom optimism had been greatest.

Thus, the adverse shock was not a fall in existing technology – which is indeed implausible – but in estimates of future technology, which affects current behaviour since firms, households and governments all make long-term plans.

Policy implications

Research on real business cycles has one vital message for macroeconomic policy. If the theory is right, it destroys the case for trying to stabilize output over the business cycle. Fluctuations in output are fluctuations in an *equilibrium* output that efficiently reconciles people's desires.

For example, in the parable of the genie, the induced effects on investment, labour supply, output and consumption implement people's preferred way to take advantage of the beneficial opportunity. Trying to prevent these ripples is misguided policy.

Although important, this caveat undermines the case for stabilization policy only if we buy totally the assumptions of complete and instant market-clearing and the absence of any externalities. For most economists these assumptions are too extreme to reflect the real world, which continues to exhibit Keynesian features in the short run. Valid reasons for stabilization policy then remain.

Even so, real business cycle theories force us all to acknowledge that there is no reason why potential output should grow as smoothly as trend output. The latter is a statistical artefact whose construction, averaging, forces it to be smooth.

Credit constraints and aggregate supply

The financial crash provided a huge adverse shock to aggregate demand, as people watched their wealth evaporate. But it would be wrong to assume the crash had no direct effect on aggregate supply. Firms need to borrow to finance the costs of production before this output can be sold.

When banks became insolvent, or people feared that banks were close to being insolvent, this had two effects. First, banks had inadequate reserves to take their normal business risks. Second, banks and all other financial market participants suddenly raised their estimate of the likely riskiness of borrowers. The result, as we saw in Chapter 18, was that interest rate spreads became huge and banks stopped lending almost completely.

This meant that many businesses found it impossible to finance production and had to cut back. Aggregate supply fell, independently of what was happening to aggregate demand.

27.4 Supply-side effects of the financial crash

We began this chapter by exploring mechanisms through which we might generate cycles in aggregate demand. These include the multiplier–accelerator model, the effects of stockbuilding, the consequences of fixed exchange rates, political cycles in the policy stimulus, and simple effects of ceilings and floors. Within such frameworks, fluctuations in aggregate demand lead to similar fluctuations in output gaps, since the trend behaviour of potential output is unaffected.

Fluctuations in aggregate demand could be largely offset by an independent central bank with perfect foresight. Eliminating fluctuations in output gaps would eliminate a key source of inflationary pressure and help stabilize inflation. The fact that there is substantial evidence that business cycles were much less marked during 1995–2007, when independent central banks were explicitly asked to conduct this task, is prima facie evidence that demand fluctuations had been the most frequent source of business cycle fluctuations. Since central banks do not have perfect foresight, and since interest rate changes take time to affect aggregate demand, even excellent central banks could never have been expected to eliminate cycles completely.

Demand is very important, but not the whole story, for four reasons. First, real business cycle theories provide a healthy antidote to an exclusive focus on demand. Sometimes, supply-side factors will cause uneven growth of potential output, and may even reduce potential output for a while. Nobody promised that technological progress would occur at an even rate.

Second, hysteresis is important, especially for large shocks. Chapter 23 explored how temporary shocks to demand can have lingering, even permanent, effects on supply, through induced effects on the capital stock, skill base and union power. Third, credit rationing by banks and other lenders can directly curtail the ability of firms to finance production.

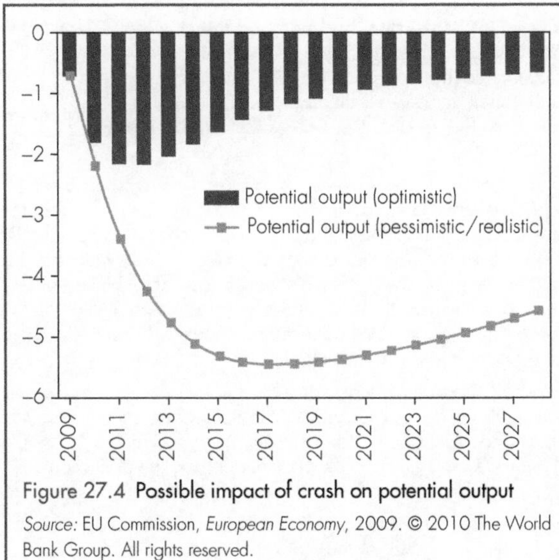

Figure 27.4 Possible impact of crash on potential output

Source: EU Commission, *European Economy*, 2009. © 2010 The World Bank Group. All rights reserved.

Research for the EU Commission has tried to model how large these effects might be.[2] Since we do not have enough evidence to give a definitive estimate, the Commission economists have produced an 'optimistic' and 'pessimistic' scenario, shown in Figure 27.4. In the optimistic scenario, the crisis leads to a fall in EU potential output by about 2 per cent in 2011, after which potential output gradually reverts to the path it would anyway have followed. However, even in the optimistic scenario, the financial crisis and subsequent recession is still casting a shadow on potential output as late as 2025. Since output cannot remain above potential output indefinitely, anything that reduces potential output for 15 years entails sacrificing considerable output cumulatively, even after the immediate crisis has been overcome.

In the pessimistic scenario, the induced effects on potential output are much, much larger and last much longer. Potential output gets worse until 2017 and is still 5 per cent worse than it would have been as late as 2025. From the perspective of a practical politician, this is as bad as a permanent reduction in potential output.

In order fully to understand business cycles, and hence to assess the consequences of the financial crash, we need to be quite sophisticated. Aggregate demand fluctuates (unless stabilized by monetary policy), but this should probably be superimposed on a path of potential output that is also capable of fluctuations. Although it is an empirical question which is larger, in normal circumstances the possible fluctuations in aggregate demand are probably more important.

In more extreme circumstances, and particularly where a financial crash is involved, aggregate supply is also capable of falling sharply for two reasons: the credit impact on the ability to finance production, and the various hysteresis effects that demand falls then induce as supply falls.

CONCEPT 27.1

DYNAMIC STOCHASTIC GENERAL EQUILIBRIUM MODELS

Now for a brief glimpse of the coal face, at which many of the top academic research economists spend their time. This approach seeks to integrate microeconomics and macroeconomics to produce a single theory of everything in macroeconomics. It begins with microeconomic descriptions of the preferences of individuals (their tastes over consumption and leisure), the technology available to firms (how combinations of inputs make output) and the institutions characterizing the economy (the solvency constraints on households, firms and governments, and the nature of the political process and policy making).

2 'Impact of the current economic and financial crisis on potential output', *European Economy*, Occasional Paper 49, June 2009.

By working with representative agents in each sector, it is possible to build up aggregate behaviour and hence *general equilibrium* in all markets simultaneously. By specifying the processes driving random shocks that hit tastes and technology, this becomes a random or *stochastic* model, in which agents form guesses about their likely futures. It is a *dynamic* model because the present and the future are connected. Consumers think about long-run income in making lifetime work and spending plans, governments and firms can also borrow to cover investments made today that generate future benefits.

These dynamic stochastic general equilibrium (DSGE) models essentially fall into two groups. The first are the real business cycle models we discussed earlier in the chapter, which focus on how real shocks (to tastes or technologies) generate short-run fluctuations within a framework of overall long-run growth. Real business cycle models have no role for stickiness of nominal prices or wages, and no role for benevolent government intervention to help the economy back to potential output. The second group of DSGE models are called New Keynesian models.

New Keynesians provide rigorous microeconomic foundations for macroeconomics with temporary price rigidity.

In earlier chapters, we developed Keynesian analysis from a series of plausible but ad hoc assumptions. The New Keynesian approach is a modern response to the claim that Keynesian economics is not properly grounded in serious microeconomics. The essential trick of New Keynesian economics is to take the DSGE model but to replace the assumption of price flexibility with the assumption that monopolistically competitive firms set prices that cannot be instantly and costlessly adjusted. This reintroduces nominal rigidities in the short run. The complicated DSGE model is then used to churn out the implications, which of course turn out to be very similar to the implications of the analysis we have adopted in the preceding chapters. In particular, demand fluctuations can generate short-run cycles. A stabilizing role for monetary policy is restored.

The elite end of the economics profession would like to show that their subject is just as scientific as physics or chemistry. Deriving behaviour from first principles is appealing, and stochastic dynamic general equilibrium models look rigorous. But there is a problem. Recall our distinction between micro and macro in Chapter 1. Our brains have chips that are too small to process everything all at once: that is why the distinction between micro and macro remains meaningful.

DSGE models appear to generate understandable solutions to complex problems, but do so largely by falling back on a different, but equally strong, simplification, that of the individual agent behaviour that is easily aggregated to describe total behaviour. Once the mix of individuals (or firms) becomes messy, it becomes impossible to aggregate easily. So DSGE models – whether real business cycle or New Keynesian – appear rigorous, but behaviour has been simplified in order to make it easily analysable within this complex setting. In that sense, it is just another shortcut, with no more (and no less) legitimacy than the shortcuts we have adopted to present the macroeconomic analysis of the previous chapters.

The ultimate test is which model policy makers used to guide their actions at the height of the financial crisis. They found insights from them all: the credit shocks of the real business cycle model, the nominal shocks in the New Keynesian framework. However, in a crisis, simple robust tools often work best. Those equipped only with the preceding macro chapters would have done just as well in understanding the evolving crisis as those seeking to interpret it through more elegant, but more complicated, DSGE models.

27.5 An international business cycle?

National politicians want all the credit when output is high but produce a cast-iron alibi when the economy turns sour. They say domestic difficulties were caused by a world recession. How good is their alibi?

Figure 27.5 plots data during 1996–2009 for the US, Japan, the UK, Germany, France and Italy. Although there were differences in the 1990s – for example, Japan continued to stagnate – it is striking how similar output growth has been across countries since 2000. Largely this reflects the fact that both the dotcom bust and the financial crisis were global events. In addition, independent central banks have pursued rather similar monetary policies, eliminating one important source of differences in national policy shocks.

These patterns warn us how interdependent the leading countries have become in the modern world. Economies are becoming more open. In product markets, protectionist policies are being removed, through global institutions like the World Trade Organization and through regional integration, as in the creation of a Single European Market.

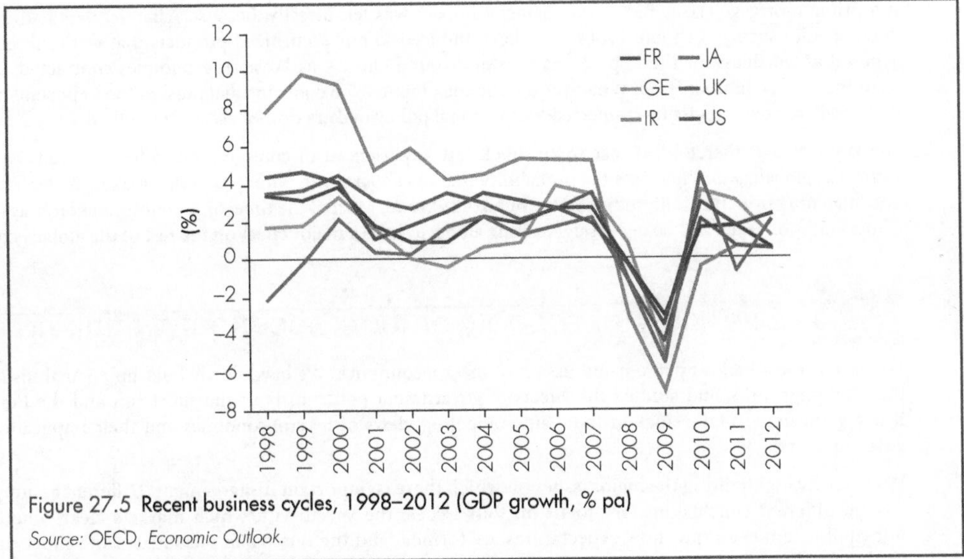

Figure 27.5 Recent business cycles, 1998–2012 (GDP growth, % pa)

Source: OECD, *Economic Outlook.*

Improvements in transport and telecommunications also favour greater integration of product markets. When R&D costs are large, producers need a global market if they are to recover their overheads. Product market integration provides an international transmission mechanism through exports and imports. Increasingly, we have a global financial market. Closer financial integration increases the likelihood that different countries pursue similar monetary policies.

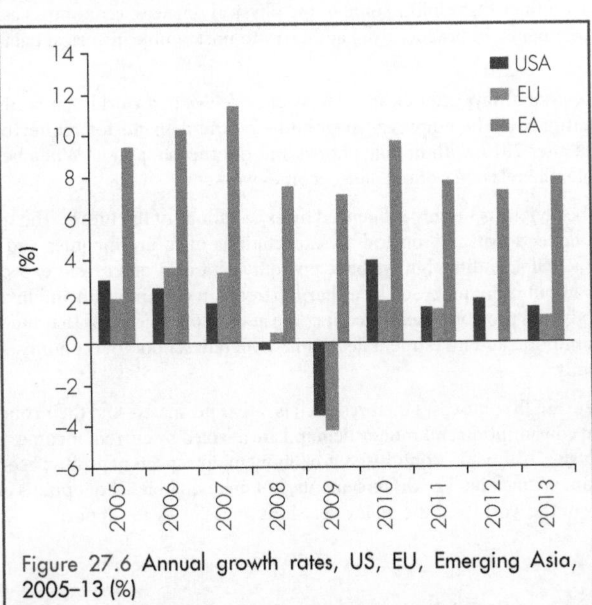

Figure 27.6 Annual growth rates, US, EU, Emerging Asia, 2005–13 (%)

Source: IMF, *World Economic Outlook*, 2012.

The business cycle is transmitted from one country to another not just through private sector decisions about imports and exports (and induced effects on labour supply, investment and consumption), but also, sometimes, through induced changes in the economic policy of other governments.

The considerable integration of advanced economies prompts a second question: are the leading emerging market economies, particularly China and India, on the way to similar integration with their longer-established partners? Figure 27.6 shows the most recent part of the answer. Prior to the crisis, Asian economies had been growing much more quickly as they caught up with the OECD. The cyclical pattern in response to the global crisis was very similar to OECD countries, albeit from a higher baseline rate of growth.

Chinese and Indian markets were not sheltered from the effects of the US sub-prime mortgage crisis. Either the financial impact was felt directly, because Asian lenders had invested in companies such as Lehman Brothers or been induced to buy securitized products that were subsequently exposed as worthless, or the impact was a second-round effect – as Western economies contracted, exports from India and China suffered. Whatever the channel, Figure 27.6 confirms that most of the important parts of the world are now sufficiently connected that national policy makers cannot escape unscathed.

The key message, therefore, is that some shocks are experienced in common, but others are not. For most countries, globalization increases the probability that the shocks with which its policy makers have to deal are not emanating from the domestic economy but from abroad. Most of the time, only countries as large as the US, China and soon India will be big enough, acting alone, to have a major effect on the rest of the global economy.

27.6 Overview of schools of macroeconomic thinking

We have come a long way in our discussion of macroeconomics. We have slowly built up an analysis of how the economy works, and studied the effects of government policy in both the short run and the long run. It is a good time to take stock of the main competing views of macroeconomics and their implications for government policy.

We begin by highlighting the major issues on which there is important disagreement. Different assumptions lead to different conclusions. We focus on four issues: the speed with which markets clear, whether or not equilibrium is unique, how expectations are formed, and the relative importance of the short run and the long run.

Against this background we then describe the four most prominent schools of macroeconomics in recent years. We encourage you to view these competing positions not as unrelated and contradictory beliefs, but as the outcome of adopting slightly different positions within the spectrum of possible views.

Areas of disagreement

Why do economists disagree at all? Surely, by looking carefully at the evidence we can say which views are correct and which are inconsistent with the facts? Unlike some of the physical sciences, economists can rarely undertake controlled laboratory experiments. In practice, we have to try to unscramble historical data to infer how the economy works.

Empirical research in economics does not always offer clear-cut answers. We live in a world that is constantly evolving. Even if we had a good estimate of the empirical magnitudes in the demand for money equation during 1950–70, would it be relevant after 2015, with mobile phones and Internet shopping? When behaviour is changing, although we get new data, the relevance of old data becomes weaker.

Taking a different example, current behaviour is heavily influenced by expectations of the future. The spending decisions of firms and households depend critically on today's expectations of future incomes and profits. Purchases and sales let us measure actual spending, but we have no equivalent data on current expectations. Suppose a sharp rise in income and output is *not* preceded by a sharp increase in consumption and investment spending: do we conclude that nobody had previously expected income and output to rise, or that the rise was foreseen but had little effect on consumption and investment decisions? Different schools of economists look at the same data but view them differently.

Empirical economists do the best they can. In some cases their research is rather persuasive and their conclusions are accepted. Few people dispute that consumption and money demand are affected by current income. In other cases, empirical research is less conclusive. Although economists agree about many aspects of positive economics, some disagreements inevitably remain. We pick out key disagreements, not mere quibbles about points of detail. They fundamentally affect one's view of the world and the policy decisions one is likely to support.

Market clearing

A market clears when desired supply equals desired demand. Whether, and if so, how quickly all markets clear is a key issue in macroeconomics. At the one extreme, the classical analysis assumes that all markets clear.

The economy is then at full employment and potential output. A monetary expansion will raise prices but not output, and a fiscal expansion will crowd out private consumption and investment until aggregate demand is restored to potential output. At the other extreme, Keynesian analysis assumes that markets, especially the labour market, do not clear. With imperfect wage flexibility, a fall in aggregate demand for goods and the demand for labour reduce output and employment. Expansionary fiscal and monetary policy can increase real output.

Do markets clear or not? Before Keynes's *General Theory*, most economists assumed that markets cleared and tried to explain periods of high unemployment within this framework. In the immediate post-war period, most economists assumed that markets did not clear continuously and interpreted macroeconomics within the Keynesian paradigm.

After 1970, the pendulum swung back again. Many economists argued that, if wage stickiness leads to involuntary unemployment, workers will find a way to make wages more flexible, avoiding involuntary unemployment. People said the Keynesian assumption of wage stickiness could not be given plausible microeconomic foundations. In the last two decades, the pendulum has been in motion again. New Keynesian economists have developed micro-foundations for wage stickiness, and fewer economists presume markets automatically clear.

The attempt by some economists to explain even short-run fluctuations with market-clearing models has spawned a new literature on what determines potential output and equilibrium unemployment, topics neglected when the focus of analysis was simply movements in aggregate demand. It is now generally accepted that movements in potential output may be significant, even in the short run. Whether they are the *only* source of short-run output fluctuations is essentially the same question as whether market clearing can be assumed, even in the short run.

Is long-run equilibrium unique?

Suppose an economy in long-run equilibrium then experiences a *temporary* shock which drives it to a different position in the short run. What happens once the shock disappears? Does the economy, sooner or later, go back to the original equilibrium or settle down in a new, *permanently different*, long-run equilibrium?

The latter case is *hysteresis*. Hysteresis exists when the path that an economy follows in the short run affects which long-run equilibrium it eventually reaches. There are then several possible equilibria in the long run. Chapter 23 discussed mechanisms that may give rise to hysteresis.

Whether hysteresis is quantitatively important is a controversial issue. If hysteresis matters, the easiest way to prevent its damaging effects is to prevent the economy from entering a recession in the first place. In contrast, economists who believe that hysteresis is unimportant take a more relaxed attitude to temporary recessions, which have no long-term consequences.

Expectations formation

Most economists accept that beliefs about the future affect behaviour today. Such beliefs certainly affect consumption and investment demand. Some disagreements between economists can be traced to different beliefs about how expectations are formed. For simplicity, we divide the possible approaches into three categories.

Exogenous expectations are determined outside the model and are an input to the analysis.

Exogenous expectations Some economists are agnostic on the vital question of how expectations are formed. They are treated as exogenous, or given, inputs to the analysis. The analysis shows *consequences* of a change in expectations – for example, a rise in expected future profits raises investment spending at each interest rate – but the analysis does not investigate the *cause* of the change in expectations. In particular, it is unrelated to other parts of the analysis. With given expectations, there is no automatic feedback from rising output to expectations of higher profits in the future.

At best, exogenous expectations give an incomplete account of how the economy works. At worst, they neglect some inevitable feedback from the variables they are analysing to the expectations that were an input to the analysis.

Extrapolative expectations A simple way to make expectations endogenous, or determined by what is going on elsewhere in the analysis, is to assume people forecast future profits by extrapolating the behaviour of profits in the recent past, or extrapolate past inflation in order to form expectations of inflation in the near future. Proponents of this approach suggest that it offers a simple rule of thumb and corresponds to what many people seem to do in the real world.

Extrapolative expectations assume that the future is an extension of the recent past.

Rational expectations guess the future correctly on average.

Rational expectations Suppose half the world oil supply is destroyed by a war. You could use simple economics (supply and demand) to guess that oil prices will jump up sharply. You should raise your forecast of oil prices immediately. If you merely extrapolate past growth of oil prices, you will keep mistakenly under-forecasting future oil prices. It is implausible to keep using a forecasting rule that makes the same mistake period after period.

Forecasting rules that systematically give too low a forecast or too high a forecast are not used. Any tendency for expectations to be systematically in error is quickly detected and put right. We live in a risky world where unforeseeable things are always happening. Expectations are fulfilled only rarely. Rational expectations make good use of information available today, and do not make forecasts that are already knowably wrong. Only genuinely unforeseeable things make present forecasts go wrong. Sometimes people under-predict; sometimes they over-predict. Any systematic tendency to do one or other gets noticed and the basis of expectations formation is amended until guesses are on average correct.

Short run and long run

Where policies have short-run benefits but long-run costs, or vice versa, different groups of economists may adopt differing value judgements about how these gains and losses should be traded off. In part, the differing policy prescriptions offered by different economists reflect differing judgements about the relative importance of the short run and the long run.

The more quickly one believes markets clear, the less scope there is for demand management in the short run and the greater the importance of supply-side policy to raise potential output in the long run. Conversely, the more one believes in the possibility of high levels of Keynesian unemployment in the short run, the more likely one is to judge that the short-run benefits of returning to full employment outweigh any tendency thus induced to reduce potential output in the long run. Similarly, the more one's horizon is short-run, the more plausible it becomes that expectations can be treated as exogenous. The more one wants to discuss the long run, the more important it is to model how expectations are changing over time. The more one believes in hysteresis, the more one must look after the short run to look after the long run.

Contemporary macroeconomic thought

Having identified four areas of disagreement, we now examine the major schools of contemporary macroeconomic thought.

New Classical macroeconomics

The analysis is *classical* because it assumes that wage and price flexibility restore the economy to its position of full employment and potential output. The analysis is *new* because it assumes that expectations adjustment, as well as wage and price adjustment, is almost instant. At best, monetary and fiscal policy affect the *composition* of full-employment aggregate demand. Its *level* is necessarily potential output. This being unique, hysteresis is unimportant.

New Classical macroeconomics is based on the twin principles of rapid market clearing and rational expectations.

Wage and price adjustment is almost instant. Whatever level of unemployment is observed is thus the natural rate of unemployment. Unemployment changes over time because microeconomic incentives alter the natural rate itself.

Because expectations are rational, the government cannot use fiscal and monetary policy systematically to fool people. Suppose the government switches to a more expansionary monetary policy. This tends to make prices rise, since the economy begins close to full employment. If the initial policy change was not foreseen, workers will not have foreseen the price rise. They have settled for too low a money wage. Firms temporarily have cheap labour and expand output. Unanticipated monetary expansion causes an unanticipated rise in output and employment, above their long-run levels.

But if everyone has rational expectations, people quickly catch on to what the government is doing. When wages are renegotiated, everyone knows the money supply is expanding and prices are rising. The next nominal wage settlement suitably reflects this and, in the absence of any further surprises, real wages are at their equilibrium level again.

It is only the fact that some variables, particularly nominal wages, must be set in advance that prevents continuous full employment and potential output. Variables set in advance are set at levels expected to produce full employment. Only unexpected developments make them temporarily inappropriate, allowing output and employment to depart temporarily from their natural rates. But the government cannot use fiscal and monetary policy to make prices unexpectedly high period after period, and thus cannot hold output systematically above potential output. Essentially, demand management through monetary and fiscal policy is completely impotent.

It only remains for the government to control the price level and to pursue supply-side policies to raise potential output. Supply-side policies include income tax cuts to increase the incentive to work. Tight monetary policy will keep inflation under control. Low government spending will prevent large government borrowing from bidding up interest rates and crowding out private investment.

Nor will tight fiscal and monetary policy cause Keynesian unemployment. Wages and prices adjust to restore aggregate demand to potential output. If a switch to tighter policy takes people by surprise, at worst it has only temporary effects on output and unemployment. As soon as wages are renegotiated, they adjust to restore full employment. Thus New Classical economists believe not merely that long-term trends but also short-run fluctuations have little to do with aggregate demand.

Real business cycle theorists belong to the same family as the New Classical macroeconomics, although their emphasis is a little different. Both believe in near-continuous market clearing and rational expectations. The New Classicals stress the effects of temporary surprises until expectations quickly catch up, thus developing a theory of fluctuations around potential output. Real business theorists take this a stage further and seek to explain all fluctuations as fluctuations in potential output itself.

Thus, the real business cycle approach is both more extreme and more general than that of New Classical macroeconomics. It is more extreme because its analysis neglects deviations from potential output even for a short time. Since changes in nominal money have no real effects in such a context, the cause of changes must be sought in shocks to real variables such as technical knowledge.

The approach is more general than that of New Classical macroeconomics because it concentrates all its powers of analysis on making explicit the microeconomic foundations for the intertemporal decisions of firms, households and governments. It is in decisions to amend intertemporal plans and reallocate them over time that real business cycle theorists believe they can explain how large movements in actual output and employment could be movements in equilibrium output and employment.

Gradualist monetarists

This school is associated with the Chicago professor, Milton Friedman (1912–2006). We use the term 'monetarist' to mean those economists espousing the classical doctrine that an increase in the money supply leads essentially to an increase in prices rather than to an increase in output. Thus, the New Classical economists believe in almost instant monetarism.

> Gradualist monetarists believe that full employment is restored within a few years, so the main effect of higher money is higher prices.

New Classical economists believe in only temporary departures from full employment as a result of unforeseeable shocks that cannot immediately be reflected in wages. **Gradualist monetarists** accept that restoration of full employment takes a little longer. Even so, they believe that within a *few* years wage and price adjustment *will* restore full employment. Like the New Classical economists, Gradualist monetarists do not believe that hysteresis matters. When the economy gets back to full employment after a temporary shock, it returns to the *same* long-run equilibrium in real terms.

The school believes in some of the arguments for wage rigidity presented in Chapter 23, but only for a short time. Different members of this school adopt different assumptions about expectations formation. Sluggish adjustment in expectations formation may provide an extra reason for slower adjustment back to full employment.

Gradualist monetarists believe that, in the short run, a fiscal or monetary stimulus *would* alter aggregate demand, output and employment, but that it is neither sensible nor desirable to undertake such policies. The short run must be subordinated to the interests of the long run.

Since wage and price adjustment take a few years to complete, expansionary monetary or fiscal policy can increase aggregate demand, output and employment in the short run. However, the Gradualists offer two reasons why policy should not be used in this way.

First, the economy will automatically return to full employment within a few years anyway. In the long run, trying to keep output above potential output leads only to inflation. Second, if instead the aim of policy is to react to shocks and reduce fluctuations around potential output, the policy may be counterproductive. By the time a shock is diagnosed and the necessary action taken, the economy may already be expanding on its own as wage and price adjustments begin to lead it back to full employment. Stabilization policy may exacerbate cycles not dampen them.

Since departures from full employment last a relatively short time, it is on the long-run classical analysis that the Gradualists place the most emphasis. The government's chief responsibility is to raise potential output through supply-side policies and the pursuit of price stability.

Moderate Keynesians

Broadly speaking, this group are short-run Keynesians and long-run monetarists.

Moderate Keynesians believe the economy will eventually return to full employment, but that this could take many years.

In the short run, a fall in aggregate demand can generate a significant recession. Although many economists in this group believe that expectations adjustment is also sluggish, some of them believe in rational expectations and hold that it is not systematic mistakes in expectations formation but sluggish wage and price adjustment that prevent rapid restoration of full employment. By sluggish we mean that they do not respond quickly to departures from potential output and equilibrium unemployment. Nominal wages may still change rapidly because of expected inflation.

Moderate Keynesians believe that recessions last a bit longer than the couple of years over which a Gradualist monetarist believes markets unaided can restore full employment. Hence, Moderate Keynesians draw a different judgement about the relative importance of the short run and the long run. Slower market adjustment reduces the danger that, by the time government has diagnosed the problem, the market is already fixing it. Slower adjustment also raises the need for stabilization policy. Thus Moderate Keynesians believe that the government should accept responsibility for stabilization policy in the short run.

Since Moderate Keynesians believe the economy will *eventually* return to full employment, they accept that persistent rapid monetary growth must eventually lead to inflation once the full employment position is reached. In the very long run, only supply-side policies can generate sustained economic growth by raising potential output. Thus many economists in this group argue that the government should not neglect two of the policy prescriptions of the monetarists. Supply-side policies are important in the long run; and, if high inflation reduces potential output, in the long run the average level of fiscal and monetary policy must be compatible with low inflation.

Moderate Keynesians see no conflict between this stance of policy in the long run and the recommendation that in the short run active stabilization policies should be undertaken. Credible policy makers can be active precisely because people trust that their actions will be temporary not permanent. If a current stimulus is reversed as soon as the crisis is over, it need not threaten price stability in the medium run.

New Keynesians

As explained in Concept 27.1 above, New Keynesians have tried to provide more rigorous micro-foundations for Keynesian analysis while espousing many of the tools (rational expectations, stochastic dynamic general equilibrium) that had been adopted by the New Classical and real business cycle attack on more primitive Keynesianism. As such, they belong in the Moderate Keynesian camp. They recognize the necessity of keeping track of aggregate demand as well as aggregate supply. But they continue to believe that many shocks have their origins (and solutions) in shifts in aggregate demand.

Extreme Keynesians

Extreme Keynesians believe markets do not clear, even in the long run.

Keynesian unemployment may persist indefinitely unless the government intervenes to boost aggregate demand. Extreme Keynesians reject the view that slumps can eventually restore full employment via downward pressure on wage growth and inflation.

Whereas hysteresis suggests that, once a recession has done its damage, supply has then been eliminated, so boosting demand no longer works, Extreme Keynesians believe that boosting aggregate demand through government policy will do the trick.

This case rests primarily on labour market rigidity. Real-wage rigidity causes excess supply in the labour market; that is, a pool of involuntarily unemployed workers that remains available at any time to be mopped up through demand expansion. Extreme Keynesians refer to this assumption of labour market inflexibility as the *real-wage hypothesis.*

Why can't all nominal variables fall, reducing inflation and allowing the central bank to reduce real interest rates, thereby eventually moving the economy to full employment? Extreme Keynesians have several answers.

First, it is impossible to co-ordinate the fall in wage growth and inflation. If all rates of wage growth could be cut together, no real wage need change. But in practice, some workers have to go first. Unless and until all other wage and price growth slows down, the first workers to reduce the growth of nominal wages also cut real wages. This may be sufficient to prevent the wage cut taking place, especially if each group of workers is very sensitive about its wages relative to other groups.

Second, the central bank can cut the nominal interest rate to zero but no further. Hence, if a recession is deep enough to induce negative inflation, it then raises real interest rates, exacerbating the recession further. Third, when times are tough and firms are losing money, they do not wish to invest, even at zero interest rates. Old Keynesians used to compare monetary policy to a string: you can pull tight on it in a boom, but pushing on it in a slump may have no effect. Thus, Extreme Keynesians stress the role of fiscal policy in getting the economy out of a serious recession.

Just as New Classical economists are optimists about both the speed of market clearing and the ability of people intelligently to form, and rapidly to adjust, expectations about the future, Extreme Keynesians are nearly as pessimistic about expectations as they are about market clearing. Keynes himself compared expectations to a beauty contest. The modern equivalent would be a TV game show where the competitor has to guess the answer most frequently chosen by the TV audience.

In such situations, what matters is not getting the right answer (which is how economists try to evaluate rational expectations): what matters is guessing what other people guess. Multiple equilibria may be common, which undermines the ease with which we can assume that people quickly adjust expectations to *the* right answer. Through Extreme Keynesian spectacles, co-ordination failures (externalities) occur as much in expectations as in wage-setting.

Summing up

We have set out the views of the competing schools of modern macroeconomics. In each case, we have sought to interpret their views against four basic assumptions: about market clearing, about expectations formation, about hysteresis and about the relative priority given to short run and long run. Table 27.2 summarizes our discussion.

We did not adjudicate between the competing views of macroeconomics, though we are probably in the Moderate Keynesian group of economists. Rather, we sought to develop a framework in which the differing positions can be interpreted. We have explained how changes in the basic assumptions, especially about the speed of adjustment, the time required for restoration of full employment and the possibility of hysteresis, allow this framework to reflect the views of the different schools of modern macroeconomics, and show why they reach differing policy recommendations.

Table 27.2 Schools of macroeconomic thought

Issue	New Classical	Gradualist Monetarist	Moderate Keynesian	Extreme Keynesian
Market clearing	Very fast	Quite fast	Quite slow	Very slow
Expectations Adjustment	Rapid	Slower	Fast or slow	Slow
Long run/short run	Little difference since adjust fast	Long run more important	Don't forget short run	Short run vital
Full employment	Always close	Never far away	Could be far away	Could stay away
Hysteresis	No problem	No problem	Might be problem	Problem
Demand management or supply side policy	Forget demand; supply side needed	Supply more important; avoid swings in demand	Demand matters too	Demand what counts

Summary

- The **trend path of output** is the long-run path after short-run fluctuations are ironed out. The **business cycle** describes fluctuations in output around this trend. Cycles last about five years but are not perfectly regular.
- A **political business cycle** arises from government manipulation of the economy to make things look good just before an election.
- **Persistence** requires either sluggish adjustment or intertemporal substitution. Persistence is necessary but not sufficient for cycles.
- The **multiplier–accelerator model** assumes investment depends on expected future profits, which reflect past output growth. The model delivers a cycle but assumes that firms are stupid: their expectations neglect the cycle implied by their own behaviour.
- Full capacity and the impossibility of negative gross investment provide **ceilings and floors** that limit the extent to which output can fluctuate.
- Fluctuations in **stockbuilding** are important in the business cycle. The need to restore stocks to original levels explains why output continues to differ from demand even during the recovery phase.
- **Real business cycles** are cycles in potential output itself. In such circumstances, it is not desirable for policy to dampen cycles.
- Some swings in potential output do occur, but many short-run fluctuations probably reflect Keynesian departures from potential output. Aggregate demand and aggregate supply both contribute to the business cycle.
- Increasing integration of world financial and product markets has made most countries heavily dependent on the wider world. Business cycles in the rich countries are closely correlated.
- There is much about which all economists agree. There are also differences of opinion, both in the positive economics of how the world actually works and in the normative economics of how the government should behave.

- Economic theories should be tested against the facts. In some cases, tests do not yield conclusive answers. Some variables, such as expectations, are unobservable. The world is also changing. It may be impossible to get enough data on the world as it is today to allow definitive empirical tests of competing theories.
- The major **schools of macroeconomic** thought can be viewed in relation to **four key issues**: the speed with which the labour market clears, how expectations are formed, the possibility of hysteresis and the relative importance of the short run and long run.
- **New Classical macroeconomists** assume market clearing is almost instant. Only predetermined contracts prevent continuous full employment. **Rational expectations** embody the best guess at the time about future values. Any foreseeable change is already built into these variables. Only pure surprises cause temporary departures from full employment until preset variables can be altered and full employment restored. With the economy near potential output, demand management is pointless. Government policy should minimize surprises. Surprises apart, movements in output reflect movements in potential output. Policy should pursue price stability and supply-side policies to raise potential output.
- **Real business cycle theorists** neglect even temporary departures from full market clearing. They argue that intertemporal decisions of households, firms and government can explain even short-term fluctuations as movements in potential output.
- **Gradualist monetarists** believe that restoration of potential output, though not instant, takes only a few years. Attempts at demand management may be counterproductive if the economy is already recovering by the time a recession is diagnosed. The government should not 'fine-tune' aggregate demand but concentrate on long-run policies to keep inflation down and promote supply-side policies to raise potential output.
- **Moderate Keynesians** believe automatic restoration of full employment can take many years but will happen eventually. Although demand management cannot raise output without limit, active stabilization policy is worth undertaking to prevent booms and slumps that could last several years and therefore are diagnosed relatively easily. In the long run, supply-side policies are still important, but eliminating big slumps is important if hysteresis has permanent effects on long-run equilibrium.
- **New Keynesians** provide microeconomic foundations for Keynesian macroeconomics, based principally on costs of changing prices and wages. Several channels for hysteresis have also been developed.
- **Extreme Keynesians** believe departures from full employment may be protracted. Keynesian unemployment does not make real wages fall, and may not even reduce inflation. Even if it does, aggregate demand may not respond to lower interest rates if pessimism is high. The first responsibility of government is not supply-side policies to raise potential output that is not attained anyway, but restoration output to potential output by expansionary fiscal and monetary policy, especially the former.

Review questions

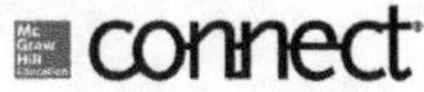

1 Would it help the world economy if all the largest countries elected governments on the same day? Why, or why not?

2 'If firms could forecast future output and profits accurately, there would not be a business cycle.' Is this true?

3 Heavily dependent on output of oil and fishing, Norway's business cycle goes the other way from that in other European countries. Why?

4 **Common fallacies** Why are these statements wrong? (a) Closer integration of national economies will abolish business cycles. (b) The more we expect cycles, the more we get them. (c) Because output and labour productivity are closely correlated, fluctuations in productivity are the main cause of business cycles.

EASY

5 Which of the following statements are correct? (a) Business cycles imply people do not expect fluctuations in the economy: if they could see a cycle coming, they would already be taking action to abolish it. (b) It is easy to explain why the economy's return to long-run equilibrium takes time, but it is not possible to explain why this return causes actual output to overshoot potential output. (c) Economic dynamics are slow and complicated. There are many models explaining the dynamics in the economy which cause business cycles.

MEDIUM

6 Why might voters care more about the direction in which the economy is heading than about the absolute level of its position at election time?

7 (a) Since central banks became independent, do you expect to see more or less evidence of a political business cycle? (b) Might there be an interest rate cycle instead? Why, or why not?

8 Suppose $Y = C + I$, $C = A + 0.6Y$ and $I = 0.1(\Delta Y)$. Does this economy converge to long-run equilibrium, explode away from long-run equilibrium or cycle forever?

9 If the multiplier–accelerator model still fits the data quite well, does this imply that people are stupid?

10 Greece, Spain, Portugal, Ireland and Italy have emerged as weak members of the Eurozone. Do you think this is because their business cycles are less correlated with France and Germany or because their political institutions are weak?

11 What do real business cycles explain?

HARD

12 Consider an economy with a fixed exchange rate. Beginning from internal and external balance, the economy experiences an adverse domestic demand shock that is not fully offset by a policy response. Draw a diagram to illustrate subsequent adjustment. Why does the requirement to get back to *both* internal and external balance generate a cyclical response?

13 Plot the data in the table below and confirm that both output and investment exhibit cyclical behaviour. Which is causing which?

The multiplier–accelerator model of the business cycle

Period	Change in last period's output $(Y_{t-1} - Y_{t-2})$	Investment I_t	Output Y_t
$t = 1$	0	10	100
$t = 2$	0	10	120
$t = 3$	20	20	140
$t = 4$	20	20	140
$t = 5$	0	10	120
$t = 6$	–20	0	100
$t = 7$	–20	0	100
$t = 8$	0	10	120
$t = 9$	20	20	140

14 **Essay question** 'The business cycle ought to last for different lengths of time depending on whether the original shocks were supply shocks or demand shocks.' Is this true?

For solutions to these questions, contact your lecturer.

CHAPTER 28

Supply-side economics and economic growth

Learning Outcomes

By the end of this chapter, you should be able to:

1 explain supply-side economics
2 understand growth in potential output
3 describe Malthus' forecast of eventual starvation
4 understand how technical progress and capital accumulation made the forecast wrong
5 describe the neoclassical model of economic growth
6 explain the convergence hypothesis
7 analyse the growth performance of rich and poor countries
8 understand whether policy can affect growth
9 understand whether growth must stop to save the environment

Much of Part Four has focused on the causes and consequences of changes in the demand for output and labour. We first introduced aggregate supply in Chapter 21. Sluggish adjustment of wages and prices induces a distinction between short-run supply and long-run supply. Chapters 21 and 27 discussed how the economy makes the transition from short run to long run.

This chapter is entirely about aggregate supply in the long run, and hence about the paths of potential output and equilibrium unemployment. We begin by analysing what actions can be taken to achieve a one-off increase in aggregate supply.

Most supply-side policies are microeconomic rather than macroeconomic. We have already referred to several, for example in Chapter 23 when discussing equilibrium unemployment. That chapter also introduced the concept of hysteresis, in which temporary macroeconomic phenomena have lasting supply-side effects. This is one case in which macroeconomics matters for aggregate supply. In this chapter, we pull together different strands to provide a comprehensive analysis of supply-side economics.

Supply-side economics analyses how to increase aggregate supply through better incentives or greater efficiency.

The longer the period that we analyse, the less important one-off changes become. In the very long run, *continuing* increases in output are much more important. The second part of the chapter analyses causes of *economic growth*, inducing increases in potential output year after year. Essentially, this requires the steady accumulation of something lasting – human capital, physical capital or technical knowledge – that provides each generation with a better inheritance than its predecessors.

28.1 Supply-side economics

We begin with one-off changes. It is useful to distinguish between those aiming to increase labour input, and those aiming to increase output per unit of labour input.

Higher labour input

Broadly, higher labour input falls into four categories: higher labour force participation, a higher fraction of the labour force accepting a job, longer hours worked on the job and more effort by workers while working. None can increase without limit – they are all sources of one-off effects.

In most advanced economies, labour force participation rates are high for men and have risen dramatically for women in the last 50 years. Governments would usually like participation to be even higher, both to boost potential output and to reduce the welfare bill that supports the old, the sick and those not bothering to look for work. However, it may also be important for young children to spend time with at least one parent. There are limits to efforts to raise labour force participation. Similar arguments apply to attempts to increase labour supply by raising the job acceptance rate or the number of hours worked.

Section 10.4 emphasized the need to consider both income and substitution effects when discussing how incentives affect both decisions to join the labour force and how many hours to work if a job offer is accepted. Higher take-home pay, relative to welfare benefits, makes working more attractive (the substitution effect) but also increases the demand for leisure (making working less attractive).

The wide range of other possible means-tested welfare benefits, from child support to housing subsidies, greatly complicates the analysis. Every government thinks it has found the secret of making work pay. In practice, they are often disappointed with the results of their policy interventions. It is difficult to be brutal and compassionate at the same time. Section 23.3 discusses in more detail the effects of welfare benefits and tax rates on decisions to join the labour force and to accept a job.

The interplay of substitution and income effects will often lead to disappointing small effects of attempts to increase incentives to work longer; the same conclusion applies to attempts to induce workers to contribute greater effort while at work.

Chapter 23 also introduced hysteresis. A temporary recession may cause capital to be scrapped, activities to be abandoned and workers to leave the labour force. Even once demand is restored, supply may be permanently reduced. Section 27.4 discussed recent estimates of the lasting adverse supply-side consequences of the financial crash and subsequent recession.

Increasing labour productivity

A second channel by which potential output can be increased is by increasing output per worker. Two important channels for increasing labour productivity are through technical progress and by providing more physical capital for each worker to use. These can be one-off or ongoing. The latter forms the basis of the long-run theory of economic growth, discussed later in the chapter.

The quantity of physical capital available depends in part on the willingness of the country to save rather than consume. The technology available depends on scientific discovery (both in universities and in research labs funded by companies or the government), converting invention to adoption through the practical process of innovation, having intellectual property laws that protect rewards for innovators, and the effectiveness of take-up of new ideas. Policies to stimulate saving and to promote research and development (R&D) can thus be viewed as supply-side policies.

However, there are many other ways in which productivity gains can be achieved. First, the human capital of each worker can be enhanced through investment in education and training. This should not be narrowly interpreted as the skills acquired at work, but much more broadly as including literacy, numeracy, IT familiarity and having acquired a work ethic. Societies that bring up young workers to have these attributes have higher productivity than those which do not.

Work and organizational practices may also have significant effects. When Japanese car companies built factories in the UK, their productivity was significantly higher than that in UK-owned factories. This was not simply because the Japanese invested in better capital for automating car production. They also organized factories differently: workers and management ate together, quality circles allowed workers' ideas for improvement to feed quickly into production improvements and the newly hired UK workforce had incentives aligned with those of the company. There were no vested interests to oppose change in order to defend people's own jobs. Social, organizational and cultural capital can sometimes be as important as physical capital.

More generally, even when it is known that a more efficient production solution exists, some particular group may lose out and have an incentive to oppose that change. Some societies are better than others at coping with change. Generally, those that change more quickly are at one end of the spectrum – either largely free market, in which case the losers from change cannot successfully oppose it, or largely centralized, in which case the powerful centre can force through change despite opposition from potential losers. The United States is close to the former, China to the latter.

Societies in the middle – such as the social democratic models of Western Europe – often create governments insufficiently powerful to force through change, while having sufficiently powerful market participants (trade unions, cartels) that can block changes not in their own interest. Europe's high level of productivity is well explained by its high levels of education and inherited capital stock. For several decades, it has not been particularly successful at increasing productivity.

Failing to allow unsuccessful companies to die inhibits 'natural selection' in which the strong do better and the weak are weeded out. Enhancing competition may have a similar effect. Yet unfettered competition and unregulated markets are not always the answer. Just think of the damage done by lightly regulated bankers, largely operating in their own self-interest, whose actions led directly to the financial crash with huge and ongoing costs for the world economy.

The right amount of regulation, effectively enforced, is desirable but hard to achieve in practice. Governments, afraid of the political consequences of high tax rates, often underfund regulatory agencies. In contrast, large companies have every incentive to invest in learning how to circumvent existing regulations.

Beginning from a heavily regulated economy, deregulation may achieve greater competition and efficient gains from natural selection. Beyond some point, further deregulation adversely affects the supply side by leading to opportunistic behaviour that is not in the general interest. Knowing exactly where to draw the line is difficult.

Summing up

Everyone wants to improve the supply side. In reality, supply-side improvement is difficult. Even a one-off increase in potential output, if truly permanent, is a considerable achievement. All of the examples above have been tried, sometimes successfully and sometimes with disappointing results. Supply-side policies are often controversial, since they usually have sharp implications for redistribution. Cutting welfare benefits may encourage incentives to work, but some people think that there are limits to how far a civilized society should proceed in this direction. Clamping down on the behaviour of private firms may prevent excesses but also risks stifling the innovation that drives productivity growth.

We now turn from the analysis of one-off changes in potential output to the analysis of continuing growth in potential output.

28.2 Economic growth: preliminary remarks

Figure 28.1 shows data on 13 OECD countries. In 1870, per capita real GDP (in 2011 US dollars) ranged from \$500–3000. By 2011, it ranged from \$18 000 to over \$30 000 per person. On average, we are richer than our grandparents, but less rich than our grandchildren will be. Figure 28.1 prompts three questions. What is long-run economic growth? What causes it? And can economic policies affect it? We focus mainly on industrial countries that have grown a lot already.

Economists are fascinated by the theory of economic growth. In 1798 Thomas Malthus' *First Essay on Population* focused on the consequence of diminishing marginal productivity. As more and more labour became available, output would increase more slowly than employment, reducing output per person, thus causing starvation. An end to population growth and output growth would be the eventual result – the origin of economics as the 'dismal science'. Some countries are still stuck in a Malthusian trap; others broke through to sustained growth and prosperity. We examine how they did so.

As Figure 28.1 implies, an extra 0.5 per cent on the annual growth rate makes a vast difference to potential output after a few decades. By the end of the 1960s, economists had worked out a theory of economic growth. It

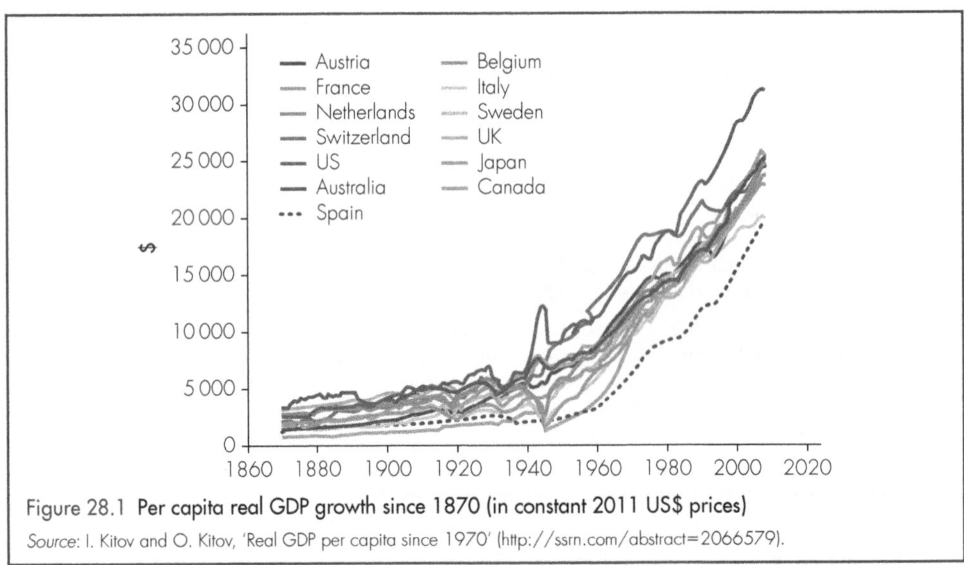

Figure 28.1 **Per capita real GDP growth since 1870 (in constant 2011 US$ prices)**

Source: I. Kitov and O. Kitov, 'Real GDP per capita since 1970' (http://ssrn.com/abstract=2066579).

yielded many insights but had one central failing. It predicted that government policy made no difference to the long-run growth rate.

In the mid-1980s, a simple insight spawned a new approach in which long-run growth is affected by private behaviour and government policy. We briefly explain this new approach to **economic growth**.

Economic growth is the rate of change of real income or real output.

Finally, we consider whether growth is good. Might it be better to grow more slowly? Can the costs of growth outweigh its benefits?

The growth rate of a variable is its percentage rise per annum. To define economic growth, we must specify both the variable to measure and the period over which to measure it. Figure 28.1 used real GDP per head. We get similar results using per capita real GNP.

GDP and GNP measure the total output and total income of an economy. But they are very incomplete measures of *economic* output and income.

GDP and economic output

GDP measures the net output or value added in an economy by measuring goods and services bought with money. It omits output not bought and sold and therefore unmeasured. Two big omissions are leisure and externalities such as pollution or congestion.

In most industrial countries, average hours of work have fallen at least ten hours a week since 1900. In choosing to work fewer hours, people reveal that the extra leisure is worth at least as much as the extra goods that could have been bought by working longer. When people swap washing machines for extra leisure, recorded GDP falls. GDP understates the true economic output of the economy. Conversely, the output of pollution reduces the net economic welfare that the economy is producing, and ideally should be subtracted from GDP.

Including leisure in GDP would have raised recorded GDP in both 1870 and 2011. Since the value of leisure probably rose less quickly than measured output, which rose 11-fold in the UK and 100-fold in Japan, a more comprehensive output measure might show a slower growth rate.

Conversely, pollution and congestion have increased rapidly. Allowing for them would also reduce true growth rates below those shown in Figure 28.1. A measure of true economic output each year would have to allow for environmental depreciation – everything from the true cost of global warming to the reduction in genetic diversity and the loss of amenities as grasslands are replaced with urban sprawl.

New products

In 1870 people had no TVs, cars or mobile phones. Statisticians do their best to compare the value of real GDP in different years, but new products make it hard to compare across time. We can estimate how much people's real income rises when a new product does an old task more cheaply. The calculation is harder when the new product allows a new activity not previously possible. A small amount of what we think of as inflation probably reflects real price increases justified by better quality or completely new products.

GDP and happiness

Even with an accurate and comprehensive measure of GDP, two problems remain. First, do we care about total GDP or GDP per capita? This depends on the question we wish to ask. Total GDP shows the size of an economy. However, if we care about the welfare of a typical individual in an economy, it is better to look at GDP per capita. Real GDP grew more quickly in Australia than in France or Sweden during 1870–2011; however, in part this reflected rapid population growth, largely through immigration. Sweden and France had faster growth in GDP per person over the period.

Real GDP per person is an imperfect indicator of the happiness of a typical citizen. When income is shared equally between citizens, a country's per capita real GDP tells us what every person gets. But some countries have very unequal income distributions. A few people earn a lot, and a lot of people earn only a little. Such countries may have fairly high per capita real income but many citizens still live in poverty.

Even when GDP is adjusted to measure leisure, pollution and so on, higher per capita GDP need not lead to greater happiness. Material goods are not everything. But they help. Movements in which people return to 'the simple life' have not had much success. Most of the poorer countries are trying to increase their GDP as quickly as possible.

A recent phenomenon

Figure 28.1 has one more implication. An annual growth rate of only 1.3 per cent in per capita GDP led to a 5.5-fold rise in UK per capita real GDP between 1870 and 2011. In 1870 UK per capita income was about £1900, measured in sterling and using 2000 prices. If its annual growth rate had always been 1.3 per cent, per capita real income would have been £370 in 1750, £75 in 1630 and £16 in 1510. This is implausible. It is only in the last 250 years that per capita real income has risen steadily.

In the long run, output fluctuations around potential output are swamped by the growth of potential output itself. If potential output rises 2 per cent a year, it will increase seven-fold in less than a century. To explain growth, we must think about changes in potential output.

28.3 Growth: an overview

The production function shows the maximum output obtainable from specified quantities of inputs, given the existing technical knowledge.

For simplicity, we assume that the economy is always at potential output. The **production function** tells us that higher potential output can be traced to more inputs of land, labour, capital and raw materials, or to technical advances that let given inputs make more output.

In the long run, population growth may be affected by per capita output, which affects the number of children people decide to have, and the health care and nutrition people then get. Nevertheless, we simplify by assuming that the rate of population growth is independent of economic factors. Anything that raises output then also raises per capita output.

Capital

Productive capital is the stock of machinery, buildings and inventories which, with other inputs, combine to make output. For a given labour input, more capital raises output. However, capital depreciates over time. Some new investment is needed just to stop the existing capital stock from shrinking. And with a growing labour force, even more investment is needed if capital per worker is to be maintained. With yet faster investment, capital per worker rises over time, increasing the output each worker can produce. Higher capital per worker is a key means of raising output per worker and per capita income.

Labour

Over a few decades, employment can rise because labour force participation is increasing or because equilibrium unemployment is falling. However, over a longer period, these one-off changes account for less and less of the total change in employment and output. However, sustained population growth is a candidate for a cause of continuing expansion of employment.

Human capital

Human capital is the skill and knowledge embodied in the minds and hands of workers. Education, training and experience allow workers to make more output. For example, much of Germany's physical capital was devastated during the Second World War but the human capital of its labour force survived. Given these skills, Germany recovered rapidly after 1945. Without its human capital, there would have been no post-war German economic miracle.

Human capital can be accumulated over time and across generations. The young can absorb quickly the lessons learned more painfully by their forebears, enhancing their productivity as workers. Human capital is a candidate for a source of ongoing growth.

Land

Land is especially important in an agricultural economy. If each worker has more land, agricultural output is higher. Land is less important in highly industrialized economies. Hong Kong and Singapore have grown rapidly despite overcrowding and a scarcity of land. Even so, more land would help.

Increases in the supply of land are pretty unimportant to growth. In theory, land is the input whose total supply to the economy is fixed. In practice, the distinction between land and capital is blurred. By applying more fertilizer per acre, the effective quantity of farming land can be increased. With investment in drainage or irrigation, marshes and deserts can be made productive. Dubai built superstar homes, hotels, and even a new airport, on land reclaimed from the sea. Increases in the supply of land are pretty unimportant to sustained growth.

Raw materials

Given the quantity of other inputs, more input of raw materials allows more output. When raw materials are scarce and expensive, workers take time and care not to waste them. With more plentiful raw materials, workers work more quickly.

When a barrel of oil has been extracted from the ground and used to fuel a machine, the world has one less barrel of oil reserves – it is a **depletable resource**. If the world has a finite stock of oil reserves, it will eventually run out of oil, though perhaps not for centuries.

> Depletable resources can be used only once.

In contrast, timber and fish, if harvested in moderation, are replaced by nature and can be used as production inputs for ever – they are **renewable resources**. However, if over-harvested they become extinct. With only a few whales left, whales find it hard to find partners with whom to breed. The stock of whales falls.

> Renewable resources can be used again if not overexploited.

Factor contributions and scale economies

The marginal product of a factor is extra output when that input rises by a unit but all other inputs are held constant. Microeconomics tells us that marginal products eventually decline as the input increases. With two workers already on each machine, another worker does little to raise output.

Instead of increasing an input in isolation, suppose all inputs are doubled together. If output exactly doubles, there are *constant returns to scale*; if output more (less) than doubles, there are *increasing (decreasing) returns to scale*.

Scale economies reinforce growth. Any rise in inputs gets an extra bonus in higher output. There may be engineering reasons for scale economies. Simple mathematics shows that it takes less than twice the steel input to build an oil tanker of twice the capacity. On the other hand, many developing countries regret that their resources are tied up in huge steel mills that are now inefficient. Bigger is not always better. In practice, economists often assume constant returns to scale.

Having discussed the different production inputs, we turn now to the role of technical knowledge.

28.4 Technical knowledge

At any given time, a society has a stock of technical knowledge about ways in which goods can be produced. Some of this knowledge is written down in books and blueprints, but much is reflected in working practices learned by hard experience.

Invention and innovation

> Technical advances in productivity come through invention, the discovery of new knowledge, and innovation, the incorporation of new knowledge into production techniques.

Major **inventions** can lead to spectacular increases in technical knowledge. The wheel, the steam engine and the modern computer are examples. Technical progress in agriculture has also been dramatic. Industrial societies began only when productivity improvements in agriculture freed some of the workforce to produce industrial goods without leaving people short of food. Before then, everyone had to work the land merely to get enough food to survive. The replacement of animal power by machines, the development of fertilizer, drainage and irrigation, and new hybrid seeds, all played a large part in improving agricultural production and enabling economic growth.

To introduce new ideas to actual production, **innovation** often requires investment in new machines. Without investment, bullocks cannot be transformed into tractors even once the know-how for building tractors is available. Major new inventions thus lead to waves of investment and innovation as the ideas are put into practice. The mid-nineteenth century was the age of the train and the mid-twentieth century the age of the car. We are now in the age of the microchip.

Human capital can matter as much as physical capital. With practice, workers get better at doing a particular job. The most famous example is known as the Horndal effect, after a Swedish steelworks built during 1835–36 and kept in the same condition for the next 15 years. With no change in the plant or the size of the labour force, output per worker-hour nevertheless rose by 2 per cent a year. Eventually, however, as skills become mastered, further productivity increases are harder to attain.

CASE 28.1

GROWTH AND COMPETITION

For centuries, per capita income growth was tiny. Most people were close to starvation. Now we take growth for granted. After 1750, industrialization changed everything. Capital and knowledge, accumulated by one generation, were inherited and augmented by the next generation. Why 1750? Mathematical and scientific ideas reached a critical mass, allowing an explosion of practical spin-offs. Yet many pioneers of the industrial revolution were commonsense artisans with little scientific training. Conversely, the ancient Greece of Pythagoras and Archimedes achieved scientific learning but not economic prosperity.

By the start of the fifteenth century, China understood hydraulic engineering, artificial fertilizers and veterinary medicine. It had blast furnaces in 200 BC, 1500 years before Europe. It had paper 1000 years before

Europe, and invented printing 400 years before Gutenberg. Yet by 1600 China had been overtaken by Western Europe, and by 1800 had been left far behind.

Economic historians continue to debate the root causes of progress, but three ingredients seem crucial: values, politics and economic institutions. Growth entails a willingness to embrace change. China's rulers liked social order, stability and isolation from foreign ideas: fine attitudes when progress was slow and domestic but a disaster when the world experienced a profusion of new technologies and applications.

Powerful Chinese rulers could enforce bans and block change in their huge empire. When individual European rulers tried to do the same, competition between small European states undermined this sovereignty and offered opportunities for growth and change. Economic competition helped separate markets from political control. Rights of merchants led to laws of contract, patent, company law and property. Competition between forms of institution allowed more effective solutions to emerge and evolve. Arbitrary intervention by heads of state was reduced. Opportunities for business, trade, invention and innovation flourished.

The making of Western Europe

Date	Per capita income (1990 prices)	Inventions
1000	400	Watermill
1100	430	Padded horse collar
1200	480	Windmill
1300	510	Compass
1400	600	Blast furnace
1500	660	Gutenberg printing press
1600	780	Telescope
1700	880	Pendulum clock, canals
1800	1280	Steam engine, spinning and weaving machines, cast iron, electric battery
1900	3400	Telegraph, telephone, electric light, wireless
2000	17 400	Steel, cars, planes, computers, nuclear energy

Source: adapted from *The Economist*, 31 December 1999.

Research and development

What determines the amount of invention and innovation? Some new ideas are the product of intellectual curiosity or frustration ('There must be a better way to do this!'). But, like most activities, the output of new ideas depends to a large extent on the resources devoted to looking for them, which in turn depends on the cost of tying up resources in this way and the prospective benefits from success. Some research activities take place in university departments, usually funded at least in part by the government, but a lot of research is privately funded through the money firms devote to R&D.

The outcome of research is risky. Research workers never know whether or not they will find anything useful. Research is like a risky investment project. The funds are committed before the benefits (if any) start to accrue, but there is one important difference. Suppose you spend a lot of money developing a better mousetrap. When you succeed, everyone copies your new mousetrap: the price is bid down, and you never recoup your initial investment. In such a world, there would be little incentive to undertake R&D.

If the invention becomes widely available, society gets the benefit but the original developer does not: there is an *externality*. Private and social gains do not coincide and the price mechanism does not provide the correct incentives. Society tries to get round this *market failure* in two ways. First, it grants *patents* to private inventors and innovators – legal monopolies for a fixed period of time that allow successful research projects to repay investments in R&D by temporarily charging higher prices than the cost of production alone. Second, the government subsidizes a good deal of basic research in universities, in its own laboratories and in private industry.

28.5 Growth and accumulation

In this section we explore the links between output growth, factor accumulation and technical progress. We organize our discussion around a simple production function:

$$Y = A \times f(K, L) \qquad (1)$$

Variable inputs capital K and labour L combine to produce a given output $f(K, L)$. The function f tells us how much we get out of particular amounts of inputs K and L. This function f never changes. We capture technical progress separately through A, which measures the extent of technical knowledge at any date. As technical progress takes place, we get more output from given inputs: a rise in A. For simplicity, we assume that land is fixed.

Malthus, land and population

Writing in 1798 and living in a largely agricultural society, Malthus worried about the fixed supply of land. As a growing population worked a fixed supply of land, the marginal product of labour would fall. Agricultural output would grow less quickly than population. The per capita food supply would fall until starvation reduced the population to the level that could be fed from the given supply of agricultural land.

In terms of equation (1), starving people consume all their income. Without savings, society cannot invest in capital, so K is zero. The production function then has diminishing returns to labour: adding more workers drives down productivity. Figure 28.2 illustrates.

Some poor countries today face this *Malthusian trap*. Agricultural productivity is so low that everyone must work the land to produce food. As the population grows and agricultural output fails to keep pace, famine sets in and people die. If better fertilizers or irrigation improve agricultural output, the population quickly expands as nutrition improves, and people are driven back to starvation levels again.

Yet Malthus' prediction was not correct for all countries. Today's rich countries broke out of the Malthusian trap. How did they do it? First, they raised agricultural productivity (without an immediate population increase) so that some workers could be switched to industrial production. The capital goods then produced included better ploughs; machinery to pump water and drain fields; and transport to distribute food more effectively. As capital was applied in agriculture, output per worker rose further, releasing more workers to industry while maintaining enough food production to feed the growing population.

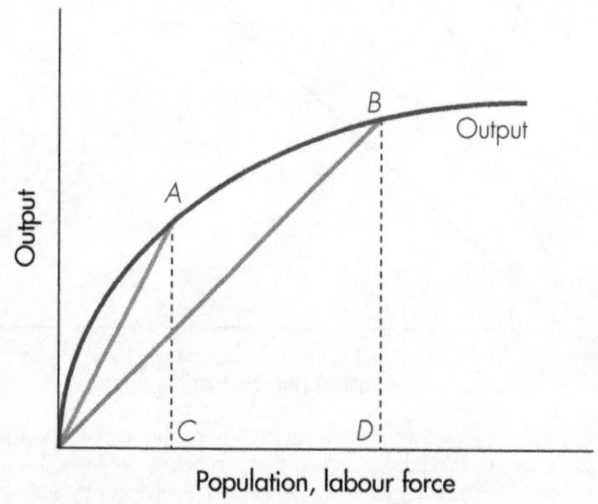

Second, the rapid technical progress in agricultural production led to large and persistent productivity increases, reinforcing the effect of moving to more capital-intensive agricultural production. In terms of equation (1), rises in A and in K let output grow faster than labour, causing a *rise* in living standards.

Thus, even the existence of a factor in fixed supply need not make sustained growth impossible. If capital can be accumulated, more and more capital can be substituted for fixed land, allowing output to grow at least as rapidly as population. Similarly, continuing technical progress allows continuing output growth even if one factor is not increasing.

The price mechanism provides the correct incentives for these processes to occur. With a given supply of land, higher agricultural production raises the price of land and the rental paid for land. This provides an incentive to switch to less land-intensive production methods (heavy fertilizer usage, battery chickens)

Output

B

Output

A

C

D

Population, labour force

The labour force grows with population, but there are diminishing returns to output. At labour force C, output is AC and output per head is given by the slope of OA. At population D, output is higher at DB but output per head has fallen from the slope OA to the slope OB. When output per head falls to starvation levels growth cannot continue.

Figure 28.2 The Malthusian trap

and an incentive to focus on technical progress that lets the economy get by with less land. A similar argument applies to any natural resource in finite supply.

Capital accumulation

Post-war theories of economic growth date back to work in the 1940s. In the late 1950s, Bob Solow of MIT assembled the nuts and bolts of neoclassical growth theory – the basis of empirical work ever since.[1]

The theory is *neoclassical* because it does not ask how actual output gets to potential output. Over a long enough period, the only question of interest is what is happening to potential output itself. Neoclassical growth theory simply assumes that actual and potential output are equal.

Along the steady-state path, output, capital and labour grow at the same rate. Hence output per worker and capital per worker are constant.

In this long run, labour and capital grow. Usually, equilibrium means that things are not changing. Now we apply equilibrium not to levels but to growth rates and ratios. The **steady state** is the long-run equilibrium in growth theory.

Assume that labour grows at a constant rate n. To keep things simple, we also assume a constant fraction s of income is saved; the rest is consumed. Aggregate capital formation (public and private) is the part of output not consumed (by both public and private sectors). Investment first **widens** and then perhaps **deepens** capital.

In a growing economy, capital widening extends the existing capital per worker to new extra workers.

Capital deepening raises capital per worker for all workers.

To keep capital per person constant, we need more investment per person the faster is population growth n (extra workers for whom capital must be provided), and the more capital per person k that has to be provided. Figure 28.3 plots the line nk along which capital per person is constant. Any investment above this line implies capital deepening is taking place, whereas below this line capital per person must be falling.

Adding more capital per worker k increases output per worker y, but with diminishing returns: hence the curve y in Figure 28.3. Since a constant amount of output is saved, sy shows the saving per person. Since saving and investment are equal, it also shows investment per person.

In the steady state, capital per person is constant. Hence investment per person sy must equal nk, the investment per person needed to keep k constant by making capital grow as fast as labour. k^* is the steady-state capital per person and y^* the steady-state output per person. Capital, output and labour all grow at the same rate n along this steady-state path.

Figure 28.3 also shows what happens away from the steady state. If capital per worker is low, the economy is left of the steady state. Per capita saving and investment sy exceed nk, the per capita investment required to keep capital in line with growing labour. So capital per person rises. Conversely, to the right of

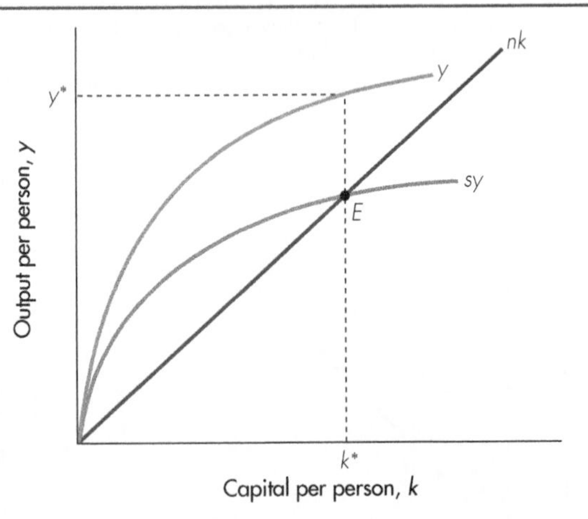

The line nk shows the investment per person that maintains capital per person while labour grows. y shows output per person, and sy is both saving and investment per person. At the steady state E, investment is just sufficient to keep capital per person constant at k^*. Per capita output is then y^*. Output and capital grow with population.

Figure 28.3 Neoclassical growth

1 Solow won a Nobel Prize for his work on long-run growth. He is also famous for his one-liners. Since, in short-run analysis, he is an unrepentant Keynesian, many of his famous barbs are aimed at those who believe that prices clear markets quickly: 'Will the olive, unassisted, always settle half way up the martini?'

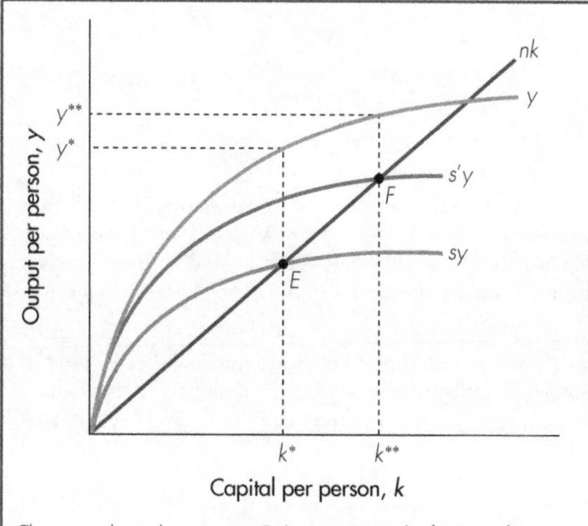

The original steady state is at E. An increase in the fraction of income saved, from s to s', leads to a steady state at F. This raises capital and output per worker, but eventually has no effect on the growth rate. Since y^{**} is constant, output and labour still grow at rate n.

Figure 28.4 A higher saving rate

the steady state, sy lies below nk and capital per person falls. Figure 28.3 shows that, from whatever level of capital the economy begins, it gradually converges to the (unique) steady state.

We could augment Figure 28.3 by also recognizing that capital depreciates over time, becoming less and less productive. Suppose the rate of depreciation is δ. In order to preserve the amount of capital per worker when the labour force is growing but inherited capital is depreciating, it now takes investment per worker of $(n + \delta)k$. Hence, to recognize depreciation, in Figure 28.3 we could replace the orange line nk by a steeper line $(n + \delta)k$. This will intersects sk at a lower level of capital per person k^*, implying also a lower level of output per person y^*. Faster depreciation increases the cost of keeping capital, and reduces steady state living standards.

A higher saving rate

Suppose people permanently increase the fraction of income saved, from s to s'. We get more saving, more investment and hence a faster rate of output growth. Oh no, we don't! Figure 28.4 explains why not.

There is no change in the production function relating output to inputs. At the original saving rate s, the steady state is at E. At the higher saving rate, $s'y$ shows saving and investment per person. At F it equals nk, the per capita investment needed to stop k rising or falling. Thus F is the new steady state.

F has more capital per worker than E. Productivity and output per worker are higher. That is the permanent effect of a higher saving rate. It affects levels, not growth rates. In *any* steady state, L, K and Y all grow at the same rate n, and that rate is determined 'outside the model': it is the rate of growth of labour and population. We return to this issue shortly.

In Figure 28.4 the higher saving rate raises output and capital per worker. To make the transition from E to F, there must be a temporary period in which capital grows faster than labour; only then can capital per worker rise as required. A higher saving rate, if successfully translated into higher investment to keep the economy at full employment, causes faster output growth for a while, but not for ever. Once capital per worker rises sufficiently, higher rates of saving and investment go entirely in capital widening, which is now more demanding than before. Further capital deepening, the basis of productivity growth, cannot continue without bound.

MATHS 28.1

NEOCLASSICAL GROWTH THEORY

Output per head is $f(k)$. With a constant saving rate s, saving per head is $sf(k)$.

In a simple economy with no government or foreign sector, at full capacity this must equal investment per head, which comprises replacement investment per head nk and capital deepening that adds to k. If $\dot{k}$ denotes the rate of change of k,

$$\dot{k} + nk = sf(k) \qquad (1)$$

In the steady state k^*, the growth of k is zero, hence $nk^* = sf(k^*)$. Elsewhere,

$$\dot{k} = sf(k) - nk \tag{2}$$

Thus,

$$\dot{k} > 0 \quad \text{if} \quad f(k)/k > n/s \qquad \text{and} \qquad \dot{k} < 0 \quad \text{if} \quad f(k)/k < n/s$$

With diminishing returns to adding extra units of k, $f(k)$ increases less quickly than k itself. Hence, for $k > k^*$ it must be the case that $f(k)/k$ is less than n/s. Conversely, for $k < k^*$, $f(k)/k$ must exceed n/s. Thus, capital deepening is positive whenever k is less than its steady-state value k^*, and is negative whenever k exceeds its steady-state value k^*, confirming that the neoclassical economy converges to its unique steady state whatever level of k it begins with.

In this steady state, $nk^* = sf(k^*)$. Hence, for given n, an exogenous increase in the saving rate s must increase $k^*/f(k^*)$. Because the function $f(k)$ has diminishing returns to increasing k, it requires a higher value of k^* to increase $k^*/f(k^*)$ when s increases. Higher saving leads to a rise in the steady-state level of capital per head.

28.6 Growth through technical progress

We have made a lot of progress, but still have some problems. First, the theory does not fit *all* the facts. So far, the theory says output, labour and capital all grow at rate n. Although capital and output do grow at similar rates, in practice both grow more rapidly than labour. That is why we are better off than our great-grandparents.

Labour-augmenting technical progress increases the effective labour supply.

The answer may lie in technical progress, which we ignored in trying to explain output growth entirely through growth in factor supplies (population growth and the accumulation of capital). **Labour-augmenting technical progress** provides the answer.

Population growth might eventually double the number of workers. Imagine instead that the number of workers is constant but that new knowledge allows the same workers to do the work of twice as many as before, as if the population had grown.

Suppose this progress occurs at rate t. Effective labour input grows at rate $(t + n)$ because of technical progress and population growth. Figure 28.5 resembles Figure 28.3 but replaces actual workers with worker-equivalents. To make this valid, we have to measure capital and output not per worker but per worker-equivalent. Worker-equivalents are created by population growth or technical progress. Otherwise the diagram is identical. Thus, investment at the rate $(t + n)k$ is now needed to ensure that capital per worker-equivalent remains constant.

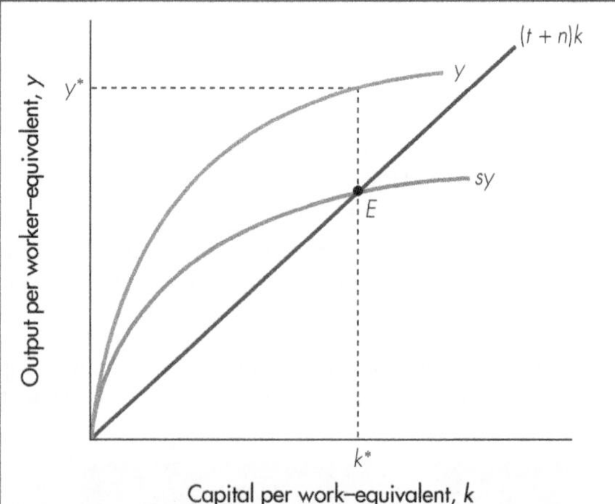

The line $(t + n)k$ shows the investment per worke–equivalent to maintain capital per worker–equivalent when effective labour input grows, sy shows saving (and thus investment) per worker–equivalent. At the steady state E, investment is just sufficient to keep capital per worker–equilent constant at k^*. Output per worker–equivalent is constant at y^*. Output and worker–equivalents grow at the rate $(t + n)$, but actual people grow only at the rate n. Hence, output per actual person grows at the rate t.

Figure 28.5 **Neoclassical growth with technical progress**

E remains the steady state. Output per worker-equivalent and capital per worker-equivalent are constant. Since worker-equivalents grow at rate $t + n$, so must capital and output. Since actual workers increase at rate n, output and capital per actual worker each increase at rate t. Now our growth theory fits all the facts. Living standards grow over time at rate t.

It is uncomfortable that the two key growth rates, n and t, are determined outside the model. For that reason, for the next 30 years the main use of this growth theory was in growth accounting: showing how to decompose actual output behaviour into the parts explained by changes in various inputs and the part residually explained by technical progress. We next examine the results of accounting for growth.

28.7 Growth in the OECD

The Organization for Economic Cooperation and Development is a club of the world's richest countries, from industrial giants like the US and Japan to smaller economies like New Zealand, Ireland and Turkey. Table 28.1 shows productivity growth of selected OECD countries since 1950.

Table 28.1 Average annual growth in real output per person employed (%)

	OECD	Japan	Germany	Italy	France	Sweden	UK	US
1950–73	3.6	8.0	5.6	5.8	4.5	3.4	3.6	2.2
1973–90	1.4	2.9	2.3	2.4	2.8	1.6	1.8	0.4
1990–2007	1.5	1.2	2.4	1.1	1.4	2.1	1.6	1.6
2008–11	0.5	0.0	−0.2	−0.7	0.0	0.5	−0.6	1.4

Sources: S. Dowrick and D. Nguyen, 'OECD comparative economic growth 1950–85', *American Economic Review* 79 (1989): 1010–1030; OECD, *Economic Outlook*.

During the post-war boom years 1950–73, productivity grew strongly in a climate of rapid trade expansion, investment and recovery. These happy days ended in 1973 in all OECD countries. Several explanations were put forward. Some stressed the rise in trade union power, resulting in their enjoying greater legal protection in the 1970s. If this explanation had been correct, the supply-side reforms of the late 1980s and 1990s should have led to high productivity growth in the 1990s. They did not.

The first OPEC oil price shock, when real oil prices quadrupled, also occurred in 1973. This had two effects. First, it diverted R&D to long-term efforts to find alternative energy-saving technologies. These efforts take decades to pay off and raise actual productivity. Second, higher energy prices made much of the capital stock economically obsolete overnight. Energy-guzzling factories were closed. The world lost part of its capital stock, which reduced output per head. In practice, scrapping took a long time, and was given renewed impetus by another sharp rise in oil prices in 1980/81. That is why its effects were drawn out over such a long period, lasting for much of the 1980s.

ACTIVITY 28.1

ABORTED TAKE-OFFS ON THE GROWTH RUNWAY

We assume people save a constant fraction s of their income. Even poor people earning only y save sy and consume $(1 - s)y$. But if y is low enough, $(1 - s)y$ is too low to stop starvation. So they consume all their income and save none. Below a critical income level y_0, saving is zero. What does the Solow diagram look like now? Look at the diagram below. Suppose k_0 is the capital per person that just generates the critical income y_0. Higher capital generates saving as in previous diagrams, and nk is still the gross investment needed to maintain a given capital–labour ratio in the face of a growing population. There are now three steady states!

If capital begins above k_1, the economy converges to the steady state at E. Between k_1 and k_2, saving and investment exceed the amount needed for capital-widening; capital-deepening also occurs and the economy grows. Above k_2, saving and investment are insufficient to maintain the capital–labour ratio, and the economy shrinks. Either way, it ends at E. This is the case analysed in Figures 28.2 and 28.3. Suppose, next, the economy begins at exactly k_1. Saving and investment just maintain the capital–labour ratio. So this is a steady state, but an unstable one. A little above k_1 the economy begins converging on E. And below k_1 there is insufficient saving and investment to provide for the growing population. Capital per person shrinks and keeps shrinking until the economy reaches $k = 0$.

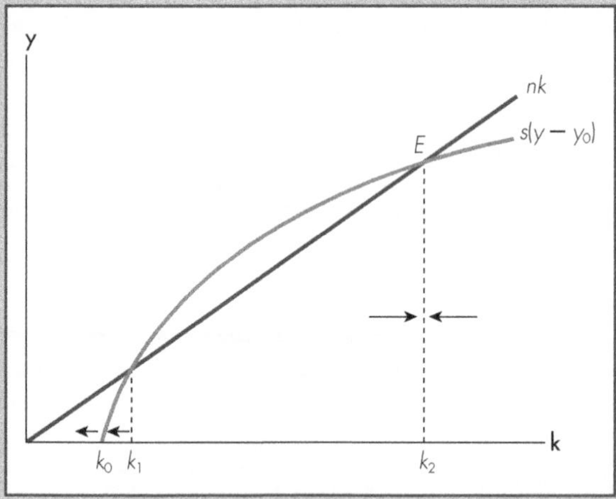

In this model, countries beginning with capital below k_1 are stuck in a poverty trap. They cannot break out. All output is consumed to prevent starvation. There is never a surplus to begin accumulation and growth. This model can also explain why convergence seems to occur within the OECD (countries already above k_1), but why simultaneously many countries are stuck in poverty. Modern growth in the last two centuries began when some key events first generated the surplus to allow saving and accumulation to begin.

Questions

(a) Why is there no poverty trap when saving is proportional to income?

(b) When a poverty trap exists, is the payoff to overseas aid from rich countries greater if it is concentrated on helping poor countries break out of the poverty trap?

(c) The poverty trap shown above is based on there being a minimum level of per capita consumption. Could we get a poverty trap based on different population growth rates above and below some critical threshold of living standards? Is this plausible?

To check your answers to these questions, go to page 682.

Neither the Internet boom nor supply-side reforms restored the productivity growth rates that the rich countries enjoyed prior to 1973. Emerging market economies, such as China, India, Brazil and Russia, are now where the action is. We turn to their story in Part Five. For rich mature economies, Table 28.1 confirms that underlying productivity growth showed a very modest improvement after 1990, until it was dramatically interrupted by recession after the financial crash.

Why was productivity growth low or negative during 2008–11? OECD countries did not mysteriously forget the skills they had learned over previous decades, nor did their capital explode. Table 28.1 is alerting us to a short-term effect, the normal fluctuation of productivity with output over the business cycles, discussed in the previous chapter. If normal output growth is resumed, we expect to see productivity growth return to normal levels again.

Having discussed differences in growth across periods, we now examine differences across countries. The one sheds light on the other. The fact that OECD countries move together across sub-periods shows that many aspects of growth are outside a country's own control. Technical progress diffuses across countries quite quickly, wherever it originates. Countries are increasingly dependent on the same global economy.

Even so, growth rates differ markedly across countries. Can growth theory explain why? First, it suggests that, if countries have access to the same technology, differences in output growth should reflect differences in labour force growth. Table 28.1 provides some degree of corroborating evidence: differences in per capita output growth are less marked than differences in output growth.

Second, we need to know how long it takes to get to the steady state, a question to which Figures 28.3 and 28.5 provide no direct answer. Is output growth over two or three decades an adjustment *towards* the steady state or can we assume that an economy has reached it within that time?

The convergence hypothesis

The convergence hypothesis asserts that poor countries grow more quickly than average and rich countries grow more slowly than average.

Figures 28.3 and 28.5 have a unique steady state at *E*. Whatever the level of capital per worker with which an economy begins, the economy eventually converges to *E*. Poor countries with low initial capital grow extra rapidly until they reach the steady-state growth rate of output and capital; rich countries with a very high inheritance of capital grow at below-average rates until capital per worker falls back to its steady-state level k^*.

When capital per worker is low, it does not take much investment to equip new workers with capital (capital-widening), so the rest of investment can go on raising capital per worker (capital-deepening). When capital per worker is already high, it takes a lot of saving and investment just to maintain capital-widening, let alone to deepen capital. This is one reason for the convergence hypothesis.

This explanation for convergence relies purely on the effect of capital accumulation. A second explanation for convergence or 'catch-up' operates through a different channel. Technical progress no longer falls out of the sky at a fixed rate. Suppose instead we have to invest real resources (universities, research labs, R&D) in trying to make technical improvements. It is rich countries that have the human and physical capital to undertake these activities, and it is in rich countries that technical progress is made. However, once discovered, new ideas are soon disseminated to other countries.

Since poorer countries do not have to use their own resources to make technical breakthroughs, they can devote their scarce investment resources to other uses, such as building machines. By slipstreaming richer countries, they can temporarily grow faster.

CASE 28.2

DOES CONVERGENCE OCCUR IN PRACTICE?

The table below shows World Bank estimates of per capita income in 1987, 2008 and the ratio of 2008 to 1987. East Asian economies such as China and South Korea grew very quickly during the last 30 years. India (not shown below) is also now growing strongly. Yet convergence cannot be a powerful force in the world or the very poorest countries would all be growing very rapidly. In reality, many poor countries stay poor and sometimes even decline in absolute terms.

Within the rich OECD countries, convergence is much more reliable. The richest OECD countries tend to grow less quickly than the poorer OECD countries.

Why did the East Asian 'tigers' grow so quickly in the post-war period? What was their secret? Professor Alwyn Young[2] of MIT has shown that there is little mystery about their rapid growth, even though they did sustain dramatic rates. These economies managed rapid growth in measured inputs – labour (via increases in participation rates), capital (via high saving and investment rates) and human capital (via substantial expenditure on education). Once we allow for the rapid growth of these inputs, Young showed that the growth of output in the tigers was not very different from what standard estimates, based on OECD and Latin American countries, would have led us to expect.

Generally, growth seems to be fostered by two conditions: absence of internal strife and openness to the world economy. Once China put insularity and the Cultural Revolution behind it, the potential for catching up was enormous. India had less internal strife, but took off only after it embraced the world economy and relaxed its more bureaucratic controls. Civil war held back Nigeria despite its oil wealth. Indeed, there is considerable evidence that mineral-rich countries without a long tradition of stable government suffer disproportionate incidence of civil war – fighting for the spoils – to the detriment of economic growth and higher living standards.

2 A. Young, 'The tyranny of numbers: Confronting the statistical realities of the East Asian growth experience, *Quarterly Journal of Economics* 110 (1995): 641–680.

Note finally that Switzerland, with much the highest living standard, has one of the slowest rates of growth of per capita GNP. The Swiss are rich today because they were rich yesterday, a secret that they discovered long ago.

Per capita GNP (2012 US$000s)

	Initially, in 1987	1987	2010	Ratio: 2010/1987
Bangladesh	Poor	0.41	0.64	1.6
Nigeria	Poor	0.57	1.18	2.1
China	Poor	0.48	4.26	9.0
Indonesia	Poor	1.06	2.58	2.4
Turkey	Middle income	4.46	9.50	2.1
South Korea	Middle income	8.46	19.90	2.4
Portugal	Middle income	13.48	21.90	1.6
Spain	Rich	20.16	31.70	1.6
Ireland	Rich	20.74	41.00	2.0
Italy	Rich	29.65	35.10	1.2
UK	Rich	28.84	38.50	1.3
France	Rich	36.85	42.38	1.1
US	Rich	40.64	47.10	1.2
Switzerland	Rich	62.72	70.40	1.1

Source: World Bank, *World Development Report*, various issues.

The figure opposite plots the final column, the ratio of per capita income in 2010 relative to 1987, on the horizontal axis, and on the vertical axis plots 1987 per capita income in ten-thousands of US dollars, obtained by dividing the third column of the table by ten in order to keep the two scales comparable. The figure conveys two messages. First, on average richer countries grow more slowly. Second, individual country performance can depart significantly from this underlying relationship.

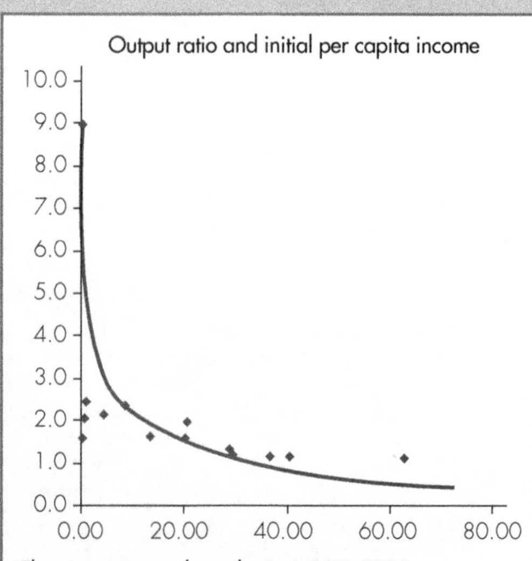

The convergence hypothesis, 1987–2010

Note: Vertical axis = ratio of 1987 to 2010 per capita income, $000 at 2012 prices; horizontal axis = 1987 per capita income at 2012 prices.

Source: World Bank, *World Development Report*, various issues.

With this understanding, what should we expect for the next 40 years, long after the consequences of the financial crash have worked themselves out? Global consultancy PricewaterhouseCoopers (PwC) makes brave projections for the future, based largely on the framework we have set out. It estimates population growth, the evolution of skills and human capital, investment in physical capital, and rates of technical progress and its dissemination across countries. From this information, it makes estimates of future growth in GDP.

The *World in 2050* chart, drawn from PwC's 2008 report, refers to the projected evolution of aggregate GDP. Who will be the economic superpowers in 2050? At present, US GDP significantly exceeds that of the second-largest economy, Japan. By 2025, China will have overhauled the US, and by 2050 will have a significant economic lead. With its much larger population, catch-up in productivity is all that is required. With an aged population, Japan will fail to keep up: old people consume but do not produce, and so attract resources away from investment and accumulation. After a slower beginning, India becomes the most exciting story of all. With the fastest population growth and the second-largest population to start with, India should start to narrow the gap on China and will overtake the US eventually, but not before 2050.

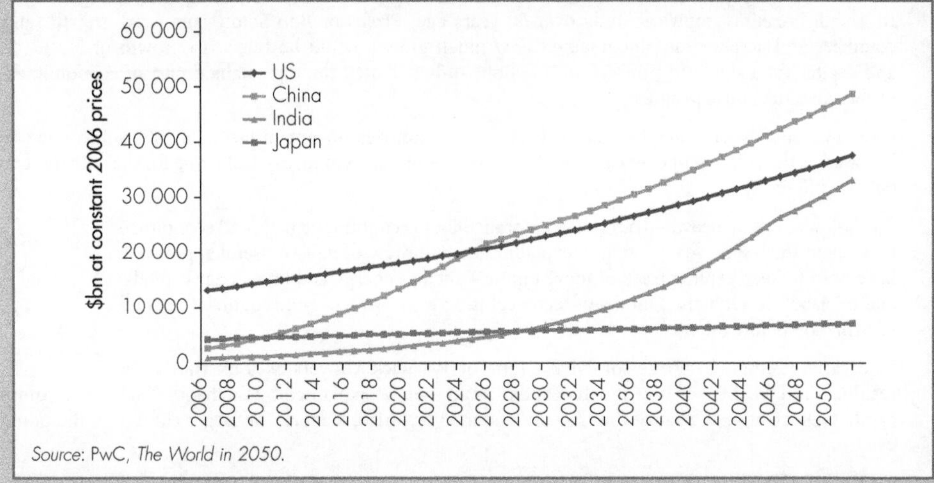

Source: PwC, *The World in 2050*.

The table below shows PwC estimates for a variety of emerging markets during 2007– 50, isolating the effect of population growth as well as the general catch-up in productivity levels implied by more rapid productivity growth in poorer countries.

	Annual real growth (%)		
	GDP	Per capita GDP	Population
Vietnam	6.8	6.0	0.8
India	5.8	5.0	0.8
Bangladesh	5.1	3.9	1.2
China	4.7	4.6	0.1
Malaysia	4.3	3.3	1.0
Turkey	4.1	3.4	0.7
Mexico	3.7	3.2	0.5
Russia	2.5	3.2	−0.6
Poland	2.1	2.7	−0.5

Source: PwC, *The World in 2050*.

The poorer countries have more rapid GDP growth not merely because they have opportunities for productivity catch-up but also because they often have more rapid population growth, except in China with its one-child per family policy. Whether this will continue until 2050, as assumed in the table, is hard to assess at this juncture. The middle-income countries (Malaysia through to Poland) are expected to have fewer opportunities for rapid productivity growth and, in the case of Eastern Europe and Russia, may actually experience falling populations. This helps their per capita growth – capital-widening is less of a burden – but not their aggregate GDP growth.

In a path-breaking empirical study over 50 years ago, Professor Bob Solow compared growth rates across countries and across time, documented how much growth could be traced to growth of inputs of labour and capital via a standard production function, and attributed the unexplained part of economic growth to unmeasured technical progress.

Case 28.2 already provides two alarm bells. First, countries do not immediately share the same technical knowledge, providing scope for catch-up by poorer countries. Second, even allowing for this, different countries behave differently.

The **Solow residual** measured our initial ignorance about economic growth, and economists have spent the last 50 years trying to explain more and more of it. Two useful approaches have been to keep explicit track of more inputs – such as energy and knowledge capital – and to elaborate a dynamic model of technical progress in which some countries get new information before others.

The part of output growth not explained by the growth of measured inputs is known as the Solow residual.

One early attempt, by Professor Nick Crafts of Warwick University, took the Solow residuals and tried to see how much of them could then be explained by catch-up. The lower a country's per capita GDP relative to that of the US (the assumed technical leader), the larger should be the potential for catch-up.

Crafts discovered that there is a systematic role for catch-up, as we would have expected from Case 28.2, but also that, after allowing for 'average catch-up' for a country of that living standard, big differences remain across countries. These may reflect the social and political framework in which the economy must operate. Change usually helps the majority but has very adverse effects on a few people whose skills are made obsolete or whose power is suddenly removed. The large number of winners should club together to buy off the few big losers, allowing change to proceed. Some societies are much better than others at organizing the deals that allow catch-up to be achieved more rapidly.

Increasingly, the effort of research economists is now focused on analysing and measuring the accumulation of knowledge capital. Amazingly, recent estimates suggest that investment in knowledge creation is even more important than investment in physical capital in generating high levels of GDP. With around 80 per cent of GDP now comprising the supply of services rather than the production of goods, perhaps this should come as no surprise. Know-how matters a lot.

This also helps explain some historical puzzles, such as why Germany and Japan grew so quickly after the Second World War. Part of the modern answer is that their advanced knowledge survived intact even if the bombs had destroyed their buildings. Conversely, if foreign aid is to help some of the world's poorest countries, supplying food and shelter may not be enough. Education and training are hugely important.

28.8 Endogenous growth

In its simplest form, Solow's theory makes economic growth depend on population growth and technical progress. Both proceed at given rates. The subsequent literature on catch-up makes technical progress respond to economic circumstances and the political and cultural environment. It would be nice to have a stronger link between economic behaviour and the rate of economic growth. We want to make growth *endogenous*; that is, determined within our theory.

Endogenous growth implies that the steady-state growth rate is affected by economic behaviour and economic policy.

The original insight is due to Professor Paul Romer. Saving, investment and capital accumulation lie at the heart of growth. In Solow's theory, applying more and more capital to a given path for population runs into the diminishing marginal product of capital. It cannot be the source of permanent growth in productivity.

We know there must be diminishing returns to capital alone at the level of individual firms; otherwise one firm would get more and more capital, become steadily more productive and gradually take over the entire world! Because diminishing returns to capital hold at the level of the firm, economists had assumed they held also at the level of the economy.

Romer's insight was the possibility (likelihood?) that there are significant externalities to capital. Higher capital in one firm increases productivity in *other* firms. When BT invests in better equipment, other firms can do things previously impossible. The Internet and the iPad have similar benefits for other technologies. The insight also applies to human capital. Training by one firm has beneficial externalities for others.

Thus the production function of each individual firm exhibits diminishing returns to its own capital input, but also depends on the capital of other firms. No firm, acting in isolation, would wish to raise its capital without limit. But when all firms expand together, the economy as a whole may face constant returns to aggregate capital.

Consider the following simple example of the aggregate economy. Per capita output y is proportional to capital per person k. To isolate the role of accumulation, suppose there is no technical progress. Thus $y = Ak$, where A is constant, and there are constant returns to accumulating more capital. Given a constant saving rate s and population growth at rate n, is there a steady state in which capital per person grows at rate g? If so, investment for capital deepening is gk and investment for capital-widening, to keep up with population growth, is nk. Hence, in per capita terms:

$$\text{Gross investment} = (g + n)k = sy = sAk = \text{gross saving}$$

Hence $gk = (sA - n)k$ and the steady-state growth rate g is

$$g = (sA - n) \qquad (2)$$

Why does this confirm the possibility of *endogenous* growth? Growth now depends on parameters that can be influenced by private behaviour or public policy. In the Solow model, without technical progress, steady-state growth is always n, whatever the saving rate s or the level of productivity A. Equation (2) says that any policy that succeeded in raising the saving rate s would *permanently* increase the *growth rate* g. Similarly, any policy achieving a one-off rise in the *level* of A, for example greater workplace efficiency, would permanently increase the growth rate of k. Since $y = Ak$, this means permanently faster output growth.

Not only can government policy affect growth in this framework, government intervention may increase efficiency. In the simple Romer model outlined above, there are externalities in capital accumulation: individual firms neglect the fact that, in raising their own capital, they also increase the productivity of *other* firms' capital. Government subsidies to investment might offset this externality.

Since Romer's original work there has been huge interest in endogenous growth. Sustaining small additions to annual growth rates eventually makes a big difference to living standards. As a result of this research we now have many potential channels of endogenous growth. For example, instead of assuming that the rate of technical progress is given, we can model the industry that undertakes R&D to produce technical progress. Constant returns in this industry will generate endogenous growth. In fact, constant returns to aggregate production of any *accumulable* factor (knowledge, capital, and so on) will suffice.

Note, too, that endogenous growth models explain why growth rates in different countries might permanently be different. This might explain why convergence does not take place and why some countries remain poor indefinitely. Different countries have different growth rates g.

While endogenous growth theory is an exciting development, it also has its critics. Most criticisms boil down to a key point. Whatever the relevant accumulatible factor, why should there be *exactly* constant returns in the aggregate? With diminishing returns, we are back in the Solow model where long-run growth is exogenous. With increasing returns, the economy would settle not on steady growth but on ever more rapid expansion of output and capital. We know this is not occurring. So for endogenous growth theory to be the answer, only constant returns to accumulation will do. Some people think this seems just too good to be true.

28.9 The costs of growth

Can the benefits of economic growth be outweighed by its costs? Pollution, climate change, congestion and a hectic lifestyle are a high price to pay for more cars, washing machines and video games.

Since GNP is an imperfect measure of the true economic value of the goods and services produced by the economy, there is no presumption we should want to maximize the growth of measured GNP. We discussed issues such as pollution in Part Three. Without government intervention, a free market economy produces too much pollution. But complete elimination of pollution is also wasteful. Society should undertake activities accompanied by pollution up to the point at which the net marginal benefit of the goods produced equals the marginal pollution cost imposed on society. Government intervention, through pollution taxes or regulation of environmental standards, can move the economy towards an efficient allocation of resources in which marginal social costs and benefits are equalized.

The full implementation of such a policy would (optimally) reduce the growth of measured GNP below the rate where there is no restriction on activities such as pollution and congestion. And this is the most sensible way in which to approach the problem. It tackles the issue directly. In contrast, the **zero-growth** solution is a blunt instrument.

The zero-growth proposal argues that, because higher measured GNP imposes environmental costs, it is best to aim for zero growth of measured GNP.

The zero-growth approach fails to distinguish between measured outputs accompanied by social costs and measured outputs without additional social costs. It does not provide the correct incentives. The principle of targeting, a key insight of the welfare economics discussed in Part Three, suggests that it is more efficient to tackle a problem directly than to adopt an indirect approach that distorts other aspects of production or consumption. Thus, when there is too much pollution, congestion, environmental damage or stress, the best solution is to provide incentives that directly reduce these phenomena. Restricting growth in measured output is a crude alternative, distinctly second-best.

Some problems might evaporate if economists and statisticians could measure true GNP more accurately, including the 'quality of life' activities (clean air, environmental beauty, sustainable climate, and so on) that yield consumption benefits but at present are omitted from measured GNP. Voters and commentators assess government performance against measurable statistics. A better measure of GNP might remove perceived conflicts between measured output and the quality of life.

This is also a good way to address 'sustainable growth'. At present, Mediterranean beauty spots become concrete jungles of hotels and bars; once the environment is spoiled, upmarket tourists move on to somewhere else. An economist's advice, however, is not to abandon being a tourist destination, but to keep track of environmental depreciation and only engage in activities that show a clear return after proper costing of environmental and other damage. Embodying these costings in actual charges also provides the market incentive to look after the environment.

This also provides the answer to those who argue that tackling climate change will hamper economic growth. Just as we want congestion charging to *reduce* some outputs (rush-hour traffic), we want environmental pricing to *reduce* some activities (greenhouse gas emissions, lax building insulation). In both cases, the objective is to get aggregate output, *properly measured*, to increase!

No matter how complete the framework, the assessment of the desirable growth rate will always be a normative question hinging on the value judgements of the assessor. Switching resources from consumption, however defined, to investment will nearly always reduce the welfare of people today but allow greater welfare for people tomorrow. Nowhere is this clearer than in the speed with which we try to deal with climate change. More sacrifice today will make life easier tomorrow; less sacrifice today will compound the problems for our children's children. The priority attached to satisfying wants of people at different points in time is always a value judgement.

Summary

- **Supply-side economics** analyses one-off changes in aggregate supply and potential output. These arise from changing the quantity of labour employed or changing the productivity of those employed.
- For a given population, the quantity of labour employed is affected by labour force participation, by incentives of the labour force to accept a job and by incentives about how long and how hard to work. Changes in incentives have income and substitution effects, often operating in different directions, somewhat mitigating their overall effectiveness.
- Productivity can be enhanced through greater competition, lighter regulation (within limits) and allowing obsolete businesses to cease (especially if accompanied by effective retraining and relocation of the workforce).
- The possibility of **hysteresis** means that temporary recessions may have permanently adverse effects on potential output. If so, demand stabilization may contribute to good long-run supply performance.
- **Economic growth** is the percentage annual increase in real GDP or per capita real GDP in the long run. It is an imperfect measure of the rate of increase of economic well-being.
- Measured GDP omits the value of leisure and of untraded goods and bads that have an impact on the quality of life. Differences in income distribution make per capita real GDP a shaky basis for comparisons of the welfare of the typical individual in different countries.
- Significant rates of **growth of per capita GDP** occurred only in the last two centuries in the advanced economies. In other countries persistent growth is even more recent.
- Potential output can be increased either by increasing the inputs of land, labour, capital and raw materials, or by increasing the output obtained from given input quantities. **Technical advances** are an important source of productivity gains.
- An apparently **fixed supply of a production input**, such as a particular raw material, need not make growth impossible in the long run. As the input becomes scarce, its price rises. This makes producers substitute other inputs, increases incentives to discover new supplies and encourages inventions that economize on the use of that resource.
- The simplest theory of growth has a **steady state** in which capital, output and labour all grow at the same rate. Whatever its initial level of capital, the economy converges on this steady-state path. This theory can explain output growth but not productivity growth.
- **Labour-augmenting technical progress** allows permanent growth of labour productivity and enables the simple growth theory to fit many of the facts.
- There is a **tendency of economies to converge**, both because **capital deepening** is easier when capital per worker is low and because of **catch-up in technology**. Implementing technical change may depend on how well society is organized to buy off (or defeat) the losers.
- Theories of **endogenous growth** are built on constant returns to accumulation. If aggregate investment does not encounter diminishing returns to capital, choices about saving and investment can affect the long-run growth rate of productivity. An externality on a giant scale provides a powerful rationale for government intervention to encourage education, training and physical capital formation.
- Nevertheless, endogenous growth rests on the presence of constant returns to accumulation. Nobody has yet explained why this should hold.

Review questions

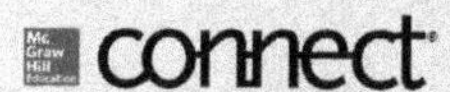

1 (a) What is the distinction between total output and per capita output? Which grows more rapidly? Why? Does it always grow? (b) What are the two channels by which potential output can be increased using supply-side policies?

2 Name two economic bads. Suggest feasible ways in which they might be measured. Should they be included in GNP? Could they be?

3 Choose the correct answer: Countries that isolate themselves from the world economy tend to grow slowly because (a) they fail to learn about technical progress elsewhere, (b) without competition, they have insufficient incentive to invest, (c) there are other adverse consequences of the political regime that took such a decision, (d) all of the above, (e) none of the above.

4 **Common fallacies** Why are these statements wrong? (a) Since the earth's resources are limited, growth cannot continue forever. (b) If we save more, we'd definitely grow faster.

5 Choose the correct answer: The empirical correlation between countries that possess extreme mineral wealth and the prevalence of civil wars suggests that: (a) wars raise the demand for resources and encourage exploration for minerals, (b) when easy wealth is available, it increases the incentive to fight over the spoils provided by nature rather than co-operate to produce goods and services, (c) mineral wealth attracts foreign predators.

EASY

6 'Because we know Malthus got it wrong, we are relaxed about the fact that some minerals are in finite supply.' Is there a connection? Explain.

7 Several decades ago, China adopted a policy of a maximum of one child per family. Using the analysis of this chapter, explain what the purpose of this might have been. Illustrate in a diagram.

8 Suppose the private sector has a given saving rate out of disposable income, but that the public sector levies taxes and utilizes all of this revenue for investment. If the private and public sector are equally efficient, what happens to the long-run growth rate? What happens to per capita incomes eventually?

9 Consider an economy in which there is constant population. Each firm's production function exhibits diminishing returns to its own capital accumulation. However, each firm creates beneficial production externalities for other firms. In the aggregate, the economy faces constant returns to capital accumulation, so that $y = 2k$. If the saving rate is 0.2, what is the permanent rate of growth of capital and output?

10 Can technical progress be negative?

11 'If the convergence hypothesis is correct, the poor African countries should have grown long ago!' Is this correct? Do newer approaches to economic growth help explain why some countries remain so poor?

MEDIUM

12 'Britain produces too many scientists, too few engineers.' What kind of evidence might help you decide if this is true? Will a free market lead people to choose the career that most benefits society?

13 Consider a planet in which population grows at the constant rate n and people save a constant fraction s of their per capita output. Output is produced by environmental capital k, which depreciates at a constant d. Gross investment is used only to improve environmental capital, and $y = f(k)$ so that output depends on environmental capital and there are diminishing returns to environmental capital. (a) Illustrate the above information in a diagram. (b) What happens to gross investment per person? (c) Suppose the rate of environmental depreciation rises. What happens to the steady state level of output per person y? (d) Is it true that if recycling were to reduce environmental depreciation, it would raise output per person in the long run?

14 **Essay question** Is it in a country's best interests to focus on economic growth? Or, in other words, is growth good?

HARD

For solutions to these questions, contact your lecturer.